The
Poetical Works
of
Elizabeth Barrett
Browning

CAMBRIDGE EDITIONS

The Poetical Works of Elizabeth Barrett Browning
The Poetical Works of Robert Browning
The Poetical Works of Burns
The Poetical Works of Byron
The Poetical Works of Dryden
The Poetical Works of Oliver Wendell Holmes
The Poetical Works of Keats
The Poetical Works of Longfellow
The Poetical Works of Amy Lowell
The Poetical Works of Shelley
The Poetical Works of Tennyson
The Selected Works of Thoreau
The Poetical Works of Whittier
The Poetical Works of Wordsworth

Elizabeth Barrett Browning

The
Poetical Works
of
Elizabeth Barrett
Browning

✠

Cambridge Edition

With a New Introduction
By Ruth M. Adams

Houghton Mifflin Company Boston

Library of Congress Cataloging in Publication Data

Browning, Elizabeth (Barrett) 1806–1861.
  The poetical works of Elizabeth Barrett Browning.

  Edited by Harriet Waters Preston.
  Edition of 1900 published under title: The complete
poetical works of Elizabeth Barrett Browning.
  I. Preston, Harriet Waters, 1836–1911, ed.
II. Title.
PR4180.F74   821'.8   73-20373
ISBN 0-395-18012-0

EDITOR'S NOTE

THIS CAMBRIDGE EDITION is without question the best single volume of the poetical works of Elizabeth Barrett Browning. When it was prepared for publication in the Cambridge series in 1900, Harriet Waters Preston followed ". . . the latest comprehensive English edition," but that was not complete in its compass. It remained for Charlotte Porter and Helen A. Clarke to edit in 1900 six volumes of *The Complete Works of Elizabeth Barrett Browning* (the Coxhoe Edition) and a year later to reissue them in a limited, deluxe edition entitled *The Complete Works of Mrs. E. B. Browning* (the Arno Edition). For the nonspecialist, however, the Cambridge Edition meets all needs.

Mrs. Preston was a sympathetic but not uncritical reader of Elizabeth Barrett Browning's poetry and her comments blend information and an intelligent reader's response in a fresh and ingratiating fashion. When the poet failed of the editor's standards, she said so. She recognized the emotionalism with which Elizabeth Barrett Browning approached the Italian question, the dubious judgment that was the basis of her enthusiasm for Napoleon III, the erratic ear that allowed bad rhymes to stand, and the temperament that forbade revisions and repeated refinements. The poet was fortunate in so sane and sensible an interpreter; today a reader can enjoy the Notes for their own sake as well as for the illumination they provide.

To annotate the poems completely would be a heroic task and would make the back of the volume disproportionate to the poetry itself. Scholars will seek their own documentation; interested readers will find enough to please and instruct them in the poems themselves.

This edition does not carry a full biographical sketch of Elizabeth Barrett Browning, as did that of 1900. Rather the Introduction identifies that part of the poetry which has proved of lasting value or interest, considers two major achievements, *Sonnets from the Portuguese* and *Aurora Leigh*, and estimates the place that Elizabeth Barrett Browning may be expected to claim in a reader's attention and in poetic evaluation.

RUTH M. ADAMS

75222

CONTENTS

CONTENTS

INTRODUCTION
BY RUTH M. ADAMS

Too FEW PEOPLE read Elizabeth Barrett's poems today. An enthusiast for the eighteenth century may turn to "Cowper's Grave"; a neo-medievalist may roll slowly through "Rhyme of the Duchess May"; the nineteenth century social historian recommends as supplementary reading "Lady Geraldine's Courtship" and "The Cry of the Children"; a devout Christian may even respond to "The Dead Pan." Her sonnets "Consolation" and "Grief" still speak directly to and for the bereaved. To her contemporary audience, however, Miss Barrett was a distinguished, erudite, modern poet, whose humanitarian dedication, classical interests, and deep feeling found expression in lucid and musical verses.

Who reads Elizabeth Barrett Browning? More people, but not a vast number. Historians seeking the expression of an emotional reaction to the cause of Italian freedom will read selectively in *Casa Guidi Windows* and *Poems Before Congress*. *Aurora Leigh* has been rediscovered by those who appreciate its vignettes of society, high and low, its concentration on women, their aspirations to independence and self-sufficiency, and its rejection of mid-Victorian taboos on subject matter. But the audience that is most assured and most numerous consists of those in love or in love with love, who find the *Sonnets from the Portuguese* a full and satisfying expression of their emotions. Certainly some of these sonnets are destined for a modest immortality, but immortality nonetheless.

Elizabeth Barrett Browning's reputation has been fading. Where once Arthur Quiller-Couch included ten of her poems in his *Oxford Book of English Verse*, of which half were from the Portuguese sonnets, Helen Gardner in 1972 reduced the representation to only three, all sonnets: "I thought once . . ." "If thou must love me . . ." and "When our two souls . . . ." Where, alas, is the much quoted — and much loved — "How do I love thee? Let me count the ways"?

One difficulty lies in the way of extended readership: too much of Mrs. Browning's poetry requires supplementary knowledge. The poems are not obscure in thought or expression, but her references to contemporary and historical personages and events make, for example, much of *Casa Guidi Windows* incomprehensible today. *Poems Before Congress* needs to be peppered with footnotes for the casual reader to comprehend the poet's strong feelings. Then, too, she is often too feverishly intense for twentieth century taste, too didactic, too hortatory, and too secure in her religious faith. She does reward a sympathetic reader, but the reward is rather in separate coins than in a golden shower.

Elizabeth Barrett Browning is at her best in brief expression of strong emotions: love, grief, joy, desolation, devotion, faith. Intensity in brief expression and immediacy of emotional response permeate her best work. This directness of communication, plus the legend of her own life, assures that she will be read both for the pleasure the poems give and from curiosity about her own romantic love affair with Robert Browning.

Fiction, drama, and film have seized upon the fairy tale of the beautiful, gifted woman, imprisoned by a cruel father, and rescued by the handsome, courageous poet, who swept aside all barriers to carry her off to the happy skies of Italy. Delightfully, there is a core of truth in this; but Elizabeth Barrett was, though an invalid, not isolated from the world, and Mr. Barrett, though perverse in his opposition to marriage for any of his children, was proudly devoted to his oldest daughter and commanded her affection.

Elizabeth Barrett was not always a resident of a dark home at 50 Wimpole Street, London. She lived her first twenty years in Herefordshire, in the beautiful country of the Malvern Hills, as the oldest of eleven children. Playmates in such number ruled out solitude and isolation. She submitted to the genteel education thought appropriate for girls — drawing, needlework, music, dancing — and sought more substantial studies, directed by her brothers' tutors and by her own exertions. She read greedily. She loved poetry and is said to have written verses even as a little girl of four. When she was fourteen her proud father arranged the private printing of her "epic," *The Battle of Marathon*. Her erudition led her at sixteen to undertake a philosophical poem, *An Essay on Mind*, showing the influence of Pope. Not all her efforts were on so large a scale; concomitantly she produced short lyrics as well. Her juvenilia is not distinguished, but her poetic commitment was more than a transient release of adolescent self-expression.

Her youth had its long shadows as well. In her teens, nervous exhaustion and disturbance undermined her health and thereafter she was never free of periods of debility and tension. When her mother died in 1828, Elizabeth moved into an even closer relationship with her father and into the responsibilities of oldest sister to the younger children. Reverses in the family fortunes dictated a change of residence, and in 1838, 50 Wimpole Street became the Barrett house. There she lived for eighteen years, reading, studying, writing her poetry and commentaries, corresponding with friends, and tending to the well-being of her brothers and sisters.

These family ties were broken in 1840 first by the death of her brother Samuel and, more painfully, by the drowning of her best loved brother, Edward. Circumstances combined to make Elizabeth feel responsible for this second tragedy (she had urged her father to allow "Bro" to keep her company at

Torquay, where the accident occurred), and her nerves gave way as she plummeted into grief, ". . . hopeless grief . . . passionless . . ." Returned to London she spent five years as an invalid, seldom leaving the house, seeing only those who could come to see her.

Although these were years of physical weakness, they were not years of apathy and literary paralysis. She already had something of a reputation as a scholar and a poet, based on her books of verse, *Prometheus Bound* (1833) and *The Seraphim* (1838). She added to her stature with the publication of a two-volume edition of her *Poems* in 1844, of which there was also an American edition with an introduction by Edgar Allan Poe. She added to her circle of friends and correspondents, which included Mary Russell Mitford, the essayist and donor of the famous spaniel, Flush; Richard Hengist Horne, the dramatist; John Kenyon, the professional man of letters; and George Ticknor, the American editor. She met Wordsworth and Landor. She corresponded with James Russell Lowell. And one correspondent initiated an exchange as a result of reading the *Poems*.

> I love your verses with all my heart, dear Miss Barrett, — and this is no off-hand complimentary letter that I shall write, — whatever else, no prompt matter-of-course recognition of your genius, and there a graceful and natural end of the thing. Since that day last week when I first read your poems, I quite laugh to remember how I have been turning and turning again in my mind what I should be able to tell you of their effect upon me, for in the first flush of delight I thought I would this once get out of my habit of purely passive enjoyment, when I do really enjoy, and thoroughly justify my admiration — perhaps even, as a loyal fellow-craftsman should, try and find fault and do you some little good to be proud of hereafter! — but nothing comes of it all — so into me has gone, and part of me has it become . . . in this addressing myself to you — your own self, and for the first time, my feeling rises altogether. I do, as I say, love these books with all my heart — and I love you too.

The correspondent was Robert Browning, six years her junior, a poet of less popular reputation but of critical consequence. Permission was sought and granted for him to visit; when he could not call, they wrote, often daily; the protestation of "love" in his first letter proved sincere and real; and Miss Barrett responded, at first hesitantly, then wholeheartedly.

Their marriage could not take place easily and openly. Edward Barrett, a jealous father, could not freely grant his children their own emotional and sexual lives. He cut himself off completely from his daughter Henrietta and his son Alfred when they married; and Bro's drowning in 1840 may have been a merciful end to that brief life, for Mr. Barrett had totally blocked his wish to marry. Mr. Barrett was most possessive of his eldest daughter, and as her attachment to Browning grew, the lovers realized that a confrontation with her father would avail them nothing by way of his sanctioning their marriage. Accordingly they were married without his consent or awareness and, leaving the proverbial letter announcing the wedding, left London for Italy, which they believed would give them sunlit years, health, and the joys of a happy marriage.

The ensuing fifteen years brought them much of what they hoped for. Life in Italy took them to Pisa, Venice, Lucca, and Rome. There were trips back to England. But their permanent residence was Florence, in the house that gave its name to Mrs. Browning's 1856 volume, *Casa Guidi Windows*. Their son was born in 1849. They loved each other, delighted in their mutual craft, respected each other's achievements. They were, however, not creatures of romance, existing in enameled harmony, but human beings. Robert Browning sardonically questioned some of his wife's greatest enthusiasms — for spiritualism and the American medium D. D. Home, who served later as the original of Browning's "Mr. Sludge, the Medium," and for Louis Napoleon and his political maneuvers. Elizabeth Browning's credo that a poet must write of the real world around him, of contemporary people, wearing contemporary clothing, meeting in contemporary drawing rooms or slum alleys, confronting contemporary problems and concerns, was not realized by her husband, whose concentration was on the timeless elements of human character. Also, like almost all parents, they disagreed on the training and education of their son. Whatever their differences, each spoke and wrote of the other in terms of mutual devotion, respect, and love.

Mrs. Browning's Italian residence made her an enthusiastic supporter of the cause of Italian independence, of Mazzini and Cavour, and she could even see hope and promise in the activities of Napoleon III. Believing that the contemporary world was a proper subject for poetic treatment, she wrote often of her aspirations for Italy, of her hope for the inspiring leader, of her irritation with her native land for not fostering her new cause. *Poems Before Congress* (1860) is a collection too preoccupied with these themes, too hectic in its expression to create the effects for which she strove. Meanwhile, in the revised edition of her *Poems* (1850), she had included the distinguished sequence, *Sonnets from the Portuguese*; and in 1856 published her largest and most ambitious work, *Aurora Leigh*.

After that year, her strength and energies diminished. She lacked the vitality to travel much, was plagued by bronchial attacks, but even so continued to write. An attack more severe than it was thought to be finally claimed her exhausted body in 1861. She was buried in her beloved city of Florence.

Her star sank toward the horizon, even as her husband's rose. He was the greater poet; but she still rightly claims a reader's serious attention and rewards sympathetic reading with lyric felicity and social perceptiveness. *Sonnets from the Portuguese* illustrates the one, and *Aurora Leigh* the other.

The sonnets were begun immediately upon her first acquaintance with Browning, and chronicle her reactions to their developing relationship. He did not know of their existence until after the birth of their son, Pen, when she confessed to him that she had written ". . . some poems about you." Each sonnet encapsulates a moment of reaction or meditation, and the constant theme is love. The sequence moves in a rising arc, from melancholy and weeping, bereavement and the habitude of grief, through wonder in the strength and joy of love, to assurance and delight in love, for the present, for the future, for eternity. Love is the inspiriting force, love finally received and given without hesitation or constraint. The sonnets tell the story of a spirit revivified.

While behind each sonnet there is an encounter or the emotional consequences of an encounter between Elizabeth Barrett and Robert Browning, appreciation of the series does not depend on a knowledge of the poets' lives. The meticulous delineation of shades of feeling, the outbursts of pain and joy, the hesitations, withdrawals and advances, all combine to produce a concentrated narrative line, a record of emotional tension. Especially powerful are individual sonnets considered in isolation, as they speak to happiness, regret, confidence, and — always — love. But the evidence of narrative development as well as the techniques used to link sonnet to sonnet indicate that the group is presented to be read as a whole.

The poet would reject a generously proffered love but acknowledges that the affection offered has changed her life for all time to come (VI). As love becomes familiar, she can accept it, can abandon her sense of returning less than she is given, and grows confident enough to demand the reassurance of his repeated vows (XXI). One last night of hesitation and insecurity (XXX) is followed by the coming of her lover and from then on all is well. She can rejoice in love given and received (XLI), rehearse the pleasures of their intimacy (XXXIII, XXXVIII), and envision a future of constant love (XLII, XLIII).

Sonnets from the Portuguese has then a narrative unity. Additional evidence of their being conceived as parts of a whole lies in the links she provides between one sonnet and another. Sonnet II's initial "but" throws us back to I; V's final "go" becomes VI's first word; VII and IX are fused by the multiple "gives"; X's "yet" looks back, while XI's "and" links the third unit; ". . . with the same heart . . ." ties XXXIII and XXXIV. Technique joins story to create the whole.

Individual sonnets must be allowed to make their special claims, however. Sonnet XXI, with its delightful demand for the voice of springtime, the repeated, reassuring "cuckoo-song" of love that brings the surety of a new season to the poet, voices a happily naive assurance of receiving the desired response. Joined to the joyous demand for speech is the wiser additional demand for silence, the tacit love of the soul. This sonnet, incidentally, represents Elizabeth Barrett Browning at the peak of her poetic competence: the chiming, accurate rhyme words, with their light, open vowels; the smooth run from the octave to the sestet; the daring and effective triple ". . . love me . . ." followed immediately by the break and subsequent imperative. Less familiar than others, it is one of her better achievements. The favorites of a hundred years retain their appeal, however, and we read and reread "If thou must love me . . ." (XIV), "First time he kissed me . . ." (XXXVIII), "When our two souls stand up erect . . ." (XXII), and "How do I love thee?" (XLIII). Elizabeth Barrett Browning is a good lyricist, strong in feeling and capable of sweetness in expression.

From *Aurora Leigh* we can expect none of the immediacy of the sonnets, nor should we; this is narrative, not lyric poetry. What it does contain is her best thinking on matters important to her as a woman, as an artist, as a human being, as an individual. She experienced what it is to be a "woman writer" and what limited expectations a male audience has of her, the areas in which they believe it impossible for her to move. She had to formulate her own theory of the art of poetry, what subjects it can appropriately treat, what conventions it can justifiably challenge. She, to her own satisfaction, held a belief that is Christian in its definitions. She found fulfillment in love and marriage. *Aurora Leigh* occupied her attention for at least four years and was her "big work." Into its melodramatic tale she wove the threads of her own preoccupations, which shine today with more immediate brilliance than for many intervening years.

In this work, Elizabeth Browning was, among the poets, an original. Tennyson had approached "the woman question" in *The Princess* (1853), but far from head-on. His idealized fable of the cloistered lady scholars, the invasion of the disguised young blades, the capitulation of the academy to the claims of love receives its most appropriate evaluation by serving as the point of departure for Gilbert and Sullivan's *Princess Ida.* Tennyson's approach is, as a whole, nonsensical, though isolated passages state with awe that women can indeed learn, think, and teach. No other poet, including Robert Browning, even attempts the theme of the independent, sensitive, intelligent woman and her dilemmas. The novelists did more: Charlotte Brontë in *Villette* (1853), Thackeray in *The Newcomes* (1855), George Eliot in *The Mill on the Floss* (1860), even Wilkie Collins in *Armadale* (1866). The later years of the nineteenth century, of course, produced many fictional studies of "the new woman"; Elizabeth Browning is a poetic original, an early voice of what was to become a chorus.

Aurora Leigh is offered as a "verse-novel." It has had a recent resurgence in popularity, though it is probably still more talked about than read. The new feminism of the seventies has seized upon the idea of *Aurora Leigh* because the protagonist is an independent woman, because another woman refuses a marriage designed only to give her illegitimate child a name. But to identify the poem as a document of women's total emancipation is to ignore the dubious quality of Aurora's self-sufficiency, to suppress the conclusion entirely, and to overlook the extended considerations the author has given topics far removed from the concerns of independent women in the last third of the twentieth century. Indeed Elizabeth Barrett Browning's aspirations and ambitions in *Aurora Leigh* are too extensive to permit the poem the limited designation of "feminist writing."

For one thing, the work carries the burden of illustrating her conviction that poetry must deal with the contemporary scene.

> Nay, if there's room for poets in this world
> A little overgrown (I think there is),
> Their sole work is to represent the age,
> Their age, not Charlemagne's, — this live, throbbing age,
> That brawls, cheats, maddens, calculates, aspires,
> And spends more passion, more heroic heat,
> Betwixt the mirrors of its drawing-rooms,
> Than Roland with his knights at Roncesvalles.
> To flinch from modern varnish, coat or flounce
> Cry out for togas and the picturesque,
> Is fatal, — foolish too.
>   Fifth Book, lines 200–210

She has already tried her hand at this in "Lady Geraldine's Courtship" (*Poems*, 1844). Now she creates as her protagonist Aurora Leigh, half Italian, half English, who despite discouragement on all sides, decides to follow a career as a writer. Hack work — plus a small income of her own — supports her more serious undertakings, and she finally publishes the poems that fully express her concept of truth, a volume quickly recognized for its inestimable value. Meanwhile she has rejected a kindly but unloving offer of marriage from her cousin Romney Leigh, who wished her to join him in service to the generality of humanity. In his cold impersonality, he turns to socialistic experiments, loses the worthy daughter of the poor whom he proposed to marry as an example of how to break class barriers, and falls victim to the shallow and wicked Lady Waldemar. Marian Erle, his lower class intended, reappears as the true victim of social inhumanity, betrayed, raped, and the mother of an illegitimate child. Aurora takes them in and informs Romney that Marian is alive, whereupon he comes to offer the girl marriage and a name for the boy. Unconventionally she refuses because she does not love him and marriage requires love. Romney, humanized as a consequence of reading Aurora's poetry, is free to offer a loving marriage to her; she recognizes that art is incomplete without love; and the ideal union is effected. This summary omits much of the melodramatic apparatus that Mrs. Browning employed: druggings and beatings, arson and riots, child prostitution, sweat shops, slums. Romney, for example, is permanently blinded by a falling timber as he attempts to rescue a portrait resembling Aurora from the holocaust of the ancestral home. Much of what she included was distasteful to mid-Victorian readers; her justification was her commitment to the contemporary, her contention that such things were part of life and mandatorily within the poet's scope. Our demurs today are not on the grounds of taste but rather of effectiveness; she did not bring it off very well.

She is better at using elements of the world around her to carry less theatrical burdens. She presents Romney as a disciple of Auguste Comte and Charles Fourier, the latter of whom theorized a pattern for ideal communal living. The poet's mocking account of Lady Waldemar among the cows, attempting to ingratiate herself with Romney, reminds us of an attribute of Elizabeth Barrett Browning too often forgotten: she did have a sense of humor. She was also something of a satirist, to which her portrait of Aurora's English aunt attests.

> I broke the copious curls upon my head
> In braids, because she liked smooth-ordered hair . . .
> She liked my father's child to speak his tongue . . .
> . . . she liked a range
> Of liberal education . . .
> She misliked women who are frivolous . . .
> . . . she liked
> A general insight into useful facts . . .
> . . . she liked accomplishments
> in girls . . .
> She liked a woman to be womanly,
> And English women, she thanked God and sighed . . .
> Were models to the universe.
> First Book, lines 384–446 *passim*

Mrs. Browning was a moralist in her illustrations of the flagrant sexuality of women, be they prostitutes or titled ladies. She was a critic, in her contemptuous evaluation of political leaders, of insolent young people. She witnessed the invasion of English drawing rooms by wealthy Americans. Her eyes were cleared of sentimental film when she looked on the greed, voracity and stupidity of the masses. Vignettes of all these and more are in *Aurora Leigh*, a poem more happily read for its parts than as a whole.

Having followed one of her own mandates in using the world about her as her material, Elizabeth Browning attempted another of her principles, the artist's responsibility to feel and to report the feeling.

> . . . Passion is
> But something suffered, after all. While Art
> Sets action on the top of suffering:
> The artist's part is both to be and do,
> Transfixing with a special, central power
> The flat experience of the common man,
> And turning outward, with a sudden wrench,
> Half agony, half ecstasy, the thing
> He feels the inmost . . .
> . . . O sorrowful great gift

> Conferred on poets, of a twofold life,
> When one life has been found enough for pain!
> Fifth Book, lines 364-382

The artist fails in *Aurora Leigh;* passion is not given effective expression. As was said of the sonnets, the poet's best realization of feeling is the brief, lyric outburst. This long narrative has only one passage that approaches the sonnets in intensity and that, interestingly enough, is the silent communion of Aurora and Romney consequent to their mutual avowal of love.

> O dark, O moon and stars, O ecstasy
> Of darkness! O great mystery of love,
> In which absorbed, loss, anguish, treason's self
> Enlarges rapture . . .
> Ninth Book, lines 814-817

Here the affinity to the sonnet sequence is emotional; one real echo is sounded as well.

> . . . 'twas granted me
> To know he loved me to the depth and height
> Of such large natures . . .
> Ninth Book, lines 753-754

But, trapped by story-telling, Elizabeth Barrett Browning cannot free her lyric gift.

The poet Aurora Leigh won her reputation by the "truth" that her book expressed.

> . . . the truth which draws
> Through all things upwards — that a two-fold world
> Must go to a perfect cosmos. Natural things
> And spiritual, — who separates those two
> In art, in morals, or the social drift,
> Tears up the bond of nature and brings death . . .
> Seventh Book, lines 763-769

For her and for her creator, the spiritual is the Christian God.

> Alas, long-suffering and most patient God,
> Thou needst be surelier God to bear with us
> Than even to have made us! Thou aspire, aspire
> From henceforth for me! thou who hast thyself
> Endured this fleshhood . . .
> Sustain me, that with thee I walk these waves,
> Resisting! — breathe me upward, thou in me
> Aspiring who art the way, the truth, the life, —
> That no truth henceforth seem indifferent,
> No way to truth laborious, and no life,
> Not even this life I live, intolerable!
> Seventh Book, lines 1027-1039

This is the ending of *Aurora Leigh*: the man has learning that systems alone will not serve — ". . . Fourier's void/And Comte absurd." The woman has learned that devotion to art is nothing if the woman-artist is unfulfilled by love and marriage.

> O Art, my Art, thou'rt much, but Love is more.
> Art symbolizes heaven, but Love is God
> And makes heaven . . .
>
> Ninth Book, lines 657–659

The Christian voice is less familiar today, but Elizabeth Barrett Browning writes from her own experience and conviction as to the most blessed security available to humanity, and has Romney sum it up.

> ". . . First, God's love."
> "And next," he smiled, "the love of wedded souls,
> . . . sweetened from one central Heart."
>
> Ninth Book, line 881ff.

Here the *Sonnets from the Portuguese* and *Aurora Leigh* are linked. The confidence and joy in love with which the sonnets concluded have been externalized and can become the emotional climax of Mrs. Browning's most ambitious work.

Yet it is not to *Aurora Leigh*, effective as parts may be, that the reader will return. It is too discursive, too tedious, too platitudinous in most of its sentiments, too much on the level of melodrama in its basic narrative to command respect or liking. The *Sonnets* on the other hand wear well, continue to express real emotion and to assert their claim to be read. It is they that give Elizabeth Barrett Browning her modest but secure place as a true lyric poet.

The
Poetical Works
of
Elizabeth Barrett
Browning

THE SERAPHIM AND OTHER POEMS

In 1833, Miss Barrett's first translation of the *Prometheus Bound* of Æschylus was published in London, — along with a score or so of miscellaneous pieces, but without her name, — by A. J. Valpy, Red Lion Court, Fleet Street. The little volume fell dead from the press — receiving only a few lines of scathing criticism in the *Athenæum*. The translator herself confessed a decade later that her version of the great Greek drama had been made in twelve days and 'should have been thrown into the fire afterward ; — the only means of giving it a little warmth.' She did her best, in fact, to suppress the volume, and subsequently executed an entire new translation of the Prometheus, which was included in the edition of her poems that appeared in 1850, and has ever since kept its place in the standard editions of her works. Meanwhile her studies in Æschylus had suggested to the young poetess the subject of the Seraphim — the first original work of hers destined to obtain anything like general recognition. 'I thought,' she says, in her own preface to *The Seraphim and other Poems* (London, Saunders J. Otley, Conduit Street, 1838), 'that, had Æschylus lived after the incarnation and crucifixion of our Lord Jesus Christ, he might have turned, if not in moral and intellectual, yet in poetic faith, from the solitudes of Caucasus to the deeper desertness of that crowded Jerusalem where none had any pity . . . to the rent rocks and darkened sun . . . to the victim whose sustaining thought beneath an unexampled agony, was not the Titanic, "I can revenge," but the celestial "I can forgive." '

THE SERAPHIM

Σῷ δὲ θρόνῳ πυροέντι παρεστᾶσιν πολύμοχθοι ᾽Αγγε-
λοι. — *Orpheus.*

' I look for Angels' songs, and hear Him cry.'
      — *Giles Fletcher.*

PART THE FIRST

[*It is the time of the Crucifixion ; and the Angels of Heaven have departed towards the Earth, except the two Seraphim,* ADOR *the Strong and* ZERAH *the Bright One. The place is the outer side of the shut Heavenly Gate.*]

Ador. O Seraph, pause no more !
Beside this gate of heaven we stand alone.
Zerah. Of heaven !
Ador. Our brother hosts are gone —
Zerah. Are gone before.
Ador. And the golden harps the angels
  bore
 To help the songs of their desire,
 Still burning from their hands of fire,
 Lie without touch or tone
  Upon the glass-sea shore.   9

Zerah. Silent upon the glass-sea shore !
Ador. There the Shadow from the
  throne
 Formless with infinity
 Hovers o'er the crystal sea
  Awfuller than light derived,
 And red with those primæval heats
  Whereby all life has lived.
Zerah. Our visible God, our heavenly
  seats !
Ador. Beneath us sinks the pomp angel-
  ical,
Cherub and seraph, powers and virtues,
  all, —
 The roar of whose descent has died 20
To a still sound, as thunder into rain.
 Immeasurable space spreads magnified
With that thick life, along the plane
The worlds slid out on. What a fall
And eddy of wings innumerous, crossed
By trailing curls that have not lost
The glitter of the God-smile shed
On every prostrate angel's head !
What gleaming up of hands that fling
 Their homage in retorted rays, 30
From high instinct of worshipping,
 And habitude of praise !

Zerah. Rapidly they drop below us:
   Pointed palm and wing and hair
     Indistinguishable show us
   Only pulses in the air
   Throbbing with a fiery beat,
   As if a new creation heard
   Some divine and plastic word,   39
   And trembling at its new-found being,
     Awakened at our feet.
Ador. Zerah, do not wait for seeing !
   His voice, his, that thrills us so
   As we our harpstrings, uttered *Go,*
   Behold the Holy in his woe !
   And all are gone, save thee and —
Zerah.   Thee !
Ador. I stood the nearest to the throne
   In hierarchical degree,
   What time the Voice said *Go !*
   And whether I was moved alone   50
   By the storm-pathos of the tone
Which swept through heaven the alien
     name of *woe,*
   Or whether the subtle glory broke
   Through my strong and shielding
     wings,
   Bearing to my finite essence
   Incapacious of their presence,
     Infinite imaginings
None knoweth save the Throned who
     spoke;
   But I who at creation stood upright
   And heard the God-breath move   60
Shaping the words that lightened, ' Be
     there light,'
   Nor trembled but with love,
   Now fell down shudderingly,
My face upon the pavement whence I had
     towered,
As if in mine immortal overpowered
     By God's eternity.
Zerah. Let me wait ! — let me wait ! —
Ador. Nay, gaze not backward through
   the gate !
God fills our heaven with God's own soli-
     tude
   Till all the pavements glow: 70
His Godhead being no more subdued,
   By itself, to glories low
     Which seraphs can sustain.
   What if thou, in gazing so,
   Shouldst behold but only one
   Attribute, the veil undone —
Even that to which we dare to press
Nearest, for its gentleness —
     Ay, his love !

How the deep ecstatic pain   80
   Thy being's strength would capture !
Without language for the rapture,
Without music strong to come
   And set the adoration free,
   For ever, ever, wouldst thou be
Amid the general chorus dumb,
God-stricken to seraphic agony.
   Or, brother, what if on thine eyes
   In vision bare should rise
The life-fount whence his hand did
   gather   90
     With solitary force
     Our immortalities !
Straightway how thine own would wither,
   Falter like a human breath,
   And shrink into a point like death,
     By gazing on its source ! —
   My words have imaged dread.
   Meekly hast thou bent thine head,
   And dropt thy wings in languishment:
   Overclouding foot and face,   100
   As if God's throne were eminent
     Before thee, in the place.
     Yet not — not so,
O loving spirit and meek, dost thou fulfil
     The supreme Will.
Not for obeisance but obedience,
Give motion to thy wings ! Depart from
   hence !
     The voice said ' Go !'
Zerah. Belovèd, I depart,
His will is as a spirit within my spirit,   110
A portion of the being I inherit.
His will is mine obedience. I resemble
A flame all undefilèd though it tremble;
I go and tremble. Love me, O beloved !
   O thou, who stronger art,
And standest ever near the Infinite,
     Pale with the light of Light,
Love me, belovèd ! me, more newly made,
     More feeble, more afraid;
And let me hear with mine thy pinions
   moved,   120
As close and gentle as the loving are,
That love being near, heaven may not seem
   so far.
Ador. I am near thee and I love thee.
   Were I loveless, from thee gone,
   Love is round, beneath, above thee,
   God, the omnipresent one.
   Spread the wing and lift the brow
   Well-beloved, what fearest thou ?
Zerah. I fear, I fear —
Ador.   What fear ?

Zerah.   The fear of earth.
Ador.   Of earth, the God-created and
    God-praised   130
  In the hour of birth ?
Where every night the moon in light
Doth lead the waters silver-faced ?
Where every day the sun doth lay
A rapture to the heart of all
The leafy and reeded pastoral,
As if the joyous shout which burst
From angel lips to see him first,
  Had left a silent echo in his ray ?
Zerah. Of earth — the God-created and
    God-curst,   140
    Where man is, and the thorn
    Where sun and moon have borne
  No light to souls forlorn:
Where Eden's tree of life no more uprears
  Its spiral leaves and fruitage, but instead
  The yew-tree bows its melancholy head
And all the undergrasses kills and seres.
Ador. Of earth the weak,
    Made and unmade ?
Where men, that faint, do strive for crowns
  that fade ?   150
Where, having won the profit which they
  seek,
They lie beside the sceptre and the gold
With fleshless hands that cannot wield or
  hold,
And the stars shine in their unwinking
  eyes ?
Zerah. Of earth the bold,
  Where the blind matter wrings
  An awful potence out of impotence,
  Bowing the spiritual things
    To the things of sense.
  Where the human will replies   160
    With ay and no,
Because the human pulse is quick or slow.
  Where Love succumbs to Change,
With only his own memories, for revenge.
And the fearful mystery —
  Ador.   Called Death ?
  Zerah. Nay, death is fearful, — but who
    saith
' To die,' is comprehensible.
What's fearfuller, thou knowest well,
Though the utterance be not for thee,
Lest it blanch thy lips from glory — 170
Ay ! the cursèd thing that moved
A shadow of ill, long time ago,
Across our heaven's own shining floor,
And when it vanished, some who were
On thrones of holy empire there,

Did reign — were seen — were — never
  more.
  Come nearer, O beloved !
Ador. I am near thee. Didst thou bear
  thee
  Ever to this earth ?
Zerah.   Before.
When thrilling from his hand along
  Its lustrous path with spheric song 181
The earth was deathless, sorrowless.
Unfearing, then, pure feet might press
The grasses brightening with their
  feet,
For God's own voice did mix its sound
In a solemn confluence oft
With the rivers' flowing round,
And the life-tree's waving soft.
Beautiful new earth and strange !
Ador. Hast thou seen it since — the
  change ?   190
Zerah. Nay, or wherefore should I fear
    To look upon it now ?
I have beheld the ruined things
Only in depicturings
Of angels from an earthly mission, —
Strong one, even upon thy brow,
When, with task completed, given
Back to us in that transition,
I have beheld thee silent stand,
Abstracted in the seraph band,   200
  Without a smile in heaven.
Ador. Then thou wast not one of those
Whom the loving Father chose
In visionary pomp to sweep
O'er Judæa's grassy places,
O'er the shepherds and the sheep,
Though thou art so tender ? — dim-
  ming
All the stars except one star
With their brighter kinder faces,
And using heaven's own tune in hymn-
  ing,   210
While deep response from earth's own
  mountains ran,
' Peace upon earth, goodwill to man.'
  Zerah. 'Glory to God.' I said amen
    afar.
And those who from that earthly mission
  are,
Within mine ears have told
That the seven everlasting Spirits did hold
With such a sweet and prodigal constraint
The meaning yet the mystery of the song
What time they sang it, on their natures
  strong,

That, gazing down on earth's dark stead-
    fastness   220.
And speaking the new peace in promises,
The love and pity made their voices faint
Into the low and tender music, keeping
The place in heaven of what on earth is
    weeping.
    Ador. ' Peace upon earth.' Come down
    to it.
    Zerah.   Ah me !
I hear thereof uncomprehendingly.
Peace where the tempest, where the sighing
    is,
And worship of the idol, 'stead of his ?
    Ador. Yea, peace, where He is.
    Zerah.   He !
Say it again.
    Ador.   Where He is.
    Zerah.   Can it be 230
That earth retains a tree
Whose leaves, like Eden foliage, can be
    swayed
By the breathing of his voice, nor shrink
    and fade ?
    Ador. There is a tree ! — it hath no leaf
    nor root;
Upon it hangs a curse for all its fruit:
    Its shadow on his head is laid.
      For he, the crownèd Son,
    Has left his crown and throne,
    Walks earth in Adam's clay,
    Eve's snake to bruise and slay —   240
    Zerah. Walks earth in clay ?
    Ador. And walking in the clay which he
    created,
    He through it shall touch death.
What do I utter ? what conceive ? did
    breath
Of demon howl it in a blasphemy ?
Or was it mine own voice, informed, dilated
By the seven confluent Spirits ? — Speak —
    answer me !
Who said man's victim was his deity ?
    Zerah. Beloved, beloved, the word came
    forth from thee.   249
Thine eyes are rolling a tempestuous light
    Above, below, around,
As putting thunder-questions without cloud,
    Reverberate without sound,
To universal nature's depth and height.
The tremor of an inexpressive thought
Too self-amazed to shape itself aloud,
O'erruns the awful curving of thy lips;
    And while thine hands are stretched
    above,

    As newly they had caught
Some lightning from the Throne, or showed
    the Lord   260
    Some retributive sword,
Thy brows do alternate with wild eclipse
    And radiance, with contrasted wrath and
    love,
As God had called thee to a seraph's part,
    With a man's quailing heart.
    Ador. O heart — O heart of man !
      O ta'en from human clay
    To be no seraph's but Jehovah's own !
      Made holy in the taking,
      And yet unseparate   270
From death's perpetual ban,
And human feelings sad and passionate:
Still subject to the treacherous forsak-
    ing
Of other hearts, and its own steadfast pain.
O heart of man — of God ! which God has
    ta'en
From out the dust, with its humanity
Mournful and weak yet innocent around
    it,
And bade its many pulses beating lie
Beside that incommunicable stir
Of Deity wherewith He interwound it.   280
O man ! and is thy nature so defiled
That all that holy Heart's devout law-keep-
    ing,
And low pathetic beat in deserts wild,
And gushings pitiful of tender weeping
For traitors who consigned it to such
    woe —
That all could cleanse thee not, without
    the flow
Of blood, the life - blood — *his* — and
    streaming *so ?*
O earth the thundercleft, windshaken,
    where
The louder voice of ' blood and blood '
    doth rise,
Hast thou an altar for this sacrifice ?   290
    O heaven ! O vacant throne !
O crownèd hierarchies that wear **your**
    crown
    When his is put away !
Are ye unshamèd that ye cannot dim
Your alien brightness to be liker him,
Assume a human passion, and down-lay
Your sweet secureness for congenial fears,
And teach your cloudless ever-burning eyes
    The mystery of his tears ?
    Zerah. I am strong, I am strong.   300
Were I never to see my heaven again,

I would wheel to earth like the tempest
    rain
Which sweeps there with an exultant sound
To lose its life as it reaches the ground.
I am strong, I am strong.
Away from mine inward vision swim
The shining seats of my heavenly birth,
I see but his, I see but Him —
The Maker's steps on his cruel earth.   309
Will the bitter herbs of earth grow sweet
To me, as trodden by his feet ?
Will the vexed, accurst humanity,
As worn by Him, begin to be
A blessèd, yea, a sacred thing
For love and awe and ministering ?
    I am strong, I am strong.
By our angel ken shall we survey
His loving smile through his woeful clay ?
    I am swift, I am strong,
The love is bearing me along.   320
  Ador. One love is bearing us along.

PART THE SECOND

Mid-air, above Judœa. ADOR *and* ZERAH
are a little apart from the visible Angelic
Hosts.

Ador. Belovèd ! dost thou see ? —
Zerah.   Thee, — thee.
  Thy burning eyes already are
  Grown wild and mournful as a star
  Whose occupation is for aye
  To look upon the place of clay
    Whereon thou lookest now.
  The crown is fainting on thy brow
  To the likeness of a cloud,   330
  The forehead's self a little bowed
  From its aspect high and holy,
  As it would in meekness meet
  Some seraphic melancholy:
  Thy very wings that lately flung
  An outline clear, do flicker here
  And wear to each a shadow hung,
    Dropped across thy feet.
  In these strange contrasting glooms
  Stagnant with the scent of tombs,   340
  Seraph faces, O my brother,
  Show awfully to one another.
Ador. Dost thou see ?
Zerah.   Even so; I see
  Our empyreal company,
  Alone the memory of their brightness
  Left in them, as in thee.

The circle upon circle, tier on tier,
  Piling earth's hemisphere
  With heavenly infiniteness,
  Above us and around,   350
Straining the whole horizon like a bow:
Their songful lips divorcèd from all sound,
A darkness gliding down their silvery
    glances, —
Bowing their steadfast solemn countenances
As if they heard God speak, and could not
    glow.
  Ador. Look downward ! dost thou see ?
  Zerah. And wouldst thou press *that*
    vision on my words ?
    Doth not earth speak enough
    Of change and of undoing,
Without a seraph's witness ? Oceans rough
With tempest, pastoral swards   361
Displaced by fiery deserts, mountains ru-
    ing
The bolt fallen yesterday,
That shake their piny heads, as who would
    say
' We are too beautiful for our decay ' —
Shall seraphs speak of these things ? Let
    alone
    Earth to her earthly moan !
Voice of all things. Is there no moan but
    hers ?
  Ador. Hearest thou the attestation
    Of the rousèd universe   370
    Like a desert-lion shaking
    Dews of silence from its mane ?
    With an irrepressive passion
      Uprising at once,
    Rising up and forsaking
    Its solemn state in the circle of suns,
      To attest the pain
    Of him who stands (O patience sweet!)
    In his own hand-prints of creation,
      With human feet ?   380
Voice of all things. Is there no moan but
    ours ?
Zerah. Forms, Spaces, Motions wide,
  O meek, insensate things,
O congregated matters ! who inherit,
    Instead of vital powers,
    Impulsions God-supplied;
    Instead of influent spirit,
    A clear informing beauty;
    Instead of creature-duty,
    Submission calm as rest.   390
    Lights, without feet or wings,
    In golden courses sliding !

Glooms, stagnantly subsiding,
Whose lustrous heart away was prest
Into the argent stars !
Ye crystal firmamental bars
That hold the skyey waters free
From tide or tempest's ecstasy !
Airs universal ! thunders lorn   399
That wait your lightnings in cloud-cave
Hewn out by the winds ! O brave
And subtle elements ! the Holy
Hath charged me by your voice with
    folly.[1]
Enough, the mystic arrow leaves its wound.
Return ye to your silences inborn,
Or to your inarticulated sound !
Ador. Zerah !
Zerah. Wilt *thou* rebuke ?
God hath rebuked me, brother. I am
    weak.
Ador. Zerah, my brother Zerah ! could
    I speak   409
Of thee, 't would be of love to thee.
Zerah.   Thy look
Is fixed on earth, as mine upon thy face.
Where shall I seek his ?
                         I have thrown
    One look upon earth, but one,
    Over the blue mountain-lines,
    Over the forests of palms and pines,
    Over the harvest-lands golden,
    Over the valleys that fold in
    The gardens and vines —
        He is not there.
    All these are unworthy   420
    Those footsteps to bear,
    Before which, bowing down
I would fain quench the stars of my crown
    In the dark of the earthy.
    Where shall I seek Him ?
                         No reply ?
Hath language left thy lips, to place
Its vocal in thine eye ?
    Ador, Ador ! are we come
To a double portent, that
Dumb matter grows articulate   430
    And songful seraphs dumb ?
    Ador, Ador !
Ador.   I constrain
    The passion of my silence. None
    Of those places gazed upon
    Are gloomy enow to fit his pain.
    Unto Him, whose forming word
    Gave to Nature flower and sward,

[1] 'His angels he charged with folly.' — *Job* iv. 18.

She hath given back again,
    For the myrtle — the thorn,
For the sylvan calm — the human scorn. 440
Still, still, reluctant seraph, gaze beneath !
There is a city —
Zerah.   Temple and tower,
Palace and purple would droop like a
    flower,
        (Or a cloud at our breath)
        If He neared in his state
        The outermost gate.
Ador.   Ah me, not so
In the state of a king did the victim go !
And THOU who hangest mute of speech
    'Twixt heaven and earth, with forehead
        yet
    Stainèd by the bloody sweat,   450
God ! man ! Thou hast forgone thy throne
    in each.
Zerah. Thine eyes behold Him ?
Ador.   Yea, below.
    Track the gazing of mine eyes,
    Naming God within thine heart
    That its weakness may depart
        And the vision rise !
    Seest thou yet, beloved ?
Zerah.   I see
Beyond the city, crosses three
And mortals three that hang thereon
'Ghast and silent to the sun.   460
Round them blacken and welter and press
Staring multitudes whose father
Adam was, whose brows are dark
With his Cain's corroded mark, —
Who curse with looks. Nay — let me
    rather
Turn unto the wilderness !
Ador. Turn not ! God dwells with men.
Zerah.   Above
He dwells with angels, and they love.
Can these love ? With the living's pride
They stare at those who die, who hang 470
In their sight and die. They bear the
    streak
Of the crosses' shadow, black not wide,
To fall on their heads, as it swerves aside
        When the victims' pang
        Makes the dry wood creak.
Ador. The cross — the cross !
Zerah.   A woman kneels
        The mid cross under,
        With white lips asunder,
        And motion on each.
        They throb, as she feels,   480

With a spasm, not a speech;
And her lids, close as sleep,
Are less calm, for the eyes
Have made room there to weep
Drop on drop —

Ador.   Weep ? Weep blood,
All women, all men !
He sweated it, He,
For your pale womanhood
And base manhood. Agree
That these water-tears, then,   490
Are vain, mocking like laughter:
Weep blood ! Shall the flood
Of salt curses, whose foam is the darkness,
     on roll
Forward, on from the strand of the storm
     beaten round,
And back from the rocks of the horrid
     hereafter,
And up, in a coil, from the present's wrath-
     spring,
Yea, down from the windows of heaven
     opening,
Deep calling to deep as they meet on his
     soul —
     And men weep only tears ?
Zerah. Little drops in the lapse !   500
     And yet, Ador, perhaps
     It is all that they can.
     Tears ! the lovingest man
     Has no better bestowed
     Upon man.
Ador.   Nor on God.
Zerah.   Do all-givers need gifts ?
If the Giver said 'Give,' the first motion
     would slay
Our Immortals, the echo would ruin away
The same worlds which he made. Why,
     what angel uplifts
     Such a music, so clear,
     It may seem in God's ear   510
Worth more than a woman's hoarse weep-
     ing ? And thus,
Pity tender as tears, I above thee would
     speak,
Thou woman that weepest ! weep un-
     scorned of us !
I, the tearless and pure, am but loving
     and weak.
Ador. Speak low, my brother, low, —
     and not of love
Or human or angelic ! Rather stand
Before the throne of that Supreme above,
In whose infinitude the secrecies

Of thine own being lie hid, and lift thine
     hand
Exultant, saying, 'Lord God, I am wise !' 520
Than utter *here*, 'I love.'
Zerah.   And yet thine eyes
Do utter it. They melt in tender light,
The tears of heaven.
Ador.   Of heaven. Ah me !
Zerah. Ador !
Ador.   Say on !
Zerah.   The crucified are three.
Beloved, they are unlike.
Ador.   Unlike.
Zerah.   For one
Is as a man who has sinned and still
     Doth wear the wicked will,
     The hard malign life-energy,
Tossed outward, in the parting soul's dis-
     dain,
On brow and lip that cannot change again.
Ador. And one —
Zerah.   Has also sinned. 531
And yet (O marvel !) doth the Spirit-wind
Blow white those waters ? Death upon
     his face
     Is rather shine than shade,
A tender shine by looks belovèd made:
He seemeth dying in a quiet place,
And less by iron wounds in hands and feet
Than heart-broke by new joy too sudden
     and sweet.
Ador. And ONE ! —
Zerah.   And ONE ! —
Ador.   Why dost thou pause ?
Zerah.   God ! God !
Spirit of my spirit ! who movest   540
Through seraph veins in burning deity
To light the quenchless pulses ! —
Ador.   But hast trod
The depths of love in thy peculiar nature,
And not in any thou hast made and lovest
In narrow seraph hearts ! —
Zerah.   Above, Creator !
Within, Upholder !
Ador.   And below, below,
The creature's and the upholden's sacri-
     fice !
Zerah. Why do I pause ? —
Ador.   There is a silentness
     That answers thee enow,
     That, like a brazen sound   550
Excluding others, doth ensheathe us
     round, —
Hear it. It is not from the visible skies

Though they are still,
Unconscious that their own dropped dews express
The light of heaven on every earthly hill.
It is not from the hills, though calm and bare
          They, since their first creation,
Through midnight cloud or morning's glittering air
Or the deep deluge blindness, toward the place
Whence thrilled the mystic word's creative grace,   560
          And whence again shall come
          The word that uncreates,
Have lift their brows in voiceless expectation.
It is not from the places that entomb
Man's dead, though common Silence there dilates
Her soul to grand proportions, worthily
          To fill life's vacant room.
          Not there: not there.
Not yet within those chambers lieth He,
A dead one in his living world; his south   570
And west winds blowing over earth and sea,
And not a breath on that creating mouth.
          But now, — a silence keeps
          (Not death's, nor sleep's)
          The lips whose whispered word
Might roll the thunders round reverbérated.
          Silent art thou, O my Lord,
          Bowing down thy stricken head !
          Fearest thou, a groan of thine
Would make the pulse of thy creation fail   580
As thine own pulse ? — would rend the veil
Of visible things and let the flood
Of the unseen Light, the essential God,
Rush in to whelm the undivine ?
Thy silence, to my thinking, is as dread.
          Zerah. O silence !
          Ador. Doth it say to thee — the NAME,
Slow-learning seraph ?
          Zerah.   I have learnt.
          Ador.   The flame
Perishes in thine eyes.
          Zerah.   He opened his,
And looked. I cannot bear —
          Ador.   Their agony ?
          Zerah. Their love. God's depth is in
          them. From his brows   590

White, terrible in meekness, didst thou see
          The lifted eyes unclose ?
He is God, seraph ! Look no more on me,
O God — I am not God.
          Ador.   The loving is
Sublimed within them by the sorrowful.
In heaven we could sustain them.
          Zerah.   Heaven is dull,
Mine Ador, to man's earth. The light that burns
          In fluent, refluent motion
          Along the crystal ocean;
The springing of the golden harps between   600
The bowery wings, in fountains of sweet sound,
The winding, wandering music that returns
Upon itself, exultingly self-bound
          In the great spheric round
          Of everlasting praises;
The God-thoughts in our midst that intervene,
Visibly flashing from the súpreme throne
          Full in seraphic faces
Till each astonishes the other, grown
More beautiful with worship and delight —   610
My heaven ! my home of heaven ! my infinite
Heaven-choirs ! what are ye to this dust and death,
This cloud, this cold, these tears, this failing breath,
Where God's immortal love now issueth
          In this MAN's woe ?
          Ador. His eyes are very deep yet calm.
          Zerah.   No more
On me, Jehovah-man —
          Ador.   Calm-deep. They show
A passion which is tranquil. They are seeing
No earth, no heaven, no men that slay and curse,
          No seraphs that adore;   620
Their gaze is on the invisible, the dread,
The things we cannot view or think or speak,
Because we are too happy, or too weak, —
The sea of ill, for which the universe,
With all its pilèd space, can find no shore,
With all its life, no living foot to tread.
But he, accomplished in Jehovah-being,
          Sustains the gaze adown,
          Conceives the vast despair,

And feels the billowy griefs come up to
    drown,   630
Nor fears, nor faints, nor fails, till all be
    finished.
    Zerah. Thus, do I find thee thus? My
    undiminished
And undiminishable God!— my God!
The echoes are still tremulous along
The heavenly mountains, of the latest
    song
Thy manifested glory swept abroad
In rushing past our lips: they echo aye
    'Creator, thou art strong!
Creator, thou art blessèd over all.'
By what new utterance shall I now re-
    call,   640
Unteaching the heaven-echoes? Dare I
    say,
'Creator, thou art feebler than thy work!
Creator, thou art sadder than thy crea-
    ture!
    A worm, and not a man,
    Yea, no worm, but a curse?'
I dare not so mine heavenly phrase re-
    verse.
Albeit the piercing thorn and thistle-fork
    (Whose seed disordered ran
From Eve's hand trembling when the curse
    did reach her)
Be garnered darklier in thy soul, the
    rod   650
That smites thee never blossoming, and
    thou
Grief-bearer for thy world, with unkinged
    brow—
I leave to men their song of Ichabod:
I have an angel-tongue — I know but
    praise.
    Ador. Hereafter shall the blood-bought
    captives raise
The passion-song of blood.
    Zerah.   And *we*, extend
Our holy vacant hands towards the Throne,
Crying 'We have no music.'
    Ador.   Rather, blend
    Both musics into one.
The sanctities and sanctified above   660
Shall each to each, with lifted looks serene,
    Their shining faces lean,
    And mix the adoring breath
And breathe the full thanksgiving.
    Zerah.   But the love —
The love, mine Ador!
    Ador.   Do we love not?
    Zerah.   Yea,

But not as man shall! not with life for
    death,
New-throbbing through the startled being;
    not
With strange astonished smiles, that ever
    may
Gush passionate like tears and fill their
    place:
Nor yet with speechless memories of
    what   670
Earth's winters were, enverduring the green
    Of every heavenly palm
    Whose windless, shadeless calm
Moves only at the breath of the Unseen.
Oh, not with this blood on us — and this
    face, —
Still, haply, pale with sorrow that it bore
In our behalf, and tender evermore
With nature all our own, upon us gazing —
Nor yet with these forgiving hands up-
    raising
Their unreproachful wounds, alone to
    bless!   680
Alas, Creator! shall we love thee less
Than mortals shall?
    Ador.   Amen! so let it be.
We love in our proportion, to the bound
Thine infinite our finite set around,
And that is finitely, — thou, infinite
And worthy infinite love! And our delight
Is, watching the dear love poured out to
    thee
From ever fuller chalice. Blessèd they,
Who love thee more than we do: blessèd
    we,
Viewing that love which shall exceed even
    this,   690
And winning in the sight a double bliss
For all so lost in love's supremacy.
The bliss is better. Only on the sad
    Cold earth there are who say
It seemeth better to be great than glad.
The bliss is better. Love him more, O
    man,
    Than sinless seraphs can!
    Zerah. Yea, love him more!
    Voices of the Angelic Multitude. Yea,
    more!
    Ador.   The loving word
Is caught by those from whom we stand
    apart.   700
For silence hath no deepness in her heart
Where love's low name low breathed would
    not be heard
By angels, clear as thunder.

Angelic Voices.   Love him more !
Ador. Sweet voices, swooning o'er
     The music which ye make !
Albeit to love there were not ever given
A mournful sound when uttered out of
     heaven,
That angel-sadness ye would fitly take.
Of love be silent now ! we gaze adown
Upon the incarnate Love who wears no
     crown.   710
   Zerah. No crown ! the woe instead
     Is heavy on his head,
     Pressing inward on his brain
     With a hot and clinging pain
     Till all tears are prest away,
     And clear and calm his vision may
     Peruse the black abyss.
     No rod, no sceptre is
     Holden in his fingers pale;
     They close instead upon the nail,   720
       Concealing the sharp dole,
     Never stirring to put by
       The fair hair peaked with blood,
     Drooping forward from the rood
     Helplessly, heavily
On the cheek that waxeth colder,
Whiter ever, and the shoulder
Where the government was laid.
His glory made the heavens afraid;
Will he not unearth this cross from its
     hole ?   730
His pity makes his piteous state;
Will he be uncompassionate
     Alone to his proper soul ?
     Yea, will he not lift up
     His lips from the bitter cup,
     His brows from the dreary weight,
     His hand from the clenching cross,
Crying, ' My Father, give to me
Again the joy I had with thee
Or ere this earth was made for loss ? '
     No stir: no sound.   741
The love and woe being interwound
     He cleaveth to the woe;
And putteth forth heaven's strength
     below,
       To bear.
   Ador. And that creates his anguish now,
     Which made his glory there.
   Zerah. Shall it need be so ?
     Awake, thou Earth ! behold.
     Thou, uttered forth of old   750
     In all thy life-emotion,
     In all thy vernal noises,
     In the rollings of thine ocean,

Leaping founts, and rivers running, —
In thy woods' prophetic heaving
Ere the rains a stroke have given,
In thy winds' exultant voices
When they feel the hills anear, —
     In the firmamental sunning,   759
     And the tempest which rejoices
Thy full heart with an awful cheer.
     Thou, uttered forth of old
     And with all thy music rolled
       In a breath abroad
       By the breathing God, —
Awake ! he is here ! behold !
Even *thou* —
         Beseems it good
To thy vacant vision dim,
That the deadly ruin should,
For thy sake, encompass him ?   770
That the Master-word should lie
A mere silence, while his own
     Processive harmony,
The faintest echo of his lightest tone,
Is sweeping in a choral triumph by ?
     Awake ! emit a cry !
And say, albeit used
From Adam's ancient years
To falls of acrid tears,
To frequent sighs unloosed,   780
Caught back to press again
On bosoms zoned with pain —
To corses still and sullen
The shine and music dulling
With closèd eyes and ears
That nothing sweet can enter,
Commoving thee no less
With that forced quietness
Than the earthquake in thy centre —
Thou hast not learnt to bear   790
This new divine despair !
These tears that sink into thee,
These dying eyes that view thee,
This dropping blood from lifted rood,
They darken and undo thee.
Thou canst not presently sustain this
     corse —
Cry, cry, thou hast not force !
Cry, thou wouldst fainer keep
Thy hopeless charnels deep,
Thyself a general tomb   800
Where the first and the second Death
Sit gazing face to face
And mar each other's breath,
While silent bones through all the place
'Neath sun and moon do faintly glisten
     And seem to lie and listen

For the tramp of the coming Doom.
 Is it not meet
That they who erst the Eden fruit did
 eat,
  Should champ the ashes ?   810
That they who wrap them in the thun-
 der-cloud
  Should wear it as a shroud,
  Perishing by its flashes ?
That they who vexed the lion should be
 rent ?
Cry, cry, 'I will sustain my punish-
 ment,
The sin being mine; but take away
 from me
This visioned Dread — this man — this
 Deity !'
 The Earth. I have groaned; I have tra-
 vailed: I am weary.
I am blind with my own grief, and cannot
 see,
As clear-eyed angels can, his agony,   820
And what I see I also can sustain,
Because his power protects me from his
 pain.
I have groaned; I have travailed: I am
 dreary,
Hearkening the thick sobs of my children's
 heart:
  How can I say 'Depart'
To that Atoner making calm and free ?
  Am I a God as he,
To lay down peace and power as willingly ?
 Ador. He looked for some to pity. There
 is none.
All pity is within him and not for him,   830
His earth is iron under him, and o'er him
  His skies are brass.
  His seraphs cry 'Alas !'
With hallelujah voices that cannot weep.
And man, for whom the dreadful work is
 done . . .
Scornful Voices from the Earth. If verily
 this *be* the Eternal's son —
 Ador. Thou hearest. Man is grateful.
 Zerah.   Can I hear
Nor darken into man and cease for ever
 My seraph-smile to wear ?
  Was it for such,   840
  It pleased him to overleap
His glory with his love and sever
From the God-light and the throne
And all angels bowing down,
For whom his every look did touch
New notes of joy on the unworn string

Of an eternal worshipping ?
 For such, he left his heaven ?
There, though never bought by blood
And tears, we gave him gratitude:
We loved him there, though unfor-
 given.   851
 Ador. The light is risen
  Above, around,
And down in lurid fragments flung,
That catch the mountain-peak and
 stream
  With momentary gleam,
Then perish in the water and the
 ground.
  River and waterfall,
  Forest and wilderness,
Mountain and city, are together wrung
Into one shape, and that is shapeless-
 ness;   861
  The darkness stands for all.
 Zerah. The pathos hath the day undone:
  The death-look of his eyes
  Hath overcome the sun
And made it sicken in its narrow skies.
 Ador. Is it to death ? He dieth.
 Zerah.   Through the dark
He still, he only, is discernible —
The naked hands and feet transfixèd stark,
The countenance of patient anguish white,
  Do make themselves a light   871
More dreadful than the glooms which round
 them dwell,
And therein do they shine.
 Ador.   God ! Father-God !
Perpetual Radiance on the radiant throne !
Uplift the lids of inward deity,
  Flashing abroad
  Thy burning Infinite !
Light up this dark where there is nought to
 see
Except the unimagined agony
Upon the sinless forehead of the Son !   880
 Zerah. God, tarry not ! Behold, enow
  Hath he wandered as a stranger,
  Sorrowed as a victim. Thou
  Appear for him, O Father !
  Appear for him, Avenger !
Appear for him, just One and holy One,
  For he is holy and just !
At once the darkness and dishonor rather
To the ragged jaws of hungry chaos rake,
  And hurl aback to ancient dust   890
These mortals that make blasphemies
 With their made breath, this earth and
 skies

That only grow a little dim,
Seeing their curse on him.
But him, of all forsaken,
Of creature and of brother,
Never wilt thou forsake!
Thy living and thy loving cannot slacken
Their firm essential hold upon each other,
And well thou dost remember how his part
Was still to lie upon thy breast and be   901
Partaker of the light that dwelt in thee
    Ere sun or seraph shone;
And how while silence trembled round the
    throne
Thou countedst by the beatings of his heart
The moments of thine own eternity.
    Awaken,
O right hand with the lightnings!   Again
    gather
His glory to thy glory!   What estranger,
What ill supreme in evil, can be thrust   910
Between the faithful Father and the Son?
    Appear for him, O Father!
    Appear for him, Avenger!
Appear for him, just One and holy One,
    For he is holy and just!
    Ador. Thy face upturned toward the
    throne is dark;
Thou hast no answer, Zerah.
    Zerah.   No reply,
O unforsaking Father?
    Ador.   Hark!
    Instead of downward voice, a cry
    Is uttered from beneath.   920
    Zerah. And by a sharper sound than
    death,
    Mine immortality is riven.
The heavy darkness which doth tent the
    sky
Floats backward as by a sudden wind:
    But I see no light behind,
    But I feel the farthest stars are all
    Stricken and shaken,
And I know a shadow sad and broad
    Doth fall — doth fall
On our vacant thrones in heaven.   930
    Voice from the Cross. MY GOD, MY GOD,
WHY HAST THOU ME FORSAKEN?
    The Earth. Ah me, ah me, ah me! the
    dreadful Why!
My sin is on thee, sinless one!   Thou art
God-orphaned, for my burden on thy head.
Dark sin, white innocence, endurance
    dread!
Be still, within your shrouds, my buried
    dead;

Nor work with this quick horror round
    mine heart.
    Zerah. He hath forsaken *him.*   I perish.
    Ador.   Hold
Upon his name!   we perish not.   Of old 940
His will —
    Zerah. I seek his will.   Seek, seraphim!
My God, my God!   where is it?   Doth that
    curse
Reverberate spare us, seraph or universe?
    He hath forsaken *him.*
    Ador. He cannot fail.
    Angel Voices. We faint, we droop,
    Our love doth tremble like fear.
    Voices of Fallen Angels from the Earth.
    Do we prevail?
Or are we lost?   Hath not the ill we did
    Been heretofore our good?   950
Is it not ill that one, all sinless, should
Hang heavy with all curses on a cross?
Nathless, that cry!   With huddled faces
    hid
Within the empty graves which men did
    scoop
To hold more damnèd dead, we shudder
    through
    What shall exalt us or undo,
    Our triumph, or our loss.
    Voice from the Cross. IT IS FINISHED.
    Zerah.   Hark, again!
    Like a victor speaks the slain.
    Angel Voices. Finished be the trembling
    vain!   960
    Ador. Upward, like a well-loved son,
    Looketh he, the orphaned one.
    Angel Voices. Finished is the mystic
    pain.
    Voices of Fallen Angels. His deathly
    forehead at the word,
    Gleameth like a seraph sword.
    Angel Voices. Finished is the demon
    reign.
    Ador. His breath, as living God, creat-
    eth,
    His breath, as dying man, completeth.
    Angel Voices. Finished work his hands
    sustain.   969
    The Earth. In mine ancient sepulchres
    Where my kings and prophets freeze,
    Adam dead four thousand years,
    Unwakened by the universe's
    Everlasting moan,
    Aye his ghastly silence mocking —
    Unwakened by his children's knocking
    At his old sepulchral stone,

'Adam, Adam, all this curse is
  Thine and on us yet ! " —
Unwakened by the ceaseless tears   980
Wherewith they made his cerement
    wet,
'Adam, must thy curse remain?' —
Starts with sudden life and hears
Through the slow dripping of the caverned
    eaves, —
Angel Voices. Finished is his bane.
Voice from the Cross. FATHER ! MY
  SPIRIT TO THINE HANDS IS GIVEN.
Ador. Hear the wailing winds that be
  By wings of unclean spirits made !
They, in that last look, surveyed
  The love they lost in losing heaven, 990
    And passionately flee
With a desolate cry that cleaves
The natural storms — though *they* are lift-
    ing
God's strong cedar-roots like leaves,
And the earthquake and the thunder,
Neither keeping either under,
Roar and hurtle through the glooms —
And a few pale stars are drifting
Past the dark, to disappear,
What time, from the splitting tombs   1000
Gleamingly the dead arise,
Viewing with their death-calmed eyes
The elemental strategies,
To witness, victory is the Lord's.
Hear the wail o' the spirits ! hear !
  Zerah. I hear alone the memory of his
    words.

EPILOGUE

I

My song is done.
My voice that long hath faltered shall be
    still.
The mystic darkness drops from Calvary's
    hill   1009
Into the common light of this day's sun.

II

I see no more thy cross, O holy Slain !
I hear no more the horror and the coil
    Of the great world's turmoil
Feeling thy countenance *too still*, — nor yell
Of demons sweeping past it to their prison.
The skies that turned to darkness with thy
    pain
Make now a summer's day;

And on my changèd ear that sabbath bell
  Records how CHRIST IS RISEN.

III

And I — ah ! what am I   1020
To counterfeit, with faculty earth-dark-
    ened,
  Seraphic brows of light
And seraph language never used nor
    hearkened ?
Ah me ! what word that seraphs say,
    could come
From mouth so used to sighs, so soon to
    lie
Sighless, because then breathless, in the
    tomb ?

IV

Bright ministers of God and grace — of
    grace
Because of God ! whether ye bow adown
In your own heaven, before the living face
Of him who died and deathless wears the
    crown,   1030
Or whether at this hour ye haply are
Anear, around me, hiding in the night
Of this permitted ignorance your light,
    This feebleness to spare, —
Forgive me, that mine earthly heart
    should dare
Shape images of unincarnate spirits
And lay upon their burning lips a thought
Cold with the weeping which mine earth
    inherits.
And though ye find in such hoarse music,
    wrought
To copy yours, a cadence all the while 1040
Of sin and sorrow — only pitying smile !
    Ye know to pity, well.

V

I too may haply smile another day
At the far recollection of this lay,
When God may call me in your midst to
    dwell,
To hear your most sweet music's miracle
And see your wondrous faces.   May it be !
For his remembered sake, the Slain on
    rood,
Who rolled his earthly garment red in
    blood
(Treading the wine-press) that the weak,
    like me,   1050
Before his heavenly throne should walk in
    white.

THE POET'S VOW

'O be wiser thou,
Instructed that true knowledge leads to love.'
—*Wordsworth.*

First printed in the *New Monthly Maga-zine* October, 1836. The author says in her preface to *The Seraphim and other Poems* that 'The Poet's Vow' 'was written to enforce the truth that the creature cannot be isolated from the creature.'

PART THE FIRST

SHOWING WHEREFORE THE VOW WAS
MADE

I

Eve is a twofold mystery;
　The stillness Earth doth keep,
The motion wherewith human hearts
　Do each to either leap
As if all souls between the poles
　Felt ' Parting comes in sleep.'

II

The rowers lift their oars to view
　Each other in the sea;
The landsmen watch the rocking boats
　In a pleasant company;
While up the hill go gladlier still
　Dear friends by two and three.

III

The peasant's wife hath looked without
　Her cottage door and smiled,
For there the peasant drops his spade
　To clasp his youngest child
Which hath no speech, but its hand can
　reach
　And stroke his forehead mild.

IV

A poet sate that eventide
　Within his hall alone,
As silent as its ancient lords
　In the coffined place of stone,
When the bat hath shrunk from the pray-
　ing monk,
　And the praying monk is gone.

V

Nor wore the dead a stiller face
　Beneath the cerement's roll:
His lips refusing out in words

Their mystic thoughts to dole,
His steadfast eye burnt inwardly,
　As burning out his soul.

VI

You would not think that brow could
　e'er
Ungentle moods express,
Yet seemed it, in this troubled world,
　Too calm for gentleness,
When the very star that shines from far
　Shines trembling ne'ertheless.

VII

It lacked, all need, the softening light
　Which other brows supply:
We should conjoin the scathèd trunks
　Of our humanity,
That each leafless spray entwining may
　Look softer 'gainst the sky.

VIII

None gazed within the poet's face,
　The poet gazed in none;
He threw a lonely shadow straight
　Before the moon and sun,
Affronting nature's heaven-dwelling crea-
　tures
　With wrong to nature done:

IX

Because this poet daringly,
　— The nature at his heart,
And that quick tune along his veins
　He could not change by art, —
Had vowed his blood of brotherhood
　To a stagnant place apart.

X

He did not vow in fear, or wrath,
　Or grief's fantastic whim,
But, weights and shows of sensual things
　Too closely crossing him,
On his soul's eyelid the pressure slid
　And made its vision dim.

XI

And darkening in the dark he strove
　'Twixt earth and sea and sky
To lose in shadow, wave and cloud,
　His brother's haunting cry:
The winds were welcome as they swept,
God's five-day work he would accept,
　But let the rest go by.

XII

He cried, 'O touching, patient Earth
That weepest in thy glee,
Whom God created very good,
And very mournful, we !
Thy voice of moan doth reach his throne,
As Abel's rose from thee.

XIII

'Poor crystal sky with stars astray !
Mad winds that howling go
From east to west ! perplexèd seas
That stagger from their blow !
O motion wild ! O wave defiled !
Our curse hath made you so.

XIV

' We ! and our curse ! do I partake
The desiccating sin ?
Have I the apple at my lips ?
The money-lust within ?
Do I human stand with the wounding
hand,
To the blasting heart akin ?

XV

' Thou solemn pathos of all things
For solemn joy designed !
Behold, submissive to your cause,
A holy wrath I find,
And, for your sake, the bondage break
That knits me to my kind.

XVI

' Hear me forswear man's sympathies,
His pleasant yea and no,
His riot on the piteous earth
Whereon his thistles grow,
His changing love — with stars above,
His pride — with graves below.

XVII

' Hear me forswear his roof by night,
His bread and salt by day,
His talkings at the wood-fire hearth,
His greetings by the way,
His answering looks, his systemed books,
All man, for aye and aye.

XVIII

'That so my purged, once human heart,
From all the human rent,
May gather strength to pledge and drink
Your wine of wonderment,

While you pardon me all blessingly
The woe mine Adam sent.

XIX

' And I shall feel your unseen looks
Innumerous, constant, deep
And soft as haunted Adam once,
Though sadder, round me creep, —
As slumbering men have mystic ken
Of watchers on their sleep.

XX

' And ever, when I lift my brow
At evening to the sun,
No voice of woman or of child
Recording " Day is done " —
Your silences shall a love express,
More deep than such an one.'

PART THE SECOND

SHOWING TO WHOM THE VOW WAS
DECLARED

I

The poet's vow was inly sworn,
The poet's vow was told.
He shared among his crowding friends
The silver and the gold,
They clasping bland his gift, — his hand
In a somewhat slacker hold.

II

They wended forth, the crowding friends,
With farewells smooth and kind.
They wended forth, the solaced friends,
And left but twain behind:
One loved him true as brothers do,
And one was Rosalind.

III

He said, 'My friends have wended forth
With farewells smooth and kind;
Mine oldest friend, my plighted bride,
Ye need not stay behind:
Friend, wed my fair bride for my sake,
And let my lands ancestral make
A dower for Rosalind.

IV

' And when beside your wassail board
Ye bless your social lot,
I charge you that the giver be

In all his gifts forgot,
Or alone of all his words recall
    The last, — Lament me not.'

V

She looked upon him silently
    With her large, doubting eyes,
Like a child that never knew but love
    Whom words of wrath surprise,
Till the rose did break from either cheek
    And the sudden tears did rise.

VI

She looked upon him mournfully,
    While her large eyes were grown
Yet larger with the steady tears,
    Till, all his purpose known,
She turnèd slow, as she would go —
    The tears were shaken down.

VII

She turnèd slow, as she would go,
    Then quickly turned again,
And gazing in his face to seek
    Some little touch of pain,
'I thought,' she said, — but shook her
        head, —
    She tried that speech in vain.

VIII

'I thought — but I am half a child
    And very sage art thou —
The teachings of the heaven and earth
    Should keep us soft and low:
They have drawn *my* tears in early years,
    Or ere I wept — as now.

IX

'But now that in thy face I read
    Their cruel homily,
Before their beauty I would fain
    Untouched, unsoftened be, —
If I indeed could look on even
The senseless, loveless earth and heaven
    As thou canst look on me!

X

'And couldest thou as coldly view
    Thy childhood's far abode,
Where little feet kept time with thine
    Along the dewy sod,
And thy mother's look from holy book
    Rose like a thought of God?

XI

'O brother, — called so, ere her last
    Betrothing words were said!
O fellow-watcher in her room,
    With hushèd voice and tread!
Rememberest thou how, hand in **hand**
O friend, O lover, we did stand,
    And knew that she was dead?

XII

'I will not live Sir Roland's bride,
    That dower I will not hold;
I tread below my feet that go,
    These parchments bought and sold:
The tears I weep are mine to keep,
    And worthier than thy gold.'

XIII

The poet and Sir Roland stood
    Alone, each turned to each,
Till Roland brake the silence left
    By that soft-throbbing speech —
'Poor heart!' he cried, 'it vainly tried
    The distant heart to reach.

XIV

'And thou, O distant, sinful heart
    That climbest up so high
To wrap and blind thee with the snows
    That cause to dream and die,
What blessing can, from lips of man,
    Approach thee with his sigh?

XV

'Ay, what from earth — create for man
    And moaning in his moan?
Ay, what from stars — revealed to man
    And man-named one by one?
Ay, more! what blessing can be given
Where the Spirits seven do show in
        heaven
    A MAN upon the throne?

XVI

'A man on earth HE wandered once,
    All meek and undefiled,
And those who loved Him said 'He
        wept' —
    None ever said He smiled;
Yet there might have been a smile un-
        seen,
When He bowed his holy face, I ween,
    To bless that happy child.

XVII

'And now He pleadeth up in heaven
  For our humanities,
Till the ruddy light on seraphs' wings
  In pale emotion dies.
They can better bear their Godhead's glare
  Than the pathos of his eyes.

XVIII

'I will go pray our God to-day
  To teach thee how to scan
His work divine, for human use
  Since earth on axle ran, —
To teach thee to discern as plain
His grief divine, the blood-drop's stain
  He left there, MAN for man.

XIX

'So, for the blood's sake shed by Him
  Whom angels God declare,
Tears like it, moist and warm with love,
  Thy reverent eyes shall wear
To see i' the face of Adam's race
  The nature God doth share.'

XX

'I heard,' the poet said, 'thy voice
  As dimly as thy breath:
The sound was like the noise of life
  To one anear his death, —
Or of waves that fail to stir the pale
  Sere leaf they roll beneath.

XXI

'And still between the sound and me
  White creatures like a mist
Did interfloat confusedly,
  Mysterious shapes unwist:
Across my heart and across my brow
I felt them droop like wreaths of snow,
  To still the pulse they kist.

XXII

'The castle and its lands are thine —
  The poor's — it shall be done.
Go, man, to love! I go to live
  In Courland hall, alone:
The bats along the ceilings cling,
The lizards in the floors do run,
And storms and years have worn and reft
The stain by human builders left
  In working at the stone.'

PART THE THIRD

SHOWING HOW THE VOW WAS KEPT

I

He dwelt alone, and sun and moon
  Were witness that he made
Rejection of his humanness
  Until they seemed to fade;
His face did so, for he did grow
  Of his own soul afraid.

II

The self-poised God may dwell alone
  With inward glorying,
But God's chief angel waiteth for
  A brother's voice, to sing;
And a lonely creature of sinful nature
  It is an awful thing.

III

An awful thing that feared itself;
  While many years did roll,
A lonely man, a feeble man,
  A part beneath the whole,
He bore by day, he bore by night
That pressure of God's infinite
  Upon his finite soul.

IV

The poet at his lattice sate,
  And downward lookèd he.
Three Christians wended by to prayers,
  With mute ones in their ee;
Each turned above a face of love
  And called him to the far chapèlle
With voice more tuneful than its bell:
  But still they wended three.

V

There journeyed by a bridal pomp,
  A bridegroom and his dame;
He speaketh low for happiness,
  She blusheth red for shame:
But never a tone of benison
  From out the lattice came.

VI

A little child with inward song,
  No louder noise to dare,
Stood near the wall to see at play
  The lizards green and rare —
Unblessed the while for his childish smile
  Which cometh unaware.

PART THE FOURTH

SHOWING HOW ROSALIND FARED BY
THE KEEPING OF THE VOW

I

In death-sheets lieth Rosalind
    As white and still as they;
And the old nurse that watched her bed
    Rose up with ' Well-a-day ! '
And oped the casement to let in
The sun, and that sweet doubtful din
Which droppeth from the grass and bough
Sans wind and bird, none knoweth how —
    To cheer her as she lay.

II

The old nurse started when she saw
    Her sudden look of woe:
But the quick wan tremblings round her
        mouth
    In a meek smile did go,
And calm she said, ' When I am dead,
    Dear nurse, it shall be so.

III

' Till then, shut out those sights and sounds,
    And pray God pardon me
That I without this pain no more
    His blessèd works can see !
And lean beside me, loving nurse,
That thou mayst hear, ere I am worse,
    What thy last love should be.'

IV

The loving nurse leant over her,
    As white she lay beneath;
The old eyes searching, dim with life,
    The young ones dim with death,
To read their look if sound forsook
    The trying, trembling breath.

V

' When all this feeble breath is done,
    And I on bier am laid,
My tresses smoothed for never a feast,
    My body in shroud arrayed,
Uplift each palm in a saintly calm,
    As if that still I prayed.

VI

' And heap beneath mine head the flowers
    You stoop so low to pull,
The little white flowers from the wood

Which grow there in the cool,
Which *he* and I, in childhood's games,
Went plucking, knowing not their names,
    And filled thine apron full.

VII

' Weep not ! *I* weep not.   Death is strong,
    The eyes of Death are dry !
But lay this scroll upon my breast
    When hushed its heavings lie,
And wait awhile for the corpse's smile
    Which shineth presently.

VIII

' And when it shineth, straightway call
    Thy youngest children dear,
And bid them gently carry me
    All barefaced on the bier;
But bid them pass my kirkyard grass
    That waveth long anear.

IX

' And up the bank where I used to sit
    And dream what life would be,
Along the brook with its sunny look
    Akin to living glee, —
O'er the windy hill, through the forest still,
    Let them gently carry me.

X

' And through the piny forest still,
    And down the open moorland
Round where the sea beats mistily
    And blindly on the foreland;
And let them chant that hymn I know,
Bearing me soft, bearing me slow,
    To the ancient hall of Courland.

XI

' And when withal they near the hall,
    In silence let them lay
My bier before the bolted door,
    And leave it for a day:
For I have vowed, though I am proud,
To go there as a guest in shroud,
    And not be turned away.'

XII

The old nurse looked within her eyes
    Whose mutual look was gone;
The old nurse stooped upon her mouth,
    Whose answering voice was done;
And nought she heard, till a little **bird**

Upon the casement's woodbine swinging
Broke out into a loud sweet singing
  For joy o' the summer sun:
' Alack ! alack !' — she watched no more,
  With head on knee she wailèd sore,
And the little bird sang o'er and o'er
  For joy o' the summer sun.

PART THE FIFTH

SHOWING HOW THE VOW WAS BROKEN

I

The poet oped his bolted door
  The midnight sky to view;
A spirit-feel was in the air
  Which seemed to touch his spirit bare
Whenever his breath he drew;
And the stars a liquid softness had,
As alone their holiness forbade
  Their falling with the dew.

II

They shine upon the steadfast hills,
  Upon the swinging tide,
Upon the narrow track of beach
  And the murmuring pebbles pied:
They shine on every lovely place,
They shine upon the corpse's face,
  As it were fair beside.

III

It lay before him, humanlike,
  Yet so unlike a thing !
More awful in its shrouded pomp
  Than any crownèd king:
All calm and cold, as it did hold
  Some secret, glorying.

IV

A heavier weight than of its clay
  Clung to his heart and knee:
As if those folded palms could strike
  He staggered groaningly,
And then o'erhung, without a groan,
The meek close mouth that smiled alone,
  Whose speech the scroll must be.

THE WORDS OF ROSALIND'S SCROLL

' I left thee last, a child at heart,
  A woman scarce in years.

I come to thee, a solemn corpse
  Which neither feels nor fears.
I have no breath to use in sighs;
They laid the dead-weights on mine eyes
  To seal them safe from tears.

' Look on me with thine own calm look:
  I meet it calm as thou.
No look of thine can change *this* smile,
  Or break thy sinful vow :
I tell thee that my poor scorned heart
Is of thine earth — thine earth, a part:
  It cannot vex thee now.

' But out, alas ! these words are writ
  By a living, loving one,
Adown whose cheeks, the proofs of life,
  The warm quick tears do run:
Ah, let the unloving corpse control
Thy scorn back from the loving soul
  Whose place of rest is won.

' I have prayed for thee with bursting sob
  When passion's course was free;
I have prayed for thee with silent lips,
  In the anguish none could see.
They whispered oft, "She sleepeth soft " —
  But I only prayed for thee.

' Go to ! I pray for thee no more:
  The corpse's tongue is still,
Its folded fingers point to heaven,
  But point there stiff and chill:
No farther wrong, no farther woe
Hath license from the sin below
  Its tranquil heart to thrill.

' I charge thee, by the living's prayer,
  And the dead's silentness,
To wring from out thy soul a cry
  Which God shall hear and bless !
Lest Heaven's own palm droop in my hand,
And pale among the saints I stand,
  A saint companionless.'

V

Bow lower down before the throne,
  Triumphant Rosalind !
He boweth on thy corpse his face,
  And weepeth as the blind:
'T was a dread sight to see them so,
For the senseless corpse rocked to and fro
  With the wail of his living mind.

VI

But dreader sight, could such be seen,
  His inward mind did lie,
Whose long-subjected humanness
  Gave out its lion-cry,
And fiercely rent its tenement
  In a mortal agony.

VII

I tell you, friends, had you heard his wail,
  'T would haunt you in court and mart,
And in merry feast until you set
  Your cup down to depart —
That weeping wild of a reckless child
  From a proud man's broken heart.

VIII

O broken heart, O broken vow,
  That wore so proud a feature !
God, grasping as a thunderbolt
  The man's rejected nature,
Smote him therewith i' the presence high
Of his so worshipped earth and sky
That looked on all indifferently —
  A wailing human creature.

IX

A human creature found too weak
  To bear his human pain —
(May Heaven's dear grace have spoken peace
  To his dying heart and brain !)
For when they came at dawn of day
To lift the lady's corpse away,
  Her bier was holding twain.

X

They dug beneath the kirkyard grass,
  For both one dwelling deep;
To which, when years had mossed the stone,
Sir Roland brought his little son
  To watch the funeral heap:
And when the happy boy would rather
  Turn upward his blithe eyes to see
  The wood-doves nodding from the tree,
'Nay, boy, look downward,' said his father,
  'Upon this human dust asleep.
  And hold it in thy constant ken
That God's own unity compresses
  (One into one) the human many,
And that his everlastingness is
  The bond which is not loosed by any:
That thou and I this law must keep,
  If not in love, in sorrow then, —

Though smiling not like other men,
Still, like them we must weep.'

THE ROMAUNT OF MARGRET

' Can my affections find out nothing best,
  But still and still remove ? ' — *Quarles.*

First printed in the *New Monthly Magazine,*
July, 1836. For this poem, as for the preceding, a distinct moral purpose was claimed by
the author, to show, namely, ' that the creature
cannot be *sustained* by the creature.'

I

I PLANT a tree whose leaf
  The yew-tree leaf will suit:
But when its shade is o'er you laid,
  Turn round and pluck the fruit.
Now reach my harp from off the wall
  Where shines the sun aslant;
The sun may shine and we be cold !
O hearken, loving hearts and bold,
  Unto my wild romaunt.
          Margret, Margret.

II

Sitteth the fair ladye
  Close to the river side
Which runneth on with a merry tone
  Her merry thoughts to guide:
It runneth through the trees,
  It runneth by the hill,
Nathless the lady's thoughts have found
  A way more pleasant still.
          Margret, Margret.

III

The night is in her hair
  And giveth shade to shade,
And the pale moonlight on her forehead white
  Like a spirit's hand is laid;
Her lips part with a smile
  Instead of speakings done:
I ween, she thinketh of a voice,
  Albeit uttering none.
          Margret, Margret.

IV

All little birds do sit
  With heads beneath their wings:
Nature doth seem in a mystic dream,
  Absorbed from her living things:

That dream by that ladye
    Is certes unpartook,
For she looketh to the high cold stars
    With a tender human look.
                Margret, Margret.

V

The lady's shadow lies
    Upon the running river;
It lieth no less in its quietness,
    For that which resteth never:
Most like a trusting heart
    Upon a passing faith,
Or as upon the course of life
    The steadfast doom of death.
                Margret, Margret.

VI

The lady doth not move,
    The lady doth not dream,
Yet she seeth her shado no longer laid
    In rest upon the stream:
It shaketh without wind,
    It parteth from the tide,
It standeth upright in the cleft moonlight,
    It sitteth at her side.
                Margret, Margret.

VII

Look in its face, ladye,
    And keep thee from thy swound;
With a spirit bold thy pulses hold
    And hear its voice's sound:
For so will sound thy voice
    When thy face is to the wall,
And such will be thy face, ladye,
    When the maidens work thy pall.
                Margret, Margret.

VIII

' Am I not like to thee ? '
    The voice was calm and low,
And between each word you might have
        heard
    The silent forests grow;
' The like may sway the like; '
    By which mysterious law
Mine eyes from thine and my lips from
        thine
    The light and breath may draw.
                Margret, Margret.

IX

' My lips do need thy breath,
    My lips do need thy smile,

And my pallid eyne, that light in thine
    Which met the stars erewhile:
Yet go with light and life
    If that thou lovest one
In all the earth who loveth thee
    As truly as the sun,
                Margret, Margret.'

X

Her cheek had waxèd white
    Like cloud at fall of snow;
Then like to one at set of sun,
    It waxèd red also;
For love's name maketh bold
    As if the loved were near.
And then she sighed the deep long sigh
    Which cometh after fear.
                Margret, Margret.

XI

' Now, sooth, I fear thee not —
    Shall never fear thee now ! '
(And a noble sight was the sudden light
    Which lit her lifted brow.)
' Can earth be dry of streams,
    Or hearts of love ? ' she said;
' Who doubteth love, can know not love:
    He is already dead.'
                Margret, Margret.

XII

' I have ' . . . and here her lips
    Some word in pause did keep,
And gave the while a quiet smile
    As if they paused in sleep, —
' I have . . . a brother dear,
    A knight of knightly fame !
I broidered him a knightly scarf
    With letters of my name
                Margret, Margret.

XIII

' I fed his gray goshawk,
    I kissed his fierce bloodhound,
I sate at home when he might come
    And caught his horn's far sound:
I sang him hunter's songs,
    I poured him the red wine,
He looked across the cup and said,
    I love thee, sister mine.'
                Margret, Margret

XIV

IT trembled on the grass
    With a low, shadowy laughter;

The sounding river which rolled, for ever
   Stood dumb and stagnant after:
'Brave knight thy brother is !
   But better loveth he
Thy chaliced wine than thy chaunted song,
   And better both than thee,
        Margret, Margret.'

xv

The lady did not heed
   The river's silence while
Her own thoughts still ran at their will,
   And calm was still her smile.
'My little sister wears
   The look our mother wore:
I smooth her locks with a golden comb,
   I bless her evermore.'
        Margret, Margret.

xvi

'I gave her my first bird
   When first my voice it knew;
I made her share my posies rare
   And told her where they grew:
I taught her God's dear name
   With prayer and praise to tell,
She looked from heaven into my face
   And said, *I love thee well.*'
        Margret, Margret.

xvii

IT trembled on the grass
   With a low, shadowy laughter;
You could see each bird as it woke and
     stared
   Through the shrivelled foliage after.
'Fair child thy sister is !
   But better loveth she
Thy golden comb than thy gathered flow-
     ers,
   And better both than thee,
        Margret, Margret.'

xviii

Thy lady did not heed
   The withering on the bough;
Still calm her smile, albeit the while
   A little pale her brow:
'I have a father old,
   The lord of ancient halls;

An hundred friends are in his court
   Yet only me he calls.
        Margret, Margret.

xix

'An hundred knights are in his court
   Yet read I by his knee;
And when forth they go to the tourney
     show
   I rise not up to see:
'T is a weary book to read,
   My tryst 's at set of sun,
But loving and dear beneath the stars
   Is his blessing when I 've done.'
        Margret, Margret.

xx

IT trembled on the grass
   With a low, shadowy laughter;
And moon and stars though bright and far
   Did shrink and darken after.
'High lord thy father is !
   But better loveth he
His ancient halls than his hundred friends,
   His ancient halls, than thee,
        Margret, Margret.'

xxi

The lady did not heed
   That the far stars did fail;
Still calm her smile, albeit the while . . .
   Nay, but she is not pale !
'I have more than a friend
   Across the mountains dim:
No other's voice is soft to me,
   Unless it nameth *him.*'
        Margret, Margret.

xxii

'Though louder beats my heart,
   I know his tread again,
And his fair plume aye, unless turned
     away,
   For the tears do blind me then:
We brake no gold, a sign
   Of stronger faith to be,
But I wear his last look in my soul,
   Which said, *I love but thee !*'
        Margret, Margret.

xxiii

IT trembled on the grass
   With a low, shadowy laughter;

And the wind did toll, as a passing soul
   Were sped by church-bell after;
And shadows, 'stead of light,
   Fell from the stars above,
In flakes of darkness on her face
   Still bright with trusting love.
          Margret, Margret.

XXIV

'He *loved* but only thee !
   That love is transient too.
The wild hawk's bill doth dabble still
   I' the mouth that vowed thee true:
Will he open his dull eyes
   When tears fall on his brow ?
Behold, the death-worm to his heart
   Is a nearer thing than *thou*,
          Margret, Margret.'

XXV

Her face was on the ground —
   None saw the agony;
But the men at sea did that night agree
   They heard a drowning cry:
And when the morning brake,
   Fast rolled the river's tide,
With the green trees waving overhead
   And a white corse laid beside.
          Margret, Margret.

XXVI

A knight's bloodhound and he
   The funeral watch did keep;
With a thought o' the chase he stroked its
   face
   As it howled to see him weep.
A fair child kissed the dead,
   But shrank before its cold.
And alone yet proudly in his hall
   Did stand a baron old.
          Margret, Margret.

XXVII

Hang up my harp again !
   I have no voice for song.
Not song but wail, and mourners pale,
   Not bards, to love belong.
O failing human love !
   O light, by darkness known !
O false, the while thou treadest earth !
   O deaf beneath the stone !
          Margret, Margret.

ISOBEL'S CHILD

   — ' so find we profit,
By losing of our prayers.'
       — *Shakespeare.*

I

To rest the weary nurse has gone:
   An eight-day watch had watchèd she,
Still rocking beneath sun and moon
   The baby on her knee,
Till Isobel its mother said
'The fever waneth — wend to bed,
   For now the watch comes round to me.'

II

Then wearily the nurse did throw
   Her pallet in the darkest place
Of that sick room, and slept and dreamed:
   For, as the gusty wind did blow   11
   The night-lamp's flare across her face,
She saw or seemed to see, but dreamed,
   That the poplars tall on the opposite hill
The seven tall poplars on the hill,
Did clasp the setting sun until
His rays dropped from him, pined and still
   As blossoms in frost,
Till he waned and paled, so weirdly
   crossed,
To the color of moonlight which doth pass
Over the dank ridged churchyard grass. 21
The poplars held the sun, and he
The eyes of the nurse that they should not
   see
— Not for a moment, the babe on her
   knee,
Though she shuddered to feel that it grew
   to be
Too chill, and lay too heavily.

III

She only dreamed; for all the while
   'T was Lady Isobel that kept
   The little baby: and it slept
Fast, warm, as if its mother's smile,   30
Laden with love's dewy weight,
And red as rose of Harpocrate
Dropt upon its eyelids, pressed
Lashes to cheek in a sealèd rest.

IV

And more and more smiled Isobel
To see the baby sleep so well —
She knew not that she smiled.
Against the lattice, dull and wild
Drive the heavy droning drops,

Drop by drop, the sound being one;   40
As momently time's segments fall
On the ear of God, who hears through all
   Eternity's unbroken monotone:
And more and more smiled Isobel
To see the baby sleep so well —
She knew not that she smiled.
The wind in intermission stops
   Down in the beechen forest,
      Then cries aloud
      As one at the sorest,   50
         Self-stung, self-driven,
And rises up to its very tops,
Stiffening erect the branches bowed,
   Dilating with a tempest-soul
The trees that with their dark hands
      break
Through their own outline, and heavy roll
   Shadows as massive as clouds in heaven
      Across the castle lake.
And more and more smiled Isobel
To see the baby sleep so well;   60
She knew not that she smiled;
She knew not that the storm was wild;
Through the uproar drear she could not
      hear
The castle clock which struck anear —
She heard the low, light breathing of her
      child.

V

O sight for wondering look !
While the external nature broke
Into such abandonment,
While the very mist, heart-rent
By the lightning, seemed to eddy   70
Against nature, with a din, —
A sense of silence and of steady
Natural calm appeared to come
From things without, and enter in
The human creature's room.

VI

So motionless she sate,
   The babe asleep upon her knees,
You might have dreamed their souls had
      gone
Away to things inanimate,
In such to live, in such to moan;   80
And that their bodies had ta'en back,
   In mystic change, all silences
That cross the sky in cloudy rack,
Or dwell beneath the reedy ground
In waters safe from their own sound:
      Only she wore

The deepening smile I named before,
And *that* a deepening love expressed;
And who at once can love and rest ?

VII

In sooth the smile that then was keeping 90
Watch upon the baby sleeping,
   Floated with its tender light
Downward, from the drooping eyes,
Upward, from the lips apart,
   Over cheeks which had grown white
With an eight-day weeping:
All smiles come in such a wise
   Where tears shall fall or have of old —
Like northern lights that fill the heart
   Of heaven in sign of cold.   100

VIII

   Motionless she sate.
Her hair had fallen by its weight
On each side of her smile, and lay
Very blackly on the arm
Where the baby nestled warm,
Pale as baby carved in stone
Seen by glimpses of the moon
   Up a dark cathedral aisle:
But, through the storm, no moonbeam fell
Upon the child of Isobel —   110
Perhaps you saw it by the ray
   Alone of her still smile.

IX

A solemn thing it is to me
   To look upon a babe that sleeps
   Wearing in its spirit-deeps
The undeveloped mystery
   Of our Adam's taint and woe,
Which, when they developed be,
   Will not let it slumber so;
Lying new in life beneath   120
The shadow of the coming death,
With that soft, low, quiet breath,
   As if it felt the sun;
Knowing all things by their blooms,
Not their roots, yea, sun and sky
Only by the warmth that comes
Out of each, earth only by
   The pleasant hues that o'er it run,
And human love by drops of sweet
   White nourishment still hanging round
   The little mouth so slumber-bound: 131
All which broken sentiency
And conclusion incomplete,
   Will gather and unite and climb
To an immortality

Good or evil, each sublime,
Through life and death to life again.
O little lids, now folded fast,
Must ye learn to drop at last
Our large and burning tears? 140
O warm quick body, must thou lie,
When the time comes round to die,
Still from all the whirl of years,
Bare of all the joy and pain?
O small frail being, wilt thou stand
At God's right hand,
Lifting up those sleeping eyes
Dilated by great destinies,
To an endless waking? thrones and
seraphim,
Through the long ranks of their solemni-
ties, 150
Sunning thee with calm looks of Heaven's
surprise,
But thine alone on Him?
Or else, self-willed, to tread the Godless
place,
(God keep thy will!) feel thine own energies
Cold, strong, objèctless, like a dead man's
clasp,
The sleepless deathless life within thee
grasp, —
While myriad faces, like one changeless
face,
With woe not love's, shall glass thee every-
where
And overcome thee with thine own despair?

X

More soft, less solemn images 160
Drifted o'er the lady's heart
Silently as snow.
She had seen eight days depart
Hour by hour, on bended knees,
With pale-wrung hands and prayings low
And broken, through which came the sound
Of tears that fell against the ground,
Making sad stops: — 'Dear Lord, dear
Lord!'
She still had prayed, (the heavenly word
Broken by an earthly sigh) 170
— 'Thou who didst not erst deny
The mother-joy to Mary mild,
Blessèd in the blessèd child
Which hearkened in meek babyhood
Her cradle-hymn, albeit used
To all that music interfused
In breasts of angels high and good!
Oh, take not, Lord, my babe away —
Oh, take not to thy songful heaven

The pretty baby thou hast given, 180
Or ere that I have seen him play
Around his father's knees and known
That he knew how my love has gone
From all the world to him.
Think, God among the cherubim,
How I shall shiver every day
In thy June sunshine, knowing where
The grave-grass keeps it from his fair
Still cheeks: and feel, at every tread,
His little body, which is dead 190
And hidden in thy turfy fold,
Doth make thy whole warm earth a-cold!
O God, I am so young, so young —
I am not used to tears at nights
Instead of slumber — not to prayer
With sobbing lips and hands out-wrung!
Thou knowest all my prayings were
'I bless thee, God, for past delights —
Thank God!' I am not used to bear
Hard thoughts of death; the earth doth
cover 200
No face from me of friend or lover:
And must the first who teaches me
The form of shrouds and funerals, be
Mine own first-born belovèd? he
Who taught me first this mother-love?
Dear Lord who spreadest out above
Thy loving, transpierced hands to meet
All lifted hearts with blessing sweet, —
Pierce not my heart, my tender heart
Thou madest tender! Thou who art 210
So happy in thy heaven alway,
Take not mine only bliss away!'

XI

She so had prayed: and God, who hears
Through seraph-songs the sound of tears
From that belovèd babe had ta'en
The fever and the beating pain.
And more and more smiled Isobel
To see the baby sleep so well,
(She knew not that she smiled, I wis)
Until the pleasant gradual thought 220
Which near her heart the smile enwrought,
Now soft and slow, itself did seem
To float along a happy dream,
Beyond it into speech like this.

XII

'I prayed for thee, my little child,
And God has heard my prayer!
And when thy babyhood is gone,
We two together undefiled
By men's repinings, will kneel down

Upon his earth which will be fair   230
(Not covering thee, sweet !) to us twain,
And give Him thankful praise.'

XIII

Dully and wildly drives the rain:
Against the lattices drives the rain.

XIV

' I thank Him now, that I can think
    Of those same future days,
Nor from the harmless image shrink
    Of what I there might see —
Strange babies on their mothers' knee,
Whose innocent soft faces might   240
From off mine eyelids strike the light,
    With looks not meant for me! '

XV

Gustily blows the wind through the rain,
As against the lattices drives the rain.

XVI

' But now, O baby mine, together,
    We turn this hope of ours again
To many an hour of summer weather,
    When we shall sit and intertwine
Our spirits, and instruct each other
    In the pure loves of child and mother!   250
Two human loves make one divine.'

XVII

The thunder tears through the wind and
    the rain,
As full on the lattices drives the rain.

XVIII

' My little child, what wilt thou choose ?
    Now let me look at thee and ponder.
What gladness, from the gladnesses
    Futurity is spreading under
Thy gladsome sight ? Beneath the trees
Wilt thou lean all day, and lose
Thy spirit with the river seen   260
Intermittently between
    The winding beechen alleys, —
Half in labor, half repose,
    Like a shepherd keeping sheep,
Thou, with only thoughts to keep
Which never a bound will overpass,
And which are innocent as those
    That feed among Arcadian valleys
    Upon the dewy grass ? '

XIX

The large white owl that with age is blind,   270
    That hath sate for years in the old tree
        hollow,
Is carried away in a gust of wind;
His wings could bear him not as fast
As he goeth now the lattice past;
    He is borne by the winds, the rains do
        follow
His white wings to the blast outflowing,
    He hooteth in going,
And still, in the lightnings, coldly glitter
    His round unblinking eyes.

XX

' Or, baby, wilt thou think it fitter   280
    To be eloquent and wise,
One upon whose lips the air
    Turns to solemn verities
For men to breathe anew, and win
A deeper-seated life within ?
    Wilt be a philosopher,
    By whose voice the earth and skies
Shall speak to the unborn ?
Or a poet, broadly spreading
    The golden immortalities   290
Of thy soul on natures lorn
    And poor of such, them all to guard
From their decay, — beneath thy treading,
Earth's flowers recovering hues of Eden, —
And stars, drawn downward by thy looks,
To shine ascendant in thy books ? '

XXI

The tame hawk in the castle-yard,
How it screams to the lightning, with its
    wet
Jagged plumes overhanging the parapet !
And at the lady's door the hound   300
Scratches with a crying sound.

XXII

' But, O my babe, thy lids are laid
    Close, fast upon thy cheek,
And not a dream of power and sheen
Can make a passage up between;
Thy heart is of thy mother's made,
    Thy looks are very meek,
And it will be their chosen place
To rest on some belovèd face,
    As these on thine, and let the noise   310
Of the whole world go on nor drown
    The tender silence of thy joys:
Or when that silence shall have grown
    Too tender for itself, the same

Yearning for sound, — to look above
And utter its one meaning, LOVE,
  That *He* may hear his name.'

XXIII

No wind, no rain, no thunder !
The waters had trickled not slowly,
The thunder was not spent   320
Nor the wind near finishing;
Who would have said that the storm was
    diminishing ?
No wind, no rain, no thunder !
Their noises dropped asunder
From the earth and the firmament,
From the towers and the lattices,
    Abrupt and echoless
As ripe fruits on the ground unshaken
    wholly —
    As life in death !
And sudden and solemn the silence fell, 330
Startling the heart of Isobel
As the tempest could not:
Against the door went panting the breath
Of the lady's hound whose cry was still,
  And she, constrained howe'er she would
    not,
Lifted her eyes and saw the moon
Looking out of heaven alone
  Upon the poplared hill, —
  A calm of God, made visible
That men might bless it at their will. 340

XXIV

The moonshine on the baby's face
  Falleth clear and cold:
The mother's looks have fallen back
  To the same place:
Because no moon with silver rack,
Nor broad sunrise in jasper skies
    Has power to hold
    Our loving eyes,
Which still revert, as ever must
Wonder and Hope, to gaze on the dust. 350

XXV

The moonshine on the baby's face
  Cold and clear remaineth;
The mother's looks do shrink away, —
The mother's looks return to stay,
  As charmèd by what paineth:
Is any glamour in the case ?
  Is it dream, or is it sight ?
Hath the change upon the wild

Elements that sign the night,
Passed upon the child ?   360
  It is not dream, but sight.

XXVI

The babe has awakened from sleep
  And unto the gaze of its mother,
Bent over it, lifted another —
  Not the baby-looks that go
Unaimingly to and fro,
But an earnest gazing deep
Such as soul gives soul at length
  When by work and wail of years
It winneth a solemn strength   370
  And mourneth as it wears.
A strong man could not brook,
  With pulse unhurried by fears,
To meet that baby's look
  O'erglazed by manhood's tears,
The tears of a man full grown,
With a power to wring our own,
In the eyes all undefiled
Of a little three-months child —
To see that babe-brow wrought   380
By the witnessing of thought
  To judgment's prodigy,
And the small soft mouth unweaned,
By mother's kiss o'erleaned,
(Putting the sound of loving
Where no sound else was moving
  Except the speechless cry)
Quickened to mind's expression,
Shaped to articulation,
Yea, uttering words, yea, naming woe, 390
  In tones that with it strangely went
  Because so baby-innocent,
As the child spake out to the mother, so: —

XXVII

' O mother, mother, loose thy prayer !
  Christ's name hath made it strong.
It bindeth me, it holdeth me
With its most loving cruelty,
  From floating my new soul along
  The happy heavenly air.
It bindeth me, it holdeth me   400
  In all this dark, upon this dull
Low earth, by only weepers trod.
It bindeth me, it holdeth me !
  Mine angel looketh sorrowful
Upon the face of God.[1]

[1] For I say unto you that in Heaven their angels do
always behold the face of my Father which is in Heaven. — *Matt.* xviii. 10.

XXVIII

'Mother, mother, can I dream
　　Beneath your earthly trees ?
I had a vision and a gleam,
　　I heard a sound more sweet than these
When rippled by the wind:　　　　　410
　　Did you see the Dove with wings
Bathed in golden glisterings
From a sunless light behind,
　　Dropping on me from the sky,
Soft as mother's kiss, until
I seemed to leap and yet was still ?
　　Saw you how his love-large eye
Looked upon me mystic calms,
　　Till the power of his divine
　　Vision was indrawn to mine ?　　420

XXIX

'Oh, the dream within the dream !
　　I saw celestial places even.
Oh, the vistas of high palms
　　Making finites of delight
　　Through the heavenly infinite,
Lifting up their green still tops
　　To the heaven of heaven !
Oh, the sweet life-tree that drops
Shade like light across the river
Glorified in its for-ever　　　　　430
　　Flowing from the Throne !
Oh, the shining holinesses
Of the thousand, thousand faces
　　God-sunned by the thronèd ONE,
And made intense with such a love
That, though I saw them turned above,
　　Each loving seemed for also me !
And, oh, the Unspeakable, the HE,
The manifest in secrecies
　　Yet of mine own heart partaker　　440
With the overcoming look
Of One who hath been once forsook
　　And blesseth the forsaker !
Mother, mother, let me go
Toward the Face that looketh so !
　　Through the mystic wingèd Four
Whose are inward, outward eyes
Dark with light of mysteries
　　And the restless evermore
"Holy, holy, holy," — through　　　450
The sevenfold Lamps that burn in view
　　Of cherubim and seraphim, —
Through the four-and-twenty crowned
Stately elders white around
　　Suffer me to go to Him !

XXX

'Is your wisdom very wise,
　　Mother, on the narrow earth,
　　Very happy, very worth
That I should stay to learn ?
Are these air-corrupting sighs　　460
　　Fashioned by unlearnèd breath ?
Do the students' lamps that burn
　　All night, illumine death ?
Mother, albeit this be so,
Loose thy prayer and let me go
Where that bright chief angel stands
Apart from all his brother bands,
Too glad for smiling, having bent
In angelic wilderment
O'er the depths of God, and brought　　470
Reeling thence one only thought
To fill his own eternity.
He the teacher is for me —
He can teach what I would know —
Mother, mother, let me go !

XXXI

'Can your poet make an Eden
　　No winter will undo,
And light a starry fire while heeding
　　His hearth's is burning too ?
Drown in music the earth's din,　　480
And keep his own wild soul within
　　The law of his own harmony ?
Mother, albeit this be so,
Let me to my heaven go !
　　A little harp me waits thereby,
A harp whose strings are golden all
And tuned to music spherical,
Hanging on the green life-tree
Where no willows ever be.
Shall I miss that harp of mine ?　　490
Mother, no ! — the Eye divine
Turned upon it, makes it shine;
And when I touch it, poems sweet
Like separate souls shall fly from it,
Each to the immortal fytte.
We shall all be poets there,
Gazing on the chiefest Fair.

XXXII

'Love ! earth's love ! and *can* we love
Fixedly where all things move ?
Can the sinning love each other ?　　500
　　Mother, mother,
I tremble in thy close embrace,
I feel thy tears adown my face,
　　Thy prayers do keep me out of bliss —

O dreary earthly love !
Loose thy prayer and let me go
  To the place which loving is
Yet not sad; and when is given
Escape to *thee* from this below,
Thou shalt behold me that I wait   510
For thee beside the happy Gate,
And silence shall be up in heaven
  To hear our greeting kiss.'

XXXIII

The nurse awakes in the morning sun,
  And starts to see beside her bed
  The lady with a grandeur spread
Like pathos o'er her face, as one
God-satisfied and earth-undone;
  The babe upon her arm was dead:
And the nurse could utter forth no cry, —
She was awed by the calm in the mother's
  eye.   521

XXXIV

' Wake, nurse ! ' the lady said;
  ' *We* are waking — he and I —
I, on earth, and he, in sky:
And thou must help me to o'erlay
With garment white this little clay
Which needs no more our lullaby.

XXXV

' I changed the cruel prayer I made,
And bowed my meekened face, and prayed
That God would do his will; and thus   530
He did it, nurse !   He parted us:
And his sun shows victorious
The dead calm face, — and *I* am calm,
And Heaven is hearkening a new psalm.

XXXVI

' This earthly noise is too anear,
Too loud, and will not let me hear
The little harp.   My death will soon
Make silence.'

                  And a sense of tune,
A satisfièd love meanwhile   540
Which nothing earthly could despoil,
Sang on within her soul.

XXXVII

                  Oh you,
Earth's tender and impassioned few,
Take courage to entrust your love
To Him so named who guards above
  Its ends and shall fulfil !

Breaking the narrow prayers that may
Befit your narrow hearts, away
  In His broad, loving will.   550

A ROMANCE OF THE GANGES

First printed in Finden's *Tableaux* for 1838.

I

SEVEN maidens 'neath the midnight
  Stand near the river-sea
Whose water sweepeth white around
  The shadow of the tree;
The moon and earth are face to face,
  And earth is slumbering deep,
The wave-voice seems the voice of dreams
  That wander through her sleep:
        The river floweth on.

II

What bring they 'neath the midnight,   10
  Beside the river-sea ?
They bring the human heart wherein
  No nightly calm can be, —
That droppeth never with the wind,
  Nor drieth with the dew:
Oh, calm in God ! thy calm is broad
  To cover spirits too.
        The river floweth on.

III

The maidens lean them over
  The waters, side by side,   20
And shun each other's deepening eyes,
  And gaze adown the tide;
For each within a little boat
  A little lamp hath put,
And heaped for freight some lily's weight
  Or scarlet rose half shut.
        The river floweth on.

IV

Of shell of cocoa carven
  Each little boat is made;
Each carries a lamp, and carries a flower,
  And carries a hope unsaid;   31
And when the boat hath carried the lamp
  Unquenched till out of sight,
The maiden is sure that love will endure;
  But love will fail with light.
        The river floweth on.

V

Why, all the stars are ready
  To symbolize the soul,
The stars untroubled by the wind,
  Unwearied as they roll;   40
And yet the soul by instinct sad
  Reverts to symbols low —
To that small flame, whose very name
  Breathed o'er it, shakes it so !
          The river floweth on.

VI

Six boats are on the river,
  Seven maidens on the shore,
While still above them steadfastly
  The stars shine evermore.
Go, little boats, go soft and safe,   50
  And guard the symbol spark !
The boats aright go safe and bright
  Across the waters dark.
          The river floweth on.

VII

The maiden Luti watcheth
  Where onwardly they float:
That look in her dilating eyes
  Might seem to drive her boat:
Her eyes still mark the constant fire,
  And kindling unawares   60
That hopeful while, she lets a smile
  Creep silent through her prayers.
          The river floweth on.

VIII

The smile — where hath it wandered ?
  She riseth from her knee,
She holds her dark, wet locks away —
  There is no light to see !
She cries a quick and bitter cry —
  'Nuleeni, launch me thine !
We must have light abroad to-night,   70
  For all the wreck of mine.'
          The river floweth on.

IX

'I do remember watching
  Beside this river-bed,
When on my childish knee was leaned
  My dying father's head;
I turned mine own to keep the tears
  From falling on his face:
What doth it prove when Death and Love
  Choose out the self-same place ? '   80
          The river floweth on.

X

'They say the dead are joyful
  The death-change here receiving:
Who say — ah me ! who dare to say
  Where joy comes to the living ?
Thy boat, Nuleeni ! look not sad —
  Light up the waters rather !
I weep no faithless lover where
  I wept a loving father.'
          The river floweth on.

XI

'My heart foretold his falsehood   91
  Ere my little boat grew dim;
And though I closed mine eyes to dream
  That one last dream of *him*,
They shall not now be wet to see
  The shining vision go:
From earth's cold love I look above
  To the holy house of snow.'
          The river floweth on.

XII

'Come thou — thou never knewest   100
  A grief, that thou shouldst fear one !
Thou wearest still the happy look
  That shines beneath a dear one:
Thy humming-bird is in the sun,
  Thy cuckoo in the grove,
And all the three broad worlds, for thee
  Are full of wandering love.'
          The river floweth on.

XIII

'Why, maiden, dost thou loiter ?
  What secret wouldst thou cover ?   110
That peepul cannot hide thy boat,
  And I can guess thy lover;
I heard thee sob his name in sleep,
  It was a name I knew:
Come, little maid, be not afraid,
  But let us prove him true ! '
          The river floweth on.

XIV

The little maiden cometh,
  She cometh shy and slow;
I ween she seeth through her lids   120
  They drop adown so low:
Her tresses meet her small bare feet,
  She stands and speaketh nought,
Yet blusheth red as if she said
  The name she only thought.
          The river floweth on.

XV

She knelt beside the water,
  She lighted up the flame,
And o'er her youthful forehead's calm
  The fitful radiance came: —   130
'Go, little boat, go soft and safe,
  And guard the symbol spark !'
Soft, safe doth float the little boat
  Across the waters dark.
        The river floweth on.

XVI

Glad tears her eyes have blinded,
  The light they cannot reach;
She turneth with that sudden smile
  She learnt before her speech —
'I do not hear his voice, the tears   140
  Have dimmed my light away,
But the symbol light will last to-night,
  The love will last for aye !'
        The river floweth on.

XVII

Then Luti spake behind her,
  Outspake she bitterly —
'By the symbol light that lasts to-night,
  Wilt vow a vow to me ?'
Nuleeni gazeth up her face,
  Soft answer maketh she —   150
'By loves that last when lights are past,
  I vow that vow to thee !'
        The river floweth on.

XVIII

An earthly look had Luti
  Though her voice was deep as prayer —
'The rice is gathered from the plains
  To cast upon thine hair:
But when *he* comes his marriage-band
  Around thy neck to throw,
Thy bride-smile raise to meet his gaze, 160
And whisper, — *There is one betrays,*
  While Luti suffers woe.'
        The river floweth on.

XIX

'And when in seasons after,
  Thy little bright-faced son
Shall lean against thy knee and ask
  What deeds his sire hath done, —
Press deeper down thy mother-smile
  His glossy curls among,
View deep his pretty childish eyes,   170

And whisper, — *There is none denies,*
  While Luti speaks of wrong.'
        The river floweth on.

XX

Nuleeni looked in wonder,
  Yet softly answered she —
'By loves that last when lights are past,
  I vowed that vow to thee:
But why glads it thee that a bride-day be
  By a word of *woe* defiled ?
That a word of *wrong* take the cradle-
      song   180
  From the ear of a sinless child ?'
'Why ?' Luti said, and her laugh was
    dread,
  And her eyes dilated wild —
'That the fair new love may her bride-
    groom prove,
  And the father shame the child !'
        The river floweth on.

XXI

'Thou flowest still, O river,
  Thou flowest 'neath the moon;
Thy lily hath not changed a leaf,
  Thy charmèd lute a tune: 190
He mixed his voice with thine and *his*
  Was all I heard around;
But now, beside his chosen bride,
  I hear the river's sound.'
        The river floweth on.

XXII

'I gaze upon her beauty
  Through the tresses that enwreathe it;
The light above thy wave, is hers —
  My rest, alone beneath it:
Oh, give me back the dying look   200
  My father gave thy water !
Give back — and let a little love
  O'erwatch his weary daughter !'
        The river floweth on.

XXIII

'Give back !' she hath departed —
  The word is wandering with her;
And the stricken maidens hear afar
  The step and cry together.
Frail symbols ? None are frail enow
  For mortal joys to borrow ! —   210
While bright doth float Nuleeni's boat,
  She weepeth dark with sorrow.
        The river floweth on.

AN ISLAND

'All goeth but Goddis will.' — Old Poet.

First printed in the *New Monthly Magazine*, January, 1837.

I

My dream is of an island-place
  Which distant seas keep lonely,
A little island on whose face
  The stars are watchers only:
Those bright still stars ! they need not
    seem
Brighter or stiller in my dream.

II

An island full of hills and dells,
  All rumpled and uneven
With green recesses, sudden swells,
  And odorous valleys driven
So deep and straight that always there
The wind is cradled to soft air.

III

Hills running up to heaven for light
  Through woods that half-way ran,
As if the wild earth mimicked right
  The wilder heart of man:
Only it shall be greener far
And gladder than hearts ever are.

IV

More like, perhaps, that mountain piece
  Of Dante's paradise,
Disrupt to an hundred hills like these,
  In falling from the skies;
Bringing within it, all the roots
Of heavenly trees and flowers and fruits:

V

For — saving where the gray rocks strike
  Their javelins up the azure,
Or where deep fissures miser-like
  Hoard up some fountain treasure,
(And e'en in them, stoop down and hear,
Leaf sounds with water in your ear,) —

VI

The place is all awave with trees,
  Limes, myrtles purple-beaded,
Acacias having drunk the lees
  Of the night-dew, faint-headed,
And wan gray olive-woods which seem
The fittest foliage for a dream.

VII

Trees, trees on all sides ! they combine
  Their plumy shades to throw,
Through whose clear fruit and blossom
    fine
Whene'er the sun may go,
The ground beneath he deeply stains,
As passing through cathedral panes.

VIII

But little needs this earth of ours
  That shining from above her,
When many Pleiades of flowers
  (Not one lost) star her over,
The rays of their unnumbered hues
Being all refracted by the dews.

IX

Wide-petalled plants that boldly drink
  The Amreeta of the sky,
Shut bells that dull with rapture sink,
  And lolling buds, half shy;
I cannot count them, but between
Is room for grass and mosses green,

X

And brooks, that glass in different strengths
  All colors in disorder,
Or, gathering up their silver lengths
  Beside their winding border,
Sleep, haunted through the slumber hidden,
By lilies white as dreams in Eden.

XI

Nor think each archèd tree with each
  Too closely interlaces
To admit of vistas out of reach,
  And broad moon-lighted places
Upon whose sward the antlered deer
May view their double image clear.

XII

For all this island's creature-full,
  (Kept happy not by halves)
Mild cows, that at the vine-wreaths pull,
  Then low back at their calves
With tender lowings, to approve
The warm mouths milking them for love,

XIII

Free gamesome horses, antelopes,
  And harmless leaping leopards,
And buffaloes upon the slopes,
  And sheep unruled by shepherds:

Hares, lizards, hedgehogs, badgers, mice,
Snakes, squirrels, frogs, and butterflies.

XIV

And birds that live there in a crowd,
　Horned owls, rapt nightingales,
Larks bold with heaven, and peacocks proud,
　Self-sphered in those grand tails;
All creatures glad and safe, I deem.
No guns nor springes in my dream !

XV

The island's edges are a-wing
　With trees that overbranch
The sea with song-birds welcoming
　The curlews to green change;
And doves from half-closed lids espy
The red and purple fish go by.

XVI

One dove is answering in trust
　The water every minute,
Thinking so soft a murmur must
　Have her mate's cooing in it:
So softly doth earth's beauty round
Infuse itself in ocean's sound.

XVII

My sanguine soul bounds forwarder
　To meet the bounding waves;
Beside them straightway I repair,
　To live within the caves:
And near me two or three may dwell
Whom dreams fantastic please as well.

XVIII

Long winding caverns, glittering far
　Into a crystal distance !
Through clefts of which shall many a star
　Shine clear without resistance,
And carry down its rays the smell
Of flowers above invisible.

XIX

I said that two or three might choose
　Their dwelling near mine own:
Those who would change man's voice and
　　use,
　For Nature's way and tone —
Man's veering heart and careless eyes,
For Nature's steadfast sympathies.

XX

Ourselves, to meet her faithfulness,
　Shall play a faithful part;
Her beautiful shall ne'er address
　The monstrous at our heart:
Her musical shall ever touch
Something within us also such.

XXI

Yet shall she not our mistress live,
　As doth the moon of ocean,
Though gently as the moon she give
　Our thoughts a light and motion:
More like a harp of many lays,
Moving its master while he plays.

XXII

No sod in all that island doth
　Yawn open for the dead;
No wind hath borne a traitor's oath;
　No earth, a mourner's tread;
We cannot say by stream or shade,
'I suffered *here*, — was *here* betrayed.'

XXIII

Our only 'farewell' we shall laugh
　To shifting cloud or hour,
And use our only epitaph
　To some bud turned a flower:
Our only tears shall serve to prove
Excess in pleasure or in love.

XXIV

Our fancies shall their plumage catch
　From fairest island-birds,
Whose eggs let young ones out at hatch,
　Born singing ! then our words
Unconsciously shall take the dyes
Of those prodigious fantasies.

XXV

Yea, soon, no consonant unsmooth
　Our smile-tuned lips shall reach;
Sounds sweet as Hellas spake in youth
　Shall glide into our speech:
(What music, certes, can you find
As soft as voices which are kind ?)

XXVI

And often, by the joy without
　And in us, overcome,
We, through our musing, shall let float
　Such poems, — sitting dumb, —
As Pindar might have writ if he
Had tended sheep in Arcady;

XXVII

Or Æschylus — the pleasant fields
  He died in, longer knowing;
Or Homer, had men's sins and shields
  Been lost in Meles flowing;
Or Poet Plato, had the undim
Unsetting Godlight broke on him.

XXVIII

Choose me the cave most worthy choice,
  To make a place for prayer,
And I will choose a praying voice
  To pour our spirits there:
How silverly the echoes run !
Thy will be done, — thy will be done.

XXIX

Gently yet strangely uttered words !
  They lift me from my dream;
The island fadeth with its swards
  That did no more than seem:
The streams are dry, no sun could find —
The fruits are fallen, without wind.

XXX

So oft the doing of God's will
  Our foolish wills undoeth !
And yet what idle dream breaks ill,
  Which morning-light subdueth ?
And who would murmur and misdoubt,
When God's great sunrise finds him out ?

THE DESERTED GARDEN

I MIND me in the days departed,
How often underneath the sun
With childish bounds I used to run
  To a garden long deserted.

The beds and walks were vanished quite;
And wheresoe'er had struck the spade,
The greenest grasses Nature laid
  To sanctify her right.

I called the place my wilderness,
For no one entered there but I;
The sheep looked in, the grass to espy,
  And passed it ne'ertheless.

The trees were interwoven wild,
And spread their boughs enough about
To keep both sheep and shepherd out,
  But not a happy child.

Adventurous joy it was for me !
I crept beneath the boughs, and found
A circle smooth of mossy ground
  Beneath a poplar tree.

Old garden rose-trees hedged it in,
Bedropt with roses waxen-white
Well satisfied with dew and light
  And careless to be seen.

Long years ago it might befall,
When all the garden flowers were trim,
The grave old gardener prided him
  On these the most of all.

Some lady, stately overmuch,
Here moving with a silken noise,
Has blushed beside them at the voice
  That likened her to such.

And these, to make a diadem,
She often may have plucked and twined,
Half-smiling as it came to mind
  That few would look at *them.*

Oh, little thought that lady proud,
A child would watch her fair white rose,
When buried lay her whiter brows,
  And silk was changed for shroud !

Nor thought that gardener, (full of scorns
For men unlearned and simple phrase,)
A child would bring it all its praise
  By creeping through the thorns !

To me upon my low moss seat,
Though never a dream the roses sent
Of science or love's compliment,
  I ween they smelt as sweet.

It did not move my grief to see
The trace of human step departed:
Because the garden was deserted,
  The blither place for me !

Friends, blame me not ! a narrow ken
Has childhood 'twixt the sun and sward;
We draw the moral afterward,
  We feel the gladness then.

And gladdest hours for me did glide
In silence at the rose-tree wall:
A thrush made gladness musical
  Upon the other side.

Nor he nor I did e'er incline
To peck or pluck the blossoms white;
How should I know but roses might
    Lead lives as glad as mine ?

To make my hermit-home complete,
I brought clear water from the spring
Praised in its own low murmuring,
    And cresses glossy wet.

And so, I thought, my likeness grew
(Without the melancholy tale)
To 'gentle hermit of the dale,'
    And Angelina too.

For oft I read within my nook
Such minstrel stories; till the breeze
Made sounds poetic in the trees,
    And then I shut the book.

If I shut this wherein I write
I hear no more the wind athwart
Those trees, nor feel that childish heart
    Delighting in delight.

My childhood from my life is parted,
My footstep from the moss which drew
Its fairy circle round: anew
    The garden is deserted.

Another thrush may there rehearse
The madrigals which sweetest are;
No more for me ! myself afar
    Do sing a sadder verse.

Ah me, ah me ! when erst I lay
In that child's-nest so greenly wrought,
I laughed unto myself and thought
    'The time will pass away.'

And still I laughed, and did not fear
But that, whene'er was past away
The childish time, some happier play
    My womanhood would cheer.

I knew the time would pass away,
And yet, beside the rose-tree wall,
Dear God, how seldom, if at all,
    Did I look up to pray !

The time is past; and now that grows
The cypress high among the trees,
And I behold white sepulchres
    As well as the white rose,—

When graver, meeker thoughts are given,
And I have learnt to lift my face,
Reminded how earth's greenest place
    The color draws from heaven, —

It something saith for earthly pain,
But more for Heavenly promise free,
That I who was, would shrink to be
    That happy child again.

THE SOUL'S TRAVELLING

'"Ηδη νοερούς
Πέτασαι ταρσούς.' — *Synesius.*

I

I DWELL amid the city ever.
The great humanity which beats
Its life along the stony streets,
Like a strong and unsunned river
In a self-made course,
I sit and hearken while it rolls.
Very sad and very hoarse
Certes is the flow of souls;
Infinitest tendencies
By the finite prest and pent,   10
In the finite, turbulent:
How we tremble in surprise
When sometimes, with an awful sound,
God's great plummet strikes the ground !

II

The champ of the steeds on the silver
        bit,
As they whirl the rich man's carriage by;
The beggar's whine as he looks at it,—
But it goes too fast for charity;
The trail on the street of the poor man's
        broom,
That the lady who walks to her palace-
        home,   20
On her silken skirt may catch no dust;
The tread of the business-men who must
Count their per-cents by the paces they take;
The cry of the babe unheard of its mother
Though it lie on her breast, while she thinks
        of her other
Laid yesterday where it will not wake;
The flower-girl's prayer to buy roses and
        pinks
Held out in the smoke, like stars by day;
The gin-door's oath that hollowly chinks
Guilt upon grief and wrong upon hate;   30

The cabman's cry to get out of the way;
The dustman's call down the area-grate;
The young maid's jest, and the old wife's
    scold,
The haggling talk of the boys at a stall,
The fight in the street which is backed for
    gold,
The plea of the lawyers in Westminster
    Hall;
The drop on the stones of the blind man's
    staff
As he trades in his own grief's sacred-
    ness,
The brothel shriek, and the Newgate
    laugh,
The hum upon 'Change, and the organ's
    grinding,   40
(The grinder's face being nevertheless
Dry and vacant of even woe
While the children's hearts are leaping
    so
At the merry music's winding;)
The black-plumed funeral's creeping train,
Long and slow (and yet they will go
As fast as Life though it hurry and strain !)
Creeping the populous houses through
And nodding their plumes at either side, —
At many a house, where an infant, new   50
To the sunshiny world, has just struggled
    and cried, —
At many a house where sitteth a bride
Trying to-morrow's coronals
With a scarlet blush to-day:
    Slowly creep the funerals,
As none should hear the noise and say
'The living, the living must go away
    To multiply the dead.'
Hark ! an upward shout is sent,
In grave strong joy from tower to steeple
    The bells ring out,   61
The trumpets sound, the people shout,
The young queen goes to her Parliament.
She turneth round her large blue eyes
More bright with childish memories
Than royal hopes, upon the people;
On either side she bows her head
    Lowly, with a queenly grace
And smile most trusting-innocent,
As if she smiled upon her mother;   70
The thousands press before each other
    To bless her to her face;
And booms the deep majestic voice
Through trump and drum, — 'May the
    queen rejoice
    In the people's liberties ! '

III

    I dwell amid the city,
And hear the flow of souls in act and speech,
For pomp or trade, for merrymake or
    folly:
I hear the confluence and sum of each,
    And that is melancholy !   80
Thy voice is a complaint, O crownèd city,
The blue sky covering thee like God's
    great pity.

IV

O blue sky ! it mindeth me
Of places where I used to see
Its vast unbroken circle thrown
From the far pale-peakèd hill
Out to the last verge of ocean,
As by God's arm it were done
Then for the first time, with the emotion
Of that first impulse on it still.   90
Oh, we spirits fly at will
Faster than the wingèd steed
Whereof in old book we read,
With the sunlight foaming back
From his flanks to a misty wrack,
And his nostril reddening proud
As he breasteth the steep thunder-cloud, —
Smoother than Sabrina's chair
Gliding up from wave to air,
While she smileth debonair   100
Yet holy, coldly and yet brightly,
Like her own mooned waters nightly,
    Through her dripping hair.

V

Very fast and smooth we fly,
Spirits, though the flesh be by;
All looks feed not from the eye
Nor all hearings from the ear:
We can hearken and espy
Without either, we can journey
Bold and gay as knight to tourney,   110
And, though we wear no visor down
To dark our countenance, the foe
Shall never chafe us as we go.

VI

I am gone from peopled town !
It passeth its street-thunder round
My body which yet hears no sound,
For now another sound, another
Vision, my soul's senses have —
O'er a hundred valleys deep
Where the hills' green shadows sleep   120

Scarce known because the valley-trees
Cross those upland images,
O'er a hundred hills each other
Watching to the western wave,
I have travelled, — I have found
The silent, lone, remembered ground.

VII

I have found a grassy niche
Hollowed in a seaside hill,
As if the ocean-grandeur which
Is aspectable from the place,   130
Had struck the hill as with a mace
Sudden and cleaving. You might fill
That little nook with the little cloud
Which sometimes lieth by the moon
To beautify a night of June;
A cavelike nook which, opening all
To the wide sea, is disallowed
From its own earth's sweet pastoral:
Cavelike, but roofless overhead
And made of verdant banks instead   140
Of any rocks, with flowerets spread
Instead of spar and stalactite,
Cowslips and daisies gold and white:
Such pretty flowers on such green sward,
You think the sea they look toward
Doth serve them for another sky
As warm and blue as that on high.

VIII

And in this hollow is a seat,
And when you shall have crept to it,
Slipping down the banks too steep   150
To be o'erbrowsèd by the sheep,
Do not think — though at your feet
The cliff's disrupt — you shall behold
The line where earth and ocean meet;
You sit too much above to view
The solemn confluence of the two:
You can hear them as they greet,
You can hear that evermore
Distance-softened noise more old
Than Nereid's singing, the tide spent   160
Joining soft issues with the shore
In harmony of discontent,
And when you hearken to the grave
Lamenting of the underwave,
You must believe in earth's communion
Albeit you witness not the union.

IX

Except that sound, the place is full
Of silences, which when you cull
By any word, it thrills you so

That presently you let them grow   170
To meditation's fullest length
Across your soul with a soul's strength:
And as they touch your soul, they borrow
Both of its grandeur and its sorrow,
That deathly odor which the clay
Leaves on its deathlessness alwày.

X

Alway ! alway ? must this be ?
Rapid Soul from city gone,
Dost thou carry inwardly
What doth make the city's moan ?   180
Must this deep sigh of thine own
Haunt thee with humanity ?
Green visioned banks that are too steep
To be o'erbrowsèd by the sheep,
May all sad thoughts adown you creep
Without a shepherd ?   Mighty sea,
Can we dwarf thy magnitude
And fit it to our straitest mood ?
O fair, fair Nature, are we thus
Impotent and querulous   190
Among thy workings glorious,
Wealth and sanctities, that still
Leave us vacant and defiled
And wailing like a soft-kissed child,
Kissed soft against his will ?

XI

God, God !
With a child's voice I cry,
Weak, sad, confidingly —
God, God !
Thou knowest, eyelids, raised not always
  up
Unto thy love, (as none of ours are)
  droop
    As ours, o'er many a tear;
Thou knowest, though thy universe is
  broad,
Two little tears suffice to cover all:
Thou knowest, Thou who art so prodigal
Of beauty, we are oft but stricken deer
Expiring in the woods, that care for none
Of those delightsome flowers they die
  upon.

XII

O blissful Mouth which breathed the
  mournful breath
We name our souls, self-spoilt ! — by that
  strong passion   210
Which paled Thee once with sighs, by that
  strong death

Which made Thee once unbreathing —
  from the wrack
Themselves have called around them, call
  them back,
Back to Thee in continuous aspiration !
  For here, O Lord,
For here they travel vainly, vainly pass
From city-pavement to untrodden sward
Where the lark finds her deep nest in the
  grass
Cold with the earth's last dew. Yea, very
  vain
The greatest speed of all these souls of men
Unless they travel upward to the throne 221
Where sittest THOU the satisfying ONE,
With help for sins and holy perfectings
For all requirements: while the archangel,
  raising
Unto thy face his full ecstatic gazing,
Forgets the rush and rapture of his wings.

SOUNDS

'"Ηκουσας ἠ οὐκ ἠκουσας.' — *Æschylus.*

I

HEARKEN, hearken !
The rapid river carrieth
Many noises underneath
  The hoary ocean:
Teaching his solemnity
Sounds of inland life and glee
Learnt beside the waving tree
When the winds in summer prank
Toss the shades from bank to bank,
And the quick rains, in emotion   10
Which rather gladdens earth than grieves,
Count and visibly rehearse
The pulses of the universe
Upon the summer leaves —
Learnt among the lilies straight
When they bow them to the weight
Of many bees whose hidden hum
Seemeth from themselves to come —
Learnt among the grasses green
Where the rustling mice are seen   20
By the gleaming, as they run,
Of their quick eyes in the sun;
And lazy sheep are browsing through
With their noses trailed in dew;
And the squirrel leaps adown
Holding fast the filbert brown;
And the lark, with more of mirth
In his song than suits the earth,

Droppeth some in soaring high,
To pour the rest out in the sky ;   30
While the woodland doves apart
In the copse's leafy heart,
Solitary, not ascetic,
Hidden and yet vocal, seem
Joining, in a lovely psalm,
Man's despondence, nature's calm,
Half mystical and half pathetic,
Like a singing in a dream.
All these sounds the river telleth,
Softened to' an undertone   40
Which ever and anon he swelleth
By a burden of his own,
  In the ocean's ear:
Ay, and ocean seems to hear
With an inward gentle scorn,
Smiling to his caverns worn.

II

Hearken, hearken !
The child is shouting at his play
Just in the tramping funeral's way;
The widow moans as she turns aside   50
To shun the face of the blushing bride
While, shaking the tower of the ancient
    church,
The marriage bells do swing;
And in the shadow of the porch
An idiot sits with his lean hands full
Of hedgerow flowers and a poet's skull,
Laughing loud and gibbering
Because it is so brown a thing,
While he sticketh the gaudy poppies red
In and out the senseless head   60
Where all sweet fancies grew instead:
And you may hear at the self-same time
Another poet who reads his rhyme,
Low as a brook in summer air,
Save when he droppeth his voice adown
To dream of the amaranthine crown
His mortal brows shall wear:
And a baby cries with a feeble sound
'Neath the weary weight of the life new-
    found,
And an old man groans, — with his testa-
    ment   70
Only half-signed, — for the life that's spent;
And lovers twain do softly say,
As they sit on a grave, 'For aye, for aye !'
And foemen twain, while Earth their mother
Looks greenly upward, curse each other;
A school-boy drones his task, with looks
Cast over the page to the elm-tree rooks:
A lonely student cries aloud

Eureka! clasping at his shroud;
A beldame's age-cracked voice doth sing 80
To a little infant slumbering;
A maid forgotten weeps alone,
Muffling her sobs on the trysting-stone;
A sick man wakes at his own mouth's wail,
A gossip coughs in her thrice-told tale,
A muttering gamester shakes the dice,
A reaper foretells goodluck from the skies,
A monarch vows as he lifts his hand to them;
A patriot, leaving his native land to them,
Cries to the world against perjured state; 90
A priest disserts
Upon linen skirts,
A sinner screams for one hope more,
A dancer's feet do palpitate
A piper's music out on the floor;
And nigh to the awful Dead, the living
Low speech and stealthy steps are giving,
Because he cannot hear;
And *he* who on that narrow bier
Has room enough, is closely wound   100
In a silence piercing more than sound.

III

Hearken, hearken !
God speaketh to thy soul,
Using the supreme voice which doth con-
      found
All life with consciousness of Deity,
      All senses into one, —
As the seer-saint of Patmos, loving John
      (For whom did backward roll
The cloud-gate of the future) turned to *see*
The Voice which spake.   It speaketh now,
Through the regular breath of the calm
      creation,   111
Through the moan of the creature's desola-
      tion
Striking, and in its stroke resembling
The memory of a solemn vow
Which pierceth the din of a festival
To one in the midst, — and he letteth fall
      The cup with a sudden trembling.

IV

Hearken, hearken !
God speaketh in thy soul,
Saying, ' O thou that movest   120
With feeble steps across this earth of Mine,
To break beside the fount thy golden bowl
      And spill its purple wine, —
Look up to heaven and see how, like a
      scroll,
My right hand hath thine immortality

In an eternal grasping ! thou, that lovest
The songful birds and grasses underfoot,
And also what change mars and tombs
      pollute —
I am the end of love ! give love to *Me* !
O thou that sinnest, grace doth more
      abound   130
Than all thy sin ! sit still beneath My rood,
And count the droppings of My victim-
      blood,
      And seek none other sound ! '

V

Hearken, hearken !
Shall we hear the lapsing river
And our brother's sighing ever,
And not the voice of God ?

NIGHT AND THE MERRY MAN

NIGHT

'NEATH my moon what doest thou,
With a somewhat paler brow
Than she giveth to the ocean ?
He, without a pulse or motion,
Muttering low before her stands,
Lifting his invoking hands
Like a seer before a sprite,
To catch her oracles of light:
But thy soul out-trembles now
Many pulses on thy brow.   10
Where be all thy laughters clear,
Others laughed alone to hear ?
Where thy quaint jests, said for fame ?
Where thy dances, mixed with game ?
Where thy festive companies,
Mooned o'er with ladies' eyes
All more bright for thee, I trow ?
'Neath my moon what doest thou ?

THE MERRY MAN

I am digging my warm heart
Till I find its coldest part;   20
I am digging wide and low,
Further than a spade will go,
Till that, when the pit is deep
And large enough, I there may heap
All my present pain and past
Joy, dead things that look aghast
By the daylight: now 't is done !
Throw them in, by one and one !
I must laugh, at rising sun.

Memories — of fancy's golden   30
Treasures which my hands have holden,
Till the chillness made them ache;
Of childhood's hopes that used to wake
If birds were in a singing strain,
And for less cause, sleep again;
Of the moss-seat in the wood
Where I trysted solitude;
Of the hill-top where the wind
Used to follow me behind,
Then in sudden rush to blind   40
Both my glad eyes with my hair,
Taken gladly in the snare;
Of the climbing up the rocks,
Of the playing 'neath the oaks
Which retain beneath them now
Only shadow of the bough;
Of the lying on the grass
While the clouds did overpass,
Only they, so lightly driven,
Seeming betwixt me and Heaven;   50
Of the little prayers serene,
Murmuring of earth and sin;
Of large-leaved philosophy
Leaning from my childish knee;
Of poetic book sublime,
Soul-kissed for the first dear time,
Greek or English, ere I knew
Life was not a poem too: —
Throw them in, by one and one !
I must laugh, at rising sun.   60

— Of the glorious ambitions
Yet unquenched by their fruitions;
Of the reading out the nights;
Of the straining at mad heights;
Of achievements, less descried
By a dear few than magnified;
Of praises from the many earned
When praise from love was undiscerned;
Of the sweet reflecting gladness
Softened by itself to sadness: —   70
Throw them in, by one and one !
I must laugh, at rising sun.

What are these ? more, more than these !
Throw in dearer memories ! —
Of voices whereof but to speak
Makes mine own all sunk and weak;
Of smiles the thought of which is sweeping
All my soul to floods of weeping;
Of looks whose absence fain would weigh
My looks to the ground for aye;   80
Of clasping hands — ah me, I wring
Mine, and in a tremble fling

Downward, downward all this paining !
Partings with the sting remaining,
Meetings with a deeper throe
Since the joy is ruined so,
Changes with a fiery burning,
(Shadows upon all the turning,)
Thoughts of . . . with a storm they came,
Them I have not breath to name: 90
Downward, downward be they cast
In the pit ! and now at last
My work beneath the moon is done,
And I shall laugh, at rising sun.

But let me pause or ere I cover
All my treasures darkly over:
I will speak not in thine ears,
Only tell my beaded tears
Silently, most silently.
When the last is calmly told,   100
Let that same moist rosary
With the rest sepulchred be,
Finished now !   The darksome mould
Sealeth up the darksome pit.
I will lay no stone on it,
Grasses I will sow instead,
Fit for Queen Titania's tread;
Flowers, encolored with the sun,
And αι αι written upon none;
Thus, whenever saileth by   110
The Lady World of dainty eye,
Not a grief shall here remain,
Silken shoon to damp or stain:
And while she lisps, 'I have not seen
Any place more smooth and clean ' . . .
Here she cometh ! — Ha, ha ! — who
Laughs as loud as I can do ?

EARTH AND HER PRAISERS

I

THE Earth is old;
Six thousand winters make her heart
     a-cold;
The sceptre slanteth from her palsied hold.
She saith, ''Las me !   God's word that I
     was " good "
          Is taken back to heaven,
From whence when any sound comes, I am
     riven
By some sharp bolt; and now no angel
     would
Descend with sweet dew-silence on my
     mountains,

To glorify the lovely river fountains
  That gush along their side: 10
I see — O weary change ! — I see instead
  This human wrath and pride,
These thrones and tombs, judicial wrong
  and blood,
And bitter words are poured upon mine
  head —
"O Earth ! thou art a stage for tricks un-
  holy,
A church for most remorseful melancholy;
Thou art so spoilt, we should forget we
  had
An Eden in thee, wert thou not so sad ! "
Sweet children, I am old ! ye, every one,
Do keep me from a portion of my sun. 20
  Give praise in change for brightness !
That I may shake my hills in infiniteness
Of breezy laughter, as in youthful mirth,
To hear Earth's sons and daughters
  praising Earth.'

II

Whereupon a child began
With spirit running up to man
As by angels' shining ladder,
(May he find no cloud above !)
Seeming he had ne'er been sadder
  All his days than now, 30
Sitting in the chestnut grove,
With that joyous overflow
Of smiling from his mouth o'er brow
And cheek and chin, as if the breeze
Leaning tricksy from the trees
To part his golden hairs, had blown
Into an hundred smiles that one.

III

'O rare, rare Earth !' he saith,
  'I will praise thee presently;
Not to-day; I have no breath: 40
  I have hunted squirrels three —
Two ran down in the furzy hollow
Where I could not see nor follow,
One sits at the top of the filbert-tree,
With a yellow nut and a mock at me:
  Presently it shall be done !
When I see which way these two have
  run,
When the mocking one at the filbert-top
Shall leap adown and beside me stop,
  Then, rare Earth, rare Earth, 50
Will I pause, having known thy worth,
  To say all good of thee !'

IV

Next a lover, — with a dream
'Neath his waking eyelids hidden,
And a frequent sigh unbidden,
And an idlesse all the day
Beside a wandering stream,
And a silence that is made
Of a word he dares not say, —
Shakes slow his pensive head: 60
  'Earth, Earth !' saith he,
'If spirits, like thy roses, grew
On one stalk, and winds austere
Could but only blow them near,
  To share each other's dew;
If, when summer rains agree
To beautify thy hills, I knew
Looking off them I might see
  Some one very beauteous too, —
  Then Earth,' saith he, 70
'I would praise . . . nay, nay — not
  thee !'

V

Will the pedant name her next ?
Crabbèd with a crabbèd text
Sits he in his study nook,
With his elbow on a book,
And with stately crossèd knees,
And a wrinkle deeply thrid
Through his lowering brow,
Caused by making proofs enow
That Plato in 'Parmenides' 80
Meant the same Spinoza did, —
Or, that an hundred of the groping
Like himself, had made one Homer,
Homeros being a misnomer.
What hath *he* to do with praise
Of Earth or aught ? Whene'er the
  sloping
Sunbeams through his window daze
His eyes off from the learnèd phrase,
Straightway he draws close the curtain.
May abstraction keep him dumb ! 90
Were his lips to ope, 't is certain
'*Derivatum est*' would come.

VI

Then a mourner moveth pale
In a silence full of wail,
Raising not his sunken head
Because he wandered last that way
With that one beneath the clay:
Weeping not, because that one,
The only one who would have said

'Cease to weep, beloved!' has gone   100
Whence returneth comfort none.
The silence breaketh suddenly, —
'Earth, I praise thee!' crieth he,
'Thou hast a grave for also *me*.'

VII

Ha, a poet! know him by
The ecstasy-dilated eye,
Not uncharged with tears that ran
Upward from his heart of man;
By the cheek, from hour to hour,
Kindled bright or sunken wan   110
With a sense of lonely power;
By the brow uplifted higher
Than others, for more low declining:
By the lip which words of fire
Overboiling have burned white
While they gave the nations light:
Ay, in every time and place
Ye may know the poet's face
  By the shade or shining.

VIII

'Neath a golden cloud he stands,   120
Spreading his impassioned hands.
'O God's Earth!' he saith, 'the sign
From the Father-soul to mine
Of all beauteous mysteries,
Of all perfect images
Which, divine in his divine,
In my human only are
Very excellent and fair!
Think not, Earth, that I would raise
Weary forehead in thy praise,   130
(Weary, that I cannot go
Farther from thy region low,)
If were struck no richer meanings
From thee than thyself. The leanings
Of the close trees o'er the brim
Of a sunshine-haunted stream
Have a sound beneath their leaves,
  Not of wind, not of wind,
Which the poet's voice achieves:
The faint mountains, heaped behind,   140
Have a falling on their tops,
  Not of dew, not of dew,
Which the poet's fancy drops:
Viewless things his eyes can view,
Driftings of his dream do light
All the skies by day and night,
And the seas that deepest roll
Carry murmurs of his soul.
Earth, I praise thee! praise thou *me*!
God perfecteth his creation   150

With this recipient poet-passion,
And makes the beautiful to be.
I praise thee, O belovèd sign,
From the God-soul unto mine!
Praise me, that I cast on thee
The cunning sweet interpretation,
The help and glory and dilation
  Of mine immortality!'

IX

There was silence. None did dare
To use again the spoken air   160
Of that far-charming voice, until
A Christian resting on the hill,
With a thoughtful smile subdued
(Seeming learnt in solitude)
Which a weeper might have viewed
Without new tears, did softly say,
And looked up unto heaven alway
While he praised the Earth —
        'O Earth,
I count the praises thou art worth,
By thy waves that move aloud,   170
By thy hills against the cloud,
By thy valleys warm and green,
By the copses' elms between,
By their birds which, like a sprite
Scattered by a strong delight
Into fragments musical,
Stir and sing in every bush;
By thy silver founts that fall,
As if to entice the stars at night
To thine heart; by grass and rush,   180
And little weeds the children pull,
Mistook for flowers!
      — Oh, beautiful
Art thou, Earth, albeit worse
Than in heaven is callèd good!
Good to us, that we may know
Meekly from thy good to go;
While the holy, crying Blood
Puts its music kind and low
'Twixt such ears as are not dull,
  And thine ancient curse!   190

X

'Praisèd be the mosses soft
In thy forest pathways oft,
And the thorns, which make us think
Of the thornless river-brink
  Where the ransomed tread:
Praisèd be thy sunny gleams,
And the storm, that worketh dreams
  Of calm unfinishèd:
Praisèd be thine active days,

And thy night-time's solemn need,   200
When in God's dear book we read
   No night shall be therein:
Praisèd be thy dwellings warm
By household fagot's cheerful blaze,
Where, to hear of pardoned sin,
Pauseth oft the merry din,
Save the babe's upon the arm
Who croweth to the crackling wood:
Yea, and, better understood,
Praisèd be thy dwellings cold,   210
Hid beneath the churchyard mould,
Where the bodies of the saints
Separate from earthly taints
Lie asleep, in blessing bound,
Waiting for the trumpet's sound
To free them into blessing; — none
Weeping more beneath the sun,
Though dangerous words of human love
Be graven very near, above.

XI

'Earth, we Christians praise thee thus,
Even for the change that comes   221
With a grief from thee to us:
For thy cradles and thy tombs,
For the pleasant corn and wine
And summer-heat; and also for
The frost upon the sycamore
And hail upon the vine!'

THE VIRGIN MARY TO THE CHILD JESUS

'But see the Virgin blest
Hath laid her babe to rest.'
   — MILTON'S *Hymn on the Nativity.*

I

  SLEEP, sleep, mine Holy One!
My flesh, my Lord! — what name? I do
    not know
A name that seemeth not too high or low,
    Too far from me or heaven:
My Jesus, *that* is best! that word being
    given
By the majestic angel whose command
Was softly as a man's beseeching said,
When I and all the earth appeared to
    stand
    In the great overflow
Of light celestial from his wings and
    head.   10
  Sleep, sleep, my saving One!

II

And art Thou come for saving, baby-
    browed
And speechless Being — art Thou come for
    saving?
The palm that grows beside our door is
    bowed
By treadings of the low wind from the
    south,
A restless shadow through the chamber
    waving:
Upon its bough a bird sings in the sun,
But Thou, with that close slumber on thy
    mouth,
Dost seem of wind and sun already weary.
Art come for saving, O my weary One?   20

III

Perchance this sleep that shutteth out the
    dreary
Earth-sounds and motions, opens on thy
    soul
    High dreams on fire with God;
High songs that make the pathways where
    they roll
More bright than stars do theirs; and vi-
    sions new
Of thine eternal Nature's old abode.
    Suffer this mother's kiss,
    Best thing that earthly is,
To glide the music and the glory through,
Nor narrow in thy dream the broad up-
    liftings   30
    Of any seraph wing.
Thus noiseless, thus. Sleep, sleep, my
    dreaming One!

IV

The slumber of his lips meseems to run
Through *my* lips to mine heart, to all its
    shiftings
Of sensual life, bringing contrariousness
In a great calm. I feel I could lie down
As Moses did, and die, — and then live
    most.
I am 'ware of you, heavenly Presences,
That stand with your peculiar light unlost,
Each forehead with a high thought for a
    crown,   40
Unsunned i' the sunshine! I am 'ware.
    Ye throw
No shade against the wall! How motion-
    less
Ye round me with your living statuary,

While through your whiteness, in and out-
 wardly,
Continual thoughts of God appear to go,
Like light's soul in itself. I bear, I bear
To look upon the dropt lids of your eyes,
Though their external shining testifies
To that beatitude within which were
Enough to blast an eagle at his sun: 50
I fall not on my sad clay face before ye, —
 I look on his. I know
My spirit which dilateth with the woe
 Of his mortality,
 May well contain your glory.
 Yea, drop your lids more low.
Ye are but fellow-worshippers with me !
Sleep, sleep, my worshipped One !

V

We sate among the stalls at Bethlehem;
The dumb kine from their fodder turning
 them, 60
 Softened their hornèd faces
 To almost human gazes
 Toward the newly Born:
The simple shepherds from the star-lit
 brooks
 Brought visionary looks,
As yet in their astonied bearing rung
 The strange sweet angel-tongue:
The magi of the East, in sandals worn,
 Knelt reverent, sweeping round,
With long pale beards, their gifts upon
 the ground, 70
 The incense, myrrh and gold
These baby hands were impotent to hold:
So let all earthlies and celestials wait
 Upon thy royal state.
 Sleep, sleep, my kingly One !

VI

I am not proud — meek angels, ye invest
New meeknesses to hear such utterance
 rest
On mortal lips, — 'I am not proud' —
 not proud !
Albeit in my flesh God sent his Son,
Albeit over Him my head is bowed 80
As others bow before Him, still mine heart
Bows lower than their knees. O centuries
That roll in vision your futurities
 My future grave athwart, —
Whose murmurs seem to reach me while I
 keep
 Watch o'er this sleep, —

Say of me as the Heavenly said — 'Thou
 art
The blessedest of women !' — blessedest,
Not holiest, not noblest, no high name
Whose height misplaced may pierce me
 like a shame 90
When I sit meek in heaven !
    For me, for me,
God knows that I am feeble like the rest !
I often wandered forth, more child than
 maiden
Among the midnight hills of Galilee
 Whose summits looked heaven-laden,
Listening to silence as it seemed to be
God's voice, so soft yet strong, so fain to
 press
Upon my heart as heaven did on the
 height,
And waken up its shadows by a light,
And show its vileness by a holiness. 100
Then I knelt down most silent like the
 night,
 Too self-renounced for fears,
Raising my small face to the boundless
 blue
Whose stars did mix and tremble in my
 tears:
God heard *them* falling after, with his dew.

VII

So, seeing my corruption, can I see
This Incorruptible now born of me,
This fair new Innocence no sun did chance
To shine on, (for even Adam was no child,)
Created from my nature all defiled, 110
This mystery, from out mine ignorance, —
Nor feel the blindness, stain corruption
 more
Than others do, or *I* did heretofore ?
Can hands wherein such burden pure has
 been,
Not open with the cry 'unclean, unclean,'
More oft than any else beneath the skies ?
 Ah King, ah Christ, ah son !
The kine, the shepherds, the abasèd wise
 Must all less lowly wait
 Than I, upon thy state. 120
 Sleep, sleep, my kingly One !

VIII

Art Thou a King, then ? Come, his uni-
 verse,
 Come, crown me Him a King !
Pluck rays from all such stars as never
 fling

Their light where fell a curse,
And make a crowning for this kingly
   brow ! —
What is my word ? Each empyreal star
   Sits in a sphere afar
   In shining ambuscade:
The child-brow, crowned by none,   130
   Keeps its unchildlike shade.
   Sleep, sleep, my crownless One !

IX

Unchildlike shade ! No other babe doth
   wear
An aspect very sorrowful, as Thou.
No small babe-smiles my watching heart
   has seen
To float like speech the speechless lips be-
   tween,
No dovelike cooing in the golden air,
No quick short joys of leaping babyhood.
   Alas, our earthly good
In heaven thought evil, seems too good for
   Thee: 140
   Yet, sleep, my weary One !

X

And then the drear sharp tongue of pro-
   phecy,
With the dread sense of things which shall
   be done,
Doth smite me inly, like a sword: a sword?
That 'smites the Shepherd.' Then, I think
   aloud
The words 'despised,' — 'rejected,' — every
   word
Recoiling into darkness as I view
   The DARLING on my knee.
Bright angels, — move not — lest ye stir the
   cloud
Betwixt my soul and his futurity !   150
I must not die, with mother's work to do,
   And could not live — and see.

XI

   It is enough to bear
   This image still and fair,
   This holier in sleep
   Than a saint at prayer,
   This aspect of a child
   Who never sinned or smiled;
   This Presence in an infant's face;
   This sadness most like love,   160
   This love than love more deep,
   This weakness like omnipotence
   It is so strong to move.

Awful is this watching place,
   Awful what I see from hence —
   A king, without regalia,
   A God, without the thunder,
   A child, without the heart for play;
   Ay, a Creator, rent asunder
   From his first glory and cast away
   On his own world, for me alone   171
To hold in hands created, crying — SON !

XII

   That tear fell not on Thee,
Beloved, yet thou stirrest in thy slumber !
THOU, stirring not for glad sounds out of
   number
Which through the vibratory palm-trees run
   From summer-wind and bird,
   So quickly hast thou heard
   A tear fall silently ?
   Wak'st thou, O loving One ? —   180

TO BETTINE

THE CHILD-FRIEND OF GOETHE

'I have the second sight, Goethe ! '
— *Letters of a Child.*

I

BETTINE, friend of Goethe,
Hadst thou the second sight —
Upturning worship and delight
   With such a loving duty
To his grand face, as women will,
The childhood 'neath thine eyelids still ?

II

— Before his shrine to doom thee,
Using the same child's smile
That heaven and earth, beheld erewhile
   For the first time, won from thee
Ere star and flower grew dim and dead
Save at his feet and o'er his head ?

III

— Digging thine heart and throwing
Away its childhood's gold,
That so its woman-depth might hold
   His spirit's overflowing ?
(For surging souls, no worlds can bound,
Their channel in the heart have found.)

IV

O child, to change appointed,
Thou hadst not second sight !

What eyes the future view aright
   Unless by tears anointed ?
Yea, only tears themselves can show
The burning ones that have to flow.

V

O woman, deeply loving,
Thou hadst not second sight !
The star is very high and bright,
   And none can see it moving.
Love looks around, below, above,
Yet all his prophecy is — love.

VI

The bird thy childhood's playing
Sent onward o'er the sea,
Thy dove of hope came back to thee
   Without a leaf: art laying
Its wet cold wing no sun can dry,
Still in thy bosom secretly ?

VII

Our Goethe's friend, Bettine,
I have the second sight !
The stone upon his grave is white,
   The funeral stone between ye;
And in thy mirror thou hast viewed
Some change as hardly understood.

VIII

Where 's childhood ? where is Goethe ?
The tears are in thine eyes.
Nay, thou shalt yet reorganize
   Thy maidenhood of beauty
In his own glory, which is smooth
Of wrinkles and sublime in youth.

IX

The poet's arms have wound thee,
He breathes upon thy brow,
He lifts thee upward in the glow
   Of his great genius round thee, —
The childlike poet undefiled
Preserving evermore THE CHILD.

FELICIA HEMANS

TO L. E. L.

REFERRING TO HER MONODY ON THE POETESS

First published with the title 'Stanzas on the Death of Mrs. Hemans.'

I

THOU bay-crowned living One that o'er the
   bay-crowned Dead art bowing,
And o'er the shadeless moveless brow the
   vital shadow throwing,
And o'er the sighless songless lips the wail
   and music wedding,
And dropping o'er the tranquil eyes the
   tears not of their shedding ! —

II

Take music from the silent Dead whose
   meaning is completer,
Reserve thy tears for living brows where
   all such tears are meeter,
And leave the violets in the grass to
   brighten where thou treadest,
No flowers for her ! no need of flowers,
   albeit 'bring flowers !' thou saidest.

III

Yes, flowers, to crown the 'cup and lute,'
   since both may come to breaking,
Or flowers, to greet the 'bride' — the
   heart's own beating works its aching;
Or flowers, to soothe the 'captive's' sight,
   from earth's free bosom gathered,
Reminding of his earthly hope, then wither-
   ing as it withered:

IV

But bring not near the solemn corse a type
   of human seeming,
Lay only dust's stern verity upon the dust
   undreaming:
And while the calm perpetual stars shall
   look upon it solely,
Her sphered soul shall look on *them* with
   eyes more bright and holy.

V

Nor mourn, O living One, because her part
   in life was mourning:
Would she have lost the poet's fire for
   anguish of the burning ?
The minstrel harp, for the strained string ?
   the tripod, for the afflated
Woe ? or the vision, for those tears in
   which it shone dilated ?

VI

Perhaps she shuddered while the world's
   cold hand her brow was wreathing,
But never wronged that mystic breath
   which breathed in all her breathing,

Which drew, from rocky earth and man,
  abstractions high and moving,
Beauty, if not the beautiful, and love, if
  not the loving.

VII

Such visionings have paled in sight; the
  Saviour she descrieth,
And little recks *who* wreathed the brow
  which on his bosom lieth:
The whiteness of his innocence o'er all her
  garments, flowing,
There learneth she the sweet ' new song '
  she will not mourn in knowing.

VIII

Be happy, crowned and living One ! and as
  thy dust decayeth
May thine own England say for thee what
  now for Her it sayeth —
' Albeit softly in our ears her silver song
  was ringing,
The foot-fall of her parting soul is softer
  than her singing.'

MEMORY AND HOPE

I

BACK-LOOKING Memory
And prophet Hope both sprang from out
  the ground;
One, where the flashing of cherubic sword
  Fell sad in Eden's ward,
And one, from Eden earth within the sound
Of the four rivers lapsing pleasantly,
What time the promise after curse was
  said,
  ' Thy seed shall bruise his head.'

II

Poor Memory's brain is wild,
As moonstruck by that flaming atmosphere
When she was born; her deep eyes shine
  and shone
  With light that conquereth sun
And stars to wanner paleness year by year:
With odorous gums she mixeth things de-
  filed,
She trampleth down earth's grasses green
  and sweet
  With her far-wandering feet.

III

She plucketh many flowers,
Their beauty on her bosom's coldness kill-
  ing;
She teacheth every melancholy sound
  To winds and waters round;
She droppeth tears with seed where man
  is tilling
The rugged soil in his exhausted hours;
She smileth — ah me ! in her smile doth go
  A mood of deeper woe.

IV

Hope tripped on out of sight,
Crowned with an Eden wreath she saw not
  wither,
And went a-nodding through the wilder-
  ness
  With brow that shone no less
Than a sea-gull's wing, brought nearer by
  rough weather,
Searching the treeless rock for fruits of
  light;
Her fair quick feet being armed from
  stones and cold
  By slippers of pure gold.

V

Memory did Hope much wrong
And, while she dreamed, her slippers stole
  away;
But still she wended on with mirth unheed-
  ing,
  Although her feet were bleeding,
Till Memory tracked her on a certain day,
And with most evil eyes did search her
  long
And cruelly, whereat she sank to ground
  In a stark deadly swound.

VI

And so my Hope were slain,
Had it not been that THOU wast standing
  near —
Oh Thou who saidest ' Live,' to creatures
  lying
  In their own blood and dying !
For Thou her forehead to thine heart didst
  rear
And make its silent pulses sing again,
Pouring a new light o'er her darkened
  eyne
  With tender tears from thine.

VII

Therefore my Hope arose
From out her swound and gazed upon thy
    face,
And, meeting there that soft subduing
    look
Which Peter's spirit shook,
Sank downward in a rapture to embrace
Thy piercèd hands and feet with kisses
    close,
And prayed Thee to assist her evermore
To 'reach the things before.'

THE SLEEP

'He giveth His beloved sleep.'
— *Psalm* cxxvii. 2.

I

OF all the thoughts of God that are
Borne inward into souls afar,
Along the Psalmist's music deep,
Now tell me if that any is,
For gift or grace, surpassing this:
'He giveth his belovèd — sleep?'

II

What would we give to our beloved?
The hero's heart to be unmoved,
The poet's star-tuned harp to sweep,
The patriot's voice to teach and rouse,
The monarch's crown to light the brows?
He giveth his belovèd — sleep.

III

What do we give to our beloved?
A little faith all undisproved,
A little dust to overweep,
And bitter memories to make
The whole earth blasted for our sake:
He giveth his belovèd — sleep.

IV

'Sleep soft,' beloved! we sometimes say,
Who have no tune to charm away
Sad dreams that through the eyelids creep:
But never doleful dream again
Shall break the happy slumber when
He giveth his belovèd — sleep.

V

O earth, so full of dreary noises!
O men, with wailing in your voices!
O delvèd gold, the wailers heap!
O strife, O curse, that o'er it fall!
God strikes a silence through you all,
And giveth his belovèd — sleep.

VI

His dews drop mutely on the hill,
His cloud above it saileth still,
Though on its slope men sow and reap:
More softly than the dew is shed,
Or cloud is floated overhead,
He giveth his belovèd — sleep.

VII

Ay, men may wonder while they scan
A living, thinking, feeling man
Confirmed in such a rest to keep;
But angels say, and through the word
I think their happy smile is *heard* —
'He giveth his belovèd — sleep.'

VIII

For me, my heart that erst did go
Most like a tired child at a show,
That sees through tears the mummers
    leap,
Would now its wearied vision close,
Would childlike on his love repose
Who giveth his belovèd — sleep.

IX

And friends, dear friends, when it shall be
That this low breath is gone from me,
And round my bier ye come to weep,
Let One, most loving of you all,
Say 'Not a tear must o'er her fall!
'He giveth his belovèd sleep.'

MAN AND NATURE

A SAD man on a summer day
Did look upon the earth and say —

'Purple cloud the hill-top binding;
Folded hills the valleys wind in;
Valleys with fresh streams among you;
Streams with bosky trees along you;
Trees with many birds and blossoms;
Birds with music-trembling bosoms;
Blossoms dropping dews that wreathe you
To your fellow flowers beneath you;
Flowers that constellate on earth;
Earth that shakest to the mirth

Of the merry Titan Ocean,
All his shining hair in motion !
Why am I thus the only one
Who can be dark beneath the sun ? '

But when the summer day was past,
He looked to heaven and smiled at last,
Self-answered so —
    ' Because, O cloud,
Pressing with thy crumpled shroud
Heavily on mountain top, —
Hills that almost seem to drop
Stricken with a misty death
To the valleys underneath, —
Valleys sighing with the torrent, —
Waters streaked with branches horrent, —
Branchless trees that shake your head
Wildly o'er your blossoms spread
Where the common flowers are found, —
Flowers with foreheads to the ground, —
Ground that shriekest while the sea
With his iron smiteth thee —
I am, besides, the only one
Who can be bright *without* the sun.'

A SEA-SIDE WALK

I

WE walked beside the sea
After a day which perished silently
Of its own glory — like the princess weird
Who, combating the Genius, scorched and
 seared,
Uttered with burning breath, ' Ho ! vic-
 tory !'
And sank adown, a heap of ashes pale:
 So runs the Arab tale.

II

The sky above us showed
A universal and unmoving cloud
On which the cliffs permitted us to see
Only the outline of their majesty,
As master-minds when gazed at by the
 crowd:
And shining with a gloom, the water gray
 Swang in its moon-taught way.

III

Nor moon, nor stars were out;
They did not dare to tread so soon about,
Though trembling, in the footsteps of the
 sun:

The light was neither night's nor day's, but
 one
Which, life-like, had a beauty in its doubt,
And silence's impassioned breathings
 round
 Seemed wandering into sound.

IV

O solemn-beating heart
Of nature ! I have knowledge that thou
 art
Bound unto man's by cords he cannot
 sever;
And, what time they are slackened by him
 ever,
So to attest his own supernal part,
Still runneth thy vibration fast and strong
 The slackened cord along:

V

For though we never spoke
Of the gray water and the shaded rock,
Dark wave and stone unconsciously were
 fused
Into the plaintive speaking that we used
Of absent friends and memories unforsook;
And, had we seen each other's face, we had
 Seen haply each was sad.

THE SEA-MEW

AFFECTIONATELY INSCRIBED TO M. E. H

I

How joyously the young sea-mew
Lay dreaming on the waters blue
Whereon our little bark had thrown
A little shade, the only one,
But shadows ever man pursue.

II

Familiar with the waves and free
As if their own white foam were he,
His heart upon the heart of ocean
Lay learning all its mystic motion,
And throbbing to the throbbing sea.

III

And such a brightness in his eye
As if the ocean and the sky
Within him had lit up and nurst
A soul God gave him not at first,
To comprehend their majesty.

IV

We were not cruel, yet did sunder
His white wing from the blue waves under,
And bound it, while his fearless eyes
Shone up to ours in calm surprise,
As deeming us some ocean wonder.

V

We bore our ocean bird unto
A grassy place where he might view
The flowers that curtsey to the bees,
The waving of the tall green trees,
The falling of the silver dew.

VI

But flowers of earth were pale to him
Who had seen the rainbow fishes swim;
And when earth's dew around him lay
He thought of ocean's wingèd spray,
And his eye waxèd sad and dim.

VII

The green trees round him only made
A prison with their darksome shade;
And drooped his wing, and mournèd he
For his own boundless glittering sea —
Albeit he knew not they could fade.

VIII

Then One her gladsome face did bring,
Her gentle voice's murmuring,
In ocean's stead his heart to move
And teach him what was human love:
He thought it a strange, mournful thing.

IX

He lay down in his grief to die,
(First looking to the sea-like sky
That hath no waves) because, alas !
Our human touch did on him pass,
And, with our touch, our agony.

THE LITTLE FRIEND

WRITTEN IN THE BOOK WHICH SHE MADE AND SENT TO ME

'— το δ'. ηδη εξ οφθαλμων απεληλυθεν.'
— *Marcus Antoninus.*

I

THE book thou givest, dear as such,
 Shall bear thy dearer name;
And many a word the leaves shall touch,
 For thee who form'dst the same !
And on them, many a thought shall grow
 'Neath memory's rain and sun,
Of thee, glad child, who dost not know
 That thought and pain are one !

II

Yes ! thoughts of thee, who satest oft,
 A while since, at my side —
So wild to tame, — to move so soft,
 So very hard to chide:
The childish vision at thine heart,
 The lesson on the knee;
The wandering looks which *would* depart,
 Like gulls, across the sea !

III

The laughter, which no half-belief
 In wrath could all suppress:
The falling tears, which looked like grief,
 And were but gentleness:
The fancies sent, for bliss, abroad,
 As Eden's were not done —
Mistaking still the cherub's sword
 For shining of the sun !

IV

The sportive speech with wisdom in 't —
 The question strange and bold —
The childish fingers in the print
 Of God's creative hold:
The praying words in whispers said,
 The sin with sobs confest;
The leaning of the young meek head
 Upon the Saviour's breast !

V

The gentle consciousness of praise,
 With hues that went and came;
The brighter blush, a word could raise,
 Were *that* — a father's name !
The shadow on thy smile for each
 That on his face could fall !
So quick hath love been, *thee* to teach,
 What soon it teacheth all.

VI

Sit still as erst beside his feet !
 The future days are dim, —
But those will seem to thee most sweet
 Which keep thee nearest *him !*
Sit at his feet in quiet mirth.

And let him see arise
A clearer sun and greener earth
Within thy loving eyes ! —

VII

Ah, loving eyes ! that used to lift
  Your childhood to my face —
That leave a memory on the gift
  I look on in your place —
May bright-eyed hosts your guardians be
  From all but thankful tears, —
While, brightly as you turn on *me*
  Ye meet th' advancing years !

MY DOVES

' O Weisheit ! Du red'st wie eine Taube ! '
                                    — *Goethe.*

My little doves have left a nest
  Upon an Indian tree
Whose leaves fantastic take their rest
  Or motion from the sea;
For ever there the sea-winds go
With sunlit paces to and fro.

The tropic flowers looked up to it,
  The tropic stars looked down,
And there my little doves did sit
  With feathers softly brown,
And glittering eyes that showed their right
To general Nature's deep delight.

And God them taught, at every close
  Of murmuring waves beyond
And green leaves round, to interpose
  Their choral voices fond,
Interpreting that love must be
The meaning of the earth and sea.

Fit ministers ! Of living loves
  Theirs hath the calmest fashion,
Their living voice the likest moves
  To lifeless intonation,
The lovely monotone of springs
And winds and such insensate things.

My little doves were ta'en away
  From that glad nest of theirs
Across an ocean rolling gray
  And tempest-clouded airs:
My little doves, who lately knew
The sky and wave by warmth and blue.

And now, within the city prison,
  In mist and chillness pent,
With sudden upward look they listen
  For sounds of past content,
For lapse of water, swell of breeze,
Or nut-fruit falling from the trees.

The stir without the glow of passion,
  The triumph of the mart,
The gold and silver as they clash on
  Man's cold metallic heart,
The roar of wheels, the cry for bread, —
These only sounds are heard instead.

Yet still, as on my human hand
  Their fearless heads they lean,
And almost seem to understand
  What human musings mean,
(Their eyes with such a plaintive shine
Are fastened upwardly to mine !) —

Soft falls their chant as on the nest
  Beneath the sunny zone;
For love that stirred it in their breast
  Has not aweary grown,
And 'neath the city's shade can keep
The well of music clear and deep.

And love, that keeps the music, fills
  With pastoral memories;
All echoings from out the hills,
  All droppings from the skies,
All flowings from the wave and wind,
Remembered in their chant, I find.

So teach ye me the wisest part,
  My little doves ! to move
Along the city-ways with heart
  Assured by holy love,
And vocal with such songs as own
A fountain to the world unknown.

'T was hard to sing by Babel's stream —
  More hard, in Babel's street:
But if the soulless creatures deem
  Their music not unmeet
For sunless walls — let *us* begin,
Who wear immortal wings within !

To me, fair memories belong
  Of scenes that used to bless,
For no regret, but present song
  And lasting thankfulness,
And very soon to break away,
Like types, in purer things than they.

I will have hopes that cannot fade,
  For flowers the valley yields;
I will have humble thoughts instead
  Of silent, dewy fields:
My spirit and my God shall be
My seaward hill, my boundless sea.

TO MARY RUSSELL MITFORD

IN HER GARDEN

WHAT time I lay these rhymes anear thy
    feet,
Benignant friend, I will not proudly say
As better poets use, ' These *flowers* I lay,'
Because I would not wrong thy roses
    sweet,
Blaspheming so their name. And yet, re-
    peat
Thou, overleaning them this springtime
    day,
With heart as open to love as theirs to
    May,
—' Low - rooted verse may reach some
    heavenly heat,
Even like my blossoms, if as nature-true
Though not as precious.' Thou art unper-
    plext —
Dear friend, in whose dear writings drops
    the dew
And blow the natural airs, — thou, who
    art next
To nature's self in cheering the world's
    view, —
To preach a sermon on so known a text !

THE STUDENT

'Τί οὖν τοῦτο πρὸς σε ; καὶ οὐδὲν λέγω ὅτι πρὸς τὸν
τεθνηκότα, ἀλλὰ πρὸς τὸν ζῶντα, τί ὁ ἔπαινος.'—*Marcus
Antoninus.*

' MY midnight lamp is weary as my soul,
And, being unimmortal, has gone out.
And now alone yon moony lamp of heaven,
Which God lit and not man, illuminates
These volumes, others wrote in weariness
As I have read them; and this cheek and
    brow,
Whose paleness, burnèd in with heats of
    thought,
Would make an angel smile to see how ill
Clay thrust from Paradise consorts with
    mind —   9
If angels could, like men, smile bitterly.

' Yet, must my brow be paler ! I have
    vowed
To clip it with the crown which cannot
    fade,
When *it* is faded.   Not in vain ye cry,
O glorious voices that survive the tongues
From whence was drawn your separate
    sovereignty —
For I would reign beside you ! I would
    melt
The golden treasures of my health and
    life
Into that name ! My lips are vowed
    apart
From cheerful words; mine ears, from
    pleasant sounds;
Mine eyes, from sights God made so beau-
    tiful, —   20
My feet, from wanderings under shady
    trees;
Mine hands, from clasping of dear-loving
    friends, —
My very heart, from feelings which move
    soft !
Vowed am I from the day's delightsome-
    ness,
And dreams of night ! and when the house
    is dumb
In sleep, which is the pause 'twixt life and
    life,
I live and waken thus; and pluck away
Slumber's sleek poppies from my painèd
    lids —
Goading my mind with thongs wrought by
    herself,
To toil and struggle along this mountain-
    path   30
Which hath no mountain-airs; until she
    sweat
Like Adam's brow, and gasp, and rend
    away
In agony, her garment of the flesh !'

And so his midnight lamp was lit anew,
And burned till morning.   But his lamp
    of life
Till morning burned not ! He was found
    embraced,
Close, cold, and stiff, by Death's compel-
    ling sleep;
His breast and brow supported on a page
Charàctered over with a praise of *fame*,
Of its divineness and beatitude —   40
Words which had often caused that heart to
    throb,

That cheek to burn; though silent lay they
    now,
Without a single beating in the pulse,
And all the fever gone !

                  I saw a hay
Spring verdant from a newly - fashioned
    grave.
The grass upon the grave was verdanter,
That being watered by the eyes of One
Who bore not to look up toward the tree !
Others looked on it — some, with passing
    glance,   49
Because the light wind stirrèd in its leaves;
And some, with sudden lighting of the soul
In admiration's ecstasy ! — Ay ! some
Did wag their heads like oracles, and say,
' 'T is very well ! ' — but none remembered
The heart which housed the root, except
    that ONE
Whose sight was lost in weeping !

                  Is it thus,
Ambition, idol of the intellect ?
Shall we drink aconite, alone to use
Thy golden bowl ? and sleep ourselves to
    death —
To dream thy visions about life ? O Power
That art a very feebleness ! — before   61
Thy clayey feet we bend our knees of clay,
And round thy senseless brow bind diadems
With paralytic hands, and shout ' a god,'
With voices mortal hoarse ! Who can
    discern
Th' infirmities they share in ? Being blind,
We cannot see thy blindness: being weak,
We cannot feel thy weakness: being low,
We cannot mete thy baseness: being unwise,
We cannot understand thy idiocy !   70

THE EXILE'S RETURN

I

WHEN from thee, weeping I removed,
    And from my land for years,
I thought not to return, Beloved,
    With those same parting tears.
I come again to hill and lea,
    Weeping for thee.

II

I clasped thine hand when standing last
    Upon the shore in sight.
The land is green, the ship is fast,

I shall be there to-night.
I shall be there — no longer *we* —
    No more with thee !

III

Had I beheld thee dead and still,
    I might more clearly know
How heart of thine could turn as chill
    As hearts by nature so;
How change could touch the falsehood-free
    And changeless *thee*.

IV

But, now thy fervid looks last-seen
    Within my soul remain,
'T is hard to think that *they* have been,
    To be no more again —
That I shall vainly wait, ah me !
    A word from thee.

V

I could not bear to look upon
    That mound of funeral clay
Where one sweet voice is silence — one
    Æthereal brow, decay;
Where all thy mortal I may see,
    But never thee.

VI

For thou art where all friends are gone
    Whose parting pain is o'er;
And I, who love and weep alone,
    Where thou wilt weep no more,
Weep bitterly and selfishly
    For *me*, not *thee*.

VII

I know, Beloved, thou canst not know
    That I endure this pain;
For saints in heaven, the Scriptures show,
    Can never grieve again:
And grief known mine, even there, would be
    Still shared by thee.

A SONG AGAINST SINGING

TO E. J. H.

I

THEY bid me sing to thee,
Thou golden-haired and silver-voiced child—
With lips by no worse sigh than sleep's
    defiled —

With eyes unknowing how tears dim the
　　sight,
And feet all trembling at the new delight
　　Treaders of earth to be !

II

Ah no ! the lark may bring
A song to thee from out the morning cloud,
The merry river from its lilies bowed,
The brisk rain from the trees, the lucky
　　wind
That half doth make its music, half doth
　　find, —
　　But *I* — I may not sing.

III

How could I think it right,
New-comer on our earth as, Sweet, thou
　　art,
To bring a verse from out a human heart
Made heavy with accumulated tears,
And cross with such amount of weary years
　　Thy day-sum of delight ?

IV

Even if the verse were said,
Thou — who wouldst clap thy tiny hands
　　to hear
The wind or rain, gay bird or river clear —
Wouldst, at that sound of sad humanities,
Upturn thy bright uncomprehending eyes
　　And bid me play instead.

V

Therefore no song of mine, —
But prayer in place of singing; prayer that
　　would
Commend thee to the new-creating God
Whose gift is childhood's heart without its
　　stain
Of weakness, ignorance, and changing
　　vain —
　　That gift of God be thine !

VI

So wilt thou aye be young,
In lovelier childhood than thy shining brow
And pretty winning accents make thee now:
Yea, sweeter than this scarce articulate
　　sound
(How sweet !) of ' father,' ' mother,' shall
　　be found
　　The ABBA on thy tongue.

VII

And so, as years shall chase
Each other's shadows, thou wilt less re-
　　semble
Thy fellows of the earth who toil and
　　tremble,
Than him thou seèst not, thine angel bold
Yet meek, whose ever-lifted eyes behold
　　The Ever-loving's face.

STANZAS

I MAY sing; but minstrel's singing
Ever ceaseth with his playing.
I may smile; but time is bringing
Thoughts for smiles to wear away in.
I may view thee, mutely loving;
But *shall* view thee so in dying !
I may sigh; but life's removing,
And with breathing endeth sighing !
　　　　Be it so !

When no song of mine comes near thee,
Will its memory fail to soften ?
When no smile of mine can cheer thee,
Will thy smile be used as often ?
When my looks the darkness boundeth,
Will thine own be lighted after ?
When my sigh no longer soundeth,
Wilt thou list another's laughter ?
　　　　Be it so !

THE YOUNG QUEEN

' This awful responsibility is imposed upon me so
suddenly and at so early a period of my life, that I
should feel myself utterly oppressed by the burden,
were I not sustained by the hope that Divine Provi-
dence, which has called me to this work, will give me
strength for the performance of it.'
　　— *The Queen's Declaration in Council.*

I

THE shroud is yet unspread
To wrap our crownèd dead;
His soul hath scarcely hearkened for the
　　thrilling word of doom;
And Death, that makes serene
Ev'n brows where crowns have been,
Hath scarcely time to meeten his for silence
　　of the tomb.

II

St. Paul's king-dirging note
The city's heart hath smote —

The city's heart is struck with thought
    more solemn than the tone !
  A shadow sweeps apace
  Before the nation's face,
Confusing in a shapeless blot the sepulchre
    and throne.

III

The palace sounds with wail —
  The courtly dames are pale —
A widow o'er the purple bows, and weeps
    its splendor dim:
  And we who hold the boon,
  A king for freedom won,
Do feel eternity rise up between our thanks
    and him.

IV

And while all things express
  All glory's nothingness,
A royal maiden treadeth firm where *that*
    departed trod !
  The deathly scented crown
  Weighs her shining ringlets down;
But calm she lifts her trusting face, and
    calleth upon God.

V

Her thoughts are deep within her:
  No outward pageants win her
From memories that in her soul are rolling
    wave on wave —
  Her palace walls enring
  The dust that was a king —
And very cold beneath her feet, she feels
    her father's grave.

VI

And One, as fair as she,
  Can scarce forgotten be, —
Who clasped a little infant dead, for all a
    kingdom's worth !
  The mournèd, blessèd One,
  Who views Jehovah's throne,
Aye smiling to the angels, that she lost a
    throne on earth.

VII

Perhaps our youthful Queen
  Remembers what has been —
Her childhood's rest by loving heart, and
    sport on grassy sod —
  Alas ! can others wear
  A mother's heart for her ?
But calm she lifts her trusting face, and
    calleth upon God.

VIII

Yea ! call on God, thou maiden
  Of spirit nobly laden,
And leave such happy days behind, for
    happy-making years !
  A nation looks to thee
  For steadfast sympathy:
Make room within thy bright clear eyes
    for all its gathered tears.

IX

And so the grateful isles
  Shall give thee back their smiles,
And as thy mother joys in thee, in them
    shalt *thou* rejoice;
  Rejoice to meekly bow
  A somewhat paler brow,
While the King of kings shall bless thee by
    the British people's voice !

VICTORIA'S TEARS

' Hark ! the reiterated clangor sounds !
Now murmurs, like the sea or like the storm,
Or like the flames on forests, move and mount
From rank to rank, and loud and louder roll,
Till all the people is one vast applause.'
      — LANDOR'S *Gebir*.

'O MAIDEN ! heir of kings !
  A king has left his place !
The majesty of Death has swept
  All other from his face !
And thou upon thy mother's breast
  No longer lean adown,
But take the glory for the rest,
And rule the land that loves thee best !'
    She heard, and wept —
  She wept, to wear a crown !

They decked her courtly halls;
  They reined her hundred steeds;
They shouted at her palace gate,
  'A noble Queen succeeds !'
Her name has stirred the mountain's sleep
  Her praise has filled the town !
And mourners God had stricken deep,
Looked hearkening up, and did not weep.
    Alone she wept,
  Who wept, to wear a crown !

She saw no purples shine,
  For tears had dimmed her eyes;
She only knew her childhood's flowers
  Were happier pageantries !

And while her heralds played the part,
    For million shouts to drown —
' God save the Queen ' from hill to mart, —
She heard through all her beating heart,
    And turned and wept —
    She wept, to wear a crown !

God save thee, weeping Queen !
    Thou shalt be well beloved !
The tyrant's sceptre cannot move,
    As those pure tears have moved !
The nature in thine eyes we see,
    That tyrants cannot own —
The love that guardeth liberties !
Strange blessing on the nation lies,
    Whose Sovereign wept —
    Yea ! wept, to wear its crown !

God bless thee, weeping Queen,
    With blessing more divine !
And fill with happier love than earth's
    That tender heart of thine !
That when the thrones of earth shall be
    As low as graves brought down,
A piercèd Hand may give to thee
The crown which angels shout to see !
    Thou wilt not *weep*,
To wear that heavenly crown !

VANITIES

' From fading things, fond men, lift your desire.'
                                    — *Drummond.*

COULD ye be very blest in hearkening
Youth's often danced-to melodies —
Hearing it piped, the midnight darkening
Doth come to show the starry skies, —
To freshen garden-flowers, the rain ? —
It is in vain, it is in vain !

Could ye be very blest in urging
A captive nation's strength to thunder
Out into foam, and with its surging
The Xerxean fetters break asunder ?
The storm is cruel as the chain ! —
It is in vain, it is in vain !

Could ye be very blest in paling
Your brows with studious nights and days,
When like your lamps your life is failing,
And sighs, not breath, are wrought from
        praise ?
Your tombs, not ye, that praise retain —
It is in vain, it is in vain !

Yea ! but ye *could* be very blest,
If some ye nearest love were nearest !
Must *they* not love when lovèd best ?
Must *ye* not happiest love when dearest ?
Alas ! how hard to feel again, —
It is in vain, it is in vain !

For those ye love are not unsighing —
They are unchanging least of all:
And ye the loved — ah ! no denying,
Will leave your lips beneath the pall,
When passioned ones have o'er it sain
' It is in vain, it is in vain ! '

BEREAVEMENT

WHEN some Beloveds, 'neath whose eye-
        lids lay
The sweet lights of my childhood, one by
        one
Did leave me dark before the natural
        sun,
And I astonied fell and could not pray, —
A thought within me to myself did say,
' Is God less God, that *thou* art left un-
        done ?
Rise, worship, bless Him, in this sackcloth
        spun,
As in that purple !' — But I answered
        Nay !
What child his filial heart in words can
        loose
If he behold his tender father raise
The hand that chastens sorely ? can he
        choose
But sob in silence with an upward gaze ? —
And *my* great Father, thinking fit to bruise,
Discerns in speechless tears both prayer
        and praise.

CONSOLATION

ALL are not taken; there are left be-
        hind
Living Belovèds, tender looks to bring
And make the daylight still a happy thing,
And tender voices, to make soft the wind:
But if it were not so — if I could find
No love in all the world for comforting,
Nor any path but hollowly did ring
Where ' dust to dust ' the love from life
        disjoined,

And if, before those sepulchres unmoving
I stood alone, (as some forsaken lamb
Goes bleating up the moors in weary
    dearth,)
Crying 'Where are ye, O my loved and
    loving ? ' —
I know a Voice would sound, 'Daughter,
    I AM.
Can I suffice for HEAVEN and not for
    earth ? '

A SUPPLICATION FOR LOVE

HYMN I

'The Lord Jesus, although gone to the Father, and we see Him no more, is still present with His Church ; and in His heavenly glory expends upon her as intense a love, as in the agony of the garden, and the crucifixion of the tree. Those eyes that wept, still gaze upon her.' — *Recalled words of an extempore Discourse, preached at Sidmouth*, 1833.

GOD, namèd Love, whose fount Thou art,
    Thy crownless Church before Thee
        stands,
With too much hating in her heart,
    And too much striving in her hands !

O loving Lord ! O slain for love !
    Thy blood upon thy garments came —
Inwrap their folds our brows above,
    Before we tell Thee all our shame !

' Love as I loved you,' was the sound
    That on thy lips expiring sate !
Sweet words, in bitter strivings drowned !
    We hated as the worldly hate.

The spear that pierced for love thy side,
    We dared for wrathful use to crave;
And with our cruel noise denied
    Its silence to thy blood-red grave !

Ah, blood ! that speaketh more of love
    Than Abel's — could we speak like Cain,
And grieve and scare that holy Dove,
    The parting love-gift of the Slain ?

Yet, Lord, thy wrongèd love fulfil !
    Thy Church, though fallen, before Thee
        stands —
Behold, the voice is Jacob's still,
    Albeit the hands are Esau's hands !

Hast Thou no tears, like those besprent
    Upon thy Zion's ancient part ?
No moving looks, like those which sent
    Their softness through a traitor's heart ?

No touching tale of anguish dear;
    Whereby like children we may creep,
All trembling, to each other near,
    And view each other's face, and weep ?

Oh, move us — THOU hast power to move —
    One in the one Beloved to be !
Teach us the heights and depths of love —
    Give THINE — that we may love like
        THEE !

THE MEDIATOR

HYMN II

' As the greatest of all sacrifices was required, we may be assured that no other would have sufficed.'— BOYD'S *Essay on the Atonement.*

How high Thou art ! our songs can own
    No music Thou couldst stoop to hear !
But still the Son's expiring groan
    Is vocal in the Father's ear.

How pure Thou art ! our hands are dyed
    With curses, red with murder's hue —
But HE hath stretched HIS hands to
        hide
    The sins that pierced them from thy
        view.

How strong Thou art ! we tremble lest
    The thunders of thine arm be moved —
But HE is lying on thy breast,
    And Thou must clasp thy best Be-
        loved !

How kind Thou art ! Thou didst not
        choose
    To joy in Him for ever so;
But that embrace Thou wilt not loose
    For vengeance, didst for love forego !

High God, and pure, and strong, and kind !
    The low, the foul, the feeble, spare !
Thy brightness in his face we find —
    Behold our darkness only *there !*

THE WEEPING SAVIOUR

HYMN III

————— tell
Whether His countenance can thee affright,
Tears in His eyes quench the amazing light.'
—Donne.

WHEN Jesus' friend had ceased to be,
　　Still Jesus' heart its friendship kept —
'Where have ye laid him ?' — 'Come and
　　see ! '
　　But ere his eyes could see, they wept.

Lord ! not in sepulchres alone
　　Corruption's worm is rank and free:
The shroud of death our bosoms own —
　　The shades of sorrow !　Come and see !

Come, Lord ! God's image cannot shine
　　Where sin's funereal darkness lowers —
Come !　Turn those weeping eyes of thine
　　Upon these sinning souls of ours !

And let those eyes with shepherd care
　　Their moving watch above us keep;
Till love the strength of sorrow wear,
　　And, as Thou weepedst, *we* may weep !

For surely we may weep to know,
　　So dark and deep our spirits' stain;
That, had thy blood refused to flow
　　Thy very tears had flowed in vain.

THE MEASURE

HYMN IV

'He comprehended the dust of the earth in a measure '
(שָׁלִישׁ). — *Isaiah* xl.
' Thou givest them tears to drink in a measure '
(שָׁלִישׁ)[1]. — *Psalm* lxxx.

I

GOD the Creator, with a pulseless hand
Of unoriginated power, hath weighed
The dust of earth and tears of man in one
　　　Measure, and by one weight:
　　　So saith his holy book.

II

Shall we, then, who have issued from the
　　dust
And there return, — shall we, who toil for
　　dust,

[1] I believe that the word occurs in no other part of
the Hebrew Scriptures.

And wrap our winnings in this dusty life,
　　　Say ' No more tears, Lord God !
　　　The measure runneth o'er ' ?

III

Oh, Holder of the balance, laughest Thou ?
Nay, Lord ! be gentler to our foolish-
　　ness,
For his sake who assumed our dust and
　　turns
　　　On Thee pathetic eyes
　　　Still moistened with our tears.

IV

And teach us, O our Father, while we weep,
To look in patience upon earth and learn —
Waiting, in that meek gesture, till it
　　last
　　　These tearful eyes be filled
　　　With the dry dust of death.

COWPER'S GRAVE

I

IT is a place where poets crowned may
　　feel the heart's decaying;
It is a place where happy saints may weep
　　amid their praying;
Yet let the grief and humbleness as low as
　　silence languish:
Earth surely now may give her calm to
　　whom she gave her anguish.

II

O poets, from a maniac's tongue was
　　poured the deathless singing !
O Christians, at your cross of hope a hope-
　　less hand was clinging !
O men, this man in brotherhood your weary
　　paths beguiling,
Groaned inly while he taught you peace,
　　and died while ye were smiling !

III

And now, what time ye all may read
　　through dimming tears his story,
How discord on the music fell and dark-
　　ness on the glory,
And how when, one by one, sweet sounds
　　and wandering lights departed,
He wore no less a loving face because so
　　broken-hearted,

IV

He shall be strong to sanctify the poet's
  high vocation,
And bow the meekest Christian down in
  meeker adoration;
Nor ever shall he be, in praise, by wise or
  good forsaken,
Named softly as the household name of
  one whom God hath taken.

V

With quiet sadness and no gloom I learn
  to think upon him,
With meekness that is gratefulness to God
  whose heaven hath won him,
Who suffered once the madness-cloud to
  his own love to blind him,
But gently led the blind along where
  breath and bird could find him;

VI

And wrought within his shattered brain
  such quick poetic senses
As hills have language for, and stars, har-
  monious influences:
The pulse of dew upon the grass kept his
  within its number,
And silent shadows from the trees refreshed
  him like a slumber.

VII

Wild timid hares were drawn from woods
  to share his home-caresses,
Uplooking to his human eyes with sylvan
  tendernesses:
The very world, by God's constraint, from
  falsehood's ways removing,
Its women and its men became, beside him,
  true and loving.

VIII

And though, in blindness, he remained un-
  conscious of that guiding,
And things provided came without the
  sweet sense of providing,
He testified this solemn truth, while phrenzy
  desolated,
— Nor man nor nature satisfies whom only
  God created.

IX

Like a sick child that knoweth not his mo-
  ther while she blesses

And drops upon his burning brow the cool-
  ness of her kisses, —
That turns his fevered eyes around, — 'My
  mother! where 's my mother?' —
As if such tender words and deeds could
  come from any other! —

X

The fever gone, with leaps of heart he sees
  her bending o'er him,
Her face all pale from watchful love, the
  unweary love she bore him!
Thus woke the poet from the dream his
  life's long fever gave him,
Beneath those deep pathetic Eyes which
  closed in death to save him.

XI

Thus? oh, not *thus*! no type of earth can
  image that awaking,
Wherein he scarcely heard the chant of
  seraphs, round him breaking,
Or felt the new immortal throb of soul
  from body parted,
But felt those eyes alone, and knew — '*My*
  Saviour! *not deserted*!'

XII

Deserted! Who hath dreamt that when
  the cross in darkness rested,
Upon the Victim's hidden face no love was
  manifested?
What frantic hands outstretched have e'er
  the atoning drops averted?
What tears have washed them from the
  soul, that *one* should be deserted?

XIII

Deserted! God could separate from his
  own essence rather;
And Adam's sins *have* swept between the
  righteous Son and Father:
Yea, once, Immanuel's orphaned cry his
  universe hath shaken —
It went up single, echoless, 'My God, I am
  forsaken!'

XIV

It went up from the Holy's lips amid his
  lost creation,
That, of the lost, no son should use those
  words of desolation!

That Earth's worst phrenzies, marring
        hope, should mar not hope's fruition,
And I, on Cowper's grave, should see his
        rapture in a vision.

THE WEAKEST THING

I

WHICH is the weakest thing of all
    Mine heart can ponder ?
The sun, a little cloud can pall
    With darkness yonder ?
The cloud, a little wind can move
    Where'er it listeth ?
The wind, a little leaf above,
    Though sere, resisteth ?

II

What time that yellow leaf was green,
    My days were gladder;
But now, whatever Spring may mean,
    I must grow sadder.
Ah me ! a *leaf* with sighs can wring
    My lips asunder ?
Then is mine heart the weakest thing
    Itself can ponder.

III

Yet, Heart, when sun and cloud are pined
    And drop together,
And at a blast which is not wind
    The forests wither,
Thou, from the darkening deathly curse
    To glory breakest, —
The Strongest of the universe
    Guarding the weakest !

THE PET-NAME

                . . . the name
Which from THEIR lips seemed a caress.'
    — MISS MITFORD'S *Dramatic Scenes.*

First printed under the title of ' The Name.'
This name, as all the world knows since the
publication of Mrs. Browning's most intimate
correspondence, was the monosyllable Bā, (pro-
nounced *bay*).

I

I HAVE a name, a little name,
    Uncadenced for the ear,
Unhonored by ancestral claim.

Unsanctified by prayer and psalm
    The solemn font anear.

II

It never did to pages wove
    For gay romance belong;
It never dedicate did move
As ' Sacharissa ' unto love,
    ' Orinda ' unto song.

III

Though I write books, it will be read
    Upon the leaves of none,
And afterward, when I am dead,
Will ne'er be graved for sight or tread,
    Across my funeral-stone.

IV

This name, whoever chance to call,
    Perhaps your smile may win:
Nay, do not smile ! mine eyelids fall
Over mine eyes and feel withal
    The sudden tears within.

V

Is there a leaf, that greenly grows
    Where summer meadows bloom,
But gathereth the winter snows
And changeth to the hue of those,
    If lasting till they come ?

VI

Is there a word, or jest, or game,
    But time incrusteth round
With sad associate thoughts the same ?
And so to me my very name
    Assumes a mournful sound.

VII

My brother gave that name to me
    When we were children twain,
When names acquired baptismally
Were hard to utter, as to see
    That life had any pain.

VIII

No shade was on us then, save one
    Of chestnuts from the hill;
And through the word our laugh did run
As part thereof: the mirth being done,
    He calls me by it still.

IX

Nay, do not smile ! I hear in it
    What none of you can hear. —

The talk upon the willow seat,
The bird and wind that did repeat
Around, our human cheer.

X

I hear the birthday's noisy bliss,
My sisters' woodland glee,
My father's praise I did not miss,
When stooping down he cared to kiss
The poet at his knee, —

XI

And voices which, to name me, aye
Their tenderest tones were keeping —
To some I never more can say
An answer till God wipes away
In heaven these drops of weeping.

XII

My name to me a sadness wears:
No murmurs cross my mind —
Now God be thanked for these thick tears
Which show, of those departed years,
Sweet memories left behind.

XIII

Now God be thanked for years enwrought
With love which softens yet:
Now God be thanked for every thought
Which is so tender it has caught
Earth's guerdon of regret.

XIV

Earth saddens, never shall remove
Affections purely given;
And e'en that mortal grief shall prove
The immortality of love,
And heighten it with Heaven.

'SINCE WITHOUT THEE WE DO NO GOOD'

HYMN

'Lord, I cry unto thee, make haste unto me.' — *Psalm* cxli.

'The Lord is nigh unto them that call upon him.' — *Psalm* cxlv.

'This hymn was included among the few fugitive pieces bound up with Miss Barrett's first and subsequently suppressed translation of the *Prometheus Bound*.'

SINCE without Thee we do no good,
And with Thee do no ill,

Abide with us in weal and woe, —
In action and in will.

In weal, — that while our lips confess
The Lord who 'gives,' we may
Remember, with an humble thought,
The Lord who 'takes away.'

In woe, — that, while to drowning tears
Our hearts their joys resign,
We may remember *who* can turn
Such water into wine.

By hours of day, — that when our feet
O'er hill and valley run,
We still may think the light of truth
More welcome than the sun.

By hours of night, — that when the air
Its dew and shadow yields,
We still may hear the voice of God
In silence of the fields.

Oh ! then sleep comes on us like death,
All soundless, deaf and deep:
Lord ! teach us so to watch and pray,
That death may come like sleep.

Abide with *us*, abide with *us*,
While flesh and soul agree;
And when our flesh is only dust,
Abide our souls with *Thee*.

QUEEN ANNELIDA AND FALSE ARCITE

(MODERNIZED FROM CHAUCER)

First published in *The Poems of Geoffrey Chaucer Modernized* (London, 1841). This volume was edited by R. H. Horne, who contributed some of the modernizations. Wordsworth, who had first suggested the scheme of turning Chaucer into modern English verse, made several contributions, as did also Leigh Hunt. Tennyson and Robert Browning were invited to coöperate in the work, but declined. Miss Barrett executed the modernization, here reprinted, of Queen Annelida's story, and gave critical assistance about the whole compilation.

I

O THOU fierce God of armies, Mars the red,
Who in thy frosty country called Thrace,

Within thy grisly temples full of dread,
Art honored as the patron of that place,
With the Bellona Pallas, full of grace !
Be present; guide, sustain this song of
    mine,
Beginning which, I cry toward thy shrine.

II

For deep the hope is sunken in my mind,
In piteous-hearted English to indite
This story old, which I in Latin find,
Of Queen Annelida and false Arcite:
Since Time, whose rust can all things fret
    and bite,
In fretting many a tale of equal fame,
Hath from our memory nigh devoured this
    same.

III

Thy favor, Polyhymnia, also deign
Who, in thy sisters' green Parnassian glade,
By Helicon, not far from Cirrha's fane,
Singest with voice memorial in the shade
Under the laurel which can never fade;
Now grant my ship, that some smooth
    haven win her !
I follow Statius first, and then Corinna.

IV

When Theseus by a long and deathly war
The hardy Scythian race had overcome,
He, laurel-crownèd, in his gold-wrought
    car,
Returning to his native city home,
The blissful people for his pomp make
    room,
And throw their shouts up to the stars,
    and bring
The general heart out for his honoring.

V

Before the Duke, in sign of victory,
The trumpets sound, and in his banner
    large
Dilates the figure of Mars — and men
    may see,
In token of glory, many a treasure charge,
Many a bright helm, and many a spear
    and targe,
Many a fresh knight, and many a blissful
    rout
On horse and foot, in all the field about.

VI

Hippolyte, his wife, the heroic queen
Of Scythia, conqueress though conquerèd,

With Emily, her youthful sister sheen,
Fair in a car of gold he with him led.
The ground about her car she overspread
With brightness from the beauty in her
    face,
Which smiled forth largesses of love and
    grace.

VII

Thus triumphing, and laurel-crownèd thus,
In all the flower of Fortune's high pro-
    viding,
I leave this noble prince, this Theseus,
Toward the walls of Athens bravely rid-
    ing, —
And seek to bring in, without more abid-
    ing,
Something of that whereof I 'gan to write
Of fair Annelida and false Arcite.

VIII

Fierce Mars, who in his furious course of
    ire,
The ancient wrath of Juno to fulfil,
Had set the nations' mutual hearts on fire
In Thebes and Argos, (so that each would
    kill
Either with bloody spears,) grew never
    still —
But rushed now here, now there, among
    them both,
Till each was slain by each, they were so
    wroth.

IX

For when Parthenopæus and Tydeus
Had perished with Hippomedon, — alsò
Amphiaraus and proud Capaneus, —
And when the wretched Theban brethren
    two
Were slain, and King Adrastus home did
    go —
So desolate stood Thebes, her halls so bare,
That no man's love could remedy his care.

X

And when the old man, Creon, 'gan espy
How darkly the blood royal was brought
    down,
He held the city in his tyranny,
And forced the nobles of that regiòn
To be his friends and dwell within the town;
Till half for love of him, and half for fear,
Those princely persons yielded, and drew
    near, —

XI

Among the rest the young Armenian queen,
Annelida, was in that city living.
She was as beauteous as the sun was sheen,
Her fame to distant lands such glory giving
That all men in the world had some heart-
    striving
To look on her. No woman, sooth, can be,
Though earth is rich in fairness, fair as she.

XII

Young was this queen, but twenty summers
    old,
Of middle stature, and such wondrous
    beauty,
That Nature, self-delighted, did behold
A rare work in her — while, in stedfast
    duty,
Lucretia and Penelope would suit ye
With a worse model — all things under-
    stood,
She was, in short, most perfect fair and
    good.

XIII

The Theban knight eke, to give all their
    due,
Was young, and therewithal a lusty knight.
But he was double in love, and nothing true,
Ay, subtler in that craft than any wight,
And with his cunning won this lady bright;
So working on her simpleness of nature,
That she him trusted above every creature.

XIV

What shall I say ? She lovèd Arcite so,
That if at any hour he parted from her,
Her heart seemed ready anon to burst in
    two;
For he with lowliness had overcome her:
She thought she knew the heart which did
    foredoom her.
But he was false, and all that softness feign-
    ing, —
I trow men need not learn such arts of
    paining.

XV

And ne'ertheless full mickle business
Had he, before he might his lady win, —
He swore that he should die of his distress,
His brain would madden with the fire
    within !
Alas, the while ! for it was ruth and sin,

That she, sweet soul, upon his grief should
    rue;
But little reckon false hearts as the true.

XVI

And she to Arcite so subjected her,
That all she did or had seemed his of right:
No creature in her house met smile or cheer,
Further than would be pleasant to Arcite;
There was no lack whereby she did despite
To his least will — for hers to his was bent,
And all things which pleased him made her
    content.

XVII

No kind of letter to her fair hands came,
Touching on love, from any kind of wight,
But him she showed it ere she burned the
    same:
So open was she, doing all she might,
That nothing should be hidden from her
    knight,
Lest he for any untruth should upbraid
    her, —
The slave of his unspoken will she made
    her.

XVIII

He played his jealous fancies over her,
And if he heard that any other man
Spoke to her, would beseech her straight to
    swear
To each word — or the speaker had his ban;
And out of her sweet wits she almost ran
For fear; but all was fraud and flattery,
Since without love he feignèd jealousy.

XIX

All which with so much sweetness suffered
    she,
Whate'er he willed she thought the wisest
    thing;
And evermore she loved him tenderly,
And did him honor as he were a king.
Her heart was wedded to him with a ring,
So eager to be faithful and intent,
That wheresoe'er he wandered, there it went.

XX

When she would eat he stole away her
    thought,
Till little thought for food, I ween, was
    kept;
And when a time for rest the midnight
    brought,

She always mused upon him till she slept, —
When he was absent, secretly she wept;
And thus lived Queen Annelida the fair,
For false Arcite, who worked her this
    despair.

XXI

This false Arcite in his new-fangleness,
Because so gentle were her ways and true,
Took the less pleasure in her stedfastness,
And saw another lady proud and new,
And right anon he clad him in her hue;
I know not whether white, or red, or green,
Betraying fair Annelida the Queen.

XXII

And yet it was no thing to wonder on,
Though he were false — It is the way of
    man,
(Since Lamech was, who flourished years
    agone,)
To be in love as false as any can;
For he was the first father who began
To love two; and I trow, indeed, that he
Invented tents as well as bigamy.

XXIII

And having so betrayed her, false Arcite
Feign'd more, that primal wrong to justify.
A vicious horse will snort besides his bite;
And so he taunted her with treachery,
Swearing he saw thro' her duplicity,
And how she was not loving, but false-
    hearted —
The perjured traitor swore thus, and de-
    parted.

XXIV

Alas, alas, what heart could suffer it,
For ruth, the story of her grief to tell?
What thinker hath the cunning and the
    wit
To image it? what hearer, strength to
    dwell
A room's length off, while I rehearse the
    hell
Suffered by Queen Annelida the fair
For false Arcite, who worked her this de-
    spair?

XXV

She weepeth, waileth, swooneth piteously;
She falleth on the earth dead as a stone;
Her graceful limbs are cramped convul-
    sively;

She speaketh out wild, as her wits were
    gone.
No color, but an ashen paleness — none —
Touched cheek or lips; and no word shook
    their white,
But 'Mercy, cruel heart! mine own
    Arcite!'

XXVI

Thus it continued, till she pinèd so,
And grew so weak, her feet no more could
    bear
Her body, languishing in ceaseless woe.
Whereof Arcite had neither ruth nor
    care —
His heart had put out new-green shoots
    elsewhere;
Therefore he deigned not on her grief to
    think,
And reckoned little, did she float or sink.

XXVII

His fine new lady kept him in such narrow
Strict limit, by the bridle, at the end
O' the whip, he feared her least word as
    an arrow, —
Her threatening made him, as a bow, to
    bend,
And at her pleasure did he turn and wend;
Seeing she never granted to this lover
A single grace he could sing 'Ios' over.

XXVIII

She drove him forth — she scarcely deigned
    to know
That he was servant to her ladyship:
But, lest he should be proud, she kept him
    low,
Nor paid his service from a smiling lip:
She sent him now to land, and now to
    ship;
And giving him all danger to his fill,
She thereby had him at her sovereign will.

XXIX

Be taught of this, ye prudent women all,
Warn'd by Annelida and false Arcite:
Because she chose, himself, 'dear heart' to
    call
And be so meek, he loved her not aright.
The nature of man's heart is to delight
In something strange — moreover, (may
    Heaven save
The wrong'd) the thing they cannot, they
    would have.

XXX

Now turn we to Annelida again,
Who pinèd day by day in languishment.
But when she saw no comfort met her
    pain,
Weeping once in a woeful unconstraint,
She set herself to fashion a complaint,
Which with her own pale hand she 'gan to
    write,
And sent it to her lover, to Arcite.

THE COMPLAINT OF ANNELIDA TO FALSE ARCITE

I

THE sword of sorrow, whetted sharp for
    me
On false delight, with point of memory
Stabb'd so mine heart, bliss-bare and black
    of hue,
That all to dread is turn'd my dance's glee,
My face's beauty to despondency —
For nothing it availeth to be true —
And, whosoever is so, she shall rue
Obeying love, and cleaving faithfully
Alway to one, and changing for no new.

II

I ought to know it well as any wight,
For I loved one with all my heart and
    might,
More than myself a hundred-thousand fold,
And callèd him my heart's dear life, my
    knight,
And was all his, as far as it was right;
His gladness did my blitheness make of
    old,
And in his least disease my death was told;
Who, on his side, had plighted lovers'
    plight,
Me, evermore, his lady and love to hold.

III

Now is he false — alas, alas! — although
Unwronged! and acting such a ruthless
    part,
That with a little word he will not deign
To bring the peace back to my mournful
    heart.
Drawn in, and caught up by another's art,
Right as he will, he laugheth at my pain;
While I — I cannot my weak heart restrain
From loving him — still, aye; yet none I
    know
To whom of all this grief I can complain.

IV

Shall I complain (ah, piteous and harsh
    sound!)
Unto my foe, who gave mine heart a
    wound,
And still desireth that the harm be more ?
Now certes, if I sought the whole earth
    round,
No other help, no better leech were found !
My destiny hath shaped it so of yore —
I would not other medicine, nor yet lore.
I would be ever where I once was bound;
And what I said, would say for evermore.

V

Alas ! and where is gone your gentillesse ?
Where gone your pleasant words, your
    humbleness ?
Where your devotion full of reverent fear,
Your patient loyalty, your busy address
To me, whom once you callèd nothing less
Than mistress, sovereign lady, i' the sphere
O' the world ? Ah me ! no word, no look
    of cheer,
Will you vouchsafe upon my heaviness !
Alas your love ! I bought it all too dear.

VI

Now certes, sweet, howe'er you be
The cause so, and so causelessly,
Of this my mortal agony,
Your reason should amend the failing !
Your friend, your true love, do you flee,
Who never in time nor yet degree
Grieved you: so may the all-knowing he
Save my lorn soul from future wailing.

VII

Because I was so plain, Arcite,
In all my doings, your delight
Seeking in all things, where I might
In honor, — meek and kind and free;
Therefore you do me such despite.
Alas ! howe'er through cruelty
My heart with sorrow's sword you smite,
You cannot kill its love. — Ah me !

VIII

Ah, my sweet foe, why do you so
                For shame ?

Think you that praise, in sooth, will raise
                              Your name,
Loving anew, and being untrue
                              For aye ?
Thus casting down your manhood's crown
                              In blame,
And working me adversity,
                              The same
Who loves you most — (O God, thou
  know'st !)
                              Alway ?
Yet turn again — be fair and plain
                              Some day;
And then shall this, that seems amiss,
                              Be game,
All being forgiv'n, while yet from heav'n
                              I stay.

IX

Behold, dear heart, I write this to obtain
Some knowledge, whether I should pray or
  'plaine:
Which way is best to force you to be true?
For either I must have you in my chain,
Or you, sweet, with the death must part us
  twain;
There is no mean, no other way more new:
And, that Heaven's mercy on my soul may
  rue
And let you slay me outright with this
  pain,
The whiteness in my cheeks may prove to
  you.

X

For hitherto mine own death have I sought;
Myself I murder with my secret thought,
In sorrow and ruth of your unkindnesses !
I weep, I wail, I fast — all helpeth nought,
I flee all joy (I mean the name of aught),
I flee all company, all mirthfulness —
Why, who can make her boast of more dis-
  tress
Than I ? To such a plight you have me
  brought,
Guiltless (I need no witness) ne'ertheless.

XI

Shall I go pray and wail my womanhood ?
Compared to such a deed, death's self were
  good.
What ! ask for mercy, and guiltless —
  where 's the need ?
And if I wailed my life so, — that you
  would

Care nothing, is less feared than under-
  stood:
And if mine oath of love I dared to plead
In mine excuse, — your scorn would be its
  meed.
Ah, love ! it giveth flowers instead of
  seed —
Full long ago I might have taken heed.

XII

And though I had you back to-morrow
  again,
I might as well hold April from the rain
As hold you to the vows you vowed me
  last.
Maker of all things, and truth's sovereign,
Where is the truth of man, who hath it
  slain,
That she who loveth him should find him
  fast
As in a tempest is a rotten mast ?
Is that a tame beast which is ever fain
To flee us when restraint and fear are
  past?

XIII

Now mercy, sweet, if I mis-say; —
Have I said aught is wrong to-day ?
I do not know — my wit 's astray —
I fare as doth the song of one who weep-
  eth;
For now I 'plaine, and now I play —
I am so 'mazed, I die away —
Arcite, you have the key for aye
Of all my world, and all the good it keep-
  eth.

XIV

And in this world there is not one
Who walketh with a sadder moan,
And bears more grief than I have done;
And if light slumbers overcome me,
Methinks your image, in the glory
Of skyey azure, stands before me,
Re-vowing the old love you bore me,
And praying for new mercy from me.

XV

Through the long night, this wondrous
  sight,
                              Bear I,
Which haunteth still, the daylight, till
                              I die:
But nought of this, your heart, I wis,
                              Can reach.

Mine eyes down-pour, they nevermore
          Are dry,
While to your ruth, and eke your truth,
          I cry —
But, weladay, too far be they
          To fetch.
Thus destiny is holding me —
          Ah, wretch !
And when I fain would break the chain,
          And try —
Faileth my wit (so weak is it)
          With speech.

XVI

Therefore I end thus, since my hope is
  o'er —
I give all up both now and evermore;
And in the balance ne'er again will lay

My safety, nor be studious in love-lore.
But like the swan who, as I heard of yore,
Singeth life's penance on his deathly day,
So I sing here my life and woes away, —
Ay, how you, cruel Arcite, wounded sore,
With memory's point, your poor Annelida.

XVII

After Annelida, the woeful queen,
Had written in her own hand in this wise,
With ghastly face, less pale than white, I
  ween,
She fell a-swooning; then she 'gan arise,
And unto Mars voweth a sacrifice
Within the temple, with a sorrowful bear-
  ing,
And in such phrase as meets your present
  hearing.

POEMS OF 1844

In 1844 appeared, *Poems. By Elizabeth Barrett Barrett, Author of The Seraphim, etc. In two volumes. (London, Edward Moxon, Dover Street.)* This edition, the last which bore Mrs Browning's maiden name, was dedicated to her father, and 'A Drama of Exile' was its initial and longest poem. Her mind, as when she wrote 'The Seraphim,' was still preoccupied by the idea of casting the stupendous incidents of the Christian story into a form approximating that of Greek tragedy.

A DRAMA OF EXILE

  ' De patrie, et de Dieu, des poëtes, de l'âme
  Qui s'élève en priant.'   *—Victor Hugo.*

PERSONS

    CHRIST, *in a Vision.*
    ADAM.
    EVE.
    GABRIEL.
    LUCIFER.

Angels, Eden Spirits, Earth Spirits, and Phantasms.

SCENE. — *The outer side of the gate of Eden shut fast with cloud, from the depth of which revolves a sword of fire self-moved. ADAM and EVE are seen in the distance flying along the glare.*

LUCIFER, *alone.*

REJOICE in the clefts of Gehenna,
  My exiled, my host !
Earth has exiles as hopeless as when a
  Heaven's empire was lost.

Through the seams of her shaken founda-
    tions,
  Smoke up in great joy !
With the smoke of your fierce exultations
  Deform and destroy !
Smoke up with your lurid revenges,
  And darken the face   10
Of the white heavens and taunt them with
    changes
  From glory and grace.
We, in falling, while destiny strangles,
  Pull down with us all.
Let them look to the rest of their angels !
  Who 's safe from a fall ?
He saves not.   Where 's Adam ?   Can
    pardon
  Requicken that sod ?
Unkinged is the King of the Garden,
  The image of God.   20
Other exiles are cast out of Eden, —
  More curse has been hurled:
Come up, O my locusts, and feed in
  The green of the world !
Come up ! we have conquered by evil;
  Good reigns not alone:

I prevail now, and, angel or devil,
Inherit a throne.
> [*In sudden apparition a watch of innum-*
> *erable* Angels, *rank above rank, slopes*
> *up from around the gate to the zenith.*
> *The* Angel GABRIEL *descends.*

Lucifer.   Hail, Gabriel, the keeper of the
gate !
Now that the fruit is plucked, prince
Gabriel,   30
I hold that Eden is impregnable
Under thy keeping.
Gabriel.   Angel of the sin,
Such as thou standest, — pale in the drear
light
Which rounds the rebel's work with
Maker's wrath, —
Thou shalt be an Idea to all souls,
A monumental melancholy gloom
Seen down all ages, whence to mark de-
spair
And measure out the distances from good.
Go from us straightway !
Lucifer.   Wherefore ?
Gabriel.   Lucifer,
Thy last step in this place trod sorrow
up.   40
Recoil before that sorrow, if not this sword.
Lucifer. Angels are in the world —
wherefore not I ?
Exiles are in the world — wherefore not I ?
The cursed are in the world — wherefore
not I ?
Gabriel. Depart !
Lucifer. And where 's the logic of ' de-
part ' ?
Our lady Eve had half been satisfied
To obey her Maker, if I had not learnt
To fix my postulate better.   Dost thou
dream
Of guarding some monopoly in heaven
Instead of earth ?   Why, I can dream with
thee   50
To the length of thy wings.
Gabriel.   I do not dream.
This is not heaven, even in a dream, nor
earth,
As earth was once, first breathed among
the stars,
Articulate glory from the mouth divine,
To which the myriad spheres thrilled au-
dibly,
Touched like a lute-string, and the sons of
God
Said AMEN, singing it.   I know that this

Is earth not new created but new cursed —
This, Eden's gate not opened but built
up
With a final cloud of sunset.   Do I
dream ?   60
Alas, not so ! this is the Eden lost
By Lucifer the serpent; this the sword
(This sword alive with justice and with
fire)
That smote, upon the forehead, Lucifer
The angel.   Wherefore, angel, go — de-
part !
Enough is sinned and suffered.
Lucifer.   By no means.
Here 's a brave earth to sin and suffer
on:
It holds fast still — it cracks not under
curse;
It holds like mine immortal.   Presently
We 'll sow it thick enough with graves as
green   70
Or greener certes, than its knowledge-tree.
We 'll have the cypress for the tree of
life,
More eminent for shadow: for the rest,
We 'll build it dark with towns and pyra-
mids,
And temples, if it please you: — we 'll
have feasts
And funerals also, merrymakes and wars,
Till blood and wine shall mix and run
along
Right o'er the edges.   And, good Gabriel
(Ye like that word in heaven), *I* too have
strength —
Strength to behold Him and not worship
Him,   80
Strength to fall from Him and not cry on
Him,
Strength to be in the universe and yet
Neither God nor his servant.   The red
sign
Burnt on my forehead, which you taunt me
with,
Is God's sign that it bows not unto God,
The potter's mark upon his work, to show
It rings well to the striker.   I and the
earth
Can bear more curse.
Gabriel.   O miserable earth,
O ruined angel !
Lucifer.   Well, and if it be !
I CHOSE this ruin; I elected it   90
Of my will, not of service.   What I do,
I do volitient, not obedient,

And overtop thy crown with my despair.
My sorrow crowns me. Get thee back to
   heaven,
And leave me to the earth, which is mine
   own
In virtue of her ruin, as I hers
In virtue of my revolt! Turn thou from
   both
That bright, impassive, passive angelhood,
And spare to read us backward any more
Of the spent hallelujahs!
  Gabriel.   Spirit of scorn, 100
I might say, of unreason! I might say,
That who despairs, acts; that who acts,
   connives
With God's relations set in time and space;
That who elects, assumes a something good
Which God made possible; that who lives,
   obeys
The law of a Life-maker . . .
  Lucifer.   Let it pass!
No more, thou Gabriel! What if I stand
   up
And strike my brow against the crystal-
   line
Roofing the creatures, — shall I say, for
   that,
My stature is too high for me to
   stand, —   110
Henceforward I must sit? Sit *thou!*
  Gabriel.   I kneel.
  Lucifer. A heavenly answer. Get thee
   to thy heaven,
And leave my earth to me!
  Gabriel.   Through heaven and earth
God's will moves freely, and I follow it,
As color follows light. He overflows
The firmamental walls with deity,
Therefore with love; his lightnings go
   abroad,
His pity may do so, his angels must,
Whene'er He gives them charges.
  Lucifer.   Verily,
I and my demons, who are spirits of
   scorn,   120
Might hold this charge of standing with a
   sword
'Twixt man and his inheritance, as well
As the benignest angel of you all.
  Gabriel. Thou speakest in the shadow of
   thy change.
If thou hadst gazed upon the face of God
This morning for a moment, thou hadst
   known

That only pity fitly can chastise;
Hate but avenges.
  Lucifer.   As it is, I know
Something of pity. When I reeled in
   heaven,
And my sword grew too heavy for my
   grasp,   130
Stabbing through matter, which it could not
   pierce
So much as the first shell of, — toward the
   throne;
When I fell back, down, — staring up as I
   fell, —
The lightnings holding open my scathed
   lids,
And that thought of the infinite of God,
Hurled after to precipitate descent;
When countless angel faces still and stern
Pressed out upon me from the level
   heavens
Adown the abysmal spaces, and I fell
Trampled down by your stillness, and struck
   blind   140
By the sight within your eyes, — 't was then
   I knew
How ye could pity, my kind angelhood!
  Gabriel. Alas, discrowned one, by the
   truth in me
Which God keeps in me, I would give
   away
All — save that truth and his love keeping
   it —
To lead thee home again into the light
And hear thy voice chant with the morning
   stars,
When their rays tremble round them with
   much song
Sung in more gladness!
  Lucifer.   Sing, my Morning Star!
Last beautiful, last heavenly, that I
   loved!   150
If I could drench thy golden locks with
   tears,
What were it to this angel?
  Gabriel.   What love is.
And now I have named God.
  Lucifer.   Yet, Gabriel,
By the lie in me which I keep myself,
Thou 'rt a false swearer. Were it other-
   wise,
What dost thou here, vouchsafing tender
   thoughts
To that earth-angel or earth-demon —
   which,

Thou and I have not solved the problem
    yet
Enough to argue, — that fallen Adam
    there, —
That red-clay and a breath, — who must,
    forsooth,   160
Live in a new apocalypse of sense,
With beauty and music waving in his trees
And running in his rivers, to make glad
His soul made perfect ? — is it not for
    hope,
A hope within thee deeper than thy truth,
Of finally conducting him and his
To fill the vacant thrones of me and mine,
Which affront heaven. with their vacu-
    ity ?
    Gabriel. Angel, there are no vacant thrones
    in heaven
To suit thy empty words.   Glory and
    life   170
Fulfil their own depletions; and if God
Sighed you far from Him, his next breath
    drew in
A compensative splendor up the vast,
Flushing the starry arteries.
    Lucifer.   What a change !
So, let the vacant thrones and gardens too
Fill as may please you ! — and be pitiful,
As ye translate that word, to the dethroned
And exiled, man or angel. The fact stands,
That I, the rebel, the cast out and down,
Am here and will not go; while there,
    along   180
The light to which ye flash the desert
    out,
Flies your adopted Adam, your red-clay
In two kinds, both being flawed. Why,
    what is this ?
Whose work is this ? Whose hand was in
    the work ?
Against whose hand ? In this last strife,
    methinks,
I am not a fallen angel !
    Gabriel.   Dost thou know
Aught of those exiles ?
    Lucifer.   Ay: I know they have fled
Silent all day along the wilderness:
I know they wear, for burden on their
    backs,
The thought of a shut gate of Paradise, 190
And faces of the marshalled cherubim
Shining against, not for them; and I know
They dare not look in one another's
    face, —
As if each were a cherub !

    Gabriel.   Dost thou know
Aught of their future ?
    Lucifer.   Only as much as this:
That evil will increase and multiply
Without a benediction.
    Gabriel.   Nothing more ?
    Lucifer. Why so the angels taunt !
    What should be more ?
    Gabriel. God is more.
    Lucifer.   Proving what ?
    Gabriel.   That he is God,
And capable of saving. Lucifer,   200
I charge thee by the solitude He kept
Ere He created, — leave the earth to God !
    Lucifer. My foot is on the earth, firm
    as my sin.
    Gabriel. I charge thee by the memory
    of heaven
Ere any sin was done, — leave earth to
    God !
    Lucifer. My sin is on the earth, to
    reign thereon.
    Gabriel. I charge thee by the choral
    song we sang,
When up against the white shore of our
    feet
The depths of the creation swelled and
    brake, —
And the new worlds, the beaded foam and
    flower   210
Of all that coil, roared outward into space
On thunder-edges, — leave the earth to
    God !
    Lucifer. My woe is on the earth, to
    curse thereby.
    Gabriel. I charge thee by that mourn-
    ful Morning Star
Which trembles . . .
    Lucifer. Enough spoken. As the pine
In norland forest drops its weight of snows
By a night's growth, so, growing toward
    my ends
I drop thy counsels. Farewell, Gabriel !
Watch out thy service; I achieve my
    will.
And peradventure in the after years,   220
When thoughtful men shall bend their
    spacious brows
Upon the storm and strife seen everywhere
To ruffle their smooth manhood and break
    up
With lurid lights of intermittent hope
Their human fear and wrong, — they may
    discern
The heart of a lost angel in the earth.

CHORUS OF EDEN SPIRITS

(*Chanting from Paradise, while* ADAM *and* EVE *fly across the Sword-glare.*)

Hearken, oh hearken! let your souls be-
    hind you
        Turn, gently moved!
Our voices feel along the Dread to find
    you,
        O lost, beloved!   230
Through the thick-shielded and strong-
    marshalled angels,
        They press and pierce:
Our requiems follow fast on our evan-
    gels,—
        Voice throbs in verse.
We are but orphaned spirits left in Eden
    A time ago:
God gave us golden cups, and we were
    bidden
        To feed you so.
But now our right hand hath no cup re-
    maining,
        No work to do,   240
The mystic hydromel is spilt, and stain-
    ing
        The whole earth through.
Most ineradicable stains, for showing
    (Not interfused!)
That brighter colors were the world's
    foregoing,
        Than shall be used.
Hearken, oh hearken! ye shall hearken
    surely
        For years and years,
The noise beside you, dripping coldly,
    purely,
        Of spirits' tears.   250
The yearning to a beautiful denied you
    Shall strain your powers;
Ideal sweetnesses shall overglide you,
    Resumed from ours.
In all your music, our pathetic minor
    Your ears shall cross;
And all good gifts shall mind you of
    diviner,
        With sense of loss.
We shall be near you in your poet-
    languors
        And wild extremes,   260
What time ye vex the desert with vain
    angers,
        Or mock with dreams.

And when upon you, weary after roam-
    ing,
        Death's seal is put,
By the foregone ye shall discern the
    coming,
        Through eyelids shut.
Spirits of the Trees.
Hark! the Eden trees are stirring,
Soft and solemn in your hearing!
Oak and linden, palm and fir,
Tamarisk and juniper,   270
Each still throbbing in vibration
Since that crowning of creation
When the God-breath spake abroad,
Let us make man like to God!
And the pine stood quivering
As the awful word went by,
Like a vibrant music-string
Stretched from mountain-peak to sky;
And the platan did expand   279
Slow and gradual, branch and head;
And the cedar's strong black shade
Fluttered brokenly and grand:
Grove and wood were swept aslant
In emotion jubilant.
Voice of the same, but softer.
Which divine impulsion cleaves
In dim movements to the leaves
Dropt and lifted, dropt and lifted,
In the sunlight greenly sifted,—
In the sunlight and the moonlight
Greenly sifted through the trees.   290
Ever wave the Eden trees
In the nightlight and the noonlight,
With a ruffling of green branches
Shaded off to resonances,
Never stirred by rain or breeze.
Fare ye well, farewell!
The sylvan sounds, no longer audible,
Expire at Eden's door.
Each footstep of your treading
Treads out some murmur which ye heard
        before.   300
Farewell! the trees of Eden
Ye shall hear nevermore.
River Spirits.
Hark! the flow of the four rivers —
    Hark the flow!
How the silence round yon shivers,
    While our voices through it go,
Cold and clear.
A softer Voice.
Think a little, while ye hear,
    Of the banks

Where the willows and the deer   310
    Crowd in intermingled ranks,
As if all would drink at once
Where the living water runs ! —
    Of the fishes' golden edges
    Flashing in and out the sedges;
Of the swans on silver thrones,
    Floating down the winding streams
With impassive eyes turned shoreward
And a chant of undertones, —
And the lotos leaning forward   320
    To help them into dreams !
Fare ye well, farewell !
The river-sounds, no longer audible,
    Expire at Eden's door.
    Each footstep of your treading
Treads out some murmur which ye heard
    before.
    Farewell ! the streams of Eden
    Ye shall hear nevermore.

Bird Spirit.

I am the nearest nightingale
    That singeth in Eden after you;   330
    And I am singing loud and true,
And sweet, — I do not fail.
I sit upon a cypress bough,
Close to the gate, and I fling my song
Over the gate and through the mail
Of   the   warden   angels   marshalled
    strong, —
    Over the gate and after you.
And the warden angels let it pass,
Because the poor brown bird, alas,
    Sings in the garden, sweet and true. 340
And I build my song of high pure notes,
    Note over note, height over height,
    Till I strike the arch of the Infinite,
And I bridge abysmal agonies
With strong, clear calms of harmonies, —
And something abides, and something
    floats,
In the song which I sing after you.
Fare ye well, farewell !
The creature-sounds, no longer audible,
    Expire at Eden's door.   350
    Each footstep of your treading
Treads out some cadence which ye heard
    before.
    Farewell ! the birds of Eden
    Ye shall hear nevermore.

Flower Spirits.

We linger, we linger,
    The last of the throng,
Like the tones of a singer
    Who loves his own song.

We are spirit-aromas
    Of blossom and bloom.   360
We call your thoughts home, — as
    Ye breathe our perfume, —
To the amaranth's splendor
    Afire on the slopes;
To the lily-bells tender,
    And gray heliotropes;
To the poppy-plains keeping
    Such dream-breath and blee
That the angels there stepping
    Grew whiter to see: 370
To the nook, set with moly,
    Ye jested one day in,
Till your smile waxed too holy
    And left your lips praying:
To the rose in the bower-place,
    That dripped o'er you sleeping;
To the asphodel flower-place,
    Ye walked ankle-deep in.
We pluck at your raiment,
    We stroke down your hair,   380
We faint in our lament
    And pine into air.
Fare ye well, farewell !
The Eden scents, no longer sensible,
    Expire at Eden's door.
    Each footstep of your treading
Treads out some fragrance which ye knew
    before.
    Farewell ! the flowers of Eden
    Ye shall smell nevermore.

> [*There is silence.* ADAM *and* EVE
> *fly on, and never look back. Only
> a colossal shadow, as of the dark
> Angel passing quickly, is cast upon
> the Sword-glare.*

SCENE. — *The extremity of the Sword-glare.*

Adam. Pausing a moment on this outer
    edge   390
Where the supernal sword-glare cuts in
    light
The   dark   exterior   desert, — hast   thou
    strength,
Beloved, to look behind us to the gate ?
    Eve. Have I not strength to look up to
    thy face ?
    Adam. We need be strong: yon spectacle
    of cloud
Which seals the gate up to the final doom,
Is God's seal manifest. There seem to
    lie

A hundred thunders in it, dark and dead;
The unmolten lightnings vein it motionless;
And, outward from its depth, the self-
    moved sword   400
Swings slow its awful gnomon of red fire
From side to side, in pendulous horror slow,
Across the stagnant ghastly glare thrown
    flat
On the intermediate ground from that to
    this.
The angelic hosts, the archangelic pomps,
Thrones, dominations, princedoms, rank on
    rank,
Rising sublimely to the feet of God,
On either side and overhead the gate,
Show like a glittering and sustainèd smoke
Drawn to an apex. That their faces shine 410
Betwixt the solemn clasping of their wings
Clasped high to a silver point above their
    heads, —
We only guess from hence, and not discern.
    Eve. Though we were near enough to
    see them shine,
The shadow on thy face were awfuller,
To me, at least, — to me — than all their
    light.
    Adam. What is this, Eve? thou drop-
    pest heavily
In a heap earthward, and thy body heaves
Under the golden floodings of thine hair!
    Eve. O Adam, Adam! by that name
    of Eve —   420
Thine Eve, thy life — which suits me little
    now,
Seeing that I now confess myself thy death
And thine undoer, as the snake was
    mine, —
I do adjure thee, put me straight away,
Together with my name! Sweet, punish
    me!
O Love, be just! and, ere we pass beyond
The light cast outward by the fiery sword,
Into the dark which earth must be to us,
Bruise my head with thy foot, — as the
    curse said
My seed shall the first tempter's! strike
    with curse,   430
As God struck in the garden! and as HE,
Being satisfied with justice and with wrath,
Did roll his thunder gentler at the close, —
Thou, peradventure, mayst at last recoil
To some soft need of mercy. Strike, my
    lord!
I, also, after tempting, writhe on the
    ground,

And I would feed on ashes from thine
    hand,
As suits me, O my tempted!
    Adam.   My beloved,
Mine Eve and life — I have no other name
For thee or for the sun than what ye are,
My utter life and light! If we have
    fallen,   441
It is that we have sinned, — we: God is
    just;
And, since his curse doth comprehend us
    both,
It must be that his balance holds the
    weights
Of first and last sin on a level. What!
Shall I who had not virtue to stand
    straight
Among the hills of Eden, here assume
To mend the justice of the perfect God,
By piling up a curse upon his curse,
Against thee — thee?
    Eve.   For so, perchance, thy God 450
Might take thee into grace for scorning
    me;
Thy wrath against the sinner giving proof
Of inward abrogation of the sin:
And so, the blessèd angels might come
    down
And walk with thee as erst, — I think they
    would, —
Because I was not near to make them sad
Or soil the rustling of their innocence.
    Adam. They know me. I am deepest
    in the guilt,
If last in the transgression.
    Eve.   Thou!
    Adam.   If God,
Who gave the right and joyaunce of the
    world   460
Both unto thee and me, — gave thee to me,
The best gift last, the last sin was the
    worst,
Which sinned against more complement of
    gifts
And grace of giving. God! I render back
Strong benediction and perpetual praise
From mortal feeble lips (as incense-smoke,
Out of a little censer, may fill heaven),
That thou, in striking my benumbèd hands
And forcing them to drop all other boons
Of beauty and dominion and delight, — 470
Hast left this well-belovèd Eve, this life
Within life, this best gift between their
    palms,
In gracious compensation!

Eve.   Is it thy voice ?
Or some saluting angel's — calling home
My feet into the garden ?
  Adam.   O my God !
I, standing here between the glory and
    dark, —
The glory of thy wrath projected forth
From Eden's wall, the dark of our dis-
    tress
Which settles a step off in that drear
    world —
Lift up to Thee the hands from whence
    hath fallen   480
Only creation's sceptre, — thanking Thee
That rather Thou hast cast me out with
    her
Than left me lorn of her in Paradise,
With angel looks and angel songs around
To show the absence of her eyes and voice,
And make society full desertness
Without her use in comfort!
  Eve.   Where is loss ?
Am I in Eden ? can another speak
Mine own love's tongue ?
  Adam.   Because with *her*, I stand
Upright, as far as can be in this fall,   490
And look away from heaven which doth
    accuse,
And look away from earth which doth con-
    vict,
Into her face, and crown my discrowned
    brow
Out of her love, and put the thought of
    her
Around me, for an Eden full of birds,
And lift her body up — thus — to my heart,
And with my lips upon her lips, — thus,
    thus, —
Do quicken and sublimate my mortal
    breath
Which cannot climb against the grave's
    steep sides
But overtops this grief.
  Eve.   I am renewed.   500
My eyes grow with the light which is in
    thine;
The silence of my heart is full of sound.
Hold me up — so ! Because I compre-
    hend
This human love, I shall not be afraid
Of any human death; and yet because
I know this strength of love, I seem to
    know
Death's strength by that same sign. Kiss
  on my lips,

To shut the door close on my rising soul, —
Lest it pass outwards in astonishment
And leave thee lonely !
  Adam.   Yet thou liest, Eve,   510
Bent heavily on thyself across mine arm,
Thy face flat to the sky.
  Eve.   Ay, and the tears
Running, as it might seem, my life from
    me,
They run so fast and warm. Let me lie
    so,
And weep so, as if in a dream or prayer,
Unfastening, clasp by clasp, the hard tight
    thought
Which clipped my heart and showed me
    evermore
Loathed of thy justice as I loathe the snake,
And as the pure ones loathe our sin. To-
    day,
All day, belovèd, as we fled across   520
This desolating radiance cast by swords
Not suns, — my lips prayed soundless **to**
    myself,
Striking against each other — 'O Lord
    God !'
('T was so I prayed) 'I ask Thee by **my**
    sin,
And by thy curse, and by thy blameless
    heavens,
Make dreadful haste to hide me from thy
    face
And from the face of my belovèd here
For whom I am no helpmeet, quick away
Into the new dark mystery of death !   529
I will lie still there, I will make no plaint,
I will not sigh, nor sob, nor speak a word,
Nor struggle to come back beneath the
    sun
Where peradventure I might sin anew
Against thy mercy and his pleasure Death,
O death, whate'er it be, is good enough
For such as I am: while for Adam here,
No voice shall say again, in heaven or
    earth,
It is not good for him to be alone.'
  Adam. And was it good for such a
    prayer to pass,
My unkind Eve, betwixt our mutual lives ?
If I am exiled, must I be bereaved ?   541
  Eve. 'T was an ill prayer: it shall be
    prayed no more;
And God did use it like a foolishness,
Giving no answer. Now my heart has
    grown

Too high and strong for such a foolish
    prayer;
Love makes it strong: and since I was the
    first
In the transgression, with a steady foot
I will be first to tread from this sword-
    glare
Into the outer darkness of the waste, —
And thus I do it.
    Adam.   Thus I follow thee,   550
As erewhile in the sin. — What sounds !
    what sounds !
I feel a music which comes straight from
    heaven,
As tender as a watering dew.
    Eve.   I think
That angels — not those guarding Para-
    dise, —
But the love-angels, who came erst to us,
And when we said 'GOD,' fainted unawares
Back from our mortal presence unto God,
(As if He drew them inward in a breath)
His name being heard of them, — I think
    that they
With sliding voices lean from heavenly
    towers,   560
Invisible but gracious. Hark — how soft !

CHORUS OF INVISIBLE ANGELS

Faint and tender.

Mortal man and woman,
  Go upon your travel !
Heaven assist the human
  Smoothly to unravel
All that web of pain
  Wherein ye are holden.
Do ye know our voices
  Chanting down the Golden ?
Do ye guess our choice is,   570
  Being unbeholden,
To be hearkened by you yet again ?

This pure door of opal
  God hath shut between us, —
Us, his shining people,
  You, who once have seen us
And are blinded new !
  Yet, across the doorway,
Past the silence reaching,
  Farewells evermore may,   580
Blessing in the teaching,
  Glide from us to you.

First Semichorus.
  Think how erst your Eden,
  Day on day succeeding,
    With our presence glowed.
We came as if the Heavens were bowed
  To a milder music rare.
Ye saw us in our solemn treading,
  Treading down the steps of cloud,
While our wings, outspreading   590
  Double calms of whiteness,
  Dropped superfluous brightness
Down from stair to stair.
Second Semichorus.
  Or oft, abrupt though tender,
    While ye gazed on space,
  We flashed our angel-splendor
    In either human face.
  With mystic lilies in our hands,
  From the atmospheric bands
    Breaking with a sudden grace,   600
  We took you unaware !
    While our feet struck glories
Outward, smooth and fair,
    Which we stood on floorwise,
Platformed in mid-air.
First Semichorus.
  Or oft, when Heaven-descended,
    Stood we in our wondering sight
    In a mute apocalypse
    With dumb vibrations on our lips
  From hosannas ended,   610
    And grand half-vanishings
    Of the empyreal things
      Within our eyes belated,
  Till the heavenly Infinite
    Falling off from the Created,
  Left our inward contemplation
  Opened into ministration.
Chorus.
  Then upon our axle turning
    Of great joy to sympathy,
  We sang out the morning   620
  Broadening up the sky.
    Or we drew
    Our music through
The noontide's hush and heat and shine,
Informed with our intense Divine:
  Interrupted vital notes
    Palpitating hither, thither,
    Burning out into the æther,
  Sensible like fiery motes.
  Or, whenever twilight drifted   630
    Through the cedar masses,
  The globèd sun we lifted,
  Trailing purple, trailing gold

Out between the passes
Of the mountains manifold,
  To anthems slowly sung:
While he, — aweary, half in swoon
For joy to hear our climbing tune
Transpierce the stars' concentric rings, —
  The burden of his glory flung   640
In broken lights upon our wings.
[*The chant dies away confusedly, and*
  ͵ LUCIFER *appears.*
Lucifer. Now may all fruits be pleasant
    to thy lips,
Beautiful Eve ! The times have somewhat
    changed
Since thou and I had talk beneath a tree,
Albeit ye are not gods yet.
  Eve.   Adam ! hold
My right hand strongly ! It is Lucifer —
And we have love to lose.
  Adam.   I' the name of God,
Go apart from us, O thou Lucifer !
And leave us to the desert thou hast made
Out of thy treason. Bring no serpent-
    slime   650
Athwart this path kept holy to our tears !
Or we may curse thee with their bitterness.
  Lucifer. Curse freely ! curses thicken.
    Why, this Eve
Who thought me once part worthy of her
    ear
And somewhat wiser than the other
    beasts, —
Drawing together her large globes of eyes,
The light of which is throbbing in and out
Their steadfast continuity of gaze, —
Knots her fair eyebrows in so hard a knot,
And down from her white heights of woman-
    hood   660
Looks on me so amazed, — I scarce should
    fear
To wager such an apple as she plucked
Against one riper from the tree of life,
That she could curse too — as a woman
    may —
Smooth in the vowels.
  Eve.   So — speak wickedly !
I like it best so. Let thy words be
    wounds, —
For, so, I shall not fear thy power to hurt.
Trench on the forms of good by open ill —
For, so, I shall wax strong and grand with
    scorn,
Scorning myself for ever trusting thee 670
As far as thinking, ere a snake ate dust,
He could speak wisdom.

  Lucifer.   Our new gods, it seems
Deal more in thunders than in courtesies.
And, sooth, mine own Olympus, which anon
I shall build up to loud-voiced imagery
From all the wandering visions of the
    world,
May show worse railing than our lady Eve
Pours o'er the rounding of her argent arm.
But why should this be ? Adam pardoned
    Eve.
  Adam. Adam loved Eve. Jehovah par-
    doned both !   680
  Eve. Adam forgave Eve — because lov-
    ing Eve.
  Lucifer. So, well. Yet Adam was un-
    done of Eve,
As both were by the snake. Therefore
    forgive,
In like wise, fellow-temptress, the poor
    snake —
Who stung there, not so poorly !   [*Aside.*
  Eve.   Hold thy wrath,
Belovèd Adam ! let me answer him;
For this time he speaks truth, which we
    should hear,
And asks for mercy, which I most should
    grant,
In like wise, as he tells us — in like
    wise !
And therefore I thee pardon, Lucifer, 690
As freely as the streams of Eden flowed
When we were happy by them. So, de-
    part;
Leave us to walk the remnant of our time
Out mildly in the desert. Do not seek
To harm us any more or scoff at us,
Or ere the dust be laid upon our face,
To find there the communion of the dust
And issue of the dust. — Go !
  Adam.   At once, go !
  Lucifer. Forgive ! and go ! Ye images
    of clay,
Shrunk somewhat in the mould, — what
    jest is this ?   700
What words are these to use ? By what a
    thought
Conceive ye of me ? Yesterday — a snake !
To-day — what ?
  Adam.   A strong spirit.
  Eve.   A sad spirit.
  Adam. Perhaps a fallen angel. — Who
    shall say !
  Lucifer. Who told thee, Adam ?
  Adam.   Thou ! The prodigy
Of thy vast brows and melancholy eyes

Which comprehend the heights of some
    great fall.
I think that thou hast one day worn a
    crown
Under the eyes of God.
   Lucifer.   And why of God?
   Adam. It were no crown else. Verily, I
    think   710
Thou 'rt fallen far. I had not yesterday
Said it so surely, but I know to-day
Grief by grief, sin by sin.
   Lucifer.   A crown, by a crown.
   Adam. Ay, mock me! now I know more
    than I knew:
Now I know that thou art fallen below
    hope
Of final re-ascent.
   Lucifer.   Because?
   Adam.   Because
A spirit who expected to see God
Though at the last point of a million years,
Could dare no mockery of a ruined man
Such as this Adam.
   Lucifer.   Who is high and bold — 720
Be it said passing! — of a good red clay
Discovered on some top of Lebanon,
Or haply of Aornus, beyond sweep
Of the black eagle's wing! A furlong
    lower
Had made a meeker king for Eden. Soh!
Is it not possible, by sin and grief
(To give the things your names) that spirits
    should rise
Instead of falling?
   Adam.   Most impossible.
The Highest being the Holy and the Glad,
Whoever rises must approach delight   730
And sanctity in the act.
   Lucifer.   Ha, my clay-king!
Thou wilt not rule by wisdom very long
The after generations. Earth, methinks,
Will disinherit thy philosophy
For a new doctrine suited to thine heirs,
And class these present dogmas with the
    rest
Of the old-world traditions, Eden fruits
And Saurian fossils.
   Eve.   Speak no more with him,
Beloved! it is not good to speak with him.
Go from us, Lucifer, and speak no more!
We have no pardon which thou dost not
    scorn,   741
Nor any bliss, thou seest, for coveting,
Nor innocence for staining. Being bereft,
We would be alone. — Go!

   Lucifer.   Ah! ye talk the same,
All of you — spirits and clay — go, and
    depart!
In Heaven they said so, and at Eden's gate,
And here, reiterant, in the wilderness.
None saith, Stay with me, for thy face is
    fair!
None saith, Stay with me, for thy voice is
    sweet!
And yet I was not fashioned out of clay. 750
Look on me, woman! Am I beautiful?
   Eve. Thou hast a glorious darkness.
   Lucifer.   Nothing more?
   Eve. I think, no more.
   Lucifer.   False Heart — thou thinkest
    more!
Thou canst not choose but think, as I praise
    God,
Unwillingly but fully, that I stand
Most absolute in beauty. As yourselves
Were fashioned very good at best, so *we*
Sprang very beauteous from the creant
    Word
Which thrilled behind us, God himself being
    moved
When that august work of a perfect shape,
His dignities of sovran angelhood,   761
Swept out into the universe, — divine
With thunderous movements, earnest looks
    of gods,
And silver-solemn clash of cymbal wings.
Whereof was I, in motion and in form,
A part not poorest. And yet, — yet, per-
    haps,
This beauty which I speak of, is not here,
As God's voice is not here, nor even my
    crown —
I do not know. What is this thought or
    thing
Which I call beauty? Is it thought, or
    thing?   770
Is it a thought accepted for a thing?
Or both? or neither? — a pretext — a
    word?
Its meaning flutters in me like a flame
Under my own breath: my perceptions reel
For evermore around it, and fall off,
As if it too were holy.
   Eve.   Which it is.
   Adam. The essence of all beauty, I call
    love.
The attribute, the evidence, and end,
The consummation to the inward sense,
Of beauty apprehended from without,   780
I still call love. As form, when colorless,

Is nothing to the eye, — that pine-tree
     there,
Without its black and green, being all a
     blank, —
So, without love, is beauty undiscerned
In man or angel.   Angel ! rather ask
What love is in thee, what love moves to
     thee,
And what collateral love moves on with
     thee;
Then shalt thou know if thou art beautiful.
     Lucifer.   Love ! what is love ?   I lose it.
     Beauty and love
I darken to the image.   Beauty — love ! 790
     [*He fades away, while a low music
     sounds.*
     Adam.   Thou art pale, Eve.
     Eve.   The precipice of ill
Down this colossal nature, dizzies me:
And, hark ! the starry harmony remote
Seems measuring the heights from whence
     he fell.
     Adam.   Think that we have not fallen so !
     By the hope
And aspiration, by the love and faith,
We do exceed the stature of this angel.
     Eve.   Happier we are than he is, by the
     death.
     Adam.   Or rather, by the life of the Lord
     God !
How dim the angel grows, as if that blast 800
Of music swept him back into the dark.
     [*The music is stronger, gathering itself
     into uncertain articulation.*
     Eve.   It throbs in on us like a plaintive
     heart,
Pressing, with slow pulsations, vibrative,
Its gradual sweetness through the yielding
     air,
To such expression as the stars may use,
Most starry-sweet and strange ! With every
     note
That grows more loud, the angel grows
     more dim,
Receding in proportion to approach,
Until he stand afar, — a shade.
     Adam.   Now, words.

SONG OF THE MORNING STAR TO LUCIFER

*He fades utterly away and vanishes, as it
     proceeds.*

     Mine orbèd image sinks   810
     Back from thee, back from thee,

As thou art fallen, methinks,
     Back from me, back from me.
     O my light-bearer,
     Could another fairer
     Lack to thee, lack to thee ?
     Ah, ah, Heosphoros !
I loved thee with the fiery love of stars
Who love by burning, and by loving move,
Too near the thronèd Jehovah not to love. 820
     Ah, ah, Heosphoros !
Their brows flash fast on me from gliding
     cars,
     Pale-passioned for my loss.
     Ah, ah, Heosphoros !

Mine orbèd heats drop cold
     Down from thee, down from thee,
As fell thy grace of old
     Down from me, down from me.
     O my light-bearer,
     Is another fairer   830
     Won to thee, won to thee ?
     Ah, ah, Heosphoros,
     Great love preceded loss,
     Known to thee, known to thee.
     Ah, ah !
Thou, breathing thy communicable grace
     Of life into my light,
Mine astral faces, from thine angel face,
     Hast inly fed,
And flooded me with radiance overmuch 840
     From thy pure height.
     Ah, ah !
Thou, with calm, floating pinions both ways
     spread,
     Erect, irradiated,
     Didst sting my wheel of glory
     On, on before thee
Along the Godlight by a quickening touch !
     Ha, ha !
Around, around the firmamental ocean
I swam expanding with delirious fire !   850
Around, around, around, in blind desire
To be drawn upward to the Infinite —
     Ha, ha !

Until, the motion flinging out the motion
     To a keen whirl of passion and avidity,
To a dim whirl of languor and delight,
I wound in gyrant orbits smooth and white
     With that intense rapidity.
     Around, around,
     I wound and interwound,   860
While all the cyclic heavens about me
     spun.

Stars, planets, suns, and moons dilated
    broad,
Then flashed together into a single sun,
And wound, and wound in one;
And as they wound I wound, — around,
    around,
In a great fire I almost took for God.
    Ha, ha, Heosphoros !

    Thine angel glory sinks
      Down from me, down from me
    My beauty falls, methinks,   870
      Down from thee, down from thee !
    O my light-bearer,
    O my path preparer,
    Gone from me, gone from me !
    Ah, ah, Heosphoros !
I cannot kindle underneath the brow
Of this new angel here, who is not thou.
All things are altered since that time
    ago, —
And if I shine at eve, I shall not know.
    I am strange — I am slow.   880
    Ah, ah, Heosphoros !
Henceforward, human eyes of lovers be
The only sweetest sight that I shall see,
With tears between the looks raised up to
    me.
    Ah, ah !
When, having wept all night, at break of
    day
Above the folded hills they shall survey
My light, a little trembling, in the gray.
    Ah, ah !
And gazing on me, such shall compre-
    hend,   890
    Through all my piteous pomp at morn
      or even,
    And melancholy leaning out of heaven,
That love, their own divine, may change
    or end,
    That love may close in loss !
    Ah, ah, Heosphoros !

SCENE. — *Farther on. A wild open country*
seen vaguely in the approaching night.

    Adam. How doth the wide and melan-
    choly earth
Gather her hills around us, gray and ghast,
And stare with blank significance of loss
Right in our faces ! Is the wind up ?
    Eve.   Nay.

    Adam. And yet the cedars and the ju-
    nipers   900
Rock slowly through the mist, without a
    sound,
And shapes which have no certainty of
    shape
Drift duskly in and out between the pines,
And loom along the edges of the hills,
And lie flat, curdling in the open ground —
Shadows without a body, which contract
And lengthen as we gaze on them.
    Eve.   O life
Which is not man's nor angel's ! What is
    this ?
    Adam. No cause for fear. The circle
    of God's life
Contains all life beside.
    Eve.   I think the earth   910
Is crazed with curse, and wanders from
    the sense
Of those first laws affixed to form and
    space
Or ever she knew sin.
    Adam.   We will not fear:
We were brave sinning.
    Eve.   Yea, I plucked the fruit
With eyes upturned to heaven and seeing
    there
Our god-thrones, as the tempter said, —
    not GOD.
My heart, which beat then, sinks. The
    sun hath sunk
Out of sight with our Eden.
    Adam.   Night is near.
    Eve. And God's curse, nearest. Let us
    travel back
And stand within the sword-glare till we
    die,   920
Believing it is better to meet death
Than suffer desolation.
    Adam.   Nay, beloved !
We must not pluck death from the Maker's
    hand,
As erst we plucked the apple: we must
    wait
Until He gives death as he gave us
    life,
Nor murmur faintly o'er the primal gift
Because we spoilt its sweetness with our
    sin.
    Eve. Ah, ah ! dost thou discern what I
    behold ?
    Adam. I see all. How the spirits in
    thine eyes

From their dilated orbits bound before 930
To meet the spectral Dread !
   Eve.   I am afraid —
Ah, ah ! the twilight bristles wild with
    shapes
Of intermittent motion, aspect vague
And mystic bearings, which o'ercreep the
    earth,
Keeping slow time with horrors in the
    blood.
How near they reach . . . and far ! How
    gray they move —
Treading upon the darkness without feet,
And fluttering on the darkness without
    wings !
Some run like dogs, with noses to the
    ground;
Some keep one path, like sheep; some rock
    like trees;   940
Some glide like a fallen leaf; and some
    flow on
Copious as rivers.
   Adam.   Some spring up like fire:
And some coil . . .
   Eve.   Ah, ah ! dost thou pause to say
Like what ? — coil like the serpent, when
    he fell
From all the emerald splendor of his height
And writhed, and could not climb against
    the curse,
Not a ring's length. I am afraid —
    afraid —
I think it is God's will to make me
    afraid, —
Permitting THESE to haunt us in the place
Of his belovèd angels — gone from us 950
Because we are not pure. Dear Pity of
    God,
That didst permit the angels to go home
And live no more with us who are not
    pure,
Save *us* too from a loathly company —
Almost as loathly in our eyes, perhaps,
As *we* are in the purest ! Pity us —
Us too ! nor shut us in the dark, away
From verity and from stability,
Or what we name such through the pre-
    cedence
Of earth's adjusted uses, — leave us not 960
To doubt betwixt our senses and our
    souls,
Which are the more distraught and full of
    pain
And weak of apprehension !
   Adam.   Courage, Sweet !

The mystic shapes ebb back from us, and
    drop
With slow concentric movement, each on
    each, —
Expressing wider spaces, — and collapsed
In lines more definite for imagery
And clearer for relation, till the throng
Of shapeless spectra merge into a few
Distinguishable phantasms vague and
    grand   970
Which sweep out and around us vastily
And hold us in a circle and a calm.
   Eve. Strange phantasms of pale shad-
    ow ! there are twelve.
Thou who didst name all lives, hast names
    for these ?
   Adam. Methinks this is the zodiac of
    the earth,
Which rounds us with a visionary dread,
Responding with twelve shadowy signs of
    earth,
In fantasque opposition and approach,
To those celestial, constellated twelve
Which palpitate adown the silent nights 980
Under the pressure of the hand of God
Stretched wide in benediction. At this
    hour,
Not a star pricketh the flat gloom of
    heaven:
But, girdling close our nether wilderness,
The zodiac - figures of the earth loom
    slow, —
Drawn out, as suiteth with the place and
    time,
In twelve colossal shades instead of stars,
Through which the ecliptic line of mystery
Strikes bleakly with an unrelenting scope,
Foreshowing life and death.
   Eve.   By dream or sense, 990
Do we see this ?
   Adam. Our spirits have climbed high
By reason of the passion of our grief,
And, from the top of sense, looked over
    sense
To the significance and heart of things
Rather than things themselves.
   Eve.   And the dim twelve . . .
   Adam. Are dim exponents of the crea-
    ture-life
As earth contains it. Gaze on them, be-
    loved !
By stricter apprehension of the sight,
Suggestions of the creatures shall assuage
The terror of the shadows, — what is
    known   1000

Subduing the unknown and taming it
From all prodigious dread. That phan-
    tasm, there,
Presents a lion, albeit twenty times
As large as any lion — with a roar
Set soundless in his vibratory jaws,
And a strange horror stirring in his mane.
And, there, a pendulous shadow seems to
    weigh —
Good against ill, perchance; and there, a
    crab
Puts coldly out its gradual shadow-claws,
Like a slow blot that spreads, — till all the
    ground,   1010
Crawled over by it, seems to crawl itself.
A bull stands hornèd here with gibbous
    glooms;
And a ram likewise: and a scorpion
    writhes
Its tail in ghastly slime and stings the
    dark.
This way a goat leaps with wild blank of
    beard;
And here, fantastic fishes duskly float,
Using the calm for waters, while their
    fins
Throb out quick rhythms along the shallow
    air.
While images more human —
    Eve.   How he stands,
That phantasm of a man — who is not *thou!*
Two phantasms of two men!
    Adam.   One that sustains, 1021
And one that strives, — resuming, so, the
    ends
Of manhood's curse of labor. Dost thou
    see
That phantasm of a woman?
    Eve.   I have seen;
But look off to those small humanities
Which draw me tenderly across my fear, —
Lesser and fainter than my womanhood,
Or yet thy manhood — with strange inno-
    cence
Set in the misty lines of head and hand.
They lean together! I would gaze on
    them   1030
Longer and longer, till my watching eyes,
As the stars do in watching anything,
Should light them forward from their out-
    line vague
To clear configuration.
    [*Two* Spirits, *of Organic and Inorganic
    Nature, arise from the ground.*
                  But what Shapes

Rise up between us in the open space,
And thrust me into horror, back from
    hope!
    Adam. Colossal Shapes — twin sovran
    images,
With a disconsolate, blank majesty
Set in their wondrous faces! with no look,
And yet an aspect — a significance   1040
Of individual life and passionate ends,
Which overcomes us gazing.
                   O bleak sound,
O shadow of sound, O phantasm of thin
    sound!
How it comes, wheeling as the pale moth
    wheels,
Wheeling and wheeling in continuous wail
Around the cyclic zodiac, and gains force,
And gathers, settling coldly like a moth,
On the wan faces of these images
We see before us, — whereby modified,
It draws a straight line of articulate
    song   1050
From out that spiral faintness of lament,
And, by one voice, expresses many griefs.
    First Spirit.
I am the spirit of the harmless earth.
God spake me softly out among the stars,
As softly as a blessing of much worth;
    And then his smile did follow unawares,
That all things fashioned so for use and
    duty
Might shine anointed with his chrism of
    beauty —
                   Yet I wail!
I drave on with the worlds exultingly, 1060
    Obliquely down the Godlight's gradual
    fall;
Individual aspect and complexity
    Of gyratory orb and interval
Lost in the fluent motion of delight
Toward the high ends of Being beyond
    sight —
                   Yet I wail!
    Second Spirit.
I am the spirit of the harmless beasts,
    Of flying things, and creeping things,
    and swimming;
Of all the lives, erst set at silent feasts,
    That found the love-kiss on the goblet
    brimming,   1070
And tasted in each drop within the mea-
    sure
The sweetest pleasure of their Lord's good
    pleasure —
                   Yet I wail!

What a full hum of life around his lips
  Bore witness to the fulness of crea-
    tion !
How all the grand words were full-laden
  ships
Each sailing onward from enunciation
To separate existence, — and each bear-
  ing
The creature's power of joying, hoping,
  fearing !
          Yet I wail !   1080
  Eve. They wail, beloved ! they speak of
    glory and God,
And they wail — wail. That burden of
  the song
Drops from it like its fruit, and heavily
  falls
Into the lap of silence.
  Adam.   Hark, again !
  First Spirit.
I was so beautiful, so beautiful,
  My joy stood up within me bold to add
A word to God's, — and, when his work
  was full,
  To ' very good ' responded ' very glad ! '
Filtered through roses did the light enclose
  me,
And bunches of the grape swam blue across
  me —   1090
          Yet I wail !
  Second Spirit.
I bounded with my panthers: I rejoiced
  In my young tumbling lions rolled to-
    gether:
My stag, the river at his fetlocks, poised
  Then dipped his antlers through the
    golden weather
In the same ripple which the alligator
Left, in his joyous troubling of the water —
          Yet I wail !
  First Spirit.
O my deep waters, cataract and flood,
  What wordless triumph did your voices
    render !   1100
O mountain-summits, where the angels
    stood
  And shook from head and wing thick
    dews of splendor !
How, with a holy quiet, did your Earthy
Accept that Heavenly, knowing ye were
  worthy !
          Yet I wail !
  Second Spirit.
O my wild wood-dogs, with your listening
  eyes !

My horses — my ground-eagles, for swift
  fleeing !
My birds, with viewless wings of harmon-
  ies,
  My calm cold fishes of a silver being,
How happy were ye, living and possess-
  ing,   1110
O fair half-souls capacious of full bless-
  ing !
          Yet I wail !
  First Spirit.
I wail, I wail ! Now hear my charge to-
  day,
  Thou man, thou woman, marked as the
    misdoers
By God's sword at your backs ! I lent my
  clay
  To make your bodies, which had grown
    more flowers:
And now, in change for what I lent, ye
  give me
The thorn to vex, the tempest-fire to cleave
  me —
          And I wail !
  Second Spirit.
I wail, I wail ! Behold ye that I fasten 1120
  My sorrow's fang upon your souls dis-
    honored ?
Accursed transgressors ! down the steep ye
  hasten, —
  Your crown's weight on the world, to
    drag it downward
Unto your ruin. Lo ! my lions, scent-
  ing
The blood of wars, roar hoarse and unre-
  lenting —
          And I wail !
  First Spirit.
I wail, I wail ! Do you hear that I wail ?
  I had no part in your transgression —
    none.
My roses on the bough did bud not pale,
  My rivers did not loiter in the sun; 1130
I was obedient. Wherefore in my cen-
  tre
Do I thrill at this curse of death and
  winter ? —
          Do I wail ?
  Second Spirit.
I wail, I wail ! I wail in the assault
  Of undeserved perdition, sorely wounded !
My nightingale sang sweet without a fault,
  My gentle leopards innocently bounded.
We were obedient. What is this con-
  vulses

Our blameless life with pangs and fever
   pulses ?
           And I wail !   1140
Eve. I choose God's thunder and his
   angels' swords
To die by, Adam, rather than such words.
Let us pass out and flee.
   Adam.   We cannot flee.
This zodiac of the creatures' cruelty
Curls round us, like a river cold and drear,
And shuts us in, constraining us to hear.
   First Spirit.
I feel your steps, O wandering sinners,
   strike
   A sense of death to me, and undug
      graves !
The heart of earth, once calm, is trem-
      bling like
The ragged foam along the ocean-waves:
The restless earthquakes rock against each
   other;   1151
The elements moan 'round me — ' Mother,
   mother ' —
          And I wail !
   Second Spirit.
Your melancholy looks do pierce me
   through;
   Corruption swathes the paleness of your
      beauty.
Why have ye done this thing ? What did
   we do
   That we should fall from bliss as ye from
      duty ?
Wild shriek the hawks, in waiting for their
   jesses,
Fierce howl the wolves along the wilder-
   nesses —
          And I wail !   1160
   Adam. To thee, the Spirit of the harm-
   less earth,
To thee, the Spirit of earth's harmless
   lives,
Inferior creatures but still innocent,
Be salutation from a guilty mouth
Yet worthy of some audience and respect
From you who are not guilty. If we have
   sinned,
God hath rebuked us, who is over us
To give rebuke or death, and if ye wail
Because of any suffering from our sin,
Ye who are under and not over us,   1170
Be satisfied with God, if not with us,
And pass out from our presence in such
   peace
As we have left you, to enjoy revenge

Such as the heavens have made you.
   Verily,
There must be strife between us, large as
   sin.
   Eve. No strife, mine Adam ! Let us
   not stand high
Upon the wrong we did to reach disdain,
Who rather should be humbler evermore
Since self-made sadder. Adam ! shall I
   speak
I who spake once to such a bitter
   end —   1180
Shall I speak humbly now who once was
   proud ?
I, schooled by sin to more humility
Than thou hast, O mine Adam, O my
   king —
My king, if not the world's ?
   Adam.   Speak as thou wilt.
   Eve. Thus, then — my hand in thine —
      . . . Sweet, dreadful Spirits !
I pray you humbly in the name of God,
Not to say of these tears, which are im-
   pure —
Grant me such pardoning grace as can go
   forth
From clean volitions toward a spotted will,
From the wronged to the wronger, this and
   no more !   1190
I do not ask more. I am 'ware, indeed,
That absolute pardon is impossible
From you to me, by reason of my sin, —
And that I cannot evermore, as once,
With worthy acceptation of pure joy,
Behold the trances of the holy hills
Beneath the leaning stars, or watch the
   vales
Dew-pallid with their morning ecstasy, —
Or hear the winds make pastoral peace be-
   tween
Two grassy uplands, — and the river-
   wells   1200
Work out their bubbling mysteries under-
   ground, —
And all the birds sing, till for joy of song
They lift their trembling wings as if to
   heave
The too-much weight of music from their
   heart
And float it up the æther. I am 'ware
That these things I can no more appre-
   hend
With a pure organ into a full delight, —
The sense of beauty and of melody
Being no more aided in me by the sense

Of personal adjustment to those heights
Of what I see well-formed or hear well-
    tuned,   1211
But rather coupled darkly and made
    ashamed
By my percipiency of sin and fall
In melancholy of humiliant thoughts.
But, oh! fair, dreadful Spirits — albeit this
Your accusation must confront my soul,
And your pathetic utterance and full gaze
Must evermore subdue me, — be content!
Conquer me gently — as if pitying me,
Not to say loving! let my tears fall
    thick   1220
As watering dews of Eden, unreproached;
And when your tongues reprove me, make
    me smooth,
Not ruffled — smooth and still with your
    reproof,
And peradventure better while more sad!
For look to it, sweet Spirits, look well to
    it,
It will not be amiss in you who kept
The law of your own righteousness, and
    keep
The right of your own griefs to mourn
    themselves, —
To pity me twice fallen, from that, and
    this,
From joy of place, and also right of
    wail,   1230
'I wail' being not for me — only 'I sin.'
Look to it, O sweet Spirits!
                          For was I not,
At that last sunset seen in Paradise,
When all the westering clouds flashed out
    in throngs
Of sudden angel-faces, face by face,
All hushed and solemn, as a thought of
    God
Held them suspended, — was I not, that
    hour,
The lady of the world, princess of life,
Mistress of feast and favor? Could I
    touch
A rose with my white hand, but it be-
    came   1240
Redder at once? Could I walk leisurely
Along our swarded garden, but the grass
Tracked me with greenness? Could I
    stand aside
A moment underneath a cornel-tree,
But all the leaves did tremble as alive
With songs of fifty birds who were made
    glad

Because I stood there? Could I turn to
    look
With these twain eyes of mine, now weep-
    ing fast,
Now good for only weeping, — upon man,
Angel, or beast, or bird, but each re-
    joiced   1250
Because I looked on him? Alas, alas!
And is not this much woe, to cry 'alas!'
Speaking of joy? And is not this more
    shame,
To have made the woe myself, from all
    that joy?
To have stretched my hand, and plucked it
    from the tree,
And chosen it for fruit? Nay, is not
    this
Still most despair, — to have halved that
    bitter fruit,
And ruined, so, the sweetest friend I have,
Turning the GREATEST to mine enemy?
    Adam. I will not hear thee speak so.
        Hearken, Spirits!   1260
Our God, who is the enemy of none
But only of their sin, hath set your hope
And my hope, in a promise, on this Head.
Show reverence, then, and never bruise her
    more
With unpermitted and extreme re-
    proach, —
Lest, passionate in anguish, she fling down
Beneath your trampling feet, God's gift to
    us
Of sovranty by reason and freewill,
Sinning against the province of the Soul
To rule the soulless. Reverence her es-
    tate,   1270
And pass out from her presence with no
    words!
    Eve. O dearest Heart, have patience
        with my heart!
O Spirits, have patience, 'stead of rever-
    ence,
And let me speak, for, not being inno-
    cent,
It little doth become me to be proud,
And I am prescient by the very hope
And promise set upon me, that hence-
    forth
Only my gentleness shall make me great,
My humbleness exalt me. Awful Spirits,
Be witness that I stand in your reproof 1280
But one sun's length off from my happi-
    ness —
Happy, as I have said, to look around,

Clear to look up ! — And now ! I need not
   speak —
Ye see me what I am; ye scorn me so,
Because ye see me what I have made my-
   self
From God's best making ! Alas, — peace
   forgone,
Love wronged, and virtue forfeit, and tears
   wept
Upon all, vainly ! Alas, me ! alas,
Who have undone myself, from all that
   best,
Fairest and sweetest, to this wretched-
   est   1290
Saddest and most defiled cast out, cast
   down —
What word metes absolute loss ? let abso-
   lute loss
Suffice you for revenge. For *I*, who lived
Beneath the wings of angels yesterday,
Wander to-day beneath the roofless world:
I, reigning the earth's empress yesterday,
Put off from me, to-day, your hate with
   prayers:
I, yesterday, who answered the Lord God,
Composed and glad as singing-birds the
   sun,
Might shriek now from our dismal desert,
   'God,'   1300
And hear him make reply, 'What is thy
   need,
Thou whom I cursed to-day ? '
  Adam.   Eve !
  Eve.   *I*, at last,
Who yesterday was helpmate and delight
Unto mine Adam, am to-day the grief
And curse-mete for him. And, so, pity
   us,
Ye gentle Spirits, and pardon him and me,
And let some tender peace, made of our
   pain,
Grow up betwixt us, as a tree might grow,
With boughs on both sides ! In the shade
   of which,
When presently ye shall behold us dead, —
For the poor sake of our humility, 1311
Breathe out your pardon on our breathless
   lips,
And drop your twilight dews against our
   brows,
And stroking with mild airs our harmless
   hands
Left empty of all fruit, perceive your love
Distilling through your pity over us,
And suffer it, self-reconciled, to pass !

        LUCIFER *rises in the circle.*

  Lucifer. Who talks here of a comple-
   ment of grief ?
Of expiation wrought by loss and fall ?
Of hate subduable to pity ? Eve ? 1320
Take counsel from thy counsellor the snake,
And boast no more in grief, nor hope from
   pain,
My docile Eve ! I teach you to despond
Who taught you disobedience. Look
   around: —
Earth spirits and phantasms hear you talk
   unmoved,
As if ye were red clay again and talked !
What are your words to them — your grief
   to them —
Your deaths, indeed, to them ? Did the
   hand pause,
For *their* sake, in the plucking of the fruit,
That they should pause for *you*, in hating
   you ?   1330
Or will your grief or death, as did your
   sin,
Bring change upon their final doom ? Be-
   hold,
Your grief is but your sin in the rebound,
And cannot expiate for it.
  Adam.   That is true.
  Lucifer. Ay, that is true. The clay-
   king testifies
To the snake's counsel, — hear him ! —
   very true.
  Earth Spirits. I wail, I wail !
  Lucifer.   And certes, *that* is true.
Ye wail, ye all wail. Peradventure I
Could wail among you. O thou universe,
That holdest sin and woe, — more room
   for wail !   1340
  Distant Starry Voice. Ah, ah, Heospho-
   ros ! Heosphoros !
  Adam. Mark Lucifer ! He changes aw-
   fully.
  Eve. It seems as if he looked from
   grief to God
And could not see him. Wretched Luci-
   fer !
  Adam. How he stands — yet an angel !
  Earth Spirits.   We all wail !
  Lucifer (after a pause). Dost thou re-
   member, Adam, when the curse
Took us in Eden ? On a mountain-peak
Half-sheathed in primal woods and glitter-
   ing
In spasms of awful sunshine at that hour,

A lion couched, part raised upon his paws,
With his calm massive face turned full on
thine,   1351
And his mane listening.   When the ended
    curse
Left silence in the world, right suddenly
He sprang up rampant and stood straight
    and stiff,
As if the new reality of death
Were dashed against his eyes, and roared
    so fierce,
(Such thick carnivorous passion in his
    throat
Tearing a passage through the wrath and
    fear)
And roared so wild, and smote from all the
    hills
Such fast keen echoes crumbling down the
    vales   1360
Precipitately, — that the forest beasts,
One after one, did mutter a response
Of savage and of sorrowful complaint
Which trailed along the gorges.   Then, at
    once,
He fell back, and rolled crashing from the
    height
Into the dusk of pines.
    Adam.   It might have been.
I heard the curse alone.
    Earth Spirits.   I wail, I wail !
    Lucifer. That lion is the type of what I
    am.
And as he fixed thee with his full-faced
    hate,
And roared, O Adam, comprehending doom,
So, gazing on the face of the Unseen,   1371
I cry out here between the Heavens and
    Earth
My conscience of this sin, this woe, this
    wrath,
Which damn me to this depth.
    Earth Spirits.   I wail, I wail !
    Eve. I wail — O God !
    Lucifer.   I scorn you that ye wail,
Who use your petty griefs for pedestals
To stand on, beckoning pity from without,
And deal in pathos of antithesis
Of what ye *were* forsooth, and what ye
    are; —
I scorn you like an angel ! Yet, one cry 1380
I, too, would drive up like a column erect,
Marble to marble, from my heart to heaven,
A monument of anguish to transpierce
And overtop your vapory complaints
Expressed from feeble woes.

    Earth Spirits.   I wail, I wail !
    Lucifer. For, O ye heavens, ye are my
    witnesses,
That *I*, struck out from nature in a blot,
The outcast and the mildew of things good,
The leper of angels, the excepted dust
Under the common rain of daily gifts, — 1390
I the snake, I the tempter, I the cursed, —
To whom the highest and the lowest alike
Say, Go from us — we have no need of
    thee, —
Was made by God like others.   Good and
    fair,
He did create me ! — ask him, if not
    fair !
Ask, if I caught not fair and silverly
His blessing for chief angels on my head
Until it grew there, a crown crystallized !
Ask, if he never called me by my name,
Lucifer — kindly said as ' Gabriel ' — 1400
Lucifer — soft as ' Michael ! ' while serene
I, standing in the glory of the lamps,
Answered ' my Father,' innocent of shame
And of the sense of thunder. Ha ! ye think,
White angels in your niches, — I repent,
And would tread down my own offences
    back
To service at the footstool ? *that 's* read
    wrong !
I cry as the beast did, that I may cry —
Expansive, not appealing ! Fallen so deep,
Against the sides of this prodigious pit 1410
I cry — cry — dashing out the hands of
    wail
On each side, to meet anguish everywhere,
And to attest it in the ecstasy
And exaltation of a woe sustained
Because provoked and chosen.
                                    Pass along
Your wilderness, vain mortals ! Puny griefs
In transitory shapes, be henceforth dwarfed
To your own conscience, by the dread ex-
    tremes
Of what I am and have been.   If ye have
    fallen,
It is but a step's fall, — the whole ground
    beneath   1420
Strewn woolly soft with promise ! if ye have
    sinned,
Your prayers tread high as angels ! if ye
    have grieved,
Ye are too mortal to be pitiable,
The power to die disproves the right to
    grieve.
Go to ! ye call this ruin ?   I half-scorn

The ill I did you ! Were ye wronged by me,
Hated and tempted and undone of me, —
Still, what 's your hurt to mine of doing
 hurt,
Of hating, tempting, and so ruining ?
This sword's *hilt* is the sharpest, and cuts
 through   1430
The hand that wields it.
     Go ! I curse you all.
Hate one another — feebly — as ye can !
I would not certes cut you short in hate,
Far be it from me ! hate on as ye can !
I breathe into your faces, spirits of earth,
As wintry blast may breathe on wintry
 leaves
And lifting up their brownness show beneath
The branches bare. Beseech you, spirits,
 give
To Eve who beggarly entreats your love
For her and Adam when they shall be dead,
An answer rather fitting to the sin 1441
Than to the sorrow — as the heavens, I
 trow,
For justice' sake gave theirs.
      I curse you both,
Adam and Eve. Say grace as after meat,
After my curses ! May your tears fall
 hot
On all the hissing scorns o' the creatures
 here, —
And yet rejoice ! Increase and multiply,
Ye in your generations, in all plagues,
Corruptions, melancholies, poverties,
And hideous forms of life and fears of
 death, —   1450
The thought of death being alway immi-
 nent,
Immovable and dreadful in your life,
And deafly and dumbly insignificant
Of any hope beyond, — as death itself,
Whichever of you lieth dead the first,
Shall seem to the survivor — yet rejoice !
My curse catch at you strongly, body and
 soul,
And HE find no redemption — nor the wing
Of seraph move your way; and yet rejoice !
Rejoice, — because ye have not, set in you,
This hate which shall pursue you — this fire-
 hate   1461
Which glares without, because it burns
 within —
Which kills from ashes — this potential
 hate,
Wherein I, angel, in antagonism
To God and his reflex beatitudes,

Moan ever, in the central universe,
With the great woe of striving against
 Love
And gasp for space amid the Infinite,
And toss for rest amid the Desertness,
Self-orphaned by my will, and self-elect 1470
To kingship of resistant agony
Toward the Good round me — hating good
 and love,
And willing to hate good and to hate love,
And willing to will on so evermore,
Scorning the past and damning the to-
 come —
   Go and rejoice ! I curse you
      [LUCIFER *vanishes.*

Earth Spirits.
And we scorn you ! there 's no pardon
 Which can lean to you aright.
When your bodies take the guerdon
 Of the death-curse in our sight, 1480
Then the bee that hummeth lowest shall
 transcend you:
Then ye shall not move an eyelid
 Though the stars look down your
  eyes;
And the earth which ye defiled
 Shall expose you to the skies, —
' Lo ! these kings of ours, who sought to
 comprehend you.'
First Spirit.
And the elements shall boldly
 All your dust to dust constrain.
Unresistedly and coldly
 I will smite you with my rain. 1490
From the slowest of my frosts is no reced-
 ing.
Second Spirit.
And my little worm, appointed
 To assume a royal part,
He shall reign, crowned and anointed,
 O'er the noble human heart.
Give him counsel against losing of that
 Eden !
Adam. Do ye scorn us? Back your
 scorn
Toward your faces gray and lorn,
 As the wind drives back the rain,
Thus I drive with passion-strife, 1500
I who stand beneath God's sun,
Made like God, and, though undone,
Not unmade for love and life.
Lo ! ye utter threats in vain.
By my free will that chose sin,
By mine agony within
Round the passage of the fire,

By the pinings which disclose
That my native soul is higher
  Than what it chose,   1510
We are yet too high, O Spirits, for your
    disdain !
Eve. Nay, beloved ! If these be low,
We confront them from no height.
We have stooped down to their level
By infecting them with evil,
And their scorn that meets our blow
  Scathes aright.
Amen.   Let it be so.
Earth Spirits.
We shall triumph — triumph greatly
  When ye lie beneath the sward.   1520
There, our lily shall grow stately
  Though ye answer not a word,
And her fragrance shall be scornful of your
    silence:
While your throne ascending calmly
  We, in heirdom of your soul,
Flash the river, lift the palm-tree,
  The dilated ocean roll,
By the thoughts that throbbed within you,
    round the islands.

Alp and torrent shall inherit
  Your significance of will,   1530
And the grandeur of your spirit
  Shall our broad savannahs fill;
In our winds, your exultations shall be
    springing !
Even your parlance which inveigles,
  By our rudeness shall be won.
Hearts poetic in our eagles
  Shall beat up against the sun
And strike downward in articulate clear
    singing.

Your bold speeches our Behemoth   1539
  With his thunderous jaw shall wield.
Your high fancies shall our Mammoth
  Breathe sublimely up the shield
Of Saint Michael at God's throne, who
    waits to speed him:
Till the heavens' smooth-groovèd thun-
    der
  Spinning back, shall leave them clear,
And the angels, smiling wonder,
  With dropt looks from sphere to
    sphere,
Shall cry 'Ho, ye heirs of Adam ! ye ex-
    ceed him.'
Adam. Root out thine eyes, Sweet, from
    the dreary ground !

Beloved, we may be overcome by God, 1550
But not by these.
  Eve.   By God, perhaps, in these.
  Adam. I think, not so.   Had God fore-
    doomed despair
He had not spoken hope.   He may destroy
Certes, but not deceive.
  Eve.   Behold this rose !
I plucked it in our bower of Paradise
This morning as I went forth, and my
    heart
Has beat against its petals all the day.
I thought it would be always red and full
As when I plucked it.   *Is* it ? — ye may
    see !
I cast it down to you that ye may see,   1560
All of you ! — count the petals lost of it,
And note the colors fainted ! ye may see!
And I am as it is, who yesterday
Grew in the same place.   O ye spirits of
    earth,
I almost, from my miserable heart,
Could here upbraid you for your cruel
    heart,
Which will not let me, down the slope of
    death,
Draw any of your pity after me,
Or lie still in the quiet of your looks,
As my flower, there, in mine.
    [*A bleak wind, quickened with indistinct*
      Human Voices, spins around the Earth-
      Zodiac, filling the circle with its pres-
      ence; and then, wailing off into the
      East, carries the rose away with it.
      EVE *falls upon her face.* ADAM
      stands erect.
  Adam.   So, verily,   1570
The last departs.
  Eve.   So Memory follows Hope,
And Life both.   Love said to me, ' Do not
    die,'
And I replied, 'O Love, I will not die.
I exiled and I will not orphan Love.'
But now it is no choice of mine to die:
My heart throbs from me.
  Adam.   Call it straightway back !
Death's consummation crowns completed
    life,
Or comes too early.   Hope being set on
    thee
For others, if for others then for thee, —
For thee and me.
    [*The wind revolves from the East, and*
      round again to the East, perfumed by
      the Eden rose, and full of Voices

which sweep out into articulation as they pass.
                    Let thy soul shake its leaves
To feel the mystic wind — hark !
Eve.   I hear life.
Infant Voices passing in the wind.
    O we live, O we live —   1582
    And this life that we receive
    Is a warm thing and a new,
    Which we softly bud into
    From the heart and from the brain, —
    Something strange that overmuch is
    Of the sound and of the sight,
    Flowing round in trickling touches,   1590
    With a sorrow and delight, —
    Yet is it all in vain ?
                    Rock us softly,
    Lest it be all in vain.
Youthful Voices passing.
    O we live, O we live —
    And this life that we achieve
    Is a loud thing and a bold
    Which with pulses manifold
    Strikes the heart out full and fain —
    Active doer, noble liver,
    Strong to struggle, sure to conquer, 1600
    Though the vessel's prow will quiver
    At the lifting of the anchor:
    Yet do we strive in vain ?
Infant Voices passing.
                    Rock us softly,
    Lest it be all in vain.
Poet Voices passing.
    O we live, O we live —
    And this life that we conceive
    Is a clear thing and a fair,
    Which we set in crystal air
    That its beauty may be plain !   1610
    With a breathing and a flooding
    Of the heaven-life on the whole,
    While we hear the forests budding
    To the music of the soul —
    Yet is it tuned in vain ?
Infant Voices passing.
                    Rock us softly,
    Lest it be all in vain.
Philosophic Voices passing.
    O we live, O we live —
    And this life that we perceive
    Is a great thing and a grave   1620
    Which for others' use we have,
    Duty-laden to remain.
    We are helpers, fellow-creatures,
    Of the right against the wrong;
    We are earnest-hearted teachers

    Of the truth which maketh strong
    Yet do we teach in vain ?
Infant Voices passing.
                    Rock us softly,
    Lest it be all in vain.
Revel Voices passing.
    O we live, O we live —   1630
    And this life that we reprieve
    Is a low thing and a light,
    Which is jested out of sight
    And made worthy of disdain !
    Strike with bold electric laughter
    The high tops of things divine —
    Turn thy head, my brother, after,
    Lest thy tears fall in my wine !
    For is all laughed in vain ?
Infant Voices passing.
                    Rock us softly,   1640
    Lest it be all in vain.
    Eve. I hear a sound of life — of life
        like ours —
Of laughter and of wailing, of grave
        speech,
Of little plaintive voices innocent,
Of life in separate courses flowing out
Like our four rivers to some outward main.
I hear life — life !
    Adam. And, so, thy cheeks have snatched
Scarlet to paleness, and thine eyes drink
        fast
Of glory from full cups, and thy moist
        lips
Seem trembling, both of them, with ear-
        nest doubts   1650
Whether to utter words or only smile.
    Eve. Shall I be mother of the coming
        life ?
Hear the steep generations, how they fall
Adown the visionary stairs of Time
Like supernatural thunders — far, yet
        near, —
Sowing their fiery echoes through the hills.
Am I a cloud to these — mother to these ?
    Earth Spirits. And bringer of the curse
        upon all these.
                    [EVE *sinks down again.*
Poet Voices passing.
    O we live, O we live —
    And this life that we conceive   1660
    Is a noble thing and high,
    Which we climb up loftily
    To view God without a stain;
    Till, recoiling where the shade is,
    We retread our steps again,
    And descend the gloomy Hades

To resume man's mortal pain.
Shall it be climbed in vain ?
Infant Voices passing.
                    Rock us softly,
Lest it be all in vain.   1670
Love Voices passing.
O we live, O we live —
And this life we would retrieve,
Is a faithful thing apart
Which we love in, heart to heart,
Until one heart fitteth twain.
' Wilt thou be one with me ? '
' I will be one with thee.'
' Ha, ha ! — we love and live ! '
Alas ! ye love and die.
Shriek — who shall reply ?   1680
For is it not loved in vain ?
Infant Voices passing.
                    Rock us softly,
Though it be all in vain.
Aged Voices passing.
O we live, O we live —
And this life we would survive,
Is a gloomy thing and brief,
Which consummated in grief,
Leaveth ashes for all gain.
Is it not *all* in vain ?
Infant Voices passing.
                    Rock us softly,   1690
Though it be *all* in vain.
                    [*Voices die away.*
Earth Spirits.   And bringer of the curse
    upon all these.
Eve. The voices of foreshown Humanity
Die off ; — so let me die.
Adam.   So let us die,
When God's will soundeth the right hour
    of death.
Earth Spirits. And bringer of the curse
    upon all these.
Eve. O Spirits ! by the gentleness ye
    use
In winds at night, and floating clouds at
    noon,
In gliding waters under lily-leaves,
In chirp of crickets, and the settling
    hush   1700
A bird makes in her nest with feet and
    wings, —
Fulfil your natures now !
Earth Spirits.   Agreed, allowed !
We gather out our natures like a cloud,
And thus fulfil their lightnings !   Thus,
    and thus !
            Hearken, oh hearken to us !

First Spirit.
As the storm-wind blows bleakly from the
    norland,
As the snow-wind beats blindly on the
    moorland,
As the simoom drive shot across the des-
    ert,
As the thunder roars deep in the Unmea-
    sured,
As the torrent tears the ocean-world to
    atoms,   1710
As the whirlpool grinds it fathoms below
    fathoms,
        Thus, — and thus !
Second Spirit.
As the yellow toad, that spits its poison
    chilly,
As the tiger, in the jungle crouching stilly,
As the wild boar, with ragged tusks of
    anger,
As the wolf-dog, with teeth of glittering
    clangor,
As the vultures, that scream against the
    thunder,
As the owlets, that sit and moan asun-
    der,
        Thus, — and thus !
Eve. Adam ! God !
Adam.   Cruel, unrelenting Spirits !   1720
By the power in me of the sovran soul
Whose thoughts keep pace yet with the
    angel's march,
I charge you into silence — trample you
Down to obedience.   I am king of you !
Earth Spirits.
        Ha, ha ! thou art king !
        With a sin for a crown,
        And a soul undone !
        Thou, the antagonized,
        Tortured and agonized,
        Held in the ring   1730
        Of the zodiac !
        Now, king, beware !
        We are many and strong
        Whom thou standest among, —
        And we press on the air,
        And we stifle thee back,
        And we multiply where
        Thou wouldst trample us down
        From rights of our own
        To an utter wrong —   1740
    And, from under the feet of thy scorn,
        O forlorn,
        We shall spring up like corn,
        And our stubble be strong.

Adam. God, there is power in thee! I
   make appeal
Unto thy kingship.
   Eve.   There is pity in THEE,
O sinned against, great God! — My seed,
   my seed,
There is hope set on THEE — I cry to thee,
Thou mystic Seed that shalt be! — leave
   us not
In agony beyond what we can bear,   1750
Fallen in debasement below thunder-mark,
A mark for scorning — taunted and per-
   plext
By all these creatures we ruled yesterday,
Whom thou, Lord, rulest alway! O my
   Seed,
Through the tempestuous years that rain
   so thick
Betwixt my ghostly vision and thy face,
Let me have token! for my soul is bruised
Before the serpent's head is.
   [*A vision of* CHRIST *appears in the midst
   of the Zodiac, which pales before the
   heavenly light. The Earth Spirits
   grow grayer and fainter.*
   CHRIST.   I AM HERE!
Adam. This is God! — Curse us not,
   God, any more!
Eve. But gazing so — so — with omnific
   eyes,   1760
Lift my soul upward till it touch thy
   feet!
Or lift it only, — not to seem too proud, —
To the low height of some good angel's
   feet,
For such to tread on when he walketh
   straight
And thy lips praise him!
   CHRIST.   Spirits of the earth,
I meet you with rebuke for the reproach
And cruel and unmitigated blame
Ye cast upon your masters. True, they
   have sinned;
And true their sin is reckoned into loss
For you the sinless. Yet, your inno-
   cence   1770
Which of you praises? since God made
   your acts
Inherent in your lives, and bound your
   hands
With instincts and imperious sanctities
From self-defacement. Which of you dis-
   dains
These sinners who in falling proved their
   height

Above you by their liberty to fall?
And which of you complains of loss by
   them,
For whose delight and use ye have your
   life
And honor in creation? Ponder it!
This regent and sublime Humanity,   1780
Though fallen, exceeds you! this shall film
   your sun,
Shall hunt your lightning to its lair of
   cloud,
Turn back your rivers, footpath all your
   seas,
Lay flat your forests, master with a look
Your lion at his fasting, and fetch down
Your eagle flying. Nay, without this law
Of mandom, ye would perish, — beast by
   beast
Devouring, — tree by tree, with strangling
   roots
And trunks set tuskwise. Ye would gaze
   on God
With imperceptive blankness up the
   stars,   1790
And mutter, 'Why, God, hast thou made
   us thus?'
And pining to a sallow idiocy
Stagger up blindly against the ends of life,
Then stagnate into rottenness and drop
Heavily — poor, dead matter — piecemeal
   down
The abysmal spaces — like a little stone
Let fall to chaos. Therefore over you
Receive man's sceptre! — therefore be con-
   tent
To minister with voluntary grace
And melancholy pardon, every rite   1800
And function in you, to the human hand!
Be ye to man as angels are to God,
Servants in pleasure, singers of delight,
Suggesters to his soul of higher things
Than any of your highest! So at last,
He shall look round on you with lids too
   straight
To hold the grateful tears, and thank you
   well,
And bless you when he prays his secret
   prayers,
And praise you when he sings his open
   songs
For the clear song-note he has learnt in
   you   1810
Of purifying sweetness, and extend
Across your head his golden fantasies
Which glorify you into soul from sense.

Go, serve him for such price !   That not in
    vain
Nor yet ignobly ye shall serve, I place
My word here for an oath, mine oath for
    act
To be hereafter.   In the name of which
Perfect redemption and perpetual grace,
I bless you through the hope and through
    the peace
Which are mine, — to the Love, which is
    myself.   1820
    Eve.   Speak on still, Christ !   Albeit
    thou bless me not
In set words, I am blessed in hearkening
    thee —
Speak, Christ !
    CHRIST.   Speak, Adam !   Bless the wo-
    man, man !
It is thine office.
    Adam.   Mother of the world,
Take heart before this Presence !   Lo, my
    voice,
Which, naming erst the creatures, did ex-
    press
(God breathing through my breath) the
    attributes
And instincts of each creature in its name,
Floats to the same afflatus, — floats and
    heaves
Like a water-weed that opens to a wave, —
A full-leaved prophecy affecting thee, 1831
Out fairly and wide.   Henceforward, arise,
    aspire
To all the calms and magnanimities,
The lofty uses and the noble ends,
The sanctified devotion and full work,
To which thou art elect for evermore,
First woman, wife, and mother !
    Eve.   And first in sin.
    Adam.   And also the sole bearer of the
    Seed
Whereby sin dieth. Raise the majesties 1839
Of thy disconsolate brows, O well-beloved,
And front with level eyelids the To-come,
And all the dark o' the world ! Rise, woman,
    rise
To thy peculiar and best altitudes
Of doing good and of enduring ill,
Of comforting for ill, and teaching good,
And reconciling all that ill and good
Unto the patience of a constant hope, —
Rise with thy daughters ! If sin came by
    thee,
And by sin, death, — the ransom-righteous-
    ness,

The heavenly life and compensative rest 1850
Shall come by means of thee. If woe by thee
Had issue to the world, thou shalt go forth
An angel of the woe thou didst achieve,
Found acceptable to the world instead
Of others of that name, of whose bright
    steps
Thy deed stripped bare the hills. Be satis-
    fied;
Something thou hast to bear through wo-
    manhood,
Peculiar suffering answering to the sin, —
Some pang paid down for each new human
    life,
Some weariness in guarding such a life, 1860
Some coldness from the guarded, some mis-
    trust
From those thou hast too well served, from
    those beloved
Too loyally some treason; feebleness
Within thy heart, and cruelty without,
And pressures of an alien tyranny
With its dynastic reasons of larger bones
And stronger sinews. But, go to ! thy love
Shall chant itself its own beatitudes
After its own life-working.   A child's kiss
Set on thy sighing lips shall make thee
    glad;   1870
A poor man served by thee shall make thee
    rich;
A sick man helped by thee shall make thee
    strong;
Thou shalt be served thyself by every sense
Of service which thou renderest.   Such a
    crown
I set upon thy head, — Christ witnessing
With looks of prompting love — to keep
    thee clear
Of all reproach against the sin forgone,
From all the generations which succeed.
Thy hand which plucked the apple I clasp
    close,
Thy lips which spake wrong counsel I kiss
    close,   1880
I bless thee in the name of Paradise
And by the memory of Edenic joys
Forfeit and lost, — by that last cypress
    tree,
Green at the gate, which thrilled as we
    came out,
And by the blessèd nightingale which threw
Its melancholy music after us, —
And by the flowers, whose spirits full of
    smells
Did follow softly, plucking us behind

Back to the gradual banks and vernal bowers
And fourfold river-courses. — By all these,
I bless thee to the contraries of these,   1891
I bless thee to the desert and the thorns,
To the elemental change and turbulence,
And to the roar of the estrangèd beasts,
And to the solemn dignities of grief, —
To each one of these ends, — and to their
      END
Of Death and the hereafter.
        Eve.   I accept
For me and for my daughters this high part
Which lowly shall be counted.   Noble work
Shall hold me in the place of garden-rest,
And in the place of Eden's lost delight 1901
Worthy endurance of permitted pain;
While on my longest patience there shall
      wait
Death's speechless angel, smiling in the east,
Whence cometh the cold wind.   I bow my-
      self
Humbly henceforward on the ill I did,
That humbleness may keep it in the shade.
Shall it be so ? shall I smile, saying so ?
O Seed ! O King ! O God, who *shall* be
      seed, —
What shall I say ?   As Eden's fountains
      swelled   1910
Brightly betwixt their banks, so swells my
      soul
Betwixt thy love and power !
                   And, sweetest thoughts
Of forgone Eden ! now, for the first time
Since God said ' Adam,' walking through
      the trees,
I dare to pluck you as I plucked erewhile
The lily or pink, the rose or heliotrope.
So pluck I you — so largely — with both
      hands,
And throw you forward on the outer earth,
Wherein we are cast out, to sweeten it.
        Adam.   As thou, Christ, to illume it,
      holdest Heaven   1920
Broadly over our heads.
        [*The* CHRIST *is gradually transfigured,
        during the following phrases of dia-
        logue, into humanity and suffering.*
        Eve.   O Saviour Christ
Thou standest mute in glory, like the sun !
        Adam.   We worship in thy silence,
      Saviour Christ !
        Eve.   Thy brows grow grander with a
      forecast woe, —
Diviner, with the possible of death.
We worship in thy sorrow, Saviour Christ !

        Adam.   How do thy clear, still eyes trans-
      pierce our souls,
As gazing *through* them toward the Father-
      throne
In a pathetical, full Deity,   1929
Serenely as the stars gaze through the air
Straight on each other !
        Eve.   O pathetic Christ,
Thou standest mute in glory, like the
      moon !
        CHRIST.   Eternity stands alway front-
      ing God;
A stern colossal image, with blind eyes
And grand dim lips that murmur evermore
God, God, God ! while the rush of life and
      death,
The roar of act and thought, of evil and
      good,
The avalanches of the ruining worlds
Tolling down space, — the new worlds'
      genesis
Budding in fire, — the gradual humming
      growth   1940
Of the ancient atoms and first forms of
      earth,
The slow procession of the swathing seas
And firmamental waters, — and the noise
Of the broad, fluent strata of pure airs, —
All these flow onward in the intervals
Of that reiterated sound of — GOD !
Which WORD innumerous angels straight-
      way lift
Wide on celestial altitudes of song
And choral adoration, and then drop   1949
The burden softly, shutting the last notes
In silver wings.   Howbeit in the noon of
      time
Eternity shall wax as dumb as Death,
While a new voice beneath the spheres
      shall cry,
' God ! why hast thou forsaken me, my
      God ? '
And not a voice in Heaven shall answer it.
        [*The transfiguration is complete in sad-
      ness.*
        Adam.   Thy speech is of the Heavenlies,
      yet, O Christ,
Awfully human are thy voice and face !
        Eve.   My nature overcomes me from
      thine eyes.
        CHRIST.   In the set noon of time shall
      one from Heaven,
An angel fresh from looking upon God, 1960
Descend before a woman, blessing her
With perfect benediction of pure love,

For all the world in all its elements,
For all the creatures of earth, air, and sea,
For all men in the body and in the soul,
Unto all ends of glory and sanctity.
    Eve.   O pale, pathetic Christ — I wor-
      ship thee !
I thank thee for that woman !
    CHRIST.   Then, at last,
I, wrapping round me your humanity,
Which, being sustained, shall neither break
    nor burn   1970
Beneath the fire of Godhead, will tread
    earth,
And ransom you and it, and set strong
    peace
Betwixt you and its creatures.   With my
    pangs
I will confront your sins; and since those
    sins
Have sunken to all Nature's heart from
    yours,
The tears of my clean soul shall follow
    them
And set a holy passion to work clear
Absolute consecration.   In my brow
Of kingly whiteness shall be crowned
    anew
Your discrowned human nature.   Look on
    me !   1980
As I shall be uplifted on a cross
In darkness of eclipse and anguish dread,
So shall I lift up in my piercèd hands,
Not into dark, but light — not unto death,
But life, — beyond the reach of guilt and
    grief,
The whole creation.   Henceforth in my
    name
Take courage, O thou woman, — man, take
    hope !
Your grave shall be as smooth as Eden's
    sward,
Beneath the steps of your prospective
    thoughts,
And, one step past it, a new Eden-gate 1990
Shall open on a hinge of harmony
And let you through to mercy.   Ye shall
    fall
No more, within that Eden, nor pass out
Any more from it.   In which hope, move
    on,
First sinners and first mourners !   Live
    and love, —
Doing both nobly because lowlily !
Live and work, strongly because patiently !
And, for the deed of death, trust it to God

That it be well done, unrepented of,
And not to loss !   And thence, with con-
    stant prayers,   2000
Fasten your souls so high, that constantly
The smile of your heroic cheer may float
Above all floods of earthly agonies,
Purification being the joy of pain !
    [*The vision of* CHRIST *vanishes.* ADAM
      and EVE *stand in an ecstasy. The*
      Earth-zodiac pales away shade by
      shade, as the stars, star by star, shine
      out in the sky; and the following chant
      from the two Earth Spirits (*as they*
      sweep back into the Zodiac and disap-
      pear with it) *accompanies the process*
      of change.
Earth Spirits.
    By the mighty word thus spoken
      Both for living and for dying,
    We our homage-oath, once broken,
      Fasten back again in sighing,
And the creatures and the elements renew
      their covenanting.

    Here, forgive us all our scorning;   2010
      Here, we promise milder duty:
    And the evening and the morning
      Shall re-organize in beauty
A sabbath day of sabbath joy, for universal
    chanting.

    And if, still, this melancholy
      May be strong to overcome us,
    If this mortal and unholy
      We still fail to cast out from us,
If we turn upon you, unaware, your own
    dark influences, —

    If ye tremble when surrounded   2020
      By our forest pine and palm trees,
    If we cannot cure the wounded
      With our gum trees and our balm
      trees,
And if your souls all mournfully sit down
    among your senses, —

    Yet, O mortals, do not fear us !
      We are gentle in our languor;
    Much more good ye shall have near us
      Than any pain or anger,
And our God's refracted blessing in our
    blessing shall be given.

    By the desert's endless vigil   2030
      We will solemnize your passions,

By the wheel of the black eagle
We will teach you exaltations,
When he sails against the wind, to the white
spot up in heaven.

Ye shall find us tender nurses
To your weariness of nature,
And our hands shall stroke the curse's
Dreary furrows from the creature,
Till your bodies shall lie smooth in death
and straight and slumberful.

Then, a couch we will provide you   2040
Where no summer heats shall dazzle,
Strewing on you and beside you
Thyme and rosemary and basil,
And the yew-tree shall grow overhead to
keep all safe and cool.

Till the Holy Blood awaited
Shall be chrism around us running,
Whereby, newly-consecrated,
We shall leap up in God's sunning,
To join the spheric company which purer
worlds assemble:

While, renewed by new evangels,   2050
Soul-consummated, made glorious,
Ye shall brighten past the angels,
Ye shall kneel to Christ victorious,
And the rays around his feet beneath your
sobbing lips shall tremble.
    [*The phantastic Vision has all passed;
    the Earth-zodiac has broken like a
    belt, and is dissolved from the Desert.
    The* Earth Spirits *vanish, and the
    stars shine out above.*

CHORUS OF INVISIBLE ANGELS

While ADAM *and* EVE *advance into the
Desert, hand in hand*

Hear our heavenly promise
Through your mortal passion!
Love, ye shall have from us,
In a pure relation.
As a fish or bird
Swims or flies, if moving,   2060
We unseen are heard
To live on by loving.
Far above the glances
Of your eager eyes,
Listen! we are loving.
Listen, through man's ignorances —

Listen, through God's mysteries —
Listen down the heart of things,
Ye shall hear our mystic wings
Murmurous with loving.   2070
Through the opal door
Listen evermore
How we live by loving!
First Semichorus.
When your bodies therefore
Reach the grave their goal,
Softly will we care for
Each enfranchised soul.
Softly and unlothly
Through the door of opal
Toward the heavenly people,   2080
Floated on a minor fine
Into the full chant divine,
We will draw you smoothly, —
While the human in the minor
Makes the harmony diviner.
Listen to our loving!
Second Semichorus.
There, a sough of glory
Shall breathe on you as you come,
Ruffling round the doorway
All the light of angeldom.   2090
From the empyrean centre
Heavenly voices shall repeat,
'Souls redeemed and pardoned, enter,
For the chrism on you is sweet!'
And every angel in the place
Lowlily shall bow his face,
Folded fair on softened sounds,
Because upon your hands and feet
He images his Master's wounds.
Listen to our loving!   2100
First Semichorus.
So, in the universe's
Consummated undoing,
Our seraphs of white mercies
Shall hover round the ruin.
Their wings shall stream upon the flame
As if incorporate of the same
In elemental fusion;
And calm their faces shall burn out
With a pale and mastering thought,
And a steadfast looking of desire   2110
From out between the clefts of fire, —
While they cry, in the Holy's name,
To the final Restitution.
Listen to our loving!
Second Semichorus.
So, when the day of God is
To the thick graves accompted,
Awaking the dead bodies,

The angel of the trumpet
Shall split and shatter the earth
  To the roots of the grave —   2120
Which never before were slackened —
And quicken the charnel birth
With his blast so clear and brave
That the Dead shall start and stand erect
And every face of the burial-place
Shall the awful, single look reflect
  Wherewith he them awakened.
  Listen to our loving !

First Semichorus.

  But wild is the horse of Death !
He will leap up wild at the clamor   2130
  Above and beneath.
  And where is his Tamer
  On that last day,
  When he crieth Ha, ha !
  To the trumpet's blare,
And paweth the earth's Aceldama ?
  When he tosseth his head,
  The drear-white steed,
And ghastlily champeth the last moon-
    ray —
  What angel there   2140
  Can lead him away,
That the living may rule for the Dead ?

Second Semichorus.

  Yet a TAMER shall be found !
  One more bright than seraph crowned,
  And more strong than cherub bold,
  Elder, too, than angel old,
  By his gray eternities.
  He shall master and surprise
  The steed of Death.
  For He is strong, and He is fain.   2150
  He shall quell him with a breath,
  And shall lead him where He will,
  With a whisper in the ear,
    Full of fear,
  And a hand upon the mane,
    Grand and still.

First Semichorus.

Through the flats of Hades where the souls
  assemble
He will guide the Death-steed calm between
  their ranks,
While, like beaten dogs, they a little moan
  and tremble
To see the darkness curdle from the horse's
  glittering flanks.   2160
Through the flats of Hades where the
  dreary shade is,
Up the steep of heaven will the Tamer
  guide the steed, —

Up the spheric circles, circle above circle,
We who count the ages shall count the toll-
  ing tread —   .
Every hoof-fall striking a blinder blanker
  sparkle
From the stony orbs, which shall show as
  they were dead.

Second Semichorus.

All the way the Death-steed with tolling
  hoofs shall travel,
Ashen-gray the planets shall be motionless
  as stones,
Loosely shall all the systems eject their parts
  coæval,
Stagnant in the spaces shall float the pallid
  moons: 2170
Suns that touch their apogees, reeling from
  their level,
Shall run back on their axles, in wild low
  broken tunes.

Chorus.

Up against the arches of the crystal ceil-
  ing,
From the horse's nostrils shall stream the
  blurting breath:
Up between the angels pale with silent
  feeling
Will the Tamer calmly lead the horse of
  Death.

Semichorus.

Cleaving all that silence, cleaving all that
  glory,
Will the Tamer lead him straightway to the
  Throne;
' Look out, O Jehovah, to this I bring be-
  fore Thee,
With a hand nail-pierc**è**d, I who am thy
  Son.'   2180
Then the Eye Divinest, from the Deepest,
  flaming,
On the mystic courser shall look out in fire:
Blind the beast shall stagger where It over-
  came him,
Meek as lamb at pasture, bloodless in
  desire.
Down the beast shall shiver, — slain amid
  the taming, —
And, by Life essential, the phantasm Death
  expire.

Chorus.

  Listen, man, through life and death,
    Through the dust and through the breath,
    Listen down the heart of things !
      Ye shall hear our mystic wings   2190
      Murmurous with loving.

A Voice from below. Gabriel, thou Gabriel !

A Voice from above. What wouldst *thou* with me ?

First Voice. I heard thy voice sound in the angels' song,
And I would give thee question.

Second Voice.   Question me !

First Voice. Why have I called thrice to my Morning Star
And had no answer ? All the stars are out,
And answer in their places. Only in vain
I cast my voice against the outer rays
Of *my* Star shut in light behind the sun.
No more reply than from a breaking string,
Breaking when touched. Or is she *not* my star ?   2201
Where *is* my Star — my Star ? Have ye cast down
Her glory like my glory ? Has she waxed
Mortal, like Adam ? Has she learnt to hate
Like any angel ?

Second Voice.   She is sad for thee.
All things grow sadder to thee, one by one.

Angel Chorus.
     Live, work on, O Earthy !
        By the Actual's tension,
     Speed the arrow worthy
        Of a pure ascension !   2210
     From the low earth round you,
        Reach the heights above you:
     From the stripes that wound you,
        Seek the loves that love you !
     God's divinest burneth plain
     Through the crystal diaphane
        Of our loves that love you.

First Voice. Gabriel, O Gabriel !

Second Voice. What wouldst *thou* with me ?

First Voice. Is it true, O thou Gabriel, that the crown
Of sorrow which I claimed, another claims ?
That HE claims THAT too ?

Second Voice. Lost one, it is true.   2221

First Voice. That HE will be an exile from his heaven,
To lead those exiles homeward ?

Second Voice.   It is true.

First Voice. That HE will be an exile by his will,
As I by mine election ?

Second Voice.   It is true.

First Voice. That *I* shall stand sole exile finally, —
Made desolate for fruition ?

Second Voice.   It is true.

First Voice. Gabriel !

Second Voice.   I hearken.

First Voice.   Is it true besides —
Aright true — that mine orient Star will give
Her name of 'Bright and Morning-Star' to HIM, —   2230
And take the fairness of his virtue back
To cover loss and sadness ?

Second Voice.   It is true.

First Voice. Untrue, *Un*true ! O Morning Star, O MINE,
Who sittest secret in a veil of light
Far up the starry spaces, say — *Untrue !*
Speak but so loud as doth a wasted moon
To Tyrrhene waters. I am Lucifer.
            [*A pause. Silence in the stars.*
All things grow sadder to me, one by one.

Angel Chorus.
     Exiled human creatures,
        Let your hope grow larger !   2240
     Larger grows the vision
        Of the new delight.
     From this chain of Nature's
        God is the Discharger,
     And the Actual's prison
        Opens to your sight.

Semichorus.
     Calm the stars and golden
        In a light exceeding:
     What their rays have measured
        Let your feet fulfil !   2250
     These are stars beholden
        By your eyes in Eden,
     Yet, across the desert,
        See them shining still !

Chorus.
     Future joy and far light
        Working such relations,
     Hear us singing gently
        Exiled is not lost !
     God, above the starlight,
        God, above the patience,   2260
     Shall at last present ye
        Guerdons worth the cost.
     Patiently enduring,
        Painfully surrounded,
     Listen how we love you,
        Hope the uttermost !
     Waiting for that curing
        Which exalts the wounded,

Hear us sing above you —
  EXILED, BUT NOT LOST !   2270
  [*The stars shine on brightly while*
    ADAM *and* EVE *pursue their way*
    into the far wilderness. There is a
    sound through the silence, as of the
    falling tears of an angel.

SONNETS

THE SOUL'S EXPRESSION

WITH stammering lips and insufficient
  sound
I strive and struggle to deliver right
That music of my nature, day and night
With dream and thought and feeling inter-
  wound,
And inly answering all the senses round
With octaves of a mystic depth and height
Which step out grandly to the infinite
From the dark edges of the sensual
  ground.
This song of soul I struggle to outbear
Through portals of the sense, sublime and
  whole,
And utter all myself into the air:
But if I did it, — as the thunder-roll
Breaks its own cloud, my flesh would per-
  ish there,
Before that dread apocalypse of soul.

THE SERAPH AND POET

THE seraph sings before the manifest
God-One, and in the burning of the Seven,
And with the full life of consummate
  Heaven
Heaving beneath him like a mother's
  breast
Warm with her first-born's slumber in that
  nest.
The poet sings upon the earth grave-riven,
Before the naughty world, soon self-for-
  given
For wronging him, — and in the darkness
  prest
From his own soul by worldly weights.
  Even so,
Sing, seraph with the glory ! heaven is high;
Sing, poet with the sorrow ! earth is low:
The universe's inward voices cry

'Amen' to either song of joy and woe:
Sing, seraph, — poet, — sing on equally !

ON A PORTRAIT OF WORDS-WORTH BY B. R. HAYDON

First printed in the *Athenæum*, October 29,
1842, as ' On Mr. Haydon's Portrait of Words-
worth.'

WORDSWORTH upon Helvellyn ! Let the
  cloud
Ebb audibly along the mountain-wind,
Then break against the rock, and show be-
  hind
The lowland valleys floating up to crowd
The sense with beauty. He with forehead
  bowed
And humble-lidded eyes, as one inclined
Before the sovran thought of his own
  mind,
And very meek with inspirations proud,
Takes here his rightful place as poet-priest
By the high altar, singing prayer and
  prayer
To the higher Heavens. A noble vision free
Our Haydon's hand has flung out from the
  mist:
No portrait this, with Academic air !
This is the poet and his poetry.

PAST AND FUTURE

MY future will not copy fair my past
On any leaf but Heaven's. Be fully done,
Supernal Will ! I would not fain be one
Who, satisfying thirst and breaking fast,
Upon the fulness of the heart at last
Says no grace after meat. My wine has run
Indeed out of my cup, and there is none
To gather up the bread of my repast
Scattered and trampled; yet I find some
  good
In earth's green herbs, and streams that
  bubble up
Clear from the darkling ground, — content
  until
I sit with angels before better food:
Dear Christ ! when thy new vintage fills
  my cup,
This hand shall shake no more, nor that
  wine spill.

IRREPARABLENESS

I HAVE been in the meadows all the day
And gathered there the nosegay that you
see,
Singing within myself as bird or bee
When such do field-work on a morn of
May.
But, now I look upon my flowers, decay
Has met them in my hands more fatally
Because more warmly clasped, — and sobs
are free
To come instead of songs. What do you
say,
Sweet counsellors, dear friends ? that I
should go
Back straightway to the fields and gather
more ?
Another, sooth, may do it, but not I !
My heart is very tired, my strength is low,
My hands are full of blossoms plucked be-
fore,
Held dead within them till myself shall
die.

TEARS

THANK God, bless God, all ye who suffer
not
More grief than ye can weep for. That is
well —
That is light grieving ! lighter, none befell
Since Adam forfeited the primal lot.
Tears ! what are tears ? The babe weeps
in its cot,
The mother singing; at her marriage-bell
The bride weeps, and before the oracle
Of high-faned hills the poet has forgot
Such moisture on his cheeks. Thank God
for grace,
Ye who weep only ! If, as some have
done,
Ye grope tear-blinded in a desert place
And touch but tombs, — look up ! those
tears will run
Soon in long rivers down the lifted face,
And leave the vision clear for stars and
sun.

GRIEF

I TELL you, hopeless grief is passionless;
That only men incredulous of despair,
Half-taught in anguish, through the mid-
night air
Beat upward to God's throne in loud access
Of shrieking and reproach. Full desert-
ness,
In souls as countries, lieth silent-bare
Under the blanching, vertical eye-glare
Of the absolute Heavens. Deep-hearted
man, express
Grief for thy Dead in silence like to
death —
Most like a monumental statue set
In everlasting watch and moveless woe
Till itself crumble to the dust beneath.
Touch it; the marble eyelids are not wet:
If it could weep, it could arise and go.

SUBSTITUTION

WHEN some belovèd voice that was to you
Both sound and sweetness, faileth sud-
denly,
And silence, against which you dare not
cry,
Aches round you like a strong disease and
new —
What hope ? what help ? what music will
undo
That silence to your sense ? Not friend-
ship's sigh,
Not reason's subtle count; not melody
Of viols, nor of pipes that Faunus blew;
Not songs of poets, nor of nightingales
Whose hearts leap upward through the
cypress-trees
To the clear moon; nor yet the spheric
laws
Self-chanted, nor the angels' sweet 'All
hails,'
Met in the smile of God: nay, none of
these.
Speak THOU, availing Christ ! — and fill
this pause.

COMFORT

SPEAK low to me, my Saviour, low and
sweet
From out the hallelujahs, sweet and low
Lest I should fear and fall, and miss Thee
so
Who art not missed by any that entreat.
Speak to me as to Mary at thy feet !

And if no precious gums my hands bestow,
Let my tears drop like amber while I go
In reach of thy divinest voice complete
In humanest affection — thus, in sooth,
To lose the sense of losing. As a child,
Whose song-bird seeks the wood for ever-
more,
Is sung to in its stead by mother's mouth
Till, sinking on her breast, love-reconciled,
He sleeps the faster that he wept before.

PERPLEXED MUSIC

AFFECTIONATELY INSCRIBED TO E. J.

EXPERIENCE, like a pale musician, holds
A dulcimer of patience in his hand,
Whence harmonies, we cannot understand,
Of God's will in his worlds, the strain un-
folds
In sad-perplexèd minors: deathly colds
Fall on us while we hear, and countermand
Our sanguine heart back from the fancy-
land
With nightingales in visionary wolds.
We murmur ' Where is any certain tune
Or measured music in such notes as
these ? '
But angels, leaning from the golden seat,
Are not so minded; their fine ear hath won
The issue of completed cadences,
And, smiling down the stars, they whisper —
SWEET.

WORK

WHAT are we set on earth for ? Say, to
toil;
Nor seek to leave thy tending of the vines
For all the heat o' the day, till it declines,
And Death's mild curfew shall from work
assoil.
God did anoint thee with his odorous oil,
To wrestle, not to reign; and He assigns
All thy tears over, like pure crystallines,
For younger fellow-workers of the soil
To wear for amulets. So others shall
Take patience, labor, to their heart and
hand,
From thy hand and thy heart and thy
brave cheer,
And God's grace fructify through thee to
all.

The least flower with a brimming cup may
stand,
And share its dew-drop with another near.

FUTURITY

AND, O belovèd voices, upon which
Ours passionately call because erelong
Ye brake off in the middle of that song
We sang together softly, to enrich
The poor world with the sense of love, and
witch
The heart out of things evil, — I am
strong,
Knowing ye are not lost for aye among
The hills, with last year's thrush. God
keeps a niche
In Heaven to hold our idols; and albeit
He brake them to our faces and denied
That our close kisses should impair their
white,
I know we shall behold them raised, com-
plete,
The dust swept from their beauty, — glori-
fied
New Memnons singing in the great God-
light.

THE TWO SAYINGS

TWO sayings of the Holy Scriptures beat
Like pulses in the Church's brow and
breast;
And by them we find rest in our unrest
And, heart deep in salt-tears, do yet en-
treat
God's fellowship as if on heavenly seat.
The first is JESUS WEPT, — whereon is
prest
Full many a sobbing face that drops its
best
And sweetest waters on the record sweet:
And one is where the Christ, denied and
scorned,
LOOKED UPON PETER. Oh, to render
plain,
By help of having loved a little and
mourned,
That look of sovran love and sovran pain
Which HE, who could not sin yet suffered,
turned
On him who could reject but not sus-
tain !

THE LOOK

THE Saviour looked on Peter. Ay, no
    word,
No gesture of reproach; the Heavens se-
    rene
Though heavy with armed justice, did not
    lean
Their thunders that way: the forsaken
    Lord
Looked only, on the traitor. None record
What that look was, none guess; for those
    who have seen
Wronged lovers loving through a death-
    pang keen,
Or pale-cheeked martyrs smiling to a
    sword,
Have missed Jehovah at the judgment-
    call.
And Peter, from the height of blas-
    phemy —
' I never knew this man ' — did quail and
    fall
As knowing straight THAT GOD; and
    turnèd free
And went out speechless from the face of
    all,
And filled the silence, weeping bitterly.

THE MEANING OF THE LOOK

I THINK that look of Christ might seem to
    say —
' Thou Peter ! art thou then a common
    stone
Which I at last must break my heart
    upon,
For all God's charge to his high angels
    may
Guard my foot better ? Did I yesterday
Wash *thy* feet, my beloved, that they
    should run
Quick to deny me 'neath the morning
    sun ?
And do thy kisses, like the rest, betray ?
The cock crows coldly. — Go, and mani-
    fest
A late contrition, but no bootless fear !
For when thy final need is dreariest,
Thou shalt not be denied, as I am here;
My voice to God and angels shall attest,
Because I KNOW *this man, let him be clear.*'

A THOUGHT FOR A LONELY DEATH-BED

INSCRIBED TO MY FRIEND E. C.

IF God compel thee to this destiny,
To die alone, with none beside thy bed
To ruffle round with sobs thy last word
    said
And mark with tears the pulses ebb from
    thee, —
Pray then alone, ' O Christ, come tenderly !
By thy forsaken Sonship in the red
Drear wine-press, — by the wilderness out-
    spread, —
And the lone garden where thine agony
Fell bloody from thy brow, — by all of
    those
Permitted desolations, comfort mine !
No earthly friend being near me, interpose
No deathly angel 'twixt my face and thine,
But stoop Thyself to gather my life's rose,
And smile away my mortal to Divine !'

WORK AND CONTEMPLATION

THE woman singeth at her spinning-wheel
A pleasant chant, ballad or barcarole;
She thinketh of her song, upon the whole,
Far more than of her flax; and yet the
    reel
Is full, and artfully her fingers feel
With quick adjustment, provident control,
The lines — too subtly twisted to unroll —
Out to a perfect thread. I hence appeal
To the dear Christian Church — that we
    may do
Our Father's business in these temples
    mirk,
Thus swift and steadfast, thus intent and
    strong;
While thus, apart from toil, our souls pur-
    sue
Some high calm spheric tune, and prove
    our work
The better for the sweetness of our song.

PAIN IN PLEASURE

A THOUGHT ay like a flower upon mine
    heart,
And drew around it other thoughts like
    bees

For multitude and thirst of sweetnesses ;
Whereat rejoicing, I desired the art
Of the Greek whistler, who to wharf and
    mart
Could lure those insect swarms from orange-
    trees,
That I might hive with me such thoughts
    and please
My soul so, always. Foolish counterpart
Of a weak man's vain wishes ! While I
    spoke,
The thought I called a flower grew nettle-
    rough,
The thoughts, called bees, stung me to fes-
    tering:
Oh, entertain (cried Reason as she woke)
Your best and gladdest thoughts but long
    enough,
And they will all prove sad enough to
    sting !

AN APPREHENSION

IF all the gentlest-hearted friends I know
Concentred in one heart their gentleness,
That still grew gentler till its pulse was
    less
For life than pity, — I should yet be slow
To bring my own heart nakedly below
The palm of such a friend, that he should
    press
Motive, condition, means, appliances,
My false ideal joy and fickle woe,
Out full to light and knowledge; I should
    fear
Some plait between the brows, some
    rougher chime
In the free voice. O angels, let your flood
Of bitter scorn dash on me ! do ye hear
What *I* say who bear calmly all the time
This everlasting face to face with GOD ?

DISCONTENT

LIGHT human nature is too lightly tost
And ruffled without cause, complaining
    on —
Restless with rest, until, being overthrown,
It learneth to lie quiet. Let a frost
Or a small wasp have crept to the inner-
    most
Of our ripe peach, or let the wilful sun

Shine westward of our window, — straight
    we run
A furlong's sigh as if the world were lost.
But what time through the heart and
    through the brain
God hath transfixed us, — we, so moved
    before,
Attain to a calm. Ay, shouldering weights
    of pain,
We anchor in deep waters, safe from
    shore,
And hear submissive o'er the stormy main
God's chartered judgments walk for ever-
    more.

PATIENCE TAUGHT BY NATURE

' O DREARY life,' we cry, ' O dreary life ! '
And still the generations of the birds
Sing through our sighing, and the flocks
    and herds
Serenely live while we are keeping strife
With Heaven's true purpose in us, as a
    knife
Against which we may struggle ! Ocean
    girds
Unslackened the dry land, savannah-
    swards
Unweary sweep, hills watch unworn, and
    rife
Meek leaves drop yearly from the forest-
    trees
To show, above, the unwasted stars that
    pass
In their old glory: O thou God of old,
Grant me some smaller grace than comes
    to these ! —
But so much patience as a blade of grass
Grows by, contented through the heat and
    cold.

CHEERFULNESS TAUGHT BY REASON

I THINK we are too ready with complaint
In this fair world of God's. Had we no
    hope
Indeed beyond the zenith and the slope
Of yon gray blank of sky, we might grow
    faint
To muse upon eternity's constraint
Round our aspirant souls; but since the
    scope

Must widen early, is it well to droop,
For a few days consumed in loss and taint?
O pusillanimous Heart, be comforted
And, like a cheerful traveller, take the
    road,
Singing beside the hedge. What if the
    bread
Be bitter in thine inn, and thou unshod
To meet the flints? At least it may be
    said
'Because the way is *short*, I thank thee,
    God.'

EXAGGERATION

WE overstate the ills of life, and take
Imagination (given us to bring down
The choirs of singing angels overshone
By God's clear glory) down our earth to
    rake
The dismal snows instead, flake following
    flake,
To cover all the corn; we walk upon
The shadow of hills across a level thrown,
And pant like climbers: near the alder
    brake
We sigh so loud, the nightingale within
Refuses to sing loud, as else she would.
O brothers, let us leave the shame and
    sin
Of taking vainly, in a plaintive mood,
The holy name of GRIEF! — holy herein,
That by the grief of ONE came all our
    good.

ADEQUACY

Now, by the verdure on thy thousand hills,
Belovèd England, doth the earth appear
Quite good enough for men to overbear
The will of God in, with rebellious wills!
We cannot say the morning-sun fulfils
Ingloriously its course, nor that the clear
Strong stars without significance insphere
Our habitation: we, meantime, our ills
Heap up against this good and lift a cry
Against this work-day world, this ill-spread
    feast,
As if ourselves were better certainly
Than what we come to. Maker and High
    Priest,
I ask thee not my joys to multiply, —
Only to make me worthier of the least.

TO GEORGE SAND

A DESIRE

THOU large-brained woman and large-
    hearted man,
Self-called George Sand! whose soul, amid
    the lions
Of thy tumultuous senses, moans defiance
And answers roar for roar, as spirits can:
I would some mild miraculous thunder ran
Above the applauded circus, in appliance
Of thine own nobler nature's strength and
    science,
Drawing two pinions, white as wings of
    swan,
From thy strong shoulders, to amaze the
    place
With holier light! that thou to woman's
    claim
And man's, mightst join beside the angel's
    grace
Of a pure genius sanctified from blame,
Till child and maiden pressed to thine em-
    brace
To kiss upon thy lips a stainless fame.

TO GEORGE SAND

A RECOGNITION

TRUE genius, but true woman! dost deny
The woman's nature with a manly scorn,
And break away the gauds and armlets
    worn
By weaker women in captivity?
Ah, vain denial! that revolted cry
Is sobbed in by a woman's voice forlorn, —
Thy woman's hair, my sister, all unshorn
Floats back dishevelled strength in agony,
Disproving thy man's name: and while be-
    fore
The world thou burnest in a poet-fire,
We see thy woman-heart beat evermore
Through the large flame. Beat purer,
    heart, and higher,
Till God unsex thee on the heavenly shore
Where unincarnate spirits purely aspire!

THE PRISONER

I COUNT the dismal time by months and
    years
Since last I felt the green sward under
    foot,

And the great breath of all things summer-
    mute
Met mine upon my lips. Now earth ap-
    pears
As strange to me as dreams of distant
    spheres
Or thoughts of Heaven we weep at. Na-
    ture's lute
Sounds on, behind this door so closely shut,
A strange wild music to the prisoner's ears,
Dilated by the distance, till the brain
Grows dim with fancies which it feels too
    fine:
While ever, with a visionary pain,
Past the precluded senses, sweep and shine
Streams, forests, glades, and many a
    golden train
Of sunlit hills transfigured to Divine.

INSUFFICIENCY

WHEN I attain to utter forth in verse
Some inward thought, my soul throbs au-
    dibly
Along my pulses, yearning to be free
And something farther, fuller, higher, re-
    hearse,
To the individual, true, and the universe,
In consummation of right harmony:
But, like a wind-exposed distorted tree,
We are blown against for ever by the curse
Which breathes through Nature. Oh, the
    world is weak !
The effluence of each is false to all,
And what we best conceive we fail to
    speak.
Wait, soul, until thine ashen garments fall,
And then resume thy broken strains, and
    seek
Fit peroration without let or thrall.

THE ROMAUNT OF THE PAGE

First printed in Finden's *Tableaux* for 1839.

I

A KNIGHT of gallant deeds
  And a young page at his side,
From the holy war in Palestine
  Did slow and thoughtful ride,
As each were a palmer and told for beads
  The dews of the eventide.

II

' O young page,' said the knight,
  ' A noble page art thou !
Thou fearest not to steep in blood
  The curls upon thy brow;
And once in the tent, and twice in the
    fight,
  Didst ward me a mortal blow.'

III

' O brave knight,' said the page,
  ' Or ere we hither came,
We talked in tent, we talked in field,
  Of the bloody battle-game;
But here, below this greenwood bough,
  I cannot speak the same.

IV

' Our troop is far behind,
  The woodland calm is new;
Our steeds, with slow grass-muffled hoofs
  Tread deep the shadows through;
And, in my mind, some blessing kind
  Is dropping with the dew.

V

' The woodland calm is pure —
  I cannot choose but have
A thought from these, o' the beechen-trees,
  Which in our England wave,
And of the little finches fine
  Which sang there while in Palestine
  The warrior-hilt we drave.

VI

' Methinks, a moment gone,
  I heard my mother pray !
I heard, sir knight, the prayer for me
  Wherein she passed away;
And I know the heavens are leaning down
  To hear what I shall say.'

VII

The page spake calm and high,
  As of no mean degree;
Perhaps he felt in nature's broad
  Full heart, his own was free:
And the knight looked up to his lifted eye,
  Then answered smilingly —

VIII

' Sir page, I pray your grace !
  Certes, I meant not so
To cross your pastoral mood, sir page,
  With the crook of the battle-bow;

But a knight may speak of a lady's face,
I ween, in any mood or place,
   If the grasses die or grow.   50

IX

' And this I meant to say —
   My lady's face shall shine
As ladies' faces use, to greet
   My page from Palestine;
Or, speak she fair or prank she gay,
   She is no lady of mine.

X

' And this I meant to fear —
   Her bower may suit thee ill;
For, sooth, in that same field and tent,
   Thy *talk* was somewhat still: 60
And fitter thy hand for my knightly spear
   Than thy tongue for my lady's will !'

XI

Slowly and thankfully
   The young page bowed his head;
His large eyes seemed to muse a smile,
   Until he blushed instead,
And no lady in her bower, pardiè,
   Could blush more sudden red:
'Sir Knight, — thy lady's bower to me
   Is suited well,' he said.   70

XII

Beati, beati, mortui !
From the convent on the sea,
One mile off, or scarce so nigh,
Swells the dirge as clear and high
As if that, over brake and lea,
Bodily the wind did carry
The great altar of Saint Mary,
And the fifty tapers burning o'er it,
And the Lady Abbess dead before it,
And the chanting nuns whom yesterweek
Her voice did charge and bless, —   81
Chanting steady, chanting meek,
Chanting with a solemn breath,
Because that they are thinking less
Upon the dead than upon death.
Beati, beati, mortui !
Now the vision in the sound
Wheeleth on the wind around;
Now it sweepeth back, away —
The uplands will not let it stay   90
To dark the western sun:
Mortui ! — away at last, —

Or ere the page's blush is past !
And the knight heard all, and the page
   heard none.

XIII

' A boon, thou noble knight,
   If ever I servèd thee !
Though thou art a knight and I am a
   page,
   Now grant a boon to me;
And tell me sooth, if dark or bright,
If little loved or loved aright   100
   Be the face of thy ladye.'

XIV

Gloomily looked the knight —
   ' As a son thou hast servèd me,
And would to none I had granted boon
   Except to only thee !
For haply then I should love aright,
For then I should know if dark or bright
   Were the face of my ladye.

XV

' Yet it ill suits my knightly tongue
   To grudge that granted boon,   110
That heavy price from heart and life
   I paid in silence down;
The hand that claimed it, cleared in fine
My father's fame: I swear by mine,
   That price was nobly won !

XVI

' Earl Walter was a brave old earl,
   He was my father's friend;
And while I rode the lists at court
   And little guessed the end,
My noble father in his shroud   120
Against a slanderer lying loud,
   He rose up to defend.

XVII

' Oh, calm below the marble gray
   My father's dust was strown !
Oh, meek above the marble gray
   His image prayed alone !
The slanderer lied: the wretch was brave :
For, looking up the minister-nave,
He saw my father's knightly glaive   130
   Was changed from steel to stone.

XVIII

' Earl Walter's glaive was steel,
   With a brave old hand to wear it,

And dashed the lie back in the mouth
Which lied against the godly truth
  And against the knightly merit:
The slanderer, 'neath the avenger's heel,
Struck up the dagger in appeal
From stealthy lie to brutal force —
  And out upon the traitor's corse
    Was yielded the true spirit.   140

XIX

' I would mine hand had fought that fight
  And justified my father !
I would mine heart had caught that wound
  And slept beside him rather !
I think it were a better thing
Than murdered friend and marriage ring
  Forced on my life together.

XX

' Wail shook Earl Walter's house;
  His true wife shed no tear;
She lay upon her bed as mute   150
  As the earl did on his bier:
Till — " Ride, ride fast," she said at last,
  " And bring the avengèd's son anear !
Ride fast, ride free, as a dart can flee,
For white of blee with waiting for me
  Is the corse in the next chambère."

XXI

' I came, I knelt beside her bed;
  Her calm was worse than strife:
" My husband, for thy father dear,
Gave freely when thou wast not here   160
  His own and eke my life.
A boon ! Of that sweet child we make
An orphan for thy father's sake,
  Make thou, for ours, a wife."

XXII

' I said, " My steed neighs in the court,
  My bark rocks on the brine,
And the warrior's vow I am under now
  To free the pilgrim's shrine;
But fetch the ring and fetch the priest
  And call that daughter of thine,   170
And rule she wide from my castle on
    Nyde
  While I am in Palestine."

XXIII

' In the dark chambère, if the bride was
    fair,
  Ye wis, I could not see,

But the steed thrice neighed, and the priest
    fast prayed,
  And wedded fast were we.
Her mother smiled upon her bed
As at its side we knelt to wed,
  And the bride rose from her knee
And kissed the smile of her mother dead,
  Or ever she kissed me.   181

XXIV

' My page, my page, what grieves thee so,
  That the tears run down thy face ? ' —
' Alas, alas ! mine own sistèr
  Was in thy lady's case:
But *she* laid down the silks she wore
And followed him she wed before,
Disguised as his true servitor,
  To the very battle-place.'

XXV

And wept the page, but laughed the knight,
  A careless laugh laughed he: 191
' Well done it were for thy sistèr,
  But not for my ladye !
My love, so please you, shall requite
No woman, whether dark or bright,
  Unwomaned if she be.'

XXVI

The page stopped weeping and smiled
    cold —
  ' Your wisdom may declare
That womanhood is proved the best
By golden brooch and glossy vest   200
  The mincing ladies wear;
Yet is it proved, and was of old,
Anear as well, I dare to hold,
  By truth, or by despair.'

XXVII

He smiled no more, he wept no more,
  But passionate he spake —
' Oh, womanly she prayed in tent,
  When none beside did wake !
Oh, womanly she paled in fight,
  For one belovèd's sake —   210
And her little hand, defiled with blood,
Her tender tears of womanhood
  Most woman-pure did make ! '

XXVIII

— ' Well done it were for thy sistèr,
  Thou tellest well her tale !
But for my lady, she shall pray
  I' the kirk of Nydesdale.

Not dread for me but love for me
  Shall make my lady pale;
No casque shall hide her woman's tear —
It shall have room to trickle clear   221
  Behind her woman's veil.'

XXIX

— 'But what if she mistook thy mind
  And followed thee to strife,
Then kneeling did entreat thy love
  As Paynims ask for life ?'
— 'I would forgive, and evermore
Would love her as my servitor,
  But little as my wife.

XXX

'Look up — there is a small bright cloud
  Alone amid the skies !   231
So high, so pure, and so apart,
  A woman's honor lies.'
The page looked up — the cloud was
  sheen —
A sadder cloud did rush, I ween,
  Betwixt it and his eyes.

XXXI

Then dimly dropped his eyes away
  From welkin unto hill —
Ha ! who rides there ? — the page is 'ware,
  Though the cry at his heart is still: 240
And the page seeth all and the knight
  seeth none,
Though banner and spear do fleck the sun,
  And the Saracens ride at will.

XXXII

He speaketh calm, he speaketh low, —
  'Ride fast, my master, ride,
Or ere within the broadening dark
  The narrow shadows hide.'
'Yea, fast, my page, I will do so,
  And keep thou at my side.'

XXXIII

'Now nay, now nay, ride on thy way,   250
  Thy faithful page precede.
For I must loose on saddle-bow
  My battle-casque that galls, I trow,
The shoulder of my steed;
And I must pray, as I did vow,
  For one in bitter need.

XXXIV

'Ere night I shall be near to thee, —
  Now ride, my master, ride !

Ere night, as parted spirits cleave
To mortals too beloved to leave,   260
  I shall be at thy side.'
The knight smiled free at the fantasy,
  And adown the dell did ride.

XXXV

Had the knight looked up to the page's face,
  No smile the word had won;
Had the knight looked up to the page's face,
  I ween he had never gone:
Had the knight looked back to the page's
  geste,
  I ween he had turned anon,   269
For dread was the woe in the face so young,
And wild was the silent geste that flung
Casque, sword to earth, as the boy down-
  sprung
  And stood — alone, alone.

XXXVI

He clenched his hands as if to hold
  His soul's great agony —
'Have I renounced my womanhood,
  For wifehood unto *thee*,
And is this the last, last look of thine
  That ever I shall see ?   279

XXXVII

'Yet God thee save, and mayst thou have
  A lady to thy mind,
More woman-proud and half as true
  As one thou leav'st behind !
And God me take with HIM to dwell —
For HIM I cannot love too well,
  As I have loved my kind.'

XXXVIII

She looketh up, in earth's despair,
  The hopeful heavens to seek;
That little cloud still floateth there,
  Whereof her loved did speak: 290
How bright the little cloud appears !
Her eyelids fall upon the tears,
  And the tears down either cheek.

XXXIX

The tramp of hoof, the flash of steel —
  The Paynims round her coming !
The sound and sight have made her
  calm, —
  False page, but truthful woman;
She stands amid them all unmoved:
A heart once broken by the loved
  Is strong to meet the foeman.   300

XL

'Ho, Christian page! art keeping sheep,
  From pouring wine-cups resting?' —
'I keep my master's noble name,
  For warring, not for feasting;
And if that here Sir Hubert were,
My master brave, my master dear,
  Ye would not stay the questing.'

XLI

'Where is thy master, scornful page,
  That we may slay or bind him?' —
'Now search the lea and search the wood,
  And see if ye can find him!   311
Nathless, as hath been often tried,
Your Paynim heroes faster ride
  Before him than behind him.'

XLII

'Give smoother answers, lying page,
  Or perish in the lying!' —
'I trow that if the warrior brand
Beside my foot, were in my hand,
  'T were better at replying!'   319
They cursed her deep, they smote her low,
They cleft her golden ringlets through;
  The Loving is the Dying.

XLIII

She felt the scimitar gleam down,
  And met it from beneath
With smile more bright in victory
  Than any sword from sheath, —
Which flashed across her lip serene,
Most like the spirit-light between
  The darks of life and death.

XLIV

Ingemisco, ingemisco!   330
From the convent on the sea,
Now it sweepeth solemnly,
As over wood and over lea
Bodily the wind did carry
The great altar of St. Mary,
And the fifty tapers paling o'er it,
And the Lady Abbess stark before it,
And the weary nuns with hearts that faintly
Beat along their voices saintly —
Ingemisco, ingemisco!   340
Dirge for abbess laid in shroud
Sweepeth o'er the shroudless dead,
Page or lady, as we said,
With the dews upon her head,
All as sad if not as loud.

Ingemisco, ingemisco!
Is ever a lament begun
By any mourner under sun,
Which, ere it endeth, suits but *one?*

THE LAY OF THE BROWN ROSARY

First printed in Finden's *Tableaux* for 1840
as, 'Legend of the Brown Rosary.'

FIRST PART

I

'ONORA, Onora,' — her mother is calling,
She sits at the lattice and hears the dew
    falling
Drop after drop from the sycamores laden
With dew as with blossom, and calls home
    the maiden,
  'Night cometh, Onora.'

II

She looks down the garden-walk caverned
    with trees,
To the limes at the end where the green
    arbor is —
'Some sweet thought or other may keep
    where it found her,
While, forgot or unseen in the dreamlight
    around her,
  Night cometh — Onora!'   10

III

She looks up the forest whose alleys shoot
    on
Like the mute minster-aisles when the
    anthem is done,
And the choristers sitting with faces aslant
Feel the silence to consecrate more than the
    chant —
  'Onora, Onora!'

IV

And forward she looketh across the brown
    heath —
'Onora, art coming?' — what is it she
    seeth?
Nought, nought but the gray border-stone
    that is wist
To dilate and assume a wild shape in the
    mist —
  'My daughter!'   Then over   20

V

The casement she leaneth, and as she doth
        so
She is 'ware of her little son playing be-
        low:
'Now where is Onora?' He hung down
        his head
And spake not, then answering blushed
        scarlet-red, —
    ' At the tryst with her lover.'

VI

But his mother was wroth: in a sternness
        quoth she,
' As thou play'st at the ball art thou play-
        ing with me ?
When we know that her lover to battle is
        gone,
And the saints know above that she loveth
        but one
    And will ne'er wed another ?'   30

VII

Then the boy wept aloud; 't was a fair
        sight yet sad
To see the tears run down the sweet blooms
        he had:
He stamped with his foot, said — 'The
        saints know I lied
Because truth that is wicked is fittest to
        hide:
    Must I utter it, mother ?'

VIII

In his vehement childhood he hurried
        within
And knelt at her feet as in prayer against
        sin,
But a child at a prayer never sobbeth as
        he —
'Oh ! she sits with the nun of the brown
        rosary,
    At nights in the ruin —   40

IX

'The old convent ruin the ivy rots off,
Where the owl hoots by day and the toad
        is sun-proof,
Where no singing-birds build and the trees
        gaunt and gray
As in stormy sea-coasts appear blasted one
        way —
    But is *this* the wind's doing ?

X

' A nun in the east wall was buried alive
Who mocked at the priest when he called
        her to shrive,
And shrieked such a curse, as the stone
        took her breath,
The old abbess fell backwards and swooned
        unto death
    With an Ave half-spoken.   50

XI

'I tried once to pass it, myself and my
        hound,
Till, as fearing the lash, down he shivered
        to ground —
A brave hound, my mother ! a brave
        hound, ye wot !
And the wolf thought the same with his
        fangs at her throat
    In the pass of the Brocken.

XII

'At dawn and at eve, mother, who sitteth
        there
With the brown rosary never used for a
        prayer ?
Stoop low, mother, low ! If we went there
        to see,
What an ugly great hole in that east wall
        must be
    At dawn and at even !   60

XIII

' Who meet there, my mother, at dawn
        and at even ?
Who meet by that wall, never looking to
        heaven ?
O sweetest my sister, what doeth with *thee*
The ghost of a nun with a brown rosary
    And a face turned from heaven ?

XIV

' Saint Agnes o'erwatcheth my dreams and
        erewhile
I have felt through mine eyelids the warmth
        of her smile;
But last night, as a sadness like pity came
        o'er her,
She whispered — " Say *two* prayers at dawn
        for Onora:
    The Tempted is sinning.'' '   70

XV

' Onora, Onora !' they heard her not com-
        ing,

Not a step on the grass, not a voice through
    the gloaming;
But her mother looked up, and she stood
    on the floor
Fair and still as the moonlight that came
    there before,
    And a smile just beginning:

XVI

It touches her lips but it dares not arise
To the height of the mystical sphere of her
    eyes,
And the large musing eyes, neither joyous
    nor sorry,
Sing on like the angels in separate glory
    Between clouds of amber;   80

XVII

For the hair droops in clouds amber-col-
    ored till stirred
Into gold by the gesture that comes with a
    word;
While — O soft ! — her speaking is so inter-
    wound
Of the dim and the sweet, 't is a twilight
    of sound
    And floats through the chamber.

XVIII

'Since thou shrivest my brother, fair mo-
    ther,' said she,
'I count on thy priesthood for marrying of
    me;
And I know by the hills that the battle is
    done,
That my lover rides on, will be here with
    the sun,
    'Neath the eyes that behold thee.'   90

XIX

Her mother sat silent — too tender, I wis,
Of the smile her dead father smiled dying
    to kiss:
But the boy started up pale with tears,
    passion-wrought —
'O wicked fair sister, the hills utter
    nought !
    If he cometh, who told thee ? '

XX

'I know by the hills,' she resumed calm
    and clear,
'By the beauty upon them, that HE is
    anear:

Did they ever look *so* since he bade me
    adieu ?
Oh, love in the waking, sweet brother, is
    true,
    As Saint Agnes in sleeping ! '   100

XXI

Half-ashamed and half-softened the boy
    did not speak,
And the blush met the lashes which fell on
    his cheek:
She bowed down to kiss him: dear saints,
    did he see
Or feel on her bosom the BROWN ROSARY,
    That he shrank away weeping ?

SECOND PART

A bed. ONORA, *sleeping.* Angels, *but*
        not near.
First Angel.
    Must we stand so far, and she
    So very fair ?
Second Angel.
             As bodies be.
First Angel.
    And she so mild ?
Second Angel.
             As spirits when
    They meeken, not to God, but men.
First Angel.
    And she so young, that I who bring
    Good dreams for saintly children,
      might   111
    Mistake that small soft face to-night,
    And fetch her such a blessèd thing
    That at her waking she would weep
    For childhood lost anew in sleep.
    How hath she sinned ?
Second Angel.
             In bartering love;
    God's love for man's.
First Angel.
             We may reprove
    The world for this, not only her:
    Let me approach to breathe away
    This dust o' the heart with holy air.
Second Angel.
    Stand off ! She sleeps, and did not
      pray.   121
First Angel.
    Did none pray for her ?
Second Angel.
             Ay, a child, —

Who never, praying, wept before;
While, in a mother undefiled,
Prayer goeth on in sleep, as true
And pauseless as the pulses do.
First Angel.
  Then I approach.
Second Angel.
                    It is not WILLED.
First Angel.
  One word: is she redeemed?
Second Angel.
                    No more!
  The place is filled.   [*Angels vanish.*
Evil Spirit (*in a Nun's garb by the bed*).
Forbear that dream — forbear that dream!
  too near to heaven it leaned.   130
Onora (*in sleep*).
Nay, leave me this — but only this! 't is
  but a dream, sweet fiend!
Evil Spirit.
It is a *thought.*
Onora (*in sleep*).
A sleeping thought — most innocent of
  good:
It doth the Devil no harm, sweet fiend! it
  cannot if it would.
I say in it no holy hymn, I do no holy
  work,
I scarcely hear the sabbath-bell that chim-
  eth from the kirk.
Evil Spirit.
Forbear that dream — forbear that dream!
Onora (*in sleep*).
Nay, let me dream at least.
That far-off bell, it may be took for viol at
  a feast:
I only walk among the fields, beneath the
  autumn-sun,
With my dead father, hand in hand, as I
  have often done.
Evil Spirit.
Forbear that dream — forbear that dream!
Onora (*in sleep*).
Nay, sweet fiend, let me go: 140
I never more can walk with *him*, oh, never
  more but so!
For they have tied my father's feet be-
  neath the kirkyard stone,
Oh, deep and straight! oh, very straight!
  they move at nights alone:
And then he calleth through my dreams,
  he calleth tenderly,
'Come forth, my daughter, my beloved,
  and walk the fields with me!'
Evil Spirit.

Forbear that dream, or else disprove its
  pureness by a sign.
Onora (*in sleep*).
Speak on, thou shalt be satisfied, my word
  shall answer thine.
I heard a bird which used to sing when I a
  child was praying,
I see the poppies in the corn I used to
  sport away in:
What shall I do — tread down the dew
  and pull the blossoms blowing?   150
Or clap my wicked hands to fright the
  finches from the rowan?
Evil Spirit.
Thou shalt do something harder still.
  Stand up where thou dost stand
Among the fields of Dreamland with thy
  father hand in hand,
And clear and slow repeat the vow, de-
  clare its cause and kind,
Which not to break, in sleep or wake thou
  bearest on thy mind.
Onora (*in sleep*).
I bear a vow of sinful kind, a vow for
  mournful cause;
I vowed it deep, I vowed it strong, the
  spirits laughed applause:
The spirits trailed along the pines low
  laughter like a breeze,
While, high atween their swinging tops,
  the stars appeared to freeze.
Evil Spirit.
More calm and free, speak out to me why
  such a vow was made.   160
Onora (*in sleep*).
Because that God decreed my death and I
  shrank back afraid.
Have patience, O dead father mine! I did
  not fear to die —
I wish I were a young dead child and had
  thy company!
I wish I lay beside thy feet, a buried three-
  year child,
And wearing only a kiss of thine upon my
  lips that smiled!
The linden-tree that covers thee might so
  have shadowed twain,
For death itself I did not fear — 't is love
  that makes the pain:
Love feareth death. I was no child, I was
  betrothed that day;
I wore a troth-kiss on my lips I could not
  give away.
How could I bear to lie content and still
  beneath a stone,   170

And feel mine own betrothed go by — alas!
    no more mine own —
Go leading by in wedding pomp some lovely
    lady brave,
With cheeks that blushed as red as rose,
    while mine were white in grave?
How could I bear to sit in heaven, on e'er
    so high a throne,
And hear him say to her — to *her!* that
    else he loveth none?
Though e'er so high I sate above, though
    e'er so low he spake,
As clear as thunder I should hear the new
    oath he might take,
That hers, forsooth, were heavenly eyes —
    ah me, while very dim
Some heavenly eyes (indeed of heaven!)
    would darken down to *him!*
    Evil Spirit.
Who told thee thou wast called to death?
    Onora (in sleep).
    I sate all night beside thee: 180
The gray owl on the ruined wall shut both
    his eyes to hide thee,
And ever he flapped his heavy wing all
    brokenly and weak,
And the long grass waved against the sky,
    around his gasping beak.
I sate beside thee all the night, while the
    moonlight lay forlorn
Strewn round us like a dead world's shroud
    in ghastly fragments torn:
And through the night, and through the
    hush, and over the flapping wing,
We heard beside the Heavenly Gate the
    angels murmuring:
We heard them say, ' Put day to day, and
    count the days to seven,
And God will draw Onora up the golden
    stairs of heaven.
And yet the Evil ones have leave that
    purpose to defer,   190
For if she has no need of HIM, He has no
    need of her.'
    Evil Spirit.
Speak out to me, speak bold and free.
    Onora (in sleep).
    And then I heard thee say —
I count upon my rosary brown the hours
    thou hast to stay!
Yet God permits us Evil ones to put by
    that decree,
Since if thou hast no need of HIM, He has
    no need of thee:
And if thou wilt forgo the sight of angels,
    verily

Thy true love gazing on thy face shall
    guess what angels be;
Nor bride shall pass, save thee ' . . . Alas!
    — my father's hand 's a-cold,
The meadows seem . . .
    Evil Spirit.
    Forbear the dream, or let the vow be
    told.
    Onora (in sleep).
I vowed upon thy rosary brown, this string
    of antique beads,   200
By charnel lichens overgrown, and dank
    among the weeds,
This rosary brown which is thine own, —
    lost soul of buried nun!
Who, lost by vow, wouldst render now all
    souls alike undone, —
I vowed upon thy rosary brown, — and, till
    such vow should break,
A pledge always of living days 't was
    hung around my neck —
I vowed to thee on rosary (dead father,
    look not so!),
I would not thank God in my weal, nor seek
    God in my woe.
    Evil Spirit.
And canst thou prove . . .
    Onora (in sleep).
    O love, my love! I felt him near
    again!
I saw his steed on mountain-head, I heard
    it on the plain!
Was this no weal for me to feel? Is
    greater weal than this?   210
Yet when he came, I wept his name — and
    the angels heard but *his.*
    Evil Spirit.
Well done, well done!
    Onora (in sleep).
    Ah me, the sun! the dreamlight 'gins
    to pine, —
Ah me, how dread can look the Dead!
    Aroint thee, father mine!

She starteth from slumber, she sitteth up-
    right,
And her breath comes in sobs, while she
    stares through the night;
There is nought; the great willow, her lat-
    tice before,
Large-drawn in the moon, lieth calm on
    the floor:
But her hands tremble fast as their pulses
    and, free
From the death-clasp, close over — the
    BROWN ROSARY.

THIRD PART

I

'T is a morn for a bridal; the merry bride-
    bell   220
Rings clear through the greenwood that
    skirts the chapelle,
And the priest at the altar awaiteth the
    bride,
And the sacristans slyly are jesting aside
      At the work shall be doing;

II

While down through the wood rides that
    fair company,
The youths with the courtship, the maids
    with the glee,
Till the chapel-cross opens to sight, and at
    once
All the maids sigh demurely and think for
    the nonce,
      ' And so endeth a wooing !'

III

And the bride and the bridegroom are
    leading the way,   230
With his hand on her rein, and a word yet
    to say;
Her dropt eyelids suggest the soft answers
    beneath,
And the little quick smiles come and go
    with her breath
      When she sigheth or speaketh.

IV

And the tender bride-mother breaks off
    unaware
From an Ave, to think that her daughter
    is fair,
Till in nearing the chapel and glancing
    before,
She seeth her little son stand at the door:
      Is it play that he seeketh?

V

Is it play, when his eyes wander innocent-
    wild   240
And sublimed with a sadness unfitting a
    child?
He trembles not, weeps not; the passion is
    done,
And calmly he kneels in their midst, with
    the sun
      On his head like a glory.

VI

' O fair-featured maids, ye are many !' he
    cried,
' But in fairness and vileness who matcheth
    the bride?
O brave-hearted youths, ye are many ! but
    whom
For the courage and woe can ye match with
    the groom
      As ye see them before ye?'

VII

Out spake the bride's mother, ' The vileness
    is thine   250
If thou shame thine own sister, a bride at
    the shrine !'
Out spake the bride's lover, ' The vileness
    be mine
If he shame mine own wife at the hearth
    or the shrine
      And the charge be unprovèd.

VIII

' Bring the charge, prove the charge, bro-
    ther ! speak it aloud:
Let thy father and hers hear it deep in his
    shroud !'
—' O father, thou seest, for dead eyes can
    see,
How she wears on her bosom a BROWN
    ROSARY,
      O my father belovèd !'

IX

Then out laughed the bridegroom, and out
    laughed withal   260
Both maidens and youths by the old chapel-
    wall:
' So she weareth no love-gift, kind brother,'
    quoth he,
' She may wear an she listeth a brown
    rosary,
      Like a pure-hearted lady.'

X

Then swept through the chapel the long
    bridal train;
Though he spake to the bride she replied
    not again;

On, as one in a dream, pale and stately she
        went
Where the altar-lights burn o'er the great
        sacrament,
        Faint with daylight, but steady.

XI

But her brother had passed in between
        them and her,   270
And calmly knelt down on the high-altar
        stair —
Of an infantine aspect so stern to the view
That the priest could not smile on the
        child's eyes of blue
        As he would for another.

XII

He knelt like a child marble-sculptured and
        white
That seems kneeling to pray on the tomb
        of a knight,
With a look taken up to each iris of stone
From the greatness and death where he
        kneeleth, but none
        From the face of a mother.

XIII

'In your chapel, O priest, ye have wedded
        and shriven   280
Fair wives for the hearth, and fair sinners
        for heaven;
But this fairest my sister, ye think now to
        wed,
Bid her kneel where she standeth, and
        shrive her instead:
        O shrive her and wed not !'

XIV

In tears, the bride's mother, — 'Sir priest,
        unto thee
Would he lie, as he lied to this fair com-
        pany.'
In wrath, the bride's lover, — 'The lie
        shall be clear !
Speak it out, boy ! the saints in their niches
        shall hear:
        Be the charge proved or said not !'

XV

Then serene in his childhood he lifted his
        face,   290
And his voice sounded holy and fit for the
        place, —
'Look down from your niches, ye still saints,
        and see

How she wears on her bosom a BROWN
        ROSARY !
        Is it used for the praying ?'

XVI

The youths looked aside — to laugh there
        were a sin —
And the maidens' lips trembled from smiles
        shut within.
Quoth the priest, 'Thou art wild, pretty
        boy ! Blessed she
Who prefers at her bridal a brown rosary
        To a worldly arraying.'

XVII

The bridegroom spake low and led onward
        the bride   300
And before the high altar they stood side
        by side:
The rite-book is opened, the rite is begun,
They have knelt down together to rise up
        as one.
        Who laughed by the altar ?

XVIII

The maidens looked forward, the youths
        looked around,
The bridegroom's eye flashed from his
        prayer at the sound;
And each saw the bride, as if no bride she
        were,
Gazing cold at the priest without gesture
        of prayer,
        As he read from the psalter.

XIX

The priest never knew that she did so, but
        still   310
He felt a power on him too strong for his
        will:
And whenever the Great Name was there
        to be read,
His voice sank to silence — THAT could not
        be said,
        Or the air could not hold it.

XX

'I have sinnèd,' quoth he, 'I have sinnèd,
        I wot'—
And the tears ran adown his old cheeks at
        the thought:
They dropped fast on the book, but he
        read on the same,

And aye was the silence where should be
    the NAME, —
      As the choristers told it.

XXI

The rite-book is closed, and the rite being
    done   320
They, who knelt down together, arise up as
    one:
Fair riseth the bride — Oh, a fair bride is
    she,
But, for all (think the maidens) that brown
    rosary,
      No saint at her praying !

XXII

What aileth the bridegroom ? He glares
    blank and wide;
Then suddenly turning he kisseth the bride;
His lips stung her with cold; she glanced
    upwardly mute:
' Mine own wife,' he said, and fell stark at
    her foot
      In the word he was saying.

XXIII

They have lifted him up, but his head sinks
    away,   330
And his face showeth bleak in the sunshine
    and gray.
Leave him now where he lieth — for oh,
    never more
Will he kneel at an altar or stand on a floor !
      Let his bride gaze upon him.

XXIV

Long and still was her gaze while they
    chaféd him there
And breathed in the mouth whose last life
    had kissed her,
But when they stood up — only *they !* with
    a start
The shriek from her soul struck her pale
    lips apart:
      She has lived, and forgone him !

XXV

And low on his body she droppeth adown —
' Didst call me thine own wife, belovèd —
    thine own ?   341
Then take thine own with thee ! thy cold-
    ness is warm
To the world's cold without thee ! Come,
    keep me from harm
      In a calm of thy teaching !'

XXVI

She looked in his face earnest-long, as in
    sooth
There were hope of an answer, and then
    kissed his mouth,
And with head on his bosom, wept, wept
    bitterly, —
' Now, O God, take pity — take pity on
    me !
      God, hear my beseeching !'

XXVII

She was 'ware of a shadow that crossed
    where she lay,   350
She was 'ware of a presence that withered
    the day:
Wild she sprang to her feet, — ' I surrender
    to *thee*
The broken vow's pledge, the accursed
    rosary, —
      I am ready for dying !'

XXVIII

She dashed it in scorn to the marble-paved
    ground
Where it fell mute as snow, and a weird
    music-sound
Crept up, like a chill, up the aisles long
    and dim, —
As the fiends tried to mock at the choristers'
    hymn
      And moaned in the trying.

FOURTH PART

Onora looketh listlessly adown the garden
    walk: 360
' I am weary, O my mother, of thy tender
    talk.
I am weary of the trees a-waving to and
    fro,
Of the steadfast skies above, the running
    brooks below.
All things are the same, but I, — only I
    am dreary,
And, mother, of my dreariness behold me
    very weary.

' Mother, brother, pull the flowers I planted
    in the spring
And smiled to think I should smile more
    upon their gathering:
The bees will find out other flowers — oh,
    pull them, dearest mine,

And carry them and carry me before Saint
    Agnes' shrine.'
— Whereat they pulled the summer flowers
    she planted in the spring,   370
And her and them all mournfully to Agnes'
    shrine did bring.

She looked up to the pictured saint and
    gently shook her head —
' The picture is too calm for *me* — too calm
    for *me*,' she said:
' The little flowers we brought with us,
    before it we may lay,
For those are used to look at heaven, — but
    I must turn away,
Because no sinner under sun can dare or
    bear to gaze
On God's or angel's holiness, except in
    Jesu's face.'

She spoke with passion after pause — ' And
    were it wisely done
If we who cannot gaze above, should walk
    the earth alone ?
If we whose virtue is so weak should have
    a will so strong,   380
And stand blind on the rocks to choose the
    right path from the wrong ?
To choose perhaps a love-lit hearth, instead
    of love and heaven, —
A single rose, for a rose-tree which beareth
    seven times seven ?
A rose that droppeth from the hand, that
    fadeth in the breast, —
Until, in grieving for the worst, we learn
    what is the best !'

Then breaking into tears, — ' Dear God,'
    she cried, 'and must we see
All blissful things depart from us or ere
    we go to THEE ?
We cannot guess Thee in the wood or hear
    Thee in the wind ?
Our cedars must fall round us ere we see
    the light behind ?
Ay sooth, we feel too strong, in weal, to
    need Thee on that road,   390
But woe being come, the soul is dumb that
    crieth not on " God." '

Her mother could not speak for tears; she
    ever musèd thus,
' *The bees will find out other flowers,* — but
    what is left for *us* ? '

But her young brother stayed his sobs and
    knelt beside her knee,
— ' Thou sweetest sister in the world, hast
    never a word for me ? '
She passed her hand across his face, she
    pressed it on his cheek,
So tenderly, so tenderly — she needed not
    to speak.

The wreath which lay on shrine that day,
    at vespers bloomed no more.
The woman fair who placed it there had
    died an hour before.
Both perished mute for lack of root, earth's
    nourishment to reach.   400
O reader, breathe (the ballad saith) some
    sweetness out of each !

THE MOURNING MOTHER

(OF THE DEAD BLIND)

First printed as ' The Mournful Mother.'

I

DOST thou weep, mourning mother,
    For thy blind boy in grave ?
That no more with each other
    Sweet counsel ye can have ?
That he, left dark by nature,
    Can never more be led
By thee, maternal creature,
    Along smooth paths instead ?
That thou canst no more show him
    The sunshine, by the heat;   10
The river's silver flowing,
    By murmurs at his feet ?
The foliage, by its coolness;
    The roses, by their smell;
And all creation's fulness,
    By Love's invisible ?
Weepest thou to behold not
    His meek blind eyes again, —
Closed doorways which were folded,
    And prayed against in vain —   20
And under which, sat smiling
    The child-mouth evermore,
As one who watcheth, wiling
    The time by, at a door ?
And weepest thou to feel not
    His clinging hand on thine —
Which now, at dream-time, will not
    Its cold touch disentwine ?
And weepest thou still ofter,

Oh, never more to mark   30
His low soft words, made softer
  By speaking in the dark ?
Weep on, thou mourning mother !

II

But since to him when living,
  Thou wast both sun and moon,
Look o'er his grave, surviving,
  From a high sphere alone:
Sustain that exaltation,
  Expand that tender light,
And hold in mother-passion   40
  Thy Blessèd in thy sight.
See how he went out straightway
  From the dark world he knew, —
No twilight in the gateway
  To mediate 'twixt the two, —
Into the sudden glory,
  Out of the dark he trod,
Departing from before thee
  At once to light and GOD ! —
For the first face, beholding   50
  The Christ's in its divine,
For the first place, the golden
  And tideless hyaline,
With trees at lasting summer
  That rock to songful sound,
While angels the new-comer
  Wrap a still smile around.
Oh, in the blessèd psalm now,
  His happy voice he tries,
Spreading a thicker palm-bough,   60
  Than others, o'er his eyes !
Yet still, in all the singing,
  Thinks haply of thy song
Which, in his life's first springing,
  Sang to him all night long;
And wishes it beside him,
  With kissing lips that cool
And soft did overglide him,
  To make the sweetness full.
Look up, O mourning mother !   70
  Thy blind boy walks in light:
Ye wait for one another
  Before God's infinite.
But thou art now the darkest,
  Thou mother left below
Thou, the sole blind, — thou markest,
  Content that it be so, —
Until ye two have meeting
  Where Heaven's pearl-gate is,
And *he* shall lead thy feet in,   80
  As once thou leddest *his*.
Wait on, thou mourning mother !

A VALEDICTION

GOD be with thee, my belovèd, — GOD be
  with thee !
  Else alone thou goest forth,
  Thy face unto the north,
Moor and pleasance all around thee and
  beneath thee
  Looking equal in one snow;
  While I, who try to reach thee,
  Vainly follow, vainly follow
  With the farewell and the hollo,
  And cannot reach thee so.
  Alas, I can but teach thee !
GOD be with thee, my belovèd, — GOD be
  with thee !

II

Can I teach thee, my belovèd, — can I
  teach thee ?
  If I said, 'Go left or right,'
  The counsel would be light,
The wisdom, poor of all that could enrich
  thee;
  My right would show like left;
  My raising would depress thee,
  My choice of light would blind thee,
  Of way — would leave behind thee,
  Of end — would leave bereft.
  Alas, I can but bless thee !
May GOD teach thee, my belovèd, — may
  GOD teach thee !

III

Can I bless thee, my belovèd, — can I bless
  thee ?
  What blessing word can I
  From mine own tears keep dry ?
What flowers grow in my field wherewith
  to dress thee ?
  My good reverts to ill;
  My calmnesses would move thee,
  My softnesses would prick thee,
  My bindings up would break thee,
  My crownings curse and kill.
  Alas, I can but love thee !
May GOD bless thee, my belovèd, — may
  GOD bless thee !

IV

Can I love thee, my belovèd, — can I love
  thee ?
  And is *this* like love, to stand

With no help in my hand,
When strong as death I fain would watch
    above thee ?
My love-kiss can deny
No tear that falls beneath it;
Mine oath of love can swear thee
From no ill that comes near thee,
And thou diest while I breathe it,
And *I* — I can but die !
May GOD love thee, my belovèd, — may
    GOD love thee !

LADY GERALDINE'S COURTSHIP

A ROMANCE OF THE AGE

A special interest attaches to this poem as the one which induced Robert Browning to seek Miss Barrett's acquaintance. She herself had been rather inclined to think lightly of it because it was, in some sense, written to order, and that with extraordinary rapidity. In a letter to H. S. Boyd, dated August 1, 1844, she gives the following account of its origin : 'Last Saturday, on its being discovered that my first volume consisted of only 208 pages, and my second of 280 pages, Mr. Moxon uttered a cry of reprehension . . . and wanted to tear away several poems from the end of the second volume, and tie them on to the end of the first ! I could not and would not hear of this because I had set my heart on having 'Dead Pan' to conclude with. So there was nothing for it but to finish a ballad poem called 'Lady Geraldine's Courtship,' which was lying by me, and I did so by writing — i. e., composing, — one hundred and forty lines last Saturday. I seemed to be in a dream all day. Long lines, too, — fifteen syllables each ! ' Elsewhere she entreats Mr. Boyd never to tell anybody in what haste the poem was written. This highly colored rhymed romance of modern life proved far more attractive to the general reader than some of the more elaborate and more truly artistic pieces in the edition of 1844. It was also a special favorite both with Carlyle and Miss Martineau.

A Poet writes to his Friend. PLACE — *A Room in Wycombe Hall*. TIME — *Late in the evening.*

I

DEAR my friend and fellow - student, I
    would lean my spirit o'er you !
Down the purple of this chamber tears
    should scarcely run at will.

I am humbled who was humble. Friend,
    I bow my head before you:
You should lead me to my peasants, but
    their faces are too still.

II

There's a lady, an earl's daughter, — she
    is proud and she is noble,
And she treads the crimson carpet and she
    breathes the perfumed air,
And a kingly blood sends glances up, her
    princely eye to trouble,
And the shadow of a monarch's crown is
    softened in her hair.

III

She has halls among the woodlands, she
    has castles by the breakers,
She has farms and she has manors, she can
    threaten and command:
And the palpitating engines snort in steam
    across her acres,
As they mark upon the blasted heaven the
    measure of the land.

IV

There are none of England's daughters
    who can show a prouder presence;
Upon princely suitors' praying she has
    looked in her disdain.
She was sprung of English nobles, I was
    born of English peasants;
What was *I* that I should love her, save
    for competence to pain ?

V

I was only a poor poet, made for singing
    at her casement,
As the finches or the thrushes, while she
    thought of other things.
Oh, she walked so high above me, she ap-
    peared to my abasement,
In her lovely silken murmur, like an angel
    clad in wings !

VI

Many vassals bow before her as her car-
    riage sweeps their doorways;
She has blessed their little children, as a
    priest or queen were she:

Far too tender, or too cruel far, her smile
  upon the poor was,
For I thought it was the same smile which
  she used to smile on *me*.

VII

She has voters in the Commons, she has
  lovers in the palace,
And, of all the fair court-ladies, few have
  jewels half as fine;
Oft the Prince has named her beauty 'twixt
  the red wine and the chalice:
Oh, and what was *I* to love her? my be-
  loved, my Geraldine!

VIII

Yet I could not choose but love her: I was
  born to poet-uses,
To love all things set above me, all of good
  and all of fair.
Nymphs of mountain, not of valley, we are
  wont to call the Muses;
And in nympholeptic climbing, poets pass
  from mount to star.

IX

And because I was a poet, and because the
  public praised me,
With a critical deduction for the modern
  writer's fault,
I could sit at rich men's tables, — though
  the courtesies that raised me,
Still suggested clear between us the pale
  spectrum of the salt.

X

And they praised me in her presence —
  'Will your book appear this sum-
  mer?'
Then returning to each other — 'Yes, our
  plans are for the moors.'
Then with whisper dropped behind me —
  'There he is! the latest comer.
Oh, she only likes his verses! what is over,
  she endures.

XI

'Quite low-born, self-educated! somewhat
  gifted though by nature,
And we make a point of asking him, — of
  being very kind.
You may speak, he does not hear you! and,
  besides, he writes no satire, —
All these serpents kept by charmers leave
  the natural sting behind.'

XII

I grew scornfuller, grew colder, as I stood
  up there among them,
Till as frost intense will burn you, the cold
  scorning scorched my brow;
When a sudden silver speaking, gravely
  cadenced, over-rung them,
And a sudden silken stirring touched my
  inner nature through.

XIII

I looked upward and beheld her: with a
  calm and regnant spirit,
Slowly round she swept her eyelids, and
  said clear before them all —
'Have you such superfluous honor, sir,
  that able to confer it
You will come down, Mister Bertram, as
  my guest to Wycombe Hall?'

XIV

Here she paused; she had been paler at the
  first word of her speaking,
But, because a silence followed it, blushed
  somewhat, as for shame;
Then, as scorning her own feeling, resumed
  calmly — 'I am seeking
More distinction than these gentlemen think
  worthy of my claim.

XV

'Ne'ertheless, you see, I seek it — not be-
  cause I am a woman,'
(Here her smile sprang like a fountain and,
  so, overflowed her mouth)
'But because my woods in Sussex have
  some purple shades at gloaming
Which are worthy of a king in state, or
  poet in his youth.

XVI

'I invite you, Mister Bertram, to no scene
  for worldly speeches —
Sir, I scarce should dare — but only where
  God asked the thrushes first:
And if *you* will sing beside them, in the
  covert of my beeches,
I will thank you for the woodlands, — for
  the human world, at worst.'

XVII

Then she smiled around right childly, then
  she gazed around right queenly,
And I bowed — I could not answer; alter-
  nated light and gloom —

While as one who quells the lions, with a
    steady eye serenely,
She, with level fronting eyelids, passed out
    stately from the room.

XVIII

Oh, the blessèd woods of Sussex, I can hear
    them still around me,
With their leafy tide of greenery still rip-
    pling up the wind !
Oh, the cursèd woods of Sussex ! where the
    hunter's arrow found me,
When a fair face and a tender voice had
    made me mad and blind !

XIX

In that ancient hall of Wycombe thronged
    the numerous guests invited,
And the lovely London ladies trod the
    floors with gliding feet;
And their voices low with fashion, not with
    feeling, softly freighted
All the air about the windows with elastic
    laughters sweet.

XX

For at eve the open windows flung their
    light out on the terrace
Which the floating orbs of curtains did with
    gradual shadow sweep,
While the swans upon the river, fed at
    morning by the heiress,
Trembled downward through their snowy
    wings at music in their sleep.

XXI

And there evermore was music, both of
    instrument and singing,
Till the finches of the shrubberies grew
    restless in the dark;
But the cedars stood up motionless, each in
    a moonlight's ringing,
And the deer, half in the glimmer, strewed
    the hollows of the park.

XXII

And though sometimes she would bind me
    with her silver-corded speeches
To commix my words and laughter with
    the converse and the jest,
Oft I sat apart and, gazing on the river
    through the beeches,
Heard, as pure the swans swam down it,
    her pure voice o'erfloat the rest.

XXIII

In the morning, horn of huntsman, hoof of
    steed and laugh of rider,
Spread out cheery from the courtyard till
    we lost them in the hills,
While herself and other ladies, and her
    suitors left beside her,
Went a-wandering up the gardens through
    the laurels and abeles.

XXIV

Thus, her foot upon the new-mown grass,
    bareheaded, with the flowing
Of the virginal white vesture gathered
    closely to her throat,
And the golden ringlets in her neck just
    quickened by her going,
And appearing to breathe sun for air, and
    doubting if to float, —

XXV

With a bunch of dewy maple, which her
    right hand held above her,
And which trembled a green shadow in be-
    twixt her and the skies,
As she turned her face in going, thus, she
    drew me on to love her,
And to worship the divineness of the smile
    hid in her eyes.

XXVI

For her eyes alone smile constantly; her
    lips have serious sweetness,
And her front is calm, the dimple rarely
    ripples on the cheek;
But her deep blue eyes smile constantly, as
    if they in discreetness
Kept the secret of a happy dream she did
    not care to speak.

XXVII

Thus she drew me the first morning, out
    across into the garden,
And I walked among her noble friends and
    could not keep behind.
Spake she unto all and unto me — ' Behold,
    I am the warden
Of the song-birds in these lindens, which
    are cages to their mind.

XXVIII

' But within this swarded circle into which
    the lime-walk brings us,
Whence the beeches, rounded greenly, stand
    away in reverent fear,

I will let no music enter, saving what the
  fountain sings us
Which the lilies round the basin may seem
  pure enough to hear.

XXIX

'The live air that waves the lilies waves
  the slender jet of water
Like a holy thought sent feebly up from
  soul of fasting saint:
Whereby lies a marble Silence, sleeping
  (Lough the sculptor wrought her),
So asleep she is forgetting to say Hush !
  — a fancy quaint.

XXX

'Mark how heavy white her eyelids ! not
  a dream between them lingers;
And the left hand's index droppeth from
  the lips upon the cheek:
While the right hand, — with the symbol-
  rose held slack within the fingers, —
Has fallen backward in the basin — yet
  this Silence will not speak !

XXXI

'That the essential meaning growing may
  exceed the special symbol,
Is the thought as I conceive it: it applies
  more high and low.
Our true noblemen will often through right
  nobleness grow humble,
And assert an inward honor by denying
  outward show.'

XXXII

'Nay, your Silence,' said I, 'truly, holds
  her symbol-rose but slackly,
Yet *she holds it*, or would scarcely be a Si-
  lence to our ken:
And your nobles wear their ermine on the
  outside, or walk blackly
In the presence of the social law as mere
  ignoble men.

XXXIII

'Let the poets dream such dreaming !
  madam, in these British islands
'T is the substance that wanes ever, 't is the
  symbol that exceeds.
Soon we shall have nought but symbol: and,
  for statues like this Silence,
Shall accept the rose's image — in another
  case, the weed's.'

XXXIV

'Not so quickly,' she retorted, — 'I con-
  fess, where'er you go, you
Find for things, names — shows for actions,
  and pure gold for honor clear:
But when all is run to symbol in the Social,
  I will throw you
The world's book which now reads dryly,
  and sit down with Silence here.'

XXXV

Half in playfulness she spoke, I thought,
  and half in indignation;
Friends, who listened, laughed her words
  off, while her lovers deemed her fair:
A fair woman, flushed with feeling, in her
  noble-lighted station
Near the statue's white reposing — and
  both bathed in sunny air !

XXXVI

With the trees round, not so distant but
  you heard their vernal murmur,
And beheld in light and shadow the leaves
  in and outward move,
And the little fountain leaping toward the
  sun-heart to be warmer,
Then recoiling in a tremble from the too
  much light above.

XXXVII

'T is a picture for remembrance. And thus,
  morning after morning,
Did I follow as she drew me by the spirit
  to her feet.
Why, her greyhound followed also ! dogs —
  we both were dogs for scorning —
To be sent back when she pleased it and
  her path lay through the wheat.

XXXVIII

And thus, morning after morning, spite of
  vows and spite of sorrow,
Did I follow at her drawing, while the
  week-days passed along, —
Just to feed the swans this noontide, or to
  see the fawns to-morrow,
Or to teach the hill-side echo some sweet
  Tuscan in a song.

XXXIX

Ay, for sometimes on the hill-side, while we
  sate down in the gowans,
With the forest green behind us and its
  shadow cast before,

And the river running under, and across it
    from the rowans
A brown partridge whirring near us till we
    felt the air it bore, —

XL

There, obedient to her praying, did I read
    aloud the poems
Made to Tuscan flutes, or instruments
    more various of our own;
Read the pastoral parts of Spenser, or the
    subtle interflowings
Found in Petrarch's sonnets — here's the
    book, the leaf is folded down !

XLI

Or at times a modern volume, Words-
    worth's solemn-thoughted idyl,
Howitt's ballad-verse, or Tennyson's en-
    chanted reverie, —
Or from Browning some ' Pomegranate,'
    which, if cut deep down the middle,
Shows a heart within blood-tinctured, of a
    veined humanity.

XLII

Or at times I read there, hoarsely, some
    new poem of my making:
Poets ever fail in reading their own verses
    to their worth,
For the echo in you breaks upon the words
    which you are speaking,
And the chariot wheels jar in the gate
    through which you drive them forth.

XLIII

After, when we were grown tired of books,
    the silence round us flinging
A slow arm of sweet compression, felt with
    beatings at the breast,
She would break out on a sudden in a gush
    of woodland singing,
Like a child's emotion in a god — a naiad
    tired of rest.

XLIV

Oh, to see or hear her singing ! scarce I
    know which is divinest,
For her looks sing too — she modulates
    her gestures on the tune,
And her mouth stirs with the song, like
    song; and when the notes are finest,
'T is the eyes that shoot out vocal light
    and seem to swell them on.

XLV

Then we talked — oh, how we talked !
    her voice, so cadenced in the talking,
Made another singing — of the soul ! a
    music without bars:
While the leafy sounds of woodlands, hum-
    ming round where we were walking,
Brought interposition worthy-sweet, — as
    skies about the stars.

XLVI

And she spake such good thoughts natural,
    as if she always thought them;
She had sympathies so rapid, open, free as
    bird on branch,
Just as ready to fly east as west, whichever
    way besought them,
In the birchen-wood a chirrup, or a cock-
    crow in the grange.

XLVII

In her utmost lightness there is truth —
    and often she speaks lightly,
Has a grace in being gay which even
    mournful souls approve,
For the root of some grave earnest thought
    is understruck so rightly
As to justify the foliage and the waving
    flowers above.

XLVIII

And she talked on — we talked, rather !
    upon all things, substance, shadow,
Of the sheep that browsed the grasses, of
    the reapers in the corn,
Of the little children from the schools, seen
    winding through the meadow,
Of the poor rich world beyond them, still
    kept poorer by its scorn.

XLIX

So, of men, and so, of letters — books are
    men of higher stature,
And the only men that speak aloud for
    future times to hear;
So, of mankind in the abstract, which
    grows slowly into nature,
Yet will lift the cry of 'progress,' as it
    trod from sphere to sphere.

L

And her custom was to praise me when I
    said, — ' The Age culls simples,
With a broad clown's back turned broadly
    to the glory of the stars.

We are gods by our own reck'ning, and
    may well shut up the temples,
And wield on, amid the incense-steam, the
    thunder of our cars.

LI

'For we throw out acclamations of self-
    thanking, self-admiring,
With, at every mile run faster, — " O the
    wondrous wondrous age ! "
Little thinking if we work our SOULS as
    nobly as our iron,
Or if angels will commend us at the goal
    of pilgrimage.

LII

'Why, what *is* this patient entrance into
    nature's deep resources
But the child's most gradual learning to
    walk upright without bane !
When we drive out, from the cloud of
    steam, majestical white horses,
Are we greater than the first men who led
    black ones by the mane ?

LIII

'If we trod the deeps of ocean, if we
    struck the stars in rising,
If we wrapped the globe intensely with one
    hot electric breath,
'T were but power within our tether, no
    new spirit-power comprising,
And in life we were not greater men, nor
    bolder men in death.'

LIV

She was patient with my talking; and I
    loved her, loved her certes
As I loved all heavenly objects, with up-
    lifted eyes and hands;
As I loved pure inspirations, loved the
    graces, loved the virtues,
In a Love content with writing his own
    name on desert sands.

LV

Or at least I thought so, purely; thought
    no idiot Hope was raising
Any crown to crown Love's silence, silent
    Love that sate alone:
Out, alas ! the stag is like me, he that tries
    to go on grazing
With the great deep gun-wound in his
    neck, then reels with sudden moan.

LVI

It was thus I reeled. I told you that her
    hand had many suitors;
But she smiles them down imperially as
    Venus did the waves,
And with such a gracious coldness that
    they cannot press their futures
On the present of her courtesy, which
    yieldingly enslaves.

LVII

And this morning as I sat alone within the
    inner chamber
With the great saloon beyond it, lost in
    pleasant thought serene,
For I had been reading Camoëns, that
    poem you remember,
Which his lady's eyes are praised in as the
    sweetest ever seen.

LVIII

And the book lay open, and my thought
    flew from it, taking from it
A vibration and impulsion to an end be-
    yond its own,
As the branch of a green osier, when a
    child would overcome it,
Springs up freely from his claspings and
    goes swinging in the sun.

LIX

As I mused I heard a murmur; it grew
    deep as it grew longer,
Speakers using earnest language — 'Lady
    Geraldine, you *would !* '
And I heard a voice that pleaded, ever on
    in accents stronger,
As a sense of reason gave it power to make
    its rhetoric good.

LX

Well I knew that voice; it was an earl's, of
    soul that matched his station,
Soul completed into lordship, might and
    right read on his brow;
Very finely courteous; far too proud to
    doubt his domination
Of the common people, he atones for gran-
    deur by a bow.

LXI

High straight forehead, nose of eagle, cold
    blue eyes of less expression
Than resistance, coldly casting off the looks
    of other men,

As steel, arrows; unelastic lips which seem
  to taste possession
And be cautious lest the common air should
  injure or distrain.

LXII

For the rest, accomplished, upright, — ay,
  and standing by his order
With a bearing not ungraceful; fond of
  art and letters too;
Just a good man made a proud man, — as
  the sandy rocks that border
A wild coast, by circumstances, in a regnant
  ebb and flow.

LXIII

Thus, I knew that voice, I heard it, and I
  could not help the hearkening:
In the room I stood up blindly, and my
  burning heart within
Seemed to seethe and fuse my senses till
  they ran on all sides darkening,
And scorched, weighed like melted metal
  round my feet that stood therein.

LXIV

And that voice, I heard it pleading, for
  love's sake, for wealth, position,
For the sake of liberal uses and great ac-
  tions to be done:
And she interrupted gently, 'Nay, my
  lord, the old tradition
Of your Normans, by some worthier hand
  than mine is, should be won.'

LXV

'Ah, that white hand!' he said quickly, —
  and in his he either drew it
Or attempted — for with gravity and in-
  stance she replied,
'Nay, indeed, my lord, this talk is vain,
  and we had best eschew it
And pass on, like friends, to other points
  less easy to decide.'

LXVI

What he said again, I know not: it is
  likely that his trouble
Worked his pride up to the surface, for
  she answered in slow scorn,
'And your lordship judges rightly. Whom
  I marry shall be noble,
Ay, and wealthy. I shall never blush to
  think how he was born.'

LXVII

There, I maddened! her words stung me.
  Life swept through me into fever,
And my soul sprang up astonished, sprang
  full-statured in an hour.
Know you what it is when anguish, with
  apocalyptic NEVER,
To a Pythian height dilates you, and de-
  spair sublimes to power?

LXVIII

From my brain the soul-wings budded,
  waved a flame about my body,
Whence conventions coiled to ashes. I felt
  self-drawn out, as man,
From amalgamate false natures, and I saw
  the skies grow ruddy
With the deepening feet of angels, and I
  knew what spirits can.

LXIX

I was mad, inspired — say either! (anguish
  worketh inspiration)
Was a man or beast — perhaps so, for the
  tiger roars when speared;
And I walked on, step by step along the
  level of my passion —
Oh my soul! and passed the doorway to
  her face, and never feared.

LXX

He had left her, peradventure, when my
  footstep proved my coming,
But for *her* — she half arose, then sate,
  grew scarlet and grew pale.
Oh, she trembled! 't is so always with a
  worldly man or woman
In the presence of true spirits; what else
  can they do but quail?

LXXI

Oh, she fluttered like a tame bird, in among
  its forest brothers
Far too strong for it; then drooping, bowed
  her face upon her hands;
And I spake out wildly, fiercely, brutal
  truths of her and others:
I, she planted in the desert, swathed her,
  windlike, with my sands.

LXXII

I plucked up her social fictions, bloody-
  rooted though leaf-verdant,
Trod them down with words of shaming, —
  all the purple and the gold.

All the 'landed stakes' and lordships, all
    that spirits pure and ardent
Are cast out of love and honor because
    chancing not to hold.

LXXIII

'For myself I do not argue,' said I, 'though
    I love you, madam,
But for better souls that nearer to the
    height of yours have trod;
And this age shows, to my thinking, still
    more infidels to Adam
Than directly, by profession, simple infidels
    to God.

LXXIV

'Yet, O God,' I said, 'O grave,' I said,
    O mother's heart and bosom,
With whom first and last are equal, saint
    and corpse and little child!
We are fools to your deductions, in these
    figments of heart-closing;
We are traitors to your causes, in these
    sympathies defiled.

LXXV

'Learn more reverence, madam, not for
    rank or wealth — that needs no
    learning:
That comes quickly, quick as sin does, ay,
    and culminates to sin;
But for Adam's seed, MAN!   Trust me,
    't is a clay above your scorning,
With God's image stamped upon it, and
    God's kindling breath within.

LXXVI

'What right have you, madam, gazing
    your palace mirror daily,
Getting so by heart your beauty which all
    others must adore,
While you draw the golden ringlets down
    your fingers, to vow gaily
You will wed no man that 's only good to
    God, and nothing more ?

LXXXVII

'Why, what right have you, made fair by
    that same God, the sweetest woman
Of all women He has fashioned, with your
    lovely spirit-face
Which would seem too near to vanish if its
    smile were not so human,
And your voice of holy sweetness, turning
    common words to grace, —

LXXVIII

'What right can you have, God's other
    works to scorn, despise, revile them
In the gross, as mere men, broadly — not
    as noble men, forsooth, —
As mere Pariahs of the outer world, for-
    bidden to assoil them
In the hope of living, dying, near that
    sweetness of your mouth ?

LXXIX

'Have you any answer, madam ?   If my
    spirit were less earthly,
If its instrument were gifted with a better
    silver string,
I would kneel down where I stand, and
    say — Behold me!   I am worthy
Of thy loving, for I love thee.   I am wor-
    thy as a king.

LXXX

'As it is — your ermined pride, I swear,
    shall feel this stain upon her,
That I, poor, weak, tost with passion,
    scorned by me and you again,
Love you, madam, dare to love you, to my
    grief and your dishonor,
To my endless desolation, and your impo-
    tent disdain ! '

LXXXI

More mad words like these — mere mad-
    ness! friend, I need not write them
    fuller,
For I hear my hot soul dropping on the
    lines in showers of tears.
Oh, a woman! friend, a woman! why, a
    beast had scarce been duller
Than roar bestial loud complaints against
    the shining of the spheres.

LXXXII

But at last there came a pause.   I stood all
    vibrating with thunder
Which my soul had used.   The silence
    drew her face up like a call.
Could you guess what word she uttered ?
    She looked up, as if in wonder,
With tears beaded on her lashes, and said —
    'Bertram!' — It was all.

LXXXIII

If she had cursed me, and she might have,
    or if even, with queenly bearing
Which at need is used by women, she had
    risen up and said,

'Sir, you are my guest, and therefore I
    have given you a full hearing:
Now, beseech you, choose a name exacting
    somewhat less, instead !'—

LXXXIV

I had borne it: but that 'Bertram'— why,
    it lies there on the paper
A mere word, without her accent, and you
    cannot judge the weight
Of the calm which crushed my passion: I
    seemed drowning in a vapor;
And her gentleness destroyed me whom her
    scorn made desolate.

LXXXV

So, struck backward and exhausted by that
    inward flow of passion
Which had rushed on, sparing nothing, into
    forms of abstract truth,
By a logic agonizing through unseemly de-
    monstration,
And by youth's own anguish turning grimly
    gray the hairs of youth,—

LXXXVI

By the sense accursed and instant, that if
    even I spake wisely
I spake basely—using truth, if what I
    spake indeed was true,
To avenge wrong on a woman— *her*, who
    sate there weighing nicely
A poor manhood's worth, found guilty of
    such deeds as I could do !—

LXXXVII

By such wrong and woe exhausted— what
    I suffered and occasioned,—
As a wild horse through a city runs with
    lightning in his eyes,
And then dashing at a church's cold and
    passive wall, impassioned,
Strikes the death into his burning brain,
    and blindly drops and dies—

LXXXVIII

So I fell, struck down before her— do you
    blame me, friend, for weakness ?
'T was my strength of passion slew me !—
    fell before her like a stone;
Fast the dreadful world rolled from me on
    its roaring wheels of blackness:
When the light came I was lying in this
    chamber and alone.

LXXXIX

Oh, of course she charged her lacqueys to
    bear out the sickly burden,
And to cast it from her scornful sight, but
    not *beyond* the gate;
She is too kind to be cruel, and too haughty
    not to pardon
Such a man as I; 't were something to be
    level to her hate.

XC

But for me— you now are conscious why,
    my friend, I write this letter,
How my life is read all backward, and the
    charm of life undone.
I shall leave her house at dawn; I would
    to-night, if I were better—
And I charge my soul to hold my body
    strengthened for the sun.

XCI

When the sun has dyed the oriel, I depart,
    with no last gazes,
No weak moanings (one word only, left in
    writing for her hands),
Out of reach of all derision, and some un-
    availing praises,
To make front against this anguish in the
    far and foreign lands.

XCII

Blame me not. I would not squander life
    in grief— I am abstemious.
I but nurse my spirit's falcon that its wing
    may soar again.
There 's no room for tears of weakness in the
    blind eyes of a Phemius:
Into work the poet kneads them, and he does
    not die *till then*.

CONCLUSION

I

Bertram finished the last pages, while along
    the silence ever
Still in hot and heavy splashes fell the tears
    on every leaf.
Having ended, he leans backward in his
    chair, with lips that quiver
From the deep unspoken, ay, and deep un-
    written thoughts of grief.

II

Soh ! how still the lady standeth ! 'T is a
 dream — a dream of mercies !
'Twixt the purple lattice-curtains how she
 standeth still and pale !
'T is a vision, sure, of mercies, sent to soften
 his self-curses,
Sent to sweep a patient quiet o'er the tossing
 of his wail.

III

' Eyes,' he said, ' now throbbing through
 me ! are ye eyes that did undo me ?
Shining eyes, like antique jewels set in
 Parian statue-stone !
Underneath that calm white forehead are
 ye ever burning torrid
O'er the desolate sand-desert of my heart
 and life undone ? '

IV

With a murmurous stir uncertain, in the
 air the purple curtain
Swelleth in and swelleth out around her
 motionless pale brows,
While the gliding of the river sends a
 rippling noise for ever
Through the open casement whitened by
 the moonlight's slant repose.

V

Said he — ' Vision of a lady ! stand there
 silent, stand there steady !
Now I see it plainly, plainly now I cannot
 hope or doubt —
There, the brows of mild repression —
 there, the lips of silent passion,
Curvèd like an archer's bow to send the
 bitter arrows out.'

VI

Ever, evermore the while in a slow silence
 she kept smiling,
And approached him slowly, slowly, in a
 gliding measured pace ;
With her two white hands extended as if
 praying one offended,
And a look of supplication gazing earnest
 in his face.

VII

Said he — ' Wake me by no gesture, —
 sound of breath, or stir of vesture !
Let the blessèd apparition melt not yet to
 its divine !

No approaching — hush, no breathing ! or
 my heart must swoon to death in
The too utter life thou bringest, O thou
 dream of Geraldine ! '

VIII

Ever, evermore the while in a slow silence
 she kept smiling,
But the tears ran over lightly from her
 eyes and tenderly : —
' Dost thou, Bertram, truly love me ?   Is
 no woman far above me
Found more worthy of thy poet-heart than
 such a one as I ? '

IX

Said he — ' I would dream so ever, like
 the flowing of that river,
Flowing ever in a shadow greenly onward
 to the sea !
So, thou vision of all sweetness, princely to
 a full completeness
Would my heart and life flow onward,
 deathward, through this dream of
 THEE ! '

X

Ever, evermore the while in a slow silence
 she kept smiling,
While the silver tears ran faster down the
 blushing of her cheeks ;
Then with both her hands enfolding both
 of his, she softly told him,
' Bertram, if I say I love thee, . . . 't is
 the vision only speaks.'

XI

Softened, quickened to adore her, on his
 knee he fell before her,
And she whispered low in triumph, ' It
 shall be as I have sworn.
Very rich he is in virtues, very noble —
 noble, certes ;
And I shall not blush in knowing that men
 call him lowly born.'

A VISION OF POETS

On September 19, 1843, Miss Barrett wrote
to her stanch friend and valued literary coun-
sellor, Hugh Stuart Boyd : ' I have just fin-
ished a poem of some eight hundred lines called
"A Vision of Poets ; " — philosophical, allegori-
cal, anything but popular. It is in stanzas

every one an octosyllabic triplet, which you will think odd, and I have not *sanguinity* enough to defend.' Elsewhere she explained that the object of the poem was to indicate 'the necessary relations of genius to suffering and self-sacrifice.' To Robert Browning, at least, the 'Vision of Poets' needed neither defence nor elucidation. Words appear almost to have failed him for the adequate expression of his enthusiasm, when he wrote to his *fiancée* on Sunday evening, August 4, 1845: 'Let me say how perfect, absolutely perfect, are those three or four pages in the Vision which present the Poets: — a line, a few words and the man there — one twang of the bow, and the arrowhead in the white — Shelley's "white ideal all statue-blind" is perfect — how can I coin words? And dear deaf old Hesiod, and all, all — are perfect — perfect.'

> 'O Sacred Essence, lighting me this hour,
>   How may I lightly stile thy great power?
>   *Echo.*   Power.
>   Power! but of whence? under the greenwood
>   spraye?
>   Or liv'st in Heaven? saye.
>   *Echo.*   In Heavens aye.
>   In Heavens aye! tell, may I it obtayne
>   By alms, by fasting, prayer, — by paine?
>   *Echo.*   By paine.
>   Show me the paine, it shall be undergone:
>   I to mine end will still go on.
>   *Echo.*   Go on.'
>   — *Britannia's Pastorals.*

A POET could not sleep aright,
For his soul kept up too much light
Under his eyelids for the night.

And thus he rose disquieted
With sweet rhymes ringing through his
        head,
And in the forest wanderèd

Where, sloping up the darkest glades,
The moon had drawn long colonnades
Upon whose floor the verdure fades

To a faint silver: pavement fair,   10
The antique wood-nymphs scarce would
        dare
To foot-print o'er, had such been there,

And rather sit by breathlessly,
With fear in their large eyes, to see
The consecrated sight. But HE —

The poet who, with spirit-kiss
Familiar, had long claimed for his
Whatever earthly beauty is,

Who also in his spirit bore
A beauty passing the earth's store, —   20
Walked calmly onward evermore.

His aimless thoughts in metre went,
Like a babe's hand without intent
Drawn down a seven-stringed instrument:

Nor jarred it with his humor as,
With a faint stirring of the grass,
An apparition fair did pass.

He might have feared another time,
But all things fair and strange did chime
With his thoughts then, as rhyme to rhyme.

An angel had not startled him,   31
Alighted from heaven's burning rim
To breathe from glory in the Dim;

Much less a lady riding slow
Upon a palfrey white as snow,
And smooth as a snow-cloud could go.

Full upon his she turned her face,
'What ho, sir poet! dost thou pace
Our woods at night in ghostly chase

'Of some fair Dryad of old tales   40
Who chants between the nightingales
And over sleep by song prevails?'

She smiled; but he could see arise
Her soul from far adown her eyes,
Prepared as if for sacrifice.

She looked a queen who seemeth gay
From royal grace alone. 'Now, nay,'
He answered, 'slumber passed away,

'Compelled by instincts in my head
That I should see to-night, instead   50
Of a fair nymph, some fairer Dread.'

She looked up quickly to the sky
And spake: 'The moon's regality
Will hear no praise; She is as I.

'She is in heaven, and I on earth;
This is my kingdom: I come forth
To crown all poets to their worth.'

He brake in with a voice that mourned;
'To their worth, lady? They are scorned
By men they sing for, till inurned.   60

'To their worth?   Beauty in the mind
Leaves the hearth cold, and love-refined
Ambitions make the world unkind.

'The boor who ploughs the daisy down,
The chief whose mortgage of renown,
Fixed upon graves, has bought a crown —

'Both these are happier, more approved
Than poets! — why should I be moved
In saying, both are more beloved?'

'The south can judge not of the north,'   70
She resumed calmly; 'I come forth
To crown all poets to their worth.

'Yea, verily, to anoint them all
With blessèd oils which surely shall
Smell sweeter as the ages fall.'

'As sweet,' the poet said, and rung
A low sad laugh, 'as flowers are, sprung
Out of their graves when they die young;

'As sweet as window-eglantine,
Some bough of which, as they decline,   80
The hired nurse gathers at their sign:

'As sweet, in short, as perfumed shroud
Which the gay Roman maidens sewed
For English Keats, singing aloud.'

The lady answered, 'Yea, as sweet!
The things thou namest being complete
In fragrance, as I measure it.

'Since sweet the death-clothes and the knell
Of him who having lived, dies well;
And wholly sweet the asphodel   90

'Stirred softly by that foot of his,
When he treads brave on all that is,
Into the world of souls, from this.

'Since sweet the tears, dropped at the door
Of tearless Death, and even before:
Sweet, consecrated evermore.

'What, dost thou judge it a strange thing
That poets, crowned for vanquishing,
Should bear some dust from out the ring?

'Come on with me, come on with me,   100
And learn in coming: let me free
Thy spirit into verity.'

She ceased: her palfrey's paces sent
No separate noises as she went;
'T was a bee's hum, a little spent.

And while the poet seemed to tread
Along the drowsy noise so made,
The forest heaved up overhead

Its billowy foliage through the air,
And the calm stars did far and spare   110
O'erswim the masses everywhere;

Save when the overtopping pines
Did bar their tremulous light with lines
All fixed and black.   Now the moon shines

A broader glory.   You may see
The trees grow rarer presently;
The air blows up more fresh and free:

Until they come from dark to light,
And from the forest to the sight   119
Of the large heaven-heart, bare with night,

A fiery throb in every star,
Those burning arteries that are
The conduits of God's life afar, —

A wild brown moorland underneath,
And four pools breaking up the heath
With white low gleamings, blank as death.

Beside the first pool, near the wood,
A dead tree in set horror stood,
Peeled and disjointed, stark as rood;

Since thunder-stricken, years ago,   130
Fixed in the spectral strain and throe
Wherewith it struggled from the blow:

A monumental tree, alone,
That will not bend in storms, nor groan,
But break off sudden like a stone.

Its lifeless shadow lies oblique
Upon the pool where, javelin-like,
The star-rays quiver while they strike.

'Drink,' said the lady, very still —
'Be holy and cold.'   He did her will   140
And drank the starry water chill.

The next pool they came near unto
Was bare of trees; there, only grew
Straight flags, and lilies just a few

Which sullen on the water sate
And leant their faces on the flat,
As weary of the starlight-state.

'Drink,' said the lady, grave and slow —
'World's use behoveth thee to know.'
He drank the bitter wave below.   150

The third pool, girt with thorny bushes
And flaunting weeds and reeds and rushes
That winds sang through in mournful
        gushes,

Was whitely smeared in many a round
By a slow slime; the starlight swound
Over the ghastly light it found.

'Drink,' said the lady, sad and slow —
'World's love behoveth thee to know.'
He looked to her commanding so;

Her brow was troubled, but her eye   160
Struck clear to his soul.   For all reply
He drank the water suddenly, —

Then, with a deathly sickness, passed
Beside the fourth pool and the last,
Where weights of shadow were down-
        cast

From yew and alder and rank trails
Of nightshade clasping the trunk-scales
And flung across the intervals

From yew to yew: who dares to stoop
Where those dank branches overdroop,   170
Into his heart the chill strikes up;

He hears a silent gliding coil,
The snakes strain hard against the soil,
His foot slips in their slimy oil,

And toads seem crawling on his hand,
And clinging bats but dimly scanned
Full in his face their wings expand.

A paleness took the poet's cheek:
'Must I drink here?' he seemed to
        seek
The lady's will with utterance meek: 180

'Ay, ay,' she said, 'it so must be;'
(And this time she spake cheerfully)
'Behoves thee know World's cruelty.'

He bowed his forehead till his mouth
Curved in the wave, and drank unloth
As if from rivers of the south;

His lips sobbed through the water rank,
His heart paused in him while he drank,
His brain beat heart-like, rose and sank,

And he swooned backward to a dream   190
Wherein he lay 'twixt gloom and gleam,
With Death and Life at each extreme:

And spiritual thunders, born of soul
Not cloud, did leap from mystic pole
And o'er him roll and counter-roll,

Crushing their echoes reboant
With their own wheels.   Did Heaven so
        grant
His spirit a sign of covenant?

At last came silence.   A slow kiss
Did crown his forehead after this;   200
His eyelids flew back for the bliss —

The lady stood beside his head,
Smiling a thought, with hair dispread;
The moonshine seemed dishevellèd

In her sleek tresses manifold
Like Danae's in the rain of old
That dripped with melancholy gold:

But SHE was holy, pale and high
As one who saw an ecstasy
Beyond a foretold agony.   210

'Rise up!' said she with voice where song
Eddied through speech, 'rise up; be
        strong:
And learn how right avenges wrong.'

The poet rose up on his feet:
He stood before an altar set
For sacrament with vessels meet

And mystic altar-lights which shine
As if their flames were crystalline
Carved flames that would not shrink or
        pine.

The altar filled the central place   220
Of a great church, and toward its face
Long aisles did shoot and interlace,

And from it a continuous mist
Of incense (round the edges kissed
By a yellow light of amethyst)

Wound upward slowly and throbbingly,
Cloud within cloud, right silverly,
Cloud above cloud, victoriously, —

Broke full against the archèd roof
And thence refracting eddied off   230
And floated through the marble woof

Of many a fine-wrought architrave,
Then, poising its white masses brave,
Swept solemnly down aisle and nave

Where, now in dark and now in light,
The countless columns, glimmering white,
Seemed leading out to the Infinite:

Plunged halfway up the shaft, they showed
In that pale shifting incense-cloud
Which flowed them by and overflowed   240

Till mist and marble seemed to blend,
And the whole temple, at the end,
With its own incense to distend, —

The arches like a giant's bow
To bend and slacken, — and below,
The nichèd saints to come and go:

Alone amid the shifting scene
That central altar stood serene
In its clear steadfast taper-sheen.

Then first, the poet was aware   250
Of a chief angel standing there
Before that altar, in the glare.

His eyes were dreadful, for you saw
That *they* saw God; his lips and jaw
Grand-made and strong, as Sinai's Law

They could enunciate and refrain
From vibratory after-pain,
And his brow's height was sovereign.

On the vast background of his wings
Rises his image, and he flings   260
From each plumed arc pale glitterings

And fiery flakes (as beateth, more
Or less, the angel-heart) before
And round him upon roof and floor,

Edging with fire the shifting fumes,
While at his side 'twixt lights and glooms
The phantasm of an organ booms.

Extending from which instrument
And angel, right and left-way bent,
The poet's sight grew sentient   270

Of a strange company around
And toward the altar; pale and bound
With bay above the eyes profound.

Deathful their faces were, and yet
The power of life was in them set —
Never forgot nor to forget:

Sublime significance of mouth,
Dilated nostril full of youth,
And forehead royal with the truth.

These faces were not multiplied   280
Beyond your count, but side by side
Did front the altar, glorified,

Still as a vision, yet exprest
Full as an action — look and gesto
Of buried saint in risen rest.

The poet knew them.   Faint and dim
His spirits seemed to sink in him —
Then, like a dolphin, change and swim

The current: these were poets true,
Who died for Beauty as martyrs do   290
For Truth — the ends being scarcely two.

God's prophets of the Beautiful
These poets were; of iron rule,
The rugged cilix, serge of wool.

Here Homer, with a broad suspense
Of thunderous brows, and lips intense
Of garrulous god-innocence.

There Shakespeare, on whose forehead climb
The crowns o' the world: O eyes sublime
With tears and laughters for all time !   300

Here Æschylus, the women swooned
To see so awful, when he frowned
As the gods did: he standeth crowned

Euripides, with close and mild
Scholastic lips, that could be wild
And laugh or sob out like a child

Even in the classes. Sophocles,
With that king's-look which down the trees
Followed the dark effigies

Of the lost Theban. Hesiod old,   310
Who, somewhat blind and deaf and cold,
Cared most for gods and bulls. And bold

Electric Pindar, quick as fear,
With race-dust on his cheeks, and clear
Slant startled eyes that seem to hear

The chariot rounding the last goal,
To hurtle past it in his soul.
And Sappho, with that gloriole

Of ebon hair on calmèd brows —
O poet-woman ! none foregoes   320
The leap, attaining the repose.

Theocritus, with glittering locks
Dropped sideway, as betwixt the rocks
He watched the visionary flocks.

And Aristophanes, who took
The world with mirth, and laughter-struck
The hollow caves of Thought and woke

The infinite echoes hid in each.
And Virgil: shade of Mantuan beech
Did help the shade of bay to reach   330

And knit around his forehead high:
For his gods wore less majesty
Than his brown bees hummed deathlessly.

Lucretius, nobler than his mood,
Who dropped his plummet down the broad
Deep universe and said 'No God — '

Finding no bottom: he denied
Divinely the divine, and died
Chief poet on the Tiber-side

By grace of God: his face is stern   340
As one compelled, in spite of scorn,
To teach a truth he would not learn.

And Ossian, dimly seen or guessed;
Once counted greater than the rest,
When mountain-winds blew out his vest.

And Spenser drooped his dreaming head
(With languid sleep-smile you had said
From his own verse engenderèd)

On Ariosto's, till they ran
Their curls in one: the Italian   350
Shot nimbler heat of bolder man

From his fine lids. And Dante stern
And sweet, whose spirit was an urn
For wine and milk poured out in turn.

Hard-souled Alfieri; and fancy-willed
Boiardo, who with laughter filled
The pauses of the jostled shield.

And Berni, with a hand stretched out
To sleek that storm. And, not with-
        out
The wreath he died in and the doubt   360

He died by, Tasso, bard and lover,
Whose visions were too thin to cover
The face of a false woman over.

And soft Racine; and grave Corneille,
The orator of rhymes, whose wail
Scarce shook his purple. And Petrarch
        pale,

From whose brain-lighted heart were
        thrown
A thousand thoughts beneath the sun,
Each lucid with the name of One.

And Camoens, with that look he had,   370
Compelling India's Genius sad
From the wave through the Lusiad, —

The murmurs of the storm-cape ocean
Indrawn in vibrative emotion
Along the verse. And, while devotion

In his wild eyes fantastic shone
Under the tonsure blown upon
By airs celestial, Calderon.

And bold De Vega, who breathed quick
Verse after verse, till death's old trick   380
Put pause to life and rhetoric.

And Goethe, with that reaching eye
His soul reached out from, far and
        high,
And fell from inner entity.

And Schiller, with heroic front
Worthy of Plutarch's kiss upon 't,
Too large for wreath of modern wont.

And Chaucer, with his infantine
Familiar clasp of things divine;
That mark upon his lip is wine.   390

Here, Milton's eyes strike piercing-dim:
The shapes of suns and stars did swim
Like clouds from them, and granted him

God for sole vision.   Cowley, there,
Whose active fancy debonair
Drew straws like amber — foul to fair.

Drayton and Browne, with smiles they drew
From outward nature, still kept new
From their own inward nature true.

And Marlowe, Webster, Fletcher, Ben,   400
Whose fire-hearts sowed our furrows when
The world was worthy of such men.

And Burns, with pungent passionings
Set in his eyes: deep lyric springs
Are of the fire-mount's issuings.

And Shelley, in his white ideal,
All statue-blind.   And Keats the real
Adonis with the hymeneal

Fresh vernal buds half sunk between
His youthful curls, kissed straight and
        sheen   410
In his Rome-grave, by Venus queen.

And poor, proud Byron, sad as grave
And salt as life; forlornly brave,
And quivering with the dart he drave.

And visionary Coleridge, who
Did sweep his thoughts as angels do
Their wings with cadence up the Blue.

These poets faced (and many more)
The lighted altar looming o'er
The clouds of incense dim and hoar: 420

And all their faces, in the lull
Of natural things, looked wonderful
With life and death and deathless rule.

All, still as stone and yet intense;
As if by spirit's vehemence
That stone were carved and not by sense.

But where the heart of each should beat,
There seemed a wound instead of it,
From whence the blood dropped to their
        feet

Drop after drop — dropped heavily   430
As century follows century
Into the deep eternity.

Then said the lady — and her word
Came distant, as wide waves were stirred
Between her and the ear that heard, —

' World's use is cold, world's love is vain,
World's cruelty is bitter bane,
But pain is not the fruit of pain.

' Hearken, O poet, whom I led
From the dark wood: dismissing dread,   440
Now hear this angel in my stead.

' His organ's clavier strikes along
These poets' hearts, sonorous, strong,
They gave him without count of wrong, —

' A diapason whence to guide
Up to God's feet, from these who died,
An anthem fully glorified —

' Whereat God's blessing, IBARAK (יברך)
Breathes back this music, folds it back
About the earth in vapory rack,   450

' And men walk in it, crying " Lo
The world is wider, and we know
The very heavens look brighter so:

' " The stars move statelier round the edge
Of the silver spheres, and give in pledge
Their light for nobler privilege:

' " No little flower but joys or grieves,
Full life is rustling in the sheaves,
Full spirit sweeps the forest-leaves."

' So works this music on the earth,   460
God so admits it, sends it forth
To add another worth to worth —

' A new creation-bloom that rounds
The old creation and expounds
His Beautiful in tuneful sounds.

'Now hearken!' Then the poet gazed
Upon the angel glorious-faced
Whose hand, majestically raised,

Floated across the organ-keys,
Like a pale moon o'er murmuring seas, 470
With no touch but with influences:

Then rose and fell (with swell and swound
Of shapeless noises wandering round
A concord which at last they found)

Those mystic keys: the tones were mixed,
Dim, faint, and thrilled and throbbed be-
    twixt
The incomplete and the unfixed:

And therein mighty minds were heard
In mighty musings, inly stirred,
And struggling outward for a word: 480

Until these surges, having run
This way and that, gave out as one
An Aphroditè of sweet tune,

A Harmony that, finding vent,
Upward in grand ascension went,
Winged to a heavenly argument,

Up, upward like a saint who strips
The shroud back from his eyes and lips,
And rises in apocalypse:

A Harmony sublime and plain, 490
Which cleft (as flying swan, the rain, —
Throwing the drops off with a strain

Of her white wing) those undertones
Of perplext chords, and soared at once
And struck out from the starry thrones

Their several silver octaves as
It passed to God. The music was
Of divine stature; strong to pass:

And those who heard it, understood
Something of life in spirit and blood, 500
Something of nature's fair and good:

And while it sounded, those great souls
Did thrill as racers at the goals
And burn in all their aureoles;

But she the lady, as vapor-bound,
Stood calmly in the joy of sound,
Like Nature with the showers around:

And when it ceased, the blood which fell
Again, alone grew audible,
Tolling the silence as a bell. 510

The sovran angel lifted high
His hand, and spake out sovranly:
'Tried poets, hearken and reply!

'Give me true answers. If we grant
That not to suffer, is to want
The conscience of the jubilant, —

'If ignorance of anguish is
But ignorance, and mortals miss
Far prospects, by a level bliss, —

'If, as two colors must be viewed 520
In a visible image, mortals should
Need good and evil, to see good, —

'If to speak nobly, comprehends
To feel profoundly, — if the ends
Of power and suffering, Nature blends, —

'If poets on the tripod must
Writhe like the Pythian to make just
Their oracles and merit trust, —

'If every vatic word that sweeps
To change the world must pale their lips
And leave their own souls in eclipse, — 531

'If to search deep the universe
Must pierce the searcher with the curse,
Because that bolt (in man's reverse)

'Was shot to the heart o' the wood and
    lies
Wedged deepest in the best, — if eyes
That look for visions and surprise

'From influent angels, must shut down
Their eyelids first to sun and moon,
The head asleep upon a stone, — 540

'If ONE who did redeem you back,
By His own loss, from final wrack,
Did consecrate by touch and track

'Those temporal sorrows till the taste
Of brackish waters of the waste
Is salt with tears He dropped too fast, —

'If all the crowns of earth must wound
With prickings of the thorns He found, —
If saddest sighs swell sweetest sound, —

'What say ye unto this ? — refuse   550
This baptism in salt water ? — choose
Calm breasts, mute lips, and labor loose ?

'Or, O ye gifted givers ! ye
Who give your liberal hearts to me
To make the world this harmony,

'Are ye resigned that they be spent
To such world's help ? '
                    The Spirits bent
Their awful brows and said ' Content.'

Content ! it sounded like *Amen*
Said by a choir of mourning men;   560
An affirmation full of pain

And patience, — ay, of glorying
And adoration, as a king
Might seal an oath for governing.

Then said the angel — and his face
Lightened abroad until the place
Grew larger for a moment's space, —

The long aisles flashing out in light,
And nave and transept, columns white
And arches crossed, being clear to sight   570

As if the roof were off and all
Stood in the noon-sun, — ' Lo, I call
To other hearts as liberal.

' This pedal strikes out in the air:
My instrument has room to bear
Still fuller strains and perfecter.

' Herein is room, and shall be room
While Time lasts, for new hearts to come
Consummating while they consume.

What living man will bring a gift   580
Of his own heart and help to lift
The tune ? — The race is to the swift.'

So asked the angel. Straight the while,
A company came up the aisle
With measured step and sorted smile;

Cleaving the incense-clouds that rise,
With winking unaccustomed eyes
And love-locks smelling sweet of spice.

One bore his head above the rest
As if the world were dispossessed,   590
And one did pillow chin on breast,

Right languid, an as he should faint;
One shook his curls across his paint
And moralized on worldly taint;

One, slanting up his face, did wink
The salt rheum to the eyelid's brink,
To think — O gods ! or — not to think.

Some trod out stealthily and slow,
As if the sun would fall in snow
If they walked to instead of fro;   600

And some, with conscious ambling free,
Did shake their bells right daintily
On hand and foot, for harmony;

And some, composing sudden sighs
In attitudes of point-device,
Rehearsed impromptu agonies.

And when this company drew near
The spirits crowned, it might appear
Submitted to a ghastly fear;

As a sane eye in master-passion   610
Constrains a maniac to the fashion
Of hideous maniac imitation

In the least geste — the dropping low
O' the lid, the wrinkling of the brow,
Exaggerate with mock and mow, —

So mastered was that company
By the crowned vision utterly,
Swayed to a maniac mockery.

One dulled his eyeballs, as they ached   619
With Homer's forehead, though he lacked
An inch of any; and one racked

His lower lip with restless tooth,
As Pindar's rushing words forsooth
Were pent behind it; one his smooth

Pink cheeks did rumple passionate
Like Æschylus, and tried to prate
On trolling tongue of fate and fate;

One set her eyes like Sappho's — or
Any light woman's; one forbore
Like Dante, or any man as poor   630

In mirth, to let a smile undo
His hard-shut lips; and one that drew
Sour humors from his mother, blew

His sunken cheeks out to the size
Of most unnatural jollities,
Because Anacreon looked jest-wise;

So with the rest: it was a sight
A great world-laughter would requite,
Or great world-wrath, with equal right.

Out came a speaker from that crowd   640
To speak for all, in sleek and proud
Exordial periods, while he bowed

His knee before the angel — 'Thus,
O angel who hast called for us,
We bring thee service emulous.

' Fit service from sufficient soul,
Hand-service to receive world's dole,
Lip-service in world's ear to roll

  Adjusted concords — soft enow
To hear the wine-cups passing, through, 650
And not too grave to spoil the show:

'Thou, certes, when thou askest more,
O sapient angel, leanest o'er
The window-sill of metaphor.

' To give our hearts up ? fie ! that rage
Barbaric antedates the age;
It is not done on any stage.

' Because your scald or gleeman went
With seven or nine-stringed instrument
Upon his back, — must ours be bent ?   660

'We are not pilgrims, by your leave;
No, nor yet martyrs; if we grieve,
It is to rhyme to — summer eve:

'And if we labor, it shall be
As suiteth best with our degree,
In after-dinner reverie.'

More yet that speaker would have said,
Poising between his smiles fair-fed
Each separate phrase till finishèd;

But all the foreheads of those born   670
And dead true poets flashed with scorn
Betwixt the bay leaves round them worn,

Ay, jetted such brave fire that they,
The new-come, shrank and paled away
Like leaden ashes when the day

Strikes on the hearth.   A spirit-blast,
A presence known by power, at last
Took them up mutely: they had passed.

And he our pilgrim-poet saw
Only their places, in deep awe,   68o
What time the angel's smile did draw

His gazing upward.   Smiling on,
The angel in the angel shone,
Revealing glory in benison;

Till, ripened in the light which shut
The poet in, his spirit mute
Dropped sudden as a perfect fruit:

He fell before the angel's feet,
Saying, 'If what is true is sweet,
In something I may compass it: 690

' For, where my worthiness is poor,
My will stands richly at the door
To pay shortcomings evermore.

' Accept me therefore: not for price
And not for pride my sacrifice
Is tendered, for my soul is nice

' And will beat down those dusty seeds
Of bearded corn if she succeeds
In soaring while the covey feeds.

' I soar, I am drawn up like the lark   7o
To its white cloud: so high my mark,
Albeit my wing is small and dark.

' I ask no wages, seek no fame:
Sew me, for shroud round face and name,
God's banner of the oriflamme.

' I only would have leave to loose
(In tears and blood if so He choose)
Mine inward music out to use;

'I only would be spent — in pain
And loss, perchance, but not in vain — 710
Upon the sweetness of that strain;

'Only project beyond the bound
Of mine own life, so lost and found,
My voice, and live on in its sound;

'Only embrace and be embraced
By fiery ends, whereby to waste,
And light God's future with my past.'

The angel's smile grew more divine,
The mortal speaking; ay, its shine
Swelled fuller, like a choir-note fine, 720

Till the broad glory round his brow
Did vibrate with the light below;
But what he said I do not know.

Nor know I if the man who prayed,
Rose up accepted, unforbade,
From the church-floor where he was laid, —

Nor if a listening life did run
Through the king-poets, one by one
Rejoicing in a worthy son:

My soul, which might have seen, grew blind
By what it looked on: I can find 731
No certain count of things behind.

I saw alone, dim, white and grand
As in a dream, the angel's hand
Stretched forth in gesture of command

Straight through the haze. And so, as erst,
A strain more noble than the first
Mused in the organ, and outburst:

With giant march from floor to roof
Rose the full notes, now parted off 740
In pauses massively aloof

Like measured thunders, now re-joined
In concords of mysterious kind
Which fused together sense and mind,

Now flashing sharp on sharp along
Exultant in a mounting throng,
Now dying off to a low song

Fed upon minors, wavelike sounds
Re-eddying into silver rounds,
Enlarging liberty with bounds: 750

And every rhythm that seemed to close
Survived in confluent underflows
Symphonious with the next that rose.

Thus the whole strain being multiplied
And greatened, with its glorified
Wings shot abroad from side to side,

Waved backward (as a wind might wave
A Brocken mist and with as brave
Wild roaring) arch and architrave,

Aisle, transept, column, marble wall, — 760
Then swelling outward, prodigal
Of aspiration beyond thrall,

Soared, and drew up with it the whole
Of this said vision, as a soul
Is raised by a thought. And as a scroll

Of bright devices is unrolled
Still upward with a gradual gold,
So rose the vision manifold,

Angel and organ, and the round
Of spirits, solemnized and crowned; 770
While the freed clouds of incense wound

Ascending, following in their track,
And glimmering faintly like the rack
O' the moon in her own light cast back.

And as that solemn dream withdrew,
The lady's kiss did fall anew
Cold on the poet's brow as dew.

And that same kiss which bound him first
Beyond the senses, now reversed
Its own law and most subtly pierced 780

His spirit with the sense of things
Sensual and present. Vanishings
Of glory with Æolian wings

Struck him and passed: the lady's face
Did melt back in the chrysopras
Of the orient morning sky that was

Yet clear of lark and there and so
She melted as a star might do,
Still smiling as she melted slow:

Smiling so slow, he seemed to see   790
Her smile the last thing, gloriously
Beyond her, far as memory.

Then he looked round: he was alone.
He lay before the breaking sun,
As Jacob at the Bethel stone.

And thought's entangled skein being wound,
He knew the moorland of his swound,
And the pale pools that smeared the
    ground;

The far wood-pines like offing ships;
The fourth pool's yew anear him drips,   800
World's cruelty attaints his lips,

And still he tastes it, bitter still;
Through all that glorious possible
He had the sight of present ill.

Yet rising calmly up and slowly
With such a cheer as scorneth folly,
A mild delightsome melancholy,

He journeyed homeward through the wood
And prayed along the solitude
Betwixt the pines, 'O God, my God!'   810

The golden morning's open flowings
Did sway the trees to murmurous bowings,
In metric chant of blessed poems.

And passing homeward through the wood,
He prayed along the solitude,
'THOU, Poet-God, art great and good!

'And though we must have, and have had
Right reason to be earthly sad,
THOU, Poet-God, art great and glad!'

CONCLUSION

Life treads on life, and heart on heart;   820
We press too close in church and mart
To keep a dream or grave apart:

And I was 'ware of walking down
That same green forest where had gone
The poet-pilgrim. One by one

I traced his footsteps. From the east
A red and tender radiance pressed
Through the near trees, until I guessed

The sun behind shone full and round;
While up the leafiness profound   830
A wind scarce old enough for sound

Stood ready to blow on me when
I turned that way, and now and then
The birds sang and brake off again

To shake their pretty feathers dry
Of the dew sliding droppingly
From the leaf-edges and apply

Back to their song: 'twixt dew and bird
So sweet a silence ministered,
God seemed to use it for a word,   840

Yet morning souls did leap and run
In all things, as the least had won
A joyous insight of the sun,

And no one looking round the wood
Could help confessing as he stood,
This Poet-God is glad and good.

But hark! a distant sound that grows,
A heaving, sinking of the boughs,
A rustling murmur, not of those,

A breezy noise which is not breeze!   850
And white-clad children by degrees
Steal out in troops among the trees,

Fair little children morning-bright,
With faces grave yet soft to sight,
Expressive of restrained delight.

Some plucked the palm-boughs within reach,
And others leapt up high to catch
The upper boughs and shake from each

A rain of dew till, wetted so,
The child who held the branch let go   860
And it swang backward with a flow

Of faster drippings. Then I knew
The children laughed; but the laugh flew
From its own chirrup as might do

A frightened song-bird; and a child
Who seemed the chief said very mild,
'Hush! keep this morning undefiled.'

His eyes rebuked them from calm spheres;
His soul upon his brow appears
In waiting for more holy years.   870

I called the child to me, and said,
'What are your palms for?' 'To be
    spread,'
He answered, 'on a poet dead.

'The poet died last month, and now
The world which had been somewhat slow
In honoring his living brow,

'Commands the palms; they must be
    strewn
On his new marble very soon,
In a procession of the town.'

I sighed and said, 'Did he foresee   880
Any such honor?' 'Verily
I cannot tell you,' answered he.

'But this I know, I fain would lay
My own head down, another day,
As *he* did, — with the fame away.

'A lily, a friend's hand had plucked,
Lay by his death-bed, which he looked
As deep down as a bee had sucked,

'Then, turning to the lattice, gazed
O'er hill and river and upraised   890
His eyes illumined and amazed

'With the world's beauty, up to God,
Re-offering on their iris broad
The images of things bestowed

'By the chief Poet. "God!" he cried,
"Be praised for anguish which has tried,
For beauty which has satisfied:

'"For this world's presence half within
And half without me — thought and
    scene —
This sense of Being and Having Been.   900

'"I thank Thee that my soul hath room
For Thy grand world: both guests may
    come —
Beauty, to soul — Body, to tomb.

'"I am content to be so weak:
Put strength into the words I speak,
And I am strong in what I seek.

'"I am content to be so bare
Before the archers, everywhere
My wounds being stroked by heavenly air.

'"I laid my soul before Thy feet   910
That images of fair and sweet
Should walk to other men on it.

'"I am content to feel the step,
Of each pure image: let those keep
To mandragore who care to sleep.

'"I am content to touch the brink
Of the other goblet, and I think
My bitter drink a wholesome drink.

'"Because my portion was assigned
Wholesome and bitter, Thou art kind,   920
And I am blessèd to my mind.

'"Gifted for giving, I receive
The maythorn and its scent outgive:
I grieve not that I once did grieve.

'"In my large joy of sight and touch
Beyond what others count for such,
I am content to suffer much.

'"*I know* — is all the mourner saith,
Knowledge by suffering entereth,
And Life is perfected by Death."'   930

The child spake nobly: strange to hear,
His infantine soft accents clear
Charged with high meanings, did appear;

And fair to see, his form and face
Winged out with whiteness and pure grace
From the green darkness of the place.

Behind his head a palm-tree grew;
An orient beam which pierced it through
Transversely on his forehead drew

The figure of a palm-branch brown   940
Traced on its brightness up and down
In fine fair lines, — a shadow-crown:

Guido might paint his angels so —
A little angel, taught to go
With holy words to saints below —

Such innocence of action yet
Significance of object met
In his whole bearing strong and sweet.

And all the children, the whole band,
Did round in rosy reverence stand,   950
Each with a palm-bough in his hand.

'And so he died,' I whispered. 'Nay,
Not *so*,' the childish voice did say,
'That poet turned him first to pray

'In silence, and God heard the rest
'Twixt the sun's footsteps down the
    west.
Then he called one who loved him best,

'Yea, he called softly through the room
(His voice was weak yet tender) —
    " Come,"
He said, "come nearer ! Let the bloom

'"Of Life grow over, undenied,   961
This bridge of Death, which is not wide —
I shall be soon at the other side.

'" Come, kiss me ! " So the one in truth
Who loved him best, — in love, not ruth,
Bowed down and kissed him mouth to
    mouth:

'And in that kiss of love was won
Life's manumission. All was done:
The mouth that kissed last, kissed *alone*.

'But in the former, confluent kiss,   970
The same was sealed, I think, by His,
To words of truth and uprightness.'

The child's voice trembled, his lips shook
Like a rose leaning o'er a brook,
Which vibrates though it is not struck.

'And who,' I asked, a little moved
Yet curious-eyed, 'was this that loved
And kissed him last, as it behooved ? '

'*I*,' softly said the child; and then
'*I*,' said he louder, once again: 980
'His son, my rank is among men:

'And now that men exalt his name
I come to gather palms with them,
That holy love may hallow fame.

'He did not die alone, nor should
His memory live so, 'mid these rude
World-praisers — a worse solitude.

'Me, a voice calleth to that tomb
Where these are strewing branch and
    bloom,
Saying, "Come nearer: " and I come.   990

'Glory to God ! ' resuméd he,
And his eyes smiled for victory
O'er their own tears which I could see

Fallen on the palm, down cheek and chin :
'That poet now has entered in
The place of rest which is not sin.

'And while he rests, his songs in troops
Walk up and down our earthly slopes,
Companioned by diviner hopes.'

'But *thou*,' I murmured to engage   1000
The child's speech farther — 'hast an age
Too tender for this orphanage.'

'Glory to God — to God ! ' he saith:
' KNOWLEDGE BY SUFFERING ENTERETH,
AND LIFE IS PERFECTED BY DEATH.'

RHYME OF THE DUCHESS MAY

Despite the irritating iteration of the refrain
Toll slowly — which most people omit in read-
ing — the 'Rhyme of the Duchess May' has
generally been accounted much the best of Mrs.
Browning's longer ballads. Yet the author
herself did not like it. On August 22, 1844,
she wrote as follows to Mr. Thomas West-
wood, — a frequent and valued correspondent ;
himself a poet of some note, author of *Beads
from a Rosary* and *The Burden of the Bell*. ' It
is curious that Duchess May is not a favorite
of mine, and that I have sighed one or two
secret wishes toward its extirpation ; but other
writers beside yourself have signalled it out for
praise, in private letters to me.' We gather
from a similarly deprecatory allusion in a letter
to her lifelong friend, Mrs. Martin, that the
nonconformist conscience of the poet pricked
her a little on account of the signal glorifica-
tion of suicide implied in the dénouement of
the Rhyme.

I

To the belfry, one by one, went the ringers
    from the sun,
        Toll slowly.
And the oldest ringer said, 'Ours is music
    for the dead
    When the rebecks are all done.'

II

Six abeles i' the churchyard grow on the
    north side in a row,
        Toll slowly.

And the shadows of their tops rock across
    the little slopes
  Of the grassy graves below.

III

On the south side and the west a small
    river runs in haste,
      Toll slowly.
And, between the river flowing and the
    fair green trees a-growing,
  Do the dead lie at their rest.

IV

On the east I sate that day, up against a
    willow gray:
      Toll slowly.
Through the rain of willow-branches I
    could see the low hill-ranges
  And the river on its way.

V

There I sate beneath the tree, and the bell
    tolled solemnly,
      Toll slowly.
While the trees' and river's voices flowed
    between the solemn noises, —
  Yet death seemed more loud to me.

VI

There I read this ancient rhyme while the
    bell did all the time
      Toll slowly.
And the solemn knell fell in with the tale
    of life and sin,
  Like a rhythmic fate sublime.

THE RHYME

I

Broad the forests stood (I read) on the
    hills of Linteged,
      Toll slowly.
And three hundred years had stood mute
    adown each hoary wood,
  Like a full heart having prayed.

II

And the little birds sang east, and the little
    birds sang west,
      Toll slowly.
And but little thought was theirs of the
    silent antique years,
  In the building of their nest.

III

Down the sun dropped large and red on the
    towers of Linteged, —
      Toll slowly.
Lance and spear upon the height, bristling
    strange in fiery light,
  While the castle stood in shade.

IV

There the castle stood up black with the
    red sun at its back —
      Toll slowly —
Like a sullen smouldering pyre with a top
    that flickers fire
  When the wind is on its track.

V

And five hundred archers tall did besiege
    the castle wall —
      Toll slowly.
And the castle, seethed in blood, fourteen
    days and nights had stood
  And to-night was near its fall.

VI

Yet thereunto, blind to doom, three months
    since, a bride did come —
      Toll slowly.
One who proudly trod the floors and softly
    whispered in the doors,
  ' May good angels bless our home.'

VII

Oh, a bride of queenly eyes, with a front of
    constancies:
      Toll slowly.
Oh, a bride of cordial mouth where the
    untired smile of youth
  Did light outward its own sighs !

VIII

'T was a Duke's fair orphan-girl, and her
    uncle's ward — the Earl —
      Toll slowly —
Who betrothed her twelve years old, for
    the sake of dowry gold,
  To his son Lord Leigh the churl.

IX

But what time she had made good all her
    years of womanhood —
      Toll slowly.
Unto both these lords of Leigh spake she
    out right sovranly,
  ' My will runneth as my blood.

X

'And while this same blood makes red this
    same right hand's veins,' she said —
       Toll slowly —
' 'T is my will, as lady free, not to wed a
    lord of Leigh,
    But Sir Guy of Linteged.'

XI

The old Earl he smilèd smooth, then he
    sighed for wilful youth —
       Toll slowly.
' Good my niece, that hand withal looketh
    somewhat soft and small
    For so large a will, in sooth.'

XII

She too smiled by that same sign, but her
    smile was cold and fine —
       Toll slowly.
' Little hand clasps muckle gold, or it were
    not worth the hold
    Of thy son, good uncle mine ! '

XIII

Then the young lord jerked his breath, and
    sware thickly in his teeth —
       Toll slowly —
' He would wed his own betrothed, an she
    loved him an she loathed,
    Let the life come or the death.'

XIV

Up she rose with scornful eyes, as her fa-
    ther's child might rise —
       Toll slowly.
' Thy hound's blood, my lord of Leigh,
    stains thy knightly heel,' quoth she,
    ' And he moans not where he lies:

XV

' But a woman's will dies hard, in the hall
    or on the sward ' —
       Toll slowly.
' By that grave, my lords, which made me
    orphaned girl and dowered lady,
    I deny you wife and ward ! '

XVI

Unto each she bowed her head and swept
    past with lofty tread.
       Toll slowly.
Ere the midnight-bell had ceased, in the
    chapel had the priest,
    Blessed her, bride of Linteged.

XVII

Fast and fain the bridal train along the
    night-storm rode amain —
       Toll slowly.
Hard the steeds of lord and serf struck
    their hoofs out on the turf,
    In the pauses of the rain.

XVIII

Fast and fain the kinsmen's train along the
    storm pursued amain —
       Toll slowly.
Steed on steed-track, dashing off, — thick-
    ening, doubling, hoof on hoof,
    In the pauses of the rain.

XIX

And the bridegroom led the flight on his
    red-roan steed of might —
       Toll slowly.
And the bride lay on his arm, still, as if
    she feared no harm,
    Smiling out into the night.

XX

' Dost thou fear ? ' he said at last. ' Nay,'
    she answered him in haste, —
       Toll slowly.
' Not such death as we could find — only
    life with one behind.
    Ride on fast as fear, ride fast ! '

XXI

Up the mountain wheeled the steed — girth
    to ground, and fetlocks spread —
       Toll slowly.
Headlong bounds, and rocking flanks, —
    down he staggered, down the banks,
    To the towers of Linteged.

XXII

High and low the serfs looked out, red the
    flambeaus tossed about —
       Toll slowly.
In the courtyard rose the cry, ' Live the
    Duchess and Sir Guy ! '
    But she never heard them shout.

XXIII

On the steed she dropped her cheek, kissed
    his mane and kissed his neck —
       Toll slowly.
' I had happier died by thee than lived on,
    a Lady Leigh,'
    Were the first words she did speak.

XXIV

But a three months' joyaunce lay 'twixt
   that moment and to-day —
     Toll slowly.
When five hundred archers tall stand beside
   the castle wall
     To recapture Duchess May.

XXV

And the castle standeth black with the red
   sun at its back —
     Toll slowly.
And a fortnight's siege is done, and, except
   the duchess, none
     Can misdoubt the coming wrack.

XXVI

Then the captain, young Lord Leigh, with
   his eyes so gray of blee —
     Toll slowly.
And thin lips that scarcely sheathe the cold
   white gnashing of his teeth,
     Gnashed in smiling, absently, —

XXVII

Cried aloud, 'So goes the day, bridegroom
   fair of Duchess May !'
     Toll slowly.
'Look thy last upon that sun ! if thou seest
   to-morrow's one
     'T will be through a foot of clay.

XXVIII

'Ha, fair bride ! dost hear no sound save
   that moaning of the hound ?'
     Toll slowly.
'Thou and I have parted troth, yet I keep
   my vengeance-oath,
     And the other may come round.

XXIX

'Ha ! thy will is brave to dare, and thy
   new love past compare' —
     Toll slowly.
'Yet thine old love's falchion brave is as
   strong a thing to have,
     As the will of lady fair.

XXX

'Peck on blindly, netted dove ! If a wife's
   name thee behove' —
     Toll slowly.
'Thou shalt wear the same to-morrow, ere
   the grave has hid the sorrow
     Of thy last ill-mated love.

XXXI

'O'er his fixed and silent mouth, thou and I
   will call back troth:'
     Toll slowly.
'He shall altar be and priest, — and he will
   not cry at least
     "I forbid you, I am loth !"'

XXXII

'I will wring thy fingers pale in the gaunt-
   let of my mail :'
     Toll slowly.
'"Little hand and muckle gold" close shall
   lie within my hold,
     As the sword did, to prevail.'

XXXIII

Oh, the little birds sang east, and the little
   birds sang west —
     Toll slowly.
Oh, and laughed the Duchess May, and her
   soul did put away
     All his boasting, for a jest.

XXXIV

In her chamber did she sit, laughing low to
   think of it, —
     Toll slowly.
'Tower is strong and will is free: thou
   canst boast, my lord of Leigh,
     But thou boastest little wit.'

XXXV

In her tire-glass gazèd she, and she blushed
   right womanly —
     Toll slowly.
She blushed half from her disdain, half her
   beauty was so plain,
     — 'Oath for oath, my lord of Leigh !'

XXXVI

Straight she called her maidens in — 'Since
   ye gave me blame herein' —
     Toll slowly —
'That a bridal such as mine should lack
   gauds to make it fine,
     Come and shrive me from that sin.

XXXVII

'It is three months gone to-day since I
   gave mine hand away:'
     Toll slowly.
'Bring the gold and bring the gem, we will
   keep bride-state in them,
     While we keep the foe at bay.

XXXVIII

'On your arms I loose mine hair; comb it
　　smooth and crown it fair'—
　　　Toll slowly.
'I would look in purple pall from this
　　lattice down the wall,
　　And throw scorn to one that's there!'

XXXIX

Oh, the little birds sang east, and the little
　　birds sang west —
　　　Toll slowly.
On the tower the castle's lord leant in silence
　　on his sword,
　　With an anguish in his breast.

XL

With a spirit-laden weight did he lean down
　　passionate:
　　　Toll slowly.
They have almost sapped the wall, — they
　　will enter therewithal
　　With no knocking at the gate.

XLI

Then the sword he leant upon, shivered,
　　snapped upon the stone —
　　　Toll slowly.
'Sword,' he thought, with inward laugh,
　　'ill thou servest for a staff
　　When thy nobler use is done!

XLII

'Sword, thy nobler use is done! tower is
　　lost, and shame begun!'—
　　　Toll slowly.
'If we met them in the breach, hilt to hilt
　　or speech to speech,
　　We should die there, each for one.

XLIII

'If we met them at the wall, we should
　　singly, vainly fall'—
　　　Toll slowly.
'But if *I* die here alone, — then I die who
　　am but one,
　　And die nobly for them all.

XLIV

'Five true friends lie for my sake in the
　　moat and in the brake'—
　　　Toll slowly.
'Thirteen warriors lie at rest with a black
　　wound in the breast,
　　And not one of these will wake.

XLV

'So, no more of this shall be! heart-blood
　　weighs too heavily'—
　　　Toll slowly.
'And I could not sleep in grave, with the
　　faithful and the brave
　　Heaped around and over me.

XLVI

'Since young Clare a mother hath, and
　　young Ralph a plighted faith'—
　　　Toll slowly.
'Since my pale young sister's cheeks blush
　　like rose when Ronald speaks,
　　Albeit never a word she saith—

XLVII

'These shall never die for me: life-blood
　　falls too heavily:'
　　　Toll slowly.
'And if *I* die here apart, o'er my dead and
　　silent heart
　　They shall pass out safe and free.

XLVIII

'When the foe hath heard it said — "Death
　　holds Guy of Linteged"'—
　　　Toll slowly.
'That new corse new peace shall bring, and
　　a blessèd, blessèd thing
　　Shall the stone be at its head.

XLIX

'Then my friends shall pass out free, and
　　shall bear my memory'—
　　　Toll slowly.
'Then my foes shall sleek their pride, sooth-
　　ing fair my widowed bride
　　Whose sole sin was love of me:

L

'With their words all smooth and sweet,
　　they will front her and entreat'—
　　　Toll slowly.
'And their purple pall will spread under-
　　neath her fainting head
　　While her tears drop over it.

LI

'She will weep her woman's tears, she will
　　pray her woman's prayers'—
　　　Toll slowly.
'But her heart is young in pain, and her
　　hopes will spring again
　　By the suntime of her years.

LII

'Ah, sweet May! ah, sweetest grief!—
 once I vowed thee my belief'—
  Toll slowly—
'That thy name expressed thy sweetness,
 — May of poets, in completeness!
Now my May-day seemeth brief.'

LIII

All these silent thoughts did swim o'er his
 eyes grown strange and dim—
  Toll slowly.
Till his true men, in the place, wished they
 stood there face to face
With the foe instead of him.

LIV

' One last oath, my friends that wear faith-
 ful hearts to do and dare!'
  Toll slowly.
' Tower must fall and bride be lost—swear
 me service worth the cost!'
Bold they stood around to swear.

LV

'Each man clasp my hand and swear by
 the deed we failed in there'—
  Toll slowly.
'Not for vengeance, not for right, will ye
 strike one blow to-night!'
Pale they stood around to swear.

LVI

'One last boon, young Ralph and Clare!
 faithful hearts to do and dare!'
  Toll slowly.
'Bring that steed up from his stall, which
 she kissed before you all:
Guide him up the turret-stair.

LVII

'Ye shall harness him aright, and lead up-
 ward to this height:'
  Toll slowly.
' Once in love and twice in war hath he
 borne me strong and far:
He shall bear me far to-night.'

LVIII

Then his men looked to and fro, when they
 heard him speaking so—
  Toll slowly.
' 'Las! the noble heart,' they thought, 'he
 in sooth is grief-distraught:
Would we stood here with the foe!'

LIX

But a fire flashed from his eye, 'twixt their
 thought and their reply—
  Toll slowly.
'Have ye so much time to waste? We
 who ride here, must ride fast
As we wish our foes to fly.'

LX

They have fetched the steed with care, in
 the harness he did wear—
  Toll slowly.
Past the court and through the doors,
 across the rushes of the floors,
But they goad him up the stair.

LXI

Then from out her bower chambère did the
 Duchess May repair:
  Toll slowly.
' Tell me now what is your need,' said the
 lady, ' of this steed,
That ye goad him up the stair?'

LXII

Calm she stood; unbodkined through, fell
 her dark hair to her shoe:
  Toll slowly.
And the smile upon her face, ere she left
 the tiring-glass,
Had not time enough to go.

LXIII

' Get thee back, sweet Duchess May! hope
 is gone like yesterday'—
  Toll slowly.
'One half-hour completes the breach; and
 thy lord grows wild of speech—
Get thee in, sweet lady, and pray!

LXIV

' In the east tower, high'st of all, loud he
 cries for steed from stall:'
  Toll slowly.
' "He would ride as far," quoth he, "as
 for love and victory,
Though he rides the castle-wall."

LXV

' And we fetch the steed from stall, up
 where never a hoof did fall'—
  Toll slowly.
' Wifely prayer meets deathly need: may
 the sweet Heavens hear thee plead
If he rides the castle-wall!'

LXVI

Low she dropped her head, and lower, till
   her hair coiled on the floor —
     Toll slowly.
And tear after tear you heard fall distinct
   as any word
   Which you might be listening for.

LXVII

'Get thee in, thou soft ladye ! here is
   never a place fcr thee !'
     Toll slowly.
'Braid thine hair and clasp thy gown, that
   thy beauty in its moan
   May find grace with Leigh of Leigh.'

LXVIII

She stood up in bitter case, with a pale yet
   steady face:
     Toll slowly.
Like a statue thunderstruck, which, though
   quivering, seems to look
   Right against the thunder-place.

LXIX

And her foot trod in, with pride, her own
   tears i' the stone beside —
     Toll slowly.
'Go to, faithful friends, go to ! judge no
   more what ladies do,
   No, nor how their lords may ride !'

LXX

Then the good steed's rein she took, and
   his neck did kiss and stroke:
     Toll slowly.
Soft he neighed to answer her, and then
   followed up the stair
   For the love of her sweet look:

LXXI

Oh, and steeply, steeply wound up the nar-
   row stair around —
     Toll slowly.
Oh, and closely, closely speeding, step by
   step beside her treading
   Did he follow, meek as hound.

LXXII

On the east tower, high'st of all, — there,
   where never a hoof did fall —
     Toll slowly.
Out they swept, a vision steady, noble steed
   and lovely lady,
   Calm as if in bower or stall.

LXXIII

Down she knelt at her lord's knee, and she
   looked up silently —
     Toll slowly.
And he kissed her twice and thrice, for
   that look within her eyes
   Which he could not bear to see.

LXXIV

Quoth he, 'Get thee from this strife, and
   the sweet saints bless thy life !'
     Toll slowly.
'In this hour I stand in need of my noble
   red-roan steed,
   But no more of my noble wife.'

LXXV

Quoth she, 'Meekly have I done all thy
   biddings under sun:'
     Toll slowly.
'But by all my womanhood, which is
   proved so, true and good,
   I will never do this one.

LXXVI

'Now by womanhood's degree and by wife-
   hood's verity' —
     Toll slowly.
'In this hour if thou hast need of thy
   noble red-roan steed,
   Thou hast also need of *me*.

LXXVII

'By this golden ring ye see on this lifted
   hand pardiè' —
     Toll slowly.
'If, this hour, on castle-wall can be room
   for steed from stall,
   Shall be also room for *me*.

LXXVIII

'So the sweet saints with me be,' (did she
   utter solemnly) —
     Toll slowly.
'If a man, this eventide, on this castle-
   wall will ride,
   He shall ride the same with *me*.'

LXXIX

Oh, he sprang up in the selle and he
   laughed out bitter-well —
     Toll slowly.
'Wouldst thou ride among the leaves, as
   we used on other eves,
   To hear chime a vesper-bell ?'

LXXX

She clung closer to his knee — ' Ay, be-
    neath the cypress-tree ! '
    Toll slowly.
' Mock me not, for otherwise than along
    the greenwood fair
Have I ridden fast with thee.

LXXXI

' Fast I rode with new-made vows from my
    angry kinsman's house: '
    Toll slowly.
' What, and would you men should reck
    that I dared more for love's sake
As a bride than as a spouse ?

LXXXII

' What, and would you it should fall, as a
    proverb, before all ' —
    Toll slowly.
' That a bride may keep your side while
    through castle-gate you ride,
Yet eschew the castle-wall ? '

LXXXIII

Ho ! the breach yawns into ruin and roars
    up against her suing —
    Toll slowly.
With the inarticulate din and the dreadful
    falling in —
Shrieks of doing and undoing !

LXXXIV

Twice he wrung her hands in twain, but
    the small hands closed again.
    Toll slowly.
Back he reined the steed — back, back !
    but she trailed along his track
With a frantic clasp and strain.

LXXXV

Evermore the foemen pour through the
    crash of window and door —
    Toll slowly.
And the shouts of Leigh and Leigh, and
    the shrieks of ' kill ! ' and ' flee ! '
Strike up clear amid the roar.

LXXXVI

Thrice he wrung her hands in twain, but
    they closed and clung again —
    Toll slowly.
While she clung, as one, withstood, clasps
    a Christ upon the rood,
In a spasm of deathly pain.

LXXXVII

She clung wild and she clung mute with
    her shuddering lips half-shut:
    Toll slowly.
Her head fallen as half in swound, hair
    and knee swept on the ground,
She clung wild to stirrup and foot.

LXXXVIII

Back he reined his steed back-thrown on
    the slippery coping-stone:
    Toll slowly.
Back the iron hoofs did grind on the bat-
    tlement behind
Whence a hundred feet went down:

LXXXIX

And his heel did press and goad on the
    quivering flank bestrode —
    Toll slowly.
' Friends and brothers, save my wife ! Par-
    don, sweet, in change for life, —
But I ride alone to God.'

XC

Straight as if the Holy name had up-
    breathed her like a flame —
    Toll slowly.
She upsprang, she rose upright, in his selle
    she sate in sight,
By her love she overcame.

XCI

And her head was on his breast where she
    smiled as one at rest —
    Toll slowly.
' Ring,' she cried, ' O vesper-bell in the
    beechwood's old chapelle —
But the passing-bell rings best ! '

XCII

They have caught out at the rein which
    Sir Guy threw loose — in vain —
    Toll slowly.
For the horse in stark despair, with his
    front hoofs poised in air,
On the last verge rears amain.

XCIII

Now he hangs, he rocks between, and his
    nostrils curdle in —
    Toll slowly.
Now he shivers head and hoof and the
    flakes of foam fall off,
And his face grows fierce and thin:

XCIV

And a look of human woe from his staring
    eyes did go:
      Toll slowly.
And a sharp cry uttered he, in a foretold
    agony
    Of the headlong death below, —

XCV

And, 'Ring, ring, thou passing-bell,' still
    she cried, 'i' the old chapelle!'
      Toll slowly.
Then, back-toppling, crashing back — a
    dead weight flung out to wrack,
    Horse and riders overfell.

CONCLUSION

I

Oh, the little birds sang east, and the little
    birds sang west —
      Toll slowly.
And I read this ancient Rhyme, in the
    churchyard, while the chime
    Slowly tolled for one at rest.

II

The abeles moved in the sun, and the river
    smooth did run —
      Toll slowly.
And the ancient Rhyme rang strange, with
    its passion and its change,
    Here, where all done lay undone.

III

And beneath a willow tree I a little grave
    did see --
      Toll slowly —
Where was graved — HERE, UNDEFILED,
    LIETH MAUD, A THREE-YEAR CHILD,
    EIGHTEEN HUNDRED FORTY-THREE.

IV

Then, O spirits, did I say, ye who rode so
    fast that day —
      Toll slowly.
Did star-wheels and angel wings with their
    holy winnowings
    Keep beside you all the way?

V

Though in passion ye would dash, with a
    blind and heavy crash —
      Toll slowly —

Up against the thick-bossed shield of God's
    judgment in the field, —
    Though your heart and brain were
    rash, —

VI

Now, your will is all unwilled; now, your
    pulses are all stilled:
      Toll slowly.
Now, ye lie as meek and mild (whereso
    laid) as Maud the child
    Whose small grave was lately filled.

VII

Beating heart and burning brow, ye are
    very patient now —
      Toll slowly.
And the children might be bold to pluck
    the kingcups from your mould
    Ere a month had let them grow.

VIII

And you let the goldfinch sing in the alder
    near in spring —
      Toll slowly.
Let her build her nest and sit all the three
    weeks out on it,
    Murmuring not at anything.

IX

In your patience ye are strong, cold and
    heat ye take not wrong —
      Toll slowly.
When the trumpet of the angel blows eter-
    nity's evangel,
    Time will seem to you not long.

X

Oh, the little birds sang east, and the little
    birds sang west —
      Toll slowly.
And I said in underbreath, — All our life
    is mixed with death,
    And who knoweth which is best?

XI

Oh, the little birds sang east, and the little
    birds sang west —
      Toll slowly.
And I smiled to think God's greatness
    flowed around our incompleteness, —
    Round our restlessness, His rest.

THE LADY'S 'YES'

I

'Yes,' I answered you last night;
  'No,' this morning, sir, I say:
Colors seen by candle-light
  Will not look the same by day.

II

When the viols played their best,
  Lamps above and laughs below,
Love me sounded like a jest,
  Fit for *yes* or fit for *no*.

III

Call me false or call me free,
  Vow, whatever light may shine, —
No man on your face shall see
  Any grief for change on mine.

IV

Yet the sin is on us both;
  Time to dance is not to woo;
Wooing light makes fickle troth,
  Scorn of *me* recoils on *you*.

V

Learn to win a lady's faith
  Nobly, as the thing is high,
Bravely, as for life and death,
  With a loyal gravity.

VI

Lead her from the festive boards,
  Point her to the starry skies;
Guard her, by your truthful words,
  Pure from courtship's flatteries.

VII

By your truth she shall be true,
  Ever true, as wives of yore;
And her *yes*, once said to you,
  Shall be Yes for evermore.

THE POET AND THE BIRD

A FABLE

I

Said a people to a poet — 'Go out from
    among us straightway !
While we are thinking earthly things,
    thou singest of divine:

There 's a little fair brown nightingale who,
    sitting in the gateway,
Makes fitter music to our ear than any
    song of thine !'

II

The poet went out weeping; the nightin-
    gale ceased chanting:
  'Now, wherefore, O thou nightingale, is
    all thy sweetness done ?'
— 'I cannot sing my earthly things, the
    heavenly poet wanting,
  Whose highest harmony includes the
    lowest under sun.'

III

The poet went out weeping, and died
    abroad, bereft there;
  The bird flew to his grave and died amid
    a thousand wails:
And when I last came by the place, I
    swear the music left there
  Was only of the poet's song, and not the
    nightingale's.

THE LOST BOWER

The scene of 'The Lost Bower' was the
wood above the garden at Hope End, among the
Malvern Hills, — the beautiful home of Eliza-
beth Barrett's girlhood, — and the incident
which it relates was an actual experience of
her juvenile years.

I

In the pleasant orchard-closes,
  'God bless all our gains,' say we,
But 'May God bless all our losses'
  Better suits with our degree.
Listen, gentle — ay, and simple ! listen,
  children on the knee !

II

Green the land is where my daily
  Steps in jocund childhood played,
Dimpled close with hill and valley,
  Dappled very close with shade:
Summer-snow of apple-blossoms running
  up from glade to glade.

III

There is one hill I see nearer
  In my vision of the rest;
And a little wood seems clearer

As it climbeth from the west,
Sideway from the tree-locked valley, to
    the airy upland crest.

IV

Small the wood is, green with hazels,
And, completing the ascent,
Where the wind blows and sun dazzles,
Thrills in leafy tremblement,
Like a heart that after climbing beateth
    quickly through content.

V

Not a step the wood advances
O'er the open hill-top's bound;
There, in green arrest, the branches
See their image on the ground:
You may walk beneath them smiling, glad
    with sight and glad with sound.

VI

For you hearken on your right hand,
How the birds do leap and call
In the greenwood, out of sight and
Out of reach and fear of all;
And the squirrels crack the filberts through
    their cheerful madrigal.

VII

On your left, the sheep are cropping
The slant grass and daisies pale,
And five apple-trees stand dropping
Separate shadows toward the vale
Over which, in choral silence, the hills look
    you their ' All hail ! '

VIII

Far out, kindled by each other,
Shining hills on hills arise,
Close as brother leans to brother
When they press beneath the eyes
Of some father praying blessings from the
    gifts of paradise.

IX

While beyond, above them mounted,
And above their woods also,
Malvern hills, for mountains counted
Not unduly, loom a-row —
Keepers of Piers Plowman's visions through
    the sunshine and the snow.

X

Yet, in chiidhood, little prized I
That fair walk and far survey;

'T was a straight walk unadvised by
The least mischief worth a nay;
Up and down — as dull as grammar on the
    eve of holiday.

XI

But the wood, all close and clenching
Bough in bough and root in root, —
No more sky (for overbranching)
At your head than at your foot, —
Oh, the wood drew me within it by a glamour
    past dispute !

XII

Few and broken paths showed through
    it,
Where the sheep had tried to run, —
Forced with snowy wool to strew it
Round the thickets, when anon
They, with silly thorn - pricked noses,
    bleated back into the sun.

XIII

But my childish heart beat stronger
Than those thickets dared to grow:
I could pierce them ! *I* could longer
Travel on, methought, than so:
Sheep for sheep-paths ! braver children
    climb and creep where they would
    go.

XIV

And the poets wander, said I,
Over places all as rude:
Bold Rinaldo's lovely lady
Sat to meet him in a wood:
Rosalinda, like a fountain, laughed out
    pure with solitude.

XV

And if Chaucer had not travelled
Through a forest by a well,
He had never dreamt nor marvelled
At those ladies fair and fell
Who lived smiling without loving in their
    island-citadel.

XVI

Thus I thought of the old singers
And took courage from their song,
Till my little struggling fingers
Tore asunder gyve and thong
Of the brambles which entrapped me, and
    the barrier branches strong.

XVII

On a day, such pastime keeping,
With a fawn's heart debonair,
Under-crawling, overleaping
Thorns that prick and boughs that bear,
I stood suddenly astonied — I was glad-
dened unaware.

XVIII

From the place I stood in, floated
Back the covert dim and close,
And the open ground was coated
Carpet-smooth with grass and moss,
And the blue-bell's purple presence signed
it worthily across.

XIX

Here a linden-tree stood, bright'ning
All adown its silver rind;
For as some trees draw the lightning,
So this tree, unto my mind,
Drew to earth the blessèd sunshine from
the sky where it was shrined.

XX

Tall the linden-tree, and near it
An old hawthorn also grew;
And wood-ivy like a spirit
Hovered dimly round the two,
Shaping thence that bower of beauty which
I sing of thus to you.

XXI

'T was a bower for garden fitter
Than for any woodland wide:
Though a fresh and dewy glitter
Struck it through from side to side,
Shaped and shaven was the freshness, as
by garden-cunning plied.

XXII

Oh, a lady might have come there,
Hooded fairly like her hawk,
With a book or lute in summer,
And a hope of sweeter talk, —
Listening less to her own music than for
footsteps on the walk !

XXIII

But that bower appeared a marvel
In the wildness of the place;
With such seeming art and travail,
Finely fixed and fitted was
Leaf to leaf, the dark-green ivy, to the
summit from the base.

XXIV

And the ivy veined and glossy
Was enwrought with eglantine;
And the wild hop fibred closely,
And the large-leaved columbine,
Arch of door and window - mullion, did
right sylvanly entwine.

XXV

Rose-trees either side the door were
Growing lithe and growing tall,
Each one set a summer warder
For the keeping of the hall, —
With a red rose and a white rose, leaning,
nodding at the wall.

XXVI

As I entered, mosses hushing
Stole all noises from my foot;
And a green elastic cushion,
Clasped within the linden's root,
Took me in a chair of silence very rare and
absolute.

XXVII

All the floor was paved with glory,
Greenly, silently inlaid
(Through quick motions made before
me)
With fair counterparts in shade
Of the fair serrated ivy - leaves which
slanted overhead.

XXVIII

' Is such pavement in a palace ? '
So I questioned in my thought:
The sun, shining through the chalice
Of the red rose hung without,
Threw within a red libation, like an answer
to my doubt.

XXIX

At the same time, on the linen
Of my childish lap there fell
Two white may-leaves, downward win-
ning
Through the ceiling's miracle,
From a blossom, like an angel, out of sight
yet blessing well.

XXX

Down to floor and up to ceiling
Quick I turned my childish face,
With an innocent appealing

For the secret of the place
To the trees, which surely knew it in par-
    taking of the grace.

XXXI

Where's no foot of human creature
How could reach a human hand?
And if this be work of Nature,
Why has Nature turned so bland,
Breaking off from other wild-work?   It
    was hard to understand.

XXXII

Was she weary of rough-doing,
Of the bramble and the thorn?
Did she pause in tender rueing
Here of all her sylvan scorn?
Or in mock of Art's deceiving was the sud-
    den mildness worn?

XXXIII

Or could this same bower (I fancied)
Be the work of Dryad strong,
Who, surviving all that chancèd
In the world's old pagan wrong,
Lay hid, feeding in the woodland on the
    last true poet's song?

XXXIV

Or was this the house of fairies,
Left, because of the rough ways,
Unassoiled by Ave Marys
Which the passing pilgrim prays,
And beyond St. Catherine's chiming on the
    blessèd Sabbath days?

XXXV

So, young muser, I sat listening
To my fancy's wildest word:
On a sudden, through the glistening
Leaves around, a little stirred,
Came a sound, a sense of music which was
    rather felt than heard.

XXXVI

Softly, finely, it inwound me;
From the world it shut me in, —
Like a fountain, falling round me,
Which with silver waters thin
Clips a little water Naiad sitting smilingly
    within.

XXXVII

Whence the music came, who knoweth?
I know nothing: but indeed
Pan or Faunus never bloweth

So much sweetness from a reed
Which has sucked the milk of waters at the
    oldest river-head.

XXXVIII

Never lark the sun can waken
With such sweetness! when the lark,
The high planets overtaking
In the half-evanished Dark,
Casts his singing to their singing, like an
    arrow to the mark.

XXXIX

Never nightingale so singeth:
Oh, she leans on thorny tree
And her poet-song she flingeth
Over pain to victory!
Yet she never sings such music, — or she
    sings it not to me.

XL

Never blackbirds, never thrushes
Nor small finches sing as sweet,
When the sun strikes through the bushes
To their crimson clinging feet,
And their pretty eyes look sideways to the
    summer heavens complete.

XLI

If it *were* a bird, it seemèd
Most like Chaucer's, which, in sooth.
He of green and azure dreamèd,
While it sat in spirit-ruth
On that bier of a crowned lady, singing
    nigh her silent mouth.

XLII

If it *were* a bird? — ah, sceptic,
Give me 'yea' or give me 'nay' —
Though my soul were nympholeptic
As I heard that virèlay,
You may stoop your pride to pardon, for
    my sin is far away!

XLIII

I rose up in exaltation
And an inward trembling heat,
And (it seemed) in geste of passion
Dropped the music to my feet
Like a garment rustling downwards — such
    a silence followed it!

XLIV

Heart and head beat through the quiet
Full and heavily, though slower:

In the song, I think, and by it,
Mystic Presences of power
Had up-snatched me to the Timeless, then
    returned me to the Hour.

XLV

In a child-abstraction lifted,
Straightway from the bower I past,
Foot and soul being dimly drifted
Through the greenwood, till, at last,
In the hill-top's open sunshine I all con-
    sciously was cast.

XLVI

Face to face with the true mountains
I stood silently and still,
Drawing strength from fancy's daunt-
    ings,
From the air about the hill,
And from Nature's open mercies and most
    debonair goodwill.

XLVII

Oh, the golden-hearted daisies
Witnessed there, before my youth,
To the truth of things, with praises
Of the beauty of the truth;
And I woke to Nature's real, laughing joy-
    fully for both.

XLVIII

And I said within me, laughing,
I have found a bower to-day,
A green lusus, fashioned half in
Chance and half in Nature's play,
And a little bird sings nigh it, I will never-
    more missay.

XLIX

Henceforth, _I_ will be the fairy
Of this bower not built by one;
I will go there, sad or merry,
With each morning's benison,
And the bird shall be my harper in the
    dream-hall I have won.

L

So I said. But the next morning,
(— Child, look up into my face —
'Ware, oh sceptic, of your scorning!
This is truth in its pure grace!)
The next morning, all had vanished, or my
    wandering missed the place.

LI

Bring an oath most sylvan-holy,
And upon it swear me true —
By the wind-bells swinging slowly
Their mute curfews in the dew,
By the advent of the snowdrop, by the
    rosemary and rue, —

LII

I affirm by all or any,
Let the cause be charm or chance,
That my wandering searches many
Missed the bower of my romance —
That I nevermore upon it turned my mortal
    countenance.

LIII

I affirm that, since I lost it,
Never bower has seemed so fair;
Never garden-creeper crossed it
With so deft and brave an air,
Never bird sung in the summer, as I saw
    and heard them there.

LIV

Day by day, with new desire,
Toward my wood I ran in faith,
Under leaf and over brier,
Through the thickets, out of breath;
Like the prince who rescued Beauty from
    the sleep as long as death.

LV

But his sword of mettle clashèd,
And his arm smote strong, I ween,
And her dreaming spirit flashèd
Through her body's fair white screen,
And the light thereof might guide him up
    the cedar alleys green:

LVI

But for me, I saw no splendor —
All my sword was my child-heart;
And the wood refused surrender
Of that bower it held apart,
Safe as Œdipus's grave-place 'mid Colonos'
    olives swart.

LVII

As Aladdin sought the basements
His fair palace rose upon,
And the four-and-twenty casements
Which gave answers to the sun;
So, in 'wilderment of gazing, I looked up
    and I looked down.

LVIII

Years have vanished since, as wholly
As the little bower did then;
And you call it tender folly
That such thoughts should come again ?
Ah, I cannot change this sighing for your
smiling, brother men !

LIX

For this loss it did prefigure
Other loss of better good,
When my soul, in spirit-vigor
And in ripened womanhood,
Fell from visions of more beauty than an
arbor in a wood.

LX

I have lost — oh, many a pleasure,
Many a hope and many a power —
Studious health and merry leisure,
The first dew on the first flower !
But the first of all my losses was the losing
of the bower.

LXI

I have lost the dream of Doing,
And the other dream of Done,
The first spring in the pursuing,
The first pride in the Begun, —
First recoil from incompletion, in the face
of what is won —

LXII

Exaltations in the far light
Where some cottage only is;
Mild dejections in the starlight,
Which the sadder-hearted miss;
And the child-cheek blushing scarlet for
the very shame of bliss.

LXIII

I have lost the sound child-sleeping
Which the thunder could not break;
Something too of the strong leaping
Of the staglike heart awake,
Which the pale is low for keeping in the
road it ought to take.

LXIV

Some respect to social fictions
Has been also lost by me;
And some generous genuflexions,
Which my spirit offered free
To the pleasant old conventions of our
false humanity.

LXV

All my losses did I tell you,
Ye perchance would look away; —
Ye would answer me, ' Farewell ! you
Make sad company to-day,
And your tears are falling faster than the
bitter words you say.'

LXVI

For God placed me like a dial
In the open ground with power,
And my heart had for its trial
All the sun and all the shower:
And I suffered many losses, — and my first
was of the bower.

LXVII

Laugh you ?   If that loss of mine be
Of no heavy-seeming weight —
When the cone falls from the pine-tree,
The young children laugh thereat;
Yet the wind that struck it, riseth, and the
tempest shall be great.

LXVIII

One who knew me in my childhood
In the glamour and the game,
Looking on me long and mild, would
Never know me for the same.
Come, unchanging recollections, where
those changes overcame !

LXIX

By this couch I weakly lie on,
While I count my memories, —
Through the fingers which, still sighing,
I press closely on mine eyes, —
Clear as once beneath the sunshine, I be-
hold the bower arise.

LXX

Springs the linden-tree as greenly,
Stroked with light adown its rind;
And the ivy-leaves serenely
Each in either intertwined;
And the rose-trees at the doorway, they
have neither grown nor pined.

LXXI

From those overblown faint roses
Not a leaf appeareth shed,
And that little bud discloses
Not a thorn's-breadth more of red,
For the winters and the summers which
have passed me overhead.

LXXII

And that music overfloweth,
  Sudden sweet, the sylvan caves:
Thrush or nightingale — who knoweth ?
  Fay or Faunus — who believes ?
But my heart still trembles in me to the
    trembling of the leaves.

LXXIII

Is the bower lost, then ? who sayeth
  That the bower indeed is lost ?
Hark ! my spirit in it prayeth
  Through the sunshine and the frost, —
And the prayer preserves it greenly, to the
    last and uttermost.

LXXIV

Till another open for me
  In God's Eden-land unknown,
With an angel at the doorway,
  White with gazing at his Throne;
And a saint's voice in the palm-trees, sing-
    ing — 'All is lost . . . and won !'

A CHILD ASLEEP

First printed in Findon's *Tableaux* for 1840
as ' The Dream.'

I

How he sleepeth, having drunken
  Weary childhood's mandragore !
From its pretty eyes have sunken
  Pleasures to make room for more;
Sleeping near the withered nosegay which
  he pulled the day before.

II

Nosegays ! leave them for the waking;
  Throw them earthward where they
    grew;
Dim are such beside the breaking
  Amaranths he looks unto:
Folded eyes see brighter colors than the
  open ever do.

III

Heaven-flowers, rayed by shadows golden
  From the palms they sprang beneath,
Now perhaps divinely holden,
  Swing against him in a wreath:
We may think so from the quickening of
  his bloom and of his breath.

IV

Vision unto vision calleth
  While the young child dreameth on:
Fair, O dreamer, thee befalleth
  With the glory thou hast won !
Darker wast thou in the garden yestermorn
  by summer sun.

V

We should see the spirits ringing
  Round thee, were the clouds away:
'T is the child-heart draws them, singing
  In the silent-seeming clay —
Singing ! stars that seem the mutest go in
  music all the way.

VI

As the moths around a taper,
  As the bees around a rose,
As the gnats around a vapor,
  So the spirits group and close
Round about a holy childhood as if drinking
  its repose.

VII

Shapes of brightness overlean thee,
  Flash their diadems of youth
On the ringlets which half screen thee,
  While thou smilest . . . not in sooth
Thy smile, but the overfair one, dropt from
  some ethereal mouth.

VIII

Haply it is angels' duty,
  During slumber, shade by shade
To fine down this childish beauty
  To the thing it must be made
Ere the world shall bring it praises, or the
  tomb shall see it fade.

IX

Softly, softly ! make no noises !
  Now he lieth dead and dumb;
Now he hears the angels' voices
  Folding silence in the room:
Now he muses deep the meaning of the
  Heaven-words as they come.

X

Speak not ! he is consecrated;
  Breathe no breath across his eyes:
Lifted up and separated
  On the hand of God he lies
In a sweetness beyond touching, held in
  cloistral sanctities.

XI

Could ye bless him, father — mother,
  Bless the dimple in his cheek ?
Dare ye look at one another
  And the benediction speak ?
Would ye not break out in weeping and
  confess yourselves too weak ?

XII

He is harmless, ye are sinful;
  Ye are troubled, he at ease;
From his slumber virtue winful
  Floweth outward with increase.
Dare not bless him ! but be blessèd by his
  peace, and go in peace.

THE CRY OF THE CHILDREN

'Φεῦ, φεῦ, τί προσδέρκεσθέ μ' ὄμμασιν, τέκνα ;'
                                      — *Medea.*

'The Cry of the Children,' first published in
Blackwood's Magazine, for August, 1843, was
called forth by Mr. Horne's report as assistant
Commissioner on the employment of children
in mines and factories.

I

Do ye hear the children weeping, O my
  brothers,
  Ere the sorrow comes with years ?
They are leaning their young heads against
  their mothers,
  And *that* cannot stop their tears.
The young lambs are bleating in the
  meadows,
  The young birds are chirping in the nest,
The young fawns are playing with the
  shadows,
  The young flowers are blowing toward
  the west —
But the young, young children, O my
  brothers,
  They are weeping bitterly !   10
They are weeping in the playtime of the
  others,
  In the country of the free.

II

Do you question the young children in the
  sorrow
  Why their tears are falling so ?
The old man may weep for his to-morrow
  Which is lost in Long Ago;

The old tree is leafless in the forest,
  The old year is ending in the frost,
The old wound, if stricken, is the sorest,
  The old hope is hardest to be lost: 20
But the young, young children, O my
  brothers,
  Do you ask them why they stand
Weeping sore before the bosoms of their
  mothers,
  In our happy Fatherland ?

III

They look up with their pale and sunken
  faces,
  And their looks are sad to see,
For the man's hoary anguish draws and
  presses
  Down the cheeks of infancy;
'Your old earth,' they say, 'is very dreary,
  Our young feet,' they say, 'are very
  weak;   30
Few paces have we taken, yet are
  weary —
  Our grave-rest is very far to seek:
Ask the aged why they weep, and not the
  children,
  For the outside earth is cold,
And we young ones stand without, in our
  bewildering,
  And the graves are for the old.

IV

'True,' say the children, ' it may happen
  That we die before our time:
Little Alice died last year, her grave is
  shapen
  Like a snowball, in the rime.   40
We looked into the pit prepared to take
  her:
  Was no room for any work in the close
  clay !
From the sleep wherein she lieth none will
  wake her,
  Crying, "Get up, little Alice ! it is day."
If you listen by that grave, in sun and
  shower,
  With your ear down, little Alice never
  cries;
Could we see her face, be sure we should
  not know her,
  For the smile has time for growing in
  her eyes:
And merry go her moments, lulled and
  stilled in
  The shroud by the kirk-chime.   50

It is good when it happens,' say the children,
  'That we die before our time.'

V

Alas, alas, the children ! they are seeking
  Death in life, as best to have:
They are binding up their hearts away from
  breaking,
    With a cerement from the grave.
Go out, children, from the mine and from
  the city,
  Sing out, children, as the little thrushes
  do;
Pluck your handfuls of the meadow-cow-
  slips pretty.
    Laugh aloud, to feel your fingers let
    them through !   60
But they answer, ' Are your cowslips of the
  meadows
  Like our weeds anear the mine ?
Leave us quiet in the dark of the coal-
  shadows,
    From your pleasures fair and fine !

VI

' For oh,' say the children, ' we are weary,
  And we cannot run or leap;
If we cared for any meadows, it were
  merely
  To drop down in them and sleep.
Our knees tremble sorely in the stooping,
  We fall upon our faces, trying to go; 70
And, underneath our heavy eyelids droop-
  ing
  The reddest flower would look as pale
  as snow.
For, all day, we drag our burden tiring
  Through the coal-dark, underground;
Or, all day, we drive the wheels of iron
  In the factories, round and round.

VII

' For all day the wheels are droning, turn-
  ing;
  Their wind comes in our faces,
Till our hearts turn, our heads with pulses
  burning,
  And the walls turn in their places: 80
Turns the sky in the high window, blank
  and reeling,
  Turns the long light that drops adown
  the wall,
Turn the black flies that crawl along the
  ceiling:

All are turning, all the day, and we with
  all.
And all day the iron wheels are droning,
  And sometimes we could pray,
" O ye wheels " (breaking out in a mad
  moaning),
  " Stop ! be silent for to-day ! " '

VIII

Ay, be silent ! Let them hear each other
  breathing
  For a moment, mouth to mouth ! 90
Let them touch each other's hands, in a
  fresh wreathing
  Of their tender human youth !
Let them feel that this cold metallic motion
  Is not all the life God fashions or re-
  veals:
Let them prove their living souls against
  the notion
  That they live in you, or under you, O
  wheels !
Still, all day, the iron wheels go onward,
  Grinding life down from its mark;
And the children's souls, which God is call-
  ing sunward,
  Spin on blindly in the dark. 100

IX

Now tell the poor young children, O my
  brothers,
  To look up to Him and pray;
So the blessèd One who blesseth all the
  others,
  Will bless them another day.
They answer, ' Who is God that He should
  hear us,
  While the rushing of the iron wheels is
  stirred ?
When we sob aloud, the human creatures
  near us
  Pass by, hearing not, or answer not a
  word.
And we hear not (for the wheels in their
  resounding)
  Strangers speaking at the door: 110
Is it likely God, with angels singing round
  Him,
  Hears our weeping any more ?

X

' Two words, indeed, of praying we re-
  member,
  And at midnight's hour of harm.

" Our Father," looking upward in the cham-
    ber,
    We say softly for a charm.
We know no other words except " Our Fa-
    ther,"
    And we think that, in some pause of
      angels' song,
God may pluck them with the silence sweet
    to gather,
    And hold both within his right hand
      which is strong.   120
" Our Father ! " If He heard us, He would
    surely
    (For they call Him good and mild)
Answer, smiling down the steep world very
    purely,
    " Come and rest with me, my child."

XI

' But, no ! ' say the children, weeping
    faster,
    ' He is speechless as a stone:
And they tell us, of His image is the
    master
    Who commands us to work on.
Go to ! ' say the children, — ' up in
    Heaven,
    Dark, wheel-like, turning clouds are all
    we find.   130
Do not mock us; grief has made us un-
    believing:
    We look up for God, but tears have made
    us blind.'
Do you hear the children weeping and dis-
    proving,
    O my brothers, what ye preach ?
For God's possible is taught by his world's
    loving,
    And the children doubt of each.

XII

And well may the children weep before
    you !
    They are weary ere they run;
They have never seen the sunshine, nor
    the glory
    Which is brighter than the sun.   140
They know the grief of man, without its
    wisdom;
    They sink in man's despair, without its
    calm;
Are slaves, without the liberty in Christ-
    dom,
    Are martyrs, by the pang without the
    palm:

Are worn as if with age, yet unretriev-
    ingly
    The harvest of its memories cannot
    reap, —
Are orphans of the earthly love and hea-
    venly.
    Let them weep ! let them weep !

XIII

They look up with their pale and sunken
    faces,
    And their look is dread to see,   150
For they mind you of their angels in high
    places,
    With eyes turned on Deity.
' How long,' they say, ' how long, O cruel
    nation,
    Will you stand, to move the world, on a
      child's heart, —
Stifle down with a mailèd heel its palpita-
    tion,
    And tread onward to your throne amid
    the mart ?
Our blood splashes upward, O gold-
    heaper,
    And your purple shows your path !
But the child's sob in the silence curses
    deeper
    Than the strong man in his wrath.'

CROWNED AND WEDDED

Queen Victoria and Prince Albert of Saxe-
Coburg-Gotha were betrothed in October,
1839, and married February 1, 1840. This
poem was first printed in the *Athenæum* for
February 15, 1840, as ' The Crowned and
Wedded Queen.'

I

When last before her people's face her own
    fair face she bent,
Within the meek projection of that shade
    she was content
To erase the child-smile from her lips,
    which seemed as if it might
Be still kept holy from the world to child-
    hood still in sight —
To erase it with a solemn vow, a princely
    vow — to rule;
A priestly vow — to rule by grace of God
    the pitiful;

A very godlike vow — to rule in right and
  righteousness
And with the law and for the land — so
  God the vower bless !

II

The minster was alight that day, but not
  with fire, I ween,
And long-drawn glitterings swept adown
  that mighty aislèd scene;   10
The priests stood stolèd in their pomp, the
  sworded chiefs in theirs,
And so, the collared knights, and so, the
  civil ministers,
And so, the waiting lords and dames, and
  little pages best
At holding trains, and legates so, from
  countries east and west;
So, alien princes, native peers, and high-
  born ladies bright,
Along whose brows the Queen's, now
  crowned, flashed coronets to light;
And so, the people at the gates with priestly
  hands on high
Which bring the first anointing to all legal
  majesty;
And so the DEAD, who lie in rows beneath
  the minster floor,
There verily an awful state maintaining
  evermore: 20
The statesman whose clean palm will kiss
  no bribe whate'er it be,
The courtier who for no fair queen will rise
  up to his knee,
The court-dame who for no court-tire will
  leave her shroud behind,
The laureate who no courtlier rhyme than
  'dust to dust' can find,
The kings and queens who having made
  that vow and worn that crown,
Descended unto lower thrones and darker,
  deep adown:
Dieu et mon droit — what is 't to them ?
  what meaning can it have ? —
The King of kings, the right of death —
  God's judgment and the grave.
And when betwixt the quick and dead the
  young fair queen had vowed,
The living shouted ' May she live ! Victoria,
  live !' aloud: 30
And as the loyal shouts went up, true
  spirits prayed between,
'The blessings happy monarchs have be
  thine, O crownèd queen !'

III

But now before her people's face she
  bendeth hers anew,
And calls them, while she vows, to be her
  witness thereunto.
She vowed to rule, and in that oath her
  childhood put away:
She doth maintain her womanhood, in vow-
  ing love to-day.
O lovely lady ! let her vow ! such lips be-
  come such vows,
And fairer goeth bridal wreath than crown
  with vernal brows.
O lovely lady ! let her vow ! yea, let her
  vow to love !
And though she be no less a queen, with
  purples hung above,   40
The pageant of a court behind, the royal
  kin around,
And woven gold to catch her looks turned
  maidenly to ground,
Yet may the bride-veil hide from her a
  little of that state,
While loving hopes for retinues about her
  sweetness wait.
SHE vows to love who vowed to rule — (the
  chosen at her side)
Let none say, God preserve the queen ! but
  rather, Bless the bride !
None blow the trump, none bend the knee,
  none violate the dream
Wherein no monarch but a wife she to her-
  self may seem.
Or if ye say, Preserve the queen ! oh,
  breathe it inward low —
She is a *woman*, and *beloved !* and 't is
  enough but so.   50
Count it enough, thou noble prince who
  tak'st her by the hand
And claimest for thy lady-love our lady of
  the land !
And since, Prince Albert, men have called
  thy spirit high and rare,
And true to truth and brave for truth as
  some at Augsburg were,
We charge thee by thy lofty thoughts and
  by thy poet-mind
Which not by glory and degree takes
  measure of mankind,
Esteem that wedded hand less dear for
  sceptre than for ring,
And hold her uncrowned womanhood to be
  the royal thing.

IV

And now, upon our queen's last vow what
    blessings shall we pray ?
None straitened to a shallow crown will
    suit our lips to-day: 60
Behold, they must be free as love, they
    must be broad as free,
Even to the borders of heaven's light and
    earth's humanity.
Long live she ! — send up loyal shouts, and
    true hearts pray between, —
' The blessings happy PEASANTS have, be
    thine, O crownèd queen ! '

CROWNED AND BURIED

First printed in the *Athenæum* for July 4,
1840, as ' Napoleon's Return.' On the 8th of the
same month Miss Barrett wrote from Beacon
Terrace, Torquay, to H. S. Boyd : ' The sub-
ject of the removal of Napoleon's ashes is a
fitter subject for you than for me. Napoleon
is no idol of mine. *I* never made a " setting
sun " of him. But my physician suggested the
subject as a noble one, and then there was some-
thing suggestive in the consideration that the
Bellerophon lay on those very bay-waters
opposite my bed.'

I

NAPOLEON ! — years ago, and that great
    word
Compàct of human breath in hate and dread
And exultation, skied us overhead —
An atmosphere whose lightning was the
    sword
Scathing the cedars of the world, — drawn
    down
In burnings, by the metal of a crown.

II

Napoleon ! — nations, while they cursed
    that name,
Shook at their own curse; and while others
    bore
Its sound, as of a trumpet, on before,
Brass-fronted legions justified its fame;
And dying men on trampled battle-sods
Near their last silence uttered it for God's.

III

Napoleon ! — sages, with high foreheads
    drooped,
Did use it for a problem; children small

Leapt up to greet it, as at manhood's call;
Priests blessed it from their altars over-
    stooped
By meek-eyed Christs; and widows with a
    moan
Spake it, when questioned why they sat
    alone.

IV

That name consumed the silence of the
    snows
In Alpine keeping, holy and cloud-hid;
The mimic eagles dared what Nature's did,
And over-rushed her mountainous repose
In search of eyries: and the Egyptian river
Mingled the same word with its grand
    ' For ever.'

V

That name was shouted near the pyramidal
Nilotic tombs, whose mummied habitants,
Packed to humanity's significance,
Motioned it back with stillness, — shouts
    as idle
As hireling artists' work of myrrh and
    spice
Which swathed last glories round the Ptole-
    mies.

VI

The world's face changed to hear it; kingly
    men
Came down in chidden babes' bewilder-
    ment
From autocratic places, each content
With sprinkled ashes for anointing: then
The people laughed or wondered for the
    nonce,
To see one throne a composite of thrones.

VII

Napoleon ! — even the torrid vastitude
Of India felt in throbbings of the air
That name which scattered by disastrous
    blare
All Europe's bound-lines, — drawn afresh
    in blood.
Napoleon ! — from the Russias west to
    Spain:
And Austria trembled till ye heard her
    chain.

VIII

And Germany was 'ware; and Italy
Oblivious of old fames — her laurel-locked,

High-ghosted Cæsars passing uninvoked —
Did crumble her own ruins with her knee,
To serve a newer: ay ! but Frenchmen
    cast
A future from them nobler than their
    past:

IX

For verily though France augustly rose
With that raised NAME, and did assume by
    such
The purple of the world, none gave so
    much
As she in purchase — to speak plain, in
    loss —
Whose hands, toward freedom stretched,
    dropped paralyzed
To wield a sword or fit an undersized

X

King's crown to a great man's head.   And
    though along
Her Paris' streets did float on frequent
    streams
Of triumph, pictured or enmarbled dreams
Dreamt right by genius in a world gone
    wrong, —
No dream of all so won was fair to see
As the lost vision of her liberty.

XI

Napoleon ! — 't was a high name lifted
    high:
It met at last God's thunder sent to clear
Our compassing and covering atmosphere
And open a clear sight beyond the sky
Of supreme empire; this of earth's was
    done —
And kings crept out again to feel the sun.

XII

The kings crept out — the peoples sat at
    home,
And finding the long-invocated peace
(A pall embroidered with worn images
Of rights divine) too scant to cover doom
Such as they suffered, cursed the corn
    that grew
Rankly, to bitter bread, on Waterloo.

XIII

A deep gloom centred in the deep repose;
The nations stood up mute to count their
    dead:

And he who owned the NAME which vi-
    brated
Through silence, — trusting to his noblest
    foes
When earth was all too gray for chivalry,
Died of their mercies 'mid the desert sea.

XIV

O wild Saint Helen ! very still she kept
    him,
With a green willow for all pyramid,
Which stirred a little if the low wind did,
A little more if pilgrims overwept him,
Disparting the lithe boughs to see the clay
Which seemed to cover his for judgment-
    day.

XV

Nay, not so long !   France kept her old
    affection
As deeply as the sepulchre the corse;
Until, dilated by such love's remorse
To a new angel of the resurrection,
She cried ' Behold, thou England ! I would
    have
The dead, whereof thou wottest, from that
    grave.'

XVI

And England answered in the courtesy
Which, ancient foes turned lovers, may
    befit:
' Take back thy dead ! and when thou
    buriest it,
Throw in all former strifes 'twixt thee and
    me.'
Amen, mine England ! 't is a courteous
    claim:
But ask a little room too — for thy shame !

XVII

Because it was not well, it was not well,
Nor tuneful with thy lofty-chanted part
Among the Oceanides, — that Heart
To bind and bare and vex with vulture fell.
I would, my noble England, men might
    seek
All crimson stains upon thy breast — not
    check !

XVIII

I would that hostile fleets had scarred Tor-
    bay,
Instead of the lone ship which waited
    moored

Until thy princely purpose was assured,
Then left a shadow, not to pass away —
Not for to-night's moon, nor to-morrow's
  sun:
Green watching hills, ye witnessed what
  was done !

XIX

But since it *was* done, — in sepulchral dust
We fain would pay back something of our
  debt
To France, if not to honor, and forget,
How through much fear we falsified the
  trust
Of a fallen foe and exile.   We return
Orestes to Electra — in his urn.

XX

A little urn — a little dust inside,
Which once outbalanced the large earth,
  albeit
To-day a four-years child might carry it
Sleek-browed and smiling, ' Let the bur-
  den 'bide ! '
Orestes to Electra ! — O fair town
Of Paris, how the wild tears will run down

XXI

And run back in the chariot-marks of
  time,
When all the people shall come forth to
  meet
The passive victor, death-still in the street
He rode through 'mid the shouting and
  bell-chime
And martial music, under eagles which
Dyed their rapacious beaks at Austerlitz !

XXII

Napoleon ! — he hath come again, borne
  home
Upon the popular ebbing heart, — a sea
Which gathers its own wrecks perpetually,
Majestically moaning.   Give him room !
Room for the dead in Paris ! welcome
  solemn
And grave-deep, 'neath the cannon-moulded
  column !

XXIII

There, weapon spent and warrior spent
  may rest
From roar of fields, — provided Jupiter
Dare trust Saturnus to lie down so near
His bolts ! — and this he may: for, dispos-
  sessed

Of any godship lies the godlike arm —
The goat, Jove sucked, as likely to do
  harm.

XXIV

And yet . . . Napoleon ! — the recovered
  name
Shakes the old casements of the world; and
  we
Look out upon the passing pageantry,
Attesting that the Dead makes good his
  claim
To a French grave, — another kingdom
  won,
The last, of few spans — by Napoleon.

XXV

Blood fell like dew beneath his sunrise —
  sooth
But glittered dew-like in the covenanted
Meridian light.   He was a despot —
  granted !
But the αὐτός of his autocratic mouth
Said yea i' the people's French; he magni-
  fied
The image of the freedom he denied:

XXVI

And if they asked for rights, he made
  reply
' Ye have my glory ! ' — and so, drawing
  round them
His ample purple, glorified and bound
  them
In an embrace that seemed identity.
He ruled them like a tyrant — true ! but
  none
Were ruled like slaves: each felt Napo-
  leon.

XXVII

I do not praise this man: the man was
  flawed
For Adam — much more, Christ ! — his
  knee unbent,
His hand unclean, his aspiration pent
Within a sword-sweep — pshaw ! — but
  since he had
The genius to be loved, why, let him have
The justice to be honored in his grave.

XXVIII

I think this nation's tears thus poured to-
  gether,
Better than shouts.   I think this funeral

Grander than crownings, though a Pope
  bless all.
I think this grave stronger than thrones.
  But whether
The crowned Napoleon or the buried clay
Be worthier, I discern not: angels may.

TO FLUSH, MY DOG

First printed in the *Athenæum*, July 22,
1843. 'This dog,' says the author, 'was the
gift of my dear and admired friend, Miss Mit-
ford, and belongs to the beautiful race she has
rendered celebrated among English and Amer-
ican readers. The Flushes have their laurels
as well as the Cæsars, — the chief difference
(at least the very head and front of it) con-
sisting, perhaps, in the bald head of the latter
under the crown.'

I

Loving friend, the gift of one
Who her own true faith has run
  Through thy lower nature,
Be my benediction said
With my hand upon thy head,
  Gentle fellow-creature !

II

Like a lady's ringlets brown,
Flow thy silken ears adown
  Either side demurely
Of thy silver-suited breast
Shining out from all the rest
  Of thy body purely.

III

Darkly brown thy body is,
Till the sunshine striking this
  Alchemize its dulness,
When the sleek curls manifold
Flash all over into gold
  With a burnished fulness.

IV

Underneath my stroking hand,
Startled eyes of hazel bland
  Kindling, growing larger,
Up thou leapest with a spring,
Full of prank and curveting,
  Leaping like a charger.

V

Leap ! thy broad tail waves a light,
Leap ! thy slender feet are bright,

Canopied in fringes,
Leap ! those tasselled ears of thine
Flicker strangely, fair and fine
  Down their golden inches.

VI

Yet, my pretty, sportive friend,
Little is 't to such an end
  That I praise thy rareness;
Other dogs may be thy peers
Haply in these drooping ears
  And this glossy fairness.

VII

But of *thee* it shall be said,
This dog watched beside a bed
  Day and night unweary,
Watched within a curtained room
Where no sunbeam brake the gloom
  Round the sick and dreary.

VIII

Roses, gathered for a vase,
In that chamber died apace,
  Beam and breeze resigning;
This dog only, waited on,
Knowing that when light is gone
  Love remains for shining.

IX

Other dogs in thymy dew
Tracked the hares and followed through
  Sunny moor or meadow;
This dog only, crept and crept
Next a languid cheek that slept,
  Sharing in the shadow.

X

Other dogs of loyal cheer
Bounded at the whistle clear,
  Up the woodside hieing;
This dog only, watched in reach
Of a faintly uttered speech
  Or a louder sighing.

XI

And if one or two quick tears
Dropped upon his glossy ears
  Or a sigh came double,
Up he sprang in eager haste,
Fawning, fondling, breathing **fast,**
  In a tender trouble.

XII

And this dog was satisfied
If a pale thin hand would glide

Down his dewlaps sloping, —
Which he pushed his nose within,
After, — platforming his chin
　　On the palm left open.

XIII

This dog, if a friendly voice
Call him now to blither choice
　　Than such chamber-keeping,
'Come out!' praying from the door, —
Presseth backward as before,
　　Up against me leaping.

XIV

Therefore to this dog will I,
Tenderly not scornfully,
　　Render praise and favor:
With my hand upon his head,
Is my benediction said
　　Therefore and for ever.

XV

And because he loves me so,
Better than his kind will do
　　Often man or woman,
Give I back more love again
Than dogs often take of men,
　　Leaning from my Human.

XVI

Blessings on thee, dog of mine,
Pretty collars make thee fine,
　　Sugared milk make fat thee!
Pleasures wag on in thy tail,
Hands of gentle motion fail
　　Nevermore, to pat thee!

XVII

Downy pillow take thy head,
Silken coverlid bestead,
　　Sunshine help thy sleeping!
No fly's buzzing wake thee up,
No man break thy purple cup
　　Set for drinking deep in.

XVIII

Whiskered cats arointed flee,
Sturdy stoppers keep from thee
　　Cologne distillations;
Nuts lie in thy path for stones,
And thy feast-day macaroons
　　Turn to daily rations!

XIX

Mock I thee, in wishing weal? —
Tears are in my eyes to feel

Thou art made so straitly,
Blessing needs must straiten too, —
Little canst thou joy or do,
　　Thou who lovest *greatly*.

XX

Yet be blessèd to the height
Of all good and all delight
　　Pervious to thy nature;
Only *loved* beyond that line,
With a love that answers thine,
　　Loving fellow-creature!

THE FOURFOLD ASPECT

I

WHEN ye stood up in the house
　　With your little childish feet,
And, in touching Life's first shows,
　　First the touch of Love did meet, —
Love and Nearness seeming one,
　　By the heartlight cast before,
And of all Beloveds, none
　　Standing farther than the door;
Not a name being dear to thought,
　　With its owner beyond call;   10
Not a face, unless it brought
　　Its own shadow to the wall;
When the worst recorded change
　　Was of apple dropt from bough,
When love's sorrow seemed more strange
　　Than love's treason can seem now; —
Then, the Loving took you up
　　Soft, upon their elder knees,
Telling why the statues droop
　　Underneath the churchyard trees,   20
And how ye must lie beneath them
　　Through the winters long and deep,
Till the last trump overbreathe them,
　　And ye smile out of your sleep.
Oh, ye lifted up your head, and it seemed as
　　　if they said
　　　　A tale of fairy ships
　　　　　With a swan-wing for a sail;
　　　Oh, ye kissed their loving lips
　　　　　For the merry merry tale —   25
So carelessly ye thought upon the Dead!

II

Soon ye read in solemn stories
　　Of the men of long ago,
Of the pale bewildering glories
　　Shining farther than we know;

Of the heroes with the laurel,
　Of the poets with the bay,
Of the two worlds' earnest quarrel
　For that beauteous Helena;
How Achilles at the portal
　Of the tent heard footsteps nigh,　40
And his strong heart, half-immortal,
　Met the keitai with a cry;
How Ulysses left the sunlight
　For the pale cidola race
Blank and passive through the dun light,
　Staring blindly in his face;
How that true wife said to Pætus,
　With calm smile and wounded heart,
'Sweet, it hurts not!' How Admetus
　Saw his blessed one depart;　50
How King Arthur proved his mission,
　And Sir Roland wound his horn,
And at Sangreal's moony vision
　Swords did bristle round like corn.
Oh, ye lifted up your head, and it seemed,
　　the while ye read,
　　　That this Death, then, must be
　　　　found
　　　A Valhalla for the crowned,
　　　The heroic who prevail:
　　　None, be sure can enter in
　　　Far below a paladin　60
　　　Of a noble noble tale —
So awfully ye thought upon the Dead!

III

Ay, but soon ye woke up shrieking,
　As a child that wakes at night
From a dream of sisters speaking
　In a garden's summer-light, —
That wakes, starting up and bounding,
　In a lonely lonely bed,
With a wall of darkness round him,
　Stifling black about his head!　70
And the full sense of your mortal
　Rushed upon you deep and loud,
And ye heard the thunder hurtle
　From the silence of the cloud.
Funeral-torches at your gateway
　Threw a dreadful light within.
All things changed: you rose up straight-
　　way,
　And saluted Death and Sin.
Since, your outward man has rallied,
　And your eye and voice grown bold;
Yet the Sphinx of Life stands pallid,　81
　With her saddest secret told.
Happy places have grown holy:
　If ye went where once ye went,

Only tears would fall down slowly,
　As at solemn sacrament.
Merry books, once read for pastime,
　If ye dared to read again,
Only memories of the last time
　Would swim darkly up the brain.　90
Household names, which used to flut-
　　ter
　Through your laughter unawares, —
God's Divinest ye could utter
　With less trembling in your prayers.
Ye have dropt adown your head, and it
　　seems as if ye tread
　　On your own hearts in the path
　　Ye are called to in His wrath,
　　And your prayers go up in wail
　　—'Dost Thou see, then, all our
　　　loss,
　　O Thou agonized on cross?　100
　　Art thou reading all its tale?'
So mournfully ye think upon the Dead!

IV

Pray, pray, thou who also weepest,
　And the drops will slacken so.
Weep, weep, and the watch thou keepest
　With a quicker count will go.
Think: the shadow on the dial
　For the nature most undone,
Marks the passing of the trial,
　Proves the presence of the sun.　110
Look, look up, in starry passion,
　To the throne above the spheres:
Learn: the spirit's gravitation
　Still must differ from the tear's.
Hope: with all the strength thou usest
　In embracing thy despair.
Love: the earthly love thou losest
　Shall return to thee more fair.
Work: make clear the forest-tangles
　Of the wildest stranger-land.　120
Trust: the blessèd deathly angels
　Whisper, 'Sabbath hours at hand!'
By the heart's wound when most gory,
　By the longest agony,
Smile! Behold in sudden glory
　The TRANSFIGURED smiles on thee!
And ye lifted up your head, and it seemed
　　as if He said,
　　　'My Belovèd, is it so?
　　　Have ye tasted of my woe?
　　　Of my Heaven ye shall not
　　　　fail!'　130
　　　He stands brightly where the
　　　　shade is,

With the keys of Death and
Hades,
And there, ends the mournful
tale —
So hopefully ye think upon the Dead !

A FLOWER IN A LETTER

I

My lonely chamber next the sea
Is full of many flowers set free
   By summer's earliest duty:
Dear friends upon the garden-walk
Might stop amid their fondest talk
   To pull the least in beauty.

II

A thousand flowers, each seeming one
That learnt by gazing on the sun
   To counterfeit his shining;
Within whose leaves the holy dew
That falls from heaven has won anew
   A glory, in declining.

III

Red roses, used to praises long,
Contented with the poet's song,
   The nightingale's being over;
And lilies white, prepared to touch
The whitest thought, nor soil it much,
   Of dreamer turned to lover.

IV

Deep violets, you liken to
The kindest eyes that look on you,
   Without a thought disloyal;
And cactuses a queen might don
If weary of a golden crown,
   And still appear as royal.

V

Pansies for ladies all, — I wis
That none who wear such brooches miss
   A jewel in the mirror;
And tulips, children love to stretch
Their fingers down, to feel in each
   Its beauty's secret nearer.

VI

Love's language may be talked with these;
To work out choicest sentences,
   No blossoms can be meeter;

And, such being used in Eastern bowers,
Young maids may wonder if the flowers
   Or meanings be the sweeter.

VII

And such being strewn before a bride,
Her little foot may turn aside,
   Their longer bloom decreeing,
Unless some voice's whispered sound
Should make her gaze upon the ground
   Too earnestly for seeing.

VIII

And such being scattered on a grave,
Whoever mourneth there may have
   A type which seemeth worthy
Of that fair body hid below,
Which bloomed on earth a time ago,
   Then perished as the earthy.

IX

And such being wreathed for worldly feast,
Across the brimming cup some guest
   Their rainbow colors viewing
May feel them, with a silent start,
The covenant, his childish heart
   With nature made, renewing.

X

No flowers our gardened England hath
To match with these, in bloom and breath,
   Which from the world are hiding
In sunny Devon moist with rills, —
A nunnery of cloistered hills,
   The elements presiding.

XI

By Loddon's stream the flowers are fair
That meet one gifted lady's care
   With prodigal rewarding:
(For Beauty is too used to run
To Mitford's bower — to want the sun
   To light her through the garden).

XII

But here, all summers are comprised,
The nightly frosts shrink exorcised
   Before the priestly moonshine;
And every wind with stolèd feet
In wandering down the alleys sweet
   Steps lightly on the sunshine.

XIII

And (having promised Harpocrate
Among the nodding roses that

No harm shall touch his daughters)
Gives quite away the rushing sound
He dares not use upon such ground
  To ever-trickling waters.

XIV

Yet, sun and wind ! what can ye do
But make the leaves more brightly show
  In posies newly gathered ?
I look away from all your best
To one poor flower unlike the rest,
  A little flower half-withered.

XV

I do not think it ever was
A pretty flower, — to make the grass
  Look greener where it reddened;
And now it seems ashamed to be
Alone, in all this company,
  Of aspect shrunk and saddened.

XVI

A chamber-window was the spot
It grew in, from a garden-pot,
  Among the city shadows:
If any, tending it, might seem
To smile, 't was only in a dream
  Of nature in the meadows.

XVII

How coldly on its head did fall
The sunshine, from the city wall
  In pale refraction driven !
How sadly plashed upon its leaves
The raindrops, losing in the eaves
  The first sweet news of heaven !

XVIII

And those who planted, gathered it
In gamesome or in loving fit,
  And sent it as a token
Of what their city pleasures be, —
For one, in Devon by the sea
  And garden blooms, to look on.

XIX

But SHE for whom the jest was meant,
With a grave passion innocent
  Receiving what was given, —
Oh, if her face she turnèd then,
Let none say 't was to gaze again
  Upon the flowers of Devon !

XX

Because, whatever virtue dwells
In genial skies, warm oracles
For gardens brightly springing, —
The flower which grew beneath your eyes,
Belovèd friends, to mine supplies
  A beauty worthier singing !

THE CRY OF THE HUMAN

First printed in *Graham's American Magazine*, 1842.

I

'THERE is no God' the foolish saith,
  But none 'There is no sorrow,'
And nature oft the cry of faith
  In bitter need will borrow:
Eyes, which the preacher could not school,
  By wayside graves are raisèd,
And lips say 'God be pitiful,'
  Who ne'er said 'God be praisèd.'
                    Be pitiful, O God !

II

The tempest stretches from the steep
  The shadow of its coming,
The beasts grow tame and near us creep,
  As help were in the human;
Yet, while the cloud-wheels roll and
    grind,
  We spirits tremble under —
The hills have echoes, but we find
  No answer for the thunder.
                    Be pitiful, O God !

III

The battle hurtles on the plains,
  Earth feels new scythes upon her;
We reap our brothers for the wains,
  And call the harvest — honor:
Draw face to face, front line to line,
  One image all inherit, —
Then kill, curse on, by that same sign,
  Clay — clay, and spirit — spirit.
                    Be pitiful, O God !

IV

The plague runs festering through the
    town,
  And never a bell is tolling,
And corpses, jostled 'neath the moon,
  Nod to the dead-cart's rolling:
The young child calleth for the cup,
  The strong man brings it weeping,
The mother from her babe looks up,

And shrieks away its sleeping.
       Be pitiful, O God !

V

The plague of gold strikes far and near,
  And deep and strong it enters;
This purple chimar which we wear
  Makes madder than the centaur's:
Our thoughts grow blank, our words grow
    strange,
  We cheer the pale gold-diggers,
Each soul is worth so much on 'Change,
  And marked, like sheep, with figures.
       Be pitiful, O God !

VI

The curse of gold upon the land
  The lack of bread enforces;
The rail-cars snort from strand to strand,
  Like more of Death's White Horses:
The rich preach 'rights' and 'future days,'
  And hear no angel scoffing,
The poor die mute, with starving gaze
  On corn-ships in the offing.
       Be pitiful, O God !

VII

We meet together at the feast,
  To private mirth betake us;
We stare down in the winecup, lest
  Some vacant chair should shake us:
We name delight, and pledge it round —
  'It shall be ours to-morrow !'
God's seraphs, do your voices sound
  As sad, in naming sorrow ?
       Be pitiful, O God !

VIII

We sit together, with the skies,
  The steadfast skies, above us,
We look into each other's eyes,
  ' And how long will you love us ? '
The eyes grow dim with prophecy,
  The voices, low and breathless, —
'Till death us part !' — O words, to be
  Our *best*, for love the deathless !
       Be pitiful, O God !

IX

We tremble by the harmless bed
  Of one loved and departed:
Our tears drop on the lips that said
  Last night ' Be stronger-hearted !'
O God — to clasp those fingers close,

And yet to feel so lonely !
To see a light upon such brows,
  Which is the daylight only !
       Be pitiful, O God !

X

The happy children come to us
  And look up in our faces;
They ask us ' Was it thus, and thus,
  When we were in their places ? '
We cannot speak; — we see anew
  The hills we used to live in,
And feel our mother's smile press through
  The kisses she is giving.
       Be pitiful, O God !

XI

We pray together at the kirk
  For mercy, mercy solely:
Hands weary with the evil work,
  We lift them to the Holy.
The corpse is calm below our knee,
  Its spirit, bright before Thee:
Between them, worse than either, we —
  Without the rest or glory.
       Be pitiful, O God !

XII

We leave the communing of men,
  The murmur of the passions,
And live alone, to live again
  With endless generations:
Are we so brave ?   The sea and sky
  In silence lift their mirrors,
And, glassed therein, our spirits high
  Recoil from their own terrors.
       Be pitiful, O God !

XIII

We sit on hills our childhood wist,
  Woods, hamlets, streams, beholding
The sun strikes through the farthest mist
  The city's spire to golden:
The city's golden spire it was,
  When hope and health were strongest,
But now it is the churchyard grass
  We look upon the longest.
       Be pitiful, O God !

XIV

And soon all vision waxeth dull;
  Men whisper ' He is dying;'
We cry no more ' Be pitiful !'
  We have no strength for crying:

No strength, no need. Then, soul of mine,
  Look up and triumph rather !
Lo, in the depth of God's Divine,
  The Son adjures the Father,
          BE PITIFUL, O GOD !

A LAY OF THE EARLY ROSE

'. . . discordance that can accord.'
          — *Romaunt of the Rose.*

A ROSE once grew within
  A garden April-green,
In her loneness, in her loneness,
And the fairer for that oneness.

A white rose delicate
  On a tall bough and straight:
Early comer, early comer,
Never waiting for the summer.

Her pretty gestes did win
  South winds to let her in,   10
In her loneness, in her loneness,
All the fairer for that oneness.

'For if I wait,' said she,
  'Till time for roses be,
For the moss-rose and the musk-rose,
Maiden-blush and royal-dusk rose,

'What glory then for me
  In such a company ? —
Roses plenty, roses plenty
And one nightingale for twenty !   20

'Nay, let me in,' said she,
  'Before the rest are free,
In my loneness, in my loneness,
All the fairer for that oneness.

'For I would lonely stand
  Uplifting my white hand,
On a mission, on a mission,
To declare the coming vision.

'Upon which lifted sign,
  What worship will be mine !   30
What addressing, what caressing,
And what thanks and praise and bless-
      ing !

'A windlike joy will rush
  Through every tree and bush,
Bending softly in affection
And spontaneous benediction.

'Insects, that only may
  Live in a sunbright ray,
To my whiteness, to my whiteness,
Shall be drawn as to a brightness, —   40

'And every moth and bee
  Approach me reverently,
Wheeling o'er me, wheeling o'er me,
Coronals of motioned glory.

'Three larks shall leave a cloud,
  To my whiter beauty vowed,
Singing gladly all the moontide,
Never waiting for the suntide.

'Ten nightingales shall flee
  Their woods for love of me,   50
Singing sadly all the suntide,
Never waiting for the moontide.

'I ween the very skies
  Will look down with surprise,
When below on earth they see me
With my starry aspect dreamy.

'And earth will call her flowers
  To hasten out of doors,
By their curtsies and sweet-smelling
To give grace to my foretelling.'   60

So praying, did she win
  South winds to let her in,
In her loneness, in her loneness,
And the fairer for that oneness.

But ah, — alas for her !
  No thing did minister
To her praises, to her praises,
More than might unto a daisy's.

No tree nor bush was seen
  To boast a perfect green,   70
Scarcely having, scarcely having
One leaf broad enough for waving.

The little flies did crawl
  Along the southern wall,
Faintly shifting, faintly shifting
Wings scarce long enough for lifting.

The lark, too high or low,
  I ween, did miss her so,

With his nest down in the gorses,
And his song in the star-courses.   80

   The nightingale did please
   To loiter beyond seas:
Guess him in the Happy Islands,
Learning music from the silence!

   Only the bee, forsooth,
   Came in the place of both,
Doing honor, doing honor
To the honey-dews upon her.

   The skies looked coldly down
   As on a royal crown;   90
Then with drop for drop, at leisure,
They began to rain for pleasure.

   Whereat the earth did seem
   To waken from a dream,
Winter-frozen, winter-frozen,
Her unquiet eyes unclosing —

   Said to the Rose, 'Ha, snow!
   And art thou fallen so?
Thou, who wast enthronèd stately
All along my mountains lately?   100

   'Holla, thou world-wide snow!
   And art thou wasted so,
With a little bough to catch thee,
And a little bee to watch thee?'

   — Poor Rose, to be misknown!
   Would she had ne'er been blown,
In her loneness, in her loneness,
All the sadder for that oneness!

   Some word she tried to say,
   Some no . . . ah, wellaway!   110
But the passion did o'ercome her,
And the fair frail leaves dropped from her.

   — Dropped from her fair and mute,
   Close to a poet's foot,
Who beheld them, smiling slowly,
As at something sad yet holy, —

   Said 'Verily and thus
   It chances too with us
Poets, singing sweetest snatches
While that deaf men keep the watches: 120

   'Vaunting to come before
   Our own age evermore,

In a loneness, in a loneness,
And the nobler for that oneness.

   'Holy in voice and heart,
   To high ends, set apart:
All unmated, all unmated,
Just because so consecrated.

   'But if alone we be,
   Where is our empery?   130
And if none can reach our stature,
Who can mete our lofty nature?

   'What bell will yield a tone,
   Swung in the air alone?
If no brazen clapper bringing,
Who can hear the chimèd ringing?

   'What angel but would seem
   To sensual eyes, ghost-dim?
And without assimilation
Vain is interpenetration.   140

   'And thus, what can we do,
   Poor rose and poet too,
Who both antedate our mission
In an unprepared season?

   'Drop, leaf! be silent, song!
   Cold things we come among:
We must warm them, we must warm them,
Ere we ever hope to charm them.

   'Howbeit' (here his face
   Lightened around the place,   150
So to mark the outward turning
Of its spirit's inward burning)

   'Something it is, to hold
   In God's worlds manifold,
First revealed to creature-duty,
Some new form of his mild Beauty.

   'Whether that form respect
   The sense or intellect,
Holy be, in mood or meadow,
The Chief Beauty's sign and shadow!   160

   'Holy, in me and thee,
   Rose fallen from the tree, —
Though the world stand dumb around us,
All unable to expound us.

   'Though none us deign to bless,
   Blessèd are we, natheless;

Blessèd still and consecrated
In that, rose, we were created.

' Oh, shame to poet's lays
  Sung for the dole of praise, —   170
Hoarsely sung upon the highway
With that *obolum da mihi !*

' Shame, shame to poet's soul
  Pining for such a dole,
When Heaven-chosen to inherit
The high throne of a chief spirit !

Sit still upon your thrones,
  O ye poetic ones !
And if, sooth, the world decry you,
Let it pass unchallenged by you.   180

' Ye to yourselves suffice,
  Without its flatteries.
Self-contentedly approve you
Unto Him who sits above you, —

' In prayers, that upward mount
  Like to a fair-sunned fount
Which, in gushing back upon you,
Hath an upper music won you, —

' In faith, that still perceives
  No rose can shed her leaves,   190
Far less, poet fall from mission,
With an unfulfilled fruition, —

' In hope, that apprehends
  An end beyond these ends,
And great uses rendered duly
By the meanest song sung truly, —

' In thanks, for all the good
  By poets understood,
For the sound of seraphs moving
Down the hidden depths of loving, —   200

' For sights of things away
  Through fissures of the clay,
Promised things which *shall* be given
And sung over, up in Heaven, —

' For life, so lovely-vain,
  For death, which breaks the chain,
For this sense of present sweetness,
And this yearning to completeness ! '

BERTHA IN THE LANE

I

Put the broidery-frame away,
  For my sewing is all done.
The last thread is used to-day,
  And I need not join it on.
Though the clock stands at the noon
I am weary. I have sewn,
Sweet, for thee, a wedding-gown.

II

Sister, help me to the bed,
  And stand near me, Dearest-sweet.
Do not shrink nor be afraid,
  Blushing with a sudden heat !
No one standeth in the street ? —
By God's love I go to meet,
Love I thee with love complete.

III

Lean thy face down; drop it in
  These two hands, that I may hold
'Twixt their palms thy cheek and chin,
  Stroking back the curls of gold:
'T is a fair, fair face, in sooth —
Larger eyes and redder mouth
Than mine were in my first youth.

IV

Thou art younger by seven years —
  Ah ! — so bashful at my gaze,
That the lashes, hung with tears,
  Grow too heavy to upraise ?
I would wound thee by no touch
Which thy shyness feels as such.
Dost thou mind me, Dear, so much ?

V

Have I not been nigh a mother
  To thy sweetness — tell me, Dear ?
Have we not loved one another
  Tenderly, from year to year,
Since our dying mother mild
Said with accents undefiled,
' Child, be mother to this child ! '

VI

Mother, mother, up in heaven,
  Stand up on the jasper sea,
And be witness I have given
  All the gifts required of me, —

Hope that blessed me, bliss that crowned,
Love that left me with a wound,
Life itself that turneth round !

VII

Mother, mother, thou art kind,
    Thou art standing in the room,
In a molten glory shrined
    That rays off into the gloom !
But thy smile is bright and bleak
Like cold waves — I cannot speak,
I sob in it, and grow weak.

VIII

Ghostly mother, keep aloof
    One hour longer from my soul,
For I still am thinking of
    Earth's warm-beating joy and dole !
On my finger is a ring
Which I still see glittering
When the night hides everything.

IX

Little sister, thou art pale !
    Ah, I have a wandering brain —
But I lose that fever-bale,
    And my thoughts grow calm again.
Lean down closer — closer still !
I have words thine ear to fill,
And would kiss thee at my will.

X

Dear, I heard thee in the spring,
    Thee and Robert — through the trees, —
When we all went gathering
    Boughs of may-bloom for the bees.
Do not start so ! think instead
How the sunshine overhead
Seemed to trickle through the shade.

XI

What a day it was, that day !
    Hills and vales did openly
Seem to heave and throb away
    At the sight of the great sky:
And the silence, as it stood
In the glory's golden flood,
Audibly did bud, and bud.

XII

Through the winding hedgerows green,
    How we wandered, I and you,
With the bowery tops shut in,
    And the gates that showed the view !
How we talked there; thrushes soft

Sang our praises out, or oft
Bleatings took them from the croft:

XIII

Till the pleasure grown too strong
    Left me muter evermore,
And, the winding road being long,
    I walked out of sight, before,
And so, wrapt in musings fond,
Issued (past the wayside pond)
On the meadow-lands beyond.

XIV

I sate down beneath the beech
    Which leans over to the lane,
And the far sound of your speech
    Did not promise any pain;
And I blessed you full and free,
With a smile stooped tenderly
O'er the may-flowers on my knee.

XV

But the sound grew into word
    As the speakers drew more near —
Sweet, forgive me that I heard
    What you wished me not to hear.
Do not weep so, do not shake,
Oh, — I heard thee, Bertha, make
Good true answers for my sake.

XVI

Yes, and HE too ! let him stand
    In thy thoughts, untouched by blame.
Could he help it, if my hand
    He had claimed with hasty claim?
That was wrong perhaps — but then
Such things be — and will, again.
Women cannot judge for men.

XVII

Had he seen thee when he swore
    He would love but me alone ?
Thou wast absent, sent before
    To our kin in Sidmouth town.
When he saw thee who art blest
Past compare, and loveliest,
He but judged thee as the rest.

XVIII

Could we blame him with grave words,
    Thou and I, Dear, if we might ?
Thy brown eyes have looks like birds
    Flying straightway to the light:
Mine are older. — Hush ! — look out —

Up the street ! Is none without ?
How the poplar swings about !

XIX

And that hour — beneath the beech,
 When I listened in a dream,
And he said in his deep speech
 That he owed me all *esteem*, —
Each word swam in on my brain
With a dim, dilating pain,
Till it burst with that last strain.

XX

I fell flooded with a dark,
 In the silence of a swoon.
When I rose, still cold and stark,
 There was night; I saw the moon
And the stars, each in its place,
And the may-blooms on the grass
Seemed to wonder what I was.

XXI

And I walked as if apart
 From myself, when I could stand,
And I pitied my own heart,
 As if I held it in my hand —
Somewhat coldly, with a sense
Of fulfilled benevolence,
And a 'Poor thing' negligence.

XXII

And I answered coldly too,
 When you met me at the door;
And I only *heard* the dew
 Dripping from me to the floor:
And the flowers, I bade you see,
Were too withered for the bee, —
As my life, henceforth, for me.

XXIII

Do not weep so — Dear, — heart-warm !
 All was best as it befell.
If I say he did me harm,
 I speak wild, — I am not well.
All his words were kind and good —
He esteemed me. Only, blood
Runs so faint in womanhood !

XXIV

Then I always was too grave, —
 Like the saddest ballad sung, —
With that look, besides, we have
 In our faces, who die young.
I had died, Dear, all the same;

Life's long, joyous, jostling game
Is too loud for my meek shame.

XXV

We are so unlike each other,
 Thou and I, that none could guess
We were children of one mother,
 But for mutual tenderness.
Thou art rose-lined from the cold,
And meant verily to hold
Life's pure pleasures manifold.

XXVI

I am pale as crocus grows
 Close beside a rose-tree's root;
Whosoe'er would reach the rose,
 Treads the crocus underfoot.
I, like may-bloom on thorn-tree,
Thou, like merry summer-bee, —
Fit that I be plucked for thee !

XXVII

Yet who plucks me ? — no one mourns,
 I have lived my season out,
And now die of my own thorns
 Which I could not live without.
Sweet, be merry ! How the light
Comes and goes ! If it be night,
Keep the candles in my sight.

XXVIII

Are there footsteps at the door ?
 Look out quickly. Yea, or nay ?
Some one might be waiting for
 Some last word that I might say.
Nay ? So best ! — so angels would
Stand off clear from deathly road,
Not to cross the sight of God.

XXIX

Colder grow my hands and feet.
 When I wear the shroud I made,
Let the folds lie straight and neat,
 And the rosemary be spread,
That if any friend should come,
(To see *thee*, Sweet !) all the room
May be lifted out of gloom.

XXX

And, dear Bertha, let me keep
 On my hand this little ring,
Which at nights, when others sleep,
 I can still see glittering !
Let me wear it out of sight,

In the grave, — where it will light
All the dark up, day and night.

XXXI

On that grave drop not a tear !
  Else, though fathom-deep the place,
Through the woollen shroud I wear
  I shall feel it on my face.
Rather smile there, blessèd one,
Thinking of me in the sun,
Or forget me — smiling on !

XXXII

Art thou near me ? nearer ! so —
  Kiss me close upon the eyes,
That the earthly light may go
  Sweetly, as it used to rise
When I watched the morning-gray
Strike, betwixt the hills, the way
He was sure to come that day.

XXXIII

So, — no more vain words be said !
  The hosannas nearer roll.
Mother, smile now on thy Dead,
  I am death-strong in my soul.
Mystic Dove alit on cross,
Guide the poor bird of the snows
Through the snow-wind above loss !

XXXIV

Jesus, Victim, comprehending
  Love's divine self-abnegation,
Cleanse my love in its self-spending,
  And absorb the poor libation !
Wind my thread of life up higher,
Up, through angels' hands of fire !
I aspire while I expire.

THAT DAY

I

I STAND by the river where both of us
    stood,
And there is but one shadow to darken the
    flood ;
And the path leading to it, where both used
    to pass,
Has the step but of one, to take dew from
    the grass, —
      One forlorn since that day.

II

The flowers of the margin are many to see;
None stoops at my bidding to pluck them
    for me.
The bird in the alder sings loudly and
    long, —
My low sound of weeping disturbs not his
    song,
      As thy vow did, that day.

III

I stand by the river, I think of the vow;
Oh, calm as the place is, vow-breaker, be
    thou !
I leave the flower growing, the bird unre-
    proved;
Would I trouble *thee* rather than *them*, my
    beloved, —
      And my lover that day ?

IV

Go, be sure of my love, by that treason for-
    given;
Of my prayers, by the blessings they win
    thee from Heaven;
Of my grief — (guess the length of the
    sword by the sheath's)
By the silence of life, more pathetic than
    death's !
      Go, — be clear of that day !

LOVED ONCE

I

    I CLASSED, appraising once,
Earth's lamentable sounds, — the wella-
    day,
    The jarring yea and nay,
The fall of kisses on unanswering clay,
The sobbed farewell, the welcome mourn-
    fuller, —
    But all did leaven the air
With a less bitter leaven of sure despair
    Than these words — ' I loved ONCE.'

II

    And who saith ' I loved ONCE ' ?
Not angels, — whose clear eyes, love, love
    foresee,
    Love, through eternity,
And by To Love do apprehend To Be.
Not God, called LOVE, his noble crown-
    name casting,

A light too broad for blasting:
The great God, changing not from ever-
    lasting,
Saith never ' I loved ONCE.'

III

Oh, never is ' Loved ONCE '
Thy word, Thou Victim-Christ, misprizèd
    friend !
Thy cross and curse may rend,
But having loved Thou lovest to the end.
This is man's saying — man's: too weak to
    move
One spherèd star above,
Man desecrates the eternal God-word Love
By his No More, and Once.

IV

How say ye ' We loved once,'
Blasphemers ? Is your earth not cold
    enow,
Mourners, without that snow ?
Ah friends, and would ye wrong each other
    so ?
And could ye say of some whose love is
    known,
Whose prayers have met your own,
Whose tears have fallen for you, whose
    smiles have shown
So long, — ' We loved them ONCE ' ?

V

Could ye ' We loved her once '
Say calm of me, sweet friends, when out of
    sight ?
When hearts of better right
Stand in between me and your happy
    light ?
Or when, as flowers kept too long in the
    shade,
Ye find my colors fade,
And all that is not love in me decayed ?
Such words — Ye loved me ONCE !

VI

Could ye ' We loved her once '
Say cold of me when further put away
In earth's sepulchral clay,
When mute the lips which deprecate to-
    day ?
Not so ! not then — least then ! When
    life is shriven
And death's full joy is given, —
Of those who sit and love you up in heaven
Say not ' We loved them once.'

VII

Say never ye loved ONCE:
God is too near above, the grave beneath,
And all our moments breathe
Too quick in mysteries of life and death,
For such a word. The eternities avenge
Affections light of range.
There comes no change to justify that
    change,
Whatever comes — Loved ONCE !

VIII

And yet that same word ONCE
Is humanly acceptive. Kings have said,
Shaking a discrowned head,
' We ruled once,' — dotards, ' We once
    taught and led,'
Cripples once danced i' the vines, and bards
    approved,
Were once by scornings moved:
But love strikes one hour — LOVE ! Those
    never loved
Who dream that they loved ONCE.

A RHAPSODY OF LIFE'S PROGRESS

' Fill all the stops of life with tuneful breath.'
   — *Poems on Man*, by CORNELIUS MATHEWS.

I

WE are born into life — it is sweet, it is
    strange.
We lie still on the knee of a mild Mystery
    Which smiles with a change;
But we doubt not of changes, we know not
    of spaces,
The Heavens seem as near as our own
    mother's face is,
And we think we could touch all the stars
    that we see;
And the milk of our mother is white on
    our mouth;
And, with small childish hands, we are
    turning around
The apple of Life which another has found;
It is warm with our touch, not with sun of
    the south,   10
And we count, as we turn it, the red side
    for four.
    O Life, O Beyond,
    Thou art sweet, thou art strange ever-
    more !

II

Then all things look strange in the pure
    golden æther;
We walk through the gardens with hands
    linked together,
    And the lilies look large as the trees;
And, as loud as the birds, sing the bloom-
    loving bees,
And the birds sing like angels, so mystical-
    fine,
And the cedars are brushing the arch-
    angels' feet,
And time is eternity, love is divine,   20
    And the world is complete.
Now, God bless the child, — father, mother,
    respond !
    O Life, O Beyond,
    Thou art strange, thou art sweet.

III

Then we leap on the earth with the armor
    of youth,
    And the earth rings again;
And' we breathe out 'O Beauty !' we
    cry out 'O truth !'
And the bloom of our lips drops with
    wine,
And our blood runs amazed 'neath the
    calm hyaline;
The earth cleaves to the foot, the sun
    burns to the brain, —   30
What is this exultation? and what this
    despair ? —
The strong pleasure is smiting the nerves
    into pain,
And we drop from the Fair as we climb to
    the Fair,
    And we lie in a trance at its feet;
And the breath of an angel cold-piercing
    the air
    Breathes fresh on our faces in swoon,
And we think him so near he is this side
    the sun,
And we wake to a whisper self-murmured
    and fond,
    O Life, O Beyond,
    Thou art strange, thou art sweet !   40

IV

And the winds and the waters in pastoral
    measures
Go winding around us, with roll upon roll,
Till the soul lies within in a circle of plea-
    sures
    Which hideth the soul:

And we run with the stag, and we leap
    with the horse,
And we swim with the fish through the
    broad watercourse,
And we strike with the falcon, and hunt
    with the hound,
And the joy which is in us flies out by a
    wound.
And we shout so aloud, ' We exult, we re-
    joice,'
That we lose the low moan of our brothers
    around: 50
And we shout so adeep down creation's
    profound,
    We are deaf to God's voice.
And we bind the rose-garland on forehead
    and ears
    Yet we are not ashamed,
And the dew of the roses that runneth un-
    blamed
    Down our cheeks, is not taken for tears.
Help us, God ! trust us, man ! love us, wo-
    man ! 'I hold
Thy small head in my hands, — with its
    grapelets of gold
Growing bright through my fingers, — like
    altar for oath,
'Neath the vast golden spaces like witness-
    ing faces   60
That watch the eternity strong in the
    troth —
    I love thee, I leave thee,
    Live for thee, die for thee !
    I prove thee, deceive thee,
    Undo evermore thee !
Help me, God ! slay me, man ! — one is
    mourning for both.'
And we stand up though young near the
    funeral-sheet
Which covers old Cæsar and old Phara-
    mond,
And death is so nigh us, life cools from its
    heat.
    O Life, O Beyond,   70
    Art thou fair, *art* thou sweet ?

V

Then we act to a purpose, we spring up
    erect :
We will tame the wild mouths of the wil-
    derness-steeds,
We will plough up the deep in the ships
    double-decked,
We will build the great cities, and do the
    great deeds,

Strike the steel upon steel, strike the soul
    upon soul,
Strike the dole on the weal, overcoming
    the dole.
Let the cloud meet the cloud in a grand
    thunder-roll !
' While the eagle of Thought rides the
    tempest in scorn,
Who cares if the lightning is burning the
    corn ?   80
    Let us sit on the thrones
      In a purple sublimity,
    And grind down men's bones
      To a pale unanimity.
Speed me, God ! serve me, man ! I am
    god over men;
When I speak in my cloud, none shall an-
    swer again;
    'Neath the stripe and the bond,
      Lie and mourn at my feet ! '
    O Life, O Beyond,
      Thou art strange, thou art sweet !

VI

Then we grow into thought, and with in-
    ward ascensions   91
    Touch the bounds of our Being.
We lie in the dark here, swathed doubly
    around
With our sensual relations and social con-
    ventions,
Yet are 'ware of a sight, yet are 'ware of
    a sound
    Beyond Hearing and Seeing, —
Are aware that a Hades rolls deep on all
    sides
    With its infinite tides
About and above us, — until the strong
    arch
Of our life creaks and bends as if ready
    for falling,   100
And through the dim rolling we hear the
    sweet calling
Of spirits that speak in a soft under-
    tongue
    The sense of the mystical march:
And we cry to them softly, 'Come nearer,
    come nearer,
And lift up the lap of this dark, and speak
    clearer,
    And teach us the song that ye sung ! '
And we smile in our thought as they an-
    swer or no,
For to dream of a sweetness is sweet as to
    know.

Wonders breathe in our face
    And we ask not their name;   110
    Love takes all the blame
Of the world's prison-place;
And we sing back the songs as we guess
    them, aloud,
And we send up the lark of our music that
    cuts
Untired through the cloud
To beat with its wings at the lattice Hea-
    ven shuts;
Yet the angels look down and the mortals
    look up
    As the little wings beat,
And the poet is blessed with their pity or
    hope.
'Twixt the heavens and the earth *can* a
    poet despond ?   120
    O Life, O Beyond,
    Thou art strange, thou art sweet !

VII

Then we wring from our souls their appli-
    cative strength,
And bend to the cord the strong bow of
    our ken,
And bringing our lives to the level of
    others,
Hold the cup we have filled, to their uses
    at length.
' Help me, God ! love me, man ! I am
    man among men,
    And my life is a pledge
    Of the ease of another's ! '
From the fire and the water we drive out
    the steam   130
With a rush and a roar and the speed of a
    dream;
And the car without horses, the car with-
    out wings,
    Roars onward and flies
    On its gray iron edge
'Neath the heat of a Thought sitting still in
    our eyes:
And our hand knots in air, with the bridge
    that it flings,
Two peaks far disrupted by ocean and
    skies,
And, lifting a fold of the smooth-flowing
    Thames,
Draws under the world with its turmoils
    and pothers,
While the swans float on softly, untouched
    in their calms   140

By humanity's hum at the root of the
    springs.
And with reachings of Thought we reach
    down to the deeps
    Of the souls of our brothers,
We teach them full words with our slow-
    moving lips,
'God,' 'Liberty,' 'Truth,' — which they
    hearken and think
And work into harmony, link upon link,
Till the silver meets round the earth gelid
    and dense,
Shedding sparks of electric responding in-
    tense
    On the dark of eclipse.
Then we hear through the silence and glory
    afar,   150
    As from shores of a star
In aphelion, the new generations that cry
Disenthralled by our voice to harmonious
    reply,
    'God,' 'Liberty,' 'Truth!'
    We are glorious forsooth,
    And our name has a seat,
Though the shroud should be donned.
    O Life, O Beyond,
Thou art strange, thou art sweet!

VIII

Help me, God! help me, man! I am low,
    I am weak: 160
Death loosens my sinews and creeps in my
    veins;
My body is cleft by these wedges of pains
    From my spirit's serene,
And I feel the externe and insensate creep
    in
    On my organized clay;
    I sob not, nor shriek,
    Yet I faint fast away:
I am strong in the spirit, —deep-thoughted,
    clear-eyed, —
I could walk, step for step, with an angel
    beside,
    On the heaven-heights of truth.   170
    Oh, the soul keeps its youth
But the body faints sore, it is tried in the
    race,
It sinks from the chariot ere reaching the
    goal,
    It is weak, it is cold,
    The rein drops from its hold,
    It sinks back, with the death in its face.
    On, chariot! on, soul!
    Ye are all the more fleet —

    Be alone at the goal
    Of the strange and the sweet!   180

IX

Love us, God! love us, man! we believe,
    we achieve:
    Let us love, let us live,
    For the acts correspond;
    We are glorious, and DIE:
And again on the knee of a mild Mystery
    That smiles with a change,
    Here we lie.
    O DEATH, O BEYOND,
    Thou art sweet, thou art strange!

L. E. L.'S LAST QUESTION

'Do you think of me as I think of you?'
        (From her poem written during
        the voyage to the Cape.)

First printed in the *Athenæum*, January 26,
1839.

I

'Do you think of me as I think of you,
My friends, my friends?'— She said it
    from the sea,
The English minstrel in her minstrelsy,
While, under brighter skies than erst she
    knew,
Her heart grew dark, and groped there as
    the blind
To reach across the waves friends left be-
    hind —
'Do you think of me as I think of you?'

II

It seemed not much to ask — 'as *I* of
    you?'
We all do ask the same; no eyelids cover
Within the meekest eyes that question
    over:
And little in the world the Loving do
But sit (among the rocks?) and listen for
The echo of their own love evermore —
'Do you think of me as I think of you?'

III

Love-learnèd she had sung of love and
    love, —
And like a child that, sleeping with dropt
    head
Upon the fairy-book he lately read,

Whatever household noises round him
 move,
Hears in his dream some elfin turbu-
 lence, —
Even so suggestive to her inward sense,
All sounds of life assumed one tune of
 love.

IV

And when the glory of her dream with-
 drew,
When knightly gestes and courtly pagean-
 tries
Were broken in her visionary eyes
By tears the solemn seas attested true, —
Forgetting that sweet lute beside her hand,
She asked not, — 'Do you praise me, O
 my land ?'
But, — 'Think ye of me, friends, as I of
 you ?'

V

Hers was the hand that played for many a
 year
Love's silver phrase for England, smooth
 and well.
Would God her heart's more inward oracle
In that lone moment might confirm her
 dear !
For when her questioned friends in agony
Made passionate response, 'We think of
 thee,'
Her place was in the dust, too deep to
 hear.

VI

Could she not wait to catch their answering
 breath ?
Was she content, content with ocean's
 sound
Which dashed its mocking infinite around
One thirsty for a little love ? — beneath
Those stars content, where last her song
 had gone, —
They mute and cold in radiant life, as
 soon
Their singer was to be, in darksome
 death ?

VII

Bring your vain answers — cry, 'We think
 of thee !'
How think ye of her ? warm in long ago
Delights ? or crowned with budding bays ?
 Not so.

None smile and none are crowned where
 lieth she,
With all her visions unfulfilled save one,
Her childhood's, of the palm-trees in the
 sun —
And lo ! their shadow on her sepulchre !

VIII

'Do ye think of me as I think of you ?'—
O friends, O kindred, O dear brotherhood
Of all the world ! what are we that we
 should
For covenants of long affection sue ?
Why press so near each other when the
 touch
Is barred by graves ?   Not much, and yet
 too much
Is this ' Think of me as I think of you.'

IX

But while on mortal lips I shape anew
A sigh to mortal issues, verily
Above the unshaken stars that see us
 die,
A vocal pathos rolls; and HE who drew
All life from dust, and for all tasted death,
By death and life and love appealing, saith
Do you think of me as I think of you ?

THE HOUSE OF CLOUDS

First printed in the *Athenæum* August 21,
1841. On August 31, 1843, Miss Barrett
wrote to R. H. Horne : 'Mr. Boyd told me
that he had read my papers on the Greek
fathers with the more satisfaction because he
had inferred from my ' House of Clouds ' that
illness had *impaired my faculties.*' But to Mr.
Boyd himself she wrote at about the same
time with her usual invincible good humor
and sweet independence : 'With regard to the
' House of Clouds,' I disagree both with you
and Miss Mitford, thinking it, comparatively
with my other poems, neither so bad nor so
good as you two account it.' And, in this in-
stance at least, her own judgment was certainly
sound.

I

I WOULD build a cloudy House
 For my thoughts to live in,
When for earth too fancy-loose,
 And too low for heaven:
Hush ! I talk my dream aloud,
 I build it bright to see, —

I build it on the moonlit cloud
　To which I looked with *thee*.

II

Cloud-walls of the morning's gray,
　Faced with amber column,
Crowned with crimson cupola
　From a sunset solemn:
May-mists, for the casements, fetch,
　Pale and glimmering,
With a sunbeam hid in each
　And a smell of spring.

III

Build the entrance high and proud,
　Darkening and then brightening,
Of a riven thunder-cloud,
　Veinèd by the lightning:
Use one with an iris-stain
　For the door so thin,
Turning to a sound like rain
　As I enter in.

IV

Build a spacious hall thereby
　Boldly, never fearing;
Use the blue place of the sky
　Which the wind is clearing:
Branched with corridors sublime,
　Flecked with winding stairs,
Such as children wish to climb
　Following their own prayers.

V

In the mutest of the house
　I will have my chamber;
Silence at the door shall use
　Evening's light of amber,
Solemnizing every mood,
　Softening in degree,
Turning sadness into good
　As I turn the key.

VI

Be my chamber tapestried
　With the showers of summer,
Close, but soundless, glorified
　When the sunbeams come here —
Wandering harpers, harping on
　Waters stringed for such,
Drawing color, for a tune,
　With a vibrant touch.

VII

Bring a shadow green and still
　From the chestnut-forest,

Bring a purple from the hill,
　When the heat is sorest;
Spread them out from wall to wall,
　Carpet-wove around,
Whereupon the foot shall fall
　In light instead of sound.

VIII

Bring fantastic cloudlets home
　From the noontide zenith,
Ranged for sculptures round the room,
　Named as Fancy weeneth;
Some be Junos, without eyes,
　Naiads, without sources,
Some be birds of paradise,
　Some, Olympian horses.

IX

Bring the dews the birds shake off
　Waking in the hedges, —
Those too perfumed, for a proof,
　From the lilies' edges:
From our England's field and moor,
　Bring them calm and white in,
Whence to form a mirror pure
　For Love's self-delighting.

X

Bring a gray cloud from the east
　Where the lark is singing,
(Something of the song at least
　Unlost in the bringing):
That shall be a morning-chair,
　Poet-dream may sit in
When it leans out on the air,
　Unrhymed and unwritten.

XI

Bring the red cloud from the sun,
　While he sinketh catch it;
That shall be a couch, — with one
　Sidelong star to watch it, —
Fit for poet's finest thought
　At the curfew-sounding;
Things unseen being nearer brought
　Than the seen, around him.

XII

Poet's thought, — not poet's sigh.
　'Las, they come together!
Cloudy walls divide and fly
　As in April weather.
Cupola and column proud,
　Structure bright to see,

Gone ! except that moonlit cloud
    To which I looked with *thee*.

XIII

Let them ! Wipe such visionings
    From the fancy's cartel:
Love secures some fairer things,
    Dowered with his immortal.
The sun may darken, heaven be bowed,
    But still unchanged shall be, —
Here, in my soul, — that moonlit cloud
    To which I looked with THEE !

CATARINA TO CAMOENS

(DYING IN HIS ABSENCE ABROAD, AND
REFERRING TO THE POEM IN WHICH
HE RECORDED THE SWEETNESS OF
HER EYES)

I

ON the door you will not enter,
    I have gazed too long: adieu !
Hope withdraws her peradventure;
    Death is near me, — and not *you*.
      Come, O lover,
      Close and cover
These poor eyes, you called, I ween,
'Sweetest eyes were ever seen !'

II

When I heard you sing that burden
    In my vernal days and bowers,
Other praises disregarding,
    I but hearkened that of yours —
      Only saying
      In heart-playing,
'Blessed eyes mine eyes have been,
If the sweetest HIS have seen !'

III

But all changes. At this vesper,
    Cold the sun shines down the door.
If you stood there, would you whisper
    'Love, I love you,' as before, —
      Death pervading
      Now, and shading
Eyes you sang of, that yestreen,
As the sweetest ever seen ?

IV

Yes. I think, were you beside them,
    Near the bed I die upon,

Though their beauty you denied them,
    As you stood there, looking down,
      You would truly
      Call them duly,
For the love's sake found therein,
'Sweetest eyes were ever seen.'

V

And if *you* looked down upon them,
    And if *they* looked up to *you*,
All the light which has forgone them
    Would be gathered back anew:
      They would truly
      Be as duly
Love-transformed to beauty's sheen,
'Sweetest eyes were ever seen.'

VI

But, ah me ! you only see me,
    In your thoughts of loving man,
Smiling soft perhaps and dreamy
    Through the wavings of my fan;
      And unweeting
      Go repeating,
In your reverie serene,
'Sweetest eyes were ever seen —'

VII

While my spirit leans and reaches
    From my body still and pale,
Fain to hear what tender speech is
    In your love to help my bale.
      O my poet,
      Come and show it !
Come, latest love, to glean
Sweetest eyes were ever seen.'

VIII

O my poet, O my prophet,
    When you praised their sweetness so,
Did you think, in singing of it,
    That it might be near to go ?
      Had you fancies
      From their glances,
That the grave would quickly screen
'Sweetest eyes were ever seen' ?

IX

No reply. The fountain's warble
    In the courtyard sounds alone.
As the water to the marble
    So my heart falls with a moan
      From love-sighing
      To this dying.

Death forerunneth Love to win
'Sweetest eyes were ever seen.'

X

Will you come ?   When I 'm departed
 Where all sweetnesses are hid,
Where thy voice, my tender-hearted,
 Will not lift up either lid.
  Cry, O lover,
  Love is over !
Cry, beneath the cypress green,
'Sweetest eyes were ever seen !'

XI

When the angelus is ringing,
 Near the convent will you walk,
And recall the choral singing
 Which brought angels down our talk?
  Spirit-shriven
  I viewed Heaven,
Till you smiled — 'Is earth unclean,
Sweetest eyes were ever seen ?'

XII

When beneath the palace-lattice
 You ride slow as you have done,
And you see a face there that is
 Not the old familiar one, —
  Will you oftly
  Murmur softly,
'Here ye watched me morn and e'en,
Sweetest eyes were ever seen !'

XIII

When the palace-ladies, sitting
 Round your gittern, shall have said,
'Poet, sing those verses written
 For the lady who is dead,'
  Will you tremble
  Yet dissemble, —
Or sing hoarse, with tears between,
'Sweetest eyes were ever seen ?'

XIV

'Sweetest eyes !' how sweet in flowings
 The repeated cadence is !
Though you sang a hundred poems,
 Still the best one would be this.
  I can hear it
  'Twixt my spirit
And the earth-noise intervene —
'Sweetest eyes were ever seen !'

XV

But the priest waits for the praying,
 And the choir are on their knees,

And the soul must pass away in
 Strains more solemn-high than these
  Miserere
 For the weary !
Oh, no longer for Catrine
'Sweetest eyes were ever seen !'

XVI

Keep my riband, take and keep it,
 (I have loosed it from my hair)
Feeling, while you overweep it,
 Not alone in your despair,
  Since with saintly
  Watch unfaintly
Out of heaven shall o'er you lean
'Sweetest eyes were ever seen.'

XVII

But — but *now* — yet unremovèd
 Up to heaven, they glisten fast;
You may cast away, Belovèd,
 In your future all my past:
  Such old phrases
  May be praises
For some fairer bosom-queen —
'Sweetest eyes were ever seen !'

XVIII

Eyes of mine, what are ye doing ?
 Faithless, faithless, — praised amiss
If a tear be of your showing,
 Dropt for any hope of HIS !
  Death has boldness
  Besides coldness,
If unworthy tears demean
'Sweetest eyes were ever seen.'

XIX

I will look out to his future;
 I will bless it till it shine.
Should he ever be a suitor
 Unto sweeter eyes than mine,
  Sunshine gild them,
  Angels shield them,
Whatsoever eyes terrene
Be the sweetest HIS have seen !

A PORTRAIT

'One name is Elizabeth.' — *Ben Jonson.*

I WILL paint her as I see her.
 Ten times have the lilies blown
Since she looked upon the sun.

And her face is lily-clear,
  Lily-shaped, and dropped in duty
  To the law of its own beauty.

Oval cheeks encolored faintly,
  Which a trail of golden hair
  Keeps from fading off to air:

And a forehead fair and saintly,
  Which two blue eyes undershine,
  Like meek prayers before a shrine.

Face and figure of a child, —
  Though too calm, you think, and tender,
  For the childhood you would lend her.

Yet child-simple, undefiled,
  Frank, obedient, waiting still
  On the turnings of your will.

Moving light, as all young things,
  As young birds, or early wheat
  When the wind blows over it.

Only, free from flutterings
  Of loud mirth that scorneth measure —
  Taking love for her chief pleasure.

Choosing pleasures, for the rest,
  Which come softly — just as she,
  When she nestles at your knee.

Quiet talk she liketh best,
  In a bower of gentle looks, —
  Watering flowers, or reading books.

And her voice, it murmurs lowly,
  As a silver stream may run,
  Which yet feels (you feel) the sun.

And her smile it seems half holy,
  As if drawn from thoughts more far
  Than our common jestings are.

And if any poet knew her,
  He would sing of her with falls
  Used in lovely madrigals.

And if any painter drew her,
  He would paint her unaware
  With a halo round the hair.

And if reader read the poem,
  He would whisper 'You have done a
  Consecrated little Una.'

And a dreamer (did you show him
  That same picture) would exclaim,
  ' 'T is my angel, with a name!'

And a stranger, when he sees her
  In the street even, smileth stilly,
  Just as you would at a lily.

And all voices that address her,
  Soften, sleeken every word,
  As if speaking to a bird.

And all fancies yearn to cover
  The hard earth, whereon she passes,
  With the thymy-scented grasses.

And all hearts do pray 'God love her!
  Ay and always, in good sooth,
  We may all be sure HE DOTH.

SLEEPING AND WATCHING

I

SLEEP on, baby, on the floor,
  Tired of all the playing:
Sleep with smile the sweeter for
  That, you dropped away in.
On your curls' full roundness stand
  Golden lights serenely;
One cheek, pushed out by the hand
  Folds the dimple inly:
Little head and little foot
  Heavy laid for pleasure,
Underneath the lids half shut
  Slants the shining azure.
Open-soul in noonday sun,
  So you lie and slumber:
Nothing evil having done,
  Nothing can encumber.

II

I, who cannot sleep as well,
  Shall I sigh to view you?
Or sigh further to foretell
  All that may undo you?
Nay, keep smiling, little child,
  Ere the sorrow neareth:
I will smile too! patience mild
  Pleasure's token weareth.
Nay, keep sleeping before loss:
  I shall sleep though losing!
As by cradle, so by cross,
  Sure is the reposing.

III

And God knows who sees us twain,
    Child at childish leisure,
I am near as tired of pain
    As you seem of pleasure.
Very soon too, by his grace
    Gently wrapt around me,
Shall I show as calm a face,
    Shall I sleep as soundly.
Differing in this, that you
    Clasp your playthings, sleeping,
While my hand shall drop the few
    Given to my keeping:
Differing in this, that I
    Sleeping shall be colder,
And in waking presently,
    Brighter to beholder:
Differing in this beside —
    (Sleeper, have you heard me ?
Do you move, and open wide
    Eyes of wonder toward me ?) —
That while you I thus recall
    From your sleep, I solely,
Me from mine an angel shall,
    With reveille holy.

WINE OF CYPRUS

GIVEN TO ME BY H. S. BOYD, AUTHOR
OF 'SELECT PASSAGES FROM THE
GREEK FATHERS,' ETC.

TO WHOM THESE STANZAS ARE ADDRESSED

I

IF old Bacchus were the speaker,
    He would tell you with a sigh
Of the Cyprus in this beaker
    I am sipping like a fly, —
Like a fly or gnat on Ida
    At the hour of goblet-pledge,
By queen Juno brushed aside, a
    Full white arm-sweep, from the edge.

II

Sooth, the drinking should be ampler
    When the drink is so divine,
And some deep-mouthed Greek exemplar
    Would become your Cyprus wine:
Cyclops' mouth might plunge aright in,
    While his one eye overleered,
Nor too large were mouth of Titan
    Drinking rivers down his beard.

III

Pan might dip his head so deep in,
    That his ears alone pricked out,
Fauns around him pressing, leaping,
    Each one pointing to his throat:
While the Naiads, like Bacchantes,
    Wild, with urns thrown out to waste,
Cry, 'O earth, that thou wouldst grant us
    Springs to keep, of such a taste !'

IV

But for me, I am not worthy
    After gods and Greeks to drink,
And my lips are pale and earthy
    To go bathing from this brink:
Since you heard them speak the last time,
    They have faded from their blooms,
And the laughter of my pastime
    Has learnt silence at the tombs.

V

Ah, my friend ! the antique drinkers
    Crowned the cup and crowned the brow.
Can I answer the old thinkers
    In the forms they thought of, now ?
Who will fetch from garden-closes
    Some new garlands while I speak,
That the forehead, crowned with roses,
    May strike scarlet down the cheek ?

VI

Do not mock me ! with my mortal
    Suits no wreath again, indeed;
I am sad-voiced as the turtle
    Which Anacreon used to feed:
Yet as that same bird demurely
    Wet her beak in cup of his,
So, without a garland, surely
    I may touch the brim of this.

VII

Go, — let others praise the Chian !
    This is soft as Muses' string,
This is tawny as Rhea's lion,
    This is rapid as his spring,
Bright as Paphia's eyes e'er met us,
    Light as ever trod her feet;
And the brown bees of Hymettus
    Make their honey not so sweet.

VIII

Very copious are my praises,
    Though I sip it like a fly !
Ah — but, sipping, — times and places

Change before me suddenly:
As Ulysses' old libation
  Drew the ghosts from every part,
So your Cyprus wine, dear Grecian,
  Stirs the Hades of my heart.

IX

And I think of those long mornings
  Which my thought goes far to seek,
When, betwixt the folio's turnings,
  Solemn flowed the rhythmic Greek:
Past the pane the mountain spreading,
  Swept the sheep's-bell's tinkling noise,
While a girlish voice was reading,
  Somewhat low for *ai*'s and *oi*'s.

X

Then, what golden hours were for us !
  While we sat together there,
How the white vests of the chorus
  Seemed to wave up a live air !
How the cothurns trod majestic
  Down the deep iambic lines,
And the rolling anapæstic
  Curled like vapor over shrines !

XI

Oh, our Æschylus, the thunderous,
  How he drove the bolted breath
Through the cloud, to wedge it ponderous
  In the gnarlèd oak beneath !
Oh, our Sophocles, the royal,
  Who was born to monarch's place,
And who made the whole world loyal
  Less by kingly power than grace !

XII

Our Euripides, the human,
  With his droppings of warm tears,
And his touches of things common
  Till they rose to touch the spheres !
Our Theocritus, our Bion,
  And our Pindar's shining goals ! —
These were cup-bearers undying
  Of the wine that 's meant for souls.

XIII

And my Plato, the divine one,
  If men know the gods aright
By their motions as they shine on
  With a glorious trail of light !
And your noble Christian bishops,
  Who mouthed grandly the last Greek !
Though the sponges on their hyssops
  Were distent with wine — too weak.

XIV

Yet, your Chrysostom, you praised him
  As a liberal mouth of gold;
And your Basil, you upraised him
  To the height of speakers old:
And we both praised Heliodorus
  For his secret of pure lies, —
Who forged first his linked stories
  In the heat of ladies' eyes.

XV

And we both praised your Synesius
  For the fire shot up his odes,
Though the Church was scarce propitious
  As he whistled dogs and gods.
And we both praised Nazianzen
  For the fervid heart and speech:
Only I eschewed his glancing
  At the lyre hung out of reach.

XVI

Do you mind that deed of Atè
  Which you bound me to so fast, —
Reading ' De Virginitate,'
  From the first line to the last ?
How I said at ending, solemn
  As I turned and looked at you,
That Saint Simeon on the column
  Had had somewhat less to do ?

XVII

For we sometimes gently wrangled,
  Very gently, be it said,
Since our thoughts were disentangled
  By no breaking of the thread !
And I charged you with extortions
  On the nobler fames of old —
Ay, and sometimes thought your Porsons
  Stained the purple they would fold.

XVIII

For the rest — a mystic moaning
  Kept Cassandra at the gate,
With wild eyes the vision shone in,
  And wide nostrils scenting fate.
And Prometheus, bound in passion
  By brute Force to the blind stone,
Showed us looks of invocation
  Turned to ocean and the sun.

XIX

And Medea we saw burning
  At her nature's planted stake:
And proud Œdipus fate-scorning

While the cloud came on to break —
While the cloud came on slow, slower,
    Till he stood discrowned, resigned ! —
But the reader's voice dropped lower
    When the poet called him BLIND.

XX

Ah, my gossip ! you were older,
    And more learnèd, and a man !
Yet that shadow, the enfolder
    Of your quiet eyelids, ran
Both our spirits to one level;
    And I turned from hill and lea
And the summer-sun's green revel,
    To your eyes that could not see.

XXI

Now Christ bless you with the one light
    Which goes shining night and day !
May the flowers which grow in sunlight
    Shed their fragrance in your way !
Is it not right to remember
    All your kindness, friend of mine,
When we two sat in the chamber,
    And the poets poured us wine ?

XXII

So, to come back to the drinking
    Of this Cyprus, — it is well,
But those memories, to my thinking,
    Make a better œnomel;
And whoever be the speaker,
    None can murmur with a sigh
That, in drinking from *that* beaker,
    I am sipping like a fly.

THE ROMANCE OF THE SWAN'S NEST

'So the dreams depart,
So the fading phantoms flee,
And the sharp reality
Now must act its part.'
    WESTWOOD'S *Beads from a Rosary.*

I

LITTLE Ellie sits alone
    'Mid the beeches of a meadow,
    By a stream-side on the grass,
And the trees are showering down
    Doubles of their leaves in shadow
    On her shining hair and face.

II

She has thrown her bonnet by,
    And her feet she has been dipping
In the shallow water's flow:
Now she holds them nakedly
    In her hands, all sleek and dripping,
    While she rocketh to and fro.

III

Little Ellie sits alone,
    And the smile she softly uses
    Fills the silence like a speech,
While she thinks what shall be done,
    And the sweetest pleasure chooses
    For her future within reach.

IV

Little Ellie in her smile
    Chooses — 'I will have a lover
    Riding on a steed of steeds:
He shall love me without guile,
    And to *him* I will discover
    The swan's nest among the reeds.

V

' And the steed shall be red-roan,
    And the lover shall be noble,
    With an eye that takes the breath:
And the lute he plays upon
    Shall strike ladies into trouble,
    As his sword strikes men to death.

VI

' And the steed it shall be shod
    All in silver, housed in azure,
    And the mane shall swim the wind;
And the hoofs along the sod
    Shall flash onward and keep measure,
    Till the shepherds look behind.

VII

' But my lover will not prize
    All the glory that he rides in,
    When he gazes in my face:
He will say, " O Love, thine eyes
    Build the shrine my soul abides in,
    And I kneel here for thy grace ! "

VIII

' Then, ay, then he shall kneel low,
    With the red-roan steed anear him
    Which shall seem to understand,
Till I answer, " Rise and go !
    For the world must love and fear him
    Whom I gift with heart and hand."

IX

'Then he will arise so pale,
  I shall feel my own lips tremble
  With a *yes* I must not say,
Nathless maiden-brave, "Farewell,"
  I will utter, and dissemble —
  "Light to-morrow with to-day !"

X

'Then he 'll ride among the hills
  To the wide world past the river,
  There to put away all wrong;
To make straight distorted wills,
  And to empty the broad quiver
  Which the wicked bear along.

XI

'Three times shall a young foot-page
  Swim the stream and climb the mountain
  And kneel down beside my feet —
"Lo, my master sends this gage,
  Lady, for thy pity's counting !
  What wilt thou exchange for it ?"

XII

'And the first time I will send
  A white rosebud for a guerdon,
  And the second time, a glove;
But the third time — I may bend
  From my pride, and answer — "Pardon
  If he comes to take my love."

XIII

'Then the young foot-page will run,
  Then my lover will ride faster,
  Till he kneeleth at my knee:
"I am a duke's eldest son,
  Thousand serfs do call me master,
  But, O Love, I love but *thee !*"

XIV

'He will kiss me on the mouth
  Then, and lead me as a lover
    Through the crowds that praise his deeds;
And, when soul-tied by one troth,
  Unto *him* I will discover
    That swan's nest among the reeds.'

XV

Little Ellie, with her smile
  Not yet ended, rose up gaily,
  Tied the bonnet, donned the shoe,

And went homeward, round a mile,
  Just to see, as she did daily,
  What more eggs were with the two.

XVI

Pushing through the elm-tree copse,
  Winding up the stream, light-hearted,
  Where the osier pathway leads,
Past the boughs she stoops — and stops.
  Lo, the wild swan had deserted,
  And a rat had gnawed the reeds !

XVII

Ellie went home sad and slow.
  If she found the lover ever,
  With his red-roan steed of steeds,
Sooth I know not; but I know
  She could never show him — never,
  That swan's nest among the reeds !

LESSONS FROM THE GORSE

> 'To win the secret of a weed's plain heart.'
>   — *Lowell.*

First printed in the *Athenæum*, October 23, 1841.

I

MOUNTAIN gorses, ever-golden,
  Cankered not the whole year long !
  Do ye teach us to be strong,
Howsoever pricked and holden
  Like your thorny blooms, and so
  Trodden on by rain and snow,
Up the hill-side of this life, as bleak as
  where ye grow ?

II

Mountain blossoms, shining blossoms,
  Do ye teach us to be glad
  When no summer can be had,
Blooming in our inward bosoms ?
  Ye, whom God preserveth still,
  Set as lights upon a hill,
Tokens to the wintry earth that Beauty
  liveth still !

III

Mountain gorses, do ye teach us
  From that academic chair
  Canopied with azure air,
That the wisest word man reaches
  Is the humblest he can speak ?

Ye, who live on mountain peak,
Yet live low along the ground, beside the
    grasses meek !

IV

Mountain gorses, since Linnæus
Knelt beside you on the sod,
For your beauty thanking God, —
For your teaching, ye should see us
    Bowing in prostration new !
Whence arisen, — if one or two
Drops be on our cheeks — O world, they
    are not tears but dew.

THE DEAD PAN

When publishing this poem, the author ac-
companied it with the following note : —
'Excited by Schiller's *Götter Griechenlands*,
and partly founded on a well-known tradition
mentioned in a treatise of Plutarch (*De Orac-
ulorum Defectu*), according to which, at the
hour of the Saviour's agony, a cry of "Great
Pan is dead!" swept across the waves in the
hearing of certain mariners, — and the oracles
ceased.
'It is in all veneration to the memory of
the deathless Schiller that I oppose a doc-
trine still more dishonoring to poetry than to
Christianity.
'As Mr. Kenyon's graceful and harmonious
paraphrase of the German poem was the first
occasion of the turning of my thoughts in
this direction, I take advantage of the pre-
tence to indulge my feelings (which overflow
on other grounds) by inscribing my lyric to
that dear friend and relative, with the earnest-
ness of appreciating esteem as well as of affec-
tionate gratitude.'
Many passages in Mrs. Browning's corre-
spondence (see *Notes* and *Illustrations* at the
end of this volume) testify to the importance
which she herself attached to 'The Dead Pan,'
— a poem which shows her at her best and
at her worst, exhibiting in an equally striking
manner her besetting faults of style and the
virile strength and splendor of her imagina-
tion. It seems to have been as a distinct and
solemn public profession of Christian faith
triumphant over pagan fancy that she insisted
on having it stand last in the collection of her
poems published in 1844.

I

Gods of Hellas, gods of Hellas,
Can ye listen in your silence ?
Can your mystic voices tell us

Where ye hide ?   In floating islands,
With a wind that evermore
Keeps you out of sight of shore ?
        Pan, Pan is dead.

II

In what revels are ye sunken
In old Æthiopia ?
Have the Pygmies made you drunken,
Bathing in mandragora
Your divine pale lips that shiver
Like the lotus in the river ?
        Pan, Pan is dead.

III

Do ye sit there still in slumber,
In gigantic Alpine rows ?
The black poppies out of number
Nodding, dripping from your brows
To the red lees of your wine,
And so kept alive and fine ?
        Pan, Pan is dead.

IV

Or lie crushed your stagnant corses
Where the silver spheres roll on,
Stung to life by centric forces
Thrown like rays out from the sun ? —
While the smoke of your old altars
Is the shroud that round you welters ?
        Great Pan is dead.

V

'Gods of Hellas, gods of Hellas'
Said the old Hellenic tongue, —
Said the hero-oaths, as well as
Poets' songs the sweetest sung:
Have ye grown deaf in a day ?
Can ye speak not yea or nay,
        Since Pan is dead ?

VI

Do ye leave your rivers flowing
All alone, O Naiades,
While your drenchèd locks dry slow in
This cold feeble sun and breeze ?
Not a word the Naiads say,
Though the rivers run for aye;
        For Pan is dead.

VII

From the gloaming of the oak-wood,
O ye Dryads, could ye flee ?
At the rushing thunderstroke, would
No sob tremble through the tree ?

Not a word the Dryads say,
Though the forests wave for aye;
    For Pan is dead.

VIII

Have ye left the mountain places,
Oreads wild, for other tryst?
Shall we see no sudden faces
Strike a glory through the mist?
Not a sound the silence thrills
Of the everlasting hills:
    Pan, Pan is dead.

IX

O twelve gods of Plato's vision,
Crowned to starry wanderings,
With your chariots in procession
And your silver clash of wings!
Very pale ye seem to rise,
Ghosts of Grecian deities,
    Now Pan is dead!

X

Jove, that right hand is unloaded
Whence the thunder did prevail,
While in idiocy of godhead
Thou art staring the stars pale!
And thine eagle, blind and old,
Roughs his feathers in the cold.
    Pan, Pan is dead.

XI

Where, O Juno, is the glory
Of thy regal look and tread?
Will they lay, for evermore, thee
On thy dim, strait, golden bed?
Will thy queendom all lie hid
Meekly under either lid?
    Pan, Pan is dead.

XII

Ha, Apollo! floats his golden
Hair all mist-like where he stands,
While the Muses hang enfolding
Knee and foot with faint wild hands?
'Neath the clanging of thy bow,
Niobe looked lost as thou!
    Pan, Pan is dead.

XIII

Shall the casque with its brown iron
Pallas' broad blue eyes eclipse,
And no hero take inspiring
From the god-Greek of her lips?
'Neath her olive dost thou sit,

Mars the mighty, cursing it?
    Pan, Pan is dead.

XIV

Bacchus, Bacchus! on the panther
He swoons, bound with his own vines;
And his Mænads slowly saunter,
Head aside, among the pines,
While they murmur dreamingly
' Evohe! — ah — evohe! —
    Ah, Pan is dead!'

XV

Neptune lies beside the trident,
Dull and senseless as a stone;
And old Pluto deaf and silent
Is cast out into the sun:
Ceres smileth stern thereat,
' We *all* now are desolate —
    Now Pan is dead.'

XVI

Aphrodite! dead and driven
As thy native foam thou art;
With the cestus long done heaving
On the white calm of thine heart!
Ai Adonis! at that shriek
Not a tear runs down her cheek —
    Pan, Pan is dead.

XVII

And the Loves, we used to know from
One another, huddled lie,
Frore as taken in a snow-storm,
Close beside her tenderly;
As if each had weakly tried
Once to kiss her as he died.
    Pan, Pan is dead.

XVIII

What, and Hermes? Time enthralleth
All thy cunning, Hermes, thus,
And the ivy blindly crawleth
Round thy brave caduceus?
Hast thou no new message for us,
Full of thunder and Jove-glories?
    Nay, Pan is dead.

XIX

Crownèd Cybele's great turret
Rocks and crumbles on her head;
Roar the lions of her chariot
Toward the wilderness, unfed:
Scornful children are not mute, —
' Mother, mother, walk afoot,
    Since Pan is dead!'

XX

In the fiery-hearted centre
Of the solemn universe,
Ancient Vesta, — who could enter
To consume thee with this curse?
Drop thy gray chin on thy knee,
O thou palsied Mystery!
    For Pan is dead.

XXI

Gods, we vainly do adjure you, —
Ye return nor voice nor sign!
Not a votary could secure you
Even a grave for your Divine:
Not a grave, to show thereby
Here these gray old gods do lie.
    Pan, Pan is dead.

XXII

Even that Greece who took your wages
Calls the obolus outworn;
And the hoarse, deep-throated ages
Laugh your godships unto scorn:
And the poets do disclaim you,
Or grow colder if they name you —
    And Pan is dead.

XXIII

Gods bereavèd, gods belated,
With your purples rent asunder!
Gods discrowned and desecrated,
Disinherited of thunder!
Now, the goats may climb and crop
The soft grass on Ida's top —
    Now Pan is dead.

XXIV

Calm, of old, the bark went onward,
When a cry more loud than wind
Rose up, deepened, and swept sunward
From the pilèd Dark behind;
And the sun shrank and grew pale,
Breathed against by the great wail —
    'Pan, Pan is dead.'

XXV

And the rowers from the benches
Fell, each shuddering on his face,
While departing Influences
Struck a cold back through the place;
And the shadow of the ship
Reeled along the passive deep —
    'Pan, Pan is dead.'

XXVI

And that dismal cry rose slowly
And sank slowly through the air,
Full of spirit's melancholy
And eternity's despair!
And they heard the words it said —
PAN IS DEAD — GREAT PAN IS DEAD —
    PAN, PAN IS DEAD.

XXVII

'T was the hour when One in Sion
Hung for love's sake on a cross;
When his brow was chill with dying
And his soul was faint with loss;
When his priestly blood dropped downward
And his kingly eyes looked throneward —
    Then, Pan was dead.

XXVIII

By the love, He stood alone in,
His sole Godhead rose complete,
And the false gods fell down moaning
Each from off his golden seat;
All the false gods with a cry
Rendered up their deity —
    Pan, Pan was dead.

XXIX

Wailing wide across the islands,
They rent, vest-like, their Divine;
And a darkness and a silence
Quenched the light of every shrine;
And Dodona's oak swang lonely
Henceforth, to the tempest only:
    Pan, Pan was dead.

XXX

Pythia staggered, feeling o'er her
Her lost god's forsaking look;
Straight her eyeballs filmed with horror
And her crispy fillets shook
And her lips gasped, through their foam,
For a word that did not come.
    Pan, Pan was dead.

XXXI

O ye vain false gods of Hellas,
Ye are silent evermore!
And I dash down this old chalice
Whence libations ran of yore.
See, the wine crawls in the dust
Wormlike — as your glories must,
    Since Pan is dead.

XXXII

Get to dust, as common mortals,
By a common doom and track !
Let no Schiller from the portals
Of that Hades call you back,
Or instruct us to weep all
At your antique funeral.
          Pan, Pan is dead.

XXXIII

By your beauty, which confesses
Some chief Beauty conquering you, —
By our grand heroic guesses
Through your falsehood at the True, —
We will weep *not !* earth shall roll
Heir to each god's aureole —
          And Pan is dead.

XXXIV

Earth outgrows the mythic fancies
Sung beside her in her youth,
And those debonair romances
Sound but dull beside the truth.
Phœbus' chariot-course is run:
Look up, poets, to the sun !
          Pan, Pan is dead.

XXXV

Christ hath sent us down the angels;
And the whole earth and the skies
Are illumed by altar-candles
Lit for blessèd mysteries;
And a Priest's hand through creation
Waveth calm and consecration:
          And Pan is dead.

XXXVI

Truth is fair: should we forgo it ?
Can we sigh right for a wrong ?
God Himself is the best Poet,
And the Real is his song.
Sing his truth out fair and full,
And secure his beautiful !
          Let Pan be dead !

XXXVII

Truth is large: our aspiration
Scarce embraces half we be.
Shame, to stand in his creation
And doubt truth's sufficiency ! —
To think God's song unexcelling
The poor tales of our own telling —
          When Pan is dead !

XXXVIII

What is true and just and honest,
What is lovely, what is pure,
All of praise that hath admonisht,
All of virtue, — shall endure;
These are themes for poets' uses,
Stirring nobler than the Muses,
          Ere Pan was dead.

XXXIX

O brave poets, keep back nothing,
Nor mix falsehood with the whole !
Look up Godward; speak the truth in
Worthy song from earnest soul:
Hold, in high poetic duty,
Truest Truth the fairest Beauty !
          Pan, Pan is dead.

POEMS OF 1850

In 1850, four years after Miss Barrett's marriage to Robert Browning, a new edition of her poems appeared under the title of *Poems by Elizabeth Barrett Browning in two volumes, London, Chapman and Hall.* This edition retained the dedication to Mr. Moulton-Barrett of the edition of 1844, and contained, beside the contents of the previous volumes, translations of the *Prometheus Bound* of Æschylus and the *Lament for Adonis* of Bion, — which will be found with other translations at the end of this volume, — and the poems which follow.

The first of these poems, 'The Runaway Slave at Pilgrim's Point,' was first printed in 1848 in *The Liberty Bell*, the annual publication issued for many years and sold at the National Anti-Slavery Bazaar held in Boston. 'The Runaway Slave' was reprinted the following year as a pamphlet for the author's own use. She says of it in a letter from Pisa to Mr. Boyd, dated December 21, 1846, 'I am just sending off an anti-slavery poem for America, too ferocious, perhaps, for the Americans to publish: but they asked for a poem, and shall have it.'

THE RUNAWAY SLAVE AT PILGRIM'S POINT

I

I STAND on the mark beside the shore
  Of the first white pilgrim's bended knee,
Where exile turned to ancestor,
  And God was thanked for liberty.
I have run through the night, my skin is as
    dark,
I bend my knee down on this mark:
  I look on the sky and the sea.

II

O pilgrim-souls, I speak to you !
  I see you come proud and slow
From the land of the spirits pale as dew
  And round me and round me ye go.
O pilgrims, I have gasped and run
All night long from the whips of one
  Who in your names works sin and woe !

III

And thus I thought that I would come
  And kneel here where ye knelt before,
And feel your souls around me hum
  In undertone to the ocean's roar;
And lift my black face, my black hand,
Here, in your names, to curse this land
  Ye blessed in freedom's, evermore.

IV

I am black, I am black,
  And yet God made me, they say:
But if He did so, smiling back
  He must have cast his work away
Under the feet of his white creatures,
With a look of scorn, that the dusky fea-
    tures
  Might be trodden again to clay.

V

And yet He has made dark things
  To be glad and merry as light:
There's a little dark bird sits and sings,
  There's a dark stream ripples out of
    sight,
And the dark frogs chant in the safe
    morass,
And the sweetest stars are made to pass
  O'er the face of the darkest night.

VI

But we who are dark, we are dark !
  Ah God, we have no stars !

About our souls in care and cark
  Our blackness shuts like prison-bars:
The poor souls crouch so far behind
That never a comfort can they find
  By reaching through the prison-bars.

VII

Indeed we live beneath the sky,
  That great smooth Hand of God stretched
    out
On all his children fatherly,
  To save them from the dread and doubt
Which would be if, from this low place,
All opened straight up to his face
  Into the grand eternity.

VIII

And still God's sunshine and his frost,
  They make us hot, they make us cold,
As if we were not black and lost;
  And the beasts and birds, in wood and
    fold,
Do fear and take us for very men:
Could the whip-poor-will or the cat of the
    glen
  Look into my eyes and be bold ?

IX

I am black, I am black !
  But, once, I laughed in girlish glee,
For one of my color stood in the track
  Where the drivers drove, and looked at
    me,
And tender and full was the look he gave —
Could a slave look so at another slave ? —
  I look at the sky and the sea.

X

And from that hour our spirits grew
  As free as if unsold, unbought:
Oh, strong enough, since we were two,
  To conquer the world, we thought.
The drivers drove us day by day;
We did not mind, we went one way,
  And no better a freedom sought.

XI

In the sunny ground between the canes,
  He said ' I love you ' as he passed;
When the shingle-roof rang sharp with the
    rains,
  I heard how he vowed it fast:
While others shook he smiled in the hut,
As he carved me a bowl of the cocoa-nut
  Through the roar of the hurricanes.

XII

I sang his name instead of a song,
  Over and over I sang his name,
Upward and downward I drew it along
  My various notes, — the same, the
    same !
I sang it low, that the slave-girls near
Might never guess, from aught they could
    hear,
  It was only a name — a name.

XIII

I look on the sky and the sea.
  We were two to love and two to pray:
Yes, two, O God, who cried to Thee,
  Though nothing didst Thou say !
Coldly Thou sat'st behind the sun:
And now I cry who am but one,
  Thou wilt not speak to-day.

XIV

We were black, we were black,
  We had no claim to love and bliss,
What marvel if each went to wrack ?
  They wrung my cold hands out of his,
They dragged him — where ? I crawled
    to touch
His blood's mark in the dust . . . not
    much,
  Ye pilgrim-souls, though plain as *this* !

XV

Wrong, followed by a deeper wrong !
  Mere grief 's too good for such as I:
So the white men brought the shame ere
    long
  To strangle the sob of my agony.
They would not leave me for my dull
Wet eyes ! — it was too merciful
  To let me weep pure tears and die.

XVI

I am black, I am black !
  I wore a child upon my breast,
An amulet that hung too slack,
  And, in my unrest, could not rest:
Thus we went moaning, child and mother,
One to another, one to another,
  Until all ended for the best.

XVII

For hark ! I will tell you low, low,
  I am black, you see, —
And the babe who lay on my bosom so,
  Was far too white, too white for me;
As white as the ladies who scorned to pray
Beside me at church but yesterday,
  Though my tears had washed a place for
    my knee.

XVIII

My own, own child ! I could not bear
  To look in his face, it was so white;
I covered him up with a kerchief there,
  I covered his face in close and tight:
And he moaned and struggled, as well
    might be,
For the white child wanted his liberty —
  Ha, ha ! he wanted the master-right.

XIX

He moaned and beat with his head and
    feet,
  His little feet that never grew;
He struck them out, as it was meet,
  Against my heart to break it through:
I might have sung and made him mild,
But I dared not sing to the white-faced
    child
  The only song I know.

XX

I pulled the kerchief very close:
  He could not see the sun, I swear,
More, then, alive, than now he does
  From between the roots of the mango
    . . . where ?
I know where. Close ! A child and mo-
    ther
Do wrong to look at one another
  When one is black and one is fair.

XXI

Why, in that single glance I had
  Of my child's face, . . . I tell you all,
I saw a look that made me mad !
  The *master's* look, that used to fall
On my soul like his lash . . . or worse !
And so, to save it from my curse,
  I twisted it round in my shawl.

XXII

And he moaned and trembled from foot to
    head,
  He shivered from head to foot;
Till after a time, he lay instead
  Too suddenly still and mute.
I felt, beside, a stiffening cold:
I dared to lift up just a fold,
  As in lifting a leaf of the mango-fruit.

XXIII

But *my* fruit . . . ha, ha ! — there, had been
(I laugh to think on 't at this hour !)
Your fine white angels (who have seen
Nearest the secret of God's power)
And plucked my fruit to make them wine,
And sucked the soul of that child of mine
As the humming-bird sucks the soul of the flower.

XXIV

Ha, ha, the trick of the angels white !
They freed the white child's spirit so.
I said not a word, but day and night
I carried the body to and fro,
And it lay on my heart like a stone, as chill.
— The sun may shine out as much as he will :
I am cold, though it happened a month ago.

XXV

From the white man's house, and the black man's hut,
I carried the little body on ;
The forest's arms did round us shut,
And silence through the trees did run :
They asked no question as I went,
They stood too high for astonishment,
They could see God sit on his throne.

XXVI

My little body, kerchiefed fast,
I bore it on through the forest, on ;
And when I felt it was tired at last,
I scooped a hole beneath the moon :
Through the forest-tops the angels far,
With a white sharp finger from every star,
Did point and mock at what was done.

XXVII

Yet when it was all done aright, —
Earth, 'twixt me and my baby, strewed, —
All, changed to black earth, — nothing white, —
A dark child in the dark ! — ensued
Some comfort, and my heart grew young ;
I sate down smiling there and sung
The song I learnt in my maidenhood.

XXVIII

And thus we two were reconciled,
The white child and black mother, thus :

For as I sang it soft and wild,
The same song, more melodious,
Rose from the grave whereon I sate :
It was the dead child singing that,
To join the souls of both of us.

XXIX

I look on the sea and the sky.
Where the pilgrims' ships first anchored lay
The free sun rideth gloriously,
But the pilgrim-ghosts have slid away
Through the earliest streaks of the morn :
My face is black, but it glares with a scorn
Which they dare not meet by day.

XXX

Ha ! — in their stead, their hunter sons !
Ha, ha ! they are on me — they hunt in a ring !
Keep off ! I brave you all at once,
I throw off your eyes like snakes that sting !
You have killed the black eagle at nest, I think :
Did you ever stand still in your triumph, and shrink
From the stroke of her wounded wing ?

XXXI

(Man, drop that stone you dared to lift ! —)
I wish you who stand there five abreast,
Each, for his own wife's joy and gift,
A little corpse as safely at rest
As mine in the mangoes ! Yes, but *she*
May keep live babies on her knee,
And sing the song she likes the best.

XXXII

I am not mad : I am black.
I see you staring in my face —
I know you staring, shrinking back,
Ye are born of the Washington-race,
And this land is the free America,
And this mark on my wrist — (I prove what I say)
Ropes tied me up here to the flogging-place.

XXXIII

You think I shrieked then ? Not a sound
I hung, as a gourd hangs in the sun ;
I only cursed them all around
As softly as I might have done

My very own child: from these sands
Up to the mountains, lift your hands,
  O slaves, and end what I begun!

XXXIV

Whips, curses; these must answer those!
  For in this UNION you have set
Two kinds of men in adverse rows,
  Each loathing each; and all forget
The seven wounds in Christ's body fair,
While HE sees gaping everywhere
  Our countless wounds that pay no debt.

XXXV

Our wounds are different. Your white
    men
  Are, after all, not gods indeed,
Nor able to make Christs again
  Do good with bleeding. We who bleed
(Stand off!) we help not in our loss!
We are too heavy for our cross,
  And fall and crush you and your seed.

XXXVI

I fall, I swoon! I look at the sky.
  The clouds are breaking on my brain;
I am floated along, as if I should die
  Of liberty's exquisite pain.
In the name of the white child waiting for
    me
In the death-dark where we may kiss and
    agree,
White men, I leave you all curse-free
  In my broken heart's disdain!

HECTOR IN THE GARDEN

First printed in *Blackwood's Magazine* for
October, 1846. The colossal design in flower-
ing annuals here described was one of the adorn-
ments of the garden at Hope End.

I

NINE years old! The first of any
  Seem the happiest years that come:
  Yet when *I* was nine, I said
  No such word! I thought instead
That the Greeks had used as many
  In besieging Ilium.

II

Nine green years had scarcely brought me
  To my childhood's haunted spring;
  I had life, like flowers and bees,
In betwixt the country trees,
And the sun the pleasure taught me
  Which he teacheth every thing.

III

If the rain fell, there was sorrow:
  Little head leant on the pane,
  Little finger drawing down it
  The long trailing drops upon it,
And the 'Rain, rain, come to-morrow,'
  Said for charm against the rain.

IV

Such a charm was right Canidian,
  Though you meet it with a jeer!
  If I said it long enough,
  Then the rain hummed dimly off,
And the thrush with his pure Lydian
  Was left only to the ear;

V

And the sun and I together
  Went a-rushing out of doors:
  We our tender spirits drew
  Over hill and dale in view,
Glimmering hither, glimmering thither
  In the footsteps of the showers.

VI

Underneath the chestnuts dripping,
  Through the grasses wet and fair,
  Straight I sought my garden-ground
  With the laurel on the mound,
And the pear-tree oversweeping
  A side-shadow of green air.

VII

In the garden lay supinely
  A huge giant wrought of spade!
  Arms and legs were stretched at length
  In a passive giant strength, —
The fine meadow turf, cut finely,
  Round them laid and interlaid.

VIII

Call him Hector, son of Priam!
  Such his title and degree.
  With my rake I smoothed his brow,
  Both his cheeks I weeded through,
But a rhymer such as I am,
  Scarce can sing his dignity.

IX

Eyes of gentianellas azure,
  Staring, winking at the skies:

Nose of gillyflowers and box;
Scented grasses put for locks,
Which a little breeze at pleasure
Set a-waving round his eyes:

X

Brazen helm of daffodillies,
  With a glitter toward the light;
  Purple violets for the mouth,
  Breathing perfumes west and south;
And a sword of flashing lilies,
  Holden ready for the fight:

XI

And a breastplate made of daisies,
  Closely fitting, leaf on leaf;
  Periwinkles interlaced
  Drawn for belt about the waist;
While the brown bees, humming praises,
  Shot their arrows round the chief.

XII

And who knows (I sometimes wondered)
  If the disembodied soul
  Of old Hector, once of Troy,
  Might not take a dreary joy
Here to enter — if it thundered,
  Rolling up the thunder-roll?

XIII

Rolling this way from Troy-ruin,
  In this body rude and rife
  Just to enter, and take rest
  'Neath the daisies of the breast —
They, with tender roots, renewing
  His heroic heart to life?

XIV

Who could know? I sometimes started
  At a motion or a sound!
  Did his mouth speak — naming Troy
  With an ὀτοτοτοτοῖ?
Did the pulse of the Strong-hearted
  Make the daisies tremble round?

XV

It was hard to answer, often:
  But the birds sang in the tree,
  But the little birds sang bold
  In the pear-tree green and old,
And my terror seemed to soften
  Through the courage of their glee

XVI

Oh, the birds, the tree, the ruddy
  And white blossoms sleek with rain!
  Oh, my garden rich with pansies!
  Oh, my childhood's bright romances!
All revive, like Hector's body,
  And I see them stir again.

XVII

And despite life's changes, chances,
  And despite the deathbell's toll,
  They press on me in full seeming
  Help, some angel! stay this dream-
      ing!
As the birds sang in the branches,
  Sing God's patience through my soul!

XVIII

That no dreamer, no neglecter
  Of the present's work unsped,
  I may wake up and be doing,
  Life's heroic ends pursuing,
Though my past is dead as Hector,
  And though Hector is twice dead.

SONNETS

FLUSH OR FAUNUS

You see this dog; it was but yesterday
I mused forgetful of his presence here,
Till thought on thought drew downward
      tear on tear:
When from the pillow where wet-cheeked
      I lay,
A head as hairy as Faunus thrust its
      way
Right sudden against my face, two golden-
      clear
Great eyes astonished mine, a drooping
      ear
Did flap me on either cheek to dry the
      spray!
I started first as some Arcadian
Amazed by goatly god in twilight grove:
But as the bearded vision closelier ran
My tears off, I knew Flush, and rose above
Surprise and sadness, — thanking the true
      PAN
Who by low creatures leads to heights of
      love.

FINITE AND INFINITE

THE wind sounds only in opposing straits,
The sea, beside the shore; man's spirit
    rends
Its quiet only up against the ends
Of wants and oppositions, loves and hates,
Where, worked and worn by passionate
    debates,
And losing by the loss it apprehends,
The flesh rocks round and every breath it
    sends
Is ravelled to a sigh. All tortured states
Suppose a straitened place. Jehovah
    Lord,
Make room for rest, around me ! out of
    sight
Now float me of the vexing land abhorred,
Till in deep calms of space my soul may
    right
Her nature, shoot large sail on lengthen-
    ing cord,
And rush exultant on the Infinite.

TWO SKETCHES

    There can be no violation of privacy now
in identifying the originals of these two
sketches as the beloved sisters of the poetess,
Henrietta and Arabella Moulton - Barrett.
These sonnets appeared in *Blackwood's Maga-
zine* during the summer of 1847.

I

H. B.

THE shadow of her face upon the wall
May take your memory to the perfect
    Greek,
But when you front her, you would call
    the cheek
Too full, sir, for your models, if withal
That bloom it wears could leave you criti-
    cal,
And that smile reaching toward the rosy
    streak;
For one who smiles so has no need to
    speak
To lead your thoughts along, as steed to
    stall.
A smile that turns the sunny side o' the
    heart
On all the world, as if herself did win
By what she lavished on an open mart !

Let no man call the liberal sweetness,
    sin, —
For friends may whisper as they stand
    apart,
'Methinks there's still some warmer place
    within.'

II

A. B.

HER azure eyes, dark lashes hold in fee;
Her fair superfluous ringlets without check
Drop after one another down her neck,
As many to each cheek as you might see
Green leaves to a wild rose; this sign out-
    wardly,
And a like woman-covering seems to deck
Her inner nature, for she will not fleck
World's sunshine with a finger. Sympa-
    thy
Must call her in Love's name ! and then, I
    know,
She rises up, and brightens as she should,
And lights her smile for comfort, and is
    slow
In nothing of high-hearted fortitude.
To smell this flower, come near it ! such
    can grow
In that sole garden where Christ's brow
    dropped blood.

MOUNTAINEER AND POET

THE simple goatherd between Alp and
    sky,
Seeing his shadow, in that awful tryst,
Dilated to a giant's on the mist,
Esteems not his own stature larger by
The apparent image, but more patiently
Strikes his staff down beneath his clenching
    fist,
While the snow-mountains lift their ame-
    thyst
And sapphire crowns of splendor, far and
    nigh,
Into the air around him. Learn from hence
Meek morals, all ye poets that pursue
Your way still onward up to eminence !
Ye are not great because creation drew
Large revelations round your earliest sense,
Nor bright because God's glory shines for
    you.

THE POET

THE poet hath the child's sight in his breast
And sees all *new*. What oftenest he has
    viewed
He views with the first glory. Fair and
    good
Pall never on him, at the fairest, best,
But stand before him holy and undressed
In week-day false conventions, such as
    would
Drag other men down from the altitude
Of primal types, too early dispossessed.
Why, God would tire of all his heavens, as
    soon
As thou, O godlike, childlike poet, didst
Of daily and nightly sights of sun and
    moon !
And therefore hath He set thee in the midst
Where men may hear thy wonder's cease-
    less tune
And praise his world for ever, as thou
    bidst.

HIRAM POWERS' 'GREEK SLAVE '

The American sculptor Hiram Powers and
his family were among the few intimate friends
of the Brownings during their first years in
Florence.

THEY say Ideal beauty cannot enter
The house of anguish. On the threshold
    stands
An alien Image with enshackled hands,
Called the Greek Slave ! as if the artist
    meant her
(That passionless perfection which he lent
    her,
Shadowed not darkened where the sill
    expands)
To so confront man's crimes in different
    lands
With man's ideal sense. Pierce to the
    centre,
Art's fiery finger, and break up ere long
The serfdom of this world. Appeal, fair
    stone,
From God's pure heights of beauty against
    man's wrong !
Catch up in thy divine face, not alone
East griefs but west, and strike and shame
    the strong,
By thunders of white silence, overthrown.

LIFE

First printed in *Blackwood's Magazine*, May,
1847.

EACH creature holds an insular point in
    space ;
Yet what man stirs a finger, breathes a
    sound,
But all the multitudinous beings round
In all the countless worlds with time and
    place
For their conditions, down to the central
    base,
Thrill, haply, in vibration and rebound,
Life answering life across the vast pro-
    found,
In full antiphony, by a common grace ?
I think this sudden joyance which illumes
A child's mouth sleeping, unaware may
    run
From some soul newly loosened from earth's
    tombs :
I think this passionate sigh, which half-
    begun
I stifle back, may reach and stir the plumes
Of God's calm angel standing in the
    sun.

LOVE

First printed in *Blackwood's Magazine*, May,
1847.

WE cannot live, except thus mutually
We alternate, aware or unaware,
The reflex act of life : and when we bear
Our virtue outward most impulsively,
Most full of invocation, and to be
Most instantly compellant, certes there
We live most life, whoever breathes most
    air
And counts his dying years by sun and
    sea.
But when a soul, by choice and conscience,
    doth
Throw out her full force on another
    soul,
The conscience and the concentration both
Make mere life, Love. For Life in perfect
    whole
And aim consummated, is Love in sooth,
As Nature's magnet-heat rounds pole with
    pole.

HEAVEN AND EARTH

'And there was silence in heaven for the space of
half an hour.'

First printed in *Blackwood*, May, 1847.

GOD, who with thunders and great voices
   kept
Beneath thy throne, and stars most silver-
   paced
Along the inferior gyres, and open-faced
Melodious angels round, canst intercept
Music with music, — yet, at will, has
   swept
All back, all back (said he in Patmos
   placed,)
To fill the heavens with silence of the waste
Which lasted half an hour ! Lo, I who have
   wept
All day and night, beseech Thee by my
   tears,
And by that dread response of curse and
   groan
Men alternate across these hemispheres,
Vouchsafe us such a half-hour's hush alone,
In compensation for our stormy years:
As heaven has paused from song, let earth
   from moan !

THE PROSPECT

First printed in *Blackwood* with the two
preceding.

METHINKS we do as fretful children do,
Leaning their faces on the window-pane
To sigh the glass dim with their own breath's
   stain,
And shut the sky and landscape from their
   view:
And thus, alas, since God the maker drew
A mystic separation 'twixt those twain, —
The life beyond us, and our souls in pain, —
We miss the prospect which we are called
   unto
By grief we are fools to use. Be still and
   strong,
O man, my brother ! Hold thy sobbing
   breath,
And keep thy soul's large window pure
   from wrong !
That so, as life's appointment issueth,
Thy vision may be clear to watch along
The sunset consummation-lights of death.

HUGH STUART BOYD

HIS BLINDNESS

To whom was inscribed, in grateful affec-
tion, my poem of 'Cyprus Wine.' There
comes a moment in life when even gratitude
and affection turn to pain, as they do now
with me. This excellent and learned man,
enthusiastic for the good and the beautiful,
and one of the most simple and upright of
human beings, passed out of his long darkness
through death in the summer of 1848 ; Dr.
Adam Clarke's daughter and biographer, Mrs.
Smith (happier in this than the absent), fulfil-
ling a doubly filial duty as she sat by the death-
bed of her father's friend and hers. — E. B. B.

GOD would not let the spheric lights ac-
   cost
This God-loved man, and bade the earth
   stand off
With all her beckoning hills whose golden
   stuff
Under the feet of the royal sun is crossed.
Yet such things were to him not wholly
   lost, —
Permitted, with his wandering eyes light-
   proof,
To catch fair visions rendered full enough
By many a ministrant accomplished
   ghost, —
Still seeing, to sounds of softly-turned
   book-leaves,
Sappho's crown - rose, and Meleager's
   Spring,
And Gregory's starlight on Greek-bur-
   nished eves:
Till Sensuous and Unsensuous seemed one
   thing,
Viewed from one level, — earth's reapers
   at the sheaves
Scarce plainer than Heaven's angels on
   the wing.

HUGH STUART BOYD

HIS DEATH, 1848

BELOVÈD friend, who living many years
With sightless eyes raised vainly to the
   sun,
Didst learn to keep thy patient soul in
   tune
To visible nature's elemental cheers !

God has not caught thee to new hemi-
spheres
Because thou wast aweary of this one; —
I think thine angel's patience first was
done,
And that he spake out with celestial tears,
' Is it enough, dear God ? then lighten so
This soul that smiles in darkness !'
       Steadfast friend,
Who never didst my heart or life mis-
know,
Nor either's faults too keenly appre-
hend, —
How can I wonder when I see thee go
To join the Dead found faithful to the
end ?

HUGH STUART BOYD

LEGACIES

THREE gifts the Dying left me, — Æschy-
lus,
And Gregory Nazianzen, and a clock
Chiming the gradual hours out like a flock
Of stars whose motion is melodious.
The books were those I used to read from,
thus
Assisting my dear teacher's soul to unlock
The darkness of his eyes; now, mine they
mock,
Blinded in turn by tears; now, murmurous
Sad echoes of my young voice, years agone
Intoning from these leaves the Grecian
phrase,
Return and choke my utterance. Books,
lie down
In silence on the shelf there, within gaze;
And thou, clock, striking the hour's pulses
on,
Chime in the day which ends these parting-
days !

CONFESSIONS

I

FACE to face in my chamber, my silent
chamber, I saw her:
God and she and I only, there I sat down
to draw her
Soul through the clefts of confession:
 ' Speak, I am holding thee fast,

As the angel of resurrection shall do at the
last !'
  ' My cup is blood-red
  With my sin,' she said,
' And I pour it out to the bitter lees,
As if the angels of judgment stood over me
strong at the last,
 Or as thou wert as these.'

II

When God smote his hands together, and
 struck out thy soul as a spark 10
Into the organized glory of things, from
 deeps of the dark, —
Say, didst thou shine, didst thou burn,
 didst thou honor the power in the
 form,
As the star does at night, or the fire-fly, or
 even the little ground-worm ?
  ' I have sinned,' she said,
  ' For my seed-light shed
 Has smouldered away from his first
 decrees.
The cypress praiseth the fire-fly, the
 ground-leaf praiseth the worm;
 I am viler than these.'

III

When God on that sin had pity, and did
 not trample thee straight
With his wild rains beating and drench-
 ing thy light found inadequate; 20
When He only sent thee the north-wind, a
 little searching and chill,
To quicken thy flame — didst thou kindle
 and flash to the heights of his will ?
  ' I have sinned,' she said,
  ' Unquickened, unspread,
 My fire dropt down, and I wept on my
 knees:
I only said of his winds of the north as I
 shrank from their chill,
 What delight is in these ?'

IV

When God on that sin had pity, and did
 not meet it as such,
But tempered the wind to thy uses, and
 softened the world to thy touch,
At least thou wast moved in thy soul,
 though unable to prove it afar, 30
Thou couldst carry thy light like a jewel,
 not giving it out like a star ?
  ' I have sinned,' she said,
  ' And not merited

The gift He gives, by the grace He
    sees !
The mine-cave praiseth the jewel, the
    hillside praiseth the star;
    I am viler than these.'

V

Then I cried aloud in my passion, — Un-
    thankful and impotent creature,
To throw up thy scorn unto God through
    the rents in thy beggarly nature !
If He, the all-giving and loving, is served
    so unduly, what then
Hast thou done to the weak and the false
    and the changing, — thy fellows of
    men ?   40
    ' I have *loved*,' she said,
    (Words bowing her head
As the wind the wet acacia-trees)
' I saw God sitting above me, but I . . . I
    sat among men,
    And I have loved these.'

VI

Again with a lifted voice, like a choral
    trumpet that takes
The lowest note of a viol that trembles,
    and triumphing breaks
On the air with it solemn and clear, —
    ' Behold ! I have sinned not in this !
Where I loved, I have loved much and
    well, — I have verily loved not
    amiss.
    Let the living,' she said,   50
    ' Inquire of the dead,
In the house of the pale-fronted images.
My own true dead will answer for me,
    that I have not loved amiss
    In my love for all these.

VII

' The least touch of their hands in the
    morning, I keep it by day and by
    night;
Their least step on the stair, at the door,
    still throbs through me, if ever so
    light;
Their least gift, which they left to my
    childhood, far off in the long-ago
    years,
Is now turned from a toy to a relic, and
    seen through the crystals of tears.
    Dig the snow,' she said,
    ' For my churchyard bed,   60

Yet I, as I sleep, shall not fear to
    freeze,
If one only of these my beloveds shall love
    me with heart-warm tears,
    As I have loved these !

VIII

' If I angered any among them, from
    thenceforth my own life was sore;
If I fell by chance from their presence, I
    clung to their memory more:
Their tender I often felt holy, their bitter
    I sometimes called sweet;
And whenever their heart has refused me,
    I fell down straight at their feet.
    I have loved,' she said, —
    ' Man is weak, God is dread,
    Yet the weak man dies with his
    spirit at ease,   70
Having poured such an unguent of love
    but once on the Saviour's feet
    As I lavished for these.'

IX

Go, I cried, thou hast chosen the Human,
    and left the Divine !
Then, at least, have the Human shared
    with thee their wild-berry wine ?
Have they loved back thy love, and when
    strangers approached thee with
    blame,
Have they covered thy fault with their
    kisses, and loved thee the same ?
    But she shrunk and said
    ' God, over my head,
    Must sweep in the wrath of his
    judgment-seas,
If *He* shall deal with me sinning, but only
    indeed the same   80
    And no gentler than these.'

A SABBATH MORNING AT SEA

First printed in *The Amaranth*, 1839, as ' A
Sabbath on the Sea.'

I

THE ship went on with solemn face;
    To meet the darkness on the deep,
    The solemn ship went onward:
I bowed down weary in the place,
    For parting tears and present sleep
    Had weighed mine eyelids downward.

II

Thick sleep which shut all dreams from me,
  And kept my inner self apart
    And quiet from emotion,
Then brake away and left me free,
  Made conscious of a human heart
    Betwixt the heaven and ocean.

III

The new sight, the new wondrous sight !
  The waters round me, turbulent,
    The skies impassive o'er me,
Calm in a moonless, sunless light,
  Half glorified by that intent
    Of holding the day-glory !

IV

Two pale thin clouds did stand upon
  The meeting line of sea and sky,
    With aspect still and mystic:
I think they did foresee the sun,
  And rested on their prophecy
    In quietude majestic,

V

Then flushed to radiance where they stood,
  Like statues by the open tomb
    Of shining saints half risen.
The sun ! — he came up to be viewed,
  And sky and sea made mighty room
    To inaugurate the vision.

VI

I oft had seen the dawnlight run
  As red wine through the hills, and break
    Through many a mist's inurning;
But, here, no earth profaned the sun:
  Heaven, ocean, did alone partake
    The sacrament of morning.

VII

Away with thoughts fantastical !
  I would be humble to my worth,
    Self-guarded as self-doubted:
Though here no earthly shadows fall,
  I, joying, grieving without earth,
    May desecrate without it.

VIII

God's sabbath morning sweeps the waves;
  I would not praise the pageant high
    Yet miss the dedicature:
I, carried toward the sunless graves
  By force of natural things, — should I
    Exult in only Nature ?

IX

And could I bear to sit alone
  'Mid Nature's fixed benignities,
    While my warm pulse was moving ?
Too dark thou art, O glittering sun,
  Too strait ye are, capacious seas,
    To satisfy the loving !

X

It seems a better lot than so,
  To sit with friends beneath the beech,
    And feel them dear and dearer;
Or follow children as they go
  In pretty pairs, with softened speech,
    As the church-bells ring nearer.

XI

Love me, sweet friends, this sabbath day !
  The sea sings round me while ye roll
    Afar the hymn unaltered,
And kneel, where once I knelt to pray,
  And bless me deeper in the soul,
    Because the voice has faltered.

XII

And though this sabbath comes to me
  Without the stolèd minister
    Or chanting congregation,
God's Spirit brings communion, He
  Who brooded soft on waters drear,
    Creator on creation.

XIII

Himself, I think, shall draw me higher
  Where keep the saints with harp and song
    An endless sabbath morning,
And on that sea commixed with fire
  Oft drop their eyelids, raised too long
    To the full Godhead's burning.

THE MASK

I

I have a smiling face, she said,
  I have a jest for all I meet,
I have a garland for my head
  And all its flowers are sweet, —
And so you call me gay, she said.

II

Grief taught to me this smile, she said,
  And Wrong did teach this jesting bold;
These flowers were plucked from garden-
    bed

While a death-chime was tolled:
And what now will you say ? — she said.

III

Behind no prison-grate, she said,
　Which slurs the sunshine half a mile,
Live captives so uncomforted
　As souls behind a smile.
God's pity let us pray, she said.

IV

I know my face is bright, she said, —
　Such brightness dying suns diffuse:
I bear upon my forehead shed
　The sign of what I lose,
The ending of my day, she said.

V

If I dared leave this smile, she said,
　And take a moan upon my mouth,
And tie a cypress round my head,
　And let my tears run smooth,
It were the happier way, she said.

VI

And since that must not be, she said,
　I fain your bitter world would leave.
How calmly, calmly smile the Dead,
　Who do not, therefore, grieve !
The yea of Heaven is yea, she said.

VII

But in your bitter world, she said,
　Face-joy 's a costly mask to wear;
'T is bought with pangs long nourishèd,
　And rounded to despair:
Grief's earnest makes life's play, she said.

VIII

Ye weep for those who weep ? she said —
　Ah fools ! I bid you pass them by.
Go, weep for those whose hearts have
　bled
　What time their eyes were dry.
Whom sadder can I say ? she said.

CALLS ON THE HEART

I

FREE Heart, that singest to-day
Like a bird on the first green spray,
Wilt thou go forth to the world

Where the hawk hath his wing unfurled
　To follow, perhaps, thy way ?
Where the tamer thine own will bind,
And, to make thee sing, will blind,
While the little lip grows for the free
　behind ?
　　Heart, wilt thou go ?
　　— 'No, no !
Free hearts are better so.'

II

The world, thou hast heard it told,
Has counted its robber-gold,
And the pieces stick to the hand;
The world goes riding it fair and grand,
　While the truth is bought and sold;
World-voices east, world-voices west,
They call thee, Heart, from thine early
　rest,
'Come hither, come hither and be our
　guest.'
　　Heart, wilt thou go ?
　　— 'No, no !
Good hearts are calmer so.'

III

Who calleth thee, Heart ? World's Strife,
With a golden heft to his knife;
World's Mirth, with a finger fine
That draws on a board in wine
　Her blood-red plans of life;
World's Gain, with a brow knit down;
World's Fame, with a laurel crown
Which rustles most as the leaves turn
　brown:
　　Heart, wilt thou go ?
　　— 'No, no !
Calm hearts are wiser so.'

IV

Hast heard that Proserpina
(Once fooling) was snatched away
To partake the dark king's seat,
And the tears ran fast on her feet
　To think how the sun shone yesterday ?
With her ankles sunken in asphodel
She wept for the roses of earth which
　fell
From her lap when the wild car drave to
　hell.
　　Heart, wilt thou go ?
　　— 'No, no !
Wise hearts are warmer so.'

V

And what is this place not seen,
Where Hearts may hide serene ?
' 'T is a fair still house well-kept
Which humble thoughts have swept
   And holy prayers made clean.
There I sit with Love in the sun,
And we two never have done
Singing sweeter songs than are guessed by
    one.'
      Heart, wilt thou go ?
       — ' No, no !
   Warm hearts are fuller so.'

VI

O Heart, O Love, — I fear
That Love may be kept too near.
Hast heard, O Heart, that tale,
How Love may be false and frail
   To a Heart once holden dear ?
— ' But this true Love of mine
Clings fast as the clinging vine,
And mingles pure as the grapes in wine.'
      Heart, wilt thou go ?
       — ' No, no !
   Full hearts beat higher so.'

VII

O Heart, O Love, beware !
Look up, and boast not there,
For who has twirled at the pin ?
'T is the World, between Death and
   Sin, —
   The World and the World's Despair !
And Death has quickened his pace
To the hearth, with a mocking face,
Familiar as Love, in Love's own place.
      Heart, wilt thou go ?
      ' Still, no !
   High hearts must grieve even so.'

VIII

The house is waste to-day,
The leaf has dropt from the spray,
The thorn, prickt through to the song:
If summer doeth no wrong,
   The winter will, they say.
Sing, Heart ! What heart replies ?
In vain we were calm and wise,
If the tears unkissed stand on in our eyes.
      Heart, wilt thou go ?
       — ' Ah, no !
   Grieved hearts must break even so.'

IX

Howbeit all is not lost.
The warm noon ends in frost,
And worldly tongues of promise
Like sheep-bells die off from us
   On the desert hills cloud-crossed:
Yet through the silence shall
Pierce the death-angel's call,
And ' Come up hither,' recover all.
      Heart, wilt thou go ?
       — ' I go !
   Broken hearts triumph so.'

WISDOM UNAPPLIED

I

If I were thou, O butterfly,
And poised my purple wing to spy
The sweetest flowers that live and die,

II

I would not waste my strength on those,
As thou, — for summer has a close,
And pansies bloom not in the snows.

III

If I were thou, O working bee,
And all that honey-gold I see
Could delve from roses easily,

IV

I would not hive it at man's door,
As thou, — that heirdom of my store
Should make him rich and leave me poor.

V

If I were thou, O eagle proud,
And screamed the thunder back aloud,
And faced the lightning from the cloud,

VI

I would not build my eyrie-throne,
As thou, — upon a crumbling stone
Which the next storm may trample down.

VII

If I were thou, O gallant steed,
With pawing hoof and dancing head,
And eye outrunning thine own speed,

VIII

I would not meeken to the rein,
As thou, — nor smooth my nostril plain
From the glad desert's snort and strain.

IX

If I were thou, red-breasted bird,
With song at shut-up window heard,
Like Love's sweet Yes too long deferred,

X

I would not overstay delight,
As thou, — but take a swallow-flight
Till the new spring returned to sight.

XI

While yet I spake, a touch was laid
Upon my brow, whose pride did fade
As thus, methought, an angel said, —

XII

'If I were *thou* who sing'st this song,
Most wise for others, and most strong
In seeing right while doing wrong,

XIII

' I would not waste my cares, and choose,
As *thou*, — to seek what thou must lose,
Such gains as perish in the use.

XIV

' I would not work where none can win,
As *thou*, — halfway 'twixt grief and sin,
But look above and judge within.

XV

'I would not let my pulse beat high,
As *thou*, — towards fame's regality,
Nor yet in love's great jeopardy.

XVI

' I would not champ the hard cold bit,
As *thou*, — of what the world thinks fit,
But take God's freedom, using it.

XVII

' I would not play earth's winter out,
As *thou*, — but gird my soul about,
And live for life past death and doubt.

XVIII

'Then sing, O singer ! — but allow,
Beast, fly and bird, called foolish now,
Are wise (for all thy scorn) as thou.'

HUMAN LIFE'S MYSTERY

I

WE sow the glebe, we reap the corn,
  We build the house where we may rest,
And then, at moments, suddenly
We look up to the great wide sky,
Inquiring wherefore we were born,
  For earnest or for jest ?

II

The senses folding thick and dark
  About the stifled soul within,
We guess diviner things beyond,
And yearn to them with yearning fond;
We strike out blindly to a mark
  Believed in, but not seen.

III

We vibrate to the pant and thrill
  Wherewith Eternity has curled
In serpent-twine about God's seat:
While, freshening upward to his feet,
In gradual growth his full-leaved will
  Expands from world to world.

IV

And, in the tumult and excess
  Of act and passion under sun,
We sometimes hear — oh, soft and far,
As silver star did touch with star,
The kiss of Peace and Righteousness
  Through all things that are done.

V

God keeps his holy mysteries
  Just on the outside of man's dream;
In diapason slow, we think
To hear their pinions rise and sink,
While they float pure beneath his eyes,
  Like swans adown a stream.

VI

Abstractions, are they, from the forms
  Of his great beauty ? — exaltations
From his great glory ? — strong previsions
Of what we shall be ? — intuitions
Of what we are — in calms and storms
  Beyond our peace and passions ?

VII

Things nameless ! which, in passing so,
  Do stroke us with a subtle grace;
We say, 'Who passes ?' — they are dumb;

We cannot see them go or come,
Their touches fall soft, cold, as snow
　Upon a blind man's face.

VIII

Yet, touching so, they draw above
　Our common thoughts to Heaven's un-
　　known;
Our daily joy and pain advance
To a divine significance
Our human love — O mortal love,
　That light is not its own !

IX

And sometimes horror chills our blood
　To be so near such mystic Things,
And we wrap round us for defence
Our purple manners, moods of sense —
As angels from the face of God
　Stand hidden in their wings.

X

And sometimes through life's heavy swound
　We grope for them, with strangled
　　breath
We stretch our hands abroad and try
To reach them in our agony;
And widen, so, the broad life-wound
　Soon large enough for death.

A CHILD'S THOUGHT OF GOD

I

THEY say that God lives very high;
　But if you look above the pines
You cannot see our God; and why ?

II

And if you dig down in the mines
　You never see Him in the gold;
Though from Him all that 's glory shines.

III

God is so good, He wears a fold
　Of heaven and earth across his face —
Like secrets kept, for love, untold.

IV

But still I feel that his embrace
　Slides down by thrills, through all things
　　made,
Through sight and sound of every place:

V

As if my tender mother laid
　On my shut lips her kisses' pressure,
Half-waking me at night, and said
　' Who kissed you through the dark, dear
　　guesser ? '

THE CLAIM

First printed in the *Athenæum*, September
17, 1842, as ' A Claim on Allegory.'

I

GRIEF sate upon a rock and sighed one
　　day,
　　(Sighing is all her rest,)
' Wellaway, wellaway, ah wellaway ! '
As ocean beat the stone, did she her
　　breast,
' Ah wellaway ! ah me ! alas, ah me ! '
　Such sighing uttered she.

II

A Cloud spake out of heaven, as soft as
　　rain
　　That falls on water, — ' Lo,
The winds have wandered from me ! I
　　remain
Alone in the sky-waste, and cannot go
To lean my whiteness on the mountain
　　blue
　Till wanted for more dew.

III

' The sun has struck my brain to weary
　　peace,
　　Whereby constrained and pale
I spin for him a larger golden fleece
Than Jason's, yearning for as full a sail.
Sweet Grief, when thou hast sighèd to thy
　　mind,
　Give me a sigh for wind,

IV

' And let it carry me adown the west ! '
　　But Love, who pròstrated
Lay at Grief's foot, his lifted eyes pos-
　　sessed
Of her full image, answered in her stead;
' Now nay, now nay ! she shall not give
　　away
What is my wealth, for any Cloud that
　flieth:

Where Grief makes moan,
Love claims his own,
And therefore do I lie here night and day,
And eke my life out with the breath she
 sigheth.'

A DEAD ROSE

First printed in *Blackwood's Magazine*,
October, 1846.

I

O ROSE, who dares to name thee ?
No longer roseate now, nor soft nor sweet,
But pale and hard and dry as stubble
 wheat, —
 Kept seven years in a drawer, thy titles
 shame thee.

II

The breeze that used to blow thee
Between the hedgerow thorns, and take
 away
An odor up the lane to last all day, —
 If breathing now, unsweetened would
 forgo thee.

III

The sun that used to smite thee,
And mix his glory in thy gorgeous urn
Till beam appeared to bloom, and flower
 to burn, —
 If shining now, with not a hue would
 light thee.

IV

The dew that used to wet thee,
And, white first, grow incarnadined be-
 cause
It lay upon thee where the crimson was, —
 If dropping now, would darken where it
 met thee.

V

The fly that 'lit upon thee
To stretch the tendrils of its tiny feet
Along thy leaf's pure edges after heat, —
 If 'lighting now, would coldly overrun
 thee.

VI

The bee that once did suck thee,
And build thy perfumed ambers up his
 hive,

And swoon in thee for joy, till scarce
 alive, —
 If passing now, would blindly overlook
 thee.

VII

The heart doth recognize thee,
Alone, alone ! the heart doth smell thee
 sweet,
Doth view thee fair, doth judge thee most
 complete,
 Perceiving all those changes that dis-
 guise thee.

VIII

Yes, and the heart doth owe thee
More love, dead rose, than to any roses
 bold
Which Julia wears at dances, smiling
 cold : —
 Lie still upon this heart which breaks
 below thee !

A WOMAN'S SHORTCOMINGS

First printed in *Blackwood's Magazine*, Oc-
tober, 1846.

I

SHE has laughed as softly as if she sighed,
 She has counted six, and over,
Of a purse well filled and a heart well
 tried —
 Oh, each a worthy lover !
They 'give her time;' for her soul must
 slip
 Where the world has set the groov-
 ing;
She will lie to none with her fair red
 lip:
 But love seeks truer loving.

II

She trembles her fan in a sweetness dumb,
 As her thoughts were beyond recalling,
With a glance for *one*, and a glance for
 some,
 From her eyelids rising and falling;
Speaks common words with a blushful air,
 Hears bold words, unreproving;
But her silence says — what she never will
 swear —
 And love seeks better loving.

III

Go, lady, lean to the night-guitar
  And drop a smile to the bringer;
Then smile as sweetly, when he is far,
  At the voice of an in-door singer.
Bask tenderly beneath tender eyes;
  Glance lightly, on their removing;
And join new vows to old perjuries —
  But dare not call it loving.

IV

Unless you can think, when the song is
    done,
  No other is soft in the rhythm;
Unless you can feel, when left by One,
  That all men else go with him;
Unless you can know, when unpraised by
    his breath,
  That your beauty itself wants proving;
Unless you can swear 'For life, for
    death !' —
  Oh, fear to call it loving !

V

Unless you can muse in a crowd all day
  On the absent face that fixed you;
Unless you can love, as the angels may,
  With the breadth of heaven betwixt
    you;
Unless you can dream that his faith is
    fast,
  Through behoving and unbehoving;
Unless you can *die* when the dream is
    past —
  Oh, never call it loving !

A MAN'S REQUIREMENTS

First printed in *Blackwood's Magazine*, October, 1846.

I

  Love me, Sweet, with all thou art,
    Feeling, thinking, seeing;
  Love me in the lightest part,
    Love me in full being.

II

Love me with thine open youth
  In its frank surrender;
With the vowing of thy mouth,
  With its silence tender.

III

Love me with thine azure eyes,
  Made for earnest granting;
Taking color from the skies,
  Can Heaven's truth be wanting ?

IV

Love me with their lids, that fall
  Snow-like at first meeting;
Love me with thine heart, that all
  Neighbors then see beating.

V

Love me with thine hand stretched out
  Freely — open-minded:
Love me with thy loitering foot, —
  Hearing one behind it.

VI

Love me with thy voice, that turns
  Sudden faint above me;
Love me with thy blush that burns
  When I murmur *Love me !*

VII

Love me with thy thinking soul,
  Break it to love-sighing;
Love me with thy thoughts that roll
  On through living — dying.

VIII

Love me in thy gorgeous airs,
  When the world has crowned thee;
Love me, kneeling at thy prayers,
  With the angels round thee.

IX

Love me pure, as musers do,
  Up the woodlands shady:
Love me gaily, fast and true,
  As a winsome lady.

X

Through all hopes that keep us brave,
  Farther off or nigher,
Love me for the house and grave,
  And for something higher.

XI

Thus, if thou wilt prove me, Dear,
  Woman's love no fable,
I will love *thee* — half a year —
  As a man is able.

A YEAR'S SPINNING

First printed in *Blackwood's Magazine*, October, 1846, as 'Maude's Spinning.'

I

HE listened at the porch that day,
  To hear the wheel go on, and on;
And then it stopped, ran back away,
  While through the door he brought the
    sun:
  But now my spinning is all done.

II

He sat beside me, with an oath
  That love ne'er ended, once begun;
I smiled — believing for us both,
  What was the truth for only one:
  And now my spinning is all done.

III

My mother cursed me that I heard
  A young man's wooing as I spun:
Thanks, cruel mother, for that word, —
  For I have, since, a harder known!
  And now my spinning is all done.

IV

I thought — O God! — my first-born's cry
  Both voices to mine ear would drown:
I listened in mine agony —
  It was the *silence* made me groan!
  And now my spinning is all done.

V

Bury me 'twixt my mother's grave,
  (Who cursed me on her death-bed lone)
And my dead baby's (God it save!)
  Who, not to bless me, would not moan.
  And now my spinning is all done.

VI

A stone upon my heart and head,
  But no name written on the stone!
Sweet neighbors, whisper low instead,
  'This sinner was a loving one —
  And now her spinning is all done.'

VII

And let the door ajar remain,
  In case he should pass by anon;
And leave the wheel out very plain, —
  That HE, when passing in the sun,
  May see the spinning is all done.

CHANGE UPON CHANGE

First printed in *Blackwood's Magazine*, October, 1846.

I

FIVE months ago the stream did flow,
  The lilies bloomed within the sedge,
And we were lingering to and fro,
Where none will track thee in this snow,
  Along the stream, beside the hedge.
Ah, Sweet, be free to love and go!
  For if I do not hear thy foot,
  The frozen river is as mute,
  The flowers have dried down to the root:
And why, since these be changed since
    May,
  Shouldst *thou* change less than *they*?

II

And slow, slow as the winter snow
  The tears have drifted to mine eyes;
And my poor cheeks, five months ago
Set blushing at thy praises so,
  Put paleness on for a disguise.
Ah, Sweet, be free to praise and go!
  For if my face is turned too pale,
  It was thine oath that first did fail, —
  It was thy love proved false and frail, —
And why, since these be changed enow,
  Should *I* change less than *thou*?

A REED

First printed in *Blackwood's Magazine*, October, 1846.

I

I AM no trumpet, but a reed;
No flattering breath shall from me lead
  A silver sound, a hollow sound:
I will not ring, for priest or king,
One blast that in re-echoing
  Would leave a bondsman faster bound.

II

I am no trumpet, but a reed, —
A broken reed, the wind indeed
  Left flat upon a dismal shore;
Yet if a little maid or child
Should sigh within it, earnest-mild
  This reed will answer evermore.

III

I am no trumpet, but a reed;
Go, tell the fishers, as they spread
  Their nets along the river's edge,
I will not tear their nets at all,
Nor pierce their hands, if they should fall:
  Then let them leave me in the sedge.

A CHILD'S GRAVE AT FLORENCE

A. A. E. C.

BORN JULY, 1848. DIED NOVEMBER, 1849

First printed in the *Athenæum*, December 22,
1849. Alice Augusta Elizabeth was the daughter
of Count and Countess Cottrell. The mother,
to whom there are many affectionate allusions
in Mrs. Browning's letters, was born Sophia Au-
gusta Tulk, the daughter of an English cler-
gyman. The father, Henry Cottrell, a young
English artist, was member of the household of
the last Duke of Lucca, and received his title
from him.

Of English blood, of Tuscan birth,
  What country should we give her?
Instead of any on the earth,
  The civic Heavens receive her.

And here among the English tombs
  In Tuscan ground we lay her,
While the blue Tuscan sky endomes
  Our English words of prayer.

A little child! — how long she lived,
  By months, not years, is reckoned: 10
Born in one July, she survived
  Alone to see a second.

Bright-featured, as the July sun
  Her little face still played in,
And splendors, with her birth begun,
  Had had no time for fading.

So, Lily, from those July hours,
  No wonder we should call her;
She looked such kinship to the flowers, —
  Was but a little taller.   20

A Tuscan Lily, — only white;
  As Dante, in abhorrence
Of red corruption, wished aright
  The lilies of his Florence.

We could not wish her whiter, — her
  Who perfumed with pure blossom
The house — a lovely thing to wear
  Upon a mother's bosom!

This July creature thought perhaps
  Our speech not worth assuming;   30
She sat upon her parents' laps
  And mimicked the gnat's humming;

Said 'father,' 'mother' — then left off,
  For tongues celestial, fitter:
Her hair had grown just long enough
  To catch heaven's jasper-glitter.

Babes! Love could always hear and see
  Behind the cloud that hid them.
'Let little children come to Me,
  And do not thou forbid them.'   40

So, unforbidding, have we met,
  And gently here have laid her,
Though winter is no time to get
  The flowers that should o'erspread her:

We should bring pansies quick with spring,
  Rose, violet, daffodilly,
And also, above everything,
  White lilies for our Lily.

Nay, more than flowers, this grave exacts, —
  Glad, grateful attestations   50
Of her sweet eyes and pretty acts,
  With calm renunciations.

Her very mother with light feet
  Should leave the place too earthy,
Saying 'The angels have thee, Sweet,
  Because we are not worthy.'

But winter kills the orange-buds,
  The gardens in the frost are,
And all the heart dissolves in floods,
  Remembering we have lost her.   60

Poor earth, poor heart, — too weak, too
      weak
  To miss the July shining!
Poor heart! — what bitter words we speak
  When God speaks of resigning!

Sustain this heart in us that faints,
  Thou God, the self-existent!
We catch up wild at parting saints
  And feel thy heaven too distant.

The wind that swept them out of sin
  Has ruffled all our vesture: 70
On the shut door that let them in
  We beat with frantic gesture,—

To us, us also, open straight !
  The outer life is chilly;
Are we too, like the earth, to wait
  Till next year for our Lily ?

— Oh, my own baby on my knees,
  My leaping, dimpled treasure,
At every word I write like these,
  Clasped close with stronger pressure ! 80

Too well my own heart understands, —
  At every word beats fuller —
My little feet, my little hands,
  And hair of Lily's color !

But God gives patience, Love learns
    strength,
  And Faith remembers promise,
And Hope itself can smile at length
  On other hopes gone from us.

Love, strong as Death, shall conquer Death,
  Through struggle made more glorious:
This mother stills her sobbing breath, 91
  Renouncing yet victorious.

Arms, empty of her child, she lifts
  With spirit unbereaven, —
' God will not all take back his gifts;
  My Lily 's mine in heaven.

' Still mine ! maternal rights serene
  Not given to another !
The crystal bars shine faint between
  The souls of child and mother. 100

' Meanwhile,' the mother cries, ' content !
  Our love was well divided;
Its sweetness following where she went,
  Its anguish stayed where I did.

' Well done of God, to halve the lot,
  And give her all the sweetness;
To us, the empty room and cot, —
  To her, the Heaven's completeness.

' To us, this grave, — to her, the rows
  The mystic palm-trees spring in; 110
To us, the silence in the house, —
  To her, the choral singing.

' For her, to gladden in God's view,
  For us, to hope and bear on.
Grow, Lily, in thy garden new,
  Beside the Rose of Sharon !

' Grow fast in heaven, sweet Lily clipped,
  In love more calm than this is,
And may the angels dewy-lipped
  Remind thee of our kisses ! 120

' While none shall tell thee of our tears,
  These human tears now falling,
Till, after a few patient years,
  One home shall take us all in.

' Child, father, mother — who, left out ?
  Not mother, and not father !
And when, our dying couch about,
  The natural mists shall gather,

' Some smiling angel close shall stand
  In old Correggio's fashion, 130
And bear a LILY in his hand,
  For death's ANNUNCIATION.'

LIFE AND LOVE

I

FAST this Life of mine was dying,
  Blind already and calm as death,
Snowflakes on her bosom lying
  Scarcely heaving with her breath.

II

Love came by, and having known her
  In a dream of fabled lands,
Gently stooped, and laid upon her
  Mystic chrism of holy hands;

III

Drew his smile across her folded
  Eyelids, as the swallow dips;
Breathed as finely as the cold did
  Through the locking of her lips.

IV

So, when Life looked upward, being
  Warmed and breathed on from above,
What sight could she have for seeing,
  Evermore . . . but only LOVE ?

A DENIAL

I

We have met late — it is too late to meet,
　O friend, not more than friend !
Death's forecome shroud is tangled round
　　my feet,
And if I step or stir, I touch the end.
　　In this last jeopardy
Can I approach thee, I, who cannot move ?
How shall I answer thy request for love ?
　　Look in my face and see.

II

I love thee not, I dare not love thee ! go
　In silence ; drop my hand.
If thou seek roses, seek them where they
　　blow
In garden-alleys, not in desert-sand.
　　Can life and death agree,
That thou shouldst stoop thy song to my
　　complaint ?
I cannot love thee.　If the word is faint,
　　Look in my face and see.

III

I might have loved thee in some former
　　days.
　Oh, then, my spirits had leapt
As now they sink, at hearing thy love-
　　praise !
Before these faded cheeks were overwept,
　Had this been asked of me,
To love thee with my whole strong heart
　　and head, —
I should have said still . . . yes, but *smiled*
　　and said,
　　‘ Look in my face and see ! ’

IV

But now . . . God sees me, God, who took
　　my heart
　And drowned it in life's surge.
In all your wide warm earth I have no
　　part —
A light song overcomes me like a dirge.
　Could Love's great harmony
The saints keep step to when their bonds
　　are loose,
Not weigh me down ? am *I* a wife to
　　choose ?
　　Look in my face and see —

V

While I behold, as plain as one who
　　dreams,
　Some woman of full worth,
Whose voice, as cadenced as a silver
　　stream's,
Shall prove the fountain-soul which sends
　　it forth ;
　One younger, more thought-free
And fair and gay, than I, thou must forget,
With brighter eyes than these . . . which
　　are not wet . . .
　　Look in my face and see !

VI

So farewell thou, whom I have known too
　　late
　To let thee come so near.
Be counted happy while men call thee
　　great,
And one belovèd woman feels thee dear ! —
　Not I ! — that cannot be.
I am lost, I am changed, — I must go
　　farther, where
The change shall take me worse, and no
　　one dare
　　Look in my face and see.

VII

Meantime I bless thee.　By these thoughts
　　of mine
　I bless thee from all such !
I bless thy lamp to oil, thy cup to wine,
Thy hearth to joy, thy hand to an equal
　　touch
　Of loyal troth.　For me,
I love thee not, I love thee not ! — away !
Here 's no more courage in my soul to say
　　‘ Look in my face and see.’

PROOF AND DISPROOF

I

Dost thou love me, my Belovèd ?
　Who shall answer yes or no ?
What is provèd or disprovèd
　When my soul inquireth so,
Dost thou love me, my Belovèd ?

II

I have seen thy heart to-day,
　Never open to the crowd,
While to love me aye and aye

Was the vow as it was vowed
By thine eyes of steadfast gray.

III

Now I sit alone, alone —
  And the hot tears break and burn,
Now, Belovèd, thou art gone,
  Doubt and terror have their turn.
Is it love that I have known ?

IV

I have known some bitter things, —
  Anguish, anger, solitude.
Year by year an evil brings,
  Year by year denies a good;
March winds violate my springs.

V

I have known how sickness bends,
  I have known how sorrow breaks, —
How quick hopes have sudden ends,
  How the heart thinks till it aches
Of the smile of buried friends.

VI

Last, I have known *thee*, my brave
  Noble thinker, lover, doer !
The best knowledge last I have.
  But thou comest as the thrower
Of fresh flowers upon a grave.

VII

Count what feelings used to move me !
  Can this love assort with those ?
Thou, who art so far above me,
  Wilt thou stoop so, for repose ?
Is it true that thou canst love me ?

VIII

Do not blame me if I doubt thee.
  I can call love by its name
When thine arm is wrapt about me;
  But even love seems not the same,
When I sit alone, without thee.

IX

In thy clear eyes I descried
  Many a proof of love, to-day;
But to-night, those unbelied
  Speechful eyes being gone away,
There 's the proof to seek, beside.

X

Dost thou love me, my Belovèd ?
  Only *thou* canst answer yes !

And, thou gone, the proof 's disprovèd,
  And the cry rings answerless —
Dost thou love me, my Belovèd ?

QUESTION AND ANSWER

I

LOVE you seek for, presupposes
  Summer heat and sunny glow.
Tell me, do you find moss-roses
  Budding, blooming in the snow ?
Snow might kill the rose-tree's root —
Shake it quickly from your foot,
  Lest it harm you as you go.

II

From the ivy where it dapples
  A gray ruin, stone by stone,
Do you look for grapes or apples,
  Or for sad green leaves alone ?
Pluck the leaves off, two or three —
Keep them for morality
  When you shall be safe and gone.

INCLUSIONS

I

OH, wilt thou have my hand, Dear, to lie
    along in thine ?
As a little stone in a running stream, it
    seems to lie and pine.
Now drop the poor pale hand, Dear, unfit
    to plight with thine.

II

Oh, wilt thou have my cheek, Dear, drawn
    closer to thine own ?
My cheek is white, my cheek is worn, by
    many a tear run down.
Now leave a little space, Dear, lest it
    should wet thine own.

III

Oh, must thou have my soul, Dear, com-
    mingled with thy soul ? —
Red grows the cheek, and warm the hand;
    the part is in the whole:
Nor hands nor cheeks keep separate, when
    soul is joined to soul.

INSUFFICIENCY

I

THERE is no one beside thee and no one
    above thee,
  Thou standest alone as the nightingale
    sings !
And my words that would praise thee
    are impotent things,
For none can express thee though all
    should approve thee.
  I love thee so, Dear, that I only can love
    thee.

II

Say, what can I do for thee ? weary thee,
    grieve thee ?
  Lean on thy shoulder, new burdens to
    add ?
Weep my tears over thee, making thee
    sad ?
Oh, hold me not — love me not ! let me
    retrieve thee.
  I love thee so, Dear, that I only can
    leave thee.

SONNETS FROM THE PORTUGUESE

It was while they were living in Pisa, soon
after their marriage, that Mrs. Browning first
showed her husband that unique sheaf of
love-poems, first published in 1850 under the
title of *Sonnets from the Portuguese.* Long
after his wife's death Robert Browning de-
scribed the scene to Mr. Edmund Gosse, who
relates the tale in his *Critical Kit-Kats,* page 2.
'Their custom was, Mr. Browning said, to
write alone, and not to show each other what
they had written. This was a rule which he
sometimes broke through, but she never. He
had the habit of working in a downstairs room,
where their meals were spread, while Mrs.
Browning studied in a room on the floor above.
One day, early in 1847, their breakfast being
over, Mrs. Browning went upstairs, while her
husband stood at the window watching the
street till the table should be cleared. He was
presently aware of some one behind him, al-
though the servant was gone. It was Mrs.
Browning, who held him by the shoulder to
prevent his turning to look at her, and at the
same time pushed a packet of papers into the
pocket of his coat. She told him to read that,
and to tear it up if he did not like it ; and then
she fled again to her own room.'

It was Robert Browning who overruled his
wife's strong initial objection to making public
these beautiful, but singularly intimate poems ;
and the fact furnishes an argument to those
who believe that he, at least, would not have
disliked the publication of the Love Letters. 'I
dared not,' he once said, 'reserve to myself the
finest Sonnets written in any language since
Shakespeare.' Mrs. Browning's reluctance once
overcome, her first fancy was to call the collec-
tion *Sonnets translated from the Bosnian* (though
why from one rather than another of the
innumerable Slavic dialects, it would be dif-
ficult to guess). But they connected them-
selves in the husband's mind with another poem
for which he had a very special admiration,
Caterina to Camoëns ; and he decreed that they
should be called *Sonnets from the Portuguese.*
A small edition was first printed for private
circulation, under the supervision of Miss
Mitford, in a slender volume entitled *Sonnets
by E. B. B.,* with the imprint Reading, 1847,
and marked *Not for Publication ;* but three
years later the Sonnets were included in the
new edition of Mrs. Browning's complete
works.

SONNETS FROM THE PORTU-GUESE

I

I THOUGHT once how Theocritus had sung
Of the sweet years, the dear and wished-
    for years,
Who each one in a gracious hand ap-
    pears
To bear a gift for mortals, old or young:

And, as I mused it in his antique tongue,
I saw, in gradual vision through my tears,
The sweet, sad years, the melancholy years,
Those of my own life, who by turns had
    flung
A shadow across me. Straightway I was
    'ware,
So weeping, how a mystic Shape did move
Behind me, and drew me backward by the
    hair;

And a voice said in mastery, while I
    strove, —
'Guess now who holds thee?' — 'Death,'
    I said. But, there,
The silver answer rang, — 'Not Death, but
    Love.'

II

But only three in all God's universe
Have heard this word thou hast said, —
    Himself, beside
Thee speaking, and me listening! and
    replied
One of us . . . *that* was God, . . . and laid
    the curse
So darkly on my eyelids, as to amerce
My sight from seeing thee, — that if I had
    died,
The deathweights, placed there, would have
    signified
Less absolute exclusion. 'Nay' is worse
From God than from all others, O my
    friend!
Men could not part us with their worldly
    jars,
Nor the seas change us, nor the tempests
    bend;
Our hands would touch for all the mountain-
    bars:
And, heaven being rolled between us at the
    end,
We should but vow the faster for the stars.

III

Unlike are we, unlike, O princely Heart!
Unlike our uses and our destinies.
Our ministering two angels look surprise
On one another, as they strike athwart
Their wings in passing. Thou, bethink
    thee, art
A guest for queens to social pageantries,
With gages from a hundred brighter eyes
Than tears even can make mine, to play
    thy part
Of chief musician. What hast *thou* to
    do
With looking from the lattice-lights at me,
A poor, tired, wandering singer, singing
    through
The dark, and leaning up a cypress tree?
The chrism is on thine head, — on mine, the
    dew, —
And Death must dig the level where these
    agree.

IV

Thou hast thy calling to some palace-floor,
Most gracious singer of high poems! where
The dancers will break footing, from the
    care
Of watching up thy pregnant lips for more.
And dost thou lift this house's latch too
    poor
For hand of thine? and canst thou think
    and bear
To let thy music drop here unaware
In folds of golden fulness at my door?
Look up and see the casement broken in,
The bats and owlets builders in the roof!
My cricket chirps against thy mandolin.
Hush, call no echo up in further proof
Of desolation! there's a voice within
That weeps . . . as thou must sing . . .
    alone, aloof.

V

I lift my heavy heart up solemnly,
As once Electra her sepulchral urn,
And, looking in thine eyes, I overturn
The ashes at thy feet. Behold and see
What a great heap of grief lay hid in me,
And how the red wild sparkles dimly burn
Through the ashen grayness. If thy foot
    in scorn
Could tread them out to darkness utterly,
It might be well perhaps. But if instead
Thou wait beside me for the wind to blow
The gray dust up, . . . those laurels on
    thine head,
O my Belovèd, will not shield thee so,
That none of all the fires shall scorch and
    shred
The hair beneath. Stand farther off then!
    go.

VI

Go from me. Yet I feel that I shall stand
Henceforward in thy shadow. Nevermore
Alone upon the threshold of my door
Of individual life, I shall command
The uses of my soul, nor lift my hand
Serenely in the sunshine as before,
Without the sense of that which I forbore —
Thy touch upon the palm. The widest land
Doom takes to part us, leaves thy heart in
    mine
With pulses that beat double. What I do
And what I dream include thee, as the
    wine

Must taste of its own grapes.   And when I
     sue
God for myself, He hears that name of
     thine,
And sees within my eyes the tears of two.

VII

THE face of all the world is changed, I
     think,
Since first I heard the footsteps of thy soul
Move still, oh, still, beside me, as they stole
Betwixt me and the dreadful outer brink
Of obvious death, where I, who thought to
     sink,
Was caught up into love, and taught the
     whole
Of life in a new rhythm.   The cup of dole
God gave for baptism, I am fain to drink,
And praise its sweetness, Sweet, with thee
     anear.
The names of country, heaven, are changed
     away
For where thou art or shalt be, there or
     here;
And this . . . this lute and song . . . loved
     yesterday,
(The singing angels know) are only dear
Because thy name moves right in what they
     say.

VIII

WHAT can I give thee back, O liberal
And princely giver, who hast brought the
     gold
And purple of thine heart, unstained, un-
     told,
And laid them on the outside of the wall
For such as I to take or leave withal,
In unexpected largesse ? am I cold,
Ungrateful, that for these most manifold
High gifts, I render nothing back at all ?
Not so; not cold, — but very poor instead.
Ask God who knows.   For frequent tears
     have run
The colors from my life, and left so dead
And pale a stuff, it were not fitly done
To give the same as pillow to thy head.
Go farther ! let it serve to trample on.

IX

CAN it be right to give what I can give ?
To let thee sit beneath the fall of tears
As salt as mine, and hear the sighing years
Re-sighing on my lips renunciative

Through those infrequent smiles which fail
     to live
For all thy adjurations ?   O my fears,
That this can scarce be right !   We are
     not peers,
So to be lovers; and I own, and grieve,
That givers of such gifts as mine are, must
Be counted with the ungenerous.   Out,
     alas !
I will not soil thy purple with my dust,
Nor breathe my poison on thy Venice-
     glass,
Nor give thee any love — which were un-
     just.
Beloved, I only love thee ! let it pass.

X

YET, love, mere love, is beautiful indeed
And worthy of acceptation.   Fire is bright,
Let temple burn, or flax; an equal light
Leaps in the flame from cedar-plank or
     weed:
And love is fire.   And when I say at need
I love thee . . . mark ! . . . *I love thee* — in
     thy sight
I stand transfigured, glorified aright,
With conscience of the new rays that pro-
     ceed
Out of my face toward thine.   There 's
     nothing low
In love, when love the lowest: meanest
     creatures
Who love God, God accepts while loving so.
And what I *feel*, across the inferior fea-
     tures
Of what I *am*, doth flash itself, and show
How that great work of Love enhances
     Nature's.

XI

AND therefore if to love can be desert,
I am not all unworthy.   Cheeks as pale
As these you see, and trembling knees that
     fail
To bear the burden of a heavy heart, —
This weary minstrel-life that once was girt
To climb Aornus, and can scarce avail
To pipe now 'gainst the valley nightingale
A melancholy music, — why advert
To these things ?   O Belovèd, it is plain
I am not of thy worth nor for thy place !
And yet, because I love thee, I obtain
From that same love this vindicating
     grace,

To live on still in love, and yet in vain, —
To bless thee, yet renounce thee to thy
    face.

XII

INDEED this very love which is my boast,
And which, when rising up from breast to
    brow,
Doth crown me with a ruby large enow
To draw men's eyes and prove the inner
    cost, —
This love even, all my worth, to the utter-
    most,
I should not love withal, unless that thou
Hadst set me an example, shown me how,
When first thine earnest eyes with mine
    were crossed,
And love called love.   And thus, I cannot
    speak
Of love even, as a good thing of my own:
Thy soul hath snatched up mine all faint
    and weak,
And placed it by thee on a golden
    throne, —
And that I love (O soul, we must be
    meek !)
Is by thee only, whom I love alone.

XIII

AND wilt thou have me fashion into speech
The love I bear thee, finding words enough,
And hold the torch out, while the winds
    are rough,
Between our faces, to cast light on
    each ? —
I drop it at thy feet.   I cannot teach
My hand to hold my spirit so far off
From myself — me — that I should bring
    thee proof
In words, of love hid in me out of reach.
Nay, let the silence of my womanhood
Commend my woman-love to thy belief, —
Seeing that I stand unwon, however wooed,
And rend the garment of my life, in brief,
By a most dauntless, voiceless fortitude,
Lest one touch of this heart convey its
    grief.

XIV

IF thou must love me, let it be for nought
Except for love's sake only.   Do not say
' I love her for her smile — her look — her
    way
Of speaking gently, — for a trick of
    thought

That falls in well with mine, and certes
    brought
A sense of pleasant ease on such a day ' —
For these things in themselves, Belovèd,
    may
Be changed, or change for thee, — and
    love, so wrought,
May be unwrought so.   Neither love me
    for
Thine own dear pity's wiping my cheeks
    dry, —
A creature might forget to weep, who bore
Thy comfort long, and lose thy love
    thereby !
But love me for love's sake, that evermore
Thou mayst love on, through love's eter-
    nity.

XV

ACCUSE me not, beseech thee, that I wear
Too calm and sad a face in front of thine;
For we two look two ways, and cannot
    shine
With the same sunlight on our brow and
    hair.
On me thou lookest with no doubting care,
As on a bee shut in a crystalline;
Since sorrow hath shut me safe in love's
    divine,
And to spread wing and fly in the outer
    air
Were most impossible failure, if I strove
To fail so.   But I look on thee — on
    thee —
Beholding, besides love, the end of love,
Hearing oblivion beyond memory;
As one who sits and gazes from above,
Over the rivers to the bitter sea.

XVI

AND yet, because thou overcomest so,
Because thou art more noble and like a
    king,
Thou canst prevail against my fears and
    fling
Thy purple round me, till my heart shall
    grow
Too close against thine heart henceforth to
    know
How it shook when alone.   Why, conquer-
    ing
May prove as lordly and complete a thing
In lifting upward, as in crushing low !
And as a vanquished soldier yields his
    sword

To one who lifts him from the bloody
  earth,
Even so, Belovèd, I at last record,
Here ends my strife. If *thou* invite me
  forth,
I rise above abasement at the word.
Make thy love larger to enlarge my worth.

XVII

MY poet, thou canst touch on all the notes
God set between his After and Before,
And strike up and strike off the general
  roar
Of the rushing worlds a melody that floats
In a serene air purely.   Antidotes
Of medicated music, answering for
Mankind's forlornest uses, thou canst pour
From thence into their ears. God's will
  devotes
Thine to such ends, and mine to wait on
  thine.
How, Dearest, wilt thou have me for most
  use ?
A hope, to sing by gladly ? or a fine
Sad memory, with thy songs to interfuse ?
A shade, in which to sing — of palm or pine?
A grave, on which to rest from singing ?
  Choose.

XVIII

I NEVER gave a lock of hair away
To a man, Dearest, except this to thee,
Which now upon my fingers thoughtfully,
I ring out to the full brown length and say
'Take it.'   My day of youth went yester-
  day;
My hair no longer bounds to my foot's glee,
Nor plant I it from rose or myrtle-tree,
As girls do, any more: it only may
Now shade on two pale cheeks the mark of
  tears,
Taught drooping from the head that hangs
  aside
Through sorrow's trick. I thought the
  funeral-shears
Would take this first, but Love is justi-
  fied, —
Take it thou, — finding pure, from all
  those years,
The kiss my mother left here when she
  died.

XIX

THE soul's Rialto hath its merchandise;
I barter curl for curl upon that mart,

And from my poet's forehead to my heart
Receive this lock which outweighs argo-
  sies, —
As purply black, as erst to Pindar's eyes
The dim purpureal tresses gloomed
  athwart
The nine white Muse-brows. For this
  counterpart,
The bay-crown's shade, . Belovèd, I surmise,
Still lingers on thy curl, it is so black !
Thus, with a fillet of smooth-kissing
  breath,
I tie the shadows safe from gliding back,
And lay the gift where nothing hindereth;
Here on my heart, as on thy brow, to lack
No natural heat till mine grows cold in
  death.

XX

BELOVED, my Belovèd, when I think
That thou wast in the world a year ago,
What time I sat alone here in the snow
And saw no footprint, heard the silence
  sink
No moment at thy voice, but, link by link,
Went counting all my chains as if that so
They never could fall off at any blow
Struck by thy possible hand, — why, thus
  I drink
Of life's great cup of wonder !   Wonder-
  ful,
Never to feel thee thrill the day or night
With personal act or speech, — nor ever
  cull
Some prescience of thee with the blossoms
  white
Thou sawest growing ! Atheists are as
  dull,
Who cannot guess God's presence out of
  sight.

XXI

SAY over again, and yet once over again,
That thou dost love me.   Though the
  word repeated
Should seem 'a cuckoo-song,' as thou dost
  treat it,
Remember, never to the hill or plain,
Valley and wood, without her cuckoo-
  strain
Comes the fresh Spring in all her green
  completed.
Belovèd, I, amid the darkness greeted
By a doubtful spirit-voice, in that doubt's
  pain

Cry, 'Speak once more — thou lovest!'
   Who can fear
Too many stars, though each in heaven
   shall roll,
Too many flowers, though each shall
   crown the year?
Say thou dost love me, love me, love me —
   toll
The silver iterance! — only minding,
   Dear,
To love me also in silence with thy soul.

XXII

WHEN our two souls stand up erect and
   strong,
Face to face, silent, drawing nigh and
   nigher,
Until the lengthening wings break into fire
At either curvèd point, — what bitter
   wrong
Can the earth do to us, that we should not
   long
Be here contented? Think. In mount-
   ing higher,
The angels would press on us and aspire
To drop some golden orb of perfect song
Into our deep, dear silence. Let us stay
Rather on earth, Belovèd, — where the un-
   fit
Contrarious moods of men recoil away
And isolate pure spirits, and permit
A place to stand and love in for a day,
With darkness and the death-hour round-
   ing it.

XXIII

Is it indeed so? If I lay here dead,
Wouldst thou miss any life in losing
   mine?
And would the sun for thee more coldly
   shine
Because of grave-damps falling round my
   head?
I marvelled, my Belovèd, when I read
Thy thought so in the letter. I am thine —
But . . . so much to thee? Can I pour
   thy wine
While my hands tremble? Then my
   soul, instead
Of dreams of death, resumes life's lower
   range.
Then, love me, Love! look on me —
   breathe on me!
As brighter ladies do not count it strange,
For love, to give up acres and degree,

I yield the grave for thy sake, and ex-
   change
My near sweet view of Heaven, for earth
   with thee!

XXIV

LET the world's sharpness, like a clasping
   knife,
Shut in upon itself and do no harm
In this close hand of Love, now soft and
   warm,
And let us hear no sound of human strife
After the click of the shutting. Life to
   life —
I lean upon thee, Dear, without alarm,
And feel as safe as guarded by a charm
Against the stab of worldlings, who if rife
Are weak to injure. Very whitely still
The lilies of our lives may reassure
Their blossoms from their roots, accessible
Alone to heavenly dews that drop not fewer,
Growing straight, out of man's reach, on
   the hill.
God only, who made us rich, can make us
   poor.

XXV

A HEAVY heart, Belovèd, have I borne
From year to year until I saw thy face,
And sorrow after sorrow took the place
Of all those natural joys as lightly worn
As the stringèd pearls, each lifted in its
   turn
By a beating heart at dance-time. Hopes
   apace
Were changed to long despairs, till God's
   own grace
Could scarcely lift above the world for-
   lorn
My heavy heart. Then thou didst bid me
   bring
And let it drop adown thy calmly great
Deep being! Fast it sinketh, as a thing
Which its own nature doth precipitate,
While thine doth close above it, mediating
Betwixt the stars and the unaccomplished
   fate.

XXVI

I LIVED with visions for my company
Instead of men and women, years ago,
And found them gentle mates, nor thought
   to know
A sweeter music than they played to me.

But soon their trailing purple was not free
Of this world's dust, their lutes did silent
    grow,
And I myself grew faint and blind below
Their vanishing eyes. Then THOU didst
    come — to be,
Belovèd, what they seemed. Their shining
    fronts,
Their songs, their splendors (better, yet
    the same,
As river-water hallowed into fonts),
Met in thee, and from out thee overcame
My soul with satisfaction of all wants:
Because God's gifts put man's best dreams
    to shame.

XXVII

MY own Belovèd, who hast lifted me
From this drear flat of earth where I was
    thrown,
And, in betwixt the languid ringlets, blown
A life-breath, till the forehead hopefully
Shines out again, as all the angels see,
Before thy saving kiss! My own, my
    own,
Who camest to me when the world was
    gone,
And I who looked for only God, found
    thee!
I find thee; I am safe, and strong, and
    glad.
As one who stands in dewless asphodel
Looks backward on the tedious time he
    had
In the upper life, — so I, with bosom-
    swell,
Make witness, here, between the good and
    bad,
That Love, as strong as Death, retrieves as
    well.

XXVIII

MY letters! all dead paper, mute and
    white !
And yet they seem alive and quivering
Against my tremulous hands which loose
    the string
And let them drop down on my knee to-
    night.
This said, — he wished to have me in his
    sight
Once, as a friend: this fixed a day in spring
To come and touch my hand . . . a simple
    thing,

Yet I wept for it ! — this, . . . the paper 's
    light . . .
Said, *Dear, I love thee;* and I sank and
    quailed
As if God's future thundered on my past.
This said, *I am thine* — and so its ink has
    paled
With lying at my heart that beat too fast.
And this . . . O Love, thy words have ill
    availed
If, what this said, I dared repeat at last !

XXIX

I THINK of thee ! — my thoughts do twine
    and bud
About thee, as wild vines, about a tree,
Put out broad leaves, and soon there 's
    nought to see
Except the straggling green which hides
    the wood.
Yet, O my palm-tree, be it understood
I will not have my thoughts instead of
    thee
Who art dearer, better ! Rather, instantly
Renew thy presence; as a strong tree
    should,
Rustle thy boughs and set thy trunk all
    bare,
And let these bands of greenery which in-
    sphere thee
Drop heavily down, — burst, shattered,
    everywhere !
Because, in this deep joy to see and hear
    thee
And breathe within thy shadow a new air,
I do not think of thee — I am too near thee.

XXX

I SEE thine image through my tears to-
    night,
And yet to-day I saw thee smiling. How
Refer the cause ? — Belovèd, is it thou
Or I, who makes me sad ? The acolyte
Amid the chanted joy and thankful rite
May so fall flat, with pale insensate brow,
On the altar-stair. I hear thy voice and
    vow,
Perplexed, uncertain, since thou art out of
    sight,
As he, in his swooning ears, the choir's
    Amen.
Belovèd, dost thou love ? or did I see all
The glory as I dreamed, and fainted when
Too vehement light dilated my ideal,

For my soul's eyes ? Will that light come
again,
As now these tears come — falling hot and
real ?

XXXI

THOU comest ! all is said without a word.
I sit beneath thy looks, as children do
In the noon-sun, with souls that tremble
through
Their happy eyelids from an unaverred
Yet prodigal inward joy. Behold, I erred
In that last doubt ! and yet I cannot rue
The sin most, but the occasion — that we
two
Should for a moment stand unministered
By a mutual presence. Ah, keep near and
close,
Thou dovelike help ! and, when my fears
would rise,
With thy broad heart serenely interpose:
Brood down with thy divine sufficiencies
These thoughts which tremble when bereft
of those,
Like callow birds left desert to the skies.

XXXII

THE first time that the sun rose on thine
oath
To love me, I looked forward to the moon
To slacken all those bonds which seemed
too soon
And quickly tied to make a lasting troth.
Quick-loving hearts, I thought, may quickly
loathe;
And, looking on myself, I seemed not one
For such man's love ! — more like an out-
of-tune
Worn viol, a good singer would be wroth
To spoil his song with, and which, snatched
in haste,
Is laid down at the first ill-sounding note.
I did not wrong myself so, but I placed
A wrong on *thee*. For perfect strains may
float
'Neath master-hands, from instruments de-
faced, —
And great souls, at one stroke, may do and
doat.

XXXIII

YES, call me by my pet-name ! let me hear
The name I used to run at, when a child,
From innocent play, and leave the cowslips
piled,
To glance up in some face that proved me
dear
With the look of its eyes. I miss the clear
Fond voices which, being drawn and recon-
ciled
Into the music of Heaven's undefiled,
Call me no longer. Silence on the bier,
While I call God — call God ! — So let thy
mouth
Be heir to those who are now exanimate.
Gather the north flowers to complete the
south,
And catch the early love up in the late.
Yes, call me by that name, — and I, in
truth,
With the same heart, will answer and not
wait.

XXXIV

WITH the same heart, I said, I 'll answer
thee
As those, when thou shalt call me by my
name —
Lo, the vain promise ! is the same, the
same,
Perplexed and ruffled by life's strategy ?
When called before, I told how hastily
I dropped my flowers or brake off from a
game,
To run and answer with the smile that
came
At play last moment, and went on with me
Through my obedience. When I answer
now,
I drop a grave thought, break from soli-
tude;
Yet still my heart goes to thee — ponder
how —
Not as to a single good, but all my good !
Lay thy hand on it, best one, and allow
That no child's foot could run fast as this
blood.

XXXV

IF I leave all for thee, wilt thou exchange
And be all to me ? Shall I never miss
Home-talk and blessing and the common
kiss
That comes to each in turn, nor count it
strange,
When I look up, to drop on a new range
Of walls and floors, another home than
this ?
Nay, wilt thou fill that place by me which
is

Filled by dead eyes too tender to know
    change?
That 's hardest. If to conquer love, has
    tried,
To conquer grief, tries more, as all things
    prove;
For grief indeed is love and grief beside.
Alas, I have grieved so I am hard to love.
Yet love me — wilt thou? Open thine
    heart wide,
And fold within the wet wings of thy dove.

XXXVI

WHEN we met first and loved, I did not
    build
Upon the event with marble. Could it
    mean
To last, a love set pendulous between
Sorrow and sorrow? Nay, I rather thrilled,
Distrusting every light that seemed to gild
The onward path, and feared to overlean
A finger even. And, though I have grown
    serene
And strong since then, I think that God
    has willed
A still renewable fear . . . O love, O
    troth . . .
Lest these enclaspèd hands should never
    hold,
This mutual kiss drop down between us
    both
As an unowned thing, once the lips being
    cold.
And Love, be false! if *he*, to keep one
    oath,
Must lose one joy, by his life's star foretold.

XXXVII

PARDON, oh, pardon, that my soul should
    make,
Of all that strong divineness which I know
For thine and thee, an image only so
Formed of the sand, and fit to shift and
    break.
It is that distant years which did not take
Thy sovranty, recoiling with a blow,
Have forced my swimming brain to under-
    go
Their doubt and dread, and blindly to for-
    sake
Thy purity of likeness and distort
Thy worthiest love to a worthless counter-
    feit:
As if a shipwrecked Pagan, safe in port,

His guardian sea-god to commemorate,
Should set a sculptured porpoise, gills
    a-snort
And vibrant tail, within the temple-gate.

XXXVIII

FIRST time he kissed me, he but only kissed
The fingers of this hand wherewith I write;
And ever since, it grew more clean and
    white,
Slow to world-greetings, quick with its 'Oh,
    list,'
When the angels speak. A ring of ame-
    thyst
I could not wear here, plainer to my sight,
Than that first kiss. The second passed in
    height
The first, and sought the forehead, and half
    missed,
Half falling on the hair. O beyond meed!
That was the chrism of love, which love's
    own crown,
With sanctifying sweetness, did precede.
The third upon my lips was folded down
In perfect, purple state; since when, in-
    deed,
I have been proud and said, 'My love, my
    own.'

XXXIX

BECAUSE thou hast the power and own'st
    the grace
To look through and behind this mask of
    me
(Against which years have beat thus blanch-
    ingly
With their rains), and behold my soul's
    true face,
The dim and weary witness of life's race, —
Because thou hast the faith and love to see,
Through that same soul's distracting
    lethargy,
The patient angel waiting for a place
In the new Heavens, — because nor sin nor
    woe,
Nor God's infliction, nor death's neighbor-
    hood,
Nor all which others viewing, turn to
    go,
Nor all which makes me tired of all, self-
    viewed, —
Nothing repels thee, . . . Dearest, teach
    me so
To pour out gratitude, as thou dost, good!

XL

Oh, yes ! they love through all this world
        of ours !
I will not gainsay love, called love forsooth.
I have heard love talked in my early youth,
And since, not so long back but that the
        flowers
Then gathered, smell still. Mussulmans
        and Giaours
Throw kerchiefs at a smile, and have no
        ruth
For any weeping. Polypheme's white tooth
Slips on the nut if, after frequent showers,
The shell is over - smooth, — and not so
        much
Will turn the thing called love, aside to
        hate
Or else to oblivion. But thou art not such
A lover, my Belovèd ! thou canst wait
Through sorrow and sickness, to bring souls
        to touch,
And think it soon when others cry 'Too
        late.'

XLI

I THANK all who have loved me in their
        hearts,
With thanks and love from mine. Deep
        thanks to all
Who paused a little near the prison-wall
To hear my music in its louder parts
Ere they went onward, each one to the
        mart's
Or temple's occupation, beyond call.
But thou, who, in my voice's sink and fall
When the sob took it, thy divinest Art's
Own instrument didst drop down at thy
        foot
To hearken what I said between my
        tears, . . .
Instruct me how to thank thee ! Oh, to
        shoot
My soul's full meaning into future years,
That *they* should lend it utterance, and
        salute
Love that endures, from Life that disap-
        pears !

XLII

This sonnet was not in the privately printed
collection of 1847, which were forty-three in
all ; but was first inserted when the sonnets
were included among Mrs. Browning's other
poems in 1856.

' *My future will not copy fair my past* ' —
I wrote that once ; and thinking at my side
My ministering life-angel justified
The word by his appealing look upcast
To the white throne of God, I turned at
        last,
And there, instead, saw thee, not unallied
To angels in thy soul ! Then I, long tried
By natural ills, received the comfort fast,
While budding, at thy sight, my pilgrim's
        staff
Gave out green leaves with morning dews
        impearled.
I seek no copy now of life's first half:
Leave here the pages with long musing
        curled,
And write me new my future's epigraph,
New angel mine, unhoped for in the world !

XLIII

How do I love thee ? Let me count the
        ways.
I love thee to the depth and breadth and
        height
My soul can reach, when feeling out of
        sight
For the ends of Being and ideal Grace.
I love thee to the level of everyday's
Most quiet need, by sun and candle-light.
I love thee freely, as men strive for Right;
I love thee purely, as they turn from
        Praise.
I love thee with the passion put to use
In my old griefs, and with my childhood's
        faith.
I love thee with a love I seemed to lose
With my lost saints, — I love thee with
        the breath,
Smiles, tears, of all my life ! — and, if God
        choose,
I shall but love thee better after death.

XLIV

BELOVÈD, thou hast brought me many
        flowers
Plucked in the garden, all the summer
        through
And winter, and it seemed as if they grew
In this close room, nor missed the sun and
        showers
So, in the like name of that love of ours,
Take back these thoughts which here un-
        folded too,
And which on warm and cold days I with-
        drew

From my heart's ground. Indeed, those
   beds and bowers
Be overgrown with bitter weeds and rue,
And wait thy weeding; yet here's eglan-
   tine,
Here's ivy ! — take them, as I used to do

Thy flowers, and keep them where they
   shall not pine.
Instruct thine eyes to keep their colors
   true,
And tell thy soul their roots are left in
   mine.

CASA GUIDI WINDOWS

Mr. and Mrs. Browning, who had passed the first winter of their married life at Pisa, moved on to Florence in May, 1847. They occupied for the first two or three months of their residence there an apartment in the Via delle Belle Donne, near the Duomo ; but on their return to Florence, after a short visit to Vallombrosa at midsummer, they installed themselves in the palace on the Via Maggio, which has ever since been associated with their names ; where the Italians have placed a tablet to Mrs. Browning's memory and which is now the property of Mr. Robert Barrett Browning. Mrs. Browning's first letter from 'Palazzo Guidi' is dated May 7, 1847. The windows of the apartment, which comprised six rooms on the *piano nobile*, overlooked the then Piazza del Gran Duca ; now the Piazza Pitti, — which was the actual theatre of many of the most picturesque events and striking demonstrations connected with the abortive Italian revolution of 1848. The first part of the poem was written in that heroic year ; the second, nearly three years later, in 1851, — the year of its first publication by Chapman & Hall. Mrs. Browning is careful to explain in her preface to this first edition, that she has attempted ' no continuous narrative, nor exposition of political philosophy,' but merely ' a simple story of personal impressions

whose only value is in the intensity with which they were received, as proving her warm attachment for a beautiful and unfortunate country.' She further apologizes for the discrepancy in tone between the two parts of the poem, which, she says, cannot be as painful to the reader as it is to the writer herself : though she thinks it should be accepted as a guaranty of her sincerity. Indeed Part II. shows a great, and much too great, revulsion of feeling from the facile sympathy and buoyant enthusiasm of Part I. Neither the optimism of 1848, nor the pessimism of 1851, was fully justified by facts ; but in either case, the writer's point of view was more that of an artist than a politician ; of a spectator at the play, than of an earnest partisan. Her wholesouled adoption of the cause of Italian independence, and passionate identification with it, date from a later period, after she had lived longer in Italy, and had begun to know Italians. The defeat of the patriots at Novara in 1849, which crushed the hopes of Italy for the time being, and was attended by peculiarly tragical circumstances, is barely mentioned in Mrs. Browning's letters. The premature peace of Villafranca, ten years later, almost broke her heart, and certainly shortened her days.

CASA GUIDI WINDOWS

A POEM, IN TWO PARTS

PART I

I HEARD last night a little child go sing-
   ing
'Neath Casa Guidi windows, by the
   church,
O bella libertà, O bella ! — stringing
   The same words still on notes he went
     in search
So high for, you concluded the upspring-
   ing

Of such a nimble bird to sky from perch
Must leave the whole bush in a tremble
   green,
And that the heart of Italy must beat,
While such a voice had leave to rise serene
   'Twixt church and palace of a Florence
     street:
A little child, too, who not long had been
   By mother's finger steadied on his feet,
And still *O bella libertà* he sang.

Then I thought, musing, of the innumer-
   ous
Sweet songs which still for Italy outrang
From older singers' lips who sang not thus

Exultingly and purely, yet, with pang
Fast sheathed in music, touched the heart
    of us
So finely that the pity scarcely pained.
I thought how Filicaja led on others,   20
Bewailers for their Italy enchained,
And how they called her childless among
    mothers,
    Widow of empires, ay, and scarce re-
        frained
Cursing her beauty to her face, as brothers
    Might a shamed sister's, — 'Had she
        been less fair
She were less wretched;' — how, evoking
    so
From congregated wrong and heaped
    despair
Of men and women writhing under blow,
Harrowed and hideous in a filthy lair,
Some personating Image wherein woe   30
    Was wrapt in beauty from offending
        much,
They called it Cybele, or Niobe,
    Or laid it corpse-like on a bier for
        such,
Where all the world might drop for It-
    aly
    Those cadenced tears which burn not
        where they touch, —
' Juliet of nations, canst thou die as we ?
    And was the violet crown that crowned
        thy head
So over-large, though new buds made it
    rough,
    It slipped down and across thine eyelids
        dead,
O sweet, fair Juliet ? ' Of such songs
    enough,   40
    Too many of such complaints ! behold,
        instead,
Void at Verona, Juliet's marble trough:
    As void as that is, are all images
Men set between themselves and actual
    wrong,
    To catch the weight of pity, meet the
        stress
Of conscience, — since 't is easier to gaze
    long
    On mournful masks and sad effigies
Than on real, live, weak creatures crushed
    by strong.

For me who stand in Italy to-day
Where worthier poets stood and sang be-
    fore,   50

I kiss their footsteps yet their words gain-
    say.
I can but muse in hope upon this shore
    Of golden Arno as it shoots away
Through Florence' heart beneath her
    bridges four:
    Bent bridges, seeming to strain off like
        bows
And tremble while the arrowy undertide
    Shoots on and cleaves the marble as it
        goes,
And strikes up palace-walls on either side,
    And froths the cornice out in glittering
        rows,
With doors and windows quaintly multi-
    plied,   60
And terrace-sweeps, and gazers upon all,
By whom if flower or kerchief were thrown
    out
    From any lattice there, the same would
        fall
Into the river underneath, no doubt,
    It runs so close and fast 'twixt wall and
        wall.
How beautiful ! the mountains from with-
    out
    In silence listen for the word said next.
What word will men say, — here where
    Giotto planted
    His campanile like an unperplexed
Fine question Heavenward, touching the
    things granted   70
    A noble people who, being greatly vexed
In act, in aspiration keep undaunted ?
    What word will God say ? Michael's
        Night and Day
And Dawn and Twilight wait in marble
    scorn
    Like dogs upon a dunghill, couched on
        clay,
From whence the Medicean stamp 's out-
    worn,
    The final putting off of all such sway
By all such hands, and freeing of the un-
    born
    In Florence and the great world outside
        Florence.
Three hundred years his patient statues
    wait   80
    In that small chapel of the dim Saint
        Lawrence:
Day's eyes are breaking bold and passion-
    ate
    Over his shoulder, and will flash abhor
        rence

On darkness and with level looks meet
　　fate,
　　When once loose from that marble film
　　　　of theirs;
The Night has wild dreams in her sleep,
　　　the Dawn
　　Is haggard as the sleepless, Twilight
　　　wears
A sort of horror; as the veil withdrawn
　　'Twixt the artist's soul and works had
　　　left them heirs
Of speechless thoughts which would not
　　quail nor fawn,　　　　　　　　　90
　　Of angers and contempts, of hope and
　　　love:
For not without a meaning did he place
The princely Urbino on the seat above
With everlasting shadow on his face,
　　While the slow dawns and twilights dis-
　　approve
The ashes of his long-extinguished race
　　Which never more shall clog the feet of
　　　men.
I do believe, divinest Angelo,
　　That winter-hour in Via Larga, when
They bade thee build a statue up in snow
　　And straight that marvel of thine art
　　again　　　　　　　　　　　　101
Dissolved beneath the sun's Italian glow,
　　Thine eyes, dilated with the plastic
　　passion,
　　Thawing too in drops of wounded man-
　　hood, since,
　　To mock alike thine art and indignation,
Laughed at the palace-window the new
　　prince, —
　　('Aha! this genius needs for exalta-
　　tion,
When all 's said and howe'er the proud
　　may wince,
　　A little marble from our princely
　　mines!')
I do believe that hour thou laughedst too
　　For the whole sad world and for thy
　　Florentines,　　　　　　　　　111
After those few tears, which were only
　　few!
　　That as, beneath the sun, the grand
　　white lines
Of thy snow-statue trembled and with-
　　drew, —
　　The head, erect as Jove's, being palsied
　　first,
The eyelids flattened, the full brow turned
　　blank,

The right-hand, raised but now as if it
　　cursed,
Dropt, a mere snowball, (till the people
　　sank
　　Their voices, though a louder laughter
　　burst
From the royal window) — thou couldst
　　proudly thank　　　　　　　　120
God and the prince for promise and
　　presage,
And laugh the laugh back, I think verily,
　　Thine eyes being purged by tears of
　　righteous rage
To read a wrong into a prophecy,
　　And measure a true great man's heri-
　　tage
Against a mere great-duke's posterity.
　　I think thy soul said then, 'I do not need
A princedom and its quarries, after all;
　　For if I write, paint, carve a word, in-
　　deed,
On book or board or dust, on floor or wall,
　　The same is kept of God who taketh
　　heed　　　　　　　　　　　　131
That not a letter of the meaning fall
　　Or ere it touch and teach his world's
　　deep heart,
Outlasting, therefore, all your lordships,
　　sir!
　　So keep your stone, beseech you, for your
　　part,
To cover up your grave-place and refer
　　The proper titles; I live by my art.
The thought I threw into this snow shall
　　stir
　　This gazing people when their gaze is
　　done;
And the tradition of your act and mine, 140
　　When all the snow is melted in the sun,
Shall gather up, for unborn men, a sign
　　Of what is the true princedom, — ay,
　　and none
Shall laugh that day, except the drunk
　　with wine.'

Amen, great Angelo! the day 's at hand.
If many laugh not on it, shall we weep?
　　Much more we must not, let us under-
　　stand.
Through rhymers sonneteering in their
　　sleep,
　　And archaists mumbling dry bones up
　　the land,
And sketchers lauding ruined towns
　　a-heap, —　　　　　　　　　　150

Through all that drowsy hum of voices
   smooth,
The hopeful bird mounts carolling from
   brake,
   The hopeful child, with leaps to catch
     his growth,
Sings open-eyed for liberty's sweet sake:
   And I, a singer also from my youth,
Prefer to sing with these who are awake,
   With birds, with babes, with men who
     will not fear
The baptism of the holy morning dew,
   (And many of such wakers now are here,
Complete in their anointed manhood, who
   Will greatly dare and greatlier perse-
     vere)   161
Than join those old thin voices with my
   new,
   And sigh for Italy with some safe sigh
Cooped up in music 'twixt an oh and ah, —
   Nay, hand in hand with that young child,
     will I
Go singing rather, ' *Bella libertà*,'
   Than, with those poets, croon the dead or
     cry
' *Se tu men bella fossi, Italia !* '

'Less wretched if less fair.'   Perhaps
   a truth
Is so far plain in this, that Italy,   170
   Long trammelled with the purple of her
     youth
Against her age's ripe activity,
   Sits still upon her tombs, without death's
     ruth
But also without life's brave energy.
   ' Now tell us what is Italy ? ' men ask:
And others answer, ' Virgil, Cicero,
   Catullus, Cæsar.'   What beside ? to
     task
The memory closer — ' Why, Boccaccio,
   Dante, Petrarca,' — and if still the flask
Appears to yield its wine by drops too
   slow, —   180
' Angelo, Raffael, Pergolese,' — all
Whose strong hearts beat through stone,
   or charged again
   The paints with fire of souls electrical,
Or broke up heaven for music.   What
   more then ?
   Why, then, no more.   The chaplet's last
     beads fall
In naming the last saintship within ken,
   And, after that, none prayeth in the land.
Alas, this Italy has too long swept

Heroic ashes up for hour-glass sand;
Of her own past, impassioned nympholept !
   Consenting to be nailed here by the hand
To the very bay-tree under which she
   stept   192
   A queen of old, and plucked a leafy
     branch;
And, licensing the world too long indeed
   To use her broad phylacteries to stanch
And stop her bloody lips, she takes no
   heed
   How one clear word would draw an
     avalanche
Of living sons around her, to succeed
   The vanished generations.   Can she
     count
These oil-eaters with large live mobile
   mouths   200
   Agape for macaroni, in the amount
Of consecrated heroes of her south's
   Bright rosary ?   The pitcher at the
     fount,
The gift of gods, being broken, she much
   loathes
   To let the ground-leaves of the place
     confer
A natural bowl.   So henceforth she would
   seem
No nation, but the poet's pensioner,
   With alms from every land of song and
     dream,
While aye her pipers sadly pipe of her
Until their proper breaths, in that extreme
   Of sighing, split the reed on which they
     played: 211
Of which, no more.   But never say ' no
   more '
To Italy's life !   Her memories undis-
     mayed
Still argue ' evermore; ' her graves implore
   Her future to be strong and not afraid;
Her very statues send their looks before.

We do not serve the dead — the past is
   past.
God lives, and lifts his glorious mornings
   up
Before the eyes of men awake at last, 219
Who put away the meats they used to sup,
   And down upon the dust of earth outcast
The dregs remaining of the ancient cup,
   Then turn to wakeful prayer and worthy
     act.
The Dead, upon their awful 'vantage
   ground,

The sun not in their faces, shall abstract
No more our strength; we will not be dis-
    crowned
    As guardians of their crowns, nor deign
      transact
A barter of the present, for a sound
Of good so counted in the foregone days.
O Dead, ye shall no longer cling to us   230
With rigid hands of dessicating praise,
And drag us backward by the garment
    thus,
    To stand and laud you in long-drawn
      virelays !
We will not henceforth be oblivious
    Of our own lives, because ye lived be-
      fore,
Nor of our acts, because ye acted well.
    We thank you that ye first unlatched
      the door,
But will not make it inaccessible
    By thankings on the threshold any more.
We hurry onward to extinguish hell   240
    With our fresh souls, our younger hope,
      and God's
Maturity of purpose.   Soon shall we
Die also ! and, that then our periods
Of life may round themselves to memory
    As smoothly as on our graves the burial-
      sods,
We now must look to it to excel as ye,
And bear our age as far, unlimited
By the last mind-mark; so, to be invoked
By future generations, as their Dead.

'T is true that when the dust of death has
    choked   250
    A great man's voice, the common words
      he said
Turn oracles, the common thoughts he
    yoked
    Like horses, draw like griffins: this is
      true
And acceptable. I, too, should desire,
    When men make record, with the flowers
      they strew,
'Savonarola's soul went out in fire
    Upon our Grand-duke's piazza, and
      burned through
A moment first, or ere he did expire,
    The veil betwixt the right and wrong, and
      showed
How near God sat and judged the judges
    there,' —   260
    Upon the self-same pavement over-
    strewed

To cast my violets with as reverent care,
    And prove that all the winters which
      have snowed
Cannot snow out the scent from stones and
    air
Of a sincere man's virtues. This was he,
Savonarola, who, while Peter sank
    With his whole boat-load, called coura-
      geously
'Wake Christ, wake Christ !' — who,
    having tried the tank
Of old church-waters used for baptistry
Ere Luther came to spill them, swore they
    stank;   270
    Who also by a princely deathbed cried,
'Loose Florence, or God will not loose thy
    soul ! '

Then fell back the Magnificent and died
Beneath the star-look shooting from the
    cowl,
    Which turned to wormwood-bitterness
      the wide
Deep sea of his ambitions. It were foul
    To grudge Savonarola and the rest
Their violets: rather pay them quick and
    fresh !
The emphasis of death makes manifest
    The eloquence of action in our flesh;   280
    And men who, living, were but dimly
      guessed,
When once free from their life's entangled
    mesh,
    Show their full length in graves, or oft
      indeed
Exaggerate their stature, in the flat,
    To noble admirations which exceed
Most nobly, yet will calculate in that
    But accurately. We, who are the seed
Of buried creatures, if we turned and
    spat
Upon our antecedents, we were vile.
Bring violets rather. If these had not
    walked   290
    Their furlong, could we hope to walk our
      mile ?
Therefore bring violets. Yet if we self-
    baulked
    Stand still, a-strewing violets all the while,
These moved in vain, of whom we have
    vainly talked.
    So rise up henceforth with a cheerful
      smile,
And having strewn the violets, reap the
    corn,

And having reaped and garnered, bring
    the plough
And draw new furrows 'neath the healthy
    morn,
And plant the great Hereafter in this
    Now.

Of old 't was so. How step by step was
    worn,   300
As each man gained on each securely ! —
    how
Each by his own strength sought his own
    Ideal, —
The ultimate Perfection leaning bright
From out the sun and stars to bless the
    leal
And earnest search of all for Fair and
    Right
Through doubtful forms by earth accounted
    real !
Because old Jubal blew into delight
The souls of men with clear-piped melodies,
If youthful Asaph were content at most
To draw from Jubal's grave, with listening
    eyes,   310
Traditionary music's floating ghost
Into the grass-grown silence, were it wise ?
And was 't not wiser, Jubal's breath being
    lost,
That Miriam clashed her cymbals to sur-
    prise
The sun between her white arms flung
    apart,
With new glad golden sounds ? that Da-
    vid's strings
O'erflowed his hand with music from his
    heart ?
So harmony grows full from many springs,
And happy accident turns holy art.

You enter, in your Florence wanderings, 320
The church of Saint Maria Novella. Pass
The left stair, where at plague-time Ma-
    chiavel
Saw One with set fair face as in a glass,
Dressed out against the fear of death and
    hell,
Rustling her silks in pauses of the mass,
To keep the thought off how her husband
    fell,
When she left home, stark dead across
    her feet, —
The stair leads up to what the Orgagnas
    save
Of Dante's dæmons; you, in passing it,

Ascend the right stair from the farther
    nave   330
To muse in a small chapel scarcely lit
By Cimabue's Virgin. Bright and brave,
    That picture was accounted, mark, of
    old:
A king stood bare before its sovran grace,
    A reverent people shouted to behold
The picture, not the king, and even the
    place
Containing such a miracle grew bold,
Named the Glad Borgo from that beauteous
    face
Which thrilled the artist, after work, to
    think
His own ideal Mary-smile should stand 340
    So very near him, — he, within the
    brink
Of all that glory, let in by his hand
    With too divine a rashness ! Yet none
    shrink
Who come to gaze here now; albeit 't was
    planned
Sublimely in the thought's simplicity:
The Lady, throned in empyreal state,
    Minds only the young Babe upon her
    knee,
While sidelong angels bear the royal
    weight,
Prostrated meekly, smiling tenderly 349
Oblivion of their wings; the Child thereat
    Stretching its hand like God. If any
    should,
Because of some stiff draperies and loose
    joints,
    Gaze scorn down from the heights of
    Raffaelhood
On Cimabue's picture, — Heaven anoints
The head of no such critic, and his blood
The poet's curse strikes full on and ap-
    points
To ague and cold spasms for evermore.
A noble picture ! worthy of the shout
    Wherewith along the streets the people
    bore
Its cherub-faces which the sun threw
    out   360
    Until they stooped and entered the
    church door.
Yet rightly was young Giotto talked about,
    Whom Cimabue found among the sheep,
And knew, as gods know gods, and carried
    home
    To paint the things he had painted, with
    a deep

And fuller insight, and so overcome
  His chapel - Lady with a heavenlier
    sweep
Of light: for thus we mount into the sum
  Of great things known or acted. I
    hold, too,
That Cimabue smiled upon the lad   370
  At the first stroke which passed what he
    could do,
Or else his Virgin's smile had never had
  Such sweetness in 't. All great men who
    foreknew
Their heirs in art, for art's sake have been
    glad,
  And bent their old white heads as if un-
    crowned,
Fanatics of their pure Ideals still
  Far more than of their triumphs, which
    were found
With some less vehement struggle of the
    will.
If old Margheritone trembled, swooned
And died despairing at the open sill   380
  Of other men's achievements (who
    achieved,
By loving art beyond the master), he
  Was old Margheritone, and conceived
Never, at first youth and most ecstasy,
  A Virgin like that dream of one, which
    heaved
The death-sigh from his heart. If wist-
    fully
Margheritone sickened at the smell
Of Cimabue's laurel, let him go !
  For Cimabue stood up very well
In spite of Giotto's, and Angelico   390
  The artist-saint kept smiling in his cell
The smile with which he welcomed the
    sweet slow
  Inbreak of angels (whitening through
    the dim
That he might paint them), while the sud-
    den sense
Of Raffael's future was revealed to him
  By force of his own fair works' compe-
    tence.
  The same blue waters where the dol-
    phins swim
Suggest the tritons. Through the blue
    Immense
  Strike out, all swimmers ! cling not in
    the way
Of one another, so to sink; but learn   400
  The strong man's impulse, catch the
    freshening spray

He throws up in his motions, and discern
  By his clear westering eye, the time of
    day.
Thou, God, hast set us worthy gifts to
    earn
  Besides thy heaven and Thee ! and when
    I say
There 's room here for the weakest man
    alive
  To live and die, there 's room too, I re-
    peat,
For all the strongest to live well, and
    strive
  Their own way, by their individual
    heat, —
Like some new bee-swarm leaving the old
    hive,   410
  Despite the wax which tempts so violet-
    sweet.
Then let the living live, the dead retain
  Their grave - cold flowers ! — though
    honor 's best supplied
By bringing actions, to prove theirs not
    vain.

  Cold graves, we say ? it shall be testi-
    fied
That living men who burn in heart and
    brain,
  Without the dead were colder. If we
    tried
To sink the past beneath our feet, be
    sure
  The future would not stand. Precipi-
    tate
This old roof from the shrine, and, inse-
    cure,   420
  The nesting swallows fly off, mate from
    mate.
How scant the gardens, if the graves were
    fewer !
  The tall green poplars grew no longer
    straight
Whose tops not looked to Troy. Would
    any fight
  For Athens, and not swear by Mara-
    thon ?
Who dared build temples, without tombs
    in sight ?
  Or live, without some dead man's beni-
    son ?
Or seek truth, hope for good, and strive
    for right,
  If, looking up, he saw not in the sun
Some angel of the martyrs all day long   430

Standing and waiting? Your last
   rhythm will need
Your earliest key-note. Could I sing this
   song,
If my dead masters had not taken heed
To help the heavens and earth to make me
   strong,
As the wind ever will find out some reed
And touch it to such issues as belong
   To such a frail thing? None may
     grudge the Dead
Libations from full cups. Unless we choose
   To look back to the hills behind us
     spread,
The plains before us sadden and confuse;
If orphaned, we are disinherited.   441

I would but turn these lachrymals to use,
   And pour fresh oil in from the olive-
     grove,
To furnish them as new lamps. Shall I
   say
What made my heart beat with exulting
   love
A few weeks back? —
          The day was such a day
As Florence owes the sun. The sky
   above,
Its weight upon the mountains seemed to
   lay,
And palpitate in glory, like a dove
Who has flown too fast, full-hearted —
   take away   450
   The image! for the heart of man beat
   higher
That day in Florence, flooding all her
   streets
And piazzas with a tumult and desire.
The people, with accumulated heats
   And faces turned one way, as if one fire
Both drew and flushed them, left their
   ancient beats
   And went up towards the palace-Pitti
   wall
To thank their Grand-duke who, not quite
   of course,
   Had graciously permitted, at their call,
The citizens to use their civic force   460
   To guard their civic homes. So, one
   and all,
The Tuscan cities streamed up to the
   source
Of this new good at Florence, taking it
As good so far, presageful of more good, —
   The first torch of Italian freedom, lit

To toss in the next tiger's face who should
   Approach too near them in a greedy
     fit, —
The first pulse of an even flow of blood
   To prove the level of Italian veins
Towards rights perceived and granted.
   How we gazed   470
   From Casa Guidi windows while, in
   trains
Of orderly procession — banners raised,
   And intermittent bursts of martial
   strains
Which died upon the shout, as if amazed
   By gladness beyond music — they passed
   on!
The Magistracy, with insignia, passed, —
   And all the people shouted in the sun,
And all the thousand windows which had
   cast
   A ripple of silks in blue and scarlet
   down
(As if the houses overflowed at last),   480
   Seemed growing larger with fair heads
   and eyes.
The Lawyers passed, — and still arose the
   shout,
   And hands broke from the windows to
   surprise
Those grave calm brows with bay-tree
   leaves thrown out.
   The Priesthood passed, — the friars
   with worldly-wise
Keen sidelong glances from their beards
   about
   The street to see who shouted; many a
   monk
Who takes a long rope in the waist, was
   there:
Whereat the popular exultation drunk
With indrawn ' vivas ' the whole sunny air,
   While through the murmuring windows
   rose and sunk   491
A cloud of kerchiefed hands, — 'The
   church makes fair
   Her welcome in the new Pope's name.'
   Ensued
The black sign of the 'Martyrs' — (name
   no name,
   But count the graves in silence). Next
   were viewed
The Artists; next, the Trades; and after
   came
   The People, — flag and sign, and rights
   as good —
And very loud the shout was for that same

Motto, 'Il popolo.' IL POPOLO, —
The word means dukedom, empire, ma-
     jesty,   500
And kings in such an hour might read it
     so.
And next, with banners, each in his degree,
Deputed representatives a-row
Of every separate state of Tuscany:
Siena's she-wolf, bristling on the fold
Of the first flag, preceded Pisa's hare,
And Massa's lion floated calm in gold,
Pienza's following with his silver stare,
     Arezzo's steed pranced clear from
     bridle-hold, —
And well might shout our Florence, greet-
     ing there   510
These, and more brethren. Last, the
     world had sent
The various children of her teeming
     flanks —
Greeks, English, French — as if to a
     parliament
Of lovers of her Italy in ranks,
Each bearing its land's symbol reverent;
At which the stones seemed breaking into
     thanks
And rattling up the sky, such sounds in
     proof
Arose; the very house-walls seemed to
     bend;
The very windows, up from door to roof,
Flashed out a rapture of bright heads, to
     mend   520
With passionate looks the gesture's
     whirling off
A hurricane of leaves. Three hours did
     end
While all these passed; and ever in the
     crowd,
Rude men, unconscious of the tears that
     kept
Their beards moist, shouted; some few
     laughed aloud,
And none asked any why they laughed and
     wept:
Friends kissed each other's cheeks, and
     foes long vowed
More warmly did it; two months' babies
     leapt
Right upward in their mother's arms,
     whose black
Wide glittering eyes looked elsewhere;
     lovers pressed   530
Each before either, neither glancing
     back;

And peasant maidens smoothly 'tired and
     tressed
Forgot to finger on their throats the
     slack
Great pearl-strings; while old blind men
     would not rest,
But pattered with their staves and slid
     their shoes
Along the stones, and smiled as if they
     saw.
O heaven, I think that day had noble use
Among God's days! So near stood Right
     and Law,
Both mutually forborne! Law would
     not bruise
Nor Right deny, and each in reverent
     awe   540
Honored the other. And if, ne'erthe-
     less,
That good day's sun delivered to the vines
No charta, and the liberal Duke's ex-
     cess
Did scarce exceed a Guelf's or Ghibel-
     line's
In any special actual righteousness
Of what that day he granted, still the signs
Are good and full of promise, we must
     say,
When multitudes approach their kings with
     prayers
And kings concede their people's right to
     pray
Both in one sunshine. Griefs are not de-
     spairs,   550
So uttered, nor can royal claims dismay
When men from humble homes and ducal
     chairs
Hate wrong together. It was well to
     view
Those banners ruffled in a ruler's face
Inscribed, 'Live freedom, union, and all
     true
Brave patriots who are aided by God's
     grace!'
Nor was it ill when Leopoldo drew
His little children to the window-place
He stood in at the Pitti, to suggest
They too should govern as the people willed.
What a cry rose then! some, who saw
     the best,   561
Declared his eyes filled up and overfilled
With good warm human tears which un-
     repressed
Ran down. I like his face; the forehead's
     build

Has no capacious genius, yet perhaps
Sufficient comprehension, — mild and sad,
And careful nobly, — not with care that
    wraps
Self-loving hearts, to stifle and make mad,
    But careful with the care that shuns a
    lapse
Of faith and duty, studious not to add   570
    A burden in the gathering of a gain.
And so, God save the Duke, I say with
    those
Who that day shouted it; and while
    dukes reign,
May all wear in the visible overflows
    Of spirit, such a look of careful pain !
For God must love it better than repose.

And all the people who went up to let
    Their hearts out to that Duke, as has
    been told —
Where guess ye that the living people met,
    Kept tryst, formed ranks, chose leaders,
    first unrolled   580
Their banners ?
            In the Loggia ? where is set
Cellini's godlike Perseus, bronze or gold,
(How name the metal, when the statue
    flings
    Its soul so in your eyes ?) with brow and
    sword
Superbly calm, as all opposing things,
    Slain with the Gorgon, were no more
    abhorred
Since ended ?
            No, the people sought no wings
From Perseus in the Loggia, nor implored
An inspiration in the place beside
    From that dim bust of Brutus, jagged
    and grand,   590
Where Buonarroti passionately tried
    From out the close-clenched marble to
    demand
The head of Rome's sublimest homicide,
    Then dropt the quivering mallet from
    his hand,
Despairing he could find no model-stuff
Of Brutus in all Florence where he found
The gods and gladiators thick enough.
    Nor there ! the people chose still holier
    ground:
The people, who are simple, blind and
    rough,
    Know their own angels, after looking
    round.   600
Whom chose they then ? where met they ?

                    On the stone
Called Dante's, — a plain flat stone scarce
    discerned
From others in the pavement, — whereupon
    He used to bring his quiet chair out,
    turned
To Brunelleschi's church, and pour alone
    The lava of his spirit when it burned:
It is not cold to-day.   O passionate
    Poor Dante who, a banished Florentine,
Didst sit austere at banquets of the great   609
    And muse upon this far-off stone of thine
And think how oft some passer used to wait
    A moment, in the golden day's decline,
With ' Good night, dearest Dante ! ' — well,
    good night !
I muse now, Dante, and think verily,
    Though chapelled in the byeway out of
    sight,
    Ravenna's bones would thrill with
    ecstasy,
Couldst know thy favorite stone's elected
    right
    As tryst-place for thy Tuscans to foresee
Their earliest chartas from.   Good night,
    good morn,
    Henceforward, Dante ! now my soul is
    sure   620
That thine is better comforted of scorn,
    And looks down earthward in completer
    cure
Than when, in Santa Croce church forlorn
    Of any corpse, the architect and hewer
Did pile the empty marbles as thy tomb.
For now thou art no longer exiled, now
Best honored: we salute thee who art come
Back to the old stone with a softer brow
Than Giotto drew upon the wall, for some
    Good lovers of our age to track and
    plough   630
Their way to, through time's ordures strati-
    fied,
    And startle broad awake into the dull
Bargello chamber: now thou 'rt milder-
    eyed, —
Now Beatrix may leap up glad to cull
Thy first smile, even in heaven and at her
    side,
Like that which, nine years old, looked
    beautiful
At May-game.   What do I say ?   I only
    meant
That tender Dante loved his Florence
    well,
While Florence, now, to love him is content;

And, mark ye, that the piercingest sweet
     smell   640
Of love's dear incense by the living sent
     To find the dead, is not accessible
To lazy livers — no narcotic, — not
     Swung in a censer to a sleepy tune, —
But trod out in the morning air by hot
     Quick spirits who tread firm to ends fore-
     shown,
And use the name of greatness unforgot,
     To meditate what greatness may be done.

For Dante sits in heaven and ye stand
     here,
     And more remains for doing, all must
     feel,   650
Than trysting on his stone from year to
     year
     To shift processions, civic toe to heel,
The town's thanks to the Pitti. Are ye
     freer
For what was felt that day ? a chariot-
     wheel
May spin fast, yet the chariot never roll.
     But if that day suggested something
     good,
And bettered, with one purpose, soul by
     soul, —
     Better means freer. A land's brother-
     hood
Is most puissant: men, upon the whole,
     Are what they can be, — nations, what
     they would.   660

Will, therefore, to be strong, thou Italy !
     Will to be noble ! Austrian Metter-
     nich
Can fix no yoke unless the neck agree;
     And thine is like the lion's when the
     thick
Dews shudder from it, and no man would
     be
     The stroker of his mane, which less
     would prick
His nostril with a reed. When nations
     roar
     Like lions, who shall tame them and de-
     fraud
Of the due pasture by the river-shore ?
     Roar, therefore ! shake your dewlaps
     dry abroad: 670
The amphitheatre with open door
     Leads back upon the benches who ap-
     plaud
The last spear-thruster.

               Yet the Heavens forbid
That we should call on passion to con-
     front
The brutal with the brutal and, amid
     This ripening world, suggest a lion-hunt
And lion's-vengeance for the wrongs men
     did
     And do now, though the spears are get-
     ting blunt.
We only call, because the sight and proof
     Of lion-strength hurts nothing; and to
     show   680
A lion-heart, and measure paw with hoof,
     Helps something, even, and will instruct
     a foe
As well as the onslaught, how to stand
     aloof:
     Or else the world gets past the mere
     brute blow
Or given or taken. Children use the fist
     Until they are of age to use the brain;
And so we needed Cæsars to assist
     Man's justice, and Napoleons to explain
God's counsel, when a point was nearly
     missed,
     Until our generations should attain   690
Christ's stature nearer. Not that we, alas,
     Attain already; but a single inch
Will raise to look down on the swordsman's
     pass,
     As knightly Roland on the coward's
     flinch:
And, after chloroform and ether-gas,
     We find out slowly what the bee and finch
Have ready found, through Nature's lamp
     in each,
     How to our races we may justify
Our individual claims and, as we reach
     Our own grapes, bend the top vines to
     supply   700
The children's uses, — how to fill a breach
     With olive-branches, — how to quench a
     lie
With truth, and smite a foe upon the cheek
     With Christ's most conquering kiss.
     Why, these are things
Worth a great nation's finding, to prove
     weak
     The 'glorious arms' of military kings.
And so with wide embrace, my England,
     seek
To stifle the bad heat and flickerings
     Of this world's false and nearly expended
     fire !
Draw palpitating arrows to the wood, 710

And twang abroad thy high hopes and thy
    higher
Resolves, from that most virtuous altitude!
Till nations shall unconsciously aspire
    By looking up to thee, and learn that
    good
And glory are not different. Announce
    law
By freedom; exalt chivalry by peace;
Instruct how clear calm eyes can overawe,
    And how pure hands, stretched simply
    to release
A bond-slave, will not need a sword to
    draw
    To be held dreadful. O my England,
    crease   720
Thy purple with no alien agonies,
    No struggles toward encroachment, no
    vile war !
Disband thy captains, change thy victories,
    Be henceforth prosperous as the angels
    are,
Helping, not humbling.

                Drums and battle-cries
Go out in music of the morning-star —
And soon we shall have thinkers in the
    place
Of fighters, each found able as a man
To strike electric influence through a race,
    Unstayed by city-wall and barbican.   730
The poet shall look grander in the face
    Than even of old (when he of Greece
    began
To sing 'that Achillean wrath which slew
    So many heroes') — seeing he shall treat
The deeds of souls heroic toward the true,
    The oracles of life, previsions sweet
And awful like divine swans gliding
    through
    White arms of Ledas, which will leave
    the heat
Of their escaping godship to undue
    The human medium with a heavenly
    flush.   740

Meanwhile, in this same Italy we want
    Not popular passion, to arise and crush,
But popular conscience, which may cove-
    nant
    For what it knows. Concede without a
    blush,
To grant the 'civic guard' is not to grant
    The civic spirit, living and awake:
Those lappets on your shoulders, citizens,

Your eyes strain after sideways till they
    ache
(While still, in admirations and amens,
    The crowd comes up on festa-days to
    take   750
The great sight in) — are not intelligence,
    Not courage even — alas, if not the sign
Of something very noble, they are nought;
    For every day ye dress your sallow kine
With fringes down their cheeks, though
    unbesought
    They loll their heavy heads and drag the
    wine
And bear the wooden yoke as they were
    taught
    The first day. What ye want is light —
    indeed
Not sunlight — (ye may well look up sur-
    prised
    To those unfathomable heavens that
    feed   760
Your purple hills) — but God's light or-
    ganized
    In some high soul, crowned capable to
    lead
The conscious people, conscious and ad-
    vised, —
    For if we lift a people like mere clay,
It falls the same. We want thee, O un-
    found
    And sovran teacher ! if thy beard be gray
Or black, we bid thee rise up from the
    ground
    And speak the word God giveth thee to
    say,
Inspiring into all this people round,
    Instead of passion, thought, which pio-
    neers   770
All generous passion, purifies from sin,
    And strikes the hour for. Rise up,
    teacher ! here's
A crowd to make a nation ! — best begin
    By making each a man, till all be peers
Of earth's true patriots and pure martyrs in
    Knowing and daring. Best unbar the
    doors
Which Peter's heirs keep locked so over-
    close
    They only let the mice across the floors,
While every churchman dangles, as he goes,
    The great key at his girdle, and abhors 780
In Christ's name, meekly. Open wide the
    house,
    Concede the entrance with Christ's liberal
    mind,

And set the tables with his wine and bread.
What ! 'commune in both kinds ?' In
    every kind —
Wine, wafer, love, hope, truth, unlimited,
    Nothing kept back. For when a man is
    blind
To starlight, will he see the rose is red ?
A bondsman shivering at a Jesuit's foot —
'Væ ! meâ culpâ !' — is not like to stand
A freedman at a despot's and dispute 790
His titles by the balance in his hand,
    Weighing them 'suo jure.' Tend the
    root
If careful of the branches, and expand
    The inner souls of men before you strive
For civic heroes.

                        But the teacher, where ?
    From all these crowded faces, all alive,
Eyes, of their own lids flashing themselves
    bare,
    And brows that with a mobile life contrive
A deeper shadow, — may we in no wise
    dare
    To put a finger out and touch a man, 800
And cry 'this is the leader' ? What, all
    these !
    Broad heads, black eyes, — yet not a soul
    that ran
From God down with a message ? All, to
    please
    The donna waving measures with her
    fan,
And not the judgment-angel on his knees
    (The trumpet just an inch off from his
    lips),
Who when he breathes next, will put out
    the sun ?

Yet mankind's self were foundered in
    eclipse,
If lacking doers, with great works to be
    done;
    And lo, the startled earth already dips 810
Back into light; a better day 's begun;
    And soon this leader, teacher, will stand
    plain,
And build the golden pipes and synthesize
    This people-organ for a holy strain.
We hold this hope, and still in all these
    eyes
    Go sounding for the deep look which
    shall drain
Suffused thought into channelled enter-
    prise.

Where is the teacher ? What now may
    he do,
Who shall do greatly ? Doth he gird his
    waist
    With a monk's rope, like Luther ? or
    pursue   820
The goat, like Tell ? or dry his nets in
    haste,
Like Masaniello when the sky was blue ?
Keep house, like other peasants, with inlaced
    Bare brawny arms about a favorite child,
And meditative looks beyond the door
    (But not to mark the kidling's teeth have
    filed
The green shoots of his vine which last
    year bore
    Full twenty bunches), or, on triple-piled
Throne-velvets sit at ease to bless the poor,
    Like other pontiffs, in the Poorest's name ?
The old tiara keeps itself aslope   831
    Upon his steady brows which, all the
    same,
Bend mildly to permit the people's hope ?

Whatever hand shall grasp this oriflamme,
Whatever man (last peasant or first pope
    Seeking to free his country) shall appear,
Teach, lead, strike fire into the masses, fill
    These empty bladders with fine air,
    insphere
These wills into a unity of will,
    And make of Italy a nation — dear 840
And blessed be that man ! the Heavens
    shall kill
No leaf the earth lets grow for him, and
    Death
Shall cast him back upon the lap of Life
To live more surely, in a clarion-breath
Of hero-music. Brutus with the knife,
    Rienzi with the fasces, throb beneath
Rome's stones, — and more who threw
    away joy's fife
Like Pallas, that the beauty of their
    souls
Might ever shine untroubled and entire:
But if it can be true that he who rolls 850
The Church's thunders will reserve her fire
    For only light, — from eucharistic bowls
Will pour new life for nations that expire,
    And rend the scarlet of his papal vest
To gird the weak loins of his countrymen, —
    I hold that he surpasses all the rest
Of Romans, heroes, patriots; and that when
    He sat down on the throne, he dis-
    possessed

The first graves of some glory. See again,
This country-saving is a glorious thing:
And if a common man achieved it ? well. 861
Say, a rich man did ? excellent. A king ?
That grows sublime. A priest ? improb-
    able.
A pope ? Ah, there we stop, and cannot
    bring
Our faith up to the leap, with history's
    bell
So heavy round the neck of it — albeit
We fain would grant the possibility
For *thy* sake, Pio Nono !

                  Stretch thy feet
In that case — I will kiss them reverently
As any pilgrim to the papal seat: 870
And, such proved possible, thy throne to
    me
Shall seem as holy a place as Pellico's
Venetian dungeon, or as Spielberg's grate
At which the Lombard woman hung the
    rose
Of her sweet soul by its own dewy weight,
To feel the dungeon round her sunshine
    close,
And pining so, died early, yet too late
For what she suffered. Yea, I will not
    choose
Betwixt thy throne, Pope Pius, and the
    spot
Marked red for ever, spite of rains and
    dews,   880
Where Two fell riddled by the Austrian's
    shot,
The brothers Bandiera, who accuse,
With one same mother-voice and face
    (that what
They speak may be invincible) the sins
Of earth's tormentors before God the just,
Until the unconscious thunderbolt begins
To loosen in his grasp.
                And yet we must
Beware, and mark the natural kiths and
    kins
Of circumstance and office, and distrust
The rich man reasoning in a poor man's
    hut,   890
The poet who neglects pure truth to
    prove
Statistic fact, the child who leaves a rut
For a smoother road, the priest who vows
    his glove
Exhales no grace, the prince who walks
    afoot,

The woman who has sworn she will not
    love,
And this Ninth Pius in Seventh Greg-
    ory's chair,
With Andrea Doria's forehead !

                Count what goes
To making up a pope, before he wear
That triple crown. We pass the world-
    wide throes
Which went to make the popedom, —
    the despair   900
Of free men, good men, wise men; the
    dread shows
Of women's faces, by the faggot's flash
Tossed out, to the minutest stir and throb
O' the white lips, the least tremble of a
    lash,
To glut the red stare of a licensed mob;
The short mad cries down oubliettes,
    and plash
So horribly far off; priests, trained to rob,
And kings that, like encouraged night-
    mares, sat
On nations' hearts most heavily dis-
    tressed
With monstrous sights and apophthegms
    of fate —   910
We pass these things, — because 'the
    times' are prest
With necessary charges of the weight
Of all this sin, and 'Calvin, for the rest,
Made bold to burn Servetus. Ah, men
    err !' —
And so do *churches !* which is all we mean
To bring to proof in any register
Of theological fat kine and lean:
So drive them back into the pens ! re-
    fer
Old sins (with pourpoint, 'quotha' and 'I
    ween')
Entirely to the old times, the old times;
Nor ever ask why this preponderant   921
Infallible pure Church could set her
    chimes
Most loudly then, just then, — most jubi-
    lant,
Precisely then, when mankind stood in
    crimes
Full heart-deep, and Heaven's judgments
    were not scant.
Inquire still less, what signifies a church
Of perfect inspiration and pure laws
Who burns the first man with a brim-
    stone-torch,

And grinds the second, bone by bone, be-
cause
  The times, forsooth, are used to rack
    and scorch!   930
What *is* a holy Church unless she awes
  The times down from their sins? Did
    Christ select
Such amiable times to come and teach
  Love to, and mercy? The whole world
    were wrecked
If every mere great man, who lives to
    reach
  A little leaf of popular respect,
Attained not simply by some special
    breach
  In the age's customs, by some prece-
    dence
In thought and act, which, having proved
    him higher
  Than those he lived with, proved his
    competence   940
In helping them to wonder and aspire.

My words are guiltless of the bigot's
    sense;
My soul has fire to mingle with the fire
Of all these souls, within or out of doors
Of Rome's church or another. I believe
  In one Priest, and one temple with its
    floors
Of shining jasper gloom'd at morn and
    eve
  By countless knees of earnest auditors,
And crystal walls too lucid to perceive,
  That none may take the measure of the
    place   950
And say 'So far the porphyry, then, the
    flint —
  To this mark mercy goes, and there
    ends grace,'
Though still the permeable crystals hint
  At some white starry distance, bathed in
    space.
I feel how nature's ice-crusts keep the
    dint
Of undersprings of silent Deity.
I hold the articulated gospels which
  Show Christ among us crucified on tree.
I love all who love truth, if poor or rich
  In what they have won of truth posses-
    sively.   960
No altars and no hands defiled with
    pitch
  Shall scare me off, but I will pray and
    eat

With all these — taking leave to choose
    my ewers —
  And say at last 'Your visible churches
    cheat
Their inward types; and, if a church as-
    sures
Of standing without failure and defeat,
The same both fails and lies.'

                          To leave which lures
  Of wider subject through past years, —
    behold,
We come back from the popedom to the
    pope,
  To ponder what he *must* be, ere we are
    bold   970
For what he *may* be, with our heavy
    hope
  To trust upon his soul. So, fold by fold,
Explore this mummy in the priestly cope,
  Transmitted through the darks of time,
    to catch
The man within the wrappage, and discern
  How he, an honest man, upon the watch
Full fifty years for what a man may learn,
  Contrived to get just there; with what
    a snatch
Of old-world oboli he had to earn
  The passage through; with what a
    drowsy sop,   980
To drench the busy barkings of his brain;
  What ghosts of pale tradition, wreathed
    with hope
'Gainst wakeful thought, he had to enter-
    tain
  For heavenly visions; and consent to
    stop
The clock at noon, and let the hour remain
  (Without vain windings-up) inviolate
Against all chimings from the belfry. Lo,
  From every given pope you must abate,
Albeit you love him, some things — good,
    you know —
  Which every given heretic you hate,   990
Assumes for his, as being plainly so.
  A pope must hold by popes a little, —
    yes,
By councils, from Nicæa up to Trent, —
  By hierocratic empire, more or less
Irresponsible to men, — he must resent
  Each man's particular conscience, and
    repress
Inquiry, meditation, argument,
  As tyrants faction. Also, he must not
Love truth too dangerously, but prefer

'The interests of the Church' (because
   a blot   1006
Is better than a rent, in miniver) —
   Submit to see the people swallow hot
Husk-porridge, which his chartered church-
   men stir
Quoting the only true God's epigraph,
'Feed my lambs, Peter!' — must consent
   to sit
   Attesting with his pastoral ring and
      staff
To such a picture of our Lady, hit
   Off well by artist-angels (though not
      half
As fair as Giotto would have painted it) —
   To such a vial, where a dead man's
      blood   1010
Runs yearly warm beneath a churchman's
   finger, —
   To such a holy house of stone and wood,
Whereof a cloud of angels was the bringer
   From Bethlehem to Loreto. Were it
      good
For any pope on earth to be a flinger
   Of stones against these high-niched
      counterfeits?
Apostates only are iconoclasts.
   He dares not say, while this false thing
      abets
That true thing, 'This is false.' He keeps
   his fasts
   And prayers, as prayer and fast were
      silver frets   1020
To change a note upon a string that lasts,
   And make a lie a virtue. Now, if he
Did more than this, higher hoped, and
      braver dared,
   I think he were a pope in jeopardy,
Or no pope rather, for his truth had barred
   The vaulting of his life, — and certainly,
If he do only this, mankind's regard
   Moves on from him at once, to seek
      some new
Teacher and leader. He is good and
   great
   According to the deeds a pope can do;
Most liberal, save those bonds; affection-
   ate,   1031
   As princes may be, and, as priests are,
      true;
But only the Ninth Pius after eight,
   When all's praised most. At best and
      hopefullest,
He's pope — we want a man! his heart
      beats warm,

But, like the prince enchanted to the
   waist,
He sits in stone and hardens by a charm
   Into the marble of his throne high-
      placed.
Mild benediction waves his saintly arm —
   So, good! but what we want's a perfect
      man,   1040
Complete and all alive: half travertine
   Half suits our need, and ill subserves
      our plan.
Feet, knees, nerves, sinews, energies di-
   vine
   Were never yet too much for men who
      ran
In such hard ways as must be this of thine,
   Deliverer whom we seek, whoe'er thou
      art,
Pope, prince, or peasant! If, indeed, the
   first,
   The noblest, therefore! since the heroic
      heart
Within thee must be great enough to burst
   Those trammels buckling to the baser
      part   1050
Thy saintly peers in Rome, who crossed
   and cursed
   With the same finger.

                  Come, appear, be found,
If pope or peasant, come! we hear the
   cock,
   The courtier of the mountains when first
      crowned
With golden dawn; and orient glories
   flock
   To meet the sun upon the highest
      ground.
Take voice and work! we wait to hear thee
   knock
   At some one of our Florentine nine gates,
On each of which was imaged a sublime
   Face of a Tuscan genius, which, for hate's
And love's sake, both, our Florence in her
      prime   1061
Turned boldly on all comers to her
   states,
As heroes turned their shields in antique
   time
   Emblazoned with honorable acts. And
      though
The gates are blank now of such images,
   And Petrarch looks no more from Nicolo
Toward dear Arezzo, 'twixt the acacia-
   trees,

Nor Dante, from gate Gallo — still we
 know,
Despite the razing of the blazonries,
Remains the consecration of the shield:
The dead heroic faces will start out   1071
  On all these gates, if foes should take the
    field,
And blend sublimely, at the earliest shout,
  With living heroes who will scorn to
    yield
A hair's-breadth even, when, gazing round
  about,
  They find in what a glorious company
They fight the foes of Florence.   Who will
  grudge
  His one poor life, when that great man
    we see
Has given five hundred years, the world
    being judge,
  To help the glory of his Italy ?   1080
Who, born the fair side of the Alps, will
  budge,
  When Dante stays, when Ariosto stays,
When Petrarch stays for ever ?   Ye bring
    swords,
  My Tuscans ? Ay, if wanted in this
    haze,
Bring swords: but first bring souls ! —
    bring thoughts and words,
  Unrusted by a tear of yesterday's,
Yet awful by its wrong, — and cut these
    cords,
  And mow this green lush falseness to
    the roots,
And shut the mouth of hell below the
    swathe !
  And, if ye can bring songs too, let the
    lute's   1090
Recoverable music softly bathe
  Some poet's hand, that, through all
    bursts and bruits
Of popular passion, all unripe and rathe
  Convictions of the popular intellect,
Ye may not lack a finger up the air,
  Annunciative, reproving, pure, erect,
To show which way your first Ideal bare
  The whiteness of its wings when (sorely
    pecked
By falcons on your wrists) it unaware
  Arose up overhead and out of sight. 1100

Meanwhile, let all the far ends of the
    world
  Breathe back the deep breath of their
    old delight,

To swell the Italian banner just unfurled.
  Help, lands of Europe ! for, if Austria
    fight,
The drums will bar your slumber. Had
    ye curled
  The laurel for your thousand artists'
    brows,
If these Italian hands had planted none ?
  Can any sit down idle in the house
Nor hear appeals from Buonarroti's stone
  And Raffael's canvas, rousing and to
    rouse ?   1110
Where 's Poussin's master ? Gallic Avig-
    non
  Bred Laura, and Vaucluse's fount has
    stirred
The heart of France too strongly, as it lets
  Its little stream out (like a wizard's
    bird
Which bounds upon its emerald wing and
    wets
  The rocks on each side), that she should
    not gird
Her loins with Charlemagne's sword when
    foes beset
  The country of her Petrarch. Spain
    may well
Be minded how from Italy she caught,
  To mingle with her tinkling Moorish
    bell,   1120
A fuller cadence and a subtler thought.
  And even the New World, the recep-
    tacle
Of freemen, may send glad men, as it
    ought,
  To greet Vespucci Amerigo's door.
While England claims, by trump of poetry,
  Verona, Venice, the Ravenna-shore,
And dearer holds John Milton's Fiesole
  Than Langland's Malvern with the stars
    in flower.

And Vallombrosa, we two went to see
  Last June, beloved companion, — where
    sublime   1130
The mountains live in holy families,
  And the slow pinewoods ever climb and
    climb
Half up their breasts, just stagger as they
    seize
  Some gray crag, drop back with it many
    a time,
And straggle blindly down the precipice.
  The Vallombrosan brooks were strewn
    as thick

That June day, knee-deep with dead
    beechen leaves,
As Milton saw them ere his heart grew
    sick
And his eyes blind. I think the monks
    and beeves
Are all the same too: scarce have they
    changed the wick   1140
On good Saint Gualbert's altar which re-
    ceives
    The convent's pilgrims; and the pool in
    front
(Wherein the hill-stream trout are cast, to
    wait
The beatific vision and the grunt
Used at refectory) keeps its weedy state,
    To baffle saintly abbots who would
    count
The fish across their breviary nor 'bate
    The measure of their steps. O water-
    falls
And forests! sound and silence! moun-
    tains bare
    That leap up peak by peak and catch
    the palls   1150
Of purple and silver mist to rend and
    share
With one another, at electric calls
Of life in the sunbeams, — till we cannot
    dare
    Fix your shapes, count your number! we
    must think
Your beauty and your glory helped to fill
The cup of Milton's soul so to the brink,
He never more was thirsty when God's
    will
    Had shattered to his sense the last
    chain-link
By which he had drawn from Nature's
    visible
    The fresh well-water. Satisfied by
    this,   1160
He sang of Adam's paradise and
    smiled,
Remembering Vallombrosa. Therefore
    is
The place divine to English man and
    child,
    And pilgrims leave their souls here in a
    kiss.

For Italy's the whole earth's treasury,
    piled
With reveries of gentle ladies, flung

Aside, like ravelled silk, from life's worn
    stuff;
    With coins of scholars' fancy, which, be-
    ing rung
On work-day counter, still sound silver-
    proof;
    In short, with all the dreams of
    dreamers young,   1170
Before their heads have time for slipping
    off
    Hope's pillow to the ground. How oft,
    indeed,
We've sent our souls out from the rigid
    north,
    On bare white feet which would not
    print nor bleed,
To climb the Alpine passes and look forth,
    Where booming low the Lombard
    rivers lead
To gardens, vineyards, all a dream is
    worth, —
    Sights, thou and I, Love, have seen
    afterward
From Tuscan Bellosguardo, wide awake,
    When, standing on the actual blessed
    sward   1180
Where Galileo stood at nights to take
    The vision of the stars, we have found it
    hard,
Gazing upon the earth and heaven, to
    make
    A choice of beauty.
                    Therefore let us all
Refreshed in England or in other land,
    By visions, with their fountain-rise and
    fall,
Of this earth's darling, — we, who under-
    stand
    A little how the Tuscan musical
Vowels do round themselves as if they
    planned   1189
    Eternities of separate sweetness, — we,
Who loved Sorrento vines in picture-book,
    Or ere in wine-cup we pledged faith or
    glee, —
Who loved Rome's wolf with demi-gods at
    suck,
    Or ere we loved truth's own divinity, —
Who loved, in brief, the classic hill and
    brook,
    And Ovid's dreaming tales and Pe-
    trarch's song,
Or ere we loved Love's self even, — let us
    give

The blessing of our souls (and wish them
strong
To bear it to the height where prayers ar-
rive,
When faithful spirits pray against a
wrong,)   1200
To this great cause of southern men who
strive
In God's name for man's rights, and
shall not fail.

Behold, they shall not fail. The shouts
ascend
Above the shrieks, in Naples, and pre-
vail.
Rows of shot corpses, waiting for the end
Of burial, seem to smile up straight and
pale
Into the azure air and apprehend
That final gun-flash from Palermo's
coast
Which lightens their apocalypse of death.
So let them die ! The world shows no-
thing lost;   1210
Therefore, not blood. Above or under-
neath,
What matter, brothers, if ye keep your
post
On duty's side ? As sword returns to
sheath,
So dust to grave, but souls find place in
Heaven.
Heroic daring is the true success,
The eucharistic bread requires no leaven;
And though your ends were hopeless, we
should bless
Your cause as holy. Strive — and, hav-
ing striven,
Take, for God's recompense, that righteous-
ness !

PART II

I wrote a meditation and a dream,
Hearing a little child sing in the street:
I leant upon his music as a theme,
Till it gave way beneath my heart's full
beat
Which tried at an exultant prophecy
But dropped before the measure was
complete —
Alas, for songs and hearts ! O Tuscany,
O Dante's Florence, is the type too
plain ?

Didst thou, too, only sing of liberty
As little children take up a high strain 10
With unintentioned voices, and break off
To sleep upon their mothers' knees again ?
Couldst thou not watch one hour ? then,
sleep enough —
That sleep may hasten manhood and
sustain
The faint pale spirit with some muscular
stuff.

But we, who cannot slumber as thou
dost,
We thinkers, who have thought for thee
and failed,
We hopers, who have hoped for thee and
lost,
We poets, wandered round by dreams, who
hailed
From this Atrides' roof (with lintel-
post   20
Which still drips blood, — the worse part
hath prevailed)
The fire-voice of the beacons to declare
Troy taken, sorrow ended, — cozened
through
A crimson sunset in a misty air,
What now remains for such as we, to do ?
God's judgments, peradventure, will He
bare
To the roots of thunder, if we kneel and
sue ?

From Casa Guidi windows I looked
forth,
And saw ten thousand eyes of Florentines
Flash back the triumph of the Lombard
north, —   30
Saw fifty banners, freighted with the signs
And exultations of the awakened earth,
Float on above the multitude in lines,
Straight to the Pitti. So, the vision went.
And so, between those populous rough
hands
Raised in the sun, Duke Leopold outleant,
And took the patriot's oath which hence-
forth stands
Among the oaths of perjurers, eminent
To catch the lightnings ripened for these
lands.

Why swear at all, thou false Duke
Leopold ?   40
What need to swear ? What need to
boast thy blood

Unspoilt of Austria, and thy heart unsold
Away from Florence? It was understood
God made thee not too vigorous or too
bold;
And men had patience with thy quiet
mood,
And women, pity, as they saw thee pace
Their festive streets with premature gray
hairs.
We turned the mild dejection of thy face
To princely meanings, took thy wrinkling
cares
For ruffling hopes, and called thee weak,
not base. 50
Nay, better light the torches for more
prayers
And smoke the pale Madonnas at the
shrine,
Being still ' our poor Grand-duke, our
good Grand-duke,
Who cannot help the Austrian in his
line,' —
Than write an oath upon a nation's book
For men to spit at with scorn's blurring
brine!
Who dares forgive what none can over-
look?

For me, I do repent me in this dust
Of towns and temples which makes It-
aly, —
I sigh amid the sighs which breathe a
gust 60
Of dying century to century
Around us on the uneven crater-crust
Of these old worlds, — I bow my soul and
knee.
Absolve me, patriots, of my woman's
fault
That ever I believed the man was true!
These sceptred strangers shun the com-
mon salt,
And, therefore, when the general board 's
in view
And they stand up to carve for blind and
halt,
The wise suspect the viands which ensue.
I much repent that, in this time and
place 70
Where many corpse-lights of experience
burn
From Cæsar's and Lorenzo's festering
race,
To enlighten groping reasoners, I could
learn

No better counsel for a simple case
Than to put faith in princes, in my turn.
Had all the death-piles of the ancient
years
Flared up in vain before me? knew I not
What stench arises from some purple
gears?
And how the sceptres witness whence they
got
Their briar-wood, crackling through the
atmosphere's 80
Foul smoke, by princely perjuries, kept
hot?
Forgive me, ghosts of patriots, — Brutus,
thou,
Who trailest downhill into life again
Thy blood-weighed cloak, to indict me
with thy slow
Reproachful eyes! — for being taught in
vain
That, while the illegitimate Cæsars show
Of meaner stature than the first full strain
(Confessed incompetent to conquer
Gaul),
They swoon as feebly and cross Rubicons
As rashly as any Julius of them all! 90
Forgive, that I forgot the mind which runs
Through absolute races, too unsceptical!
I saw the man among his little sons,
His lips were warm with kisses while he
swore;
And I, because I am a woman — I,
Who felt my own child's coming life be-
fore
The prescience of my soul, and held faith
high, —
I could not bear to think, whoever bore,
That lips, so warmed, could shape so cold a
lie.

From Casa Guidi windows I looked
out, 100
Again looked, and beheld a different sight.
The Duke had fled before the people's
shout
'Long live the Duke!' A people, to speak
right,
Must speak as soft as courtiers, lest a
doubt
Should curdle brows of gracious sovereigns,
white.
Moreover that same dangerous shouting
meant
Some gratitude for future favors, which
Were only promised, the Constituent

Implied, the whole being subject to the
  hitch
In 'motu proprios,' very incident   110
To all these Czars, from Paul to Paulo-
  vitch.
Whereat the people rose up in the dust
Of the ruler's flying feet, and shouted still
  And loudly; only, this time, as was just,
Not 'Live the Duke,' who had fled for
  good or ill,
  But ' Live the People,' who remained and
  must,
The unrenounced and unrenounceable.
  Long live the people ! How they lived !
  and boiled
And bubbled in the cauldron of the street:
  How the young blustered, nor the old
  recoiled,   120
And what a thunderous stir of tongues and
  feet
Trod flat the palpitating bells and foiled
The joy-guns of their echo, shattering it !
  How down they pulled the Duke's arms
  everywhere !
How up they set new café-signs, to show
  Where patriots might sip ices in pure
  air —
(The fresh paint smelling somewhat) ! To
  and fro
  How marched the civic guard, and
  stopped to stare
When boys broke windows in a civic glow !
  How rebel songs were sung to loyal
  tunes,   130
And bishops cursed in ecclesiastic metres:
  How all the Circoli grew large as moons,
And all the speakers, moonstruck, — thank-
  ful greeters
  Of prospects which struck poor the ducal
  boons,
A mere free Press, and Chambers ! —
  frank repeaters
  Of great Guerazzi's praises — ' There 's
  a man,
The father of the land, who, truly great,
  Takes off that national disgrace and ban,
The farthing tax upon our Florence-gate,
  And saves Italia as he only can !'   140
How all the nobles fled, and would not
  wait,
  Because they were most noble, — which
  being so,
How Liberals vowed to burn their palaces,
  Because free Tuscans were not free to
  go !

How grown men raged at Austria's wicked-
  ness,
  And smoked, — while fifty striplings in
  a row
Marched straight to Piedmont for the
  wrong's redress !
  You say we failed in duty, we who wore
Black velvet like Italian democrats,
  Who slashed our sleeves like patriots,
  nor forswore   150
The true republic in the form of hats ?
  We chased the archbishop from the
  Duomo door,
We chalked the walls with bloody caveats
  Against all tyrants. If we did not fight
Exactly, we fired muskets up the air
  To show that victory was ours of right.
We met, had free discussion everywhere
  (Except perhaps i' the Chambers) day
  and night.
We proved the poor should be employed,
  . . . that 's fair, —
  And yet the rich not worked for any-
  wise, —   160
Pay certified, yet payers abrogated, —
  Full work secured, yet liabilities
To overwork excluded, — not one bated
  Of all our holidays, that still, at twice
Or thrice a week, are moderately rated.
  We proved that Austria was dislodged,
  or would
Or should be, and that Tuscany in arms
  Should, would dislodge her, ending the
  old feud;
And yet, to leave our piazzas, shops, and
  farms,
  For the simple sake of fighting, was not
  good —   170
We proved that also. ' Did we carry
  charms
  Against being killed ourselves, that we
  should rush
On killing others ? what, desert herewith
  Our wives and mothers ? — was that
  duty ? tush !'
At which we shook the sword within the
  sheath
  Like heroes — only louder; and the flush
Ran up the cheek to meet the future
  wreath.
  Nay, what we proved, we shouted — how
  we shouted
(Especially the boys did), boldly planting
  That tree of liberty, whose fruit is
  doubted,   180

Because the roots are not of nature's grant-
ing !
A tree of good and evil: none, without it,
Grow gods; alas and, with it, men are
wanting !

O holy knowledge, holy liberty,
O holy rights of nations ! If I speak
These bitter things against the jugglery
Of days that in your names proved blind
and weak,
It is that tears are bitter. When we see
The brown skulls grin at death in church-
yards bleak,
We do not cry ' This Yorick is too light,'
For death grows deathlier with that mouth
he makes. 191
So with my mocking: bitter things I
write
Because my soul is bitter for your sakes,
O freedom ! O my Florence !

Men who might
Do greatly in a universe that breaks
And burns, must ever *know* before they do.
Courage and patience are but sacrifice;
And sacrifice is offered for and to
Something conceived of. Each man pays a
price
For what himself counts precious,
whether true 200
Or false the appreciation it implies.
But here, — no knowledge, no conception,
nought !
Desire was absent, that provides great deeds
From out the greatness of prevenient
thought:
And action, action, like a flame that needs
A steady breath and fuel, being caught
Up, like a burning reed from other reeds,
Flashed in the empty and uncertain air,
Then wavered, then went out. Behold, who
blames
A crooked course, when not a goal is
there 210
To round the fervid striving of the games ?
An ignorance of means may minister
To greatness, but an igorance of aims
Makes it impossible to be great at all.
So with our Tuscans ! Let none dare to
say,
' Here virtue never can be national;
Here fortitude can never cut a way
Between the Austrian muskets, out of
thrall:'

I tell you rather that, whoever may
Discern true ends here, shall grow pure
enough 220
To love them, brave enough to strive for
them,
And strong to reach them though the
roads be rough:
That having learnt — by no mere apoph-
thegm —
Not just the draping of a graceful stuff
About a statue, broidered at the hem, —
Not just the trilling on an opera-stage
Of ' libertà ' to bravos — (a fair word,
Yet too allied to inarticulate rage
And breathless sobs, for singing, though
the chord
Were deeper than they struck it) but
the gauge 230
Of civil wants sustained and wrongs ab-
horred,
The serious sacred meaning and full use
Of freedom for a nation, — then, indeed,
Our Tuscans, underneath the bloody dews
Of some new morning, rising up agreed
And bold, will want no Saxon souls or
thews
To sweep their piazzas clear of Austria's
breed.

Alas, alas ! it was not so this time.
Conviction was not, courage failed, and
truth
Was something to be doubted of. The
mime 240
Changed masks, because a mime. The tide
as smooth
In running in as out, no sense of crime
Because no sense of virtue, — sudden ruth
Seized on the people: they would have
again
Their good Grand-duke and leave Guerazzi,
though
He took that tax from Florence. ' Much
in vain
He takes it from the market-carts, we
trow,
While urgent that no market-men remain,
But all march off and leave the spade and
plough,
To die among the Lombards. Was it
thus 250
The dear paternal Duke did ? Live the
Duke !'
At which the joy-bells multitudinous,
Swept by an opposite wind, as loudly shook.

Call back the mild archbishop to his
    house,
To bless the people with his frightened
    look, —
    He shall not yet be hanged, you compre-
        hend !
Seize on Guerazzi; guard him in full view,
    Or else we stab him in the back, to end !
Rub out those chalked devices, set up new
    The Duke's arms, doff your Phrygian
        caps, and mend   260
The pavement of the piazzas broke into
    By barren poles of freedom: smooth the
        way
For the ducal carriage, lest his highness
        sigh
'Here trees of liberty grew yesterday !'
'Long live the Duke !' — how roared the
        cannonry,
    How rocked the bell-towers, and through
        thickening spray
Of nosegays, wreaths, and kerchiefs tossed
        on high,
    How marched the civic guard, the people
        still
Being good at shouts, especially the boys !
    Alas, poor people, of an unfledged will 270
Most fitly expressed by such a callow voice !
    Alas, still poorer Duke, incapable
Of being worthy even of so much noise !

You think he came back instantly, with
        thanks
And tears in his faint eyes, and hands ex-
        tended
    To stretch the franchise through their
        utmost ranks ?
That having, like a father, apprehended,
    He came to pardon fatherly those pranks
Played out and now in filial service
        ended ? —
    That some love-token, like a prince, he
        threw   280
To meet the people's love-call, in return ?
    Well, how he came I will relate to you;
And if your hearts should burn, why, hearts
        must burn,
    To make the ashes which things old and
        new
Shall be washed clean in — as this Duke
        will learn.

From Casa Guidi windows gazing, then,
I saw and witness how the Duke came
    back.

The regular tramp of horse and tread of
        men
Did smite the silence like an anvil black
    And sparkless. With her wide eyes at
        full strain,   290
Our Tuscan nurse exclaimed ' Alack, alack,
    Signora ! these shall be the Austrians.'
        ' Nay,
Be still,' I answered, 'do not wake the
        child !'
    — For so, my two-months' baby sleeping
        lay
In milky dreams upon the bed and smiled,
    And I thought ' He shall sleep on, while
        he may,
Through the world's baseness: not being
        yet defiled,
    Why should he be disturbed by what is
        done ?'
Then, gazing, I beheld the long-drawn
        street
    Live out, from end to end, full in the
        sun,   300
With Austria's thousand; sword and
        bayonet,
    Horse, foot, artillery, — cannons rolling
        on
Like blind slow storm-clouds gestant with
        the heat
    Of undeveloped lightnings, each bestrode
By a single man, dust-white from head to
        heel,
    Indifferent as the dreadful thing he rode,
Like a sculptured Fate serene and terrible.
    As some smooth river which has over-
        flowed
Will slow and silent down its current wheel
    A loosened forest, all the pines erect, 310
So swept, in mute significance of storm,
    The marshalled thousands; not an eye
        deflect
To left or right, to catch a novel form
    Of Florence city adorned by architect
And carver, or of Beauties live and warm
    Scared at the casements, — all, straight-
        forward eyes
And faces, held as steadfast as their swords,
    And cognizant of acts, not imageries.
The key, O Tuscans, too well fits the wards !
    Ye asked for mimes, — these bring you
        tragedies: 320
For purple, — these shall wear it as your
        lords.
    Ye played like children, — die like inno-
        cents.

Ye mimicked lightnings with a torch, — the crack
  Of the actual bolt, your pastime circumvents.
Ye called up ghosts, believing they were slack
  To follow any voice from Gilboa's tents, . . .
Here 's Samuel ! — and, so, Grand-dukes come back !

And yet, they are no prophets though they come:
That awful mantle, they are drawing close,
  Shall be searched, one day, by the shafts of Doom   330
Through double folds now hoodwinking the brows.
  Resuscitated monarchs disentomb
Grave-reptiles with them, in their new life-throes.
  Let such beware. Behold, the people waits,
Like God: as He, in his serene of might,
  So they, in their endurance of long straits.
Ye stamp no nation out, though day and night
  Ye tread them with that absolute heel which grates
And grinds them flat from all attempted height.
  You kill worms sooner with a garden-spade   340
Than you kill peoples: peoples will not die;
  The tail curls stronger when you lop the head:
They writhe at every wound and multiply
  And shudder into a heap of life that 's made
Thus vital from God's own vitality.
  'T is hard to shrivel back a day of God's
Once fixed for judgment; 't is as hard to change
  The peoples, when they rise beneath their loads
And heave them from their backs with violent wrench
  To crush the oppressor: for that judgment-rod 's   350
The measure of this popular revenge.

Meanwhile, from Casa Guidi windows, we
Beheld the armament of Austria flow

Into the drowning heart of Tuscany:
And yet none wept, none cursed, or, if 't was so,
  They wept and cursed in silence. Silently
Our noisy Tuscans watched the invading foe;
  They had learnt silence. Pressed against the wall,
And grouped upon the church-steps opposite,
  A few pale men and women stared at all.   360
God knows what they were feeling, with their white
  Constrained faces, they, so prodigal
Of cry and gesture when the world goes right,
  Or wrong indeed. But here was depth of wrong,
And here, still water; they were silent here;
  And through that sentient silence, struck along
That measured tramp from which it stood out clear,
  Distinct the sound and silence, like a gong
At midnight, each by the other awfuller, —
  While every soldier in his cap displayed
A leaf of olive. Dusty, bitter thing !   371
Was such plucked at Novara, is it said ?

A cry is up in England, which doth ring
  The hollow world through, that for ends of trade
And virtue and God's better worshipping,
  We henceforth should exalt the name of Peace
And leave those rusty wars that eat the soul, —
  Besides their clippings at our golden fleece.
I, too, have loved peace, and from bole to bole
  Of immemorial undeciduous trees   380
Would write, as lovers use upon a scroll,
  The holy name of Peace and set it high
Where none could pluck it down. On trees, I say, —
  Not upon gibbets ! — With the greenery
Of dewy branches and the flowery May,
  Sweet mediation betwixt earth and sky
Providing, for the shepherd's holiday.

Not upon gibbets ! though the vulture
  leaves
The bones to quiet, which he first picked
  bare.
Not upon dungeons ! though the wretch
  who grieves   390
And groans within less stirs the outer
  air
Than any little field-mouse stirs the
  sheaves.
Not upon chain-bolts ! though the slave's
  despair
Has dulled his helpless miserable brain
And left him blank beneath the freeman's
  whip
To sing and laugh out idiocies of pain.
Nor yet on starving homes ! where many a
  lip
Has sobbed itself asleep through curses
  vain.
I love no peace which is not fellowship
And which includes not mercy. I would
  have   400
Rather the raking of the guns across
  The world, and shrieks against Heaven's
  architrave;
Rather the struggle in the slippery fosse
Of dying men and horses, and the wave
Blood-bubbling. . . . Enough said ! — by
  Christ's own cross,
And by this faint heart of my woman-
  hood,
Such things are better than a Peace that
  sits
Beside a hearth in self-commended mood,
And takes no thought how wind and rain
  by fits
Are howling out of doors against the
  good   410
Of the poor wanderer. What ! your peace
  admits
Of outside anguish while it keeps at
  home ?
I loathe to take its name upon my tongue.
'T is nowise peace: 't is treason, stiff with
  doom, —
'T is gagged despair and inarticulate
  wrong, —
Annihilated Poland, stifled Rome,
Dazed Naples, Hungary fainting 'neath the
  thong,
And Austria wearing a smooth olive-leaf
On her brute forehead, while her hoofs out-
  press
The life from these Italian souls, in brief.

O Lord of Peace, who art Lord of Right-
  eousness,   421
Constrain the anguished worlds from sin
  and grief,
Pierce them with conscience, purge them
  with redress,
And give us peace which is no counter-
  feit !

But wherefore should we look out any
  more
From Casa Guidi windows ? Shut them
  straight,
And let us sit down by the folded door,
And veil our saddened faces and, so,
  wait
What next the judgment-heavens make
  ready for.
I have grown too weary of these win-
  dows. Sights   430
Come thick enough and clear enough in
  thought,
Without the sunshine; souls have inner
  lights.
And since the Grand-duke has come back
  and brought
This army of the North which thus re-
  quites
His filial South, we leave him to be taught.
His South, too, has learnt something
  certainly,
Whereof the practice will bring profit
  soon;
And peradventure other eyes may see,
From Casa Guidi windows, what is done
Or undone. Whatsoever deeds they be,
Pope Pius will be glorified in none.   441
Record that gain, Mazzini ! — it shall
  top
Some heights of sorrow. Peter's rock, so
  named,
Shall lure no vessel any more to drop
Among the breakers. Peter's chair is
  shamed
Like any vulgar throne the nations lop
To pieces for their firewood unreclaimed, —
And, when it burns too, we shall see as
  well
In Italy as elsewhere. Let it burn.
The cross, accounted still adorable,   450
Is Christ's cross only ! — if the thief's
  would earn
Some stealthy genuflexions, we rebel;
And here the impenitent thief's has had its
  turn,

As God knows; and the people on their
knees
Scoff and toss back the crosiers stretched
like yokes
To press their heads down lower by de-
grees.
So Italy, by means of these last strokes,
Escapes the danger which preceded
these,
Of leaving captured hands in cloven
oaks, —
Of leaving very souls within the
buckle 460
Whence bodies struggled outward, — of
supposing
That freemen may like bondsmen kneel
and truckle,
And then stand up as usual, without losing
An inch of stature.
Those whom she-wolves suckle
Will bite as wolves do in the grapple-clos-
ing
Of adverse interests. This at last is
known
(Thank Pius for the lesson), that albeit
Among the popedom's hundred heads of
stone
Which blink down on you from the roof's
retreat
In Siena's tiger-striped cathedral, Joan
And Borgia 'mid their fellows you may
greet, 471
A harlot and a devil, — you will see
Not a man, still less angel, grandly set
With open soul to render man more
free.
The fishers are still thinking of the net,
And, if not thinking of the hook too, we
Are counted somewhat deeply in their
debt;
But that's a rare case — so, by hook
and crook
They take the advantage, agonizing Christ
By rustier nails than those of Cedron's
brook, 480
I' the people's body very cheaply priced, —
And quote high priesthood out of Holy
book,
While buying death-fields with the sacri-
ficed.

Priests, priests, — there's no such
name ! — God's own, except
Ye take most vainly. Through heaven's
lifted gate

The priestly ephod in sole glory swept
When Christ ascended, entered in, and
sate
(With victor face sublimely overwept)
At Deity's right hand, to mediate,
He alone, He for ever. On his
breast 490
The Urim and the Thummim, fed with
fire
From the full Godhead, flicker with the
unrest
Of human pitiful heart-beats. Come up
higher,
All Christians ! Levi's tribe is dispos-
sest.
That solitary alb ye shall admire,
But not cast lots for. The last chrism,
poured right,
Was on that Head, and poured for burial
And not for domination in men's sight.
What are these churches ? The old
temple-wall
Doth overlook them juggling with the
sleight 500
Of surplice, candlestick and altar-pall;
East church and west church, ay, north
church and south,
Rome's church and England's, — let them
all repent,
And make concordats 'twixt their soul
and mouth,
Succeed Saint Paul by working at the tent,
Become infallible guides by speaking
truth,
And excommunicate their pride that bent
And cramped the souls of men.
Why, even here
Priestcraft burns out, the twinèd linen
blazes;
Not, like asbestos, to grow white and
clear, 510
But all to perish ! — while the fire-smell
raises
To life some swooning spirits who, last
year,
Lost breath and heart in these church-
stifled places.
Why, almost, through this Pius, we be-
lieved,
The priesthood could be an honest thing,
he smiled
So saintly while our corn was being
sheaved
For his own granaries ! Showing now de-
filed

His hireling hands, a better help's
 achieved
Than if they blessed us shepherd-like and
 mild.
False doctrine, strangled by its own
 amen, 520
Dies in the throat of all this nation. Who
 Will speak a pope's name as they rise
 again?
What woman or what child will count him
 true?
What dreamer praise him with the voice
 or pen?
What man fight for him? — Pius takes
 his due.

Record that gain, Mazzini! — Yes, but
 first
Set down thy people's faults; set down the
 want
 Of soul-conviction; set down aims dis-
 persed,
And incoherent means, and valor scant
 Because of scanty faith, and schisms ac-
 cursed 530
That wrench these brother-hearts from
 covenant
 With freedom and each other. Set
 down this,
And this, and see to overcome it when
 The seasons bring the fruits thou wilt
 not miss
If wary. Let no cry of patriot men
 Distract thee from the stern analysis
Of masses who cry only! keep thy ken
 Clear as thy soul is virtuous. Heroes'
 blood
Splashed up against thy noble brow in
 Rome; 539
 Let such not blind thee to an inter-
 lude
Which was not also holy, yet did come
 'Twixt sacramental actions, — brother-
 hood
Despised even there, and something of the
 doom
 Of Remus in the trenches. Listen
 now —
Rossi died silent near where Cæsar died.
HE did not say 'My Brutus, is it thou?'
But Italy unquestioned testified
 'I killed him! I am Brutus. — I avow.'
At which the whole world's laugh of scorn
 replied
 'A poor maimed copy of Brutus!'

 Too much like, 550
Indeed, to be so unlike! too unskilled
 At Philippi and the honest battle-pike,
To be so skilful where a man is killed
 Near Pompey's statue, and the daggers
 strike
At unawares i' the throat. Was thus ful-
 filled
 An omen once of Michael Angelo? —
When Marcus Brutus he conceived com-
 plete,
 And strove to hurl him out by blow on
 blow
Upon the marble, at Art's thunderheat,
 Till haply (some pre-shadow rising
 slow 560
Of what his Italy would fancy meet
 To be called BRUTUS) straight his plastic
 hand
Fell back before his prophet-soul, and
 left
 A fragment, a maimed Brutus, — but
 more grand
Than this, so named at Rome, was!
 'Let thy weft
 Present one woof and warp, Mazzini!
 Stand
With no man hankering for a dagger's
 heft,
 No, not for Italy! — nor stand apart,
No, not for the Republic! — from those
 pure
 Brave men who hold the level of thy
 heart 570
In patriot truth, as lover and as doer,
 Albeit they will not follow where thou
 art
As extreme theorist. Trust and distrust
 fewer;
 And so bind strong and keep unstained
 the cause
Which (God's sign granted) war-trumps
 newly blown
 Shall yet annunciate to the world's ap-
 plause.

But now, the world is busy; it has grown
 A Fair-going world. Imperial England
 draws
The flowing ends of the earth from Fez,
 Canton,
 Delhi and Stockholm, Athens and
 Madrid, 580
The Russias and the vast Americas,
 As if a queen drew in her robes amid

Her golden cincture, — isles, peninsulas,
 Capes, continents, far inland countries
  hid
By jasper-sands and hills of chrysopras,
 All trailing in their splendors through
  the door
Of the gorgeous Crystal Palace. Every
  nation,
 To every other nation strange of yore,
Gives face to face the civic salutation,
 And holds up in a proud right hand be-
  fore   590
That congress the best work which she can
  fashion
By her best means. ' These corals, will
  you please
To match against your oaks ? They grow
  as fast
Within my wilderness of purple seas.' —
' This diamond stared upon me as I passed
 (As a live god's eye from a marble
  frieze)
Along a dark of diamonds. Is it
  classed ? ' —
 ' I wove these stuffs so subtly that the
  gold
Swims to the surface of the silk like cream
 And curdles to fair patterns. Ye be-
  hold ! ' —   600
' These delicatest muslins rather seem
 Than be, you think ? Nay, touch them
  and be bold,
Though such veiled Chakhi's face in Hafiz'
  dream.' —
 ' These carpets — you walk slow on them
  like kings,
Inaudible like spirits, while your foot
 Dips deep in velvet roses and such
  things.' —
' Even Apollonius might commend this
  flute:
 The music, winding through the stops,
  upsprings
To make the player very rich : com-
  pute ! '
 ' Here's goblet-glass, to take in with
  your wine   610
The very sun its grapes were ripened
  under:
 Drink light and juice together, and each
  fine.' —
' This model of a steamship moves your
  wonder ?
 You should behold it crushing down the
  brine

Like a blind Jove who feels his way with
  thunder.' —
 ' Here's sculpture ! Ah, *we* live too !
  why not throw
Our life into our marbles ? Art has place
 For other artists after Angelo.' —
' I tried to paint out here a natural face;
 For nature includes Raffael, as we know,
Not Raffael nature. Will it help my
  case ? ' —   621
 ' Methinks you will not match this steel
  of ours ! ' —
' Nor you this porcelain ! One might
  dream the clay
Retained in it the larvæ of the flowers,
 They bud so, round the cup, the old Spring-
  way.' —
 ' Nor you these carven woods, where
  birds in bowers
With twisting snakes and climbing cupids,
  play.'

O Magi of the east and of the west,
 Your incense, gold and myrrh are ex-
  cellent ! —
What gifts for Christ, then, bring ye
  with the rest ?   630
Your hands have worked well: is your
  courage spent
 In handwork only ? Have you nothing
  best,
Which generous souls may perfect and
  present,
 And He shall thank the givers for ? no
  light
Of teaching, liberal nations, for the poor
 Who sit in darkness when it is not night ?
No cure for wicked children ? Christ, — no
  cure !
No help for women sobbing out of sight
 Because men made the laws ? no brothel-
  lure
Burnt out by popular lightnings ? Hast
  thou found   640
No remedy, my England, for such woes ?
 No outlet, Austria, for the scourged and
  bound,
No entrance for the exiled ? no repose,
 Russia, for knouted Poles worked under-
  ground,
And gentle ladies bleached among the
  snows ?
 No mercy for the slave, America ?
No hope for Rome, free France, chivalric
  France ?

Alas, great nations have great shames, I
   say.
No pity, O world, no tender utterance
   Of benediction, and prayers stretched
     this way   650
For poor Italia, baffled by mischance ?
   O gracious nations, give some ear to
     me !
You all go to your Fair, and I am one
   Who at the roadside of humanity
Beseech your alms, — God's justice to be
   done.
So, prosper !

In the name of Italy,
Meantime, her patriot Dead have benison.
   They only have done well; and, what
     they did
Being perfect, it shall triumph. Let them
   slumber:
   No king of Egypt in a pyramid   660
Is safer from oblivion, though he number
Full seventy cerements for a coverlid.
These Dead be seeds of life, and shall en-
   cumber
The sad heart of the land until it loose
The clammy clods and let out the Spring-
   growth
In beatific green through every bruise.
The tyrant should take heed to what he
   doth,
Since every victim-carrion turns to use,
And drives a chariot, like a god made wroth,
   Against each piled injustice. Ay, the
     least,   670
Dead for Italia, not in vain has died;
   Though many vainly, ere life's struggle
     ceased,
To mad dissimilar ends have swerved aside;
   Each grave her nationality has pieced
By its own majestic breadth, and fortified
And pinned it deeper to the soil. Forlorn
Of thanks be, therefore, no one of these
   graves !
   Not Hers, — who, at her husband's side,
     in scorn,
Outfaced the whistling shot and hissing
   waves,
Until she felt her little babe unborn   680
Recoil, within her, from the violent staves
   And bloodhounds of the world, — at
     which, her life
Dropt inwards from her eyes and followed
   it
Beyond the hunters. Garibaldi's wife

And child died so. And now, the seaweeds
   fit
   Her body, like a proper shroud and coif,
And murmurously the ebbing waters grit
   The little pebbles while she lies interred
In the sea-sand. Perhaps, ere dying thus,
   She looked up in his face (which never
     stirred   690
From its clenched anguish) as to make
   excuse
For leaving him for his, if so she erred.
He well remembers that she could not
   choose.
A memorable grave ! Another is
At Genoa. There, a king may fitly lie,
   Who, bursting that heroic heart of his
At lost Novara, that he could not die
   (Though thrice into the cannon's eyes for
     this
He plunged his shuddering steed, and felt
   the sky
   Reel back between the fire-shocks),
     stripped away   700
The ancestral ermine ere the smoke had
   cleared,
   And, naked to the soul, that none might
     say
His kingship covered what was base and
   bleared
   With treason, went out straight an exile,
     yea,
An exiled patriot. Let him be revered.

Yea, verily, Charles Albert has died well;
   And if he lived not all so, as one spoke,
The sin pass softly with the passing-bell:
For he was shriven, I think, in cannon-
   smoke,   709
   And, taking off his crown, made visible
A hero's forehead. Shaking Austria's yoke
   He shattered his own hand and heart.
     'So best,'
His last words were upon his lonely bed,
   'I do not end like popes and dukes at
     least —
Thank God for it.' And now that he is
   dead,
   Admitting it is proved and manifest
That he was worthy, with a discrowned
   head,
   To measure heights with patriots, let
     them stand
Beside the man in his Oporto shroud,
   And each vouchsafe to take him by the
     hand,   720

And kiss him on the cheek, and say aloud, —
    ' Thou, too, hast suffered for our native
        land !
My brother, thou art one of us ! be proud.'

Still, graves, when Italy is talked upon.
Still, still, the patriot's tomb, the stranger's
    hate.
Still Niobe ! still fainting in the sun,
By whose most dazzling arrows violate
    Her beauteous offspring perished ! has
        she won
Nothing but garlands for the graves, from
    Fate ?
    Nothing but death-songs ? — Yes, he it
        understood   730
Life throbs in noble Piedmont ! while the
    feet
    Of Rome's clay image, dabbled soft in
        blood,
Grow flat with dissolution and, as meet,
    Will soon be shovelled off like other
        mud,
To leave the passage free in church and
    street.
    And I, who first took hope up in this
        song,
Because a child was singing one . . . be-
        hold,
    The hope and omen were not, haply,
        wrong !
Poets are soothsayers still, like those of
    old
    Who studied flights of doves; and crea-
        tures young   740
And tender, mighty meanings may unfold.

The sun strikes, through the windows,
    up the floor;
Stand out in it, my own young Florentine,
    Not two years old, and let me see thee
        more !
It grows along thy amber curls, to shine
    Brighter than elsewhere. Now, look
        straight before,
And fix thy brave blue English eyes on
    mine,
    And from my soul, which fronts the fu-
        ture so,
With unabashed and unabated gaze,
    Teach me to hope for, what the angels
        know   750
When they smile clear as thou dost. Down
    God's ways
    With just alighted feet, between the snow

And snowdrops, where a little lamb may
    graze,
    Thou hast no fear, my lamb, about the
        road,
Albeit in our vainglory we assume
    That, less than we have, thou hast
        learnt of God.
Stand out, my blue-eyed prophet ! — thou,
    to whom
    The earliest world-day light that ever
        flowed,
Through Casa Guidi Windows chanced to
    come !
    Now shake the glittering nimbus of thy
        hair,   760
And be God's witness that the elemental
    New springs of life are gushing every-
        where
To cleanse the watercourses, and prevent
    all
    Concrete obstructions which infest the
        air !
That earth 's alive, and gentle or ungentle
    Motions within her, signify but
        growth ! —
The ground swells greenest o'er the labor-
    ing moles.

Howe'er the uneasy world is vexed and
    wroth,
Young children, lifted high on parent souls,
    Look round them with a smile upon the
        mouth,   770
And take for music every bell that tolls;
    (Who said we should be better if like
        these ?)
But *we* sit murmuring for the future
    though
    Posterity is smiling on our knees,
Convicting us of folly. Let us go —
    We will trust God. The blank inter-
        stices
Men take for ruins, He will build into
    With pillared marbles rare, or knit
        across
With generous arches, till the fane 's com-
    plete.
    This world has no perdition, if some
        loss.   780

Such cheer I gather from thy smiling,
    Sweet !
    The self-same cherub-faces which em-
        boss
The Vail, lean inward to the Mercy-seat.

AURORA LEIGH

A POEM IN NINE BOOKS

From the time when Mrs. Browning dashed off the greater part of 'Lady Geraldine's Courtship' in response to a demand from her publisher for 'more copy,' she had cherished the design of writing a complete poetical romance, of which the scene should be laid in the present time amid the seemingly unromantic surroundings of modern society. When, therefore, she had become a little wonted to married life in Italy and had delivered her soul of the first ardent though fluctuating emotions excited by the earlier stages of the Italian struggle for independence, she set about the execution of her previous project. The narrative poem of *Aurora Leigh*, her most sustained and considerable if not her most symmetrical and beautiful work, was begun in Florence, or at the Baths of Lucca, in the early fifties, and continued during the summers of 1855 and 1856, which the Brownings passed in England, and the intervening winter, when they were living in Paris, in a small apartment on the Rue du Colisée. It was finally completed in England, in the London house of John Kenyon, Mrs. Browning's generous cousin, and the faithful friend of both poets, who lived only a few weeks after *Aurora Leigh* had received its dedication to him, in October, 1856. The first edition appeared at the Christmas holidays of that year, and bears the imprint London: Chapman & Hall, 1857.

DEDICATION

TO

JOHN KENYON, Esq.

The words 'cousin' and 'friend' are constantly recurring in this poem, the last pages of which have been finished under the hospitality of your roof, my own dearest cousin and friend; — cousin and friend, in a sense of less equality and greater disinterestedness than 'Romney''s.

Ending, therefore, and preparing once more to quit England, I venture to leave in your hands this book, the most mature of my works, and the one into which my highest convictions upon Life and Art have entered; that as, through my various efforts in Literature and steps in life, you have believed in me, borne with me, and been generous to me, far beyond the common uses of mere relationship or sympathy of mind, so you may kindly accept, in sight of the public, this poor sign of esteem, gratitude, and affection from — Your unforgetting
E. B. B.

39 DEVONSHIRE PLACE: *October* 17, 1856.

AURORA LEIGH

FIRST BOOK

OF writing many books there is no end;
And I who have written much in prose and verse
For others' uses, will write now for mine, —
Will write my story for my better self,
As when you paint your portrait for a friend,
Who keeps it in a drawer and looks at it
Long after he has ceased to love you, just
To hold together what he was and is.

I, writing thus, am still what men call young;
I have not so far left the coasts of life   10
To travel inland, that I cannot hear
That murmur of the outer Infinite
Which unweaned babies smile at in their sleep
When wondered at for smiling; not so far,
But still I catch my mother at her post
Beside the nursery door, with finger up,
'Hush, hush — here's too much noise!' while her sweet eyes
Leap forward, taking part against her word
In the child's riot. Still I sit and feel
My father's slow hand, when she had left us both,   20
Stroke out my childish curls across his knee,
And hear Assunta's daily jest (she knew
He liked it better than a better jest)
Inquire how many golden scudi went
To make such ringlets. O my father's hand,
Stroke heavily, heavily the poor hair down,
Draw, press the child's head closer to thy knee!
I 'm still too young, too young, to sit alone.

I write. My mother was a Florentine,
Whose rare blue eyes were shut from see-
    ing me 30
When scarcely I was four years old, my
    life
A poor spark snatched up from a failing
    lamp
Which went out therefore. She was weak
    and frail;
She could not bear the joy of giving life,
The mother's rapture slew her. If her
    kiss
Had left a longer weight upon my lips
It might have steadied the uneasy breath,
And reconciled and fraternized my soul
With the new order. As it was, indeed,
I felt a mother-want about the world, 40
And still went seeking, like a bleating
    lamb
Left out at night in shutting up the
    fold, —
As restless as a nest-deserted bird
Grown chill through something being away,
    though what
It knows not. I, Aurora Leigh, was born
To make my father sadder, and myself
Not overjoyous, truly. Women know
The way to rear up children (to be just),
They know a simple, merry, tender knack
Of tying sashes, fitting baby-shoes, 50
And stringing pretty words that make no
    sense,
And kissing full sense into empty words,
Which things are corals to cut life upon,
Although such trifles: children learn by
    such,
Love's holy earnest in a pretty play
And get not over-early solemnized,
But seeing, as in a rose-bush, Love's
    Divine
Which burns and hurts not, — not a single
    bloom, —
Become aware and unafraid of Love.
Such good do mothers. Fathers love as
    well 60
— Mine did, I know, — but still with
    heavier brains,
And wills more consciously responsible,
And not as wisely, since less foolishly;
So mothers have God's license to be missed.

My father was an austere Englishman,
Who, after a dry lifetime spent at home
In college-learning, law, and parish talk,
Was flooded with a passion unaware,

His whole provisioned and complacent past
Drowned out from him that moment. As
    he stood 70
In Florence, where he had come to spend
    a month
And note the secret of Da Vinci's drains,
He musing somewhat absently perhaps
Some English question . . . whether men
    should pay
The unpopular but necessary tax
With left or right hand — in the alien sun
In that great square of the Santissima
There drifted past him (scarcely marked
    enough
To move his comfortable island scorn)
A train of priestly banners, cross and
    psalm, 80
The white-veiled rose-crowned maidens
    holding up
Tall tapers, weighty for such wrists, aslant
To the blue luminous tremor of the air,
And letting drop the white wax as they
    went
To eat the bishop's wafer at the church;
From which long trail of chanting priests
    and girls,
A face flashed like a cymbal on his face
And shook with silent clangor brain and
    heart,
Transfiguring him to music. Thus, even
    thus,
He too received his sacramental gift 90
With eucharistic meanings; for he loved.

And thus beloved, she died. I've heard it
    said
That but to see him in the first surprise
Of widower and father, nursing me,
Unmothered little child of four years old,
His large man's hands afraid to touch my
    curls,
As if the gold would tarnish, — his grave
    lips
Contriving such a miserable smile
As if he knew needs must, or I should die,
And yet 't was hard, — would almost make
    the stones 100
Cry out for pity. There's a verse he set
In Santa Croce to her memory, —
'Weep for an infant too young to weep
    much
When death removed this mother' — stops
    the mirth
To-day on women's faces when they walk
With rosy children hanging on their gowns.

Under the cloister to escape the sun
That scorches in the piazza.   After which
He left our Florence and made haste to
  hide
Himself, his prattling child, and silent
  grief,   110
Among the mountains above Pelago;
Because unmothered babes, he thought, had
  need
Of mother nature more than others use,
And Pan's white goats, with udders warm
  and full
Of mystic contemplations, come to feed
Poor milkless lips of orphans like his
  own —
Such scholar-scraps he talked, I 've heard
  from friends,
For even prosaic men who wear grief long
Will get to wear it as a hat aside
With a flower stuck in 't.   Father, then,
  and child,   120
We lived among the mountains many years,
God's silence on the outside of the house,
And we who did not speak too loud within,
And old Assunta to make up the fire,
Crossing herself whene'er a sudden flame
Which lightened from the firewood, made
  alive
That picture of my mother on the wall.

The painter drew it after she was dead,
And when the face was finished, throat
  and hands,
Her cameriera carried him, in hate   130
Of the English-fashioned shroud, the last
  brocade
She dressed in at the Pitti; 'he should
  paint
No sadder thing than that,' she swore, 'to
  wrong
Her poor signora.'   Therefore very strange
The effect was.   I, a little child, would
  crouch
For hours upon the floor with knees drawn
  up,
And gaze across them, half in terror, half
In adoration, at the picture there, —
That swan-like supernatural white life
Just sailing upward from the red stiff
  silk   140
Which seemed to have no part in it nor
  power
To keep it from quite breaking out of
  bounds.
For hours I sat and stared.   Assunta's awe

And my poor father's melancholy eyes
Still pointed that way.   That way went my
  thoughts
When wandering beyond sight.   And as I
  grew
In years, I mixed, confused, unconsciously,
Whatever I last read or heard or dreamed,
Abhorrent, admirable, beautiful,
Pathetical, or ghastly, or grotesque,   150
With still that face . . . which did not
  therefore change,
But kept the mystic level of all forms,
Hates, fears, and admirations, was by turns
Ghost, fiend, and angel, fairy, witch, and
  sprite,
A dauntless Muse who eyes a dreadful
  Fate,
A loving Psyche who loses sight of Love,
A still Medusa with mild milky brows
All curdled and all clothed upon with
  snakes
Whose slime falls fast as sweat will; or
  anon
Our Lady of the Passion, stabbed with
  swords   160
Where the Babe sucked; or Lamia in her
  first
Moonlighted pallor, ere she shrunk and
  blinked
And shuddering wriggled down to the un-
  clean;
Or my own mother, leaving her last smile
In her last kiss upon the baby-mouth
My father pushed down on the bed for
  that, —
Or my dead mother, without smile or
  kiss,
Buried at Florence.   All which images,
Concentred on the picture, glassed them-
  selves
Before my meditative childhood, as   170
The incoherencies of change and death
Are represented fully, mixed and merged,
In the smooth fair mystery of perpetual
  Life.
And while I stared away my childish
  wits
Upon my mother's picture (ah, poor
  child!),
My father, who through love had suddenly
Thrown off the old conventions, broken
  loose
From chin-bands of the soul, like Lazarus,
Yet had no time to learn to talk and walk
Or grow anew familiar with the sun, — 180

Who had reached to freedom, not to action, lived,
But lived as one entranced, with thoughts, not aims, —
Whom love had unmade from a common man,
But not completed to an uncommon man, —
My father taught me what he had learnt the best
Before he died and left me, — grief and love.
And, seeing we had books among the hills,
Strong words of counselling souls confederate
With vocal pines and waters, — out of books
He taught me all the ignorance of men, 190
And how God laughs in heaven when any man
Says 'Here I 'm learned; this I understand;
In that, I am never caught at fault or doubt.'
He sent the schools to school, demonstrating
A fool will pass for such through one mistake,
While a philosopher will pass for such,
Through said mistakes being ventured in the gross
And heaped up to a system.
　　　　　　　　　　I am like,
They tell me, my dear father. Broader brows
Howbeit, upon a slenderer undergrowth 200
Of delicate features, — paler, near as grave;
But then my mother's smile breaks up the whole,
And makes it better sometimes than itself.
So, nine full years, our days were hid with God
Among his mountains: I was just thirteen,
Still growing like the plants from unseen roots
In tongue-tied Springs, — and suddenly awoke
To full life and life's needs and agonies
With an intense, strong, struggling heart beside
A stone-dead father. Life, struck sharp on death, 210

Makes awful lightning. His last word was 'Love —'
'Love, my child, love, love !' — (then he had done with grief)
'Love, my child.' Ere I answered he was gone,
And none was left to love in all the world.
There, ended childhood. What succeeded next
I recollect as, after fevers, men
Thread back the passage of delirium,
Missing the turn still, baffled by the door;
Smooth endless days, notched here and there with knives,
A weary, wormy darkness, spurred i' the flank 220
With flame, that it should eat and end itself
Like some tormented scorpion. Then at last
I do remember clearly how there came
A stranger with authority, not right
(I thought not), who commanded, caught me up
From old Assunta's neck; how, with a shriek,
She let me go, — while I, with ears too full
Of my father's silence to shriek back a word,
In all a child's astonishment at grief
Stared at the wharf-edge where she stood and moaned, 230
My poor Assunta, where she stood and moaned !
The white walls, the blue hills, my Italy,
Drawn backward from the shuddering steamer-deck,
Like one in anger drawing back her skirts
Which suppliants catch at. Then the bitter sea
Inexorably pushed between us both
And, sweeping up the ship with my despair,
Threw us out as a pasture to the stars.

Ten nights and days we voyaged on the deep;
Ten nights and days without the common face 240
Of any day or night; the moon and sun
Cut off from the green reconciling earth,
To starve into a blind ferocity
And glare unnatural; the very sky

(Dropping its bell-net down upon the sea,
As if no human heart should 'scape alive)
Bedraggled with the desolating salt,
Until it seemed no more that holy heaven
To which my father went. All new and
    strange;
The universe turned stranger, for a
    child.   250

Then, land! — then, England! oh, the
    frosty cliffs
Looked cold upon me. Could I find a
    home
Among those mean red houses through the
    fog ?
And when I heard my father's language
    first
From alien lips which had no kiss for mine
I wept aloud, then laughed, then wept,
    then wept,
And some one near me said the child was
    mad
Through much sea-sickness. The train
    swept us on:
Was this my father's England ? the great
    isle ?
The ground seemed cut up from the fel-
    lowship   260
Of verdure, field from field, as man from
    man;
The skies themselves looked low and posi-
    tive,
As almost you could touch them with a
    hand,
And dared to do it they were so far off
From God's celestial crystals; all things
    blurred
And dull and vague. Did Shakespeare
    and his mates
Absorb the light here ? — not a hill or
    stone
With heart to strike a radiant color up
Or active outline on the indifferent air.

I think I see my father's sister stand   270
Upon the hall-step of her country-house
To give me welcome. She stood straight
    and calm,
Her somewhat narrow forehead braided
    tight
As if for taming accidental thoughts
From possible pulses; brown hair pricked
    with gray
By frigid use of life (she was not old,
Although my father's elder by a year),

A nose drawn sharply, yet in delicate
    lines;
A close mild mouth, a little soured about
The ends, through speaking unrequited
    loves   280
Or peradventure niggardly half-truths;
Eyes of no color, — once they might have
    smiled,
But never, never have forgot themselves
In smiling; cheeks, in which was yet a
    rose
Of perished summers, like a rose in a
    book,
Kept more for ruth than pleasure, — if past
    bloom,
Past fading also.
                      She had lived, we 'll say,
A harmless life, she called a virtuous
    life,
A quiet life, which was not life at all
(But that, she had not lived enough to
    know),   290
Between the vicar and the county squires,
The lord-lieutenant looking down some-
    times
From the empyrean to assure their souls
Against chance vulgarisms, and, in the
    abyss,
The apothecary, looked on once a year
To prove their soundness of humility.
The poor - club exercised her Christian
    gifts
Of knitting stockings, stitching petticoats,
Because we are of one flesh, after all,
And need one flannel (with a proper sense
Of difference in the quality) — and still 301
The book-club, guarded from your modern
    trick
Of shaking dangerous questions from the
    crease,
Preserved her intellectual. She had lived
A sort of cage-bird life, born in a cage,
Accounting that to leap from perch to
    perch
Was act and joy enough for any bird.
Dear heaven, how silly are the things that
    live
In thickets, and eat berries !
                                    I, alas,
A wild bird scarcely fledged, was brought
    to her cage,   310
And she was there to meet me. Very
    kind.
Bring the clean water, give out the fresh
    seed.

She stood upon the steps to welcome me,
Calm, in black garb. I clung about her
   neck, —
Young babes, who catch at every shred of
   wool
To draw the new light closer, catch and
   cling
Less blindly. In my ears my father's
   word
Hummed ignorantly, as the sea in shells,
'Love, love, my child' She, black there
   with my grief,
Might feel my love — she was his sister
   once —   320
I clung to her. A moment she seemed
   moved,
Kissed me with cold lips, suffered me to
   cling,
And drew me feebly through the hall
   into
The room she sat in.
          There, with some strange spasm
Of pain and passion, she wrung loose my
   hands
Imperiously, and held me at arm's length,
And with two gray-steel naked-bladed
   eyes
Searched through my face, — ay, stabbed it
   through and through,
Through brows and cheeks and chin, as if
   to find
A wicked murderer in my innocent
   face,   330
If not here, there perhaps. Then, drawing
   breath,
She struggled for her ordinary calm —
And missed it rather, — told me not to
   shrink,
As if she had told me not to lie or
   swear, —
'She loved my father and would love me
   too
As long as I deserved it.' Very kind.

I understood her meaning afterward;
She thought to find my mother in my
   face,
And questioned it for that. For she, my
   aunt,
Had loved my father truly, as she
   could,   340
And hated, with the gall of gentle souls,
My Tuscan mother who had fooled away
A wise man from wise courses, a good
   man

From obvious duties, and, depriving her,
His sister, of the household precedence,
Had wronged his tenants, robbed his native
   land,
And made him mad, alike by life and
   death,
In love and sorrow. She had pored for
   years
What sort of woman could be suitable
To her sort of hate, to entertain it with, 350
And so, her very curiosity
Became hate too, and all the idealism
She ever used in life was used for hate,
Till hate, so nourished, did exceed at last
The love from which it grew, in strength
   and heat,
And wrinkled her smooth conscience with a
   sense
Of disputable virtue (say not, sin)
When Christian doctrine was enforced at
   church.

And thus my father's sister was to me
My mother's hater. From that day she
   did   360
Her duty to me (I appreciate it
In her own word as spoken to herself),
Her duty, in large measure, well pressed
   out,
But measured always. She was generous,
   bland,
More courteous than was tender, gave me
   still
The first place, — as if fearful that God's
   saints
Would look down suddenly and say
   'Herein
You missed a point, I think, through lack of
   love.'
Alas, a mother never is afraid
Of speaking angerly to any child,   370
Since love, she knows, is justified of love.

And I, I was a good child on the whole,
A meek and manageable child. Why
   not?
I did not live, to have the faults of life:
There seemed more true life in my father's
   grave
Than in all England Since that threw me
   off
Who fain would cleave (his latest will, they
   say,
Consigned me to his land), I only thought
Of lying quiet there where I was thrown

Like sea-weed on the rocks, and suffering
   her　　　　　　　　　　　　　　　380
To prick me to a pattern with her pin,
Fibre from fibre, delicate leaf from leaf,
And dry out from my drowned anatomy
The last sea-salt left in me.
　　　　　　　　　　So it was.
I broke the copious curls upon my head
In braids, because she liked smooth-
   ordered hair.
I left off saying my sweet Tuscan words
Which still at any stirring of the heart
Came up to float across the English phrase
As lilies (*Bene* or *Che che*), because　　390
She liked my father's child to speak his
   tongue.
I learnt the collects and the catechism,
The creeds, from Athanasius back to Nice,
The Articles, the Tracts *against* the times
(By no means Buonaventure's 'Prick of
   Love '),
And various popular synopses of
Inhuman doctrines never taught by John,
Because she liked instructed piety.
I learnt my complement of classic French
(Kept pure of Balzac and neologism)　　400
And German also, since she liked a range
Of liberal education, — tongues, not books.
I learnt a little algebra, a little
Of the mathematics, — brushed with ex-
   treme flounce
The circle of the sciences, because
She misliked women who are frivolous.
I learnt the royal genealogies
Of Oviedo, the internal laws
Of the Burmese empire, — by how many
   feet
Mount Chimborazo outsoars Teneriffe,　410
What navigable river joins itself
To Lara, and what census of the year five
Was taken at Klagenfurt, — because she
   liked
A general insight into useful facts.
I learnt much music, — such as would
   have been
As quite impossible in Johnson's day
As still it might be wished — fine sleights
   of hand
And unimagined fingering, shuffling off
The hearer's soul through hurricanes of
   notes
To a noisy Tophet; and I drew . . . cos-
   tumes　　　　　　　　　　　　　420
From French engravings, nereids neatly
   draped

(With smirks of simmering godship): I
   washed in
Landscapes from nature (rather say,
   washed out).
I danced the polka and Cellarius,
Spun glass, stuffed birds, and modelled
   flowers in wax,
Because she liked accomplishments in
   girls.
I read a score of books on womanhood
To prove, if women do not think at all,
They may teach thinking (to a maiden
   aunt
Or else the author), — books that boldly
   assert　　　　　　　　　　　　430
Their right of comprehending husband's
   talk
When not too deep, and even of answering
With pretty 'may it please you,' or 'so it
   is,' —
Their rapid insight and fine aptitude,
Particular worth and general missionari-
   ness,
As long as they keep quiet by the fire
And never say 'no' when the world says
   'ay,'
For that is fatal, — their angelic reach
Of virtue, chiefly used to sit and darn,
And fatten household sinners, — their, in
   brief,　　　　　　　　　　　　440
Potential faculty in everything
Of abdicating power in it: she owned
She liked a woman to be womanly,
And English women, she thanked God
   and sighed
(Some people always sigh in thanking
   God),
Were models to the universe. And last
I learnt cross-stitch, because she did not
   like
To see me wear the night with empty
   hands
A-doing nothing. So, my shepherdess
Was something after all (the pastoral
   saints　　　　　　　　　　　　450
Be praised for 't), leaning lovelorn with
   pink eyes
To match her shoes, when I mistook the
   silks;
Her head uncrushed by that round weight
   of hat
So strangely similar to the tortoise shell
Which slew the tragic poet.
　　　　　　　　　　By the way,
The works of women are symbolical.

We sew, sew, prick our fingers, dull our
    sight,
Producing what ? A pair of slippers, sir,
To put on when you 're weary — or a stool
To stumble over and vex you . . . 'curse
    that stool ! '   460
Or else at best, a cushion, where you lean
And sleep, and dream of something we are
    not
But would be for your sake. Alas, alas !
This hurts most, this — that, after all, we
    are paid
The worth of our work, perhaps.
                 In looking down
Those years of education (to return)
I wonder if Brinvilliers suffered more
In the water-torture . . . flood succeed-
    ing flood
To drench the incapable throat and split
    the veins . . .   469
Than I did. Certain of your feebler souls
Go out in such a process; many pine
To a sick, inodorous light; my own en-
    dured :
I had relations in the Unseen, and drew
The elemental nutriment and heat
From nature, as earth feels the sun at
    nights,
Or as a babe sucks surely in the dark.
I kept the life thrust on me, on the out-
    side
Of the inner life with all its ample room
For heart and lungs, for will and intellect,
Inviolable by conventions. God,   480
I thank thee for that grace of thine !
                 At first
I felt no life which was not patience, — did
The thing she bade me, without heed to a
    thing
Beyond it, sat in just the chair she placed,
With back against the window, to ex-
    clude
The sight of the great lime-tree on the
    lawn,
Which seemed to have come on purpose
    from the woods
To bring the house a message, — ay, and
    walked
Demurely in her carpeted low rooms,
As if I should not, hearkening my own
    steps,   490
Misdoubt I was alive. I read her
Was civil to her cousin, Romney Leigh,
Gave ear to her vicar, tea to her visitors,

And heard them whisper, when I changed
    a cup
(I blushed for joy at that), — 'The
    Italian child,
For all her blue eyes and her quiet ways,
Thrives ill in England: she is paler yet
Than when we came the last time; she
    will die.'

'Will die.' My cousin, Romney Leigh,
    blushed too,
With sudden anger, and approaching me 500
Said low between his teeth, 'You 're
    wicked now ?
You wish to die and leave the world a-dusk
For others, with your naughty light blown
    out ? '
I looked into his face defyingly;
He might have known that, being what I
    was,
'T was natural to like to get away
As far as dead folk can: and then indeed
Some people make no trouble when they
    die.
He turned and went abruptly, slammed
    the door,
And shut his dog out.
              Romney, Romney Leigh.
I have not named my cousin hitherto, 511
And yet I used him as a sort of friend;
My elder by few years, but cold and shy
And absent . . . tender, when he thought
    of it,
Which scarcely was imperative, grave be-
    times,
As well as early master of Leigh Hall,
Whereof the nightmare sat upon his youth,
Repressing all its seasonable delights,
And agonizing with a ghastly sense
Of universal hideous want and wrong 520
To incriminate possession. When he
    came
From college to the country, very oft
He crossed the hill on visits to my aunt,
With gifts of blue grapes from the hot-
    houses,
A book in one hand, — mere statistics (if
I chanced to lift the cover), count of all
The goats whose beards grow sprouting
    down toward hell
Against God's separative judgment-hour.
And she, she almost loved him, — even al-
    lowed
That sometimes he should seem to sigh my
    way;   530

It made him easier to be pitiful,
And sighing was his gift. So, undisturbed,
At whiles she let him shut my music up
And push my needles down, and lead me
    out
To see in that south angle of the house
The figs grow black as if by a Tuscan
    rock,
On some light pretext. She would turn
    her head
At other moments, go to fetch a thing,
And leave me breath enough to speak with
    him,
For his sake; it was simple.
                              Sometimes too
He would have saved me utterly, it
    seemed,   541
He stood and looked so.
                        Once, he stood so near,
He dropped a sudden hand upon my head
Bent down on woman's work, as soft as
    rain —
But then I rose and shook it off as fire,
The stranger's touch that took my father's
    place
Yet dared seem soft.
                      I used him for a friend
Before I ever knew him for a friend.
'T was better, 't was worse also, afterward:
We came so close, we saw our differ-
    ences   550
Too intimately. Always Romney Leigh
Was looking for the worms, I for the
    gods.
A godlike nature his; the gods look down,
Incurious of themselves; and certainly
'T is well I should remember, how, those
    days,
I was a worm too, and he looked on me.

A little by his act perhaps, yet more
By something in me, surely not my will,
I did not die. But slowly, as one in swoon,
To whom life creeps back in the form of
    death,   560
With a sense of separation, a blind pain
Of blank obstruction, and a roar i' the
    ears
Of visionary chariots which retreat
As earth grows clearer . . . slowly, by de-
    grees,
I woke, rose up . . . where was I ? in the
    world;
For uses therefore I must count worth
    while.

I had a little chamber in the house,
As green as any privet-hedge a bird
Might choose to build in, though the nest
    itself
Could show but dead-brown sticks and
    straws; the walls   570
Were green, the carpet was pure green,
    the straight
Small bed was curtained greenly, and the
    folds
Hung green about the window which let in
The out-door world with all its greenery.
You could not push your head out and es-
    cape
A dash of dawn-dew from the honeysuckle,
But so you were baptized into the grace
And privilege of seeing. . . .
                              First, the lime
(I had enough there, of the lime, be
    sure, —
My morning-dream was often hummed
    away   580
By the bees in it); past the lime, the lawn,
Which, after sweeping broadly round the
    house,
Went trickling through the shrubberies in
    a stream
Of tender turf, and wore and lost itself
Among the acacias, over which you saw
The irregular line of elms by the deep lane
Which stopped the grounds and dammed
    the overflow
Of arbutus and laurel. Out of sight
The lane was; sunk so deep, no foreign
    tramp
Nor drover of wild ponies out of Wales 590
Could guess if lady's hall or tenant's lodge
Dispensed such odors, — though his stick
    well-crooked
Might reach the lowest trail of blossoming
    briar
Which dipped upon the wall. Behind the
    elms,
And through their tops, you saw the folded
    hills
Striped up and down with hedges (burly
    oaks
Projecting from the line to show them-
    selves),
Through which my cousin Romney's chim-
    neys smoked
As still as when a silent mouth in frost
Breathes, showing where the woodlands
    hid Leigh Hall;   600
While, far above, a jut of table-land,

A promontory without water, stretched, —
You could not catch it if the days were
thick,
Or took it for a cloud; but, otherwise,
The vigorous sun would catch it up at eve
And use it for an anvil till he had filled
The shelves of heaven with burning thun-
derbolts,
Protesting against night and darkness: —
then,
When all his setting trouble was resolved
To a trance of passive glory, you might
see   610
In apparition on the golden sky
(Alas, my Giotto's background!) the sheep
run
Along the fine clear outline, small as mice
That run along a witch's scarlet thread.

Not a grand nature. Not my chestnut-
woods
Of Vallombrosa, cleaving by the spurs
To the precipices. Not my headlong leaps
Of waters, that cry out for joy or fear
In leaping through the palpitating pines,
Like a white soul tossed out to eternity 620
With thrills of time upon it. Not indeed
My multitudinous mountains, sitting in
The magic circle, with the mutual touch
Electric, panting from their full deep
hearts
Beneath the influent heavens, and waiting
for
Communion and commission. Italy
Is one thing, England one.
                    On English ground
You understand the letter, — ere the fall
How Adam lived in a garden. All the
fields
Are tied up fast with hedges, nosegay like;
The hills are crumpled plains, the plains
parterres,   631
The trees, round, woolly, ready to be
clipped,
And if you seek for any wilderness
You find, at best, a park. A nature tamed
And grown domestic like a barn-door fowl,
Which does not awe you with its claws and
beak,
Nor tempt you to an eyrie too high up,
But which, in cackling, sets you thinking of
Your eggs to-morrow at breakfast, in the
pause
Of finer meditation.
                    Rather say,   640

A sweet familiar nature, stealing in
As a dog might, or child, to touch your
hand
Or pluck your gown, and humbly mind you
so
Of presence and affection, excellent
For inner uses, from the things without.

I could not be unthankful, I who was
Entreated thus and holpen. In the room
I speak of, ere the house was well awake,
And also after it was well asleep,
I sat alone, and drew the blessing in   650
Of all that nature. With a gradual step,
A stir among the leaves, a breath, a ray,
It came in softly, while the angels made
A place for it beside me. The moon
came,
And swept my chamber clean of foolish
thoughts.
The sun came, saying, 'Shall I lift this
light
Against the lime-tree, and you will not
look?
I make the birds sing — listen! but, for
you,
God never hears your voice, excepting
when
You lie upon the bed at nights and weep.'

Then, something moved me. Then, I
wakened up   661
More slowly than I verily write now,
But wholly, at last, I wakened, opened
wide
The window and my soul, and let the airs
And out-door sights sweep gradual gospels
in,
Regenerating what I was. O Life,
How oft we throw it off and think, —
'Enough,
Enough of life in so much! — here's a
cause
For rupture; — herein we must break with
Life,
Or be ourselves unworthy; here we are
wronged,   670
Maimed, spoiled for aspiration: farewell,
Life!'
And so, as froward babes, we hide our
eyes
And think all ended. — Then, Life calls to
us
In some transformed, apocalyptic voice,
Above us, or below us, or around:

Perhaps we name it Nature's voice, or
    Love's,
Tricking ourselves, because we are more
    ashamed
To own our compensations than our griefs:
Still, Life's voice ! — still, we make our
    peace with Life.

And I, so young then, was not sullen.
    Soon   680
I used to get up early, just to sit
And watch the morning quicken in the
    gray,
And hear the silence open like a flower
Leaf after leaf, — and stroke with listless
    hand
The woodbine through the window, till at
    last
I came to do it with a sort of love,
At foolish unaware: whereat I smiled, —
A melancholy smile, to catch myself
Smiling for joy.
              Capacity for joy
Admits temptation. It seemed, next,
    worth while   690
To dodge the sharp sword set against my
    life;
To slip down stairs through all the sleepy
    house,
As mute as any dream there, and escape
As a soul from the body, out of doors,
Glide through the shrubberies, drop into
    the lane,
And wander on the hills an hour or two,
Then back again before the house should
    stir.

Or else I sat on in my chamber green,
And lived my life, and thought my
    thoughts, and prayed
My prayers without the vicar; read my
    books,   700
Without considering whether they were fit
To do me good. Mark, there. We get no
    good
By being ungenerous, even to a book,
And calculating profits, — so much help
By so much reading. It is rather when
We gloriously forget ourselves and plunge
Soul-forward, headlong, into a book's pro-
    found,
Impassioned for its beauty and salt of
    truth —
'T is then we get the right good from a
    book.

I read much. What my father taught be-
    fore   710
From many a volume, Love re-emphasized
Upon the self-same pages: Theophrast
Grew tender with the memory of his eyes,
And Ælian made mine wet. The trick of
    Greek
And Latin he had taught me, as he would
Have taught me wrestling or the game of
    fives
If such he had known, — most like a ship-
    wrecked man
Who heaps his single platter with goats'
    cheese
And scarlet berries; or like any man
Who loves but one, and so gives all at
    once,   720
Because he has it, rather than because
He counts it worthy. Thus, my father
    gave:
And thus, as did the women formerly
By young Achilles, when they pinned a
    veil
Across the boy's audacious front, and swept
With tuneful laughs the silver-fretted
    rocks,
He wrapt his little daughter in his large
Man's doublet, careless did it fit or no.

But, after I had read for memory,
I read for hope. The path my father's
    foot   730
Had trod me out (which suddenly broke
    off
What time he dropped the wallet of the
    flesh
And passed), alone I carried on, and set
My child-heart 'gainst the thorny under-
    wood,
To reach the grassy shelter of the trees.
Ah babe i' the wood, without a brother-
    babe !
My own self-pity, like the red-breast bird,
Flies back to cover all that past with
    leaves.

Sublimest danger, over which none weeps,
When any young wayfaring soul goes
    forth   740
Alone, unconscious of the perilous road,
The day-sun dazzling in his limpid eyes,
To thrust his own way, he an alien,
    through
The world of books ! Ah, you ! — you
    think it fine,

You clap hands — 'A fair day ! ' — you
    cheer him on,
As if the worst, could happen, were to rest
Too long beside a fountain. Yet, behold,
Behold ! — the world of books is still the
    world,
And worldings in it are less merciful
And more puissant.   For the wicked
    there   750
Are winged like angels; every knife that
    strikes
Is edged from elemental fire to assail
A spiritual life; the beautiful seems right
By force of beauty, and the feeble wrong
Because of weakness; power is justified
Though armed against Saint Michael; many
    a crown
Covers bald foreheads.   In the book-world,
    true,
There 's no lack, neither, of God's saints
    and kings,
That shake the ashes of the grave aside
From their calm locks and undiscom-
    fited   760
Look steadfast truths against Time's chan-
    ging mask.
True, many a prophet teaches in the roads;
True, many a seer pulls down the flaming
    heavens
Upon his own head in strong martyrdom
In order to light men a moment's space.
But stay ! — who judges ? — who distin-
    guishes
'Twixt Saul and Nahash justly, at first
    sight,
And leaves king Saul precisely at the sin,
To serve king David ? who discerns at
    once
The sound of the trumpets, when the trum-
    pets blow   770
For Alaric as well as Charlemagne ?
Who judges wizards, and can tell true
    seers
From conjurers ? the child, there ? Would
    you leave
That child to wander in a battle-field
And push his innocent smile against the
    guns;
Or even in a catacomb, — his torch
Grown ragged in the fluttering air, and all
The dark a-mutter round him ? not a
    child.

    I read books bad and good — some bad
        and good

At once (good aims not always make good
    books: 780
Well-tempered spades turn up ill-smelling
    soils
In digging vineyards even); books that
    prove
God's being so definitely, that man's doubt
Grows self-defined the other side the line,
Made atheist by suggestion; moral books,
Exasperating to license; genial books,
Discounting from the human dignity;
And merry books, which set you weeping
    when
The sun shines, — ay, and melancholy
    books,
Which make you laugh that any one should
    weep   790
In this disjointed life for one wrong more.

The world of books is still the world, I
    write,
And both worlds have God's providence,
    thank God,
To keep and hearten: with some struggle,
    indeed,
Among the breakers, some hard swimming
    through
The deeps — I lost breath in my soul some-
    times
And cried 'God save me if there 's any
    God,'
But, even so, God saved me; and, being
    dashed
From error on to error, every turn
Still brought me nearer to the central
    truth.   800

I thought so.   All this anguish in the thick
Of men's opinions . . . press and counter-
    press,
Now up, now down, now underfoot, and
    now
Emergent . . . all the best of it, perhaps,
But throws you back upon a noble trust
And use of your own instinct, — merely
    proves
Pure reason stronger than bare inference
At strongest.   Try it, — fix against heaven's
    wall
The scaling-ladders of school logic —
    mount
Step by step ! — sight goes faster; that still
    ray   810
Which strikes out from you, how, you can-
    not tell.

And why, you know not (did you eliminate,
That such as you indeed should analyze ?)
Goes straight and fast as light, and high as
   God.

The cygnet finds the water, but the man
Is born in ignorance of his element
And feels out blind at first, disorganized
By sin i' the blood, — his spirit-insight
   dulled
And crossed by his sensations. Presently
He feels it quicken in the dark sometimes,
When, mark, be reverent, be obedient, 821
For such dumb motions of imperfect life
Are oracles of vital Deity
Attesting the Hereafter. Let who says
'The soul's a clean white paper,' rather
   say,
A palimpsest, a prophet's holograph
Defiled, erased and covered by a monk's; —
The apocalypse, by a Longus ! poring on
Which obscene text, we may discern per-
   haps
Some fair, fine trace of what was written
   once, 830
Some upstroke of an alpha and omega
Expressing the old scripture.
             Books, books, books !
I had found the secret of a garret-room
Piled high with cases in my father's name,
Piled high, packed large, — where, creep-
   ing in and out
Among the giant fossils of my past,
Like some small nimble mouse between the
   ribs
Of a mastodon, I nibbled here and there
At this or that box, pulling through the gap,
In heats of terror, haste, victorious joy, 840
The first book first. And how I felt it beat
Under my pillow, in the morning's dark,
An hour before the sun would let me read !
My books ! At last because the time was
   ripe,
I chanced upon the poets.
               As the earth
Plunges in fury, when the internal fires
Have reached and pricked her heart, and,
   throwing flat
The marts and temples, the triumphal gates
And towers of observation, clears herself
To elemental freedom — thus, my soul, 850
At poetry's divine first finger-touch,
Let go conventions and sprang up surprised,
Convicted of the great eternities
Before two worlds.

           What's this, Aurora Leigh,
You write so of the poets, and not laugh ?
Those virtuous liars, dreamers after dark,
Exaggerators of the sun and moon,
And soothsayers in a tea-cup ?
                  I write so
Of the only truth-tellers now left to God,
The only speakers of essential truth, 860
Opposed to relative, comparative,
And temporal truths; the only holders by
His sun-skirts, through conventional gray
   glooms;
The only teachers who instruct mankind
From just a shadow on a charnel-wall
To find man's veritable stature out
Erect, sublime, — the measure of a man,
And that's the measure of an angel, says
The apostle. Ay, and while your common
   men
Lay telegraphs, gauge railroads, reign,
   reap, dine, 870
And dust the flaunty carpets of the world
For kings to walk on, or our president,
The poet suddenly will catch them up
With his voice like a thunder, — 'This is
   soul,
This is life, this word is being said in
   heaven,
Here's God down on us ! what are you
   about ?'
How all those workers start amid their
   work,
Look round, look up, and feel, a moment's
   space,
That carpet-dusting, though a pretty trade,
Is not the imperative labor after all. 880

My own best poets, am I one with you,
That thus I love you, — or but one through
   love ?
Does all this smell of thyme about my
   feet
Conclude my visit to your holy hill
In personal presence, or but testify
The rustling of your vesture through my
   dreams
With influent odors ? When my joy and
   pain,
My thought and aspiration, like the stops
Of pipe or flute, are absolutely dumb
Unless melodious, do you play on me 890
My pipers, — and if, sooth, you did not
   blow,
Would no sound come ? or is the music
   mine,

As a man's voice or breath is called his own,
Inbreathed by the Life-breather? There's
   a doubt
For cloudy seasons!
          But the sun was high
When first I felt my pulses set themselves
For concord; when the rhythmic turbulence
Of blood and brain swept outward upon
   words,
As wind upon the alders, blanching them
By turning up their under-natures till   900
They trembled in dilation. O delight
And triumph of the poet, who would say
A man's mere 'yes,' a woman's common
   'no,'
A little human hope of that or this,
And says the word so that it burns you
   through
With a special revelation, shakes the heart
Of all the men and women in the world,
As if one came back from the dead and
   spoke,
With eyes too happy, a familiar thing
Become divine i' the utterance! while for
   him   910
The poet, speaker, he expands with joy;
The palpitating angel in his flesh
Thrills inly with consenting fellowship
To those innumerous spirits who sun them-
   selves
Outside of time.
          O life, O poetry,
— Which means life in life! cognizant of
   life
Beyond this blood-beat, passionate for truth
Beyond these senses! — poetry, my life,
My eagle, with both grappling feet still
   hot
From Zeus's thunder, who hast ravished
   me   920
Away from all the shepherds, sheep, and
   dogs,
And set me in the Olympian roar and round
Of luminous faces for a cup-bearer,
To keep the mouths of all the godheads
   moist
For everlasting laughters, — I myself
Half drunk across the beaker with their
   eyes!
How those gods look!
          Enough so, Ganymede,
We shall not bear above a round or two.
We drop the golden cup at Herè's foot
And swoon back to the earth, — and find
   ourselves   930

Face-down among the pine-cones, cold with
   dew,
While the dogs bark, and many a shepherd
   scoffs,
'What's come now to the youth?' Such
   ups and downs
Have poets.
        Am I such indeed? The name
Is royal, and to sign it like a queen
Is what I dare not, — though some royal
   blood
Would seem to tingle in me now and then,
With sense of power and ache, — with
   imposthumes
And manias usual to the race. Howbeit
I dare not: 't is too easy to go mad   940
And ape a Bourbon in a crown of straws;
The thing's too common.
          Many fervent souls
Strike rhyme on rhyme, who would strike
   steel on steel
If steel had offered, in a restless heat
Of doing something. Many tender souls
Have strung their losses on a rhyming
   thread,
As children cowslips: — the more pains
   they take,
The work more withers. Young men, ay,
   and maids,
Too often sow their wild oats in tame
   verse,
Before they sit down under their own
   vine   950
And live for use. Alas, near all the birds
Will sing at dawn, — and yet we do not
   take
The chaffering swallow for the holy lark.
In those days, though, I never analyzed,
Not even myself. Analysis comes late.
You catch a sight of Nature, earliest,
In full front sun-face, and your eyelids
   wink
And drop before the wonder of 't; you
   miss
The form, through seeing the light. I
   lived, those days,
And wrote because I lived — unlicensed
   else;   960
My heart beat in my brain. Life's violent
   flood
Abolished bounds, — and, which my neigh-
   bor's field,
Which mine, what mattered? it is thus in
   youth!
We play at leap-frog over the god Term;

The love within us and the love without
Are mixed, confounded; if we are loved or
love,
We scarce distinguish: thus, with other
power;
Being acted on and acting seem the same:
In that first onrush of life's chariot-wheels,
We know not if the forests move or we. 970

And so, like most young poets, in a flush
Of individual life I poured myself
Along the veins of others, and achieved
Mere lifeless imitations of live verse,
And made the living answer for the dead,
Profaning nature. ' Touch not, do not
taste,
Nor handle,' — we 're too legal, who write
young:
We beat the phorminx till we hurt our
thumbs,
As if still ignorant of counterpoint;
We call the Muse, — ' O Muse, benignant
Muse,' —   980
As if we had seen her purple-braided head,
With the eyes in it, start between the
boughs
As often as a stag's.   What make-believe,
With so much earnest ! what effete re-
sults
From virile efforts ! what cold wire-drawn
odes
From such white heats ! — bucolics, where
the cows
Would scare the writer if they splashed
the mud
In lashing off the flies, — didactics, driven
Against the heels of what the master said;
And counterfeiting epics, shrill with
trumps   990
A babe might blow between two straining
cheeks
Of bubbled rose, to make his mother laugh;
And elegiac griefs, and songs of love,
Like cast-off nosegays picked up on the
road,
The worse for being warm: all these things,
writ
On happy mornings, with a morning heart,
That leaps for love, is active for resolve,
Weak for art only.   Oft, the ancient
forms
Will thrill, indeed, in carrying the young
blood.
The wine-skins, now and then, a little
warped,   1000

Will crack even, as the new wine gurgles
in.
Spare the old bottles ! — spill not the new
wine.

By Keats's soul, the man who never stepped
In gradual progress like another man,
But, turning grandly on his central self,
Ensphered himself in twenty perfect years
And died, not young (the life of a long
life
Distilled to a mere drop, falling like a
tear
Upon the world's cold cheek to make it
burn   1009
For ever); by that strong excepted soul,
I count it strange and hard to understand
That nearly all young poets should write
old,
That Pope was sexagenary at sixteen,
And beardless Byron academical,
And so with others. It may be perhaps
Such have not settled long and deep
enough
In trance, to attain to clairvoyance, — and
still
The memory mixes with the vision, spoils,
And works it turbid.
                        Or perhaps, again,
In order to discover the Muse-Sphinx, 1020
The melancholy desert must sweep round,
Behind you as before. —
                        For me, I wrote
False poems, like the rest, and thought
them true
Because myself was true in writing them.
I peradventure have writ true ones since
With less complacence.
                        But I could not hide
My quickening inner life from those at
watch.
They saw a light at a window, now and
then,
They had not set there: who had set it
there ?
My father's sister started when she caught
My soul agaze in my eyes.   She could not
say   1031
I had no business with a sort of soul,
But plainly she objected, — and demurred
That souls were dangerous things to carry
straight
Through all the spilt saltpetre of the world.
She said sometimes, ' Aurora, have you
done

Your task this morning? have you read
that book?
And are you ready for the crochet here?' —
As if she said, 'I know there's something
wrong;
I know I have not ground you down
enough 1040
To flatten and bake you to a wholesome
crust
For household uses and proprieties,
Before the rain has got into my barn
And set the grains a-sprouting. What,
you're green
With out-door impudence? you almost
grow?'
To which I answered, 'Would she hear
my task,
And verify my abstract of the book?
Or should I sit down to the crochet work?
Was such her pleasure?' Then I sat and
teased
The patient needle till it split the thread,
Which oozed off from it in meandering
lace 1051
From hour to hour. I was not, therefore,
sad;
My soul was singing at a work apart
Behind the wall of sense, as safe from
harm
As sings the lark when sucked up out of
sight
In vortices of glory and blue air.

And so, through forced work and spontane-
ous work,
The inner life informed the outer life,
Reduced the irregular blood to a settled
rhythm,
Made cool the forehead with fresh-sprin-
kling dreams, 1060
And, rounding to the spheric soul the thin,
Pined body, struck a color up the cheeks
Though somewhat faint. I clenched my
brows across
My blue eyes greatening in the looking-
glass,
And said 'We'll live, Aurora! we'll be
strong.
The dogs are on us — but we will not
die.'

Whoever lives true life will love true love.
I learnt to love that England. Very oft,
Before the day was born, or otherwise
Through secret windings of the afternoons,

I threw my hunters off and plunged my-
self 1071
Among the deep hills, as a hunted stag
Will take the waters, shivering with the
fear
And passion of the course. And when at
last
Escaped, so many a green slope built on
slope
Betwixt me and the enemy's house behind,
I dared to rest, or wander, in a rest
Made sweeter for the step upon the grass,
And view the ground's most gentle dimple-
ment
(As if God's finger touched but did not
press 1080
In making England), such an up and down
Of verdure, — nothing too much up or
down,
A ripple of land; such little hills, the
sky
Can stoop to tenderly and the wheatfields
climb;
Such nooks of valleys lined with orchises,
Fed full of noises by invisible streams;
And open pastures where you scarcely
tell
White daisies from white dew, — at inter-
vals
The mythic oaks and elm-trees standing
out
Self-poised upon their prodigy of shade, —
I thought my father's land was worthy
too 1091
Of being my Shakespeare's.
Very oft alone,
Unlicensed; not unfrequently with leave
To walk the third with Romney and his
friend
The rising painter, Vincent Carrington,
Whom men judge hardly as bee-bonneted,
Because he holds that, paint a body well,
You paint a soul by implication, like
The grand first Master. Pleasant walks!
for if
He said 'When I was last in Italy,' 1100
It sounded as an instrument that's played
Too far off for the tune — and yet it's
fine
To listen.
Ofter we walked only two
If cousin Romney pleased to walk with
me.
We read, or talked, or quarrelled, as it
chanced.

We were not lovers, nor even friends well-
matched:
Say rather, scholars upon different tracks,
And thinkers disagreed: he, overfull
Of what is, and I, haply, overbold
For what might be.
        But then the thrushes sang,
And shook my pulses and the elms' new
leaves: 1111
At which I turned, and held my finger
up,
And bade him mark that, howsoe'er the
world
Went ill, as he related, certainly
The thrushes still sang in it. At the word
His brow would soften, — and he bore with
me
In melancholy patience, not unkind,
While breaking into voluble ecstasy
I flattered all the beauteous country
round,
As poets use, the skies, the clouds, the
fields,   1120
The happy violets hiding from the roads
The primroses run down to, carrying gold;
The tangled hedgerows, where the cows
push out
Impatient horns and tolerant churning
mouths
'Twixt dripping ash-boughs, — hedgerows
all alive
With birds and gnats and large white but-
terflies
Which look as if the may-flower had caught
life
And palpitated forth upon the wind;
Hills, vales, woods, netted in a silver mist,
Farms, granges, doubled up among the
hills;   1130
And cattle grazing in the watered vales,
And cottage-chimneys smoking from the
woods,
And cottage-gardens smelling everywhere,
Confused with smell of orchards. 'See,' I
said,
'And see! is God not with us on the
earth?
And shall we put Him down by aught we
do?
Who says there's nothing for the poor and
vile
Save poverty and wickedness? behold!'
And ankle-deep in English grass I leaped
And clapped my hands, and called all very
fair.   1140

In the beginning when God called all good,
Even then was evil near us, it is writ;
But we indeed who call things good and
fair,
The evil is upon us while we speak;
Deliver us from evil, let us pray.

SECOND BOOK

Times followed one another. Came a
morn
I stood upon the brink of twenty years,
And looked before and after, as I stood
Woman and artist, — either incomplete,
Both credulous of completion. There I
held
The whole creation in my little cup,
And smiled with thirsty lips before I
drank
'Good health to you and me, sweet neigh-
bor mine,
And all these peoples.'
      I was glad, that day;
The June was in me, with its multitudes 10
Of nightingales all singing in the dark,
And rosebuds reddening where the calyx
split.
I felt so young, so strong, so sure of God!
So glad, I could not choose be very wise!
And, old at twenty, was inclined to pull
My childhood backward in a childish jest
To see the face of 't once more, and fare-
well!
In which fantastic mood I bounded forth
At early morning, — would not wait so
long
As even to snatch my bonnet by the
strings,   20
But, brushing a green trail across the lawn
With my gown in the dew, took will and
way
Among the acacias of the shrubberies,
To fly my fancies in the open air
And keep my birthday, till my aunt awoke
To stop good dreams. Meanwhile I mur-
mured on
As honeyed bees keep humming to them-
selves,
'The worthiest poets have remained un-
crowned
Till death has bleached their foreheads to
the bone;
And so with me it must be unless I prove
Unworthy of the grand adversity,   31

And certainly I would not fail so much.
What, therefore, if I crown myself to-day
In sport, not pride, to learn the feel of it,
Before my brows be numbed as Dante's own
To all the tender pricking of such leaves?
Such leaves! what leaves?'
                I pulled the branches down
To choose from.
           'Not the bay! I choose no bay
(The fates deny us if we are overbold),
Nor myrtle — which means chiefly love; and love   40
Is something awful which one dares not touch
So early o' mornings. This verbena strains
The point of passionate fragrance; and hard by,
This guelder-rose, at far too slight a beck
Of the wind, will toss about her flower-apples.
Ah — there's my choice, — that ivy on the wall,
That headlong ivy! not a leaf will grow
But thinking of a wreath. Large leaves, smooth leaves,
Serrated like my vines, and half as green.
I like such ivy, bold to leap a height   50
'T was strong to climb; as good to grow on graves
As twist about a thyrsus; pretty too
(And that's not ill) when twisted round a comb.'
Thus speaking to myself, half singing it,
Because some thoughts are fashioned like a bell
To ring with once being touched, I drew a wreath
Drenched, blinding me with dew, across my brow,
And fastening it behind so, turning faced
. . . My public! — cousin Romney — with a mouth
Twice graver than his eyes.
              I stood there fixed, —
My arms up, like the caryatid, sole   61
Of some abolished temple, helplessly
Persistent in a gesture which derides
A former purpose. Yet my blush was flame,
As if from flax, not stone.
              'Aurora Leigh,
The earliest of Auroras!'
             Hand stretched out

I clasped, as shipwrecked men will clasp a hand,
Indifferent to the sort of palm. The tide
Had caught me at my pastime, writing down
My foolish name too near upon the sea   70
Which drowned me with a blush as foolish.
              'You,
My cousin!'
            The smile died out in his eyes
And dropped upon his lips, a cold dead weight,
For just a moment, 'Here's a book I found!
No name writ on it — poems, by the form;
Some Greek upon the margin, — lady's Greek
Without the accents. Read it? Not a word.
I saw at once the thing had witchcraft in 't,
Whereof the reading calls up dangerous spirits: 79
I rather bring it to the witch.'
              'My book.
You found it' . . . .
           'In the hollow by the stream
That beech leans down into — of which you said
The Oread in it has a Naiad's heart
And pines for waters.'
             'Thank you.'
               'Thanks to *you*
My cousin! that I have seen you not too much
Witch, scholar, poet, dreamer, and the rest,
To be a woman also.'
           With a glance
The smile rose in his eyes again and touched
The ivy on my forehead, light as air.
I answered gravely, 'Poets needs must be   90
Or men or women — more's the pity.'
              'Ah,
But men, and still less women, happily,
Scarce need be poets. Keep to the green wreath,
Since even dreaming of the stone and bronze
Brings headaches, pretty cousin, and defiles
The clean white morning dresses.'
           'So you judge!
Because I love the beautiful I must
Love pleasure chiefly, and be overcharged

For ease and whiteness ! well, you know
    the world,
And only miss your cousin, 't is not
    much.   100
But learn this; I would rather take my
    part
With God's Dead, who afford to walk in
    white
Yet spread his glory, than keep quiet here
And gather up my feet from even a step
For fear to soil my gown in so much dust.
I choose to walk at all risks. — Here, if
    heads
That hold a rhythmic thought, must ache
    perforce,
For my part I choose headaches, — and to-
    day 's
My birthday.'
            ' Dear Aurora, choose instead
To cure them. You have balsams.'
                        ' I perceive.
The headache is too noble for my sex.   111
You think the heartache would sound de-
    center,
Since that 's the woman's special, proper
    ache,
And altogether tolerable, except
To a woman.'
          Saying which, I loosed my wreath,
And swinging it beside me as I walked,
Half-petulant, half-playful, as we walked,
I sent a sidelong look to find his thought, —
As falcon set on falconer's finger may,
With sidelong head, and startled, braving
    eye,   120
Which means, ' You 'll see — you 'll see !
    I 'll soon take flight,
You shall not hinder.'   He, as shaking out
His hand and answering ' Fly then,' did not
    speak,
Except by such a gesture.   Silently
We paced, until, just coming into sight
Of the house-windows, he abruptly caught
At one end of the swinging wreath, and
    said
' Aurora ! '   There I stopped short, breath
    and all.

' Aurora, let 's be serious, and throw by
This game of head and heart. Life means,
    be sure,   130
Both heart and head, — both active, both
    complete,
And both in earnest. Men and women
    make

The world, as head and heart make human
    life.
Work man, work woman, since there 's work
    to do
In this beleaguered earth, for head and
    heart,
And thought can never do the work of
    love:
But work for ends, I mean for uses, not
For such sleek fringes (do you call them
    ends,
Still less God's glory ?) as we sew ourselves
Upon the velvet of those baldaquins   140
Held 'twixt us and the sun. That book of
    yours,
I have not read a page of; but I toss
A rose up — it falls calyx down, you see !
The chances are that, being a woman, young
And pure, with such a pair of large, calm
    eyes,
You write as well . . . and ill . . . upon
    the whole,
As other women. If as well, what then ?
If even a little better, . . . still, what
    then ?
We want the Best in art now, or no art.
The time is done for facile settings up   150
Of minnow gods, nymphs here and tritons
    there;
The polytheists have gone out in God,
That unity of Bests. No best, no God !
And so with art, we say. Give art's divine,
Direct, indubitable, real as grief,
Or leave us to the grief we grow ourselves
Divine by overcoming with mere hope
And most prosaic patience. You, you are
    young
As Eve with nature's daybreak on her face,
But this same world you are come to, dearest
    coz,   160
Has done with keeping birthdays, saves her
    wreaths
To hang upon her ruins, — and forgets
To rhyme the cry with which she still beats
    back
Those savage, hungry dogs that hunt her
    down
To the empty grave of Christ. The world 's
    hard pressed:
The sweat of labor in the early curse
Has (turning acrid in six thousand years)
Become the sweat of torture. Who has
    time,
An hour's time . . . think ! — to sit upon
    a bank

And hear the cymbal tinkle in white hands?
When Egypt 's slain, I say, let Miriam
   sing!—   171
Before — where 's Moses?'
                'Ah, exactly that.
Where 's Moses?—is a Moses to be found?
You 'll seek him vainly in the bulrushes,
While I in vain touch cymbals. Yet con-
   cede,
Such sounding brass has done some actual
   good
(The application in a woman's hand,
If that were credible, being scarcely spoilt,)
In colonizing beehives.'
              'There it is!—
You play beside a death-bed like a child, 180
Yet measure to yourself a prophet's place
To teach the living. None of all these
   things
Can women understand. You generalize
Oh, nothing,—not even grief! Your
   quick-breathed hearts,
So sympathetic to the personal pang,
Close on each separate knife-stroke, yield-
   ing up
A whole life at each wound, incapable
Of deepening, widening a large lap of life
To hold the world-full woe. The human
   race
To you means, such a child, or such a
   man,   190
You saw one morning waiting in the cold,
Beside that gate, perhaps. You gather up
A few such cases, and when strong some-
   times
Will write of factories and of slaves, as if
Your father were a negro, and your son
A spinner in the mills. All 's yours and
   you,
All, colored with your blood, or otherwise
Just nothing to you. Why, I call you hard
To general suffering. Here 's the world
   half blind
With intellectual light, half brutalized 200
With civilization, having caught the plague
In silks from Tarsus, shrieking east and
   west
Along a thousand railroads, mad with pain
And sin too!... does one woman of you
   all
(You who weep easily) grow pale to see
This tiger shake his cage?—does one of
   you
Stand still from dancing, stop from string-
   ing pearls,

And pine and die because of the great sum
Of universal anguish?— Show me a tear
Wet as Cordelia's, in eyes bright as yours,
Because the world is mad. You cannot
   count,   211
That you should weep for this account, not
   you!
You weep for what you know. A red-
   haired child
Sick in a fever, if you touch him once,
Though but so little as with a finger-tip,
Will set you weeping; but a million
   sick ...
You could as soon weep for the rule of
   three
Or compound fractions. Therefore, this
   same world,
Uncomprehended by you, must remain
Uninfluenced by you.— Women as you are,
Mere women, personal and passionate, 221
You give us doating mothers, and perfect
   wives,
Sublime Madonnas, and enduring saints!
We get no Christ from you,— and verily
We shall not get a poet, in my mind.'
'With which conclusion you conclude' ...
                   'But this,
That you, Aurora, with the large live brow
And steady eyelids, cannot condescend
To play at art, as children play at swords,
To show a pretty spirit, chiefly admired 230
Because true action is impossible.
You never can be satisfied with praise
Which men give women when they judge a
   book
Not as mere work but as mere woman's
   work,
Expressing the comparative respect
Which means the absolute scorn. "Oh,
   excellent,
What grace, what facile turns, what fluent
   sweeps,
What delicate discernment ... almost
   thought!
The book does honor to the sex, we hold.
Among our female authors we make room
For this fair writer, and congratulate 241
The country that produces in these times
Such women, competent to ... spell."'
                 'Stop there,'
I answered, burning through his thread of
   talk
With a quick flame of emotion,—'You
   have read
My soul, if not my book, and argue well

I would not condescend . . . we will not
    say
To such a kind of praise (a worthless
    end
Is praise of all kinds), but to such a use
Of holy art and golden life. I am young, 250
And peradventure weak — you tell me
    so —
Through being a woman. And, for all the
    rest,
Take thanks for justice. I would rather
    dance
At fairs on tight-rope, till the babies
    dropped
Their gingerbread for joy, — than shift the
    types
For tolerable verse, intolerable
To men who act and suffer. Better far
Pursue a frivolous trade by serious means,
Than a sublime art frivolously.'
                        ' You,
Choose nobler work than either, O moist
    eyes   260
And hurrying lips and heaving heart ! We
    are young,
Aurora, you and I. The world, — look
    round, —
The world, we 're come to late, is swollen
    hard
With perished generations and their sins:
The civilizer's spade grinds horribly
On dead men's bones, and cannot turn up
    soil
That 's otherwise than fetid. All success
Proves partial failure; all advance implies
What 's left behind; all triumph, some-
    thing crushed
At the chariot-wheels; all government,
    some wrong: 270
And rich men make the poor, who curse
    the rich,
Who agonize together, rich and poor,
Under and over, in the social spasm
And crisis of the ages. Here 's an age
That makes its own vocation ! here we
    have stepped
Across the bounds of time ! here 's nought
    to see,
But just the rich man and just Lazarus,
And both in torments, with a mediate gulf,
Though not a hint of Abraham's bosom. Who
Being man, Aurora, can stand calmly by 280
And view these things, and never tease his
    soul

For some great cure ? No physic for this
    grief,
In all the earth and heavens too ? '
                            ' You believe
In God, for your part ? — ay ? that He
    who makes
Can make good things from ill things, best
    from worst,
As men plant tulips upon dunghills when
They wish them finest ? '
                        ' True. A death-heat is
The same as life-heat, to be accurate,
And in all nature is no death at all,
As men account of death, so long as
    God   290
Stands witnessing for life perpetually,
By being just God. That 's abstract truth,
    I know,
Philosophy, or sympathy with God:
But I, I sympathize with man, not God
(I think I was a man for chiefly this),
And when I stand beside a dying bed,
'T is death to me. Observe, — it had not
    much
Consoled the race of mastodons to know,
Before they went to fossil, that anon
Their place would quicken with the ele-
    phant.   300
They were not elephants but mastodons;
And I, a man, as men are now and not
As men may be hereafter, feel with men
In the agonizing present.'
                        ' Is it so,'
I said, ' my cousin ? is the world so
    bad,
While I hear nothing of it through the
    trees ?
The world was always evil, — but so
    bad ? '

' So bad, Aurora. Dear, my soul is gray
With poring over the long sum of ill;
So much for vice, so much for discontent,
So much for the necessities of power,   311
So much for the connivances of fear,
Coherent in statistical despairs
With such a total of distracted life, . . .
To see it down in figures on a page,
Plain, silent, clear, as God sees through
    the earth
The sense of all the graves, — that 's ter-
    rible
For one who is not God, and cannot right
The wrong he looks on. May I choose in-
    deed,

But vow away my years, my means, my
    aims, 320
Among the helpers, if there 's any help
In such a social strait? The common
    blood
That swings along my veins is strong
    enough
To draw me to this duty.'
                       Then I spoke.
'I have not stood long on the strand of
    life,
And these salt waters have had scarcely
    time
To creep so high up as to wet my feet:
I cannot judge these tides — I shall, per-
    haps.
A woman 's always younger than a man
At equal years, because she is disal-
    lowed 330
Maturing by the outdoor sun and air,
And kept in long-clothes past the age to
    walk.
Ah well, I know you men judge otherwise!
You think a woman ripens, as a peach,
In the cheeks chiefly. Pass it to me now;
I 'm young in age, and younger still, I
    think,
As a woman. But a child may say amen
To a bishop's prayer and feel the way it
    goes,
And I, incapable to loose the knot
Of social questions, can approve, applaud
August compassion, Christian thoughts
    that shoot 341
Beyond the vulgar white of personal aims.
Accept my reverence.'
              There he glowed on me
With all his face and eyes. 'No other
    help?'
Said he — 'no more than so?'
                  'What help?' I asked.
'You 'd scorn my help, — as Nature's
    self, you say,
Has scorned to put her music in my mouth
Because a woman's. Do you now turn
    round
And ask for what a woman cannot give?'

'For what she only can, I turn and
    ask,' 350
He answered, catching up my hands in his,
And dropping on me from his high-eaved
    brow
The full weight of his soul, — 'I ask for
    love,

And that, she can; for life in fellowship
Through bitter duties — that, I know she
    can;
For wifehood — will she?'
                'Now,' I said, 'may God
Be witness 'twixt us two!' and with the
    word,
Meseemed I floated into a sudden light
Above his stature, — 'am I proved too
    weak
To stand alone, yet strong enough to
    bear 360
Such leaners on my shoulder? poor to
    think,
Yet rich enough to sympathize with
    thought?
Incompetent to sing, as blackbirds can,
Yet competent to love, like HIM?'
                    I paused;
Perhaps I darkened, as the lighthouse
    will
That turns upon the sea. 'It 's always so.
Anything does for a wife.'
                'Aurora, dear,
And dearly honored,' — he pressed in at
    once
With eager utterance, — 'you translate
    me ill.
I do not contradict my thought of you 370
Which is most reverent, with another
    thought
Found less so. If your sex is weak for
    art
(And I, who said so, did but honor you
By using truth in courtship), it is strong
For life and duty. Place your fecund
    heart
In mine, and let us blossom for the
    world
That wants love's color in the gray of
    time.
My talk, meanwhile, is arid to you, ay,
Since all my talk can only set you where
You look down coldly on the arena-
    heaps 380
Of headless bodies, shapeless, indistinct!
The Judgment-Angel scarce would find
    his way
Through such a heap of generalized dis-
    tress
To the individual man with lips and eyes,
Much less Aurora. Ah, my sweet, come
    down,
And hand in hand we 'll go where yours
    shall touch

These victims, one by one! till, one by one,
The formless, nameless trunk of every man
Shall seem to wear a head with hair you know,   389
And every woman catch your mother's face
To melt you into passion.'

      'I am a girl,'
I answered slowly; 'you do well to name
My mother's face. Though far too early, alas,
God's hand did interpose 'twixt it and me,
I know so much of love as used to shine
In that face and another. Just so much;
No more indeed at all. I have not seen
So much love since, I pray you pardon me,
As answers even to make a marriage with
In this cold land of England. What you love   400
Is not a woman, Romney, but a cause:
You want a helpmate, not a mistress, sir,
A wife to help your ends, — in her no end.
Your cause is noble, your ends excellent,
But I, being most unworthy of these and that,
Do otherwise conceive of love. Farewell.'

'Farewell, Aurora? you reject me thus?'
He said.
    'Sir, you were married long ago.
You have a wife already whom you love,
Your social theory. Bless you both, I say.
For my part, I am scarcely meek enough 411
To be the handmaid of a lawful spouse.
Do I look a Hagar, think you?'
       'So you jest.'

'Nay, so, I speak in earnest,' I replied.
'You treat of marriage too much like, at least,
A chief apostle: you would bear with you
A wife . . . a sister . . . shall we speak it out?
A sister of charity.'
      'Then, must it be
Indeed farewell? And was I so far wrong
In hope and in illusion, when I took 420
The woman to be nobler than the man,
Yourself the noblest woman, in the use
And comprehension of what love is, — love,
That generates the likeness of itself
Through all heroic duties? so far wrong,

In saying bluntly, venturing truth on love,
"Come, human creature, love and work with me," —
Instead of "Lady, thou art wondrous fair,
And, where the Graces walk before, the Muse
Will follow at the lightning of their eyes,
And where the Muse walks, lovers need to creep: 431
Turn round and love me, or I die of love."'

With quiet indignation I broke in.
'You misconceive the question like a man,
Who sees the woman as the complement
Of his sex merely. You forget too much
That every creature, female as the male,
Stands single in responsible act and thought
As also in birth and death. Whoever says
To a loyal woman, "Love and work with me,"   440
Will get fair answers if the work and love,
Being good themselves, are good for her — the best
She was born for. Women of a softer mood,
Surprised by men when scarcely awake to life,
Will sometimes only hear the first word, love,
And catch up with it any kind of work,
Indifferent, so that dear love go with it.
I do not blame such women, though, for love,
They pick much oakum; earth's fanatics make
Too frequently heaven's saints. But *me* your work   450
Is not the best for, — nor your love the best,
Nor able to commend the kind of work
For love's sake merely. Ah, you force me, sir,
To be overbold in speaking of myself:
I too have my vocation, — work to do,
The heavens and earth have set me since I changed
My father's face for theirs, and, though your world
Were twice as wretched as you represent,
Most serious work, most necessary work
As any of the economists'. Reform, 460
Make trade a Christian possibility,
And individual right no general wrong;

Wipe out earth's furrows of the Thine and
    Mine,
And leave one green for men to play at
    bowls,
With innings for them all ! . . . What
    then, indeed,
If mortals are not greater by the head
Than any of their prosperities ? what then,
Unless the artist keep up open roads
Betwixt the seen and unseen, — bursting
    through
The best of your conventions with his
    best, 470
The speakable, imaginable best
God bids him speak, to prove what lies be-
    yond
Both speech and imagination ? A starved
    man
Exceeds a fat beast: we 'll not barter, sir,
The beautiful for barley. — And, even so,
I hold you will not compass your poor
    ends
Of barley-feeding and material ease,
Without a poet's individualism
To work your universal. It takes a soul,
To move a body: it takes a high-souled
    man, 480
To move the masses, even to a cleaner
    stye:
It takes the ideal, to blow a hair's-breadth
    off
The dust of the actual. — Ah, your Fouriers
    failed,
Because not poets enough to understand
That life develops from within. — For me,
Perhaps I am not worthy, as you say,
Of work like this: perhaps a woman's soul
Aspires, and not creates: yet we aspire,
And yet I 'll try out your perhapses, sir,
And if I fail . . . why, burn me up my
    straw 490
Like other false works — I 'll not ask for
    grace;
Your scorn is better, cousin Romney. I
Who love my art, would never wish it
    lower
To suit my stature. I may love my art.
You 'll grant that even a woman may love
    art,
Seeing that to waste true love on anything
Is womanly, past question.'
                I retain
The very last word which I said that day,
As you the creaking of the door, years
    past,

Which let upon you such disabling news 500
You ever after have been graver. He,
His eyes, the motions in his silent mouth,
Were fiery points on which my words were
    caught,
Transfixed for ever in my memory
For his sake, not their own. And yet I
    know
I did not love him . . . nor he me . . .
    that 's sure . . .
And what I said is unrepented of,
As truth is always. Yet . . . a princely
    man ! —
If hard to me, heroic for himself !
He bears down on me through the slanting
    years, 510
The stronger for the distance. If he had
    loved,
Ay, loved me, with that retributive
    face, . . .
I might have been a common woman now
And happier, less known and less left alone,
Perhaps a better woman after all,
With chubby children hanging on my neck
To keep me low and wise. Ah me, the
    vines
That bear such fruit are proud to stoop
    with it.
The palm stands upright in a realm of
    sand.

And I, who spoke the truth then, stand up-
    right, 520
Still worthy of having spoken out the
    truth,
By being content I spoke it though it set
Him there, me here. — O woman's vile re-
    morse,
To hanker after a mere name, a show,
A supposition, a potential love !
Does every man who names love in our
    lives
Become a power for that ? is love's true
    thing
So much best to us, that what personates
    love
Is next best ? A potential love, forsooth !
I 'm not so vile. No, no — he cleaves, I
    think, 530
This man, this image, — chiefly for the
    wrong
And shock he gave my life, in finding me
Precisely where the devil of my youth
Had set me, on those mountain-peaks of
    hope

All glittering with the dawn-dew, all erect
And famished for the noon, — exclaiming,
  while
I looked for empire and much tribute,
  'Come,
I have some worthy work for thee below.
Come, sweep my barns and keep my hos-
  pitals,
And I will pay thee with a current coin 540
Which men give women.'
            As we spoke, the grass
Was trod in haste beside us, and my aunt,
With smile distorted by the sun, — face,
  voice
As much at issue with the summer-day
As if you brought a candle out of doors,
Broke in with ' Romney here ! — My child,
  entreat
Your cousin to the house, and have your
  talk,
If girls must talk upon their birthdays.
  Come.'

He answered for me calmly, with pale lips
That seemed to motion for a smile in vain,
' The talk is ended, madam, where we
  stand. 551
Your brother's daughter has dismissed me
  here;
And all my answer can be better said
Beneath the trees, than wrong by such a
  word
Your house's hospitalities.   Farewell.'

With that he vanished.   I could hear his
  heel
Ring bluntly in the lane, as down he leapt
The short way from us. — Then a measured
  speech
Withdrew me.   ' What means this, Aurora
  Leigh ?
My brother's daughter has dismissed my
  guests ? '   560

The lion in me felt the keeper's voice
Through all its quivering dew-laps; I was
  quelled
Before her, — meekened to the child she
  knew:
I prayed her pardon, said ' I had little
  thought
To give dismissal to a guest of hers,
In letting go a friend of mine who came
To take me into service as a wife, —
No more than that, indeed.'

            ' No more, no more ?
Pray Heaven,' she answered, ' that I was
  not mad.
I could not mean to tell her to her face 570
That Romney Leigh had asked me for a
  wife,
And I refused him ? '
            ' Did he ask ? ' I said;
' I think he rather stooped to take me up
For certain uses which he found to do
For something called a wife.   He never
  asked.'

' What stuff ! ' she answered; ' are they
  queens, these girls ?
They must have mantles, stitched with
  twenty silks,
Spread out upon the ground, before they 'll
  step
One footstep for the noblest lover born.'
' But I am born,' I said with firmness, ' I,
To walk another way than his, dear aunt.'

' You walk, you walk !   A babe at thirteen
  months   582
Will walk as well as you,' she cried in
  haste,
' Without a steadying finger.   Why, you
  child,
God help you, you are groping in the dark,
For all this sunlight.   You suppose, per-
  haps,
That you, sole offspring of an opulent
  man,
Are rich and free to choose a way to
  walk ?
You think, and it 's a reasonable thought,
That I, beside, being well to do in life, 590
Will leave my handful in my niece's hand
When death shall paralyze these fingers ?
  Pray,
Pray, child, albeit I know you love me
  not,
As if you loved me, that I may not die !
For when I die and leave you, out you
  go
(Unless I make room for you in my grave),
Unhoused, unfed, my dear poor brother's
  lamb
(Ah heaven ! — that pains !) — without a
  right to crop
A single blade of grass beneath these trees,
Or cast a lamb's small shadow on the
  lawn,   600
Unfed, unfolded !   Ah, my brother, here 's

The fruit you planted in your foreign
   loves ! —
Ay, there's the fruit he planted ! never
   look
Astonished at me with your mother's eyes,
For it was they who set you where you are,
An undowered orphan. Child, your
   father's choice
Of that said mother disinherited
His daughter, his and hers. Men do not
   think
Of sons and daughters, when they fall in
   love,
So much more than of sisters; otherwise 610
He would have paused to ponder what he
   did,
And shrunk before that clause in the entail
Excluding offspring by a foreign wife
(The clause set up a hundred years ago
By a Leigh who wedded a French dancing-
   girl
And had his heart danced over in return);
But this man shrank at nothing, never
   thought
Of you, Aurora, any more than me —
Your mother must have been a pretty
   thing,
For all the coarse Italian blacks and
   browns, 620
To make a good man, which my brother
   was,
Unchary of the duties to his house;
But so it fell indeed. Our cousin Vane,
Vane Leigh, the father of this Romney,
   wrote
Directly on your birth, to Italy,
" I ask your baby daughter for my son,
In whom the entail now merges by the law.
Betroth her to us out of love, instead
Of colder reasons, and she shall not lose
By love or law from henceforth,' — so he
   wrote; 630
A generous cousin was my cousin Vane.
Remember how he drew you to his knee
The year you came here, just before he
   died,
And hollowed out his hands to hold your
   cheeks,
And wished them redder, — you remember
   Vane.
And now his son, who represents our
   house,
And holds the fiefs and manors in his
   place,
To whom reverts my pittance when I die

(Except a few books and a pair of shawls),
The boy is generous like him, and pre-
   pared 640
To carry out his kindest word and thought
To you, Aurora. Yes, a fine young man
Is Romney Leigh; although the sun of
   youth
Has shone too straight upon his brain, I
   know,
And fevered him with dreams of doing
   good
To good-for-nothing people. But a wife
Will put all right, and stroke his temples
   cool
With healthy touches.' . . .
           I broke in at that.
I could not lift my heavy heart to breathe
Till then, but then I raised it, and it fell
In broken words like these — ' No need to
   wait: 651
The dream of doing good to . . . me, at
   least,
Is ended, without waiting for a wife
To cool the fever for him. We've escaped
That danger, — thank Heaven for it.'
           ' You,' she cried,
' Have got a fever. What, I talk and talk
An hour long to you, — I instruct you
   how
You cannot eat or drink or stand or sit
Or even die, like any decent wretch
In all this unroofed and unfurnished
   world, 660
Without your cousin, — and you still main-
   tain
There's room 'twixt him and you for flirt-
   ing fans
And running knots in eyebrows ? You
   must have
A pattern lover sighing on his knee ?
You do not count enough, a noble heart
(Above book-patterns) which this very
   morn
Unclosed itself in two dear fathers' names
To embrace your orphaned life ? Fie, fie !
   But stay,
I write a word, and counteract this sin.'

She would have turned to leave me, but I
   clung. 670
' O sweet my father's sister, hear my word
Before you write yours. Cousin Vane did
   well,
And cousin Romney well, — and I well
   too,

In casting back with all my strength and
    will
The good they meant me.   O my God, my
    God !
God meant me good, too, when He hindered
    me
From saying "yes" this morning.   If you
    write
A word, it shall be "no."   I say no, no !
I tie up "no" upon his altar-horns,
Quite out of reach of perjury !   At least 680
My soul is not a pauper; I can live
At least my soul's life, without alms from
    men;
And if it must be in heaven instead of
    earth,
Let heaven look to it, — I am not afraid.'

She seized my hands with both hers, strained
    them fast,
And drew her probing and unscrupulous
    eyes
Right through me, body and heart.   'Yet,
    foolish Sweet,
You love this man.   I 've watched you when
    he came,
And when he went, and when we 've talked
    of him:
I am not old for nothing; I can tell   690
The weather-signs of love: you love this
    man.'

Girls blush sometimes because they are
    alive,
Half wishing they were dead to save the
    shame.
The sudden blush devours them, neck and
    brow;
They have drawn too near the fire of life,
    like gnats,
And flare up bodily, wings and all.   What
    then ?
Who 's sorry for a gnat . . . or girl ?
                        I blushed.
I feel the brand upon my forehead now
Strike hot, sear deep, as guiltless men may
    feel
The felon's iron, say, and scorn the
    mark   700
Of what they are not.   Most illogical
Irrational nature of our womanhood,
That blushes one way, feels another way,
And prays, perhaps, another !   After all,
We cannot be the equal of the male
Who rules his blood a little.

                              For although
I blushed indeed, as if I loved the man,
And her incisive smile, accrediting
That treason of false witness in my blush,
Did bow me downward like a swathe of
    grass   710
Below its level that struck me, — I attest
The conscious skies and all their daily
    suns,
I think I loved him not, — nor then, nor
    since,
Nor ever.   Do we love the schoolmaster,
Being busy in the woods ? much less, being
    poor,
The overseer of the parish ?   Do we keep
Our love to pay our debts with ?
                        White and cold
I grew next moment.   As my blood re-
    coiled
From that imputed ignominy, I made
My heart great with it.   Then, at last, I
    spoke,   720
Spoke veritable words but passionate,
Too passionate perhaps . . . ground up with
    sobs
To shapeless endings.   She let fall my
    hands
And took her smile off, in sedate disgust,
As peradventure she had touched a
    snake, —
A dead snake, mind ! — and, turning round,
    replied,
'We 'll leave Italian manners, if you
    please.
I think you had an English father, child,
And ought to find it possible to speak   729
A quiet "yes" or "no," like English girls,
Without convulsions.   In another month
We 'll take another answer — no, or yes.'
With that, she left me in the garden-
    walk.

I had a father ! yes, but long ago —
How long it seemed that moment. Oh, how
    far,
How far and safe, God, dost thou keep thy
    saints
When once gone from us !   We may call
    against
The lighted windows of thy fair June-
    heaven
Where all the souls are happy, — and not
    one,
Not even my father, look from work or
    play   740

To ask, ' Who is it that cries after us,
Below there, in the dusk ? ' Yet formerly
He turned his face upon me quick enough,
If I said ' father.' Now I might cry loud;
The little lark reached higher with his
    song
Than I with crying. Oh, alone, alone, —
Not troubling any in heaven, nor any on
    earth,
I stood there in the garden, and looked up
The deaf blue sky that brings the roses
    out
On such June mornings.
            You who keep account
Of crisis and transition in this life,   751
Set down the first time Nature says plain
    ' no '
To some ' yes ' in you, and walks over you
In gorgeous sweeps of scorn. We all be-
    gin
By singing with the birds, and running
    fast
With June days, hand in hand: but once,
    for all,
The birds must sing against us, and the
    sun
Strike down upon us like a friend's sword
    caught
By an enemy to slay us, while we read
The dear name on the blade which bites at
    us ! —   760
That 's bitter and convincing: after that,
We seldom doubt that something in the
    large
Smooth order of creation, though no more
Than haply a man's footstep, has gone
    wrong.
Some tears fell down my cheeks, and then
    I smiled,
As those smile who have no face in the
    world
To smile back to them. I had lost a
    friend
In Romney Leigh; the thing was sure —
    a friend,
Who had looked at me most gently now
    and then,
And spoken of my favorite books, ' our
    books,'   770
With such a voice ! Well, voice and look
    were now
More utterly shut out from me, I felt,
Than even my father's. Romney now
    was turned
To a benefactor, to a generous man,

Who had tied himself to marry . . . me,
    instead
Of such a woman, with low timorous lids
He lifted with a sudden word one day,
And left, perhaps, for my sake. — Ah,
    self-tied
By a contract, male Iphigenia bound
At a fatal Aulis for the winds to change 780
(But loose him, they 'll not change), he
    well might seem
A little cold and dominant in love !
He had a right to be dogmatical,
This poor, good Romney. Love, to him,
    was made
A simple law-clause. If I married
    him,
I should not dare to call my soul my own
Which so he had bought and paid for:
    every thought
And every heart-beat down there in the
    bill;
Not one found honestly deductible
From any use that pleased him ! He
    might cut   790
My body into coins to give away
Among his other paupers; change my
    sons,
While I stood dumb as Griseld, for black
    babes
Or piteous foundlings; might unquestioned
    set
My right hand teaching in the Ragged
    Schools,
My left hand washing in the Public Baths,
What time my angel of the Ideal stretched
Both his to me in vain. I could not claim
The poor right of a mouse in a trap, to
    squeal,
And take so much as pity from myself. 800

Farewell, good Romney ! if I loved you
    even,
I could but ill afford to let you be
So generous to me. Farewell, friend,
    since friend
Betwixt us two, forsooth, must be a word
So heavily overladen. And, since help
Must come to me from those who love me
    not,
Farewell, all helpers — I must help my-
    self.
And am alone from henceforth. — Then I
    stooped
And lifted the soiled garland from the
    earth,

And set it on my head as bitterly   810
As when the Spanish monarch crowned the
      bones
Of his dead love. So be it. I preserve
That crown still, — in the drawer there !
      't was the first.
The rest are like it; — those Olympian
      crowns,
We run for, till we lose sight of the sun
In the dust of the racing chariots !
                              After that,
Before the evening fell, I had a note,
Which ran, — ' Aurora, sweet Chaldean,
      you read
My meaning backward like your eastern
      books,
While I am from the west, dear. Read
      me now   820
A little plainer. Did you hate me quite
But yesterday ? I loved you for my part;
I love you. If I spoke untenderly
This morning, my beloved, pardon it;
And comprehend me that I loved you so
I set you on the level of my soul,
And overwashed you with the bitter brine
Of some habitual thoughts. Henceforth,
      my flower,
Be planted out of reach of any such,
And lean the side you please, with all your
      leaves !   830
Write woman's verses and dream woman's
      dreams;
But let me feel your perfume in my home
To make my sabbath after working-days.
Bloom out your youth beside me, — be my
      wife.'

I wrote in answer — ' We Chaldeans dis-
      cern
Still farther than we read. I know your
      heart,
And shut it like the holy book it is,
Reserved for mild-eyed saints to pore
      upon
Betwixt their prayers at vespers. Well,
      you 're right,
I did not surely hate you yesterday;   840
And yet I do not love you enough to-day
To wed you, cousin Romney. Take this
      word,
And let it stop you as a generous man
From speaking farther. You may tease,
      indeed,
And blow about my feelings, or my
      leaves,

And here 's my aunt will help you with
      east winds
And break a stalk, perhaps, tormenting
      me;
But certain flowers grow near as deep as
      trees,
And, cousin, you 'll not move my root, not
      you,
With all your confluent storms. Then let
      me grow   850
Within my wayside hedge, and pass your
      way !
This flower has never as much to say to
      you
As the antique tomb which said to travel-
      lers, "Pause,
Siste, viator." ' Ending thus, I sighed.

The next week passed in silence, so the
      next,
And several after: Romney did not come
Nor my aunt chide me. I lived on and on,
As if my heart were kept beneath a glass,
And everybody stood, all eyes and ears,
To see and hear it tick. I could not sit,
Nor walk, nor take a book, nor lay it
      down,   861
Nor sew on steadily, nor drop a stitch,
And a sigh with it, but I felt her looks
Still cleaving to me, like the sucking asp
To Cleopatra's breast, persistently
Through the intermittent pantings. Being
      observed,
When observation is not sympathy,
Is just being tortured. If she said a word,
A ' thank you,' or an ' if it please you,
      dear,'
She meant a commination, or, at best, 870
An exorcism against the devildom
Which plainly held me. So with all the
      house.
Susannah could not stand and twist my
      hair
Without such glancing at the looking-glass
To see my face there, that she missed the
      plait.
And John, — I never sent my plate for
      soup,
Or did not send it, but the foolish John
Resolved the problem, 'twixt his napkined
      thumbs,
Of what was signified by taking soup
Or choosing mackerel. Neighbors who
      dropped in   880
On morning visits, feeling a joint wrong,

Smiled admonition, sat uneasily,
And talked, with measured, emphasized re-
    servc,
Of parish news, like doctors to the sick,
When not called in, — as if, with leave to
    speak,
They might say something. Nay, the very
    dog
Would watch me from his sun-patch on the
    floor,
In alternation with the large black fly
Not yet in reach of snapping. So I lived.

A Roman died so; smeared with honey,
    teased   890
By insects, stared to torture by the noon:
And many patient souls 'neath English
    roofs
Have died like Romans. I, in looking
    back,
Wish only, now, I had borne the plague of
    all
With meeker spirits than were rife at
    Rome.

For, on the sixth week, the dead sea broke
    up,
Dashed suddenly through beneath the heel
    of Him
Who stands upon the sea and earth and
    swears
Time shall be nevermore. The clock struck
    nine
That morning too, — no lark was out of
    tune,   900
The hidden farms among the hills breathed
    straight
Their smoke toward heaven, the lime-tree
    scarcely stirred
Beneath the blue weight of the cloudless
    sky,
Though still the July air came floating
    through
The woodbine at my window, in and out,
With touches of the out-door country
    news
For a bending forehead. There I sat, and
    wished
That morning-truce of God would last till
    eve,
Or longer. 'Sleep,' I thought, 'late
    sleepers, — sleep,
And spare me yet the burden of your
    eyes.'   910

Then, suddenly, a single ghastly shriek
Tore upward from the bottom of the house.
Like one who wakens in a grave and
    shrieks,
The still house seemed to shriek itself alive,
And shudder through its passages and
    stairs
With slam of doors and clash of bells. —
I sprang,
I stood up in the middle of the room,
And there confronted at my chamber-door
A white face, — shivering, ineffectual lips.

'Come, come,' they tried to utter, and I
    went: 920
As if a ghost had drawn me at the point
Of a fiery finger through the uneven dark,
I went with reeling footsteps down the
    stair,
Nor asked a question.
                    There she sat, my aunt, —
Bolt upright in the chair beside her bed,
Whose pillow had no dint ! she had used
    no bed
For that night's sleeping, yet slept well.
    My God,
The dumb derision of that gray, peaked
    face
Concluded something grave against the sun,
Which filled the chamber with its July
    burst   930
When Susan drew the curtains ignorant
Of who sat open-eyed behind her. There
She sat . . . it sat . . . we said 'she'
    yesterday . . .
And held a letter with unbroken seal
As Susan gave it to her hand last night:
All night she had held it. If its news re-
    ferred
To duchies or to dunghills, not an inch
She 'd budge, 't was obvious, for such worth-
    less odds:
Nor, though the stars were suns and over-
    burned
Their spheric limitations, swallowing up
Like wax the azure spaces, could they
    force   941
Those open eyes to wink once. What last
    sight
Had left them blank and flat so, — draw-
    ing out
The faculty of vision from the roots,
As nothing more, worth seeing, remained
    behind ?

Were those the eyes that watched me,
      worried me ?
That dogged me up and down the hours
      and days,
A beaten, breathless, miserable soul ?
And did I pray, a half-hour back, but so,
To escape the burden of those eyes . . .
      those eyes ?   950
'Sleep late,' I said ? —
            Why, now, indeed, they sleep.
God answers sharp and sudden on some
      prayers,
And thrusts the thing we have prayed for
      in our face,
A gauntlet with a gift in 't.   Every wish
Is like a prayer, with God.

                              I had my wish,
To read and meditate the thing I would,
To fashion all my life upon my thought,
And marry or not marry.   Henceforth none
Could disapprove me, vex me, hamper me.
Full ground-room, in this desert newly
      made,   960
For Babylon or Baalbec, — when the breath,
Now choked with sand, returns for building
      towns.

The heir came over on the funeral day,
And we two cousins met before the dead,
With two pale faces.   Was it death or life
That moved us ?   When the will was read
      and done,
The official guests and witnesses withdrawn,
We rose up in a silence almost hard,
And looked at one another.   Then I said,
'Farewell, my cousin.'
                  But he touched, just touched
My hatstrings, tied for going (at the door
The carriage stood to take me), and said
      low,   972
His voice a little unsteady through his
      smile,
'Siste, viator.'
                  'Is there time,' I asked,
'In these last days of railroads, to stop
      short
Like Cæsar's chariot (weighing half a ton)
On the Appian road, for morals ? '
                              'There is time,'
He answered grave, 'for necessary words,
Inclusive, trust me, of no epitaph   979
On man or act, my cousin.   We have read
A will, which gives you all the personal
      goods
And funded moneys of your aunt.'

                                    'I thank
Her memory for it.   With three hundred
      pounds
We buy, in England even, clear standing-
      room
To stand and work in.   Only two hours
      since,
I fancied I was poor.'
                        'And, cousin, still
You 're richer than you fancy.   The will
      says,
Three hundred pounds, and any other sum
Of which the said testatrix dies possessed.
I say she died possessed of other sums.'   990

'Dear Romney, need we chronicle the
      pence ?
I 'm richer than I thought — that 's evident.
Enough so.'
                  'Listen rather.   You 've to do
With business and a cousin,' he resumed,
'And both, I fear, need patience.   Here 's
      the fact.
The other sum (there *is* another sum,
Unspecified in any will which dates
After possession, yet bequeathed as much
And clearly as those said three hundred
      pounds)
Is thirty thousand.   You will have it paid
When ? . ._. where ?   My duty troubles
      you with words.'   1001

He struck the iron when the bar was hot;
No wonder if my eyes sent out some sparks.
'Pause there !   I thank you.   You are deli-
      cate
In glozing gifts; — but I, who share your
      blood,
Am rather made for giving, like yourself,
Than taking, like your pensioners.   Fare-
      well.'

He stopped me with a gesture of calm
      pride.
'A Leigh,' he said, 'gives largesse and
      gives love,   1009
But glozes never: if a Leigh could gloze,
He would not do it, moreover, to a Leigh,
With blood trained up along nine centu-
      ries
To hound and hate a lie from eyes like
      yours.
And now we 'll make the rest as clear: your
      aunt
Possessed these moneys.'

'You will make it clear,
My cousin, as the honor of us both,
Or one of us speaks vainly ! that's not I.
My aunt possessed this sum, — inherited
From whom, and when ? bring documents,
  prove dates.'

' Why, now indeed you throw your bonnet
  off   1020
As if you had time left for a logarithm !
The faith's the want. Dear cousin, give
  me faith,
And you shall walk this road with silken
  shoes,
As clean as any lady of our house
Supposed the proudest. Oh, I compre-
  hend
The whole position from your point of sight.
I oust you from your father's halls and
  lands
And make you poor by getting rich —
  that's laws;
Considering which, in common circum-
  stance,
You would not scruple to accept from me
Some compensation, some sufficiency   1031
Of income — that were justice; but, alas,
I love you, — that's mere nature; you re-
  ject
My love, — that's nature also; and at once,
You cannot, from a suitor disallowed,
A hand thrown back as mine is, into yours
Receive a doit, a farthing, — not for the
  world !
That's woman's etiquette, and obviously
Exceeds the claim of nature, law, and right,
Unanswerable to all. I grant, you see,   1040
The case as you conceive it, — leave you
  room
To sweep your ample skirts of womanhood,
While, standing humbly squeezed against
  the wall,
I own myself excluded from being just,
Restrained from paying indubitable debts,
Because denied from giving you my soul.
That's my misfortune ! — I submit to it
As if, in some more reasonable age,
'T would not be less inevitable. Enough.
You'll trust me, cousin, as a gentleman, 1050
To keep your honor, as you count it, pure,
Your scruples (just as if I thought them
  wise)
Safe and inviolate from gifts of mine.'
I answered mild but.earnest. ' I believe
In no one's honor which another keeps,

Nor man's nor woman's. As I keep, my-
  self,
My truth and my religion, I depute
No father, though I had one this side death,
Nor brother, though I had twenty, much
  less you,
Though twice my cousin, and once Romney
  Leigh,   1060
To keep my honor pure. You face, to-
  day,
A man who wants instruction, mark me,
  not
A woman who wants protection. As to a
  man,
Show manhood, speak out plainly, be pre-
  cise
With facts and dates. My aunt inherited
This sum, you say ' —
              ' I said she died possessed
Of this, dear cousin.'
                ' Not by heritage.
Thank you: we're getting to the facts at
  last.
Perhaps she played at commerce with a
  ship
Which came in heavy with Australian
  gold ?   1070
Or touched a lottery with her finger-end,
Which tumbled on a sudden into her lap
Some old Rhine tower or principality ?
Perhaps she had to do with a marine
Sub-transatlantic railroad, which pre-pays
As well as pre-supposes ? or perhaps
Some stale ancestral debt was after-paid
By a hundred years, and took her by sur-
  prise ? —
You shake your head, my cousin; I guess
  ill.'

' You need not guess, Aurora, nor deride;
The truth is not afraid of hurting you.   1081
You'll find no cause, in all your scruples,
  why
Your aunt should cavil at a deed of gift
'Twixt her and me.'
            ' I thought so — ah ! a gift.'

' You naturally thought so,' he resumed.
' A very natural gift.'
              ' A gift, a gift !
Her individual life being stranded high
Above all want, approaching opulence,
Too haughty was she to accept a gift
Without some ultimate aim: ah, ah, I
  see, —   1090

A gift intended plainly for her heirs,
And so accepted . . . if accepted . . . ah,
Indeed that might be; I am snared per-
    haps
Just so. But, cousin, shall I pardon you,
If thus you have caught me with a cruel
    springe ? '

He answered gently, ' Need you tremble
    and pant
Like a netted lioness ? is 't my fault,
    mine,
That you 're a grand wild creature of the
    woods
And hate the stall built for you ? Any
    way,
Though triply netted, need you glare at
    me ?   1100
I do not hold the cords of such a net;
You 're free from me, Aurora ! '
                              ' Now may God
Deliver me from this strait ! This gift of
    yours
Was tendered . . . when ? accepted . . .
    when ? ' I asked.
' A month . . . a fortnight since ? Six
    weeks ago
It was not tendered; by a word she
    dropped
I know it was not tendered nor received.
When was it ? bring your dates.'
                          ' What matters when ?
A half-hour ere she died, or a half-year,
Secured the gift, maintains the heritage
Inviolable with law. As easy pluck   1111
The golden stars from heaven's embroid-
    ered stole
To pin them on the gray side of this earth,
As make you poor again, thank God.'
                                      ' Not poor
Nor clean again from henceforth, you
    thank God ?
Well, sir — I ask you — I insist at
    need, —
Vouchsafe the special date, the special
    date.'

' The day before her death-day,' he re-
    plied,
' The gift was in her hands. We 'll find
    that deed,
And certify that date to you.'
                              As one   1120
Who has climbed a mountain-height and
    carried up

His own heart climbing, panting in his
    throat
With the toil of the ascent, takes breath at
    last,
Looks back in triumph — so I stood and
    looked.
' Dear cousin Romney, we have reached the
    top
Of this steep question, and may rest, I
    think.
But first, — I pray you pardon, that the
    shock
And surge of natural feeling and event
Has made me oblivious of acquainting you
That this, this letter (unread, mark, still
    sealed),   1130
Was found enfolded in the poor dead
    hand:
That spirit of hers had gone beyond the
    address,
Which could not find her though you wrote
    it clear, —
I know your writing, Romney, — recog-
    nize
The open-hearted A, the liberal sweep
Of the G. Now listen, — let us under-
    stand:
You will not find that famous deed of gift,
Unless you find it in the letter here,
Which, not being mine, I give you back. —
    Refuse
To take the letter ? well then — you and
    I,   1140
As writer and as heiress, open it
Together, by your leave. — Exactly so:
The words in which the noble offering 's
    made
Are nobler still, my cousin; and, I own,
The proudest and most delicate heart
    alive,
Distracted from the measure of the gift
By such a grace in giving, might accept
Your largesse without thinking any more
Of the burthen of it, than King Solomon
Considered, when he wore his holy ring 1150
Charactered over with the ineffable spell,
How many carats of fine gold made up
Its money-value: so, Leigh gives to Leigh !
Or rather, might have given, observe, —
    for that 's
The point we come to. Here 's a proof of
    gift,
But here 's no proof, sir, of acceptancy,
But, rather, disproof. Death's black dust,
    being blown,

Infiltrated through every secret fold
Of this sealed letter by a puff of fate,
Dried up for ever the fresh-written ink,
Annulled the gift, disutilized the grace, 1161
And left these fragments.'
                    As I spoke, I tore
The paper up and down, and down and up
And crosswise, till it fluttered from my
    hands,
As forest-leaves, stripped suddenly and
    rapt
By a whirlwind on Valdarno, drop again,
Drop slow, and strew the melancholy
    ground
Before the amazèd hills . . . why, so, in-
    deed,
I 'm writing like a poet, somewhat large
In the type of the image, and exagger-
    ate   1170
A small thing with a great thing, topping
    it: —
But then I 'm thinking how his eyes looked,
    his,
With what despondent and surprised re-
    proach !
I think the tears were in them as he
    looked;
I think the manly mouth just trembled.
    Then
He broke the silence.
                    'I may ask, perhaps,
Although no stranger . . . only Romney
    Leigh,
Which means still less . . . than Vincent
    Carrington,
Your plans in going hence, and where you
    go.
This cannot be a secret.'
                    'All my life 1180
Is open to you, cousin. I go hence
To London, to the gathering-place of souls,
To live mine straight out, vocally, in
    books;
Harmoniously for others, if indeed
A woman's soul, like man's, be wide
    enough
To carry the whole octave (that 's to
    prove).
Or, if I fail, still purely for myself.
Pray God be with me, Romney.'
                    'Ah, poor child,
Who fight against the mother's 'tiring
    hand,
And choose the headsman's ! May God
    change his world   1190

For your sake, sweet, and make it mild as
    heaven,
And juster than I have found you.'
                    But I paused.
' And you, my cousin ? ' —
                    ' I,' he said, — ' you ask ?
You care to ask ?   Well, girls have curious
    minds
And fain would know the end of every-
    thing,
Of cousins therefore with the rest.   For
    me,
Aurora, I 've my work; you know my
    work;
And, having missed this year some personal
    hope,
I must beware the rather that I miss
No reasonable duty.   While you sing   1200
Your happy pastorals of the meads and
    trees,
Bethink you that I go to impress and
    prove
On stifled brains and deafened ears, stunned
    deaf,
Crushed dull with grief, that nature sings
    itself,
And needs no mediate poet, lute or voice,
To make it vocal.   While you ask of men
Your audience, I may get their leave per-
    haps
For hungry orphans to say audibly
" We 're hungry, see," — for beaten and
    bullied wives
To hold their unweaned babies up in
    sight,   1210
Whom orphanage would better, and for all
To speak and claim their portion . . . by no
    means
Of the soil, . . . but of the sweat in tilling
    it;
Since this is nowadays turned privilege,
To have only God's curse on us, and not
    man's.
Such work I have for doing, elbow-deep
In social problems, — as you tie your
    rhymes,
To draw my uses to cohere with needs
And bring the uneven world back to its
    round,
Or, failing so much, fill up, bridge at
    least   1220
To smoother issues some abysmal cracks
And feuds of earth, intestine heats have
    made
To keep men separate, — using sorry shifts

Of hospitals, almshouses, infant schools,
And other practical stuff of partial good
You lovers of the beautiful and whole
Despise by system.'
　　　　　　　' I despise ?　The scorn
Is yours, my cousin.　Poets become such
Through scorning nothing.　You decry them
　　for
The good of beauty sung and taught by
　　them,　　　　　　　　　　　　1230
While they respect your practical partial
　　good
As being a part of beauty's self.　Adieu !
When God helps all the workers for his
　　world,
The singers shall have help of Him, not
　　last.'

He smiled as men smile when they will not
　　speak
Because of something bitter in the thought;
And still I feel his melancholy eyes
Look judgment on me.　It is seven years
　　since:
I know not if 't was pity or 't was scorn
Has made them so far-reaching: judge it
　　ye　　　　　　　　　　　　　　1240
Who have had to do with pity more than
　　love
And scorn than hatred.　I am used, since
　　then,
To other ways, from equal men.　But so,
Even so, we let go hands, my cousin and I,
And in between us rushed the torrent-
　　world
To blanch our faces like divided rocks,
And bar for ever mutual sight and touch
Except through swirl of spray and all that
　　roar.

THIRD BOOK

' To-day thou girdest up thy loins thyself
And goest where thou wouldest: presently
Others shall gird thee,' said the Lord, ' to
　　go
Where thou wouldst not.'　He spoke to
　　Peter thus,
To signify the death which he should die
When crucified head downward.
　　　　　　　　　　If He spoke
To Peter then, He speaks to us the same;
The word suits many different martyr-
　　doms,

And signifies a multiform of death,
Although we scarcely die apostles, we,　10
And have mislaid the keys of heaven and
　　earth.

For 't is not in mere death that men die
　　most,
And, after our first girding of the loins
In youth's fine linen and fair broidery
To run up hill and meet the rising sun,
We are apt to sit tired, patient as a fool,
While others gird us with the violent
　　bands
Of social figments, feints, and formalisms,
Reversing our straight nature, lifting up
Our base needs, keeping down our lofty
　　thoughts,　　　　　　　　　　20
Head downward on the cross-sticks of the
　　world.
Yet He can pluck us from that shameful
　　cross.
God, set our feet low and our forehead
　　high,
And show us how a man was made to
　　walk !

Leave the lamp, Susan, and go up to bed.
The room does very well; I have to write
Beyond the stroke of midnight.　Get away;
Your steps, for ever buzzing in the room,
Tease me like gnats.　Ah, letters ! throw
　　them down
At once, as I must have them, to be sure,
Whether I bid you never bring me such　31
At such an hour, or bid you.　No excuse;
You choose to bring them, as I choose per-
　　haps
To throw them in the fire.　Now get to
　　bed,
And dream, if possible, I am not cross.

Why what a pettish, petty thing I grow, —
A mere mere woman, a mere flaccid nerve,
A kerchief left out all night in the rain,
Turned soft so, — overtasked and over-
　　strained
And overlived in this close London life !　40
And yet I should be stronger.
　　　　　　　　　　　Never burn
Your letters, poor Aurora ! for they stare
With red seals from the table, saying each,
' Here 's something that you know not.'
　　　　　Out, alas,
'T is scarcely that the world 's more good
　　and wise

Or even straighter and more consequent
Since yesterday at this time — yet, again,
If but one angel spoke from Ararat
I should be very sorry not to hear:
So open all the letters ! let me read.   50
Blanche Ord, the writer in the 'Lady's
   Fan,'
Requests my judgment on . . . that, after-
   wards.
Kate Ward desires the model of my cloak,
And signs 'Elisha to you.' Pringle
   Sharpe
Presents his work on 'Social Conduct,'
   craves
A little money for his pressing debts . . .
From me, who scarce have money for my
   needs;
Art's fiery chariot which we journey in
Being apt to singe our singing-robes to
   holes,
Although you ask me for my cloak, Kate
   Ward !   60
Here 's Rudgely knows it, — editor and
   scribe;
He 's 'forced to marry where his heart is
   not,
Because the purse lacks where he lost his
   heart.'
Ah, — lost it because no one picked it up;
That 's really loss, — (and passable impu-
   dence).
My critic Hammond flatters prettily,
And wants another volume like the last.
My critic Belfair wants another book
Entirely different, which will sell (and
   live ?),
A striking book, yet not a startling book,
The public blames originalities   71
(You must not pump spring-water una-
   wares
Upon a gracious public full of nerves):
Good things, not subtle, new yet ortho-
   dox,
As easy reading as the dog-eared page
That 's fingered by said public fifty years,
Since first taught spelling by its grand-
   mother,
And yet a revelation in some sort:
That 's hard, my critic Belfair. So —
   what next ?
My critic Stokes objects to abstract
   thoughts;   80
'Call a man John, a woman Joan,' says
   he,
'And do not prate so of *humanities :*'

Whereat I call my critic simply, Stokes.
My critic Jobson recommends more mirth
Because a cheerful genius suits the times,
And all true poets laugh unquenchably
Like Shakespeare and the gods. That 's
   very hard.
The gods may laugh, and Shakespeare;
   Dante smiled
With such a needy heart on two pale lips,
We cry 'Weep rather, Dante.' Poems
   are   90
Men, if true poems: and who dares exclaim
At any man's door, 'Here, 't is understood
The thunder fell last week and killed a
   wife
And scared a sickly husband — what of
   that ?
Get up, be merry, shout and clap your
   hands,
Because a cheerful genius suits the
   times — ' ?
None says so to the man, and why indeed
Should any to the poem ? A ninth seal;
The apocalypse is drawing to a close.
Ha, — this from Vincent Carrington, —
   'Dear friend,   100
I want good counsel. Will you lend me
   wings
To raise me to the subject, in a sketch
I 'll bring to-morrow — may I ? at eleven ?
A poet 's only born to turn to use:
So save you ! for the world . . . and Car-
   rington.'
' (Writ after.) Have you heard of Rom-
   ney Leigh,
Beyond what 's said of him in newspapers,
His phalansteries there, his speeches here,
His pamphlets, pleas, and statements,
   everywhere ?   109
He dropped *me* long ago, but no one drops
A golden apple — though indeed one day
You hinted that, but jested. Well, at
   least
You know Lord Howe who sees him . . .
   whom he sees
And *you* see and I hate to see, — for Howe
Stands high upon the brink of theories,
Observes the swimmers and cries "Very
   fine,"
But keeps dry linen equally, — unlike
That gallant breaster, Romney. Strange
   it is,
Such sudden madness seizing a young man
To make earth over again, — while I 'm
   content   120

To make the pictures. Let me bring the
      sketch.
A tiptoe Danae, overbold and hot,
Both arms aflame to meet her wishing
      Jove
Halfway, and burn him faster down; the
      face
And breasts upturned and straining, the
      loose locks
All glowing with the anticipated gold.
Or here's another on the self-same theme.
She lies here — flat upon her prison-floor,
The long hair swathed about her to the
      heel
Like wet seaweed. You dimly see her
      through   130
The glittering haze of that prodigious rain,
Half blotted out of nature by a love
As heavy as fate. I 'll bring you either
      sketch.
I think, myself, the second indicates
More passion.'
                    Surely. Self is put away,
And calm with abdication. She is Jove,
And no more Danae — greater thus. Per-
      haps
The painter symbolizes unaware
Two states of the recipient artist-soul,
One, forward, personal, wanting reverence,
Because aspiring only. We 'll be calm, 141
And know that, when indeed our Joves
      come down,
We all turn stiller than we have ever been.

Kind Vincent Carrington. I 'll let him
      come.
He talks of Florence, — and may say a
      word
Of something as it chanced seven years
      ago,
A hedgehog in the path, or a lame bird,
In those green country walks, in that good
      time
When certainly I was so miserable . . .
I seem to have missed a blessing ever
      since.   150

The music soars within the little lark,
And the lark soars. It is not thus with
      men.
We do not make our places with our
      strains, —
Content, while they rise, to remain behind
Alone on earth instead of so in heaven.
No matter; I bear on my broken tale.

When Romney Leigh and I had parted
      thus,
I took a chamber up three flights of stairs
Not far from being as steep as some larks
      climb,
And there, in a certain house in Kensing-
      ton,   160
Three years I lived and worked. Get
      leave to work
In this world — 't is the best you get at all;
For God, in cursing, gives us better gifts
Than men in benediction. God says,
      'Sweat
For foreheads,' men say 'crowns,' and so
      we are crowned,
Ay, gashed by some tormenting circle of
      steel
Which snaps with a secret spring. Get
      work, get work;
Be sure 't is better than what you work to
      get.

Serene and unafraid of solitude,
I worked the short days out, — and watched
      the sun   170
On lurid morns or monstrous afternoons
(Like some Druidic idol's fiery brass
With fixed unflickering outline of dead
      heat,
From which the blood of wretches pent in-
      side
Seems oozing forth to incarnadine the air)
Push out through fog with his dilated disk,
And startle the slant roofs and chimney-
      pots
With splashes of fierce color. Or I saw
Fog only, the great tawny weltering fog
Involve the passive city, strangle it   180
Alive, and draw it off into the void,
Spires, bridges, streets, and squares, as if
      a sponge
Had wiped out London, — or as noon and
      night
Had clapped together and utterly struck
      out
The intermediate time, undoing themselves
In the act. Your city poets see such
      things
Not despicable. Mountains of the south,
When drunk and mad with elemental
      wines
They rend the seamless mist and stand up
      bare,
Make fewer singers, haply. No one sings,
Descending Sinai: on Parnassus mount 191

You take a mule to climb and not a muse
Except in fable and figure: forests chant
Their anthems to themselves, and leave you
    dumb.
But sit in London at the day's decline,
And view the city perish in the mist
Like Pharaoh's armaments in the deep Red
    Sea,
The chariots, horsemen, footmen, all the
    host,
Sucked down and choked to silence —then,
    surprised
By a sudden sense of vision and of tune, 200
You feel as conquerors though you did not
    fight,
And you and Israel's other singing girls,
Ay, Miriam with them, sing the song you
    choose.
I worked with patience, which means
    almost power:
I did some excellent things indifferently,
Some bad things excellently. Both were
    praised,
The latter loudest. And by such a time
That I myself had set them down as sins
Scarce worth the price of sackcloth, week
    by week
Arrived some letter through the sedulous
    post, 210
Like these I've read, and yet dissimilar,
With pretty maiden seals, — initials twined
Of lilies, or a heart marked *Emily*
(Convicting Emily of being all heart);
Or rarer tokens from young bachelors,
Who wrote from college with the same
    goose-quill,
Suppose, they had just been plucked of,
    and a snatch
From Horace, 'Collegisse juvat,' set
Upon the first page. Many a letter, signed
Or unsigned, showing the writers at
    eighteen 220
Had lived too long, although a muse should
    help
Their dawn by holding candles, — compli-
    ments
To smile or sigh at. Such could pass with
    me
No more than coins from Moscow circulate
At Paris: would ten roubles buy a tag
Of ribbon on the boulevard, worth a sou ?
I smiled that all this youth should love me,
    — sighed
That such a love could scarcely raise them
    up

To love what was more worthy than my-
    self;
Then sighed again, again, less generously,
To think the very love they lavished so 231
Proved me inferior. The strong loved me
    not,
And he . . . my cousin Romney . . . did
    not write.
I felt the silent finger of his scorn
Prick every bubble of my frivolous fame
As my breath blew it, and resolve it back
To the air it came from. Oh, I justified
The measure he had taken of my height:
The thing was plain — he was not wrong a
    line;
I played at art, made thrusts with a toy-
    sword, 240
Amused the lads and maidens.
                     Came a sigh
Deep, hoarse with resolution, — I would
    work
To better ends, or play in earnest.
    'Heavens,
I think I should be almost popular
If this went on !' — I ripped my verses up,
And found no blood upon the rapier's
    point;
The heart in them was just an embryo's
    heart
Which never yet had beat, that it should
    die;
Just gasps of make-believe galvanic life;
Mere tones, inorganized to any tune. 250

And yet I felt it in me where it burnt,
Like those hot fire-seeds of creation held
In Jove's clenched palm before the worlds
    were sown, —
But I — I was not Juno even ! my hand
Was shut in weak convulsion, woman's ill,
And when I yearned to loose a finger — lo,
The nerve revolted. 'T is the same even
    now:
This hand may never, haply, open large,
Before the spark is quenched, or the palm
    charred,
To prove the power not else than by the
    pain. 260

It burnt, it burns — my whole life burnt
    with it,
And light, not sunlight and not torchlight,
    flashed
My steps out through the slow and diffi
    cult road.

I had grown distrustful of too forward
    Springs,
The season's books in drear significance
Of morals, dropping round me. Lively
    books ?
The ash has livelier verdure than the yew;
And yet the yew 's green longer, and alone
Found worthy of the holy Christmas time:
We 'll plant more yews if possible, albeit 270
We plant the graveyards with them.
                  Day and night
I worked my rhythmic thought, and fur-
    rowed up
Both watch and slumber with long lines of
    life
Which did not suit their season.   The rose
    fell
From either cheek, my eyes globed lumi-
    nous
Through orbits of blue shadow, and my
    pulse
Would shudder along the purple-veinèd
    wrist
Like a shot bird.   Youth's stern, set face
    to face
With youth's ideal: and when people came
And said 'You work too much, you are
    looking ill,'   280
I smiled for pity of them who pitied me,
And thought I should be better soon per-
    haps
For those ill looks.   Observe — 'I,' means
    in youth
Just *I*, the conscious and eternal soul
With all its ends, and not the outside
    life,
The parcel-man, the doublet of the flesh,
The so much liver, lung, integument,
Which make the sum of 'I' hereafter
    when
World-talkers talk of doing well or ill.
I prosper if I gain a step, although   290
A nail then pierced my foot: although my
    brain
Embracing any truth froze paralyzed,
I prosper: I but change my instrument;
I break the spade off, digging deep for
    gold,
And catch the mattock up.
                  I worked on, on.
Through all the bristling fence of nights
    and days
Which hedges time in from the eternities,
I struggled, — never stopped to note the
    stakes

Which hurt me in my course.   The mid-
    night oil
Would stink sometimes; there came some
    vulgar needs: 300
I had to live that therefore I might work,
And, being but poor, I was constrained,
    for life,
To work with one hand for the book-
    sellers
While working with the other for myself
And art: you swim with feet as well as
    hands,
Or make small way.   I apprehended
    this, —
In England no one lives by verse that
    lives;
And, apprehending, I resolved by prose
To make a space to sphere my living verse.
I wrote for cyclopædias, magazines,   310
And weekly papers, holding up my name
To keep it from the mud.   I learnt the
    use
Of the editorial 'we' in a review
As courtly ladies the fine trick of trains,
And swept it grandly through the open
    doors
As if one could not pass through doors at
    all
Save so encumbered.   I wrote tales be-
    side,
Carved many an article on cherry-stones
To suit light readers, — something in the
    lines
Revealing, it was said, the mallet-hand, 320
But that, I 'll never vouch for: what you
    do
For bread will taste of common grain, not
    grapes,
Although you have a vineyard in Cham-
    pagne;
Much less in Nephelococcygia
As mine was, peradventure.
                  Having bread
For just so many days, just breathing-
    room
For body and verse, I stood up straight
    and worked
My veritable work.   And as the soul
Which grows within a child makes the
    child grow, —
Or as the fiery sap, the touch from God, 330
Careering through a tree, dilates the bark
And roughs with scale and knob, before
    it strikes
The summer foliage out in a green flame —

So life, in deepening with me, deepened all
The course I took, the work I did. Indeed
The academic law convinced of sin;
The critics cried out on the falling off,
Regretting the first manner. But I felt
My heart's life throbbing in my verse to show
It lived, it also — certes incomplete,   340
Disordered with all Adam in the blood,
But even its very tumors, warts and wens
Still organized by and implying life.

A lady called upon me on such a day.
She had the low voice of your English dames,
Unused, it seems, to need rise half a note
To catch attention, — and their quiet mood,
As if they lived too high above the earth
For that to put them out in anything:
So gentle, because verily so proud;   350
So wary and afraid of hurting you,
By no means that you are not really vile,
But that they would not touch you with their foot
To push you to your place; so self-possessed
Yet gracious and conciliating, it takes
An effort in their presence to speak truth:
You know the sort of woman, — brilliant stuff,
And out of nature. 'Lady Waldemar.'
She said her name quite simply, as if it meant
Not much indeed, but something, — took my hands,   360
And smiled as if her smile could help my case,
And dropped her eyes on me and let them melt.
'Is this,' she said, 'the Muse'?
                    'No sybil even,'
I answered, 'since she fails to guess the cause
Which taxed you with this visit, madam.'
                    'Good,'
She said; 'I value what's sincere at once.
Perhaps if I had found a literal Muse,
The visit might have taxed me. As it is,
You wear your blue so chiefly in your eyes,
My fair Aurora, in a frank good way,   370
It comforts me entirely for your fame,
As well as for the trouble of ascent
To this Olympus.'
                    There, a silver laugh
Ran rippling through her quickened little breaths
The steep stair somewhat justified.
                    'But still
Your ladyship has left me curious why
You dared the risk of finding the said Muse?'

'Ah, keep me, notwithstanding, to the point,
Like any pedant? Is the blue in eyes
As awful as in stockings after all,   380
I wonder, that you'd have my business out
Before I breathe — exact the epic plunge
In spite of gasps? Well, naturally you think
I've come here, as the lion-hunters go
To deserts, to secure you with a trap
For exhibition in my drawing-rooms
On zoologic soirées? Not in the least.
Roar softly at me; I am frivolous,
I dare say; I have played at wild-beast shows
Like other women of my class, — but now
I meet my lion simply as Androcles   391
Met his . . . when at his mercy.'
                    So, she bent
Her head, as queens may mock, — then lifting up
Her eyelids with a real grave queenly look,
Which ruled and would not spare, not even herself, —
'I think you have a cousin: — Romney Leigh.'

'You bring a word from him?' — my eyes leapt up
To the very height of hers, — 'a word from him?'

'I bring a word about him, actually.
But first' (she pressed me with her urgent eyes),   400
'You do not love him, — you?'
                    'You're frank at least
In putting questions, madam,' I replied;
'I love my cousin cousinly — no more.'

'I guessed as much. I'm ready to be frank
In answering also, if you'll question me,
Or even for something less. You stand outside,
You artist women, of the common sex;
You share not with us, and exceed us so

Perhaps by what you 're mulcted in, your
    hearts
Being starved to make your heads: so run
    the old   410
Traditions of you. I can therefore speak
Without the natural shame which creatures
    feel
When speaking on their level, to their like.
There 's many a papist she, would rather
    die
Than own to her maid she put a ribbon on
To catch the indifferent eye of such a man,
Who yet would count adulteries on her
    beads
At holy Mary's shrine and never blush; 418
Because the saints are so far off, we lose
All modesty before them. Thus, to-day.
'T is _I_, love Romney Leigh.'
                ' Forbear,' I cried.
' If here 's no Muse, still less is any saint;
Nor even a friend, that Lady Waldemar
Should make confessions ' . . .
             ' That 's unkindly said:
If no friend, what forbids to make a friend
To join to our confession ere we have done ?
I love your cousin. If it seems unwise
To say so, it 's still foolisher (we 're frank)
To feel so. My first husband left me young,
And pretty enough, so please you, and rich
    enough,   430
To keep my booth in Mayfair with the rest
To happy issues. There are marquises
Would serve seven years to call me wife, I
    know,
And, after seven, I might consider it,
For there 's some comfort in a marquisate
When all 's said, — yes, but after the seven
    years;
I, now, love Romney. You put up your
    lip,
So like a Leigh ! so like him ! — Pardon
    me,
I 'm well aware I do not derogate
In loving Romney Leigh. The name is
    good,   440
The means are excellent, but the man, the
    man —
Heaven help us both, — I am near as mad
    as he,
In loving such an one.'
                She slowly swung
Her heavy ringlets till they touched her
    smile,
As reasonably sorry for herself,
And thus continued.

                ' Of a truth, Miss Leigh,
I have not, without struggle, come to this.
I took a master in the German tongue,
I gamed a little, went to Paris twice;
But, after all, this love ! . . . you eat of
    love,   450
And do as vile a thing as if you ate
Of garlic — which, whatever else you eat,
Tastes uniformly acrid, till your peach
Reminds you of your onion. Am I coarse ?
Well, love 's coarse, nature 's coarse — ah,
    there 's the rub.
We fair fine ladies, who park out our lives
From common sheep-paths, cannot help the
    crows
From flying over, — we 're as natural still
As Blowsalinda.   Drape us perfectly
In Lyons velvet, — we are not, for that, 460
Lay - figures, look you: we have hearts
    within,
Warm, live, improvident, indecent hearts,
As ready for outrageous ends and acts
As any distressed sempstress of them all
That Romney groans and toils for. We
    catch love,
And other fevers, in the vulgar way:
Love will not be outwitted by our wit,
Nor outrun by our equipages: — mine
Persisted, spite of efforts. All my cards
Turned up but Romney Leigh; my German
    stopped   470
At germane Wertherism; my Paris rounds
Returned me from the Champs Elysées
    just
A ghost, and sighing like Dido's. I came
    home
Uncured, — convicted rather to myself
Of being in love . . . in love ! That 's
    coarse, you 'll say,
I 'm talking garlic.'
                Coldly I replied:
' Apologize for atheism, not love !
For me, I do believe in love, and God.
I know my cousin: Lady Waldemar
I know not: yet I say as much as this, —
Whoever loves him, let her not excuse 481
But cleanse herself, that, loving such a man,
She may not do it with such unworthy
    love
He cannot stoop and take it.'
                ' That is said
Austerely, like a youthful prophetess,
Who knits her brows across her pretty eyes
To keep them back from following the gray
    flight

Of doves between the temple-columns. Dear,
Be kinder with me; let us two be friends.
I'm a mere woman, — the more weak perhaps 490
Through being so proud; you're better; as for him,
He's best. Indeed he builds his goodness up
So high, it topples down to the other side
And makes a sort of badness; there's the worst
I have to say against your cousin's best!
And so be mild, Aurora, with my worst
For his sake, if not mine.'
　　　　　　　' I own myself
Incredulous of confidence like this
Availing him or you.'
　　　　　　　' And I, myself,
Of being worthy of him with any love: 500
In your sense I am not so — let it pass.
And yet I save him if I marry him;
Let that pass too.'
　　　　　　　' Pass, pass! we play police
Upon my cousin's life, to indicate
What may or may not pass?' I cried.
' He knows
What's worthy of him; the choice remains with *him;*
And what he chooses, act or wife, I think
I shall not call unworthy, I, for one.'

' 'T is somewhat rashly said,' she answered slow;
' Now let's talk reason, though we talk of love. 510
Your cousin Romney Leigh's a monster; there,
The word's out fairly, let me prove the fact.
We'll take, say, that most perfect of antiques
They call the Genius of the Vatican
(Which seems too beauteous to endure itself
In this mixed world), and fasten it for once
Upon the torso of the Dancing Faun
(Who might limp surely, if he did not dance),
Instead of Buonarroti's mask: what then?
We show the sort of monster Romney is, 520
With godlike virtues and heroic aims
Subjoined to limping possibilities

Of mismade human nature. Grant the man
Twice godlike, twice heroic, — still he limps,
And here's the point we come to.'
　　　　　　　' Pardon me,
But, Lady Waldemar, the point's the thing
We never come to.'
　　　　　　　' Caustic, insolent
At need! I like you' — (there, she took my hands)
' And now, my lioness, help Androcles,
For all your roaring. Help me! for myself 530
I would not say so — but for him. He limps
So certainly, he'll fall into the pit
A week hence, — so I lose him — so he is lost!
For when he's fairly married, he a Leigh,
To a girl of doubtful life, undoubtful birth,
Starved out in London till her coarse-grained hands
Are whiter than her morals, — even you
May call his choice unworthy.'
　　　　　　　' Married! lost!
He . . . Romney!'
　　　　　　　' Ah, you're moved at last,' she said.
' These monsters, set out in the open sun,
Of course throw monstrous shadows: those who think 541
Awry, will scarce act straightly. Who but he?
And who but you can wonder? He has been mad,
The whole world knows, since first, a nominal man,
He soured the proctors, tried the gownsmen's wits,
With equal scorn of triangles and wine,
And took no honors, yet was honorable.
They'll tell you he lost count of Homer's ships
In Melbourne's poor-bills, Ashley's factory bills, —
Ignored the Aspasia we all dare to praise,
For other women, dear, we could not name
Because we're decent. Well, he had some right 551
On his side probably; men always have
Who go absurdly wrong. The living boor
Who brews your ale exceeds in vital worth
Dead Cæsar who "stops bungholes" in the cask;

And also, to do good is excellent,
For persons of his income, even to boors:
I sympathize with all such things. But he
Went mad upon them . . . madder and
    more mad   560
From college times to these, — as, going
    down hill,
The faster still, the farther. You must
    know
Your Leigh by heart: he has sown his
    black young curls
With bleaching cares of half a million men
Already. If you do not starve, or sin,
You 're nothing to him: pay the income-
    tax
And break your heart upon 't, he 'll scarce
    be touched;
But come upon the parish, qualified
For the parish stocks, and Romney will be
    there
To call you brother, sister, or perhaps   570
A tenderer name still. Had I any chance
With Mister Leigh, who am Lady Walde-
    mar
And never committed felony ? '
                     ' You speak
Too bitterly,' I said, ' for the literal truth.'

' The truth is bitter. Here 's a man who
    looks
For ever on the ground ! you must be low,
Or else a pictured ceiling overhead,
Good painting thrown away. For me, I 've
    done
What women may — we 're somewhat
    limited,
We modest women — but I 've done my
    best.   580
— How men are perjured when they swear
    our eyes
Have meaning in them ! they 're just blue
    or brown,
They just can drop their lids a little. And
    yet
Mine did more, for I read half Fourier
    through,
Proudhon, Considérant, and Louis Blanc,
With various others of his socialists,
And, if I had been a fathom less in love,
Had cured myself with gaping. As it
    was,
I quoted from them prettily enough,   589
Perhaps, to make them sound half rational
To a saner man than he whene'er we talked

(For which I dodged occasion) — learnt by
    heart
His speeches in the Commons and else-
    where
Upon the social question; heaped reports
Of wicked women and penitentiaries
On all my tables (with a place for Sue),
And gave my name to swell subscription
    lists
Toward keeping up the sun at nights in
    heaven,
And other possible ends. All things I did,
Except the impossible . . . such as wear-
    ing gowns   600
Provided by the Ten Hours' movement:
    there
I stopped — we must stop somewhere.
    He, meanwhile
Unmoved as the Indian tortoise 'neath the
    world,
Let all that noise go on upon his back:
He would not disconcert or throw me out,
'T was well to see a woman of my class
With such a dawn of conscience. For the
    heart,
Made firewood for his sake, and flaming
    up
To his face, — he merely warmed his feet
    at it:
Just deigned to let my carriage stop him
    short   610
In park or street, — he leaning on the
    door
With news of the committee which sat last
On pickpockets at suck.'
               ' You jest — you jest.'

' As martyrs jest, dear (if you read their
    lives),
Upon the axe which kills them. When
    all 's done
By me, . . . for him — you 'll ask him
    presently
The color of my hair — he cannot tell,
Or answers " dark " at random; while, be
    sure,
He 's absolute on the figure, five or ten,
Of my last subscription. Is it bearable, 620
And I a woman ? '
                 ' Is it reparable,
Though I were a man ? '
                  ' I know not. That 's to prove.
But, first, this shameful marriage ? '
                     ' Ay ? ' I cried.
' Then really there 's a marriage ? '

                      ' Yesterday
I held him fast upon it. " Mister Leigh,"
Said I, " shut up a thing, it makes more
    noise.
The boiling town keeps secrets ill; I 've
    known
Yours since last week. Forgive my know-
    ledge so:
You feel I 'm not the woman of the world
The world thinks; you have borne with
    me before   630
And used me in your noble work, our
    work,
And now you shall not cast me off be-
    cause
You 're at the difficult point, the *join*.
    'T is true
Even I can scarce admit the cogency
Of such a marriage . . . where you do
    not love
(Except the class), yet marry and throw
    your name
Down to the gutter, for a fire-escape
To future generations ! 't is sublime,
A great example, a true Genesis
Of the opening social era. But take
    heed,   640
This virtuous act must have a patent
    weight,
Or loses half its virtue. Make it tell,
Interpret it, and set it in the light,
And do not muffle it in a winter-cloak
As a vulgar bit of shame, — as if, at best,
A Leigh had made a misalliance and
    blushed
A Howard should know it." Then, I
    pressed him more:
" He would not choose," I said, " that even
    his kin, . . .
Aurora Leigh, even . . . should conceive
    his act
Less sacrifice, more fantasy." At which 650
He grew so pale, dear, . . . to the lips, I
    knew
I had touched him. "Do you know her,"
    he inquired,
" My cousin Aurora ? " " Yes," I said, and
    lied
(But truly we all know you by your books),
And so I offered to come straight to
    you,
Explain the subject, justify the cause,
And take you with me to Saint Margaret's
    Court
To see this miracle, this Marian Erle,

This drover's daughter (she 's not pretty,
    he swears),
Upon whose finger, exquisitely pricked 660
By a hundred needles, we 're to hang the
    tie
'Twixt class and class in England, — thus
    indeed
By such a presence, yours and mine, to
    lift
The match up from the doubtful place.
    At once
He thanked me sighing, murmured to him-
    self
" She 'll do it perhaps, she 's noble," —
    thanked me twice,
And promised, as my guerdon, to put off
His marriage for a month.'
                       I answered then.
' I understand your drift imperfectly.
You wish to lead me to my cousin's be-
    trothed,   670
To touch her hand if worthy, and hold her
    hand
If feeble, thus to justify his match.
So be it then. But how this serves your
    ends,
And how the strange confession of your
    love
Serves this, I have to learn — I cannot
    see.'

She knit her restless forehead. ' Then,
    despite,
Aurora, that most radiant morning name,
You 're dull as any London afternoon.
I wanted time, and gained it, — wanted
    you,
And gain you ! you will come and see the
    girl   680
In whose most prodigal eyes the lineal
    pearl
And pride of all your lofty race of Leighs
Is destined to solution. Authorized
By sight and knowledge, then, you 'll
    speak your mind,
And prove to Romney, in your brilliant
    way,
He 'll wrong the people and posterity
(Say such a thing is bad for me and
    you,
And you fail utterly), by concluding thus
An execrable marriage. Break it up,
Disroot it — peradventure presently   690
We 'll plant a better fortune in its place.
Be good to me, Aurora, scorn me less

For saying the thing I should not. Well
    I know
I should not. I have kept, as others have,
The iron rule of womanly reserve
In lip and life, till now: I wept a week
Before I came here.' — Ending, she was
    pale;
The last words, haughtily said, were trem-
    ulous.
This palfrey pranced in harness, arched
    her neck,
And, only by the foam upon the bit,   700
You saw she champed against it.
                     Then I rose.
'I love love: truth 's no cleaner thing
    than love.
I comprehend a love so fiery hot
It burns its natural veil of august shame,
And stands sublimely in the nude, as
    chaste
As Medicean Venus. But I know,
A love that burns through veils will burn
    through masks
And shrivel up treachery. What, love
    and lie!
Nay — go to the opera! your love 's cur-
    able.'

'I love and lie?' she said — 'I lie, for-
    sooth?'   710
And beat her taper foot upon the floor,
And smiled against the shoe, — 'You 're
    hard, Miss Leigh,
Unversed in current phrases. — Bowling
    greens
Of poets are fresher than the world's high-
    ways:
Forgive me that I rashly blew the dust
Which dims our hedges even, in your eyes,
And vexed you so much. You find, prob-
    ably,
No evil in this marriage, — rather good
Of innocence, to pastoralize in song:
You 'll give the bond your signature, per-
    haps,   720
Beneath the lady's work, — indifferent
That Romney chose a wife could write
    her name,
In witnessing he loved her.'
                 'Loved!' I cried;
'Who tells you that he wants a wife to
    love?
He gets a horse to use, not love, I think:
There 's work for wives as well, — and
    after, straw,

When men are liberal. For myself, you
    err
Supposing power in me to break this
    match.
I could not do it to save Romney's life,
And would not to save mine.'
                 'You take it so,'
She said, 'farewell then. Write your books
    in peace,   731
As far as may be for some secret stir
Now obvious to me, — for, most obviously,
In coming hither I mistook the way.'
Whereat she touched my hand and bent her
    head,
And floated from me like a silent cloud
That leaves the sense of thunder.
                    I drew breath,
Oppressed in my deliverance. After all,
This woman breaks her social system up
For love, so counted — the love possi-
    ble   740
To such, — and lilies are still lilies, pulled
By smutty hands, though spotted from their
    white;
And thus she is better haply, of her kind,
Than Romney Leigh, who lives by dia-
    grams,
And crosses out the spontaneities
Of all his individual, personal life
With formal universals. As if man
Were set upon a high stool at a desk
To keep God's books for Him in red and
    black,
And feel by millions! What, if even
    God   750
Were chiefly God by living out Himself
To an individualism of the Infinite,
Eterne, intense, profuse, — still throwing
    up
The golden spray of multitudinous worlds
In measure to the proclive weight and
    rush
Of his inner nature, — the spontaneous
    love
Still proof and outflow of spontaneous
    life?
Then live, Aurora.
                 Two hours afterward,
Within Saint Margaret's Court I stood
    alone,
Close-veiled. A sick child, from an ague-
    fit,   760
Whose wasted right hand gambled 'gainst
    his left
With an old brass button in a blot of sun,

Jeered weakly at me as I passed across
The uneven pavement; while a woman, rouged
Upon the angular cheek-bones, kerchief torn,
Thin dangling locks, and flat lascivious mouth,
Cursed at a window both ways, in and out,
By turns some bed-rid creature and myself, —
'Lie still there, mother! liker the dead dog
You 'll be to-morrow. What, we pick our way, 770
Fine madam, with those damnable small feet!
We cover up our face from doing good,
As if it were our purse! What brings you here,
My lady? Is 't to find my gentleman
Who visits his tame pigeon in the eaves?
Our cholera catch you with its cramps and spasms,
And tumble up your good clothes, veil and all,
And turn your whiteness dead-blue.' I looked up;
I think I could have walked through hell that day,
And never flinched. 'The dear Christ comfort you,' 780
I said, 'you must have been most miserable
To be so cruel,' — and I emptied out
My purse upon the stones: when, as I had cast
The last charm in the cauldron, the whole court
Went boiling, bubbling up, from all its doors
And windows, with a hideous wail of laughs
And roar of oaths, and blows perhaps . . .
I passed
Too quickly for distinguishing . . . and pushed
A little side-door hanging on a hinge,
And plunged into the dark, and groped and climbed 790
The long, steep, narrow stair 'twixt broken rail
And mildewed wall that let the plaster drop
To startle me in the blackness. Still, up, up!

So high lived Romney's bride. I paused at last
Before a low door in the roof, and knocked.
There came an answer like a hurried dove —
'So soon? can that be Mister Leigh? so soon?'
And, as I entered, an ineffable face
Met mine upon the threshold. 'Oh, not you,
Not you!' — the dropping of the voice implied; 800
'Then, if not you, for me not any one.'
I looked her in the eyes, and held her hands,
And said 'I am his cousin, — Romney Leigh's;
And here I come to see my cousin too.'
She touched me with her face and with her voice,
This daughter of the people. Such soft flowers
From such rough roots? The people, under there,
Can sin so, curse so, look so, smell so . . . faugh!
Yet have such daughters?
                              Nowise beautiful
Was Marian Erle. She was not white nor brown, 810
But could look either, like a mist that changed
According to being shone on more or less:
The hair, too, ran its opulence of curls
In doubt 'twixt dark and bright, nor left you clear
To name the color. Too much hair perhaps
(I 'll name a fault here) for so small a head,
Which seemed to droop on that side and on this,
As a full-blown rose uneasy with its weight
Though not a wind should trouble it.
Again,
The dimple in the cheek had better gone 820
With redder, fuller rounds; and somewhat large
The mouth was, though the milky little teeth
Dissolved it to so infantine a smile.
For soon it smiled at me; the eyes smiled too,

But 't was as if remembering they had wept,
And knowing they should, some day, weep again.

We talked. She told me all her story out,
Which I 'll re-tell with fuller utterance,
As colored and confirmed in after times
By others and herself too.   Marian Erle 830
Was born upon the ledge of Malvern Hill,
To eastward, in a hut built up at night,
To evade the landlord's eye, of mud and turf,
Still liable, if once he looked that way,
To being straight levelled, scattered by his foot,
Like any other anthill.   Born, I say;
God sent her to his world, commissioned right,
Her human testimonials fully signed,
Not scant in soul — complete in lineaments;
But others had to swindle her a place 840
To wail in when she had come.   No place for her,
By man's law! born an outlaw was this babe;
Her first cry in our strange and strangling air,
When cast in spasms out by the shuddering womb,
Was wrong against the social code, — forced wrong: —
What business had the baby to cry there ?

I tell her story and grow passionate.
She, Marian, did not tell it so, but used
Meek words that made no wonder of herself
For being so sad a creature.   'Mister Leigh 850
Considered truly that such things should change.
They will, in heaven — but meantime, on the earth,
There 's none can like a nettle as a pink,
Except himself.   We 're nettles, some of us,
And give offence by the act of springing up;
And, if we leave the damp side of the wall,
The hoes, of course, are on us.'   So she said.

Her father earned his life by random jobs
Despised by steadier workmen — keeping swine
On commons, picking hops, or hurrying on
The harvest at wet seasons, or, at need, 861
Assisting the Welsh drovers, when a drove
Of startled horses plunged into the mist
Below the mountain-road, and sowed the wind
With wandering neighings.   In between the gaps
Of such irregular work he drank and slept,
And cursed his wife because, the pence being out,
She could not buy more drink.   At which she turned
(The worm), and beat her baby in revenge
For her own broken heart.   There 's not a crime 870
But takes its proper change out still in crime
If once rung on the counter of this world:
Let sinners look to it.
                              Yet the outcast child,
For whom the very mother's face forwent
The mother's special patience, lived and grew;
Learnt early to cry low, and walk alone,
With that pathetic vacillating roll
Of the infant body on the uncertain feet
(The earth being felt unstable ground so soon),
At which most women's arms unclose at once 880
With irrepressive instinct.   Thus, at three,
This poor weaned kid would run off from the fold,
This babe would steal off from the mother's chair,
And, creeping through the golden walls of gorse,
Would find some keyhole toward the secrecy
Of Heaven's high blue, and, nestling down, peer out —
Oh, not to catch the angels at their games, —
She had never heard of angels, — but to gaze
She knew not why, to see she knew not what,
A-hungering outward from the barren earth 890
For something like a joy.   She liked, she said,

To dazzle black her sight against the sky,
For then, it seemed, some grand blind
    Love came down,
And groped her out, and clasped her with
    a kiss;
She learnt God that way, and was beat for
    it
Whenever she went home, — yet came
    again,
As surely as the trapped hare, getting free,
Returns to his form. This grand blind
    Love, she said,
This skyey father and mother both in one,
Instructed her and civilized her more   900
Than even Sunday-school did afterward,
To which a lady sent her to learn books
And sit upon a long bench in a row
With other children. Well, she laughed
    sometimes
To see them laugh and laugh and maul
    their texts;
But often she was sorrowful with noise
And wondered if their mothers beat them
    hard
That ever they should laugh so. There
    was one
She loved indeed, — Rose Bell, a seven
    years' child,
So pretty and clever, who read syllables 910
When Marian was at letters; *she* would
    laugh
At nothing — hold your finger up, she
    laughed,
Then shook her curls down over eyes and
    mouth
To hide her make-mirth from the school-
    master:
And Rose's pelting glee, as frank as rain
On cherry-blossoms, brightened Marian
    too,
To see another merry whom she loved.
She whispered once (the children side by
    side,
With mutual arms entwined about their
    necks)
'Your mother lets you laugh so?' 'Ay,'
    said Rose,   920
'She lets me. She was dug into the
    ground
Six years since, I being but a yearling
    wean.
Such mothers let us play and lose our
    time,
And never scold nor beat us! Don't you
    wish

You had one like that?' There, Marian
    breaking off
Looked suddenly in my face. 'Poor Rose,'
    said she,
'I heard her laugh last night in Oxford
    Street.
I'd pour out half my blood to stop that
    laugh.
Poor Rose, poor Rose!' said Marian.
              She resumed.
It tried her, when she had learnt at Sun-
    day-school   930
What God was, what He wanted from us
    all,
And how in choosing sin we vexed the
    Christ,
To go straight home and hear her father
    pull
The Name down on us from the thunder-
    shelf,
Then drink away his soul into the dark
From seeing judgment. Father, mother,
    home,
Were God and heaven reversed to her:
    the more
She knew of Right, the more she guessed
    their wrong:
Her price paid down for knowledge, was to
    know
The vileness of her kindred: through her
    heart,   940
Her filial and tormented heart, henceforth,
They struck their blows at virtue. Oh, 't is
    hard
To learn you have a father up in heaven
By a gathering certain sense of being, on
    earth,
Still worse than orphaned: 't is too heavy
    a grief,
The having to thank God for such a joy!

And so passed Marian's life from year to
    year.
Her parents took her with them when they
    tramped,
Dodged lanes and heaths, frequented towns
    and fairs,   949
And once went farther and saw Manches-
    ter,
And once the sea, that blue end of the
    world,
That fair scroll-finis of a wicked book, —
And twice a prison, — back at intervals,
Returning to the hills. Hills draw like
    heaven,

And stronger sometimes, holding out their
 hands
To pull you from the vile flats up to them.
And though perhaps these strollers still
 strolled back,
As sheep do, simply that they knew the way,
They certainly felt bettered unaware
Emerging from the social smut of towns 960
To wipe their feet clean on the mountain
 turf.
In which long wanderings, Marian lived
 and learned,
Endured and learned.   The people on the
 roads
Would stop and ask her why her eyes out-
 grew
Her cheeks, and if she meant to lodge the
 birds
In all that hair; and then they lifted her,
The miller in his cart, a mile or twain,
The butcher's boy on horseback.   Often too
The pedler stopped, and tapped her on the
 head   969
With absolute forefinger, brown and ringed,
And asked if peradventure she could read,
And when she answered 'ay,' would toss
 her down
Some stray odd volume from his heavy pack,
A Thomson's Seasons, mulcted of the
 Spring,
Or half a play of Shakespeare's torn across
(She had to guess the bottom of a page
By just the top sometimes, — as difficult,
As, sitting on the moon, to guess the
 earth !),
Or else a sheaf of leaves (for that small
 Ruth's
Small gleanings) torn out from the heart of
 books,   980
From Churchyard Elegies and Edens Lost,
From Burns, and Bunyan, Selkirk, and Tom
 Jones, —
'T was somewhat hard to keep the things
 distinct,
And oft the jangling influence jarred the
 child
Like looking at a sunset full of grace
Through a pothouse window while the
 drunken oaths
Went on behind her.   But she weeded out
Her book-leaves, threw away the leaves
 that hurt
(First tore them small, that none should
 find a word),   989
And made a nosegay of the sweet and good

To fold within her breast, and pore upon
At broken moments of the noontide glare,
When leave was given her to untie her
 cloak
And rest upon the dusty highway's bank
From the road's dust: or oft, the journey
 done,
Some city friend would lead her by the
 hand
To hear a lecture at an institute.
And thus she had grown, this Marian Erle
 of ours,   998
To no book-learning, — she was ignorant
Of authors, — not in earshot of the things
Outspoken o'er the heads of common men
By men who are uncommon, — but within
The cadenced hum of such, and capable
Of catching from the fringes of the wing
Some fragmentary phrases, here and there,
Of that fine music, — which, being carried
 in
To her soul, had reproduced itself afresh
In finer motions of the lips and lids.

She said, in speaking of it, ' If a flower 1009
Were thrown you out of heaven at intervals,
You 'd soon attain to a trick of looking
 up, —
And so with her.'   She counted me her
 years,
Till *I* felt old; and then she counted me
Her sorrowful pleasures, till I felt ashamed.
She told me she was fortunate and calm
On such and such a season, sat and sewed,
With no one to break up her crystal
 thoughts,
While rhymes from lovely poems span
 around
Their ringing circles of ecstatic tune,   1019
Beneath the moistened finger of the Hour.
Her parents called her a strange, sickly
 child,
Not good for much, and given to sulk and
 stare,
And smile into the hedges and the clouds,
And tremble if one shook her from her
 fit
By any blow, or word even.   Out-door jobs
Went ill with her, and household quiet
 work
She was not born to.   Had they kept the
 north,
They might have had their pennyworth out
 of her,
Like other parents, in the factories

(Your children work for you, not you for
them,   1030
Or else they better had been choked with
air
The first breath drawn); but, in this tramp-
ing life,
Was nothing to be done with such a child
But tramp and tramp. And yet she knitted
hose
Not ill, and was not dull at needlework;
And all the country people gave her pence
For darning stockings past their natural
age,
And patching petticoats from old to new,
And other light work done for thrifty wives.

One day, said Marian — the sun shone that
day —   1040
Her mother had been badly beat, and felt
The bruises sore about her wretched soul
(That must have been): she came in
suddenly,
And snatching in a sort of breathless rage
Her daughter's headgear comb, let down
the hair
Upon her like a sudden waterfall,
Then drew her drenched and passive by the
arm
Outside the hut they lived in. When the
child
Could clear her blinded face from all that
stream
Of tresses . . . there, a man stood, with
beast's eyes   1050
That seemed as they would swallow her
alive
Complete in body and spirit, hair and
all, —
And burning stertorous breath that hurt
her cheek,
He breathed so near. The mother held
her tight,
Saying hard between her teeth — 'Why
wench, why wench,
The squire speaks to you now — the
squire's too good:
He means to set you up and comfort us.
Be mannerly at least.' The child turned
round
And looked up piteous in the mother's face
(Be sure that mother's death-bed will not
want   1060
Another devil to damn, than such a look),
'Oh, mother !' then, with desperate glance
to heaven,

'God, free me from my mother,' she
shrieked out,
'These mothers are too dreadful.' And,
with force
As passionate as fear, she tore her hands,
Like lilies from the rocks, from hers and
his,
And sprang down, bounded headlong down
the steep,
Away from both — away, if possible,
As far as God, — away ! They yelled at
her,
As famished hounds at a hare. She heard
them yell;   1070
She felt her name hiss after her from the
hills,
Like shot from guns. On, on. And now
she had cast
The voices off with the uplands. On. Mad
fear
Was running in her feet and killing the
ground;
The white roads curled as if she burnt
them up,
The green fields melted, wayside trees fell
back
To make room for her. Then her head
grew vexed;
Trees, fields, turned on her and ran after
her;
She heard the quick pants of the hills be-
hind,
Their keen air pricked her neck: she had
lost her feet,   1080
Could run no more, yet somehow went as
fast,
The horizon red 'twixt steeples in the east
So sucked her forward, forward, while her
heart
Kept swelling, swelling, till it swelled so
big
It seemed to fill her body, — when it burst
And overflowed the world and swamped
the light;
'And now I am dead and safe,' thought
Marian Erle —
She had dropped, she had fainted.
                    As the sense returned,
The night had passed — not life's night.
She was 'ware
Of heavy tumbling motions, creaking
wheels,   1090
The driver shouting to the lazy team
That swung their rankling bells against
her brain,

While, through the wagon's coverture and
     chinks,
The cruel yellow morning pecked at her
Alive or dead upon the straw inside, —
At which her soul ached back into the
     dark
And prayed, 'no more of that.' A wag-
     oner
Had found her in a ditch beneath the
     moon,
As white as moonshine save for the oozing
     blood.
At first he thought her dead; but when he
     had wiped   1100
The mouth and heard it sigh, he raised her
     up,
And laid her in his wagon in the straw,
And so conveyed her to the distant town
To which his business called himself, and
     left
That heap of misery at the hospital.

She stirred; — the place seemed new and
     strange as death.
The white strait bed, with others strait and
     white,
Like graves dug side by side at measured
     lengths,
And quiet people walking in and out
With wonderful low voices and soft steps
And apparitional equal care for each,   1111
Astonished her with order, silence, law.
And when a gentle hand held out a cup,
She took it, as you do at sacrament,
Half awed, half melted, — not being used,
     indeed,
To so much love as makes the form of
     love
And courtesy of manners.   Delicate drinks
And rare white bread, to which some dying
     eyes
Were turned in observation.   O my God,
How sick we must be, ere we make men
     just !   1120
I think it frets the saints in heaven to see
How many desolate creatures on the earth
Have learnt the simple dues of fellowship
And social comfort, in a hospital,
As Marian did.   She lay there, stunned,
     half tranced,
And wished, at intervals of growing sense,
She might be sicker yet, if sickness made
The world so marvellous kind, the air so
     hushed,
And all her wake-time quiet as a sleep;

For now she understood (as such things
     were)   1130
How sickness ended very oft in heaven
Among the unspoken raptures: — yet more
     sick,
And surelier happy.   Then she dropped
     her lids,
And, folding up her hands as flowers at
     night,
Would lose no moment of the blessèd time.

She lay and seethed in fever many weeks,
But youth was strong and overcame the
     test;
Revolted soul and flesh were reconciled
And fetched back to the necessary day
And daylight duties.   She could creep
     about   1140
The long bare rooms, and stare out drearily
From any narrow window on the street,
Till some one who had nursed her as a
     friend
Said coldly to her, as an enemy,
'She had leave to go next week, being well
     enough'
(While only her heart ached).   'Go next
     week,' thought she:
'Next week ! how would it be with her
     next week,
Let out into that terrible street alone
Among the pushing people, . . . to go . . .
     where ?'

One day, the last before the dreaded last,
Among the convalescents, like herself   1151
Prepared to go next morning, she sat
     dumb,
And heard half absently the women
     talk, —
How one was famished for her baby's
     cheeks,
'The little wretch would know her ! a
     year old
And lively, like his father !' — one was
     keen
To get to work, and fill some clamorous
     mouths;
And one was tender for her dear goodman
Who had missed her sorely, — and one,
     querulous . . .
'Would pay backbiting neighbors who had
     dared   1160
To talk about her as already dead,' —
And one was proud . . . 'and if her sweet-
     heart Luke

Had left her for a ruddier face than hers
(The gossip would be seen through at a
    glance),
Sweet riddance of such sweethearts — let
    him hang !
'T were good to have been sick for such an
    end.'

And while they talked, and Marian felt the
    worse
For having missed the worst of all their
    wrongs,
A visitor was ushered through the wards
And paused among the talkers. ' When
    he looked   1170
It was as if he spoke, and when he spoke
He sang perhaps,' said Marian; ' could she
    tell ?
She only knew ' (so much she had chron-
    icled,
As seraphs might the making of the sun)
' That he who came and spake was Rom-
    ney Leigh,
And then and there she saw and heard him
    first.'

And when it was her turn to have the face
Upon her, all those buzzing pallid lips
Being satisfied with comfort — when he
    changed
To Marian, saying ' And *you ?* you 're go-
    ing, where ? ' —   1180
She, moveless as a worm beneath a stone
Which some one's stumbling foot has
    spurned aside,
Writhed suddenly, astonished with the
    light,
And, breaking into sobs, cried ' Where I
    go ?
None asked me till this moment. Can I
    say
Where *I* go, — when it has not seemed
    worth while
To God Himself, who thinks of every one,
To think of me and fix where I shall go ? '

' So young,' he gently asked her, ' you
    have lost
Your father and your mother ? '
                ' Both,' she said,
' Both lost ! my father was burnt up with
    gin   1191
Or ever I sucked milk, and so is lost.
My mother sold me to a man last month,
And so my mother 's lost, 't is manifest.

And I, who fled from her for miles and
    miles,
As if I had caught sight of the fire of hell
Through some wild gap (she was my
    mother, sir),
It seems I shall be lost too, presently,
And so we end, all three of us.'
                          ' Poor child,'
He said, — with such a pity in his voice,
It soothed her more than her own tears, —
    ' poor child !   1201
'T is simple that betrayal by mother's love
Should bring despair of God's too. Yet be
    taught,
He 's better to us than many mothers are,
And children cannot wander beyond reach
Of the sweep of his white raiment. Touch
    and hold !
And if you weep still, weep where John
    was laid
While Jesus loved him.
                    ' She could say the words,'
She told me, ' exactly as he uttered them
A year back, since in any doubt or dark
They came out like the stars, and shone on
    her   1211
With just their comfort. Common words,
    perhaps;
The ministers in church might say the
    same;
But *he,* he made the church with what he
    spoke, —
The difference was the miracle,' said she.

Then catching up her smile to ravishment,
She added quickly, ' I repeat his words,
But not his tones: can any one repeat
The music of an organ, out of church ?
And when he said " poor child," I shut my
    eyes   1220
To feel how tenderly his voice broke
    through,
As the ointment-box broke on the Holy feet
To let out the rich medicative nard.'

She told me how he had raised and rescued
    her
With reverent pity, as, in touching grief,
He touched the wounds of Christ, — and
    made her feel
More self-respecting. Hope he called be-
    lief
In God, — work, worship, — therefore let
    us pray !
And thus, to snatch her soul from atheism,

And keep it stainless from her mother's
    face,   1230
He sent her to a famous sempstress-house
Far off in London, there to work and hope.

With that they parted. She kept sight of
    Heaven,
But not of Romney. He had good to do
To others: through the days and through
    the nights
She sewed and sewed and sewed. She
    drooped sometimes,
And wondered, while along the tawny
    light
She struck the new thread into her needle's
    eye,
How people without mothers on the hills
Could choose the town to live in ! — then
    she drew   1240
The stitch, and mused how Romney's face
    would look,
And if 't were likely he 'd remember hers
When they two had their meeting after
    death.

FOURTH BOOK

They met still sooner. 'T was a year from
    thence
That Lucy Gresham, the sick sempstress
    girl,
Who sewed by Marian's chair so still and
    quick,
And leant her head upon its back to cough
More freely, when, the mistress turning
    round,
The others took occasion to laugh out,
Gave up at last. Among the workers,
    spoke
A bold girl with black eyebrows and red
    lips:
'You know the news ? Who 's dying, do
    you think ?
Our Lucy Gresham. I expected it   10
As little as Nell Hart's wedding. Blush
    not, Nell,
Thy curls be red enough without thy
    cheeks,
And, some day, there 'll be found a man to
    dote
On red curls. — Lucy Gresham swooned
    last night,
Dropped sudden in the street while going
    home;

And now the baker says, who took her up
And laid her by her grandmother in bed,
He 'll give her a week to die in. Pass the
    silk.
Let 's hope he gave her a loaf too, within
    reach,
For otherwise they 'll starve before they
    die,   20
That funny pair of bedfellows ! Miss
    Bell,
I 'll thank you for the scissors. The old
    crone
Is paralytic — that 's the reason why
Our Lucy's thread went faster than her
    breath,
Which went too quick, we all know. Marian
    Erle,
Why, Marian Erle, you 're not the fool to
    cry ?
Your tears spoil Lady Waldemar's new
    dress,
You piece of pity !'
                 Marian rose up straight,
And, breaking through the talk and through
    the work,
Went outward, in the face of their sur-
    prise,   30
To Lucy's home, to nurse her back to life
Or down to death. She knew, by such an
    act,
All place and grace were forfeit in the
    house,
Whose mistress would supply the missing
    hand
With necessary, not inhuman haste,
And take no blame. But pity, too, had
    dues:
She could not leave a solitary soul
To founder in the dark, while she sat still
And lavished stitches on a lady's hem
As if no other work were paramount.   40
'Why, God,' thought Marian, 'has a miss-
    ing hand
This moment; Lucy wants a drink, per-
    haps.
Let others miss me ! never miss me,
    God !'

So Marian sat by Lucy's bed, content
With duty, and was strong, for recom-
    pense,
To hold the lamp of human love arm-high,
To catch the death-strained eyes and com-
    fort them,
Until the angels, on the luminous side

Of death, had got theirs ready. And she
   said,
If Lucy thanked her sometimes, called her
   kind,   50
It touched her strangely. 'Marian Erle
   called kind!
What, Marian, beaten and sold, who could
   not die!
'T is verily good fortune to be kind.
Ah you,' she said, 'who are born to such a
   grace,
Be sorry for the unlicensed class, the poor,
Reduced to think the best good fortune
   means
That others, simply, should be kind to
   them.'

From sleep to sleep when Lucy had slid
   away
So gently, like the light upon a hill,
Of which none names the moment that it
   goes   60
Though all see when 't is gone, — a man
   came in
And stood beside the bed. The old idiot
   wretch
Screamed feebly, like a baby overlain,
'Sir, sir, you won't mistake me for the
   corpse?
Don't look at *me*, sir! never bury *me!*
Although I lie here, I 'm alive as you,
Except my legs and arms, — I eat and
   drink
And understand, — (that you 're the gentle-
   man
Who fits the funerals up, Heaven speed you,
   sir),
And certainly I should be livelier still   70
If Lucy here . . . sir, Lucy is the corpse . . .
Had worked more properly to buy me
   wine;
But Lucy, sir, was always slow at work,
I shan't lose much by Lucy. Marian Erle,
Speak up and show the gentleman the
   corpse.'

And then a voice said 'Marian Erle.' She
   rose;
It was the hour for angels — there, stood
   hers!
She scarcely marvelled to see Romney
   Leigh.
As light November snows to empty nests,
As grass to graves, as moss to mildewed
   stones,   80

As July suns to ruins, through the rents,
As ministering spirits to mourners, through
   a loss,
As Heaven itself to men, through pangs of
   death,
He came uncalled wherever grief had
   come.
'And so,' said Marian Erle, 'we met
   anew,'
And added softly, 'so, we shall not part.'

He was not angry that she had left the
   house
Wherein he placed her. Well — she had
   feared it might
Have vexed him. Also, when he found her
   set
On keeping, though the dead was out of
   sight,   90
That half-dead, half-alive body left behind
With cankerous heart and flesh, which took
   your best
And cursed you for the little good it did
(Could any leave the bed-rid wretch alone,
So joyless she was thankless even to God,
Much more to you?), he did not say 't was
   well,
Yet Marian thought he did not take it
   ill, —
Since day by day he came, and every
   day
She felt within his utterance and his eyes
A closer, tenderer presence of the soul, 100
Until at last he said 'We shall not part.'

On that same day was Marian's work com-
   plete:
She had smoothed the empty bed, and
   swept the floor
Of coffin sawdust, set the chairs anew
The dead had ended gossip in, and stood
In that poor room so cold and orderly,
The door-key in her hand, prepared to go
As *they* had, howbeit not their way. He
   spoke.

'Dear Marian, of one clay God made us
   all,
And though men push and poke and pad-
   dle in 't   110
(As children play at fashioning dirt-pies)
And call their fancies by the name of facts,
Assuming difference, lordship, privilege,
When all 's plain dirt, — they come back
   to it at last,

The first grave-digger proves it with a
  spade,
And pats all even. Need we wait for this,
You, Marian, and I, Romney ? '
                          She, at that,
Looked blindly in his face, as when one
  looks
Through driving autumn-rains to find the
  sky.   119
He went on speaking.
                  ' Marian, I being born
What men call noble, and you, issued from
The noble people, — though the tyrannous
  sword,
Which pierced Christ's heart, has cleft the
  world in twain
'Twixt class and class, opposing rich to
  poor,
Shall *we* keep parted ? Not so. Let us
  lean
And strain together rather, each to each,
Compress the red lips of this gaping
  wound
As far as two souls can, — ay, lean and
  league,
I from my superabundance, — from your
  want
You, — joining in a protest 'gainst the
  wrong   130
On both sides.'
                All the rest, he held her hand
In speaking, which confused the sense of
  much.
Her heart against his words beat out so
  thick,
They might as well be written on the
  dust
Where some poor bird, escaping from
  hawk's beak,
Has dropped and beats its shuddering
  wings, — the lines
Are rubbed so, — yet 't was something like
  to this,
— ' That they two, standing at the two
  extremes
Of social classes, had received one seal,
Been dedicate and drawn beyond them-
  selves   140
To mercy and ministration, — he, indeed,
Through what he knew, and she, through
  what she felt,
He, by man's conscience, she, by woman's
  heart,
Relinquishing their several 'vantage posts
Of wealthy ease and honorable toil,

To work with God at love. And since
  God willed
That putting out his hand to touch this ark
He found a woman's hand there, he 'd
  accept
The sign too, hold the tender fingers fast,
And say " My fellow - worker, be my
  wife ! " '   150

She told the tale with simple, rustic
  turns, —
Strong leaps of meaning in her sudden
  eyes
That took the gaps of any imperfect phrase
Of the unschooled speaker: I have rather
  writ
The thing I understood so, than the thing
I heard so.   And I cannot render right
Her quick gesticulation, wild yet soft,
Self-startled from the habitual mood she
  used,
Half sad, half languid, — like dumb crea-
  tures (now
A rustling bird, and now a wandering
  deer,   160
Or squirrel 'gainst the oak-gloom flashing
  up
His sidelong burnished head, in just her
  way
Of savage spontaneity), that stir
Abruptly the green silence of the woods,
And make it stranger, holier, more pro-
  found;
As Nature's general heart confessed itself
Of life, and then fell backward on repose.

I kissed the lips that ended. — ' So indeed
He loves you, Marian ? '
                  ' Loves me ! ' She looked up
With a child's wonder when you ask him
  first   170
Who made the sun — a puzzled blush, that
  grew,
Then broke off in a rapid radiant smile
Of sure solution. ' Loves me ! he loves
  all, —
And me, of course. He had not asked me
  else
To work with him for ever and be his wife.'

Her words reproved me. This perhaps
  was love —
To have its hands too full of gifts to give,
For putting out a hand to take a gift;
To love so much, the perfect round of love

Includes, in strict conclusion, being
    loved; 180
As Eden-dew went up and fell again,
Enough for watering Eden. Obviously
She had not thought about his love at all:
The cataracts of her soul had poured them-
    selves,
And risen self-crowned in rainbow: would
    she ask
Who crowned her? — it sufficed that she
    was crowned.
With women of my class 't is otherwise:
We haggle for the small change of our
    gold,
And so much love accord for so much love,
Rialto-prices. Are we therefore wrong? 190
If marriage be a contract, look to it then,
Contracting parties should be equal, just;
But if, a simple fealty on one side,
A mere religion, — right to give, is all,
And certain brides of Europe duly ask
To mount the pile as Indian widows do,
The spices of their tender youth heaped
    up,
The jewels of their gracious virtues worn,
More gems, more glory, — to consume en-
    tire
For a living husband: as the man's
    alive, 200
Not dead, the woman's duty by so much
Advanced in England beyond Hindostan.

I sat there musing, till she touched my
    hand
With hers, as softly as a strange white bird
She feared to startle in touching. 'You
    are kind,
But are you, peradventure, vexed at heart
Because your cousin takes me for a wife?
I know I am not worthy — nay, in truth,
I'm glad on 't, since, for that, he chooses
    me.
He likes the poor things of the world the
    best; 210
I would not therefore, if I could, be rich.
It pleasures him to stoop for buttercups;
I would not be a rose upon the wall
A queen might stop at, near the palace-
    door,
To say to a courtier, "Pluck that rose for
    me,
It's prettier than the rest." O Romney
    Leigh!
I'd rather far be trodden by his foot,
Than lie in a great queen's bosom.'

Out of breath,
She paused.
        'Sweet Marian, do you disavow
The roses with that face?'
              She dropped her head
As if the wind had caught that flower of
    her 221
And bent it in the garden, — then looked
    up
With grave assurance. 'Well, you think
    me bold!
But so we all are, when we 're praying
    God.
And if I 'm bold — yet, lady, credit me,
That, since I know myself for what I
    am,
Much fitter for his handmaid than his wife,
I'll prove the handmaid and the wife at
    once,
Serve tenderly, and love obediently,
And be a worthier mate, perhaps, than
    some 230
Who are wooed in silk among their learned
    books,
While I shall set myself to read his eyes,
Till such grow plainer to me than the
    French
To wisest ladies. Do you think I'll miss
A letter, in the spelling of his mind?
No more than they do when they sit and
    write
Their flying words with flickering wild-fowl
    tails,
Nor ever pause to ask how many t's,
Should that be y or i, they know 't so well:
I 've seen them writing, when I brought a
    dress 240
And waited, — floating out their soft white
    hands
On shining paper. But they 're hard,
    sometimes,
For all those hands! — we 've used out
    many nights,
And worn the yellow daylight into shreds
Which flapped and shivered down our ach-
    ing eyes
Till night appeared more tolerable, just
That pretty ladies might look beautiful,
Who said at last . . . "You 're lazy in that
    house!
You 're slow in sending home the work, —
    I count
I 've waited near an hour for 't." Pardon
    me, 250
I do not blame them, madam, nor misprize;

They are fair and gracious; ay, but not
    like you,
Since none but you has Mister Leigh's own
    blood,
Both noble and gentle, — and, without it
    . . . well,
They are fair, I said; so fair, it scarce
    seems strange
That, flashing out in any looking-glass
The wonder of their glorious brows and
    breasts,
They 're charmed so, they forget to look
    behind
And mark how pale we 've grown, we piti-
    ful
Remainders of the world. And so perhaps
If Mister Leigh had chosen a wife from
    these,   261
She might, although he 's better than her
    best
And dearly she would know it, steal a
    thought
Which should be all his, an eye-glance from
    his face,
To plunge into the mirror opposite
In search of her own beauty's pearl; while
    I . . .
Ah, dearest lady, serge will outweigh silk
For winter-wear when bodies feel a-cold,
And I 'll be a true wife to your cousin
    Leigh.'   269

Before I answered he was there himself.
I think he had been standing in the room
And listened probably to half her talk,
Arrested, turned to stone, — as white as
    stone.
Will tender sayings make men look so
    white?
He loves her then profoundly.
                     ' You are here,
Aurora? Here I meet you!' — We
    clasped hands.

'Even so, dear Romney. Lady Waldemar
Has sent me in haste to find a cousin of
    mine
Who shall be.'
                ' Lady Waldemar is good.'

'Here 's one, at least, who is good,' I
    sighed, and touched   280
Poor Marian's happy head, as doglike she,
Most passionately patient, waited on,
A-tremble for her turn of greeting words;

'I 've sat a full hour with your Marian
    Erle,
And learnt the thing by heart, — and from
    my heart
Am therefore competent to give you thanks
For such a cousin.'
                ' You accept at last
A gift from me, Aurora, without scorn?
At last I please you?' — How his voice
    was changed.

'You cannot please a woman against her
    will,   290
And once you vexed me.   Shall we speak
    of that?
We 'll say, then, you were noble in it all,
And I not ignorant — let it pass! And
    now
You please me, Romney, when you please
    yourself;
So, please you, be fanatical in love,
And I 'm well pleased. Ah, cousin! at
    the old hall,
Among the gallery portraits of our Leighs,
We shall not find a sweeter signory
Than this pure forehead's.'
                   Not a word he said.
How arrogant men are! — Even philan-
    thropists,   300
Who try to take a wife up in the way
They put down a subscription-cheque, — if
    once
She turns and says ' I will not tax you so,
Most charitable sir,' — feel ill at ease
As though she had wronged them somehow.
    I suppose
We women should remember what we are,
And not throw back an obolus inscribed
With Cæsar's image, lightly.   I resumed.

'It strikes me, some of those sublime Van-
    dykes
Were not too proud to make good saints in
    heaven;   310
And if so, then they 're not too proud to-day,
To bow down (now the ruffs are off their
    necks)
And own this good, true, noble Marian,
    yours,
And mine, I 'll say! — For poets (bear the
    word),
Half-poets even, are still whole demo-
    crats, —
Oh, not that we 're disloyal to the high,
But loyal to the low, and cognizant

Of the less scrutable majesties. For me,
I comprehend your choice, I justify 319
Your right in choosing.'
          'No, no, no,' he sighed,
With a sort of melancholy, impatient scorn,
As some grown man who never had a child
Puts by some child who plays at being a
          man,
'You did not, do not, cannot comprehend
My choice, my ends, my motives, nor my-
          self:
No matter now; we 'll let it pass, you say.
I thank you for your generous cousinship
Which helps this present; I accept for
          her
Your favorable thoughts. We 're fallen on
          days,
We two who are not poets, when to wed 330
Requires less mutual love than common
          love
For two together to bear out at once
Upon the loveless many. Work in pairs,
In galley-couplings or in marriage-rings,
The difference lies in the honor, not the
          work, —
And such we 're bound to, I and she. But
          love
(You poets are benighted in this age,
The hour 's too late for catching even moths,
You 've gnats instead), love ! — love's fool-
          paradise
Is out of date, like Adam's. Set a swan 340
To swim the Trenton, rather than true love
To float its fabulous plumage safely down
The cataracts of this loud transition-time, —
Whose roar for ever henceforth in my ears
Must keep me deaf to music.'
                    There, I turned
And kissed poor Marian, out of discon-
          tent.
The man had baffled, chafed me, till I flung
For refuge to the woman, — as, sometimes,
Impatient of some crowded room's close
          smell,
You throw a window open and lean out 350
To breathe a long breath in the dewy night
And cool your angry forehead. She, at
          least,
Was not built up as walls are, brick by
          brick,
Each fancy squared, each feeling ranged by
          line,
The very heat of burning youth applied
To indurate form and system ! excellent
          bricks,

A well-built wall, — which stops you on the
          road,
And into which you cannot see an inch
Although you beat your head against it —
          pshaw !

'Adieu,' I said, 'for this time, cousins
          both, 360
And, cousin Romney, pardon me the word,
Be happy ! — oh, in some esoteric sense
Of course ! — I mean no harm in wishing
          well.
Adieu, my Marian: — may she come to me,
Dear Romney, and be married from my
          house ?
It is not part of your philosophy
To keep your bird upon the blackthorn ?'
                              'Ay,'
He answered, 'but it is. I take my wife
Directly from the people, — and she comes,
As Austria's daughter to imperial France,
Betwixt her eagles, blinking not her race, 371
From Margaret's Court at garret-height, to
          meet
And wed me at Saint James's, nor put off
Her gown of serge for that. The things we
          do,
We do: we 'll wear no mask, as if we
          blushed.'
'Dear Romney, you 're the poet,' I replied,
But felt my smile too mournful for my
          word,
And turned and went. Ay, masks, I
          thought, — beware
Of tragic masks we tie before the glass,
Uplifted on the cothurn half a yard 380
Above the natural stature ! we would play
Heroic parts to ourselves, — and end, per-
          haps,
As impotently as Athenian wives
Who shrieked in fits at the Eumenides.

His foot pursued me down the stair. 'At
          least
You 'll suffer me to walk with you beyond
These hideous streets, those graves, where
          men alive
Packed close do walk with earthworms, burr uncon-
          sciously
About the plague that slew them; let me
          go,
The very women pelt their souls in mud 390
At any woman who walks here alone.
How came you here alone ? — you are ig-
          norant.'

We had a strange and melancholy walk:
The night came drizzling downward in
　dark rain,
And, as we walked, the color of the time,
The act, the presence, my hand upon his
　arm,
His voice in my ear, and mine to my own
　sense,
Appeared unnatural. We talked modern
　books
And daily papers, Spanish marriage-
　schemes
And English climate — was't so cold last
　year?　　　　　　　　　　　　　　400
And will the wind change by to-morrow
　morn?
Can Guizot stand? is London full? is
　trade
Competitive? has Dickens turned his
　hinge
A-pinch upon the fingers of the great?
And are potatoes to grow mythical
Like moly? will the apple die out too?
Which way is the wind to-night? south-
　east? due east?

We talked on fast, while every common
　word
Seemed tangled with the thunder at one
　end,
And ready to pull down upon our heads 410
A terror out of sight. And yet to pause
Were surelier mortal: we tore greedily
　up
All silence, all the innocent breathing-
　points,
As if, like pale conspirators in haste,
We tore up papers where our signatures
Imperilled us to an ugly shame or death.

I cannot tell you why it was. 'T is plain
We had not loved nor hated: wherefore
　dread
To spill gunpowder on ground safe from
　fire?
Perhaps we had lived too closely, to di-
　verge　　　　　　　　　　　　　420
So absolutely: leave two clocks, they say,
Wound up to different hours, upon one
　shelf,
And slowly, through the interior wheels of
　each,
The blind mechanic motion sets itself
A-throb to feel out for the mutual time.
It was not so with us, indeed: while he

Struck midnight, I kept striking six at
　dawn;
While he marked judgment, I, redemption-
　day;
And such exception to a general law
Imperious upon inert matter even,　　430
Might make us, each to either, insecure,
A beckoning mystery or a troubling fear.

I mind me, when we parted at the door,
How strange his good-night sounded, —
　like good-night
Beside a deathbed, where the morrow's sun
Is sure to come too late for more good-
　days:
And all that night I thought . . . 'Good-
　night,' said he.

And so, a month passed. Let me set it
　down
At once, — I have been wrong, I have been
　wrong.
We are wrong always when we think too
　much
Of what we think or are: albeit our
　thoughts　　　　　　　　　　　440
Be verily bitter as self-sacrifice,
We 're no less selfish. If we sleep on
　rocks
Or roses, sleeping past the hour of noon
We 're lazy. This I write against my-
　self.
I had done a duty in the visit paid
To Marian, and was ready otherwise
To give the witness of my presence and
　name
Whenever she should marry. — Which, I
　thought,
Sufficed. I even had cast into the scale 450
An overweight of justice toward the
　match;
The Lady Waldemar had missed her tool,
Had broken it in the lock as being too
　straight
For a crooked purpose, while poor Marian
　Erle
Missed nothing in my accents or my acts:
I had not been ungenerous on the whole,
Nor yet untender; so, enough. I felt
Tired, overworked: this marriage some-
　what jarred;
Or, if it did not, all the bridal noise,
The pricking of the map of life with pins,
In schemes of . . . 'Here we 'll go,' and
　'There we 'll stay,'　　　　　　461

And 'Everywhere we'll prosper in our
 love,'
Was scarce my business: let them order it;
Who else should care? I threw myself
 aside,
As one who had done her work and shuts
 her eyes
To rest the better.
                    I, who should have known,
Forereckoned mischief! Where we disa-
 vow
Being keeper to our brother, we're his
 Cain.

I might have held that poor child to my
 heart
A little longer! 't would have hurt me
 much   470
To have hastened by its beats the marriage
 day,
And kept her safe meantime from tamper-
 ing hands
Or, peradventure, traps. What drew me
 back
From telling Romney plainly the designs
Of Lady Waldemar, as spoken out
To me . . . me? Had I any right, ay,
 right,
With womanly compassion and reserve,
To break the fall of woman's impu-
 dence? —
To stand by calmly, knowing what I knew,
And hear him call her *good?*
                        Distrust that word.
'There is none good save God,' said Jesus
 Christ.   481
If He once, in the first creation-week,
Called creatures good, — for ever, after-
 ward,
The Devil only has done it, and his heirs,
The knaves who win so, and the fools who
 lose;
The word's grown dangerous. In the
 middle age,
I think they called malignant fays and
 imps
Good people. A good neighbor, even in
 this,
Is fatal sometimes, — cuts your morning
 up
To mincemeat of the very smallest talk, 490
Then helps to sugar her bohea at night
With your reputation. I have known good
 wives,
As chaste, or nearly so, as Potiphar's;

And good, good mothers, who would use a
 child
To better an intrigue; good friends, be-
 side
(Very good), who hung succinctly round
 your neck
And sucked your breath, as cats are fabled
 to do
By sleeping infants. And we all have
 known
Good critics who have stamped out poet's
 hope,
Good statesmen who pulled ruin on the
 state,   500
Good patriots who for a theory risked a
 cause,
Good kings who disembowelled for a tax,
Good popes who brought all good to jeop-
 ardy,
Good Christians who sat still in easy chairs
And damned the general world for stand-
 ing up. —
Now may the good God pardon all good
 men!

How bitterly I speak, — how certainly
The innocent white milk in us is turned,
By much persistent shining of the sun! —
Shake up the sweetest in us long
 enough,   510
With men, it drops to foolish curd, too
 sour
To feed the most untender of Christ's
 lambs.

I should have thought, — a woman of the
 world
Like her I'm meaning, centre to herself,
Who has wheeled on her own pivot half a
 life
In isolated self-love and self-will,
As a windmill seen at distance radiating
Its delicate white vans against the sky,
So soft and soundless, simply beautiful,
Seen nearer, — what a roar and tear it
 makes,   520
How it grinds and bruises! — if she loves
 at last,
Her love's a readjustment of self-love,
No more, — a need felt of another's use
To her one advantage, as the mill wants
 grain,
The fire wants fuel, the very wolf wants
 prey,
And none of these is more unscrupulous

Than such a charming woman when she
    loves.
She 'll not be thwarted by an obstacle
So trifling as . . . her soul is, . . . much less
    yours ! —
Is God a consideration ? — she loves
    you,   530
Not God; she will not flinch for Him in-
    deed:
She did not for the Marchioness of Perth,
When wanting tickets for the fancy ball.
She loves you, sir, with passion, to lunacy;
She loves you like her diamonds . . .
    almost.
            Well,
A month passed so, and then the notice
    came,
On such a day the marriage at the church.
I was not backward.
            Half Saint Giles in frieze
Was bidden to meet Saint James in cloth
    of gold,
And, after contract at the altar, pass   540
To eat a marriage-feast on Hampstead
    Heath.
Of course the people came in uncompelled,
Lame, blind, and worse — sick, sorrowful,
    and worse —
The humors of the peccant social wound
All pressed out, poured down upon Pim-
    lico,
Exasperating the unaccustomed air
With a hideous interfusion. You 'd sup-
    pose
A finished generation, dead of plague,
Swept outward from their graves into the
    sun,
The moil of death upon them. What a
    sight !   550
A holiday of miserable men
Is sadder than a burial-day of kings.
They clogged the streets, they oozed into
    the church
In a dark slow stream, like blood. To see
    that sight,
The noble ladies stood up in their pews,
Some pale for fear, a few as red for hate,
Some simply curious, some just insolent,
And some in wondering scorn, — ' What
    next ? what next ? '
These crushed their delicate rose-lips from
    the smile
That misbecame them in a holy place, 560
With broidered hems of perfumed hand-
    kerchiefs;

Those passed the salts, with confidence of
    eyes
And simultaneous shiver of moiré silk:
While all the aisles, alive and black with
    heads,
Crawled slowly toward the altar from the
    street,
As bruised snakes crawl and hiss out of a
    hole
With shuddering involution, swaying slow
From right to left, and then from left to
    right,
In pants and pauses. What an ugly crest
Of faces rose upon you everywhere   570
From that crammed mass ! you did not
    usually
See faces like them in the open day:
They hide in cellars, not to make you mad
As Romney Leigh is. — Faces ! — O my
    God,
We call those, faces ? men's and women's
    . . . ay,
And children's; — babies, hanging like a
    rag
Forgotten on their mother's neck, — poor
    mouths,
Wiped clean of mother's milk by mother's
    blow
Before they are taught her cursing. Faces ?
    . . . phew,
We 'll call them vices, festering to de-
    spairs,   580
Or sorrows, petrifying to vices: not
A finger-touch of God left whole on them,
All ruined, lost — the countenance worn
    out
As the garment, the will dissolute as the
    act,
The passions loose and draggling in the
    dirt
To trip a foot up at the first free step !
Those, faces ? 't was as if you had stirred
    up hell
To heave its lowest dreg-fiends upper-
    most
In fiery swirls of slime, — such strangled
    fronts,
Such obdurate jaws were thrown up con-
    stantly   590
To twit you with your race, corrupt your
    blood,
And grind to devilish colors all your
    dreams
Henceforth, — though, haply, you should
    drop asleep

By clink of silver waters, in a muse
On Raffael's mild Madonna of the Bird.

I 've waked and slept through many nights
    and days
Since then, — but still that day will catch
    my breath
Like a nightmare. There are fatal days,
    indeed,   598
In which the fibrous years have taken root
So deeply, that they quiver to their tops
Whene'er you stir the dust of such a day.

My cousin met me with his eyes and hand,
And then, with just a word, . . . that
    ' Marian Erle
Was coming with her bridesmaids pre-
    sently,'
Made haste to place me by the altar-stair
Where he and other noble gentlemen
And high-born ladies waited for the bride.

We waited. It was early: there was time
For greeting and the morning's compli-
    ment,   609
And gradually a ripple of women's talk
Arose and fell and tossed about a spray
Of English s's, soft as a silent hush,
And, notwithstanding, quite as audible
As louder phrases thrown out by the men.
— ' Yes, really, if we need to wait in
    church,
We need to talk there.' — ' She ? 't is
    Lady Ayr,
In blue — not purple ! that 's the dowager.'
— ' She looks as young ' — ' She flirts as
    young, you mean.
Why, if you had seen her upon Thursday
    night,
You 'd call Miss Norris modest.' — ' You
    again !   620
I waltzed with you three hours back. Up
    at six,
Up still at ten; scarce time to change
    one's shoes:
I feel as white and sulky as a ghost,
So pray don't speak to me, Lord Belcher.'
    — ' No,
I 'll look at you instead, and it 's enough
While you have that face.' ' In church,
    my lord ! fie, fie !'
— ' Adair, you stayed for the Division ? ' —
    ' Lost
By one.' ' The devil it is ! I 'm sorry
    for 't.

And if I had not promised Mistress
    Grove ' . . .
' You might have kept your word to Liver-
    pool.'   630
— ' Constituents must remember, after all,
We 're mortal.' — ' We remind them of it.'
    — ' Hark,
The bride comes ! here she comes, in a
    stream of milk !'
— ' There ? Dear, you are asleep still;
    don't you know
The five Miss Granvilles ? always dressed
    in white
To show they 're ready to be married.' —
    ' Lower !
The aunt is at your elbow.' — ' Lady
    Maud,
Did Lady Waldemar tell you she had seen
This girl of Leigh's ? ' ' No, — wait !
    't was Mistress Brookes,   639
Who told me Lady Waldemar told her —
No, 't was n't Mistress Brookes.' — ' She 's
    pretty ? ' — ' Who ?
Mistress Brookes ? Lady Waldemar ? ' —
    ' How hot !
Pray is 't the law to-day we 're not to
    breathe ?
You 're treading on my shawl — I thank
    you, sir.'
— ' They say the bride 's a mere child,
    who can't read,
But knows the things she should n't, with
    wide-awake
Great eyes. I 'd go through fire to look
    at her.'
— ' You do, I think.' — ' And Lady Walde-
    mar
(You see her; sitting close to Romney
    Leigh.   649
How beautiful she looks, a little flushed !)
Has taken up the girl, and methodized
Leigh's folly. Should I have come here,
    you suppose,
Except she 'd asked me ? ' — ' She 'd have
    served him more
By marrying him herself.'
                 ' Ah — there she comes,
The bride, at last !'
                    ' Indeed, no. Past eleven.
She puts off her patched petticoat to-day
And puts on Mayfair manners, so begins
By setting us to wait.' — ' Yes, yes, this
    Leigh
Was always odd; it 's in the blood, I think;
His father's uncle's cousin's second son   660

Was, was . . . you understand me; and
     for him,
He's stark, — has turned quite lunatic
     upon
This modern question of the poor — the
     poor.
An excellent subject when you're moder-
     ate;
You've seen Prince Albert's model lodging-
     house ?
Does honor to his Royal Highness. Good !
But would he stop his carriage in Cheap-
     side
To shake a common fellow by the fist
Whose name was . . . Shakespeare ? No.
     We draw a line,
And if we stand not by our order, we   670
In England, we fall headlong. Here's a
     sight, —
A hideous sight, a most indecent sight !
My wife would come, sir, or I had kept her
     back.
By heaven, sir, when poor Damiens' trunk
     and limbs
Were torn by horses, women of the court
Stood by and stared, exactly as to-day
On this dismembering of society,
With pretty, troubled faces.'
                         ' Now, at last.
She comes now.'
     ' Where ? who sees ? you push me, sir,
Beyond the point of what is mannerly.   680
You're standing, madam, on my second
     flounce.
I do beseech you . . . '
                    ' No — it's not the bride.
Half-past eleven. How late. The bride-
     groom, mark,
Gets anxious and goes out.'
                         ' And as I said,
These Leighs ! our best blood running in
     the rut !
It's something awful. We had pardoned
     him
A simple misalliance got up aside
For a pair of sky-blue eyes; the House of
     Lords
Has winked at such things, and we've all
     been young;
But here's an intermarriage reasoned out,
A contract (carried boldly to the light   691
To challenge observation, pioneer
Good acts by a great example) 'twixt the
     extremes
Of martyrized society, — on the left

The well-born, on the right the merest mob,
To treat as equals ! — 't is anarchical;
It means more than it says; 't is damnable.
Why, sir, we can't have even our coffee
     good,
Unless we strain it.'
               ' Here, Miss Leigh !'
                         ' Lord Howe.
You're Romney's friend. What's all this
     waiting for ?'   700

' I cannot tell. The bride has lost her head
(And way, perhaps !) to prove her sympathy
With the bridegroom.'
               ' What, — you also, disapprove !'

' Oh, I approve of nothing in the world,'
He answered, ' not of you, still less of me,
Nor even of Romney, though he's worth
     us both.
We're all gone wrong. The tune in us is
     lost;
And whistling down back alleys to the
     moon
Will never catch it.'
               Let me draw Lord Howe.
A born aristocrat, bred radical,   710
And educated socialist, who still
Goes floating, on traditions of his kind,
Across the theoretic flood from France,
Though, like a drenched Noah on a rotten
     deck,
Scarce safer for his place there. He, at
     least,
Will never land on Ararat, he knows,
To recommence the world on the new plan:
Indeed, he thinks, said world had better
     end.
He sympathizes rather with the fish
Outside, than with the drowned paired
     beasts within   720
Who cannot couple again or multiply, —
And that's the sort of Noah he is, Lord
     Howe.
He never could be anything complete,
Except a loyal, upright gentleman,
A liberal landlord, graceful diner-out,
And entertainer more than hospitable,
Whom authors dine with and forget the
     hock.
Whatever he believes, and it is much,
But nowise certain, now here and now there,
He still has sympathies beyond his creed 730
Diverting him from action. In the House,
No party counts upon him, while for all

His speeches have a noticeable weight.
Men like his books too (he has written
  books),
Which, safe to lie beside a bishop's chair,
At times outreach themselves with jets of
  fire
At which the foremost of the progressists
May warm audacious hands in passing by.
Of stature over-tall, lounging for ease;
Light hair, that seems to carry a wind in
  it,
And eyes that, when they look on you, will
  lean   741
Their whole weight, half in indolence and
  half
In wishing you unmitigated good,
Until you know not if to flinch from him
Or thank him. — 'T is Lord Howe.
                  ' We 're all gone wrong,'
Said he; ' and Romney, that dear friend
  of ours,
Is nowise right. There 's one true thing
  on earth,
That 's love ! he takes it up, and dresses it,
And acts a play with it, as Hamlet did,
To show what cruel uncles we have been, 750
And how we should be uneasy in our minds
While he, Prince Hamlet, weds a pretty
  maid
(Who keeps us too long waiting, we 'll con-
  fess)
By symbol, to instruct us formally
To fill the ditches up 'twixt class and class,
And live together in phalansteries.
What then ? — he 's mad, our Hamlet ! clap
  his play,
And bind him.'
            ' Ah, Lord Howe, this spectacle
Pulls stronger at us than the Dane's. See
  there !
The crammed aisles heave and strain and
  steam with life.   760
Dear Heaven, what life ! '
                ' Why, yes, — a poet sees;
Which makes him different from a common
  man.
I, too, see somewhat, though I cannot sing;
I should have been a poet, only that
My mother took fright at the ugly world,
And bore me tongue-tied. If you 'll grant
  me now
That Romney gives us a fine actor-piece
To make us merry on his marriage-morn,
The fable 's worse than Hamlet's I 'll con-
  cede.

The terrible people, old and poor and
  blind,   770
Their eyes eat out with plague and pov-
  erty
From seeing beautiful and cheerful sights,
We 'll liken to a brutalized King Lear,
Led out, — by no means to clear scores
  with wrongs —
His wrongs are so far back, he has for-
  got
(All 's past like youth); but just to witness
  here
A simple contract, — he, upon his side,
And Regan with her sister Goneril
And all the dappled courtiers and court-
  fools
On their side. Not that any of these would
  say   780
They 're sorry, neither. What is done, is
  done,
And violence is now turned privilege,
As cream turns cheese, if buried long
  enough.
What could such lovely ladies have to do
With the old man there, in those ill-odor-
  ous rags,
Except to keep the wind-side of him ?
  Lear
Is flat and quiet, as a decent grave;
He does not curse his daughters in the
  least:
Be these his daughters ? Lear is thinking
  of
His porridge chiefly . . . is it getting cold
At Hampstead ? will the ale be served in
  pots ?   791
Poor Lear, poor daughters ! Bravo, Rom-
  ney's play ! '

A murmur and a movement drew around,
A naked whisper touched us. Something
  wrong.
What 's wrong ? The black crowd, as an
  overstrained
Cord, quivered in vibration, and I saw . . .
Was that *his* face I saw ? . . . his . . .
  Romney Leigh's
Which tossed a sudden horror like a sponge
Into all eyes, — while himself stood white
  upon   799
The topmost altar-stair and tried to speak,
And failed, and lifted higher above his
  head
A letter, . . . as a man who drowns and
  gasps.

'My brothers, bear with me! I am very
    weak.
I meant but only good. Perhaps I meant
Too proudly, and God snatched the circum-
    stance
And changed it therefore. There's no
    marriage — none.
She leaves me, — she departs, — she disap-
    pears, —
I lose her. Yet I never forced her " ay,"
To have her " no " so cast into my teeth
In manner of an accusation, thus.   810
My friends, you are dismissed. Go, eat
    and drink
According to the programme, — and fare-
    well !'
He ended. There was silence in the
    church.
We heard a baby sucking in its sleep
At the farthest end of the aisle. Then
    spoke a man:
'Now, look to it, coves, that all the beef
    and drink
Be not filched from us like the other fun,
For beer's spilt easier than a woman's
    lost !
This gentry is not honest with the poor;
They bring us up, to trick us.' — ' Go it,
    Jim,'   820
A woman screamed back, — ' I 'm a tender
    soul,
I never banged a child at two years old
And drew blood from him, but I sobbed
    for it
Next moment, — and I 've had a plague of
    seven.
I 'm tender; I 've no stomach even for
    beef,
Until I know about the girl that 's lost,
That 's killed, mayhap. I did misdoubt, at
    first,
The fine lord meant no good by her or us.
He, maybe, got the upper hand of her
By holding up a wedding - ring, and
    then . . .   830
A choking finger on her throat last night,
And just a clever tale to keep us still,
As she is, poor lost innocent. " Disap-
    pear ! "
Who ever disappears except a ghost ?
And who believes a story of a ghost ?
I ask you, — would a girl go off, instead
Of staying to be married ? a fine tale !
A wicked man, I say, a wicked man !
For my part, I would rather starve on gin

Than make my dinner on his beef and
    beer.' —   840
At which a cry rose up — ' We 'll have our
    rights.
We 'll have the girl, the girl ! Your ladies
    there
Are married safely and smoothly every
    day,
And *she* shall not drop through into a trap
Because she 's poor and of the people:
    shame !
We 'll have no tricks played off by gentle-
    folk;
We 'll see her righted.'
              Through the rage and roar
I heard the broken words which Romney
    flung
Among the turbulent masses, from the
    ground
He held still with his masterful pale
    face, —   850
As huntsmen throw the ration to the pack,
Who, falling on it headlong, dog on dog
In heaps of fury, rend it, swallow it up
With yelling hound-jaws, — his indignant
    words,
His suppliant words, his most pathetic
    words,
Whereof I caught the meaning here and
    there
By his gesture . . . torn in morsels, yelled
    across,
And so devoured. From end to end, the
    church
Rocked round us like the sea in storm, and
    then
Broke up like the earth in earthquake.
    Men cried out   860
' Police ' — and women stood and shrieked
    for God,
Or dropped and swooned; or, like a herd
    of deer
(For whom the black woods suddenly grow
    alive,
Unleashing their wild shadows down the
    wind
To hunt the creatures into corners, back
And forward), madly fled, or blindly fell,
Trod screeching underneath the feet of
    those
Who fled and screeched.
              The last sight left to me
Was Romney's terrible calm face above
The tumult ! — the last sound was ' Pull
    him down !   87

Strike — kill him !' Stretching my un-
    reasoning arms,
As men in dreams, who vainly interpose
'Twixt gods and their undoing, with a cry
I struggled to precipitate myself
Head-foremost to the rescue of my soul
In that white face, . . . till some one
    caught me back,
And so the world went out, — I felt no
    more.

What followed was told after by Lord
    Howe,
Who bore me senseless from the strangling
    crowd
In church and street, and then returned
    alone   880
To see the tumult quelled. The men of
    law
Had fallen as thunder on a roaring fire,
And made all silent, — while the people's
    smoke
Passed eddying slowly from the emptied
    aisles.

Here's Marian's letter, which a ragged
    child
Brought running, just as Romney at the
    porch
Looked out expectant of the bride. He
    sent
The letter to me by his friend Lord Howe
Some two hours after, folded in a sheet
On which his well-known hand had left a
    word.   890
Here's Marian's letter.
           'Noble friend, dear saint,
Be patient with me. Never think me vile
Who might to-morrow morning be your
    wife
But that I loved you more than such a
    name.
Farewell, my Romney. Let me write it
    once, —
My Romney.
        ''T is so pretty a coupled word,
I have no heart to pluck it with a blot.
We say " my God " sometimes, upon our
    knees,
Who is not therefore vexed: so bear with
    it . . .
And me. I know I 'm foolish, weak, and
    vain: 900
Yet most of all I 'm angry with myself
For losing your last footstep on the stair

That last time of your coming, — yester-
    day !
The very first time I lost step of yours
(Its sweetness comes the next to what you
    speak),
But yesterday sobs took me by the throat
And cut me off from music.
           'Mister Leigh,
You 'll set me down as wrong in many
    things.
You 've praised me, sir, for truth, — and
    now you 'll learn
I had not courage to be rightly true.   910
I once began to tell you how she came,
The woman . . . and you stared upon the
    floor
In one of your fixed thoughts . . . which
    put me out
For that day. After, some one spoke of
    me,
So wisely, and of you, so tenderly,
Persuading me to silence for your
    sake . . .
Well, well ! it seems this moment I was
    wrong
In keeping back from telling you the
    truth:
There might be truth betwixt us two, at
    least,
If nothing else. And yet 't was danger-
    ous.   920
Suppose a real angel came from heaven
To live with men and women ! he 'd go
    mad,
If no considerate hand should tie a blind
Across his piercing eyes. 'T is thus with
    you:
You see us too much in your heavenly
    light;
I always thought so, angel, — and indeed
There 's danger that you beat yourself to
    death
Against the edges of this alien world,
In some divine and fluttering pity.
           'Yes,
It would be dreadful for a friend of
    yours,   930
To see all England thrust you out of doors
And mock you from the windows. You
    might say,
Or think (that 's worse) " There 's some
    one in the house
I miss and love still." Dreadful !
           'Very kind,
I pray you mark, was Lady Waldemar.

She came to see me nine times, rather
    ten —
So beautiful, she hurts one like the day
Let suddenly on sick eyes.
                'Most kind of all,
Your cousin! — ah, most like you! Ere
    you came
She kissed me mouth to mouth: I felt her
    soul   940
Dip through her serious lips in holy fire.
God help me, but it made me arrogant;
I almost told her that you would not
    lose
By taking me to wife: though ever since
I 've pondered much a certain thing she
    asked . . .
"He loves you, Marian?" . . . in a sort
    of mild
Derisive sadness . . . as a mother asks
Her babe, "You 'll touch that star, you
    think?"
              'Farewell!
I know I never touched it.
                  'This is worst:
Babes grow and lose the hope of things
    above;   950
A silver threepence sets them leaping
    high —
But no more stars! mark that.
              'I 've writ all night
Yet told you nothing. God, if I could
    die,
And let this letter break off innocent
Just here! But no — for your sake.
             'Here 's the last:
I never could be happy as your wife,
I never could be harmless as your friend,
I never will look more into your face
Till God says "Look!" I charge you,
    seek me not,   959
Nor vex yourself with lamentable thoughts
That peradventure I have come to grief;
Be sure I 'm well, I 'm merry, I 'm at ease,
But such a long way, long way, long way
    off,
I think you 'll find me sooner in my grave,
And that 's my choice, observe. For what
    remains,
An over-generous friend will care for me
And keep me happy . . . happier . . .
             'There 's a blot!
This ink runs thick . . . we light girls lightly
    weep . . .
And keep me happier . . . was the thing to
    say,

Than as your wife I could be. — O, my
    star,   970
My saint, my soul! for surely you 're my
    soul,
Through whom God touched me! I am not
    so lost
I cannot thank you for the good you did,
The tears you stopped, which fell down
    bitterly,
Like these — the times you made me weep
    for joy
At hoping I should learn to write your
    notes
And save the tiring of your eyes, at night;
And most for that sweet thrice you kissed
    my lips
Saying "Dear Marian."
            'T would be hard to read,
This letter, for a reader half as learn'd; 980
But you 'll be sure to master it in spite
Of ups and downs. My hand shakes, I am
    blind;
I 'm poor at writing at the best, — and yet
I tried to make my g's the way you
    showed.
Farewell. Christ love you. — Say "poor
    Marian" now.'

Poor Marian! — wanton Marian! — was it
    so,
Or so? For days, her touching, foolish
    lines
We mused on with conjectural fantasy,
As if some riddle of a summer-cloud
On which one tries unlike similitudes 990
Of now a spotted Hydra-skin cast off,
And now a screen of carven ivory
That shuts the heavens' conventual secrets
    up
From mortals overbold. We sought the
    sense:
She loved him so perhaps (such words mean
    love),
That, worked on by some shrewd perfidious
    tongue
(And then I thought of Lady Waldemar),
She left him, not to hurt him; or per-
    haps
She loved one in her class, — or did not
    love,
But mused upon her wild bad tramping
    life   1000
Until the free blood fluttered at her heart,
And black bread eaten by the roadside
    hedge

Seemed sweeter than being put to Romney's
　　school
Of philanthropical self-sacrifice
Irrevocably. — Girls are girls, beside,
Thought I, and like a wedding by one
　　rule.
You seldom catch these birds except with
　　chaff:
They feel it almost an immoral thing
To go out and be married in broad day,
Unless some winning special flattery
　　should　　　　　　　　　　　　1010
Excuse them to themselves for 't, . . . 'No
　　one parts
Her hair with such a silver line as you,
One moonbeam from the forehead to the
　　crown!'
Or else . . . 'You bite your lip in such a
　　way
It spoils me for the smiling of the rest,'
And so on. Then a worthless gaud or
　　two
To keep for love, — a ribbon for the neck,
Or some glass pin, — they have their weight
　　with girls.
And Romney sought her many days and
　　weeks:
He sifted all the refuse of the town,　　1020
Explored the trains, inquired among the
　　ships,
And felt the country through from end to
　　end;
No Marian! — Though I hinted what I
　　knew, —
A friend of his had reasons of her own
For throwing back the match — he would
　　not hear:
The lady had been ailing ever since,
The shock had harmed her.　Something in
　　his tone
Repressed me; something in me shamed my
　　doubt
To a sigh repressed too.　He went on to
　　say
That, putting questions where his Marian
　　lodged,　　　　　　　　　　　　1030
He found she had received for visitors,
Besides himself and Lady Waldemar
And, that once, me — a dubious woman
　　dressed
Beyond us both: the rings upon her hands
Had dazed the children when she threw
　　them pence;
'She wore her bonnet as the queen might
　　hers,

To show the crown,' they said, — 'a scarlet
　　crown
Of roses that had never been in bud.'

When Romney told me that, — for now and
　　then
He came to tell me how the search ad-
　　vanced,　　　　　　　　　　　　1040
His voice dropped: I bent forward for the
　　rest:
The woman had been with her, it ap-
　　peared,
At first from week to week, then day by
　　day,
And last, 't was sure . . .
　　　　　　　　I looked upon the ground
To escape the anguish of his eyes, and
　　asked
As low as when you speak to mourners
　　now
Of those they cannot bear yet to call dead,
'If Marian had as much as named to him
A certain Rose, an early friend of hers,
A ruined creature.'
　　　　　　　'Never.' — Starting up
He strode from side to side about the
　　room,　　　　　　　　　　　　1051
Most like some prisoned lion sprung
　　awake,
Who has felt the desert sting him through
　　his dreams.
'What was I to her, that she should tell
　　me aught?
A friend! was I a friend? I see all clear.
Such devils would pull angels out of hea-
　　ven,
Provided they could reach them; 't is their
　　pride;
And that's the odds 'twixt soul and body
　　plague!
The veriest slave who drops in Cairo's
　　street
Cries "Stand off from me" to the passen-
　　gers;　　　　　　　　　　　　1060
While these blotched souls are eager to
　　infect,
And blow their bad breath in a sister's
　　face
As if they got some ease by it.'
　　　　　　　　　　I broke through.
'Some natures catch no plagues. I've read
　　of babes
Found whole and sleeping by the spotted
　　breast
Of one a full day dead. I hold it true,

As I 'm a woman and know womanhood,
That Marian Erle, however lured from
　　place,
Deceived in way, keeps pure in aim and
　　heart
As snow that 's drifted from the garden-
　　bank　　　　　　　　　　　　　　1070
To the open road.'
　　　　　　　'T was hard to hear him laugh.
' The figure 's happy. Well — a dozen
　　carts
And trampers will secure you presently
A fine white snow-drift. Leave it there,
　　your snow:
'T will pass for soot ere sunset. Pure in
　　aim ?
She 's pure in aim, I grant you, — like my-
　　self,
Who thought to take the world upon my
　　back
To carry it o'er a chasm of social ill,
And end by letting slip through impotence
A single soul, a child's weight in a soul, 1080
Straight down the pit of hell ! yes, I and
　　she
Have reason to be proud of our pure aims.'
Then softly, as the last repenting drops
Of a thunder-shower, he added, ' The poor
　　child,
Poor Marian ! 't was a luckless day for her
When first she chanced on my philan-
　　thropy.'

He drew a chair beside me, and sat down;
And I, instinctively, as women use
Before a sweet friend's grief, — when, in
　　his ear,
They hum the tune of comfort though
　　themselves　　　　　　　　　　1090
Most ignorant of the special words of such,
And quiet so and fortify his brain
And give it time and strength for feeling
　　out
To reach the availing sense beyond that
　　sound, —
Went murmuring to him what, if written
　　here,
Would seem not much, yet fetched him
　　better help
Than peradventure if it had been more.

I 've known the pregnant thinkers of our
　　time,
And stood by breathless, hanging on their
　　lips,

When some chromatic sequence of fine
　　thought　　　　　　　　　　　1100
In learned modulation phrased itself
To an unconjectured harmony of truth:
And yet I 've been more moved, more
　　raised, I say,
By a simple word . . . a broken easy
　　thing
A three-years' infant might at need repeat,
A look, a sigh, a touch upon the palm,
Which meant less than ' I love you,' than
　　by all
The full-voiced rhetoric of those master-
　　mouths.

' Ah, dear Aurora,' he began at last,
His pale lips fumbling for a sort of smile,
' Your printer's devils have not spoilt
　　your heart:　　　　　　　　　　1111
That 's well. And who knows but, long
　　years ago
When you and I talked, you were some-
　　what right
In being so peevish with me ? You, at
　　least,
Have ruined no one through your dreams.
　　Instead,
You 've helped the facile youth to live
　　youth's day
With innocent distraction, still perhaps
Suggestive of things better than your
　　rhymes.
The little shepherd-maiden, eight years
　　old,　　　　　　　　　　　　1119
I 've seen upon the mountains of Vaucluse,
Asleep i' the sun, her head upon her knees,
The flocks all scattered, — is more laudable
Than any sheep-dog, trained imperfectly,
Who bites the kids through too much zeal.'
　　　　　　　　　　　　　　' I look
As if I had slept, then ? '
　　　　　　　　　　　He was touched at once
By something in my face. Indeed 't was
　　sure
That he and I, — despite a year or two
Of younger life on my side, and on his
The heaping of the years' work on the
　　days,
The three-hour speeches from the member's
　　seat,　　　　　　　　　　　1130
The hot committees in and out of doors,
The pamphlets, ' Arguments,' ' Collective
　　Views,'
Tossed out as straw before sick houses,
　　just

To show one's sick and so be trod to dirt
And no more use, — through this world's
    underground,
The burrowing, groping effort, whence the
    arm
And heart come torn, — 't was sure that he
    and I
Were, after all, unequally fatigued;
That he, in his developed manhood, stood
A little sunburnt by the glare of life,   1140
While I . . . it seemed no sun had shone
    on me,
So many seasons I had missed my Springs.
My cheeks had pined and perished from
    their orbs,
And all the youth-blood in them had grown
    white
As dew on autumn cyclamens: alone
My eyes and forehead answered for my
    face.

He said, 'Aurora, you are changed — are
    ill!'

'Not so, my cousin, — only not asleep,'
I answered, smiling gently.   'Let it be.
You scarcely found the poet of Vaucluse
As drowsy as the shepherds.   What is
    art   1151
But life upon the larger scale, the higher,
When, graduating up in a spiral line
Of still expanding and ascending gyres,
It pushes toward the intense significance
Of all things, hungry for the Infinite?
Art's life, — and where we live, we suffer
    and toil.'

He seemed to sift me with his painful
    eyes.
'You take it gravely, cousin; you refuse
Your dreamland's right of common, and
    green rest.   1160
You break the mythic turf where danced
    the nymphs,
With crooked ploughs of actual life, — let
    in
The axes to the legendary woods,
To pay the poll-tax.   You are fallen in-
    deed
On evil days, you poets, if yourselves
Can praise that art of yours no otherwise;
And, if you cannot, . . . better take a
    trade
And be of use: 't were cheaper for your
    youth.'

'Of use!'   I softly echoed, 'there's the
    point
We sweep about for ever in argument,   1170
Like swallows which the exasperate, dying
    year
Sets spinning in black circles, round and
    round,
Preparing for far flights o'er unknown seas.
And we, where tend we?'
            'Where?' he said, and sighed.
'The whole creation, from the hour we are
    born,
Perplexes us with questions.   Not a stone
But cries behind us, every weary step,
"Where, where?" I leave stones to reply
    to stones.
Enough for me and for my fleshly heart
To hearken the invocations of my kind,   1180
When men catch hold upon my shuddering
    nerves
And shriek "What help? what hope?
    what bread i' the house,
What fire i' the frost?"   There must be
    some response,
Though mine fail utterly.   This social
    Sphinx
Who sits between the sepulchres and stews,
Makes mock and mow against the crystal
    heavens,
And bullies God, — exacts a word at least
From each man standing on the side of
    God,
However paying a sphinx-price for it.
We pay it also if we hold our peace,   1190
In pangs and pity.   Let me speak and die.
Alas, you'll say I speak and kill instead.'
I pressed in there.   'The best men, doing
    their best,
Know peradventure least of what they do:
Men usefullest i' the world are simply used;
The nail that holds the wood must pierce it
    first,
And He alone who wields the hammer sees
The work advanced by the earliest blow.
Take heart.'

'Ah, if I could have taken yours!' he
    said,
'But that's past now.'   Then rising, — 'I
    will take   1200
At least your kindness and encouragement.
I thank you.   Dear, be happy.   Sing your
    songs,
If that's your way! but sometimes slum-
    ber too,

Nor tire too much with following, out of
  breath,
The rhymes upon your mountains of De-
  light.
Reflect, if Art be in truth the higher life,
You need the lower life to stand upon
In order to reach up unto that higher;
And none can stand a-tiptoe in the place
He cannot stand in with two stable feet. 1210
Remember then ! — for Art's sake, hold
  your life.'

We parted so. I held him in respect.
I comprehended what he was in heart
And sacrificial greatness. Ay, but he
Supposed me a thing too small, to deign to
  know:
He blew me, plainly, from the crucible
As some intruding, interrupting fly,
Not worth the pains of his analysis
Absorbed on nobler subjects. Hurt a fly !
He would not for the world: he 's pitiful 1220
To flies even. 'Sing,' says he, 'and tease
  me still,
If that 's your way, poor insect.' That 's
  your way !

FIFTH BOOK

Aurora Leigh, be humble. Shall I hope
To speak my poems in mysterious tune
With man and nature ? — with the lava-
  lymph
That trickles from successive galaxies
Still drop by drop adown the finger of
  God
In still new worlds ? — with summer-days
  in this
That scarce dare breathe they are so beau-
  tiful ?
With spring's delicious trouble in the
  ground,
Tormented by the quickened blood of roots,
And softly pricked by golden crocus-sheaves
In token of the harvest-time of flowers ? 11
With winters and with autumns, — and be-
  yond
With the human heart's large seasons, when
  it hopes
And fears, joys, grieves, and loves ? — with
  all that strain
Of sexual passion, which devours the flesh
In a sacrament of souls ? with mother's
  breasts

Which, round the new-made creatures
  hanging there,
Throb luminous and harmonious like pure
  spheres ? —
With multitudinous life, and finally
With the great escapings of ecstatic souls, 20
Who, in a rush of too long prisoned flame,
Their radiant faces upward, burn away
This dark of the body, issuing on a world
Beyond our mortal ? — can I speak my
  verse
So plainly in tune to these things and the
  rest
That men shall feel it catch them on the
  quick
As having the same warrant over them
To hold and move them if they will or no,
Alike imperious as the primal rhythm
Of that theurgic nature ? — I must fail, 30
Who fail at the beginning to hold and move
One man, — and he my cousin, and he my
  friend,
And he born tender, made intelligent,
Inclined to ponder the precipitous sides
Of difficult questions; yet, obtuse to *me*,
Of *me*, incurious ! likes me very well,
And wishes me a paradise of good,
Good looks, good means, and good digestion,
  — ay,
But otherwise evades me, puts me off
With kindness, with a tolerant gentleness,—
Too light a book for a grave man's read-
  ing ! Go,   41
Aurora Leigh: be humble.
                              There it is,
We women are too apt to look to one,
Which proves a certain impotence in art.
We strain our natures at doing something
  great,
Far less because it 's something great to do,
Than haply that we, so, commend ourselves
As being not small, and more appreciable
To some one friend. We must have medi-
  ators
Betwixt our highest conscience and the
  judge;   50
Some sweet saint's blood must quicken in
  our palms,
Or all the life in heaven seems slow and
  cold:
Good only being perceived as the end of
  good,
And God alone pleased, — that 's too poor,
  we think,
And not enough for us by any means.

Ay — Romney, I remember, told me once
We miss the abstract when we compre-
hend.
We miss it most when we aspire, — and fail.

Yet, so, I will not. — This vile woman's
way
Of trailing garments shall not trip me up:
I'll have no traffic with the personal
thought 61
In Art's pure temple. Must I work in
vain,
Without the approbation of a man ?
It cannot be; it shall not. Fame itself,
That approbation of the general race,
Presents a poor end (though the arrow
speed
Shot straight with vigorous finger to the
white),
And the highest fame was never reached
except
By what was aimed above it. Art for art,
And good for God Himself, the essential
Good ! 70
We'll keep our aims sublime, our eyes
erect,
Although our woman-hands should shake
and fail;
And if we fail . . . But must we ? —
Shall I fail ?
The Greeks said grandly in their tragic
phrase,
'Let no one be called happy till his death.'
To which I add, — Let no one till his
death
Be called unhappy. Measure not the work
Until the day's out and the labor done,
Then bring your gauges. If the day's
work's scant,
Why, call it scant; affect no compromise;
And, in that we have nobly striven at
least, 81
Deal with us nobly, women though we be,
And honor us with truth if not with praise.

My ballads prospered; but the ballad's
race
Is rapid for a poet who bears weights
Of thought and golden image. He can
stand
Like Atlas, in the sonnet, — and support
His own heavens pregnant with dynastic
stars;
But then he must stand still, nor take a
step.

In that descriptive poem called ' The
Hills,' 90
The prospects were too far and indistinct.
'Tis true my critics said ' A fine view,
that ! '
The public scarcely cared to climb my book
For even the finest, and the public's right;
A tree's mere firewood, unless human-
ized, —
Which well the Greeks knew when they
stirred its bark
With close-pressed bosoms of subsiding
nymphs,
And made the forest-rivers garrulous
With babble of gods. For us, we are
called to mark
A still more intimate humanity 100
In this inferior nature, or ourselves
Must fall like dead leaves trodden under-
foot
By veritable artists. Earth (shut up
By Adam, like a fakir in a box
Left too long buried) remained stiff and
dry,
A mere dumb corpse, till Christ the Lord
came down,
Unlocked the doors, forced open the blank
eyes,
And used his kingly chrism to straighten
out
The leathery tongue turned back into the
throat;
Since when, she lives, remembers, palpi-
tates 110
In every limb, aspires in every breath,
Embraces infinite relations. Now
We want no half-gods, Panomphæan Joves,
Fauns, Naiads, Tritons, Oreads and the
rest,
To take possession of a senseless world
To unnatural vampire-uses. See the earth,
The body of our body, the green earth,
Indubitably human like this flesh
And these articulated veins through which
Our heart drives blood. There's not a
flower of spring 120
That dies ere June but vaunts itself al-
lied
By issue and symbol, by significance
And correspondence, to that spirit-world
Outside the limits of our space and time,
Whereto we are bound. Let poets give it
voice
With human meanings, — else they miss
the thought,

And henceforth step down lower, stand confessed
Instructed poorly for interpreters,
Thrown out by an easy cowslip in the text.
Even so my pastoral failed: it was a book
Of surface-pictures — pretty, cold, and false
With literal transcript, — the worse done, I think,   132
For being not ill-done: let me set my mark
Against such doings, and do otherwise.
This strikes me. — If the public whom we know
Could catch me at such admissions, I should pass
For being right modest. Yet how proud we are,
In daring to look down upon ourselves !

The critics say that epics have died out
With Agamemnon and the goat - nursed gods;   140
I 'll not believe it. I could never deem,
As Payne Knight did (the mythic mountaineer
Who travelled higher than he was born to live,
And showed sometimes the goitre in his throat
Discoursing of an image seen through fog),
That Homer's heroes measured twelve feet high.
They were but men: — his Helen's hair turned gray
Like any plain Miss Smith's who wears a front;
And Hector's infant whimpered at a plume
As yours last Friday at a turkey-cock.   150
All actual heroes are essential men,
And all men possible heroes: every age,
Heroic in proportions, double-faced,
Looks backward and before, expects a morn
And claims an epos.
                    Ay, but every age
Appears to souls who live in 't (ask Carlyle)
Most unheroic. Ours, for instance, ours:
The thinkers scout it, and the poets abound
Who scorn to touch it with a finger-tip:
A pewter age, — mixed metal, silver-washed;   160
An age of scum, spooned off the richer past,

An age of patches for old gaberdines,
An age of mere transition, meaning nought
Except that what succeeds must shame it quite
If God please. That 's wrong thinking, to my mind,
And wrong thoughts make poor poems.
                                  Every age,
Through being beheld too close, is ill-discerned
By those who have not lived past it. We 'll suppose
Mount Athos carved, as Alexander schemed,
To some colossal statue of a man.   170
The peasants, gathering brushwood in his ear,
Had guessed as little as the browsing goats
Of form or feature of humanity
Up there, — in fact, had travelled five miles off
Or ere the giant image broke on them,
Full human profile, nose and chin distinct,
Mouth, muttering rhythms of silence up the sky
And fed at evening with the blood of suns;
Grand torso, — hand, that flung perpetually
The largesse of a silver river down   180
To all the country pastures. 'T is even thus
With times we live in, — evermore too great
To be apprehended near.
                        But poets should
Exert a double vision; should have eyes
To see near things as comprehensively
As if afar they took their point of sight,
And distant things as intimately deep
As if they touched them. Let us strive for this.
I do distrust the poet who discerns
No character or glory in his times,   190
And trundles back his soul five hundred years,
Past moat and drawbridge, into a castle-court,
To sing — oh, not of lizard or of toad
Alive i' the ditch there, — 't were excusable,
But of some black chief, half knight, half sheep-lifter,
Some beauteous dame, half chattel and half queen,
As dead as must be, for the greater part,

The poems made on their chivalric bones;
And that's no wonder: death inherits
    death.

Nay, if there's room for poets in this
    world   200
A little overgrown (I think there is),
Their sole work is to represent the age,
Their age, not Charlemagne's, — this live,
    throbbing age,
That brawls, cheats, maddens, calculates,
    aspires,
And spends more passion, more heroic
    heat,
Betwixt the mirrors of its drawing-rooms,
Than Roland with his knights at Ronces-
    valles.
To flinch from modern varnish, coat or
    flounce,
Cry out for togas and the picturesque,
Is fatal, — foolish too. King Arthur's
    self   210
Was commonplace to Lady Guenever;
And Camelot to minstrels seemed as flat
As Fleet Street to our poets.
                Never flinch,
But still, unscrupulously epic, catch
Upon the burning lava of a song
The full-veined, heaving, double-breasted
    Age:
That, when the next shall come, the men
    of that
May touch the impress with reverent hand,
    and say
'Behold, — behold the paps we all have
    sucked !
This bosom seems to beat still, or at
    least   220
It sets ours beating: this is living art,
Which thus presents and thus records true
    life.'

What form is best for poems? Let me
    think
Of forms less, and the external. Trust
    the spirit,
As sovran nature does, to make the form;
For otherwise we only imprison spirit
And not embody. Inward evermore
To outward, — so in life, and so in art
Which still is life.
             Five acts to make a play.
And why not fifteen? why not ten? or
    seven?   230
What matter for the number of the leaves,

Supposing the tree lives and grows?
    exact
The literal unities of time and place,
When 't is the essence of passion to ignore
Both time and place? Absurd. Keep
    up the fire,
And leave the generous flames to shape
    themselves.

'T is true the stage requires obsequiousness
To this or that convention; 'exit' here
And 'enter' there; the points for clap-
    ping, fixed,
Like Jacob's white-peeled rods before the
    rams,   240
And all the close-curled imagery clipped
In manner of their fleece at shearing-time.
Forget to prick the galleries to the heart
Precisely at the fourth act, — culminate
Our five pyramidal acts with one act
    more, —
We 're lost so: Shakespeare's ghost could
    scarcely plead
Against our just damnation. Stand aside;
We 'll muse for comfort that, last cen-
    tury,
On this same tragic stage on which we
    have failed,
A wigless Hamlet would have failed the
    same.   250

And whosoever writes good poetry,
Looks just to art. He does not write for
    you
Or me, — for London or for Edinburgh;
He will not suffer the best critic known
To step into his sunshine of free thought
And self-absorbed conception and exact
An inch-long swerving of the holy lines.
If virtue done for popularity
Defiles like vice, can art, for praise or hire,
Still keep its splendor and remain pure
    art?   260
Eschew such serfdom. What the poet
    writes,
He writes: mankind accepts it if it suits,
And that 's success; if not, the poem's
    passed
From hand to hand, and yet from hand to
    hand
Until the unborn snatch it, crying out
In pity on their fathers' being so dull,
And that 's success too.
             I will write no plays;
Because the drama, less sublime in this,

Makes lower appeals, submits more me-
    nially,
Adopts the standard of the public taste 270
To chalk its height on, wears a dog-chain
    round
Its regal neck, and learns to carry and
    fetch
The fashions of the day to please the day,
Fawns close on pit and boxes, who clap
    hands
Commending chiefly its docility
And humor in stage-tricks, — or else indeed
Gets hissed at, howled at, stamped at like
    a dog,
Or worse, we 'll say. For dogs, unjustly
    kicked,
Yell, bite at need; but if your dramatist
(Being wronged by some five hundred no-
    bodies   280
Because their grosser brains most naturally
Misjudge the fineness of his subtle wit)
Shows teeth an almond's breadth, protests
    the length
Of a modest phrase, — 'My gentle coun-
    trymen,
There 's something in it haply of your
    fault,' —
Why then, besides five hundred nobodies,
He 'll have five thousand and five thousand
    more
Against him, — the whole public, — all the
    hoofs
Of King Saul's father's asses, in full drove,
And obviously deserve it.   He appealed
To these, — and why say more if they con-
    demn,   291
Than if they praise him ? — Weep, my
    Æschylus,
But low and far, upon Sicilian shores !
For since 't was Athens (so I read the
    myth)
Who gave commission to that fatal weight
The tortoise, cold and hard, to drop on thee
And crush thee, — better cover thy bald
    head;
She 'll hear the softest hum of Hyblan
    bee
Before thy loudest protestation !
                                    Then
The risk 's still worse upon the modern
    stage.   300
I could not, for so little, accept success,
Nor would I risk so much, in ease and
    calm,
For manifester gains: let those who prize,

Pursue them: I stand off. And yet, forbid
That any irreverent fancy or conceit
Should litter in the Drama's throne-room
    where
The rulers of our art, in whose full veins
Dynastic glories mingle, sit in strength
And do their kingly work, — conceive, com-
    mand,   309
And, from the imagination's crucial heat,
Catch up their men and women all a-flame
For action, all alive and forced to prove
Their life by living out heart, brain, and
    nerve,
Until mankind makes witness, ' These be
    men
As we are,' and vouchsafes the greeting
    due
To Imogen and Juliet — sweetest kin
On art's side.
              'T is that, honoring to its worth
The drama, I would fear to keep it down
To the level of the footlights. Dies no
    more
The sacrificial goat, for Bacchus slain, 320
His filmed eyes fluttered by the whirling
    white
Of choral vestures, — troubled in his blood,
While tragic voices that clanged keen as
    swords,
Leapt high together with the altar-flame
And made the blue air wink.   The waxen
    mask,
Which set the grand still front of Themis'
    son
Upon the puckered visage of a player, —
The buskin, which he rose upon and moved,
As some tall ship first conscious of the wind
Sweeps slowly past the piers, — the mouth-
    piece, where   330
The mere man's voice with all its breaths
    and breaks
Went sheathed in brass, and clashed on
    even heights
Its phrasèd thunders, — these things are no
    more,
Which once were. And concluding, which
    is clear,
The growing drama has outgrown such toys
Of simulated stature, face, and speech,
It also peradventure may outgrow
The simulation of the painted scene,
Boards, actors, prompters, gaslight, and
    costume,
And take for a worthier stage the soul it-
    self,   340

Its shifting fancies and celestial lights,
With all its grand orchestral silences
To keep the pauses of its rhythmic sounds.

Alas, I still see something to be done,
And what I do falls short of what I see,
Though I waste myself on doing. Long
    green days,
Worn bare of grass and sunshine, — long
    calm nights
From which the silken sleeps were fretted
    out,
Be witness for me, with no amateur's
Irreverent haste and busy idleness   350
I set myself to art ! What then ? what 's
    done ?
What 's done, at last ?
                Behold, at last, a book.
If life-blood 's necessary, which it is, —
(By that blue vein athrob on Mahomet's
    brow,
Each prophet-poet's book must show man's
    blood !)
If life-blood 's fertilizing, I wrung mine
On every leaf of this, — unless the drops
Slid heavily on one side and left it dry.
That chances often: many a fervid man
Writes books as cold and flat as graveyard
    stones   360
From which the lichen 's scraped; and if
    Saint Preux
Had written his own letters, as he might,
We had never wept to think of the little
    mole
'Neath Julie's drooping eyelid. Passion is
But something suffered, after all.
                    While Art
Sets action on the top of suffering:
The artist's part is both to be and do,
Transfixing with a special, central power
The flat experience of the common man,
And turning outward, with a sudden
    wrench,   370
Half agony, half ecstasy, the thing
He feels the inmost, — never felt the less
Because he sings it. Does a torch less
    burn
For burning next reflectors of blue steel,
That *he* should be the colder for his place
Twixt two incessant fires, — his personal
    life's
And that intense refraction which burns
    back
Perpetually against him from the round
Of crystal conscience he was born into

If artist-born ? O sorrowful great gift 380
Conferred on poets, of a twofold life,
When one life has been found enough for
    pain !
We, staggering 'neath our burden as mere
    men,
Being called to stand up straight as demi-
    gods,
Support the intolerable strain and stress
Of the universal, and send clearly up,
With voices broken by the human sob,
Our poems to find rhymes among the
    stars !
But soft, — a ' poet ' is a word soon said,
A book 's a thing soon written. Nay, in-
    deed,   390
The more the poet shall be questionable,
The more unquestionably comes his book.
And this of mine — well, granting to my-
    self
Some passion in it, — furrowing up the
    flats,
Mere passion will not prove a volume
    worth
Its gall and rags even. Bubbles round a
    keel
Mean nought, excepting that the vessel
    moves.
There 's more than passion goes to make a
    man
Or book, which is a man too.
                  I am sad. 399
I wonder if Pygmalion had these doubts
And feeling the hard marble first relent,
Grow supple to the straining of his arms,
And tingle through its cold to his burning
    lip,
Supposed his senses mocked, supposed the
    toil
Of stretching past the known and seen to
    reach
The archetypal Beauty out of sight,
Had made his heart beat fast enough for
    two,
And with his own life dazed and blinded
    him !
Not so Pygmalion loved, — and whoso
    loves
Believes the impossible.
              But I am sad: 410
I cannot thoroughly love a work of mine,
Since none seems worthy of my thought
    and hope
More highly mated. He has shot them
    down,

My Phœbus Apollo, soul within my soul,
Who judges, by the attempted, what 's at-
    tained,
And with the silver arrow from his height
Has struck down all my works before my
    face
While I said nothing. Is there aught to
    say ?
I called the artist but a greatened man.
He may be childless also, like a man.   420

I labored on alone. The wind and dust
And sun of the world beat blistering in my
    face;
And hope, now for me, now against me,
    dragged
My spirits onward, as some fallen balloon,
Which, whether caught by blossoming tree
    or bare,
Is torn alike. I sometimes touched my
    aim,
Or seemed, — and generous souls cried out
    ' Be strong,
Take courage; now you 're on our level, —
    now !
The next step saves you ! ' I was flushed
    with praise,   429
But, pausing just a moment to draw breath,
I could not choose but murmur to myself
' Is this all ? all that 's done ? and all
    that 's gained ?
If this then be success, 't is dismaller
Than any failure.'
                    O my God, my God,
O supreme Artist, who as sole return
For all the cosmic wonder of thy work,
Demandest of us just a word . . . a name,
' My Father ! ' thou hast knowledge, only
    thou,
How dreary 't is for women to sit still,
On winter nights by solitary fires,   440
And hear the nations praising them far off,
Too far ! ay, praising our quick sense of
    love,
Our very heart of passionate womanhood,
Which could not beat so in the verse with-
    out
Being present also in the unkissed lips
And eyes undried because there 's none to
    ask
The reason they grew moist.
                    To sit alone
And think for comfort how, that very
    night,
Affianced lovers, leaning face to face

With sweet half-listenings for each other's
    breath,   450
Are reading haply from a page of ours,
To pause with a thrill (as if their cheeks
    had touched)
When such a stanza, level to their mood,
Seems floating their own thought out — ' So
    I feel
For thee,' — ' And I, for thee: this poet
    knows
What everlasting love is ! ' — how, that
    night,
Some father, issuing from the misty roads
Upon the luminous round of lamp and
    hearth
And happy children, having caught up
    first
The youngest there until it shrink and
    shriek   46
To feel the cold chin prick its dimples
    through
With winter from the hills, may throw i
    the lap
Of the eldest (who has learnt to drop her
    lids
To hide some sweetness newer than las
    year's)
Our book and cry, . . . ' Ah you, you car
    for rhymes;
So here be rhymes to pore on under trees,
When April comes to let you ! I 've beer
    told
They are not idle as so many are,
But set hearts beating pure as well as fast
'T is yours, the book; I 'll write your nam
    in it,   47
That so you may not lose, however lost
In poet's lore and charming reverie,
The thought of how your father thought o
    you
In riding from the town.'
                    To have our book
Appraised by love, associated with love,
While we sit loveless ! is it hard, yo
    think ?
At least 't is mournful. Fame, indeed
    't was said,
Means simply love. It was a man sa
    that:
And then, there 's love and love: the lov
    of all
(To risk in turn a woman's paradox)
Is but a small thing to the love of one.
You bid a hungry child be satisfied
With a heritage of many corn-fields: nay

He says he's hungry, — he would rather
    have
That little barley-cake you keep from
    him
While reckoning up his harvests. So with
    us
(Here, Romney, too, we fail to generalize):
We're hungry.
                    Hungry ! but it's pitiful
To wail like unweaned babes and suck
    our thumbs
Because we're hungry. Who, in all this
    world   490
(Wherein we are haply set to pray and
    fast
And learn what good is by its opposite),
Has never hungered ? Woe to him who has
    found
The meal enough ! if Ugolino's full,
His teeth have crunched some foul unnatural
    thing,
For here satiety proves penury
More utterly irremediable. And since
We needs must hunger, — better, for man's
    love,
Than God's truth ! better, for companions
    sweet,
Than great convictions ! let us bear our
    weights,   500
Preferring dreary hearths to desert souls.
Well, well ! they say we're envious, we
    who rhyme;
But I, because I am a woman perhaps
And so rhyme ill, am ill at envying.
    never envied Graham his breadth of
    style,
Which gives you, with a random smutch or
    two
    Near-sighted critics analyze to smutch),
Such delicate perspectives of full life:
Nor Belmore, for the unity of aim
To which he cuts his cedarn poems, fine 510
As sketchers do their pencils: nor Mark
    Gage,
For that caressing color and trancing tone
Whereby you're swept away and melted
    in
The sensual element, which with a back
    wave
Restores you to the level of pure souls
And leaves you with Plotinus. None of
    these,
For native gifts or popular applause,
I've envied; but for this, — that when by
    chance

Says some one, — 'There goes Belmore, a
    great man !
He leaves clean work behind him, and re-
    quires   520
No sweeper up of the chips,' . . . a girl I
    know,
Who answers nothing, save with her brown
    eyes,
Smiles unaware as if a guardian saint
Smiled in her: — for this, too, — that Gage
    comes home
And lays his last book's prodigal review
Upon his mother's knee, where, years ago,
He laid his childish spelling-book and
    learned
To chirp and peck the letters from her
    mouth,
As young birds must. 'Well done,' she
    murmured then;
She will not say it now more wonder-
    ingly: 530
And yet the last 'Well done' will touch
    him more,
As catching up to-day and yesterday
In a perfect chord of love: and so, Mark
    Gage,
I envy you your mother ! — and you, Gra-
    ham,
Because you have a wife who loves you so,
She half forgets, at moments, to be proud
Of being Graham's wife, until a friend ob-
    serves,
'The boy here has his father's massive
    brow
Done small in wax . . . if we push back the
    curls.'
Who loves me ? Dearest father, — mother
    sweet, —   540
I speak the names out sometimes by my-
    self,
And make the silence shiver. They sound
    strange,
As Hindostanee to an Ind-born man
Accustomed many years to English
    speech;
Or lovely poet-words grown obsolete,
Which will not leave off singing. Up in
    heaven
I have my father, — with my mother's
    face
Beside him in a blotch of heavenly light;
No more for earth's familiar, household
    use,
No more. The best verse written by this
    hand   550

Can never reach them where they sit, to
　　seem
Well done to *them*.　Death quite unfellows
　　us,
Sets dreadful odds betwixt the live and
　　dead,
And makes us part as those at Babel did
Through sudden ignorance of a common
　　tongue.
A living Cæsar would not dare to play
At bowls with such as my dead father is.

And yet this may be less so than appears,
This change and separation.　Sparrows
　　five
For just two farthings, and God cares for
　　each.　　　　　　　　　　　　　　　560
If God is not too great for little cares,
Is any creature, because gone to God ?
I 've seen some men, veracious, nowise
　　mad,
Who have thought or dreamed, declared
　　and testified
They heard the Dead a-ticking like a
　　clock
Which strikes the hours of the eternities,
Beside them, with their natural ears, — and
　　known
That human spirits feel the human way
And hate the unreasoning awe which waves
　　them off
From possible communion.　It may be.　570
At least, earth separates as well as heaven.
For instance, I have not seen Romney
　　Leigh
Full eighteen months . . . add six, you get
　　two years.
They say he 's very busy with good
　　works, —
Has parted Leigh Hall into almshouses.
He made one day an almshouse of his
　　heart,
Which ever since is loose upon the latch
For those who pull the string. — I never
　　did.

It always makes me sad to go abroad,
And now I 'm sadder that I went to-
　　night　　　　　　　　　　　　　　580
Among the lights and talkers at Lord
　　Howe's.
His wife is gracious, with her glossy
　　braids,
And even voice, and gorgeous eyeballs,
　　calm

As her other jewels.　If she 's somewhat
　　cold,
Who wonders, when her blood has stood so
　　long
In the ducal reservoir she calls her line
By no means arrogantly ? she 's not proud;
Not prouder than the swan is of the lake
He has always swum in; — 't is her ele-
　　ment;
And so she takes it with a natural
　　grace,　　　　　　　　　　　　　　590
Ignoring tadpoles.　She just knows per-
　　haps
There *are* who travel without outriders,
Which is n't her fault.　Ah, to watch her
　　face,
When good Lord Howe expounds his the-
　　ories
Of social justice and equality !
'T is curious, what a tender, tolerant bend
Her neck takes: for she loves him, likes his
　　talk,
' Such clever talk — that dear, odd Alger-
　　non ! '
She listens on, exactly as if he talked
Some Scandinavian myth of Lemures,　600
Too pretty to dispute, and too absurd.
She 's gracious to me as her husband's
　　friend,
And would be gracious were I not a Leigh,
Being used to smile just so, without her
　　eyes,
On Joseph Strangways the Leeds mesmer-
　　ist,
And Delia Dobbs the lecturer from ' the
　　States '
Upon the ' Woman's question.'　Then, for
　　him,
I like him; he 's my friend.　And all the
　　rooms
Were full of crinkling silks that swept
　　about
The fine dust of most subtle courtesies.　610
What then ? — why then, we come home to
　　be sad.

How lovely One I love not looked to-
　　night !
She 's very pretty, Lady Waldemar.
Her maid must use both hands to twist
　　that coil
Of tresses, then be careful lest the rich
Bronze rounds should slip: — she missed,
　　though, a gray hair,
A single one, — I saw it; otherwise

The woman looked immortal. How they
    told,
Those alabaster shoulders and bare breasts,
On which the pearls, drowned out of sight
    in milk,   620
Were lost, excepting for the ruby-clasp !
They split the amaranth velvet - bodice
    down
To the waist or nearly, with the audacious
    press
Of full - breathed beauty. If the heart
    within
Were half as white ! — but, if it were, per-
    haps
The breast were closer covered and the
    sight
Less aspectable by half, too.
                        I heard
The young man with the German student's
    look —
A sharp face, like a knife in a cleft stick,
Which shot up straight against the parting
    line   630
So equally dividing the long hair, —
Say softly to his neighbor (thirty-five
And mediæval), ' Look that way, Sir
    Blaise.
She 's Lady Waldemar — to the left — in
    red —
Whom Romney Leigh, our ablest man just
    now,
Is soon about to marry.'
                        Then replied
Sir Blaise Delorme, with quiet, priestlike
    voice,
Too used to syllable damnations round
To make a natural emphasis worth while:
' Is Leigh your ablest man ? the same, I
    think,   640
Once jilted by a recreant pretty maid
Adopted from the people ?   Now, in
    change,
He seems to have plucked a flower from
    the other side
Of the social hedge.'
            ' A flower, a flower,' exclaimed
My German student, — his own eyes full-
    blown
Bent on her. He was twenty, certainly.

Sir Blaise resumed with gentle arrogance,
As if he had dropped his alms into a hat
And gained the right to counsel, — ' My
    young friend,
I doubt your ablest man's ability   650

To get the least good or help meet for
    him,
For pagan phalanstery or Christian home,
From such a flowery creature.'
                            ' Beautiful ! '
My student murmured rapt, — ' Mark how
    she stirs !
Just waves her head, as if a flower indeed,
Touched far off by the vain breath of our
    talk.'

At which that bilious Grimwald (he who
    writes
For the Renovator), who had seemed ab-
    sorbed
Upon the table-book of autographs   659
(I dare say mentally he crunched the bones
Of all those writers, wishing them alive
To feel his tooth in earnest), turned short
    round
With low carnivorous laugh, — ' A flower,
    of course !
She neither sews nor spins, — and takes no
    thought
Of her garments . . . falling off.'
                            The student flinched;
Sir Blaise, the same; then both, drawing
    back their chairs
As if they spied black-beetles on the floor,
Pursued their talk, without a word being
    thrown
To the critic.
            Good Sir Blaise's brow is high
And noticeably narrow: a strong wind   670
You fancy, might unroof him suddenly,
And blow that great top attic off his head
So piled with feudal relics.   You admire
His nose in profile, though you miss his
    chin;
But, though you miss his chin, you seldom
    miss
His ebon cross worn innermostly (carved
For penance by a saintly Styrian monk
Whose flesh was too much with him), slip-
    ping through
Some unaware unbuttoned casualty
Of the under-waistcoat.   With an absent
    air   680
Sir Blaise sat fingering it and speaking
    low,
While I, upon the sofa, heard it all.

' My dear young friend, if we could bear
    our eyes,
Like blessedest Saint Lucy, on a plate,

They would not trick us into choosing
   wives,
As doublets, by the color. Otherwise
Our fathers chose, — and therefore, when
   they had hung
Their household keys about a lady's waist,
The sense of duty gave her dignity;
She kept her bosom holy to her babes, 690
And, if a moralist reproved her dress,
'T was "Too much starch !" — and not
   "Too little lawn ! " '

'Now, pshaw !' returned the other in a
   heat,
A little fretted by being called 'young
   friend,'
Or so I took it, — 'for Saint Lucy's sake,
If she 's the saint to swear by, let us leave
Our fathers, — plagued enough about our
   sons !'
(He stroked his beardless chin) 'yes,
   plagued, sir, plagued:
The future generations lie on us
As heavy as the nightmare of a seer; 700
Our meat and drink grow painful prophecy:
I ask you, — have we leisure, if we liked,
To hollow out our weary hands to keep
Your intermittent rushlight of the past
From draughts in lobbies ? Prejudice of
   sex
And marriage-law . . . the socket drops
   them through
While we two speak, — however may pro-
   test
Some over-delicate nostrils like your own,
'Gainst odors thence arising.'
                 'You are young,'
Sir Blaise objected.
          'If I am,' he said 710
With fire, — 'though somewhat less so than
   I seem,
The young run on before, and see the thing
That 's coming. Reverence for the young,
   I cry.
In that new church for which the world 's
   near ripe,
You 'll have the younger in the Elder's
   chair,
Presiding with his ivory front of hope
O'er foreheads clawed by cruel carrion-birds
Of life's experience.'
             'Pray your blessing, sir,'
Sir Blaise replied good-humoredly, — 'I
   plucked 719
A silver hair this morning from my beard,

Which left me your inferior. Would I
   were
Eighteen and worthy to admonish you !
If young men of your order run before
To see such sights as sexual prejudice
And marriage-law dissolved, — in plainer
   words,
A general concubinage expressed
In a universal pruriency, — the thing
Is scarce worth running fast for, and you 'd
   gain
By loitering with your elders.'
                    'Ah,' he said,
'Who, getting to the top of Pisgah-hill, 730
Can talk with one at bottom of the view,
To make it comprehensible ? Why, Leigh
Himself, although our ablest man, I said,
Is scarce advanced to see as far as this,
Which some are: he takes up imperfectly
The social question — by one handle —
   leaves
The rest to trail. A Christian socialist
Is Romney Leigh, you understand.'
                       'Not I
I disbelieve in Christian-pagans, much
As you in women-fishes. If we mix 740
Two colors, we lose both, and make a third
Distinct from either. Mark you ! to mis
   take
A color is the sign of a sick brain,
And mine, I thank the saints, is clear an
   cool:
A neutral tint is here impossible.
The church, — and by the church I mea
   of course,
The catholic, apostolic, mother-church, —
Draws lines as plain and straight as her ow
   walls,
Inside of which are Christians, obviously.
And outside . . . dogs.'
             'We thank you. Well I kno
The ancient mother-church would fain sti
   bite, 7
For all her toothless gums, — as Leigh hi
   self
Would fain be a Christian still, for all b
   wit.
Pass that; you two may settle it, for me.
You 're slow in England. In a month
   learnt
At Göttingen enough philosophy
To stock your English schools for fif
   years;
Pass that, too. Here alone, I stop y
   short,

— Supposing a true man like Leigh could
  stand
Unequal in the stature of his life   760
To the height of his opinions. Choose a
  wife
Because of a smooth skin ? — not he, not
  he !
He 'd rail at Venus' self for creaking shoes,
Unless she walked his way of righteousness:
And if he takes a Venus Meretrix
(No imputation on the lady there),
Be sure that, by some sleight of Christian
  art,
He has metamorphosed and converted her
To a Blessed Virgin.'
            'Soft !' Sir Blaise drew breath
As if it hurt him, — 'Soft ! no blasphemy,
I pray you !'
      'The first Christians did the thing:
Why not the last ? ' asked he of Göttingen,
With just that shade of sneering on the lip
Compensates for the lagging of the beard, —
And so the case is. If that fairest fair
Is talked of as the future wife of Leigh,
She 's talked of too, at least as certainly,
As Leigh's disciple. You may find her
  name
On all his missions and commissions,
  schools,
Asylums, hospitals, — he had her down, 780
With other ladies whom her starry lead
Persuaded from their spheres, to his
  country-place
In Shropshire, to the famed phalanstery
At Leigh Hall, christianized from Fourier's
  own
In which he has planted out his sapling
  stocks
Of knowledge into social nurseries),
And there, they say, she has tarried half a
  week,
And milked the cows, and churned, and
  pressed the curd,
And said " my sister " to the lowest drab 789
Of all the assembled castaways; such girls !
Ay, sided with them at the washing-tub —
Conceive, Sir Blaise, those naked perfect
  arms,
Round glittering arms, plunged elbow-deep
  in suds,
Like wild swans hid in lilies all a-shake.'

Lord Howe came up. 'What, talking
  poetry
So near the image of the unfavoring Muse ?

That 's you, Miss Leigh: I 've watched you
  half an hour
Precisely as I watched the statue called
A Pallas in the Vatican; — you mind
The face, Sir Blaise ? — intensely calm and
  sad,   800
As wisdom cut it off from fellowship, —
But that spoke louder. Not a word from
  you !
And these two gentlemen were bold, I
  marked,
And unabashed by even your silence.'
                              'Ah,'
Said I, 'my dear Lord Howe, you shall not
  speak
To a printing woman who has lost her place
(The sweet safe corner of the household
  fire
Behind the heads of children), compliments,
As if she were a woman. We who have
  clipt   809
The curls before our eyes may see at least
As plain as men do. Speak out, man to
  man;
No compliments, beseech you.'
                      'Friend to friend,
Let that be. We are sad to-night, I saw
(— Good night, Sir Blaise ! ah, Smith — he
  has slipped away),
I saw you across the room, and stayed,
  Miss Leigh,
To keep a crowd of lion-hunters off,
With faces toward your jungle. There
  were three;
A spacious lady, five feet ten and fat,
Who has the devil in her (and there 's
  room)
For walking to and fro upon the earth, 820
From Chippewa to China; she requires
Your autograph upon a tinted leaf
'Twixt Queen Pomare's and Emperor Sou-
  louque's.
Pray give it; she has energies, though
  fat:
For me, I 'd rather see a rick on fire
Than such a woman angry. Then a youth
Fresh from the backwoods, green as the
  underboughs,
Asks modestly, Miss Leigh, to kiss your
  shoe,
And adds, he has an epic in twelve parts,
Which when you 've read, you 'll do it for
  his boot: 830
All which I saved you, and absorb next
  week

Both manuscript and man, — because a
    lord
Is still more potent than a poetess
With any extreme republican.   Ah, ah,
You smile, at last, then.'
                    'Thank you.'
                         ' Leave the smile.
I 'll lose the thanks for 't, — ay, and throw
    you in
My transatlantic girl, with golden eyes,
That draw you to her splendid whiteness
    as
The pistil of a water-lily draws,
Adust with gold.   Those girls across the
    sea   840
Are tyrannously pretty, — and I swore
(She seemed to me an innocent, frank
    girl)
To bring her to you for a woman's kiss,
Not now, but on some other day or week:
— We 'll call it perjury; I give her up.'

' No, bring her.'
              ' Now,' said he, ' you make it hard
To touch such goodness with a grimy palm.
I thought to tease you well, and fret you
    cross,
And steel myself, when rightly vexed with
    you,
For telling you a thing to tease you
    more.'   850

' Of Romney ? '
          ' No, no; nothing worse,' he cried,
' Of Romney Leigh than what is buzzed
    about, —
That he is taken in an eye-trap too,
Like many half as wise.   The thing I
    mean
Refers to you, not him.'
                    ' Refers to me.'
He echoed, — ' Me !   You sound it like a
    stone
Dropped down a dry well very listlessly
By one who never thinks about the toad
Alive at the bottom.   Presently perhaps
You 'll sound your " me " more proudly —
    till I shrink.'   860

' Lord Howe 's the toad, then, in this
    question ? '
                  ' Brief,
We 'll take it graver.   Give me sofa-room,
And quiet hearing.   You know Eglinton,
John Eglinton, of Eglinton in Kent ? '

' Is he the toad ? — he 's rather like the
    snail,
Known chiefly for the house upon his back:
Divide the man and house — you kill the
    man;
That 's Eglinton of Eglinton, Lord Howe.'

He answered grave.   ' A reputable man,
An excellent landlord of the olden
    stamp,   870
If somewhat slack in new philanthropies,
Who keeps his birthdays with a tenants'
    dance,
Is hard upon them when they miss the
    church
Or hold their children back from cate-
    chism,
But not ungentle when the agèd poor
Pick sticks at hedge-sides: nay, I 've heard
    him say
" The old dame has a twinge because she
    stoops;
That 's punishment enough for felony." '

' O tender-hearted landlord !   may I take
My long lease with him, when the time
    arrives   880
For gathering winter-fagots !'
                              'He likes art,
Buys books and pictures . . . of a certain
    kind;
Neglects no patent duty; a good son ' . . .

' To a most obedient mother.   Born to
    wear
His father's shoes, he wears her husband's
    too:
Indeed I 've heard it 's touching.   Dear
    Lord Howe,
You shall not praise me so against your
    heart,
When I 'm at worst for praise and fag-
    ots.'
                    ' Be
Less bitter with me, for . . . in short,' he
    said,
' I have a letter, which he urged me so   890
To bring you . . . I could scarcely choose
    but yield;
Insisting that a new love, passing through
The hand of an old friendship, caught
    from it
Some reconciling odor.'
                         ' Love, you say
My lord, I cannot love: I only find

The rhyme for love, — and that's not love,
my lord.
Take back your letter.'
'Pause: you 'll read it first?'

'I will not read it: it is stereotyped;
The same he wrote to, — anybody's name,
Anne Blythe the actress, when she died so
true,   900
A duchess fainted in a private box:
Pauline the dancer, after the great *pas*
In which her little feet winked overhead
Like other fire-flies, and amazed the pit:
Or Baldinacci, when her F in alt
Had touched the silver tops of heaven it-
self
With such a pungent spirit-dart, the
Queen
Laid softly, each to each, her white-gloved
palms,
And sighed for joy: or else (I thank your
friend)
Aurora Leigh, — when some indifferent
rhymes,   910
Like those the boys sang round the holy ox
On Memphis-highway, chance perhaps to
set
Our Apis-public lowing. Oh, he wants,
Instead of any worthy wife at home,
A star upon his stage of Eglinton?
Advise him that he is not overshrewd
In being so little modest: a dropped star
Makes bitter waters, says a Book I 've
read, —
And there 's his unread letter.'
'My dear friend,'
Lord Howe began . . .
In haste I tore the phrase.
'You mean your friend of Eglinton, or
me?'   921

'I mean you, you,' he answered with some
fire.
'A happy life means prudent compromise;
The tare runs through the farmer's gar-
nered sheaves,
And though the gleaner's apron holds
pure wheat
We count her poorer. Tare with wheat,
we cry,
And good with drawbacks. You, you love
your art,
And, certain of vocation, set your soul
On utterance. Only, in this world we have
made

(They say God made it first, but if He
did   930
'T was so long since, and, since, we have
spoiled it so,
He scarce would know it, if He looked this
way,
From hells we preach of, with the flames
blown out),
— In this bad, twisted, topsy-turvy world
Where all the heaviest wrongs get upper-
most, —
In this uneven, unfostering England here,
Where ledger-strokes and sword-strokes
count indeed,
But soul-strokes merely tell upon the flesh
They strike from, — it is hard to stand for
art,
Unless some golden tripod from the sea 940
Be fished up, by Apollo's divine chance,
To throne such feet as yours, my prophet-
ess,
At Delphi. Think, — the god comes down
as fierce
As twenty bloodhounds, shakes you, stran-
gles you,
Until the oracular shriek shall ooze in
froth!
At best 't is not all ease, — at worst too
hard:
A place to stand on is a 'vantage gained,
And here 's your tripod. To be plain, dear
friend,
You 're poor, except in what you richly
give;   949
You labor for your own bread painfully
Or ere you pour our wine. For art's sake,
pause.'

I answered slow, — as some wayfaring man,
Who feels himself at night too far from
home,
Makes steadfast face against the bitter
wind.
'Is art so less a thing than virtue is,
That artists first must cater for their ease
Or ever they make issue past themselves
To generous use? Alas, and is it so
That we, who would be somewhat clean,
must sweep
Our ways as well as walk them, and no
friend   960
Confirm us nobly, — "Leave results to
God,
But you, be clean?" What! "prudent
compromise

Makes acceptable life," you say instead,
You, you, Lord Howe ? — in things indif-
ferent, well.
For instance, compromise the wheaten
bread
For rye, the meat for lentils, silk for serge,
And sleep on down, if needs, for sleep on
straw;
But there, end compromise. I will not
bate
One artist-dream on straw or down, my
lord,
Nor pinch my liberal soul, though I be
poor,   970
Nor cease to love high, though I live thus
low.'

So speaking, with less anger in my voice
Than sorrow, I rose quickly to depart;
While he, thrown back upon the noble
shame
Of such high-stumbling natures, murmured
words,
The right words after wrong ones. Ah,
the man
Is worthy, but so given to entertain
Impossible plans of superhuman life, —
He sets his virtues on so raised a shelf,
To keep them at the grand millennial height,
He has to mount a stool to get at them;
And, meantime, lives on quite the common
way,   982
With everybody's morals.
                            As we passed,
Lord Howe insisting that his friendly arm
Should oar me across the sparkling brawl-
ing stream
Which swept from room to room, — we
fell at once
On Lady Waldemar. 'Miss Leigh,' she
said,
And gave me such a smile, so cold and
bright,
As if she tried it in a 'tiring glass
And liked it, ' all to-night I 've strained at
you   990
As babes at baubles held up out of reach
By spiteful nurses (" Never snatch," they
say),
And there you sat, most perfectly shut in
By good Sir Blaise and clever Mister Smith
And then our dear Lord Howe ! at last
indeed
I almost snatched. I have a world to
speak

About your cousin's place in Shropshire,
where
I 've been to see his work . . . our work, —
you heard
I went ? . . . and of a letter yesterday,
In which if I should read a page or two
You might feel interest, though you 're
locked of course   1001
In literary toil. — You 'll like to hear
Your last book lies at the phalanstery,
As judged innocuous for the elder girls
And younger women who still care for
books.
We all must read, you see, before we live,
Till slowly the ineffable light comes up
And, as it deepens, drowns the written
word, —
So said your cousin, while we stood and
felt   1009
A sunset from his favorite beech-tree seat,
He might have been a poet if he would,
But then he saw the higher thing at once
And climbed to it. I think he looks well
now,
Has quite got over that unfortunate . . .
Ah, ah . . . I know it moved you. Ten-
der-heart !
You took a liking to the wretched girl.
Perhaps you thought the marriage suit-
able,
Who knows ? a poet hankers for romance,
And so on. As for Romney Leigh, 't is
sure
He never loved her, — never. By the
way,   1020
You have not heard of her ? . . . quite
out of sight,
And out of saving ? lost in every sense ? '

She might have gone on talking half an
hour
And I stood still, and cold, and pale, I
think,
As a garden-statue a child pelts with snow
For pretty pastime. Every now and then
I put in ' yes ' or ' no,' I scarce knew
why;
The blind man walks wherever the dog
pulls,
And so I answered. Till Lord Howe broke
in:
' What penance takes the wretch who in-
terrupts   1030
The talk of charming women ? I, at last,
Must brave it. Pardon, Lady Waldemar,

The lady on my arm is tired, unwell,
And loyally I 've promised she shall say
No harder word this evening than . . .
   good-night;
The rest her face speaks for her.' — Then
   we went.

And I breathe large at home. I drop my
   cloak,
Unclasp my girdle, loose the band that
   ties
My hair . . . now could I but unloose my
   soul !
We are sepulchred alive in this close
   world,   1040
And want more room.
        The charming woman there —
This reckoning up and writing down her
   talk
Affects me singularly. How she talked
To pain me ! woman's spite. — You wear
   steel-mail:
A woman takes a housewife from her
   breast
And plucks the delicatest needle out
As 't were a rose, and pricks you carefully
'Neath nails, 'neath eyelids, in your nos-
   trils, — say,
A beast would roar so tortured, — but a
   man,
A human creature, must not, shall not
   flinch,   1050
No, not for shame.
          What vexes, after all,
Is just that such as she, with such as I,
Knows how to vex. Sweet heaven, she
   takes me up
As if she had fingered me and dog-eared
   me
And spelled me by the fireside half a life !
She knows my turns, my feeble points. —
   What then ?
The knowledge of a thing implies the
   thing;
Of course, she found *that* in me, she saw
   that,
Her pencil underscored *this* for a fault,
And I, still ignorant. Shut the book up,
   — close !   1060
And crush that beetle in the leaves.
           O heart,
At last we shall grow hard too, like the
   rest,
And call it self-defence because we are
   soft.

And after all, now . . . why should I be
   pained
That Romney Leigh, my cousin, should
   espouse
This Lady Waldemar ? And, say, she
   held
Her newly - blossomed gladness in my
   face, . . .
'T was natural surely, if not generous,
Considering how, when winter held her
   fast,
I helped the frost with mine, and pained
   her more   1070
Than she pains me. Pains me ! — but
   wherefore pained ?
'T is clear my cousin Romney wants a
   wife, —
So, good ! — The man's need of the wo-
   man, here,
Is greater than the woman's of the man,
And easier served; for where the man dis-
   cerns
A sex (ah, ah, the man can generalize,
Said he), we see but one, ideally
And really: where we yearn to lose our-
   selves
And melt like white pearls in another's
   wine,
He seeks to double himself by what he
   loves,   1080
And make his drink more costly by our
   pearls.
At board, at bed, at work and holiday,
It is not good for man to be alone,
And that 's his way of thinking, first and
   last,
And thus my cousin Romney wants a
   wife.
But then my cousin sets his dignity
On personal virtue. If he understands
By love, like others, self-aggrandizement,
It is that he may verily be great
By doing rightly and kindly. Once he
   thought,   1090
For charitable ends set duly forth
In Heaven's white judgment-book, to
   marry . . . ah,
We 'll call her name Aurora Leigh, al-
   though
She 's changed since then ! — and once, for
   social ends,
Poor Marian Erle, my sister Marian Erle,
My woodland sister, sweet maid Marian,
Whose memory moans on in me like the
   wind

Through ill-shut casements, making me
 more sad
Than ever I find reasons for.   Alas,
Poor pretty plaintive face, embodied ghost !
He finds it easy then, to clap thee off   1101
From pulling at his sleeve and book and
 pen, —
He locks thee out at night into the cold
Away from butting with thy horny eyes
Against his crystal dreams, that now he 's
 strong
To love anew ? that Lady Waldemar
Succeeds my Marian ?
      After all, why not ?
He loved not Marian, more than once he
 loved
Aurora.   If he loves at last that Third,
Albeit she prove as slippery as spilt oil   1110
On marble floors, I will not augur him
Ill-luck for that.   Good love, howe'er ill-
 placed,
Is better for a man's soul in the end,
Than if he loved ill what deserves love
 well.
A pagan, kissing for a step of Pan
The wild-goat's hoof-print on the loamy
 down,
Exceeds our modern thinker who turns
 back
The strata . . . granite, limestone, coal,
 and clay,
Concluding coldly with ' Here 's law !
 where 's God ? '

And then at worst, — if Romney loves her
 not, —   1120
At worst — if he 's incapable of love,
Which may be — then indeed, for such a
 man
Incapable of love, she 's good enough;
For she, at worst too, is a woman still
And loves him . . . as the sort of woman
 can.

My loose long hair began to burn and
 creep,
Alive to the very ends, about my knees:
I swept it backward as the wind sweeps
 flame,
With the passion of my hands.   Ah, Rom-
 ney laughed
One day . . . (how full the memories come
 up !)   1130
— ' Your Florence fire-flies live on in your
 hair,'

He said, ' it gleams so.'   Well, I wrung
 them out,
My fire-flies; made a knot as hard as life
Of those loose, soft, impracticable curls,
And then sat down and thought . . . ' She
 shall not think
Her thought of me,' — and drew my desk
 and wrote.

' Dear Lady Waldemar, I could not speak
With people round me, nor can sleep to-
 night
And not speak, after the great news I
 heard
Of you and of my cousin.   May you be   1140
Most happy; and the good he meant the
 world
Replenish his own life.   Say what I say,
And let my word be sweeter for your
 mouth,
As you are *you* . . . I only Aurora Leigh.'
That 's quiet, guarded: though she hold it
 up
Against the light, she 'll not see through it
 more
Than lies there to be seen.   So much for
 pride;
And now for peace, a little.   Let me stop
All writing back . . . ' Sweet thanks, my
 sweetest friend,
You 've made more joyful my great joy
 itself.'   1150
— No, that 's too simple ! she would twist
 it thus,
' My joy would still be as sweet as thyme
 in drawers,
However shut up in the dark and dry;
But violets, aired and dewed by love like
 yours,
Out-smell all thyme: we keep that in our
 clothes,
But drop the other down our bosoms till
They smell like — ' . . . ah, I see her
 writing back
Just so.   She 'll make a nosegay of her
 words,
And tie it with blue ribbons at the end
To suit a poet; — pshaw !
      And then we 'll have
The call to church, the broken, sad, bad
 dream   1161
Dreamed out at last, the marriage-vow
 complete
With the marriage breakfast; praying in
 white gloves,

Drawn off in haste for drinking pagan
   toasts
In somewhat stronger wine than any sipped
By gods since Bacchus had his way with
   grapes.

A postscript stops all that and rescues me.
'You need not write. I have been over-
   worked,
And think of leaving London, England
   even,
And hastening to get nearer to the sun 1170
Where men sleep better. So, adieu.'— I
   fold
And seal, — and now I'm out of all the
   coil;
I breathe now, I spring upward like a
   branch
The ten-years school-boy with a crooked
   stick
May pull down to his level in search of
   nuts,
But cannot hold a moment. How we
   twang
Back on the blue sky, and assert our
   height,
While he stares after! Now, the wonder
   seems
That I could wrong myself by such a
   doubt.
We poets always have uneasy hearts, 1180
Because our hearts, large-rounded as the
   globe,
Can turn but one side to the sun at once.
We are used to dip our artist-hands in gall
And potash, trying potentialities
Of alternated color, till at last
We get confused, and wonder for our skin
How nature tinged it first. Well — here's
   the true
Good flesh-color; I recognize my hand, —
Which Romney Leigh may clasp as just a
   friend's, 1189
And keep his clean.
              And now, my Italy.
Alas, if we could ride with naked souls
And make no noise and pay no price at all,
I would have seen thee sooner, Italy,
For still I have heard thee crying through
   my life,
Thou piercing silence of ecstatic graves,
Men call that name!

             But even a witch to-day
Must melt down golden pieces in the nard

Wherewith to anoint her broomstick ere
   she rides;
And poets evermore are scant of gold,
And if they find a piece behind the
   door 1200
It turns by sunset to a withered leaf.
The Devil himself scarce trusts his pa-
   tented
Gold-making art to any who make rhymes,
But culls his Faustus from philosophers
And not from poets. 'Leave my Job,'
   said God;
And so the Devil leaves him without
   pence,
And poverty proves plainly special grace.
In these new, just, administrative times
Men clamor for an order of merit: why?
Here's black bread on the table and no
   wine! 1210

At least I am a poet in being poor,
Thank God. I wonder if the manuscript
Of my long poem, if 't were sold outright,
Would fetch enough to buy me shoes to go
Afoot (thrown in, the necessary patch
For the other side the Alps)? It cannot
   be.
I fear that I must sell this residue
Of my father's books, although the Elze-
   virs
Have fly-leaves overwritten by his hand
In faded notes as thick and fine and
   brown 1220
As cobwebs on a tawny monument
Of the old Greeks — *conferenda hæc cum
   his* —
Corruptè citat — lege potiùs,
And so on, in the scholar's regal way
Of giving judgment on the parts of speech,
As if he sat on all twelve thrones up-piled,
Arraigning Israel. Ay, but books and
   notes
Must go together. And this Proclus too,
In these dear quaint contracted Grecian
   types,
Fantastically crumpled like his thoughts 1230
Which would not seem too plain; you go
   round twice
For one step forward, then you take it back
Because you're somewhat giddy; there's
   the rule
For Proclus. Ah, I stained this middle
   leaf
With pressing in 't my Florence iris-bell,
Long stalk and all: my father chided me

For that stain of blue blood, — I recollect
The peevish turn his voice took, 'Silly
    girls,
Who plant their flowers in our philosophy
To make it fine, and only spoil the book !
No more of it, Aurora.'   Yes — no more !
Ah, blame of love, that 's sweeter than all
    praise   1242
Of those who love not ! 't is so lost to
    me,
I cannot, in such beggared life, afford
To lose my Proclus, — not for Florence
    even.

The kissing Judas, Wolff, shall go instead,
Who builds us such a royal book as this
To honor a chief-poet, folio-built,
And writes above ' The house of Nobody ! '
Who floats in cream, as rich as any sucked
From Juno's breasts, the broad Homeric
    lines,   1251
And, while with their spondaic prodigious
    mouths
They lap the lucent margins as babe-gods,
Proclaims them bastards.   Wolff 's an
    atheist:
And if the Iliad fell out, as he says,
By mere fortuitous concourse of old
    songs,
Conclude as much too for the universe.

That Wolff, those Platos: sweep the upper
    shelves
As clean as this, and so I am almost rich,
Which means, not forced to think of being
    poor   1260
In sight of ends.   To-morrow: no delay.
I 'll wait in Paris till good Carrington
Dispose of such and, having chaffered for
My book's price with the publisher, direct
All proceeds to me.   Just a line to ask
His help.
        And now I come, my Italy,
My own hills ! Are you 'ware of me, my
    hills,
How I burn toward you ? do you feel to-
    night
The urgency and yearning of my soul,
As sleeping mothers feel the sucking babe
And smile ? — Nay, not so much as when
    in heat   1271
Vain lightnings catch at your inviolate
    tops
And tremble while ye are steadfast.   Still
    ye go

Your own determined, calm, indifferent
    way
Toward sunrise, shade by shade, and light
    by light,
Of all the grand progression nought left
    out,
As if God verily made you for yourselves
And would not interrupt your life with
    ours.

SIXTH BOOK

The English have a scornful insular way
Of calling the French light.   The levity
Is in the judgment only, which yet stands,
For say a foolish thing but oft enough
(And here 's the secret of a hundred
    creeds,
Men get opinions as boys learn to spell,
By reiteration chiefly), the same thing
Shall pass at last for absolutely wise,
And not with fools exclusively.   And so
We say the French are light, as if we
    said   10
The cat mews or the milch-cow gives us
    milk:
Say rather, cats are milked and milch-cows
    mew;
For what is lightness but inconsequence,
Vague fluctuation 'twixt effect and cause
Compelled by neither ?   Is a bullet light
That dashes from the gun-mouth, while
    the eye
Winks and the heart beats one, to flatten
    itself
To a wafer on the white speck on a wall
A hundred paces off ?   Even so direct,
So sternly undivertible of aim,   20
Is this French people.
               All, idealists
Too absolute and earnest, with them all
The idea of a knife cuts real flesh;
And still, devouring the safe interval
Which Nature placed between the thought
    and act
With those two fiery and impatient souls,
They threaten conflagration to the world,
And rush with most unscrupulous logic
    on
Impossible practice.   Set your orators
To blow upon them with loud windy
    mouths,   30
Through watchword phrases, jest or senti-
    ment,

Which drive our burly brutal English
   mobs
Like so much chaff, whichever way they
   blow, —
This light French people will not thus be
   driven.
They turn indeed, — but then they turn
   upon
Some central pivot of their thought and
   choice,
And veer out by the force of holding fast.
That 's hard to understand, for English-
   men
Unused to abstract questions, and untrained
To trace the involutions, valve by valve, 40
In each orbed bulb-root of a general truth,
And mark what subtly fine integument
Divides opposed compartments. Freedom's
   self
Comes concrete to us, to be understood,
Fixed in a feudal form incarnately
To suit our ways of thought and rever-
   ence,
The special form, with us, being still the
   thing.
With us, I say, though I 'm of Italy
By mother's birth and grave, by father's
   grave
And memory; let it be — a poet's heart 50
Can swell to a pair of nationalities,
However ill-lodged in a woman's breast.

And so I am strong to love this noble
   France,
This poet of the nations, who dreams on
And wails on (while the household goes to
   wreck)
For ever, after some ideal good, —
Some equal poise of sex, some unvowed
   love
Inviolate, some spontaneous brotherhood,
Some wealth that leaves none poor and
   finds none tired,
Some freedom of the many that respects 60
The wisdom of the few. Heroic dreams !
Sublime, to dream so; natural, to wake:
And sad, to use such lofty scaffoldings,
Erected for the building of a church,
To build instead a brothel or a prison —
May God save France !
              And if at last she sighs
Her great soul up into a great man's face,
To flush his temples out so gloriously
That few dare carp at Cæsar for being
   bald,

What then ? — this Cæsar represents, not
   reigns, 70
And is no despot, though twice absolute:
This Head has all the people for a heart;
This purple 's lined with the democracy, —
Now let him see to it ! for a rent within
Would leave irreparable rags without.

A serious riddle: find such anywhere
Except in France; and when 't is found in
   France,
Be sure to read it rightly. So, I mused
Up and down, up and down, the terraced
   streets,
The glittering boulevards, the white colon-
   nades 80
Of fair fantastic Paris who wears trees
Like plumes, as if man made them, spire
   and tower
As if they had grown by nature, tossing
   up
Her fountains in the sunshine of the
   squares,
As if in beauty's game she tossed the dice,
Or blew the silver down-balls of her
   dreams
To sow futurity with seeds of thought
And count the passage of her festive hours.

The city swims in verdure, beautiful
As Venice on the waters, the sea-swan. 90
What bosky gardens dropped in close-
   walled courts
Like plums in ladies' laps who start and
   laugh:
What miles of streets that run on after
   trees,
Still carrying all the necessary shops,
Those open caskets with the jewels seen !
And trade is art, and art 's philosophy,
In Paris. There 's a silk for instance, there,
As worth an artist's study for the folds
As that bronze opposite ! nay, the bronze
   has faults, 99
Art 's here too artful, — conscious as a maid
Who leans to mark her shadow on the wall
Until she lose a vantage in her step.
Yet Art walks forward, and knows where to
   walk;
The artists also are idealists,
Too absolute for nature, logical
To austerity in the application of
The special theory, — not a soul content
To paint a crooked pollard and an ass,
As the English will because they find it so

And like it somehow. — There the old
  Tuileries   110
Is pulling its high cap down on its eyes,
Confounded,   conscience - stricken,   and
  amazed
By the apparition of a new fair face
In those devouring mirrors. Through the
  grate
Within the gardens, what a heap of babes,
Swept up like leaves beneath the chestnut-
  trees
From every street and alley of the town,
By ghosts perhaps that blow too bleak this
  way
A-looking for their heads ! dear pretty
  babes,
I wish them luck to have their ball-play
  out   120
Before the next change. Here the air is
  thronged
With statues poised upon their columns
  fine,
As if to stand a moment were a feat,
Against that blue ! What squares, — what
  breathing-room
For a nation that runs fast, — ay, runs
  against
The dentist's teeth at the corner in pale
  rows,
Which grin at progress, in an epigram.

I walked the day out, listening to the chink
Of the first Napoleon's bones in his second
  grave,
By victories guarded 'neath the golden
  dome   130
That caps all Paris like a bubble. 'Shall
These dry bones live ?' thought Louis
  Philippe once,
And lived to know. Herein is argument
For kings and politicians, but still more
For poets, who bear buckets to the well
Of ampler draught.
                    These crowds are very good
For meditation (when we are very strong)
Though love of beauty makes us timorous,
And draws us backward from the coarse
  town-sights
To count the daisies upon dappled fields 140
And hear the streams bleat on among the
  hills
In innocent and indolent repose,
While still with silken elegiac thoughts
We wind out from us the distracting world
And die into the chrysalis of a man,

And leave the best that may, to come of us,
In some brown moth. I would be bold and
  bear
To look into the swarthiest face of things,
For God's sake who has made them.

                              Six days' work;
The last day shutting 'twixt its dawn and
  eve   150
The whole work bettered of the previous
  five !
Since God collected and resumed in man
The firmaments, the strata, and the lights,
Fish, fowl, and beast, and insect, — all
  their trains
Of various life caught back upon his arm,
Reorganized, and constituted MAN,
The microcosm, the adding up of works, —
Within whose fluttering nostrils, then at
  last
Consummating Himself the Maker sighed,
As some strong winner at the foot-race
  sighs   160
Touching the goal.
                    Humanity is great;
And, if I would not rather pore upon
An ounce of common, ugly, human dust,
An artisan's palm or a peasant's brow,
Unsmooth, ignoble, save to me and God,
Than track old Nilus to his silver roots,
Or wait on all the changes of the moon
Among the mountain-peaks of Thessaly
(Until her magic crystal round itself
For many a witch to see in) — set it down
As weakness, — strength by no means.
  How is this,   171
That men of science, osteologists
And surgeons, beat some poets in respect
For nature, — count nought common or
  unclean,
Spend raptures upon perfect specimens
Of indurated veins, distorted joints,
Or beautiful new cases of curved spine,
While we, we are shocked at nature's fall-
  ing off,
We dare to shrink back from her warts
  and blains,
We will not, when she sneezes, look at
  her,   180
Not even to say 'God bless her' ? That 's
  our wrong;
For that, she will not trust us often with
Her larger sense of beauty and desire,
But tethers us to a lily or a rose
And bids us diet on the dew inside,

Left ignorant that the hungry beggar-boy
(Who stares unseen against our absent
    eyes,
And wonders at the gods that we must
    be,
To pass so careless for the oranges !)
Bears yet a breastful of a fellow-world 190
To this world, undisparaged, undespoiled,
And (while we scorn him for a flower or
    two,
As being, Heaven help us, less poetical)
Contains himself both flowers and firma-
    ments
And surging seas and aspectable stars
And all that we would push him out of
    sight
In order to see nearer. Let us pray
God's grace to keep God's image in repute,
That so, the poet and philanthropist
(Even I and Romney) may stand side by
    side,   200
Because we both stand face to face with
    men,
Contemplating the people in the rough,
Yet each so follow a vocation, his
And mine.   I walked on, musing with myself
On life and art, and whether after all
A larger metaphysics might not help
Our physics, a completer poetry
Adjust our daily life and vulgar wants
More fully than the special outside plans,
Phalansteries, material institutes,   210
The civil conscriptions and lay monasteries
Preferred by modern thinkers, as they
    thought
The bread of man indeed made all his life,
And washing seven times in the 'People's
    Baths'
Were sovereign for a people's leprosy,
Still leaving out the essential prophet's
    word
That comes in power. On which, we thun-
    der down,
We prophets, poets, — Virtue's in the
    word !
The maker burnt the darkness up with
    his,
To inaugurate the use of vocal life;   220
And, plant a poet's word even, deep enough
In any man's breast, looking presently
For offshoots, you have done more for the
    man
Than if you dressed him in a broadcloth
    coat

And warmed his Sunday pottage at your
    fire.
Yet Romney leaves me . . .
                God ! what face is that ?
O Romney, O Marian !
                   Walking on the quays
And pulling thoughts to pieces leisurely,
As if I caught at grasses in a field   229
And bit them slow between my absent lips
And shred them with my hands . . .
                  What face is that ?
What a face, what a look, what a likeness !
    Full on mine
The sudden blow of it came down, till all
My blood swam, my eyes dazzled. Then
    I sprang . . .

It was as if a meditative man
Were dreaming out a summer afternoon
And watching gnats a-prick upon a pond,
When something floats up suddenly, out
    there,
Turns over . . . a dead face, known once
    alive . . .
So old, so new ! it would be dreadful now
To lose the sight and keep the doubt of
    this: 241
He plunges — ha ! he has lost it in the
    splash.

I plunged — I tore the crowd up, either
    side,
And rushed on, forward, forward, after
    her.
Her ? whom ?
            A woman sauntered slow in front,
Munching an apple, — she left off amazed
As if I had snatched it: that 's not she, at
    least.
A man walked arm-linked with a lady
    veiled,
Both heads dropped closer than the need
    of talk: 250
They started; he forgot her with his face,
And she, herself, and clung to him as if
My look were fatal. Such a stream of
    folk,
And all with cares and business of their
    own !
I ran the whole quay down against their
    eyes;
No Marian; nowhere Marian. Almost,
    now,
I could call Marian, Marian, with the
    shriek

Of desperate creatures calling for the
    Dead.
Where is she, was she ? was she any-
    where ?
I stood still, breathless, gazing, straining
    out
In every uncertain distance, till at last 260
A gentleman abstracted as myself
Came full against me, then resolved the
    clash
In voluble excuses, — obviously
Some learned member of the Institute
Upon his way there, walking, for his
    health
While meditating on the last ' Discourse;'
Pinching the empty air 'twixt finger and
    thumb,
From which the snuff being ousted by that
    shock
Defiled his snow - white waistcoat duly
    pricked
At the button-hole with honorable red; 270
' Madame, your pardon,' — there he
    swerved from me
A metre, as confounded as he had heard
That Dumas would be chosen to fill up
The next chair vacant, by his ' men *in us*.'
Since when was genius found respectable ?
It passes in its place, indeed, — which
    means
The seventh floor back, or else the hospital:
Revolving pistols are ingenious things,
But prudent men (Academicians are)
Scarce keep them in the cupboard next the
    prunes. 280

And so, abandoned to a bitter mirth,
I loitered to my inn. O world, O world,
O jurists, rhymers, dreamers, what you
    please,
We play a weary game of hide-and-seek !
We shape a figure of our fantasy,
Call nothing something, and run after it
And lose it, lose ourselves too in the search,
Till clash against us comes a somebody
Who also has lost something and is lost,
Philosopher against philanthropist, 290
Academician against poet, man
Against woman, against the living the
    dead, —
Then home, with a bad headache and worse
    jest !

To change the water for my heliotropes
And yellow roses. Paris has such flowers;

But England, also. 'T was a yellow rose,
By that south window of the little house,
My cousin Romney gathered with his hand
On all my birthdays for me, save the last;
And then I shook the tree too rough, too
    rough, 300
For roses to stay after.
              Now, my maps.
I must not linger here from Italy
Till the last nightingale is tired of song,
And the last fire-fly dies off in the maize.
My soul's in haste to leap into the sun
And scorch and seethe itself to a finer
    mood,
Which here, in this chill north, is apt to
    stand
Too stiffly in former moulds.
               That face persists,
It floats up, it turns over in my mind,
As like to Marian as one dead is like 310
The same alive. In very deed a face
And not a fancy, though it vanished so;
The small fair face between the darks of
    hair,
I used to liken, when I saw her first,
To a point of moonlit water down a well:
The low brow, the frank space between the
    eyes,
Which always had the brown, pathetic
    look
Of a dumb creature who had been beaten
    once
And never since was easy with the world.
Ah, ah — now I remember perfectly 320
Those eyes, to-day, — how overlarge they
    seemed,
As if some patient, passionate despair
(Like a coal dropped and forgot on tapes-
    try,
Which slowly burns a widening circle out)
Had burnt them larger, larger. And those
    eyes,
To-day, I do remember, saw me too,
As I saw them, with conscious lids astrain
In recognition. Now a fantasy,
A simple shade or image of the brain,
Is merely passive, does not retro-act, 330
Is seen, but sees not.
              'T was a real face,
Perhaps a real Marian.
              Which being so,
I ought to write to Romney, ' Marian's
    here;
Be comforted for Marian.'
               My pen fell,

My hands struck sharp together, as hands
    do
Which hold at nothing. Can I write to
    him
A half-truth? can I keep my own soul
    blind
To the other half, . . . the worse? What
    are our souls,
If still, to run on straight a sober pace
Nor start at every pebble or dead leaf, 340
They must wear blinkers, ignore facts, sup-
    press
Six tenths of the road?   Confront the
    truth, my soul!
And oh, as truly as that was Marian's face,
The arms of that same Marian clasped a
    thing
. . . Not hid so well beneath the scanty
    shawl,
I cannot name it now for what it was.

A child.   Small business has a castaway
Like Marian with that crown of prosper-
    ous wives
At which the gentlest she grows arrogant
And says 'My child.'   Who finds an
    emerald ring   350
On a beggar's middle finger and requires
More testimony to convict a thief?
A child's too costly for so mere a wretch;
She filched it somewhere, and it means,
    with her,
Instead of honor, blessing, merely shame.

I cannot write to Romney, 'Here she is,
Here's Marian found! I 'll set you on her
    track:
I saw her here, in Paris, . . . and her
    child.
She put away your love two years ago,
But, plainly, not to starve. You suffered
    then;   360
And, now that you 've forgot her utterly
As any last year's annual, in whose place
You 've planted a thick-flowering ever-
    green,
I choose, being kind, to write and tell you
    this
To make you wholly easy — she's not
    dead,
But only . . . damned.'
                    Stop there: I go too fast;
I 'm cruel like the rest, — in haste to
    take
The first stir in the arras for a rat,

And set my barking, biting thoughts
    upon 't.
— A child! what then? Suppose a neigh-
    bor's sick,   370
And asked her, 'Marian, carry out my
    child
In this Spring air,' — I punish her for
    that?
Or say, the child should hold her round the
    neck
For good child-reasons, that he liked it so
And would not leave her — she had win-
    ning ways —
I brand her therefore that she took the
    child?
Not so.
        I will not write to Romney Leigh,
For now he's happy, — and she may in-
    deed
Be guilty, — and the knowledge of her
    fault
Would draggle his smooth time. But I,
    whose days   380
Are not so fine they cannot bear the rain,
And who moreover having seen her face
Must see it again, . . . *will* see it, by my
    hopes
Of one day seeing heaven too. The police
Shall track her, hound her, ferret their own
    soil;
We 'll dig this Paris to its catacombs
But certainly we 'll find her, have her out,
And save her, if she will or will not —
    child
Or no child, — if a child, then one to
    save!

The long weeks passed on without conse-
    quence.   390
As easy find a footstep on the sand
The morning after spring-tide, as the trace
Of Marian's feet between the incessant
    surfs
Of this live flood. She may have moved
    this way, —
But so the star-fish does, and crosses out
The dent of her small shoe. The foiled
    police
Renounced me. 'Could they find a girl
    and child,
No other signalment but girl and child?
No data shown but noticeable eyes   399
And hair in masses, low upon the brow,
As if it were an iron crown and pressed?
Friends heighten, and suppose they specify:

Why, girls with hair and eyes are every-
        where
In Paris; they had turned me up in vain
No Marian Erle indeed, but certainly
Mathildes, Justines, Victoires, . . . or, if
        I sought
The English, Betsis, Saras, by the score.
They might as well go out into the fields
To find a speckled bean, that 's somehow
        specked,
And somewhere in the pod.' — They left
        me so.   410
Shall *I* leave Marian ? have I dreamed a
        dream ?

— I thank God I have found her ! I must
        say
'Thank God,' for finding her, although 't is
        true
I find the world more sad and wicked for 't.
But she —
        I 'll write about her, presently.
My hand 's a-tremble, as I had just caught
        up
My heart to write with, in the place of it.
At least you 'd take these letters to be
        writ
At sea, in storm ! — wait now . . .
                A simple chance
Did all.   I could not sleep last night, and,
        tired   420
Of turning on my pillow and harder
        thoughts,
Went out at early morning, when the air
Is delicate with some last starry touch,
To wander through the Market-place of
        Flowers
(The prettiest haunt in Paris), and make
        sure
At worst that there were roses in the
        world.
So wandering, musing, with the artist's eye
That keeps the shade-side of the thing it
        loves,
Half-absent, whole - observing, while the
        crowd
Of young, vivacious, and black-braided
        heads   430
Dipped, quick as finches in a blossomed
        tree,
Among the nosegays, cheapening this and
        that
In such a cheerful twitter of rapid
        speech, —
My heart leapt in me, startled by a voice

That slowly, faintly, with long breaths
        that marked
The interval between the wish and word,
Inquired in stranger's French, 'Would
        that be much,
That branch of flowering mountain-gorse ? '
        — 'So much ?
Too much for me, then ! ' turning the face
        round
So close upon me that I felt the sigh   440
It turned with.
        'Marian, Marian ! ' — face to face —
'Marian ! I find you. Shall I let you go ? '
I held her two slight wrists with both my
        hands;
'Ah Marian, Marian, can I let you go ? '
— She fluttered from me like a cyclamen,
As white, which taken in a sudden wind
Beats on against the palisade. — 'Let pass,'
She said at last. 'I will not,' I replied;
'I lost my sister Marian many days,
And sought her ever in my walks and
        prayers,   450
And, now I find her . . . do we throw
        away
The bread we worked and prayed for, —
        crumble it
And drop it, . . . to do even so by thee
Whom still I 've hungered after more than
        bread,
My sister Marian ? — can I hurt thee,
        dear ?
Then why distrust me ? Never tremble
        so.
Come with me rather where we 'll talk and
        live,
And none shall vex us. I 've a home for
        you
And me and no one else.' . . .
                She shook her head.
'A home for you and me and no one else
Ill suits one of us: I prefer to such,   461
A roof of grass on which a flower might
        spring,
Less costly to me than the cheapest here;
And yet I could not, at this hour, afford
A like home even. That you offer yours,
I thank you. You are good as heaven it-
        self —
As good as one I knew before. . . . Fare-
        well.'
I loosed her hands: — 'In *his* name, no fare-
        well ! '
(She stood as if I held her.) 'For his
        sake,

For his sake, Romney's ! by the good he
    meant, 470
Ay, always ! by the love he pressed for
    once, —
And by the grief, reproach, abandonment,
He took in change ' . . .
    ' He ? — Romney ! who grieved *him ?*
Who had the heart for 't ? what reproach
    touched *him ?*
Be merciful, — speak quickly.'
           ' Therefore come,'
I answered with authority. — ' I think
We dare to speak such things and name
    such names
In the open squares of Paris !'
           Not a word
She said, but in a gentle humbled way
(As one who had forgot herself in grief)
Turned round and followed closely where
    I went, 481
As if I led her by a narrow plank
Across devouring waters, step by step;
And so in silence we walked on a mile.

And then she stopped: her face was white
    as wax.
' We go much farther ? '
           ' You are ill,' I asked,
' Or tired ? '
    She looked the whiter for her smile.
' There 's one at home,' she said, ' has need
    of me
By this time, — and I must not let him
    wait.'

' Not even,' I asked, ' to hear of Romney
    Leigh ? ' 490

' Not even,' she said, ' to hear of Mister
    Leigh.'

' In that case,' I resumed, ' I go with you,
And we can talk the same thing there as
    here.
None waits for me: I have my day to
    spend.'

Her lips moved in a spasm without a
    sound, —
But then she spoke. ' It shall be as you
    please;
And better so — 't is shorter seen than
    told:
And though you will not find me worth
    your pains,

That, even, may be worth some pains to
    know
For one as good as you are.'
           Then she led
The way, and I, as by a narrow plank 501
Across devouring waters, followed her,
Stepping by her footsteps, breathing by her
    breath,
And holding her with eyes that would not
    slip;
And so, without a word, we walked a mile,
And so, another mile, without a word.

Until the peopled streets being all dis-
    missed,
House-rows and groups all scattered like a
    flock,
The market-gardens thickened, and the
    long
White walls beyond, like spiders' outside
    threads, 510
Stretched, feeling blindly toward the coun-
    try-fields,
Through half-built habitations and half-dug
Foundations, — intervals of trenchant
    chalk
That bit betwixt the grassy uneven turfs
Where goats (vine-tendrils trailing from
    their mouths)
Stood perched on edges of the cellarage
Which should be, staring as about to leap
To find their coming Bacchus. All the
    place
Seemed less a cultivation than a waste.
Men work here, only, — scarce begin to
    live: 520
All 's sad, the country struggling with the
    town,
Like an untamed hawk upon a strong man's
    fist,
That beats its wings and tries to get away,
And cannot choose be satisfied so soon
To hop through court-yards with its right
    foot tied,
The vintage plains and pastoral hills in
    sight.

We stopped beside a house too high and
    slim
To stand there by itself, but waiting till
Five others, two on this side, three on
    that,
Should grow up from the sullen second
    floor 530
They pause at now, to build it to a row.

The upper windows partly were unglazed
Meantime, — a meagre, unripe house: a
line
Of rigid poplars elbowed it behind,
And, just in front, beyond the lime and
bricks
That wronged the grass between it and the
road,
A great acacia with its slender trunk
And overpoise of multitudinous leaves
(In which a hundred fields might spill their
dew
And intense verdure, yet find room
enough)   540
Stood reconciling all the place with green.
I followed up the stair upon her step.
She hurried upward, shot across a face,
A woman's, on the landing, — 'How now,
now !
Is no one to have holidays but you ?
You said an hour, and stayed three hours, I
think,
And Julie waiting for your betters here ?
Why if he had waked he might have waked,
for me.'
— Just murmuring an excusing word, she
passed
And shut the rest out with the chamber-
door,   550
Myself shut in beside her.
                      'T was a room
Scarce larger than a grave, and near as
bare;
Two stools, a pallet-bed; I saw the room:
A mouse could find no sort of shelter in 't,
Much less a greater secret; curtainless, —
The window fixed you with its torturing
eye,
Defying you to take a step apart
If peradventure you would hide a thing.
I saw the whole room, I and Marian there
Alone.
        Alone ?   She threw her bonnet off,
Then, sighing as 't were sighing the last
time,   561
Approached the bed, and drew a shawl
away:
You could not peel a fruit you fear to
bruise
More calmly and more carefully than so, —
Nor would you find within, a rosier flushed
Pomegranate —
              There he lay upon his back,
The yearling creature, warm and moist with
life

To the bottom of his dimples, — to the
ends
Of the lovely tumbled curls about his
face;
For since he had been covered over-
much   570
To keep him from the light-glare, both his
cheeks
Were hot and scarlet as the first live rose
The shepherd's heart-blood ebbed away
into
The faster for his love.   And love was
here
As instant; in the pretty baby-mouth,
Shut close as if for dreaming that it
sucked,
The little naked feet, drawn up the way
Of nestled birdlings; everything so soft
And tender, — to the tiny holdfast hands,
Which, closing on a finger into sleep,   580
Had kept the mould of 't.
                      While we stood there dumb,
For oh, that it should take such innocence
To prove just guilt, I thought, and stood
there dumb, —
The light upon his eyelids pricked them
wide,
And, staring out at us with all their blue,
As half perplexed between the angelhood
He had been away to visit in his sleep,
And our most mortal presence, gradually
He saw his mother's face, accepting it
In change for heaven itself with such a
smile   590
As might have well been learnt there, —
never moved,
But smiled on, in a drowse of ecstasy,
So happy (half with her and half with
heaven)
He could not have the trouble to be stirred,
But smiled and lay there.   Like a rose, I
said ?
As red and still indeed as any rose,
That blows in all the silence of its leaves,
Content in blowing to fulfil its life.

She leaned above him (drinking him as
wine)
In that extremity of love, 't will pass   600
For agony or rapture, seeing that love
Includes the whole of nature, rounding it
To love . . . no more, — since more can
never be
Than just love.   Self-forgot, cast out of
self,

And drowning in the transport of the
    sight,
Her whole pale passionate face, mouth,
    forehead, eyes,
One gaze, she stood: then, slowly as he
    smiled
She smiled too, slowly, smiling unaware,
And drawing from his countenance to hers
A fainter red, as if she watched a flame 610
And stood in it aglow. 'How beautiful,'
Said she.

        I answered, trying to be cold.
(Must sin have compensations, was my
    thought,
As if it were a holy thing like grief ?
And is a woman to be fooled aside
From putting vice down, with that woman's
    toy
A baby ?) — 'Ay ! the child is well
    enough,'
I answered. 'If his mother's palms are
    clean
They need be glad of course in clasping
    such;
But if not, I would rather lay my hand, 620
Were I she, on God's brazen altar-bars
Red-hot with burning sacrificial lambs,
Than touch the sacred curls of such a
    child.'

She plunged her fingers in his clustering
    locks,
As one who would not be afraid of fire;
And then with indrawn steady utterance
    said,
'My lamb, my lamb ! although, through
    such as thou,
The most unclean got courage and approach
To God, once, — now they cannot, even
    with men,
Find grace enough for pity and gentle
    words.'
                      630

'My Marian,' I made answer, grave and
    sad,
'The priest who stole a lamb to offer him,
Was still a thief. And if a woman steals
(Through God's own barrier-hedges of
    true love,
Which fence out license in securing love)
A child like this, that smiles so in her face,
She is no mother, but a kidnapper,
And he 's a dismal orphan, not a son,
Whom all her kisses cannot feed so full
He will not miss hereafter a pure home 640

To live in, a pure heart to lean against,
A pure good mother's name and memory
To hope by, when the world grows thick
    and bad
And he feels out for virtue.'
               'Oh,' she smiled
With bitter patience, 'the child takes his
    chance;
Not much worse off in being fatherless
Than I was, fathered. He will say, belike,
His mother was the saddest creature born;
He 'll say his mother lived so contrary
To joy, that even the kindest, seeing
    her,   650
Grew sometimes almost cruel: he 'll not
    say
She flew contrarious in the face of God
With bat-wings of her vices. Stole my
    child, —
My flower of earth, my only flower on
    earth,
My sweet, my beauty !' . . . Up she
    snatched the child,
And, breaking on him in a storm of tears,
Drew out her long sobs from their shiver-
    ing roots,
Until he took it for a game, and stretched
His feet and flapped his eager arms like
    wings
And crowed and gurgled through his in-
    fant laugh: 660
'Mine, mine,' she said. 'I have as sure a
    right
As any glad proud mother in the world,
Who sets her darling down to cut his teeth
Upon her church-ring. If she talks of law,
I talk of law ! I claim my mother-dues
By law, — the law which now is para-
    mount, —
The common law, by which the poor and
    weak
Are trodden underfoot by vicious men,
And loathed for ever after by the good.
Let pass ! I did not filch, — I found the
    child.'   670
'You found him, Marian ?'
                'Ay, I found him where
I found my curse, — in the gutter, with
    my shame !
What have you, any of you, to say to that,
Who all are happy, and sit safe and high,
And never spoke before to arraign my
    right
To grief itself ? What, what, . . . being
    beaten down

By hoofs of maddened oxen into a ditch,
Half-dead, whole mangled, when a girl at
  last
Breathes, sees . . . and finds there, bedded
  in her flesh
Because of the extremity of the shock, 680
Some coin of price ! . . . and when a good
  man comes
(That 's God ! the best men are not quite
  as good)
And says " I dropped the coin there: take
  it you,
And keep it, — it shall pay you for the
  loss," —
You all put up your finger — " See the
  thief !
Observe what precious thing she has come
  to filch.
How bad those girls are ! " Oh, my flower,
  my pet,
I dare forget I have you in my arms
And fly off to be angry with the world,
And fright you, hurt you with my tempers,
  till   690
You double up your lip ? Why, that in-
  deed
Is bad: a naughty mother ! '
                          ' You mistake,'
I interrupted; ' if I loved you not,
I should not, Marian, certainly be here.'

' Alas,' she said, ' you are so very good;
And yet I wish indeed you had never come
To make me sob until I vex the child.
It is not wholesome for these pleasure-plats
To be so early watered by our brine.
And then, who knows ? he may not like
  me now   700
As well, perhaps, as ere he saw me fret, —
One 's ugly fretting ! he has eyes the same
As angels, but he cannot see as deep,
And so I 've kept for ever in his sight
A sort of smile to please him, — as you
  place
A green thing from the garden in a cup,
To make believe it grows there. Look,
  my sweet,
My cowslip-ball ! we 've done with that
  cross face,
And here 's the face come back you used
  to like.
Ah, ah ! he laughs ! he likes me. Ah,
  Miss Leigh,   710
You 're great and pure; but were you
  purer still, —

As if you had walked, we 'll say, no other-
  where
Than up and down the New Jerusalem,
And held your trailing lutestring up your-
  self
From brushing the twelve stones, for fear
  of some
Small speck as little as a needle-prick,
White stitched on white, — the child
  would keep to *me*,
Would choose his poor lost Marian, like me
  best,
And, though you stretched your arms, cry
  back and cling,
As we do when God says it 's time to die
And bids us go up higher. Leave us,
  then;   721
We two are happy. Does *he* push me off ?
He 's satisfied with me, as I with him.'

' So soft to one, so hard to others ! Nay,'
I cried, more angry that she melted me,
' We make henceforth a cushion of our
  faults
To sit and practise easy virtues on ?
I thought a child was given to sanctify
A woman, — set her in the sight of all
The clear-eyed heavens, a chosen minister
To do their business and lead spirits up 731
The difficult blue heights. A woman lives,
Not bettered, quickened toward the truth
  and good
Through being a mother ? . . . then she 's
  none ! although
She damps her baby's cheeks by kissing
  them,
As we kill roses.'
                    ' Kill ! O Christ,' she said,
And turned her wild sad face from side to
  side
With most despairing wonder in it,
  ' What,
What have you in your souls against me
  then,
All of you ? am I wicked, do you think ?
God knows me, trusts me with the child;
  but you,   741
You think me really wicked ? '
                              ' Complaisant,'
I answered softly, ' to a wrong you 've
  done,
Because of certain profits, — which is
  wrong
Beyond the first wrong, Marian. When
  you left

The pure place and the noble heart, to
take
The hand of a seducer ' . . .
                        ' Whom ? whose hand ?
I took the hand of ' . . .
                        Springing up erect,
And lifting up the child at full arm's
length,
As if to bear him like an oriflamme   750
Unconquerable to armies of reproach, —
' By *him*,' she said, ' my child's head and
its curls,
By these blue eyes no woman born could
dare
A perjury on, I make my mother's oath,
That if I left that Heart, to lighten it,
The blood of mine was still, except for
grief !
No cleaner maid than I was took a step
To a sadder end, — no matron-mother now
Looks backward to her early maidenhood
Through chaster pulses. I speak steadily;
And if I lie so, . . . if, being fouled in
will   761
And paltered with in soul by devil's lust,
I dared to bid this angel take my part, . . .
Would God sit quiet, let us think, in hea-
ven,
Nor strike me dumb with thunder ? Yet
I speak:
He clears me therefore. What, " seduced "
's your word !
Do wolves seduce a wandering fawn in
France ?
Do eagles, who have pinched a lamb with
claws,
Seduce it into carrion ? So with me.
I was not ever, as you say, seduced,   770
But simply, murdered.'
                        There she paused, and sighed
With such a sigh as drops from agony
To exhaustion, — sighing while she let the
babe
Slide down upon her bosom from her
arms,
And all her face's light fell after him
Like a torch quenched in falling. Down
she sank,
And sat upon the bedside with the child.

But I, convicted, broken utterly,
With woman's passion clung about her
waist
And kissed her hair and eyes, — ' I have
been wrong,   780

Sweet Marian ' . . . (weeping in a tender
rage) . . .
' Sweet holy Marian ! And now, Marian,
now,
I 'll use your oath although my lips are
hard,
And by the child, my Marian, by the child,
I swear his mother shall be innocent
Before my conscience, as in the open Book
Of Him who reads for judgment. Inno-
cent,
My sister ! let the night be ne'er so dark
The moon is surely somewhere in the sky;
So surely is your whiteness to be found   790
Through all dark facts. But pardon, par-
don me,
And smile a little, Marian, — for the child,
If not for me, my sister.'
                        The poor lip
Just motioned for the smile and let it go:
And then, with scarce a stirring of the
mouth,
As if a statue spoke that could not breathe,
But spoke on calm between its marble
lips, —
' I 'm glad, I 'm very glad you clear me so.
I should be sorry that you set me down
With harlots, or with even a better name
Which misbecomes his mother. For the
rest,   801
I am not on a level with your love,
Nor ever was, you know, — but now am
worse,
Because that world of yours has dealt with
me
As when the hard sea bites and chews a
stone
And changes the first form of it. I 've
marked
A shore of pebbles bitten to one shape
From all the various life of madrepores;
And so, that little stone, called Marian
Erle,
Picked up and dropped by you and another
friend,   810
Was ground and tortured by the incessant
sea
And bruised from what she was, — changed?
death 's a change,
And she, I said, was murdered; Marian 's
dead.
What can you do with people when they
are dead
But, if you are pious, sing a hymn and go;
Or, if you are tender heave a sigh and go;

But go by all means, — and permit the grass
To keep its green feud up 'twixt them and you?
Then leave me, — let me rest. I 'm dead, I say,
And if, to save the child from death as well,   820
The mother in me has survived the rest,
Why, that 's God's miracle you must not tax,
I 'm not less dead for that: I 'm nothing more
But just a mother. Only for the child
I 'm warm, and cold, and hungry, and afraid,
And smell the flowers a little and see the sun,
And speak still, and am silent, — just for him!
I pray you therefore to mistake me not
And treat me haply as I were alive;
For though you ran a pin into my soul, 830
I think it would not hurt nor trouble me.
Here 's proof, dear lady, — in the market-place
But now, you promised me to say a word
About . . . a friend, who once, long years ago,
Took God's place toward me, when He leans and loves
And does not thunder, . . . whom at last I left,
As all of us leave God. You thought perhaps
I seemed to care for hearing of that friend?
Now, judge me! we have sat here half an hour
And talked together of the child and me,
And I not asked as much as ' What 's the thing   841
"You had to tell me of the friend . . . the friend?"
He 's sad, I think you said, — he 's sick perhaps?
'T is nought to Marian if he 's sad or sick.
Another would have crawled beside your foot
And prayed your words out. Why, a beast, a dog,
A starved cat, if he had fed it once with milk,
Would show less hardness. But I 'm dead, you see,
And that explains it.'

Poor, poor thing, she spoke
And shook her head, as white and calm as frost   850
On days too cold for raining any more,
But still with such a face, so much alive,
I could not choose but take it on my arm
And stroke the placid patience of its cheeks, —
Then told my story out, of Romney Leigh,
How, having lost her, sought her, missed her still,
He, broken-hearted for himself and her,
Had drawn the curtains of the world awhile
As if he had done with morning. There I stopped,
For when she gasped, and pressed me with her eyes,   860
' And now . . . how is it with him? tell me now,'
I felt the shame of compensated grief,
And chose my words with scruple — slowly stepped
Upon the slippery stones set here and there
Across the sliding water. 'Certainly,
As evening empties morning into night,
Another morning takes the evening up
With healthful, providential interchange;
And, though he thought still of her —'
                    'Yes, she knew,
She understood: she had supposed indeed   870
That, as one stops a hole upon a flute,
At which a new note comes and shapes the tune,
Excluding her would bring a worthier in,
And, long ere this, that Lady Waldemar
He loved so' . . .
                'Loved,' I started, — 'loved her so!
Now tell me' . . .
                'I will tell you,' she replied:
'But since we 're taking oaths, you 'll promise first
That he in England, he, shall never learn
In what a dreadful trap his creature here,
Round whose unworthy neck he had meant to tie   880
The honorable ribbon of his name,
Fell unaware and came to butchery:
Because, — I know him, — as he takes to heart
The grief of every stranger, he 's not like
To banish mine as far as I should choose
In wishing him most happy. Now he leaves

To think of me, perverse, who went my
    way,
Unkind, and left him, — but if once he
    knew . . .
Ah, then, the sharp nail of my cruel wrong
Would fasten me for ever in his sight, 890
Like some poor curious bird, through each
    spread wing
Nailed high up over a fierce hunter's fire,
To spoil the dinner of all tenderer folk
Come in by chance. Nay, since your
    Marian's dead,
You shall not hang her up, but dig a hole
And bury her in silence ! ring no bells.'

I answered gayly, though my whole voice
    wept,
'We'll ring the joy-bells, not the funeral-
    bells,
Because we have her back, dead or alive.'

She never answered that, but shook her
    head; 900
Then low and calm, as one who, safe in
    heaven,
Shall tell a story of his lower life,
Unmoved by shame or anger, — so she
    spoke.
She told me she had loved upon her knees,
As others pray, more perfectly absorbed
In the act and inspiration. She felt his
For just his uses, not her own at all, —
His stool, to sit on or put up his foot,
His cup, to fill with wine or vinegar,
Whichever drink might please him at the
    chance, 910
For that should please her always: let him
    write
His name upon her . . . it seemed natural;
It was most precious, standing on his shelf,
To wait until he chose to lift his hand.
Well, well, — I saw her then, and must
    have seen
How bright her life went floating on her
    love,
Like wicks the housewives send afloat on
    oil
Which feeds them to a flame that lasts the
    night.

To do good seemed so much his business,
That, having done it, she was fain to think,
Must fill up his capacity for joy. 921
At first she never mooted with herself
If he was happy, since he made her so,

Or if he loved her, being so much beloved.
Who thinks of asking if the sun is light,
Observing that it lightens ? who's so bold
To question God of his felicity ?
Still less. And thus she took for granted
    first
What first of all she should have put to
    proof,
And sinned against him so, but only so.
'What could you hope,' she said, 'of such
    as she ? 931
You take a kid you like, and turn it out
In some fair garden: though the creature's
    fond
And gentle, it will leap upon the beds
And break your tulips, bite your tender
    trees;
The wonder would be if such innocence
Spoiled less: a garden is no place for
    kids.'
And, by degrees, when he who had chosen
    her
Brought in his courteous and benignant
    friends
To spend their goodness on her, which she
    took 940
So very gladly, as a part of his, —
By slow degrees it broke on her slow
    sense
That she too in that Eden of delight
Was out of place, and, like the silly kid,
Still did most mischief where she meant
    most love.
A thought enough to make a woman mad
(No beast in this but she may well go
    mad),
That saying, 'I am thine to love and use'
May blow the plague in her protesting
    breath
To the very man for whom she claims to
    die, — 950
That, clinging round his neck, she pulls
    him down
And drowns him, — and that, lavishing her
    soul,
She halos perdition on him. 'So, being
    mad,'
Said Marian . . .
    'Ah — who stirred such thoughts, you
    ask ?
Whose fault it was, that she should have
    such thoughts ?
None's fault, none's fault. The light
    comes, and we see:
But if it were not truly for our eyes,

There would be nothing seen, for all the
   light.
And so with Marian: if she saw at last,
The sense was in her, — Lady Walde-
   mar   960
Had spoken all in vain else.'
                                 ' O my heart,
O prophet in my heart,' I cried aloud,
' Then Lady Waldemar spoke !'
                                 ' _Did_ she speak,'
Mused Marian softly, ' or did she only
   sign ?
Or did she put a word into her face
And look, and so impress you with the
   word ?
Or leave it in the foldings of her gown,
Like rosemary smells a movement will
   shake out
When no one 's conscious ? who shall say,
   or guess ?
One thing alone was certain — from the
   day   970
The gracious lady paid a visit first,
She, Marian, saw things different, — felt
   distrust
Of all that sheltering roof of circumstance
Her hopes were building into with clay
   nests:
Her heart was restless, pacing up and
   down
And fluttering, like dumb creatures before
   storms,
Not knowing wherefore she was ill at
   ease.'

' And still the lady came,' said Marian
   Erle,
' Much oftener than _he_ knew it Mister
   Leigh.   979
She bade me never tell him she had come,
She liked to love me better than he knew,
So very kind was Lady Waldemar:
And every time she brought with her more
   light,
And every light made sorrow clearer . . .
   Well,
Ah, well ! we cannot give her blame for
   that;
'T would be the same thing if an angel
   came,
Whose right should prove our wrong. And
   every time
The lady came, she looked more beautiful
And spoke more like a flute among green
   trees,

Until at last, as one, whose heart being
   sad   990
On hearing lovely music, suddenly
Dissolves in weeping, I brake out in tears
Before her, asked her counsel, — " Had I
   erred
In being too happy ? would she set me
   straight ?
For she, being wise and good and born
   above
The flats I had never climbed from, could
   perceive
If such as I might grow upon the hills;
And whether such poor herb sufficed to
   grow,
For Romney Leigh to break his fast
   upon 't, —
Or would he pine on such, or haply
   starve ? "   1000
She wrapped me in her generous arms at
   once,
And let me dream a moment how it feels
To have a real mother, like some girls:
But when I looked, her face was younger
   . . . ay,
Youth 's too bright not to be a little hard,
And beauty keeps itself still uppermost,
That 's true ! — Though Lady Waldemar
   was kind
She hurt me, hurt, as if the morning-sun
Should smite us on the eyelids when we
   sleep,
And wake us up with headache. Ay, and
   soon   1010
Was light enough to make my heart ache
   too:
She told me truths I asked for, — 't was my
   fault, —
" That Romney could not love me, if he
   would,
As men call loving: there are bloods that
   flow
Together like some rivers and not mix,
Through contraries of nature. He in-
   deed
Was set to wed me, to espouse my class,
Act out a rash opinion, — and, once wed,
So just a man and gentle could not
   choose
But make my life as smooth as marriage-
   ring,   1020
Bespeak me mildly, keep me a cheerful
   house,
With servants, brooches, all the flowers I
   liked,

And pretty dresses, silk the whole year
 round " . . .
At which I stopped her, — "This for me.
 And now
For *him*." — She hesitated, — truth grew
 hard;
She owned "'T was plain a man like Rom-
 ney Leigh
Required a wife more level to himself.
If day by day he had to bend his height
To pick up sympathies, opinions, thoughts,
And interchange the common talk of
 life   1030
Which helps a man to live as well as
 talk,
His days were heavily taxed. Who buys
 a staff
To fit the hand, that reaches but the knee ?
He 'd feel it bitter to be forced to miss
The perfect joy of married suited pairs,
Who, bursting through the separating
 hedge
Of personal dues with that sweet eglan-
 tine
Of equal love, keep saying, 'So *we* think,
It strikes *us*, — that's *our* fancy'" — When
 I asked
If earnest will, devoted love, employed 1040
In youth like mine, would fail to raise me
 up
As two strong arms will always raise a
 child
To a fruit hung overhead, she sighed and
 sighed . . .
" That could not be," she feared. " You
 take a pink,
You dig about its roots and water it
And so improve it to a garden-pink,
But will not change it to a heliotrope,
The kind remains. And then, the harder
 truth —
This Romney Leigh, so rash to leap a
 pale,
So bold for conscience, quick for martyr-
 dom,   1050
Would suffer steadily and never flinch,
But suffer surely and keenly, when his
 class
Turned shoulder on him for a shameful
 match,
And set him up as nine-pin in their talk
To bowl him down with jestings." — There,
 she paused.
And when I used the pause in doubting
 that

We wronged him after all in what we
 feared —
" Suppose such things could never touch
 him more
In his high conscience (if the things should
 be)
Than, when the queen sits in an upper
 room   1060
The horses in the street can spatter her ! " —
A moment, hope came, — but the lady
 closed
That door and nicked the lock and shut it
 out,
Observing wisely that " the tender heart
Which made him over-soft to a lower
 class,
Would scarcely fail to make him sensitive
To a higher, — how they thought and what
 they felt."

' Alas, alas !' said Marian, rocking slow
The pretty baby who was near asleep,
The eyelids creeping over the blue balls, —
'She made it clear, too clear — I saw the
 whole !   1071
And yet who knows if I had seen my
 way
Straight out of it by looking, though 't was
 clear,
Unless the generous lady, 'ware of this,
Had set her own house all afire for me
To light me forwards ? Leaning on my
 face
Her heavy agate eyes which crushed my
 will,
She told me tenderly (as when men come
To a bedside to tell people they must die),
" She knew of knowledge, — ay, of know-
 ledge knew,   1080
That Romney Leigh had loved *her* for-
 merly.
And *she* loved *him*, she might say, now the
 chance
Was past, — but that, of course, he never
 guessed, —
For something came between them, some-
 thing thin
As a cobweb, catching every fly of doubt
To hold it buzzing at the window-pane
And help to dim the daylight. Ah, man's
 pride
Or woman's — which is greatest ? most
 averse
To brushing cobwebs ? Well, but she and
 he

Remained fast friends; it seemed not more
    than so,   1090
Because he had bound his hands and could
    not stir.
An honorable man, if somewhat rash;
And she, not even for Romney, would she
    spill
A blot . . . as little even as a tear . . .
Upon his marriage-contract, — not to gain
A better joy for two than came by that:
For, though I stood between her heart and
    heaven,
She loved me wholly." '
                Did I laugh or curse ?
I think I sat there silent, hearing all,
Ay, hearing double, — Marian's tale, at
    once,   1100
And Romney's marriage vow, ' *I 'll keep to*
    THEE,'
Which means that woman-serpent. Is it
    time
For church now ?
          'Lady Waldemar spoke more,'
Continued Marian, ' but, as when a soul
Will pass out through the sweetness of a
    song
Beyond it, voyaging the uphill road,
Even so mine wandered from the things I
    heard
To those I suffered. It was afterward
I shaped the resolution to the act.
For many hours we talked. What need to
    talk ?   1110
The fate was clear and close; it touched
    my eyes;
But still the generous lady tried to keep
The case afloat, and would not let it go,
And argued, struggled upon Marian's side,
Which was not Romney's ! though she
    little knew
What ugly monster would take up the
    end, —
What griping death within the drowning
    death
Was ready to complete my sum of death.'

I thought, — Perhaps he 's sliding now the
    ring   1119
Upon that woman's finger . . .
                She went on:
'The lady, failing to prevail her way,
Upgathered my torn wishes from the
    ground
And pieced them with her strong benevo-
    lence;

And, as I thought I could breathe freer
    air
Away from England, going without pause,
Without farewell, just breaking with a
    jerk
The blossomed offshoot from my thorny
    life, —
She promised kindly to provide the means,
With instant passage to the colonies
And full protection, — " would commit me
    straight   1130
To one who once had been her waiting-
    maid
And had the customs of the world, intent
On changing England for Australia
Herself, to carry out her fortune so."
For which I thanked the Lady Waldemar,
As men upon their death-beds thank last
    friends
Who lay the pillow straight: it is not much,
And yet 't is all of which they are capa-
    ble,
This lying smoothly in a bed to die.
And so, 't was fixed; — and so, from day to
    day,   1140
The woman named came in to visit me.'

Just then the girl stopped speaking, — sat
    erect,
And stared at me as if I had been a ghost
(Perhaps I looked as white as any ghost),
With large-eyed horror. 'Does God
    make,' she said,
' All sorts of creatures really, do you
    think ?
Or is it that the Devil slavers them
So excellently, that we come to doubt
Who 's stronger, He who makes, or he who
    mars ?
I never liked the woman's face or voice 1150
Or ways: it made me blush to look at
    her;
It made me tremble if she touched my
    hand;
And when she spoke a fondling word I
    shrank
As if one hated me who had power to hurt;
And, every time she came, my veins ran
    cold
As somebody were walking on my grave.
At last I spoke to Lady Waldemar:
" Could such an one be good to trust ? " I
    asked.
Whereat the lady stroked my cheek and
    laughed

Her silver laugh (one must be born to
    laugh, 1160
To put such music in it), — " Foolish girl,
Your scattered wits are gathering wool
    beyond
The sheep-walk reaches ! — leave the thing
    to me."
And therefore, half in trust, and half in
    scorn
That I had heart still for another fear
In such a safe despair, I left the thing.

' The rest is short. I was obedient:
I wrote my letter which delivered *him*
From Marian to his own prosperities,
And followed that bad guide. The lady ?
    — hush, 1170
I never blame the lady. Ladies who
Sit high, however willing to look down,
Will scarce see lower than their dainty
    feet;
And Lady Waldemar saw less than I
With what a Devil's daughter I went forth
Along the swine's road, down the preci-
    pice,
In such a curl of hell-foam caught and
    choked,
No shriek of soul in anguish could pierce
    through
To fetch some help. They say there 's
    help in heaven
For all such cries. But if one cries from
    hell . . . 1180
What then ? — the heavens are deaf upon
    that side.

' A woman . . . hear me, let me make it
    plain, . . .
A woman . . . not a monster . . . both
    her breasts
Made right to suckle babes . . . she took
    me off
A woman also, young and ignorant
And heavy with my grief, my two poor
    eyes
Near washed away with weeping, till the
    trees,
The blessed unaccustomed trees and fields
Ran either side the train like stranger
    dogs
Unworthy of any notice, — took me off 1190
So dull, so blind, so only half-alive,
Not seeing by what road, nor by what
    ship,

Nor toward what place, nor to what end of
    all.
Men carry a corpse thus, — past the door-
    way, past
The garden-gate, the children's playground,
    up
The green lane, — then they leave it in the
    pit,
To sleep and find corruption, cheek to
    cheek
With him who stinks since Friday.
              ' But suppose;
To go down with one's soul into the grave,
To go down half-dead, half-alive, I say, 1200
And wake up with corruption, . . . cheek
    to cheek
With him who stinks since Friday ! There
    it is
And that 's the horror of 't, Miss Leigh.
              ' You feel ?
You understand ? — no, do not look at me,
But understand. The blank, blind, weary
    way,
Which led, where'er it led, away at least;
The shifted ship, to Sydney or to France,
Still bound, wherever else, to another
    land;
The swooning sickness on the dismal sea,
The foreign shore, the shameful house, the
    night, 1210
The feeble blood, the heavy-headed
    grief, . . .
No need to bring their damnable drugged
    cup,
And yet they brought it. Hell 's so prodi-
    gal
Of devil's gifts, hunts liberally in packs,
Will kill no poor small creature of the
    wilds
But fifty red wide throats must smoke at
    it,
As HIS at me . . . when waking up at
    last . . .
I told you that I waked up in the grave.

' Enough so ! — it is plain enough so.
    True,
We wretches cannot tell out all our wrong
Without offence to decent happy folk. 1221
I know that we must scrupulously hint
With half-words, delicate reserves, the
    thing
Which no one scrupled we should feel in
    full.

Let pass the rest, then; only leave my
    oath
Upon this sleeping child, — man's violence,
Not man's seduction, made me what I am,
As lost as . . . I told *him* I should be
    lost.
When mothers fail us, can we help our-
    selves ?
That 's fatal ! — And you call it being lost,
That down came next day's noon and
    caught me there,   1231
Half-gibbering and half-raving on the
    floor,
And wondering what had happened up in
    heaven,
That suns should dare to shine when God
    Himself
Was certainly abolished.

                 ' I was mad,
How many weeks, I know not, — many
    weeks.
I think they let me go when I was mad,
They feared my eyes and loosed me, as
    boys might
A mad dog which they had tortured. Up
    and down
I went, by road and village, over tracts 1240
Of open foreign country, large and strange,
Crossed everywhere by long thin poplar-
    lines
Like fingers of some ghastly skeleton
    Hand
Through sunlight and through moonlight
    evermore
Pushed out from hell itself to pluck me
    back,
And resolute to get me, slow and sure;
While every roadside Christ upon his
    cross
Hung reddening through his gory wounds
    at me,
And shook his nails in anger, and came
    down
To follow a mile after, wading up   1250
The low vines and green wheat, crying
    " Take the girl !
She 's none of mine from henceforth."
    Then I knew
(But this is somewhat dimmer than the
    rest)
The charitable peasants gave me bread
And leave to sleep in straw: and twice they
    tied,
At parting, Mary's image round my
    neck —

How heavy it seemed ! as heavy as a
    stone;
A woman has been strangled with less
    weight:
I threw it in a ditch to keep it clean
And ease my breath a little, when none
    looked;   1260
I did not need such safeguards: — brutal
    men
Stopped short, Miss Leigh, in insult, when
    they had seen
My face, — I must have had an awful
    look.
And so I lived: the weeks passed on, — I
    lived.
'T was living my old tramp-life o'er again,
But, this time, in a dream, and hunted
    round
By some prodigious Dream-fear at my
    back,
Which ended yet: my brain cleared pre-
    sently;
And there I sat, one evening, by the road,
I, Marian Erle, myself, alone, undone, 1270
Facing a sunset low upon the flats
As if it were the finish of all time,
The great red stone upon my sepulchre,
Which angels were too weak to roll away.

SEVENTH BOOK

' The woman's motive ? shall we daub our-
    selves
With finding roots for nettles ? 't is soft
    clay
And easily explored. She had the means,
The moneys, by the lady's liberal grace,
In trust for that Australian scheme and
    me,
Which so, that she might clutch with both
    her hands
And chink to her naughty uses undisturbed,
She served me (after all it was not
    strange,
'T was only what my mother would have
    done)
A motherly, right damnable good turn.   10

' Well, after. There are nettles every-
    where,
But smooth green grasses are more com-
    mon still;
The blue of heaven is larger than the
    cloud;

A miller's wife at Clichy took me in
And spent her pity on me, — made me
    calm
And merely very reasonably sad.
She found me a servant's place in Paris,
    where
I tried to take the cast-off life again,
And stood as quiet as a beaten ass
Who, having fallen through overloads,
    stands up   20
To let them charge him with another pack.

'A few months, so. My mistress, young
    and light,
Was easy with me, less for kindness than
Because she led, herself, an easy time
Betwixt her lover and her looking-glass,
Scarce knowing which way she was praised
    the most.
She felt so pretty and so pleased all day
She could not take the trouble to be cross,
But sometimes, as I stooped to tie her
    shoe,
Would tap me softly with her slender
    foot   30
Still restless with the last night's dancing
    in 't,
And say "Fie, pale-face! are you English
    girls
All grave and silent? mass-book still, and
    Lent?
And first - communion pallor on your
    cheeks,
Worn past the time for 't? little fool, be
    gay!"
At which she vanished like a fairy,
    through
A gap of silver laughter.
                'Came an hour
When all went otherwise. She did not
    speak,
But clenched her brows, and clipped me
    with her eyes
As if a viper with a pair of tongs,   40
Too far for any touch, yet near enough
To view the writhing creature, — then at
    last,
"Stand still there, in the holy Virgin's
    name,
Thou Marian; thou 'rt no reputable girl,
Although sufficient dull for twenty saints!
I think thou mock'st me and my house,"
    she said;
"Confess thou 'lt be a mother in a month,
Thou mask of saintship."

                'Could I answer her?
The light broke in so. It meant *that* then,
    that?
I had not thought of that, in all my
    thoughts,   50
Through all the cold, dumb aching of my
    brow,
Through all the heaving of impatient life
Which threw me on death at intervals, —
    through all
The upbreak of the fountains of my heart
The rains had swelled too large: it could
    mean *that?*
Did God make mothers out of victims,
    then,
And set such pure amens to hideous deeds?
Why not? He overblows an ugly grave
With violets which blossom in the spring.
And *I* could be a mother in a month?   60
I hope it was not wicked to be glad.
I lifted up my voice and wept, and
    laughed,
To heaven, not her, until it tore my throat.
"Confess, confess!" — what was there to
    confess,
Except man's cruelty, except my wrong?
Except this anguish, or this ecstasy?
This shame or glory? The light woman
    there
Was small to take it in: an acorn-cup
Would take the sea in sooner.
                ' "Good," she cried;
"Unmarried and a' mother, and she
    laughs!   70
These unchaste girls are always impudent.
Get out, intriguer! leave my house and
    trot.
I wonder you should look me in the face,
With such a filthy secret."
                'Then I rolled
My scanty bundle up and went my way,
Washed white with weeping, shuddering
    head and foot
With blind hysteric passion, staggering
    forth
Beyond those doors. 'T was natural of
    course
She should not ask me where I meant to
    sleep;
I might sleep well beneath the heavy
    Seine,   80
Like others of my sort; the bed was laid
For us. But any woman, womanly,
Had thought of him who should be in a
    month,

The sinless babe that should be in a month,
And if by chance he might be warmer
housed
Than underneath such dreary dripping
eaves.'

I broke on Marian there. ' Yet she her-
self,
A wife, I think, had scandals of her own, —
A lover not her husband.'
      ' Ay,' she said,
' But gold and meal are measured other-
wise;   90
I learnt so much at school,' said Marian
Erle.

' O crooked world,' I cried, ' ridiculous
If not so lamentable ! 'T is the way
With these light women of a thrifty vice,
My Marian, — always hard upon the rent
In any sister's virtue ! while they keep
Their own so darned and patched with
perfidy,
That, though a rag itself, it looks as well
Across a street, in balcony or coach,
As any perfect stuff might. For my
part,   100
I'd rather take the wind-side of the stews
Than touch such women with my finger-
end !
They top the poor street-walker by their
lie
And look the better for being so much
worse:
The devil's most devilish when respect-
able.
But you, dear, and your story.'
       ' All the rest
Is here,' she said, and signed upon the
child.
' I found a mistress-sempstress who was
kind
And let me sew in peace among her girls.
And what was better than to draw the
threads   110
All day and half the night for him and
him ?
And so I lived for him, and so he lives,
And so I know, by this time, God lives
too.'

She smiled beyond the sun and ended so,
And all my soul rose up to take her part
Against the world's successes, virtues,
fames.

' Come with me, sweetest sister,' I re-
turned,
' And sit within my house and do me good
From henceforth, thou and thine ! ye are
my own
From henceforth. I am lonely in the
world,   120
And thou art lonely, and the child is half
An orphan. Come, — and henceforth thou
and I
Being still together will not miss a friend,
Nor he a father, since two mothers shall
Make that up to him. I am journeying
south,
And in my Tuscan home I'll find a niche
And set thee there, my saint, the child and
thee,
And burn the lights of love before thy
face,
And ever at thy sweet look cross myself
From mixing with the world's prosperi-
ties;   130
That so, in gravity and holy calm,
We two may live on toward the truer
life.'

She looked me in the face and answered
not,
Nor signed she was unworthy, nor gave
thanks,
But took the sleeping child and held it
out
To meet my kiss, as if requiting me
And trusting me at once. And thus, at
once,
I carried him and her to where I live;
She's there now, in the little room, asleep,
I hear the soft child-breathing through the
door,   140
And all three of us, at to-morrow's break,
Pass onward, homeward, to our Italy.
Oh, Romney Leigh, I have your debts to
pay,
And I'll be just and pay them.
        But yourself
To pay your debts is scarcely difficult,
To buy your life is nearly impossible,
Being sold away to Lamia. My head aches
I cannot see my road along this dark;
Nor can I creep and grope, as fits the dark
For these foot-catching robes of woman-
hood: 150
A man might walk a little . . . but I ! —
He loves
The Lamia-woman, — and I, write to him

What stops his marriage, and destroys his
    peace, —
Or what perhaps shall simply trouble him,
Until she only need to touch his sleeve
With just a finger's tremulous white flame,
Saying ' Ah, — Aurora Leigh ! a pretty
    tale,
A very pretty poet ! I can guess
The motive ' — then, to catch his eye in
    hers
And vow she does not wonder, — and they
    two   160
To break in laughter as the sea along
A melancholy coast, and float up higher,
In such a laugh, their fatal weeds of love !
Ay, fatal, ay. And who shall answer me
Fate has not hurried tides, — and if to-
    night
My letter would not be a night too late,
An arrow shot into a man that 's dead,
To prove a vain intention ? Would I
    show
The new wife vile, to make the husband
    mad ?
No, Lamia ! shut the shutters, bar the
    doors   170
From every glimmer on thy serpent-skin !
I will not let thy hideous secret out
To agonize the man I love — I mean
The friend I love . . . as friends love.
                            It is strange,
To-day while Marian told her story like
To absorb most listeners, how I listened
    chief
To a voice not hers, nor yet that enemy's,
Nor God's in wrath, . . . but one that
    mixed with mine
Long years ago among the garden trees,
And said to me, to me too, ' Be my wife, 180
Aurora.' It is strange with what a swell
Of yearning passion, as a snow of ghosts
Might beat against the impervious door of
    heaven,
I thought, ' Now, if I had been a woman,
    such
As God made women, to save men by
    love,
By just my love I might have saved this
    man,
And made a nobler poem for the world
Than all I have failed in.' But I failed
    besides
In this; and now he 's lost ! through me
    alone !
And, by my only fault, his empty house 190

Sucks in, at this same hour, a wind from
    hell
To keep his hearth cold, make his case-
    ments creak
For ever to the tune of plague and sin —
O Romney, O my Romney, O my friend,
My cousin and friend ! my helper, when
    I would,
My love, that might be ! mine !
                        Why, how one weeps
When one 's too weary ! Were a witness
    by,
He 'd say some folly . . . that I loved the
    man,
Who knows ? . . . and make me laugh
    again for scorn.   199
At strongest, women are as weak in flesh,
As men, at weakest, vilest, are in soul:
So, hard for women to keep pace with men !
As well give up at once, sit down at once,
And weep as I do. Tears, tears ! why we
    weep ?
'T is worth inquiry ? — that we 've shamed
    a life,
Or lost a love, or missed a world, per-
    haps ?
By no means. Simply, that we 've walked
    too far,
Or talked too much, or felt the wind i' the
    east, —
And so we weep, as if both body and soul
Broke up in water — this way.
                        Poor mixed rags
Forsooth we 're made of, like those other
    dolls   211
That lean with pretty faces into fairs.
It seems as if I had a man in me,
Despising such a woman.
                        Yet indeed,
To see a wrong or suffering moves us all
To undo it though we should undo our-
    selves,
Ay, all the more, that we undo ourselves ;
That 's womanly, past doubt, and not ill-
    moved.
A natural movement therefore, on my
    part,
To fill the chair up of my cousin's wife, 220
And save him from a devil's company !
We 're all so, — made so — 't is our wo-
    man's trade
To suffer torment for another's ease.
The world's male chivalry has perished
    out,
But women are knights-errant to the last;

And if Cervantes had been Shakespeare too,
He had made his Don a Donna.
                                        So it clears,
And so we rain our skies blue.
                                        Put away
This weakness. If, as I have just now said,
A man's within me, — let him act himself,   230
Ignoring the poor conscious trouble of blood
That's called the woman merely. I will write
Plain words to England, — if too late, too late,
If ill-accounted, then accounted ill;
We'll trust the heavens with something.
                          'Dear Lord Howe,
You'll find a story on another leaf
Of Marian Erle, — what noble friend of yours
She trusted once, through what flagitious means,
To what disastrous ends; — the story's true.
I found her wandering on the Paris quays,
A babe upon her breast, — unnatural,   241
Unseasonable outcast on such snow
Unthawed to this time. I will tax in this
Your friendship, friend, if that convicted She
Be not his wife yet, to denounce the facts
To himself, — but, otherwise, to let them pass
On tip-toe like escaping murderers,
And tell my cousin merely — Marian lives,
Is found, and finds her home with such a friend,
Myself, Aurora. Which good news, "She's found,"   250
Will help to make him merry in his love:
I send it, tell him, for my marriage-gift,
As good as orange-water for the nerves,
Or perfumed gloves for headache, — though aware
That he, except of love, is scarcely sick:
I mean the new love this time, . . . since last year.
Such quick forgetting on the part of men !
Is any shrewder trick upon the cards
To enrich them ? pray instruct me how 't is done:
First, clubs, — and while you look at clubs,
        't is spades;   260

That's prodigy. The lightning strikes a man,
And when we think to find him dead and charred . . .
Why, there he is on a sudden, playing pipes
Beneath the splintered elm-tree ! Crime and shame
And all their hoggery trample your smooth world,
Nor leave more foot-marks than Apollo's kine
Whose hoofs were muffled by the thieving god
In tamarisk leaves and myrtle. I'm so sad,
So weary and sad to-night, I'm somewhat sour, —
Forgive me. To be blue and shrew at once   270
Exceeds all toleration except yours,
But yours, I know, is infinite. Farewell.
To-morrow we take train for Italy.
Speak gently of me to your gracious wife,
As one, however far, shall yet be near
In loving wishes to your house.'
                                        I sign.
And now I loose my heart upon a page,
This —
        'Lady Waldemar, I'm very glad
I never liked you; which you knew so well
You spared me, in your turn, to like me much: 280
Your liking surely had done worse for me
Than has your loathing, though the last appears
Sufficiently unscrupulous to hurt,
And not afraid of judgment. Now, there's space
Between our faces, — I stand off, as if
I judged a stranger's portrait and pronounced
Indifferently the type was good or bad.
What matter to me that the lines are false,
I ask you ? did I ever ink my lips
By drawing your name through them as a friend's,   290
Or touch your hands as lovers do ? Thank God
I never did: and since you're proved so vile,
Ay, vile, I say, — we'll show it presently, —
I'm not obliged to nurse my friend in you,

Or wash out my own blots, in counting
yours,
Or even excuse myself to honest souls
Who seek to press my lip or clasp my
palm, —
" Alas, but Lady Waldemar came first ! "

'T is true, by this time you may near me
so
That you 're my cousin's wife. You 've
gambled deep   300
As Lucifer, and won the morning star
In that case, — and the noble house of
Leigh
Must henceforth with its good roof shelter
you:
I cannot speak and burn you up between
Those rafters, I who am born a Leigh, —
nor speak
And pierce your breast through Romney's,
I who live,
His friend and cousin, — so, you 're safe.
You two
Must grow together like the tares and wheat
Till God's great fire. — But make the best
of time.   309

' And hide this letter: let it speak no more
Than I shall, how you tricked poor Marian
Erle,
And set her own love digging its own grave
Within her green hope's pretty garden-
ground, —
Ay, sent her forth with some one of your
sort
To a wicked house in France, from which
she fled
With curses in her eyes and ears and
throat,
Her whole soul choked with curses, — mad
in short,
And madly scouring up and down for weeks
The foreign hedgeless country, lone and
lost, —   319
So innocent, male-fiends might slink within
Remote hell-corners, seeing her so defiled.

' But you, — you are a woman and more
bold.
To do you justice, you 'd not shrink to
face . . .
We 'll say, the unfledged life in the other
room,
Which, treading down God's corn, you trod
in sight

Of all the dogs, in reach of all the guns, —
Ay, Marian's babe, her poor unfathered
child,
Her yearling babe ! — you 'd face him when
he wakes
And opens up his wonderful blue eyes:
You 'd meet them and not wink perhaps,
nor fear   330
God's triumph in them and supreme revenge
When righting his creation's balance-scale
(You pulled as low as Tophet) to the top
Of most celestial innocence.   For me,
Who am not as bold, I own those infant
eyes
Have set me praying.
                    ' While they look at heaven,
No need of protestation in my words
Against the place you 've made them ! let
them look.
They 'll do your business with the heavens,
be sure·   339
I spare you common curses.
                    ' Ponder this;
If haply you 're the wife of Romney Leigh
(For which inheritance beyond your birth
You sold that poisonous porridge called
your soul),
I charge you, be his faithful and true
wife !
Keep warm his hearth and clean his board,
and, when
He speaks, be quick with your obedience;
Still grind your paltry wants and low
desires
To dust beneath his heel; though, even
thus,
The ground must hurt him, — it was writ
of old,   349
" Ye shall not yoke together ox and ass,"
The nobler and ignobler. Ay, but you
Shall do your part as well as such ill
things
Can do aught good. You shall not vex
him, — mark,
You shall not vex him, jar him when he 's
sad,
Or cross him when he 's eager. Under-
stand
To trick him with apparent sympathies,
Nor let him see thee in the face too near
And unlearn thy sweet seeming. Pay the
price
Of lies, by being constrained to lie on still:
'T is easy for thy sort: a million more   360
Will scarcely damn thee deeper.

'Doing which
You are very safe from Marian and myself;
We'll breathe as softly as the infant here,
And stir no dangerous embers. Fail a point,
And show our Romney wounded, ill-con-
tent,
Tormented in his home, we open mouth,
And such a noise will follow, the last
trump's
Will scarcely seem more dreadful, even to
you;
You'll have no pipers after: Romney will
(I know him) push you forth as none of his,
All other men declaring it well done,   371
While women, even the worst, your like,
will draw
Their skirts back, not to brush you in the
street,
And so I warn you. I'm . . . Aurora
Leigh.'

The letter written, I felt satisfied.
The ashes, smouldering in me, were thrown
out
By handfuls from me : I had writ my heart
And wept my tears, and now was cool and
calm;
And, going straightway to the neighboring
room,
I lifted up the curtains of the bed   380
Where Marian Erle, the babe upon her arm,
Both faces leaned together like a pair
Of folded innocences self-complete,
Each smiling from the other, smiled and
slept.
There seemed no sin, no shame, no wrath,
no grief.
I felt she too had spoken words that night,
But softer certainly, and said to God,
Who laughs in heaven perhaps that such
as I
Should make ado for such as she. — 'De-
filed'   389
I wrote ? 'defiled' I thought her ? Stoop,
Stoop lower, Aurora ! get the angels' leave
To creep in somewhere, humbly, on your
knees,
Within this round of sequestration white
In which they have wrapped earth's found-
lings, heaven's elect.

The next day we took train to Italy
And fled on southward in the roar of steam.
The marriage-bells of Romney must be
loud,

To sound so clear through all: I was not
well,
And truly, though the truth is like a jest,
I could not choose but fancy, half the
way,   400
I stood alone i' the belfry, fifty bells
Of naked iron, mad with merriment
(As one who laughs and cannot stop him-
self),
All clanking at me, in me, over me,
Until I shrieked a shriek I could not hear,
And swooned with noise, — but still, along
my swoon,
Was 'ware the baffled changes backward
rang
Prepared, at each emerging sense, to beat
And crash it out with clangor. I was
weak;
I struggled for the posture of my soul   410
In upright consciousness of place and time,
But evermore, 'twixt waking and asleep,
Slipped somehow, staggered, caught at
Marian's eyes
A moment (it is very good for strength
To know that some one needs you to be
strong),
And so recovered what I called myself,
For that time.
          I just knew it when we swept
Above the old roofs of Dijon: Lyons
dropped
A spark into the night, half trodden out
Unseen. But presently the winding Rhone
Washed out the moonlight large along his
banks   421
Which strained their yielding curves out
clear and clean
To hold it, — shadow of town and castle
blurred
Upon the hurrying river. Such an air
Blew thence upon the forehead — half an
air
And half a water — that I leaned and
looked,
Then, turning back on Marian, smiled to
mark
That she looked only on her child, who
slept,
His face toward the moon too.
                    So we passed
The liberal open country and the close,   430
And shot through tunnels, like a lightning-
wedge
By great Thor-hammers driven through
the rock,

Which, quivering through the intestine
blackness, splits,
And lets it in at once: the train swept in
Athrob with effort, trembling with resolve,
The fierce denouncing whistle wailing on
And dying off smothered in the shudder-
ing dark,
While we, self - awed, drew troubled
breath, oppressed
As other Titans underneath the pile
And nightmare of the mountains. Out, at
last, 440
To catch the dawn afloat upon the land !
— Hills, slung forth broadly and gauntly
everywhere,
Not cramped in their foundations, pushing
wide
Rich outspreads of the vineyards and the
corn
(As if they entertained i' the name of
France),
While down their straining sides streamed
manifest
A soil as red as Charlemagne's knightly
blood,
To consecrate the verdure. Some one
said
'Marseilles !' And lo, the city of Mar-
seilles,
With all her ships behind her, and be-
yond, 450
The scimitar of ever-shining sea
For right-hand use, bared blue against the
sky !

That night we spent between the purple
heaven
And purple water: I think Marian slept;
But I, as a dog awatch for his master's
foot,
Who cannot sleep or eat before he hears,
I sat upon the deck and watched the night
And listened through the stars for Italy.
Those marriage-bells I spoke of sounded
far,
As some child's go-cart in the street be-
neath 460
To a dying man who will not pass the
day,
And knows it, holding by a hand he loves.
I too sat quiet, satisfied with death,
Sat silent: I could hear my own soul
speak,
And had my friend, — for Nature comes
sometimes

And says, 'I am ambassador for God.'
I felt the wind soft from the land of souls;
The old miraculous mountains heaved in
sight,
One straining past another along the shore,
The way of grand dull Odyssean ghosts, 470
Athirst to drink the cool blue wine of
seas
And stare on voyagers. Peak pushing
peak
They stood: I watched, beyond that Tyr-
ian belt
Of intense sea betwixt them and the ship,
Down all their sides the misty olive-woods
Dissolving in the weak, congenial moon
And still disclosing some brown convent
tower
That seems as if it grew from some brown
rock,
Or many a little lighted village, dropped
Like a fallen star upon so high a point, 480
You wonder what can keep it in its place
From sliding headlong with the waterfalls
Which powder all the myrtle and orange
groves
With spray of silver. Thus my Italy
Was stealing on us. Genoa broke with
day,
The Doria's long pale palace striking out,
From green hills in advance of the white
town,
A marble finger dominant to ships,
Seen glimmering through the uncertain
gray of dawn.

And then I did not think, 'My Italy,' 490
I thought 'My father !' O my father's
house,
Without his presence ! — Places are too
much,
Or else too little, for immortal man —
Too little, when love's May o'ergrows
the ground;
Too much, when that luxuriant robe of
green
Is rustling to our ankles in dead leaves.
'T is only good to be or here or there,
Because we had a dream on such a stone,
Or this or that, — but, once being wholly
waked
And come back to the stone without the
dream, 500
We trip upon 't, — alas, and hurt our-
selves;
Or else it falls on us and grinds us flat,

The heaviest gravestone on this burying
    earth.
— But while I stood and mused, a quiet
    touch
Fell light upon my arm, and, turning
    round,
A pair of moistened eyes convicted mine.
' What, Marian! is the babe astir so soon?'
' He sleeps,' she answered; ' I have crept
    up thrice,
And seen you sitting, standing, still at
    watch.
I thought it did you good till now, but
    now ' . . .   510
  But now,' I said, ' you leave the child
    alone.'
'And you 're alone,' she answered, — and
    she looked
As if I too were something. Sweet the
    help
Of one we have helped ! Thanks, Marian,
    for such help.

I found a house at Florence on the hill
Of Bellosguardo. 'T is a tower which
    keeps
A post of double observation o'er
That valley of Arno (holding as a hand
The outspread city) straight toward Fie-
    sole   519
And Mount Morello and the setting sun,
The Vallombrosan mountains opposite,
Which sunrise fills as full as crystal cups
Turned red to the brim because their wine
    is red.
No sun could die nor yet be born unseen
By dwellers at my villa: morn and eve
Were magnified before us in the pure
Illimitable space and pause of sky,
Intense as angels' garments blanched with
    God,
Less blue than radiant. From the outer
    wall
Of the garden, drops the mystic floating
    gray   530
Of olive-trees (with interruptions green
From maize and vine), until 't is caught
    and torn
Upon the abrupt black line of cypresses
Which signs the way to Florence. Beauti-
    ful
The city lies along the ample vale,
Cathedral, tower and palace, piazza and
    street,
The river trailing like a silver cord

Through all, and curling loosely, both be-
    fore
And after, over the whole stretch of land
Sown whitely up and down its opposite
    slopes   540
With farms and villas.
                Many weeks had passed,
No word was granted. — Last, a letter
    came
From Vincent Carrington: — ' My dear
    Miss Leigh,
You 've been as silent as a poet should,
When any other man is sure to speak.
If sick, if vexed, if dumb, a silver piece
Will split a man's tongue, — straight he
    speaks and says
" Received that cheque." But you! . . .
    I send you funds
To Paris, and you make no sign at all.
Remember, I 'm responsible and wait   550
A sign of you, Miss Leigh.
                ' Meantime your book
Is eloquent as if you were not dumb;
And common critics, ordinarily deaf
To such fine meanings, and, like deaf men,
    loth
To seem deaf, answering chance-wise, yes
    or no,
" It must be " or " it must not " (most pro-
    nounced
When least convinced), pronounce for once
    aright:
You 'd think they really heard, — and so
    they do . . .
The burr of three or four who really hear
And praise your book aright: Fame's
    smallest trump   560
Is a great ear-trumpet for the deaf as
    posts,
No other being effective. Fear not, friend;
We think here you have written a good
    book,
And you, a woman ! It was in you, — yes,
I felt 't was in you: yet I doubted half
If that od-force of German Reichenbach,
Which still from female finger-tips burns
    blue,
Could strike out as our masculine white
    heats
To quicken a man. Forgive me. All my
    heart
Is quick with yours since, just a fortnight
    since,   570
I read your book and loved it.
                 ' Will you love

My wife, too ?   Here 's my secret I might
   keep
A month more from you ! but I yield it up
Because I know you 'll write the sooner
   for 't,
Most women (of your height even) count-
   ing love
Life's only serious business   Who 's my
   wife
That shall be in a month ? you ask, nor
   guess ?
Remember what a pair of topaz eyes
You once detected, turned against the wall,
That morning in my London painting-
   room;   580
The face half-sketched, and slurred; the
   eyes alone !
But you . . . you caught them up with
   yours, and said
" Kate Ward's eyes, surely." — Now I own
   the truth:
I had thrown them there to keep them
   safe from Jove,
They would so naughtily find out their
   way
To both the heads of both my Danaës
Where just it made me mad to look at
   them.
Such eyes ! I could not paint or think of
   eyes
But those, — and so I flung them into
   paint
And turned them to the wall's care. Ay,
   but now   590
I 've let them out, my Kate's: I 've painted
   her
(I change my style and leave mythologies),
The whole sweet face; it looks upon my
   soul
Like a face on water, to beget itself.
A half-length portrait, in a hanging cloak
Like one you wore once ; 't is a little
   frayed, —
I pressed too for the nude harmonious arm;
But she, she 'd have her way, and have her
   cloak —
She said she could be like you only so,
And would not miss the fortune. Ah, my
   friend,   600
You 'll write and say she shall not miss
   your love
Through meeting mine ? in faith, she
   would not change.
She has your books by heart more than
   my words,

And quotes you up against me till I 'm
   pushed
Where, three months since, her eyes were:
   nay, in fact,
Nought satisfied her but to make me paint
Your last book folded in her dimpled
   hands
Instead of my brown palette as I wished,
And, grant me, the presentment had been
   newer;
She 'd grant me nothing: I compounded
   for   610
The naming of the wedding - day next
   month,
And gladly too. 'T is pretty to remark
How women can love women of your sort,
And tie their hearts with love-knots to
   your feet,
Grow insolent about you against men,
And put us down by putting up the lip,
As if a man — there *are* such, let us own,
Who write not ill — remains a man, poor
   wretch,
While you ! — Write weaker than Aurora
   Leigh,   619
And there 'll be women who believe of you
(Besides my Kate) that if you walked on
   sand
You would not leave a foot-print.
                   ' Are you put
To wonder by my marriage, like poor
   Leigh ?
" Kate Ward ! " he said. " Kate Ward ! "
   he said anew.
" I thought " . . . he said, and stopped — " I
   did not think " . . .
And then he dropped to silence.
                  ' Ah, he 's changed.
I had not seen him, you 're aware, for long,
But went of course. I have not touched on
   this
Through all this letter — conscious of your
   heart,
And writing lightlier for the heavy fact, 630
As clocks are voluble with lead.
                   ' How poor,
To say I 'm sorry ! dear Leigh, dearest
   Leigh.
In those old days of Shropshire — pardon
   me —
When he and you fought many a field of
   gold
On what you should do, or you should not
   do,
Make bread or verses (it just came to that),

I thought you'd one day draw a silken
    peace
Through a golden ring. I thought so:
    foolishly,
The event proved; for you went more
    opposite
To each other, month by month, and year
    by year,   640
Until this happened. God knows best, we
    say,
But hoarsely. When the fever took him
    first,
Just after I had writ to you in France,
They tell me, Lady Waldemar mixed drinks
And counted grains, like any salaried nurse,
Excepting that she wept too. Then Lord
    Howe,
You're right about Lord Howe, Lord
    Howe's a trump,
And yet, with such in his hand, a man like
    Leigh
May lose as *he* does. There's an end to all,
Yes, even this letter, though this second
    sheet   650
May find you doubtful. Write a word for
    Kate:
She reads my letters always, like a wife,
And if she sees her name I'll see her smile
And share the luck. So, bless you, friend
    of two !
I will not ask you what your feeling is
At Florence with my pictures; I can hear
Your heart a-flutter over the snow-hills:
And, just to pace the Pitti with you once,
I'd give a half-hour of to-morrow's walk
With Kate . . . I think so. Vincent Car-
    rington.'   660

The noon was hot; the air scorched like the
    sun,
And was shut out. The closed persiani
    threw
Their long-scored shadows on my villa-floor,
And interlined the golden atmosphere
Straight, still, — across the pictures on the
    wall,
The statuette on the console (of young Love
And Psyche made one marble by a kiss),
The low couch where I leaned, the table
    near,
The vase of lilies Marian pulled last night
(Each green leaf and each white leaf ruled
    in black   670
As if for writing some new text of fate),
And the open letter, rested on my knee,

But there the lines swerved, trembled,
    though I sat
Untroubled, plainly, reading it again,
And three times. Well, he's married;
    that is clear.
No wonder that he's married, nor much
    more
That Vincent's therefore 'sorry.' Why, of
    course
The lady nursed him when he was not well,
Mixed drinks, — unless nepenthe was the
    drink
'T was scarce worth telling. But a man in
    love   680
Will see the whole sex in his mistress' hood,
The prettier for its lining of fair rose,
Although he catches back and says at last,
'I'm sorry.' Sorry. Lady Waldemar
At prettiest, under the said hood, pre-
    served
From such a light as I could hold to her
    face
To flare its ugly wrinkles out to shame,
Is scarce a wife for Romney, as friends
    judge,
Aurora Leigh or Vincent Carrington,
That's plain. And if he's 'conscious of
    my heart' . . .   690
It may be natural, though the phrase is
    strong
(One's apt to use strong phrases, being in
    love) ;
And even that stuff of ' fields of gold,' ' gold
    rings,'
And what he ' thought,' poor Vincent, what
    he ' thought,'
May never mean enough to ruffle me.
— Why, this room stifles. Better burn than
    choke;
Best have air, air, although it comes with
    fire,
Throw open blinds and windows to the noon,
And take a blister on my brow instead
Of this dead weight ! best, perfectly be
    stunned   700
By those insufferable cicale, sick
And hoarse with rapture of the summer-
    heat,
That sing, like poets, till their hearts break,
    — sing
Till men say ' It's too tedious.'
                      Books succeed,
And lives fail. Do I feel it so, at last ?
Kate loves a worn-out cloak for being like
    mine,

While I live self-despised for being myself,
And yearn toward some one else, who yearns
    away
From what he is, in his turn. Strain a
    step
For ever, yet gain no step? Are we such,
We cannot, with our admirations even, 711
Our tip-toe aspirations, touch a thing
That 's higher than we? is all a dismal flat,
And God alone above each, as the sun
O'er level lagunes, to make them shine and
    stink —
Laying stress upon us with immediate flame,
While we respond with our miasmal fog,
And call it mounting higher because we
    grow
More highly fatal?
             Tush, Aurora Leigh!
You wear your sackcloth looped in Cæsar's
    way, 720
And brag your failings as mankind's. Be
    still.
There *is* what 's higher, in this very world,
Than you can live, or catch at. Stand
    aside
And look at others — instance little Kate!
She 'll make a perfect wife for Carrington.
She always has been looking round the
    earth
For something good and green to alight
    upon
And nestle into, with those soft-winged
    eyes,
Subsiding now beneath his manly hand
'Twixt trembling lids of inexpressive joy.
I will not scorn her, after all, too much,
That so much she should love me: a wise
    man 732
Can pluck a leaf, and find a lecture in 't;
And I, too, . . . God has made me, — I 've
    a heart
That 's capable of worship, love, and loss;
We say the same of Shakespeare's. I 'll
    be meek
And learn to reverence, even this poor
    myself.

The book, too — pass it. 'A good book,'
    says he,
'And you a woman.' I had laughed at
    that, 739
But long since. I 'm a woman, it is true;
Alas, and woe to us, when we feel it most!
Then, least care have we for the crowns
    and goals

And compliments on writing our good
    books.
The book has some truth in it, I believe,
And truth outlives pain, as the soul does
    life.
I know we talk our Phædons to the end,
Through all the dismal faces that we make,
O'erwrinkled with dishonoring agony
From decomposing drugs. I have written
    truth,
And I a woman, — feebly, partially, 750
Inaptly in presentation, Romney 'll add,
Because a woman. For the truth itself,
That 's neither man's nor woman's, but just
    God's,
None else has reason to be proud of truth:
Himself will see it sifted, disenthralled,
And kept upon the height and in the light,
As far as and no farther than 't is truth;
For, now He has left off calling firma-
    ments
And strata, flowers and creatures, very
    good, 759
He says it still of truth, which is his own.

Truth, so far, in my book; the truth which
    draws
Through all things upwards — that a two-
    fold world
Must go to a perfect cosmos. Natural
    things
And spiritual, — who separates those two
In art, in morals, or the social drift,
Tears up the bond of nature and brings
    death,
Paints futile pictures, writes unreal verse,
Leads vulgar days, deals ignorantly with
    men,
Is wrong, in short, at all points. We di-
    vide
This apple of life, and cut it through the
    pips: 770
The perfect round which fitted Venus'
    hand
Has perished as utterly as if we ate
Both halves. Without the spiritual, ob-
    serve,
The natural 's impossible — no form,
No motion: without sensuous, spiritual
Is inappreciable, — no beauty or power:
And in this twofold sphere the twofold
    man
(For still the artist is intensely a man)
Holds firmly by the natural, to reach
The spiritual beyond it, — fixes still 780

The type with mortal vision, to pierce
through,
With eyes immortal, to the antitype
Some call the ideal, — better called the
real,
And certain to be called so presently
When things shall have their names. Look
long enough
On any peasant's face here, coarse and
lined,
You 'll catch Antinous somewhere in that
clay,
As perfect featured as he yearns at Rome
From marble pale with beauty; then per-
sist, 789
And, if your apprehension 's competent,
You 'll find some fairer angel at his back,
As much exceeding him as he the boor,
And pushing him with empyreal disdain
For ever out of sight. Ay, Carrington
Is glad of such a creed; an artist must,
Who paints a tree, a leaf, a common stone,
With just his hand, and finds it suddenly
A-piece with and conterminous to his soul.
Why else do these things move him, leaf
or stone ?
The bird 's not moved that pecks at a
spring-shoot; 800
Nor yet the horse, before a quarry agraze:
But man, the twofold creature, appre-
hends
The twofold manner, in and outwardly,
And nothing in the world comes single to
him,
A mere itself, — cup, column, or candle-
stick,
All patterns of what shall be in the Mount;
The whole temporal show related royally,
And built up to eterne significance
Through the open arms of God. 'There 's
nothing great
Nor small,' has said a poet of our day, 810
Whose voice will ring beyond the curfew
of eve
And not be thrown out by the matin's bell:
And truly, I reiterate, nothing 's small !
No lily-muffled hum of a summer-bee,
But finds some coupling with the spinning
stars;
No pebble at your foot, but proves a
sphere;
No chaffinch, but implies the cherubim;
And (glancing on my own thin, veinèd
wrist)
In such a little tremor of the blood

The whole strong clamor of a vehement
soul 820
Doth utter itself distinct. Earth 's
crammed with heaven,
And every common bush afire with God;
But only he who sees, takes off his shoes —
The rest sit round it and pluck black-
berries,
And daub their natural faces unaware
More and more from the first similitude.

Truth, so far, in my book ! a truth which
draws
From all things upward. I, Aurora, still
Have felt it hound me through the wastes
of life
As Jove did Io; and, until that Hand 830
Shall overtake me wholly and on my head
Lay down its large unfluctuating peace,
The feverish gad-fly pricks me up and
down.
It must be. Art 's the witness of what
Is
Behind this show. If this world's show
were all,
Then imitation would be all in Art;
There, Jove's hand gripes us ! — For we
stand here, we,
If genuine artists, witnessing for God's
Complete, consummate, undivided work;
That every natural flower which grows on
earth 840
Implies a flower upon the spiritual side,
Substantial, archetypal, all aglow
With blossoming causes, — not so far
away,
But we, whose spirit-sense is somewhat
cleared,
May catch at something of the bloom and
breath, —
Too vaguely apprehended, though indeed
Still apprehended, consciously or not,
And still transferred to picture, music,
verse,
For thrilling audient and beholding souls
By signs and touches which are known to
souls. 850
How known, they know not, — why, they
cannot find,
So straight call out on genius, say ' A man
Produced this,' when much rather they
should say
' 'T is insight and he saw this.'
Thus is Art
Self-magnified in magnifying a truth

Which, fully recognized, would change the
    world
And shift its morals. If a man could feel,
Not one day, in the artist's ecstasy,
But every day, feast, fast, or working-day,
The spiritual significance burn through 860
The hieroglyphic of material shows,
Henceforward he would paint the globe
    with wings,
And reverence fish and fowl, the bull, the
    tree,
And even his very body as a man —
Which now he counts so vile, that all the
    towns
Make offal of their daughters for its use,
On summer-nights, when God is sad in
    heaven
To think what goes on in his recreant
    world
He made quite other; while that moon He
    made
To shine there, at the first love's cove-
    nant,   870
Shines still, convictive as a marriage-ring
Before adulterous eyes.
                        How sure it is,
That, if we say a true word, instantly
We feel 't is God's, not ours, and pass it
    on
Like bread at sacrament we taste and pass
Nor handle for a moment, as indeed
We dared to set up any claim to such !
And I — my poem, — let my readers talk.
I 'm closer to it — I can speak as well:
I 'll say with Romney, that the book is
    weak,   880
The range uneven, the points of sight ob-
    scure,
The music interrupted.
                        Let us go.
The end of woman (or of man, I think)
Is not a book. Alas, the best of books
Is but a word in Art, which soon grows
    cramped,
Stiff, dubious-statured with the weight of
    years,
And drops an accent or digamma down
Some cranny of unfathomable time,
Beyond the critic's reaching. Art itself,
We 've called the larger life, must feel the
    soul   890
Live past it. For more 's felt than is per-
    ceived,
And more 's perceived than can be inter-
    preted,

And Love strikes higher with his lambent
    flame
Than Art can pile the fagots.
                                Is it so ?
When Jove's hand meets us with compos-
    ing touch,
And when at last we are hushed and satis-
    fied,
Then Io does not call it truth, but love ?
Well, well ! my father was an English-
    man:
My mother's blood in me is not so strong
That I should bear this stress of Tuscan
    noon   900
And keep my wits. The town, there,
    seems to seethe
In this Medæan boil-pot of the sun,
And all the patient hills are bubbling
    round
As if a prick would leave them flat.
    Does heaven
Keep far off, not to set us in a blaze ?
Not so, — let drag your fiery fringes,
    heaven,
And burn us up to quiet. Ah, we know
Too much here, not to know what 's best
    for peace;
We have too much light here, not to want
    more fire
To purify and end us. We talk, talk, 910
Conclude upon divine philosophies,
And get the thanks of men for hopeful
    books,
Whereat we take our own life up, and . . .
    pshaw !
Unless we piece it with another's life
(A yard of silk to carry out our lawn)
As well suppose my little handkerchief
Would cover Samminiato, church and all,
If out I threw it past the cypresses,
As, in this ragged, narrow life of mine,
Contain my own conclusions.
                                But at least
We 'll shut up the persiani and sit down,
And when my head 's done aching, in the
    cool,   922
Write just a word to Kate and Carrington.
May joy be with them ! she has chosen
    well,
And he not ill.
                I should be glad, I think,
Except for Romney. Had *he* married
    Kate,
I surely, surely, should be very glad.
This Florence sits upon me easily,

With native air and tongue. My graves
are calm,
And do not too much hurt me. Marian's
good,   930
Gentle and loving, — lets me hold the
child,
Or drags him up the hills to find me
flowers
And fill these vases ere I'm quite
awake, —
My grandiose red tulips, which grow wild,
Or Dante's purple lilies, which he blew
To a larger bubble with his prophet
breath,
Or one of those tall flowering reeds that
stand
In Arno, like a sheaf of sceptres left
But some remote dynasty of dead gods
To suck the stream for ages and get
green,   940
And blossom wheresoe'er a hand divine
Had warmed the place with ichor. Such
I find
At early morning laid across my bed,
And wake up pelted with a childish laugh
Which even Marian's low precipitous
'hush'
Has vainly interposed to put away, —
While I, with shut eyes, smile and motion
for
The dewy kiss that's very sure to come
From mouth and cheeks the whole child's
face at once   949
Dissolved on mine, — as if a nosegay burst
Its string with the weight of roses over-
blown,
And dropped upon me. Surely I should be
glad.
The little creature almost loves me now,
And calls my name, ' Alola,' stripping off
The r's like thorns, to make it smooth
enough
To take between his dainty, milk-fed lips,
God love him ! I should certainly be glad,
Except, God help me, that I'm sorrowful
Because of Romney.
                 Romney, Romney ! Well,
This grows absurd ! — too like a tune that
runs   960
I' the head, and forces all things in the
world,
Wind, rain, the creaking gnat, or stuttering
fly,
To sing itself and vex you, — yet perhaps
A paltry tune you never fairly liked,

Some ' I'd be a butterfly,' or ' C'est
l'amour: '
We 're made so, — not such tyrants to our-
selves
But still we are slaves to nature. Some of
us
Are turned, too, overmuch like some poor
verse
With a trick of ritournelle: the same thing
goes   969
And comes back ever.
                 Vincent Carrington
Is ' sorry,' and I'm sorry; but he's strong
To mount from sorrow to his heaven of
love,
And when he says at moments, ' Poor, poor
Leigh,
Who'll never call his own so true a heart,
So fair a face even,' — he must quickly lose
The pain of pity, in the blush he makes
By his very pitying eyes. The snow, for
him,
Has fallen in May and finds the whole
earth warm,
And melts at the first touch of the green
grass.
But Romney, — he has chosen, after all. 980
I think he had as excellent a sun
To see by, as most others, and perhaps
Has scarce seen really worse than some of
us
When all 's said. Let him pass. I'm not
too much
A woman, not to be a man for once
And bury all my Dead like Alaric,
Depositing the treasures of my soul
In this drained watercourse, then letting flow
The river of life again with commerce-ships
And pleasure-barges full of silks and songs.
Blow, winds, and help us.
                 Ah, we mock ourselves
With talking of the winds; perhaps as
much   992
With other resolutions. How it weighs,
This hot, sick air ! and how I covet here
The Dead's provision on the river-couch,
With silver curtains drawn on tinkling
rings !
Or else their rest in quiet crypts, — laid by
From heat and noise; — from those cicale,
say,
And this more vexing heart-beat.
                 So it is:
We covet for the soul, the body's part, 1000
To die and rot. Even so, Aurora, ends

Our aspiration who bespoke our place
So far in the east. The occidental flats
Had fed us fatter, therefore? we have
climbed
Where herbage ends? we want the beast's
part now
And tire of the angel's? — Men define a man,
The creature who stands frontward to the
stars,
The creature who looks inward to himself,
The tool-wright, laughing creature. 'T is
enough:
We'll say instead, the inconsequent crea-
ture, man,   1010
For that's his specialty. What creature else
Conceives the circle, and then walks the
square?
Loves things proved bad, and leaves a thing
proved good?
You think the bee makes honey half a year,
To loathe the comb in winter and desire
The little ant's food rather? But a man —
Note men! — they are but women after all,
As women are but Auroras! there are
men
Born tender, apt to pale at a trodden worm,
Who paint for pastime, in their favorite
dream,   1020
Spruce auto-vestments flowered with crocus-
flames.
There are, too, who believe in hell, and lie;
There are, too, who believe in heaven, and
fear:
There are, who waste their souls in working
out
Life's problem on these sands betwixt two
tides,
Concluding, — 'Give us the oyster's part,
in death.'

Alas, long-suffering and most patient God,
Thou needst be surelier God to bear with
us
Than even to have made us! thou aspire,
aspire
From henceforth for me! thou who hast
thyself   1030
Endured this fleshhood, knowing how as a
soaked
And sucking vesture it can drag us down
And choke us in the melancholy Deep,
Sustain me, that with thee I walk these
waves,
Resisting! — breathe me upward, thou in
me

Aspiring who art the way, the truth, the
life, —
That no truth henceforth seem indifferent,
No way to truth laborious, and no life,
Not even this life I live, intolerable!

The days went by. I took up the old days,
With all their Tuscan pleasures worn and
spoiled,   1041
Like some lost book we dropped in the long
grass
On such a happy summer afternoon
When last we read it with a loving friend,
And find in autumn when the friend is gone,
The grass cut short, the weather changed,
too late,
And stare at, as at something wonderful
For sorrow, — thinking how two hands be-
fore
Had held up what is left to only one,
And how we smiled when such a vehement
nail   1050
Impressed the tiny dint here which pre-
sents
This verse in fire forever. Tenderly
And mournfully I lived. I knew the birds
And insects, — which looked fathered by
the flowers
And emulous of their hues: I recognized
The moths, with that great overpoise of
wings
Which make a mystery of them how at all
They can stop flying: butterflies, that bear
Upon their blue wings such red embers
round,
They seem to scorch the blue air into holes
Each flight they take: and fireflies, that
suspire   1061
In short soft lapses of transported flame
Across the tingling Dark, while overhead
The constant and inviolable stars
Outburn those light-of-love: melodious
owls
(If music had but one note and was sad,
'T would sound just so), and all the silent
swirl
Of bats that seem to follow in the air
Some grand circumference of a shadowy
dome
To which we are blind: and then the night-
ingales,   1070
Which pluck our heart across a garden-
wall
(When walking in the town) and carry it
So high into the bowery almond-trees

We tremble and are afraid, and feel as if
The golden flood of moonlight unaware
Dissolved the pillars of the steady earth
And made it less substantial. And I knew
The harmless opal snakes, the large-
    mouthed frogs
(Those noisy vaunters of their shallow
    streams);
And lizards, the green lightnings of the
    wall,   1080
Which, if you sit down quiet, nor sigh loud,
Will flatter you and take you for a stone,
And flash familiarly about your feet
With such prodigious eyes in such small
    heads ! —
I knew them (though they had somewhat
    dwindled from
My childish imagery), and kept in mind
How last I sat among them equally,
In fellowship and mateship, as a child
Feels equal still toward insect, beast, and
    bird,
Before the Adam in him has forgone   1090
All privilege of Eden, — making friends
And talk with such a bird or such a goat,
And buying many a two-inch-wide rush-
    cage
To let out the caged cricket on a tree,
Saying ' Oh my dear grillino, were you
    cramped ?
And are you happy with the ilex-leaves ?
And do you love me who have let you
    go ?
Say *yes* in singing, and I 'll understand.'

But now the creatures all seemed farther
    off,
No longer mine, nor like me, only *there*,   1100
A gulf between us. I could yearn indeed,
Like other rich men, for a drop of dew
To cool this heat, — a drop of the early
    dew,
The irrecoverable child-innocence
(Before the heart took fire and withered
    life)
When childhood might pair equally with
    birds;
But now . . . the birds were grown too
    proud for us,
Alas, the very sun forbids the dew.
And I, I had come back to an empty nest,
Which every bird 's too wise for. How I
    heard   1110
My father's step on that deserted ground,
His voice along that silence, as he told

The names of bird and insect, tree and
    flower,
And all the presentations of the stars
Across Valdarno, interposing still
My child,' ' my child.' When fathers say
    ' my child,'
'T is easier to conceive the universe,
And life's transitions down the steps of
    law.

I rode once to the little mountain-house
As fast as if to find my father there,   1120
But, when in sight of 't, within fifty yards,
I dropped my horse's bridle on his neck
And paused upon his flank. The house's
    front
Was cased with lingots of ripe Indian
    corn
In tessellated order and device
Of golden patterns, not a stone of wall
Uncovered, — not an inch of room to grow
A vine-leaf. The old porch had disap-
    peared;
And right in the open doorway sat a girl
At plaiting straws, her black hair strained
    away   1130
To a scarlet kerchief caught beneath her
    chin
In Tuscan fashion, — her full ebon eyes,
Which looked too heavy to be lifted so,
Still dropped and lifted toward the mul-
    berry-tree
On which the lads were busy with their
    staves
In shout and laughter, stripping every
    bough
As bare as winter, of those summer leaves
My father had not changed for all the
    silk
In which the ugly silkworms hide them-
    selves.
Enough. My horse recoiled before my
    heart;   1140
I turned the rein abruptly. Back we went
As fast, to Florence.
                That was trial enough
Of graves. I would not visit, if I could,
My father's, or my mother's any more,
To see if stone cutter or lichen beat
So early in the race, or throw my flowers,
Which could not out-smell heaven or
    sweeten earth.
They live too far above, that I should
    look
So far below to find them: let me think

That rather they are visiting my grave, 1150
Called life here (undeveloped yet to life),
And that they drop upon me, now and
    then,
For token or for solace, some small weed
Least odorous of the growths of paradise,
To spare such pungent scents as kill with
    joy.

My old Assunta, too, was dead, was dead —
O land of all men's past ! for me alone,
It would not mix its tenses. I was past,
It seemed, like others, — only not in
    heaven.   1159
And many a Tuscan eve I wandered down
The cypress alley like a restless ghost
That tries its feeble ineffectual breath
Upon its own charred funeral-brands put
    out
Too soon, where black and stiff stood up
    the trees
Against the broad vermilion of the skies.
Such skies ! — all clouds abolished in a
    sweep
Of God's skirt, with a dazzle to ghosts and
    men,
As down I went, saluting on the bridge
The hem of such before 't was caught
    away
Beyond the peaks of Lucca. Under-
    neath,   1170
The river, just escaping from the weight
Of that intolerable glory, ran
In acquiescent shadow murmurously;
While, up beside it, streamed the festa-
    folk
With fellow-murmurs from their feet and
    fans,
And *issimo* and *ino* and sweet poise
Of vowels in their pleasant scandalous
    talk;
Returning from the grand-duke's dairy-
    farm
Before the trees grew dangerous at eight
(For 'trust no tree by moonlight,' Tus-
    cans say),   1180
To eat their ice at Donay's tenderly, —
Each lovely lady close to a cavalier
Who holds her dear fan while she feeds
    her smile
On meditative spoonfuls of vanille
And listens to his hot-breathed vows of
    love
Enough to thaw her cream and scorch his
    beard.

'T was little matter. I could pass them
    by
Indifferently, not fearing to be known.
No danger of being wrecked upon a friend,
And forced to take an iceberg for an
    isle !   1190
The very English, here, must wait and
    learn
To hang the cobweb of their gossip out
To catch a fly. I 'm happy. It 's sub-
    lime,
This perfect solitude of foreign lands !
To be, as if you had not been till then,
And were then, simply that you chose to
    be:
To spring up, not be brought forth from
    the ground,
Like grasshoppers at Athens, and skip
    thrice
Before a woman makes a pounce on you
And plants you in her hair ! — possess,
    yourself,   1200
A new world all alive with creatures new,
New sun, new moon, new flowers, new
    people — ah,
And be possessed by none of them ! no
    right
In one, to call your name, inquire your
    where,
Or what you think of Mister Someone's
    book,
Or Mister Other's marriage or decease,
Or how 's the headache which you had last
    week,
Or why you look so pale still, since it 's
    gone ?
— Such most surprising riddance of one's
    life
Comes next one's death; 't is disembodi-
    ment   1210
Without the pang. I marvel, people
    choose
To stand stock-still like fakirs, till the
    moss
Grows on them and they cry out, self-ad-
    mired,
'How verdant and how virtuous ! ' Well,
    I 'm glad;
Or should be, if grown foreign to myself
As surely as to others.   Musing so,
I walked the narrow unrecognizing streets,
Where many a palace-front peers gloomily
Through stony visors iron-barred (pre-
    pared

Alike, should foe or lover pass that
    way,   1220
For guest or victim), and came wandering
    out
Upon the churches with mild open doors
And plaintive wail of vespers, where a
    few,
Those chiefly women, sprinkled round in
    blots
Upon the dusky pavement, knelt and
    prayed
Toward the altar's silver glory. Oft a ray
(I liked to sit and watch) would tremble
    out,
Just touch some face more lifted, more in
    need
(Of course a woman's), — while I dreamed
    a tale
To fit its fortunes. There was one who
    looked   1230
As if the earth had suddenly grown too
    large
For such a little humpbacked thing as
    she;
The pitiful black kerchief round her neck
Sole proof she had had a mother. One,
    again,
Looked sick for love, — seemed praying
    some soft saint
To put more virtue in the new fine scarf
She spent a fortnight's meals on, yester-
    day,
That cruel Gigi might return his eyes
From Giuliana. There was one, so old,
So old, to kneel grew easier than to
    stand, —   1240
So solitary, she accepts at last
Our Lady for her gossip, and frets on
Against the sinful world which goes its
    rounds
In marrying and being married, just the
    same
As when 't was almost good and had the
    right
(Her Gian alive, and she herself eighteen).
'And yet, now even, if Madonna willed,
She'd win a tern in Thursday's lottery
And better all things. Did she dream for
    nought,
That, boiling cabbage for the fast-day's
    soup,   1250
It smelt like blessèd entrails? such a
    dream
For nought? would sweetest Mary cheat
    her so,

And lose that certain candle, straight and
    white
As any fair grand-duchess in her teens,
Which otherwise should flare here in a
    week?
Benigna sis, thou beauteous Queen of
    Heaven!'

I sat there musing, and imagining
Such utterance from such faces: poor
    blind souls
That writhe toward heaven along the
    devil's trail, —
Who knows, I thought, but He may stretch
    his hand   1260
And pick them up? 't is written in the
    Book
He heareth the young ravens when they
    cry,
And yet they cry for carrion. — O my God,
And we, who make excuses for the rest,
We do it in our measure. Then I knelt,
And dropped my head upon the pavement
    too,
And prayed, since I was foolish in desire
Like other creatures, craving offal-food,
That He would stop his ears to what I
    said,
And only listen to the run and beat   1270
Of this poor, passionate, helpless blood —
                      And then
I lay, and spoke not: but He heard in
    heaven.

So many Tuscan evenings passed the same.
I could not lose a sunset on the bridge,
And would not miss a vigil in the church,
And liked to mingle with the outdoor crowd
So strange and gay and ignorant of my
    face,
For men you know not are as good as trees.
And only once, at the Santissima,
I almost chanced upon a man I knew,   1280
Sir Blaise Delorme. He saw me certainly,
And somewhat hurried, as he crossed him-
    self,
The smoothness of the action, — then half
    bowed,
But only half, and merely to my shade,
I slipped so quick behind the porphyry
    plinth
And left him dubious if 't was really I
Or peradventure Satan's usual trick
To keep a mounting saint uncanonized.
But he was safe for that time, and I too;

The argent angels in the altar-flare   1290
Absorbed his soul next moment. The good
   man !
In England we were scarce acquaintances,
That here in Florence he should keep my
   thought
Beyond the image on his eye, which came
And went: and yet his thought disturbed
   my life:
For, after that, I oftener sat at home
On evenings, watching how they fined them-
   selves
With gradual conscience to a perfect night,
Until the moon, diminished to a curve,
Lay out there like a sickle for his hand   1300
Who cometh down at last to reap the earth.
At such times, ended seemed my trade of
   verse;
I feared to jingle bells upon my robe
Before the four-faced silent cherubim.
With God so near me, could I sing of God ?
I did not write, nor read, nor even think,
But sat absorbed amid the quickening
   glooms,
Most like some passive broken lump of salt
Dropped in by chance to a bowl of œnomel,
To spoil the drink a little and lose itself, 1310
Dissolving slowly, slowly, until lost.

EIGHTH BOOK

One eve it happened, when I sat alone,
Alone, upon the terrace of my tower,
A book upon my knees to counterfeit
The reading that I never read at all,
While Marian, in the garden down below,
Knelt by the fountain I could just hear
   thrill
The drowsy silence of the exhausted day,
And peeled a new fig from that purple heap
In the grass beside her, turning out the red
To feed her eager child(who sucked at it   10
With vehement lips across a gap of air
As he stood opposite, face and curls a-flame
With that last sun-ray, crying 'Give me,
   give,'
And stamping with imperious baby-feet,
We 're all born princes) — something star-
   tled me,
The laugh of sad and innocent souls, that
   breaks
Abruptly, as if frightened at itself.
'Twas Marian laughed. I saw her glance
   above

In sudden shame that I should hear her
   laugh,
And straightway dropped my eyes upon my
   book,   20
And knew, the first time, 't was Boccaccio's
   tale,
The Falcon's, of the lover who for love
Destroyed the best that loved him. Some
   of us
Do it still, and then we sit and laugh no
   more.
Laugh *you*, sweet Marian, — you 've the
   right to laugh,
Since God Himself is for you, and a child !
For me there 's somewhat less, — and so I
   sigh.

The heavens were making room to hold the
   night,
The sevenfold heavens unfolding all their
   gates
To let the stars out slowly (prophesied   30
In close-approaching advent, not discerned),
While still the cuc-owls from the cypresses
Of the Poggio called and counted every
   pulse
Of the skyey palpitation. Gradually
The purple and transparent shadows slow
Had filled up the whole valley to the brim,
And flooded all the city, which you saw
As some drowned city in some enchanted
   sea,
Cut off from nature, — drawing you who
   gaze,
With passionate desire, to leap and plunge 40
And find a sea-king with a voice of waves,
And treacherous soft eyes, and slippery
   locks
You cannot kiss but you shall bring away
Their salt upon your lips. The duomo bell
Strikes ten, as if it struck ten fathoms
   down,
So deep; and twenty churches answer it
The same, with twenty various instances.
Some gaslights tremble along squares and
   streets;
The Pitti's palace-front is drawn in fire;
And, past the quays, Maria Novella Place, 50
In which the mystic obelisks stand up
Triangular, pyramidal, each based
Upon its four-square brazen tortoises,
To guard that fair church, Buonarroti's
   Bride,
That stares out from her large blind dial-
   eyes,

(Her quadrant and armillary dials, black
With rhythms of many suns and moons) in
    vain
Inquiry for so rich a soul as his.
Methinks I have plunged, I see it all so
    clear . . .
And, O my heart, . . . the sea-king !
                                In my ears
The sound of waters.   There he stood, my
    king !   61

I felt him, rather than beheld him.   Up
I rose, as if he were my king indeed,
And then sat down, in trouble at myself,
And struggling for my woman's empery.
'T is pitiful; but women are so made:
We'll die for you perhaps, — 't is proba-
    ble;
But we'll not spare you an inch of our full
    height:
We'll have our whole just stature, — five
    feet four,
Though laid out in our coffins: pitiful.   70
— 'You, Romney ! — Lady Waldemar is
    here ? '

He answered in a voice which was not his.
'I have her letter; you shall read it soon.
But first, I must be heard a little, I,
Who have waited long and travelled far for
    that,
Although you thought to have shut a tedi-
    ous book
And farewell.   Ah, you dog-eared such a
    page,
And here you find me.'
                            Did he touch my hand,
Or but my sleeve ?   I trembled, hand and
    foot, —
He must have touched me. — 'Will you
    sit ? ' I asked,   80
And motioned to a chair; but down he sat,
A little slowly, as a man in doubt,
Upon the couch beside me, — couch and
    chair
Being wheeled upon the terrace.
                            ' You are come,
My cousin Romney ? — this is wonderful.
But all is wonder on such summer-nights;
And nothing should surprise us any more,
Who see that miracle of stars.   Behold.'

I signed above, where all the stars were
    out,
As if an urgent heat had started there   90

A secret writing from a sombre page,
A blank, last moment, crowded suddenly
With hurrying splendors.
                    'Then you do not know ' —
He murmured.
                        ' Yes, I know,' I said, ' I know.
I had the news from Vincent Carrington.
And yet I did not think you 'd leave the
    work
In England, for so much even, — though
    of course
You 'll make a work-day of your holiday,
And turn it to our Tuscan people's use, —
Who much need helping since the Aus-
    trian boar   100
(So bold to cross the Alp to Lombardy
And dash his brute front unabashed against
The steep snow-bosses of that shield of
    God
Who soon shall rise in wrath and shake it
    clear)
Came hither also, raking up our grape
And olive gardens with his tyrannous tusk,
And rolling on our maize with all his
    swine.'

'You had the news from Vincent Carring-
    ton,'
He echoed, — picking up the phrase be-
    yond,
As if he knew the rest was merely talk   110
To fill a gap and keep out a strong wind;
'You had, then, Vincent's personal news ? '
                                    'His own,'
I answered. 'All that ruined world of
    yours
Seems crumbling into marriage.   Carring-
    ton
Has chosen wisely.'
                        'Do you take it so ? '
He cried, ' and is it possible at last ' . . .
He paused there, — and then, inward to
    himself,
' Too much at last, too late ! — yet cer-
    tainly ' . . .
(And there his voice swayed as an Alpine
    plank
That feels a passionate torrent under-
    neath)   120
'The knowledge, had I known it first o
    last,
Could scarce have changed the actual cas
    for me.
And best for her at this time.'
                            Nay, I thought

He loves Kate Ward, it seems, now, like a
man,
Because he has married Lady Waldemar !
Ah, Vincent's letter said how Leigh was
moved
To hear that Vincent was betrothed to
Kate.
With what cracked pitchers go we to deep
wells
In this world ! Then I spoke, — 'I did
not think,
My cousin, you had ever known Kate
Ward.'   130

'In fact, I never knew her. 'T is enough
That Vincent did, and therefore chose his
wife
For other reasons than those topaz eyes
We 've heard of. Not to undervalue them,
For all that. One takes up the world with
eyes.'

— Including Romney Leigh, I thought
again,
Albeit he knows them only by repute.
How vile must all men be since *he*'s a
man.   138

His deep pathetic voice, as if he guessed
I did not surely love him, took the word;
'You never got a letter from Lord Howe
A month back, dear Aurora ?'
                                    'None,' I said.

'I felt it was so,' he replied: 'yet,
strange !
Sir Blaise Delorme has passed through
Florence ?'
                              'Ay,
By chance I saw him in Our Lady's church
(I saw him, mark you, but he saw not me),
Clean-washed in holy water from the
count
Of things terrestrial, — letters, and the
rest;
He had crossed us out together with his
sins.
Ay, strange; but only strange that good
Lord Howe   150
Preferred him to the post because of pauls.
For me I 'm sworn to never trust a man —
At least with letters.'
                        'There were facts to tell,
To smooth with eye and accent. Howe
supposed . . .

Well, well, no matter ! there was dubious
need;
You heard the news from Vincent Carring-
ton.
And yet perhaps you had been startled less
To see me, dear Aurora, if you had read
That letter.'
                — Now he sets me down as vexed.
I think I 've draped myself in woman's
pride   160
To a perfect purpose. Oh, I 'm vexed, it
seems !
My friend Lord Howe deputes his friend
Sir Blaise
To break as softly as a sparrow's egg
That lets a bird out tenderly, the news
Of Romney's marriage to a certain saint;
To *smooth with eye and accent*, — indicate
His possible presence. Excellently well
You 've played your part, my Lady Walde-
mar, —
As I 've played mine.
                      'Dear Romney,' I began,
'You did not use, of old, to be so like   170
A Greek king coming from a taken Troy,
'T was needful that precursors spread your
path
With three-piled carpets, to receive your
foot
And dull the sound of 't. For myself, be
sure,
Although it frankly grinds the gravel here,
I still can bear it. Yet I 'm sorry too
To lose this famous letter, which Sir Blaise
Has twisted to a lighter absently
To fire some holy taper: dear Lord Howe
Writes letters good for all things but to
lose;   180
And many a flower of London gossipry
Has dropped wherever such a stem broke
off.
Of course I feel that, lonely among my
vines,
Where nothing 's talked of, save the blight
again,
And no more Chianti ! Still the letter 's
use
As preparation . . . Did I start, indeed ?
Last night I started at a cockchafer,
And shook a half-hour after. Have you
learnt
No more of women, 'spite of privilege,
Than still to take account too seriously 190
Of such weak flutterings ? Why, we like
it, sir,

We get our powers and our effects that
    way:
The trees stand stiff and still at time of
    frost,
If no wind tears them; but, let summer
    come,
When trees are happy, — and a breath
    avails
To set them trembling through a million
    leaves
In luxury of emotion. Something less
It takes to move a woman: let her start
And shake at pleasure, — nor conclude at
    yours,
The winter's bitter, — but the summer's
    green.'   200

He answered: 'Be the summer ever green
With you, Aurora! — though you sweep
    your sex
With somewhat bitter gusts from where
    you live
Above them, — whirling downward from
    your heights
Your very own pine-cones, in a grand dis-
    dain
Of the lowland burrs with which you scatter
    them.
So high and cold to others and yourself,
A little less to Romney were unjust,
And thus, I would not have you. Let it
    pass:
I feel content so. You can bear indeed 210
My sudden step beside you: but for me,
'Twould move me sore to hear your
    softened voice, —
Aurora's voice, — if softened unaware
In pity of what I am.'
                  Ah friend, I thought,
As husband of the Lady Waldemar
You 're granted very sorely pitiable!
And yet Aurora Leigh must guard her
    voice
From softening in the pity of your case,
As if from lie or license. Certainly   219
We 'll soak up all the slush and soil of life
With softened voices, ere we come to *you*.

At which I interrupted my own thought
And spoke out calmly, 'Let us ponder,
    friend,
Whate'er our state we must have made it
    first;
And though the thing displease us, ay,
    perhaps

Displease us warrantably, never doubt
That other states, thought possible once,
    and then
Rejected by the instinct of our lives,
If then adopted had displeased us more
Than this in which the choice, the will, the
    love,   230
Has stamped the honor of a patent act
From henceforth. What we choose may
    not be good,
But, that we choose it, proves it good for *us*
Potentially, fantastically, now
Or last year, rather than a thing we saw,
And saw no need for choosing. Moths
    will burn
Their wings, — which proves that light is
    good for moths,
Who else had flown not where they agonize.'

'Ay, light is good,' he echoed, and there
    paused;
And then abruptly, . . . 'Marian. Ma-
    rian's well?'   240

I bowed my head but found no word.
    'T was hard
To speak of *her* to Lady Waldemar's
New husband. How much did he know,
    at last?
How much! how little! — He would take
    no sign,
But straight repeated, — 'Marian. Is she
    well?'

'She 's well,' I answered.
                 She was there in sight
An hour back, but the night had drawn her
    home,
Where still I heard her in an upper room,
Her low voice singing to the child in bed,
Who, restless with the summer-heat and
    play   250
And slumber snatched at noon, was long
    sometimes
In falling off, and took a score of songs
And mother-hushes ere she saw him sound.

'She 's well,' I answered.
                'Here?' he asked.
                      'Yes, here.'

He stopped and sighed. 'That shall be
    presently,
But now this must be. I have words to
    say,

And would be alone to say them, I with
  you,
And no third troubling.'
              'Speak then,' I returned,
'She will not vex you.'
              At which, suddenly
He turned his face upon me with its
  smile   260
As if to crush me. 'I have read your
  book,
Aurora.'
        'You have read it,' I replied,
'And I have writ it, — we have done with
  it.
And now the rest?'
            'The rest is like the first,'
He answered, — 'for the book is in my
  heart,
Lives in me, wakes in me, and dreams in
  me;
My daily bread tastes of it, — and my
  wine
Which has no smack of it, I pour it out,
It seems unnatural drinking.'
                      Bitterly
I took the word up; 'Never waste your
  wine.   270
The book lived in me ere it lived in you;
I know it closer than another does,
And how it's foolish, feeble, and afraid,
And all unworthy so much compliment.
Beseech you, keep your wine, — and, when
  you drink,
Still wish some happier fortune to a friend,
Than even to have written a far better
  book.'

He answered gently, 'That is consequent:
The poet looks beyond the book he has
  made,
Or else he had not made it. If a man 280
Could make a man, he'd henceforth be a
  god
In feeling what a little thing is man:
It is not my case. And this special book,
I did not make it, to make light of it:
It stands above my knowledge, draws me
  up;
'T is high to me. It may be that the
  book
Is not so high, but I so low, instead;
Still high to me. I mean no compliment:
I will not say there are not, young or
  old,
Male writers, ay, or female, let it pass, 290

Who 'll write us richer and completer
  books.
A man may love a woman perfectly,
And yet by no means ignorantly maintain
A thousand women have not larger eyes:
Enough that she alone has looked at him
With eyes that, large or small, have won
  his soul.
And so, this book, Aurora, — so, your
  book.'

'Alas,' I answered, 'is it so, indeed?'
And then was silent.
            'Is it so, indeed,'
He echoed, ' that alas is all your word?' 300
I said, 'I'm thinking of a far-off June,
When you and I, upon my birthday once,
Discoursed of life and art, with both un-
  tried.
I'm thinking, Romney, how 't was morn-
  ing then,
And now 't is night.'
          'And now,' he said, ''t is night.'

'I'm thinking,' I resumed, ''t is some-
  what sad,
That if I had known, that morning in the
  dew,
My cousin Romney would have said such
  words
On such a night at close of many years, 310
In speaking of a future book of mine
It would have pleased me better as a hope,
Than as an actual grace it can at all:
That's sad, I'm thinking.'
          'Ay,' he said, ''t is night.'

'And there,' I added lightly, 'are the
  stars!
And here, we'll talk of stars and not of
  books.'
'You have the stars,' he murmured, — 'it
  is well:
Be like them! shine, Aurora, on my dark,
Though high and cold and only like a star,
And for this short night only, — you, who
  keep   319
The same Aurora of the bright June day
That withered up the flowers before my
  face,
And turned me from the garden evermore
Because I was not worthy. Oh, deserved,
Deserved! that I, who verily had not
  learnt
God's lesson half, attaining as a dunce

To obliterate good words with fractious
    thumbs
And cheat myself of the context, — I should
    push
Aside, with male ferocious impudence,
The world's Aurora who had conned her
    part   329
On the other side the leaf! ignore her so,
Because she was a woman and a queen,
And had no beard to bristle through her
    song,
My teacher, who has taught me with a
    book,
My Miriam whose sweet mouth, when
    nearly drowned
I still heard singing on the shore! De-
    served,
That here I should look up unto the stars
And miss the glory ' . . .
                  ' Can I understand ? '
I broke in. ' You speak wildly, Romney
    Leigh,
Or I hear wildly. In that morning-time
We recollect, the roses were too red,   340
The trees too green, reproach too natural
If one should see not what the other saw:
And now, it 's night, remember; we have
    shades
In place of colors; we are now grown cold,
And old, my cousin Romney. Pardon
    me, —
I 'm very happy that you like my book,
And very sorry that I quoted back
A ten years' birthday. 'T was so mad a
    thing
In any woman, I scarce marvel much
You took it for a venturous piece of spite,
Provoking such excuses as indeed   351
I cannot call you slack in.'
                    ' Understand,'
He answered sadly, ' something, if but
    so.
This night is softer than an English day,
And men may well come hither when
    they 're sick,
To draw in easier breath from larger air.
'T is thus with me; I come to you, — to
    you
My Italy of women, just to breathe
My soul out once before you, ere I go,
As humble as God makes me at the last 360
(I thank Him), quite out of the way of
    men
And yours, Aurora, — like a punished
    child,

His cheeks all blurred with tears and
    naughtiness,
To silence in a corner. I am come
To speak, beloved ' . . .
                ' Wisely, cousin Leigh,
And worthily of us both ! '
                      ' Yes, worthily,
For this time I must speak out and con-
    fess
That I, so truculent in assumption once,
So absolute in dogma, proud in aim,
And fierce in expectation, — I, who felt 370
The whole world tugging at my skirts for
    help,
As if no other man than I could pull,
Nor woman but I led her by the hand,
Nor cloth hold but I had it in my coat,
Do know myself to-night for what I was
On that June day, Aurora. Poor bright
    day,
Which meant the best . . . a woman and a
    rose,
And which I smote upon the cheek with
    words
Until it turned and rent me ! Young you
    were,
That birthday, poet, but you talked the
    right: 380
While I, . . . I built up follies like a wall
To intercept the sunshine and your face.
Your face ! that 's worse.'
                ' Speak wisely, cousin Leigh.'

' Yes, wisely, dear Aurora, though too late:
But then, not wisely. I was heavy then,
And stupid, and distracted with the cries
Of tortured prisoners in the polished brass
Of that Phalarian bull, society,
Which seems to bellow bravely like ten
    bulls,
But, if you listen, moans and cries instead
Despairingly, like victims tossed and
    gored   391
And trampled by their hoofs. I heard the
    cries
Too close: I could not hear the angels lift
A fold of rustling air, nor what they said
To help my pity. I beheld the world
As one great famishing carnivorous
    mouth, —
A huge, deserted, callow, blind bird Thing,
With piteous open beak that hurt my
    heart,
Till down upon the filthy ground I dropped,
And tore the violets up to get the worms.

Worms, worms, was all my cry: an open mouth, 401
A gross want, bread to fill it to the lips,
No more. That poor men narrowed their demands
To such an end, was virtue, I supposed,
Adjudicating that to see it so
Was reason. Oh, I did not push the case
Up higher, and ponder how it answers when
The rich take up the same cry for themselves,
Professing equally, — "An open mouth,
A gross need, food to fill us, and no more."
Why that 's so far from virtue, only vice 411
Can find excuse for 't! that makes libertines,
And slurs our cruel streets from end to end
With eighty thousand women in one smile,
Who only smile at night beneath the gas,
The body's satisfaction and no more,
Is used for argument against the soul's,
Here too; the want, here too, implies the right.
— How dark I stood that morning in the sun,
My best Aurora (though I saw your eyes),
When first you told me . . . oh, I recollect 421
The sound, and how you lifted your small hand,
And how your white dress and your burnished curls
Went greatening round you in the still blue air,
As if an inspiration from within
Had blown them all out when you spoke the words,
Even these, — "You will not compass your poor ends
Of barley-feeding and material ease,
Without the poet's individualism
To work your universal. It takes a soul
To move a body, — it takes a high-souled man 431
To move the masses, even to a cleaner stye:
It takes the ideal, to blow an inch inside
The dust of the actual: and your Fouriers failed,
Because not poets enough to understand
That life develops from within." I say
Your words, — I could say other words of yours,

For none of all your words will let me go;
Like sweet verbena which, being brushed against,
Will hold us three hours after by the smell
In spite of long walks upon windy hills. 441
But these words dealt in sharper perfume, — these
Were ever on me, stinging through my dreams,
And saying themselves for ever o'er my acts
Like some unhappy verdict. That I failed,
Is certain. Stye or no stye, to contrive
The swine's propulsion toward the precipice,
Proved easy and plain. I subtly organized
And ordered, built the cards up high and higher,
Till, some one breathing, all fell flat again;
In setting right society's wide wrong, 451
Mere life 's so fatal. So I failed indeed
Once, twice, and oftener, — hearing through the rents
Of obstinate purpose, still those words of yours,
"You will not compass your poor ends, not you!"
But harder than you said them; every time
Still farther from your voice, until they came
To overcrow me with triumphant scorn
Which vexed me to resistance. Set down this
For condemnation, — I was guilty here; 460
I stood upon my deed and fought my doubt,
As men will, — for I doubted, — till at last
My deed gave way beneath me suddenly
And left me what I am: — the curtain dropped,
My part quite ended, all the footlights quenched,
My own soul hissing at me through the dark,
I ready for confession, — I was wrong,
I 've sorely failed, I 've slipped the ends of life, 468
I yield, you have conquered.'
                    'Stay,' I answered him;
'I 've something for your hearing, also. I
Have failed too.'
          'You !' he said, 'you 're very great;
The sadness of your greatness fits you well:
As if the plume upon a hero 's casque
Should nod a shadow upon his victor face.'

I took him up austerely, — 'You have read
My book, but not my heart; for recollect,

'T is writ in Sanscrit, which you bungle at.
I 've surely failed, I know, if failure means
To look back sadly on work gladly done, —
To wander on my Mountains of Delight, 480
So called (I can remember a friend's words
As well as you, sir), weary and in want
Of even a sheep-path, thinking bitterly . . .
Well, well ! no matter. I but say so much,
To keep you, Romney Leigh, from saying
 more,
And let you feel I am not so high indeed,
That I can bear to have you at my foot, —
Or safe, that I can help you. That June
 day,
Too deeply sunk in craterous sunsets now
For you or me to dig it up alive, —   490
To pluck it out all bleeding with spent flame
At the roots, before those moralizing stars
We have got instead, — that poor lost day,
 you said
Some words as truthful as the thing of
 mine
You cared to keep in memory; and I hold
If I, that day, and being the girl I was,
Had shown a gentler spirit, less arrogance,
It had not hurt me. You will scarce
 mistake
The point here: I but only think, you see,
More justly, that 's more humbly, of my-
 self,   500
Than when I tried a crown on and sup-
 posed . . .
Nay, laugh, sir, — I 'll laugh with you ! —
 pray you, laugh,
I 've had so many birthdays since that day
I 've learnt to prize mirth's opportunities,
Which come too seldom. Was it you who
 said
I was not changed ? the same Aurora ?
 Ah,
We could laugh there, too ! Why, Ulysses'
 dog
Knew *him*, and wagged his tail and died:
 but if
I had owned a dog, I too, before my Troy,
And if you brought him here, . . . I war-
 rant you   510
He 'd look into my face, bark lustily,
And live on stoutly, as the creatures will
Whose spirits are not troubled by long
 loves.
A dog would never know me, I 'm so
 changed,
Much less a friend . . . except that you 're
 misled

By the color of the hair, the trick of the
 voice,
Like that Aurora Leigh's.'
     'Sweet trick of voice !
I would be a dog for this, to know it at
 last,
And die upon the falls of it. O love,
O best Aurora ! are you then so sad   520
You scarcely had been sadder as my wife ?'

'Your wife, sir ! I must certainly be
 changed,
If I, Aurora, can have said a thing
So light, it catches at the knightly spurs
Of a noble gentleman like Romney Leigh,
And trips him from his honorable sense
Of what befits ' . . .
    'You wholly misconceive,'
He answered.
    I returned, — 'I 'm glad of it.
But keep from misconception, too, your-
 self:
I am not humbled to so low a point,   530
Not so far saddened. If I am sad at all,
Ten layers of birthdays on a woman's head
Are apt to fossilize her girlish mirth,
Though ne'er so merry: I 'm perforce more
 wise,
And that, in truth, means sadder. For the
 rest,
Look here, sir: I was right upon the whole
That birthday morning. 'T is impossible
To get at men excepting through their
 souls,
However open their carnivorous jaws;
And poets get directlier at the soul   540
Than any of your œconomists — for which
You must not overlook the poet's work
When scheming for the world's necessi-
 ties.
The soul 's the way. Not even Christ
 Himself
Can save man else than as He holds man's
 soul;
And therefore did He come into our flesh,
As some wise hunter creeping on his knees,
With a torch, into the blackness of a cave,
To face and quell the beast there — take
 the soul,
And so possess the whole man, body and
 soul.   550
I said, so far, right, yes: not farther,
 though:
We both were wrong that June day —
 both as wrong

As an east wind had been. I who talked
of art,
And you who grieved for all men's griefs
. . . what then ?
We surely made too small a part for God
In these things. What we are, imports us
more
Than what we eat ; and life, you 've
granted me,
Develops from within. But innermost
Of the inmost, most interior of the interne,
God claims his own, Divine humanity   560
Renewing nature, or the piercingest verse
Pressed in by subtlest poet, still must keep
As much upon the outside of a man
As the very bowl in which he dips his
beard.
— And then, . . . the rest; I cannot surely
speak:
Perhaps I doubt more than you doubted
then,
If I the poet's veritable charge
Have borne upon my forehead. If I have,
It might feel somewhat liker to a crown,
The foolish green one even. — Ah, I
think,   570
And chiefly when the sun shines, that I 've
failed.
But what then, Romney ? Though we
fail indeed,
You . . . I . . . a score of such weak
workers, . . . He
Fails never. If He cannot work by us,
He will work over us. Does He want a
man,
Much less a woman, think you ? Every
time
The star winks there, so many souls are
born,
Who all shall work too. Let our own be
calm:
We should be ashamed to sit beneath those
stars,   579
Impatient that we 're nothing.'
                              'Could we sit
Just so for ever, sweetest friend,' he said,
'My failure would seem better than suc-
cess.
And yet indeed your book has dealt with
me
More gently, cousin, than you ever will !
Your book brought down entire the bright
June day,
And set me wandering in the garden-walks,
And let me watch the garland in a place

You blushed so . . . nay, forgive me, do
not stir, —
I only thank the book for what it taught,
And what permitted. Poet, doubt your-
self,   590
But never doubt that you 're a poet to me
From henceforth. You have written poems,
sweet,
Which moved me in secret, as the sap is
moved
In still March-branches, signless as a stone:
But this last book o'ercame me like soft
rain
Which falls at midnight, when the tight-
ened bark
Breaks out into unhesitating buds
And sudden protestations of the spring.
In all your other books, I saw but you :
A man may see the moon so, in a pond,   600
And not be nearer therefore to the moon,
Nor use the sight . . . except to drown
himself:
And so I forced my heart back from the
sight,
For what had I, I thought, to do with
her,
Aurora . . . Romney ? But, in this last
book,
You showed me something separate from
yourself,
Beyond you, and I bore to take it in
And let it draw me. You have shown me
truths,
O June-day friend, that help me now at
night,
When June is over ! truths not yours, in-
deed,   610
But set within my reach by means of you,
Presented by your voice and verse the way
To take them clearest. Verily I was
wrong;
And verily many thinkers of this age,
Ay, many Christian teachers, half in
heaven,
Are wrong in just my sense who under-
stood
Our natural world too insularly, as if
No spiritual counterpart completed it,
Consummating its meaning, rounding all
To justice and perfection, line by line,   620
Form by form, nothing single nor alone,
The great below clenched by the great
above,
Shade here authenticating substance there,
The body proving spirit, as the effect

The cause: we meantime being too grossly
   apt
To hold the natural, as dogs a bone
(Though reason and nature beat us in the
   face),
So obstinately, that we 'll break our teeth
Or ever we let go.   For everywhere
We 're too materialistic, — eating clay   630
(Like men of the west) instead of Adam's
   corn
And Noah's wine — clay by handfuls, clay
   by lumps,
Until we 're filled up to the throat with
   clay,
And grow the grimy color of the ground
On which we are feeding.   Ay, materialist
The age's name is.   God Himself, with
   some,
Is apprehended as the bare result
Of what his hand materially has made,
Expressed in such an algebraic sign
Called God — that is, to put it otherwise, 640
They add up nature to a nought of God
And cross the quotient.   There are many
   even,
Whose names are written in the Christian
   Church
To no dishonor, diet still on mud
And splash the altars with it.   You might
   think
The clay Christ laid upon their eyelids
   when,
Still blind, He called them to the use of
   sight,
Remained there to retard its exercise
With clogging incrustations.   Close to
   heaven,
They see for mysteries, through the open
   doors,   650
Vague puffs of smoke from pots of earthen-
   ware,
And fain would enter, when their time
   shall come,
With quite another body than Saint Paul
Has promised — husk and chaff, the whole
   barley-corn
Or where 's the resurrection ? '
                              ' Thus it is,'
I sighed.   And he resumed with mournful
   face,
' Beginning so, and filling up with clay
The wards of this great key, the natural
   world,
And fumbling vainly therefore at the lock
Of the spiritual, we feel ourselves shut in

With all the wild-beast roar of struggling
   life,   661
The terrors and compunctions of our souls,
As saints with lions, — we who are not
   saints,
And have no heavenly lordship in our stare
To awe them backward.   Ay, we are
   forced, so pent,
To judge the whole too partially, . . . con-
   found
Conclusions.   Is there any common phrase
Significant, with the adverb heard alone,
The verb being absent, and the pronoun
   out ?
But we, distracted in the roar of life,   670
Still insolently at God's adverb snatch,
And bruit against Him that his thought is
   void,
His meaning hopeless, — cry, that every-
   where
The government is slipping from his hand,
Unless some other Christ (say Romney
   Leigh)
Come up and toil and moil and change the
   world,
Because the First has proved inadequate,
However we talk bigly of his work
And piously of his person.   We blaspheme
At last, to finish our doxology,   680
Despairing on the earth for which He died.'

'So now,' I asked, 'you have more hope
   of men ? '

'I hope,' he answered.   'I am come to
   think
That God will have his work done, as you
   said,
And that we need not be disturbed too
   much
For Romney Leigh or others having failed
With this or that quack nostrum — recipes
For keeping summits by annulling depths,
For wrestling with luxurious lounging
   sleeves,
And acting heroism without a scratch,   69.
We fail, — what then ?   Aurora, if
   smiled
To see you, in your lovely morning-pride,
Try on the poet's wreath which suits the
   noon
(Sweet cousin, walls must get the weathe
   stain
Before they grow the ivy !), certainly
I stood myself there worthier of contemp

Self-rated, in disastrous arrogance,
As competent to sorrow for mankind,
And even their odds. A man may well
   despair   699
Who counts himself so needful to success.
I failed: I throw the remedy back on God,
And sit down here beside you, in good
   hope.'

'And yet take heed,' I answered, 'lest we
   lean
Too dangerously on the other side,
And so fail twice. Be sure, no earnest
   work
Of any honest creature, howbeit weak,
Imperfect, ill-adapted, fails so much,
It is not gathered as a grain of sand
To enlarge the sum of human action used
For carrying out God's end. No creature
   works   710
So ill, observe, that therefore he's cash-
   iered.
The honest, earnest man must stand and
   work,
The woman also — otherwise she drops
At once below the dignity of man,
Accepting serfdom. Free men freely
   work.
Whoever fears God, fears to sit at ease.'

He cried: 'True. After Adam, work was
   curse:
The natural creature labors, sweats, and
   frets.   718
But, after Christ, work turns to privilege,
And henceforth, one with our humanity,
The Six-day Worker working still in us
Has called us freely to work on with Him
In high companionship. So, happiest!
I count that heaven itself is only work
To a surer issue. Let us work, indeed,
But no more work as Adam, — nor as
   Leigh
Erewhile, as if the only man on earth,
Responsible for all the thistles blown
And tigers couchant, struggling in amaze
Against disease and winter, snarling on   730
For ever that the world's not paradise.
O cousin, let us be content, in work,
To do the thing we can, and not presume
To fret because it's little. 'T will employ
Seven men, they say, to make a perfect
   pin:
Who makes the head, content to miss the
   point;

Who makes the point, agreed to leave the
   join:
And if a man should cry "I want a pin,
And I must make it straightway, head and
   point,"
His wisdom is not worth the pin he wants.
Seven men to a pin, — and not a man too
   much!   741
Seven generations, haply, to this world,
To right it visibly a finger's breadth,
And mend its rents a little. Oh, to storm
And say "This world here is intolerable;
I will not eat this corn, nor drink this wine,
Nor love this woman, flinging her my soul
Without a bond for 't as a lover should,
Nor use the generous leave of happiness
As not too good for using generously" —
(Since virtue kindles at the touch of joy
Like a man's cheek laid on a woman's
   hand,   752
And God, Who knows it, looks for quick
   returns
From joys) — to stand and claim to have a
   life
Beyond the bounds of the individual man,
And raze all personal cloisters of the soul
To build up public stores and magazines,
As if God's creatures otherwise were lost,
The builder surely saved by any means I
To think, — I have a pattern on my nail, 760
And I will carve the world new after it
And solve so these hard social questions —
   nay,
Impossible social questions, since their
   roots
Strike deep in Evil's own existence here,
Which God permits because the question's
   hard
To abolish evil nor attaint free-will.
Ay, hard to God, but not to Romney Leigh!
For Romney has a pattern on his nail
(Whatever may be lacking on the Mount),
And, not being over-nice to separate   770
What's element from what's convention,
   hastes
By line on line to draw you out a world,
Without your help indeed, unless you take
His yoke upon you, and will learn of him,
So much he has to teach! so good a world!
The same the whole creation's groaning
   for!
No rich nor poor, no gain nor loss nor
   stint;
No pottage in it able to exclude
A brother's birthright, and no right of birth

The pottage — both secured to every man,
And perfect virtue dealt out like the rest
Gratuitously, with the soup at six,   782
To whoso does not seek it.'
                              ' Softly, sir,'
I interrupted, — ' I had a cousin once
I held in reverence. If he strained too
    wide,
It was not to take honor, but give help;
The gesture was heroic. If his hand
Accomplished nothing . . . (well, it is not
    proved)
That empty hand thrown impotently out
Were sooner caught, I think, by One in
    heaven,   790
Than many a hand that reaped a harvest in,
And keeps the scythe's glow on it. Pray
    you, then,
For my sake merely, use less bitterness
In speaking of my cousin.'
                              ' Ah,' he said,
' Aurora ! when the prophet beats the ass,
The angel intercedes.' He shook his head —
' And yet to mean so well and fail so foul,
Expresses ne'er another beast than man;
The antithesis is human. Hearken, dear;
There 's too much abstract willing, pur-
    posing,   800
In this poor world. We talk by aggre-
    gates,
And think by systems, and, being used to
    face
Our evils in statistics, are inclined
To cap them with unreal remedies
Drawn out in haste on the other side the
    slate.'
' That 's true,' I answered, fain to throw up
    thought
And make a game of 't. ' Yes, we gener-
    alize
Enough to please you. If we pray at all,
We pray no longer for our daily bread, 809
But next centenary's harvests. If we give,
Our cup of water is not tendered till
We lay down pipes and found a Company
With Branches. Ass or angel, 't is the
    same:
A woman cannot do the thing she ought,
Which means whatever perfect thing she
    can,
In life, in art, in science, but she fears
To let the perfect action take her part,
And rest there: she must prove what she
    can do
Before she does it, prate of woman's rights,

Of woman's mission, woman's function, till
The men (who are prating too on their side)
    cry,   821
" A woman's function plainly is . . . to
    talk."
Poor souls, they are very reasonably vexed;
They cannot hear each other talk.'
                                    ' And you,
An artist, judge so ? '
                              ' I, an artist — yes:
Because, precisely, I 'm an artist, sir,
And woman, if another sat in sight,
I 'd whisper, — Soft, my sister ! not a word !
By speaking we prove only we can speak,
Which he, the man here, never doubted.
    What   830
He doubts is, whether we can do the thing
With decent grace we 've not yet done at
    all.
Now, do it; bring your statue, — you have
    room !
He 'll see it even by the starlight here;
And if 't is e'er so little like the god
Who looks out from the marble silently
Along the track of his own shining dart
Through the dusk of ages, there 's no need
    to speak;
The universe shall henceforth speak for
    you,
And witness, " She who did this thing was
    born   840
To do it — claims her license in her work."
And so with more works. Whoso cures the
    plague,
Though twice a woman, shall be called a
    leech;
Who rights a land's finances is excused
For touching coppers, though her hands be
    white.
But we, we talk !'
                              ' It is the age's mood,'
He said; ' we boast, and do not. We put
    up
Hostelry signs where'er we lodge a day, —
Some red colossal cow with mighty paps
A Cyclops' fingers could not strain to
    milk, —   850
Then bring out presently our saucerful
Of curds. We want more quiet in our
    works,
More knowledge of the bounds in which we
    work;
More knowledge that each individual man
Remains an Adam to the general race,
Constrained to see, like Adam, that he keep

His personal state's condition honestly,
Or vain all thoughts of his to help the
    world,
Which still must be developed from its
    one
If bettered in its many. We indeed,   860
Who think to lay it out new like a park,
We take a work on us which is not man's,
For God alone sits far enough above
To speculate so largely. None of us
(Not Romney Leigh) is mad enough to
    say,
We 'll have a grove of oaks upon that slope
And sink the need of acorns. Government,
If veritable and lawful, is not given
By imposition of the foreign hand,
Nor chosen from a pretty pattern-book   870
Of some domestic idealogue who sits
And coldly chooses empire, where as well
He might republic. Genuine government
Is but the expression of a nation, good
Or less good — even as all society,
Howe'er unequal, monstrous, crazed and
    cursed,
Is but the expression of men's single lives,
The loud sum of the silent units. What,
We 'd change the aggregate and yet retain
Each separate figure ? whom do we cheat
    by that ?   880
Now, not even Romney.'
                        'Cousin, you are sad.
Did all your social labor at Leigh Hall,
And elsewhere, come to nought, then ? '
                        ' It *was* nought,'
He answered mildly. ' There is room, in-
    deed,
For statues still in this large world of
    God's,
But not for vacuums; so I am not sad —
Not sadder than is good for what I am.
My vain phalanstery dissolved itself;
My men and women of disordered lives
I brought in orderly to dine and sleep,
Broke up those waxen masks I made them
    wear,   891
With fierce contortions of the natural face,
And cursed me for my tyrannous con-
    straint
In forcing crooked creatures to live
    straight;
And set the country hounds upon my back
To bite and tear me for my wicked deed
Of trying to do good without the church
Or even the squires, Aurora. Do you
    mind

Your ancient neighbors ? The great book-
    club teems
With "sketches," "summaries," and "last
    tracts " but twelve,   900
On socialistic troublers of close bonds
Betwixt the generous rich and grateful
    poor
The vicar preached from " Revelations "
    (till
The doctor woke), and found me with "the
    frogs "
On three successive Sundays; ay, and
    stopped
To weep a little (for he 's getting old)
That such perdition should o'ertake a
    man
Of such fair acres — in the parish, too !
He printed his discourses " by request,"
And if your book shall sell as his did,
    then   910
Your verses are less good than I suppose.
The women of the neighborhood subscribed,
And sent me a copy, bound in scarlet silk,
Tooled edges, blazoned with the arms of
    Leigh:
I own that touched me.'
                        ' What, the pretty ones ?
Poor Romney ! '
                        ' Otherwise the effect was small:
I had my windows broken once or twice
By liberal peasants naturally incensed
At such a vexer of Arcadian peace,
Who would not let men call their wives
    their own   920
To kick like Britons, and made obstacles
When things went smoothly as a baby
    drugged,
Toward freedom and starvation — bring-
    ing down
The wicked London tavern - thieves and
    drabs
To affront the blessed hillside drabs and
    thieves
With mended morals, quotha — fine new
    lives ! —
My windows paid for 't. I was shot at,
    once,
By an active poacher who had hit a hare
From the other barrel (tired of springe-
    ing game
So long upon my acres, undisturbed,   930
And restless for the country's virtue — yet
He missed me); ay, and pelted very oft
In riding through the village. " There he
    goes

Who 'd drive away our Christian gentle-
    folk,
To catch us undefended in the trap
He baits with poisonous cheese, and lock
    us up
In that pernicious prison of Leigh Hall
With all his murderers! Give another
    name
And say Leigh Hell, and burn it up with
    fire."
And so they did, at last, Aurora.'
                     'Did?'

'You never heard it, cousin? Vincent's
    news   941
Came stinted, then.'
      'They did? they burnt Leigh Hall?'

'You 're sorry, dear Aurora? Yes, indeed,
They did it perfectly: a thorough work,
And not a failure, this time. Let us grant
'T is somewhat easier, though, to burn a
    house
Than build a system; yet that 's easy too
In a dream. Books, pictures — ay, the
    pictures! What,
You think your dear Vandykes would give
    them pause?
Our proud ancestral Leighs, with those
    peaked beards,   950
Or bosoms white as foam thrown up on
    rocks
From the old-spent wave. Such calm de-
    fiant looks
They flared up with! now nevermore to
    twit
The bones in the family vault with ugly
    death.
Not one was rescued, save the Lady Maud,
Who threw you down, that morning you
    were born,
The undeniable lineal mouth and chin
To wear for ever for her gracious sake,
For which good deed I saved her; the rest
    went:
And you, you 're sorry, cousin. Well, for
    me,   960
With all my phalansterians safely out
  Poor hearts, they helped the burners, it
    was said,
And certainly a few clapped hands and
    yelled),
The ruin did not hurt me as it might —
As when for instance I was hurt one day
A certain letter being destroyed. In fact,

To see the great house flare so . . . oaken
    floors
Our fathers made so fine with rushes once
Before our mothers furbished them with
    trains,
Carved wainscots, panelled walls, the fa-
    vorite slide   970
For draining off a martyr (or a rogue),
The echoing galleries, half a half-mile
    long,
And all the various stairs that took you
    up
And took you down, and took you round
    about
Upon their slippery darkness, recollect,
All helping to keep up one blazing jest!
The flames through all the casements
    pushing forth,
Like red-hot devils crinkled into snakes,
All signifying "Look you, Romney Leigh,
We save the people from your saving,
    here,   980
Yet so as by fire! we make a pretty show
Besides — and that 's the best you 've ever
    done."
— To see this, almost moved myself to
    clap!
The " vale et plaude " came too with effect
When in the roof fell, and the fire that
    paused,
Stunned momently beneath the stroke of
    slates
And tumbling rafters, rose at once and
    roared,
And wrapping the whole house (which dis-
    appeared
In a mounting whirlwind of dilated flame),
Blew upward, straight, its drift of fiery
    chaff   990
In the face of Heaven, which blenched,
    and ran up higher.'

'Poor Romney!'
    'Sometimes when I dream,' he said
'I hear the silence after, 't was so still.
For all those wild beasts, yelling, cursing
    round,
Were suddenly silent, while you counted
    five,
So silent, that you heard a young bird fall
From the top nest in the neighboring rook-
    ery,
Through edging over-rashly toward the
    light.
The old rooks had already fled too far

To hear the screech they fled with, though
you saw   1000
Some flying still, like scatterings of dead
leaves
In autumn-gusts, seen dark against the
sky, —
All flying, — ousted, like the House of
Leigh.'

'Dear Romney!'
       'Evidently 't would have been
A fine sight for a poet, sweet, like you,
To make the verse blaze after. I myself,
Even I, felt something in the grand old
trees,
Which stood that moment like brute Druid
gods
Amazed upon the rim of ruin, where,
As into a blackened socket, the great
fire   1010
Had dropped, still throwing up splinters
now and then
To show them gray with all their centu-
ries,
Left there to witness that on such a day
The House went out.'
      'Ah!'
      'While you counted five,
I seemed to feel a little like a Leigh, —
But then it passed, Aurora. A child cried,
And I had enough to think of what to do
With all those houseless wretches in the
dark,
And ponder where they 'd dance the next
time, they   1019
Who had burnt the viol.'
      'Did you think of that?
Who burns his viol will not dance, I know,
To cymbals, Romney.'
      'O my sweet, sad voice!'
He cried, — 'O voice that speaks and over-
comes!
The sun is silent, but Aurora speaks.'

'Alas,' I said, 'I speak I know not what:
I 'm back in childhood, thinking as a child,
A foolish fancy — will it make you smile?
I shall not from the window of my room
Catch sight of those old chimneys any
more.'

'No more,' he answered. 'If you pushed
one day   1030
Through all the green hills to our fathers'
house,

You 'd come upon a great charred circle,
where
The patient earth was singed an acre
round;
With one stone stair, symbolic of my life,
Ascending, winding, leading up to nought!
'T is worth a poet's seeing. Will you go?'

I made no answer. Had I any right
To weep with this man, that I dared to
speak?
A woman stood between his soul and mine,
And waved us off from touching ever-
more,   1040
With those unclean white hands of hers.
Enough.
We had burnt our viols, and were silent.
      So,
The silence lengthened till it pressed. I
spoke,
To breathe: 'I think you were ill after-
ward.'

'More ill,' he answered, 'had been scarcely
ill.
I hoped this feeble fumbling at life's knot
Might end concisely, — but I failed to die,
As formerly I failed to live, — and thus
Grew willing, having tried all other ways,
To try just God's. Humility 's so good,
When pride 's impossible. Mark us, how
we make   1051
Our virtues, cousin, from our worn-out sins,
Which smack of them from henceforth.
Is it right,
For instance, to wed here while you love
there?
And yet because a man sins once, the sin
Cleaves to him, in necessity to sin,
That if he sin not so to damn himself,
He sins so, to damn others with himself:
And thus, to wed here, loving there, be-
comes
A duty. Virtue buds a dubious leaf   1060
Round mortal brows; your ivy 's better,
dear.
— Yet she, 't is certain, is my very wife,
The very lamb left mangled by the wolves
Through my own bad shepherding: and
could I choose
But take her on my shoulder past this
stretch
Of rough, uneasy wilderness, poor lamb,
Poor child, poor child? — Aurora, my
beloved,

I will not vex you any more to-night,
But, having spoken what I came to say,
The rest shall please you. What she can,
     in me —   1070
Protection, tender liking, freedom, ease —
She shall have surely, liberally, for her
And hers, Aurora. Small amends they 'll
     make
For hideous evils which she had not known
Except by me, and for this imminent loss,
This forfeit presence of a gracious friend,
Which also she must forfeit for my sake,
Since, . . . drop your hand in mine a
     moment, sweet,
We 're parting ! — Ah, my snowdrop, what
     a touch,
As if the wind had swept it off ! You
     grudge   1080
Your gelid sweetness on my palm but so,
A moment ? Angry, that I could not
     bear
You . . . speaking, breathing, living, side
     by side
With some one called my wife . . . and
     live, myself ?
Nay, be not cruel — you must understand !
Your lightest footfall on a floor of mine
Would shake the house, my lintel being
     uncrossed
'Gainst angels: henceforth it is night with
     me,
And so, henceforth, I put the shutters up:
Auroras must not come to spoil my dark.'

He smiled so feebly, with an empty hand
Stretched sideway from me — as indeed he
     looked   1092
To any one but me to give him help;
And, while the moon came suddenly out
     full,
The double-rose of our Italian moons,
Sufficient plainly for the heaven and earth
(The stars struck dumb and washed away
     in dews
Of golden glory, and the mountains steeped
In divine languor), he, the man, appeared
So pale and patient, like the marble man 1100
A sculptor puts his personal sadness in
To join his grandeur of ideal thought,
As if his mallet struck me from my height
Of passionate indignation, I who had risen
Pale, doubting paused . . . Was Romney
     mad indeed ?
Had all this wrong of heart made sick the
     brain ?

Then quiet, with a sort of tremulous pride,
' Go, cousin,' I said coldly; ' a farewell
Was sooner spoken 'twixt a pair of friends
In those old days, than seems to suit you
     now.   1110
Howbeit, since then, I 've writ a book or
     two,
I 'm somewhat dull still in the manly art
Of phrase and metaphrase. Why, any man
Can carve a score of white Loves out of
     snow,
As Buonarroti in my Florence there,
And set them on the wall in some safe
     shade,
As safe, sir, as your marriage ! very good;
Though if a woman took one from the ledge
To put it on the table by her flowers
And let it mind her of a certain friend, 1120
'T would drop at once (so better), would
     not bear
Her nail-mark even, where she took it up
A little tenderly, — so best, I say:
For me, I would not touch the fragile thing
And risk to spoil it half an hour before
The sun shall shine to melt it: leave it
     there.
I 'm plain at speech, direct in purpose:
     when
I speak, you 'll take the meaning as it is,
And not allow for puckerings in the silk
By clever stitches. I 'm a woman, sir — 1130
I use the woman's figures naturally,
As you the male license. So, I wish you
     well.
I 'm simply sorry for the griefs you 've had,
And not for your sake only, but mankind's.
This race is never grateful: from the first,
One fills their cup at supper with pure wine,
Which back they give at cross-time on a
     sponge,
In vinegar and gall.'
                     ' If gratefuller,'
He murmured, ' by so much less pitiable !
God's self would never have come down to
     die,   1140
Could man have thanked Him for it.'
                         ' Happily
'T is patent that, whatever,' I resumed,
' You suffered from this thanklessness of
     men,
You sink no more than Moses' bulrush-boat
When once relieved of Moses, — for you 're
     light,
You 're light, my cousin ! which is well for
     you,

And manly. For myself, now mark me,
    sir,
They burnt Leigh Hall; but if, consum-
    mated
To devils, heightened beyond Lucifers,
They had burnt, instead, a star or two of
    those   1150
We saw above there just a moment back,
Before the moon abolished them, — de-
    stroyed
And riddled them in ashes through a sieve
On the head of the foundering universe —
    what then?
If you and I remained still you and I,
It could not shift our places as mere friends,
Nor render decent you should toss a phrase
Beyond the point of actual feeling! Nay,
You shall not interrupt me: as you said,
We're parting. Certainly, not once nor
    twice   1160
To-night you've mocked me somewhat, or
    yourself,
And I, at least, have not deserved it so
That I should meet it unsurprised. But
    now,
Enough: we're parting . . . parting.
    Cousin Leigh,
I wish you well through all the acts of life
And life's relations, wedlock not the least,
And it shall "please me," in your words, to
    know
You yield your wife protection, freedom,
    ease,
And very tender liking. May you live
So happy with her, Romney, that your
    friends   1170
Shall praise her for it! Meantime some of
    us
Are wholly dull in keeping ignorant
Of what she has suffered by you, and what
    debt
Of sorrow your rich love sits down to pay:
But if 't is sweet for love to pay its debt,
'T is sweeter still for love to give its gift,
And you, be liberal in the sweeter way,
You can, I think. At least, as touches me,
You owe her, cousin Romney, no amends:
She is not used to hold my gown so fast, 1180
You need entreat her now to let it go;
The lady never was a friend of mine,
Nor capable — I thought you knew as
    much —
Of losing for your sake so poor a prize
As such a worthless friendship. Be con-
    tent,

Good cousin, therefore, both for her and
    you!
I'll never spoil your dark, nor dull your
    noon,
Nor vex you when you're merry, or at rest:
You shall not need to put a shutter up
To keep out this Aurora, — though your
    north   1190
Can make Auroras which vex nobody,
Scarce known from night, I fancied! let
    me add,
My larks fly higher than some windows.
    Well,
You've read your Leighs. Indeed, 't would
    shake a house,
If such as I came in with outstretched hand,
Still warm and thrilling from the clasp of
    one . . .
Of one we know, . . . to acknowledge,
    palm to palm,
As mistress there, the Lady Waldemar.'
'Now God be with us' . . . with a sudden
    clash
Of voice he interrupted. 'What name's
    that?   1200
You spoke a name, Aurora.'
                     'Pardon me;
I would that, Romney, I could name your
    wife
Nor wound you, yet be worthy.'
                     'Are we mad?'
He echoed. 'Wife! mine! Lady Walde-
    mar!
I think you said my wife.' He sprang to
    his feet,
And threw his noble head back toward the
    moon
As one who swims against a stormy sea,
Then laughed with such a helpless, hopeless
    scorn,
I stood and trembled.
                'May God judge me so,'
He said at last, — 'I came convicted here,
And humbled sorely if not enough. I
    came,   1211
Because this woman from her crystal soul
Had shown me something which a man
    calls light:
Because too, formerly, I sinned by her
As then and ever since I have, by God,
Through arrogance of nature, — though I
    loved . . .
Whom best, I need not say, since that is
    writ
Too plainly in the book of my misdeeds:

And thus I came here to abase myself,
And fasten, kneeling, on her regent brows
A garland which I startled thence one
   day   1221
Of her beautiful June-youth. But here
   again
I 'm baffled, — fail in my abasement as
My aggrandizement: there 's no room left
   for me
At any woman's foot who misconceives
My nature, purpose, possible actions.
   What !
Are you the Aurora who made large my
   dreams
To frame your greatness ? you conceive so
   small ?
You stand so less than woman through
   being more
And lose your natural instinct (like a
   beast)   1230
Through intellectual culture ? since indeed
I do not think that any common she
Would dare adopt such monstrous forger-
   ies
For the legible life signature of such
As I, with all my blots — with all my
   blots !
At last, then, peerless cousin, we are
   peers —
At last we 're even. Ay, you 've left your
   height,
And here upon my level we take hands,
And here I reach you to forgive you, sweet,
And that 's a fall, Aurora. Long ago 1240
You seldom understood me, — but before,
I could not blame you. Then, you only
   seemed
So high above, you could not see below;
But now I breathe, — but now I pardon !
   — nay,
We 're parting. Dearest, men have burnt
   my house,
Maligned my motives; but not one, I
   swear,
Has wronged my soul as this Aurora has
Who called the Lady Waldemar my wife.'

'Not married to her ! yet you said ' . . .
                       ' Again ?
Nay, read the lines ' (he held a letter out)
'She sent you through me.'
                By the moonlight there
I tore the meaning out with passionate
   haste   1252
Much rather than I read it. Thus it ran.

NINTH BOOK

Even thus. I pause to write it out at
   length,
The letter of the Lady Waldemar.

'I prayed your cousin Leigh to take you
   this:
He says he 'll do it. After years of love,
Or what is called so, when a woman frets
And fools upon one string of a man's name,
And fingers it for ever till it breaks, —
He may perhaps do for her such a thing,
And she accept it without detriment
Although she should not love him any
   more.   10
And I, who do not love him, nor love
   you,
Nor you, Aurora, — choose you shall re-
   pent
Your most ungracious letter and confess,
Constrained by his convictions (he 's con-
   vinced),
You 've wronged me foully. Are you made
   so ill,
You woman, to impute such ill to *me?*
We both had mothers, — lay in their bosom
   once.
And after all, I thank you, Aurora Leigh,
For proving to myself that there are things
I would not do — not for my life, nor
   him,
Though something I have somewhat over-
   done, —   21
For instance, when I went to see the gods
One morning on Olympus, with a step
That shook the thunder from a certain
   cloud,
Committing myself vilely. Could I think,
The Muse I pulled my heart out from my
   breast
To soften, had herself a sort of heart,
And loved my mortal ? He at least loved
   her, —
I heard him say so: 't was my recompense,
When, watching at his bedside fourteen
   days,   30
He broke out ever like a flame at whiles
Between the heats of fever, — " Is it thou ?
Breathe closer, sweetest mouth ! " and
   when at last,
The fever gone, the wasted face extinct,
As if it irked him much to know me there
He said " 'T was kind, 't was good, 't was
   womanly,"

(And fifty praises to excuse no love);
" But was the picture safe he had ventured
    for ? "
And then, half wandering, " I have loved
    her well,
Although she could not love me." — " Say,
    instead,"   40
I answered, "she does love you." — 'T was
    my turn
To rave: I would have married him so
    changed,
Although the world had jeered me properly
For taking up with Cupid at his worst,
The silver quiver worn off on his hair.
" No, no," he murmured; " no, she loves me
    not;
Aurora Leigh does better: bring her book
And read it softly, Lady Waldemar,
Until I thank your friendship more for
    that
Than even for harder service." So I
    read   50
Your book, Aurora, for an hour that day:
I kept its pauses, marked its emphasis;
My voice, impaled upon its hooks of rhyme,
Not once would writhe, nor quiver, nor
    revolt;
I read on calmly, — calmly shut it up,
Observing, " There 's some merit in the
    book;
And yet the merit in 't is thrown away,
As chances still with women if we write
Or write not: we want string to tie our
    flowers,
So drop them as we walk, which serves to
    show   60
The way we went. Good morning, Mister
    Leigh;
You 'll find another reader the next time.
A woman who does better than to love,
I hate; she will do nothing very well:
Male poets are preferable, straining less
And teaching more." I triumphed o'er
    you both,
And left him.
           ' When I saw him afterward
I had read your shameful letter, and my
    heart.
He came with health recovered, strong
    though pale,
Lord Howe and he, a courteous pair of
    friends,   70
To say what men dare say to women, when
Their debtors. But I stopped them with
    a word,

And proved I had never trodden such a
    road
To carry so much dirt upon my shoe.
Then, putting into it something of disdain,
I asked, forsooth, his pardon, and my own,
For having done no better than to love,
And that not wisely, — though 't was long
    ago,
And had been mended radically since.
I told him, as I tell you now, Miss Leigh, 80
And proved, I took some trouble for his
    sake
(Because I knew he did not love the girl)
To spoil my hands with working in the
    stream
Of that poor bubbling nature, — till she
    went,
Consigned to one I trusted, my own maid
Who once had lived full five months in my
    house
(Dressed hair superbly), with a lavish
    purse,
To carry to Australia, where she had left
A husband, said she. If the creature lied,
The mission failed: we all do fail and
    lie   90
More or less — and I 'm sorry — which is
    all
Expected from us when we fail the most
And go to church to own it. What I
    meant,
Was just the best for him, and me, and
    her . . .
Best even for Marian ! — I am sorry for 't,
And very sorry. Yet my creature said
She saw her stop to speak in Oxford Street
To one . . . no matter ! I had sooner cut
My hand off (though 't were kissed the
    hour before,
And promised a duke's troth-ring for the
    next)   100
Than crush her silly head with so much
    wrong.
Poor child ! I would have mended it
    with gold,
Until it gleamed like Saint Sophia's dome
When all the faithful troop to morning
    prayer:
But he, he nipped the bud of such a thought
With that cold Leigh look which I fancied
    once,
And broke in, " Henceforth she was called
    his wife:
His wife required no succor: he was bound
To Florence, to resume this broken bond;

Enough so. Both were happy, he and
   Howe,   110
To acquit me of the heaviest charge of
   all ” —
— At which I shot my tongue against my
   fly
And struck him: “ Would he carry — he
   was just —
A letter from me to Aurora Leigh,
And ratify from his authentic mouth
My answer to her accusation ? ” — “ Yes,
If such a letter were prepared in time.”
— He ’s just, your cousin, — ay, abhor-
   rently:
He ’d wash his hands in blood, to keep
   them clean.   119
And so, cold, courteous, a mere gentleman,
He bowed, we parted.
         ‘ Parted. Face no more,
Voice no more, love no more ! — wiped
   wholly out
Like some ill scholar’s scrawl from heart
   and slate, —
Ay, spit on, and so wiped out utterly
By some coarse scholar ! I have been too
   coarse,
Too human. Have we business, in our
   rank,
With blood i’ the veins ? I will have
   henceforth none,
Not even to keep the color at my lip.
A rose is pink and pretty without blood:
Why not a woman ? When we ’ve played
   in vain   130
The game, to adore, — we have resources
   still,
And can play on at leisure, being adored:
Here ’s Smith already swearing at my feet
That I ’m the typic She. Away with
   Smith ! —
Smith smacks of Leigh, — and henceforth
   I ’ll admit
No socialist within three crinolines,
To live and have his being. But for you,
Though insolent your letter and absurd,
And though I hate you frankly, — take my
   Smith !
For when you have seen this famous mar-
   riage tied,   140
A most unspotted Erle to a noble Leigh
(His love astray on one he should not love),
Howbeit you may not want his love, be-
   ware,
You ’ll want some comfort. So I leave you
   Smith,

Take Smith ! — he talks Leigh’s subjects,
   somewhat worse;
Adopts a thought of Leigh’s, and dwindles
   it;
Goes leagues beyond, to be no inch behind;
Will mind you of him, as a shoe-string
   may
Of a man: and women, when they are
   made like you,
Grow tender to a shoe-string, footprint
   even,   150
Adore averted shoulders in a glass,
And memories of what, present once, was
   loathed.
And yet, you loathed not Romney, —
   though you played
At “ fox and goose ” about him with your
   soul;
Pass over fox, you rub out fox, — ignore
A feeling, you eradicate it, — the act ’s
Identical.
         ‘ I wish you joy, Miss Leigh;
You ’ve made a happy marriage for your
   friend,
And all the honor well-assorted love
Derives from you who love him, whom he
   loves !   160
You need not wish me joy to think of it;
I have so much. Observe, Aurora Leigh,
Your droop of eyelid is the same as his,
And, but for you, I might have won his
   love,
And, to you, I have shown my naked heart;
For which three things, I hate, hate, hate
   you. Hush !
Suppose a fourth ! — I cannot choose but
   think
That, with him, I were virtuouser than you
Without him: so I hate you from this
   gulf
And hollow of my soul, which opens out 170
To what, except for you, had been my
   heaven,
And is, instead, a place to curse by ! LOVE.’

An active kind of curse. I stood there
   cursed,
Confounded. I had seized and caught the
   sense
Of the letter, with its twenty stinging
   snakes,
In a moment’s sweep of eyesight, and I
   stood
Dazed. — ‘ Ah ! not married.’
         ‘ You mistake,’ he said:

'I 'm married. Is not Marian Erle my
   wife ?
As God sees things, I have a wife and child;
And I, as I 'm a man who honors God, 180
Am here to claim them as my child and
   wife.'

I felt it hard to breathe, much less to speak.
Nor word of mine was needed. Some one
   else
Was there for answering. ' Romney,' she
   began,
' My great good angel, Romney.'
                  Then at first,
I knew that Marian Erle was beautiful.
She stood there, still and pallid as a saint,
Dilated, like a saint in ecstasy,
As if the floating moonshine interposed
Betwixt her foot and the earth, and raised
   her up   190
To float upon it. ' I had left my child,
Who sleeps,' she said, ' and having drawn
   this way,
I heard you speaking, . . . friend ! — Con-
   firm me now.
You take this Marian, such as wicked men
Have made her, for your honorable wife ? '

The thrilling, solemn, proud, pathetic voice.
He stretched his arms out toward that
   thrilling voice,
As if to draw it on to his embrace.
— ' I take her as God made her, and as men
Must fail to unmake her, for my honored
   wife.'   200

She never raised her eyes, nor took a step,
But stood there in her place, and spoke
   again.
— ' You take this Marian's child, which is
   her shame
In sight of men and women, for your child,
Of whom you will not ever feel ashamed ? '

The thrilling, tender, proud, pathetic voice.
He stepped on toward it, still with out-
   stretched arms,
As if to quench upon his breast that voice.
— ' May God so father me, as I do him,
And so forsake me, as I let him feel   210
He 's orphaned haply. Here I take the
   child
To share my cup, to slumber on my knee,
To play his loudest gambol at my foot,
To hold my finger in the public ways,

Till none shall need inquire " Whose child
   is this ? "
The gesture saying so tenderly " My
   own." '

She stood a moment silent in her place;
Then turning toward me very slow and
   cold: —
' And you, — what say you ? — will you
   blame me much,
If, careful for that outcast child of mine, 220
I catch this hand that 's stretched to me and
   him,
Nor dare to leave him friendless in the
   world
Where men have stoned me ?   Have I not
   the right
To take so mere an aftermath from life,
Else found so wholly bare ? Or is it wrong
To let your cousin, for a generous bent,
Put out his ungloved fingers among briars
To set a tumbling bird's nest somewhat
   straight ?
You will not tell him, though we 're in-
   nocent,
We are not harmless, . . . and that both
   our harms   230
Will stick to his good, smooth, noble life
   like burrs,
Never to drop off though he shakes the
   cloak ?
You 've been my friend: you will not now
   be his ?
You 've known him that he 's worthy of a
   friend,
And you 're his cousin, lady, after all,
And therefore more than free to take his
   part,
Explaining, since the nest is surely spoilt
And Marian what you know her — though
   a wife,
The world would hardly understand her
   case
Of being just hurt and honest; while, for
   him,   240
'T would ever twit him with his bastard
   child
And married harlot. Speak, while yet
   there 's time.
You would not stand and let a good man's
   dog
Turn round and rend him, because his, and
   reared
Of a generous breed, — and will you let his
   act,

Because it 's generous ? Speak. I 'm bound
to you,
And I 'll be bound by only you, in this.'

The thrilling, solemn voice, so passionless,
Sustained, yet low, without a rise or fall,
As one who had authority to speak,   250
And not as Marian.
                          I looked up to feel
If God stood near me, and beheld his
heaven
As blue as Aaron's priestly robe appeared
To Aaron when he took it off to die.
And then I spoke: ' Accept the gift, I say,
My sister Marian, and be satisfied.
The hand that gives has still a soul behind
Which will not let it quail for having
given,
Though foolish worldlings talk they know
not what —
Of what they know not. Romney 's strong
enough   260
For this: do you be strong to know he 's
strong:
He stands on Right's side; never flinch for
him,
As if he stood on the other. You 'll be
bound
By me ? I am a woman of repute;
No fly-blow gossip ever specked my life;
My name is clean and open as this hand,
Whose glove there 's not a man dares blab
about
As if he had touched it freely. Here 's
my hand
To clasp your hand, my Marian, owned as
pure !   269
As pure — as I 'm a woman and a Leigh ! —
And, as I 'm both, I 'll witness to the world
That Romney Leigh is honored in his
choice
Who chooses Marian for his honored wife.'

Her broad wild woodland eyes shot out a
light,
Her smile was wonderful for rapture.
' Thanks,
My great Aurora.' Forward then she
sprang,
And dropping her impassioned spaniel head
With all its brown abandonment of curls
On Romney's feet, we heard the kisses
drawn
Through sobs upon the foot, upon the
ground —   280

'O Romney ! O my angel ! O unchanged
Though since we 've parted I have passed
the grave !
But Death itself could only better *thee*,
Not change thee ! — *Thee* I do not thank
at all:
I but thank God who made thee what thou
art,
So wholly godlike.'
                          When he tried in vain
To raise her to his embrace, escaping
thence
As any leaping fawn from a huntsman's
grasp,
She bounded off and 'lighted beyond reach,
Before him, with a staglike majesty   290
Of soft, serene defiance, — as she knew
He could not touch her, so was tolerant
He had cared to try. She stood there with
her great
Drowned eyes, and dripping cheeks, and
strange, sweet smile
That lived through all, as if one held a
light
Across a waste of waters — shook her
head
To keep some thoughts down deeper in
her soul, —
Then, white and tranquil like a summer-
cloud
Which, having rained itself to a tardy
peace,
Stands still in heaven as if it ruled the
day,   300
Spoke out again, — ' Although, my gener-
ous friend,
Since last we met and parted you 're un-
changed,
And having promised faith to Marian Erle,
Maintain it, as she were not changed at
all;
And though that 's worthy, though that 's
full of balm
To any conscious spirit of a girl
Who once has loved you as I loved you
once —
Yet still it will not make her . . . if she 's
dead,
And gone away where none can give or
take
In marriage — able to revive, return   310
And wed you — will it, Romney ? Here 's
the point,
My friend, we 'll see it plainer: you and I
Must never, never, never join hands so.

Nay, let me say it — for I said it first
To God, and placed it, rounded to an oath,
Far, far above the moon there, at his feet,
As surely as I wept just now at yours —
We never, never, never join hands so.
And now, be patient with me; do not think
I 'm speaking from a false humility.   320
The truth is, I am grown so proud with grief,
And He has said so often through his nights
And through his mornings, " Weep a little still,
Thou foolish Marian, because women must,
But do not blush at all except for sin " —
That I, who felt myself unworthy once
Of virtuous Romney and his high-born race,
Have come to learn, — a woman, poor or rich,
Despised or honored, is a human soul,   329
And what her soul is, that she is herself,
Although she should be spit upon of men,
As is the pavement of the churches here,
Still good enough to pray in. And being chaste
And honest, and inclined to do the right,
And love the truth, and live my life out green
And smooth beneath his steps, I should not fear
To make him thus a less uneasy time
Than many a happier woman. Very proud
You see me. Pardon, that I set a trap
To hear a confirmation in your voice,   340
Both yours and yours. It is so good to know
'T was really God who said the same before;
And thus it is in heaven, that first God speaks,
And then his angels. Oh, it does me good,
It wipes me clean and sweet from devil's dirt,
That Romney Leigh should think me worthy still
Of being his true and honorable wife !
Henceforth I need not say, on leaving earth,
I had no glory in it. For the rest,   349
The reason 's ready (master, angel, friend,
Be patient with me) wherefore you and I
Can never, never, never join hands so.

I know you 'll not be angry like a man
(For *you* are none) when I shall tell the truth,
Which is, I do not love you, Romney Leigh,
I do not love you. Ah well ! catch my hands,
Miss Leigh, and burn into my eyes with yours —
I swear I do not love him. Did I once ?
'T is said that women have been bruised to death
And yet, if once they loved, that love of theirs   360
Could never be drained out with all their blood:
I 've heard such things and pondered. Did I indeed
Love once; or did I only worship ? Yes,
Perhaps, O friend, I set you up so high
Above all actual good or hope of good
Or fear of evil, all that could be mine,
I haply set you above love itself,
And out of reach of these poor woman's arms,
Angelic Romney. What was in my thought ?
To be your slave, your help, your toy, your tool.   370
To be your love . . . I never thought of that:
To give you love . . . still less. I gave you love ?
I think I did not give you anything;
I was but only yours — upon my knees,
All yours, in soul and body, in head and heart,
A creature you had taken from the ground
Still crumbling through your fingers to your feet
To join the dust she came from. Did I love,
Or did I worship ? judge, Aurora Leigh !
But, if indeed I loved, 't was long ago — 380
So long ! before the sun and moon were made,
Before the hells were open, — ah, before
I heard my child cry in the desert night,
And knew he had no father. It may be
I 'm not as strong as other women are,
Who, torn and crushed, are not undone from love:
It may be I am colder than the dead,
Who, being dead, love always. But for me,

Once killed, this ghost of Marian loves no
  more,
No more . . . except the child ! . . . no
  more at all.   390
I told your cousin, sir, that I was dead;
And now, she thinks I 'll get up from my
  grave,
And wear my chin-cloth for a wedding-veil,
And glide along the churchyard like a
  bride
While all the dead keep whispering through
  the withes,
" You would be better in your place with
  us,
You pitiful corruption ! " At the thought,
The damps break out on me like leprosy
Although I 'm clean. Ay, clean as Marian
  Erle !
As Marian Leigh, I know, I were not
  clean: 400
Nor have I so much life that I should love,
Except the child. Ah God ! I could not
  bear
To see my darling on a good man's knees,
And know, by such a look, or such a sigh,
Or such a silence, that he thought some-
  times,
" This child was fathered by some cursèd
  wretch " . . .
For, Romney, angels are less tender-wise
Than God and mothers: even *you* would
  think
What *we* think never. He is ours, the
  child;
And we would sooner vex a soul in
  heaven   410
By coupling with it the dead body's thought,
It left behind it in a last month's grave,
Than, in my child, see other than . . . my
  child.
We only never call him fatherless
Who has God and his mother. O my
  babe,
My pretty, pretty blossom, an ill wind
Once blew upon my breast ! can any think
I 'd have another — one called happier,
A fathered child, with father's love and
  race
That 's worn as bold and open as a smile, 420
To vex my darling when he 's asked his
  name
And has no answer ? What ! a happier
  child
Than mine, my best — who laughed so
  loud to-night

He could not sleep for pastime ? Nay, I
  swear,
By life and love, that, if I lived like some,
And loved like . . . *some*, ay, loved you,
  Romney Leigh,
As some love (eyes that have wept so
  much, see clear),
I 've room for no more children in my
  arms,
My kisses are all melted on one mouth,
I would not push my darling to a stool 430
To dandle babies. Here 's a hand shall
  keep
For ever clean without a marriage-ring,
To tend my boy until he cease to need
One steadying finger of it, and desert
(Not miss) his mother's lap, to sit with
  men.
And when I miss him (not he me), I 'll
  come
And say " Now give me some of Romney's
  work,
To help your outcast orphans of the world
And comfort grief with grief." For you,
  meantime,
Most noble Romney, wed a noble wife, 440
And open on each other your great souls —
I need not farther bless you. If I dared
But strain and touch her in her upper
  sphere,
And say " Come down to Romney — pay
  my debt ! "
I should be joyful with the stream of joy
Sent through me. But the moon is in my
  face . . .
I dare not — though I guess the name he
  loves;
I 'm learned with my studies of old days,
Remembering how he crushed his under-
  lip
When some one came and spoke, or did
  not come.   450
Aurora, I could touch her with my hand,
And fly because I dare not.'
                              She was gone.

He smiled so sternly that I spoke in haste.
' Forgive her — she sees clearly for her-
  self:
Her instinct 's holy.'
                        ' *I* forgive ! ' he said,
' I only marvel how she sees so sure,
While others ' . . . there he paused —
  then hoarse, abrupt,
' Aurora ! you forgive us, her and me ?

For her, the thing she sees, poor, loyal
 child,
If once corrected by the thing I know, 460
Had been unspoken, since she loves you
 well,
Has leave to love you: — while for me,
 alas !
If once or twice I let my heart escape
This night, . . . remember, where hearts
 slip and fall,
They break beside: we 're parting — part-
 ing — ah !
You do not love, that you should surely
 know
What that word means. Forgive, be tol-
 erant:
It had not been, but that I felt myself
So safe in impuissance and despair,
I could not hurt you though I tossed my
 arms 470
And sighed my soul out. The most utter
 wretch
Will choose his postures when he comes to
 die,
However in the presence of a queen;
And you 'll forgive me some unseemly
 spasms
Which meant no more than dying. Do you
 think
I had ever come here in my perfect mind
Unless I had come here in my settled
 mind
Bound Marian's, bound to keep the bond
 and give
My name, my house, my hand, the things I
 could,
To Marian ? For even *I* could give as
 much: 480
Even I, affronting her exalted soul
By a supposition that she wanted these,
Could act the husband's coat and hat set
 up
To creak i' the wind and drive the world-
 crows off
From pecking in her garden. Straw can
 fill
A hole to keep out vermin. Now, at last,
I own heaven's angels round her life suffice
To fight the rats of our society
Without this Romney: I can see it at last;
And here is ended my pretension which 490
The most pretended. Over-proud of
 course,
Even so ! — but not so stupid . . . blind
 . . . that I,

Whom thus the great Taskmaster of the
 world
Has set to meditate mistaken work,
My dreary face against a dim blank wall
Throughout man's natural lifetime — could
 pretend
Or wish . . . O love, I have loved you ! O
 my soul,
I have lost you ! — but I swear by all your-
 self,
And all you might have been to me these
 years,
If that June morning had not failed my
 hope — 500
I 'm not so bestial, to regret that day —
This night — this night, which still to you
 is fair !
Nay, not so blind, Aurora. I attest
Those stars above us which I cannot
 see ' . . .

' You cannot ' . . .
   ' That if Heaven itself should stoop,
Re-mix the lots, and give me another
 chance,
I 'd say "No other !" — I 'd record my
 blank.
Aurora never should be wife of mine."

' Not see the stars ? '
   ''T is worse still, not to see,
To find your hand, although we 're parting,
 dear. 510
A moment let me hold it ere we part;
And understand my last words — these, at
 last !
I would not have you thinking when I 'm
 gone
That Romney dared to hanker for your
 love
In thought or vision, if attainable
(Which certainly for me it never was),
And wished to use it for a dog to-day
To help the blind man stumbling. God
 forbid !
And now I know He held you in his palm,
And kept you open-eyed to all my
 faults, 520
To save you at last from such a dreary
 end.
Believe me, dear, that, if I had known like
 Him
What loss was coming on me, I had done
As well in this as He has. — Farewell,
 you

Who are still my light, — farewell ! How
　　late it is:
I know that, now.　You 've been too patient,
　　sweet.
I will but blow my whistle toward the
　　lane,
And some one comes — the same who
　　brought me here.
Get in — Good-night.'
　　　　'A moment.　Heavenly Christ !
A moment.　Speak once, Romney.　'T is
　　not true.　　　　　　　　　　530
I hold your hands, I look into your face —
You see me ? '
　　　　' No more than the blessèd stars.
Be blessèd too, Aurora.　Nay, my sweet,
You tremble.　Tender-hearted !　Do you
　　mind
Of yore, dear, how you used to cheat old
　　John,
And let the mice out slyly from his traps,
Until he marvelled at the soul in mice
Which took the cheese and left the
　　snare ?　The same
Dear soft heart always !　'T was for this I
　　grieved
Howe's letter never reached you.　Ah, you
　　had heard　　　　　　　　　540
Of illness — not the issue, not the extent:
My life, long sick with tossings up and
　　down,
The sudden revulsion in the blazing house,
The strain and struggle both of body and
　　soul,
Which left fire running in my veins for
　　blood,
Scarce lacked that thunderbolt of the fall-
　　ing beam
Which nicked me on the forehead as I
　　passed
The gallery-door with a burden.　Say
　　heaven's bolt,
Not William Erle's, not Marian's fa-
　　ther's, — tramp
And poacher, whom I found for what he
　　was,　　　　　　　　　　550
And, eager for her sake to rescue him,
Forth swept from the open highway of the
　　world,
Road-dust and all — till, like a woodland
　　boar
Most naturally unwilling to be tamed,
He notched me with his tooth.　But not a
　　word
To Marian ! and I do not think, besides,

He turned the tilting of the beam my way;
And if he laughed, as many swear, poor
　　wretch,　　　　　　　　　　558
Nor he nor I supposed the hurt so deep.
We 'll hope his next laugh may be mer-
　　rier,
In a better cause.'
　　　　' Blind, Romney ? '
　　　　　　　　　' Ah, my friend,
You 'll learn to say it in a cheerful voice;
I, too, at first desponded.　To be blind,
Turned out of nature, mulcted as a man,
Rèfused the daily largesse of the sun
To humble creatures !　When the fever's
　　heat
Dropped from me, as the flame did from
　　my house,
And left me ruined like it, stripped of all
The hues and shapes of aspectable life,
A mere bare blind stone in the blaze of
　　day,　　　　　　　　　　570
A man, upon the outside of the earth,
As dark as ten feet under, in the grave, —
Why, that seemed hard.'
　　　　　　　' No hope ? '
　　　　　　　　　' A tear ! you weep,
Divine Aurora ? tears upon my hand !
I 've seen you weeping for a mouse, a
　　bird, —
But, weep for me, Aurora ?　Yes, there 's
　　hope.
Not hope of sight, — I could be learned,
　　dear,
And tell you in what Greek and Latin
　　name
The visual nerve is withered to the root,
Though the outer eyes appear indiffer-
　　ent,　　　　　　　　　　580
Unspotted in their crystals.　But there 's
　　hope.
The spirit, from behind this dethroned
　　sense,
Sees, waits in patience till the walls break
　　up
From which the bas-relief and fresco have
　　dropped:
There 's hope.　The man here, once so
　　arrogant
And restless, so ambitious, for his part,
Of dealing with statistically packed
Disorders (from a pattern on his nail),
And packing such things quite another
　　way, —
Is now contented.　From his personal
　　loss　　　　　　　　　　590

He has come to hope for others when they
lose,
And wear a gladder faith in what we
gain . . .
Through bitter experience, compensation
sweet,
Like that tear, sweetest. I am quiet now,
As tender surely for the suffering world,
But quiet, — sitting at the wall to learn,
Content henceforth to do the thing I can:
For, though as powerless, said I, as a
stone,
A stone can still give shelter to a worm,
And it is worth while being a stone for
that: 600
There 's hope, Aurora.'
    ' Is there hope for me ?
For me ? — and is there room beneath the
stone
For such a worm ? — And if I came and
said . . .
What all this weeping scarce will let me
say,
And yet what women cannot say at all
But weeping bitterly . . . (the pride keeps
up,
Until the heart breaks under it) . . . I
love, —
I love you, Romney ' . . .
    ' Silence !' he exclaimed.
' A woman's pity sometimes makes her
mad. 609
A man's distraction must not cheat his soul
To take advantage of it. Yet, 't is hard
Farewell, Aurora.'
    ' But I love you, sir;
And when a woman says she loves a man,
The man must hear her, though he love her
not,
Which . . . hush ! . . . he has leave to
answer in his turn;
She will not surely blame him. As for
me,
You call it pity, — think I 'm generous ?
'T were somewhat easier, for a woman
proud
As I am, and I 'm very vilely proud,
To let it pass as such, and press on you 620
Love born of pity, — seeing that excellent
loves
Are born so, often, nor the quicklier
die, —
And this would set me higher by the head
Than now I stand. No matter: let the
truth

Stand high; Aurora must be humble: no,
My love 's not pity merely. Obviously
I 'm not a generous woman, never was,
Or else, of old, I had not looked so near
To weights and measures, grudging you the
power
To give, as first I scorned your power to
judge 630
For me, Aurora. I would have no gifts,
Forsooth, but God's, — and I would use
them too
According to my pleasure and my choice,
As He and I were equals, you below,
Excluded from that level of interchange
Admitting benefaction. You were wrong
In much ? you said so. I was wrong in
most.
Oh, most ! You only thought to rescue
men
By half-means, half-way, seeing half their
wants,
While thinking nothing of your personal
gain. 640
But I, who saw the human nature broad
At both sides, comprehending too the soul's,
And all the high necessities of Art,
Betrayed the thing I saw, and wronged my
own life
For which I pleaded. Passioned to exalt
The artist's instinct in me at the cost
Of putting down the woman's, I forgot
No perfect artist is developed here
From any imperfect woman. Flower from
root,
And spiritual from natural, grade by
grade 650
In all our life. A handful of the earth
To make God's image ! the despised poor
earth,
The healthy, odorous earth, — I missed
with it
The divine Breath that blows the nostrils
out
To ineffable inflatus, — ay, the breath
Which love is. Art is much, but Love is
more.
O Art, my Art, thou 'rt much, but Love is
more !
Art symbolizes heaven, but Love is God
And makes heaven. I, Aurora, fell from
mine.
I would not be a woman like the rest, 660
A simple woman who believes in love
And owns the right of love because she
loves,

And, hearing she 's beloved, is satisfied
With what contents God: I must ana-
lyze,
Confront, and question; just as if a fly
Refused to warm itself in any sun
Till such was *in Leone :* I must fret,
Forsooth, because the month was only
May,
Be faithless of the kind of proffered love,
And captious, lest it miss my dignity,   670
And scornful, that my lover sought a wife
To use . . . to use! O Romney, O my
love,
I am changed since then, changed wholly, —
for indeed
If now you 'd stoop so low to take my
love
And use it roughly, without stint or spare,
As men use common things with more
behind
(And, in this, ever would be more behind)
To any mean and ordinary end, —
The joy would set me like a star, in hea-
ven,
So high up, I should shine because of
height   680
And not of virtue. Yet in one respect,
Just one, beloved, I am in nowise changed:
I love you, loved you . . . loved you first
and last,
And love you on for ever. Now I know
I loved you always, Romney. She who
died
Knew that, and said so; Lady Waldemar
Knows that; . . . and Marian. I had known
the same,
Except that I was prouder than I knew,
And not so honest. Ay, and, as I live,
I should have died so, crushing in my
hand   690
This rose of love, the wasp inside and all,
Ignoring ever to my soul and you
Both rose and pain — except for this great
loss,
This great despair — to stand before your
face
And know you do not see me where I stand.
You think, perhaps, I am not changed from
pride
And that I chiefly bear to say such words,
Because you cannot shame me with your
eyes?
O calm, grand eyes, extinguished in a
storm,
Blown out like lights o'er melancholy seas,

Though shrieked for by the shipwrecked, —
O my Dark,   701
My Cloud, — to go before me every day
While I go ever toward the wilderness, —
I would that you could see me bare to the
soul !
If this be pity, 't is so for myself,
And not for Romney ! *he* can stand alone;
A man like *him* is never overcome:
No woman like me counts him pitiable
While saints applaud him. He mistook the
world;
But I mistook my own heart, and that
slip
Was fatal. Romney, — will you leave me
here ?   711
So wrong, so proud, so weak, so unconsoled,
So mere a woman ! — and I love you so,
I love you, Romney ' —
                        Could I see his face,
I wept so ? Did I drop against his breast,
Or did his arms constrain me ? were my
cheeks
Hot, overflooded, with my tears — or his ?
And which of our two large explosive hearts
So shook me ? That, I know not. There
were words
That broke in utterance . . . melted, in the
fire, —   720
Embrace, that was convulsion, . . . then a
kiss
As long and silent as the ecstatic night,
And deep, deep, shuddering breaths, which
meant beyond
Whatever could be told by word or kiss.
But what he said . . . I have written day
by day,
With somewhat even writing. Did I think
That such a passionate rain would intercept
And dash this last page ? What he said,
indeed,
I fain would write it down here like the
rest,
To keep it in my eyes, as in my ears,   730
The heart's sweet scripture, to be read at
night
When weary, or at morning when afraid,
And lean my heaviest oath on when I swear
That, when all 's done, all tried, all counted
here,
All great arts, and all good philosophies,
This love just puts its hand out in a dream
And straight outstretches all things.
                        What he said,
I fain would write. But if an angel spoke

In thunder, should we haply know much
    more
Than that it thundered ? If a cloud came
    down   740
And wrapped us wholly, could we draw its
    shape,
As if on the outside and not overcome ?
And so he spake. His breath against my
    face
Confused his words, yet made them more
    intense
(As when the sudden finger of the wind
Will wipe a row of single city-lamps
To a pure white line of flame, more lumi-
    nous
Because of obliteration), more intense,
The intimate presence carrying in itself
Complete communication, as with souls 750
Who, having put the body off, perceive
Through simply being. Thus, 't was granted
    me
To know he loved me to the depth and
    height
Of such large natures, ever competent,
With grand horizons by the sea or land,
To love's grand sunrise. Small spheres
    hold small fires,
But he loved largely, as a man can love
Who, baffled in his love, dares live his
    life,
Accept the ends which God loves, for his
    own,
And lift a constant aspect.
                  From the day
I brought to England my poor searching
    face   761
(An orphan even of my father's grave),
He had loved me, watched me, watched his
    soul in mine,
Which in me grew and heightened into
    love.
For he, a boy still, had been told the tale
Of how a fairy bride from Italy
With smells of oleanders in her hair,
Was coming through the vines to touch his
    hand;
Whereat the blood of boyhood on the palm
Made sudden heats. And when at last I
    came,   770
And lived before him — lived, and rarely
    smiled —
He smiled and loved me for the thing I
    was,
As every child will love the year's first
    flower

(Not certainly the fairest of the year,
But, in which, the complete year seems to
    blow),
The poor sad snowdrop, — growing between
    drifts,
Mysterious medium 'twixt the plant and
    frost,
So faint with winter while so quick with
    spring,
And doubtful if to thaw itself away
With that snow near it. Not that Romney
    Leigh   780
Had loved me coldly. If I thought so
    once,
It was as if I had held my hand in fire
And shook for cold. But now I under-
    stood,
For ever, that the very fire and heat
Of troubling passion in him burned him
    clear,
And shaped, to dubious order, word and
    act:
That, just because he loved me over all,
All wealth, all lands, all social privilege,
To which chance made him unexpected heir,
And, just because on all these lesser gifts, 790
Constrained by conscience and the sense of
    wrong,
He had stamped with steady hand God's
    arrow-mark
Of dedication to the human need,
He thought it should be so too, with his
    love.
He, passionately loving, would bring down
His love, his life, his best (because the
    best),
His bride of dreams, who walked so still
    and high
Through flowery poems as through mea-
    dow-grass,
The dust of golden lilies on her feet,
That *she* should walk beside him on the
    rocks   800
In all that clang and hewing out of men,
And help the work of help which was his
    life,
And prove he kept back nothing, — not his
    soul.
And when I failed him, — for I failed him,
    I,
And when it seemed he had missed my
    love, he thought
' Aurora makes room for a working-noon,'
And so, self-girded with torn strips of
    hope,

Took up his life as if it were for death
(Just capable of one heroic aim),
And threw it in the thickest of the
    world, —   810
At which men laughed as if he had drowned
    a dog.
No wonder, — since Aurora failed him
    first !
The morning and the evening made his
    day.

But oh, the night ! oh, bitter-sweet ! oh,
    sweet !
O dark, O moon and stars, O ecstasy
Of darkness !   O great mystery of love,
In which absorbed, loss, anguish, treason's
    self
Enlarges rapture, — as a pebble dropped
In some full wine-cup overbrims the wine !
While we two sat together, leaned that
    night   820
So close my very garments crept and
    thrilled
With strange electric life, and both my
    cheeks
Grew red, then pale, with touches from my
    hair
In which his breath was, — while the gold-
    en moon
Was hung before our faces as the badge
Of some sublime inherited despair,
Since ever to be seen by only one, —
A voice said, low and rapid as a sigh,
Yet breaking, I felt conscious, from a
    smile,
'Thank God, who made me blind, to make
    me see !   830
Shine on, Aurora, dearest light of souls,
Which rul'st for evermore both day and
    night !
I am happy.'
                I flung closer to his breast,
As sword that, after battle, flings to
    sheath;
And, in that hurtle of united souls,
The mystic motions which in common
    moods
Are shut beyond our sense, broke in on
    us,
And, as we sat, we felt the old earth spin,
And all the starry turbulence of worlds
Swing round us in their audient circles,
    till,   840
If that same golden moon were overhead
Or if beneath our feet, we did not know.

And then calm, equal, smooth with weights
    of joy,
His voice rose, as some chief musician's
    song
Amid the old Jewish temple's Selah-pause,
And bade me mark how we two met at
    last
Upon this moon - bathed promontory of
    earth,
To give up much on each side, then take
    all.
' Beloved,' it sang, ' we must be here to
    work;   849
And men who work can only work for men,
And, not to work in vain, must comprehend
Humanity and so work humanly,
And raise men's bodies still by raising souls,
As God did first.'
                    ' But stand upon the earth,'
I said, ' to raise them (this is human too,
There 's nothing high which has not first
    been low;
My humbleness, said One, has made me
    great !)
As God did last.'
                    ' And work all silently
And simply,' he returned, ' as God does all;
Distort our nature never for our work, 860
Nor count our right hands stronger for
    being hoofs.
The man most man, with tenderest human
    hands,
Works best for men, — as God in Naza-
    reth.'

He paused upon the word, and then re-
    sumed:
' Fewer programmes, we who have no pre-
    science.
Fewer systems, we who are held and do
    not hold.
Less mapping out of masses to be saved,
By nations or by sexes. Fourier 's void,
And Comte absurd, — and Cabet puerile.
Subsist no rules of life outside of life, 870
No perfect manners without Christian
    souls:
The Christ Himself had been no Lawgiver
Unless He had given the life, too, with the
    law.'

I echoed thoughtfully: ' The man, most
    man,
Works best for men, and, if most man
    indeed,

He gets his manhood plainest from 'his
    soul:
While obviously this stringent soul itself
Obeys the old law of development,
The Spirit ever witnessing in ours,
And Love, the soul of soul, within the
    soul,   880
Evolving it sublimely. First, God's love.'

'And next,' he smiled, 'the love of wedded
    souls,
Which still presents that mystery's coun-
    terpart.
Sweet shadow-rose, upon the water of life,
Of such a mystic substance, Sharon gave
A name to ! human, vital, fructuous rose,
Whose calyx holds the multitude of leaves,
Loves filial, loves fraternal, neighbor-loves
And civic - all fair petals, all good scents,
All reddened, sweetened from one central
    Heart !'   890

'Alas,' I cried, 'it was not long ago
You swore this very social rose smelt ill.'

'Alas,' he answered, 'is it a rose at all ?
The filial 's thankless, the fraternal 's hard,
The rest is lost. I do but stand and think,
Across the waters of a troubled life
This Flower of Heaven so vainly overhangs,
What perfect counterpart would be in
    sight
If tanks were clearer. Let us clean the
    tubes,
And wait for rains. O poet, O my love, 900
Since *I* was too ambitious in my deed
And thought to distance all men in success
(Till God came on me, marked the place,
    and said
" Ill-doer, henceforth keep within this line,
Attempting less than others," — and I
    stand
And work among Christ's little ones, con-
    tent),
Come thou, my compensation, my dear
    sight,
My morning-star, my morning, — rise and
    shine,
And touch my hills with radiance not their
    own.
Shine out for two, Aurora, and fulfil   910
My falling-short that must be ! work for
    two,
As I, though thus restrained, for two shall
    love !

Gaze on, with inscient vision toward the
    sun,
And, from his visceral heat, pluck out the
    roots
Of light beyond him. Art's a service, —
    mark:
A silver key is given to thy clasp,
And thou shalt stand unwearied, night and
    day,
And fix it in the hard, slow-turning wards,
To open, so, that intermediate door
Betwixt the different planes of sensuous
    form   920
And form insensuous, that inferior men
May learn to feel on still through these to
    those,
And bless thy ministration. The world
    waits
For help. Beloved, let us love so well,
Our work shall still be better for our
    love,
And still our love be sweeter for our work,
And both commended, for the sake of each,
By all true workers and true lovers born.
Now press the clarion on thy woman's lip
(Love's holy kiss shall still keep conse-
    crate)   930
And breathe thy fine keen breath along the
    brass,
And blow all class-walls level as Jericho's
Past Jordan, — crying from the top of
    souls,
To souls that, here assembled on earth's
    flats,
They get them to some purer eminence
Than any hitherto beheld for clouds !
What height we know not, — but the way
    we know,
And how by mounting ever we attain,
And so climb on. It is the hour for souls,
That bodies, leavened by the will and love,
Be lightened to redemption. The world 's
    old,   941
But the old world waits the time to be
    renewed,
Toward which, new hearts in individual
    growth
Must quicken, and increase to multitude
In new dynasties of the race of men;
Developed whence, shall grow spontane-
    ously
New churches, new œconomies, new laws,
Admitting freedom, new societies
Excluding falsehood: HE shall make all
    new.'

My Romney! — Lifting up my hand in
  his,   950
As wheeled by Seeing spirits toward the
  east,
He turned instinctively, where, faint and far,
Along the tingling desert of the sky,
Beyond the circle of the conscious hills,
Were laid in jasper-stone as clear as glass
The first foundations of that new, near
  Day
Which should be builded out of heaven to
  God.

He stood a moment with erected brows,
In silence, as a creature might who
  gazed, —
Stood calm, and fed his blind, majestic
  eyes   960
Upon the thought of perfect noon: and
  when
I saw his soul saw, — 'Jasper first,' I
  said;
'And second, sapphire; third, chalced-
  ony;
The rest in order: — last, an amethyst.'

POEMS BEFORE CONGRESS

The small volume entitled *Poems before
Congress* (*London: Chapman and Hall*, 1860)
which appeared about a year before Mrs.
Browning's death, was the last of her pub-
lished works to receive her personal super-
vision. Of the eight pieces which it contains,
the first, *Napoleon III. in Italy*, is much the
longest and most elaborate; but all are dis-
tinctly and even fiercely controversial: — *sir-
ventes*, the Troubadours would have called
them, rather than songs; and the entire vol-
ume a pamphlet, rather than a collection of
poems. They were sharply criticised, at the
time of their appearance, for their passionate
one-sidedness and reckless glorification of the
French emperor; while their severe strictures
on the vacillating, and, indeed, hardly ingen-
uous policy of England toward Italy in her
hour of supreme struggle, were bitterly re-
sented by Mrs. Browning's fellow-countrymen.
No apology for the vehemence of these indig-
nant cries, need, however, be offered here,
other than the author's own rather haughty
one, prefixed to the first edition of the *Poems
before Congress* and dated Rome, February,
1860. 'These poems were written under the
pressure of the events they indicate, after a
residence in Italy of so many years that the
present triumph of great principles is height-
ened, to the writer's feelings, by the disastrous
issue of the last movement witnessed from
"Casa Guidi windows" in 1849. Yet if the
verses should appear to English readers too
pungently rendered to admit of a patriotic
respect to the English sense of things, I will
not excuse myself on such grounds, nor on the
ground of my attachment to the Italian peo-
ple, and my admiration for their heroic con-
stancy and union. What I have written has
simply been written, because I love truth and
justice, *quand même*, "more than Plato and
Plato's country, more than Dante and Dante's
country," more even than Shakespeare, and
Shakespeare's country.'

NAPOLEON III. IN ITALY

I

EMPEROR, Emperor!
From the centre to the shore,
  From the Seine back to the Rhine,
Stood eight millions up and swore
  By their manhood's right divine
So to elect and legislate,
  This man should renew the line
Broken in a strain of fate
And leagued kings at Waterloo,
When the people's hands let go.   10
      Emperor
      Evermore.

II

With a universal shout
They took the old regalia out
From an open grave that day;
  From a grave that would not close,
Where the first Napoleon lay
  Expectant, in repose,
As still as Merlin, with his conquering face
  Turned up in its unquenchable appeal 20
To men and heroes of the advancing
      race, —
  Prepared to set the seal
Of what has been on what shall be.
      Emperor
      Evermore.

III

The thinkers stood aside
  To let the nation act.
Some hated the new-constituted fact
Of empire, as pride treading on their
    pride.
Some quailed, lest what was poisonous in
    the past   30
  Should graft itself in that Druidic bough
    On this green Now.
Some cursed, because at last
The open heavens to which they had looked
    in vain
For many a golden fall of marvellous rain
Were closed in brass; and some
Wept on because a gone thing could not
    come;
And some were silent, doubting all things
    for
That popular conviction, — evermore
      Emperor.   40

IV

That day I did not hate
  Nor doubt, nor quail nor curse.
I, reverencing the people, did not bate
My reverence of their deed and oracle,
  Nor vainly prate
    Of better and of worse
Against the great conclusion of their will.
  And yet, O voice and verse,
Which God set in me to acclaim and sing
Conviction, exaltation, aspiration,   50
We gave no music to the patent thing,
  Nor spared a holy rhythm to throb and
    swim
    About the name of him
Translated to the sphere of domination
  By democratic passion !
I was not used, at least,
  Nor can be, now or then,
To stroke the ermine beast
  On any kind of throne
('Though builded by a nation for its
    own),   60
And swell the surging choir for kings of
    men
      'Emperor
      Evermore.'

V

But now, Napoleon, now
That, leaving far behind the purple throng
  Of vulgar monarchs, thou

Tread'st higher in thy deed
Than stair of throne can lead,
To help in the hour of wrong
The broken hearts of nations to be
    strong, —   70
Now, lifted as thou art
To the level of pure song,
We stand to meet thee on these Alpine
    snows !
And while the palpitating peaks break
    out
Ecstatic from somnambular repose
  With answers to the presence and the
    shout,
We, poets of the people, who take part
  With elemental justice, natural right,
Join in our echoes also, nor refrain.   79
  We meet thee, O Napoleon, at this height
At last, and find thee great enough to
    praise,
Receive the poet's chrism, which smells
    beyond
  The priest's, and pass thy ways; —
An English poet warns thee to maintain
God's word, not England's: — let his truth
    be true
And all men liars ! with his truth respond
To all men's lie. Exalt the sword and smite
On that long anvil of the Apennine
Where Austria forged the Italian chain in
    view
Of seven consenting nations, sparks of fine
    Admonitory light,   91
Till men's eyes wink before convictions
    new.
Flash in God's justice to the world's amaze,
Sublime Deliverer ! — after many days
Found worthy of the deed thou art come to
    do —
      Emperor
      Evermore.

VI

But Italy, my Italy,
  Can it last, this gleam ?
Can she live and be strong,   100
  Or is it another dream
Like the rest we have dreamed so long ?
  And shall it, must it be,
That after the battle-cloud has broken
  She will die off again
    Like the rain,
  Or like a poet's song
    Sung of her, sad at the end

Because her name is Italy, —
    Die and count no friend ?   110
Is it true, — may it be spoken, —
    That she who has lain so still,
With a wound in her breast,
And a flower in her hand,
And a grave-stone under her head,
    While every nation at will
Beside her has dared to stand,
And flout her with pity and scorn,
    Saying, 'She is at rest,
She is fair, she is dead,   120
And, leaving room in her stead
To Us who are later born,
    This is certainly best !'
Saying, 'Alas, she is fair,
Very fair, but dead, — give place,
And so we have room for the race.'
-- Can it be true, be true,
That she lives anew ?
That she rises up at the shout of her sons,
    At the trumpet of France,   130
And lives anew ? — is it true
    That she has not moved in a trance,
As in Forty-eight ?
    When her eyes were troubled with blood
Till she knew not friend from foe,
Till her hand was caught in a strait
Of her cerement and baffled so
    From doing the deed she would;
And her weak foot stumbled across
The grave of a king,   140
And down she dropt at heavy loss,
    And we gloomily covered her face and
        said,
'We have dreamed the thing;
    She is not alive, but dead.'

VII

Now, shall we say
    Our Italy lives indeed ?
And if it were not for the beat and bray
Of drum and trump of martial men,
Should we feel the underground heave and
        strain,
    Where heroes left their dust as a seed   150
Sure to emerge one day ?
And if it were not for the rhythmic march
    Of France and Piedmont's double hosts,
    Should we hear the ghosts
Thrill through ruined aisle and arch,
    Throb along the frescoed wall,
Whisper an oath by that divine
They left in picture, book, and stone,
    That Italy is not dead at all ?

Ay, if it were not for the tears in our
    eyes,   160
These tears of a sudden passionate joy,
    Should we see her arise
From the place where the wicked are over-
        thrown,
Italy, Italy — loosed at length
    From the tyrant's thrall,
Pale and calm in her strength ?
Pale as the silver cross of Savoy
When the hand that bears the flag is brave,
And not a breath is stirring, save
    What is blown   170
Over the war-trump's lip of brass,
Ere Garibaldi forces the pass !

VIII

Ay, it is so, even so.
Ay, and it shall be so.
Each broken stone that long ago
She flung behind her as she went
In discouragement and bewilderment
Through the cairns of Time, and missed
        her way
Between to-day and yesterday,
    Up springs a living man,   180
And each man stands with his face in the
        light
Of his own drawn sword,
Ready to do what a hero can.
    Wall to sap, or river to ford,
Cannon to front, or foe to pursue,
Still ready to do, and sworn to be true,
    As a man and a patriot can.
Piedmontese, Neapolitan,
Lombard, Tuscan, Romagnole,
Each man's body having a soul, —   190
Count how many they stand,
All of them sons of the land,
    Every live man there
Allied to a dead man below,
    And the deadest with blood to spare
To quicken a living hand
In case it should ever be slow.
Count how many they come
To the beat of Piedmont's drum,
    With faces keener and grayer   200
    Than swords of the Austrian slayer,
All set against the foe.
        'Emperor
        Evermore.'

IX

Out of the dust where they ground them;
    Out of the holes where they dogged them;

Out of the hulks where they wound them
  In iron, tortured and flogged them; 208
Out of the streets where they chased them,
  Taxed them, and then bayonetted them;
Out of the homes where they spied on them
  (Using their daughters and wives);
Out of the church where they fretted
    them,
Rotted their souls and debased them,
  Trained them to answer with knives,
Then cursed them all at their prayers! —
Out of cold lands, not theirs,
Where they exiled them, starved them, lied
    on them;
Back they come like a wind, in vain
  Cramped up in the hills, that roars its
    road 220
The stronger into the open plain,
Or like a fire that burns the hotter
  And longer for the crust of cinder,
Serving better the ends of the potter;
  Or like a restrainèd word of God,
  Fulfilling itself by what seems to hinder.
      'Emperor
      Evermore.'

          X

Shout for France and Savoy!
  Shout for the helper and doer. 230
Shout for the good sword's ring,
  Shout for the thought still truer.
Shout for the spirits at large
Who passed for the dead this spring,
  Whose living glory is sure.
Shout for France and Savoy!
Shout for the council and charge!
  Shout for the head of Cavour;
And shout for the heart of a King
That's great with a nation's joy! 240
  Shout for France and Savoy!

          XI

Take up the child, Macmahon, though
  Thy hand be red
  From Magenta's dead,
And riding on, in front of the troop,
  In the dust of the whirlwind of war
Through the gate of the city of Milan, stoop
And take up the child to thy saddle-bow,
  Nor fear the touch as soft as a flower of
    his smile as clear as a star!
Thou hast a right to the child, we say, 250
Since the women are weeping for joy as
    they
Who, by thy help and from this day,

Shall be happy mothers indeed.
They are raining flowers from terrace and
    roof:
  Take up the flower in the child.
While the shout goes up of a nation freed
  And heroically self-reconciled,
Till the snow on that peaked Alp aloof
Starts, as feeling God's finger anew,
And all those cold white marble fires 260
Of mounting saints on the Duomo-spires
  Flicker against the Blue.
      'Emperor
      Evermore.'

          XII

Ay, it is He,
Who rides at the King's right hand!
Leave room to his horse and draw to the
    side,
Nor press too near in the ecstasy
Of a newly delivered impassioned land:
  He is moved, you see, 270
He who has done it all.
They call it a cold stern face;
  But this is Italy
Who rises up to her place! —
For this he fought in his youth,
Of this he dreamed in the past;
The lines of the resolute mouth
Tremble a little at last.
Cry, he has done it all!
      'Emperor 280
      Evermore.'

          XIII

It is not strange that he did it,
  Though the deed may seem to strain
To the wonderful, unpermitted,
  For such as lead and reign.
But he is strange, this man:
  The people's instinct found him
(A wind in the dark that ran
Through a chink where was no door),
  And elected him and crowned him 290
      Emperor
      Evermore.

          XIV

Autocrat? let them scoff,
  Who fail to comprehend
That a ruler incarnate of
  The people must transcend
All common king-born kings;
  These subterranean springs
A sudden outlet winning

Have special virtues to spend.   300
The people's blood runs through him,
  Dilates from head to foot,
  Creates him absolute,
And from this great beginning
Evokes a greater end
To justify and renew him —
        Emperor
        Evermore.

XV

What ! did any maintain
That God or the people (think !)   310
Could make a marvel in vain ? —
  Out of the water-jar there
Draw wine that none could drink ?
Is this a man like the rest,
  This miracle, made unaware
  By a rapture of popular air,
And caught to the place that was best ?
You think he could barter and cheat
  As vulgar diplomates use,
With the people's heart in his breast ?   320
Prate a lie into shape
Lest truth should cumber the road;
  Play at the fast and loose
Till the world is strangled with tape;
Maim the soul's complete
  To fit the hole of a toad;
And filch the dogman's meat
  To feed the offspring of God ?

XVI

Nay, but he, this wonder,
  He cannot palter nor prate,   330
Though many around him and under,
With intellects trained to the curve,
Distrust him in spirit and nerve
  Because his meaning is straight.
Measure him ere he depart
  With those who have governed and led;
Larger so much by the heart,
  Larger so much by the head.
        Emperor
        Evermore.   340

XVII

He holds that, consenting or dissident,
  Nations must move with the time;
Assumes that crime with a precedent
  Doubles the guilt of the crime;
— Denies that a slaver's bond,
  Or a treaty signed by knaves
(*Quorum magna pars* and beyond

Was one of an honest name)
Gives an inexpugnable claim
  To abolish men into slaves.   350
        Emperor
        Evermore.

XVIII

He will not swagger nor boast
  Of his country's meeds, in a tone
Missuiting a great man most
  If such should speak of his own;
Nor will he act, on her side,
  From motives baser, indeed,
Than a man of a noble pride
  Can avow for himself at need;   360
Never, for lucre or laurels,
  Or custom, though such should be rife,
Adapting the smaller morals
  To measure the larger life.
He, though the merchants persuade,
  And the soldiers are eager for strife,
Finds not his country in quarrels
  Only to find her in trade, —
While still he accords her such honor
  As never to flinch for her sake   370
Where men put service upon her,
  Found heavy to undertake
And scarcely like to be paid:
Believing a nation may act
  Unselfishly — shiver a lance
(As the least of her sons may, in fact)
  And not for a cause of finance.
        Emperor
        Evermore.

XIX

  Great is he   380
Who uses his greatness for all.
His name shall stand perpetually
  As a name to applaud and cherish,
Not only within the civic wall
For the loyal, but also without
  For the generous and free.
  Just is he,
Who is just for the popular due
  As well as the private debt.
The praise of nations ready to perish   390
Fall on him, — crown him in view
  Of tyrants caught in the net,
And statesmen dizzy with fear and doubt !
And though, because they are many,
  And he is merely one,
And nations selfish and cruel
Heap up the inquisitor's fuel

To kill the body of high intents,
And burn great deeds from their place,
Till this, the greatest of any, 400
  May seem imperfectly done;
  Courage, whoever circumvents !
Courage, courage, whoever is base !
The soul of a high intent, be it known,
Can die no more than any soul
Which God keeps by Him under the throne;
And this, at whatever interim,
  Shall live, and be consummated
Into the being of deeds made whole.
Courage, courage ! happy is he, 410
  Of whom (himself among the dead
  And silent) this word shall be said:
— That he might have had the world with
    him,
  But chose to side with suffering men,
  And had the world against him when
He came to deliver Italy.
          Emperor
          Evermore.

THE DANCE

Mrs. Browning told Mrs. Jameson in a letter
dated Rome, February 22, 1860, that the hero-
ine of the poem called 'The Dance' was a cer-
tain Madame de Laiatico.

I

You remember down at Florence our Cas-
    cine,
  Where the people on the feast-days walk
    and drive,
And, through the trees, long-drawn in
    many a green way,
  O'er-roofing hum and murmur like a
    hive,
  The river and the mountains look alive ?

II

You remember the piazzone there, the
    stand-place
  Of carriages abrim with Florence Beau-
    ties,
Who lean and melt to music as the band
    plays,
  Or smile and chat with some one who
    afoot is,
  Or on horseback, in observance of male
    duties ?

III

'T is so pretty, in the afternoons of summer,
  So many gracious faces brought to-
    gether !
Call it rout, or call it concert, they have
    come here,
  In the floating of the fan and of the
    feather,
  To reciprocate with beauty the fine
    weather.

IV

While the flower-girls offer nosegays (be-
    cause *they* too
  Go with other sweets) at every carriage-
    door;
Here, by shake of a white finger, signed
    away to
  Some next buyer, who sits buying score
    on score,
  Piling roses upon roses evermore.

V

And last season, when the French camp
    had its station
  In the meadow-ground, things quickened
    and grew gayer
Through the mingling of the liberating
    nation
  With this people; groups of Frenchmen
    everywhere,
  Strolling, gazing, judging lightly — 'who
    was fair.'

VI

Then the noblest lady present took upon her
  To speak nobly from her carriage for
    the rest:
'Pray these officers from France to do us
    honor
  By dancing with us straightway.' The
    request
  Was gravely apprehended as addressed.

VII

And the men of France, bareheaded, bow-
    ing lowly,
  Led out each a proud signora to the
    space
Which the startled crowd had rounded for
    them — slowly,
  Just a touch of still emotion in his face,
  Not presuming, through the symbol, on
    the grace.

VIII

There was silence in the people: some lips
    trembled,
    But none jested.   Broke the music, at a
    glance:
And the daughters of our princes, thus as-
    sembled,
    Stepped the measure with the gallant
    sons of France,
    Hush ! it might have been a Mass, and
    not a dance.

IX

And they danced there till the blue that
    over-skied us
    Swooned with passion, though the foot-
    ing seemed sedate;
And the mountains, heaving mighty hearts
    beside us,
    Sighed a rapture in a shadow, to di-
    late,
    And touch the holy stone where Dante
    sate.

X

Then the sons of France, bareheaded, lowly
    bowing,
    Led the ladies back where kinsmen of
    the south
Stood, received them; till, with burst of
    overflowing
    Feeling — husbands, brothers, Florence's
    male youth,
    Turned and kissed the martial strangers
    mouth to mouth.

XI

And a cry went up, a cry from all that
    people !
    — You have heard a people cheering,
    you suppose,
For the Member, mayor . . . with chorus
    from the steeple ?
    This was different: scarce as loud, per-
    haps (who knows ?),
    For we saw wet eyes around us ere the
    close.

XII

And we felt as if a nation, too long borne
    in
    By hard wrongers, — comprehending in
    such attitude

That God had spoken somewhere since the
    morning,
    That men were somehow brothers, by no
    platitude, —
    Cried exultant in great wonder and free
    gratitude.

A TALE OF VILLAFRANCA

TOLD IN TUSCANY

First printed in the *Athenæum*, September
24, 1859.

I

My little son, my Florentine,
    Sit down beside my knee,
And I will tell you why the sign
    Of joy which flushed our Italy
Has faded since but yesternight;
And why your Florence of delight
    Is mourning as you see.

II

A great man (who was crowned one
    day)
    Imagined a great Deed:
He shaped it out of cloud and clay,
    He touched it finely till the seed
Possessed the flower: from heart and brain
He fed it with large thoughts humane,
    To help a people's need.

III

He brought it out into the sun —
    They blessed it to his face:
' O great pure Deed, that hast undone
    So many bad and base !
O generous Deed, heroic Deed,
Come forth, be perfected, succeed,
    Deliver by God's grace.'

IV

Then sovereigns, statesmen, north and
    south,
    Rose up in wrath and fear,
And cried, protesting by one mouth,
    What monster have we here ?
A great Deed at this hour of day ?
A great just Deed — and not for pay ?
    Absurd, — or insincere.'

V

'And if sincere, tho heavier blow
  In that case we shall bear,
For where 's our blessed "status quo,"
  Our holy treaties, where, —
Our rights to sell a race, or buy,
Protect and pillage, occupy,
  And civilize despair ?'

VI

Some muttered that the great Deed meant
  A great pretext to sin;
And others, the pretext, so lent,
  Was heinous (to begin).
Volcanic terms of 'great' and 'just' ?
Admit such tongues of flame, the crust
  Of time and law falls in.

VII

A great Deed in this world of ours ?
  Unheard of the pretence is:
It threatens plainly the great Powers;
  Is fatal in all senses.
A just Deed in the world ? — call out
The rifles ! be not slack about
  The national defences.

VIII

And many murmured, 'From this source
  What red blood must be poured !'
And some rejoined, ''T is even worse;
  What red tape is ignored !'
All cursed the Doer for an evil
Called here, enlarging on the Devil, —
  There, monkeying the Lord !

IX

Some said it could not be explained,
  Some, could not be excused;
And others, 'Leave it unrestrained,
  Gehenna's self is loosed.'
And all cried, 'Crush it, maim it, gag it !
Set dog-toothed lies to tear it ragged,
  Truncated and traduced !'

X

But He stood sad before the sun
  (The peoples felt their fate).
'The world is many, — I am one;
  My great Deed was too great.
God's fruit of justice ripens slow:
Men's souls are narrow, let them grow.
  My brothers, we must wait.'

XI

The tale is onded, child of mine,
  Turned graver at my knee.
They say your eyes, my Florentine,
  Are English: it may be.
And yet I 've marked as blue a pair
Following the doves across the square
  At Venice by the sea.

XII

Ah child ! ah child ! I cannot say
  A word more. You conceive
The reason now, why just to-day
  We see our Florence grieve.
Ah child, look up into the sky !
In this low world, where great Deeds
  die,
  What matter if we live ?

A COURT LADY

We have Mrs. Browning's word for it, that
the Court Lady was a type, not an individual.
Quite a number of the *grandes dames* of Milan
in 1859 indulged in the sincere, if slightly
theatrical, display of patriotism here described.

Her hair was tawny with gold, her eyes
    with purple were dark,
Her cheeks' pale opal burnt with a red
    and restless spark.

Never was lady of Milan nobler in name
    and in race;
Never was lady of Italy fairer to see in
    the face.

Never was lady on earth more true as
    woman and wife,
Larger in judgment and instinct, prouder
    in manners and life.

She stood in the early morning, and said to
    her maidens 'Bring
That silken robe made ready to wear at the
    Court of the King.

'Bring me the clasps of diamond, lucid,
    clear of the mote,
Clasp me the large at the waist, and clasp
    me the small at the throat.   10

' Diamonds to fasten the hair, and diamonds
      to fasten the sleeves,
Laces to drop from their rays, like a pow-
      der of snow from the eaves.'

Gorgeous she entered the sunlight which
      gathered her up in a flame,
While, straight in her open carriage, she
      to the hospital came.

In she went at the door, and gazing from
      end to end,
' Many and low are the pallets, but each is
      the place of a friend.'

Up she passed through the wards, and
      stood at a young man's bed:
Bloody the band on his brow, and livid the
      droop of his head.

' Art   thou a Lombard, my brother ?
      Happy art thou,' she cried,.
And smiled like Italy on him: he dreamed
      in her face and died.   20

Pale with his passing soul, she went on
      still to a second:
He was a grave hard man, whose years by
      dungeons were reckoned.

Wounds in his body were sore, wounds in
      his life were sorer.
' Art   thou a Romagnole ? '   Her eyes
      drove lightnings before her.

' Austrian and priest had joined to double
      and tighten the cord
Able to bind thee, O strong one, — free by
      the stroke of a sword.

' Now be grave for the rest of us, using
      the life overcast
To ripen our wine of the present (too new)
      in glooms of the past.'

Down she stepped to a pallet where lay a
      face like a girl's,
Young, and pathetic with dying, — a deep
      black hole in the curls.   30

' Art thou from Tuscany, brother ? and
      seest thou, dreaming in pain,
Thy mother stand in the piazza, searching
      the list of the slain ? '

Kind as a mother herself, she touched his
      cheeks with her hands:
' Blessed is she who has borne thee, al-
      though she should weep as she
      stands.'

On she passed to a Frenchman, his arm
      carried off by a ball:
Kneeling, — ' O more than my brother !
      how shall I thank thee for all ?

' Each of the heroes around us has fought
      for his land and line,
But thou hast fought for a stranger, in hate
      of a wrong not thine.

' Happy are all free peoples, too strong to
      be dispossessed.
But blessed are those among nations who
      dare to be strong for the rest ! '   40

Ever she passed on her way, and came to a
      couch where pined
One with a face from Venetia, white with
      a hope out of mind.

Long she stood and gazed, and twice she
      tried at the name,
But two great crystal tears were all that
      faltered and came.

Only a tear for Venice ? — she turned as in
      passion and loss,
And stooped to his forehead and kissed it,
      as if she were kissing the cross.

Faint with that strain of heart she moved
      on then to another,
Stern and strong in his death.   ' And dost
      thou suffer, my brother ? '

Holding his hands in hers : — ' Out of the
      Piedmont lion
Cometh the sweetness of freedom ! sweet-
      est to live or to die on.'   50

Holding his cold rough hands, — ' Well,
      oh well have ye done
In noble, noble Piedmont, who would not
      be noble alone.'

Back he fell while she spoke. She rose to
      her feet with a spring, —
' That was a Piedmontese ! and this is the
      Court of the King.'

AN AUGUST VOICE

' Una voce augusta.' — MONITORE TOSCANO.

I

You 'LL take back your Grand-duke ?
  I made the treaty upon it.
Just venture a quiet rebuke;
  Dall' Ongaro write him a sonnet;
Ricasoli gently explain
  Some need of the constitution:
He 'll swear to it over again,
  Providing an ' easy solution.'
You 'll call back the Grand-duke.

II

You 'll take back your Grand-duke ?
  I promised the Emperor Francis
To argue the case by his book,
  And ask you to meet his advances.
The Ducal cause, we know
  (Whether you or he be the wronger),
Has very strong points; — although
  Your bayonets, there, have stronger.
You 'll call back the Grand-duke.

III

You 'll take back your Grand-duke ?
  He is not pure altogether.
For instance, the oath which he took
  (In the Forty-eight rough weather)
He 'd ' nail your flag to his mast,'
  Then softly scuttled the boat you
Hoped to escape in at last,
  And both by a ' Proprio motu.'
You 'll call back the Grand-duke.

IV

You 'll take back your Grand-duke ?
  The scheme meets nothing to shock it
In this smart letter, look,
  We found in Radetsky's pocket;
Where his Highness in sprightly style
  Of the flower of his Tuscans wrote,
' These heads be the hottest in file;
  Pray shoot them the quickest.' Quote,
And call back the Grand-duke.

V

You 'll take back your Grand-duke ?
  There *are* some things to object to.
He cheated, betrayed, and forsook,
  Then called in the foe to protect you.
He taxed you for wines and for meats
  Throughout that eight years' pastime
Of Austria's drum in your streets —
  Of course you remember the last time
You called back your Grand-duke ?

VI

You 'll take back the Grand-duke ?
  It is not race he is poor in,
Although he never could brook
  The patriot cousin at Turin.
His love of kin you discern,
  By his hate of your flag and me —
So decidedly apt to turn
  All colors at the sight of the Three.
You 'll call back the Grand-duke.

VII

You 'll take back your Grand-duke ?
  'T was weak that he fled from the Pitti;
But consider how little he shook
  At thought of bombarding your city !
And, balancing that with this,
  The Christian rule is plain for us;
. . . Or the Holy Father's Swiss
  Have shot his Perugians in vain for us.
You 'll call back the Grand-duke.

VIII

Pray take back your Grand-duke.
  — I, too, have suffered persuasion.
All Europe, raven and rook,
  Screeched at me armed for your nation.
Your cause in my heart struck spurs;
  I swept such warnings aside for you:
My very child's eyes, and Hers,
  Grew like my brother's who died for
    you.
You 'll call back the Grand-duke ?

IX

You 'll take back your Grand-duke ?
  My French fought nobly with reason, —
Left many a Lombardy nook
  Red as with wine out of season.
Little we grudged what was done there,
  Paid freely your ransom of blood:
Our heroes stark in the sun there
  We would not recall if we could.
You 'll call back the Grand-duke ?

X

You 'll take back your Grand-duke ?
  His son rode fast as he got off
That day on the enemy's hook,
  When *I* had an epaulet shot off.
Though splashed (as I saw him afar — no,

Near) by those ghastly rains,
The mark, when you 've washed him in
    Arno,
Will scarcely be larger than Cain's.
You 'll call back the Grand-duke ?

XI

You 'll take back your Grand-duke ?
    'T will be so simple, quite beautiful:
The shepherd recovers his crook,
    . . . If you should be sheep, and dutiful.
I spoke a word worth chalking
    On Milan's wall — but stay,
Here 's Poniatowsky talking, —
    You 'll listen to *him* to-day,
And call back the Grand-duke.

XII

You 'll take back your Grand-duke ?
    Observe, there 's no one to force it, —
Unless the Madonna, Saint Luke
    Drew for you, choose to endorse it.
I charge you, by great Saint Martino
    And prodigies quickened by wrong,
Remember your Dead on Ticino;
    Be worthy, be constant, be strong —
Bah ! — call back the Grand-duke ! !

CHRISTMAS GIFTS

'ὡς βασιλεῖ, ὡς θεῷ, ὡς νεκρῷ.'
— GREGORY NAZIANZEN.

I

THE Pope on Christmas Day
    Sits in Saint Peter's chair;
But the peoples murmur and say
    'Our souls are sick and forlorn,
And who will show us where
    Is the stable where Christ was born ? '

II

The star is lost in the dark;
    The manger is lost in the straw,
The Christ cries faintly . . . hark ! . . .
    Through bands that swaddle and stran-
        gle —
But the Pope in the chair of awe
    Looks down the great quadrangle.

III

The Magi kneel at his foot,
    Kings of the East and West,

But, instead of the angels (mute
    Is the 'Peace on earth' of their song),
The peoples, perplexed and opprest,
    Are sighing 'How long, how long ? '

IV

And, instead of the kine, bewilder in
    Shadow of aisle and dome,
The bear who tore up the children,
    The fox who burnt up the corn,
And the wolf who suckled at Rome
    Brothers to slay and to scorn.

V

Cardinals left and right of him,
    Worshippers round and beneath,
The silver trumpets at sight of him
    Thrill with a musical blast:
But the people say through their teeth,
    'Trumpets ? we wait for the Last ! '

VI

He sits in the place of the Lord,
    And asks for the gifts of the time;
Gold, for the haft of a sword
    To win back Romagna averse,
Incense, to sweeten a crime,
    And myrrh, to embitter a curse.

VII

Then a king of the West said 'Good ! —
    I bring thee the gifts of the time;
Red, for the patriot's blood,
    Green, for the martyr's crown,
White, for the dew and the rime,
    When the morning of God comes down

VIII

— O mystic tricolor bright !
    The Pope's heart quailed like a man's;
The cardinals froze at the sight,
    Bowing their tonsures hoary:
And the eyes in the peacock-fans
    Winked at the alien glory.

IX

But the peoples exclaimed in hope,
    'Now blessed be he who has brought
These gifts of the time to the Pope,
    When our souls were sick and forlorn.
— And *here* is the star we sought,
    To show us where Christ was born ! '

ITALY AND THE WORLD

I

FLORENCE, Bologna, Parma, Modena:
  When you named them a year ago,
So many graves reserved by God, in a
  Day of Judgment, you seemed to know,
To open and let out the resurrection.

II

And meantime (you made your reflection
  If you were English), was nought to be
    done
But sorting sables, in predilection
  For all those martyrs dead and gone,
Till the new earth and heaven made ready.

III

And if your politics were not heady,
  Violent, . . . 'Good,' you added, 'good
In all things! Mourn on sure and steady.
  Churchyard thistles are wholesome food
For our European wandering asses.

IV

'The date of the resurrection passes
  Human foreknowledge: men unborn
Will gain by it (even in the lower classes),
  But none of these. It is not the morn
Because the cock of France is crowing.

V

'Cocks crow at midnight, seldom knowing
  Starlight from dawn-light! 't is a mad
Poor creature.' Here you paused, and
    growing
  Scornful, — suddenly, let us add,
The trumpet sounded, the graves were
    open.

VI

Life and life and life! agrope in
  The dusk of death, warm hands, stretched
    out
For swords, proved more life still to hope
    in,
  Beyond and behind. Arise with a shout,
Nation of Italy, slain and buried!

VII

Hill to hill and turret to turret
  Flashing the tricolor, — newly created
Beautiful Italy, calm, unhurried,
  Rise heroic and renovated,
Rise to the final restitution.

VIII

Rise; prefigure the grand solution
  Of earth's municipal, insular schisms, —
Statesmen draping self-love's conclusion
  In cheap vernacular patriotisms,
Unable to give up Judæa for Jesus.

IX

Bring us the higher example; release us
  Into the larger coming time:
And into Christ's broad garment piece
    us
  Rags of virtue as poor as crime,
National selfishness, civic vaunting.

X

No more Jew nor Greek then, — taunting
  Nor taunted; — no more England nor
    France!
But one confederate brotherhood planting
  One flag only, to mark the advance,
Onward and upward, of all humanity.

XI

For civilization perfected
  Is fully developed Christianity.
'Measure the frontier,' shall it be said,
  'Count the ships,' in national vanity?
— Count the nation's heart-beats sooner.

XII

For, though behind by a cannon or
    schooner,
  That nation still is predominant
Whose pulse beats quickest in zeal to
    oppugn or
  Succor another, in wrong or want,
Passing the frontier in love and abhor-
    rence.

XIII

Modena, Parma, Bologna, Florence,
  Open us out the wider way!
Dwarf in that chapel of old Saint Lawrence
  Your Michel Angelo's giant Day,
With the grandeur of this Day breaking
    o'er us!

XIV

Ye who, restrained as an ancient chorus,
  Mute while the coryphæus spake,
Hush your separate voices before us,
  Sink your separate lives for the sake
Of one sole Italy's living for ever!

XV

Givers of coat and cloak too, — never
  Grudging that purple of yours at the
    best, —
By your heroic will and endeavor
  Each sublimely dispossessed,
That all may inherit what each surrenders!

XVI

Earth shall bless you, O noble emenders
  On egotist nations! Ye shall lead
The plough of the world, and sow new
  splendors
  Into the furrow of things for seed, —
Ever the richer for what ye have given.

XVII

Lead us and teach us, till earth and heaven
  Grow larger around us and higher above.
Our sacrament-bread has a bitter leaven;
  We bait our traps with the name of love,
Till hate itself has a kinder meaning.

XVIII

Oh, this world: this cheating and screen-
  ing
  Of cheats! this conscience for candle-
    wicks,
Not beacon-fires! this overweening
  Of underhand diplomatical tricks,
Dared for the country while scorned for
    the counter!

XIX

Oh, this envy of those who mount here,
  And oh, this malice to make them trip!
Rather quenching the fire there, drying
    the fount here,
  To frozen body and thirsty lip,
Than leave to a neighbor their ministra-
  tion.

XX

I cry aloud in my poet-passion,
  Viewing my England o'er Alp and sea.
I loved her more in her ancient fashion:
  She carries her rifles too thick for me
Who spares them so in the cause of a bro-
  ther.

XXI

Suspicion, panic? end this pother.
  The sword, kept sheathless at peace-
    time, rusts.
None fears for himself while he feels for
    another:

The brave man either fights or trusts,
And wears no mail in his private chamber.

XXII

Beautiful Italy! golden amber
  Warm with the kisses of lover and
    traitor!
Thou who hast drawn us on to remember,
  Draw us to hope now: let us be greater
By this new future than that old story.

XXIII

Till truer glory replaces all glory,
  As the torch grows blind at the dawn of
    day;
And the nations, rising up, their sorry
  And foolish sins shall put away,
As children their toys when the teacher
  enters.

XXIV

Till Love's one centre devour these centres
  Of many self-loves; and the patriot's
    trick
To better his land by egotist ventures,
  Defamed from a virtue, shall make men
    sick,
As the scalp at the belt of some red hero.

XXV

For certain virtues have dropped to zero,
  Left by the sun on the mountain's dewy
    side;
Churchman's charities, tender as Nero,
  Indian suttee, heathen suicide,
Service to rights divine, proved hollow:

XXVI

And Heptarchy patriotisms must follow. —
  National voices, distinct yet dependent,
Ensphering each other, as swallow does
    swallow,
  With circles still widening and ever as-
    cendant,
In multiform life to united progression, —

XXVII

These shall remain. And when, in the ses-
  sion
  Of nations, the separate language is
    heard,
Each shall aspire, in sublime indiscretion,
  To help with a thought or exalt with a
    word
Less her own than her rival's honor.

XXVIII

Each Christian nation shall take upon
 her
The law of the Christian man in vast:
The crown of the getter shall fall to the
 donor,
 And last shall be first while first shall be
  last,
And to love best shall still be, to reign un-
 surpassed.

A CURSE FOR A NATION

PROLOGUE

I HEARD an angel speak last night,
 And he said 'Write !
Write a Nation's curse for me,
And send it over the Western Sea.'

I faltered, taking up the word:
 'Not so, my lord !
If curses must be, choose another
To send thy curse against my brother.

'For I am bound by gratitude,
 By love and blood,
To brothers of mine across the sea,
Who stretch out kindly hands to me.'

'Therefore,' the voice said, 'shalt thou
 write
  My curse to-night.
From the summits of love a curse is driven,
As lightning is from the tops of heaven.'

'Not so,' I answered. 'Evermore
 My heart is sore
For my own land's sins: for little feet
Of children bleeding along the street:

'For parked-up honors that gainsay
 The right of way;
For almsgiving through a door that is
Not open enough for two friends to kiss:

'For love of freedom which abates
 Beyond the Straits:
For patriot virtue starved to vice on
Self-praise, self-interest, and suspicion:

'For an oligarchic parliament,
 And bribes well-meant.

What curse to another land assign,
When heavy-souled for the sins of mine ?'

'Therefore,' the voice said, 'shalt thou
 write
  My curse to-night.
Because thou hast strength to see and hate
A foul thing done *within thy gate.*'

'Not so,' I answered once again.
 'To curse, choose men.
For I, a woman, have only known
How the heart melts and the tears run
 down.'

'Therefore,' the voice said, 'shalt thou
 write
  My curse to-night.
Some women weep and curse, I say
(And no one marvels), night and day.

'And thou shalt take their part to-night,
 Weep and write.
A curse from the depths of womanhood
Is very salt, and bitter, and good.'

So thus I wrote, and mourned indeed,
 What all may read.
And thus, as was enjoined on me,
I send it over the Western Sea.

THE CURSE

I

BECAUSE ye have broken your own chain
 With the strain
Of brave men climbing a Nation's height,
Yet thence bear down with brand and thong
On souls of others, — for this wrong
 This is the curse. Write.

Because yourselves are standing straight
 In the state
Of Freedom's foremost acolyte,
Yet keep calm footing all the time
On writhing bond slaves, — for this crime
 This is the curse. Write.

Because ye prosper in God's name,
 With a claim
To honor in the old world's sight,
Yet do the fiend's work perfectly
In strangling martyrs, — for this lie
 This is the curse. Write.

II

Ye shall watch while kings conspire
Round the people's smouldering fire,
  And, warm for your part,
Shall never dare — O shame !
To utter the thought into flame
  Which burns at your heart.
        This is the curse. Write.

Ye shall watch while nations strive
With the bloodhounds, die or survive,
  Drop faint from their jaws,
Or throttle them backward to death;
And only under your breath
  Shall favor the cause.
        This is the curse. Write.

Ye shall watch while strong men draw
The nets of feudal law
  To strangle the weak;
And, counting the sin for a sin,
Your soul shall be sadder within
  Than the word ye shall speak.
        This is the curse. Write.

When good men are praying erect
That Christ may avenge his elect
  And deliver the earth,
The prayer in your ears, said low,

Shall sound like the tramp of a foe
  That 's driving you forth.
        This is the curse. Write.

When wise men give you their praise,
They shall pause in the heat of the phrase,
  As if carried too far.
When ye boast your own charters kept
    true,
Ye shall blush; for the thing which ye
    do
  Derides what ye are.
        This is the curse. Write.

When fools cast taunts at your gate,
Your scorn ye shall somewhat abate
  As ye look o'er the wall;
For your conscience, tradition, and name
Explode with a deadlier blame
  Than the worst of them all.
        This is the curse. Write.

Go, wherever ill deeds shall be done,
Go, plant your flag in the sun
  Beside the ill-doers !
And recoil from clenching the curse
Of God's witnessing Universe
  With a curse of yours.
        THIS is the curse. Write.

LAST POEMS

TO 'GRATEFUL FLORENCE,'

TO THE MUNICIPALITY, HER REPRESENTATIVE, AND TO TOMMASEO, ITS SPOKESMAN,

MOST GRATEFULLY

The last winter of Mrs. Browning's life was passed at No. 16 Via Felice, now the Via Sistina, Rome. She died in Florence on the evening of June 29, 1861, leaving behind her a short list of unpublished poems which she herself had drawn up, doubtless with a view to another volume. A few of these had already appeared in periodicals. One, 'De Profundis,' had been written twenty years before. These poems her husband brought out in London in the ensuing February (London, Chapman and Hall, 193 Piccadilly, 1862), adding the translations which here accompany them ; concerning which last he says : ' They were intended many years ago to accompany and explain certain engravings after ancient Gems, in the projected works of a friend by whose kindness they are now recovered ; but as two of the original series (the " Adonis of Bion and the " Song to the Rose " from Achilles Tatius) have subsequently appeared, it is presumed that the remainder may not improperly follow. A single recent version (from Heine) is added.'

The words 'grateful Florence,' '*grata Firenze*,' in the dedication to this last volume, are a quotation from the memorial tablet to Mrs. Browning's memory, inserted in the wall of Casa Guidi by the municipality of Florence.

LITTLE MATTIE

First printed in the *Cornhill Magazine*, June, 1861.

I

DEAD! Thirteen a month ago!
  Short and narrow her life's walk;
Lover's love she could not know
  Even by a dream or talk:
Too young to be glad of youth,
  Missing honor, labor, rest,
And the warmth of a babe's mouth
  At the blossom of her breast.
Must you pity her for this
And for all the loss it is,   10
You, her mother, with wet face,
Having had all in your case?

II

Just so young but yesternight,
  Now she is as old as death.
Meek, obedient in your sight,
  Gentle to a beck or breath
Only on last Monday! Yours,
  Answering you like silver bells
Lightly touched! An hour matures:
  You can teach her nothing else.   20
She has seen the mystery hid
Under Egypt's pyramid:
By those eyelids pale and close
Now she knows what Rhamses knows.

III

Cross her quiet hands, and smooth
  Down her patient locks of silk,
Cold and passive as in truth
  You your fingers in spilt milk
Drew along a marble floor;
  But her lips you cannot wring   30
Into saying a word more,
  'Yes,' or 'No,' or such a thing:
Though you call and beg and wreak
Half your soul out in a shriek,
She will lie there in default
And most innocent revolt.

IV

Ay, and if she spoke, maybe
  She would answer, like the Son,
'What is now 'twixt thee and me?'
  Dreadful answer! better none.   40

Yours on Monday, God's to-day!
  Yours, your child, your blood, your
    heart,
Called . . . you called her, did you say,
  'Little Mattie' for your part?
Now already it sounds strange,
And you wonder, in this change,
What He calls his angel-creature,
Higher up than you can reach her.

V

'T was a green and easy world
  As she took it; room to play   50
(Though one's hair might get uncurled
  At the far end of the day).
What she suffered she shook off
  In the sunshine; what she sinned
She could pray on high enough
  To keep safe above the wind.
If reproved by God or you,
'T was to better her, she knew;
And if crossed, she gathered still
'T was to cross out something ill.   60

VI

You, you had the right, you thought,
  To survey her with sweet scorn,
Poor gay child, who had not caught
  Yet the octave-stretch forlorn
Of your larger wisdom! Nay,
  Now your places are changed so,
In that same superior way
  She regards you dull and low
As you did herself exempt
From life's sorrows. Grand contempt 70
Of the spirits risen awhile,
Who look back with such a smile!

VII

There's the sting of 't. That, I think,
  Hurts the most a thousandfold!
To feel sudden, at a wink,
  Some dear child we used to scold,
Praise, love both ways, kiss and tease,
  Teach and tumble as our own,
All its curls about our knees,
  Rise up suddenly full-grown.   80
Who could wonder such a sight
Made a woman mad outright?
Show me Michael with the sword
Rather than such angels, Lord!

A FALSE STEP

SWEET, thou hast trod on a heart.
  Pass; there 's a world full of men;
And women as fair as thou art
  Must do such things now and then.

Thou hast only stepped unaware, —
  Malice, not one can impute;
And why should a heart have been there
  In the way of a fair woman's foot?

It was not a stone that could trip,
  Nor was it a thorn that could rend:
Put up thy proud under-lip!
  'T was merely the heart of a friend.

And yet peradventure one day
  Thou, sitting alone at the glass,
Remarking the bloom gone away,
  Where the smile in its dimplement was,

And seeking around thee in vain
  From hundreds who flattered before,
Such a word as ' Oh, not in the main
  Do I hold thee less precious, but
    more!' . . .

Thou 'lt sigh, very like, on thy part,
  ' Of all I have known or can know,
I wish I had only that Heart
  I trod upon ages ago!'

VOID IN LAW

I

SLEEP, little babe, on my knee,
  Sleep, for the midnight is chill,
And the moon has died out in the tree,
  And the great human world goeth ill.
Sleep, for the wicked agree:
  Sleep, let them do as they will.
    Sleep.

II

Sleep, thou hast drawn from my breast
  The last drop of milk that was good;
And now, in a dream, suck the rest,
  Lest the real should trouble thy blood.
Suck, little lips dispossessed,
  As we kiss in the air whom we would.
    Sleep.

III

O lips of thy father! the same,
  So like! Very deeply they swore
When he gave me his ring and his name,
  To take back, I imagined, no more!
And now is all changed like a game,
  Though the old cards are used as of
    yore?
    Sleep.

IV

' Void in law,' said the Courts. Some-
    thing wrong
  In the forms? Yet, ' Till death part us
    two,
I, James, take thee, Jessie,' was strong,
  And ONE witness competent. True
Such a marriage was worth an old song,
  Heard in Heaven though, as plain as the
    New.
    Sleep.

V

Sleep, little child, his and mine!
  Her throat has the antelope curve,
And her cheek just the color and line
  Which fade not before him nor swerve:
Yet *she* has no child! — the divine
  Seal of right upon loves that deserve.
    Sleep.

VI

My child! though the world take her part,
  Saying ' She was the woman to choose;
He had eyes, was a man in his heart,' —
  We twain the decision refuse:
We . . . weak as I am, as thou art, . . .
  Cling on to him, never to loose.
    Sleep.

VII

He thinks that, when done with this place,
  All 's ended! he 'll new-stamp the ore?
Yes, Cæsar's — but not in our case.
  Let him learn we are waiting before
The grave's mouth, the heaven's gate, God's
    face,
  With implacable love evermore.
    Sleep.

VIII

He 's ours, though he kissed her but now,
  He 's ours, though she kissed in reply:
He 's ours, though himself disavow,

And God's universe favor the lie;
Ours to claim, ours to clasp, ours below,
Ours above, . . . if we live, if we die.
Sleep.

IX

Ah baby, my baby, too rough
Is my lullaby ?   What have I said ?
Sleep !   When I 've wept long enough
I shall learn to weep softly instead,
And piece with some alien stuff
My heart to lie smooth for thy head.
Sleep.

X

Two souls met upon thee, my sweet;
Two loves led thee out to the sun:
Alas, pretty hands, pretty feet,
If the one who remains (only one)
Set her grief at thee, turned in a heat
To thine enemy, — were it well done ?
Sleep.

XI

May He of the manger stand near
And love thee !   An infant He came
To his own who rejected Him here,
But the Magi brought gifts all the same.
I hurry the cross on my Dear !
My gifts are the griefs I declaim !
Sleep.

LORD WALTER'S WIFE

This poem, to Mrs. Browning's deep chagrin,
was rejected (with a thousand apologies) by
Thackeray, as editor of the *Cornhill Magazine*,
on account of the *risqué* character of its subject.

' BUT why do you go ? ' said the lady,
while both sat under the yew,
And her eyes were alive in their depth, as
the kraken beneath the sea-blue.

' Because I fear you,' he answered; — ' be-
cause you are far too fair,
And able to strangle my soul in a mesh of
your gold-colored hair.'

' Oh, that,' she said, ' is no reason !   Such
knots are quickly undone,
And too much beauty, I reckon, is nothing
but too much sun.'

' Yet farewell so,' he answered; — ' the
sunstroke 's fatal at times.
I value your husband, Lord Walter, whose
gallop rings still from the limes.'

' Oh, that,' she said, ' is no reason.   You
smell a rose through a fence:
If two should smell it, what matter ? who
grumbles, and where 's the pre-
tence ? '   10

' But I,' he replied, ' have promised another,
when love was free,
To love her alone, alone, who alone and
afar loves me.'

' Why, that,' she said, ' is no reason.
Love 's always free, I am told.
Will you vow to be safe from the head-
ache on Tuesday, and think it will
hold ? '

' But you,' he replied, ' have a daughter, a
young little child, who was laid
In your lap to be pure; so I leave you
the angels would make me afraid.'

' Oh, that,' she said, ' is no reason.   The
angels keep out of the way;
And Dora, the child, observes nothing, al-
though you should please me and
stay.'

At which he rose up in his anger, — ' Why,
now, you no longer are fair !
Why, now, you no longer are fatal, but
ugly and hateful, I swear.'   20

At which she laughed out in her scorn:
' These men !   Oh, these men over-
nice,
Who are shocked if a color not virtuous is
frankly put on by a vice.'

Her eyes blazed upon him — ' And *you !*
You bring us your vices so near
That we smell them !   You think in our
presence a thought 't would defame
us to hear !

' What reason had you, and what right, —
I appeal to your soul from my life, —
To find me too fair as a woman ?   Why,
sir, I am pure, and a wife.

' Is the day-star too fair up above you ?   It
   burns you not.   Dare you imply
I brushed you more close than the star does,
   when Walter had set me as high ?

' If a man finds a woman too fair, he means
   simply adapted too much
To uses unlawful and fatal.   The praise ! —
   shall I thank you for such ?   30

' Too fair ? — not unless you misuse us !
   and surely if, once in a while,
You attain to it, straightway you call us no
   longer too fair, but too vile.

' A moment, — I pray your attention ! — I
   have a poor word in my head
I must utter, though womanly custom
   would set it down better unsaid.

' You grew, sir, pale to impertinence, once
   when I showed you a ring.
You kissed my fan when I dropped it.   No
   matter ! — I 've broken the thing.

' You did me the honor, perhaps, to be
   moved at my side now and then
In the senses — a vice, I have heard, which
   is common to beasts and some men.

' Love 's a virtue for heroes ! — as white as
   the snow on high hills,
And immortal as every great soul is that
   struggles, endures, and fulfils.   40

' I love my Walter profoundly, — you,
   Maude, though you faltered a week,
For the sake of . . . what was it — an eye-
   brow ?   or, less still, a mole on a
   cheek ?

' And since, when all 's said, you 're too
   noble to stoop to the frivolous cant
About crimes irresistible, virtues that swin-
   dle, betray, and supplant,

' I determined to prove to yourself that,
   whate'er you might dream or avow
By illusion, you wanted precisely no more
   of me than you have now.

' There ! Look me full in the face ! — in
   the face.   Understand, if you can,
That the eyes of such women as I am are
   clean as the palm of a man.

' Drop his hand, you insult him.   Avoid us
   for fear we should cost you a scar —
You take us for harlots, I tell you, and not
   for the women we are.   50

' You wronged me: but then I considered
   . . . there 's Walter !   And so at
   the end
I vowed that he should not be mulcted, by
   me, in the hand of a friend.

' Have I hurt you indeed ?   We are quits
   then.   Nay, friend of my Walter,
   be mine !
Come, Dora, my darling, my angel, and
   help me to ask him to dine.'

BIANCA AMONG THE NIGHTINGALES

I

THE cypress stood up like a church
   That night we felt our love would hold,
And saintly moonlight seemed to search
   And wash the whole world clean as gold;
The olives crystallized the vales'
   Broad slopes until the hills grew strong:
The fireflies and the nightingales
   Throbbed each to either, flame and song.
The nightingales, the nightingales !

II

Upon the angle of its shade
   The cypress stood, self-balanced high;
Half up, half down, as double-made,
   Along the ground, against the sky;
And we, too ! from such soul-height went
   Such leaps of blood, so blindly driven,
We scarce knew if our nature meant
   Most passionate earth or intense heaven
The nightingales, the nightingales !

III

We paled with love, we shook with love,
   We kissed so close we could not vow;
Till Giulio whispered ' Sweet, above
   God's Ever guaranties this Now.'
And through his words the nightingales
   Drove straight and full their long clear
   call,
Like arrows through heroic mails,
   And love was awful in it all.
The nightingales, the nightingales !

IV

O cold white moonlight of the north,
  Refresh these pulses, quench this hell !
O coverture of death drawn forth
  Across this garden-chamber . . . well !
But what have nightingales to do
  In gloomy England, called the free . . .
(Yes, free to die in ! . . .) when we two
  Are sundered, singing still to me ?
And still they sing, the nightingales !

V

I think I hear him, how he cried
  ' My own soul's life !' between their
    notes.
Each man has but one soul supplied,
  And that 's immortal. Though his
    throat 's
On fire with passion now, to *her*
  He can't say what to me he said !
And yet he moves her, they aver.
  The nightingales sing through my
    head, —
The nightingales, the nightingales !

VI

He says to her what moves her most.
  He would not name his soul within
Her hearing, — rather pays her cost
  With praises to her lips and chin.
Man has but one soul, 't is ordained,
  And each soul but one love, I add;
Yet souls are damned and love 's profaned;
  These nightingales will sing me mad !
The nightingales, the nightingales !

VII

I marvel how the birds can sing.
  There 's little difference, in their view,
Betwixt our Tuscan trees that spring
  As vital flames into the blue,
And dull round blots of foliage meant,
  Like saturated sponges here
To suck the fogs up. As content
  Is he too in this land, 't is clear.
And still they sing, the nightingales.

VIII

My Native Florence ! dear, forgone !
  I see across the Alpine ridge
How the last feast-day of Saint John
  Shot rockets from Carraia bridge.
The luminous city, tall with fire,
  Trod deep down in that river of ours,
While many a boat with lamp and choir
Skimmed birdlike over glittering towers.
I will not hear these nightingales.

IX

I seem to float, *we* seem to float
  Down Arno's stream in festive guise;
A boat strikes flame into our boat,
  And up that lady seems to rise
As then she rose. The shock had flashed
  A vision on us ! What a head,
What leaping eyeballs ! — beauty dashed
  To splendor by a sudden dread.
And still they sing, the nightingales.

X

Too bold to sin, too weak to die;
  Such women are so. As for me,
I would we had drowned there, he and I,
  That moment, loving perfectly.
He had not caught her with her loosed
  Gold ringlets . . . rarer in the
    south . . .
Nor heard the ' Grazie tanto ' bruised
  To sweetness by her English mouth.
And still they sing, the nightingales.

XI

She had not reached him at my heart
  With her fine tongue, as snakes indeed
Kill flies; nor had I, for my part,
  Yearned after, in my desperate need,
And followed him as he did her
  To coasts left bitter by the tide,
Whose very nightingales, elsewhere
  Delighting, torture and deride !
For still they sing, the nightingales.

XII

A worthless woman; mere cold clay
  As all false things are: but so fair,
She takes the breath of men away
  Who gaze upon her unaware.
I would not play her larcenous tricks
  To have her looks ! She lied and stole,
And spat into my love's pure pyx
  The rank saliva of her soul.
And still they sing, the nightingales.

XIII

I would not for her white and pink,
  Though such he likes — her grace of
    limb,
Though such he has praised — nor yet, I
    think,
  For life itself, though spent with him,

Commit such sacrilege, affront
  God's nature which is love, intrude
'Twixt two affianced souls, and hunt
  Like spiders, in the altar's wood.
I cannot bear these nightingales.

XIV

If she chose sin, some gentler guise
  She might have sinned in, so it seems:
She might have pricked out both my eyes,
  And I still seen him in my dreams!
— Or drugged me in my soup or wine,
  Nor left me angry afterward:
To die here with his hand in mine,
  His breath upon me, were not hard.
(Our Lady hush these nightingales!)

XV

But set a springe for *him,* 'mio ben,'
  My only good, my first last love! —
Though Christ knows well what sin is, when
  He sees some things done they must
    move
Himself to wonder. Let her pass.
  I think of her by night and day.
Must *I* too join her . . . out, alas! . . .
  With Giulio, in each word I say?
And evermore the nightingales!

XVI

Giulio, my Giulio! — sing they so,
  And you be silent? Do I speak,
And you not hear? An arm you throw
  Round some one, and I feel so weak?
— Oh, owl-like birds! They sing for spite,
  They sing for hate, they sing for doom,
They'll sing through death who sing
    through night,
  They'll sing and stun me in the tomb —
The nightingales, the nightingales!

MY KATE

I

SHE was not as pretty as women I know,
And yet all your best made of sunshine and
    snow
Drop to shade, melt to nought in the long-
    trodden ways,
While she 's still remembered on warm and
    cold days —
        My Kate.

II

Her air had a meaning, her movements a
    grace;
You turned from the fairest to gaze on her
    face:
And when you had once seen her forehead
    and mouth,
You saw as distinctly her soul and her
    truth —
        My Kate.

III

Such a blue inner light from her eyelids
    outbroke,
You looked at her silence and fancied she
    spoke:
When she did, so peculiar yet soft was
    the tone,
Though the loudest spoke also, you heard
    her alone —
        My Kate.

IV

I doubt if she said to you much that could
    act
As a thought or suggestion: she did not
    attract
In the sense of the brilliant or wise: I
    infer
'T was her thinking of others made you
    think of her —
        My Kate.

V

She never found fault with you, never im-
    plied
Your wrong by her right; and yet men at
    her side
Grew nobler, girls purer, as through the
    whole town
The children were gladder that pulled at
    her gown —
        My Kate.

VI

None knelt at her feet confessed lovers in
    thrall;
They knelt more to God than they used, —
    that was all:
If you praised her as charming, some asked
    what you meant,
But the charm of her presence was felt
    when she went —
        My Kate.

VII

The weak and the gentle, the ribald and
  rude,
She took as she found them, and did them
  all good;
It always was so with her — see what you
  have !
She has made the grass greener even here
  . . . with her grave —
My Kate.

VIII

My dear one ! — when thou wast alive with
  the rest,
I held thee the sweetest and loved thee the
  best :
And now thou art dead, shall I not take thy
  part
As thy smiles used to do for thyself, my
  sweet Heart —
My Kate ?

A SONG FOR THE RAGGED SCHOOLS OF LONDON

WRITTEN IN ROME

The 'Song for the Ragged Schools' was writ-
ten in 1854 for the table at a Charity Bazaar in
London presided over by Mrs. Browning's sis-
ter, Arabel Barrett. Mr. Browning also con-
tributed a poem called 'The Twins' (later in-
cluded in his *Dramatic Romances*), and the
two were printed with the names of husband
and wife, in a thin pamphlet, price 6*d*.

I AM listening here in Rome.
  'England 's strong,' say many speakers,
'If she winks, the Czar must come,
  Prow and topsail, to the breakers.'

'England 's rich in coal and oak,'
  Adds a Roman, getting moody;
'If she shakes a travelling cloak,
  Down our Appian roll the scudi.'

'England 's righteous,' they rejoin:
  'Who shall grudge her exaltations,   10
When her wealth of golden coin
  Works the welfare of the nations ? '

I am listening here in Rome.
  Over Alps a voice is sweeping —
'England 's cruel, save us some
  Of these victims in her keeping !'

As the cry beneath the wheel
  Of an old triumphant Roman
Cleft the people's shouts like steel,
  While the show was spoilt for no man,   20

Comes that voice. Let others shout,
  Other poets praise my land here:
I am sadly sitting out,
  Praying, 'God forgive her grandeur.'

Shall we boast of empire, where
  Time with ruin sits commissioned ?
In God's liberal blue air
  Peter's dome itself looks wizened;

And the mountains, in disdain,
  Gather back their lights of opal   30
From the dumb despondent plain
  Heaped with jawbones of a people.

Lordly English, think it o'er,
  Cæsar's doing is all undone !
You have cannons on your shore,
  And free Parliaments in London;

Princes' parks, and merchants' homes,
  Tents for soldiers, ships for seamen, —
Ay, but ruins worse than Rome's
  In your pauper men and women.   40

Women leering through the gas
  (Just such bosoms used to nurse you),
Men, turned wolves by famine — pass !
  Those can speak themselves, and curse
    you.

But these others — children small,
  Spilt like blots about the city,
Quay, and street, and palace-wall —
  Take them up into your pity !

Ragged children with bare feet,
  Whom the angels in white raiment   50
Know the names of, to repeat
  When they come on you for payment.

Ragged children, hungry-eyed,
  Huddled up out of the coldness
On your doorsteps, side by side,
  Till your footman damns their boldness.

In the alleys, in the squares,
  Begging, lying little rebels;
In the noisy thoroughfares,
  Struggling on with piteous trebles.   60

Patient children — think what pain
　Makes a young child patient — ponder !
Wronged too commonly to strain
　After right, or wish, or wonder.

Wicked children, with peaked chins,
　And old foreheads ! there are many
With no pleasures except sins,
　Gambling with a stolen penny.

Sickly children, that whine low
　To themselves and not their mothers,　70
From mere habit, — never so
　Hoping help or care from others.

Healthy children, with those blue
　English eyes, fresh from their Maker,
Fierce and ravenous, staring through
　At the brown loaves of the baker.

I am listening here in Rome,
　And the Romans are confessing,
'English children pass in bloom
　All the prettiest made for blessing.　80

' Angli angeli !' (resumed
　From the mediæval story)
' Such rose angelhoods, emplumed
　In such ringlets of pure glory !'

Can we smooth down the bright hair,
　O my sisters, calm, unthrilled in
Our heart's pulses ?　Can we bear
　The sweet looks of our own children,

While those others, lean and small,
　Scurf and mildew of the city,　90
Spot our streets, convict us all
　Till we take them into pity ?

' Is it our fault ? ' you reply,
　' When, throughout civilization,
Every nation's empery
　Is asserted by starvation ?

' All these mouths we cannot feed,
　And we cannot clothe these bodies.'
Well, if man 's so hard indeed,
　Let them learn at least what God is !　100

Little outcasts from life's fold,
　The grave's hope they may be joined in,
By Christ's covenant consoled
　For our social contract's grinding.

If no better can be done,
　Let us do but this, — endeavor
That the sun behind the sun
　Shine upon them while they shiver !

On the dismal London flags,
　Through the cruel social juggle,　110
Put a thought beneath their rags
　To ennoble the heart's struggle.

O my sisters, not so much
　Are we asked for — not a blossom
From our children's nosegay, such
　As we gave it from our bosom, —

Not the milk left in their cup,
　Not the lamp while they are sleeping,
Not the little cloak hung up
　While the coat 's in daily keeping, —　120

But a place in RAGGED SCHOOLS,
　Where the outcasts may to-morrow
Learn by gentle words and rules
　Just the uses of their sorrow.

O my sisters ! children small,
　Blue-eyed, wailing through the city —
Our own babes cry in them all:
　Let us take them into pity.

MAY'S LOVE

I

You love all, you say,
　Round, beneath, above me:
Find me then some way
　Better than to love me,
Me, too, dearest May !

II

O world-kissing eyes
　Which the blue heavens melt to;
I, sad, overwise,
　Loathe the sweet looks dealt to
All things — men and flies.

III

You love all, you say:
　Therefore, Dear, abate me
Just your love, I pray !
　Shut your eyes and hate me —
Only me — fair May !

AMY'S CRUELTY

FAIR Amy of the terraced house,
　Assist me to discover
Why you who would not hurt a mouse
　Can torture so your lover.

You give your coffee to the cat,
　You stroke the dog for coming,
And all your face grows kinder at
　The little brown bee's humming.

But when *he* haunts your door . . . the town
　Marks coming and marks going . . .
You seem to have stitched your eyelids
　　down
　To that long piece of sewing !

You never give a look, not you,
　Nor drop him a ' Good morning,'
To keep his long day warm and blue,
　So fretted by your scorning.

She shook her head　' The mouse and bee
　For crumb or flower will linger:
The dog is happy at my knee,
　The cat purrs at my finger.

' But *he* . . . to *him*, the least thing given
　Means great things at a distance;
He wants my world, my sun, my heaven,
　Soul, body, whole existence.

' They say love gives as well as takes;
　But I 'm a simple maiden, —
My mother's first smile when she wakes
　I still have smiled and prayed in.

' I only know my mother's love
　Which gives all and asks nothing;
And this new loving sets the groove
　Too much the way of loathing.

' Unless he gives me all in change,
　I forfeit all things by him:
The risk is terrible and strange —
　I tremble, doubt, . . . deny him.

' He 's sweetest friend or hardest foe,
　Best angel or worst devil;
I either hate or . . . love him so,
　I can't be merely civil !

' You trust a woman who puts forth
　Her blossoms thick as summer's ?

You think she dreams what love is worth,
　Who casts it to new-comers ?

' Such love 's a cowslip-ball to fling,
　A moment's pretty pastime;
I give . . . all me, if anything,
　The first time and the last time.

' Dear neighbor of the trellised house,
　A man should murmur never,
Though treated worse than dog and mouse,
　Till doated on for ever ! '

MY HEART AND I

I

ENOUGH ! we 're tired, my heart and I.
　We sit beside the headstone thus,
　And wish that name were carved for us.
The moss reprints more tenderly
　The hard types of the mason's knife,
　As heaven's sweet life renews earth's life
With which we 're tired, my heart and I.

II

You see we 're tired, my heart and I.
　We dealt with books, we trusted men,
　And in our own blood drenched the
　　pen,
As if such colors could not fly.
　We walked too straight for fortune's end,
　We loved too true to keep a friend;
At last we 're tired, my heart and I.

III

How tired we feel, my heart and I !
　We seem of no use in the world;
　Our fancies hang gray and uncurled
About men's eyes indifferently;
　Our voice which thrilled you so, will
　　let
　You sleep; our tears are only wet:
What do we here, my heart and I ?

IV

So tired, so tired, my heart and I !
　It was not thus in that old time
　When Ralph sat with me 'neath the lime
To watch the sunset from the sky.
　' Dear love, you 're looking tired,' he
　　said;
　I, smiling at him, shook my head:
'T is now we 're tired, my heart and I.

V

So tired, so tired, my heart and I !
　Though now none takes me on his arm
　To fold me close and kiss me warm
Till each quick breath end in a sigh
　Of happy languor.　Now, alone,
　We lean upon this graveyard stone,
Uncheered, unkissed, my heart and I.

VI

Tired out we are, my heart and I.
　Suppose the world brought diadems
　To tempt us, crusted with loose gems
Of powers and pleasures ?　Let it try.
　We scarcely care to look at even
　A pretty child, or God's blue heaven,
We feel so tired, my heart and I.

VII

Yet who complains ?　My heart and I ?
　In this abundant earth no doubt
　Is little room for things worn out:
Disdain them, break them, throw them by !
　And if before the days grew rough
　We *once* were loved, used, — well
　　enough,
I think, we 've fared, my heart and I.

THE BEST THING IN THE WORLD

WHAT 's the best thing in the world ?
June-rose, by May-dew impearled;
Sweet south-wind, that means no rain;
Truth, not cruel to a friend;
Pleasure, not in haste to end;
Beauty, not self-decked and curled
Till its pride is over-plain;
Light, that never makes you wink;
Memory, that gives no pain;
Love, when, *so*, you 're loved again.
What 's the best thing in the world ?
— Something out of it, I think.

WHERE 'S AGNES ?

I

NAY, if I had come back so,
　And found her dead in her grave,
And if a friend I know
　Had said, ' Be strong, nor rave:
She lies there, dead below:

II

' I saw her, I who speak,
　White, stiff, the face one blank:
The blue shade came to her cheek
　Before they nailed the plank,
For she had been dead a week.'

III

Why, if he had spoken so,
　I might have believed the thing,
Although her look, although
　Her step, laugh, voice's ring
Lived in me still as they do.

IV

But dead that other way,
　Corrupted thus and lost ?
That sort of worm in the clay ?
　I cannot count the cost,
That I should rise and pay.

V

My Agnes false ? such shame ?
　She ?　Rather be it said
That the pure saint of her name
　Has stood there in her stead,
And tricked you to this blame.

VI

Her very gown, her cloak
　Fell chastely: no disguise,
But expression ! while she broke
　With her clear gray morning-eyes
Full upon me and then spoke.

VII

She wore her hair away
　From her forehead, — like a cloud
Which a little wind in May
　Peels off finely: disallowed
Though bright enough to stay.

VIII

For the heavens must have the place
　To themselves, to use and shine in,
As her soul would have her face
　To press through upon mine, in
That orb of angel grace.

IX

Had she any fault at all,
　'T was having none, I thought too —
There seemed a sort of thrall;
　As she felt her shadow ought to
Fall straight upon the wall.

X

Her sweetness strained the sense
Of common life and duty;
And every day's expense
Of moving in such beauty
Required, almost, defence.

XI

What good, I thought, is done
By such sweet things, if any ?
This world smells ill i' the sun
Though the garden-flowers are many,
She is only one.

XII

Can a voice so low and soft
Take open actual part
With Right, — maintain aloft
Pure truth in life or art,
Vexed always, wounded oft ? —

XIII

She fit, with that fair pose
Which melts from curve to curve,
To stand, run, work with those
Who wrestle and deserve,
And speak plain without glose ?

XIV

But I turned round on my fear
Defiant, disagreeing —
What if God has set her here
Less for action than for Being ? —
For the eye and for the ear.

XV

Just to show what beauty may,
Just to prove what music can, —
And then to die away
From the presence of a man,
Who shall learn, henceforth, to pray ?

XVI

As a door, left half ajar
In heaven, would make him think
How heavenly-different are
Things glanced at through the chink,
Till he pined from near to far.

XVII

That door could lead to hell ?
That shining merely meant
Damnation ?   What !   She fell
Like a woman, who was sent
Like an angel, by a spell ?

XVIII

She, who scarcely trod the earth,
Turned   mere   dirt ?   My   Agnes, —
mine !
Called so ! felt of too much worth
To be used so ! too divine
To be breathed near, and so forth !

XIX

Why, I dared not name a sin
In her presence : I went round,
Clipped its name and shut it in
Some mysterious crystal sound, —
Changed the dagger for the pin.

XX

Now you name herself *that word ?*
O my Agnes !   O my saint !
Then the great joys of the Lord
Do not last ?   Then all this paint
Runs off nature ? leaves a board ?

XXI

Who 's dead here ?   No, not she:
Rather I ! or whence this damp
Cold corruption's misery ?
While my very mourners stamp
Closer in the clods on me.

XXII

And my mouth is full of dust
Till I cannot speak and curse —
Speak and damn him . . . 'Blame 's un-
just ' ?
Sin blots out the universe,
All because she would and must ?

XXIII

She, my white rose, dropping off
The high rose-tree branch ! and not
That the night-wind blew too rough,
Or the noon-sun burnt too hot,
But, that being a rose — 't was enough !

XXIV

Then henceforth may earth grow trees !
No more roses ! — hard straight lines
To score lies out ! none of these
Fluctuant curves, but firs and pines,
Poplars, cedars, cypresses !

DE PROFUNDIS

It was commonly supposed, at the time of its publication, that the poem ' De Profundis' was called forth by the death of Mrs. Browning's sister Henrietta, — Mrs. Surtees Cook, — which occurred only a few months before her own. In reality it had been written not long after the tragic death by drowning at Torquay, of her brother Edward, on July 11, 1840. The difficulty which Mrs. Browning experienced, for many years, about making any allusion to that sharp calamity, which nearly cost her her own life, doubtless caused her to withhold from publication almost to the last these peculiarly intimate verses.

I

THE face which, duly as the sun,
Rose up for me with life begun,
To mark all bright hours of the day
With hourly love, is dimmed away, —
And yet my days go on, go on.

II

The tongue which, like a stream, could run
Smooth music from the roughest stone,
And every morning with ' Good day '
Make each day good, is hushed away, —
And yet my days go on, go on.

III

The heart which, like a staff, was one
For mine to lean and rest upon,
The strongest on the longest day
With steadfast love, is caught away, —
And yet my days go on, go on.

IV

And cold before my summer 's done,
And deaf in Nature's general tune,
And fallen too low for special fear,
And here, with hope no longer here, —
While the tears drop, my days go on.

V

The world goes whispering to its own,
' This anguish pierces to the bone;'
And tender friends go sighing round,
' What love can ever cure this wound ? '
My days go on, my days go on.

VI

The past rolls forward on the sun
And makes all night. O dreams begun,

Not to be ended ! Ended bliss,
And life that will not end in this !
My days go on, my days go on.

VII

Breath freezes on my lips to moan:
As one alone, once not alone,
I sit and knock at Nature's door,
Heart-bare, heart-hungry, very poor,
Whose desolated days go on.

VIII

I knock and cry, — Undone, undone !
Is there no help, no comfort, — none ?
No gleaning in the wide wheat-plains
Where others drive their loaded wains ?
My vacant days go on, go on.

IX

This Nature, though the snows be down,
Thinks kindly of the bird of June:
The little red hip on the tree
Is ripe for such. What is for me,
Whose days so winterly go on ?

X

No bird am I, to sing in June,
And dare not ask an equal boon.
Good nests and berries red are Nature's
To give away to better creatures, —
And yet my days go on, go on.

XI

I ask less kindness to be done, —
Only to loose these pilgrim-shoon,
(Too early worn and grimed) with sweet
Cool deathly touch to these tired feet.
Till days go out which now go on.

XII

Only to lift the turf unmown
From off the earth where it has grown,
Some cubit-space, and say ' Behold,
Creep in, poor Heart, beneath that fold,
Forgetting how the days go on.'

XIII

What harm would that do ? Green anon
The sward would quicken, overshone
By skies as blue; and crickets might
Have leave to chirp there day and night
While my new rest went on, went on.

XIV

From gracious Nature have I won
Such liberal bounty ? may I run
So, lizard-like, within her side,
And there be safe, who now am tried
By days that painfully go on ?

XV

— A Voice reproves me thereupon,
More sweet than Nature's when the drone
Of bees is sweetest, and more deep
Than when the rivers overleap
The shuddering pines, and thunder on.

XVI

God's Voice, not Nature's ! Night and
    noon
He sits upon the great white throne
And listens for the creatures' praise.
What babble we of days and days ?
The Day-spring He, whose days go on.

XVII

He reigns above, He reigns alone;
Systems burn out and leave his throne;
Fair mists of seraphs melt and fall
Around Him, changeless amid all, —
Ancient of Days, whose days go on.

XVIII

He reigns below, He reigns alone,
And, having life in love forgone,
Beneath the crown of sovran thorns,
He reigns the Jealous God. Who mourns
Or rules with Him, while days go on ?

XIX

By anguish which made pale the sun,
I hear Him charge his saints that none
Among his creatures anywhere
Blaspheme against Him with despair,
However darkly days go on.

XX

Take from my head the thorn-wreath
    brown !
No mortal grief deserves that crown.
O supreme Love, chief misery,
The sharp regalia are for THEE
Whose days eternally go on !

XXI

For us, — whatever 's undergone,
Thou knowest, willest what is done.

Grief may be joy misunderstood;
Only the Good discerns the good.
I trust Thee while my days go on.

XXII

Whatever 's lost, it first was won;
We will not struggle nor impugn.
Perhaps the cup was broken here,
That Heaven's new wine might show more
    clear.
I praise Thee while my days go on.

XXIII

I praise Thee while my days go on;
I love Thee while my days go on:
Through dark and dearth, through fire and
    frost,
With emptied arms and treasure lost,
I thank Thee while my days go on.

XXIV

And having in thy life-depth thrown
Being and suffering (which are one),
As a child drops his pebble small
Down some deep well, and hears it fall
Smiling — so I. THY DAYS GO ON.

A MUSICAL INSTRUMENT

First printed in the *Cornhill Magazine*, July,
1860.

I

WHAT was he doing, the great god Pan,
    Down in the reeds by the river ?
Spreading ruin and scattering ban,
Splashing and paddling with hoofs of a
    goat,
And breaking the golden lilies afloat
    With the dragon-fly on the river.

II

He tore out a reed, the great god Pan,
    From the deep cool bed of the river:
The limpid water turbidly ran,
And the broken lilies a-dying lay,
And the dragon-fly had fled away,
    Ere he brought it out of the river.

III

High on the shore sat the great god Pan
    While turbidly flowed the river;
And hacked and hewed as a great god can,

With his hard bleak steel at the patient
    reed,
Till there was not a sign of the leaf indeed
    To prove it fresh from the river.

IV

He cut it short, did the great god Pan,
    (How tall it stood in the river !)
Then drew the pith, like the heart of a
    man,
Steadily from the outside ring,
And notched the poor dry empty thing
    In holes, as he sat by the river.

V

'This is the way,' laughed the great god
    Pan
    (Laughed while he sat by the river),
'The only way, since gods began
To make sweet music, they could succeed.'
Then, dropping his mouth to a hole in the
    reed,
    He blew in power by the river.

VI

Sweet, sweet, sweet, O Pan !
    Piercing sweet by the river !
Blinding sweet, O great god Pan !
The sun on the hill forgot to die,
And the lilies revived, and the dragon-fly
    Came back to dream on the river.

VII

Yet half a beast is the great god Pan,
    To laugh as he sits by the river,
Making a poet out of a man:
The true gods sigh for the cost and pain, —
For the reed which grows nevermore again
    As a reed with the reeds in the river.

FIRST NEWS FROM VILLA-
FRANCA

I

PEACE, peace, peace, do you say ?
    What ! — with the enemy's guns in our
        ears ?
    With the country's wrong not rendered
        back ?
What ! — while Austria stands at bay
    In Mantua, and our Venice bears
    The cursed flag of the yellow and
        black ?

II

Peace, peace, peace, do you say ?
    And this the Mincio ? Where's the
        fleet,
    And where's the sea ? Are we all
        blind
Or mad with the blood shed yesterday,
    Ignoring Italy under our feet,
    And seeing things before, behind ?

III

Peace, peace, peace, do you say ?
    What ! — uncontested, undenied ?
    Because we triumph, we succumb ?
A pair of Emperors stand in the way
    (One of whom is a man, beside),
    To sign and seal our cannons dumb ?

IV

No, not Napoleon ! — he who mused
    At Paris, and at Milan spake,
    And at Solferino led the fight:
Not he we trusted, honored, used
    Our hopes and hearts for . . . till they
        break
    Even so, you tell us . . . in his sight.

V

Peace, peace, is still your word ?
    We say you lie then ! — that is plain.
    There *is* no peace, and shall be none.
Our very Dead would cry ' Absurd ! '
    And clamor that they died in vain,
    And whine to come back to the sun.

VI

Hush ! more reverence for the Dead !
    They 've done the most for Italy
    Evermore since the earth was fair.
Now would that *we* had died instead,
    Still dreaming peace meant liberty,
    And did not, could not, mean despair.

VII

Peace, you say ? — yes, peace, in truth !
    But such a peace as the ear can achieve
    'Twixt the rifle's click and the rush of
        the ball,
'Twixt the tiger's spring and the crunch of
        the tooth,
    'Twixt the dying atheist's negative
    And God's Face — waiting, after all !

KING VICTOR EMANUEL ENTER-
ING FLORENCE, APRIL, 1860

I

KING of us all, we cried to thee, cried to
    thee,
  Trampled to earth by the beasts im-
    pure,
Dragged by the chariots which shame
    as they roll:
The dust of our torment far and wide to
    thee
  Went up, dark'ning thy royal soul.
  Be witness, Cavour,
That the King was sad for the people in
    thrall,
    This King of us all !

II

King, we cried to thee ! Strong in reply-
    ing,
  Thy word and thy sword sprang rapid
    and sure,
Cleaving our way to a nation's place.
Oh, first soldier of Italy ! — crying
  Now grateful, exultant, we look in thy
    face.
  Be witness, Cavour,
That, freedom's first soldier, the freed
    should call
    First King of them all !

III

This is our beautiful Italy's birthday;
  High-thoughted souls, whether many or
    fewer,
Bring her the gift, and wish her the
    good,
While Heaven presents on this sunny
    earthday
The noble King to the land renewed:
  Be witness, Cavour !
Roar, cannon-mouths ! Proclaim, install
    The King of us all !

IV

Grave he rides through the Florence gate-
    way,
  Clenching his face into calm, to immure
His struggling heart till it half disap-
    pears;
If he relaxed for a moment, straightway
  He would break out into passionate
    tears —

  Be witness, Cavour !)
While rings the cry without interval,
    ' Live, King of us all ! '

V

Cry, free peoples ! Honor the nation
  By crowning the true man — and none is
    truer:
Pisa is here, and Livorno is here,
And thousands of faces, in wild exultation,
  Burn over the windows to feel him
    near —
  (Be witness, Cavour !)
Burn over from terrace, roof, window and
    wall,
    On this King of us all.

VI

Grave ! A good man 's ever the graver
  For bearing a nation's trust secure;
And he, he thinks of the Heart, beside,
Which broke for Italy, failing to save
    her,
  And pining away by Oporto's tide:
  Be witness, Cavour,
That he thinks of his vow on that royal
    pall,
    This King of us all.

VII

Flowers, flowers, from the flowery city !
  Such innocent thanks for a deed so
    pure,
As, melting away for joy into flowers,
The nation invites him to enter his Pitti
  And evermore reign in this Florence of
    ours.
  Be witness, Cavour !
He 'll stand where the reptiles were used
    to crawl,
    This King of us all.

VIII

Grave, as the manner of noble men is —
  Deeds unfinished will weigh on the doer:
And, baring his head to those crape-
    veiled flags.
He bows to the grief of the South and
    Venice.
  Oh, riddle the last of the yellow to
    rags,
  And swear by Cavour
That the King shall reign where the ty-
    rants fall,
    True King of us all !

THE SWORD OF CASTRUCCIO CASTRACANI

'Questa è per me.' — KING VICTOR EMANUEL.

I

WHEN Victor Emanuel the King
  Went down to his Lucca that day,
The people, each vaunting the thing
  As he gave it, gave all things away, —
In a burst of fierce gratitude, say,
As they tore out their hearts for the King.

II

— Gave the green forest-walk on the wall,
  With the Apennine blue through the
    trees;
Gave the palaces, churches, and all
  The great pictures which burn out of
    these;
  But the eyes of the King seemed to
    freeze
As he gazed upon ceiling and wall.

III

'Good,' said the King as he passed.
  Was he cold to the arts ? — or else coy
To possession ? or crossed, at the last
  (Whispered some), by the vote in Savoy ?
  Shout ! Love him enough for his joy !
'Good,' said the King as he passed.

IV

He, travelling the whole day through
    flowers
  And protesting amenities, found
At Pistoia, betwixt the two showers
  Of red roses, the 'Orphans' (renowned
  As the heirs of Puccini) who wound
With a sword through the crowd and the
    flowers.

V

''T is the sword of Castruccio, O King, —
  In that strife of intestinal hate,
Very famous ! Accept what we bring,
  We who cannot be sons, by our fate,
  Rendered citizens by thee of late,
And endowed with a country and king.

VI

'Read ! Puccini has willed that this
  sword
  (Which once made in an ignorant feud
Many orphans) remain in our ward

Till some patriot its pure civic blood
Wipe away in the foe's and make good,
In delivering the land by the sword.'

VII

Then the King exclaimed 'This is for *me !*'
  And he dashed out his hand on the hilt,
While his blue eye shot fire openly,
  And his heart overboiled till it spilt
  A hot prayer, — 'God ! the rest as Thou
    wilt !
But grant me this ! — *This* is for *me.*'

VIII

O Victor Emanuel, the King,
  The sword is for *thee*, and the deed,
And nought for the alien, next spring,
  Nought for Hapsburg and Bourbon
    agreed —
  But, for us, a great Italy freed,
With a hero to head us, — our King !

SUMMING UP IN ITALY

(INSCRIBED TO INTELLIGENT PUBLICS
OUT OF IT)

I

OBSERVE how it will be at last,
  When our Italy stands at full stature,
A year ago tied down so fast
  That the cord cut the quick of her na-
    ture !
You 'll honor the deed and its scope,
  Then, in logical sequence upon it,
Will use up the remnants of rope
  By hanging the men who have done it.

II

The speech in the Commons, which hits you
  A sketch off, how dungeons must feel, —
The official despatch, which commits you
  From stamping out groans with your
    heel, —
Suggestions in journal or book for
  Good efforts, — are praised as is meet:
But what in this world can men look for,
  Who only achieve and complete ?

III

True, you 've praise for the fireman who
  sets his
  Brave face to the axe of the flame,

Disappears in the smoke, and then fetches
  A babe down, or idiot that 's lame, —
For the boor even, who rescues through
    pity
A sheep from the brute who would kick
    it:
But saviours of nations ! — 't is pretty,
  And doubtful: they *may* be so wicked :

IV

Azeglio, Farini, Mamiani,
  Ricasoli, — doubt by the dozen ! —
    here 's
Pepoli too, and Cipriani,
  Imperial cousins and cozeners —
Aresc, Laiatico, — courtly
Of manners, if stringent of mouth:
Garibaldi ! we 'll come to him shortly
  (As soon as he *ends* in the South).

V

Napoleon — as strong as ten armies,
  Corrupt as seven devils — a fact
You accede to, then seek where the harm
    is
Drained off from the man to his act,
And find — a free nation ! Suppose
  Some hell-brood in Eden's sweet green-
    ery,
Convoked for creating — a rose !
  Would it suit the infernal machinery ?

VI

Cavour, — to the despot's desire,
  Who his own thought so craftily mar-
    ries —
What is he but just a thin wire
  For conducting the lightning from Paris ?
Yes, write down the two as compeers,
  Confessing (you would not permit a lie)
He bore up his Piedmont ten years
  Till she suddenly smiled and was Italy.

VII

And the King, with that ' stain on his
    scutcheon,'
  Savoy — as the calumny runs;
(If it be not his blood, — with his clutch on
  The sword, and his face to the guns.)
O first, where the battle-storm gathers,
  O loyal of heart on the throne,
Let those keep the ' graves of their fa-
    thers '
  Who quail, in a nerve, from their own !

VIII

For *thee* — through the dim Hades-por-
    tal
  The dream of a voice — ' Blessed thou
Who hast made all thy race twice im-
    mortal !
  No need of the sepulchres now !
— Left to Bourbons and Hapsburgs, who
    fester
  Above-ground with worm-eaten souls,
While the ghost of some pale feudal jester
  Before them strews treaties in holes.'

IX

But hush ! — am I dreaming a poem
  Of Hades, Heaven, Justice ? Not I;
I began too far off, in my proem,
  With what men believe and deny:
And on earth, whatsoever the need is
  (To sum up as thoughtful reviewers),
The moral of every great deed is —
  The virtue of slandering the doers.

'DIED . . .'

(The Times Obituary)

I

WHAT shall we add now ? He is dead.
  And I who praise and you who blame,
  With wash of words across his name,
Find suddenly declared instead —
' *On Sunday, third of August, dead.*'

II

Which stops the whole we talked to-
    day.
  I, quickened to a plausive glance
  At his large general tolerance
By common people's narrow way,
Stopped short in praising. Dead, they
    say.

III

And you, who had just put in a sort
  Of cold deduction — ' rather, large
  Through weakness of the continent
    marge,
Than greatness of the thing contained ' —
Broke off. Dead ! — there, you stood re-
    strained.

IV

As if we had talked in following one
  Up some long gallery. ' Would you
    choose
An air like that ? The gait is loose —
Or noble.' Sudden in the sun
An oubliette winks. Where *is* he ? Gone.

V

Dead. Man's ' I was ' by God's ' I am ' —
  All hero-worship comes to that.
  High heart, high thought, high fame, as
    flat
As a gravestone. Bring your *Jacet jam* —
The epitaph 's an epigram.

VI

Dead. There 's an answer to arrest
  All carping. Dust 's his natural place ?
He 'll let the flies buzz round his face
And, though you slander, not protest ?
— From such an one, exact the Best ?

VII

Opinions gold or brass are null.
  We chuck our flattery or abuse,
  Called Cæsar's due, as Charon's dues,
I' the teeth of some dead sage or fool,
To mend the grinning of a skull.

VIII

Be abstinent in praise and blame.
  The man 's still mortal, who stands first,
  And mortal only, if last and worst.
Then slowly lift so frail a fame,
Or softly drop so poor a shame.

THE FORCED RECRUIT

SOLFERINO, 1859

First printed in the *Cornhill Magazine*, October, 1860.

In the ranks of the Austrian you found
    him,
  He died with his face to you all;
Yet bury him here where around him
  You honor your bravest that fall.

Venetian, fair-featured and slender,
  He lies shot to death in his youth,
With a smile on his lips over-tender
  For any mere soldier's dead mouth.

No stranger, and yet not a traitor,
  Though alien the cloth on his breast,
Underneath it how seldom a greater
  Young heart has a shot sent to rest !

By your enemy tortured and goaded
  To march with them, stand in their file,
His musket (see) never was loaded,
  He facing your guns with that smile !

As orphans yearn on to their mothers,
  He yearned to your patriot bands;—
' Let me die for our Italy, brothers,
  If not in your ranks, by your hands !

' Aim straightly, fire steadily ! spare me
  A ball in the body which may
Deliver my heart here, and tear me
  This badge of the Austrian away !'

So thought he, so died he this morning.
  What then ? many others have died.
Ay, but easy for men to die scorning
  The death-stroke, who fought side by
    side —

One tricolor floating above them;
  Struck down 'mid triumphant acclaims
Of an Italy rescued to love them
  And blazon the brass with their names.

But he, — without witness or honor,
  Mixed, shamed in his country's regard,
With the tyrants who march in upon
    her,
  Died faithful and passive: 't was hard.

'T was sublime. In a cruel restriction
  Cut off from the guerdon of sons,
With most filial obedience, conviction,
  His soul kissed the lips of her guns.

That moves you ? Nay, grudge not to show
    it,
  While digging a grave for him here:
The others who died, says your poet,
  Have glory, — let *him* have a tear.

GARIBALDI

I

He bent his head upon his breast
  Wherein his lion-heart lay sick; —

'Perhaps we are not ill-repaid;
Perhaps this is not a true test;
Perhaps this was not a foul trick;
Perhaps none wronged, and none be-
trayed.

II

'Perhaps the people's vote which here
United, there may disunite,
And both be lawful as they think;
Perhaps a patriot statesman, dear
For chartering nations, can with right
Disfranchise those who hold the ink.

III

'Perhaps men's wisdom is not craft;
Men's greatness, not a selfish greed;
Men's justice, not the safer side;
Perhaps even women, when they laughed,
Wept, thanked us that the land was
freed,
Not wholly (though they kissed us) lied.

IV

Perhaps no more than this we meant,
When up at Austria's guns we flew,
And quenched them with a cry apiece,
Italia! — Yet a dream was sent . . .
The little house my father knew,
The olives and the palms of Nice.'

V

He paused, and drew his sword out slow,
Then pored upon the blade intent,
As if to read some written thing;
While many murmured, — 'He will go
In that despairing sentiment
And break his sword before the King.'

VI

He poring still upon the blade,
His large lid quivered, something fell.
'Perhaps,' he said, 'I was not born
With such fine brains to treat and
trade, —
And if a woman knew it well,
Her falsehood only meant her scorn.

VII

Yet through Varese's cannon-smoke
My eye saw clear: men feared this man
At Como, where this sword could seal
Death's protocol with every stroke:

And now . . . the drop there scarcely
can
Impair the keenness of the steel.

VIII

'So man and sword may have their use;
And if the soil beneath my foot
In valor's act is forfeited,
I'll strike the harder, take my dues
Out nobler, and all loss confute
From ampler heavens above my head.

IX

'My King, King Victor, I am thine!
So much Nice-dust as what I am
(To make our Italy) must cleave.
Forgive that.' Forward with a sign
He went.
You 've seen the telegram?
Palermo's taken, we believe.

ONLY A CURL

I

FRIENDS of faces unknown and a land
Unvisited over the sea,
Who tell me how lonely you stand
With a single gold curl in the hand
Held up to be looked at by me, —

II

While you ask me to ponder and say
What a father and mother can do,
With the bright fellow-locks put away
Out of reach, beyond kiss, in the clay
Where the violets press nearer than you.

III

Shall I speak like a poet, or run
Into weak woman's tears for relief?
Oh, children! — I never lost one, —
Yet my arm's round my own little son,
And Love knows the secret of Grief.

IV

And I feel what it must be and is,
When God draws a new angel so
Through the house of a man up to his,
With a murmur of music you miss,
And a rapture of light you forgo.

V

How you think, staring on at the door,
Where the face of your angel flashed in,

That its brightness, familiar before,
Burns off from you ever the more
   For the dark of your sorrow and sin.

VI

'God lent him and takes him,' you sigh;
  — Nay, there let me break with your
     pain:
God's generous in giving, say I, —
And the thing which He gives, I deny
   That He ever can take back again.

VII

He gives what He gives. I appeal
  To all who bear babes — in the hour
When the veil of the body we feel
Rent round us, — while torments reveal
   The motherhood's advent in power,

VIII

And the babe cries! — has each of us
   known
  By apocalypse (God being there
Full in nature) the child is our own,
Life of life, love of love, moan of moan,
   Through all changes, all times, every-
     where.

IX

He's ours and for ever. Believe,
  O father! — O mother, look back
To the first love's assurance! To give
Means with God not to tempt or deceive
   With a cup thrust in Benjamin's sack.

X

He gives what He gives. Be content!
  He resumes nothing given, — be sure!
God lend? Where the usurers lent
In his temple, indignant He went
   And scourged away all those impure.

XI

He lends not; but gives to the end,
  As He loves to the end. If it seem
That He draws back a gift, comprehend
'T is to add to it rather, — amend,
   And finish it up to your dream, —

XII

Or keep, — as a mother will toys
  Too costly, though given by herself,
Till the room shall be stiller from noise,

And the children more fit for such joys,
  Kept over their heads on the shelf.

XIII

So look up, friends! you, who indeed
  Have possessed in your house a sweet
    piece
Of the Heaven which men strive for, must
    need
Be more earnest than others are, — speed
  Where they loiter, persist where they
   cease.

XIV

You know how one angel smiles there:
  Then weep not. 'T is easy for you
To be drawn by a single gold hair
Of that curl, from earth's storm and de-
    spair,
  To the safe place above us. Adieu.

A VIEW ACROSS THE ROMAN CAMPAGNA

1861

I

OVER the dumb Campagna-sea,
  Out in the offing through mist and rain,
Saint Peter's Church heaves silently
  Like a mighty ship in pain,
   Facing the tempest with struggle and
    strain.

II

Motionless waifs of ruined towers,
  Soundless breakers of desolate land:
The sullen surf of the mist devours
  That mountain-range upon either hand,
   Eaten away from its outline grand.

III

And over the dumb Campagna-sea
  Where the ship of the Church heaves on
    to wreck,
Alone and silent as God must be,
  The Christ walks. Ay, but Peter's neck
   Is stiff to turn on the foundering deck.

IV

Peter, Peter! if such be thy name,
  Now leave the ship for another to steer,
And proving thy faith evermore the same,

Come forth, tread out through the dark
          and drear,
Since He who walks on the sea is here.

V

Peter, Peter! He does not speak;
He is not as rash as in old Galilee:
Safer a ship, though it toss and leak,
     Than a reeling foot on a rolling sea !
     And he 's got to be round in the girth,
          thinks he.

VI

Peter, Peter! He does not stir;
     His nets are heavy with silver fish;
He reckons his gains, and is keen to in-
          fer
     — 'The broil on the shore, if the Lord
          should wish;
     But the sturgeon goes to the Cæsar's
          dish.'

VII

Peter, Peter! thou fisher of men,
     Fisher of fish wouldst thou live instead ?
Haggling for pence with the other Ten,
     Cheating the market at so much a head,
     Griping the Bag of the traitor Dead ?

VIII

At the triple crow of the Gallic cock
     Thou weep'st not, thou, though thine
          eyes be dazed:
What bird comes next in the tempest-
          shock ?
     — Vultures ! see, — as when Romulus
          gazed, —
     To   inaugurate   Rome   for   a   world
          amazed !

THE KING'S GIFT

I

     TERESA, ah, Teresita !
Now what has the messenger brought her,
Our Garibaldi's young daughter,
     To make her stop short in her sing-
          ing ?
Will she not once more repeat a
Verse from that hymn of our hero's,
     Setting the souls of us ringing ?
Break off the song where the tear rose ?
     Ah, Teresita !

II

A young thing, mark, is Teresa:
Her eyes have caught fire, to be sure, in
That necklace of jewels from Turin,
     Till blind their regard to us men is.
But still she remembers to raise a
Sly look to her father, and note —
     'Could she sing on as well about Ven-
          ice,
Yet wear such a flame at her throat ?
     Decide for Teresa.'

III

     Teresa, ah, Teresita !
His right hand has paused on her head —
' Accept it, my daughter,' he said;
     ' Ay, wear it, true child of thy mother !
Then sing, till all start to their feet, a
New verse ever bolder and freer !
     King Victor's no king like another,
But verily noble as *we* are,
          Child, Teresita !'

PARTING LOVERS

SIENA, 1860

I

I LOVE thee, love thee, Giulio;
     Some call me cold, and some demure;
And if thou hast ever guessed that so
     I loved thee . . . well, the proof was
          poor
          And no one could be sure.

II

Before thy song (with shifted rhymes
     To suit my name) did I undo
The persian ? If it stirred sometimes,
     Thou hast not seen a hand push through
          A foolish flower or two.

III

My mother listening to my sleep,
     Heard nothing but a sigh at night, —
The short sigh rippling on the deep,
     When hearts run out of breath and sight
          Of men, to God's clear light.

IV

When others named thee, — thought thy
          brows
     Were straight, thy smile was tender —
          ' Here

He comes between the vineyard-rows ! '
  I said not ' Ay,' nor waited, Dear,
    To feel thee step too near.

V

I left such things to bolder girls, —
  Olivia or Clotilda. Nay,
When that Clotilda, through her curls,
  Held both thine eyes in hers one day,
    I marvelled, let me say.

VI

I could not try the woman's trick:
  Between us straightway fell the blush
Which kept me separate, blind and sick.
  A wind came with thee in a flush,
    As blown through Sinai's bush.

VII

But now that Italy invokes
  Her young men to go forth and chase
The foe or perish, — nothing chokes
  My voice, or drives me from the place.
    I look thee in the face.

VIII

I love thee ! It is understood,
  Confest: I do not shrink or start.
No blushes ! all my body's blood
  Has gone to greaten this poor heart.
    That, loving, we may part.

IX

Our Italy invokes the youth
  To die if need be. Still there 's room,
Though earth is strained with dead in
    truth:
  Since twice the lilies were in bloom
    They have not grudged a tomb.

X

And many a plighted maid and wife
  And mother, who can say since then
' My country,' — cannot say through life
  ' My son,' ' my spouse,' ' my flower of
    men,'
    And not weep dumb again.

XI

Heroic males the country bears, —
  But daughters give up more than sons:
Flags wave, drums beat, and unawares

You flash your souls out with the guns,
  And take your Heaven at once.

XII

But we ! — we empty heart and home
  Of life's life, love ! We bear to think
You 're gone, — to feel you may not
    come, —
  To hear the door-latch stir and clink,
    Yet no more you ! . . . nor sink.

XIII

Dear God ! when Italy is one,
  Complete, content from bound to bound
Suppose, for my share, earth 's undone
  By one grave in 't — as one small wound
    Will kill a man, 't is found.

XIV

What then ? If love's delight must end,
  At least we 'll clear its truth from flaws
I love thee, love thee, sweetest friend !
  Now take my sweetest without pause,
    And help the nation's cause.

XV

And thus, of noble Italy
  We 'll both be worthy ! Let her show
The future how we made her free,
  Not sparing life . . . nor Giulio,
    Nor this . . . this heartbreak ! Go.

MOTHER AND POET

TURIN, AFTER NEWS FROM GAETA, 1861

  The mother was Laura Savio of Turin, both
poet and patriot, whose two sons were killed
Ancona and Gaeta.

I

DEAD ! One of them shot by the sea in the
    east,
  And one of them shot in the west by the
    sea.
Dead ! both my boys ! When you sit
    the feast
  And are wanting a great song for Italy
    free,
    Let none look at me !

II

Yet I was a poetess only last year,
  And good at my art, for a woman, men
    said;

But *this* woman, *this,* who is agonized here,
— The east sea and west sea rhyme on in
  her head
For ever instead.

III

What art can a woman be good at ? Oh,
  vain !
What art *is* she good at, but hurting her
  breast
With the milk-teeth of babes, and a smile
  at the pain ?
Ah boys, how you hurt ! you were strong
  as you pressed,
And I proud, by that test.

IV

What art 's for a woman ? To hold on her
  knees
Both darlings ! to feel all their arms
  round her throat,
Cling, strangle a little ! to sew by degrees
And 'broider the long-clothes and neat
  little coat;
To dream and to doat.

V

To teach them . . . It stings there ! *I*
  made them indeed
Speak plain the word *country.* I taught
  them, no doubt,
That a country 's a thing men should die
  for at need.
I prated of liberty, rights, and about
  The tyrant cast out.

VI

And when their eyes flashed . . . O my
  beautiful eyes ! . . .
I exulted; nay, let them go forth at the
  wheels
Of the guns, and denied not. But then the
  surprise
When one sits quite alone ! Then one
  weeps, then one kneels !
God, how the house feels !

VII

At first, happy news came, in gay letters
  moiled
With my kisses, — of camp-life and
  glory, and how
They both loved me; and, soon coming
  home to be spoiled

In return would fan off every fly from my
  brow
With their green laurel-bough.

VIII

Then was triumph at Turin: 'Ancona was
  free !'
And some one came out of the cheers in
  the street,
With a face pale as stone, to say something
  to me.
My Guido was dead ! I fell down at his
  feet,
While they cheered in the street.

IX

I bore it; friends soothed me; my grief
  looked sublime
As the ransom of Italy. One boy re-
  mained
To be leant on and walked with, recalling
  the time
When the first grew immortal, while
  both of us strained
To the height he had gained.

X

And letters still came, shorter, sadder,
  more strong,
Writ now but in one hand, 'I was not to
  faint, —
One loved me for two — would be with me
  ere long:
And *Viva l' Italia! — he* died for, our
  saint,
Who forbids our complaint.'

XI

My Nanni would add, 'he was safe, and
  aware
Of a presence that turned off the balls, —
  was imprest
It was Guido himself, who knew what I
  could bear,
And how 't was impossible, quite dis-
  possessed
To live on for the rest.'

XII

On which, without pause, up the telegraph-
  line
Swept smoothly the next news from
  Gaeta: — *Shot.*
Tell his mother. Ah, ah, 'his,' 'their' mother,
  — not 'mine,'

No voice says 'My mother' again to me.
　　What !
　　You think Guido forgot ?

XIII

Are souls straight so happy that, dizzy
　　with Heaven,
　　They drop earth's affections, conceive
　　　not of woe ?
I think not.　Themselves were too lately
　　forgiven
　　Through THAT Love and Sorrow which
　　　reconciled so
　　The Above and Below.

XIV

O Christ of the five wounds, who look'dst
　　through the dark
　　To the face of thy mother !　consider, I
　　　pray,
How we common mothers stand desolate,
　　mark,
　　Whose sons, not being Christs, die with
　　　eyes turned away,
　　And no last word to say !

XV

Both boys dead ?　but that's out of nature.
　　We all
　　Have been patriots, yet each house must
　　　always keep one.
Twere imbecile, hewing out roads to a
　　wall;
　　And, when Italy's made, for what end
　　　is it done
　　If we have not a son ?

XVI

Ah, ah, ah !　when Gaeta's taken, what
　　then ?
　　When the fair wicked queen sits no more
　　　at her sport
Of the fire-balls of death crashing souls
　　out of men ?
　　When the guns of Cavalli with final re-
　　　tort
　　Have cut the game short ?

XVII

When Venice and Rome keep their new
　　jubilee,
　　When your flag takes all heaven for its
　　　white, green, and red,
When you have your country from moun-
　　tain to sea,

When King Victor has Italy's crown on
　　his head,
　　(And I have my Dead) —

XVIII

What then ?　Do not mock me.　Ah, ring
　　your bells low,
　　And burn your lights faintly !　My
　　　country is there,
Above the star pricked by the last peak of
　　snow:
　　My Italy's THERE, with my brave civic
　　　Pair,
　　To disfranchise despair !

XIX

Forgive me.　Some women bear children
　　in strength,
　　And bite back the cry of their pain in
　　　self-scorn;
But the birth-pangs of nations will wring
　　us at length
　　Into wail such as this — and we sit on
　　　forlorn
　　When the man-child is born.

XX

Dead !　One of them shot by the sea in
　　the east,
　　And one of them shot in the west by
　　　the sea.
Both !　both my boys !　If in keeping the
　　feast
　　You want a great song for your Italy
　　　free,
　　Let none look at me!

NATURE'S REMORSES

ROME, 1861

I

HER soul was bred by a throne, and fed
　　From the sucking-bottle used in her
　　　race
　　　On starch and water (for mother's
　　　　milk
　　Which gives a larger growth instead),
　　And, out of the natural liberal grace,
　　　Was swaddled away in violet silk.

II

And young and kind, and royally blind,
　　Forth she stepped from her palace-door

On three-piled carpet of compliments,
Curtains of incense drawn by the wind
In between her for evermore
And daylight issues of events.

III

On she drew, as a queen might do,
To meet a Dream of Italy, —
Of magical town and musical wave,
Where even a god, his amulet blue
Of shining sea, in an ecstasy
Dropt and forgot in a Nereid's cave.

IV

Down she goes, as the soft wind blows,
To live more smoothly than mortals can,
To love and to reign as queen and wife,
To wear a crown that smells of a rose,
And still, with a sceptre as light as a fan,
Beat sweet time to the song of life.

V

What is this? As quick as a kiss
Falls the smile from her girlish mouth!
The lion-people has left its lair,
Roaring along her garden of bliss,
And the fiery underworld of the South
Scorched a way to the upper air.

VI

And a fire-stone ran in the form of a man,
Burningly, boundingly, fatal and fell,
Bowling the kingdom down! Where was the King?
She had heard somewhat, since life began,
Of terrors on earth and horrors in hell,
But never, never of such a thing.

VII

You think she dropped when her dream was stopped,
When the blotch of Bourbon blood inlay,
Lividly rank, her new lord's cheek?
Not so. Her high heart overtopped
The royal part she had come to play.
Only the men in that hour were weak.

VIII

And twice a wife by her ravaged life,
And twice a queen by her kingdom lost,
She braved the shock and the counter-shock
Of hero and traitor, bullet and knife,

While Italy pushed, like a vengeful ghost,
That son of the Cursed from Gaeta's rock.

IX

What will ye give her, who could not deliver,
German Princesses? A laurel-wreath
All over-scored with your signatures,
Graces, Serenities, Highnesses ever?
Mock her not, fresh from the truth of Death,
Conscious of dignities higher than yours.

X

What will ye put in your casket shut,
Ladies of Paris, in sympathy's name?
Guizot's daughter, what have you brought her?
Withered immortelles, long ago cut
For guilty dynasties perished in shame,
Putrid to memory, Guizot's daughter?

XI

Ah poor queen! so young and serene!
What shall we do for her, now hope's done,
Standing at Rome in these ruins old,
She too a ruin and no more a queen?
Leave her that diadem made by the sun
Turning her hair to an innocent gold.

XII

Ay! bring close to her, as 't were a rose, to her,
Yon free child from an Apennine city
Singing for Italy, — dumb in the place!
Something like solace, let us suppose, to her
Given, in that homage of wonder and pity,
By his pure eyes to her beautiful face.

XIII

Nature, excluded, savagely brooded;
Ruined all queendom and dogmas of state:
Then, in reaction remorseful and mild,
Rescues the womanhood, nearly eluded,
Shows her what's sweetest in womanly fate —
Sunshine from Heaven, and the eyes of a child.

THE NORTH AND THE SOUTH

THE LAST POEM

ROME, MAY, 1861

The occasion of Mrs. Browning's last poem was a visit of the Danish novelist Hans Christian Andersen to Rome in the spring of 1861.

I

' Now give us lands where the olives grow,'
    Cried the North to the South,
' Where the sun with a golden mouth can
    blow
Blue bubbles of grapes down a vineyard-
    row ! '
    Cried the North to the South.

' Now give us men from the sunless plain,'
    Cried the South to the North,
' By need of work in the snow and the rain,
Made strong, and brave by familiar pain ! '
    Cried the South to the North.

II

' Give lucider hills and intenser seas,'
    Said the North to the South.
' Since ever by symbols and bright degrees
Art, childlike, climbs to the dear Lord's
    knees,'
    Said the North to the South.

' Give strenuous souls for belief and prayer,'
    Said the South to the North,
' That stand in the dark on the lowest stair,
While affirming of God, " He is certainly
    there," '
    Said the South to the North.

III

' Yet oh for the skies that are softer and
    higher ! '
    Sighed the North to the South;
For the flowers that blaze, and the trees
    that aspire,
And the insects made of a song or a
    fire ! '
    Sighed the North to the South.

' And oh for a seer to discern the same ! '
    Sighed the South to the North;
' For a poet's tongue of baptismal flame.
To call the tree or the flower by its
    name ! '
    Sighed the South to the North.

IV

The North sent therefore a man of men
    As a grace to the South;
And thus to Rome came Andersen.
— ' Alas, but must you take him again ? '
    Said the South to the North.

TRANSLATIONS

PROMETHEUS BOUND

The translation which follows of the *Prometheus Bound* of Æschylus is the revised version first published by Mrs. Browning among the *Poems of 1850.* She herself called it a retranslation rather than a revision, and was very severe in her own strictures on the earlier version which had been published without her name, along with a few occasional pieces in 1833. The present is undoubtedly a much better piece of work than the ambitious first attempt, which the author wished to have it entirely supersede. Yet a certain special interest will always attach to the previous rendering as having been the one which Robert and Elizabeth Browning discussed so fully in some of the earlier letters of their famous correspondence. (Vide *Letters of Robert and Elizabeth Barrett Browning*, vol. i. pp. 34–46.)

PERSONS

PROMETHEUS.
OCEANUS.
HERMES.
HEPHÆSTUS.
IO, *daughter of* Inachus.
STRENGTH *and* FORCE.
Chorus of Sea Nymphs.

SCENE. — STRENGTH *and* FORCE, HEPHÆSTUS *and* PROMETHEUS, *at the Rocks.*

Strength. We reach the utmost limit of
    the earth,
The Scythian track, the desert without man.
And now, Hephæstus, thou must needs fulfil
The mandate of our Father, and with links
Indissoluble of adamantine chains
Fasten against this beetling precipice
This guilty god. Because he filched away

Thine own bright flower, the glory of plas-
tic fire,
And gifted mortals with it, — such a sin
It doth behove he expiate to the gods,   10
Learning to accept the empery of Zeus
And leave off his old trick of loving man.
  Hephæstus. O Strength and Force, for
you, our Zeus's will
Presents a deed for doing, no more ! —
but I,
I look your daring, up this storm - rent
chasm
To fix with violent hands a kindred god,
Howbeit necessity compels me so
That I must dare it, and our Zeus com-
mands
With a most inevitable word. Ho, thou !
High-thoughted son of Themis who is sage !
Thee loth, I loth must rivet fast in chains 21
Against this rocky height unclomb by man,
Where never human voice nor face shall
find
Out thee who lov'st them, and thy beauty's
flower,
Scorched in the sun's clear heat, shall fade
away.
Night shall come up with garniture of
stars
To comfort thee with shadow, and the sun
Disperse with retrickt beams the morning-
frosts,
But through all changes sense of present
woe
Shall vex thee sore, because with none of
them   30
There comes a hand to free. Such fruit is
plucked
From love of man ! and in that thou, a
god,
Didst brave the wrath of gods and give
away
Undue respect to mortals, for that crime
Thou art adjudged to guard this joyless
rock,
Erect, unslumbering, bending not the knee,
And many a cry and unavailing moan
To utter on the air. For Zeus is stern,
And new-made kings are cruel.
  Strength.   Be it so.
Why loiter in vain pity ? Why not hate 40
A god the gods hate ? one too who betrayed
Thy glory unto men ?
  Hephæstus.   An awful thing
Is kinship joined to friendship.
  Strength.   Grant it be;

Is disobedience to the Father's word
A possible thing ? Dost quail not more for
that ?
  Hephæstus. Thou, at least, art a stern
one: ever bold.
  Strength. Why, if I wept, it were no
remedy ;
And do not thou spend labor on the air
To bootless uses.
  Hephæstus.   Cursed handicraft !
I curse and hate thee, O my craft !
  Strength.   Why hate
Thy craft most plainly innocent of all   51
These pending ills ?
  Hephæstus. I would some other hand
Were here to work it !
  Strength.   All work hath its pain,
Except to rule the gods. There is none
free
Except King Zeus.
  Hephæstus.   I know it very well:
I argue not against it.
  Strength.   Why not, then,
Make haste and lock the fetters over HIM
Lest Zeus behold thee lagging ?
  Hephæstus.   Here be chains.
Zeus may behold these.
  Strength.   Seize him: strike amain:
Strike with the hammer on each side his
hands —   60
Rivet him to the rock.
  Hephæstus.   The work is done,
And thoroughly done.
  Strength.   Still faster grapple him ;
Wedge him in deeper : leave no inch to
stir.
He's terrible for finding a way out
From the irremediable.
  Hephæstus.   Here's an arm, at least,
Grappled past freeing.
  Strength.   Now then, buckle me
The other securely. Let this wise one
learn
He's duller than our Zeus.
  Hephæstus.   Oh, none but he
Accuse me justly.
  Strength.   Now, straight through
the chest,
Take him and bite him with the clenching
tooth   70
Of the adamantine wedge, and rivet him.
  Hephæstus. Alas, Prometheus, what thou
sufferest here
I sorrow over.
  Strength.   Dost thou flinch again

And breathe groans for the enemies of
    Zeus ?
Beware lest thine own pity find thee out.
    Hephœstus. Thou dost behold a spectacle
        that turns
The sight o' the eyes to pity.
    Strength.   I behold
A sinner suffer his sin's penalty.
But lash the thongs about his sides.
    Hephœstus.   So much,
I must do.   Urge no farther than I must. 80
    Strength. Ay, but I *will* urge ! — and,
        with shout on shout,
Will hound thee at this quarry. Get thee
    down
And ring amain the iron round his legs.
    Hephœstus. That work was not long
        doing.
    Strength.   Heavily now
Let fall the strokes upon the perforant
    gyves:
For He who rates the work has a heavy
    hand.
    Hephœstus. Thy speech is savage as thy
        shape.
    Strength.   Be thou
Gentle and tender ! but revile not me
For the firm will and the untruckling
    hate.
    Hephœstus. Let us go. He is netted
    round with chains.   90
    Strength. Here, now, taunt on ! and hav-
    ing spoiled the gods
Of honors, crown withal thy mortal men
Who live a whole day out. Why how could
    they
Draw off from thee one single of thy
    griefs ?
Methinks the Dæmons gave thee a wrong
    name,
'Prometheus,' which means Providence, —
    because
Thou dost thyself need providence to see
Thy roll and ruin from the top of doom.
    Prometheus (*alone*). O holy Æther, and
    swift-wingèd Winds,
And River-wells, and laughter innumer-
    ous   100
Of yon sea-waves ! Earth, mother of us
    all,
And all-viewing cyclic Sun, I cry on you, —
Behold me, a god, what I endure from
    gods !
        Behold, with throe on throe,
        How, wasted by this woe,

I wrestle down the myriad years of time !
    Behold, how fast around me,
The new King of the happy ones sublime
Has flung the chain he forged, has shamed
    and bound me !
Woe, woe ! to-day's woe and the coming
    morrow's   110
I cover with one groan. And where is
    found me
    A limit to these sorrows ?
And yet what word do I say ? I have fore-
    known
Clearly all things that should be ; nothing
    done
Comes sudden to my soul ; and I must bear
What is ordained with patience, being aware
    Necessity doth front the universe
With an invincible gesture. Yet this
    curse
Which strikes me now, I find it hard to
    brave   119
In silence or in speech. Because I gave
Honor to mortals, I have yoked my soul
To this compelling fate. Because I stole
The secret fount of fire, whose bubbles
    went
Over the ferule's brim, and manward
    sent
Art's mighty means and perfect rudi-
    ment,
That sin I expiate in this agony,
Hung here in fetters, 'neath the blanch-
    ing sky.
        Ah, ah me ! what a sound,
What a fragrance sweeps up from a pinion
    unseen
Of a god, or a mortal, or nature between, 130
Sweeping up to this rock where the earth
    has her bound,
To have sight of my pangs or some guer-
    don obtain.
Lo, a god in the anguish, a god in the
    chain !
        The god, Zeus hateth sore
        And his gods hate again,
As many as tread on his glorified floor,
Because I loved mortals too much ever-
    more.
Alas me ! what a murmur and motion I
    hear,
        As of birds flying near !
        And the air undersings   140
        The light stroke of their wings —
And all life that approaches I wait for in
    fear.

Chorus of Sea Nymphs, 1st Strophe

    Fear nothing! our troop
    Floats lovingly up
    With a quick-oaring stroke
    Of wings steered to the rock,
Having softened the soul of our father
    below.
For the gales of swift-bearing have sent me
    a sound,
And the clank of the iron, the malleted
    blow,
    Smote down the profound   150
    Of my caverns of old,
And struck the red light in a blush from
    my brow, —
Till I sprang up unsandalled, in haste to
    behold,
And rushed forth on my chariot of wings
    manifold.

Prometheus. Alas me! — alas me!
Ye offspring of Tethys who bore at her
    breast
Many children, and eke of Oceanus, he
Coiling still around earth with perpetual
    unrest!
    Behold me and see
    How transfixed with the fang 160
    Of a fetter I hang
On the high-jutting rocks of this fissure
    and keep
An uncoveted watch o'er the world and the
    deep.

Chorus, 1st Antistrophe.

I behold thee, Prometheus; yet now, yet
    now,
A terrible cloud whose rain is tears
Sweeps over mine eyes that witness how
    Thy body appears
Hung awaste on the rocks by infrangible
    chains:
For new is the Hand, new the rudder that
    steers
The ship of Olympus through surge and
    wind —   170
And of old things passed, no track is be-
    hind.

Prometheus. Under earth, under Hades
    Where the home of the shade is,
    All into the deep, deep Tartarus,
    I would he had hurled me adown.
I would he had plunged me, fastened thus
In the knotted chain with the savage clang,

All into the dark where there should be
    none,
Neither god nor another, to laugh and
    see.
    But now the winds sing through and
    shake   180
    The hurtling chains wherein I hang,
    And I, in my naked sorrows, make
    Much mirth for my enemy.

Chorus, 2d Strophe.

Nay! who of the gods hath a heart so
    stern
    As to use thy woe for a mock and
    mirth?
Who would not turn more mild to
    learn
    Thy sorrows? who of the heaven and
    earth
      Save Zeus? But he
      Right wrathfully
Bears on his sceptral soul unbent 190
And rules thereby the heavenly seed,
Nor will he pause till he content
His thirsty heart in a finished deed;
Or till Another shall appear,
To win by fraud, to seize by fear
The hard-to-be-captured government.

Prometheus. Yet even of *me* he shall
    have need,
That monarch of the blessed seed,
Of me, of me, who now am cursed
    By his fetters dire, —   200
To wring my secret out withal
    And learn by whom his sceptre shall
Be filched from him — as was, at first,
    His heavenly fire.
But he never shall enchant me
    With his honey-lipped persuasion;
Never, never shall he daunt me
    With the oath and threat of passion
    Into speaking as they want me,
    Till he loose this savage chain, 210
    And accept the expiation
    Of my sorrow, in his pain.

Chorus, 2d Antistrophe.

    Thou art, sooth, a brave god,
      And, for all thou hast borne
    From the stroke of the rod,
      Nought relaxest from scorn.
    But thou speakest unto me
      Too free and unworn;
    And a terror strikes through me

And festers my soul   220
And I fear, in the roll
Of the storm, for thy fate
In the ship far from shore :
Since the son of Saturnus is hard in his hate
And unmoved in his heart evermore.

Prometheus.   I know that Zeus is stern ;
I know he metes his justice by his will ;
And yet, his soul shall learn
More softness when once broken by this
    ill :
And curbing his unconquerable vaunt   230
He shall rush on in fear to meet with me
Who rush to meet with him in agony,
To issues of harmonious covenant.
    Chorus. Remove the veil from all things
     and relate
The story to us, — of what crime accused,
Zeus smites thee with dishonorable pangs.
Speak : if to teach us do not grieve thy-
    self.
    Prometheus. The utterance of these
     things is torture to me,
But so, too, is their silence ; each way lies
Woe strong as fate.
         When gods began with wrath,
And war rose up between their starry
    brows,   241
Some choosing to cast Chronos from his
    throne
That Zeus might king it there, and some
    in haste
With opposite oaths that they would have
    no Zeus
To rule the gods forever, — I, who brought
The counsel I thought meetest, could not
    move
The Titans, children of the Heaven and
    Earth,
What time, disdaining in their rugged souls
My subtle machinations, they assumed
It was an easy thing for force to take   250
The mastery of fate. My mother, then,
Who is called not only Themis but Earth
    too,
(Her single beauty joys in many names)
Did teach me with reiterant prophecy
What future should be, and how conquer-
    ing gods
Should not prevail by strength and vio-
    lence
But by guile only. When I told them so,
They would not deign to contemplate the
    truth

On all sides round ; whereat I deemed it
    best
To lead my willing mother upwardly   260
And set my Themis face to face with Zeus
As willing to receive her. Tartarus,
With its abysmal cloister of the Dark,
Because I gave that counsel, covers up
The antique Chronos and his siding hosts,
And, by that counsel helped, the king of
    gods
Hath recompensed me with these bitter
    pangs :
For kingship wears a cancer at the heart, —
Distrust in friendship. Do ye also ask
What crime it is for which he tortures
    me ?   270
That shall be clear before you. When at
    first
He filled his father's throne, he instantly
Made various gifts of glory to the gods
And dealt the empire out. Alone of men,
Of miserable men, he took no count,
But yearned to sweep their track off from
    the world
And plant a newer race there. Not a god
Resisted such desire except myself.
I dared it ! *I* drew mortals back to light
From meditated ruin deep as hell !   28
For which wrong, I am bent down in these
    pangs
Dreadful to suffer, mournful to behold,
And I, who pitied man, am thought my-
    self
Unworthy of pity ; while I render out
Deep rhythms of anguish 'neath the harping
    hand
That strikes me thus — a sight to sham
    your Zeus !
    Chorus. Hard as thy chains and cold a
     all these rocks
Is he, Prometheus, who withholds his hea
From joining in thy woe. I yearned befor
To fly this sight ; and, now I gaze o
    it,   29
I sicken inwards.
    Prometheus.   To my friends, indee
I must be a sad sight.
    Chorus.   And didst thou si
No more than so ?
    Prometheus.   I did restrain beside
My mortals from premeditating death.
    Chorus. How didst thou medicine th
     plague-fear of death ?
    Prometheus. I set blind Hopes to inhab
    in their house.

Chorus. By that gift thou didst help thy
  mortals well.
Prometheus. I gave them also fire.
Chorus.   And have they now,
Those creatures of a day, the red-eyed
  fire ?
Prometheus. They have: and shall learn
  by it many arts.   300
Chorus. And truly for such sins Zeus
  tortures thee
And will remit no anguish ? Is there
  set
No limit before thee to thine agony ?
Prometheus. No other: only what seems
  good to HIM.
Chorus. And how will it seem good ?
  what hope remains ?
Seest thou not that thou hast sinned ? But
  that thou hast sinned
It glads me not to speak of, and grieves
  thee:
Then let it pass from both, and seek thy-
  self
Some outlet from distress.
Prometheus.   It is in truth
An easy thing to stand aloof from pain 310
And lavish exhortation and advice
On one vexed sorely by it. I have known
All in prevision. By my choice, my
  choice,
  freely sinned — I will confess my sin —
And helping mortals, found my own de-
  spair.
I did not think indeed that I should pine
Beneath such pangs against such skyey
  rocks,
Doomed to this drear hill and no neighbor-
  ing
Of any life: but mourn not ye for griefs
I bear to-day: hear rather, drooping down
To the plain, how other woes creep on to
  me,   321
And learn the consummation of my doom.
Beseech you, nymphs, beseech you, grieve
  for me
Who now am grieving; for Grief walks the
  earth,
And sits down at the foot of each by
  turns.
Chorus. We hear the deep clash of thy
  words,
        Prometheus, and obey.
And I spring with a rapid foot away
From the rushing car and the holy air,
        The track of birds;   330

And I drop to the rugged ground and
  there
  Await the tale of thy despair.

OCEANUS *enters.*

Oceanus. I reach the bourn of my weary
  road,
  Where I may see and answer thee,
  Prometheus, in thine agony.
On the back of the quick-winged bird I
  glode,
  And I bridled him in
  With the will of a god.
Behold, thy sorrow aches in me
  Constrained by the force of kin.   340
Nay, though that tie were all undone,
For the life of none beneath the sun
Would I seek a larger benison
  Than I seek for thine.
And thou shalt learn my words are
  truth, —
That no fair parlance of the mouth
Grows falsely out of mine.
Now give me a deed to prove my faith;
For no faster friend is named in breath
  Than I, Oceanus, am thine.   350
Prometheus. Ha ! what has brought thee ?
  Hast thou also come
To look upon my woe ? How hast thou
  dared
To leave the depths called after thee, the
  caves
Self-hewn and self-roofed with spontaneous
  rock,
To visit earth, the mother of my chain ?
Hast come indeed to view my doom and
  mourn
That I should sorrow thus ? Gaze on, and
  see
How I, the fast friend of your Zeus, —
  how I
The erector of the empire in his hand,
Am bent beneath that hand, in this despair.
Oceanus. Prometheus, I behold: and I
  would fain   361
Exhort thee, though already subtle enough,
To a better wisdom. Titan, know thy-
  self,
And take new softness to thy manners
  since
A new king rules the gods. If words like
  these,
Harsh words and trenchant, thou wilt fling
  abroad,
Zeus haply, though he sit so far and high,

May hear thee do it, and so, this wrath of
    his
Which now affects thee fiercely, shall ap-
    pear
A mere child's sport at vengeance.
    Wretched god, 370
Rather dismiss the passion which thou
    hast,
And seek a change from grief. Perhaps I
    seem
To address thee with old saws and outworn
    sense, —
Yet such a curse, Prometheus, surely waits
On lips that speak too proudly : thou, mean-
    time,
Art none the meeker, nor dost yield a jot
To evil circumstance, preparing still
To swell the account of grief with other
    griefs
Than what are borne. Beseech thee, use
    me then
For counsel : do not spurn against the
    pricks, — 380
Seeing that who reigns, reigns by cruelty
Instead of right. And now, I go from
    hence,
And will endeavor if a power of mine
Can break thy fetters through. For thee,
    — be calm,
And smooth thy words from passion.
    Knowest thou not
Of perfect knowledge, thou who knowest
    too much,
That where the tongue wags, ruin never
    lags ?
    Prometheus. I gratulate thee who hast
    shared and dared
All things with me, except their penalty.
Enough so ! leave these thoughts. It can-
    not be 390
That thou shouldst move HIM. HE may *not*
    be moved;
And *thou*, beware of sorrow on this road.
    Oceanus. Ay ! ever wiser for another's
    use
Than thine ! the event, and not the pro-
    phecy,
Attests it to me. Yet where now I rush,
Thy wisdom hath no power to drag me
    back;
Because I glory, glory, to go hence
And win for thee deliverance from thy
    pangs,
As a free gift from Zeus.
    Prometheus. Why there, again,

I give thee gratulation and applause. 400
Thou lackest no goodwill. But, as for
    deeds,
Do nought ! 't were all done vainly; help-
    ing nought,
Whatever thou wouldst do. Rather take
    rest
And keep thyself from evil. If I grieve,
I do not therefore wish to multiply
The griefs of others. Verily, not so !
For still my brother's doom doth vex my
    soul, —
My brother Atlas, standing in the west,
Shouldering the column of the heaven and
    earth,
A difficult burden ! I have also seen, 410
And pitied as I saw, the earth-born one,
The inhabitant of old Cilician caves,
The great war-monster of the hundred
    heads,
(All taken and bowed beneath the violent
    Hand,)
Typhon the fierce, who did resist the
    gods,
And, hissing slaughter from his dreadful
    jaws,
Flash out ferocious glory from his eyes
As if to storm the throne of Zeus. Where-
    at,
The sleepless arrow of Zeus flew straight at
    him,
The headlong bolt of thunder breathing
    flame, 420
And struck him downward from his emi-
    nence
Of exultation; through the very soul
It struck him, and his strength was with-
    ered up
To ashes, thunder-blasted. Now he lies
A helpless trunk supinely, at full length
Beside the strait of ocean, spurred into
By roots of Ætna; high upon whose tops
Hephæstus sits and strikes the flashing
    ore.
From thence the rivers of fire shall burst
    away
Hereafter, and devour with savage jaws 43
The equal plains of fruitful Sicily,
Such passion he shall boil back in ho
    darts
Of an insatiate fury and sough of flame,
Fallen Typhon, — howsoever struck an
    charred
By Zeus's bolted thunder. But for thee,
Thou art not so unlearned as to need

My teaching — let thy knowledge save thy-
self.
I quaff the full cup of a present doom,
And wait till Zeus hath quenched his will in
wrath.
   Oceanus. Prometheus, art thou ignorant
    of this,   440
That words do medicine anger ?
   Prometheus.   If the word
With seasonable softness touch the soul
And, where the parts are ulcerous, sear
    them not
By any rudeness.
   Oceanus.   With a noble aim
To dare as nobly — is there harm in *that ?*
Dost thou discern it ?   Teach me.
   Prometheus.   I discern
Vain aspiration, unresultive work.
   Oceanus. Then suffer me to bear the
    brunt of this !
Since it is profitable that one who is wise
Should seem not wise at all.
   Prometheus.   And such would seem 450
My very crime.
   Oceanus.   In truth thine argument
Sends me back home.
   Prometheus.   Lest any lament for me
Should cast thee down to hate.
   Oceanus.   The hate of him
Who sits a new king on the absolute throne ?
   Prometheus. Beware of him, lest thine
    heart grieve by him.
   Oceanus. Thy doom, Prometheus, be my
    teacher !
   Prometheus.   Go.
Depart — beware — and keep the mind
    thou hast.
   Oceanus. Thy words drive after, as I rush
    before.
Lo ! my four-footed bird sweeps smooth
    and wide
The flats of air with balanced pinions,
    glad   460
To bend his knee at home in the ocean-
    stall.
              [OCEANUS *departs.*

      Chorus, 1st Strophe.

I moan thy fate, I moan for thee,
   Prometheus ! From my eyes too ten-
    der,
Drop after drop incessantly
   The tears of my heart's pity render
My cheeks wet from their fountains
   free;

Because that Zeus, the stern and cold,
   Whose law is taken from his breast,
   Uplifts his sceptre manifest
    Over the gods of old.   470

     1st Antistrophe.
  All the land is moaning
With a murmured plaint to-day;
  All the mortal nations
  Having habitations
  In the holy Asia
  Are a dirge entoning
For thine honor and thy brothers',
  Once majestic beyond others
   In the old belief, —
Now are groaning in the groaning   480
  Of thy deep-voiced grief.

     2d Strophe.
Mourn the maids inhabitant
  Of the Colchian land,
Who with white, calm bosoms stand
  In the battle's roar:
Mourn the Scythian tribes that haunt
The verge of earth, Mæotis' shore.

    2d Antistrophe.
Yea ! Arabia's battle-crown,
And dwellers in the beetling town
Mount Caucasus sublimely nears, — 490
An iron squadron, thundering down
  With the sharp-prowed spears.

But one other before, have I seen to re-
    main
   By invincible pain
Bound and vanquished, — one Titan ! 't was
    Atlas, who bears
In a curse from the gods, by that strength
    of his own
    Which he evermore wears,
The weight of the heaven on his shoulder
    alone,
    While he sighs up the stars;
And the tides of the ocean wail bursting their
    bars, —   500
    Murmurs still the profound,
And black Hades roars up through the
    chasm of the ground,
And the fountains of pure-running rivers
    moan low
    In a pathos of woe.

   Prometheus. Beseech you, think not I am
    silent thus

Through pride or scorn. I only gnaw my
      heart
With meditation, seeing myself so wronged.
For see — their honors to these new-made
      gods,
What other gave but I, and dealt them out
With distribution ?   Ay — but here I am
      dumb !   510
For here, I should repeat your knowledge
      to you,
If I spake aught.   List rather to the deeds
I did for mortals; how, being fools before,
I made them wise and true in aim of soul.
And let me tell you — not as taunting men,
But teaching you the intention of my gifts,
How, first beholding, they beheld in vain,
And hearing, heard not, but, like shapes in
      dreams,
Mixed all things wildly down the tedious
      time,
Nor knew to build a house against the
      sun   520
With wickered sides, nor any woodcraft
      knew,
But lived, like silly ants, beneath the
      ground
In hollow caves unsunned.   There, came to
      them
No steadfast sign of winter, nor of spring
Flower-perfumed, nor of summer full of
      fruit,
But blindly and lawlessly they did all
      things,
Until I taught them how the stars do rise
And set in mystery, and devised for them
Number, the inducer of philosophies,
The synthesis of Letters, and, beside,   530
The artificer of all things, Memory,
That sweet Muse-mother.   I was first to
      yoke
The servile beasts in couples, carrying
An heirdom of man's burdens on their backs.
I joined to chariots, steeds, that love the
      bit
They champ at — the chief pomp of golden
      ease.
And none but I originated ships,
The seaman's chariots, wandering on the
      brine
With linen wings.   And I — oh, miser-
      able ! —
Who did devise for mortals all these arts,
Have no device left now to save myself 541
From the woe I suffer.
      Chorus.   Most unseemly woe

Thou sufferest, and dost stagger from the
      sense
Bewildered ! like a bad leech falling sick
Thou art faint at soul, and canst not find
      the drugs
Required to save thyself.
      Prometheus.   Hearken the rest,
And marvel further, what more arts and
      means
I did invent, — this, greatest: if a man
Fell sick, there was no cure, nor esculent
Nor chrism nor liquid, but for lack of
      drugs   550
Men pined and wasted, till I showed them
      all
Those mixtures of emollient remedies
Whereby they might be rescued from dis-
      ease.
I fixed the various rules of mantic art,
Discerned the vision from the common
      dream,
Instructed them in vocal auguries
Hard to interpret, and defined as plain
The wayside omens, — flights of crook-
      clawed birds, —
Showed which are, by their nature, fortu-
      nate,
And which not so, and what the food of
      each,   560
And what the hates, affections, social needs,
Of all to one another, — taught what
      sign
Of visceral lightness, colored to a shade,
May charm the genial gods, and what fair
      spots
Commend the lung and liver.   Burning so
The limbs encased in fat, and the long
      chine,
I led my mortals on to an art abstruse,
And cleared their eyes to the image in the
      fire,
Erst filmed in dark.   Enough said now of
      this.
For the other helps of man hid under-
      ground,   570
The iron and the brass, silver and gold,
Can any dare affirm he found them out
Before me ? none, I know ! unless he
      choose
To lie in his vaunt.   In one word learn the
      whole, —
That all arts came to mortals from Prome-
      theus.
      Chorus.   Give mortals now no inexpedient
      help,

Neglecting thine own sorrow. I have hope
  still
To see thee, breaking from the fetter
  here,
Stand up as strong as Zeus.
  Prometheus.　　　　　This ends not thus,
The oracular fate ordains. I must be
  bowed　　　　　　　　　　　　580
By infinite woes and pangs, to escape this
  chain.
Necessity is stronger than mine art.
  Chorus. Who holds the helm of that Ne-
  cessity ?
  Prometheus. The threefold Fates and the
  unforgetting Furies.
  Chorus. Is Zeus less absolute than these
  are ?
  Prometheus.　　　　　　　　　Yea,
And therefore cannot fly what is or-
  dained.
  Chorus. What is ordained for Zeus, ex-
  cept to be
A king forever ?
  Prometheus.　　'T is too early yet
For thee to learn it: ask no more.
  Chorus　　　　　　　　　Perhaps
Thy secret may be something holy ?
  Prometheus.　　　　　　　　Turn
To another matter: this, it is not time　591
To speak abroad, but utterly to veil
In silence. For by that same secret kept,
I 'scape this chain's dishonor and its woe.

Chorus, 1st Strophe.

Never, oh never
May Zeus, the all-giver,
Wrestle down from his throne
In that might of his own
To antagonize mine !
Nor let me delay　　　　　　600
As I bend on my way
Toward the gods of the shrine
Where the altar is full
Of the blood of the bull,
Near the tossing brine
Of Ocean my father.
May no sin be sped in the word that is
  said,
But my vow be rather
  Consummated,
Nor evermore fail, nor evermore pine.　610

1st Antistrophe.

'T is sweet to have
Life lengthened out

With hopes proved brave
By the very doubt,
Till the spirit enfold
Those manifest joys which were foretold.
But I thrill to behold
Thee, victim doomed,
By the countless cares
And the drear despairs　　　　620
Forever consumed, —
And all because thou, who art fearless
  now
Of Zeus above,
Didst overflow for mankind below
With a free-souled, reverent love.
Ah friend, behold and see !
What 's all the beauty of humanity ?
  Can it be fair ?
What 's all the strength ? is it strong ?
  And what hope can they bear,　　630
These dying livers — living one day long ?
  Ah, seest thou not, my friend,
  How feeble and slow
  And like a dream, doth go
This poor blind manhood, drifted from its
  end ?
  And how no mortal wranglings can con-
  fuse
  The harmony of Zeus ?
Prometheus, I have learnt these things
From the sorrow in thy face.
  Another song did fold its wings　　640
Upon my lips in other days,
When round the bath and round the bed
The hymeneal chant instead
  I sang for thee, and smiled, —
And thou didst lead, with gifts and vows,
  Hesione, my father's child,
  To be thy wedded spouse.

Io *enters.*

Io. What land is this ? what people is
  here ?
And who is he that writhes, I see,
  In the rock-hung chain ?　　　650
Now what is the crime that hath brought
  thee to pain ?
Now what is the land — make answer free—
Which I wander through, in my wrong and
  fear ?
  Ah ! ah ! ah me !
The gad-fly stingeth to agony !
O Earth, keep off that phantasm pale
Of earth-born Argus ! — ah ! — I quail
  When my soul descries
That herdsman with the myriad eyes

Which seem, as he comes, one crafty
 eye.   660
Graves hide him not, though he should
 die,
But he doggeth me in my misery
From the roots of death, on high — on
 high —
And along the sands of the siding deep,
All famine-worn, he follows me,
And his waxen reed doth undersound
  The waters round
And giveth a measure that giveth sleep.

   Woe, woe, woe !
Where shall my weary course be done ? 670
What wouldst thou with me, Saturn's son ?
And in what have I sinned, that I should
 go
Thus yoked to grief by thine hand forever ?
  Ah ! ah ! dost vex me so
   That I madden and shiver
   Stung through with dread ?
  Flash the fire down to burn me !
  Heave the earth up to cover me !
Plunge me in the deep, with the salt waves
 over me,
  That the sea-beasts may be fed ! 680
  O king, do not spurn me
   In my prayer !
For this wandering, everlonger, ever-
 more,
   Hath overworn me,
 And I know not on what shore
 I may rest from my despair.

Chorus. Hearest thou what the ox-horned
  maiden saith ?
Prometheus. How could I choose but
  hearken what she saith,
The frenzied maiden ? — Inachus's child ? —
Who love-warms Zeus's heart, and now is
 lashed   690
By Herè's hate along the unending ways ?

Io. Who taught thee to articulate that
 name, —
  My father's ? · Speak to his child
  By grief and shame defiled !
Who art thou, victim, thou who dost ac-
 claim
Mine anguish in true words on the wide
 air,
And callest too by name the curse that came
  From Herè unaware,

To waste and pierce me with its maddening
 goad ?
  Ah — ah — I leap   700
With the pang of the hungry — I bound on
 the road —
  I am driven by my doom —
  I am overcome
By the wrath of an enemy strong and
 deep !
Are any of those who have tasted pain,
  Alas ! as wretched as I ?
Now tell me plain, doth aught remain
For my soul to endure beneath the sky ?
Is there any help to be holpen by ?
If knowledge be in thee, let it be said ! 710
  Cry aloud — cry
To the wandering, woeful maid !

Prometheus. Whatever thou wouldst learn
 I will declare, —
No riddle upon my lips, but such straight
 words
As friends should use to each other when
 they talk.
Thou seest Prometheus, who gave mortals
 fire.
 Io. O common Help of all men, known of
 all,
O miserable Prometheus, — for what cause
Dost thou endure thus ?
 Prometheus.   I have done with wail
For my own griefs, but lately.
 Io.   Wilt thou not 720
Vouchsafe the boon to me ?
 Prometheus.   Say what thou wilt,
For I vouchsafe all.
 Io.   Speak then, and reveal
Who shut thee in this chasm.
 Prometheus.   The will of Zeus,
The hand of his Hephæstus.
 Io.   And what crime
Dost expiate so ?
 Prometheus. Enough for thee I have told
In so much only.
 Io.   Nay, but show besides
The limit of my wandering, and the
 time
Which yet is lacking to fulfil my grief.
 Prometheus. Why, not to know were bet-
  ter than to know   729
For such as thou.
 Io.   Beseech thee, blind me not
To that which I must suffer.
 Prometheus.   If I do,
The reason is not that I grudge a boon.

Io. What reason, then, prevents thy
speaking out ?
Prometheus. No grudging ; but a fear to
break thine heart.
Io. Less care for me, I pray thee. Cer-
tainty
I count for advantage.
Prometheus. Thou wilt have it so,
And therefore I must speak. Now hear —
Chorus. Not yet.
Give half the guerdon my way. Let us learn
First, what the curse is that befell the
maid, —
Her own voice telling her own wasting
woes : 740
The sequence of that anguish shall await
The teaching of thy lips.
Prometheus. It doth behove
That thou, Maid Io, shouldst vouchsafe to
these
The grace they pray, — the more, because
they are called
Thy father's sisters : since to open out
And mourn out grief where it is possible
To draw a tear from the audience, is a work
That pays its own price well.
Io. I cannot choose
But trust you, nymphs, and tell you all ye
ask,
In clear words — though I sob amid my
speech 750
In speaking of the storm-curse sent from
Zeus,
And of my beauty, from what height it took
Its swoop on me, poor wretch ! left thus
deformed
And monstrous to your eyes. For evermore
Around my virgin-chamber, wandering went
The nightly visions which entreated me
With syllabled smooth sweetness. — 'Bless-
ed maid,
Why lengthen out thy maiden hours when
fate
Permits the noblest spousal in the world ?
When Zeus burns with the arrow of thy
love 760
And fain would touch thy beauty ? —
Maiden, thou
Despise not Zeus ! depart to Lerné's mead
That 's green around thy father's flocks and
stalls,
Until the passion of the heavenly Eye
Be quenched in sight.' Such dreams did all
night long
Constrain me — me, unhappy !—till I dared

To tell my father how they trod the dark
With visionary steps. Whereat he sent
His frequent heralds to the Pythian fane,
And also to Dodona, and inquired 770
How best, by act or speech, to please the
gods.
The same returning brought back oracles
Of doubtful sense, indefinite response,
Dark to interpret ; but at last there came
To Inachus an answer that was clear,
Thrown straight as any bolt, and spoken
out —
This — ' he should drive me from my home
and land,
And bid me wander to the extreme verge
Of all the earth — or, if he willed it not,
Should have a thunder with a fiery eye 780
Leap straight from Zeus to burn up all his
race
To the last root of it.' By which Loxian
word
Subdued, he drove me forth and shut me out,
He loth, me loth, — but Zeus's violent bit
Compelled him to the deed : when instantly
My body and soul were changèd and dis-
traught,
And, hornèd as ye see, and spurred along
By the fanged insect, with a maniac leap
I rushed on to Cenchrea's limpid stream
And Lerné's fountain-water. There, the 790
earth-born,
The herdsman Argus, most immitigable
Of wrath, did find me out, and track me out
With countless eyes set staring at my steps:
And though an unexpected sudden doom
Drew him from life, I, curse-tormented still,
Am driven from land to land before the
scourge
The gods hold o'er me. So thou hast heard
the past,
And if a bitter future thou canst tell,
Speak on. I charge thee, do not flatter me
Through pity, with false words; for, in my
mind, 800
Deceiving works more shame than tortur-
ing doth.

Chorus.

Ah ! silence here !
Nevermore, nevermore
Would I languish for
The stranger's word
To thrill in mine ear —
Nevermore for the wrong and the woe
and the fear

So hard to behold,
So cruel to bear,
Piercing my soul with a double-edged
sword   810
Of a sliding cold.
Ah Fate ! ah me !
I shudder to see
This wandering maid in her agony.

Prometheus. Grief is too quick in thee and
fear too full :
Be patient till thou hast learnt the rest.
Chorus.   Speak : teach.
To those who are sad already, it seems
sweet,
By clear foreknowledge to make perfect,
pain.
Prometheus. The boon ye asked me first
was lightly won, —
For first ye asked the story of this maid's
grief   820
As her own lips might tell it.   Now re-
mains
To list what other sorrows she so young
Must bear from Herè.   Inachus's child,
O thou ! drop down thy soul my weighty
words,
And measure out the landmarks which are
set
To end thy wandering.   Toward the orient
sun
First turn thy face from mine and journey
on
Along the desert flats till thou shalt come
Where Scythia's shepherd peoples dwell
aloft,
Perched in wheeled wagons under woven
roofs,   830
And twang the rapid arrow past the bow —
Approach them not; but siding in thy course
The rugged shore-rocks resonant to the sea,
Depart that country.   On the left hand
dwell
The iron-workers, called the Chalybes,
Of whom beware, for certes they are un-
couth
And nowise bland to strangers.   Reaching so
The stream Hybristes (well the *scorner*
called),
Attempt no passage, — it is hard to pass, —
Or ere thou come to Caucasus itself,   840
That highest of mountains, where the river
leaps
The precipice in his strength.   Thou must
toil up

Those mountain-tops that neighbor with
the stars,
And tread the south way, and draw near, at
last,
The Amazonian host that hateth man,
Inhabitants of Themiscyra, close
Upon Thermodon, where the sea's rough jaw
Doth gnash at Salmydessa and provide
A cruel host to seamen, and to ships   849
A stepdame.   They with unreluctant hand
Shall lead thee on and on, till thou arrive
Just where the ocean-gates show narrowest
On the Cimmerian isthmus.   Leaving which,
Behoves thee swim with fortitude of soul
The strait Mæotis.   Ay, and evermore
That traverse shall be famous on men's lips,
That strait, called Bosphorus, the horned
one's road,
So named because of thee, who so wilt go
From Europe's plain to Asia's continent.
How think ye, nymphs ? the king of gods
appears   860
Impartial in ferocious deeds ?   Behold !
The god desirous of this mortal's love
Hath cursed her with these wanderings.
Ah, fair child,
Thou hast met a bitter groom for bridal
troth !
For all thou yet hast heard can only prove
The incompleted prelude of thy doom.
Io. Ah, ah !
Prometheus. Is 't thy turn, now, to shriek
and moan ?
How wilt thou, when thou hast hearkened
what remains ?
Chorus. Besides the grief thou hast told
can aught remain ?
Prometheus. A sea — of foredoomed evil
worked to storm.   870
Io. What boots my life, then ? why not
cast myself
Down headlong from this miserable rock,
That, dashed against the flats, I may re-
deem
My soul from sorrow ?   Better once to die
Than day by day to suffer.
Prometheus.   Verily,
It would be hard for thee to bear my woe
For whom it is appointed not to die.
Death frees from woe: but I before me see
In all my far prevision not a bound
To all I suffer, ere that Zeus shall fall   880
From being a king.
Io.   And can it ever be
That Zeus shall fall from empire ?

Prometheus.   *Thou,* methinks,
Wouldst take some joy to see it.
   Io.   Could I choose ?
I who endure such pangs now, by that god !
   Prometheus. Learn from me, therefore,
      that the event shall be.
   Io. By whom shall his imperial sceptred
      hand
Be emptied so ?
   Prometheus. Himself shall spoil himself,
Through his idiotic counsels.
   Io.   How ? declare :
Unless the word bring evil.
   Prometheus.   He shall wed;
And in the marriage-bond be joined to
      grief.   890
   Io. A heavenly bride — or human ?
      Speak it out
If it be utterable.
   Prometheus. Why should I say which ?
It ought not to be uttered, verily.
   Io.   Then
It is his wife shall tear him from his throne ?
   Prometheus. It is his wife shall bear a son
      to him,
More mighty than the father.
   Io.   From this doom
Hath he no refuge ?
   Prometheus.   None: or ere that I,
Loosed from these fetters —
   Io.   Yea   but who shall loose
While Zeus is adverse ?
   Prometheus.   One who is born of thee:
It is ordained so.
   Io.   What is this thou sayest ?
A son of mine shall liberate thee from woe ?
   Prometheus. After ten generations, count
      three more,   902
And find him in the third.
   Io.   The oracle
Remains obscure.
   Prometheus. And search it not, to learn
Thine own griefs from it.
   Io.   Point me not to a good,
To leave me straight bereaved.
   Prometheus.   I am prepared
To grant thee one of two things.
   Io.   But which two ?
Set them before me; grant me power to
      choose.
   Prometheus. I grant it; choose now: shall
      I name aloud
What griefs remain to wound thee, or what
      hand   910
Shall save me out of mine ?

   Chorus.   Vouchsafe, O god,
The one grace of the twain to her who prays;
The next to me; and turn back neither
      prayer
Dishonor'd by denial. To herself
Recount the future wandering of her feet;
Then point me to the looser of thy chain,
Because I yearn to know him.
   Prometheus.   Since ye will,
Of absolute will, this knowledge, I will set
No contrary against it, nor keep back
A word of all ye ask for. Io, first   920
To thee I must relate thy wandering course
Far winding. As I tell it, write it down
In thy soul's book of memories. When
      thou hast past
The refluent bound that parts two conti-
      nents,
Track on the footsteps of the orient sun
In his own fire, across the roar of seas, —
Fly till thou hast reached the Gorgonæan
      flats
Beside Cisthené. There, the Phorcides,
Three ancient maidens, live, with shape of
      swan,
One tooth between them, and one common
      eye: 930
On whom the sun doth never look at all
With all his rays, nor evermore the moon
When she looks through the night. Anear
      to whom
Are the Gorgon sisters three, enclothed with
      wings,
With twisted snakes for ringlets, man-ab-
      horred:
There is no mortal gazes in their face
And gazing can breathe on. I speak of such
To guard thee from their horror. Ay, and
      list
Another tale of a dreadful sight; beware
The Griffins, those unbarking dogs of Zeus,
Those sharp-mouthed dogs ! — and the Ari-
      maspian host   941
Of one-eyed horsemen, habiting beside
The river of Pluto that runs bright with
      gold:
Approach them not, beseech thee ! Pre-
      sently
Thou 'lt come to a distant land, a dusky tribe
Of dwellers at the fountain of the Sun,
Whence flows the river Æthiops; wind along
Its banks and turn off at the cataracts,
Just as the Nile pours from the Bybline hills
His holy and sweet wave; his course shall
      guide   950

Thine own to that triangular Nile-ground
Where, Io, is ordained for thee and thine
A lengthened exile. Have I said in this
Aught darkly or incompletely ? — now re-
    peat
The question, make the knowledge fuller ! Lo,
I have more leisure than I covet, here.
    Chorus. If thou canst tell us aught that's
    left untold,
Or loosely told, of her most dreary flight,
Declare it straight: but if thou hast uttered
    all,
Grant us that latter grace for which we
    prayed, 960
Remembering how we prayed it.
    Prometheus.   She has heard
The uttermost of her wandering. There it
    ends.
But that she may be certain not to have
    heard
All vainly, I will speak what she endured
Ere coming hither, and invoke the past
To prove my prescience true. And so — to
    leave
A multitude of words and pass at once
To the subject of thy course — when thou
    hadst gone
To those Molossian plains which sweep
    around
Dodona shouldering Heaven, whereby the
    fane 970
Of Zeus Thesprotian keepeth oracle,
And, wonder past belief, where oaks do
    wave
Articulate adjurations — (ay, the same
Saluted thee in no perplexèd phrase
But clear with glory, noble wife of Zeus
That shouldst be, — there some sweetness
    took thy sense !)
Thou didst rush further onward, stung along
The ocean-shore, toward Rhea's mighty bay
And, tost back from it, wast tost to it again
In stormy evolution: — and, know well, 980
In coming time that hollow of the sea
Shall bear the name Ionian and present
A monument of Io's passage through
Unto all mortals. Be these words the signs
Of my soul's power to look beyond the veil
Of visible things. The rest, to you and her
I will declare in common audience, nymphs,
Returning thither where my speech brake
    off.
There is a town Canobus, built upon
The earth's fair margin at the mouth of Nile

And on the mound washed up by it; Io,
    there 991
Shall Zeus give back to thee thy perfect
    mind,
And only by the pressure and the touch
Of a hand not terrible; and thou to Zeus
Shalt bear a dusky son who shall be called
Thence, Epaphus, *Touched.* That son shall
    pluck the fruit
Of all that land wide-watered by the flow
Of Nile; but after him, when counting out
As far as the fifth full generation, then
Full fifty maidens, a fair woman-race, 1000
Shall back to Argos turn reluctantly,
To fly the proffered nuptials of their kin,
Their father's brothers. These being pas-
    sion-struck,
Like falcons bearing hard on flying doves,
Shall follow, hunting at a quarry of love
They should not hunt; till envious Heaven
    maintain
A curse betwixt that beauty and their de-
    sire,
And Greece receive them, to be overcome
In murtherous woman-war, by fierce red
    hands 1009
Kept savage by the night. For every wife
Shall slay a husband, dyeing deep in blood
The sword of a double edge — (I wish in-
    deed
As fair a marriage-joy to all my foes !)
One bride alone shall fail to smite to death
The head upon her pillow, touched with
    love,
Made impotent of purpose and impelled
To choose the lesser evil, — shame on her
    cheeks,
Than blood-guilt on her hands : which bride
    shall bear
A royal race in Argos. Tedious speech
Were needed to relate particulars 1020
Of these things; 't is enough that from her
    seed
Shall spring the strong He, famous with the
    bow,
Whose arm shall break my fetters off. Be-
    hold,
My mother Themis, that old Titaness,
Delivered to me such an oracle, —
But how and when, I should be long to
    speak,
And thou, in hearing, wouldst not gain at
    all.
    Io.   Eleleu, eleleu !
           How the spasm and the pain

And the fire on the brain   1030
   Strike, burning me through !
How the sting of the curse, all aflame as it
   flew,
   Pricks me onward again !
How my heart in its terror is spurning my
   breast,
And my eyes, like the wheels of a chariot,
   roll round !
I am whirled from my course, to the east,
   to the west,
In the whirlwind of frenzy all madly in-
   wound —
And my mouth is unbridled for anguish and
   hate,
And my words beat in vain, in wild storms
   of unrest,
   On the sea of my desolate fate.   1040
               [Io *rushes out.*

Chorus. — Strophe.

Oh, wise was he, oh, wise was he
Who first within his spirit knew
And with his tongue declared it true
That love comes best that comes unto
   The equal of degree !
And that the poor and that the low
Should seek no love from those above,
Whose souls are fluttered with the flow
Of airs about their golden height,
Or proud because they see arow   1050
   Ancestral crowns of light.

Antistrophe.

Oh, never, never may ye, Fates,
   Behold me with your awful eyes
   Lift mine too fondly up the skies
Where Zeus upon the purple waits !
   Nor let me step too near — too near
To any suitor, bright from heaven :
   Because I see, because I fear
This loveless maiden vexed and lad
By this fell curse of Herè, driven   1060
   On wanderings dread and drear.

Epode.

Nay, grant an equal troth instead
   Of nuptial love, to bind me by !
It will not hurt, I shall not dread
   To meet it in reply.
But let not love from those above
Revert and fix me, as I said,
   With that inevitable Eye !
I have no sword to fight that fight,
I have no strength to tread that path,
I know not if my nature hath   1071

The power to bear, I cannot see
Whither from Zeus's infinite
I have the power to flee.

Prometheus. Yet Zeus, albeit most abso-
   lute of will,
Shall turn to meekness, — such a marriage-
   rite
He holds in preparation, which anon
Shall thrust him headlong from his gerent
   seat
Adown the abysmal void, and so the curse
His father Chronos muttered in his fall, 1080
As he fell from his ancient throne and
   cursed,
Shall be accomplished wholly.   No escape
From all that ruin shall the filial Zeus
Find granted to him from any of his gods,
Unless I teach him.   I the refuge know,
And I, the means.   Now, therefore, let him sit
And brave the imminent doom, and fix his
   faith
On his supernal noises, hurtling on
With restless hand the bolt that breathes
   out fire;
For these things shall not help him, none
   of them,   1090
Nor hinder his perdition when he falls
To shame, and lower than patience: such a
   foe
He doth himself prepare against himself,
A wonder of unconquerable hate,
An organizer of sublimer fire
Than glares in lightnings, and of grander
   sound
Than aught the thunder rolls, out-thunder-
   ing it,
With power to shatter in Poseidon's fist
The trident-spear which, while it plagues
   the sea,
Doth shake the shores around it.   Ay, and
   Zeus,   1100
Precipitated thus, shall learn at length
The difference betwixt rule and servitude.
   Chorus. Thou makest threats for Zeus of
   thy desires.
   Prometheus. I tell you, all these things
   shall be fulfilled.
Even so as I desire them.
   Chorus.   Must we then
Look out for one shall come to master Zeus ?
   Prometheus. These chains weigh lighter
   than his sorrows shall.
   Chorus. How art thou not afraid to utter
   such words ?

Prometheus. What should *I* fear who cannot die ?

Chorus. But *he*
Can visit thee with dreader woe than death's.

Prometheus. Why, let him do it ! I am here, prepared   1111
For all things and their pangs.

Chorus. The wise are they
Who reverence Adrasteia.

Prometheus. Reverence thou,
Adore thou, flatter thou, whomever reigns,
Whenever reigning ! but for me, your Zeus
Is less than nothing. Let him act and reign
His brief hour out according to his will —
He will not, therefore, rule the gods too long.
But lo ! I see that courier-god of Zeus,
That new-made menial of the new-crowned king :   1120
He doubtless comes to announce to us something new.

HERMES *enters.*

Hermes. I speak to thee, the sophist, the talker-down
Of scorn by scorn, the sinner against gods,
The reverencer of men, the thief of fire, —
I speak to thee and adjure thee ! Zeus requires
Thy declaration of what marriage-rite
Thus moves thy vaunt and shall hereafter cause
His fall from empire. Do not wrap thy speech
In riddles, but speak clearly ! Never cast
Ambiguous paths, Prometheus, for my feet,
Since Zeus, thou mayst perceive, is scarcely won   1131
To mercy by such means.

Prometheus. A speech well-mouthed
In the utterance, and full-minded in the sense,
As doth befit a servant of the gods !
New gods, ye newly reign, and think forsooth
Ye dwell in towers too high for any dart
To carry a wound there ! — have I not stood by
While two kings fell from thence ? and shall I not
Behold the third, the same who rules you now,
Fall, shamed to sudden ruin ? — Do I seem
To tremble and quail before your modern gods ?   1141
Far be it from me ! — For thyself, depart,

Re-tread thy steps in haste. To all thou hast asked
I answer nothing.

Hermes. Such a wind of pride
Impelled thee of yore full-sail upon these rocks.

Prometheus. I would not barter — learn thou soothly that ! —
My suffering for thy service. I maintain
It is a nobler thing to serve these rocks
Than live a faithful slave to father Zeus.
Thus upon scorners I retort their scorn.   1150

Hermes. It seems that thou dost glory in thy despair.

Prometheus. I glory ? would my foes did glory so,
And I stood by to see them ! — naming whom,
Thou art not unremembered.

Hermes. Dost thou charge
Me also with the blame of thy mischance ?

Prometheus. I tell thee I loathe the universal gods,
Who for the good I gave them rendered back
The ill of their injustice.

Hermes. Thou art mad —
Thou art raving, Titan, at the fever-height.

Prometheus. If it be madness to abhor my foes,   1160
May I be mad !

Hermes. If thou wert prosperous
Thou wouldst be unendurable.

Prometheus. Alas !

Hermes. Zeus knows not that word.

Prometheus. But maturing Time
Teaches all things.

Hermes. Howbeit, thou hast not learnt
The wisdom yet, thou needest.

Prometheus. If I had,
I should not talk thus with a slave like thee.

Hermes. No answer thou vouchsafest, I believe,
To the great Sire's requirement.

Prometheus. Verily
I owe him grateful service, — and should pay it.

Hermes. Why, thou dost mock me, Titan, as I stood   1170
A child before thy face.

Prometheus. No child, forsooth,
But yet more foolish than a foolish child,
If thou expect that I should answer aught
Thy Zeus can ask. No torture from his hand
Nor any machination in the world

Shall force mine utterance ere he loose, him-
    self,
These cankerous fetters from me. For the
    rest,
Let him now hurl his blanching lightnings
    down,
And with his white-winged snows and mut-
    terings deep   1179
Of subterranean thunders mix all things,
Confound them in disorder. None of this
Shall bend my sturdy will and make me
    speak
The name of his dethroner who shall come.
    Hermes. Can this avail thee ? Look to it !
    Prometheus.   Long ago
It was looked forward to, precounselled of.
    Hermes. Vain god, take righteous cour-
    age ! dare for once
To apprehend and front thine agonies
With a just prudence.
    Prometheus.   Vainly dost thou chafe
My soul with exhortation, as yonder sea
Goes beating on the rock. Oh, think no
    more   1190
That I, fear-struck by Zeus to a woman's
    mind,
Will supplicate him, loathèd as he is,
With feminine upliftings of my hands,
To break these chains. Far from me be the
    thought !
    Hermes. I have indeed, methinks, said
    much in vain,
For still thy heart beneath my showers of
    prayers
Lies dry and hard — nay, leaps like a young
    horse
Who bites against the new bit in his teeth,
And tugs and struggles against the new-
    tried rein, —
Still fiercest in the feeblest thing of all, 1200
Which sophism is ; since absolute will dis-
    joined
From perfect mind is worse than weak.
    Behold,
Unless my words persuade thee, what a blast
And whirlwind of inevitable woe
Must sweep persuasion through thee ! For
    at first
The Father will split up this jut of rock
With the great thunder and the bolted
    flame
And hide thy body where a hinge of stone
Shall catch it like an arm; and when thou
    hast passed   1209
A long black time within, thou shalt come out

To front the sun while Zeus's wingèd hound,
The strong carnivorous eagle, shall wheel
    down
To meet thee, self-called to a daily feast,
And set his fierce beak in thee and tear off
The long rags of thy flesh and batten deep
Upon thy dusky liver. Do not look
For any end moreover to this curse
Or ere some god appear, to accept thy pangs
On his own head vicarious, and descend
With unreluctant step the darks of hell 1220
And gloomy abysses around Tartarus.
Then ponder this — this threat is not a
    growth
Of vain invention; it is spoken and meant;
King Zeus's mouth is impotent to lie,
Consummating the utterance by the act;
So, look to it, thou ! take heed, and never-
    more
Forget good counsel, to indulge self-will.
    Chorus. Our Hermes suits his reasons to
    the times;
At least I think so, since he bids thee
    drop
Self-will for prudent counsel. Yield to him!
When the wise err, their wisdom makes
    their shame.   1231
    Prometheus. Unto me the foreknower,
    this mandate of power
He cries, to reveal it.
What's strange in my fate, if I suffer from
    hate
At the hour that I feel it ?
Let the locks of the lightning, all bristling
    and whitening,
    Flash, coiling me round,
While the æther goes surging 'neath thun-
    der and scourging
    Of wild winds unbound !
Let the blast of the firmament whirl from its
    place   1240
    The earth rooted below,
And the brine of the ocean, in rapid emotion,
    Be driven in the face
Of the stars up in heaven, as they walk to
    and fro !
Let him hurl me anon into Tartarus — on —
    To the blackest degree,
With Necessity's vortices strangling me
    down;
But he cannot join death to a fate meant
    for *me !*
    Hermes. Why, the words that he speaks
    and the thoughts that he thinks
Are maniacal ! — add,   1250

If the Fate who hath bound him should
  loose not the links,
    He were utterly mad.
    Then depart ye who groan with him,
    Leaving to moan with him, —
Go in haste! lest the roar of the thunder
  anearing
Should blast you to idiocy, living and hear-
  ing.
    Chorus. Change thy speech for another,
    thy thought for a new,
  If to move me and teach me indeed be
    thy care!
For thy words swerve so far from the loyal
  and true
That the thunder of Zeus seems more easy
  to bear.   1260
How! couldst teach me to venture such
  vileness? behold!
I *choose*, with this victim, this anguish
  foretold!
I recoil from the traitor in hate and dis-
  dain,
And I know that the curse of the treason is
  worse
    Than the pang of the chain.
    Hermes. Then remember, O nymphs,
    what I tell you before,
Nor, when pierced by the arrows that Até
  will throw you,
Cast blame on your fate and declare ever-
  more
That Zeus thrust you on anguish he did
  not foreshow you.
Nay, verily, nay! for ye perish anon   1270
  For your deed — by your choice. By no
  blindness of doubt,
No abruptness of doom, but by madness
  alone,
  In the great net of Até, whence none com-
  eth out,
    Ye are wound and undone.
    Prometheus. Ay! in act now, in word now
    no more,
    Earth is rocking in space.
And the thunders crash up with a roar
  upon roar,
  And the eddying lightnings flash fire in
  my face,
And the whirlwinds are whirling the dust
  round and round,
And the blasts of the winds universal leap
  free   1280
And blow each upon each with a passion of
  sound,

And æther goes mingling in storm with
  the sea.
Such a curse on my head, in a manifest
  dread,
  From the hand of your Zeus has been
  hurtled along.
O my mother's fair glory! O Æther, en-
  ringing
All eyes with the sweet common light of
  thy bringing!
  Dost see how I suffer this wrong?

A LAMENT FOR ADONIS

FROM THE GREEK OF BION

I

I MOURN for Adonis — Adonis is dead,
  Fair Adonis is dead and the Loves are
  lamenting.
Sleep, Cypris, no more on thy purple-
  strewed bed:
  Arise, wretch stoled in black; beat thy
  breast unrelenting,
And shriek to the worlds, 'Fair Adonis is
  dead!'

II

I mourn for Adonis — the Loves are la-
  menting,
  He lies on the hills in his beauty and
  death;
The white tusk of a boar has transpierced
  his white thigh.
  Cytherea grows mad at his thin gasping
  breath,
While the black blood drips down on the
  pale ivory,   10
  And his eyeballs lie quenched with the
  weight of his brows,
The rose fades from his lips, and upon them
  just parted
  The kiss dies the goddess consents not
  to lose,
Though the kiss of the Dead cannot make
  her glad-hearted:
  He knows not who kisses him dead in the
  dews.

III

I mourn for Adonis — the Loves are la-
  menting.
  Deep, deep in the thigh is Adonis's
  wound,

But a deeper, is Cypris's bosom presenting.
  The youth lieth dead while his dogs howl
    around,
And the nymphs weep aloud from the
  mists of the hill,   20
    And the poor Aphrodité, with tresses un-
      bound,
All dishevelled, unsandaled, shrieks mourn-
    ful and shrill
  Through the dusk of the groves. The
    thorns, tearing her feet,
Gather up the red flower of her blood which
  is holy,
    Each footstep she takes; and the valleys
      repeat
The sharp cry she utters and draw it out
  slowly.
  She calls on her spouse, her Assyrian, on
    him
Her own youth, while the dark blood
  spreads over his body,
  The chest taking hue from the gash in
    the limb,   29
And the bosom, once ivory, turning to ruddy.

IV

Ah, ah, Cytherea! the Loves are lamenting.
  She lost her fair spouse and so lost her
    fair smile:
When he lived she was fair, by the whole
  world's consenting,
  Whose fairness is dead with him: woe
    worth the while!
All the mountains above and the oaklands
  below
  Murmur, ah, ah, Adonis! the streams
    overflow
Aphrodité's deep wail; river-fountains in
  pity
  Weep soft in the hills, and the flowers as
    they blow
Redden outward with sorrow, while all hear
  her go
  With the song of her sadness through
    mountain and city.   40

V

Ah, ah, Cytherea! Adonis is dead,
  Fair Adonis is dead — Echo answers,
    Adonis!
Who weeps not for Cypris, when bowing
  her head
  She stares at the wound where it gapes
    and astonies?
— When, ah, ah! — she saw how the blood
    ran away

And empurpled the thigh, and, with wild
  hands flung out,
Said with sobs: 'Stay, Adonis! unhappy
  one, stay,
  Let me feel thee once more, let me ring
    thee about
With the clasp of my arms, and press kiss
  into kiss!
  Wait a little, Adonis, and kiss me again,
For the last time, beloved, — and but so
  much of this   51
  That the kiss may learn life from the
    warmth of the strain!
— Till thy breath shall exude from thy soul
  to my mouth,
  To my heart, and, the love-charm I once
    more receiving
May drink thy love in it and keep of a
  truth
  That one kiss in the place of Adonis the
    living.
Thou fliest me, mournful one, fliest me far,
  My Adonis, and seekest the Acheron
    portal, —
To Hell's cruel King goest down with a scar,
  While I weep and live on like a wretched
    immortal,   60
And follow no step! O Persephoné, take
  him,
  My husband! — thou 'rt better and
    brighter than I,
So all beauty flows down to thee: *I* cannot
  make him
  Look up at my grief; there's despair in
    my cry,
Since I wail for Adonis who died to me —
  died to me —
  Then, I fear *thee!* — Art thou dead, my
    Adored?
Passion ends like a dream in the sleep
  that's denied to me,
  Cypris is widowed, the Loves seek their
    lord
All the house through in vain. Charm of
  cestus has ceased
  With thy clasp! O too bold in the hunt
    past preventing,   70
Ay, mad, thou so fair, to have strife with a
  beast!'
  Thus the goddess wailed on — and the
    Loves are lamenting.

VI

Ah, ah, Cytherea! Adonis is dead.
She wept tear after tear with the blood
  which was shed,

And both turned into flowers for the earth's garden-close,
Her tears, to the windflower; his blood, to the rose.

VII

I mourn for Adonis — Adonis is dead.
  Weep no more in the woods, Cytherea, thy lover !
So, well: make a place for his corse in thy bed,
  With the purples thou sleepest in, under and over.   80
He 's fair though a corse — a fair corse, like a sleeper.
  Lay him soft in the silks he had pleasure to fold
When, beside thee at night, holy dreams deep and deeper
  Enclosed his young life on the couch made of gold.
Love him still, poor Adonis; cast on him together
  The crowns and the flowers: since he died from the place,
Why, let all die with him; let the blossoms go wither,
  Rain myrtles and olive-buds down on his face.
Rain the myrrh down, let all that is best fall a-pining,
  Since the myrrh of his life from thy keeping is swept.   90
Pale he lay, thine Adonis, in purples reclining;
  The Loves raised their voices around him and wept.
They have shorn their bright curls off to cast on Adonis;
  One treads on his bow, — on his arrows, another, —
One breaks up a well-feathered quiver, and one is
  Bent low at a sandal, untying the strings,
And one carries the vases of gold from the springs,
  While one washes the wound, — and behind them a brother
  Fans down on the body sweet air with his wings.

VIII

Cytherea herself now the Loves are lamenting.   100
  Each torch at the door Hymenæus blew out;

And, the marriage-wreath dropping its leaves as repenting,
  No more 'Hymen, Hymen,' is chanted about,
But the *ai ai* instead — 'Ai alas !' is begun
  For Adonis, and then follows 'Ai Hymenæus !'
The Graces are weeping for Cinyris's son,
  Sobbing low each to each, ' His fair eyes cannot see us !'
Their wail strikes more shrill than the sadder Dioné's.
The Fates mourn aloud for Adonis, Adonis,
  Deep chanting; he hears not a word that they say: 110
  He *would* hear, but Persephoné has him in keeping.
— Cease moan, Cytherea ! leave pomps for to-day,
  And weep new when a new year refits thee for weeping.

SONG OF THE ROSE

ATTRIBUTED TO SAPPHO

FROM 'ACHILLES TATIUS'

IF Zeus chose us a King of the flowers in his mirth,
  He would call to the Rose and would royally crown it;
For the Rose, ho, the Rose ! is the grace of the earth,
  Is the light of the plants that are growing upon it:
For the Rose, ho, the Rose ! is the eye of the flowers,
  Is the blush of the meadows that feel themselves fair,
Is the lightning of beauty that strikes through the bowers
  On pale lovers who sit in the glow unaware.
Ho, the Rose breathes of love ! ho, the Rose lifts the cup
  To the red lips of Cypris invoked for a guest !
Ho, the Rose, having curled its sweet leaves for the world,
  Takes delight in the motion its petals keep up,
As they laugh to the wind as it laughs from the west !

FROM THEOCRITUS

THE CYCLOPS

(IDYL XI)

AND so an easier life our Cyclops drew,
The ancient Polyphemus, who in youth
Loved Galatea while the manhood grew
  Adown his cheeks and darkened round
    his mouth.
No jot he cared for apples, olives, roses;
  Love made him mad: the whole world
    was neglected,
The very sheep went backward to their
    closes
  From out the fair green pastures, self-
    directed,
And singing Galatea, thus, he wore
The sunrise down along the weedy shore, 10
  And pined alone, and felt the cruel
    wound
Beneath his heart, which Cypris' arrow
    bore,
  With a deep pang; but, so, the cure was
    found;
And sitting on a lofty rock he cast
His eyes upon the sea, and sang at last: —
' O whitest Galatea, can it be
  That thou shouldst spurn me off who love
    thee so ?
More white than curds, my girl, thou art to
    see,
More meek than lambs, more full of leaping
    glee
  Than kids, and brighter than the early
    glow 20
On grapes that swell to ripen, — sour like
    thee !
Thou comest to me with the fragrant
    sleep,
  And with the fragrant sleep thou goest
    from me;
Thou fliest . . . fliest, as a frightened
    sheep
  Flies the gray wolf ! — yet Love did over-
    come me,
So long, — I loved thee, maiden, first of
    all
  When down the hills (my mother fast
    beside thee)
I saw thee stray to pluck the summer-
    fall
  Of hyacinth bells, and went myself to
    guide thee:

And since my eyes have seen thee, they can
    leave thee 30
No more, from that day's light ! But thou
    . . . by Zeus,
Thou wilt not care for *that*, to let it grieve
    thee !
  I know thee, fair one, why thou springest
    loose
From my arm round thee. Why ? I tell
    thee, Dear !
  One shaggy eyebrow draws its smudging
    road
Straight through my ample front, from ear
    to ear, —
  One eye rolls underneath; and yawning,
    broad
Flat nostrils feel the bulging lips too near.
Yet . . . ho, ho ! — I, — whatever I ap-
    pear, —
  Do feed a thousand oxen ! When I have
    done, 40
I milk the cows, and drink the milk that 's
    best !
  I lack no cheese, while summer keeps the
    sun;
And after, in the cold, it 's ready prest !
  And then, I know to sing, as there is none
Of all the Cyclops can, . . . a song of thee,
Sweet apple of my soul, on love's fair tree,
And of myself who love thee . . . till the
    West
Forgets the light, and all but I have rest.
I feed for thee, besides, eleven fair does,
  And all in fawn; and four tame whelps
    of bears. 50
Come to me, Sweet ! thou shalt have all of
    those
  In change for love ! I will not halve the
    shares.
Leave the blue sea, with pure white arms
    extended
  To the dry shore; and, in my cave's re-
    cess,
Thou shalt be gladder for the noonlight
    ended, —
  For here be laurels, spiral cypresses,
Dark ivy, and a vine whose leaves enfold
Most luscious grapes; and here is water
    cold,
  The wooded Ætna pours down through
    the trees
From the white snows, — which gods were
    scarce too bold 60
  To drink in turn with nectar. Who with
    these

Would choose the salt wave of the luke-
    warm seas ?
Nay, look on me ! If I am hairy and
    rough,
  I have an oak's heart in me; there's a
    fire
In these gray ashes which burns hot
    enough;
  And when I burn for *thee*, I grudge the
    pyre
No fuel . . . not my soul, nor this one
    eye, —
Most precious thing I have, because
    thereby
I see thee, Fairest ! Out, alas ! I wish
My mother had borne me finnèd like a
    fish,   70
That I might plunge down in the ocean near
    thee,
  And kiss thy glittering hand between the
    weeds,
If still thy face were turned; and I would
    bear thee
  Each lily white, and poppy fair that
    bleeds
Its red heart down its leaves ! — one gift,
    for hours
  Of summer, — one, for winter; since, to
    cheer thee,
I could not bring at once all kinds of flow-
    ers.
Even now, girl, now, I fain would learn to
    swim,
  If stranger in a ship sailed nigh, I
    wis, —
That I may know how sweet a thing it is
To live down with you in the Deep and
    Dim !   81
Come up, O Galatea, from the ocean,
  And, having come, forget again to go !
As I, who sing out here my heart's emo-
    tion,
  Could sit for ever. Come up from be-
    low !
Come, keep my flocks beside me, milk my
    kine, —
  Come, press my cheese, distrain my whey
    and curd !
Ah, mother ! she alone . . . that mother
    of mine . . .
  Did wrong me sore ! I blame her ! —
    Not a word
Of kindly intercession did she address   90
Thine ear with for my sake; and ne'erthe-
    less

She saw me wasting, wasting, day by
    day:
  Both head and feet were aching, I will
    say,
All sick for grief, as I myself was sick.
  O Cyclops, Cyclops, whither hast thou
    sent
Thy soul on fluttering wings ? If thou
    wert bent
On turning bowls, or pulling green and
    thick
  The sprouts to give thy lambkins, — thou
    wouldst make thee
A wiser Cyclops than for what we take
    thee.
Milk dry the present ! Why pursue too
    quick   100
That future which is fugitive aright ?
  Thy Galatea thou shalt haply find, —
  Or else a maiden fairer and more kind;
For many girls do call me through the
    night,
  And, as they call, do laugh out silverly.
I, too, am something in the world, I
    see !'

While thus the Cyclops love and lambs did
    fold,
Ease came with song he could not buy with
    gold.

FROM APULEIUS

PSYCHE GAZING ON CUPID

(Metamorph., Lib. IV.)

Then Psyche, weak in body and soul, put
    on
The cruelty of Fate, in place of strength:
She raised the lamp to see what should be
    done,
  And seized the steel, and was a man at
    length
In courage, though a woman ! Yes, but
    when
  The light fell on the bed whereby she
    stood
To view the '*beast*' that lay there, —
    certes, then,
  She saw the gentlest, sweetest beast in
    wood —
Even Cupid's self, the beauteous god !
    more beauteous

For that sweet sleep across his eyelids
dim,
The light, the lady carried as she viewed,
Did blush for pleasure as it lighted
him,
The dagger trembled from its aim undute-
ous;
And *she* . . . oh, *she* — amazed and soul-
distraught,
And fainting in her whiteness like a veil,
Slid down upon her knees, and, shudder-
ing, thought
To hide — though in her heart — the
dagger pale !
She would have done it, but her hands did
fail
To hold the guilty steel, they shivered
so, —
And feeble, exhausted, unawares she took
To gazing on the god, — till, look by look,
Her eyes with larger life did fill and
glow.
She saw his golden head alight with
curls, —
She might have guessed their brightness
in the dark
By that ambrosial smell of heavenly
mark !
She saw the milky brow, more pure than
pearls,
The purple of the cheeks, divinely sun-
dered
By the globed ringlets, as they glided
free,
Some back, some forwards, — all so radi-
antly,
That, as she watched them there, she
never wondered
To see the lamplight, where it touched
them, tremble:
On the god's shoulders, too, she marked
his wings
Shine faintly at the edges and resemble
A flower that 's near to blow. The poet
sings
And lover sighs, that Love is fugitive;
And certes, though these pinions lay re-
posing,
The feathers on them seemed to stir and
live
As if by instinct, closing and unclosing.
Meantime the god's fair body slumbered
deep,
All worthy of Venus, in his shining
sleep;

While at the bed's foot lay the quiver,
bow,
And darts, — his arms of godhead. Psyche
gazed
With eyes that drank the wonders in, —
said, — 'Lo,
Be these my husband's arms ? ' — and
straightway raised
An arrow from the quiver-case, and
tried
Its point against her finger, — trembling
till
She pushed it in too deeply (foolish
bride !)
And made her blood some dewdrops small
distil,
And learnt to love Love, of her own good-
will.

PSYCHE WAFTED BY ZEPHYRUS

(Metamorph., Lib. IV.)

While Psyche wept upon the rock forsa-
ken,
Alone, despairing, dreading, — gradu-
ally
By Zephyrus she was enwrapt and taken
Still trembling, — like the lilies planted
high, —
Through all her fair white limbs. Her
vesture spread,
Her very bosom eddying with sur-
prise, —
He drew her slowly from the mountain-
head,
And bore her down the valleys with wet
eyes,
And laid her in the lap of a green dell
As soft with grass and flowers as any
nest,
With trees beside her, and a limpid well:
Yet Love was not far off from all that
Rest.

PSYCHE AND PAN

(Metamorph., Lib. V.)

The gentle River, in her Cupid's honor,
Because he used to warm the very wave,
Did ripple aside, instead of closing on
her,

And cast up Psyche, with a refluence
 brave,
Upon the flowery bank, — all sad and sin-
 ning.
Then Pan, the rural god, by chance was
 leaning
 Along the brow of waters as they wound,
 Kissing the reed-nymph till she sank to
 ground,
And teaching, without knowledge of the
 meaning,
 To run her voice in music after his
Down many a shifting note; (the goats
 around,
 In wandering pasture and most leaping
 bliss,
Drawn on to crop the river's flowery
 hair).
And as the hoary god beheld her there,
 The poor, worn, fainting Psyche ! —
 knowing all
 The grief she suffered, he did gently
 call
Her name, and softly comfort her de-
 spair: —

' O wise, fair lady, I am rough and rude
And yet experienced through my weary
 age !
 And if I read aright, as soothsayer
 should,
Thy faltering steps of heavy pilgrimage,
Thy paleness, deep as snow we cannot see
The roses through, — thy sighs of quick
 returning,
Thine eyes that seem, themselves, two souls
 in mourning, —
 Thou lovest, girl, too well, and bitterly !
But hear me: rush no more to a headlong
 fall:
 Seek no more deaths ! leave wail, lay
 sorrow down,
And pray the sovran god; and use withal
 Such prayer as best may suit a tender
 youth,
Well-pleased to bend to flatteries from thy
 mouth,
 And feel them stir the myrtle of his
 crown.'

— So spake the shepherd-god; and an-
 swer none
Gave Psyche in return: but silently
She did him homage with a bended knee,
And took the onward path. —

PSYCHE PROPITIATING CERES

(METAMORPH., LIB. VI.)

THEN mother Ceres from afar beheld her,
 While Psyche touched, with reverent
 fingers meek,
The temple's scythes; and with a cry com-
 pelled her: —
 ' O wretched Psyche, Venus roams to
 seek
Thy wandering footsteps round the weary
 earth,
Anxious and maddened, and adjures thee
 forth
 To accept the imputed pang, and let her
 wreak
Full vengeance with full force of deity !
 Yet *thou*, forsooth, art in my temple
 here,
Touching my scythes, assuming my degree,
 And daring to have thoughts that are not
 fear ! '
— But Psyche clung to her feet, and as
 they moved
 Rained tears along their track, tear
 dropped on tear,
And drew the dust on in her trailing locks,
 And still, with passionate prayer, the
 charge disproved : —
' Now, by thy right hand's gathering from
 the shocks
Of golden corn, — and by thy gladsome
 rites
Of harvest, — and thy consecrated sights
Shut safe and mute in chests, — and by the
 course
Of thy slave-dragons, — and the driving
 force
Of ploughs along Sicilian glebes pro-
 found, —
By thy swift chariot, — by thy steadfast
 ground, —
By all those nuptial torches that departed
 With thy lost daughter, — and by those
 that shone
Back with her, when she came again glad-
 hearted, —
 And by all other mysteries which are
 done
In silence at Eleusis, — I beseech thee,
 O Ceres, take some pity, and abstain
 From giving to my soul extremer pain
Who am the wretched Psyche ! Let me
 teach thee

A little mercy, and have thy leave to
spend
A few days only in thy garnered corn,
 Until that wrathful goddess, at the end,
Shall feel her hate grow mild the longer
 borne, —
Or till, alas ! — this faintness at my breast
Pass from me, and my spirit apprehend
From life-long woe a breath-time hour of
 rest !'
 But Ceres answered ' I am moved indeed
 By prayers so moist with tears, and
 would defend
The poor beseecher from more utter need:
 But where old oaths, anterior ties, com-
 mend,
I cannot fail to a sister, lie to a friend,
As Venus is to *me*.   Depart with speed !'

PSYCHE AND THE EAGLE

(METAMORPH., LIB. VI.)

BUT sovran Jove's rapacious Bird, the regal
High percher on the lightning, the great
 eagle,
Drove down with rushing wings; and, —
 thinking how,
By Cupid's help, he bore from Ida's brow
A cup-boy for his master, — he inclined
To yield, in just return, an influence kind;
The god being honored in his lady's woe.
And thus the Bird wheeled downward from
 the track,
Gods follow gods in, to the level low
Of that poor face of Psyche left in wrack.
— 'Now fie, thou simple girl !' the Bird
 began;
' For if thou think to steal and carry back
A drop of holiest stream that ever ran,
No simpler thought, methinks, were found
 in man.
What ! know'st thou not these Stygian
 waters be
Most holy, even to Jove ? that as, on earth,
Men swear by gods, and by the thunder's
 worth,
Even so the heavenly gods do utter forth
Their oaths by Styx's flowing majesty ?
And yet, one little urnful, I agree
To grant thy need !' Whereat, all has-
 tily,
He takes it, fills it from the willing wave,
And bears it in his beak, incarnadined

By the last Titan-prey he screamed to
 have;
And, striking calmly out, against the wind,
Vast wings on each side, — there, where
 Psyche stands,
He drops the urn down in her lifted hands.

PSYCHE AND CERBERUS

(METAMORPH., LIB. VI.)

A MIGHTY dog with three colossal necks,
 And heads in grand proportion; vast as
 fear,
With jaws that bark the thunder out that
 breaks
 In most innocuous dread for ghosts anear,
Who are safe in death from sorrow: he re-
 clines
Across the threshold of queen Proserpine's
Dark-sweeping halls, and, there, for Pluto's
 spouse,
Doth guard the entrance of the empty
 house.
When Psyche threw the cake to him, once
 again
He howled up wildly from his hunger-pain,
And was still, after. —

PSYCHE AND PROSERPINE

(METAMORPH., LIB. VI.)

THEN Psyche entered in to Proserpine
In the dark house, and straightway did de-
 cline
With meek denial the luxurious seat,
 The liberal board for welcome strangers
 spread,
But sat down lowly at the dark queen's
 feet,
 And told her tale, and brake her oaten
 bread.
And when she had given the pyx in humble
 duty,
 And told how Venus did entreat the
 queen
To fill it up with only one day's beauty
 She used in Hades, star-bright and
 serene,
To beautify the Cyprian, who had been
 All spoilt with grief in nursing her sick
 boy, —

Then Proserpine, in malice and in joy,
  Smiled in the shade and took the pyx,
    and put
A secret in it; and so, filled and shut,
Gave it again to Psyche. Could she tell
It held no beauty, but a dream of hell?

PSYCHE AND VENUS

(METAMORPH., LIB. VI.)

AND Psyche brought to Venus what was
    sent
By Pluto's spouse; the paler, that she went
So low to seek it, down the dark descent.

MERCURY CARRIES PSYCHE TO OLYMPUS

(METAMORPH., LIB. VI.)

THEN Jove commanded the god Mercury
To float up Psyche from the earth. And
    she
Sprang at the first word, as the fountain
    springs,
And shot up bright and rustling through
    his wings.

MARRIAGE OF PSYCHE AND CUPID

(METAMORPH., LIB. VI.)

AND Jove's right hand approached the
    ambrosial bowl
  To Psyche's lips, that scarce dared yet
    to smile, —
'Drink, O my daughter, and acquaint thy
    soul
  With deathless uses, and be glad the
    while!
No more shall Cupid leave thy lovely side;
  Thy marriage-joy begins for never-end-
    ing.'
While yet he spake, — the nuptial feast
    supplied, —
  The bridegroom on the festive couch
    was bending
O'er Psyche in his bosom — Jove; the
    same,
  On Juno, and the other deities,

Alike ranged round. The rural cup-boy
    came
  And poured Jove's nectar out with shin-
    ing eyes,
While Bacchus, for the others, did as much,
  And Vulcan spread the meal; and all
    the Hours
Made all things purple with a sprinkle
    of flowers,
Or roses chiefly, not to say the touch
  Of their sweet fingers; and the Graces
    glided
Their balm around, and the Muses, through
    the air,
  Struck out clear voices, which were still
    divided
By that divinest song Apollo there
  Intoned to his lute; while Aphroditè fair
Did float her beauty along the tune, and
    play
  The notes right with her feet. And
    thus, the day
Through every perfect mood of joy was
    carried.
  The Muses sang their chorus; Satyrus
Did blow his pipes; Pan touched his reed;
  — and thus
At last were Cupid and his Psyche married.

FROM NONNUS

HOW BACCHUS FINDS ARIADNE SLEEPING

(DIONYSIACA, LIB. XLVII.)

WHEN Bacchus first beheld the desolate
And sleeping Ariadne, wonder straight
Was mixed with love in his great golden
    eyes;
He turned to his Bacchantes in surprise,
And said with guarded voice, — 'Hush!
    strike no more
  Your brazen cymbals; keep those voices
    still
Of voice and pipe; and since ye stand
    before
  Queen Cypris, let her slumber as she
    will!
And yet the cestus is not here in proof.
A Grace, perhaps, whom sleep has stolen
    aloof: 10
In which case, as the morning shines in
    view,

Wake this Aglaia ! — yet in Naxos, who
Would veil a Grace so ? Hush ! And if
   that she
Were Hebe, which of all the gods can be
The pourer-out of wine ? or if we think
She 's like the shining moon by ocean's
   brink,
The guide of herds, — why, could she sleep
   without
Endymion's breath on her cheek ? or if I
   doubt
Of silver-footed Thetis, used to tread
These shores, — even *she* (in reverence be
   it said)   20
Has no such rosy beauty to dress deep
   With the blue waves.   The Loxian god-
   dess might
Repose so from her hunting-toil aright
Beside the sea, since toil gives birth to
   sleep,
   But who would find her with her tunic
   loose,
Thus ?   Stand off, Thracian ! stand off !
   Do not leap,
   Not this way !   Leave that piping, since
   I choose,
O dearest Pan, and let Athenè rest !
And yet if she be Pallas . . . truly
   guessed . . .
Her lance is — where ? her helm and ægis
   — where ? '   30
— As Bacchus closed, the miserable Fair
   Awoke at last, sprang upward from the
   sands,
   And gazing wild on that wild throng that
   stands
Around, around her, and no Theseus
   there ! —
Her voice went moaning over shore and
   sea,
   Beside the halcyon's cry; she called her
   love;
She named her hero, and raged madden-
   ingly
   Against the brine of waters; and, above,
Sought the ship's track, and cursed the
   hours she slept;
And still the chiefest execration swept   40
Against queen Paphia, mother of the ocean;
And cursed and prayed by times in her
   emotion
The winds all round. . . .

. . . .

Her grief did make her glorious; her de-
   spair

Adorned her with its weight.   Poor wail-
   ing child !
She looked like Venus when the goddess
   smiled
At liberty of godship, debonair;
Poor Ariadne ! and her eyelids fair
Hid looks beneath them lent her by Per-
   suasion.
And every Grace, with tears of Love's own
   passion   50
She wept long; then she spake: — 'Sweet
   sleep did come
While sweetest Theseus went.   Oh, glad
   and dumb,
I wish he had left me still ! for in my sleep
I saw his Athens, and did gladly keep
My new bride-state within my Theseus'
   hall;
And heard the pomp of Hymen, and the
   call
Of " Ariadne, Ariadne," sung
In choral joy; and there, with joy I hung
Spring-blossoms round love's altar ! — ay,
   and wore
A wreath myself; and felt *him* evermore 60
Oh, evermore beside me, with his mighty
Grave head bowed down in prayer to
   Aphroditè !
Why, what a sweet, sweet dream ! *He*
   went with it,
And left me here unwedded where I sit !
Persuasion help me ! The dark night did
   make me
A brideship, the fair morning takes away;
My Love had left me when the Hour did
   wake me;
   And while I dreamed of marriage, as I
   say,
And blest it well, my blessèd Theseus left
   me:
And thus the sleep, I loved so, has bereft
   me.   70
Speak to me, rocks, and tell my grief to-
   day,
Who stole my love of Athens ? ' . . .

HOW BACCHUS COMFORTS
ARIADNE

(DIONYSIACA, LIB. XLVII.)

THEN Bacchus' subtle speech her sorrow
   crossed: —
'O maiden, dost thou mourn for having
   lost

The false Athenian heart ? and dost thou still
Take thought of Theseus, when thou mayst at will
Have Bacchus for a husband ? Bacchus bright !
A god in place of mortal ! Yes, and though
The mortal youth be charming in thy sight,
That man of Athens cannot strive below,
In beauty and valor, with my deity !
Thou 'lt tell me of the labyrinthine dweller,   10
The fierce man-bull he slew: I pray thee, be,
Fair Ariadne, the true deed's true teller,
And mention thy clue's help ! because, forsooth,
Thine armed Athenian hero had not found
A power to fight on that prodigious ground,
Unless a lady in her rosy youth
Had lingered near him: not to speak the truth
Too definitely out till names be known —
Like Paphia's — Love's — and Ariadne's own.
Thou wilt not say that Athens can compare
With Æther, nor that Minos rules like Zeus,   21
Nor yet that Gnossus has such golden air
As high Olympus. Ha ! for noble use
We came to Naxos ! Love has well intended
To change thy bridegroom ! Happy thou, defended
From entering in thy Theseus' earthly hall,
That thou mayst hear the laughters rise and fall
Instead, where Bacchus rules ! Or wilt thou choose
A still-surpassing glory ? — take it all, —
A heavenly house, Kronion's self for kin, —
A place where Cassiopea sits within   31
Inferior light, for all her daughter's sake,
Since Perseus, even amid the stars, must take
Andromeda in chains æthereal !
But *I* will wreathe *thee*, sweet, an astral crown,

And as my queen and spouse thou shalt be known —
Mine, the crown-lover's ! ' Thus, at length, he proved
His comfort on her; and the maid was moved;
And casting Theseus' memory down the brine,
She straight received the troth of her divine
Fair Bacchus; Love stood by to close the rite;   41
The marriage-chorus struck up clear and light,
Flowers sprouted fast about the chamber green,
And with spring-garlands on their heads, I ween,
The Orchomenian dancers came along
And danced their rounds in Naxos to the song.
A Hamadryad sang a nuptial dit
Right shrilly: and a Naiad sat beside   48
A fountain, with her bare foot shelving it,
And hymned of Ariadne, beauteous bride,
Whom thus the god of grapes had deified.
Ortygia sang out, louder than her wont,
An ode which Phœbus gave her to be tried,
And leapt in chorus, with her steadfast front,
While prophet Love, the stars have called a brother,
Burnt in his crown, and twined in one another
His love-flower with the purple roses, given
In type of that new crown assigned in heaven.

FROM HESIOD

BACCHUS AND ARIADNE

(Theog. 947.)

THE golden-hairèd Bacchus did espouse
That fairest Ariadne, Minos' daughter,
And made her wifehood blossom in the house;
Where such protective gifts Kronion brought her,
Nor Death nor Age could find her when they sought her.

FROM EURIPIDES

AURORA AND TITHONUS

(TROADES, ANTISTROPHE, 853)

LOVE, Love, who once didst pass the Dardan
  portals,
Because of Heavenly passion !
Who once didst lift up Troy in exulta-
  tion,
To mingle in thy bond the high Im-
  mortals ! —
Love, turned from his own name
  To Zeus's shame,
  Can help no more at all.
And Eos' self, the fair, white-steeded
  Morning, —
Her light which blesses other lands, return-
  ing,
Has changed to a gloomy pall !
She looked across the land with eyes of
  amber, —
  She saw the city's fall, —
  She who, in pure embraces,
Had held there, in the hymeneal cham-
  ber,
Her children's father, bright Tithonus old,
Whom the four steeds with starry brows
  and paces
Bore on, snatched upward, on the car of
  gold,
And with him, all the land's full hope of
  joy !
The love-charms of the gods are vain for
  Troy.

FROM HOMER

HECTOR AND ANDROMACHE

(ILIAD, LIB. VI.)

SHE rushed to meet him: the nurse follow-
  ing
Bore on her bosom the unsaddened child,
A simple babe, prince Hector's well-loved
  son,
Like a star shining when the world is dark.
Scamandrius, Hector called him; but the
  rest
Named him Astyanax, the city's prince,
Because that Hector only had saved Troy.
He, when he saw his son, smiled silently;

While, dropping tears, Andromache
  pressed on,
And clung to his hand, and spake, and
  named his name.   10

'Hector, my best one, — thine own noble-
  ness
Must needs undo thee. Pity hast thou none
For this young child, and this most sad
  myself,
Who soon shall be thy widow — since
  that soon
The Greeks will slay thee in the general
  rush —
And then, for me, what refuge, 'reft of *thee*,
But to go graveward ?   Then, no comfort
  more
Shall touch me, as in the old sad times thou
  know'st —
Grief only — grief ! I have no father now,
No mother mild ! Achilles the divine,   20
He slew my father, sacked his lofty Thebes,
Cilicia's populous city, and slew its king,
Eëtion — father ! — did not spoil the corse,
Because the Greek revered him in his soul,
But burnt the body with its dædal arms,
And poured the dust out gently. Round
  that tomb
The Oreads, daughters of the goat-nursed
  Zeus,
Tripped in a ring, and planted their green
  elms.
There were seven brothers with me in the
  house,
Who all went down to Hades in one day, —
For *he* slew all, Achilles the divine,   31
Famed for his swift feet, — slain among
  their herds
Of cloven-footed bulls and flocking sheep !
My mother too, who queened it o'er the
  woods
Of Hippoplacia, he, with other spoil,
Seized, — and, for golden ransom, freed too
  late, —
Since, as she went home, arrowy Artemis
Met her and slew her at my father's door.
But — oh my Hector, — thou art still to me
Father and mother ! — yes, and brother
  dear,
O thou, who art my sweetest spouse be-
  side !   40
Come now, and take me into pity ! Stay
I' the town here with us ! Do not make
  thy child
An orphan, nor a widow thy poor wife !

Call up the people to the fig-tree, where
The city is most accessible, the wall
Most easy of assault ! — for thrice thereby
The boldest Greeks have mounted to the
breach, —
Both Ajaxes, the famed Idomeneus,
Two sons of Atreus, and the noble one   50
Of Tydeus, — whether taught by some
wise seer,
Or by their own souls prompted and in-
spired.'

Great Hector answered: — 'Lady, for these
things
It is my part to care.   And *I* fear most
My Trojans, and their daughters, and their
wives,
Who through their long veils would glance
scorn at me
If, coward-like, I shunned the open war.
Nor doth my own soul prompt me to that
end !
I learnt to be a brave man constantly,
And to fight foremost where my Trojans
fight,   60
And vindicate my father's glory and
mine —
Because I know, by instinct and my soul,
The day comes that our sacred Troy must
fall,
And Priam and his people. Knowing
which,
I have no such grief for all my Trojans'
sake,
For Hecuba's, for Priam's, our old king,
Not for my brothers', who so many and
brave
Shall bite the dust before our enemies, —
As, sweet for *thee !* — to think some mailèd
Greek
Shall lead thee weeping and deprive thy
life   70
Of the free sun-sight — that, when gone
away
To Argos, thou shalt throw the distaff there,
Not for thy uses — or shalt carry instead
Upon thy loathing brow, as heavy as doom,
The water of Greek wells — Messeis' own,
Or Hyperea's ! — that some stander-by,
Marking my tears fall, shall say, " This is
She,
The wife of that same Hector who fought
best
Of all the Trojans, when all fought for
Troy " —

Ay ! — and, so speaking, shall renew thy
pang   80
That, 'reft of Him so named, thou shouldst
survive
To a slave's life ! But earth shall hide
my corse
Ere that shriek sound, wherewith thou art
dragged from Troy.'

Thus Hector spake, and stretched his arms
to his child.
Against the nurse's breast, with childly
cry,
The boy clung back, and shunned his
father's face,
And feared the glittering brass and waving
hair
Of the high helmet, nodding horror down.
The father smiled, the mother could not
choose
But smile too. Then he lifted from his
brow   90
The helm, and set it on the ground to
shine:
Then, kissed his dear child — raised him
with both arms,
And thus invoked Zeus and the general
gods: —

' Zeus, and all godships ! grant this boy of
mine
To be the Trojans' help, as I myself, —
To live a brave life and rule well in
Troy !
Till men shall say, " The son exceeds the
sire
By a far glory." Let him bring home
spoil
Heroic, and make glad his mother's heart.'

With which prayer, to his wife's extended
arms   100
He gave the child; and she received him
straight
To her bosom's fragrance — smiling up her
tears.
Hector gazed on her till his soul was
moved;
Then softly touched her with his hand and
spake.
' My best one — 'ware of passion and ex-
cess
In any fear. There 's no man in the world
Can send me to the grave apart from
fate, —

And no man . . . Sweet, I tell thee . . .
can fly fate —
No good nor bad man. Doom is self-ful-
filled.
But now, go home, and ply thy woman's
task   110
Of wheel and distaff! bid thy maidens
haste
Their occupation. War 's a care for men —
For all men born in Troy, and chief for
me.'
Thus spake the noble Hector, and resumed
His crested helmet, while his spouse went
home;
But as she went, still looked back lov-
ingly,
Dropping the tears from her reverted face.

THE DAUGHTERS OF PAN-DARUS

(ODYSS., LIB. XX.)

AND so these daughters fair of Pandarus
The whirlwinds took. The gods had
slain their kin:
They were left orphans in their father's
house.
And Aphroditè came to comfort them
With incense, luscious honey, and fragrant
wine;
And Herè gave them beauty of face and
soul
Beyond all women; purest Artemis
Endowed them with her stature and white
grace;
And Pallas taught their hands to flash
along
Her famous looms. Then, bright with
deity,
Toward far Olympus, Aphroditè went
To ask of Zeus (who has his thunder-
joys
And his full knowledge of man's mingled
fate)
How best to crown those other gifts with
love
And worthy marriage: but, what time she
went,
The ravishing Harpies snatched the maids
away,
And gave them up, for all their loving
eyes,
To serve the Furies who hate constantly.

ANOTHER VERSION

So the storms bore the daughters of Pan-
darus out into thrall —
The gods slew their parents; the orphans
were left in the hall.
And there, came, to feed their young lives,
Aphroditè divine,
With the incense, the sweet-tasting honey,
the sweet-smelling wine;
Herè brought them her wit above woman's,
and beauty of face;
And pure Artemis gave them her stature,
that form might have grace:
And Athenè instructed their hands in her
works of renown;
Then, afar to Olympus, divine Aphroditè
moved on :
To complete other gifts, by uniting each
girl to a mate,
She sought Zeus, who has joy in the thun-
der and knowledge of fate,
Whether mortals have good chance or ill.
But the Harpies a-late
In the storm came, and swept off the maid-
ens, and gave them to wait,
With that love in their eyes, on the Furies
who constantly hate.

FROM ANACREON

ODE TO THE SWALLOW

THOU indeed, little Swallow,
A sweet yearly comer,
Art building a hollow
New nest every summer,
And straight dost depart
Where no gazing can follow,
Past Memphis, down Nile !
Ah ! but Love all the while
Builds his nest in my heart,
Through the cold winter-weeks:
And as one Love takes flight,
Comes another, O Swallow,
In an egg warm and white,
And another is callow.
And the large gaping beaks
Chirp all day and all night:
And the Loves who are older
Help the young and the poor Loves,
And the young Loves grown bolder
Increase by the score Loves —

Why, what can be done?
If a noise comes from one
Can I bear all this rout of a hundred and
    more Loves?

FROM HEINE

THE LAST TRANSLATION

ROME, 1860

I

I

OUT of my own great woe
I make my little songs,
Which rustle their feathers In throngs
And beat on her heart even so.

II

They found the way, for their part,
Yet come again, and complain:
Complain, and are not fain
To say what they saw in her heart.

II

I

Art thou indeed so adverse?
Art thou so changed indeed?   10
Against the woman who wrongs me
I cry to the world in my need.

II

O recreant lips unthankful,
How could ye speak evil, say,
Of the man who so well has kissed you
On many a fortunate day?

III

I

My child, we were two children,
Small, merry by childhood's law;
We used to crawl to the hen-house
And hide ourselves in the straw.   20

II

We crowed like cocks, and whenever
The passers near us drew —
Cock-a-doodle! they thought
'T was a real cock that crew.

III

The boxes about our courtyard
We carpeted to our mind,
And lived there both together —
Kept house in a noble kind.

IV

The neighbor's old cat often
Came to pay us a visit;   30
We made her a bow and curtsey,
Each with a compliment in it.

V

After her health we asked
Our care and regard to evince —
(We have made the very same speeches
To many an old cat since).

VI

We also sat and wisely
Discoursed, as old folk do,
Complaining how all went better
In those good times we knew, —   40

VII

How love and truth and believing
Had left the world to itself,
And how so dear was the coffee,
And how so rare was the pelf.

VIII

The children's games are over,
The rest is over with youth —
The world, the good games, the good times,
The belief, and the love, and the truth.

IV

I

Thou lovest me not, thou lovest me not!
    'T is scarcely worth a sigh;   50
Let me look in thy face, and no king in his
      place
    Is a gladder man than I.

II

Thou hatest me well, thou hatest me
    well —
    Thy little red mouth has told:
Let it reach me a kiss, and, however it
    is,
    My child, I am well consoled.

V

I

My own sweet Love, if thou in the grave,
  The darksome grave, wilt be,
Then will I go down by the side, and
      crave
  Love-room for thee and me.

II

I kiss and caress and press thee wild,
  Thou still, thou cold, thou white !
I wail, I tremble, and weeping mild,
  Turn to a corpse at the right.

III

The Dead stand up, the midnight calls,
  They dance in airy swarms —
We two keep still where the grave-shade
      falls,
  And I lie on in thine arms.

IV

The Dead stand up, the Judgment-day 70
  Bids such to weal or woe —
But nought shall trouble us where we stay
  Embraced and embracing below.

VI

I

The years they come and go,
  The races drop in the grave,
Yet never the love doth so
  Which here in my heart I have.

II

Could I see thee but once, one day,
  And sink down so on my knee,
And die in thy sight while I say,
  'Lady, I love but thee !' 80

APPENDIX

I. JUVENILIA

I

THE BATTLE OF MARATHON

On October 5, 1843, Elizabeth Barrett wrote as follows to Mr. R. H. Horne, who had requested biographical details for the sketch which he wished to embody in *A New Spirit of the Age*, concerning her first considerable poetical production : ' My great epic of eleven or twelve years old, in four books, and called *The Battle of Marathon*, and of which fifty copies were printed because papa was bent upon spoiling me, is simply Pope's Homer done over again, or rather undone ; for although a curious production for a child, it gives evidence only of an imitative faculty, and an ear, and a good deal of reading in a peculiar direction.' This privately printed edition dedicated to the father of the poetess (LONDON : printed for W. Lindsell, 87 Wimpole St., Cavendish Square, 1820) was first reprinted for publication in London in 1891.

BOOK I

THE war of Greece with Persia's haughty King,
No vulgar strain, eternal Goddess, sing !
What dreary ghosts to glutted Pluto fled,
What nations suffered, and what heroes bled :
Sing Asia's powerful Prince, who envious saw
The fame of Athens, and her might in war ;
And scorns her power, at Cytherea's call
Her ruin plans, and meditates her fall ;
How Athens, blinded to the approaching chains
By Vulcan's artful spouse, unmoved remains ;   10
Deceived by Venus thus, unconquered Greece
Forgot her glories in the lap of peace ;
While Asia's realms, and Asia's lord prepare
T' ensnare her freedom, by the wiles of war :
Hippias t' exalt upon th' Athenian throne,
Where once Pisistratus his father shone.
For yet her son Æneas' wrongs impart
Revenge and grief to Cytherea's heart ;
And still from smoking Troy's once sacred wall,
Does Priam's reeking shade for vengeance call.   20
Minerva saw, and Paphia's Queen defied,
A boon she begged, nor Jove the boon denied ;

That Greece should rise, triumphant o'er her foe,
Disarm th' invaders, and their power o'erthrow.
Her prayer obtained, the blue-eyed Goddess flies
As the fierce eagle, thro' the radiant skies.
To Aristides then she stood confessed,
Shews Persia's arts, and fires his warlike breast :
Then pours celestial ardor o'er his frame
And points the way to glory and to fame.   30
Awe struck the Chief, and swells his troubled soul,
In pride and wonder thoughts progressive roll.
He inly groaned and smote his laboring breast,
At once by Pallas, and by care opprest.
Inspired he moved, earth echoed where he trod,
All full of Heaven, all burning with the God.
Th' Athenians viewed with awe the mighty man,
To whom the Chief impassioned thus began :
' Hear, all ye Sons of Greece ! Friends, Fathers, hear !
The Gods command it, and the Gods revere !   40
No madness mine, for mark, oh favored Greeks !
That by my mouth the martial Goddess speaks !
This know, Athenians, that proud Persia now
Prepares to twine thy laurels on her brow ;
Behold her princely Chiefs their weapons wield
By Venus fired, and shake the brazen shield.
I hear their shouts that echo to the skies,
I see their lances blaze, their banners rise,
I hear the clash of arms, the battle's roar,
And all the din and thunder of the war !   50
I know that Greeks shall purchase just renown,
And fame impartial, shall Athena crown.
Then Greeks, prepare your arms ! award the yoke,
Thus Jove commands ' — sublime the hero spoke ;
The Greeks assent with shouts, and rend the skies
With martial clamor, and tumultuous cries.
So struggling winds with rage indignant sweep
The azure waters of the silent deep,
Sudden the seas rebellowing, frightful rise,
And dash their foaming surges to the skies ;   60
Burst the firm sand, and boil with dreadful roar,

Lift their black waves, and combat with the shore.
So each brave Greek in thought aspires to fame,
Stung by his words, and dread of future shame ;
Glory's own fires within their bosom rise
And shouts tumultuous thunder to the skies.

But Love's celestial Queen resentful saw
The Greeks (by Pallas warned) prepare for war ;
Th' indignant Goddess of the Paphian bower
Deceives Themistocles with heavenly power; 70
The hero rising spoke, ' Oh rashly blind,
What sudden fury thus has seized thy mind ?
Boy as thou art, such empty dreams beware !
Shall we, for griefs and wars unsought, prepare ?
The will of mighty Jove, whate'er it be,
Obey, and own th' Omnipotent decree.
If our disgrace and fall the fates employ,
Why did we triumph o'er perfidious Troy ?
Why, say, oh Chief, in that eventful hour
Did Grecian heroes crush Dardanian power ? '
Him eyeing sternly, thus the Greek replies, 81
Renowned for truth, and as Minerva wise,
' Oh Son of Greece, no heedless boy am I,
Despised in battle's toils, nor first to fly,
Nor dreams or phrenzy call my words astray,
The heaven-sent mandate pious I obey.
If Pallas did not all my words inspire,
May heaven pursue me with unceasing ire !
But if (oh grant my prayer, almighty Jove)
I bear a mandate from the Courts above, 90
Then thro' yon heaven, let awful thunder roar
Till Greeks believe my mission, and adore ! '

He ceased — and thro' the host one murmur ran,
With eyes transfixed upon the godlike man.
But hark ! o'er earth expands the solemn sound,
It lengthening grows — heaven's azure vaults resound,
While peals of thunder beat the echoing ground.
Prostrate, convinc'd, divine Themistocles
Embraced the hero's hands, and clasped his knees :
' Behold me here,' (the awe-struck Chieftain cries 100
While tears repentant glisten in his eyes,)
' Behold me here, thy friendship to entreat,
Themistocles, a suppliant at thy feet.
Before no haughty despot's royal throne
This knee has bent — it bends to thee alone
Thy mission to adore, thy truth to own.
Behold me Jove, and witness what I swear
By all on earth I love, by all in heav'n I fear,
Some fiend inspired my words, of dark design,
Some fiend concealed beneath a robe divine ; 110
Then aid me in my prayer, ye Gods above,
Bid Aristides give me back his love ! '
He spake and wept ; benign the godlike man
Felt tears descend and paused, then thus began,

' Thrice worthy Greek, for this shall we contend ?
Ah no ! I feel thy worth, thou more than friend,
Pardon sincere, Themistocles, receive ;
The heart declares 'tis easy to forgive.'
He spake divine, his eye with Pallas burns,
He spoke and sighed, and sighed and wept by turns. 120
Themistocles beheld the Chief opprest,
Awe-struck he paused, then rushed upon his breast,
Whom sage Miltiades with joy addressed.
' Hero of Greece, worthy a hero's name
Adored by Athens, fav'rite child of fame !
Glory's own spirit does with truth combine
To form a soul, so godlike, so divine !
Oh Aristides rise, our Chief ! to save
The fame, the might of Athens from the grave.
Nor then refuse thy noble arm to lend 130
To guard Athena, and her state defend.
First I, obedient, 'customed homage pay
To own a hero's and a leader's sway.'
He said, and would have knelt ; the man divine
Perceived his will, and stayed the Sire's design.
' Not mine, oh Sage, to lead this gallant band,'
He generous said, and grasped his aged hand,
' Proud as I am in glory's arms to rise,
Athenian Greeks, to shield your liberties,
Yet 't is not mine to lead your powerful state, 140
Enough it is to tempt you to be great ;
Be 't for Miltiades, experienced sage,
To curb your ardor, and restrain your rage,
Your souls to temper — by his skill prepare
To succor Athens, and conduct the war.
More fits my early youth to purchase fame,
By deeds in arms t' immortalize my name.'
Firmly he spake, his words the Greek inspire,
And all were hushed to listen and admire.
The Sage thus — ' Most Allied to Gods ! the fame, 150
The pride, the glory of the Grecian name,
E'en by thee, Chief, I swear, to whom is given
The sacred mandate of yon marble heaven —
To lead, not undeserving of thy love,
T' avert the yoke, if so determines Jove.'
Amidst the host imagination rose
And paints the combat, but disdains the woes.
And heaven-born fancy, with dishevelled hair,
Points to the ensanguined field, and victory there.
But soon, too soon, these empty dreams are driven 160
Forth from their breasts — but soothing hope is given,
Hope sprung from Jove, man's sole, and envied heav'n.
Then all his glory, Aristides felt,
And begged the Chieftain's blessing as he knelt :
Miltiades his pious arms outspread,
Called Jove's high spirit on the hero's head,
Nor called unheard — sublime in upper air

The bird of Jove appeared to bless his prayer,
Lightning he breathed, not harsh, not fiercely
    bright,
But one pure stream of heaven-collected light:
Jove's sacred smile lulls every care to rest,   171
Calms every woe, and gladdens every breast.
But what shrill blast thus bursts upon the ear;
What banners rise, what heralds' forms ap-
    pear?
That haughty mien, and that commanding face
Bespeak them Persians, and of noble race;
One on whose hand Darius' signet beamed,
Superior to the rest, a leader seemed,
With brow contracted, and with flashing eye
Thus threatening spoke, in scornful majesty:
' Know Greeks that I, a sacred herald, bring
The awful mandate of the Persian King,   182
To force allegiance from the Sons of Greece,
Then earth and water give, nor scorn his peace.
For, if for homage, back reproof I bear,
To meet his wrath, his vengeful wrath, prepare,
For not in vain ye scorn his dread command
When Asia's might comes thundering in his
    hand.'
To whom Miltiades with kindling eye,
' We scorn Darius, and his threats defy;   190
And now, proud herald, shall we stoop to
    shame?
Shall Athens tremble at a tyrant's name?
Persian away! such idle dreams forbear,
And shun our anger and our vengeance fear.'
' Oh! vain thy words,' the herald fierce began;
' Thrice vain thy dotaged words, oh powerless
    man,
Sons of a desert, hoping to withstand
All the joint forces of Darius' hand,
Fools, fools, the King of millions to defy,
For freedom's empty name, to ask to die!   200
Yet stay, till Persia's powers their banners ⎫
    rear,   ⎬
Then shall ye learn our forces to revere,   ⎪
And ye, oh impotent, shall deign to fear!' ⎭
To whom great Aristides: rising ire
Boiled in his breast, and set his soul on fire:
' Oh wretch accurst,' the hero cried, ' to seek
T' insult experienced age, t' insult a Greek!
Inglorious slave! whom truth and heaven deny,
Unfit to live, yet more unfit to die:
But, trained to pass the goblet at the board 210
And servile kiss the footsteps of thy lord,
Whose wretched life no glorious deeds beguile,
Who lives upon the semblance of a smile,
Die! thy base shade to gloomy regions fled,
Join there the shivering phantoms of the dead.
Base slave, return to dust ' — his victim then
In fearful accents cried, ' Oh best of men,
Most loved of Gods, most merciful, most just,
Behold me humbled, grovelling in the dust:
Not mine th' offence, the mandate stern I
    bring   220
From great Darius, Asia's tyrant King.
Oh strike not, Chief, not mine the guilt, not ⎫
    mine,   ⎬
Ah o'er those brows severe, let mercy shine, ⎪
So dear to heav'n, of origin divine!   ⎭
Tributes, lands, gold, shall wealthy Persia
    give,

All, and yet more, but bid me, wretched, live!'
He trembling, thus persuades with fond en-
    treat
And nearer prest, and clasped the hero's feet.
Forth from the Grecian's breast, all rage is
    driv'n,   229
He lifts his arms, his eyes, his soul to heav'n.
' Hear, Jove omnipotent, all wise, all great,
To whom all fate is known; whose will is fate;
Hear thou all-seeing one, hear Sire divine,
Teach me thy will, and be thy wisdom mine!
Behold this suppliant! life or death decree;
Be thine the judgment, for I bend to thee.'
And thus the Sire of Gods and men replies,
While pealing thunder shakes the groaning
    skies.
The awful voice thro' spheres unknown was
    driv'n
Resounding thro' the dark'ning realms of hea-
    ven.   240
Aloft in air sublime the echo rode,
And earth resounds the glory of the God:
' Son of Athena, let the coward die,
And his pale ghost, to Pluto's empire fly;
Son of Athena, our command obey,
Know thou our might, and then adore our
    sway.'
Th' Almighty spake — the heavens convulsive
    start,
From the black clouds the whizzing lightnings
    dart
And dreadful dance along the troubled sky
Struggling with fate in awful mystery.   250
The hero heard, and Jove his breast inspired
Nor now by pity touched, but anger fired;
While his big heart within his bosom burns,
Off from his feet the clinging slave he spurns.
Vain were his cries, his prayers 'gainst fate
    above,
Jove wills his fall, and who can strive with
    Jove?
To whom the hero — ' Hence to Pluto's sway,
To realms of night, ne'er lit by Cynthia's ray,
Hence, from yon gulph the earth and water
    bring
And crown with victory your mighty King.'
He said — and where the gulph of death ap-
    peared   261
Where raging waves, with rocks sublimely
    reared,
He hurled the wretch at once of hope be-
    reaved;
Struggling he fell, the roaring flood received.
E'en now for life his shrieks, his groans im- ⎫
    plore,   ⎬
And now death's latent agony is o'er,   ⎪
He struggling sinks, and sinks to rise no more. ⎭
The train amaz'd, behold their herald die,
And Greece in arms — they tremble and they
    fly;
So some fair herd upon the verdant mead   270
See by the lion's jaws their foremost bleed,
Fearful they fly, lest what revolving fate
Had doomed their leader, should themselves
    await.
Then shouts of glorious war, and fame resound,
Athena's brazen gates receive the lofty sound.

But she whom Paphia's radiant climes adore
From her own bower the work of Pallas saw :
Tumultuous thoughts within her bosom rise,
She calls her car, and at her will it flies.
Th' eternal car with gold celestial burns,   280
Its polished wheel on brazen axle turns : .
This to his spouse by Vulcan's self was given
An offering worthy of the forge of heav'n.
The Goddess mounts the seat, and seized the
  reins,
The doves celestial cut the aerial plains,
Before the sacred birds and car of gold
Self-moved the radiant gates of heav'n unfold.
She then dismounts, and thus to mighty Jove
Begins the Mother and the Queen of Love.
'And is it thus, oh Sire, that fraud should
  spring   290
From the pure breast of heaven's eternal King ?
Was it for this, Saturnius' word was given
That Greece should fall 'mong nations curst of
  heaven ?
Thou swore by hell's black flood, and heaven
  above,
Is this, oh say, is this the faith of Jove ?
Behold stern Pallas, Athens' Sons alarms,
Darius' herald crushed, and Greece in arms.
E'en now behold her crested streamers fly,
Each Greek resolved to triumph or to die :   299
Ah me unhappy ! when shall sorrow cease ;
Too well I know the fatal might of Greece ;
Was 't not enough, imperial Troy should fall,
That Argive hands should raze the god-built
  wall ?
Was 't not enough Anchises' Son should roam
Far from his native shore and much loved home ?
All this unconscious of thy fraud I bore,
For thou, oh Sire, t' allay my vengeance, swore
That Athens towering in her might should fall
And Rome should triumph on her prostrate
  wall ;
But oh, if haughty Greece should captive bring
The great Darius, Persia's mighty King,   311
What power her pride, what power her might
  shall move ?
Not e'en the Thunderer, not eternal Jove,
E'en to thy heav'n shall rise her towering fame,
And prostrate nations will adore her name.
Rather on me thy instant vengeance take ⎫
Than all should fall for Cytherea's sake ! ⎬
Oh ! hurl me flaming in the burning lake, ⎭
Transfix me there unknown to Olympian calm,
Launch thy red bolt, and bare thy crimson arm.
I 'd suffer all — more — bid my woes increase 321
To hear but one sad groan from haughty Greece.'
She thus her grief with fruitless rage expressed,
And pride and anger swelled within her breast.
But he whose thunders awe the troubled sky
Thus mournful spake, and curbed the rising
  sigh :
'And it is thus celestial pleasures flow ?
E'en here shall sorrow reach and mortal woe ?
Shall strife the heavenly powers for ever move
And e'en insult the sacred ear of Jove ?   330
Know, oh rebellious, Greece shall rise sublime
In fame the first, nor, daughter, mine the crime,
In valor foremost, and in virtue great,
Fame's highest glories shall attend her state.

So fate ordains, nor all my boasted power
Can raise those virtues, or those glories low'r :
But rest secure, destroying time must come
And Athens' self must own imperial Rome.'
Then the great Thunderer, and with visage mild,
Shook his ambrosial curls before his child,   340
And bending awful gave the eternal nod ;
Heav'n quaked, and fate adored the parent
  God.
Joy seized the Goddess of the smiles and loves,
Nor longer, care, her heavenly bosom moves.
Hope rose, and o'er her soul its powers dis-
  played,
Nor checked by sorrow, nor by grief dismayed.
She thus — ' Oh thou, whose awful thunders roll
Thro' heaven's etherial vaults and shake the
  Pole,
Eternal Sire, so wonderfully great,
To whom is known the secret page of fate,   350
Say, shall great Persia, next to Rome most dear
To Venus' breast, shall Persia learn to fear ?
Say, shall her fame, and princely glories cease ?
Shall Persia, servile, own the sway of Greece ? '
To whom the Thunderer bent his brow divine
And thus in accents heavenly and benign ;
' Daughter, not mine the secrets to relate,
The mysteries of all-revolving fate.   358
But ease thy breast ; enough for thee to know,
What powerful fate decrees, will Jove bestow ! '
He then her griefs, and anxious woes beguiled,
And in his sacred arms embraced his child.
Doubt clouds the Goddess' breast — she calls
  her car,
And lightly sweeps the liquid fields of air.
When sable night midst silent nature springs,
And o'er Athena shakes her drowsy wings,
The Paphian Goddess from Olympus flies,
And leaves the starry senate of the skies ;
To Athens' heaven-blest towers, the Queen re-
  pairs
To raise more sufferings, and to cause more
  cares ;   370
The Pylian Sage she moved so loved by fame,
In face, in wisdom, and in voice the same.
Twelve Chiefs in sleep absorbed and grateful
  rest
She first beheld, and them she thus addrest.
' Immortal Chiefs,' the fraudful Goddess cries,
While all the hero kindled in her eyes,
' For you, these aged arms did I employ,
For you, we razed the sacred walls of Troy,
And now for you, my shivering shade is driven
From Pluto's dreary realms by urgent Heaven ;
Then, oh be wise, nor tempt th' unequal fight
In open fields, but wait superior might   382
Within immortal Athens' sacred wall,
There strive, there triumph, nor there fear to
  fall ;
To own the Thunderer's sway, then Greeks pre-
  pare.'
Benign she said, and melted into air.

BOOK II

When from the briny deep, the orient morn
Exalts her purple light, and beams unshorn ;
And when the flaming orb of infant day   38

Glares o'er the earth, and re illumes the sky;
The twelve deceived, with souls on fire arose,
While the false vision fresh in memory glows,
The Senate first they sought, whose lofty wall
Midst Athens rises, and o'ershadows all;
The pride of Greece, it lifts its front sublime
Unbent amidst the ravages of time:
High on their towering seats, the heroes found
The Chiefs of Athens solemn ranged around;
One of the twelve, the great Clombrotus, then,
Renowned for piety, and loved by men: 400
'Assembled heroes, Chief to Pallas dear,
All great in battle, and in virtue, hear!
When night with sable wings extended rose
And wrapt our weary limbs in sweet repose,
I and my friends, Cydoon famed in song,
Thelon the valiant, Herocles the strong,
Cleon and Thermosites, in battle great
By Pallas loved, and blest by partial fate,
To us and other six, while day toils steep
Our eyes in happy dreams, and grateful
sleep, 410
The Pylian Sage appeared, but not as when
On Troy's last dust he stood, the pride of
men;
Driven from the shore of Acheron he came
From lower realms to point the path to fame,
"Oh glorious Chiefs," the sacred hero said,
"For you and for your fame, all Troy has
bled;
Hither for you, my shivering shade is driv'n
From Pluto's dreary realms by urgent Heav'n;
Then oh be wise, nor tempt th' unequal fight
In open field, but wait superior might 420
Within immortal Athens' sacred wall;
There strive, there triumph, nor there fear to
fall!
To own the Thunderer's sway, then Greeks
prepare."
Benign he said, and melted into air.
"Leave us not thus," I cried, "Oh Pylian
Sage,
Experienced Nestor, famed for reverend age,
Say first, great hero, shall the trump of fame
Our glory publish, or disclose our shame?
Oh what are Athens' fates?" In vain I said;
E'en as I spoke the shadowy Chief had fled. 430
Then here we flew, to own the vision's sway
And heaven's decrees to adore and to obey.'
He thus — and as before the blackened skies,
Sound the hoarse breezes, murmuring as they
rise,
So thro' th' assembled Greeks, one murmur
rose,
One long dull echo lengthening as it goes.
Then all was hushed in silence — breathless
awe
Opprest each tongue, and trembling they
adore.
But now uprising from th' astonished Chiefs,
Divine Miltiades exposed his griefs. 440
For well the godlike warrior Sage had seen
The frauds deceitful of the Paphian Queen,
And feared for Greece, for Greece to whom
is given
Eternal fame, the purest gift of heaven.
And yet he feared — the pious hero rose

Majestic in his sufferings, in his woes;
Grief clammed his tongue, but soon his spirit
woke,
Words burst aloft, and all the Patriot spoke.
'Oh Athens, Athens! all the snares I view;
Thus shalt thou fall, and fall inglorious
too! 450
Are all thy boasted dignities no more?
Is all thy might, are all thy glories o'er?
Oh woe on woe, unutterable grief!
Not Nestor's shade, that cursed phantom
chief,
But in that reverend air, that lofty mien,
Behold the frauds of Love's revengeful Queen.
Not yet, her thoughts does vengeance cease t'
employ;
Her son Æneas' wrongs, and burning Troy
Not yet forgotten lie within her breast,
Nor soothed by time, nor by despair de-
prest. 460
Greeks still extolled by glory and by fame,
For yet, oh Chiefs! ye bear a Grecian name,
If in these walls, these sacred walls we wait
The might of Persia, and the will of fate,
Before superior force will Athens fall
And one o'erwhelming ruin bury all.
Then in the open plain your might essay,
Rush on to battle, crush Darius' sway;
The frauds of Venus, warrior Greeks, beware,
Disdain the Persian foes, nor stoop to fear.' 470
This said, Clombrotus him indignant heard,
Nor felt his wisdom, nor his wrath he feared.
With rage the Chief, the godlike Sage beheld,
And passion in his stubborn soul rebelled.
'Thrice impious man,' th' infuriate Chieftain
cries,
(Flames black and fearful, flashing from his
eyes,)
'Where lies your spirit, Greeks? and can ye
bow
To this proud upstart of your power so low?
What! does his aspect awe ye! is his eye
So full of haughtiness and majesty? 480
Behold the impious soul, that dares defy
The power of Gods and Sovereign of the sky!
And can your hands no sacred weapon wield,
To crush the tyrant, and your country shield?
On, Greeks! — your sons, your homes, your
country free
From such usurping Chiefs and tyranny!'
He said, and grasped his weapon — at his
words
Beneath the horizon gleamed ten thousand
swords,
Ten thousand swords e'en in one instant raised,
Sublime they danced aloft, and midst the Senate
blazed. 490
Nor wisdom checked, nor gratitude represt,
They rose, and flashed before the Sage's
breast.
With pride undaunted, greatness unsubdued,
Gainst him in arms, the impetuous Greeks he
viewed,
Unarmed, unawed, before th' infuriate bands,
Nor begged for life, nor stretched his suppliant
hands.
He stood astounded, riveted, oppressed

By grief unspeakable, which swelled his
    breast;
Life, feeling, being, sense forgotten lie,
Buried in one wide waste of misery.   500
Can this be Athens! this her Senate's pride?
He asked but gratitude, — was this denied?
Tho' Europe's homage at his feet were hurled
Athens forsakes him — Athens was his world.
Unutterable woe! by anguish stung
All his full soul rushed heaving to his tongue,
And thoughts of power, of fame, of greatness
    o'er,
He cried 'Athenians!' and he could no more.
Awed by that voice of agony, that word,
Hushed were the Greeks, and sheathed the
    obedient sword,   510
They stood abashed — to them the ancient
    Chief
Began — and thus relieved his swelling grief:
'Athenians! warrior Greeks! my words revere!
Strike me, but listen — bid me die, but hear!
Hear not Clombrotus, when he bids you wait,
At Athens' walls, Darius and your fate;
I feel that Pallas' self, my soul inspires
My mind she strengthens, and my bosom fires;
Strike, Greeks! but hear me; think not to
    this heart
Yon thirsty swords, one breath of fear impart!
Such slavish, low born thoughts, to Greeks un-
    known,   521
A Persian feels, and cherishes alone!
Hear me, Athenians! hear me, and believe,
See Greece mistaken! e'en the Gods deceive.
But fate yet wavers — yet may wisdom move
These threatening woes and thwart the Queen
    of Love.
Obey my counsels, and invoke for aid
The cloud-compelling God, and blue-eyed
    maid;
I fear not for myself the silent tomb,
Death lies in every shape, and death must
    come.   530
But ah! ye mock my truth, traduce my fame,
Ye blast my honor, stigmatize my name!
Ye call me tyrant when I wish thee free,
Usurper, when I live but, Greece, for thee!'
And thus the Chief — and boding silence
    drowned
Each clam'rous tongue, and sullen reigned
    around.
'Oh Chief!' great Aristides first began,
'Mortal yet perfect, godlike and yet man!
Boast of ungrateful Greece! my prayer attend,
Oh! be my Chieftain, Guardian, Father,
    Friend!   540
And ye, oh Greeks! impetuous and abhorred,
Again presumptuous, lift the rebel sword,
Again your weapons raise, in hateful ire,
To crush the Leader, Hero, Patriot, Sire!
Not such was Greece, when Greeks united
    stood
To bathe perfidious Troy in hostile blood,
Not such were Greeks inspired by glory; then
As Gods they conquered, now they 're less
    than men!
Degenerate race! now lost to once loved fame,
Traitors to Greece, and to the Grecian name!

Who now your honors, who your praise will
    seek?   551
Who now shall glory in the name of Greek?
But since such discords your base souls divide,
Procure the lots, let Jove and Heaven decide.'
To him Clombrotus thus admiring cries,
'Thy thoughts how wondrous, and thy words
    how wise!
So let it be, avert the threatened woes,
And Jove be present, and the right disclose;
But give me, Sire of Gods and powers above,
The heavenly vision, and my truth to prove! 560
Give me t' avenge the breach of all thy laws,
T' avenge myself, then aid my righteous cause!
If this thou wilt, I 'll to thine altars lead
Twelve bulls which to thy sacred name shall
    bleed,
Six snow-white heifers of a race divine
Prostrate shall fall, and heap the groaning
    shrine.
Nor this the most — six rams that fearless
    stray
Untouched by man, for thee this arm shall
    slay.'
Thus prayed the Chief, with shouts the hea-
    vens resound;
Jove weighs the balance and the lots go
    round!   570
Declare, oh muse! for to thy piercing eyes
The book of fate irrevocably lies;
What lots leapt forth, on that eventful day
Who won, who lost, all seeing Goddess, say!
First great Clombrotus all his fortune tried
And strove with fate, but Jove his prayer de-
    nied.
Infuriate to the skies his arms are driven,
And raging thus upbraids the King of Heaven.
'Is this the virtue of the blest abodes,
And this the justice of the God of Gods?   580
Can he who hurls the bolt, and shakes the
    sky
The prayer of truth, unblemished truth, deny?
Has he no faith by whom the clouds are riven,
Who sits superior on the throne of Heaven?
No wonder earth-born men are prone to fall
In sin, or listen to dishonor's call,
When Gods, th' immortal Gods, transgress the
    laws
Of truth, and sin against a righteous cause.'
Furious he said, by anger's spirit fired,
Then sullen from the Senate walls retired. 590
'T is now Miltiades' stern fate to dare,
But first he lifts his pious soul in prayer.
'Daughter of Jove!' the mighty Chief began,
'Without thy wisdom, frail and weak is man.
A phantom Greece adores; oh show thy power,
And prove thy love in this eventful hour!
Crown all thy glory, all thy might declare!'
The Chieftain prayed, and Pallas heard his
    prayer.
Swayed by the presence of the power divine,
The fated lot, Miltiades, was thine!   600
That hour the swelling trump of partial fame
Diffused eternal glory on thy name!
'Daughter of Jove,' he cries, 'unconquered
    maid!
Thy power I own, and I confess thy aid,

For this twelve ewes upon thy shrine shall
smoke
Of milk-white fleece, the comellest of their
flock.
While hecatombs and generous sacrifice
Shall fume and blacken half th' astonished
skies.'
And thus the Chief — the shouting Greeks ad-
mire,
While truth's bright spirit sets their souls on
fire. 610
Then thus Themistocles, ' Ye Grecian host,
Not now the time for triumph or for boast.
Now, Greeks! for graver toils your minds pre-
pare,
Not for the strife, but council of the war.
Behold the sacred herald ! sent by Greece
To Sparta's vales now hushed in leagues of
peace ;
Her Chiefs, to aid the common cause, t' im-
plore,
And bid Darius shun the Argive shore ;
Behold him here ! then let the leader Greek
Command the bearer of our hopes to speak.'
And thus the Sage, 'Where'er the herald
stands, 621
Bid him come forth, 't is Athens' Chief com-
mands,
And bid him speak with freedom uncontrolled,
His thoughts deliver and his charge unfold.'
He said and sat — the Greeks impatient wait
The will of Sparta, and Athena's fate.
Silent they sat — so ere the whirlwinds rise
Ere billows foam and thunder to the skies,
Nature in death-like calm her breath suspends,
And hushed in silent awe, th' approaching
storm attends. 630
Now midst the Senate's walls the herald
stands:
' Ye Greeks,' he said, and stretched his sacred
hands.
' Assembled heroes, ye Athenian bands,
And thou beloved of Jove, our Chief, oh Sage,
Renowned for wisdom, as renowned for age,
And all ye Chiefs in battle rank divine !
No joyful mission swayed by Pallas mine.
The hardy Spartans, with one voice declare
Their will to aid our freedom and our war,
Instant they armed, by zeal and impulse
driven, 640
But on the plains of the mysterious heaven
Comets and fires were writ — and awful sign,
And dreadful omen of the wrath divine :
While threatened plagues upon their shores ap-
pear,
They curb their valor, all subdued by fear ;
The oracles declare the will above,
And of the sister and the wife of Jove,
That not until the moon's bright course was
o'er
The Spartan warriors should desert their shore.
Threats following threats succeed the mandate
dire, 650
Plagues to themselves, and to their harvest
fire.
The Spartan Chiefs desist, their march delay
To wait th' appointed hour and heaven obey.

Grief smote my heart, my hopes and mission
vain ;
Their town I quitted for my native plain,
And when an eminence I gained, in woe
I gazed upon the verdant fields below,
Where nature's ample reign extending wide,
Displays her graces with commanding pride ;
Where cool Eurotas winds her limpid floods 660
Thro' verdant valleys, and thro' shady woods ;
And crowned in majesty o'ertowering all
In bright effulgence, Sparta's lofty wall.
To these I looked farewell, and humbled,
bowed
In chastened sorrow, to the thundering God.
'T was thus I mused, when from a verdant
grove
That wafts delicious perfume from above,
The monster Pan his form gigantic reared,
And dreadful to my awe-struck sight appeared.
I hailed the God who reigns supreme below,
Known by the horns that started from his
brow ; 671
Up to the hips a goat, but man's his face
Tho' grim, and stranger to celestial grace.
Within his hand a shepherd's crook he bore
The gift of Dian, on th' Arcadian shore ;
Before th' immortal power I, fearing, bowed
Congealed with dread, and thus addressed the
God :
" Comes Hermes' Son, as awful as his Sire,
To vent upon the Greeks immortal ire ?
Is 't not enough, the mandate stern I bring 680
From Sparta's Chiefs, and Sparta's royal King,
That heaven enjoins them to refrain from fight
Till Dian fills again her horns with light ?
Then vain their aid, ere then may Athens fall
And Persia's haughty Chiefs invest her wall."
I said and sighed, the God in accents mild
My sorrow thus and rigid griefs beguiled :
" Not to destroy I come, oh chosen Greek,
Not Athens' fall, but Athens' fame I seek.
Then give again to honor and to fame 690
My power despised, and my forgotten name.
At Sparta's doom, no longer, Chief, repine,
But learn submission to the will divine ;
Behold e'en now, within this fated hour
On Marathonian plains, the Persian power !
E'en Hippias' self inspires th' embattled host,
Th' Athenian's terror, as the Persian's boast.
Bid Athens rise and glory's powers attest.
Enough — no more — the fates conceal the rest."
He said, his visage burned with heavenly
light ; 700
He spoke and, speaking, vanished from my
sight ;
And awed, I sought where those loved walls
invite.
But think not, warrior Greeks, the fault is
mine,
If Athens fall — it is by wrath divine.
I vainly, vainly grieve, the evil springs
From him — the God of Gods, the King of
Kings ! '
The Herald said, and bent his sacred head,
While cherished hope from every bosom fled.
Each dauntless hero, by despair deprest 709
Felt the deep sorrow, swelling in his breast.

They mourn for Athens, friendless and alone ;
Cries followed cries, and groan succeeded groan.
Th' Athenian matrons, startled at the sound,
Rush from their looms and anxious crowd
    around.
They ask the cause, the fatal cause is known
By each fond sigh, and each renewing groan,
While in their arms some infant love they bear
At once for which they joy, for which they fear.
Hushed on its mother's breast, the cherished
    child   719
Unconscious midst the scene of terror smiled ;
On rush the matrons, they despairing seek
Miltiades, adored by every Greek ;
Him found at length, his counsels they entreat,
Hang on his knees and clasp his sacred feet.
Their babes before him on the ground they
    throw
In all the maddening listlessness of woe.
First Delopeia, of the matrons chief,
Thus vents her bursting soul in frantic grief,
While her fond babe she holds aloft in air ;
Thus her roused breast prefers a mother's
    prayer :   730
' Oh Son of Cimon, for the Grecians raise
To heaven, thy fame, thy honor, and thy praise.
Thus — thus — shall Athens and her heroes fall,
Shall thus one ruin seize and bury all ?
Say, shall these babes be strangers then to fame,
And be but Greeks in spirit and in name ?
Oh first, ye Gods ! and hear a mother's prayer,
First let them glorious fall in ranks of war !
If Asia triumph, then shall Hippias reign
And Athens' free-born Sons be slaves again ! 740
Oh Son of Cimon ! let thy influence call
The souls of Greeks to triumph or to fall !
And guard their own, their children's, country's
    name,
From foul dishonor, and eternal shame ! '
Thus thro' her griefs, the love of glory broke,
The mother wept, but 't was the Patriot spoke :
And as before the Greek she bowed with
    grace,
The lucid drops bedewed her lovely face.
Their shrieks and frantic cries the matrons
    cease,
And death-like silence awes the Sons of
    Greece.   750
Thrice did the mighty Chief of Athens seek
To curb his feelings and essay to speak,
'T was vain — the ruthless sorrow wrung his
    breast,
His mind disheartened, and his soul opprest.
He thus — while o'er his cheek the moisture
    stole,
' Retire ye matrons, nor unman my soul !
Tho' little strength this aged arm retains,
My swelling soul Athena's foe disdains ;
Hushed be your griefs, to heav'n for victory
    cry,
Assured we 'll triumph, or with freedom
    die.   760
And ye, oh Chiefs, when night disowns her
    sway
And pensive Dian yields her power to day,
To quit these towers for Marathon prepare,
And brave Darius in the ranks of war.

For yet may Jove protect the Grecian name
And crown, in unborn ages, Athens' fame.'
He said — and glowing with the warlike fire,
And cheered by hope, the Godlike Chiefs re-
    tire.
Now Cynthia rules the earth, the flaming God
In ocean sinks, green Neptune's old abode : 770
Black Erebus on drowsy pinions springs,
And o'er Athena cowers his sable wings.

BOOK III

When from the deep the hour's eternal sway
Impels the coursers of the flaming day,
The long haired Greeks, with brazen arms pre-
    pare,
Their freedom to preserve and wage the war.
First Aristides from the couch arose,
While his great mind with all Minerva glows ;
His mighty limbs, his golden arms invest,
The cuirass blazes on his ample breast,   780
The glittering cuisses both his legs enfold,
And the huge shield 's on fire with burnished
    gold ;
His hands two spears uphold of equal size,
And fame's bright glories kindle in his eyes ;
Upon his helmet, plumes of horse hair nod,
And forth he moved, majestic as a God !
Upon his snorting steed the warrior sprung,
The courser neighed, the brazen armor rung ;
From heaven's etherial heights the martial
    maid
With conscious pride, the hero's might sur-
    veyed.   790
Him as she eyed, she shook the gorgon shield ;
' Henceforth to me,' she cried, ' let all th' im-
    mortals yield.
Let monster Mars, the Latian regions own,
For Attica, Minerva stands alone.'
And now, th' unconquered Chief of Justice
    gains
The Senate's walls, and there the steed de-
    tains,
Whence he dismounts — Miltiades he seeks,
Beloved of Jove, the leader of the Greeks,
Nor sought in vain ; there clad in armor bright
The Chieftain stood, all eager for the fight. 800
Within his aged hands two lances shine,
The helmet blazed upon his brows divine,
And as he bends beneath th' unequal weight
Youth smiles again, when with gigantic might
His nervous limbs, immortal arms could wield,
Crush foe on foe, and raging, heap the field.
Yet tho' such days were past, and ruthless age
Transformed the warrior to the thoughtful
    sage ;
Tho' the remorseless hand of silent time
Impaired each joint, and stiffened every
    limb ;   810
Yet thro' his breast, the fire celestial stole,
Throbbed in his veins, and kindled in his soul.
In thought, the Lord of Asia threats no more,
And Hippias bites the dust, mid seas of gore.
Him as he viewed, the youthful hero's breast
Heaved high with joy, and thus the Sage ad-
    dressed :

'Chief, best beloved of Pallas,' he began,
'In fame allied to Gods, oh wondrous man!
Behold Apollo gilds th' Athenian wall,
Our freedom waits, and fame and glory call 820
To battle! Asia's King and myriads dare,
Swell the loud trump, and swell the din of
　　war.'
He said impatient; then the warrior sage
Began, regardless of the fears of age:
' Not mine, oh youth, with caution to control
The fire and glory of thy eager soul;
So was I wont in brazen arms to shine,
Such strength, and such impatient fire were
　　mine.'
He said, and bade the trumpet's peals rebound,
High, and more high, the echoing war notes
　　sound:　　　　　　　　　　　　　　830
Sudden one general shout the din replies,
A thousand lances blazing as they rise,
And Athens' banners wave, and float along
　　the skies.
So from the marsh, the cranes embodied fly,
Clap their glad wings, and cut the liquid sky.
With thrilling cries they mount their joyful
　　way,
Vig'rous they spring, and hail the new born
　　day.
So rose the shouting Greeks, inspired by fame
T' assert their freedom, and maintain their
　　name.
First came Themistocles in arms renowned, 840
Whose steed impatient, tore the trembling
　　ground.
High o'er his helmet snowy plumes arise
And shade that brow, which Persia's might
　　defies;
A purple mantle graceful waves behind,
Nor hides his arms but floats upon the wind.
His mighty form two crimson belts enfold
Rich in embroidery, and stiff with gold.
Callimachus the Polemarch next came,
The theme of general praise and general fame.
Cynagirus, who e'en the Gods would dare, 850
Heap ranks on ranks and thunder thro' the war;
His virtues godlike; man's his strength sur-
　　passed,
In battle foremost, and in flight the last:
His ponderous helm 's a shaggy lion's hide.
And the huge war axe clattered at his side,
The mighty Chief, a brazen chariot bore,
While fame and glory hail him and adore.
Antenor next his aid to Athens gave,
Like Paris youthful, and like Hector brave;
Cleon, Minerva's priest, experienced sage, 860
Advanced in wisdom, as advanced in age.
Agregoras, Delenus' favorite child;
The parent's cares, the glorious son beguiled.
But now he leaves his sire to seek his doom,
His country's freedom, or a noble tomb.
And young Aratus moved with youthful pride,
And heart elated at the hero's side.
Next thou, Cleones, thou triumphant moved
By Athens honored, by the Greeks beloved:
And Sthenelus the echoing pavements trod,
From youth devoted to the martial God. 871
Honor unspotted crowned the hero's name,
Unbounded virtue, and unbounded fame.

Such heroes shone the foremost of the host,
All Athens' glory, and all Athens' boast.
Behind a sable cloud of warriors rise
With ponderous arms, and shouting rend the
　　skies.
These bands with joy Miltiades inspire,
Fame fills his breast, and sets his soul on fire.
Aloft he springs into the gold-wrought car, 880
While the shrill blast resounds, to war! to war!
The coursers plunge as conscious of their load
And proudly neighing, feel they bear a God.
The snow white steeds by Pallas' self were
　　given,
Which sprung from the immortal breed of
　　heaven.
The car was wrought of brass and burnished
　　gold,
And divers figures on its bulk were told,
Of heroes who in plunging to the fight
Shrouded Troy's glories in eternal night:
Of fierce Pelides, who relenting gave, 890
At Priam's prayer, to Hector's corpse a grave;
Here Spartan Helen flies her native shore,
To bid proud Troy majestic stand no more;
There Hector clasps his consort to his breast,
Consoles his sufferings, tho' himself oppressed;
And there he rushes to the embattled field
For victory or death, nor e'en in death to yield:
Here Ilium prostrate feels the Argive ire,
Her heroes perished, and her towers on fire.
And here old Priam breathes his last drawn
　　sigh,　　　　　　　　　　　　　　900
And feels 't is least of all his griefs to die.
There his loved sire, divine Æneas bears,
And leaves his own with all a patriot's tears;
While in one hand he holds his weeping boy,
And looks his last on lost unhappy Troy.
The warrior seized the reins, the impatient
　　steeds
Foam at the mouth and spring where glory
　　leads.
The gates, the heroes pass, th' Athenian dames
Bend from their towers, and bid them save from
　　flames
Their walls, their infant heirs, and fill the
　　skies　　　　　　　　　　　　　　910
With shouts, entreaties, prayers, and plaintive
　　cries:
Echo repeats their words, the sounds impart
New vigor to each Greek's aspiring heart.
Forward with shouts they press, and hastening
　　on
Try the bold lance and dream of Marathon.
Meanwhile the Persians on th' embattled plain
Prepare for combat, and the Greeks disdain.
Twice twenty sable bulls they daily pay,
Unequalled homage, to the God of day; 919
Such worthy gifts, the wealthy warriors bring,
And such the offerings of the Persian King;
While the red wine around his altars flowed
They beg protection from the flaming God.
But the bright Patron of the Trojan war
Accepts their offerings, but rejects their prayer:
The power of love alone dares rigid fate,
To vent on Greece her vengeance and her hate;
Not love for Persia prompts the vengeful dame,
But hate for Athens, and the Grecian name:

In Phœbus' name, the fraudful Queen receives
The hecatombs, and happy omens gives.   931
And now the heralds with one voice repeat
The will of Datis echoing thro' the fleet,
To council, to convene the Persian train,
That Athens' Chiefs should brave their might
   in vain.
The Chiefs and Hippias' self his will obey,
And seek the camp, the heralds lead the way.
There on the couch, their leader Datis sat
In ease luxurious, and in kingly state ;
Around his brow, pride deep and scornful
   played,   940
A purple robe, his slothful limbs arrayed,
Which o'er his form, its silken draperies fold,
Majestic sweeps the ground, and glows with
   gold ;
While Artaphernes resting at his side
Surveys th' advancing train with conscious
   pride.
The Elder leader, mighty Datis, then,
' Assembled Princes, great and valiant men,
And thou thrice glorious Hippias, loved by
   heav'n,
To whom, as to thy Sire, is Athens giv'n ;
Behold the Grecian banners float afar,   950
Shouting they hail us, and provoke the war.
Then, mighty Chiefs and Princes, be it yours
To warm and fire the bosoms of our powers,
That when the morn has spread her saffron
   light,
The Greeks may own and dread Darius' might ;
For know, oh Chiefs, when once proud Athens
   falls,
When Persian flames shall reach her haughty
   walls,
From her depression, wealth to you shall spring,
And honor, fame, and glory to your King.'
He said ; his words the Princes' breasts inspire,
Silent they bend, and with respect retire.   961
And now the Greeks in able marches gain,
By Pallas fired, the Marathonian plain.
Before their eyes th' unbounded ocean rolls
And all Darius' fleet — unawed their souls,
They fix their banners, and the tents they
   raise
And in the sun, their polished javelins blaze.
Their leader's self within the brazen car
Their motions orders, and prepares for war ;
Their labors o'er, the aged hero calls   970
The Chiefs to council midst the canvas walls,
And then the Sage, ' How great the Persian
   host !
But let them not their strength or numbers
   boast.
Their slothful minds to love of fame unknown,
Sigh not for war, but for the spoil alone.
Strangers to honor's pure immortal light,
They not as heroes, but as women fight ;
Grovelling as proud, and cowardly as vain,
The Greeks they fear, their numbers they dis-
   dain.
And now Athenians ! fired by glory, rise   980
And lift your fame unsullied to the skies,
Your victim Persia, liberty your prize.
And now twice twenty sable bullocks bring
To heap the altars of the thundering King,

Bid twelve white heifers of gigantic breed
To Jove's great daughter, wise Minerva, bleed,
And then in sleep employ the solemn night
Nor till Apollo reigns, provoke the fight.'
The hero said ; the warlike council o'er
They raise the lofty altars on the shore.   990
They pile in heaps the pride of all the wood ;
They fall the first, who first in beauty stood :
The pine that soars to heaven, the sturdy
   oak,
And cedars crackle at each hero's stroke.
And now two altars stand of equal size
And lift their forms majestic to the skies,
The heroes then twice twenty bullocks bring,
A worthy offering to the thundering King.
The aged leader seized the sacred knife,
Blow followed blow, out gushed the quivering
   life ;   1000
Thro' their black hides the ruthless steel is
   driven
The victims groan — Jove thunders from his
   heaven.
And then their bulks upon the pile they lay,
The flames rush upward, and the armies pray.
Driven by the wind, the roaring fires ascend,
And now they hiss in air, and now descend ;
With all their sap, the new cut faggots raise
Their flames to heaven, and crackle as they
   blaze ;
And then the Sage, ' Oh, thou of powers above
The first and mightiest, hear, eternal Jove ! 1010
Give us, that Athens in her strength may rise
And lift our fame and freedom to the skies ! '
This said, he ceased — th' assembled warriors
   pour
The sacred incense, and the God adore ;
Then partial Jove propitious heard their
   prayer,
Thrice shook the heavens, and thundered thro'
   the air ;
With joy, the Greeks, the favoring sign in-
   spires,
And their breasts glow with all the warlike
   fires :
And now twelve heifers white as snow they
   lead
To great Minerva's sacred name to bleed.   1020
They fall — their bulks upon the pile are laid
Sprinkled with oil, and quick in flame arrayed.
And now descending midst the darkening skies
Behold the Goddess of the radiant eyes.
The ground she touched, beneath the mighty
   load
Earth groaning rocks, and nature hails the
   God.
Within her hand her father's lightnings shone,
And shield that blazes near th' eternal throne ;
The Greeks with fear, her dauntless form sur-
   veyed,
And trembling bowed before the blue-eyed
   maid.   1030
Then favoring, thus began the power divine,
While in her eyes celestial glories shine ;
' Ye sons of Athens, loved by heaven,' she
   cries
' Revered by men, be valiant and be wise.
When morn awakes, Darius' numbers dare,

Clang your loud arms, and rouse the swelling
   war:
But first to yon proud fleet a herald send
To bid the Persians yield, and fight suspend,
For vainly to their God they suppliant call,
Jove favors Greece, and Pallas wills their
   fall.'   1040
She said, and thro' the depths of air she flies,
Mounts the blue heaven, and scales the liquid
   skies.
The Greeks rejoicing thank the powers above
And Jove's great daughter, and eternal Jove.
And now a herald to the fleet they send
To bid the Persians yield, and war suspend.
Thro' the divided troops the herald goes
Thro' Athens' host, and thro' th' unnumbered
   foes.
Before the holy man, the Persian bands
Reverend give way, and ask what Greece de-
   mands: 1050
He tells not all, but that he, chosen, seeks
Datis their Chief, by order of the Greeks.
The mission but in part he sage reveals,
And what his prudence prompts him, he con-
   ceals.
Then to their Chief they lead him, where he
   sat
With pomp surrounded, and in gorgeous state;
Around his kingly couch, his arms were spread
Flaming in gold, by forge Cyclopean made;
And then stern Datis frowning thus began,
'What hopes deceive thee, miserable man?
What treacherous fate allures thee thus to
   stray   1061
Thro' all our hosts? What Gods beguile the
   way?
Think'st thou to 'scape the Persian steel, when
   Greece
Our herald crushed, and banished hopes of
   peace?
But speak, what will the Greeks? and do they
   dare
To prove our might, and tempt th' unequal
   war?
Or do they deign to own Darius' sway
And yield to Persia's might th' embattled
   day?'
To thus th' Athenian herald made reply
'The Greeks disdain your terms, and scorn to
   fly.   1070
Unknown to heroes and to sons of Greece
The shameful slavery of a Persian peace;
Defiance stern, not servile gifts I bring,
Your bonds detested, and despised your King;
Of equal size, the Greeks two altars raise
To Jove's high glory, and Minerva's praise.
The God propitious heard, and from the skies
Descends the Goddess of the azure eyes,
And thus began — "Assembled Greeks, give
   ear
Attend my wisdom, nor my glory fear; 1080
When morn awakes, Darius' numbers dare,
Clang your loud arms, and rouse the swelling
   war:
But first to yon proud fleet a herald send
To bid the Persians yield, and war suspend,
For vainly to their God they suppliant call,

Jove favors Greece, and Pallas wills their fall,'
The Goddess spoke; th' Athenians own her
   sway.
I seek the fleet, and heaven's command obey.
The Greeks disdain your millions in the war,
Nor I, oh Chief, your promised vengeance
   fear.   1090
Strike! but remember that the God on high
Who rules the heavens, and thunders thro' the
   sky,
Not unrevenged will see his herald slain,
Nor shall thy threats his anger tempt in vain.'
And thus the Greek: then Datis thus replies,
Flames black and fearful scowling from his
   eyes,
'Herald away! and Asia's vengeance fear;
Back to your phrenzied train my mandate
   bear,
That Greece and Grecian Gods may threat in
   vain,
We scorn their anger, and their wrath dis-
   dain: 1100
For he who lights the earth and rules the skies
With happy omens to our vows replies.
When morn uprising breathes her saffron
   light,
Prepare to dare our millions in the fight.
Thy life I give, Darius' will to say
And Asia's hate — hence, Chief, no more,
   away!'
He said, and anger filled the Grecian's breast,
But prudent, he the rising wrath suppressed;
Indignant, thro' the canvas tents he strode
And silently invoked the thundering God. 1110
Fears for his country in his bosom rose,
As on he wandered midst unnumbered foes;
He strikes his swelling breast and hastens on
O'er the wide plains of barren Marathon.
And now he sees the Grecian banners rise,
And well-armed warriors blaze before his eyes.
Then thus he spoke — 'Ye Grecian bands, give
   ear,
Ye warrior Chiefs and Attic heroes hear!
Your will to Asia's other Prince I told,
All which you bade me, Chieftains, to un-
   fold,   1120
But Pallas' vengeance I denounced in vain,
Your threats he scorned, and heard with proud
   disdain.
The God, he boasts, who lights the earth and
   skies,
With happy omens to his vows replies;
Then when the uprising morn extends her
   light
Prepare, ye Greeks, to dare his powers in
   fight.'
He said — the Greeks for instant strife declare
Their will, and arm impatient for the war.
Then he, their godlike Chief, as Pallas sage,
'Obey my counsels, and repress your rage, 1130
Ye Greeks,' he cried, 'the sacred night displays
Her shadowy veil, and earth in gloom arrays;
Her sable shades, e'en Persia's Chiefs obey,
And wait the golden mandate of the day:
Such is the will of Jove, and Gods above,
And such the order of the loved of Jove.'
He said — the Greeks their leader's word obey.

They seek their tents, and wait th' approaching
day,
O'er either host celestial Somnus reigns,
And solemn silence lulls th' embattled
plains.   1140

BOOK IV

And now the morn by Jove to mortals given
With rosy fingers opes the gates of heaven.
The Persian Princes and their haughty Lord
Gird on their arms, and seize the flaming
sword:
Forth, forth they rush to tempt the battle's
roar,
Earth groans, and shouts rebellowing shake the
shore.
As when the storm the heavenly azure shrouds
With sable night, and heaps on clouds, the
clouds,
The Persians rose, and crowd th' embattl'd
plain
And stretch their warlike millions to the
main;   1150
And now th' Athenians throng the fatal field
By fame inspired, and swords and bucklers
wield;
In air sublime their floating banners rise,
The lances blaze; the trumpets rend the skies.
And then Miltiades — 'Athenians, hear,
Behold the Persians on the field appear
Dreadful in arms; remember, Greeks, your
fame,
Rush to the war, and vindicate your name;
Forward! till low in death the Persians lie,
For freedom triumph or for freedom die.'   1160
He said; his visage glows with heavenly light;
He spoke sublime, and rush'd into the fight.
And now the fury of the way [1] began —
Lance combats lance, and man 's opposed to
man;
Beneath their footsteps, groans the laboring
plain
And shouts re-echoing bellow to the main;
Mars rages fierce; by heroes, heroes die;
Earth rocks, Jove thunders, and the wounded
cry.
What mighty Chiefs by Aristides fell,
What heroes perished, heavenly Goddess,
tell,   1170
First thou, oh Peleus! felt his conquering
hand,
Stretched in the dust and weltering in the
sand,
Thro' thy bright shield, the forceful weapon
went,
Thyself in arms o'erthrown, thy corslet rent;
Next rash Antennes met an early fate,
And feared, alas! th' unequal foe too late;
And Delucus the sage, and Philo fell,
And Crotan sought the dreary gates of hell,
And Mnemon's self with wealth and honor
crowned,
Revered for virtue, and for fame re-
nowned;   1180

[1] [So the original; query, *day* or *fray* ?]

He, great in battle, feared the hero's hand,
Groaning he fell, and spurned the reeking
sand.
But what bold chief thus rashly dares advance?
Tho' not in youth, he shakes the dreadful lance,
Proudly the earth the haughty warrior trod,
He looked a Monarch and he moved a God:
Then on the Greek with rage intrepid flew
And with one blow th' unwary Greek o'er-
threw;
That hour, oh Chief, and that eventful day
Had bade thee pass a shivering ghost away,
But Pallas, fearful for her fav'rite's life,   1191
Sudden upraised thee to renew the strife;
Then Aristides with fresh vigor rose,
Shame fired his breast, his soul with anger
glows,
With all his force he rushes on the foe,
The warrior bending disappoints the blow,
And thus with rage contemptuous, 'Chieftain,
know,
Hippias, the loved of heaven, thine eyes be-
hold,
Renowned for strength of arm, in battle bold,
But tell thy race, and who the man whose
might   1200
Dares cope with rebel Athens' King in fight.'
Stung to the soul, 'Oh Slave,' the Greek returns,
While his big heart within his bosom burns,
'Perfidious Prince, to faith and truth unknown;
On Athens' ashes, raise thy tyrant throne,
When Grecia's chiefs, and Grecia's heroes fall,
When Persia's fires invest her lofty wall,
When nought but slaves within her towers re-
main,
Then, nor till then, shalt thou, oh Hippias,
reign,
Then, nor till then, will Athens yield her ⎫
fame   1210 ⎪
To foul dishonor, and eternal shame;   ⎬
Come on! no matter what my race or name; ⎪
For this, oh Prince, this truth unerring know, ⎭
That in a Greek, you meet a noble foe.'
Furious he said, and on the Prince he sprung
With all his force, the meeting armor rung,
Struggling they raged, and both together fell.
That hour the tyrant's ghost had entered hell,
But partial fate prolonged the Prince's breath,
Renewed the combat, and forbad the death.
Meanwhile the hosts, the present war sus-
pend,   1221
Silent they stand, and heaven's decree attend.
First the bright lance majestic Hippias threw
But erringly the missile weapon flew;
Then Aristides hurled the thirsty dart,
Struck the round shield, and nearly pierced his
heart,
But the bright arms, that shone with conscious
pride,
Received the blow, and turned the point aside.
And thus, the Greek, 'Whom your enquiring
eyes
Behold, oh Prince,' th' Athenian hero cries,
'Is Aristides, called the just, a name   1231
By Athens honored, nor unknown to fame.'
Scared at the sound, and seized by sudden
fright,

The Prince starts back, in mean, inglorious
   flight.
And now Bellona rages o'er the field,
All strive elated, all disdain to yield ;
And great Themistocles in arms renowned,
Stretched heaps of heroes on the groaning
   ground.
First by his hand fell Delos' self, divine,
The last loved offspring of a noble line,   1240
Straight thro' his neck the reeking dart was
   driven,
Prostrate he sinks, and vainly calls to heaven.
Next godlike Phanes, midst the Persians just,
Leucon and mighty Caudos bit the dust ;
And now the Greek, with pride imprudent,
   dares
Victorious Mandrocles renowned in wars.
The agile Persian swift avoids the blow
Furious disarms and grasps th' unequal foe !
Th' intrepid Greek, with godlike calm awaits
His instant fall, and dares th' impending
   fates,   1250
But great Cynœgirus his danger spies
And lashed his steeds, the ponderous chariot
   flies,
Then from its brazen bulk, he leaps to ground,
Beneath his clanging arms the plains resound,
And on the Persian rushes fierce, and raised
The clattering axe on high, which threatening
   blazed,
And lopped his head ; out spouts the smoking
   gore
And the huge trunk rolled bleeding on the
   shore.
And then Cynœgirus, ' Thus, Persian, go
And boast thy victory in the shades below, 1260
A headless form, and tell who bade thee bleed,
For know a Greek performed the wonderous
   deed :
But thou, Themistocles, oh hero ! say
Who bade thee rush, to tempt th' unequal
   fray ?
But learn from this, thy daring to restrain,
And seek less mighty foes upon the plain.'
With secret wrath the youthful hero burned
And thus impetuous to the Chief returned ;
' Such thoughts as these, unworthy those who
   dare
The battle's rage, and tempt the toils of
   war ;   1270
Heedless of death, and by no fears opprest,
Conquest my aim, I leave to heaven the rest.'
He said, and glowed with an immortal light,
Plunged 'midst the foes, and mingled in the
   fight.
Zeno the bravest of the Persian youth
Renowned for filial piety and truth ;
His mother's only joy ; she loved to trace
His father's features in his youthful face ;
That Sire, in fight o'erwhelmed, mid seas of
   gore
Slept unentombed, and cared for fame no
   more.   1280
And now as youth in opening manhood glows,
All his loved father in his visage rose,
Like him, regardful of his future fame,
Resolved like him to immortalize his name,

At glory's call, he quits his native shore
And feeble parent, to return no more ;
Oh ! what prophetic griefs her bosom wrung
When on his neck in agony she hung !
When on that breast she hid her sorrowing
   face,
And feared to take, or shun, the last em-
   brace !   1290
Unhappy youth ! the fates decree thy doom,
Those flowers, prepared for joy, shall deck thy
   tomb.
Thy mother now no more shall hail thy name
So high enrolled upon the lists of fame,
Nor check the widow's tear, the widow's sigh,
For e'en her son, her Zeno's doom to die.
Zeno, e'en thou ! for so the Gods decree,
A parents' threshold opes no more for thee !
On him the hero turned his eye severe
Nor on his visage saw one mark of fear ;   1300
There manly grace improved each separate
   part,
And joined by ties of truth, the face and heart.
The supple javelin then the Grecian tries
With might gigantic, and the youth defies
Its point impetuous, at his breast he flung,
The brazen shield received, and mocking rung ;
Then Zeno seized the lance, the Chief defied,
And scoffing, thus began, in youthful pride ;
' Go, mighty Greek ! to weaker warriors go,
And fear this arm, and an unequal foe ;   1310
A mother gave the mighty arms I bear,
Nor think with such a gift, I cherish fear.'
He hurled the lance, but Pallas' self was
   there,
And turned the point, it passed in empty air.
With hope renewed, again the hero tries
His boasted might, the thirsty weapon flies
In Zeno's breast it sinks, and drank the gore,
And stretched the hero vanquished on the
   shore ;
Gasping for utterance, and life, and breath,
For fame he sighs, nor fears approaching
   death.   1320
Themistocles perceived, and bending low
Thought of his friends, and tears began to
   flow
That washed the bleeding bosom of his foe.
Young Zeno then, the Grecian hero eyed
Rejects his offered aid, and all defied,
Breathed one disdainful sigh, and turned his
   head and died.
Such Persians did the godlike warrior slay,
And bade their groaning spirits pass away.
Epizelus, the valiant and the strong,
Thundered in fight, and carried death along ;
Him not a Greek in strength of arms sur-
   passed,   1331
In battle foremost, but in virtue last.
He, impious man, to combat dared defy
The Gods themselves, and senate of the sky,
E'en earth and heaven, and heaven's eternal
   sire,
He mocks his thunders, and disdains his ire.
But now the retributive hour is come,
And rigid justice seals the Boaster's doom,
Theseus he sees, within the fight, revealed
To him alone — to all the rest concealed.   1340

To punish guilt, he leaves the shades below
And quits the seat of never ending woe.
Pale as in death, upon his hands he bore
Th' infernal serpent of the dreadful shore,
To stay his progress should he strive to fly
From Tart'rus far, and gain the upper sky.
This (dreadful sight!) with slippery sinews
   now
Wreathed round his form, and clasped his
   ghastly brow;
With horror struck, and seized with sudden
   awe
The Greek beheld, nor mingled in the war. 1350
Withheld from combat by the force of fear,
He trembling thus — ' Oh say, what God draws
   near ?
But speak thy will, if 't is a God, oh speak!
Nor vent thy vengeance on a single Greek.'
Vainly he suppliant said — o'erpowered with
   fright,
And instant from his eyeballs fled the sight;
Confused, distracted, to the skies he throws
His frantic arms, and thus bewails his woes:
' Almighty! thou by whom the bolts are
   driven!'
He said, and cast his sightless balls to
   heav'n,   1360
' Restore my sight, unhappy me, restore
My own loved offspring, to behold once more!
So will I honor thy divine abodes,
And learn how dreadful th' avenging Gods!
And if — but oh forbid! you mock my prayer
And cruel fate me ever cursed declare,
Give me, to yield to fame alone my life
And fall immortalized, — in glorious strife!'
He said — the God who thunders thro' the
   air,
Frowns on his sufferings and rejects his
   prayer.   1370
Around his form the dreadful Ægis spread
And darts fall harmless on his wretched head;
Condemned by fate in ceaseless pain to groan,
Friendless, in grief, in agony alone.
Now Mars and death pervade on every side
And heroes fall, and swell the crimson tide.
Not with less force th' Athenian leader shone
In strife conspicuous, nor to fame unknown,
Advanced in wisdom, and in honored years,
He nor for life, but for the battle fears.   1380
Borne swift as winds within the flying car
Now here, now there, directs the swelling war,
On every side the foaming coursers guides,
Here praises valor, and there rashness chides;
While from his lips persuasive accents flow
T' inspire th' Athenians, or unman the foe.
The glorious Greeks rush on, with daring
   might
And shout and thunder, and encrease the fight.
Nor yet inglorious do the Persians shine,
In battle's ranks they strength and valor
   join.   1390
Datis himself impels the ponderous car
Thro' broken ranks, conspicuous in the war,
In armor sheathed, and terror round him
   spread
He whirls his chariot over heaps of dead;
Where'er he dreadful rushes, warriors fly,

Ghosts seek their hell, and chiefs and heroes
   die.
All pale with rage he ranks on ranks o'er-
   throws,
For blood he gasps, and thunders midst his
   foes.
Callimachus the mighty leader found
In fight conspicuous, bearing death around. 1400
The lance wheeled instant from the Persian's
   hand
Transfixed the glorious Grecian in the sand.
Fate ends the hero's life, and stays his breath
And clouds his eyeballs with the shade of
   death:
Erect in air the cruel javelin stood,
Pierced thro' his breast, and drank the spouting
   blood.
Released from life's impending woes and care,
The soul immerges in the fields of air:
Then, crowned with laurels, seeks the blest
   abodes
Of awful Pluto, and the Stygian floods.   1410
And now with joy great Aristides saw
Again proud Hippias thundering thro' the war,
And mocking thus, ' Oh tyrant, now await
The destined blow, behold thy promised fate!
Thrice mighty King, obey my javelin's call
For e'en thy godlike self 's decreed to fall;'
He said, and hurled the glittering spear on
   high,
The destined weapon hissed along the sky;
Winged by the hero's all-destroying hand
It pierced the Prince, and stretched him on
   the sand.   1420
Then thro' the air the awful peals were driven
And lightnings blazed along the vast of hea-
   ven.
The Persian hosts behold their bulwark die,
Fear chills their hearts, and all their numbers
   fly,
And reached the fleet; the shouting Greeks
   pursue
All Asia's millions, flying in their view.
On, on, they glorious rush, and side by side
Yet red with gore, they plunge into the tide;
For injured freedom's sake, th' indignant main
With swelling pride receives the crimson
   stain;   1430
The Persians spread the sail, nor dare delay, ⎫
And suppliant call upon the King of day, ⎬
But vainly to their Gods the cowards pray. ⎟
Some of the ships th' Athenian warriors stay ⎭
And fire their bulks; the flames destroying
   rise,
Rushing they swell, and mount into the skies.
Foremost Cynœgirus with might divine,
While midst the waves his arms majestic
   shine;
With blood-stained hand a Persian ship he
   seized,
The vessel vainly strove to be released;   1440
With fear the crew the godlike man beheld,
And pride and shame their troubled bosoms
   swelled.
They lop his limb: then Pallas fires his frame
With scorn of death, and hope of future fame:
Then with the hand remaining seized the prize,

A glorious spirit kindling in his eyes.
Again the Persians wield the unmanly blow
And wreck their vengeance on a single foe.
The fainting Greek by loss of blood opprest
Still feels the patriot rise within his breast. 1450
Within his teeth the shattered ship he held,
Nor in his soul one wish for life rebelled.
But strength decaying, fate suppress his breath,
And o'er his brows expand the dews of death.
The Elysium plains his generous spirit trod,
' He lived a Hero and he died a God.'
By vengeance fired, the Grecians from the
   deep
With rage and shouting, scale the lofty ship,
Then in the briny bosom of the main
They hurl in heaps the living and the slain.
Thro' the wide shores resound triumphant
   cries, 1461
Fill all the seas, and thunder thro' the skies.

II

AN ESSAY ON MIND

' My narrow leaves cannot in them contayne
The large discourse.' — *Spenser.*

In 1826, when Elizabeth Barrett was twenty, her first volume of verse was offered to the public under the title of *An Essay on Mind, with Other Poems.* (LONDON, James Duncan.) Nineteen years later she said of it, in deprecation, to Robert Browning, whose growing interest in the poetess disposed him to regard with reverential interest everything that bore her signature, that it was only a ' girlish exercise,' and, ' after all, more printed than published.' This probably means that her father, Mr. Moulton-Barrett, bore more than half the cost of production. In the notes for her biography which Mrs. Browning furnished to Mr. Horne in 1853, she mentions the ' Essay on Mind ' as ' long repented of, and worthy of all repentance ; ' ' and yet,' she adds, ' it is not without traces of an individual thinking and feeling. The bird pecks through the shell in it.' The ' Other Poems ' consisted of fourteen miscellaneous pieces, mostly occasional verses or personal tributes, — ' On the Death of Lord Byron,' ' To My Father on his Birthday,' etc., of small intrinsic merit, and no permanent significance.

ANALYSIS OF THE FIRST BOOK

THE poem commences by remarking the desire, natural to the mind, of investigating its own qualities — qualities the more exalted, as their development has seldom been impeded by external circumstances — The various dispositions of different minds are next considered, and are compared to the varieties of scenic nature ; inequalities in the spiritual not being more wonderful than inequalities in the natural — Byron and Campbell contrasted — The varieties of genius having been thus treated, the art of criticism is briefly alluded to, as generally independent of genius, but always useful to its productions — Jeffrey — The various stages of life in which genius appears, and the different causes by which its influence is discovered — Cowley, Alfieri — Allusion to the story of the emotion of Thucydides on hearing Herodotus recite his History at the Olympic Games — The elements of Mind are thus arranged, Invention, Judgment, Memory, and Association — The creations of mind are next noticed, among which we first behold Philosophy — History, Science, and Metaphysics are included in the studies of Philosophy.

Of History, it is observed, that though on a cursory view her task of recalling the past may appear of little avail, it is in reality one of the highest importance — The living are sent for a lesson to the grave — The present state of Rome alluded to ; and the future state of England anticipated — Condemnation of those who deprive historical facts of their moral inference, and only make use of their basis to render falsehood more secure — Gibbon — Condemnation of those who would color the political conduct of past ages with their own political feelings — Hume, Mitford — From the writers, we turn to the readers of history — Their extreme scepticism, or credulity — They are recommended to be guided by no faction ; but to measure facts by their consistency with reason — to study the personal character and circumstances of an historian, before they give entire credit to his representations — The influence of private feeling and prejudice — Miller — Science is introduced — Apostrophe to man — Episode of Archimedes — Parallel between history and science — The pride of the latter considered most excessive — The risk attending knowledge — Buffon, Leibnitz — The advantageous experience to be derived from the errors of others, illustrated by an allusion to Southey's Hexameters — Utility the object of science — An exclusive attention to parts deprecated, since it is impossible even to have a just idea of PARTS, without acquiring a knowledge of their relative situation in the whole — The extreme difficulty of enlarging the contemplations of a mind long accustomed to contracted views — The scale of knowledge — every science being linked with the one preceding and succeeding — giving and receiving reciprocal support — Why this system is not calculated, as might be conjectured, either to render scientific men superficial, or to intrude on the operations of genius — That the danger of knowledge originates in PARTIAL knowledge — Apostrophe to Newton.

BOOK I

SINCE Spirit first inspir'd, pervaded all,
And Mind met Matter, at th' Eternal call —
Since dust weigh'd Genius down, or Genius
   gave
Th' immortal halo to the mortal's grave ;

Th' ambitious soul her essence hath defin'd,
And Mind hath eulogiz'd the pow'rs of Mind.
Ere Revelation's holy light began
To strengthen Nature, and illumine Man —
When Genius, on Icarian pinions, flew,   9
And Nature's pencil, Nature's portrait, drew ;
When Reason shudder'd at her own wan beam,
And Hope turn'd pale beneath the sickly
    gleam —
Ev'n then hath Mind's triumphant influence
    spoke,
Dust own'd the spell, and Plato's spirit woke —
Spread her eternal wings, and rose sublime
Beyond th' expanse of circumstance and time :
Blinded, but free, with faith instinctive, soar'd,
And found her home, where prostrate saints
    ador'd !

Thou thing of light ! that warm'st the breasts
    of men,
Breath'st from the lips, and tremblest from the
    pen !   20
Thou, form'd at once t' astonish, fire, be-
    guile, —
With Bacon reason, and with Shakespeare
    smile !
The subtle cause, ethereal essence ! say,
Why dust rules dust, and clay surpasses clay ;
Why a like mass of atoms should combine
To form a Tully, and a Catiline ?
Or why, with flesh perchance of equal weight,
One cheers a prize-fight, and one frees a state ?
Why do not I the muse of Homer call,
Or why, indeed, did Homer sing at all ?   30
Why wrote not Blackstone upon love's delusion,
Or Moore, a libel on the Constitution ?
Why must the faithful page refuse to tell
That Dante, Laura sang, and Petrarch, Hell —
That Tom Paine argued in the throne's de-
    fence —
That Byron nonsense wrote, and Thurlow
    sense —
That Southey sigh'd with all a patriot's cares,
While Locke gave utterance to Hexameters ?
Thou thing of light ! instruct my pen to find
Th' unequal pow'rs, the various forms of
    Mind !   40

O'er Nature's changeful face direct your sight ;
View light meet shade, and shade dissolve in
    light !
Mark, from the plain, the cloud-capp'd moun-
    tain soar ;
The sullen ocean spurn the desert shore !
Behold, afar, the playmate of the storm,
Wild Niagara lifts his awful form —
Spits his black foam above the madd'ning
    floods,
Himself the savage of his native woods —
See him, in air, his smoking torrents wheel,
While the rocks totter, and the forests reel —
Then, giddy, turn ! lo ! Shakespeare's Avon
    flows,   51
Charm'd, by the green-sward's kiss, to soft re-
    pose ;
With tranquil brow reflects the smile of fame,
And, 'midst her sedges, sighs her Poet's name.

Thus, in bright sunshine, and alternate storms,
Is various mind express'd in various forms.
In equal men, why burns not equal fire ?
Why are not valleys hills, — or mountains
    higher ?
Her destin'd way, hath destin'd Nature trod ;
While Matter, Spirit rules, and Spirit, God. 60

Let outward scenes, for inward sense design'd,
Call back our wand'rings to the world of
    Mind !
Where Reason, o'er her vasty realms, may
    stand,
Convene proud thoughts, and stretch her scep-
    ter'd hand.
Here, classic recollections breathe around ;
Here, living Glory consecrates the ground ;
And here, Mortality's deep waters span
The shores of Genius, and the paths of Man !

O'er this imagin'd land, your soul direct —
Mark Byron, the Mont Blanc of intellect,   70
'Twixt earth and heav'n exalt his brow sub-
    lime,
O'erlook the nations, and shake hands with
    Time !
Stretch'd at his feet do Nature's beauties
    throng,
The flow'rs of love, the gentleness of song ;
Above, the Avalanche's thunder speaks,
While Terror's spirit walks abroad, and
    shrieks !

To some Utopian strand, some fairy shore,
Shall soft-eyed Fancy waft her Campbell o'er !
Wont, o'er the lyre of Hope, his hand to fling,
And never waken a discordant string ;   80
Who ne'er grows awkward by affecting grace,
Or ' Common sense confounds with common-
    place ; '
To bright conception, adds expression chaste,
And human feeling joins to classic taste.
For still, with magic art, he knows, and knew,
To touch the heart, and win the judgment
    too !

Thus, in uncertain radiance, Genius glows,
And fitful gleams on various mind reposes :
While Mind, exulting in th' admitted day,
On various themes, reflects its kindling ray. 90
Unequal forms receive an equal light ;
And Klopstock wrote what Kepler could not
    write.

Yet Fame hath welcom'd a less noble few,
And Glory hail'd whom Genius never knew ;
Art labor'd, Nature's birthright, to secure,
And forg'd, with cunning hand, her signa-
    ture.
The scale of life is link'd by close degrees ;
Motes float in sunbeams, mites exist in cheese ;
Critics seize half the fame which bards re-
    ceive, —
And Shakespeare suffers that his friends may
    live ;   100
While Bentley leaves, on stilts, the beaten
    track,

And peeps at glory from some ancient's back.
But, though to hold a lantern to the sun
Be not too wise, and were as well undone —
Though, e'en in this inventive age, alas !
A moral darkness can't be cur'd by gas —
And, though we may not reasonably deem
How poets' craniums can be turn'd by steam —
Yet own we, in our juster reasonings,
That lanterns, gas, and steam, are useful things —   110
And oft, this truth, Reflection ponders o'er —
Bards would write worse, if critics wrote no more.

Let Jeffrey's praise, our willing pen, engage,
The letter'd critic of a letter'd age !
Who justly judges, rightfully discerns,
With wisdom teaches, and with candor learns.
His name on Scotia's brightest tablet lives,
And proudly claims the laurel that it gives.

Eternal Genius ! fashion'd like the sun,
To make all beautiful thou look'st upon !   120
Prometheus of our earth ! whose kindling smile
May warm the things of clay a little while ;
Till, by thy touch inspir'd, thine eyes survey'd,
Thou stoop'st to love the glory thou hast made ;
And weepest, human-like, the mortal's fall,
When, by-and-bye, a breath disperses all.
Eternal Genius ! mystic essence ! say,
How, on 'the chosen breast,' descends thy day !   128
Breaks it at once in Thought's celestial dream,
While Nature trembles at the sudden gleam?
Or steals it, gently, like the morning's light,
Shedding, unmark'd, an influence soft and bright,
Till all the landscape gather on the sight ?

As different talents, different breasts, inspire,
So different causes wake the latent fire.
The gentle Cowley of our native clime,
Lisp'd his first accents in Aonian rhyme.
Alfieri's startling muse tun'd not her strings,
And dumbly look'd ' unutterable things ;'   139
Till, when six lustrums o'er his head had past,
Conception found expression's voice at last ;
Broke the bright light, uprose the smother'd flame, —
And Mind and Nature own'd their poet's fame!
To some the waving woods, the harp of spring,
A gently-breathing inspiration bring !
Some hear, from Nature's haunts, her whisper'd call ;
And Mind hath triumph'd by an apple's fall.

Wave Fancy's picturing wand ! recall the scene
Which Mind hath hallow'd — where her sons have been —
Where, 'midst Olympia's concourse, simply great,   150
Th' historic sage, the son of Lyxes, sate,
Grasping th' immortal scroll — he breath'd no sound,

But, calm in strength, an instant look'd around,
And rose — the tone of expectation rush'd
Through th' eager throng — he spake, and Greece was hush'd !
See, in that breathless crowd, Olorus stand,
While one fair boy hangs, list'ning, on his hand —
The young Thucydides ! with upward brow
Of radiance, and dark eye, that beaming now
Full on the speaker, drinks th' inspirëd air —
Gazing entranc'd, and turn'd to marble there !
Yet not to marble — for the wild emotion   162
Is kindling on his cheek, like light on ocean,
Coming to vanish ; and his pulses throb
With transport, and the inarticulate sob
Swells to his lip — internal nature leaps
To glorious life, and all th' historian weeps !
The mighty master mark'd the favor'd child —
Did Genius linger there ?   She did, and smil'd !
Still, on itself, let Mind its eye direct,   170
To view the elements of intellect —
How wild Invention (darling artist !) plies
Her magic pencil, and creating dies ;
And Judgment, near the living canvass, stands,
To blend the colors for her airy hands ;
While Memory waits, with twilight mists o'er-cast,
To mete the length'ning shadows of the past :
And bold Association, not untaught,
The links of fact, unites, with links of thought ;
Forming th' electric chains, which, mystic, bind
Scholastic learning, and reflective mind.   181

Let reasoning Truth's unerring glance survey
The fair creations of the mental ray ;
Her holy lips, with just discernment, teach
The forms, the attributes, the modes of each,
And tell, in simple words, the narrow span
That circles intellect, and fetters man ;
Where darkling mists, o'er Time's last foot-step, creep,
And Genius drops her languid wing — to weep.

See first Philosophy's mild spirit, nigh,   190
Raise the rapt brow, and lift the thoughtful eye ;
Whether the glimmering lamp, that Hist'ry gave,
Light her enduring steps to some lone grave ;
The while she dreams on him, asleep beneath,
And conjures mystic thoughts of life and death —
Whether, on Science' rushing wings, she sweep
From concave heav'n to earth — and search the deep ;
Shewing the pensile globe attraction's force,
The tides their mistress, and the stars their course :
Or whether (task with nobler object fraught)
She turn the pow'rs of thinking back on thought —   201
With mind, delineate mind ; and dare define
The point, where human mingles with divine :
Majestic still, her solemn form shall stand,
To shew the beacon on the distant land —
Of thought, and nature, chronicler sublime !
The world her lesson, and her teacher Time !

And when, with half a smile, and half a sigh,
She lifts old History's faded tapestry,
I' the dwelling of past years — she, aye, is seen
Point to the shades, where bright'ning tints had
    been —   211
The shapeless forms outworn, and mildew'd
    o'er —
And bids us rev'rence what was lov'd before ;
Gives the dank wreath and dusty urn to fame,
And lends its ashes — all she can — a name.
Think'st thou, in vain, while pale Time glides
    away,
She rakes cold graves, and chronicles their
    clay ?
Think'st thou, in vain, she counts the boney
    things,
Once lov'd as patriots, or obey'd as kings ?
Lifts she, in vain, the past's mysterious veil ?
Seest thou no moral in her awful tale ?   221
Can man, the crumbling pile of nations, scan, —
And is their mystic language mute for man ?

Go ! let the tomb its silent lesson give,
And let the dead instruct thee how to live !
If Tully's page hath bade thy spirit burn,
And lit the raptur'd cheek — behold his urn !
If Maro's strains, thy soaring fancy, guide,
That hail ' th' eternal city ' in their pride —
Then turn to mark, in some reflective hour,
The immortality of mortal pow'r !   231
See the crush'd column, and the ruin'd dome —
'T is all Eternity has left of Rome !
While travell'd crowds, with curious gaze, re-
    pair,
To read the littleness of greatness there !

Alas ! alas ! so, Albion shall decay,
And all my country's glory pass away !
So shall she perish, as the mighty must,
And be Italia's rival — in the dust ;
While her ennobled sons, her cities fair,   240
Be dimly thought of 'midst the things that
    were !
Alas ! alas ! her fields of pleasant green,
Her woods of beauty, and each well-known
    scene !
Soon, o'er her plains, shall grisly Ruin haste,
And the gay vale become the silent waste !
Ah ! soon perchance, our native tongue for-
    got —
The land may hear strange words it knoweth
    not ;
And the dear accents which our bosoms move,
With sounds of friendship, or with tones of
    love,
May pass away ; or, conn'd on mould'ring
    page,   250
Gleam 'neath the midnight lamp, for unborn
    sage ;
To tell our dream-like tale to future years,
And wake th' historian's smile, and schoolboy's
    tears !

Majestic task ! to join, though plac'd afar,
The things that have been, with the things that
    are !
Important trust ! the awful dead, to scan,

And teach mankind to moralize from man !
Stupendous charge ! when, on the record true,
Depend the dead, and hang the living too !
And, oh ! thrice impious he, who dares abuse
That solemn charge, and good and ill con-
    fuse !   261
Thrice guilty he who, false with ' words of
    sooth,'
Would pay, to Prejudice, his debt to Truth ;
The hallow'd page of fleeting Time prophane,
And prove to Man that man has liv'd in vain ;
Pass the cold grave, with colder jestings, by ;
And use the truth to illustrate a lie !

Let Gibbon's name be trac'd, in sorrow,
    here, —
Too great to spurn, too little to revere !
Who follow'd Reason, yet forgot her laws,   270
And found all causes, but the ' great first
    Cause : '
The paths of time, with guideless footsteps,
    trod ;
Blind to the light of nature and of God ;
Deaf to the voice, amid the past's dread hour,
Which sounds his praise, and chronicles his
    pow'r !
In vain for him was Truth's fair tablet spread,
When Prejudice, with jaundiced organs, read.
In vain for us the polish'd periods flow,
The fancy kindles, and the pages glow ;
When one bright hour, and startling transport
    past,   280
The musing soul must turn — to sigh at last.
Still let the page be luminous and just,
Nor private feeling war with public trust ;
Still let the pen from narrowing views forbear,
And modern faction ancient freedom spare.
But, ah ! too oft th' historian bends his mind
To flatter party — not to serve mankind ;
To make the dead, in living feuds, engage,
And give all time, the feelings of his age.
Great Hume hath stoop'd, the Stuarts' fame,
    t' increase ;   290
And ultra Mitford soar'd to libel Greece !

Yet must the candid muse, impartial, learn
To trace the errors which her eyes discern ;
View ev'ry side, investigate each part,
And get the holy scroll of Truth by heart ;
No blame misplac'd, and yet no fault forgot —
Like ink employ'd to write with — not to blot.
Hence, while historians, just reproof, incur,
We find some readers, with their authors, err ;
And soon discover, that as few excel   300
In reading justly, as in writing well.
For prejudice, or ignorance, is such,
That men believe too little, or too much ;
Too apt to cavil, or too glad to trust,
With confidence misplac'd, or blame unjust.

Seek out no faction — no peculiar school —
But lean on Reason, as your safest rule.
Let doubtful facts, with patient hand, be led,
To take their place on this Procrustian bed !
What, plainly, fits not, may be thrown aside, 310
Without the censure of pedantic pride :
For nature still, to just proportion, clings ;

And human reason judges natural things.
Moreover, in th' historian's bosom look,
And weigh his feelings ere you trust his book;
His private friendships, private wrongs, de-
    scry,
Where tend his passions, where his int'rests
    lie —
And, while his proper faults your mind engage,
Discern the ruling foibles of his age.
Hence, when on deep research, the work you
    find   320
A too obtrusive transcript of his mind;
When you perceive a fact too highly wrought,
Which kindly seems to prove a fav'rite
    thought;
Or some opposing truth trac'd briefly out,
With hand of careless speed — then turn to
    doubt!
For private feeling, like the taper, glows,
And here a light, and there a shadow, throws.

If some gay picture, vilely daubed, were seen
With grass of azure, and a sky of green,
Th' impatient laughter we'd suppress in
    vain,   330
And deem the painter jesting, or insane.
But, when the sun of blinding prejudice
Glares in our faces, it deceives our eyes;
Truth appears falsehood to the dazzled sight,
The comment apes the fact, and black seems
    white;
Commingled hues, their separate colors lost,
Dance wildly on, in bright confusion tost;
And, midst their drunken whirl, the giddy
    eye
Beholds one shapeless blot for earth and sky.

Of such delusions let the mind take heed,   340
And learn to think, or wisely cease to read;
And, if a style of labor'd grace display
Perverted feelings, in a pleasing way;
False tints, on real objects, brightly laid,
Facts in disguise, and Truth in masquerade —
If cheating thoughts in beauteous dress appear,
With magic sound, to captivate the ear —
Th' enchanting poison of that page decline,
Or drink Circean draughts — and turn to
    swine!

We hail with British pride, and ready
    praise,   350
Enlightened Miller of our modern days!
Too firm though temp'rate, liberal though exact,
To give too much to argument or fact,
To love details, and draw no moral thence,
Or seek the comment, and forget the sense,
He leaves all vulgar aims, and strives alone
To find the ways of Truth, and make them
    known!

Spirit of life! for aye, with heav'nly breath,
Warm the dull clay, and cold abodes of death!
Clasp in its urn the consecrated dust,   360
And bind a laurel round the broken bust;
While mid decaying tombs, thy pensive choice,
Thou bidst the silent utter forth a voice,
To prompt the actors of our busy scene,

And tell what *is*, the tale of what *has been!*
Yet turn, Philosophy! with brow sublime,
Shall Science follow on the steps of Time!
As, o'er Thought's measureless depths, we
    bend to hear
The whispered sound, which stole on Descartes'
    ear,
Hallowing the sunny visions of his youth   370
With that eternal mandate, 'Search for
    Truth!'
Yes! search for Truth — the glorious path is
    free;
Mind shews her dwelling — Nature holds the
    key —
Yes! search for Truth — her tongue shall bid
    thee scan
The book of knowledge, for the use of Man!

Man! Man! thou poor antithesis of power!
Child of all time! yet creature of an hour!
By turns, camelion of a thousand forms,
The lord of empires, and the food of worms!
The little conqueror of a petty space,   380
The more than mighty, or the worse than
    base!
Thou ruin'd landmark, in the desert way,
Betwixt the all of glory, and decay!
Fair beams the torch of Science in thine hand,
And sheds its brightness o'er the glimmering
    land;
While, in thy native grandeur, bold, and free,
Thou bid'st the wilds of nature smile for thee,
And treadest Ocean's paths full royally!
Earth yields her treasures up — celestial air
Receives thy globe of life   when, journeying
    there,   390
It bounds from dust, and bends its course on
    high,
And walks, in beauty, through the wondering
    sky.
And yet, proud clay! thine empire is a span,
Nor all thy greatness makes thee more than
    man!
While Knowledge, Science, only serve t' im-
    part
The god thou *would'st* be, and the thing thou
    art!

Where stands the Syracusan — while the roar
Of men, and engines, echoes through the
    shore?
Where stands the Syracusan? haggard Fate,
With ghastly smile, is sitting at the gate;   400
And Death forgets his silence 'midst the crash
Of rushing ruins — and the torches' flash
Waves redly on the straggling forms that
    die;
And masterless steeds, beneath that gleam,
    dart by,
Scared into madness, by the battle cry —
And sounds are hurtling in the angry air,
Of hate, and pain, and vengeance, and de-
    spair —
The smothered voice of babes — the long wild
    shriek
Of mothers — and the curse the dying speak!
Where stands the Syracusan? tranquil sage,

He bends, sublime, o'er Science' splendid page ; 411
Walks the high circuit of extended mind,
Surpasses man, and dreams not of mankind ;
While, on his listless ear, the battle shout
Falls senseless — as if echo breath'd about
The hum of many words, the laughing glee,
Which linger'd there, when Syracuse was free.
Away ! away ! for louder accents fall —
But not the sounds of joy from marble hall !
Quick steps approach — but not of sylphic feet, 420
Whose echo heralded a smile more sweet,
Coming, all sport, th' indulgent sage, t' upbraid
For lonely hours, to studious musing, paid —
Be hushed ! Destruction bares the flickering blade !
He asked to live, th' unfinished lines to fill,
And died — to solve a problem deeper still.
He died, the glorious ! who, with soaring sight,
Sought some new world, to plant his foot of might ;
Thereon, in solitary pride, to stand,
And lift our planet, with a master's hand ! 430
He sank in death — Creation only gave
That thorn-encumbered space which forms his grave —
An unknown grave, till Tully chanced to stray,
And named the spot where Archimedes lay !
Genius ! behold the limit of thy power !
Thou fir'st the soul — but, when life's dream is o'er,
Giv'st not the silent pulse one throb the more :
And mighty beings come, and pass away,
Like other comets, and like other — clay.

Though analyzing Truth must still divide 440
Historic state, and scientific pride ;
Yet one stale fact, our judging thoughts infer —
Since each is human, each is prone to err !
Oft, in the night of Time, doth History stray,
And lift her lantern, and proclaim it day !
And oft, when day's eternal glories shine,
Doth Science, boasting, cry — 'The light is mine !'
So hard to bear, with unobstructed sight,
Th' excess of darkness, or th' extreme of light.

Yet, to be just, though faults belong to each,
The themes of one, an humbler moral, teach :
And, 'midst th' historian's eloquence, and skill, 452
The human chronicler is human still.
If on past power, his eager thoughts be cast,
It brings an awful antidote — 't is past !
If, deathless fame, his ravish'd organs scan,
The deathless fame exists for buried man :
Power, and decay, at once he turns to view;
And, with the strength, beholds the weakness too.
Not so, doth Science' musing son aspire ; 460
And pierce creation, with his eye of fire.
Yon mystic pilgrims of the starry way,
No humbling lesson, to his soul, convey ;

No tale of change, their changeless course hath taught ;
And works divine excite no earthward thought.
And still, he, reckless, builds the splendid dream ;
And still, his pride increases with his theme ;
And still, the cause is slighted in th' effect ;
And still, self-worship follows self-respect.
Too apt to watch the engines of the scene, 470
And lose the hand, which moves the vast machine ;
View Matter's form, and not its moving soul ;
Interpret parts, and misconceive the whole :
While, darkly musing 'twixt the earth, and sky,
His heart grows narrow, as his hopes grow high ;
And quits, for aye, with unavailing loss,
The sympathies of earth, but not the dross ;
Till Time sweeps down the fabric of his trust ;
And life, and riches, turn to death, and dust.

And such is Man ! 'neath Error's foul assaults, 480
His noblest moods beget his grossest faults !
When Knowledge lifts her hues of varied grace,
The fair exotic of a brighter place,
To keep her stem, from mundane blasts, enshrin'd,
He makes a fatal hot-bed of his mind ;
Too oft adapted, in their growth, to spoil
The natural beauties of a generous soil.
Ah ! such is Man ! thus strong, and weak withal,
His rise oft renders him too prone to fall !
The loftiest hills' fresh tints, the soonest, fade ; 490
And highest buildings cast the deepest shade !

So Buffon err'd ; amidst his chilling dream,
The judgment grew material as the theme :
Musing on Matter, till he called away
The modes of Mind, to form the modes of clay ;
And made, confusing each, with judgment blind,
Mind stoop to dust, and dust ascend to Mind.
So Leibnitz err'd ; when, in the starry hour,
He read no weakness, where was written, 'Power ;'
Beheld the verdant earth, the circling sea ; 500
Nor dreamt so fair a world could cease to be !
Yea ! but he heard the Briton's awful name,
As, scattering darkness, in his might, he came,
Girded with Truth, and earnest to confute
What gave to Matter, Mind's best attribute.
Sternly they strove — th' unequal race was run !
The owlet met the eagle at the sun !

While such defects, their various forms, unfold ;
And rust, so foul, obscures the brightest gold —
Let Science' soaring sons, the ballast, cast, 510
But judge their present errors, by their past.

As some poor wanderer, in the darkness, goes,
When fitful wind, in hollow murmur, blows;
Hailing, with trembling joy, the lightning's
    ray,
Which threats his safety, but illumes his way.

Gross faults buy deep experience. Sages tell
That Truth, like Æsop's fox, is in a well;
And, like the goat, his fable prates about,
Fools must stay in, that wise men may get
    out.
What thousand scribblers, of our age, would
    choose   520
To throw a toga round the English muse;
Rending her garb of ease, which graceful grew
From Dryden's loom, beprankt with varied
    hue!
In that dull aim, by Mind unsanctified,
What thousand Wits would have their wits
    belied,
Devoted Southey! if thou had'st not tried!
Use is the aim of Science; this the end
The wise appreciate, and the good commend.
For not, like babes, the flaming torch, we prize,
That sparkling lustre may attract our eyes;
But that, when evening shades impede the
    sight,   531
It casts, on objects round, a useful light.

Use is the aim of Science! give again
A golden sentence to the faithful pen —
Dwell not on parts! for parts contract the
    mind;
And knowledge still is useless, when confined.
The yearning soul, inclosed in narrow bound,
May be ingenious, but is ne'er profound:
Spoil'd of its strength, the fettered thought
    grows tame;
And want of air extinguishes the flame!   540
And as the sun, beheld in mid-day blaze,
Seems turned to darkness, as we strive to
    gaze;
So mental vigor, on one object, cast,
That object's self becomes obscured at last.
'T is easy, as Experience may aver,
To pass from general to particular.
But most laborious to direct the soul
From studying parts, to reason on the whole:
Thoughts, train'd on narrow subjects, to let
    fall;
And learn the unison of each with all.   550

In Nature's reign, a scale of life, we find:
A scale of knowledge, we behold, in mind;
With each progressive link, our steps ascend,
And traverse all, before they reach the end:
Searching, while Reason's powers may farther
    go,
The things we know not, by the things we
    know.

But hold! methinks some sons of Thought
    demand,
'Why strive to form the Trajan's vase in
    sand?
Are Reason's paths so few, that Mind may call
Her finite energies, to tread them all?   560

Lo! Learning's waves, in bounded channel,
    sweep;
When they flow wider, shall they run as deep?
Shall that broad surface, no dull shallow, hide,
Growing dank weeds of superficial pride?
Then Heaven may leave our giant powers
    alone;
Nor give each soul a focus of its own!
Genius bestows, in vain, the chosen page,
If all the tome, the minds of all, engage!'

Nay! I reply — with free congenial breast,
Let each peruse the part, which suits him
    best!   570
But, lest contracting prejudice mislead,
Regard the context, as he turns to read!
Hence, liberal feeling gives th' enlighten'd
    soul,
The spirit, with the letter of the scroll.

With what triumphant joy, what glad surprise,
The dull behold the dullness of the wise!
What insect tribes of brainless impudence
Buzz round the carcase of perverted sense!
What railing ideots hunt, from classic school,
Each flimsy sage, and scientific fool,   580
Crying, ' 'T is well! we see the blest effect
Of watchful night, and toiling intellect!'
Yet let them pause, and tremble — vainly glad;
For too much learning maketh no man mad!
Too *little* dims the sight, and leads us o'er
The twilight path, where fools have been be-
    fore;
With not enough of Reason's radiance seen,
To track the footsteps, where those fools have
    been.

Divinest Newton! if my pen may shew
A name so mighty, in a verse so low, —   590
Still let the sons of Science, joyful, claim
The bright example of that splendid name!
Still let their lips repeat, my page bespeak,
The sage how learned! and the man how
    meek!
Too wise, to think his human folly less;
Too great, to doubt his proper littleness;
Too strong, to deem his weakness past away;
Too high in soul, to glory in his clay:
Rich in all nature, but her erring side:
Endow'd with all of Science — but its pride.

ANALYSIS OF THE SECOND BOOK

METAPHYSICS — Address to Metaphysicians
— The most considerable portion of their errors
conceived to arise from difficulties attending
the use of words — That on one hand, thoughts
become obscure without the assistance of lan-
guage, while on the other, language from its
material analogy deteriorates from spiritual
meaning — Allusion to a probable mode of com-
munication between spirits after death — That
a limited respect, though not a servile submis-
sion, is due to verbal distinctions — Clearness
of style peculiarly necessary to Metaphysical
subjects — The graces of Composition not in-

consistent with them — Plato, Bacon, Boling-
broke — The extremes into which Philosophers
have fallen with regard to sensation, and re-
flection — Berkeley, Condillac — That subject
briefly considered — Abstractions — Longinus,
Burke, Price, Payne Knight — Blind submis-
sion to authorities deprecated — The Pytha-
gorean saying opposed, and Cicero's unphilo-
sophical assertion alluded to — That, however,
it partakes of injustice to love Truth, and yet
refuse our homage to the advocates of Truth —
How the names of great writers become en-
deared to us by early recollections — Descrip-
tion of the School-boy's first intellectual grati-
fications — That even without reference to the
past, some immortal names are entitled to our
veneration, since they are connected with Truth
— Bacon — Apostrophe to Locke.

Poetry is introduced — More daring than
Philosophy, she personifies abstractions, and
brings the things unseen before the eye of the
Mind — How often reason is indebted to poetic
imagery — Irving — The poetry of prose —
Plato's ingratitude — Philosophers and Poets
contrasted — An attempt to define Poetry —
That the passions make use of her language —
Nature the poet's study — Shakespeare — Hu-
man nature as seen in cities — Scenic nature,
and how the mind is affected thereby — That
Poetry exists not in the object contemplated,
but is created by the contemplating mind — The
ideal — Observations on the structure of verse,
as adapted to the subject treated — Milton,
Horace, Pope — The French Drama — Corneille,
Racine — Harmony and chasteness of versifi-
cation — The poem proceeds to argue, that the
muse will refuse her inspiration to a soul unat-
tuned to generous sympathy, unkindled by the
deeds of Virtue, or the voice of Freedom —
Contemptuous notice of those prompted only
by interest to aspire to poetic eminence — What
should be the Poet's best guerdon — From the
contemplation of motives connected with Free-
dom, we are led by no unnatural transition to
Greece — Her present glorious struggle — An-
ticipation of her ultimate independence, and
the restoration of the Muses to their ancient
seats — Allusion to the death of Byron — Re-
flections on Mortality — The terrors of death as
beheld by the light of Nature — The consola-
tions of death as beheld with reference to a
future state — Contemplation of the immor-
tality of Mind, and her perfected powers —
Conclusion.

BOOK II

But now to higher themes ! no more confin'd 601
To copy Nature, Mind returns to Mind.
We leave the throng, so nobly, and so well,
Tracing, in Wisdom's book, things visible, —
And turn to things unseen ; where, greatly
    wrought,
Soul questions soul, and thought revolves on
    thought.
My spirit loves, my voice shall hail ye, now,

Sons of the patient eye, and passionless brow !
Students sublime ! Earth, man, unmov'd, ye
    view,   609
Time, circumstance ; for what are they to you ?
What is the crash of worlds, — the fall of
    kings, —
When worlds and monarchs are such brittle
    things !
What the tost, shatter'd bark, that blindly
    dares
A sea of storm ? Ye sketch the wave which
    bears !
The cause, and not th' effect, your thoughts
    state ;
The principle of action, not the act, —
The soul ! the soul ! and, 'midst so grand a
    task,
Ye call her rushing passions, and ye ask
Whence are ye ? and each mystic thing re-
    sponds !
I would be all *ye* are — except those bonds ! 620

Except those bonds ! ev'n here is oft descried
The love to parts, the poverty of pride !
Ev'n here, while Mind, in Mind's horizon,
    springs,
Her 'native mud ' is weighing on her wings !
Ev'n here, while Truth invites the ardent crowd,
Ixion-like, they rush t' embrace a cloud !
Ev'n here, oh ! foul reproach to human wit !
A Hobbes hath reasoned, and Spinosa writ !

Rank pride does much ! and yet we justly
    cry,
Our greatest errors in our weakness lie.   630
For thoughts uncloth'd by language are, at best,
Obscure ; while grossness injures· those ex-
    prest —
Through words, — in whose analysis, we find
Th' analogies of Matter, not of Mind :
Hence, when the use of words is graceful
    brought,
As physical dress to metaphysic thought,
The thought, howe'er sublime its pristine
    state,
Is by th' expression made degenerate ;
Its spiritual essence changed, or cramp'd ; and
    hence
Some hold by words, who cannot hold by
    sense ;   640
And leave the thought behind, and take th'
    attire —
Elijah's mantle — but without his fire !
Yet spurn not words ! 't is needful to confess
They give ideas, a body and a dress !
Behold them traverse Learning's region round,
The vehicles of thought on wheels of sound ;
Mind's winged strength, wherewith the height
    is won,
Unless she trust their frailty to the sun.
Destroy the body ! — will the spirit stay ?
Destroy the car ! — will Thought pursue her
    way ?   650
Destroy the wings — let Mind their aid forego !
Do no Icarian billows yawn below ?
Ah ! spurn not words with reckless insolence ;
But still admit their influence with the sense,

And fear to slight their laws ! Perchance we
    find
No perfect code transmitted to mankind ;
And yet mankind, till life's dark sands are
    run,
Prefers imperfect government to none.
Thus Thought must bend to words ! — Some
    sphere of bliss,
Ere long, shall free her from th' alloy of
    this : 660
Some kindred home for Mind — some holy
    place,
Where spirits look on spirits, ' face to face,' —
Where souls may see, as they themselves are
    seen,
And voiceless intercourse may pass between,
All pure — all free ! as light, which doth ap-
    pear
In its own essence, incorrupt and clear !
One service, praise ! one age, eternal youth !
One tongue, intelligence ! one subject, truth !

Till then, no freedom, Learning's search
    affords,
Of soul from body, or of thought from
    words. 670
For thought may lose, in struggling to be
    hence,
The gravitating power of Common-sense ;
Through all the depths of space with Phaeton
    hurl'd,
T' impair our reason, as he scorch'd our world.
Hence, this preceptive truth, my page af-
    firms —
Respect the technicality of terms !
Yet not in base submission — lest we find
That, aiding clay, we crouch too low for Mind ;
Too apt conception's essence to forget,
And place all wisdom in the alphabet. 680

Still let appropriate phrase the sense invest ;
That what is well conceived be well exprest !
Nor e'er the reader's wearied brain engage,
In hunting meaning down the mazy page,
With three long periods tortured into one,
The sentence ended, with the sense begun ;
Nor in details, which schoolboys know by
    heart,
Perplex each turning with the terms of art.
To understand, we deem no common good ;
And 't is less easy to be *understood*. 690
But let not clearness be your only praise,
When style may charm a thousand different
    ways ;
In Plato glow, to life and glory wrought,
By high companionship with noblest thought ;
In Bacon, warm abstraction with a breath,
Catch Poesy's bright beams, and smile be-
    neath ;
In St. John roll, a generous stream, along,
Correctly free, and regularly strong.
Nor scornful deem the effort out of place,
With taste to reason, and convince with
    grace ; 700
But ponder wisely, ere you know, too late,
Contempt of trifles will not prove us great !
The Cynics, not their tubs, respect engage ;

And dirty tunic never made a sage.
E'en Cato — had he own'd the Senate's will,
And wash'd his toga — had been Cato still.
Justly we censure — yet are free to own,
That indecision is a crime unknown.
For, never faltering, seldom reasoning long,
And still most positive whene'er most wrong,
No theoretic sage is apt to fare 711
Like Mah'met's coffin — hung in middle air !
No ! fenc'd by Error's all-sufficient trust,
These stalk ' in nubibus ' — those crawl in dust.
From their proud height, the first demand to
    know,
If spiritual essence should descend more low ?
The last, as vainly, from their dunghill, cry,
Can body's grossness hope t' aspire more high ?
And while Reflection's empire, these disclose,
Sensation's sovereign right is told by those. 720
Lo ! Berkeley proves an old hypothesis !
' Out on the senses ! ' (he was out of his !)
' All is idea ! and nothing real springs
But God, and Reason ' — (not the right of
    kings ?)
' Hold ! ' says Condillac with profound sur-
    prise —
' Why prate of Reason ? we have ears and
    eyes ! '

Condillac ! while the dangerous periods fall
Upon thy page, to stamp sensation *all;*
While (coldly studious !) thine ingenious
    scroll
Endows the mimic statue with a soul 730
Compos'd of sense — behold the generous
    hound —
His piercing eye, his ear awake to sound,
His scent, most delicate organ ! and declare
What triumph hath the ' Art of thinking '
    there !
What Gall, or Spurzheim, on his front hath
    sought
The mystic bumps indicative of Thought ?
Or why, if Thought *do* there maintain her
    throne,
Will reasoning curs leave logic for a bone ?

Mind is imprison'd in a lonesome tower :
Sensation is its window — hence herb, flower,
Landscapes all sun, the rush of thousand
    springs, 741
Waft in sweet scents, fair sights, soft murmur-
    ings ;
And in her joy, she gazeth — yet ere long,
Reason awaketh in her, bold and strong,
And o'er the scene exerting secret laws,
First seeks th' efficient, then the final cause,
Abstracts from forms their hidden accidents,
And marks in outward substance, inward sense.

Our first perceptions formed — we search, to
    find
The operations of the forming mind ; 750
And turn within by Reason's certain route,
To view the shadows of the things without
Discern'd, retain'd, compar'd, combin'd, and
    brought
To mere abstraction, by abstracting Thought.

Hence to discern, retain, compare, connect,
We deem the faculties of Intellect;
The which, mus'd on, exert a new control,
And fresh ideas are open'd on the soul.

Sensation is a stream with dashing spray,
That shoots in idle speed its arrowy way;   760
When lo! the mill arrests its waters' course,
Turning to use their unproductive force:
The cunning wheels by foamy currents sped,
Reflection triumphs, — and mankind is fed!

Since Pope hath shewn, and Learning still
    must shew,
'We cannot reason but from what we
    know,' —
Unfold the scroll of Thought; and turn to
    find
The undeceiving signature of Mind!
There, judge her nature by her nature's course,
And trace her actions upwards to their source.
So when the property of Mind we call   771
An essence, or a substance spiritual,
We name her thus, by marking how she clings
Less to the forms than essences of things;
For body clings to body — objects seen
And substance sensible alone have been
Sensation's study; while reflective Mind,
Essence unseen in objects seen may find;
And, tracing whence her known impressions
    came,
Give single forms an universal name.   780

So, when particular sounds in concord rise,
Those sounds as *melody*, we generalize;
When pleasing shapes and colors blend, the
    soul
Abstracts th' idea of *beauty* from the whole,
Deducting thus, by Mind's enchanting spell,
The intellectual from the sensible.
Hence bold Longinus' splendid periods grew,
'Who was himself the great sublime he
    drew: '
Hence Burke, the poet-reasoner, learn'd to
    trace
His glowing style of energetic grace: 790
Hence thoughts, perchance, some favor'd
    bosoms move,
Which Price might own, and classic Knight
    approve!

Go! light a rushlight, ere the day is done,
And call its glimm'ring brighter than the sun!
Go! while the stars in midnight glory beam,
Prefer their cold reflection in the stream!
But be not that dull slave, who only looks
On Reason, 'through the spectacles of books! '
Rather by Truth determine what is true, —
And reasoning works, through Reason's me-
    dium, view;   800
For authors can't monopolize her light:
'T is your's to read, as well as their's to write.
To judge is your's! — then why submissive
    call,
'The master said so? ' — 't is no rule at all!
Shall passive sufferance e'en to mind belong,
When right divine in man is human wrong?

Shall a high name a low idea enhance,
When all may fail, as some succeed — by
    chance?
Shall fix'd chimeras unfix'd reason shock?
And if Locke err, must thousands err with
    Locke?   810
Men! claim your charter! spurn th' unjust
    control,
And shake the bondage from the free-born
    soul!
Go walk the porticoes! and teach your youth
All names are bubbles, but the name of
    Truth!
If fools, by chance, attend to Wisdom's rules,
'T is no dishonor to be right with fools,
If human faults to Plato's page belong,
Not ev'n with Plato, willingly go wrong.
But though the judging page declare it well
To love Truth better than the lips which tell;
Yet 't were an error, with injustice class'd,   821
T' adore the former, and neglect the last.

Oh! beats there, Heav'n! a heart of human
    frame,
Whose pulses throb not at some kindling
    name?
Some sound, which brings high musings in its
    track,
Or calls perchance the days of childhood back,
In its dear echo, — when, without a sigh,
Swift hoop, and bounding ball, were first laid
    by,
To clasp in joy, from school-room tyrant, free,
The classic volume on the little knee,   830
And con sweet sounds of dearest minstrelsy,
Or words of sterner lore; the young brow
    fraught
With a calm brightness which might mimic
    thought,
Leant on the boyish hand — as, all the while,
A half-heav'd sigh, or aye th' unconscious
    smile
Would tell how, o'er that page, the soul was
    glowing,
In an internal transport, past the knowing!
How feelings, erst unfelt, did then appear,
Give forth a voice, and murmur, 'We are
    here! '
As lute-strings, which a strong hand plays
    upon;   840
Or Memnon's statue singing 'neath the sun.
Ah me! for such are pleasant memories —
And call the tears of fondness to our eyes
Reposing on this gone-by dream — when thus,
One marbled book was all the world to us;
The gentlest bliss our innocent thoughts could
    find —
The happiest cradle of our infant mind!
And though such hours be past, we shall not
    less
Think on their joy with grateful tenderness;
And bless the page which bade our reason
    wake, —   850
And love the prophet, for his mission's sake.
But not alone doth Memory's smouldering
    flame
Reflect a radiance on a glorious name;

For there are names of pride ; and they who
bear
Have walked with Truth, and turn'd their
footsteps where
We walk not — their beholdings aye have
been
O'er Mind's far countries which we have not
seen —
Our thoughts are not their thoughts ! — and oft
we dream
That light upon the awful brow doth gleam,
From that high converse ; as when Moses
trod   860
Towards the people, from the mount of God,
His lips were silent, but his face was bright,
And prostrate Israel trembled at the sight.

What tongue can syllable our Bacon's name,
Nor own a heart exulting in his fame ?
Where prejudice' wild blasts were wont to
blow ;
And waves of ignorance roll'd dark below,
He raised his sail — and left the coast be-
hind, —
Sublime Columbus of the realms of Mind !
Dared folly's mists, opinion's treacherous
sands,   870
And walk'd, with godlike step, th' untrodden
lands !
But ah ! our Muse of Britain, standing near,
Hath dimm'd my tablet with a pensive tear !
Thrice, the proud theme, her free-born voice
essays, —
And thrice that voice is faltering in his praise —
Yea ! till her eyes in silent triumph turn
To mark afar her Locke's sepulchral urn !
Oh urn ! where students rapturous vigils keep,
Where sages envy, and where patriots weep !
Oh Name ! that bids my glowing spirit
wake —   880
To freemen's hearts endeared for Freedom's
sake !
Oh soul ! too bright in life's corrupting hour,
To rise by faction, or to crouch to power !
While radiant Genius lifts her heav'nward
wing,
And human bosoms own the Mind I sing ;
While British writers British thoughts record,
And England's press is fearless as her sword ;
While, 'mid the seas which gird our favor'd
isle,
She clasps her charter'd rights with conscious
smile ;
So long be *thou* her glory, and her guide,   890
Thy page her study, and thy name her pride !
Oh ! ever thus, immortal Locke, belong,
First to my heart, as noblest in my song ;
And since in thee, the muse enraptured find
A moral greatness, and creating mind,
Still may thine influence, which with honor'd
light
Beams when I read, illume me as I write !
The page too guiltless, and the soul too free,
To call a frown from Truth, or blush from
thee !
But where Philosophy would fear to soar,   900
Young Poesy's elastic steps explore !

Her fairy foot, her daring eye pursues
The light of faith — nor trembles as she views !
Wont o'er the Psalmist's holy harp to hang,
And swell the sacred note when Milton sang ;
Mingling reflection's chords with fancy's lays,
The tones of music with the voice of praise !

And while Philosophy, in spirit, free,
Reasons, believes, yet cannot plainly *see*,
Poetic Rapture, to her dazzled sight,   910
Portrays the shadows of the things of light ;
Delighting o'er the unseen worlds to roam,
And waft the pictures of perfection home.
Thus Reason oft the aid of fancy seeks,
And strikes Pierian chords — when Irving
speaks !

Oh ! silent be the withering tongue of those
Who call each page, bereft of measure, prose ;
Who deem the Muse possest of such faint
spells,
That like poor fools, she glories in her *bells ;*
Who hear her voice alone in tinkling chime, 920
And find a line's whole magic in its rhyme ;
Forgetting, if the gilded shrine be fair,
What purer spirit may inhabit there !
For such, — indignant at her questioned might,
Let Genius cease to charm — and Scott to
write !

Ungrateful Plato ! o'er thy cradled rest,
The Muse hath hung, and all her love exprest :
Thy first imperfect accents fondly taught,
And warm'd thy visions with poetic thought !
Ungrateful Plato ! should her deadliest foe 930
Be found within the breast she tended so ?
Spoil'd of her laurels, should she weep to
find
The best belov'd become the most unkind ?
And was it well or generous, Brutus like,
To pierce the hand that gave the power to
strike ?

Sages, by reason, reason's powers direct ;
Bards, through the heart, convince the intel-
lect.
Philosophy majestic brings to view
Mind's perfect modes, and fair proportions
too ;
Enchanting Poesy bestows the while,   940
Upon its sculptured grace, her magic smile,
Bids the cold form, with living radiance glow,
And stamps existence on its marble brow !
For Poesy's whole essence, when defined,
Is elevation of the reasoning mind,
When inward sense from Fancy's page is
taught,
And moral feeling ministers to Thought.
And hence, the natural passions all agree
In seeking Nature's language — poetry.   949
When Hope, in soft perspective, from afar,
Sees lovely scenes more lovely than they are ;
To deck the landscape, tiptoe Fancy brings
Her plastic shapes, and bright imaginings.
Or when man's breast by torturing pangs is
stung,
If fearful silence cease t' enchain his tongue,

In metaphor, the feelings seek relief,
And all the soul grows eloquent with grief.

Poetic fire, like Vesta's, pure and bright,
Should draw from Nature's sun, its holy light.
With Nature, should the musing poet roam, 960
And steal instruction from her classic tome ;
When 'neath her guidance, least inclin'd to
    err —
The ablest painter when he copies *her*.

Beloved   Shakespeare !   England's   dearest
    fame !
Dead is the breast that swells not at thy name !
Whether thine Ariel skim the seas along,
Floating on wings etherial as his song —
Lear rave amid the tempest — or Macbeth
Question the hags of hell on midnight heath —
Immortal Shakespeare ! still, thy lips im-
    part   970
The noblest comment on the human heart.
And as fair Eve, in Eden newly placed,
Gazed on her form, in limpid waters traced,
And stretch'd her gentle arms, with pleased
    surprise,
To meet the image of her own bright eyes —
So Nature, on thy magic page, surveys
Her sportive graces, and untutored ways !
Wondering, the soft reflection doth she see,
Then laughing owns she loves herself in thee !

Shun not the haunts of crowded cities then ;
Nor e'er, as man, forget to study men !   981
What though the tumult of the town intrude
On the deep silence, and the lofty mood ;
'T will make thy human sympathies rejoice,
To hear the music of a human voice —
To watch strange brows by various reason
    wrought,
To claim the interchange of thought with
    thought ;
T' associate mind with mind, for Mind's own
    weal,
As steel is ever sharpen'd best by steel.
T' impassion'd bards, the scenic world is
    dear, —   990
But Nature's glorious masterpiece is here !
All poetry is beauty, but exprest
In inward essence, not in outward vest.
Hence lovely scenes, reflective poets find,
Awake their lovelier images in Mind :
Nor doth the pictur'd earth, the bard invite,
The lake of azure, or the heav'n of light,
But that his swelling breast arouses there,
Something less visible, and much more fair !
There is a music in the landscape round, —
A silent voice, that speaks without a sound —
A witching spirit, that reposing near,   1002
Breathes to the heart, but comes not to the ear !
These softly steal, his kindling soul t' embrace,
And natural beauty, gild with moral grace.
Think not, when summer breezes tell their tale,
The poet's thoughts are with the summer gale ;
Think not his Fancy builds her elfin dream
On painted floweret, or on sighing stream :
No single objects cause his raptured starts, 1010
For Mind is narrow'd, not inspir'd by parts ;

But o'er the scene the poet's spirit broods,
To warm the thoughts that form his noblest
    moods ;
Peopling his solitude with faëry play,
And beckoning shapes that whisper him
    away, —
While lilied fields, and hedge-row blossoms
    white,
And hills, and glittering streams, are full in
    sight —
The forests wave, the joyous sun beguiles,
And all the poetry of Nature smiles !

Such poetry is formed by Mind, and not   1020
By scenic grace of one peculiar spot.
The artist lingers in the moon-lit glade,
And light and shade, with him, are — light and
    shade.
The philosophic chymist wandering there,
Dreams of the soil, and nature of the air.
The rustic marks the young herbs' fresh'ning
    hue,
And only thinks — his scythe may soon pass
    through !
None ' muse on nature with a Poet's eye,'
None read, but Poets, Nature's poetry !
Its characters are trac'd in mystic hand,   1030
And all may gaze, but few can understand.

Nor here alone the Poet's dwelling rear,
Though Beauty's voice perchance is sweetest
    here !
Bind not his footsteps to the sylvan scene,
To heathy banks, fair woods, and valleys green,
When Mind is all his own ! her dear impress
Shall throw a magic o'er the wilderness,
As o'er the blossoming vale, and aye recall
Its shadowy plane, and silvery waterfall,
Or sleepy crystal pool, reposing by,   1040
To give the earth a picture of the sky !
Such, gazed on by the spirit, are, I ween,
Lovelier than ever prototype was seen ;
For Fancy teacheth Memory's hand to trace
Nature's ideal form in Nature's place.

In every theme by lofty Poet sung,
The thought should seem to speak, and not the
    tongue.
When godlike Milton lifts th' exalted song,
The subject bears the burning words along —
Resounds the march of Thought, th' o'erflowing
    line,   1050
Full cadence, solemn pause, and strength di-
    vine !
When Horace chats his neighbor's faults away,
The sportive measures, like his muse, are gay ;
For once Good-humor Satire's by-way took,
And all his soul is laughing in his book !
On moral Pope's didactic page is found,
Sound rul'd by sense, and sense made clear by
    sound ;
The power to reason, and the taste to please,
While, as the subject varies in degrees,   1059
He stoops with dignity, and soars with ease.

Hence let our Poets, with discerning glance,
Forbear to imitate the stage of France.

What though Corneille arouse the thrilling
    chords,
And walk with Genius o'er th' inspirëd boards ;
What though his rival bring, with calmer grace,
The classic unities of time and place, —
All polish, and all eloquence — 't were mean
To leave the path of Nature for Racine ;
When Nero's parent, 'midst her woe, defines
The wrong that tortures — in two hundred
    lines :   1070
Or when Orestes, madden'd by his crime,
Forgets life, joy, and every thing — but rhyme.

While thus to character and nature, true,
Still keep the harmony of verse in view ;
Yet not in changeless concord, — it should
    be
Though graceful, nervous, — musical, though
    free ;
Not clogg'd by useless drapery, not beset
By the superfluous word, or epithet,
Wherein Conception only dies in state,
As Draco, smother'd by the garments' weight —
But join, Amphion-like, (whose magic fire   1081
Won the deep music of the Maian lyre,
To call Bœotia's city from the ground,)
The just in structure, with the sweet in sound.

Nor this the whole — the poet's classic strain
May flow in smoothest numbers, yet in vain ;
And Taste may please, and Fancy sport awhile,
And yet Aonia's muse refuse to smile !
For lo ! her heavenly lips these words reveal —
'The sage may coldly *think*, the bard must
    feel !   1090
And if his writings, to his heart untrue,
Would ape the fervent throb it never knew ;
If generous deeds, and Virtue's noblest part,
And Freedom's voice, could never warm that
    heart ;
If Interest tax'd the produce of the brain,
And fetter'd Genius follow'd in her train,
Weeping as each unwilling word she spoke, —
Then hush the lute — its master string is
    broke !
In vain, the skilful hand may linger o'er —
Concord is dead, and music speaks no more ! '

There are, and have been such — they were for-
    got   1101
If shame could veil their page, if tears could
    blot !
There are, and have been, whose dishonor'd
    lay
Aspired t' enrapture that the world might —
    pay !
Whose life was one long bribe, oft counted
    o'er, —
Brib'd to think on, and brib'd to think no
    more ;
Brib'd to laugh, weep, nor ask the reason
    why ;
Brib'd to tell truth, and brib'd to gild a lie !
Oh Man ! for this, the sensual left behind,
We boast our empire o'er the vast of Mind ?
Oh Mind ! reported valueless, till sold,   1111
Thought dross till metamorphos'd into gold

By Midas' touch — breath'st thou immortal
    verse
To throw a ducat in an empty purse ?
To walk the market at a belman's cry,
For knaves to sell, and wond'ring fools to
    buy ?
Can Heav'n-born bards, undone by lucre's
    lust,
Crouch thus, like Heav'n-born ministers, to
    dust ?
Alas ! to dust indeed — yet wherefore blame ?
They keep their profits, though they lose their
    fame.   1120

Leave to the dross they seek, the grovelling
    throng,
And swell with nobler aim th' Aonian song !
Enough for thee uninfluenc'd and unhir'd,
If Truth reward the strain herself inspir'd !
Enough for thee, if grateful Man commend,
If Genius love, and Virtue call thee friend !
Enough for thee, to wake th' exalted mood,
Reprove the erring, and confirm the good ;
Excite the tender smile, the generous tear,
Or rouse the thought to loftiest Nature dear,
Which rapturous greets amidst the fervent
    line   1131
Thy name, O Freedom ! glorious Hellas,
    thine !

I love my own dear land — it doth rejoice
The soul, to stretch my arms, and lift my
    voice,
To tell her of my love ! I love her green
And bowery woods, her hills in mossy sheen,
Her silver running waters — there 's no spot
In all her dwelling, which my breast loves
    not —
No place not heart-enchanted ! Sunnier skies,
And calmer waves, may meet another's eyes ;
I love the sullen mist, the stormy sea,   1141
The winds of rushing strength which, like the
    land, are free !
Such is my love — yet turning thus to thee,
Oh Græcia ! I must hail with hardly less
Of joy, and pride, and deepening tenderness,
And feelings wild, I know not to control,
My other country — country of my soul !
For so, to me, thou art ! my lips have sung
Of thee with childhood's lisp, and harp un-
    strung !
In thee, my Fancy's pleasant walks have been,
Telling her tales, while Memory wept be-
    tween !   1151
And now *for* thee I joy, with heart beguiled,
As if a dying friend looked up, and smiled.

Lo ! o'er Ægæa's waves, the shout hath
    ris'n !
Lo ! Hope hath burst the fetters of her prison !
And Glory sounds the trump along the shore,
And Freedom walks where Freedom walk'd
    before !
Ipsara glimmers with heroic light,
Redd'ning the waves that lash her flaming
    height ;   1159
And Ægypt hurries from that dark blue sea !

Lo! o'er the cliffs of fam'd Thermopylæ,
And voiceful Marathon, the wild winds sweep,
Bearing this message to the brave who sleep —
'They come! they come! with their embat-
  tled shock,
From Pelion's steep, and Paros' foam-dash'd
  rock!
They come from Tempe's vale, and Helicon's
  spring,
And proud Eurotas' banks, the river king!
They come from Leuctra, from the waves that
  kiss
Athena — from the shores of Salamis;   1169
From Sparta, Thebes, Eubœa's hills of blue —
To live with Hellas — or to sleep with you!'

  Smile — smile, beloved land! and though no
    lay
From Doric pipe, may charm thy glades to-
  day —
Though dear Ionic music murmur not
Adown the vale — its echo all forgot!
Yet smile, beloved land! for soon, around,
Thy silent earth shall utter forth a sound,
As whilom — and, its pleasant groves among,
The Grecian voice shall breathe the Grecian
  song,
While the exilèd muse shall 'habit still   1180
The happy haunts of her Parnassian hill.
Till then, behold the cold dumb sepulchre —
The ruin'd column — ocean, earth, and air,
Man, and his wrongs — thou hast Tyrtæus
  there!
And pardon, if across the heaving main,
Sound the far melody of minstrel strain,
In wild and fitful gust from England's shore,
For *his* immortal sake, who never more
Shall tread with living foot, and spirit free,
Her fields, or breathe her passionate poetry —
The pilgrim bard, who lived, and died for
  thee,
Oh land of Memory! loving thee no less   1192
Than parent — with the filial tenderness,
And holy ardor of the Argive son,
Straining each nerve to bear thy chariot on —
Till when its wheels the place of glory swept,
He laid him down before the shrine — and
  slept.

So be it! at his cold unconscious bier,
We fondly sate, and dropp'd the natural tear —
Yet wept not wisely, for he sank to rest   1200
On the dear earth his waking thoughts loved
  best,
And gently life's last pulses stole away!
No Moschus sang a requiem o'er his clay,
But Greece was sad! and breathed above, be-
  low,
The warrior's sigh, the silence, and the woe!

  And is this all? Is this the little sum
For which we toil — to which our glories come?
Doth History bend her mouldering pages o'er,
And Science stretch her bulwark from the
  shore,
And Sages search the mystic paths of Thought,
And Poets charm with lays that Genius taught —

For this? to labor through their little day, 1212
To weep an hour, then want the tear they pay —
To ask the urn, their death and life to tell,
When the dull dust would give that tale as
  well!

Man! hast thou seen the gallant vessel sweep,
Borrowing her moonlight from the jealous deep,
And gliding with mute foot, and silver wing,
Over the waters like a soul-mov'd thing?
Man, hast thou gazed on this — then look'd
  again,   1220
And seen no speck on all that desolate main,
And heard no sound, — except the gurgling
  cry,
The winds half stifled in their mockery?

Woe unto thee! for, thus, thy course is run,
And, in the fulness of thy noon-day sun,
The darkness cometh — yea! thou walk'st
  abroad
In glory, Child of Mind, Creation's Lord —
And wisdom's music from thy lips hath gush'd!
Then comes the *Selah!* and the voice is hush'd,
And the light past! we seek where thou hast
  been   1230
In beauty — but thy beauty is not seen!
We breathe the air thou breath'dst, we tread
  the spot
Thy feet were wont to tread, but find thee
  not!
Beyond, sits Darkness with her haggard face,
Brooding fiend-like above thy burying-place —
Beneath, let wildest Fancy take her fill!
Shall we seek on? we shudder and are still!
Yet weep not unto thee, thou child of Earth!
Though moonlight sleep on thy deserted hearth,
We will not cry ' Alas!' above thy clay!   1240
It was, perchance, thy joyous pride to stray
On Mind's lone shore, and linger by the
  way:
But now thy pilgrim's staff is laid aside,
And on thou journeyest o'er the sullen tide,
To bless thy wearied sight, and glad thine
  heart
With all that Mind's serener skies impart;
Where Wisdom suns the day no shades de-
  stroy,
And Learning ends in Truth, as hope in joy:
While *we* stand mournful on the desert beach,
And wait, and wish, thy distant bark, to reach,
And weep to watch it passing from our sight,
And sound the gun's salute, and sigh our last
  ' good night!'   1252

  And oh! while thus the spirit glides away, —
Give to the world its memory with its clay!
Some page our country's grateful eyes may
  scan;
Some useful truth to bless surviving man;
Some name to honest bosoms justly dear;
Some grave t' exalt the thought, and claim the
  tear;
So when the pilgrim Sun is travelling o'er
The last blue hill, to gild a distant shore,   1260
He leaves a freshness in the evening scene,
That tells Creation where his steps have been!

II. SOME ACCOUNT OF THE GREEK CHRISTIAN POETS

The series of papers on the Greek Christian Poets appeared first in the *Athenæum* between the months of February and August, 1842. They were reprinted along with a second series of papers on the English poets — contributed to the same periodical — in a small separate volume, two years after Mrs. Browning's death. (*The Greek Christian Poets and The English Poets, by Elizabeth Barrett Browning, London. Chapman and Hall,* 1863.) As a mere girl, Miss Barrett had read the Greek Fathers in the original, under the guidance of the blind scholar, Hugh Stuart Boyd, who was deeply versed in them and could repeat from memory pages of their works both in prose and verse. A playful allusion to his especial enthusiasm for Saint Gregory Nazianzen occurs in Mrs. Browning's poem ' Wine of Cyprus,' which was dedicated to Mr. Boyd.

> ' Do you mind that deed of Atè
>   Which you bound me to so fast,
> Reading " *De Virginitate*,"
>   From the first line to the last ?
> How I said, at ending solemn,
>   As I turned and looked at you,
> That Saint Simeon on the column
>   Had had somewhat less to do ? '

The Greek language was a strong intellectual life, stronger than any similar one which has lived in the breath of 'articulately speaking men,' and survived it. No other language has lived so long and died so hard, — pang by pang, each with a dolphin color — yielding reluctantly to that doom of death and silence which must come at last to the speaker and the speech. Wonderful it is to look back fathoms down the great Past, thousands of years away — where whole generations lie unmade to dust — where the sounding of their trumpets, and the rushing of their scythed chariots, and that great shout which brought down the birds stone dead from beside the sun, are more silent than the dog breathing at our feet, or the fly's paces on our window-pane ; and yet, from the heart of which silence, to feel *words* rise up like a smoke — words of men, even words of women, uttered at first, perhaps, in ' excellent low voices,' but audible and distinct to our times, through ' the dreadful pother ' of life and death, the hissing of the steam-engine and the cracking of the cerement ! It is wonderful to look back and listen. Blind Homer spoke this Greek after blind Demodocus, with a quenchless light about his brows, which he felt through his blindness. Pindar rolled his chariots in it, prolonging the clamor of the games. Sappho's heart beat through it, and heaved up the world's. Æschylus strained it to the stature of his high thoughts. Plato crowned it with his divine peradventures. Aristophanes made it

drunk with the wine of his fantastic merriment. The latter Platonists wove their souls away in it, out of sight of other souls. The first Christians heard in it God's new revelation, and confessed their Christ in it from the suppliant's knee, and presently from the bishop's throne. To all times, and their transitions, the language lent itself. Through the long summer of above two thousand years, from the grasshopper Homer sang of, to that grasshopper of Manuel Phile, which might indeed have been ' a burden,' we can in nowise mistake the chirping of the bloodless, deathless, wondrous creature. It chirps on in Greek still. At the close of that long summer, though Greece lay withered to her root, her academic groves and philosophic gardens all leafless and bare, still from the depth of the desolation rose up the voice —

> O cuckoo, shall I call thee bird,
> Or but a wandering voice ?

which did not grow hoarse, like other cuckoos, but sang not unsweetly, if more faintly than before. Strangely vital was this Greek language —

> Some straggling spirits were behind, to be
> Laid out with most thrift on its memory.

It seemed as if nature could not part with so lovely a tune, as if she felt it ringing on still in her head — or as if she hummed it to herself, as the watchman used to do, with ' night wandering round ' him, when he watched wearily on the palace roof of the doomed house of Atreus. But, although it is impossible to touch with a thought the last estate of Greek poetical literature without the wonder occurring of its being still Greek, still poetry, — though we are startled by the phenomenon of lifelike sounds coming up from the ashes of a mighty people — at the aspect of an Alcestis returned from the dead, *veiled* but identical, — we are forced to admit, after the first pause of admiration, that a change has passed upon the great thing we recognize, a change proportionate to the greatness, and involving a caducity. Therefore, in adventuring some imperfect account of the Greek ecclesiastical poets, it is right to premise it with the full and frank admission, that they are not accomplished poets, — that they do not, in fact, reach with their highest lifted hand, the lowest foot of those whom the world has honored as Greek poets, but who have honored the world more by their poetry. The instrument of the Greek tongue was, at the Christian era, an antique instrument, somewhat worn, somewhat stiff in the playing, somewhat deficient in notes which it had once, somewhat feeble and uncertain in such as it retained. The subtlety of the ancient music, the variety of its cadences, the intersections of sweetness in the rise and fall of melodies, rounded and contained in the unity of its harmony, are as utterly lost to this later period as the digamma was to an earlier one. We must not seek for them; we shall not find them; their place knows them no more. Not only was there a lack in the instrument, — there was also a deficiency in the players. Thrown aside, after the old flute-story, by a goddess, it was taken up by a mortal hand — by the hand of men gifted and noble in their generation, but belonging to it intellectually, even by their gifts and their nobleness. Another immortal, a true genius, might — nay, would — have asserted himself, and wrung a poem of almost the ancient force from the infirm instrument. It is easy to fancy, and to wish that it had been so — that some martyr or bishop, when bishops were martyrs, and the earth was still warm with the Sacrificial blood, had been called to the utterance of his soul's devotion, with the emphasis of a great poet's power. No one, however, was so called. Of all the names which shall presently be reckoned, and of which it is the object of this sketch to give some account, beseeching its readers to hold several in honorable remembrance, not one can be crowned with a steady hand as a true complete poet's name. Such a crown is a sacred dignity, and, as it should not be touched idly, it must not be used here. A born Warwick could find, here, no head for a crown.

Yet we shall reckon names 'for remembrance,' and speak of things not ignoble — of meek heroic Christians, and heavenward faces washed serene by tears — strong knees bending humbly for the very strength's sake — bright intellects burning often to the winds in fantastic shapes, but oftener still with an honest inward heat, vehement on heart and brain — most eloquent fallible lips that convince us less than they persuade — a divine loquacity of human falsities — poetical souls, that are not souls of poets! Surely not ignoble things! And the reader will perceive at once that the writer's heart is not laid beneath the wheels of a cumbrous ecclesiastical antiquity — that its intent is to love what is lovable, to honor what is honorable, and to kiss both through the dust of centuries, but by no means to recognize a *hierarchy*, whether in the church or in literature.

If, indeed, an opinion on the former relation might be regarded here, it would be well to suggest, that to these ' Fathers,' as we call them filially, with heads turned away, we owe more reverence for the grayness of their beards than theological gratitude for the outstretching of their hands. Devoted and disinterested as many among them were, they, themselves, were at most times evidently and consciously surer of their *love*, in a theologic sense, than of their knowledge in any. It is no place for a reference to religious controversy; and if it were, we are about to consider them simply as poets, without trenching on the very wide ground of their prose works and ecclesiastical opinions. Still one passing remark may be admissible, since the fact *is* so remarkable — how any body of Christian men can profess to derive their opinions from ' the opinions of the Fathers,' when *all* bodies might do so equally. These fatherly opinions are, in truth, multiform, and multitudinous as the fatherly ' sublime gray hairs.' There is not only a father apiece for every child, but, not to speak it unfilially, a piece of every father for every child. Justin Martyr would, of himself, set up a wilderness of sects, besides ' something over ' for the future ramifications of each several one. What then should be done with our ' Fathers '? Leave them to perish by the time-Ganges, as old men innocent and decrepit, and worthy of no use or honor? Surely not. We may learn of them, if God will let us, *love*, and love is much — we may learn devotedness of them and warm our hearts by theirs; and this, although we rather distrust them as commentators, and utterly refuse them the reverence of our souls, in the capacity of theological oracles.

Their place in literature, which we have to do with to-day, may be found, perhaps, by a like moderation. That place is not, it has been admitted, of the highest; and that it is not of the lowest the proof will presently be attempted. There is a mid-air kingdom of the birds called Nephelococcygia, of which Aristophanes tells us something; and we might stand there a moment so as to measure the local adaptitude, putting up the Promethean umbrella to hide us from the ' Gods,' if it were not for the ' men and columns' lower down. But as it is, the very suggestion, if persisted in, would sink all the ecclesiastical antiquity it is desirable to find favor for, to all eternity, in the estimation of the kindest reader. No! the mid-air kingdom of the birds will not serve the wished-for purpose even illustratively, and by grace of the nightingale. ' May the sweet saints pardon us ' for wronging them by an approach to such a sense, which, if attained and determined, would have consigned them so certainly to what St. Augustine called — when *he* was moderate too — *mitissima damnatio*, a very mild species of damnation.

It would be, in fact, a rank injustice to the beauty we are here to recognize, to place these writers in the rank of mediocrities, supposing the harsh sense. They may be called mediocrities as poets among poets, but not so as no poets at all. Some of them may sing before gods and men, and in front of any column from Trajan's to that projected one in Trafalgar Square, to which is promised the miraculous distinction of making the National Gallery sink lower than we see it now. They may, as a body, sing exultingly, holding the relation of column to gallery, in front of the whole ' corpus of Latin ecclesiastical poetry, and claim the world's ear and the poet's palm. That the modern Latin poets have been more read by scholars, and are better known by reputation to the general reader, is unhappily true: but the truth involves no good reason why it should be so, nor much marvel that it is so. Beside the greater accessibility of Latin literature, the vicissitude of life is extended to posthumous fame, and Time, who is Justice to the poet, i sometimes too busy in pulverizing bones to give the due weight to memories. The modern Latin poets, ' elegant,' — which is the critic's word to spend upon them, — elegant as they are occasionally, polished and accurate as they are comparatively, stand cold and lifeless, with statue-eyes, near these good, fervid, faulty Greeks of ours — and we do not care to look again. Our Greeks do, in their degree, claim their ancestral advantage, not the mere advantage of language, — nay, least the advantage of language — a comparative elegance and accuracy of expression being ceded to the Latins — but that higher distinction inherent in brain and breast, of vivid thought and quick sensibility. What if we swamp for a moment the Tertullians and Prudentiuses, and touch, by a permitted anachronism, with one hand VIDA, with the other GREGORY NAZIANZEN, what then? What though the Italian poet be smooth as the Italian Canova — working like him out of stone — smooth and cold, disdaining to ruffle his dactyls with the beating of his pulses — what then? Would we change for him our sensitive Gregory, with all his defects in the glorious ' scientia metrica'? We would not — perhaps we should not, even if those defects were not attributable, as Mr. Boyd, in the preface to his work on the Fathers, most justly intimates, to the changes incident to a declining language.

It is, too, as religious poets that we are called upon to estimate these neglected Greeks — as religious poets, of whom the universal church and the world's literature would gladly embrace more names than can be counted to either. For it is strange that, although Wilhelm Meister's uplooking and downlooking aspects, the reverence to things above and things below, the religious all-clasping spirit, be, and must be, in degree and measure, the grand necessity of every true poet's soul, — of religious poets, strictly so called, the earth is very bare. Religious ' parcel-poets' we have, indeed, more than enough ; writers of hymns, translators of scripture into prose, or of prose generally into rhymes, of whose heart-devotion a higher faculty were worthy. Also there have been poets, not a few, singing as if earth were still Eden ; and poets, many, singing as if in the first hour of exile, when the echo of the curse was louder than the whisper of the promise. But the right ' genius of Christianism' has done little up to this moment, even for Chateaubriand. We want the touch of Christ's hand upon our literature, as it touched other dead things — we want the sense of the saturation of Christ's blood upon the souls of our poets, that it may cry *through* them in answer to the ceaseless wail of the Sphinx of our humanity, expounding agony into renovation. Something of this has been perceived in art when its glory was at the fullest. Something of a yearning after this may be seen among the Greek Christian poets, something which would have been *such* with a stronger faculty. It will not harm us in any case, as lovers of literature and honest

judges, if we breathe away, or peradventure *besom* away, the thick dust which lies upon their heavy folios, and besom away, or peradventure *breathe* away, the inward intellectual dust, which must be confessed to lie thickly, too, upon the heavy poems, and make our way softly and meekly into the heart of such hidden beauties (hidden and scattered) as our good luck, or good patience, or, to speak more reverently, the intrinsic goodness of the Fathers of Christian Poetry, shall permit us to discover. May gentle readers favor the endeavor, with ' gentle airs,' if any ! readers not too proud to sleep, were it only for Homer's sake ; nor too passionate, at their worst displeasure, to do worse than growl in their sleeves, after the manner of ' most delicate monsters.' It is not intended to crush this forbearing class with folios nor even with a folio ; only to set down briefly in their sight what shall appear to the writer the characteristics of each poet, and to illustrate the opinion by the translation of a few detached passages, or, in certain possible cases, of short entire poems. And so much has been premised, simply that too much be not expected.

It has the look of an incongruity, to begin an account of the Greek Christian poets with a Jew ; and EZEKIEL is a Jew in his very name, and a ' poet of the Jews' by profession. Moreover he is wrapt in such a mystery of chronology, that nobody can be quite sure of his not having lived before the Christian era — and one whole whisper establishes him as a unit of the famous seventy or seventy-two, under Ptolemy Philadelphus. Let us waive the chronology in favor of the mystery. He is brought out into light by Clemens Alexandrinus ; and being associated with Greek poets, and a writer himself of Greek verses, we may receive him in virtue of the τοτοτοτοτοτοτοτοτιξ, with little fear, in his case, of implying an injustice in that middle bird-locality of Nephelococcygia. The reader must beware of confounding him with the prophet ; and the circumstance of the latter's inspiration is sufficiently distinguishing. Our Greek Ezekiel is, indeed, whatever his chronology may be, no *vates* in the ancient sense. A Greek tragedy (and some fragments of a tragedy are all that we hold of him), by a Jew, and on a Jewish subject, ' The Exodus from Egypt,' may startle the most serene of us into curiosity — with which curiosity begins and ends the only strong feeling we can bring to bear upon the work ; since, if the execution of it is somewhat curious too, there is a gentle collateral dulness which effectually secures us from feverish excitement. Moses prologizes after the worst manner of Euripides (worse than the worse), compendiously relating his adventures among the bulrushes and in Pharaoh's household, concluded by his slaying an Egyptian, *because nobody was looking.* So saith the poet. Then follows an interview between the Israelite and Zipporah, and her companions, wherein he puts to her certain geographical questions, and she (as far as we can make out through fragmentary cracks) rather *brusquely* proposes their mutual marriage; on which subject he does not venture an opinion; but we find him next confiding his dreams in a family fashion to her father, who considers them satisfactory. Here occurs a broad crack down the tragedy — and we are suddenly called to the revelation from the bush by an extraordinarily ordinary dialogue, between Deity and Moses. It is a surprising specimen of the kind of composition adverted to some lines ago, as the translation of Scripture into prose; and the sublime simplicity of the scriptural narrative being thus done (away) into Greek for a certain time, the following reciprocation — to which our old moralities can scarcely do more, or less, than furnish a parallel — prays for an English — exposure. The Divine Being is supposed to address Moses: —

But what is this thou holdest in thine hand? —
Let thy reply be sudden.
   Moses.   'T is my rod —
I chasten with it quadrupeds and men.
   Voice from the Bush. Cast it upon the ground — and
       straight recoil;
For it shall be, to move thy wonderment,
A terrible serpent.
   Moses.   It is cast. But THOU,
Be gracious to me, Lord. How terrible!
How monstrous! Oh, be pitiful to me!
I shudder to behold it, my limbs shake.

The reader is already consoled for the destiny which mutilated the tragedy, without requiring the last words of the analysis. Happily characteristic of the 'meekest of men' is Moses's naïve admission of the uses of his rod — to beat men and animals withal — of course 'when nobody is looking.'

CLEMENS ALEXANDRINUS, to whom we owe whatever gratitude is due for our fragmentary Ezekiel, was originally an Athenian philosopher, afterwards a converted Christian, a Presbyter of the Church at Alexandria, and preceptor of the famous Origen. Clemens flourished at the close of the second century. As a prose writer — and we have no prose writings of his, except such as were produced subsequently to his conversion — he is learned and various. His 'Pedagogue' is a wanderer, to universal intents and purposes; and his 'Tapestry,' if the 'Stromata' may be called so, is embroidered in all crossstitches of philosophy, with not much scruple as to the shading of colors. In the midst of all is something, ycleped a dithyrambic ode, addressed to the Saviour, composite of fantastic epithets in the mode of the old litanies, and almost as bald of merit as the Jew-Greek drama, though Clemens himself (worthier in worthier places) be the poet. Here is the opening, which is less fanciful than what follows it: —

      Curb for wild horses,
      Wing for bird-courses
      Never yet flown!
      Helm, safe for weak ones,
      Shepherd, bespeak once,
      The young lambs thine own.

      Rouse up the youth,
      Shepherd and feeder,
      So let them bless thee,
      Praise and confess thee, —
      Pure words on pure mouth, —
      Christ, the child-leader!
      O, the saints' Lord,
      All-dominant word!
      Holding, by Christdom,
      God's highest wisdom!
      Column in place
      When sorrows seize us, —
      Endless in grace
      Unto man's race,
      Saving one, Jesus!
      Pastor and ploughman,
      Helm, curb, together, —
      Pinion that now can
      (Heavenly of feather)
      Raise and release us, —
      Fisher who catcheth
      Those whom he watcheth . . .

It goes on; but we need not do so. 'By the pricking of our thumbs,' we know that the reader has had enough of it.

Passing rapidly into the fourth century, we would offer our earliest homage to Gregory Nazianzen,

    That name must ever be to us a friend,

when the two APOLINARII cross our path and intercept the 'all hail.' Apolinarius the grammarian, formerly of Alexandria, held the office of presbyter in the church of Laodicæa, and his son Apolinarius, an accomplished rhetorician, that of *reader*, an ancient ecclesiastical office, in the same church. This younger Apolinarius was a man of indomitable energies and most practical inferences; and when the edict of Julian forbade to the Christians the study of Grecian letters, he, assisted perhaps by his father's hope and hand, stood strong in the gap, not in the attitude of supplication, not with the gesture of consolation, but in power and sufficiency to fill up the void and baffle the tyrant. Both father and son were in the work, by some testimony; the younger Apolinarius standing out, by all, as the chief worker, and only one in any extensive sense. 'Does Julian deny us Homer?' said the brave man in his armed soul — 'I am Homer!' and straightway he turned the whole Biblical history, down to Saul's accession, into Homeric hexameters, — dividing the work, so as to clench the identity of first and second Homers, into twenty-four books, each superscribed by a letter of the alphabet, and the whole acceptable, according to the expression of Sozomen ἀντὶ τῆς Ὁμήρου ποιήσεως, in the place of Homer's poetry. 'Does Julian deny us Euripides?' said Apolinarius again — 'I am Euripides!' and up he sprang, — as good an Euripides (who can doubt it?) as he ever was a Homer. 'Does Julian forbid us Menander? — Pindar? — Plato? — I am Menander! — I am Pindar! — I am Plato!' And comedies, lyrics, philosophics, flowed fast at the word; and the gospel and epistles adapted themselves naturally to the rules of Socratic disputation. A brave man, forsooth, was our Apolinarius of Laodicæa, and literally a man of men — for observe, says Sozomen, with a venerable innocence, at which the gravest may smile gravely, — as at a doublet worn awry at the Council of Nice, — that the old authors did each man his own work, whereas this Apolinarius did every man's work in addition to his own — and so admirably intimates the ecclesiastical critic, — that if it were not for the common prejudice in favor of antiquity, no ancient could be missed in the all-comprehensive representativeness of the Laodicæan writer. So excellent was his ability, to 'outbrave the stars in several kinds of light,' besides the Cæsar! Whether Julian, naturally mortified to witness this germination of illustrious heads under the very iron of his searing, vowed vengeance against the Hydra-spirit, by the sacred memory of the animation of his own beard, we do not exactly know. To embitter the wrong, Apolinarius sent him a treatise upon truth — a confutation of the pagan doctrine, apart from the scriptural argument, — the Emperor's notice of which is both worthy of his Cæsarship, and a good model-notice for all sorts of critical dignities. Ἀνέγνων ἔγνων κατέγνων, is the Greek of it; so that, turning from the letter to catch something of the point, we may write it down — 'I have perused, I have mused, I have abused:' which provoked as imperious a retort — 'Thou mayest have perused, but thou hast not mused; for hadst thou mused, thou wouldst not have abused.' Brave Laodicæan! Apolinarius's laudable *double* of Greek literature has perished, the reader will be concerned to hear, from the face of the earth, being, like other *lusus*, or marvels, or monsters, brief of days. One only tragedy remains, with which the memory of Gregory Nazianzen has been right tragically affronted, and which Gregory, — εἴ τις αἴσθησις, as he said of Constantine, — would cast off with the scorn and anger befitting an Apolinarian heresy. For Apolinarius, besides being an epoist, dramatist, lyrist, philosopher, and rhetorician, was, we are sorry to add, in the eternal bustle of his soul, a heretic, — possibly for the advantage of something additional to do. He not only intruded into the churches hymns which were not authorized, being his own composition — so that reverend brows grew dark to hear women with musical voices sing them softly to the turning of their distaff, — but he fell into the heresy of denying a human soul to the perfect MAN, and of leaving the Divinity in bare combination with the Adamic dust. No wonder that a head so beset with many thoughts and individualities should at last turn round! — that eyes rolling in fifty-nine frenzies of twenty-five fine poets should at last turn blind! — that a determination to rival all geniuses should be followed by a disposition more baleful in its exercise, to understand 'all mysteries'! Nothing can be plainer than the step after step, whereby, through excess of vain-glory and morbid mental activity, Apolinarius, the vice-poet of Greece, subsided into Apolinarius the chief heretic of Christendom.

To go back sighingly to the tragedy, where we shall have to sigh again — the only tragedy left to us of all the tragic works of Apolinarius (but we do not sigh for *that*!) — let no voice ever more attribute it to Gregory Nazianzen. How could Mr. Alford do so, however hesitatingly, in his 'Chapters,' attaching to it, without the hesitation, a charge upon the writer, whether Gregory or another man, that *he*, whoever he was, had, of his own free will and choice, destroyed the old Greek originals out of which his tragedy was constructed, and left it a monument of their sacrifice as of the blood on his barbarian hand? The charge passes, not only before a breath, but before its own breath. The tragedy is, in fact, a specimen of *centoism*, which is the adaptation of the phraseology of one work to the construction of another; and we have only to glance at it to perceive the Medæa of Euripides dislocated into the CHRISTUS PATIENS. Instead of the ancient opening —

> Oh, would ship Argo had not sailed away
> To Colchos by the rough Symplegades!
> Nor ever had been felled in Pelion's grove
> The pine, hewn for her side! . . .
>   So she my queen,
> Medæa, had not touched this fatal shore,
> Soul-struck by love of Jason!

Apolinarius opens it thus —

> Oh, would the serpent had not glode along
> To Eden's garden-land, — nor ever had
> The crafty dragon planted in that grove
> A slimy snare! So she, rib-born of man,
> The wretched misled mother of our race,
> Had dared not to dare on beyond worst daring,
> Soul-struck by love of — apples!

'Let us alone for keeping our countenance' — and at any rate we are bound to ask gravely of Mr. Alford, *is the Medæa destroyed?* — and if not, did the author of the 'Christus Patiens' destroy his originals? and if not, may we not say of Mr. Alford's charge against that author, 'Oh, would he had not made it!' So far from Apolinarius being guilty of destroying his originals, it was his reverence for them which struggled with the edict of the persecutor, and accomplished this dramatic adventure; — and this adventure, the only remaining specimen of his adventurousness, may help us to the secret of his wonderful fertility and omni-representativeness, which is probably this — that the great majority of his works, tragic, comic, lyric, and philosophic, consisted simply of *centos*. Yet we pray for justice to Apolinarius: we pray for honor to his motives and energies. Without pausing to inquire whether it had been better and wiser to let poetry and literature depart at once before the tyranny of the edict, than to drag them back by the hair into attitudes grotesquely ridiculous — better and wiser for the Greek Christian schools to let them forgo altogether the poems of their Euripides, than adapt to the meek sorrows of the tender Virgin-mother, the bold, bad, cruel frenzy of Medæa, in such verses as these —

She howls out ancient oaths, invokes the faith
Of pledged right-hands, and calls, for witness, God !

— we pray straightforwardly for justice and honor to the motives and energies of Apolinarius. 'Oh, would that' many lived *now* as appreciative of the influences of poetry on our schools and country, as impatient of their contraction, as self-devoted in the great work of extending them ! There remains of his poetical labors, besides the tragedy, a translation of David's Psalms into 'heroic verse,' which the writer of these remarks has not seen, — and of which those critics who desire to deal gently with Apolinarius seem to begin their indulgence by doubting the authenticity.

It is pleasant to turn shortly round, and find ourselves face to face, not with the author of 'Christus Patiens,' but with one antagonistical both to his poetry and his heresy, GREGORY NAZIANZEN. A noble and tender man was this Gregory, and so tender, because so noble ; a man to lose no cubit of his stature for being looked at steadfastly, or struck at reproachfully. 'You may cast me down,' he said, 'from my bishop's throne, but you cannot banish me from before God's.' And bishop as he was, his saintly crown stood higher than his tiara, and his loving martyr-smile, the crown of a nature more benign than his fortune, shone up toward both. Son of the bishop of Nazianzen, and holder of the diocese which was his birthplace, previous to his elevation to the level of the storm in the bishopric of Constantinople, little did he care for bishoprics or high places of any kind, — the desire of his soul being for solitude, quietude, and that silent religion which should 'rather be than seem.' But his father's head bent whitely before him, even in the chamber of his brother's death, — and Basil, his beloved friend, the 'half of his soul,' pressed on him with the weight of love ; and Gregory, feeling their tears upon his cheeks, did not count his own, but took up the priestly office. Poor Gregory ! not merely as a priest, but as a man, he had a sighing life of it. His student days at Athens, where he and Basil read together poems and philosophies, and holier things, or talked low and *misopogonistically* of their fellow-student Julian's bearded boding smile, were his happiest days. He says of himself,

As many stones
Were thrown at *me*, as other men had flowers.

Nor was persecution the worst evil ; for friend after friend, beloved after beloved, passed away from before his face, and the voice which charmed them living spoke brokenly beside their graves, — his funeral orations marked severally the wounds of his heart, — and his genius served, as genius often does, to lay an emphasis on his grief. The passage we shall venture to translate is rather a cry than a song —

Where are my wingèd words ? Dissolved in air.
Where is my flower of youth ? All withered. Where
My glory ? Vanished. Where the strength I knew
From comely limbs ? Disease hath changed it too,
And bent them. Where the riches and the lands ?
GOD HATH THEM ! Yea, and sinners' snatching hands
Have grudged the rest. Where is my father, mother,
And where my blessed sister, my sweet brother ?
Gone to the grave ! — There did remain for me
Alone my fatherland, till destiny,
Malignly stirring a black tempest, drove
My foot from that last rest. And now I rove
Estranged and desolate a foreign shore,
And drag my mournful life and age all hoar
Throneless and cityless, and childless save
This father-care for children, which I have,
Living from day to day on wandering feet.
Where shall I cast this body ? What will greet
My sorrows with an end ? What gentle ground
And hospitable grave will wrap me round ?
Who last my dying eyelids stoop to close —
Some saint, the Saviour's friend ? or one of those
Who do not know Him ? The air interpose,
And scatter these words too.

The return upon the first thought is highly pathetic ; and there is a restlessness of anguish about the whole passage which consecrates it with the cross of nature. His happy Athenian associations gave a color, unwashed out by tears, to his mind and works. Half apostolical he was, and half scholastical ; and while he mused, on his bishop's throne, upon the mystic tree of twelve fruits, and the shining of the river of life, he carried, as Milton did, with a gentle and not ungraceful distraction, both hands full of green trailing branches from the banks of the Cephissus, nay, from the very plane-tree which Socrates sat under with Phædrus, when they two talked about beauty to the rising and falling of its leaves. As an orator, he is greater, all must feel if some do not think, than his contemporaries ; and the 'golden mouth' might confess it meekly. Erasmus compares him to Isocrates, but the unlikeness is obvious : Gregory was not excellent at an artful blowing of the pipes. He spoke grandly as the wind does, in gusts ; and, as in a mighty wind, which combines unequal noises, the creaking of trees and rude swinging of doors as well as the sublime sovereign rush along the valleys, we gather the idea, from his eloquence less of music than of power. Not that he is cold as the wind is — the metaphor goes no further : Gregory cannot be cold, even by dis favor of his antithetic points. He is various in his oratory, full and rapid in allusion, briefly graphic in metaphor, equally sufficient for in dignation or pathos, and gifted peradventure with a keener dagger of sarcasm than should hang in a saint's girdle. His orations against Julian have all these characteristics, but they are not poetry, and we must pass down lower and quite over his beautiful letters, to Gregory the poet.

He wrote *thirty thousand verses*, among the which are several long poems, severally defec tive in a defect common but not necessary to short occasional poems, and lamentable anywhere, a want of unity and completeness. The excellences of his prose are transcribed, with whatever faintness, in his poetry — the exaltation, the devotion, the sweetness, the pathos, even to the playing of satirical power about the graver meanings. But although noble thoughts break up the dulness of the groundwork, — although, with the instinct of greater poets, he bares his heart in his poetry, and the heart is worth baring, still monotony of construction without unity of intention is the most wearisome of monotonies, and, except in the case of a few short poems, we find it everywhere in Gregory. The lack of variety is extended to the cadences, and the pauses fall stiffly 'come corpo morto cade.' Melodious lines we have often: harmonious passages scarcely ever — the music turning heavily on its own axle, as inadequate to living evolution. The poem on his own life ('De Vitâ suâ') is, in many places, interesting and affecting, yet faulty with all these faults. The poem on Celibacy, which state is commended by Gregory as becometh a bishop, has occasionally graphic touches, but is dull enough generally to suit the fairest spinster's view of that melancholy subject. If Hercules could have read it, he must have rested in the middle — from which the reader is entreated to forbear the inference that the poem has not been read through by the writer of the present remarks, seeing that that writer marked the grand concluding moment with a white stone, and laid up the memory of it among the chief triumphs, to say nothing of the fortunate deliverances, *vitæ suæ*. In Gregory's elegiac poems, our ears, at least, are better contented, because the sequence of pentameter to hexameter necessarily excludes the various cadence which they yearn for under other circumstances. His anacreontics are sometimes nobly written, with a certain brave recklessness, as if the thoughts despised the measure — and we select from this class a specimen of his poetry, both because three of his hymns have already appeared in the 'Athenæum,' and because the anacreontic in question includes to a remarkable extent the various qualities we have attributed to Gregory, not omitting that play of satirical humor with which he delights to ripple the abundant flow of his thoughts. The writer, though also a translator, feels less misgiving than usual in offering to the reader, in such English as is possible, this spirited and beautiful poem.

SOUL AND BODY

WHAT wilt thou possess or be ?
O my soul, I ask of thee.
What of great, or what of small,
Counted precious therewithal ?
Be it only rare, and want it,
I am ready, soul, to grant it.
Wilt thou choose to have and hold
Lydian Gyges' charm of old,
So to rule us with a ring,

Turning round the jewelled thing,
Hidden by its face concealed,
And revealed by its revealed ?
Or preferrest Midas' fate —
He who died in golden state,
All things being changed to gold ?
Of a golden hunger dying,
Through a surfeit of 'would I '-ing !
Wilt have jewels brightly cold,
  Or may fertile acres please ?
Or the sheep of many a fold,
Camels, oxen, for the wold ?
  Nay ! I will not give thee these !
These to take thou hast not will,
These to give I have not skill;
Since I cast earth's cares abroad,
That day when I turned to God.

Wouldst a throne, a crown sublime,
Bubble blown upon the time ?
So thou mayest sit to-morrow
Looking downward in meek sorrow,
Some one walking by thee scorning
Who adored thee yester morning,
Some malign one ? Wilt be bound
Fast in marriage (joy unsound !)
And be turnéd round and round
As the time turns ? Wilt thou catch it,
That sweet sickness ? and to match it
Have babies by the hearth, bewildering ?
And if I tell thee the best children
Are none — what answer ?
                    Wilt thou thunder
Thy rhetorics, move the people under ?
Covetest to sell the laws
With no justice in thy cause,
And bear on, or else be borne,
Before tribunals worthy scorn ?
Wilt thou shake a javelin rather
Breathing war ? or wilt thou gather
Garlands from the wrestler's ring ?
Or kill beasts for glorying ?
Covetest the city's shout,
And to be in brass struck out ?
Cravest thou that shade of dreaming,
Passing air of shifting seeming,
Rushing of a printless arrow,
  Clapping echo of a hand ?
  What to those who understand
Are to-day's enjoyments narrow
Which to-morrow go again,
Which are shared with evil men
And of which no man in his dying
Taketh aught for softer lying ?
What then wouldst thou, if thy mood
  Choose not these ? what wilt thou be
  O my soul — a deity ?
A God before the face of God,
Standing glorious in His glories,
Choral in His angels' chorus ?

Go ! upon thy wing arise,
Pluméd by quick energies,
Mount in circles up the skies :
And I will bless thy wingéd passion,
Help with words thine exaltation,
And, like a bird of rapid feather,
Outlaunch thee, Soul, upon the æther

But thou, O fleshly nature, say,
Thou with odors from the clay,
Since thy presence I must have
As a lady with a slave,
What wouldst thou possess or be,
That thy breath may stay with thee ?
Nay ! I owe thee nought beside,
Though thine hands be open wide.

Would a table suit thy wishes,
Fragrant with sweet oils and dishes
Wrought to subtle niceness? where
Stringèd music strokes the air,
And blithe hand-clappings, and the smooth
Fine postures of the tender youth
And virgins wheeling through the dance
With an unveiled countenance, —
Joys for drinkers, who love shame,
And the maddening wine-cup's flame.
Wilt thou such, howe'er decried?
Take them, — and a rope beside!

Nay! this boon I give instead
Unto friend insatiated, —
May some rocky house receive thee,
Self-roofed, to conceal thee chiefly;
Or if labor there must lurk,
Be it by a short day's work!
And for garment, camel's hair,
As the righteous clothèd were,
Clothe thee! or the bestial skin
Adam's bareness hid within, —
Or some green thing from the way,
   Leaf of herb, or branch of vine,
Swelling, purpling as it may,
   Fearless to be drunk for wine!
Spread a table there beneath thee,
Which a sweetness shall upbreathe thee,
And which the dearest earth is giving,
Simple present to all living!
When that we have placed thee near it,
We will feed thee with glad spirit.
Wilt thou eat? soft, take the bread,
Oaten cake, if that bested;
Salt will season all aright,
And thine own good appetite,
Which we measure not, nor fetter:
'T is an uncooked condiment,
Famine's self the only better.
   Wilt thou drink? why, here doth bubble
Water from a cup unspent,
   Followed by no tipsy trouble,
Pleasure sacred from the grape!
Wilt thou have it in some shape
More like luxury? we are
No grudgers of wine-vinegar!
But if all will not suffice thee,
   And thou covetest to draw
   In that pitcher with a flaw,
Brimful pleasures heaven denies thee —
Go, and seek out, by that sign,
Other help than this of mine!
For me, I have not leisure so
To warm thee, Sweet, my household foe,
Until, like a serpent frozen,
New maddened with the heat, thou loosen
   Thy rescued fang within mine heart!
Wilt have measureless delights
Of gold-roofed palaces, and sights
   From pictured or from sculptured art,
With motion near their life; and splendor
Of bas-relief, with tracery tender,
And varied and contrasted hues?
Wilt thou have, as nobles use,
Broidered robes to flow about thee?
Jewelled fingers? Need we doubt thee?
Gauds for which the wise will flout thee?
I most, who, of all beauty, know
It must be inward, to be so!
And thus I speak to mortals low,
Living for the hour, and o'er
Its shadow, seeing nothing more;
But for those of nobler bearing,
Who live more worthily of wearing
A portion of the heavenly nature —
To low estate of clayey creature,

See, I bring the beggar's meed,
Nutriment beyond the need!
O, beholder of the Lord,
Prove on me the flaming sword!
Be mine husbandman, to nourish
Holy plants, that words may flourish
Of which mine enemy would spoil me,
Using pleasurehood to foil me!
Lead me closer to the tree
Of all life's eternity;
Which, as I have pondered, is
The knowledge of God's greatnesses:
Light of One, and shine of Three,
Unto whom all things that be
Flow and tend!
            In such a guise,
Whoever on the earth is wise
Will speak unto himself: and who
Such inner converse would eschew, —
We say perforce of that poor wight,
'He lived in vain!' and if *aright*,
It is not the worst word we might.

AMPHILOCHIUS, bishop of Iconium, was beloved and much appreciated by Gregory, and often mentioned in his writings. Few of the works of Amphilochius are extant, and of these only one is a poem. It is a didactic epistle to Seleucus, 'On the Right Direction of his Studies and Life,' and has been attributed to Gregory Nazianzen by some writers, upon very inadequate evidence, — that adduced (the similar phraseology which conveys, in this poem and a poem of Gregory's, the catalogue of canonical scriptures), being as easily explained by the imitation of one poet, as by the identity of two. They differ, moreover, upon ground more important than phraseology: Amphilochius appearing to reject, or at least to receive doubtfully, Jude's epistle, and the Second of Peter. And there is a harsh force in the whole poem which does not remind us of our Nazianzen, while it becomes, in the course of dissuading Seleucus from the amusements of the amphitheatre, graphic and effective. We hear, through the description, the grinding of the tigers' teeth, the sympathy of the people with the tigers showing still more savage.

They sit unknowing of these agonies,
Spectators at a show. When a man flies
From a beast's jaw, they groan, as if at least
They missed the ravenous pleasure, like the beast,
And sat there vainly. When, in the next spring,
The victim is attained, and, uttering
The deep roar or quick shriek between the fangs,
Beats on the dust the passion of his pangs,
All pity dieth in that glaring look.
They clap to see the blood run like a brook;
They stare with hungry eyes, which tears should fill,
And cheer the beasts on with their soul's good will;
And wish more victims to their maw, and urge
And lash their fury, as they shared the surge,
Gnashing their teeth, like beasts, on flesh of men.

There is an appalling reality in this picture. The epistle consists of 333 lines, which we mention specifically, because the poet takes advantage of the circumstance to illustrate or enforce an important theological doctrine: —

Three hundred lines, three decads, monads three,
Comprise my poem. *Love the Trinity.*

It would be almost a pain, and quite a regret, to pass from this fourth century without speaking a word which belongs to it — a word which rises to our lips, a word worthy of honor — HELIODORUS. Though a bishop and an imaginative writer, his 'Æthiopica' has no claim on our attention, either by right of Christianity or poetry; and yet we may be pardoned on our part for love's sake, and on account of the false position into which, by negligence of readers or insufficiency of translators, his beautiful romance has fallen, if we praise it heartily and faithfully even here. Our tears praised it long ago, our recollection does so now, and its own pathetic eloquence and picturesque descriptiveness are ripe for any praise. It has, besides, a vivid Arabian Night charm, almost as charming as Scheherazade herself, suggestive of an Arabian Night story drawn out 'in many a winding bout,' and not merely on the ground of extemporaneous loving and methodical (must we say it?) lying. In good sooth — no, not in good sooth, but in evil leasing — every hero and heroine of them all, from Abou Hassan to 'the divine Chariclæa,' does lie most vehemently and abundantly by gift of nature and choice of author, whether bishop or sultana. 'It is,' as Pepys observes philosophically of the comparative destruction of gin-shops and churches in the Great Fire of London, 'pretty to observe' how they all lie. And although the dearest of story-tellers, our own Chaucer, has told us that 'some leasing is, of which there cometh none advauntage to no wight,' even that species is used by them magnanimously in its turn, for the bare glory's sake, and without caring for the 'advauntage.' With equal liberality, but more truth, we write down the bishop of Tricca's romance charming, and wish the charm of it (however we may be out of place in naming him among poets,) upon any poet who has not yet felt it, and whose eyes, giving honor, may wander over these Remarks. The poor bishop thought as well of his book as we do, perhaps better; for when commanded, under ecclesiastical censure, to burn it or give up his bishopric, he gave up the bishopric. And who blames Heliodorus? He thought well of his romance; he was angry with those who did not; he was weak with the love of it. Let whosoever blames, speak low. Romance-writers are not educated for martyrs, and the exacted martyrdom was very very hard. Think of that English bishop who burnt his hand by an act of volition — only his hand, and which was sure to be burnt afterwards; and how he was praised for it! Heliodorus had to do with a dearer thing — — handwriting, not hands. Authors will pardon him, if bishops do not.

NONNUS of Panopolis, the poet of the 'Dionysiaca,' a work of some twenty-two thousand verses, on some twenty-two thousand subjects shaken together, flourished, as people say of many a dry-rooted soul, at the commencement of the fifth century. He was converted from paganism, but we are sorry to make the melancholy addition, that he was never converted from the 'Dionysiaca.' The only Christian poem we owe to him — a paraphrase, in hexameters, of the apostle John's gospel — does all that a bald verbosity and an obscure tautology can do or undo, to quench the divinity of that divine narrative. The two well-known words, bearing on their brief vibration the whole passion of a world saved through pain from pain, are thus traduced : —

<blockquote>
They answered him
'Come and behold.' Then Jesus himself groaned,
Dropping strange tears from eyes unused to weep.
</blockquote>

'Unused to weep!' Was it so of the Man of Sorrows? Oh, obtuse poet! We had translated the opening passage of the Paraphrase, and laid it by for transcription, but are repelled. Enough is said. Nonnus was never converted from the 'Dionysiaca.'

SYNESIUS of Cyrene learnt Plato's philosophy so well of Hypatia of Alexandria at the commencement of the fifth century, or rather before, that, to the obvious honor of that fair and learned teacher, he never, as bishop of Ptolemais, could attain to unlearning it. He did not wish to be bishop of Ptolemais; he had divers objections to the throne and the domination. He loved his dogs, he loved his wife; he loved Hypatia and Plato as well as he loved truth; and he loved beyond all things, under the womanly instruction of the former, to have his own way. He was a poet, too; the chief poet, we do not hesitate to record our opinion, — the chief, for true and natural gifts, of all our Greek Christian poets; and it was his choice to pray lyrically between the dew and the cloud rather than preach dogmatically between the doxies. If Gregory shrank from the episcopal office through a meek self-distrust and a yearning for solitude, Synesius repulsed the invitation to it through an impatience of control over heart and life, and for the earnest joy's sake of thinking out his own thought in the hunting-grounds, with no deacon or disciple astuter than his dog to watch the thought in his face, and trace it backward or forward, as the case might be, into something more or less than what was orthodox. Therefore he, a man of many and wandering thoughts, refused the bishopric, —not weepingly, indeed, as Gregory did, nor feigning madness with another of the 'nolentes episcopari' of that earnest period, — but with a sturdy enunciation of resolve, more likely to be effectual, of keeping his wife by his side as long as he lived, and of doubting as long as he pleased to doubt upon the resurrection of the body. But Synesius was a man of genius, and of all such true energies as are taken for granted in the name; and the very sullenness of his 'nay' being expressive to grave judges of the faithfulness of his 'yea and amen,' he was considered too noble a man not to be made a bishop of in his own despite, and on his own terms. The fact proves the latitude of discipline, and even of doctrine, permitted to the churches of that age; and it does not appear that the church at Ptolemais suffered any wrong as its result, seeing that Synesius, recovering from the shock militant of his ordination, in the course of which his ecclesiastical friends had ' laid hands upon him ' in the roughest sense of the word, performed his new duties willingly; was no sporting bishop otherwise than as a ' fisher of men ' — sent his bow to the dogs, and his dogs to Jericho, that nearest Coventry to Ptolemais, silencing his ' staunch hound's authentic voice ' as soon as ever any importance became attached to the authenticity of his own. And if, according to the bond, he retained his wife and his Platonisms, we may honor him by the inference, that he did so for conscience' sake still more than love's, since the love was inoperative in other matters. For spiritual fervor and exaltation, he has honor among men and angels; and however intent upon spiritualizing away the most glorified material body from ' the heaven of his invention,' he held fast and earnestly, as anybody's clenched hand could a horn of the altar, the Homoousion doctrine of the Christian heaven, and other chief doctrines emphasizing the divine sacrifice. But this poet has a higher place among poets than this bishop among bishops; the highest, we must repeat our conviction, of all yet named or to be named by us as ' Greek Christian poets.' Little, indeed, of his poetry has reached us, but this little is great in a nobler sense than of quantity; and when of his odes, Anacreontic for the most part, we cannot say praisefully that ' they smell of Anacreon,' it is because their fragrance is holier and more abiding; it is because the human soul burning in the censer effaces from our spiritual perceptions the attar of a thousand rose-trees whose roots are in Teos. These odes have, in fact, a wonderful rapture and ecstasy. And if we find in them the phraseology of Plato or Plotinus, for he leant lovingly to the later Platonists, — nay, if we find in them oblique references to the out-worn mythology of paganism, even so have we beheld the mixed multitude of unconnected motes wheeling, rising in a great sunshine, as the sunshine were a motive energy, — and even so the burning, adoring poet-spirit sweeps upward the motes of world-fancies (as if, being in the world, their tendency was Godward) upward in a strong stream of sunny light, while she rushes into the presence of ' the Alone.' We say the *spirit* significantly in speaking of this poet's aspiration. His is an ecstasy of abstract intellect, of pure spirit, cold though impetuous; the heart does not beat in it, nor is the human voice heard; the poet is true to the heresy of the ecclesiastic, and there is no resurrection of the body. We shall attempt a translation of the ninth ode, closer if less graceful and polished than Mr. Boyd's, helping our hand to courage by the persuasion that the genius of its poetry must look through the thickest blanket of our dark.

> Well-beloved and glory-laden,
> Born of Solyma's pure maiden !
> I would hymn Thee, blessed Warden,
> Driving from Thy Father's garden
> Blinking serpent's crafty lust,

> With his bruised head in the dust !
> Down Thou camest, low as earth,
> Bound to those of mortal birth ;
> Down Thou camest, low as hell,
> Where shepherd-Death did tend and keep
> A thousand nations like to sheep,
> While weak with age old Hades fell
> Shivering through his dark to view Thee,
> And the Dog did backward yell
> With jaws all gory to let through Thee !
> So, redeeming from their pain
> Choirs of disembodied ones,
> Thou didst lead whom Thou didst gather,
> Upward in ascent again,
> With a great hymn to the Father,
> Upward to the pure white thrones !
> King, the dæmon tribes of air
> Shuddered back to feel Thee there !
> And the holy stars stood breathless,
> Trembling in their chorus deathless;
> A low laughter fillèd æther —
> Harmony's most subtle sire
> From the seven strings of his lyre
> Stroked a measured music hither —
> Io pæan ! victory !
> Smiled the star of morning — he
> Who smileth to foreshow the day !
> Smilèd Hesperus the golden,
> Who smileth soft for Venus gay !
> While that hornèd glory holden
> Brimful from the fount of fire,
> The white moon, was leading higher
> In a gentle pastoral wise
> All the nightly deities !
> Yea, and Titan threw abroad
> The far shining of his hair
> 'Neath Thy footsteps holy-fair,
> Owning Thee the Son of God;
> The Mind artificer of all,
> And his own fire's original.

> And THOU upon Thy wing of will
> Mounting, — Thy God-foot uptill
> The neck of the blue firmament, —
> Soaring, didst alight content
> Where the spirit-spheres were singing,
> And the fount of good was springing,
> In the silent heaven !
> Where Time is not with his tide
> Ever running, never weary,
> Drawing earth-born things aside
> Against the rocks : nor yet are given
> The plagues death-bold that ride the dreary
> Tost matter-depths. Eternity
> Assumes the places which they yield !
> Not aged, howsoe'er she held
> Her crown from everlastingly —
> At once of youth, at once of eld,
> While in that mansion which is hers
> To God and gods she ministers !

How the poet rises in his ' singing clothes,' embroidered all over with the mythos and the philosophy ! Yet his eye is to the Throne : and we must not call him half a heathen by reason of a Platonic idiosyncrasy, seeing that the esoteric of the most suspicious turnings of his phraseology is ' Glory to the true God.' For another ode, Paris should be here to choose it — we are puzzled among the beautiful. Here is one with a thought in it from Gregory's prose, which belongs to Synesius by right of conquest : —

> O my deathless, O my blessed,
> Maid-born, glorious son confessed,

O my Christ of Solyma!
I who earliest learnt to play
This measure for Thee, fain would bring
Its new sweet tune to citern-string —
Be propitious, O my King!
Take this music which is mine
Anthem'd from the songs divine!

We will sing thee, deathless One,
God himself and God's great Son —
Of sire of endless generations,
Son of manifold creations!
Nature mutually endued,
Wisdom in infinitude!
God, before the angels burning —
Corpse, among the mortals mourning!
What time Thou wast pourèd mild
From an earthy vase defiled,
Magi with fair arts besprent,
At Thy new star's orient,
Trembled inly, wondered wild,
Questioned with their thoughts abroad —
'What then is the new-born child?
WHO the hidden God?
God, or corpse, or king?
Bring your gifts, oh hither bring
Myrrh for rite — for tribute, gold —
Frankincense for sacrifice!
God! Thine incense take and hold!
King! I bring thee gold of price!
Myrrh with tomb will harmonize!

For Thou, entombed, hast purified
Earthly ground and rolling tide,
And the path of dæmon nations,
And the free air's fluctuations,
And the depth below the deep!
Thou God, helper of the dead,
Low as Hades didst Thou tread!
Thou King, gracious aspect keep,
Take this music which is mine,
Anthem'd from the songs divine.

EUDOCIA — in the twenty-first year of the fifth century — wife of Theodosius, and empress of the world, thought good to extend her sceptre —

(Hac claritate gemina
O gloriosa fœmina!) —

over Homer's poems, and cento-ize them into an epic on the Saviour's life. She was the third fair woman accused of sacrificing the world for an apple, having moved her husband to wrath, by giving away his imperial gift of a large one to her own philosophic friend Paulinus; and being unhappily more learned than her two predecessors in the sin, in the course of her exile to Jerusalem she took ghostly comfort by separating Homer's εἴδωλον from his φρένες. There she sat among the ruins of the holy city, addressing herself most unholily, with whatever good intentions and delicate fingers, to pulling Homer's gold to pieces bit by bit, even as the ladies of France devoted what remained to them of virtuous energy 'pour parfiler' under the benignant gaze of Louis Quinze. She, too, who had no right of the purple to literary ineptitude — she, born no empress of Rome, but daughter of Leontius the Athenian, what had she to do with Homer, 'parfilant'? Was it not enough for Homer that he was turned once,

like her own cast imperial mantle, by Apolinarius into a Jewish epic, but that he must be unpicked again by Eudocia for a Christian epic? The reader, who has heard enough of centos, will not care to hear how she did it. That she did it was too much; and the deed recoiled. For mark the poetical justice of her destiny; let all readers mark it, and all writers, especially female writers, who may be half as learned, and not half as fair, — that although she wrote many poems, one 'On the Persian War,' whose title and merit are recorded, not one, except this cento, has survived. The obliterative sponge, we hear of in Æschylus, has washed out every verse except this cento's 'damned spot.' This remains. This is called Eudocia: this stands for the daughter of Leontius, and this only in the world. O fair mischief! she is punished by her hand.

And yet, are we born critics any more than she was born an empress, that we should not have a heart? and is our heart stone, that it should not wax soft within us while the vision is stirred 'between our eyelids and our eyes,' of this beautiful Athenais, baptized once by Christian waters, and once by human tears, into Eudocia, the imperial mourner? — this learned pupil of a learned father, crowned once by her golden hair, and once by her golden crown, yet praised more for poetry and learning than for beauty and greatness by such grave writers as Socrates and Evagrius, the ecclesiastical historians? — this world's empress, pale with the purple of her palaces, an exile even on the throne from her Athens, and soon twice an exile, from father's grave and husband's bosom? We relent before such a vision. And what if, relentingly, we declare her innocent of the Homeric cento? — what if we find her 'a whipping boy' to take the blame? — what if we write down a certain Proba 'improba,' and bid her bear it? For Eudocia, having been once a mark to slander, may have been so again; and Falconia Proba, having committed centoism upon Virgil, must have been capable of anything. The Homeric cento has been actually attributed to her by certain critics, with whom we would join in all earnestness our most sour voices, gladly, for Eudocia's sake, who is closely dear to us, and not malignly for Proba's, who was 'improba' without our help. So shall we impute evil to only one woman, and she not an Athenian; while our worst wish, even to her, assumes this innoxious shape, that she had used a distaff rather than a stylus, though herself and the yet more 'Sleeping Beauty' had owned one horoscope between them! Amen to our wish! A busy distaff and a sound sleep to Proba!

And now, that golden-haired, golden-crowned daughter of Leontius, for whom neither the much learning nor the much sorrow drove Hesperus from her sovran eyes — let her pass on unblenched. Be it said of her, softly as she goes, by all gentle readers — 'She is innocent, whether for centos or for apples! She wrote only such Christian Greek poems as Christians and poets might rejoice to read, but which

perished with her beauty, as being of one seed
with it.'

Midway in the sixth century we encounter
PAUL SILENTIARIUS, called so in virtue of the
office held by him in the court of Justinian, and
chiefly esteemed for his descriptive poem on
the Byzantine church of St. Sophia, which, after
the Arian conflagration, was rebuilt gorgeously
by the emperor. This church was not dedi-
cated to a female saint, according to the suppo-
sition of many persons, but to the second person
of the Trinity, the ἁγία σοφία — holy wisdom;
while the poem being recited in the imperial
presence, and the poet's gaze often forgetting
to rise higher than the imperial smile, Paul
Silentiarius dwelt less on the divine dedication
and the spiritual uses of the place, than on the
glory of the dedicator and the beauty of the
structure. We hesitate, moreover, to grant to
his poem the praise which has been freely
granted to it by more capable critics, of its
power to realize this beauty of structure to the
eyes of the reader. It is highly elaborate and
artistic; but the elaboration and art appear
to us architectural far more than picturesque.
There is no sequency, no congruity, no keeping,
no light and shade. The description has refer-
ence to the working as well as to the work, to
the materials as well as to the working. The
eyes of the reader are suffered to approach the
whole only in analysis, or rather in analysis
analyzed. Every part, part by part, is re-
counted to him excellently well — is brought
close till he may touch it with his eyelashes;
but when he seeks for the general effect, it is
in pieces — there is none of it. Byron shows
him more in the passing words —

> I have beheld Sophia's bright roofs swell
> Their glittering mass i' the sun —

than Silentiarius in all his poem. Yet the
poem has abundant merit in diction and har-
mony; and, besides higher noblenesses, the
pauses are modulated with an artfulness not
commonly attained by these later Greeks, and
the ear exults in an unaccustomed rhythmic
pomp which the inward critical sense is inclined
to murmur at, as an expletive verbosity.

> Whoever looketh with a mortal eye
> To heaven's emblazoned forms, not steadfastly
> With unreverted neck can bear to measure
> That meadow-round of star-apparelled pleasure,
> But drops his eyelids to the verdant hill,
> Yearning to see the river run at will,
> With flowers on each side, — and the ripening corn,
> And grove thick set with trees, and flocks at morn
> Leaping against the dews, — and olives twined,
> And green vine-branches, trailingly inclined, —
> And the blue calmness skimmed by dripping oar
> Along the Golden Horn.
>   But if he bring
> His foot across this threshold, never more
> Would he withdraw it; fain, with wandering
> Moist eyes, and ever-turning head, to stay,
> Since all satiety is driven away
> Beyond the noble structure. Such a fane
> Of blameless beauty hath our Cæsar raised
> By God's perfective grace, and not in vain!

> O emperor, these labors we have praised,
> Draw down the glorious Christ's perpetual smile;
> For thou, the high-peaked Ossa didst not pile
> Upon Olympus' head, nor Pelion throw
> Upon the neck of Ossa, opening so
> The æther to the steps of mortals! no!
> Having achieved a work more high than hope,
> Thou didst not need these mountains as a slope
> Whereby to scale the heaven! Wings take thee thither
> From purest piety to highest æther.

The following passage, from the same 'De-
scription,' is hard to turn into English, through
the accumulative riches of the epithets. Greek
words atone for their vainglorious redundancy
by their beauty, but we cannot think so of
these our own pebbles: —

> Who will unclose me Homer's sounding lips,
> And sing the marble meed that oversweeps
> The mighty walls and pavements spread around
> Of this tall temple, which the sun has crowned?
> The hammer with its iron tooth was loosed
> Into Carystus' summit green, and bruised
> The Phrygian shoulder of the dædal stone; —
> This marble, colored after roses found
> In a white air, and that, with flowers thereon
> Both purple and silver, shining tenderly!
> And that which in the broad fair Nile sank low
> The barges to their edge, the porphyry's glow
> Sown thick with little stars! and thou mayst see
> The green stone of Laconia glitter free!
> And all the Carian hill's deep bosom brings,
> Streaked bow-wise, with a livid white and red, —
> And all the Lydian chasm keeps coverèd,
> A hueless blossom with a ruddier one
> Soft mingled! all, besides, the Libyan sun
> Warms with his golden splendor, till he make
> A golden yellow glory for his sake,
> Along the roots of the Maurusian height;
> And all the Celtic mountains give to sight
> From crystal clefts: black marbles dappled fair
> With milky distillations here and there!
> And all the onyx yields in metal-shine
> Of precious greenness! — all that land of thine,
> Ætolia, hath on even plains engendered
> But not on mountain-tops, — a marble rendered
> Here nigh to green, of tints which emeralds use,
> Here with a sombre purple in the hues!
> Some marbles are like new-dropt snow, and some
> Alight with blackness! Beauty's rays have come,
> So congregate, beneath this holy dome!

And thus the poet takes us away from the
church and dashes our senses and admirations
down these marble quarries! Yet it is right
for us to admit the miracle of a poem made out
of stones! and when he spoke of unclosing
Homer's lips on such a subject, he was probably
thinking of Homer's ships, and meant to inti-
mate that one catalogue was as good for him as
another.

JOHN GEOMETRA arose in no propitious orient
probably with the seventh century, although
the time of his 'elevation' appears to be uncer-
tain within a hundred years.

> He riseth slowly, as his sullen car
> Had all the weights of sleep and death hung on it.

Plato, refusing his divine fellowship to any
one who was not a geometrician or who was a
poet, might have kissed our Johannes, who was

not divine, upon both cheeks, in virtue of his other name and in vice of his verses. He was the author of certain hymns to the Virgin Mary, as accumulative of epithets and admirations as ten of her litanies, inclusive of a pious compliment, which, however geometrically exact in its proportions, sounds strangely.

O health to thee! new living car of the sky,
　Afire on the wheels of four virtues at once!
O health to thee! Seat, than the cherubs more high,
　More pure than the seraphs, *more broad than the
　　thrones!*

Towards the close of the last hymn, the exhausted poet empties back something of the ascription into his own lap, by a remarkable 'mihi quoque.'

O health to me, royal one! if there belong
　Any grace to my singing, that grace is from thee.
O health to me, royal one! if in my song
　Thou hast pleasure, oh, thine is the grace of the
　　glee!

We may mark the time of GEORGE PISIDA, about thirty years deep in the seventh century. He has been confounded with the rhetorical archbishop of Nicomedia, but held the office of scævophylax, only lower than the highest, in the metropolitan church of St. Sophia, and was a poet, singing half in the church and half in the court, and considerably nearer to the feet of the Emperor Heraclius than can please us in any measure. Hoping all things, however, in our poetical charity, we are willing to hope even this, — that the man whom Heraclius carried about with him as a singing-man when he went to fight the Persians, and who sang and recited accordingly, and provided notes of admiration for all the imperial notes of interrogation, and gave his admiring poems the appropriate and suggestive name of *acroases* — auscultations, things intended to be heard, — might nevertheless love Heraclius the fighting-man, not slave-wise or flatterer-wise, but man-wise or dog-wise, in good truth, and up to the brim of his praise; and so hoping, we do not dash the praise down as a libation to the infernal task-masters. Still it is an impotent conclusion to a free-hearted poet's musing on the 'Six Days' Work,' to wish God's creation under the sceptre of his particular friend! It looks as if the particular friend had an ear like Dionysius, and the poet — ah, the poet! — a mark as of a chain upon his brow in the shadow of his court laurel.

We shall not revive the question agitated among his contemporaries, whether Euripides or George Pisida wrote the best iambics; but that our George knew the secret of beauty, and that, having noble thoughts, he could utter them nobly, is clear, despite of Heraclius. That he is, besides, unequal; often coldly perplexed when he means to be ingenious, only violent when he seeks to be inspired; that he premeditates ecstasies, and is inclined to the attitudes of the orators; in brief, that he 'not only'

(and not seldom) 'sleeps but *snores*' — are facts as true of him as the praise is. His Hexaëmeron, to which we referred as his chief work, is rather a meditation or rhythmetical speech upon the finished creation, than a retrospection of the six days; and also there is more of Plato in it than of Moses. It has many fine things, and whole passages of no ordinary eloquence, though difficult to separate and select.

Whatever eyes seek God to view His Light,
As far as they behold Him close in night!
Whoever searcheth with insatiate balls
Th' abysmal glare, or gazeth on Heaven's walls
Against the fire-disk of the sun, the same
According to the vision he may claim,
Is dazzled from his sense.　What soul of flame
Is called sufficient to view onward thus
The way whereby the sun's light came to us?

O distant Presence in fixed motion!　Known
To all men, and inscrutable to one:
Perceived — uncomprehended! unexplained
To all the spirits, yet by each attained,
Because its God-sight is Thy work!　O Presence,
Whatever holy greatness of Thine essence
Lie virtue-hidden, Thou hast given our eyes
The vision of Thy plastic energies —
Not shown in angels only (those create
All fiery-hearted, in a mystic state
Of bodiless body) but, if order be
Of natures more sublime than they or we,
In highest Heaven, or mediate æther, or
This world now seen, or one that came before
Or one to come, — quick in Thy purpose, *there!*
Working in fire and water, earth and air —
In every tuneful star, and tree, and bird —
In all the swimming, creeping life unheard,
In all green herbs, and chief of all, in MAN.

There are other poems of inferior length, 'On the Persian War,' in three books, or, alas, 'auscultations,' — 'The Heracliad,' again on the Persian war, and in two (of course) auscultations again, — 'Against Severus,' 'On the Vanity of Life,' 'The War of the Huns,' and others. From the 'Vanity of Life,' which has much beauty and force, we shall take a last specimen: —

Some yearn to rule the state, to sit above,
And touch the cares of hate as near as love;
Some their own reason for tribunal take,
And for all thrones the humblest prayers they make;
Some love the orator's vain-glorious art, —
The wise love silence and the hush of heart, —
Some to ambition's spirit-curse are fain,
That golden apple with a bloody stain;
While some do battle in her face (more rife
Of noble ends) and conquer strife with strife:
And while your groaning tables gladden these,
Satiety's quick chariot to disease,
Hunger the wise man helps, to water, bread,
And light wings to the dreams about his head.

The truth becomes presently obvious, that —

The sage o'er all the world his sceptre waves,
And earth is common ground to thrones and graves.

JOHN DAMASCENUS, to whom we should not give by any private impulse of admiration the title of Chrysorrhoas, accorded to him by his times, lived at Damascus, his native city, early in the eighth century, holding an unsheathed sword of controversy until the point drew down the lightning. He retired before the affront rather than the injury; and in company with his beloved friend and fellow poet, Cosmas of Jerusalem (whose poetical remains the writer of these Remarks has vainly sought the sight of, and therefore can only, as by hearsay, ascribe some value to them), hid the remnant of his life in the monastery of Saba, where Phocas of the twelfth century looked upon the tomb of either poet. John Damascenus wrote several acrostics on the chief festivals of the churches, which are not much better, although very much longer, than acrostics need be. When he writes out of his heart, without looking to the first letters of his verses, — as indeed, in his Anacreontic his eyes are too dim for iota hunting, — he is another man, and almost a strong man; for the heart being sufficient to speak, we want no Delphic oracle — 'Pan is NOT dead.' In our selection from the Anacreontic hymn, the tears seem to trickle audibly; we welcome them as a Castalia, or, rather, 'as Siloa's brook,' flowing by an oracle more divine than any Grecian one: —

> From my lips in their defilement,
> From my heart in its beguilement,
> From my tongue which speaks not fair,
> From my soul stained everywhere,
> O my Jesus, take my prayer!
> Spurn me not for all it says,
> Not for words and not for ways,
> Not for shamelessness endued!
> Make me brave to speak my mood,
> O my Jesus, as I would!
> Or teach me, which I rather seek,
> What to do and what to speak.

> I have sinnèd more than she,
> Who learning where to meet with Thee,
>   And bringing myrrh, the highest-priced,
> Anointed bravely, from her knee,
> Thy blessed feet accordingly,
>   My God, my Lord, my Christ!
> As Thou saidest not 'Depart'
> To that suppliant from her heart,
> Scorn me not, O Word, that art
> The gentlest one of all words said!
> But give Thy feet to me instead
> That tenderly I may them kiss
> And clasp them close, and never miss
> With over-dropping tears, as free
> And precious as that myrrh could be,
> T' anoint them bravely from my knee!
> Wash me with Thy tears: draw nigh me,
> That their salt may purify me.
> THOU remit my sins who knowest
> All the sinning to the lowest —
> Knowest all my wounds, and seest
> All the stripes Thyself decreest;
> Yea, but knowest all my faith,
> Seest all my force to death,
> Hearest all my wailings low,
> That mine evil should be so!
> Nothing hidden but appears
> In Thy knowledge, O Divine,
> O Creator, Saviour mine —
> Not a drop of falling tears,

> Not a breath of inward moan,
> Not a heart-beat — which is gone!

After this deep pathos of Christianity, we dare not say a word; we dare not even praise it as poetry: our heart is stirred, and not 'idly.' The only sound which can fitly succeed the cry of the contrite soul is that of Divine condonation or of angelic rejoicing. Let us who are sorrowful still, be silent too.

Although doubts, as broad as four hundred years, separate the earliest and latest period talked of as the age of SIMEON METAPHRASTES by those 'viri illustrissimi' the classical critics, we may set him down, without much peril to himself or us, at the close of the tenth century, or very early in the eleventh. He is chiefly known for his 'Lives of the Saints,' which have been lifted up as a mark both for honor and dishonor; which Psellus hints at as a favorite literature of the angels, which Leo Allatius exalts as chafing the temper of the heretics, and respecting which we, in an exemplary serenity, shall straightway accede to one half of the opinion of Bellarmine — that the work speaketh not as things actually happened, but as they might have happened — 'non ut res gestæ fuerunt, sed ut geri potuerant.' Our half of this weighty opinion is the first clause — we demur upon 'ut geri potuerant,' — and we need not go further than the former to win a light of commentary for the term 'metaphrases,' applied to the saintly biographies in otherwise a doubtful sense, and worn obliquely upon the sleeve of the biographer Metaphrastes, in no doubtful token of his skill in metamorphosing things as they were into things as they might have been. And Simeon having received from Constantinople the honor of his birth within her walls, and returning to her the better honor of the distinctions and usefulness of his life, — so writeth Psellus, his encomiast, with a graceful turn of thought, — expired in an 'odor of sanctity' befitting the biographer of all the saints, — breathing out from his breathless remains such an incense of celestial sweetness, that if it had not been for the maladroitness of certain unfragrant persons whose desecration of the next tomb acted incontinently as a stopper, the whole earth might at this day be *metaphrased* to our nostrils, as steeped in an attar-gul of Eden or Ede! — we might be dwelling in a phœnix-nest at this day. Through the maladroitness, however, in question, there is lost to us every sweeter influence from the life and death of Simeon Metaphrastes than may result from the lives and deaths of his saints, and from other works of his, whether commentaries, orations, or poems; and we cannot add that the aroma from his writings bears any proportion in value to the fragrance from his sepulchre. Little of his poetry has reached us, and we are satisfied with the limit. There were three Simeons, who did precede our Simeon, as the world knoweth, and whose titles were Stylitæ or Columnarii, because it pleased them in their saintly volition to take the highest place and live out their natural lives supernaturally, each upon the top of a column. Peradventure the columns which our Simeon refused to live upon conspired against his poetry ; peradventure it is on their account that we find ourselves between two alphabetic acrostics, written solemnly by his hand, and take up one wherein every alternate line begins with a letter of the alphabet ; its companion in the couplet being left to run behind it, out of livery and sometimes out of breath. Will the public care to look upon such a curiosity ? Will our verse-writers care to understand what harm may be done by a conspiration of columns — gods and men quite on one side ? And will candid readers care to confess at last, that there is an earnestness in the poem, acrostic as it is — a leaning to beauty's side — which is above the acrosticism ? Let us try : —

Ah, tears upon mine eyelids, sorrow on mine heart,
  I bring Thee soul-repentance, Creator as Thou art !
Bounding joyous actions, deep as arrows go ;
  Pleasures self-revolving, issue into woe !
Creatures of our mortal, headlong rush to sin :
  I have seen them ; of them — ah me, — I have been !
Duly pitying Spirits, from your spirit-frame,
  Bring your cloud of weeping, — worthy of the same !
Else I would be bolder ; if that light of Thine,
  Jesus, quell the evil, let it on me shine !
Fail me truth, is living, less than death forlorn,
  When the sinner readeth — ' better be unborn ' ?
God, I raise toward Thee both eyes of my heart,
  With a sharp cry — ' Help me ! ' — while mine hopes depart.
Help me ! Death is bitter, all hearts comprehend ;
  But I fear beyond it — end beyond the end.
Inwardly behold me, how my soul is black :
  Sympathize in gazing, do not spurn me back !
Knowing that Thy pleasure is not to destroy,
  That Thou fain wouldst save me — this is all my joy.
Lo, the lion, hunting spirits in their deep,
  (Stand beside me !) roareth — (help me !) nears to leap.
Mayst Thou help me, Master ! Thou art pure alone,
  Thou alone art sinless, one Christ on a throne.
Nightly deeds I loved them, hated day's instead ;
  Hence this soul-involving darkness on mine head.
O Word, who constrainest things estranged and curst,
  If Thy hand can save me, that work were the first !
Pensive o'er my sinning, counting all its ways,
  Terrors shake me, waiting adequate dismays.
Quenchless glories many, hast Thou — many a rod —
  Thou, too, hast Thy measures. Can I bear Thee, God ?
Rend away my counting from my soul's decline,
  Show me of the portion of those saved of Thine !
Slow drops of my weeping to Thy mercy run :
  Let its rivers wash me, by that mercy won !
Tell me what is worthy, in our dreary now,
  As the future glory ? (madness !) what, as Thou ?
Union, oh, vouchsafe me to Thy fold beneath,
  Lest the wolf across me gnash his gory teeth !
View me, judge me gently ! spare me, Master bland
  Brightly lift Thine eyelids, kindly stretch Thine hand !
Winged and choral angels ! 'twixt my spirit lone,
  And all deathly visions, interpose your own !
Yea, my soul, remember death and woe inwrought —
  After-death affliction, wringing earth's to nought !
Zone me, Lord, with graces ! Be foundations built
  Underneath me ; save me ! as Thou know'st and wilt !

The omission of our X (in any case too sullen a letter to be employed in the service of an acrostic) has permitted us to write line for line with the Greek ; and we are able to infer to the honor of the Greek poet, that although he did not live upon a column, he was not far below one, in the virtue of self-mortification. We are tempted to accord him some more gracious and serious justice, by breaking away a passage from his 'Planctus Mariæ,' the lament of Mary on embracing the Lord's body ; and giving a moment's insight into a remarkable composition, which, however deprived of its poetical right of measure, is, in fact, nearer to a poem, both in purpose and achievement, than any versified matter we have looked upon from this metaphrastic hand : —

' O, uncovered corse, yet Word of the Living One ! self-doomed to be uplifted on the cross for the drawing of all men unto Thee, — what member of Thine hath no wound ? O my blessed brows, embraced by the thorn-wreath which is pricking at my heart ! O beautiful and priestly One, who hadst not where to lay Thine head and rest, and now wilt lay it only in the tomb, resting *there ;* sleeping, as Jacob said, a lion's sleep ! O cheeks turned to the smiter ! O lips, new hive for bees, yet fresh from the sharpness of vinegar and bitterness of gall ! O mouth, wherein was no guile, yet betrayed by the traitor's kiss ! O hand, creative of man, yet nailed to the cross, and since stretched out unto Hades, with help for the first transgressor ! O feet, once walking on the deep to hallow the waters of nature ! O me, my son ! . . . Where is thy chorus of sick ones ? — those whom Thou didst cure of their diseases, and bring back from the dead ? Is none here, but only Nicodemus, to draw the nails from those hands and feet ? — none here, but only Nicodemus, to lift Thee from the cross heavily, heavily, and lay Thee in these mother-arms, which bore Thee long ago, in thy babyhood, and were glad *then ?* These hands, which swaddled Thee then, let them bind Thy grave-clothes now. And yet, — O bitter funerals ! — O Giver of life from the dead, liest Thou dead before mine eyes ? Must *I*, who said " hush " beside Thy cradle, wail this passion upon Thy grave ? *I*, who washed Thee in Thy first bath, must I drop on Thee these hotter tears ? I, who raised Thee high in my maternal arms, — but *then* Thou leapedst, — *then* Thou sprangest up in Thy child-play ! '

It is better to write so than to stand upon a column. And, although the passage does, both generally and specifically, in certain of its ideas, recall the antithetic eloquence of that Gregory Nazianzen before whom this Simeon must be dumb, we have touched his ' oration,' so called, nearer than our subject could permit us to do any of Gregory's, because the ' Planctus' involves an imagined situation, is poetical in its design. Moreover, we must prepare to look downwards ; the poets were descending from the gorgeous majesty of the hexameter and the severe simplicity of iambics down through the mediate *versus politici*, a loose metre, adapted to the popular ear, to the lowest deep of a 'measured prose,'— which has been likened, but which *we* will not liken, to the blank verse of our times. Presently, we may offer an example from Psellus of a prose acrostic — the reader being delighted with the prospect! 'A whole silver threepence, mistress.'

MICHAEL PSELLUS lived midway in the eleventh century, and appears to have been a man of much aspiration toward the higher places of the earth. A senator of no ordinary influence, preceptor of the Emperor Michael previous to that accession, he is supposed to have included in his instructions the advantages of sovereignty, and in his precepts the most subtle means of securing them. We were about to add, that his acquirements as a scholar were scarcely less imperial than those of his pupil as a prince ; but the expression might have been inappropriate. There are cases not infrequent, not entirely opposite to the present case, and worthy always of all meditation by such intelligent men as affect extensive acquisition, — when acquirements are not ruled by the man, but rule him. Whatever originates from the mind cannot obstruct her individual faculty ; nay, whatever she receives inwardly and marks her power over by creating out of it a *tertium quid*, according to the law of the perpetual generation of spiritual verities, is not obstructive but impulsive to the evolution of faculty ; but the erudition, whether it be erudition as the world showed it formerly, or miscellaneous literature, as the world shows it now, the accumulated acquirement of whatever character, which remains *extraneous* to the mind, is and must be in the same degree an obstruction and deformity. How many are there, from Psellus to Bayle, bound hand and foot intellectually with the rolls of their own papyrus — men whose erudition has grown stronger than their souls ! How many whom we would gladly see washed in the clean waters of a little ignorance, and take our own part in their refreshment ! Not that knowledge is bad, but that wisdom is better ; and that it is better and wiser in the sight of the angels of knowledge to think out one true thought with a thrush's song and a green light for all lexicon (or to think it without the light and without the song — because truth is beautiful, where they are not seen or heard) — than to mummy our benumbed souls with the circumvolutions of twenty thousand books. And so Michael Psellus was a learned man.

We have sought earnestly, yet in vain, — and the fact may account for our ill-humor,— a sight of certain iambics upon vices and virtues, and Tantalus and Sphinx, which are attributed to this writer, and cannot be in the moon after all : — earnestly, yet with no fairer encouragement to our desire than what befalls it from his *poems* 'On the Councils,' the first of which, and only the first, through the softness of our charities, we bring to confront the reader : —

Know the holy councils, King, to their utmost number,
Such as roused the impious ones from their world-wide slumber !

Seven in all those councils were : Nice the first containing,
When the godly master-soul Constantine was reigning,
What time at Byzantium, hallowed with the hyssop,
In heart and word, Metrophanes presided as archbishop !
It cut away Arius' tongue's maniacal delusion,
Which cut off from the Trinity the blessed Homoousion —
Blasphemed (O miserable man !) the maker of the creature,
And low beneath the Father cast the equal Filial nature.

The prose acrostic, contained in an office written by Psellus to the honor of Simeon, is elaborated on the words 'I sing thee who didst write the metaphrases ;' every sentence being insulated, and beginning with a charmed letter.

Say in a dance how we shall go,
Who never could a measure know ?

why, thus — (and yet Psellus, who did *know* everything, wrote a synopsis of the metres !) — why, thus : —

'Inspire me, Word of God, with a rhythmetic chant, for I am borne onward to praise Simeon Metaphrastes and Logothetes, as he is fitly called, the man worthy of admiration !

'Solemnly from the heavenly heights did the Blessed Ghost descend on thee, wise one, and finding thine heart pure, rested there, there verily in the body !'

Surely we need not write any more. But Michael Psellus was a very learned man.

JOHN of EUCHAITA (or Euchania, or Theodoropolis, — the three names do appear through the twilight to belong to one city) was a bishop, probably contemporary with Psellus — is only a poet now : we turn to see the voice which speaks to us. It is a voice with a soul in it, clear and sweet and living : and we who have walked long in the desert, leap up to its sound as to the dim flowing of a stream, and would take a deep breath by its side both for the weariness which is gone and the repose which is coming. But it is a rarer thing than a stream in the desert ; it is a voice in the desert — the only voice of a city. The city may have three names, as we have said, or the three names may more fitly appertain to three cities — scholars knit their brows and wax doubtful as they talk ; but a city denuded of its multitudes it surely is, ruined even of its ruins it surely is : no exhalation arises from its tombs, the foxes have lost their way to it, the bittern's cry is as dumb as the vanished population — only the Voice remains. John Mauropus, of Euchaita, Euchania, Theodoropolis — one living man among many dead, as the Arabian tale goes of the city of enchantment — one speechful voice among the silent, sole survivor of the breath which maketh words. effluence of the soul replacing the bittern's cry —speak to us ! And thou shalt be to us as a poet ; we will salute thee by that high name. For have we not stood face to face with Michael Psellus and him of the metaphrases ? Surely as a poet may we salute *thee* !

His poetry has, as if in contrast to the scenery of circumstances in which we find it, or to the fatality of circumstances in which it has *not* been found (and even Mr. Clarke in his learned work upon Sacred Literature, which is, however, incommunicative generally upon sacred poetry, appears unconscious of his being and his bishopric) — his poetry has a character singularly vital, fresh, and serene. There is nothing in it of the rapture of inspiration, little of the operativeness of art — nothing of imagination in a high sense, or of ear-service in any: he is not, he says, of those —

Who rain hard with redundancies of words,
And thunder and lighten out of eloquence.

His Greek being opposed to that of the Silentiarii and the Pisidæ by a peculiar simplicity and ease of collocation which the reader feels lightly in a moment, the thoughts move through its transparency with a certain calm nobleness and sweet living earnestness, with holy upturned eyes and human tears beneath the lids, till the reader feels lovingly too. We startle him from his reverie with an octave note on a favorite literary fashion of the living London, drawn from the voice of the lost city; discovering by that sound the first serial illustrator of pictures by poems, in the person of our Johannes. Here is a specimen from an annual of Euchaita, or Euchania, or Theodoropolis — we may say 'annual' although the pictures were certainly not in a book, but were probably ornaments of the beautiful temple in the midst of the city, concerning which there is a tradition. Here is a specimen selected for love's sake, because it 'illustrates' a portrait of Gregory Nazianzen: —

What meditates thy thoughtful gaze, my father?
To tell me some new truth? Thou canst not so!
For all that mortal hands are weak to gather
Thy blessed books unfolded long ago.

These are striking verses, upon the Blessed among women, weeping: —

O Lady of the passion, dost thou weep?
    What help can we then through our tears survey,
If such as thou a cause for wailing keep?
    What help, what hope, for us, sweet Lady, say?
' Good man, it doth befit thine heart to lay
More courage next it, having seen me so.
    All other hearts find other balm to-day —
The whole world's consolation is my woe! '

Would any hear what can be said of a Transfiguration before Raffael's: —

Tremble, spectator, at the vision won thee!
    Stand afar off, look downward from the height,
Lest Christ too nearly seen should lighten on thee,
    And from thy fleshly eyeballs strike the sight,
    As Paul fell ruined by that glory white!
Lo, the disciples prostrate, each apart,
    Each impotent to bear the lamping light!
And all that Moses and Elias might,
The darkness caught the grace upon her heart
And gave them strength for! *Thou*, if evermore
A God-voice pierce thy dark. — rejoice, adore!

Our poet was as unwilling a bishop as the most sturdy of the ' nolentes ; ' and there are poems written both in depreciation of, and in retrospective regret for, the ordaining dignity, marked by noble and holy beauties which we are unwilling to pass without extraction. Still we are constrained for space, and must come at last to his chief individual characteristic — to the gentle humanities which, strange to say, preponderate in the solitary voice — to the familiar smiles and sighs which go up and down in it, to our ear. We will take the poem ' To his Old House,' and see how the house survives by his good help, when the sun shines no more on the golden statue of Constantine: —

O be not angry with me, gentle house,
    That I have left thee empty and deserted!
Since thou thyself that evil didst arouse,
    In being to thy masters so false-hearted,
In loving none of those who did possess thee,
    In minist'ring to no one to an end,
In no one's service caring to confess thee,
    But loving still the change of friend for friend,
And sending the last, plague-wise, to the door!
    And so, or ere thou canst betray and leave me,
I, a wise lord, dismiss thee, servitor,
    And antedate the wrong thou mayst achieve me
Against my will, by what my will allows;
Yet not without some sorrow, gentle house!

For oh, beloved house, what time I render
    My last look back on thee I grow more tender!
Pleasant possession, hearth for father's age,
Dear gift of buried hands, sole heritage!
My blood is stirred; and love, that learnt its play
From all sweet customs, moves mine heart thy way!
For thou wast all my nurse and helpful creature,
For thou wast all my tutor and my teacher;
In thee through lengthening toils I struggled deep,
In thee I watched all night without its sleep,
In thee I worked the wearier daytime out,
Exalting truth, or trying by a doubt.

. . . .

And oh, my father's roof, the memory leaves
Such pangs as break mine heart, beloved eaves!
But God's word conquers all.

He is forced to a strange land, reverting with this benediction to the ' dearest house: ' —

Farewell, farewell, mine own familiar one,
Estranged for evermore from this day's sun,
Fare-thee-well so! Farewell, O second mother,
O nurse and help, — remains there not another!
My bringer-up to some sublimer measure
Of holy childhood and perfected pleasure!
Now other spirits must thou tend and teach,
And minister thy quiet unto each,
For reasoning uses, if they love such use,
But nevermore to me. God keep thee, house,
God keep thee, faithful corner, where I drew
So calm a breath of life! And God keep you,
Kind neighbors! Though I leave you by His grace,
Let no grief bring a shadow to your face;
Because whate'er He willeth to be done
His will makes easy, makes the distant — one,
And soon brings all embraced before His throne!

We pass PHILIP SOLITARIUS, who lived at the close of this eleventh century, even as we have passed one or two besides of his fellow-poets ; because they, having hidden themselves beyond the reach of our eyes and the endeavor of our hands, and we being careful to speak by knowledge rather than by testimony, nothing remains to us but this same silent passing — this regretful one, as our care to do better must testify — albeit our fancy will not, by any means, account them, with all their advantages of absence, ' the best part of the solemnity.'

Early in the twelfth century we are called to the recognition of THEODORE PRODROMUS, theologian, philosopher, and poet. His poems are unequal, consisting principally of a series of tetrastichs (Greek epigrams for lack of point, French epigrams for lack of poetry) upon the Old and New Testaments, and the Life of Chrysostom, — all nearly as bare of the rags of literary merit as might be expected from the design ; and three didactic poems upon Love, Providence, and against Bareus the heretic, into which the poet has cast the recollected life of his soul. The soul deports herself as a soul should, with a vivacity and energy which work outward and upward into eloquence. The sentiments are lofty, the expression free ; there is an instinct to a middle and an end. Music we miss, even to the elementary melody: the poet thinks his thoughts, and speaks them ; not indeed what all poets, so called, do esteem a necessary effort, and indeed what we should thank him for doing ; but he *sings* them in nowise, and they are not of that divine order which are crowned by right of their divinity with an inseparable aureole of sweet sound. His poem upon Love, — φιλία says the Greek word, but friendship does not answer to it, — is a dialogue between the personification and a stranger. It opens thus dramatically, the stranger speaking : —

Love ! Lady diademed with honor, whence
And whither goest thou ? Thy look presents
Tears to the lid, thy mien is vext and low,
Thy locks fall wildly from thy drooping brow,
  Thy blushes are all pale, thy garb is fit
For mourning in, and shoon and zone are loose !
  So changed thou art to sadness every whit,
And all that pomp and purple thou didst use,
  That seemly sweet, that new rose on the mouth,
Those fair-smoothed tresses, and that graceful zone,
Bright sandals, and the rest thou haddest on,
  Are all departed, gone to nought together !
And now thou walkest mournful in the train
Of mourning women ! — where and whence, again ?
  Love. From earth to God my Father.
  Stranger.   Dost thou say
That earth of Love is desolated ?
  Love.   Yea !
It so much scorned me.
  Stranger.   Scorned ?
  Love.   And cast me out
From its door.
  Stranger.   From its door ?
  Love.   As if without
I had my lot to die !

Love consents to give her confidence to the wondering stranger ; whereupon, as they sit in the shadow of a tall pine, she tells a Platonic story of all the good she had done in heaven before the stars, and the angels, and the throned Triad, and of all her subsequent sufferings on the melancholy and ungrateful earth. The poem, which includes much beauty, ends with a quaint sweetness in the troth-plighting of the stranger and the lady. Mayst thou have been faithful to that oath, O Theodore Prodromus ! but thou didst swear ' too much to be believed — so *much.*' —

The poems ' On Providence ' and ' Against Bareus ' exceed the ' Love,' perhaps, in power and eloquence to the full measure of the degree in which they fall short of the interest of the latter's design. Whereupon we dedicate the following selection from the ' Providence ' to Mr. Carlyle's ' gigmen ' and all ' respectable persons : ' —

Ah me! what tears mine eyes are welling forth,
To witness in this synagogue of earth
Wise men speak wisely while the scoffers sing,
And rich men folly, for much honoring !
Melitus trifles, — Socrates decrees
Our further knowledge ! Death to Socrates,
And long life to Melitus ! . . .

. . . . . .

Chiefdom of evil, gold ! blind child of clay,
Gnawing with fixèd tooth earth's heart away !
Go ! perish from us ! objurgation vain
To soulless nature, powerless to contain
One ill unthrust upon it ! Rather perish
That turpitude of crowds, by which they cherish
Bad men for their good fortune, or condemn,
Because of evil fortune, virtuous men !

. . . . . .

Oh, for a trumpet mouth ! an iron tongue
Sufficient for all speech ! foundations hung
High on Parnassus' top to bear my feet !
So from that watch-tower, words which shall be meet,
I may out-thunder to the nations near me —
' Ye worshippers of gold, poor rich men, hear me !
Where do ye wander ? — for what object stand ?
That gold is earth's ye carry in your hand,
And floweth earthward ; bad men have its curse
The most profusely : would yourselves be worse
So to be richer ? — better in your purse ?
Your royal purple — 't was a dog that found it !
Your pearl of price — a sickened oyster owned it !
Your glittering gems are pebbles, dust-astray ;
Your palace pomp was wrought of wood and clay,
Smoothed rock and moulded plinth ! earth's clay, earth's wood,
Earth's common-hearted stones ! Is this your mood,
To honor *earth*, to worship *earth*, nor blush ? '
What dost thou murmur, savage mouth ? Hush, hush,
Thy wrath is vainly breathed. The depth to tread
Of God's deep judgments, was not Paul's, he said.

The ' savage mouth ' speaks in power, with whatever harshness : and we are tempted to contrast with this vehement utterance another short poem by the same poet, a little quaint withal, but light, soft, almost tuneful, — as written for a ' Book of Beauty,' and that not of Euchaita ! The subject is ' LIFE.'

Oh, take me, thou mortal, — thy LIFE for thy praiser !
Thou hast met, found and seized me, and know'st what my ways are.

Nor leave me for slackness, nor yield me for plea-
sure,
Nor look up too saintly, nor muse beyond measure!
There's the veil from my head — see the worst of my
mourning!
There are wheels to my feet — have a dread of their
turning!
There are wings round my waist — I may flatter and
flee thee!
There are yokes on my hands — fear the chains I de-
cree thee!
Hold *me!* hold a shadow, the winds as they quiver;
Hold *me!* hold a dream, smoke, a track on the river.

Oh! take me, thou mortal, — thy Life for thy praiser,
Thou hast met not, and seized not, nor know'st what
my ways are!
Nay, frown not, and shrink not, nor call me an as-
pen;
There's the veil from my head! I have dropped from
thy clasping!
A fall-back within it I soon may afford thee;
There are wheels to my feet — I may roll back toward
thee!
There are wings round my waist — I may flee back and
clip thee!
There are yokes on my hands — I may soon cease to
whip thee!
Take courage! I rather would hearten than hip thee!

JOHN TZETZA divides the twelfth century
with his name, which is not a great one. In
addition to an iambic fragment upon educa-
tion, he has written indefatigably in the metre
politicus, what must be read, if read at all,
with a corresponding energy, — thirteen 'chili-
ads,' of 'vario historiæ,' so called after
Ælian's, — Ælian's without the 'honey tongue,'
— very various histories indeed, about croco-
diles and flies, and Plato's philosophy and
Cleopatra's nails, and Samson and Phidias,
and the resurrection from the dead, and the
Calydonian boar, — 'everything under the sun'
being, in fact, their imperfect epitome. The
omission is simply POETRY! there is no appar-
ent consciousness of her entity in the mind of
this versifier; no aspiration towards her pre-
sence, not so much as a sigh upon her absence.
We do not, indeed, become aware, in the whole
course of this laborious work, of much unfold-
ing of faculty — take it lower than the poetical;
of nothing much beyond an occasional dry, sly,
somewhat boorish humor, which being good
humor besides, would not be a bad thing were
its traces only more extended. But the general
level of the work is a dull talkativeness, a prosy
adversity, who is no 'Daughter of Jove,' and a
slumberousness without a dream. We adjudge
to our reader the instructive history of the
Phœnix.

A phœnix is a single bird and synchronous with na-
ture;
The peacock cannot equal him in beauty or in stat-
ure.
In radiance he outshines the gold; the world in wonder
yieldeth;
His nest he fixeth in the trees, and all of spices build-
eth.
And when he dies, a little worm, from out his body
twining,

Doth generate him back again whence'er the sun is
shining.
He lives in Ægypt, and he dies in Æthiopia only, as
Asserts Philostratus, who wrote the Life of Apollonius.
And (as the wise Ægyptian scribe, the holy scribe,
Chæremon,
Hath entered on these Institutes, all centre their esteem
on)
Seven thousand years and six of age, this phœnix of the
story
Expireth from the fair Nile side, whereby he had his
glory.

In the early part of the fourteenth century,
MANUEL PHILE, pricked emulously to the
heart by the successful labors of Tzetza, em-
braced into identity with himself the remaining
half of Ælian, and developed in his poetical
treatise 'On the Properties of Animals,' to
which Isachimus Camerarius provided a con-
clusion — the 'Natural History' of that in-
dustrious and amusing Greek-Roman. The
Natural History is translated into verse, but
by no means glorified; and yet the poet of
animals, Phile, has carried away far more of
the Ælian honey clinging to the edges of his
patera than the poet of the Chiliads did ever
wot of. What we find in him is not beauty,
what we hear in him is not music, but there
is an open feeling for the beautiful which stirs
at a word, and we have a scarcely confessed
contentment in hearkening to those twice-
told stories of birds and beasts and fishes, mea-
sured out to us in the low monotony of his
chanting voice. Our selections shall say no-
thing of the live grasshopper, called, with the
first breath of this paper, an emblem of the
vital Greek tongue; because the space left to
us closes within our sight, and the science of
the age does not thirst to receive, through our
hands, the history of grasshoppers, according to
Ælian or Phile either. Everybody knows what
Phile tells us here, that grasshoppers live upon
morning dew, and cannot sing when it is dry.
Everybody knows that the lady grasshopper
sings not at all. And if the moral, drawn by
Phile from this latter fact, of the advantage of
silence in the female sex generally, be true and
important, it is also too obvious to exact our
enforcement of it. Therefore we pass by the
grasshopper, and the nightingale too, for all
her fantastic song; and hasten to introduce to
European naturalists a Philhellenic species of
heron, which has escaped the researches of
Cuvier, and the peculiarities of which may
account for the philosophic reader for that in-
stinct of the 'wisdom of our forefathers,'
which established an English university in
approximation with the Fens. It is earnestly
to be hoped that the nice ear in question for
the Attic dialect may still be preserved among
the herons of Cambridgeshire : —

A Grecian island nourisheth to bless
A race of herons in all nobleness.
If some barbarian bark approach the shore,
They hate, they flee, — no eagle can outsoar!
But if by chance an Attic voice be wist,
They grow softhearted straight, philhellenist;

Press on in earnest flocks along the strand,
And stretch their wings out to the comer's hand.
Perhaps he nears them with a gentle mind, —
They love his love, though foreign to their kind !
For so the island giveth wingèd teachers,
In true love lessons, to all wingless creatures.

He has written, besides, ' A Dialogue between
Mind and Phile,' and other poems ; and we can-
not part without taking from him a more sol-
emn tone, which may sound as an 'Amen' to
the good we have said of him. The following
address to the Holy Spirit is concentrated in
expression : —

O living Spirit, O falling of God-dew,
O Grace which dost console us and renew,
O vital light, O breath of angelhood,
O generous ministration of things good,
Creator of the visible, and best
Upholder of the great unmanifest
Power infinitely wise, new boon sublime
Of science and of art, constraining might,
In whom I breathe, live, speak, rejoice, and write, —
Be with us in all places, for all time !

' And now,' saith the patientest reader of
all, ' you have done. Now we have watched
out the whole night of the world with you, by
no better light than these poetical rushlights,
and the wicks fail, and the clock of the uni-
versal hour is near upon the stroke of the sev-
enteenth century, and you have surely done ! '
Surely *not*, we answer; for we see a hand which
the reader sees not, which beckons us over to
Crete, and clasps within its shadowy fingers a
roll of hymns Anacreontical, written by MAXI-
MUS MARGUNIUS: and not for the last of our
readers would we lose this last of the Greeks,
owing him salutation. Yet the hymns have,
for the true Anacreontic fragrance, a musty
odor, and we have scant praise for them in our
nostrils. Their inspiration is from Gregory
Nazianzen, whose 'Soul and Body' are renewed
in them by a double species of transmigration ;
and although we kiss the feet of Gregory's
high excellences, we cannot admit any one of
them to be a safe conductor of poetical inspi-
ration. And, in union with Margunius's plagi-
aristic tendencies, there is a wearisome lengthi-
ness, harder to bear. He will knit you to the
whole length of a ' Honi soit qui mal y pense,'
till you fall asleep to the humming of the stitches
what time you should be reading the ' moral.'
We ourselves once dropped into a ' distraction,'
as the French say, — for nothing could be more
different from what the English say, than our
serene state of self-abnegation, — at the begin-
ging of a house-building by this Maximus Mar-
gunius : when, reading on some hundred lines
with our bare bodily eyes, and our soul starting
up on a sudden to demand a measure of the
progress, behold, he was building it still, with
trowel in the same hand: it was not forwarder
by a brick. The swallows had time to hatch
two nestfuls in a chimney while he finished the
chimney-pot ! Nevertheless he has moments of
earnestness, and they leave beauties in their
trace. Let us listen to this extract from his
fifth hymn : –

Take me as a hermit lone
With a desert life and moan ;
Only Thou anear to mete
Slow or quick my pulse's beat;
Only Thou, the night to chase
With the sunlight in Thy face !
Pleasure to the eyes may come
From a glory seen afar,
But if life concentre gloom
Scattered by no little star,
Then, how feeble, God, we are !
Nay, whatever bird there be,
(Æther by his flying stirred),
He, in this thing, must be free —
And I, Saviour, am Thy bird,
Pricking with an open beak
At the words that Thou dost speak !
Leave a breath upon my wings,
That above these nether things
I may rise to where Thou art,
I may flutter next Thine heart !
For if a light within me burn,
It must be darkness in an urn,
Unless, within its crystalline,
That unbeginning light of Thine
Shine ! oh Saviour, *let* it shine !

He is the last of our Greeks. The light
from Troy city, with which all Greek glory be-
gan, ' threw three-times six,' said Æschylus,
that man with a soul, — beacon after beacon,
into the heart of Greece. ' Three-times six,'
too, threw the light from Greece, when her
own heart-light had gone out like Troy's, on-
ward along the ridges of time. Three-times
six — but what faint beacons are the last ! —
sometimes only a red brand ; sometimes only a
small trembling flame ; sometimes only a white
glimmer as of ashes breathed on by the wind ;
faint beacons and far ! How far ! We have
watched them along the cloudy tops of the
great centuries, through the ages dark but for
them, — and now stand looking with eyes of
farewell upon the last pale sign on the last mist-
bound hill. But it is the sixteenth century.
Beyond the ashes on the hill a red light is
gathering ; above the falling of the dews a great
sun is rising : there is a rushing of life and
song upward — let it still be UPWARD ! Shake-
speare is in the world ! And the Genius of
English Poetry, she who only of all the earth
is worthy (Goethe's spirit may hear us say so,
and smile), stooping, with a royal gesture, to
kiss the dead lips of the Genius of Greece,
stands up her successor in the universe, by vir-
tue of that chrism, and in right of her own
crown.

III. NOTES AND ILLUSTRATIONS

[The task of annotating Mrs. Browning's
text is greatly simplified by the fact of her
constitutional unwillingness to change the form
of any thought that she had once expressed
fairly to her own satisfaction. It belonged,
perhaps, to her very serious conception of the
Poet's ' divine mission,' and of her own, as
a poet by predestination, however unworthy,

that her thought, as first visibly, and often painfully *enfanté*, seemed to her a species of organism, — which might be clumsy and unfortunate in shape, but which could not be altered without mutilation. She said a good deal about Art, — particularly in her later days, when she lived nearer to the *grand monde* of letters than she had done in her earlier and more productive period. But in truth, she was much more a moralist than an artist, and had very little of the consuming passion for mere beauty, and the unresting pursuit of external perfection, which characterize the poets of supremely artistic temperament, like Tennyson and Keats. Even her extensive classical studies, — and they were extensive, though not analytic, nor what would now be considered profound, failed, curiously enough, to develop her sense of form; and Greek was to her, if such a thing be possible, almost too much like a living language. No great writer was ever more humble and reasonable about the intrinsic worth of her own productions than Mrs. Browning ; but the words in which she said her say seemed to her essential, and preëminently her own affair ; and when once she had called the Seer of Patmos ' apolyptic John,' it required a good deal of argument on the part of persons whose judgment she deeply respected to convince her that the adjective would not do. She altered (see note, p. 516), at Wordsworth's own request, a line in her sonnet on Haydon's portrait, without very materially improving it ; and she made a change also — it may be presumed upon representation — in one of the more dithyrambic stanzas of *Lady Geraldine's Courtship*. In the earlier editions of that florid poetical romance, we have, as illustrating the extent of the heroine's landed possessions, and the material interests which she controlled, the statement that —

> the resonant steam-eagles
> Follow far on the direction of her little dove-like hand.

Both the eagle and the dove were banished subsequently, and the verse now reads —

> And the palpitating engines snort in steam across her acres —

which comes a little nearer to scientific truth, no doubt ; though it must be confessed that both these attempted impersonations of the locomotive remind the reader unpleasantly of the ear-splitting melodies of the ' Siren.'

When a fourth edition of *Aurora Leigh* was called for, in January, 1859, two years after its original publication, Robert Browning wrote from Rome to Mr. Ruskin that a corrected edition of *Aurora Leigh* had just been sent off to London which had cost ' us ' (Mrs. Browning and himself) ' a great deal of pains ; ' and Mrs. Browning wrote to a friend at the same time that she had ' dizzied herself with " *ifs* " and " *ands*." ' The labor which irked her so was indeed almost confined to the ' ifs ' and ' ands ; ' that is to say, to those minute corrections in grammar and punctuation which leave, for the most part, the thought and imagery of a passage unchanged, but which ought, in fairness to the author, to be accepted without question, as annulling the previous reading. Not one of the more important and memorable passages in the poem was noticeably modified. In looking through the letters of both poets for passages calculated to throw light on the origin and growth of Mrs. Browning's principal works, we find enough and to spare in her own, but are disappointed to discover so little in her husband's. The slight reference in the note to Ruskin mentioned above is almost solitary ; and even there, it will be observed, he speaks in no wise as a critic, but rather as one partner in a firm with unlimited liability. We know, in a general way, how exalted was the rank which Robert Browning assigned to his wife's genius ; that he thought the Portuguese Sonnets the finest written in any language since Shakespeare's ; that it was through the charm and power over him of her earlier writings that he first came to adore her. We have the eloquent dedications of *Men and Women* to her living self, and of the *Ring and the Book* to her memory, and we have the conjecture, not very well supported, however, of Mr. Browning's biographer that he intended to portray Mrs. Browning in the beautiful character of Pompilia. But for any more specific judgment or intimate commentary, we shall seek the husband's published correspondence in vain. It is to be remembered, of course, that he himself destroyed, some years before his death, all those letters to members of his own family in which he would have been most likely, perhaps, to speak of his wife's work without reserve ; and also that from the time, beginning with the publication of *Casa Guidi Windows*, when Mrs. Browning's muse began to occupy itself so much more than formerly with political events, and social and philanthropic speculations, he may purposely have refrained from any allusion to what she published, for the reason that while bating not one jot of his loyal admiration for her character and gifts, he did not always entirely agree with her opinions.]

A ROMANCE OF THE GANGES.
Page 30, line 98. *To the holy house of snow.*
The Hindoo heaven is localized on the summit of Mount Meru — one of the mountains of Himalaya or Himmaleh, which signifies, I be-

lieve, in Sanscrit, the abode of snow, winter, or coldness.

Line 104. *The humming-bird is in the sun.*

Himadeva, the Indian god of love, is imagined to wander through the three worlds, accompanied by the humming-bird, cuckoo, and gentle breezes.

Page 31, line 157. *To cast upon thine hair.*

The casting of rice upon the head, and the fixing of the band or tali about the neck, are parts of the Hindoo marriage ceremonial.

Line 189. *Thy lily hath not changed a leaf.*

The Ganges is represented as a white woman, with a water-lily in her right hand, and in her left a lute.

SOUNDS.

Page 38, line 38. *Like a singing in a dream.*

> While floating up bright forms ideal,
> Mistress or friend, around me stream;
> Half sense-supplied, and half unreal,
> Like music mingling with a dream.
> — *John Kenyon.*

I do not doubt that the 'music' of the two concluding lines mingled, though very unconsciously, with my own 'dream' and gave their form and pressure to the above distich. The ideas however being sufficiently distinct, I am satisfied with sending this note to the press after my verses, and with acknowledging another obligation to the valued friend to whom I already owe so many. — 1844.

Page 39, line 107. *As the seer-saint of Patmos, loving John.*

[This line, as first printed in 1838, contained an extraordinary abbreviation: 'As erst in Patmos *apolyptic* John.' Miss Barrett had to be convinced by Mr. Boyd and others that the word was inadmissible before she substituted the above reading.]

THE VIRGIN MARY TO THE CHILD JESUS.
Page 43, line 37. *As Moses did, and die, — and then live most.*

It is a Jewish tradition that Moses died of the kisses of God's lips.

A DRAMA OF EXILE.
Page 81, line 1023. *Of manhood's curse of labor.*

Adam recognizes in *Aquarius*, the Water-bearer, and *Sagittarius*, the Archer, distinct types of the man bearing and the man combating, — the passive and active forms of human labor. I hope that the preceding zodiacal signs — transferred to the earthly shadow and representative purpose — of Aries, Taurus, Cancer, Leo, Libra, Scorpio, Capricornus, and Pisces, are sufficiently obvious to the reader.

Line 1025. *But look off to those small humanities.*

Her maternal instinct is excited by Gemini.

ON A PORTRAIT OF WORDSWORTH BY B. R. HAYDON.
Page 98. [On October 31st, 1842, Miss Barrett wrote to Hugh Stuart Boyd that she had had

a 'letter from *the great poet*' and was better pleased with it than were ever 'King John's barons with their charter.' The highly characteristic communication was as follows : —

RYDAL MOUNT : Oct. 26, '42.

DEAR MISS BARRETT, — Through our common friend Mr. Haydon I have received a sonnet which his portrait of me suggested. I should have thanked you sooner for that effusion of a feeling towards myself, with which I am much gratified, but I have been absent from home and much occupied.

The conception of your sonnet is in full accordance with the painter's intended work, and the expression vigorous ; yet the word 'ebb,' though I do not myself object to it, nor wish to have it altered, will I fear prove obscure to nine readers out of ten.

> A vision free
> And noble, Haydon, hath thine art released.

Owing to the want of inflections in our language the construction here is obscure. Would it not be a little [better] thus ? — I was going to write a small change in the order of the words, but I find it would not remove the objection. The verse, as I take it, would be somewhat clearer thus, if you would tolerate the redundant syllable : —

> By a vision free
> And noble, Haydon, is thine art released.

I had the gratification of receiving, a good while ago, two copies of a volume of your writing, which I have read with much pleasure, and beg that the thanks which I charged a friend to offer may be repeated [to] you.

It grieved me much to hear from Mr. Kenyon that your health is so much deranged. But for that cause I should have presumed to call upon you when I was in London last spring.

With every good wish, I remain, dear Miss Barrett, your much obliged

WM. WORDSWORTH.

[Postmark : Ambleside, Oct. 28, 1842.]
Letters of Mrs. Browning, vol. i. p. 113.

A poet whose gravity of spirit had been less profound than Wordsworth's would hardly have known how to suggest alterations in the lines written by another poet on his own personal appearance. It may be added that although Miss Barrett altered the passage criticised by the Laureate, she did not accept his amendment. The lines now read : —

> A noble vision free
> Our Haydon's hand has flung out from the mist.]

THE LOST BOWER.
Page 150, stanza ix. *Keepers of Piers Plowman's visions through the sunshine and the snow.*

The Malvern Hills of Worcestershire are the scene of Langland's Visions, and thus present the earliest classic ground of English poetry.

THE CRY OF THE CHILDREN.

Page 158, line 115. *'Our Father,' looking upward in the chamber.*

A fact rendered pathetically historical by Mr. Horne's report of his Commission. The name of the poet of 'Orion' and 'Cosmo de' Medici' has, however, a change of associations, and comes in time to remind me that we have some noble poetic heat of literature still, — however open to the reproach of being somewhat gelid in our humanity. — 1844.

CROWNED AND BURIED.

Page 162, stanza xviii. *Green watching hills, ye witnessed what was done.*

Written at Torquay.

Stanza xxii. *And grave-deep 'neath the cannon-moulded column.*

It was the first intention to bury him under the column.

L. E. L.'s LAST QUESTION.

Page 179, stanza vi. *Their singer was to be, in darksome death.*

Her lyric on the Polar Star came home with her latest papers.

CATARINA TO CAMOENS.

Page 182, stanza xvi. *Keep my riband, take and keep it.*

She left him the riband from her hair.

Page 188. THE DEAD PAN.

[The subject of 'The Dead Pan' was first suggested to Miss Barrett by John Kenyon's translation of Schiller's *Gods of Greece.* We have seen what importance she attached to its position at the end of the Poems published, in two volumes, in 1844. She wished it to be her last and most emphatic word to the public upon this occasion, for it represented a tremendous intellectual effort on her part, — nothing less than an attempted synthesis of Paganism and Christianity. The poem was, however, criticised with very special severity, not merely for its flagrant faults of rhyme and rhythm, but for the free and, as it seemed to many, irreverent use made, in the concluding stanzas, of the name or names of the Christian Deity. Even Mr. Kenyon remonstrated with the poetess, and begged her to alter or suppress those last verses, but found her intractable and able to defend the faith was in her very passionately. See *Letters of Mrs. Browning,* vol. i. pp. 127–130.]

Page 207. A DEAD ROSE AND OTHER POEMS.

[In October, 1846, only a few weeks after Mrs. Browning's romantic marriage, there appeared in *Blackwood's Magazine* seven poems by her, some of which had been in the editor's hands for a considerable time. It illustrates the excessive tenderness of the bride's filial conscience, that she was deeply distressed for fear her father should give a too literal interpretation to these poems, and see in some of their expressions a calculated defiance of himself. 'I am so vexed,' she wrote to Miss Mitford on the 9th of November, 'about these poems appearing just now in Blackwood. Papa must think it *impudent* of me. It is unfortunate.' The poems were: 'A Woman's Shortcomings,' 'A Man's Requirements,' 'Maud's Spinning' (published among her poems as 'A Year's Spinning'), 'A Dead Rose,' 'Change upon Change,' and 'Hector in the Garden.' To one who re-reads them now, there seems to be very little in any of these pieces which could have been offensive, even to so morbid and biased a reader as Mr. Moulton-Barrett. The secret of the writer's heart, which already had been confided with magnificent *abandon* to the Portuguese Sonnets, is assuredly not betrayed in these poems.]

Page 214. SONNETS FROM THE PORTUGUESE.

[Miss Barrett's daring innovations in rhyme (they were less frequent and conspicuous in the work of *Mrs. Browning*) were never the result of carelessness. She was always very much grieved at any such suggestion, and, as far as it was in her gentle nature to do so, she resented it. She honestly believed that in making *panther* rhyme with *saunter*, *virtues* with *certes*, and *turret* with *chariot*, she was 'widening the artistic capabilities of the English language.' It was just the species of fond delusion to which an original mind whose early development has been solitary, is especially prone. Yet it is a curious fact that, whenever she was under the stress of an emotion strong enough to make her forget herself, her 'mission' as a poet, and her supposed moral and artistic responsibilities, her versification became almost flawless. It was so in 'Cowper's Grave,' in the matchless Portuguese Sonnets, and even in *Casa Guidi Windows,* which, though weak enough as a political pamphlet, still glows with the fresh inspiration which her sensitive soul inevitably received from its first contact with Italy.]

Page 224. CASA GUIDI WINDOWS.

[There is a singular felicity about the title chosen by Mrs. Browning for her initial poem on Italy. She herself says of *Casa Guidi Windows* that it was 'a meditation and a dream,' and the very name seems to confess a certain superficiality in her first outlook upon that stern secular struggle for national independence, which began in the early years of the nineteenth century, and has hardly reached, even as yet, a securely triumphant conclusion. The events of 1847 and 1848 were a spectacle to the newly arrived poetess; one part only though undoubtedly the most vivid and affecting part of the pageant which all Italy presented to a learned and visionary spectator who had never been out of England before, and who had passed years of her life immured in the dim dungeon of a London bedchamber. See *Letters of Mrs. Browning*, vol. i. pp. 386–388.

The second part of the poem, dated two years later than the first, is vaguely denunciatory in tone, and on the whole very despondent concerning the future of Italy. Yet it contains one or two of Mrs. Browning's noblest bits of versification, such as the tribute to Carlo Alberto, and the pathetic passage near the close beginning —

> Still graves, where Italy is talked upon !
> Still, still, the patriot's tomb, the stranger's hate !

and one does not quite understand upon what grounds the author anticipated for *Casa Guidi Windows* a peculiarly hostile reception in England. 'I have a book coming out,' she wrote to Miss Isa Blagden on May 1, 1851, ' which will prevent everybody else except you from ever speaking to me again ! ']

Page 225, line 42. *Void at Verona, Juliet's marble trough.*

They show at Verona, as the tomb of Juliet, an empty trough of stone.

Line 73. *And Dawn and Twilight wait in marble scorn.*

These famous statues recline in the Sagrestia Nuova, on the tombs of Giuliano de' Medici, third son of Lorenzo the Magnificent, and Lorenzo of Urbino, his grandson. Strozzi's epigram on the Night, with Michel Angelo's rejoinder, is well known.

Page 228, line 100. *They bade thee build a statue up in snow.*

This mocking task was set by Pietro, the unworthy successor of Lorenzo the Magnificent.

Page 228, lines 256, 257.

> *Savonarola's soul went out in fire*
> *Upon our Grand-duke's piazza.*

Savonarola was burnt for his testimony against papal corruptions as early as March, 1498 : and, as late as our own day, it has been a custom in Florence to strew with violets the pavement where he suffered, in grateful recognition of the anniversary.

Page 229, lines 321–323.

> *Pass*
> *The left stair, where at plague time Machiavel*
> *Saw One with set fair face as in a glass.*

See his description of the plague of Florence.

Line 334. *A king stood bare before its sovran grace.*

Charles of Anjou, in his passage through Florence, was permitted to see this picture while yet in Cimabue's ' bottega.' The populace followed the royal visitor, and, from the universal delight and admiration, the quarter of the city in which the artist lived was called ' Borgo Allegri.' The picture was carried in triumph to the church, and deposited there.

Line 363. *Whom Cimabue found among the sheep.*

How Cimabue found Giotto, the shepherd-boy, sketching a ram of his flock upon a stone, is prettily told by Vasari, — who also relates that the elder artist Margheritone died 'infastidito' of the successes of the new school.

Page 233, line 625. *Did pile the empty marbles as thy tomb.*

The Florentines, to whom the Ravennese refused the body of Dante (demanded of them 'in a late remorse of love '), have given a cenotaph in this church to their divine poet. Something less than a grave !

Line 630. *Good lovers of our age to track and plough.*

In allusion to Mr. Kirkup's discovery of Giotto's fresco portrait of Dante.

Page 241, line 1179. *From Tuscan Bellosguardo, wide awake.*

Galileo's villa, close to Florence, is built on an eminence called Bellosguardo.

Page 242, line 19. *We poets, wandered round by dreams, who hailed.*

See the opening passage of the *Agamemnon* of Æschylus.

Page 251, line 607. *Even Apollonius might commend this flute.*

Philostratus relates of Apollonius how he objected to the musical instrument of Linus the Rhodien that it could not enrich or beautify. The history of music in our day would satisfy the philosopher on one point at least.

Page 254. AURORA LEIGH.

[The inspiration and the main purport of *Aurora Leigh* were frankly socialistic, — as socialism was understood by disinterested dreamers half a century ago.

The poem, or novel, ' I flatter myself it 's a novel,' Mrs. Browning wrote to one friend, was begun under the immediate impulse of certain studies in the works of Louis Blanc, Prudhon, and other theorists which she and her husband had made together and continued with great enthusiasm during the winter of 1855–56, when the Brownings were once more living in Paris. Mr. Browning, to whom solitude, stillness, and reasonably congenial surroundings were essential to composition, was immensely struck by the power of mental abstraction which his wife displayed during that winter of work at high pressure. ' She wrote in pencil,' Robert Browning's biographer tells us, ' as she lay on the sofa in her sitting-room open to interruption from chance visitors, or from her little omnipresent son ; simply hiding the paper beside her if any one came in, and taking it up again when she was free. And if this process was conceivable, in the large, comparatively silent spaces of their Italian home, and amidst habits of life which reserved social intercourse to the close of the working-day, it baffles belief when one thinks of it as carried on in the conditions of a Parisian winter, and the little salon of the apartment in the Rue du Colisée, where those months were spent.' (*Life of Robert Browning*, by Mrs. Sutherland-Orr, vol. i. p. 302.)

The villa on Bellosguardo where the final scene of the poem passes was, in the main, the Villa Briochion, which had been taken on a long lease by Miss Isa Blagden, and concerning the view from which Mrs. Browning wrote, after having tea upon the terrace there one day in early April: 'You seem to be lifted above the world, in a divine ecstasy. Oh, what a vision!' The vision which must indeed haunt the memory of all who have ever seen it, is painted as faithfully as words can paint, in that passage of the seventh book of *Aurora Leigh* which begins,

I found a house in Florence on the hill.

The great popularity of *Aurora Leigh* on its first appearance was apparently due to the fact that, while it embodied some of the most revolutionary sentiments concerning social matters which chanced to be rife at the time, the story was interesting and sensational enough to bear the average reader smoothly and rapidly above the dark places of the intrigue. Nevertheless, the daring character of the plot, and the absolute freedom with which many of the more obscure and painful questions connected with the greatest of social evils were handled, exposed the author once more to ruthless criticism in some highly respectable quarters. But if, in the entire singleness of her intention, Mrs. Browning was amazed and distressed to learn that men of letters who were also men of the world, such as Thackeray, strongly demurred to her experiment, while a cynical recluse like Edward Fitzgerald fiercely condemned, and the editor of the *Tablet* did not hesitate to qualify the poem as 'grossly indecent;' she could comfort herself with the knowledge that her American publisher 'shed tears of sympathy' over the proof, and that to so lofty and uncompromising a moralist as John Ruskin it was 'the finest poem written in any language in this century.']

Page 410. POEMS BEFORE CONGRESS.
[During the decade of suspense and enforced inaction, so trying to all true Italian patriots, which intervened between 1849 and 1859, both Mr. and Mrs. Browning had come to identify themselves much more deeply with the National Cause than they had done when they were newcomers in Tuscany. When that most intemperate of Mrs. Browning's publications the *Poems before Congress* first appeared, about six months after the sharp disappointment of Villafranca, she wrote to her sister-in-law, Miss Sariana Browning, that she and her husband had begun writing on the Italian question together at his suggestion, meaning to publish jointly, but that he subsequently abandoned the project, which she carried on alone.
It is made clear enough by later events and publications of Robert Browning's own that the point where he differed most widely from his wife's conclusions on the Italian question was in his estimate of the character and the mission to Italy of Louis Napoleon Bonaparte. He could not echo the rapture of hero-worship, — the extravagant adulation of that high-strung Ode which stood at the head of the *Poems before Congress*, under the title of 'Napoleon III. and Italy,' but neither would he dissent from his wife before the world. To us, who have long known on

how shallow and unsteady a foundation the imposing fabric of the second French Empire was reared, and how often, when it appeared boldest, the policy of Napoleon III. was merely desperate, it is even more difficult to understand Mrs. Browning's adoring faith in the French Emperor.

Her frenzied devotion withstood even the staggering blow dealt by the summary Peace of Villafranca, and enabled her speedily to rally her hopes, though her health never recovered from that shock. She had an attack of severe illness in consequence; but the moment she was able to hold a pen she wrote from Siena to Miss Browning, that what had so prostrated her was — 'the blow on the *heart* about the peace after all that excitement and exultation, that walking on the clouds for weeks and months, and then the sudden stroke and fall, and the impotent rage against all the nations of the earth — selfish, inhuman, wicked — who forced the hand of Napoleon, and truncated his great intentions.' (*Letters of Mrs. Browning*, vol. ii. p. 320.)

The truth is that, while Mrs. Browning possessed, as clever women often do, a certain amount of political insight and an enormous capacity for political passion, of sound judgment in matters political she had none whatever: she could do nothing better for her own country, during the sharp, successive agonies of the Crimean War and the Indian Mutiny, when initial mistakes were made, no doubt, but which proved in the end so glorious a vindication of English valor and school of English character, than belabor the home government with the most opprobrious epithets which even her vast vocabulary could furnish. It was all 'dismal' and 'full of horror and despair,' — 'the alliance with France the only consolation' (!) She can even dismiss Florence Nightingale with a cold word of commendation, adding that she does not consider that *the best use to which we can put a gifted and accomplished woman is to make her a hospital nurse!*

We ourselves got, and indeed richly deserved, a sharp taste of Mrs. Browning's denunciatory eloquence in the piece entitled 'A Curse for a Nation,' which stands at the end of the *Poems before Congress*. In the prologue to the 'Curse,' Mrs. Browning seems for a moment almost to confuse herself with 'Apolyptic John.'

'I heard an angel speak last night
　　And he said "Write!"
Write a Nation's Curse for me
　And send it over the Western Sea.'

She begins by protesting her unwillingness. 'Not so, my lord!

for I am bound by gratitude,
By love and blood
To brothers of mine across the sea.'

But the god overpowers the pythoness and the curse follows. No doubt we were in mortal sin when these words were written, and escaped only by a speedy and terrible purgation the greater part of the woes which they denounced.

But the oddest and most inexplicable part of the whole matter is that many people in England, including the astute Mr. Chorley, who himself reviewed the *Poems before Congress* in the *Athenœum*, understood the Curse to be launched against England.]

Page 427. LORD WALTER'S WIFE.
Page 441, stanza vii. *And the King, with that stain on his scutcheon.*
Blue Book : Diplomatical Correspondence.

Page 499. AN ESSAY ON MIND.
Page 501, line 102. *And peeps at glory from some ancient's back.*
'The reason which the learned Bentley gave his daughter for not himself becoming an original writer, instead of wasting his talents on the works of others, is probably the cause of many not attempting original composition. Bentley seemed embarrassed at her honest question, and remained for a considerable time thoughtful. At length he observed : Child, I am sensible I have not always turned my talents to the proper use for which they were given me ; yet I have done something : but the wit and genius of the old authors beguiled me, and as I despaired of raising myself up to their standard upon fair ground, I thought the only chance I had of looking over their heads was to get upon their shoulders.' — *Curiosities of Literature*, vol. i.
Lines 136, 137.
  The gentle Cowley of our native clime
  Lisp'd his first accents in Aonian rhyme.
A volume of Cowley's poems was published in his fifteenth year ; and contains 'The Tragical History of Pyramus and Thispe,' written in his tenth.
Lines 138–141.
Alfieri's startling muse tuned not her strings,
And dumbly look'd 'unutterable things,'
Till when five lustrums o'er his head had past —
This poet's great mind exhibited no precocity. His 'Cleopatra,' written at the age of twenty-five years, first discovered its author's dramatic genius to himself and to the world.
Lines 156–158.
See in that breathless crowd Olorus stand,
While one fair boy hangs listening on his hand —
The young Thucydides.
It is said that Thucydides, in early youth, was present at the Olympic games when Herodotus recited his History ; and that a burst of tears spoke his admiration. 'Take care of that boy,' observed the sage, turning to Olorus ; 'he will one day make a great man ! '
Page 502, line 229. *That hail 'th' eternal city ' in their pride.*
'Imperium sine fine dedi,' says Virgil's Jupiter. How little did the writer of those four words dream of their surviving the Glory, whose eternity they were intended to predict ! Horace too, in the most exulting of his odes, boldly proclaims that his fame will live as long as
  Capitolium
Scandet cum tacitâ virgine Pontifex.

Yes ! his fame *will live !* — but where now is the Pontifex, and the silent vestal ? where now is the Capitol ? Such passages are, to my mind, preëminently more affecting than all the ruins in the world !
Line 291. *And ultra Mitford soar'd to libel Greece.*
Mr. Mitford's acknowledged learning, and accuracy in detail, have a claim on our consideration, which we admit with readiness and pleasure ; but prejudices, arising probably from early habits and associations, have deformed his work. He is evidently so afraid of taking the mob for the people, that he constantly takes the people for the mob — a perversion much in vogue among despots of Europe in the nineteenth century. He considers the Athenian Democracy as he would a classical kind of Radicalism ; and generously endows Philip of Macedon with a 'right divine,' not only over his own possessions, but over those of his neighbors. Mr. Mitford lets his readers look at facts : but, whether shortsighted as himself or not, he will not allow them to enjoy that privilege unless they make use of his political glasses ; which, by the way, are No. 20, — 'ne plus ultra ! '
Lines 307–309.
  But lean on Reason, as your safest rule !
  Let doubtful facts, with patient hand be led
  To take their place on this Procrustian bed.
We shall find some clever and animated observations on this subject, in Voltaire's preface to his Charles XII. I should extract them, but the book is too well known for me to doubt their having come to the knowledge of most readers ; and a new publication is perhaps the only place in which we are not glad to meet an old acquaintance.
Page 503, line 351. *Enlighten'd Miller of our modern days !*
Those who may think this praise excessive are referred to the *Philosophy of Modern History*, given to the world by Dr. Miller ; and thence are requested to judge of the reality of the merit.
Lines 369–371.
The whisper'd sound which stole on Descartes' ear,
Hallowing the sunny visions of his youth,
With that eternal mandate, 'Search for Truth ! '
'Descartes, when young, and in a country seclusion, his brain exhausted by meditation and his imagination heated to excess, heard a voice in the air, which called him to pursue the search of Truth : he never doubted the vision, and this dream, in the delirium of Genius, charmed him even in his after studies.' — *D'Israeli's Literary Character.*
Page 504, lines 427, 428.
He died, the glorious ! who, with soaring sight,
Sought some new world to plant his foot of might.
Archimedes wrote to Hiero, that, if he had another world to stand on, he could move this by the power of his machinery. When Cicero stumbled on his grave, he found it, 'Septum undique et vestitum vepribus et dumetis.' What a homily !

Lines 448, 449.
So hard to bear with unobstructed sight,
Th' excess of darkness, or th' extreme of light.

Gray ingeniously asks, 'Must I plunge into metaphysics?' (he might in some cases have said history). 'Alas! I cannot see in the dark ; Nature has not furnished me with the optics of a cat. Must I pore upon mathematics? Alas! I cannot see in too much light; I am no eagle.'

Lines 492, 493.
So Buffon erred — amidst his chilling dream
The judgment grew material as the theme.

Buffon was a materialist upon principle, though a Catholic by observance. Upon reading a poem on the immortality of the soul, he exclaimed, 'Religion would be a noble present if this were true.'

Line 506. *Sternly they strove — th' unequal race was run —*

Leibnitz attacked with violence Sir Isaac Newton's opinion, that the seeds of mortality would be developed in the fabric of the universe if unrenewed by its divine Maker. Such an opinion he considered 'impious ;' and, in opposition to it, maintained, that as Creation proceeded from the hand of Perfection, it is perfect — and as perfect, immutable.

Page 505, line 526. *Devoted Southey! if thou had'st not tried.*

Few are ready to bear a more respectful tribute to Dr. Southey's poetical talents than the writer of this Work, who however begs to be allowed to admire his genius, without extending that admiration either to his politics or Hexameters.

Line 535. *Dwell not on parts, for parts contract the mind.*

Lord Bacon thus expresses himself — 'Sciences distinguished have a dependence upon universal knowledge, to be augmented, and rectified by the superior light thereof ; as well as the parts and members of a science have upon the maxims of the same science, and the mutual light and consent which one part receiveth of another.' — *Interpretatio Naturæ.*

Line 584. *For too much learning maketh no man mad.*

Perhaps, after all, the great danger of knowing is in not knowing enough ; and certainly 'il pie fermo' is not 'il piu basso.' 'It is true,' says Lord Bacon, 'that a little philosophy inclineth men's minds to atheism, but depth in philosophy bringeth their minds about to religion.' This is an acute observation, and if generalized will be found equally so. The errors attending Intellectual Elevation I have alluded to and allowed ; but that elevation is only comparative. 'Alps on Alps arise !' and the *ars longa vita brevis* prevents our attaining the topmost height. In our progress towards it then is our risk, lest we rejoice to have gone a yard, without remembering we have a mile to go. Like the princess, in the pretty Arabian tale, who was ascending the mountain in search of her talking bird and golden water, if during

the ascent we turn back to gaze, we are transformed into black stones — capable of impeding others, though not of advancing ourselves.

Line 594. *The sage how learned, and the man how meek!*

The character of Sir Isaac Newton forms a sublime comment on the foregoing note. 'I don't know,' said that greatest and humblest of men, 'what I may seem to the world ; but as to myself, I seem to have been only like a boy playing on the seashore, and diverting myself in now and then finding a smoother pebble or a prettier shell than ordinary, whilst the great ocean of Truth lay all undiscovered before me.' — We find the anecdote in Spence.

Page 507, lines 705, 706.
Ev'n Cato, had he own'd the senate's will,
And wash'd his toga — had been Cato still!

Plutarch relates that Cato Uticensis was thought to disgrace the Prætorship by the meanness of his dress. To couple 'disgrace' with the name of Cato revolts the soul ; and yet who would call his 'exigua toga' a *proof* of the loftiness of his virtue, or think him less a patriot if he had kept on his shoes ?

Lines 723, 724.
'*All is idea, and nothing real springs*
But God and Reason!' (*not the right of kings ?*)

An obvious question. Pyrrho the Elean, founder of the Ideal Philosophy, on the near approach of carts and carriages, did not think it worth while to turn aside or change his posture. Dr. Berkeley, with less consistency but more prudence, found time (and conscience) to write three sermons in vindication of passive obedience.

Lines 729-731.
'*While (coldly studious !) thine ingenious scroll*
Endows the mimic statue with a soul,
Compos'd of sense.'

It is the object of Condillac's work, 'Sur la Sensation,' to prove 'que la reflexion n'est dans son principe que la sensation même,' and that our ideas are only sensation transformed. His statue is very cleverly put together, but is a statue after all.

Line 734. *What triumph hath the 'Art of Thinking' there ?*

'L'Art de penser' — title to one of Condillac's works.

Page 508, lines 803, 804.
To judge is yours — then why submissive call,
'*The master said so ?*'

An 'argumentum ad verecundiam' used by the Pythagoreans. I so much admire a passage in Plato's Phædo, illustrative of these lines, that the reader must forgive my referring to it. Cebes supports with animation an opinion in opposition to Socrates, who, turning a gratified countenance ('ἡσθῆναί τέ μοι ἔδοξε,' says the narrator) to his other disciples, benignly observes: 'Cebes always looks into principles ; neither will he admit, without examination, the sentiments of any man.'

We find in Dr. Reid the following striking precept, 'Let us, as becomes philosophers, lay aside authority.'

Lines 817, 818.
If human faults to Plato's page belong,
Not ev'n with Plato willingly go wrong.
Cicero's assertion, 'errare mehercule malo cum Platone quam cum istis vera sentire,' is more boldly said than singularly thought. How many are there, among the canaille of readers, prepared to praise an inferior volume, with the Waverley magic on its *titlepage;* to commend a commonplace by Rogers or a far-fetched allusion by Moore. Even among the more critical of us, have the names of Scott, and Moore, and Rogers no secret influence? Do we not so devoutly admire the noisy slippered Venus that at length we begin to reverence, abstractedly, the noisy slippers? This is so, and I will not quarrel with it ; since to forget the trifling faults of a great writer is the gratitude we owe to his perfections. But what, in subjects of taste and sentiment, may be tolerated as pardonable enthusiasm, must in grave discussion be condemned as unpardonable weakness. If, therefore, we judge Cicero only by the above-cited passage, we shall pronounce him to be a good Platonist (in one sense of the word), but a very bad philosopher. It is not with him, 'Amicus Plato sed magis amica veritas:' he loves truth less than he loves Plato.
Line 841. *Or Memnon's statue singing 'neath the sun.*
The statue of Memnon, the Ethiopian king, was said to utter musical sounds at the rising of the sun. Strabo witnessed this singular phenomenon, but could only explain it by conjecture.
Page 509, lines 872, 873.
But, ah! our Muse of Britain standing near,
Hath dimm'd my tablet with a pensive tear!
It is a practice too common, but manifestly unjust, to visit on the memory of distinguished authors their individual failings. I wish therefore to state expressly, that the Muse of Britain is not here supposed to animadvert on Lord Bacon's character as a statesman, with which she has nothing to do in this place. It is with regard to his writings that I cannot avoid expressing a regret — and I do so reverentially — that pages so glorious should be polluted by passages so servile. 'As men, we share his fame ;' as Englishmen, we feel his degradation. If, indeed, the *Novum Organum* and *Advancement of Learning* kindled our souls into a less proud consciousness of intellectual dignity, we might better brook hearing a king called 'a mortal god upon earth,' and James the First compared to Solomon. But Lord Bacon first teaches us how high Philosophy can soar, and then how low a philosopher can stoop.
Line 915. *And strikes Pierian chords — when Irving speaks!*
There is a pleasure in being benefited by the labors of Genius : there is a pride in possessing powers capable of benefiting. The pride Mr. Irving may justly feel ; and which of his readers, or hearers, cannot boast the pleasure? It gratifies me to be enabled to express in this place my admiration of his talents, and my respect for their direction.

Lines 926, 927.
Ungrateful Plato! o'er thy cradled rest
The Muse hath hung, and all her love exprest.
Plato wrote poetry in his youth ; and when indeed did not Plato write poetry? Longinus numbers him among the imitators of Homer —

Πάντων δὲ τούτων μάλιστα ὁ Πλάτων ἀπὸ τοῦ Ὁμηρικοῦ ἐκείνου νάματος εἰς αὑτὸν μυρίας ὅσας παρατροπὰς ἀποχετευσάμενος.

Page 510, lines 972, 973.
And as fair Eve, in Eden newly placed,
Gaz'd on her form, in limpid waters traced —
The reader will here perceive an allusion to that beautiful passage in *Paradise Lost,* book the fourth, where Eve describes to Adam her emotions on first beholding her own reflection in 'the clear smooth lake' —

A shape within the watery gleam appeared,
Bending to look on me — I started back —
It started back, etc.

Lines 1022, 1023.
The artist lingers in the moon-lit glade,
And light and shade, with him, are — light and shade.
'Quam multa vident Pictores in umbris et eminentia quæ nos non videmus,' is the motto to Mr. Price's admirable essay on the Picturesque. Dugald Stewart proposes its reversion —'Quam multa videmus nos quæ Pictores non vident,' which if it be as true as ingenious, will go a great way in assisting my position.
Lines 1044, 1045.
—— *to trace*
Nature's ideal form in Nature's place.
Lord Bacon says of Poetry, that 'it was ever thought to have some participation of divineness, because it doth raise and erect the mind, by submitting the shews of things to the desires of the mind ; whereas Reason doth buckle and bow the mind unto the nature of things.' — *Advancement of Learning,* Book 2.
Page 511, lines 1079, 1080.
Wherein Conception only dies in state,
As Draco smother'd by the garments' weight.
The Athenian people being accustomed to testify their approbation by the casting of their garments on the approved individual, Draco was honorably smothered through excess of popularity.
Page 512, lines 1182–1184.
—— *behold the cold, dumb sepulchre,*
The ruined column — ocean, earth and air,
Man and his wrongs! — thou hast Tyrtæus there!
The inspiriting effect of the productions of this Greek poet, during the war between the Lacedæmonians and Messenians, is well known.
Line 1197. *He laid him down before the shrine — and slept!*
Herodotus relates of Cleobis and Bito, Argive brothers, that on a festival of Juno they themselves, in default of oxen, drew the chariot of the priestess, their mother, forty-five stadia to the temple. Amidst the shouts of an admiring multitude, their grateful parent asked of the

gods the best boon mortals could receive, wherewith to reward the piety of her sons. The young men fell asleep within the temple, and woke no more.

Line 1203. *No Moschus sang a requiem o'er his clay!*

That exquisite effusion of Moschus over the grave of Bion, his ' vatis amici ' — his brother in poetry and love — will occur to the reader's recollection.

Line 1229. *Then comes the* SELAH *— and the voice is hush'd!*

Respecting this Hebrew word, which is found ' seventy times in the Psalms, and three times in Habakkuk,' Calmet observes: ' One conjecture is, that it means the end or a pause, and that the ancient musicians put it occasionally in the margin of their psalters, to shew where a musical pause was to be made, and where the tune ended.'

IV. CHRONOLOGY

1806   Birth, Coxhoe Hall, County Durham, March 6

1809   Move to Hope End, Herefordshire

1814   Early attempts at writing poetry

1815   Visit to Paris

1820   *The Battle of Marathon* privately printed

1821   First nervous collapse

1826   *An Essay on Mind, with Other Poems*

1828   Death of Mrs. Barrett

1833   *Prometheus Bound . . . and Miscellaneous Poems*

1837   Move to 50 Wimpole Street, London

1838   *The Seraphim and Other Poems*

1840   Death of favorite brother, Edward ("Bro")

1844   *Poems* (2 vols.)

1845   First letter from Robert Browning, January; first meeting, May; begins *Sonnets from the Portuguese*

1846   Marriage to Robert Browning, September 12; journeys to France, Pisa, Florence

1849   Birth of Robert Wiedeman Barrett-Browning, March

1850   *Poems* (2 vols.), revision of 1844 edition includes *Sonnets from the Portuguese*

1856   *Casa Guidi Windows, Aurora Leigh*

1860   *Poems Before Congress*

1861   Death, Florence; buried in Protestant Cemetery there

INDEX OF FIRST LINES

[Including the first lines of songs contained in poems and dramas.]

INDEX OF TITLES

[The titles of major works and of general divisions are set in SMALL CAPITALS.]